Magill's
Cinema
Annual
2 0 0 9

Magill's Cinema Annual 2009

28th Edition
A Survey of the films of 2008

Hilary White, Editor

**With an Introduction by
Barry Keith Grant**

A VideoHound® Reference

GALE
CENGAGE Learning™

Detroit • New York • San Francisco • New Haven, Conn • Waterville, Maine • London

Magill's Cinema Annual 2009

Hilary White, Editor

Project Editor: Michael J. Tyrkus

Editorial: Laura Avery, Jim Craddock, Margaret Mazurkiewicz, Katherine H. Nemeh

Editorial Support Services: Wayne Fong

Composition and Electronic Prepress: Gary Leach, Evi Seoud

Manufacturing: Rhonda Dover

For product information and technology assistance, contact us at **Gale Customer Support, 1-800-877-4253.**
For permission to use material from this text or product, submit all requests online at **www.cengage.com/permissions.**
Further permissions questions can be emailed to **permissionrequest@cengage.com**

Gale
27500 Drake Rd.
Farmington Hills, MI, 48331-3535

ISBN-13: 978-1-55862-632-4
ISBN-10: 1-55862-632-8

ISSN: 0739-2141

Printed in the United States of America
1 2 3 4 5 6 7 13 12 11 10 09

Contents

Preface

Magill's Cinema Annual 2009 continues the fine film reference tradition that defines the VideoHound® series of entertainment industry products published by Gale. The twenty-eighth annual volume in a series that developed from the twenty-one-volume core set, *Magill's Survey of Cinema,* the *Annual* was formerly published by Salem Press. Gale's fourteenth volume, as with the previous Salem volumes, contains essay-reviews of significant domestic and foreign films released in the United States during the preceding year.

The *Magill's* editorial staff at Gale, comprising the VideoHound® team and a host of *Magill's* contributors, continues to provide the enhancements that were added to the *Annual* when Gale acquired the line. These features include:

- More essay-length reviews of significant films released during the year
- Obituaries and book review sections
- Trivia and "fun facts" about the reviewed movies, their stars, the crew, and production
- Quotes and dialogue "soundbites" from reviewed movies, or from stars and crew about the film
- More complete awards and nominations listings, including the American Academy Awards®, the Golden Globes, and others (see the User's Guide for more information on awards coverage)
- Box office grosses, including year-end and other significant totals
- Publicity taglines featured in film reviews and advertisements

In addition to these elements, *Magill's Cinema Annual 2009* still features:

- An obituaries section profiling major contributors to the film industry who died in 2008
- An annotated list of selected film books published in 2008
- Nine indexes: Director, Screenwriter, Cinematographer, Editor, Art Director, Music Director, Performer, Subject, and Title (now cumulative)

COMPILATION METHODS

The *Magill's* editorial staff reviews a variety of entertainment industry publications, including trade magazines and newspapers, as well as online sources, on a daily and weekly basis to select significant films for review in *Magill's Cinema Annual*. *Magill's* staff and other contributing reviewers, including film scholars and university faculty, write the reviews included in the *Annual*.

MAGILL'S CINEMA ANNUAL: A VIDEOHOUND® REFERENCE

The *Magill's Survey of Cinema* series, now supplemented by the *Annual*, is the recipient of the Reference Book of the Year Award in Fine Arts by the American Library Association. Gale, an award-winning publisher of reference products, is proud to offer *Magill's Cinema Annual* as part of its popular VideoHound® product line, which includes *VideoHound®'s Golden Movie Retriever* and *The Video Source Book*. Other Gale film-related products include the four-volume *International Dictionary of Films and Filmmakers, Women Filmmakers & Their Films*, the *Contemporary Theatre, Film, and Television* series, and the four-volume *Schirmer Encyclopedia of Film*. Also, be sure to visit Video-Hound on the web at *www.MovieRetriever.com*.

ACKNOWLEDGMENTS

The editor would like to thank all of the contributors for their expertise and professionalism. *Magill's Cinema Annual* is honored again this year with a Guest Introduction by Barry Keith Grant, Professor of Film Studies and Popular Culture at Brock University (St. Catherines, Ontario), author, and editor-in-chief of the *Schirmer Encyclopedia of Film*. Thank you to Gary Leach for his typesetting expertise, and Wayne Fong for his invaluable technical assistance. For their invaluable assistance and unflagging efforts, *Magill's* would also like to thank Mike Tyrkus, Senior Content Project Editor at Gale and Project Editor for *Magill's Cinema Annual;* Jim Craddock, Editor of *VideoHound®'s Golden Movie Retriever;* and Tom Burns, Project Editor of *Children's Literature Review,* all of whom generously contributed their time and resources to *Magill's*.

We at *Magill's* look forward to another exciting year in film and preparing the next edition of *Magill's Cinema Annual*. As always, we invite your comments, questions, and suggestions. Please direct them to:

Editor
Magill's Cinema Annual
Gale, a part of Cengage Learning
27500 Drake Road
Farmington Hills, MI 48331-3535
Phone: (248) 699-4253
Toll-Free: (800) 347-GALE (4253)
Fax: (248) 699-8865

The Year in Film: An Introduction

Two thousand and eight once again saw the number of films attaining official blockbuster status continue to grow, with fifty-seven movies earning more than $100 million, nine more than in the previous year, and twelve of these reaching international blockbuster status by earning more than $400 million, also an increase over the previous two years and setting a new record established last year by one. As the economy began to nosedive, action and superhero movies soared to the top of the box office. *Hancock* and *Iron Man* took fourth and fifth place in the year's returns, pulling in more than $600 million and $500 million for Columbia and Paramount, respectively.

Animated films continued to perform well at the box office, with DreamWorks' *Kung Fu Panda* and *Madagascar: Escape 2 Africa,* and the Pixar/Disney *Wall-E* all placing in the top ten successes of the year, while the more modest but respectable performance of the French *Persepolis*, about a young woman's memory of growing up in Iran, served as a poignant reminder that good animation is not limited to children or family fare. But towering over all others, like the Batman looming over Gotham City from atop its tallest skyscraper, was *The Dark Knight,* the most recent installment of the caped crusader once again starring Christian Bale. Propelled by Heath Ledger's striking interpretation of the villainous Joker, as well as by his untimely death shortly before the film's release, *The Dark Knight* earned $1 billion worldwide and more than $158 million on its opening weekend alone, surpassing last year's biggest performer, *Pirates of the Caribbean: At World's End,* dominating the box-office for most of the summer, and breaking a number of box office records.

Remakes, sequels, and spinoffs continued to be a strong trend in Hollywood, indicating either creative exhaustion or dynamic corporate synergy, depending on one's point of view. *The Women* was a remake of George Cukor's classic melodrama, *The Incredible Hulk* was the second adaptation of the comic book character, and *Get Smart* and *Sex and the City* were based on popular television shows. Some of the biggest releases of the year were sequels, including *The Chronicles of Narnia: Prince Caspian, The Mummy: Tomb of the Dragon Emperor, Star Wars: The Clone Wars, The X-Files: I Want to Believe,* and *Quantum of Solace,* marking the reprise of Daniel Craig as Agent 007 in the James Bond series' highest octane offering to date. Other sequels included *The Sisterhood of the Traveling Pants 2, Hellboy 2: The Golden Army, Step Up 2 the Streets, High School Musical 3: Senior Year, Transporter 3,* and *Saw V.* Harold and Kumar escaped from Guantanamo Bay, *Rambo* returned for retribution for the fourth time, and *Indiana Jones and the*

Kingdom of the Crystal Skull, the fourth installment of the Lucas-Spielberg franchise, was the second-highest grossing film of the year, earning almost $800 million worldwide, despite the fact that poor old Indy (Harrison Ford) and the entire enterprise seemed enervated.

More original and challenging films such as *Frozen River, The Reader, Synecdoche, New York, The Wrestler,* and *Milk* received relatively limited release, although the latter two featured Oscar®-nominated performances by, respectively, Mickey Rourke and Sean Penn, who won the Oscar® Award for Best Actor. *Doubt,* an adaptation by John Patrick Shanley of his own stage play with Meryl Streep and Philip Seymour Hoffman, and Ron Howard's *Frost/Nixon,* featuring a terrific performance by Frank Langella as Richard Nixon, attained wide release. While some outstanding non-English language films such as *The Class* (France), *Gomorrah* (Italy), *The Band's Visit* (Israel), and *Two-Legged Horse* (Iran) received only limited distribution, Danny Boyle's *Slumdog Millionaire,* about a homeless orphan from Mumbai who wins the Indian version of television's *Who Wants to Be a Millionaire,* began by grabbing audiences at international film festivals and eventually managed to move into wide release by year's end and then winning the Oscar® for Best Film of the Year. No documentaries loomed large on the cultural landscape in 2008, although *Religulous,* combining the slapdash approach to directing of Larry Charles with the opinionated humor of Bill Maher, tried hard with an aggressive advertising campaign but nonetheless alienated audiences with its self-righteous cynicism.

As always, genre films comprised the bulk of production. The musical *Mamma Mia!* was the sixth top grossing film of the year, and *The Duchess* delivered the sumptuous spectacle of the best costume dramas along with a mild feminist message. Thrillers and crime films continued to be popular with, among others, *Bangkok Dangerous, The Bank Job, Untraceable, Burn After Reading,* and *Righteous Kill,* the much-touted but ultimately disappointing pairing of Robert De Niro and Al Pacino. Jonathan Demme's *Rachel Getting Married* took a fresh, neorealist approach to the romantic comedy, but Mike Nichols' *The Bucket List* and Michael Myers' *The Love Guru* flopped, as did *Zack and Miri Make a Porno,* despite the presence of the seemingly ubiquitous Seth Rogen, in part because of a poor advertising campaign by the Weinstein Company that unaccountably failed to play up the contribution of cult director Kevin Smith. Several of the year's comedies were genre parodies, including *Disaster Movie, Meet the Spartans,* and the most successful, *Tropic Thunder.*

Horror, fantasy, and science fiction continued to dominate mainstream cinema. Two of the year's best horror films, *Cloverfield* and George Romero's *Diary of the Dead,* effectively employed the first person, hand-hand style pioneered in 1999 by the surprise independent horror hit *The Blair Witch Project. Journey to the Center of the Earth 3-D, 10,000 BC, Blindness,* and M. Night Shamalyan's *The Happening* ranged from serious to silly, and *Jumper* was yet another attempt to turn a video game into a movie. Only these genres' commercial appeal could explain such remakes as *The Day the Earth Stood Still, Death Race, Prom Night, Shutter,* and *Quarantine.* Michael Haneke remade his own disturbing *Funny Games,* originally in German, in English with Naomi Watts and Tim Roth as the unfortunate victims of a home invasion, a theme also shared with *The Strangers.* The most commercially successful horror film of the year was *Twilight,* based on the popular novel by Stephenie Meyer, which captured the book's steamy adolescent romanticism sufficiently well to gross $188 million domestically, mostly from teenage girls.

Almost alone working the middle ground between genre and art cinema, prestige and popularity, like a high plains drifter in the desert, Clint Eastwood carried on the tradition of the classic Hollywood cinema of social significance. *Changeling,* with its exposure of the corruption at the heart of early Los Angeles recalling Roman Polanski's *Chinatown* (1974), was undoubtedly the handsomest American film of the year, evoking, also like Polanski's film, the polished look of the classic studio era; and *Gran Torino,* also directed by Eastwood, offered in its story about a white man's initial resistance to multi-cultural integration, not only a meditation on Eastwood's own screen persona but also a parable about the inevitably changing face of global cinema.

Barry Keith Grant
St. Catharines, Ontario

Contributing Reviewers

Michael Adams
Publishing Professional, Associate Professor, City University of New York Graduate Center

Richard Baird
Freelance Reviewer

Michael Betzold
Author, Publishing Professional

John Boaz
Publishing Professional

David L. Boxerbaum
Freelance Reviewer

Tom Burns
Publishing Professional

Marisa Carroll
Publishing Professional

Peter N. Chumo II
Professional Film Critic

Beth Fhaner
Publishing Professional

David Flanagin
Educator, Freelance Reviewer

Jaye Furlonger
Author, Publishing Professional

David Hodgson
Professional Film Critic

Glenn Hopp
Author, Film Critic, Department Head, Howard Payne University

Heather Hughes
Publishing Professional

Eric Monder
Professional Film Critic

David Metz Roberts
Freelance Reviewer

Brian Tallerico
Professional Film Critic

John C. Tibbetts
Author, Film Critic, Associate Professor, University of Kansas

Christine Tomassini
Publishing Professional

James M. Welsh
Author, Film Critic, Professor, Salisbury State University

Michael White
Freelance Reviewer

User's Guide

ALPHABETIZATION

Film titles and reviews are arranged on a word-by-word basis, including articles and prepositions. English leading articles (A, An, The) are ignored, as are foreign leading articles (El, Il, La, Las, Le, Les, Los). Other considerations:

- Acronyms appear alphabetically as if regular words.
- Common abbreviations in titles file as if they are spelled out, so *Mr. Death* will be found as if it was spelled *Mister Death*.
- Proper names in titles are alphabetized beginning with the individual's first name, for instance, *Gloria* will be found under "G."
- Titles with numbers, for instance, *200 Cigarettes,* are alphabetized as if the numbers were spelled out, in this case, "Two-Hundred." When numeric titles gather in close proximity to each other, the titles will be arranged in a low-to-high numeric sequence.

SPECIAL SECTIONS

The following sections that are designed to enhance the reader's examination of film are arranged alphabetically, they include:

- *List of Awards.* An annual list of awards bestowed upon the year's films by the following: Academy of Motion Picture Arts and Sciences, British Academy of Film and Television Arts Awards, Directors Guild of America Awards, Golden Globe Awards, Golden Raspberry Awards, Independent Spirit Awards, the Screen Actors Guild Awards, and the Writer's Guild Awards.
- *Obituaries.* Profiles major contributors to the film industry who died in 2008.
- *Selected Film Books of 2008.* An annotated list of selected film books published in 2008.

INDEXES

Film titles and artists are separated into nine indexes, allowing the reader to effectively approach a film from any one of several directions, including not only its credits but its subject matter.

- *Director, Screenwriter, Cinematographer, Editor, Art Director, Music Director,* and *Performer* indexes are arranged alphabetically according to artists appearing in this volume, followed by a list of the films on which they worked. In the *Performer* index, a (V) beside a movie title indicates voice-only work and an (N) beside a movie title indicates work as narrator.

- *Subject Index.* Films may be categorized under several of the subject terms arranged alphabetically in this section.

- *Title Index.* The title index is a cumulative alphabetical list of films covered in the twenty-eight volumes of the *Magill's Cinema Annual,* including the films covered in this volume. Films reviewed in past volumes are cited with the year in which the film appeared in the *Annual;* films reviewed in this volume are cited with the film title in boldface with a bolded Arabic numeral indicating the page number on which the review begins. Original and alternate titles are cross-referenced to the American release title in the Title Index. Titles of retrospective films are followed by the year, in brackets, of their original release.

SAMPLE REVIEW

Each *Magill's* review contains up to sixteen items of information. A fictionalized composite sample review containing all the elements of information that may be included in a full-length review follows the outline on the facing page. The circled number following each element in the sample review designates an item of information that is explained in the outline.

1. **Title:** Film title as it was released in the United States.

2. **Foreign or alternate title(s):** The film's original title or titles as released outside the United States, or alternate film title or titles. Foreign and alternate titles also appear in the Title Index to facilitate user access.

3. **Taglines:** Up to ten publicity taglines for the film from advertisements or reviews.

4. **Box office information:** Year-end or other box office domestic revenues for the film.

5. **Film review:** A signed review of the film, including an analytic overview of the film and its critical reception.

6. **Reviewer byline:** The name of the reviewer who wrote the full-length review. A complete list of this volume's contributors appears in the "Contributing Reviewers" section which follows the Introduction.

7. **Principal characters:** Listings of the film's principal characters and the names of the actors who play them in the film.

8. **Country of origin:** The film's country or countries of origin.

9. **Release date:** The year of the film's first general release.

10. **Production information:** This section typically includes the name(s) of the film's producer(s), production company, and distributor; director(s); screenwriter(s); cinematographer(s) (if the film is animated, this will be replaced with Animation or Animation direction, or it will not be listed); editor(s); art director(s); production designer(s); music composer(s); and other credits such as visual effects, sound, costume design, and song(s) and songwriter(s).

11. **MPAA rating:** The film's rating by the Motion Picture Association of America. If there is no rating given, the line will read, "Unrated."

12. **Running time:** The film's running time in minutes.

13. **Reviews:** A list of brief citations of major newspaper and journal reviews of the film, including publication title, date of review, and page number (when available).

14. **Film quotes:** Memorable dialogue directly from the film, attributed to the character who spoke it, or comment from cast or crew members or reviewers about the film.

15. **Film trivia:** Interesting tidbits about the film, its cast, or production crew.

16. **Awards information:** Awards won by the film, followed by category and name of winning cast or crew member. Listings of the film's nominations follow the wins on a separate line for each award. Awards are arranged alphabetically. Information is listed for films that won or were nominated for the following awards: American Academy Awards®, British Academy of Film and Television Arts Awards, Directors Guild of America Awards, Golden Globe Awards, Golden Raspberry Awards, Independent Spirit Awards, the Screen Actors Guild Awards, and the Writers Guild of America Awards.

THE GUMP DIARIES ①

(Los Diarios del Gump) ②

Love means never having to say you're stupid.
—Movie tagline ③

Box Office: $10 million ④

In writer/director Robert Zemeckis' *Back to the Future* trilogy (1985, 1989, 1990), Marty McFly (Michael J. Fox) and his scientist sidekick Doc Brown (Christopher Lloyd) journey backward and forward in time, attempting to smooth over some rough spots in their personal histories in order to remain true to their individual destinies. Throughout their time-travel adventures, Doc Brown insists that neither he nor Marty influence any major historical events, believing that to do so would result in catastrophic changes in humankind's ultimate destiny. By the end of the trilogy, however, Doc Brown has revised his thinking and tells Marty that, "Your future hasn't been written yet. No one's has. Your future is whatever you make it. So make it a good one."

In *Forrest Gump*, Zemeckis once again explores the theme of personal destiny and how an individual's life affects and is affected by his historical time period. This time, however, Zemeckis and screenwriter Eric Roth chronicle the life of a character who does nothing but meddle in the historical events of his time without even trying to do so. By the film's conclusion, however, it has become apparent that Zemeckis' main concern is something more than merely having fun with four decades of American history. In the process of re-creating significant moments in time, he has captured on celluloid something eternal and timeless—the soul of humanity personified by a nondescript simpleton from the deep South.

The film begins following the flight of a seemingly insignificant feather as it floats down from the sky and brushes against various objects and people before finally coming to rest at the feet of Forrest Gump (Tom Hanks). Forrest, who is sitting on a bus-stop bench, reaches down and picks up the feather, smooths it out, then opens his traveling case and carefully places the feather between the pages of his favorite book, *Curious George*.

In this simple but hauntingly beautiful opening scene, the filmmakers illustrate the film's principal concern: Is life a series of random events over which a person has no control, or is there an underlying order to things that leads to the fulfillment of an individual's destiny? The rest of the film is a humorous and moving attempt to prove that, underlying the random, chaotic events that make up a person's life, there exists a benign and simple order.

Forrest sits on the bench throughout most of the film, talking about various events of his life to others who happen to sit down next to him. It does not take long, however, for the audience to realize that Forrest's seemingly random chatter to a parade of strangers has a perfect chronological order to it. He tells his first story after looking down at the feet of his first bench partner and observing, "Mama always said that you can tell a lot about a person by the shoes they wear." Then, in a voice-over narration, Forrest begins the story of his life, first by telling about the first pair of shoes he can remember wearing.

The action shifts to the mid-1950s with Forrest as a young boy (Michael Humphreys) being fitted with leg braces to correct a curvature in his spine. Despite this traumatic handicap, Forrest remains unaffected, thanks to his mother (Sally Field) who reminds him on more than one occasion that he is no different from anyone else. Although this and most of Mrs. Gump's other words of advice are in the form of hackneyed cliches, Forrest, whose intelligence quotient is below normal, sincerely believes every one of them, namely because he instinctively knows they are sincere expressions of his mother's love and fierce devotion. ⑤

John Byline ⑥

CREDITS ⑦

Forrest Gump: Tom Hanks
Forrest's Mother: Sally Field
Young Forrest: Michael Humphreys
Origin: United States ⑧
Language: English, Spanish
Released: 1994 ⑨
Production: Liz Heller, John Manulis; New Line Cinema; released by Island Pictures ⑩
Directed by: Robert Zemeckis
Written by: Eric Roth
Cinematography by: David Phillips
Music by: Graeme Revell
Editing: Dana Congdon
Production Design: Danny Nowak
Sound: David Sarnoff
Costumes: David Robinson
MPAA rating: R ⑪
Running time: 102 minutes ⑫

REVIEWS ⑬

Entertainment Weekly. July 15, 1994, p. 42.
Hollywood Reporter. June 29, 1994, p. 7.
Los Angeles Times. July 6, 1994, p. F1.
New York Times Online. July 15, 1994.

QUOTES ⑭

Forrest Gump (Tom Hanks): "The state of existence may be likened unto a receptacle containing cocoa-based confections, in that one may never predict that which one may receive."

TRIVIA ⑮

Hanks was the first actor since Spencer Tracy to win back-to-back Oscars® for Best Actor. Hanks received the award in 1993 for his performance in *Philadelphia.* Tracy won Oscars® in 1937 for *Captains Courageous* and in 1938 for *Boys Town.*

AWARDS ⑯

Academy Awards 1994: Film, Actor (Hanks), Special Effects, Cinematography

Nomination:

Golden Globes 1994: Film, Actor (Hanks), Supporting Actress (Field), Music.

A

THE AIR I BREATHE

*Sometimes the things we can't change...end up
   changing us.*
   —Movie tagline
Happiness. Sorrow. Pleasure. Love.
   —Movie tagline

With *The Air I Breathe,* novice director Jieho Lee attempted to fashion a psychologically and artistically stimulating study of human nature, but unfortunately the attempt often falls flat as a result of his trying to cover too much of an emotional canvas and failing to convey a clear, coherent, and consistent message.

Supposedly inspired by a Chinese proverb that says that life is composed of four emotions (happiness, pleasure, sorrow, and love), the film is constructed as a series of vignettes that tell a continuous story, probing the interconnections between an ensemble of four characters. Each "chapter" is labeled with one of the emotions, and the main character in each is supposed to represent the corresponding emotion, though none of the four is actually named in the film (only the end credits clarify that they are, in fact, named Happiness, Pleasure, Sorrow, and Love. For some reason, in devising a story that draws connections between these four characters, the writers chose to create another character who touches the lives of all of them, and this person is a murderous, vile gangster named Fingers (Andy Garcia).

The first main character to be introduced is Happiness (Forest Whitaker), a discontented bank worker who literally decides to take a risky gamble and winds up in debt to the cruel Fingers. In desperation, Happiness robs the very bank where he works but is pursued by the police and ultimately shot to death. The second character, Pleasure (Brendan Fraser), an enforcer/collector for Fingers, happens to have the gift of precognition. Ironically, he derives no pleasure from life, living a melancholy existence in which he bemoans the fact (via voiceover monologue) that he knows the future but cannot change it. The third major character is Sorrow (Sarah Michelle Gellar), a pop singer whose stage name is Trista and whose fame is on the rise but who becomes ensnared in Fingers's web when her manager turns her contract over to the gangster as payment for a debt. When Pleasure discovers that Sorrow is the only person whose future he cannot see, he is attracted to her. At the same time, he finds that his gift has started to fail in general. Pleasure then offers sanctuary to Sorrow when she decides to flee rather than have her life dictated by Fingers, and the two fall in love. However, Fingers discovers this "betrayal" and kills Pleasure. Finally, the fourth major character is Love (Kevin Bacon), a doctor who desperately tries to save the life of his true love, Gina (Julie Delpy), after she is bitten by a poisonous snake. Gina needs a blood transfusion but has an extremely rare blood type, yet Love learns by chance that Trista (Sorrow) has same blood type. After Sorrow saves Gina's life by agreeing to a transfusion, Love helps her leave Fingers behind by loaning her a car. Finally, in a surprise ending that reveals that the first chapter in the story is really part of the last, Sorrow happens upon an unexpected turn of luck when a bag full of money drops on her car—it is the moneybag Happiness had stolen from the bank and tossed from the rooftop of a building just as he was shot by the police. The money enables Sorrow to start a new, presumably happier life.

While there are some interesting philosophical aphorisms scattered throughout the film ("Sometimes things you can't change end up changing you"), along with many clichéd ones ("Scars are a window to the soul"), overall the film contains a hodgepodge of ideas that do not connect as the story suggests. The filmmaker wants to make a statement about the emotions represented as main characters; however, these characters do not genuinely represent those emotions. For example, Happiness is certainly not happy, and surely the filmmakers are not suggesting that he only finds happiness by throwing away everything he has, including his own life. Although Happiness seems to experience an epiphany when he is about to be shot, this event suggests that he has been experiencing deep depression or psychosis, rather than happiness. As stated before, Pleasure definitely finds no joy or even pleasure in anything. Consequently, it is very unclear what the filmmakers intend to say about the connection between happiness and pleasure as they exist in real life. There is also what appears to be a butterfly motif in the beginning of the film, but its relevancy is lost in the story. Happiness ponders whether a butterfly that has just emerged from its cocoon realizes that it has been transformed into a beautiful creature, or if it still believes itself to be a caterpillar—a thought that would seem important to the theme. Overall, the film does not draw clear connections between the imagery and any of the characters. Possibly this butterfly image refers to Sorrow, who does get a chance to transform, but if the image was meant to refer also to Happiness or Pleasure, it fails in that their transformations are not "beautiful." Like many of the plot points in the film, this episode seems contrived.

In general, plot plausibility is an issue in this film because the storyline relies on too many unrealistic coincidences that undermine whatever themes the film hopes to convey. The surprise ending is not really a twist, nor does it reveal significant details about the characters or plot. Therefore, tying the ending to the beginning seems like an attempt to be clever for cleverness' sake.

Several actors give strong performances, however: Brendan Fraser and Sarah Michelle Gellar portray the two characters who are most fully developed and most likely to elicit the audience's sympathy. Gellar especially adds emotional depth and complexity to the character of Sorrow. Unfortunately, the performances alone do not rescue the film. It is an interesting effort, but the effort seems to have gotten in the way of the story and the underlying meaning.

David Flanagin

CREDITS

Happiness: Forest Whitaker
Pleasure: Brendan Fraser
Sorrow: Sarah Michelle Gellar
Love: Kevin Bacon
Fingers: Andy Garcia
Tony: Emile Hirsch
Gina: Julie Delpy
Origin: USA
Language: English
Released: 2007
Production: Paul Schiff, Darlene Caamano Loquet, Emilo Deiz Barroso; Nala Films; released by ThinkFilm
Directed by: Jieho Lee
Written by: Jieho Lee, Bob DeRosa
Cinematography by: Walt Lloyd
Music by: Marcelo Zarvos
Sound: Alec St. John, Robert Getty
Editing: Robert Hoffman
Costumes: Michele Michel
Production Design: Bernardo Trujillo
MPAA rating: R
Running time: 97 minutes

REVIEWS

Hollywood Reporter Online. January 25, 2008.
Los Angeles Times Online. January 25, 2008.
New York Times Online. January 25, 2008.
Variety Online. May 15, 2007.
Village Voice Online. January 22, 2008.

QUOTES

Sorrow: "Did you know that scars are the roadmap to the soul?"
Happiness: "So where does change come from? And how do we recognize it when it happens?"

TRIVIA

Although Sarah Michelle Gellar plays a pop star, she does not do her own singing. The songs are performed by Kim Wayman.

AN AMERICAN CAROL

Laugh like your country depends on it.
—Movie tagline

Box Office: $7 million

Director David Zucker (*Airplane!* [1980]) recruited some of Hollywood's highest profile and most talented Republican actors and icons—Kelsey Grammer, Jon Voight, James Woods, Dennis Hopper, and Bill O'Reilly—and used many of his time-tested sight gags and comic acting for this slapstick satire against the liberal left, *An American Carol*. Despite this and an overripe left target—the highly lampoonable Michael Moore—the film fails largely because of the unrelenting political aggressiveness and unwarranted preachiness that is often at odds with the light, farcical humor. Much of the film is also poorly made, with cheap looking sets and visual effects and out-of-sync sound. Perhaps the film's most serious mistake, however, is in its utter unmarketability. Aimed at conservatives who will certainly appreciate the patriotic, pro-war message, the type of crude, over-the-top humor Zucker normally employs is also offensive to this same demographic. Box office records concur, with *An American Carol* recouping a mere $3.6 million of its $20 million budget.

Narrated by Zucker regular Leslie Neilson, *An American Carol* tells the cautionary tale of Michael Malone (Kevin Farley, Chris Farley's look-a-like brother), a documentary filmmaker, whose credits include, *Die, You American Pigs!* and who is in the midst of organizing a rally to ban the Fourth of July. As in Charles Dickens's short story *A Christmas Carol*, Malone is visited by three ghosts; they attempt to teach him the error of his ways, which primarily involves repeatedly slapping him in the face, and although not entirely unfunny, like most of the gags in the film, this one looses luster in its repetitiveness. At the same time, three jihadists from Afghanistan are on a mission to recruit a director who hates America as much as they do to remake their dated and amateurish recruitment videos; they find Malone to be the perfect candidate. Malone has no qualms working with the Middle Eastern "filmmakers"—the bumbling Mohammed (Geoffrey Arend), Ahmed (Serdar Kalsin) and their stone-faced superior Aziz (Robert Davi)—for the right price. The jihadists then see an opportunity to use Malone's all-access passes gain entrance to and bomb his war veteran-filled rally.

Malone is first visited by the ghost of patriots past, General Patton (Kelsey Grammer) who takes him to pre-World War II negotiations with Hitler to illustrate that talking to terrorists is never a successful strategy. In several scenes Malone's idol, President John F. Kennedy (Chriss Anglin), emerges from the television to dispel Malone of his delusion that if Kennedy were alive today, he would somehow approve of his anti-American sentiment. The visitors become increasingly less friendly, with George Washington (Jon Voight) turning up to give Malone a stern civics lesson, and the strapping Angel of Death (Trace Adkins) has little patience for the whining liberal. The ghosts/angels serve as messengers, constantly hitting Malone and the audience over the head repeatedly with their message: liberals are wimpy tree-huggers and Anti-American troop-haters.

Although *An American Carol* fails overall, it is not the performances that are at fault. Farley is a capable, if somewhat restrained, lead. Grammer is thoroughly likable and completely convincing in his portrayal of Patton, and Voight brings much-needed austerity and dignity to the proceedings as our Founding Father. In smaller cameos, Dennis Hopper as a judge, along with James Woods, as Michael's agent add credibility. Less successful, however, is Anglin as Kennedy, for the actor's unauthentic accent lapses and his bearing is far from presidential.

Nevertheless, veteran Zucker and co-writers Myrna Sokoloff and Lewis Friedman elicit their fair share of chuckles. For instance, Malone's visit to Cuba touting its superior health care system and culture as a paradise compared with America is humorously dispelled as desperate citizens being shot by soldiers rush to mob his tiny, America-bound raft. A futuristic Hollywood after Muslim extremists have won the war on terror features a hilarious "Victoria's Burkas" billboard. Finally, *Airplane!* is certainly called to mind as women and invalid children are dragged overboard by the oblivious documentarian.

The performances and rare bright spots of humor, however, cannot mend the strained marriage of slapstick to politics, sloppy writing and directing, and overarching preachiness.

Hilary White

CREDITS

Michael Malone: Kevin Farley
George S. Patton: Kelsey Grammer
George Washington: Jon Voight
Aziz: Robert Davi
John F. Kennedy: Chriss Anglin
Osama Bin Nielsen: Leslie Nielsen
Jane Wagstaff: Gail O'Grady
Angel of Death: Trace Adkins
Michael's Agent: James Woods
Origin: USA
Language: English
Released: 2008
Production: David Zucker, John Shepherd, Stephen McEveety; Mpower Pictures; released by Vivendi Entertainment
Directed by: David Zucker
Written by: David Zucker, Lewis Freidman, Myrna Sokoloff
Cinematography by: Brian Baugh
Music by: James L. Venable
Sound: Mark Steinberg
Editing: Vashi Nedomansky

Art Direction: Aaron Haye
Costumes: Rachel Good
Production Design: Patrick M. Sullivan Jr.
MPAA rating: PG-13
Running time: 84 minutes

REVIEWS

Boston Globe Online. October 4, 2008.
Entertainment Weekly Online. October 3, 2008.
Hollywood Reporter Online. October 3, 2008.
Los Angeles Times Online. October 4, 2008.
New York Times Online. October 4, 2008.
Variety Online. October 6, 2008.

QUOTES

Michael Malone: "Who are these people?"
General George S. Patton: "They're not people, they're the ACLU!"

TRIVIA

The date on the headstone lists Micheal Malone's birthdate as April 20, 1952 which is also the birthdate of Adolf Hitler albeit in a different year.

AMERICAN TEEN

In high school, the toughest thing to be…is yourself.
—Movie tagline

Director/producer Nanette Burstein's entertaining, occasionally poignant documentary *American Teen* follows five students during their senior year of high school in Warsaw, Indiana. Using shorthand from John Hughes's teen classic *The Breakfast Club* (1985), she introduces her main characters as the rebel (Hannah Bailey), the jock (Colin Clemens), the princess (Megan Krizmanich), the geek (Jake Tusing), and the heartthrob (Mitch Reinhold). Mitch strays the furthest from the formula—there is no pot-smoking "criminal" in steel-toed boots, à la John Bender, in *American Teen*—so he comes across as a mere placeholder in the *Breakfast Club*-styled promotional materials.

Burstein and her crew capture the five kids before, during, and after their school day: taking class, cheering on the Warsaw basketball team, and hanging out in the local Bob Evans. From a year's worth of footage, she creates a "quest arc" for each of her characters: Hannah aims to attend film school in San Francisco, much to the chagrin of her parents; Colin attempts to earn an athletic scholarship to an NCAA university; Megan awaits an acceptance letter from her family's alma mater, Notre Dame; Jake tries to find a girlfriend; and Mitch (again fitting loosely into the film's structure) would simply like to romance his somewhat unlikely crush, Hannah Bailey, before graduation. That they all believe their lives will be set once they achieve these goals is touching.

The teenagers confront obstacles, some of their own making, and Burstein effectively shows how much pressure they are under to succeed. Megan believes that if she cannot enroll at Notre Dame, her father "will be heartbroken," and Colin anticipates that "the community's going to go nuts" if his basketball team does not win. Burstein also illustrates how their parents, though well-intentioned, sabotage the teenagers' most audacious plans. For example, Hannah's mother tells her daughter that she is "not special" enough for film school and that if she moves to San Francisco, she will simply become a target for predatory men.

Hannah, Colin, Megan, Jake, and Mitch all have *American Teen*-related Facebook pages, so there was clearly an attempt by the film's marketers to reach a younger audience. Yet because the film relies so heavily on the *Breakfast Club*'s formula, viewers cannot help wonder about the intended audience: contemporary teenagers or adults who were in high school when Hughes's movie was first released. Although *The Breakfast Club* has received play on cable over the years, it is more likely a touchstone for nostalgic Generation Xers (viewers born after 1965) than the current teen audience. After all, once the film's trailer lists the rebel, jock, princess, geek, and heartthrob archetypes, it pointedly inquires of the audience, "Who were you?" By employing this strategy, the movie's project is two-fold: First, and most simply, it invites older viewers to empathize with the characters who remind them of themselves (or at least the perception they had of themselves in high school); second, it seeks to reassure these older viewers. By showing Generation Xers that they have more perspective on life than their younger onscreen counterparts, the film validates this growth in maturity. Burstein's movie surrogate is clearly the aspiring filmmaker Hannah, whose narration begins the film and whose contented face forms the film's parting image.

The film contains many high school tropes to which older viewers can relate, but it also shows ways in which new technologies have made the landscape even more treacherous than it was in the 1980s. For instance, when a classmate's nude digital photograph falls into the hands of Megan, she laughingly sends it to her friends, who pass it on to their friends, and so on. Soon the photo has been posted on MySpace pages, and everyone in the school is privy to it. Tools for humiliating classmates are faster and more far-reaching than ever before.

Burstein includes on-screen titles to document these text messages as they are being passed back and forth. While informative, this technique threatens the film's verisimilitude. As John Anderson of *Newsday* noted, "Burstein's camera always seems to be in the room when someone gets a devastating e-mail; the sense of orchestration is all over the movie." There are also flights of fantasy, like several animated sequences that illustrate the students' dreams or, in Hannah's case, nightmares. That said, the cinematographic style is not as flashy as Burstein's previous effort *The Kid Stays in the Picture* (2002). She mainly observes the cast members in their "natural habitats" and conducts the requisite close-up interviews, staying discreetly off screen.

Although parts of *American Teen* are theatrical, the stories are compelling, and the cast Burstein assembled is a likable one. (Megan's mean-girl antics may seem implausible, but a mid-film revelation indicates a potential reason for them.) The audience cannot help rooting for these teenagers and may even want to reassure them that they will overcome the challenges of their high school years.

Marisa Carroll

CREDITS

Origin: USA
Language: English
Released: 2008
Production: Nanette Burstein, Jordan Roberts, Eli Gonda, Chris Huddleston; Firehouse Films, Quasiworld Entertainment, 57th and Irving; released by Paramount Advantage
Directed by: Nanette Burstein
Cinematography by: Laela Kilbourn, Wolfgang Held, Robert Hanna
Music by: Michael Penn
Sound: Mike Chock
Music Supervisor: Chris Douridas
Editing: Nanette Burstein, Mary Manhardt, Tom Haneke
MPAA rating: PG-13
Running time: 95 minutes

REVIEWS

Christian Science Monitor Online. July 25, 2008.
Entertainment Weekly. August 1, 2008, p. 38.
Hollywood Reporter Online. January 31, 2008.
Los Angeles Times Online. July 25, 2008.
New York Times Online. July 25, 2008.
Rolling Stone Online. August 7, 2008.
Variety Online. January 20, 2008.
Village Voice Online. July 23, 2008.

APPALOOSA

Feelings get you killed.
—Movie tagline

Box Office: $20.2 million

Since the debut of Edwin S. Porter's pioneering classic *The Great Train Robbery* (1903), Americans have felt nostalgia for the Western. Rife with symbolism (the hero wearing the white hat) and a simple moral code, the Western represents America's romantic pulse, some commentators argue. It is usually set between the Civil War and the Reconstruction Era, though the genre is often idealized as taking place in a harsher yet more lucid, unambiguous time. These established traits make Westerns the perfect vehicle for escape from the contemporary world full of twenty-first century dangers.

Appaloosa delivers on all levels as a temporary reprieve from modern societal ills. The film uses an time-tested formula that works: the laconic, tough cowboy in conflict with a predatory extortionist of a small town culminates in a shootout. Adapted from Robert B. Parker's 2005 novel, the story is narrated by Everett Hitch (played in understated fashion by Viggo Mortensen). Like most of the characters he develops, Parker (primarily a crime novelist), likes to pen men who are both rugged and fearless. He frames them within an unwavering moral construct coupled with an unyielding resolve to remain true to themselves. It is an equation that has served Parker well with his *Spenser for Hire* books and Jesse Stone novels and television movies.

Ed Harris brought the novel to life by co-writing the screenplay and by producing and directing the film, in which he reunites with Mortensen, his co-star in *A History of Violence* (2005). Viewers will find few similarities in this work and Harris's directorial debut, *Pollock* (2000), a biopic about the haunted abstract expressionist painter. In *Appaloosa* Harris plays a lawman for hire, Virgil Cole, who travels from town to town in need of law enforcement with his partner, Hitch. Although Hitch is a seasoned West Point educated soldier who fought in both the Civil War and the U.S. Calvary's campaign against various Indian tribes, he is content with being Cole's calm, reflective sidekick. He reveres the stoic Cole, who appears to him like a grizzled gunslinger-god poured into a weathered pair of Lucchese boots.

There exists unspoken mutual respect and understanding between these two men that transcends the nooses found in many conventional friendships. Although an impression is formed that neither man would consider betraying the other, this bond appears to be challenged by the arrival of Allie French (Renée Zellweger). Wearing a silk dress and exuding high-cultured charm, Allie shatters that common western archetype of women as either the sagacious prostitute or saloon proprietor. Arriving in town with a dollar and marginal piano skills, she quickly throws a wrench into the plot by affirming that the keyboard is not the only instrument she plays. Immediately smitten, Cole becomes the most animated when around Allie. Thus far, Cole's experience with women has been limited to "whores and Squaws," and it is clear that they are possibly his sole weakness. Unlike the other women, Allie is driven by an inner compass that draws her to whomever she perceives to be the alpha male. Allie is not evil like Randall Bragg, the sociopathic murderous rancher played with panache by Jeremy Irons; she is acting on a warped survival predisposition.

Whether malevolent or instinctual, swiveling her hips against powerful suitors proves to be dangerous to all those involved. For example, Allie lies to Cole, telling him that Everett tried to seduce her in the house Cole was building for the couple, when in fact she attempted to seduce life-weary Everett. After the composed sidekick denies this accusation, an incensed Allie asks Cole, "Would you believe Everett over me?" and, straying from formula, Cole replies, "That would be correct."

In New Mexico Territory in the 1880s, the two gunmen have been placed on the town of Appaloosa's payroll as the law, an intangible concept in a town being consumed by Bragg, who killed the previous sheriff and his deputies in the first scene. Armed with a hard-set angular jaw and an eight-gauge shotgun, Hitch resolves to give Cole a chance with Allie by restoring his leading status, which was usurped by Bragg once he was given a presidential pardon for the murders he committed. (Ed Harris's father, Bob Harris, presides over Bragg's trial in a small but excellent performance as Judge Callison.)

The climax follows a predictable path as Hitch severs his partnership with Cole and challenges Bragg to a duel by slapping his face in Bragg's own hotel lobby. Yet Hitch meets Bragg on Appaloosa's dusty road for the showdown in an atypical stance for a western draw, with one arm behind his back, so that though the outcome is certain, the means to that end retain suspense. Similar to the denouements of golden age Westerns, Hitch departs alone, riding into the desert sunset.

With resplendent cinematography mainly shot in Santa Fe by Dean Semler, *Appaloosa* hails the classics by John Ford. While it is not a revision of the genre, it avoids the pitfalls of recent releases: It eschews the excessive violence relied upon in *3:10 to Yuma* (2007), yet recoils from the digressive, meditative doldrums that are meant to convey depth in *The Assassination of Jesse James by the Coward Robert Ford* (2007). With its outstanding dialogue interlaced with ironic humor, *Appaloosa* stands out as the best big screen western since Clint Eastwood's *Unforgiven* (1992).

David Metz Roberts

CREDITS

Virgil Cole: Ed Harris
Everett Hitch: Viggo Mortensen
Allison French: Renee Zellweger
Randall Bragg: Jeremy Irons
Sheriff Stringer: Rex Linn
Abner Raines: Tom Bower
Phil Olson: Timothy Spall
Earl May: James Gammon
Ring Shelton: Lance Henriksen
Katie: Ariadna Gil
Origin: USA
Language: English
Released: 2008
Production: Ed Harris, Robert Knott, Ginger Sledge; Groundswell Productions, Axon Films; released by New Line Cinema
Directed by: Ed Harris
Written by: Ed Harris, Robert Knott
Cinematography by: Dean Semler
Music by: Jeff Beal
Sound: John Pritchett
Editing: Kathryn Himoff
Art Direction: Steve Arnold
Costumes: David C. Robinson
Production Design: Waldemar Kalinowski
MPAA rating: R
Running time: 114 minutes

REVIEWS

Entertainment Weekly Online. September 16, 2008.
Hollywood Reporter Online. September 6, 2008.
Los Angeles Times Online. September 19, 2008.
New York Times Online. September 19, 2008.
Rolling Stone Online. September 18, 2008.
Time Online. September 19, 2008.
Variety Online. September 6, 2008.
Village Voice Online. September 16, 2008.
Wall Street Journal Online. September 19, 2008.

QUOTES

Virgil: "I don't kill people for a living. I enforce the law. Killing is sometimes a byproduct."
Everett: " Life has a way of making the foreseeable that which never happens...and the unforeseeable that which your life becomes."

Ed Harris originally intended his character to have hair and even selected a wig and screen tested it before deciding to play the part bald.

ASHES OF TIME REDUX

Two facts about *Ashes of Time Redux* are noteworthy. Because Wong Kar Wai is best known as a writer-director of lushly romantic films (e.g. *In the Mood for Love* [2000], his approach to a martial arts saga is interesting, as is his desire to reinvent one of his earliest films. The original *Ashes of Time* (1994) began shooting in 1992 after Wong had directed only two previous films, so when he discovered several versions, some pirated, for sale in Asian DVD markets, Wong decided to create a definitive version, enhancing the images and adding a new musical score. The result is definitely a Wong Kar Wai film: elliptical, visually ravishing at times, and frequently strange. *Ashes of Time Redux* is primarily an experience for the eyes and ears, but it often engages emotions as well.

The main fault of *Ashes of Time Redux,* noted by both admiring and disappointed reviewers, is that its plot lacks coherence. The film is loosely based on the novel *The Eagle-Shooting Heroes* (1957-1959), a sword epic by Louis Cha, the world's best-selling martial arts novelist. Because the novel had already been adapted several times, Wong uses only the names of Cha's characters, creating a view of their earlier lives. Set in a Chinese desert sometime in the distant past, *Ashes of Time Redux* presents Ouyang Feng (Leslie Cheung), an agent for hired killers living a self-imposed exile after the woman (Maggie Cheung) he loves spurns him to marry his brother. Ouyang narrates accounts of the adventures of his swordsmen in five chapters that correspond to the five seasons of the Chinese almanac, with the second spring section bringing the story full circle.

His rival, Huang Yaoshi (Tony Leung Ka Fai), and two of his killers, Hong Qi (Jacky Cheung) and the Blind Swordsman (Tony Leung Chiu Wai), have also been unlucky in love. Huang promises Murong Yang (Brigitte Lin) that he will marry the man's sister, Murong Yin (also played by Brigitte Lin), only to abandon her. Murong Yang wants Ouyang to have Huang killed, while Murong Yin wants her brother killed to protect Huang. Murong Yin eventually reveals that she has been pretending to be her brother. A young peasant woman (Charlie Young) who can pay only in eggs wants revenge against the bandits who killed her brother. The Blind Swordsman and Hong Qi take up her cause, with disastrous results causing the film's two main martial arts sequences. There are also glimpses of the Blind Swords-

man's lost love (Carina Lau), involving remarkably lit shots of her hugging her horse while standing in a stream. Throughout *Ashes of Time Redux*, it is often difficult to determine the characters' interactions and motivations because the various strands of the story overlap and intertwine. The plot arc and character motivations become clearer, however, upon a second viewing.

In 1998 Wong retrieved his original negatives of *Ashes of Time* from a bankrupt Hong Kong film-processing laboratory, where they had been stored only to be shocked by how the neglected negatives were disintegrating. He then spent five years tracking down other prints of the film, which he restored and re-edited while digitally altering the color images shot by Christopher Doyle, his longtime cinematographer. *Ashes of Times Redux* is ten minutes shorter than the original version partly because of the unavailability of usable footage. Wong is notorious for endlessly tinkering with his films, taking five years to shoot *2046* (2004). He took two years to make the original *Ashes of Time*, which was shown in the United States only in Chinese-language theaters, revising the screenplay to accommodate the availability of his actors and taking three months off to write and direct *Chungking Express* (1994), his breakthrough film with international audiences.

The swordfights in *Ashes of Time Redux* are not typical of those in Asian action films. Instead of placing the camera so that it will catch all the movements of the combatants, Wong thrusts it into the action, comparable to what Orson Welles did in *Chimes at Midnight* (1967). These shots are presented in an odd slow motion, sometimes resembling a series of still shots rather than continuous motion. The images are also blurred, with streaks of color seemingly added to magnify the overall chaotic effect.

The Wong-Doyle collaborations are known for their saturated colors. In his restoration, Wong has enhanced the original colors to make them seem even more unearthly. For example, the sands of the Gobi Desert take on a variety of unnatural shades of orange and yellow, and a cloudy sky becomes a mixture of blue tones. Much of *Ashes of Time Redux* suggests that Wong and Doyle are treating the film primarily as a palette on which to impose striking images. One of the most unusual images is made up of shadows created by a spinning bird cage, with an elaborate pattern of constantly changing lines playing across Murong Yin's face. Because the image is more compelling than the lines being delivered by Murong Yin and Ouyang, Wong seems to suggest that his visual artistry has supplanted the significance of the narrative. In other words, it is not particularly important that *Ashes of Time Redux* is difficult to understand. Lin told Scarlet Cheng of the *New*

York Times that she did not understand the film in 1994 but realized in 2008 that it is about love.

Wong has also altered Frankie Chan's original score by adding pieces by Roel García, Chan's frequent collaborator. Many martial arts films have been heavily influenced by westerns, and this new score often echoes the music Ennio Morricone composed for Sergio Leone westerns, particularly *Once Upon a Time in the West* (1968). Wong has described the film as a synthesis of both Leone and William Shakespeare. As acknowledged by Cha, the assumed and blurred identities of the characters derive specifically from Shakespeare. The score features performances by world-renowned cellist Yo-Yo Ma, who recorded a collection of Morricone's music in 2004. The plaintive sound of Ma's cello contributes to the otherworldliness of *Ashes of Time Redux* and underscores the essential loneliness of its characters.

Ashes of Time Redux will likely disappoint martial arts fans because the action is too abstract and the violence not graphic enough, though Wong's fans may find the spurts of blood too gory. Yet this film is unlike any other in its genre or in Wong's own oeuvre. It is "a hallucination masquerading as motion picture," noted John Anderson of the *Washington Post*. The images are consistently breathtaking, and few directors have Wong's skill at eliciting a range of emotions simply by training the camera on the faces of the actors; the long, forlorn gaze at Maggie Cheung near the end of the film is especially noteworthy. While *Ashes of Time Redux* may be enigmatic, it is nevertheless a fascinating look at memory, love, loss, and betrayal.

Michael Adams

CREDITS

Ouyang Feng: Leslie Cheung
Brother's Wife: Maggie Cheung
Murong Yin/Murong Yang: Brigitte Lin
Peach Blossom: Carina Lau
Huang Yaoshi: Tony Leung Ka-Fai
Hung Qi: Jacky Cheung
Blind Swordsman: Tony Leung Chiu-Wai
Origin: Hong Kong
Language: Chinese
Released: 2008
Production: Jeff Lau, Kar-Wai Wong; Block 2 Pictures Inc., Jet Tone Productions, Beijing Film Studio, Scholar Film Co.; released by Sony Pictures Classics
Directed by: Wong Kar-Wai
Written by: Wong Kar-Wai
Cinematography by: Christopher Doyle
Music by: Wu Tong

Editing: Patrick Tam
Production Design: William Chang
MPAA rating: R
Running time: 93 minutes

REVIEWS

Entertainment Weekly Online. October 7, 2008.
Hollywood Reporter Online. May 19, 2008.
Los Angeles Times Online. October 10, 2008.
New York Times Online. October 5, 10, 2008.
Variety Online. May 20, 2008.
Village Voice Online. October 8, 2008.

QUOTES

Ouyang Feng: "The root of man's problems is memory."

AUSTRALIA

Box Office: $49.3 million

As wondrous as the world seemed over the rainbow, what Dorothy Gale learned while there was that "there's no place like home." To Baz Luhrmann, however, Oz is home, an endlessly enchanting, magnificent place unlike any other, where the dreams that he dared to dream really did begin to come true. For those unfamiliar with nicknames for Australia other than "The Land Down Under," the country is also referred to as Oz, a shortened version of the correctly pronounced term for its citizens. Luhrmann's beloved homeland is the only nation that is also a continent, so it is not entirely surprising that his cinematic ode to it also covers a large territory.

Remembering sweeping epics that awed, exhilarated, and ultimately influenced him, Luhrmann wanted to apply that grand treatment to a story set upon his nation's red soils and steeped in its rich history and fascinating multiculturalism. The director-writer-producer repeatedly—and absolutely correctly—peppered descriptions of the film *Australia* with words like "heightened" and "amplified," as it attempts to thrill viewers with the following and more: a romance sealed with clinches in the pouring rain and silhouetted against colorful sunsets; a rough-hewn, dashing hero stirringly astride a rearing steed; blatantly evil, land-grabbing, moneyed schemers who will stop at nothing; an obviously computer-generated sea of cattle thunderously stampeding toward a cliff; nightmarish destruction and chaos caused by barbarous Japanese invaders; and a heart-melting little member of Australia's "Stolen Generation," who is outrageously dragged off to a mission to have the virtues of his white ancestors enhanced and the black bred out of him. All this is captured by a camera that repeatedly swoops down, glides across, and/or soars upward to reveal a landscape that is sometimes brutally desolate, at other times beautifully resplendent, but always breathtakingly stunning.

All of *Australia*'s purposefully-rousing components are from a time and place, viewers are told, that simply brimmed with "adventure and romance," and they are crammed into a tightly edited, three-hour film. The film repeatedly mentions the Aboriginal coming-of-age tradition known as "walkabout," and more than a few viewers may have needed a little walking of their own. However, despite its long-windedness and machinations that make the outcome thoroughly predictable if the viewer has seen any of the many movies (including *The Wizard of Oz* [1939]) from which Luhrmann has drawn inspiration, *Australia* offers viewers sustained (if superficial) old-style entertainment.

Repeated, long shots of windblown sands remind viewers not only of David Lean's *Lawrence of Arabia* (1962) but also of how often *Australia*'s tone shifts. The film is unified by the engaging voiceover narration of Nullah (new discovery Brandon Walters), a boy who is half-Caucasian and half-Aborigine, and entirely frightened of being taken away from his mother to be made into "a white fella." The film partly aims to educate its viewers about the Australian government's long-time policy of seizing children born from illegal biracial relationships, a practice thought to be morally and socially positive because it involved "salvaging" those considered to be semi-savages. Amazingly, this practice did not stop until 1973, and was not apologized for until 2008, so as a sort of cinematic mea culpa for such shamefulness, the indigenous inhabitants who were treated as subhuman are presented by Luhrmann as almost superhuman, majestic possessors of special, even magical, abilities. The primary representative of that culture and purveyor of such powers is Nullah's spear-carrying, flamingo-stanced Aboriginal grandfather and ever-present guardian angel, King George (David Gulpilil, who starred in Nicolas Roeg's moving tale of the Outback, *Walkabout* [1971]). Early on, as possible abductors approach, King George protectively urges the child to hide in a stream whose waters turn a sickening crimson after an impaled man falls in near the poor child. Especially when Nullah is portrayed by doe-eyed, adorable Walters, the challenges he faces appear to be quite sobering.

Australia often veers toward comedy, some of it broad—the last word to describe aristocratically upright and uptight Lady Sarah Ashleigh (Nicole Kidman) in her presence. Arriving in Australia from England in 1939 to speak to her husband about finances (and possibly also philandering) at their massive, isolated cattle ranch appropriately called Faraway Downs, the comely woman receives a gently but not exactly gentlemanly boost to her bottom while disembarking. Looking ridiculously overdressed in her parasol-shaded finery and possessing a crisp manner, her back ramrod-straight and her walk brisk, Sarah is a chortle-inducing fish out of water. (Nullah calls her "the strangest woman I've ever seen," who is obviously "not from this land.") When Sarah makes connections with the Drover (well-cast Hugh Jackman), the ruggedly handsome, steadfastly independent freelance cattle driver utilized in season by her husband, he is in the midst of a less-than-decorous barroom brawl, during which a piece in her parade of luggage bursts open to mortifyingly reveal stuffy Sarah's stash of undies for all to see. She sputters, utterly aghast; he merely welcomes her to Australia and spits.

As their subsequent trek out to Faraway Downs quickly and humorously sketches, these two as polar opposites, each with a fairly equal amount of disdain for the other. The viewer cannot help but think of the early interactions between Katharine Hepburn's Rose Sayer and Humphrey Bogart's Charlie Allnut as they traversed another continent's inhospitable environs in *The African Queen* (1951). In that film as in this one, sparks caused by friction precede those that ignite love. When Sarah gets an eyeful of the Drover's impressively-sculpted musculature during an open-air shower, it appears the seeds for adoration's eventual bloom have been successfully planted.

Upon finding out that her husband was the aforementioned skewered individual erroneously reported to have been killed by King George, Sarah takes command, firing traitorous, treacherous station manager Neil Fletcher (an especially over-the-top David Wenham) and defiantly declaring that she will not let greedy meanie King Carney (Bryan Brown) add Faraway Downs to his near-monopolistic cattle ranching empire. (Nullah now smilingly refers to her as "Mrs. Boss.") After the lovable boy's mother drowns while trying to hide him in a water tank, Sarah's heart and general iciness begin to melt. Kidman is particularly effective and affecting as her character, who will never be able to have offspring of her own, awkwardly presses forward in attempting to console the newly orphaned child, revealing hitherto undetected warmth as she does her best to relate the story of *The Wizard of Oz* and sing its most famous song. As the *Wall Street Journal*'s Joe Morgenstern rightly pointed out, Luhrmann goes on to belabor the *Oz* stuff at least as badly as Steven Spielberg did with his Pinocchio references in *Artificial Intelligence: A.I.* (2001).

Next, with its cattle drive to outmaneuver Carney and Fletcher across extremely hazardous, arid expanses, *Australia* echoes the great Hollywood Westerns by directors like John Ford and Howard Hawks, particularly the latter's *Red River* (1948). Working together with (and earning the surprised admiration of) the Drover as part of a stopgap, eclectic crew that also includes an enthusiastic little Nullah, Sarah is further transformed, her flawless, alabaster skin now a healthy tan and grimy, her hair and her attitude now noticeably, appealingly more relaxed. When they succeed against all odds (with key help from Nullah's mystical gifts), their triumph is accompanied by emotive music that has swelled up before and will do so numerous times again. Later, the rains come and Faraway Downs greens back up, representing how Sarah, along with the still-bitter, widowed Drover, has been transformed by love, Australian beauty, and providence.

Other films might have ended with Sarah as a new woman and with the cattle ranch's solvency secured, but *Australia* continues with scenes reminiscent of the ups and finally downs of Scarlett and Rhett in *Gone with the Wind* (1939), on its way to becoming yet another genre: war drama. Luhrmann, with camera shaking as it captures explosions and confusion, gives a full-bodied (if formulaic) recreation of the February 1942 Japanese air bombardment that decimated the Northern Australian settlement of Darwin. A heartsick Sarah went there to be closer to Nullah, who had been taken to a nearby island mission that was also attacked. This event allows the Drover to heroically find and rescue his pseudo-son (suspense about Nullah's survival is nullified if the viewer remembers that he is the narrator), and sets up their pleasantly-moving reunification with Sarah, three members of a makeshift family who feared they would never see the others again.

One of *Australia*'s most powerful and haunting shots is that in which primitive-looking King George incredulously surveys the destruction the bombers have wrought, an apparent questioning by Luhrmann of the nature of civility. One doubts it is an accident that the Aboriginal man is often seen perched higher than the other characters, as if Luhrmann aims to reverentially place him upon a pedestal of honor. In the end, Sarah tearfully relents to being separated once again from Nullah as he leaves for his walkaboutl She does not want to ressemble in any way those people who so reprehensibly tried to cut off such children from their Aboriginal roots.

To some, Luhrmann's epic increasingly lagged, like a New York-Sydney flight. Indeed, even in its last minutes, there are multiple times when the viewer is certain that the film has come to a satisfactory conclusion, only to have it continue. Perhaps because of its intimidating length or the mixed reviews it received, *Australia*, made on a budget that ballooned to $130 million, struggled to gross a third of that amount. While the alcoholic Faraway Downs accountant (Jack Thomp-

son) suffers early on from having taken too much in, Luhrmann's epic homage, many thought, predominantly suffers in the end from having taken too much on.

David L. Boxerbaum

CREDITS

Lady Sarah Ashley: Nicole Kidman
The Drover: Hugh Jackman
Neil Fletcher: David Wenham
King Carney: Bryan Brown
Kipling Flynn: Jack Thompson
Dutton: Ben Mendelsohn
King George: David Gulpilil
Magarri: David Ngoombujarra
Sing Song: Yuen Wah
Administrator Allsop: Barry Otto
Dr. Barker: Bruce Spence
Nullah: Brandon Walters
Brandy: Lillian Crombie
Origin: Australia, USA, Great Britain
Language: English
Released: 2008
Production: Baz Luhrmann, G. Mac Brown, Catherine Knapman; Bazmark, Dune Entertainment, Ingenious Film Partners; released by 20th Century-Fox
Directed by: Baz Luhrmann
Written by: Baz Luhrmann, Stuart Beattie, Ronald Harwood, Richard Flanagan
Cinematography by: Mandy Walker
Music by: David Hirschfelder
Sound: Guntis Sics
Editing: Dody Dorn, Michael McCusker
Art Direction: Karen Murphy
Costumes: Catherine Martin
Production Design: Catherine Martin
MPAA rating: PG-13
Running time: 165 minutes

REVIEWS

Boston Globe Online. November 26, 2008.
Chicago Sun-Times Online. November 25, 2008.
Entertainment Weekly Online. November 25, 2008.
Hollywood Reporter Online. November 18, 2008.
Los Angeles Times Online. November 26, 2008.
New York Times Online. November 26, 2008.
Rolling Stone Online. December 11, 2008.
San Francisco Chronicle. November 26, 2008, p. E1.
Time Online. November 25, 2008.
Variety Online. November 19, 2008.
Washington Post. November 26, 2008, p. C1.

QUOTES

Lady Sarah Ashley: "A woman? I suppose you think I should be back in Darwin, at the church fete or a lady's whatever you call it. Well I will have you know, I am as capable as any man."

TRIVIA

No less than fifteen production babies were born to cast and crew, one being Kidman's own daughter, during the lengthy shoot.

AWARDS

Nomination:

Oscars 2008: Costume Des.

B

BABY MAMA

Would you put your eggs...in this basket?
—Movie tagline

Box Office: $60.4 million

Tina Fey will be better remembered for her inspired impersonation of groundbreaking Republican Vice-Presidential nominee Sarah Palin in 2008 than for the release of the pedestrian romantic comedy *Baby Mama*. The film deals with issue of working women delaying motherhood to the point that they may no longer be able to conceive naturally and the modern solution of paying a surrogate mother—the ultimate in "outsourcing," as one character puts it, in a nation consumed by it. Much of the humor that could be wrung from the timely and widespread topic, however, is overshadowed by the over-the-top culture clash comedy that the film favors.

The amusing title is urban slang for an unmarried woman who has child, and the film has fun gender-bending the definition, which usually involves a man writing a check to the mother of his child rather than a woman paying her female surrogate, as in this case. Tina Fey plays the upscale Philadelphia, organic foods executive Kate Holbrook and her "baby mama" is Amy Poehler's working-class Angie Ostrowiski, whom she hires through the exclusive Chaffee Bicknell agency. Fey and Poehler, both extremely funny and talented, have innate chemistry and a familiarity from their years together on *Saturday Night Live*. Fey is the more conservative of the two in acting and comedy style and, accordingly, her character Kate is the more believable and more realistically written. Poehler's more raucous comedic approach

is not well served by her two-dimensional character Angie, who is reduced to being defined by her typical, no-good, cheating common law husband and her devotion to *America's Funniest Home Videos*. Her extremely flimsy character also undermines the emotional impact of the bonding the women are supposed to experience during the pregnancy.

While the main thrust of the plot is that these two very different women are united by the universal miracle of birth, the film requires more conflict and takes a wrong turn by inserting a ill-conceived and half-heartedly executed plot twist. After Angie is implanted with Kate's fertilized eggs, she does not become pregnant but reluctantly pretends as if she is so that she and her common law husband Carl (Dax Shepard) can cash the hefty checks. Angie's guilt is further exacerbated by the fact that she has moved in with Kate after leaving Carl for cheating on her. Only Oscar (an excellent Romany Malco), the building's impudent-but-wise doorman suspects the truth. Angie almost confesses to Kate during her first ultrasound examination but to her surprise, finds that she is, in fact, pregnant—after learning Kate's embryo failed to impregnate her, she and Carl had sex. Angie finally tells the truth at Kate's family gathering, and they all wind up in court to determine paternity and discover Carl is the father. The final plot thread has the despondent Kate finding out that she inadvertantly became pregnant after sleeping with her budding love interest (an underused Greg Kinnear), and the final credits roll to a montage of Angie and Kate on an outing with their newborns.

Former *Saturday Night Live* writer and contributor to the *Austin Powers* franchise, writer-director Michael

McCullers too often falls back on polarizing stereotypes to underscore the clash of cultures humor. The scenes showing the two women living together at Kate's home are of the typical, banal "odd couple" variety. Super-organized Kate brings home organic fare for Angie to eat and is shocked to see her eating junk food and chugging Red Bull. While Kate frets over which high-end baby carriage to buy and the nuances of natural childbirth, Angie watches *America's Funniest Home Videos* and sticks gum under Kate's expensive reclaimed barn wood table.

The film is at its funniest during scenes that include its venerable supporting actors with whom both Fey and Poehler have a winning rapport. Sigourney Weaver plays the far over-the-hill agency head Chaffee Bicknell who, despite being in her fifties, is still more than able to conceive naturally, much to the horror of the younger women around her. When she announces she is expecting again, Kate mumbles, "Expecting what? A Social Security check?" When Chaffee tells her the cost of a surrogate is $100,000, Kate quips, "It costs more to have someone born than to have someone killed!," and Chaffee replies, "It takes longer." Steve Martin delivers the biggest laughs, though, donning a hilarious wig with a long, gray ponytail as Kate's uber-New Age boss Barry. When Kate performs particularly well, Barry says earnestly, "Congratulations, Kate. I want to reward you with five minutes of uninterrupted eye contact." Seeing writer-actor Martin locking eyes with writer-actor Fey for seconds on end feels like a sort of passing of the comedic torch.

Hilary White

CREDITS

Kate Holbrook: Tina Fey
Angie Ostrowiski: Amy Poehler
Rob: Greg Kinnear
Carl: Dax Shepard
Oscar: Romany Malco
Rose: Holland Taylor
Chaffee Bicknell: Sigourney Weaver
Caroline: Maura Tierney
Barry: Steve Martin
Birthing Teacher: Siobhan Fallon Hogan
Origin: USA
Language: English
Released: 2008
Production: Lorne Michaels, John Goldwyn; Relativity Media; released by Universal
Directed by: Michael McCullers
Written by: Michael McCullers

Cinematography by: Daryn Okada
Music by: Jeff Richmond
Sound: Allan Byer
Music Supervisor: Kathy Nelson
Editing: Bruce Green
Art Direction: David Swayze
Costumes: Renee Ehrlich Kalfus
Production Design: Jess Gonchor
MPAA rating: PG-13
Running time: 99 minutes

REVIEWS

Boston Globe Online. April 24, 2008.
Chicago Sun-Times Online. April 25, 2008.
Hollywood Reporter Online. April 21, 2008.
Los Angeles Times Online. April 25, 2008.
New York Times Online. April 25, 2008.
New Yorker Online. April 28, 2008.
San Francisco Chronicle. April 25, 2008, p. E1.
Variety Online. April 20, 2008.
Washington Post. April 25, 2008, p. C1.

QUOTES

Angie Ostrowiski: "Can I just spray a little PAM down there right before the baby comes out?"

TRIVIA

When Angie goes into labor, Kate drives her to the hospital and they can be seen driving over the Benjamin Franklin Bridge to Camden, New Jersey. Later, they arrive at the University of Pennsylvania Hospital.

BABYLON A.D.

Box Office: $22.5 million

The quick-paced storyline and confusing denouement of *Babylon A.D.* did not help this film compete against such summer box office blockbusters as *The Dark Knight* and *Iron Man*. In fact, some viewers wondered if they were watching the top contender for the Razzie Awards.

Mercenary bad boy Toorop (Vin Diesel) lives in a post-apocalyptic Slavic dystopia where chaos is the norm and inhabitants wander around aimlessly in a seemingly endless, dirty third world market. He has been conscripted by Russian underworld heavy Gorsky (Gérard Depardieu) to protect and transport a "package," which turns out to be a gifted young woman named Aurora (French actress Mélanie Thierry). The mysterious girl has been brought up in a convent by a religious order of nuns, the Noelites, and Gorsky has strong-armed Toorop to guide Aurora, accompanied by a nun, Sister Rebeka (Michelle Yeoh) to New York City, where the young woman is to be given over to a strange new cult. Gorsky informs Toorop that he will be paid a high commission for his services—enough to leave the anarchic slum behind him. This serves as Toorop's sole motivation. Toorop is portrayed as a cold, efficient killing machine, but as the story progresses, he begins to thaw. The rough on the outside, soft on the inside characterization is given a clichéd gloss in this film, and Diesel's delivery is bereft of subtlety and nuance.

During their travel, Toorop discovers that Aurora is a human anomaly, a product of genetic engineering. She exhibits precognition and displays inexplicable abilities given her sheltered upbringing in the convent; for example, she is able to operate a submarine when distraught about seeing refugees being slaughtered who were attempting to gain transport like herself. Sister Rebeka informs Toorop that Aurora was able to speak at age two. This does not impress Toorop, who tells her that in and of itself he does not consider speaking at such a young age unusual. The nun adds that as a tot Aurora spoke nineteen languages without being formally exposed to them.

Once arriving in New York City, the trio discovers that the convent in Kazakhstan was bombed shortly after their departure. Aurora also informs them that she is pregnant with twins despite being a virgin—knowledge the girl simply intuits. Outside their hotel room, they see two groups of heavily armed men: Gorsky's thugs as well as a brigade of Noelites. The High Priestess of the Noelite Church (Charlotte Rampling) commands Toorop to bring the girl to a waiting convoy outside. Using his extensive fighting skills, Toorop initiates a battle. and soon the city street erupts into a barrage of automatic gunfire and explosions. During the battle Sister Rebeka is mortally wounded. Sustaining a fatal wound himself, Toorop is "cybernetically resurrected" and rebuilt by Dr. Arthur Darquandier (Lambert Wilson), who the viewer learns is Aurora's father. Originally working for the Noelites, he had Aurora programmed to become pregnant at a specific time because the cult intended to use Aurora's miraculous virgin birth to validate their faith and thus elevate it to the status of a legitimate religion.

During the film, the viewer feels a distinct sense of cinematic déjà vu—for good reason. The plot brazenly follows the same ideas and progression as Alfonso Cuarón's *Children of Men* (2006). Moreover, while the visual of a futuristic New York City is stunning, complete with its array of glutted neon signs and anachronistic architecture, it is only a slight tweaking of the Los Angeles setting in Ridley Scott's *Blade Runner*

(1982). Perhaps the most blatant piracy is in the film's ending, when Toorop approaches the late Aurora's twin girls who are enjoying a beautiful summer day on a pastoral landscape. Taking them by the hand, he walks them to an idyllic countryside cottage and tells them, "There's a storm coming." The exact same last line was used by Sarah Conner in James Cameron's *The Terminator* (1984). It is as if *Babylon A.D.* director Mathieu Kassovitz decided to simply cut and paste sections of past science fiction films he admired onto his own work and pass it off as an original.

David Metz Roberts

CREDITS

Toorop: Vin Diesel
Aurora: Melanie Thierry
Gorsky: Gerard Depardieu
Neolite Priestess: Charlotte Rampling
Finn: Mark Strong
Darquandier: Lambert Wilson
Sister Rebecca: Michelle Yeoh
Killa: Jerome Le Banner
Origin: France, USA
Language: English
Released: 2008
Production: Ilan Goldman; StudioCanal, M6 Films; released by 20th Century-Fox
Directed by: Mathieu Kassovitz
Written by: Mathieu Kassovitz, Eric Besnard
Cinematography by: Thierry Arbogast
Music by: Atli Örvarsson
Sound: John Rodda
Editing: Benjamin Weill
Art Direction: John King
Costumes: Chattoune
Production Design: Sonja Klaus, Paul Cross
MPAA rating: PG-13
Running time: 90 minutes

REVIEWS

Boston Globe Online. August 30, 2008.
Entertainment Weekly Online. August 29, 2008.
Hollywood Reporter Online. August 29, 2008.
New York Times Online. August 30, 2008.
Variety Online. August 20, 2008.

QUOTES

Toorop: "Look lady, I'm just a delivery boy and to me you're just a package. I'm not your friend, I'm not your brother,

I'm not your boyfriend. In six days I'm gonna deliver you and never see you again."

TRIVIA

The studio supposedly apparently cut 70 minutes from the film, against director Mathieu Kassovitz's wishes to get to a running time of 93 minutes.

BALLAST

Watching Lance Hammer's highly acclaimed debut film *Ballast* is a dark, painful experience, but one that is ultimately rewarding enough, or at least haunting enough, to recommend. There is less joy and hope on display in this talented new voice's examination of the often-ignored residents of the United States than arguably any film released in 2008. Hammer's film is a memorable visit with the people who live near the freeway exits that most drivers speed by on their way to somewhere else. A deep sadness pervades the characters of *Ballast,* a melancholy that feels completely genuine and never manipulative. Thus Hammer gives resonance to the forgotten people of the country in a way that very few writer-directors have been able to do. Yet while these people be forgotten, Hammer's film is surely memorable.

Just before the action of *Ballast* begins, an overweight man named Lawrence (Micheal J. Smith, Sr.) has suffered the emotional tragedy of his twin brother's suicide. Silently, Lawrence sits in the small living room of his brother's home as his sibling's body decays in the adjacent bedroom. It seems possible that Lawrence would sit there until he himself died, if not for the concern of a neighbor, who comes to check on him. Forced to face the reality of what has happened, Lawrence, who ran a convenience store with his twin brother, immediately goes next door to his own house and shoots himself in the chest.

Lawrence survives the attempted suicide and decides to contact his deceased brother's ex-wife Marlee (Tarra Riggs) to let her know about his brother's death and that she now has some rights to the property he co-owned and the store they worked in together. Marlee has some serious problems of her own. She has a very troubled pre-teen son named James (JimMyron Ross), who has become so bored by his lackluster life that he has decided to experiment with crack and gotten into some trouble with local drug dealers. Marlee works cleaning toilets and can barely make ends meet.

When James discovers Lawrence's existence, he robs his uncle at gunpoint, but, recognizing the pain in his nephew's eyes, Lawrence does not overreact. After a violent encounter with drug dealers looking for the James, Marlee and her son move into the home owned by her ex-husband. Here these three incredibly damaged souls—Lawrence, Marlee, and James—try to deal with depression, boredom, poverty, and the demons of their past. The three primary characters in *Ballast* are not looking for what could be called "typical movie happiness." Like many people, they are merely looking for a reason to keep going. They are the "ballast" of humanity. They are weight, not cargo, on this ship called Earth, and they are looking for a reason to stay on board.

Lance Hammer has made a poetic film that offers very little hope or redemption and is almost erringly bleak in its depiction of life without even a hint of a smile. *Ballast* is a brutal, depressing film that borders on audience torture. Because he strives for cinematic poetry over traditional prose, the result is one of the most depressing films in years but also one that has undeniable lingering power that often fails to register in many similarly bleak motion pictures. Reminiscent of David Gordon Green's *George Washington* (2000), *Ballast* sometimes gives the impression that Hammer is trying a little too hard to be "dramatically important" by sacrificing consistency for poetry's sake. Although the film is too consciously artistic to be considered straight realism, the material is so dark that it certainly would never be categorized as escapist entertainment.

Despite the sensation that Hammer may be trying too hard when it comes to the film's more depressing beats, for lack of a less critically overused phrase, *Ballast* works because the film is ultimately so incredibly haunting. Lawrence, Marlee, and James linger in the mind much longer than most movie characters. It is ironic that a film about forgotten convenience store workers and bathroom cleaners in the United States would be so memorable, but *Ballast* is just such a film. After hundreds of other films from 2008 have come and gone from the collective movie consciousness, the gentle voice of Lawrence, the sad eyes of James, and damaged psyche of Marlee will linger for years to come.

Brian Tallerico

CREDITS

Marlee: Tarra Riggs
James: JimMyron Ross
Lawrence: Michael J. Smith Sr.
John: Johnny McPhail
Origin: USA
Language: English

Released: 2008

Production: Lance Hammer, Nina Parikh; released by Alluvial Film Company

Directed by: Lance Hammer

Written by: Lance Hammer

Cinematography by: Lol Crawley

Sound: Sam Watson

Editing: Lance Hammer

Costumes: Caroline Eselin

Production Design: Jerel Levanway

MPAA rating: Unrated

Running time: 96 minutes

REVIEWS

Chicago Sun-Times Online. October 29, 2008.
Hollywood Reporter Online. January 20, 2008.
Los Angeles Times Online. November 7, 2008.
New York Times Online. October 1, 2008.
San Francisco Chronicle. October 17, 2008, p. E13.
Variety Online. January 19, 2008.
Village Voice Online. September 30, 2008.

AWARDS

Nomination:

Ind. Spirit 2009: Support. Actor (Ross), Actress (Riggs), Cinematog., Director (Hammer), Film, First Screenplay.

THE BAND'S VISIT
(Bikur Ha-Tizmoret)

Once—not long ago—a small Egyptian police band arrived in Israel. Not many remember this…It wasn't that important.
—Movie tagline

They came, they saw, they bridged a divide.
—Movie tagline

Box Office: $3 million

Eran Kolirin's *The Band's Visit* (also known as *Bikur Ha-Tizmoret*) was a small arthouse sensation after winning audience awards at the Munich and Warsaw Film Festivals in 2007 and getting a limited release in early 2008, but this heartfelt and believable gem deserved a much larger following and is likely to find one on DVD. Falling just short of perfection, *The Band's Visit* features the kind of heartwarming and cheerful story that builds positive word-of-mouth publicity. Only a small final act decision by Kolirin keeps *The Band's Visit* from becoming a true classic, but even that is a minor complaint for a very good film, one that is likely to find a loyal audience over the years.

The poignant *The Band's Visit* opens with the arrival of a very formal and almost old-fashioned Egyptian police band in Israel to play at the Arab Cultural Center. When no one is there to pick up the strangers in a strange land, a misunderstanding over the name of the small town that they are supposed to go to by bus takes the formal heroes to what is essentially the middle of nowhere. Stuck in a lonely, nearly desolate town named Bet Hatikva (as opposed to Petha Tiqva, which is where they should be), the eight men that make up the Alexandria Ceremonial Police Orchestra must spend the night in the middle of the Negev Desert. There are no hotels in this city, but the band is lucky enough to meet the lovely Dina (Ronit Elkabetz), who cooks them dinner in the restaurant she owns and arranges for the group to sleep at her apartment, her friend's apartment, and in the restaurant itself. Two of the band members, including the noble and polite leader Lieutenant-Colonel Tawfiq Zacharya (Sasson Gabai) and the younger, more rebellious Haled (Saleh Bakri) form a bond with Dina, while others share meals with their new cross-cultural friends and even go out dancing.

The Band's Visit is an exercise in subtlety. It could have easily become a generic fish-out-of-water comedy, but Kolirin refuses to take the easy outs of his genre, choosing to focus instead on comedic details instead of the broad strokes. Issues of age, sexuality, loneliness, and, of course, music come to the foreground, but they never feel forced. None of *The Band's Visit* feels overdone, and the entire cast, particularly Elkabetz and Gabai, are remarkably believable. There are wonderful moments in *The Band's Visit*—for example, a conversation on a park bench is one of the best scenes of the year—because both the script and the performances have a truthfulness that is absent from many contemporary films. Rare in modern cinema is a film that is truly heartwarming without ever being manipulative, and Kolirin achieves this quality with *The Band's Visit*. Despite such accolades, the film is not flawless. For instance, in the final act, a decision made by Dina simply does not ring true, yet it is a small misstep in an otherwise excellent screenplay.

Israel originally submitted *The Band's Visit* as the country's candidate for Foreign Language Film to the 80th Academy Awards®, but the film was deemed ineligible by the Academy of Motion Pictures Arts and Sciences because so much of it takes place in the English language. As in real life, the Egyptians in the band and the Israeli townspeople of Bet Hatikva speak English, so that is how they communicate through most of *The Band's Visit*. However, the film is clearly the type of movie that could have benefited from a major Academy Award® nomination, and the decision seemed somewhat arbitrary.

The Academy may have said no, but critics and audiences fell in love with *The Band's Visit*. Ray Bennett of the *Hollywood Reporter* put the film in the second slot on his best of 2007 list, and it also made lists for the *New York Post*, *LA Weekly*, and the *Associated Press*. Kolirin's heartfelt comedy has won over a dozen awards at festivals and the Awards of the Israeli Film Academy, which named the film the best of the year. At the website *Rotten Tomatoes*, which gathers the reviews of critics from around the world and assigns films a percentage of positive reviews, *The Band's Visit* garnered a stunningly rare ninety-eight percent. Although *The Band's Visit* may not have made the cut for the Academy of Motion Pictures Arts and Sciences, it has been accurately praised by nearly everyone else who has seen it.

Brian Tallerico

CREDITS

Tawfiq: Sasson Gabai
Dina: Ronit Elkabetz
Khaled: Saleh Bakri
Papi: Shlomi Avraham
Simon: Khalifa Natour
Itzik: Rubi Muscovich
Origin: France, Israel, USA
Language: English, Arabic, Hebrew
Released: 2007
Production: Eilon Ratzkovsky, Ehud Bleiberg, Yossi Uzrad, Kobi Gal-Raday, Guy Jacoel; July August Productions, Sophie Dulac Productions, Bleiberg Entertainment; released by Sony Pictures Classics
Directed by: Eran Kolirin
Written by: Eran Kolirin
Cinematography by: Shai Goldman
Music by: Habib Shehadeh Hanna
Sound: Itai Eloav
Editing: Arik Lahav Leibovitz
Costumes: Doron Ashkenzai
Production Design: Eitan Levi
MPAA rating: PG-13
Running time: 89 minutes

REVIEWS

Entertainment Weekly. January 15, 2008, p. 48.
Guardian Online. November 9, 2007.
Hollywood Reporter Online. May 20, 2007.
Los Angeles Times Online. December 7, 2007.
New York Times Online. December 7, 2007.
New Yorker Online. February 11, 2008.
Observer Online. November 11, 2007.

Variety Online. January 20, 2007.
Village Voice Online. December 4, 2007.
Wall Street Journal. February 8, 2008, p. W1.

BANGKOK DANGEROUS

There's only one way out.
　—Movie tagline
It's all in the execution.
　—Movie tagline

Box Office: $15.2 million

There is nothing wrong with filmmakers remaking their own films. Alfred Hitchcock drastically improved on *The Man Who Knew Too Much* (1934) with his 1956 remake because he was a much better director, as well as having a considerably larger budget. Although Danny Pang and Oxide Pang Chun, who appear in the credits as the Pang Brothers, have remade *Bangkok Dangerous* (1999) with an American movie star and a much larger budget, they appear to have had no motive beyond the financial.

As he explains in his voiceover narration, Joe (Nicolas Cage), an American hit man, goes to Bangkok following an assassination in Prague to complete his last assignment. Although screenwriter Jason Richman somewhat avoids the cliché of the killer who wants to relinquish his trade by assigning Joe four targets, most of the action that occurs upon Joe's arrival in Thailand is predictable.

Despite having worked alone in the past, Joe hires a local pickpocket, Kong (Shahkrit Yamnarm), to gather information about his hits from a dancer (Panward Hemmanee) at a nightclub. At the beginning of *Bangkok Dangerous*, Joe stated the four rules by which a paid assassin must operate, yet he violates them with ease. In addition, for no obvious reason he decides to make Kong his protégé, training him in hand-to-hand combat and shooting between the assignments. (The Pangs are rather vague about the passage of time.)

After Joe cuts his arm fleeing the scene of a hit, he meets and falls for Fon (Charlie Young), a deaf pharmacist, thereby violating another of his rules. Scenes of the two eating spicy food, feeding an elephant, and meeting Fon's mother are especially tedious. While the Pangs have some skill with action sequences, they are at a loss with domesticity. Because Joe recites his four rules twice, it becomes all too clear that his violations of them will have consequences, but, unfortunately, these consequences are not especially interesting.

In the 1999 version, Kong is the protagonist and deaf. Thus the audience watches Kong evolve into a killer and become torn between his violent and peaceful sides. Joe, on the other hand, seems such a hardened killer that it is difficult to reconcile his affection for Fon. Part of this lack of character plausibility resides with Cage, who while quite effective and charming in such films as *Raising Arizona* (1987) and *Adaptation* (2002), seems not be emotionally invested in other works, especially in his big-budget action films. It is easy to see why *Bangkok Dangerous* appealed to Cage, who is also one of the film's producers, because it offers another chance for him to play two characters (the killer and the lover) at once. In *Raising Arizona* he is both a career criminal and a would-be typical husband and father, and in *Adaptation* he plays brothers with conflicting personalities, while in *Face/Off* (1997) he is again both a ruthless criminal and an FBI agent posing as a criminal. Yet in *Bangkok Dangerous,* Joe's good-bad dichotomy is more sentimentality imposed upon a bloody action film than a philosophical statement about people's dual natures. Cage as Joe is simply not as interesting or as sympathetic as is Kong in the original version.

Alhough Owen Gleiberman of *Entertainment Weekly* gave *Bangkok Dangerous* an F rating, the film's major defect is not poor quality acting, but a lack of originality and energy. Even the chases and shootouts are mediocre. For example, a chase involving two boats and one motorcycle in a canal, meant to be a highpoint, is poorly edited, so that the viewer cannot easily follow the action. Decha Srimantra photographed both versions of the *Bangkok Dangerous,* giving a distinctive blue-gray sheen to the 2008 film, yet even his lighting is inconsistent during the canal scene. This overall cinematographic sloppiness is surprising because Danny Pang and Curran Pang previously co-edited one of the best Asian crime films, *Infernal Affairs* (2002). Fans of Asian crime are better off with the 1999 *Bangkok Dangerous,* which is not simply a payday for its participants.

Michael Adams

CREDITS

Joe London: Nicolas Cage
Fon: Charlie Yeung
Kong: Shahkrit Yamnarm
Aom: Panward Hemmanee
Chicago: James With
Aran: Dom Hetrakul
Police Van Driver: Philip Waley
Joe's Father: Shaun Delaney
Origin: USA
Language: English
Released: 2008

Production: William Sherak, Jason Shuman, Nicolas Cage, Norm Golightly; Blue Star Entertainment, Saturn Films, IEG Virtual Studios; released by Lionsgate
Directed by: Danny Pang, Oxide Pang
Written by: Jason Richman
Cinematography by: Decha Srimantra
Music by: Brian Tyler
Sound: Paul Clark
Editing: Mike Jackson, Curran Pang
Art Direction: Arin Pinijvararak
Costumes: Kristen M. Burke
Production Design: James William Newport
MPAA rating: R
Running time: 100 minutes

REVIEWS

Boston Globe Online. September 6, 2008.
Entertainment Weekly Online. September 5, 2008.
Hollywood Reporter Online. September 5, 2008.
New Yorker Online. September 8, 2008.
Variety Online. August 27, 2008.

QUOTES

Joe: "I was taught four rules…One: Don't ask questions. There is no such thing as right and wrong. Two: Don't take an interest in people outside of work. There is no such thing as trust. Three: Erase every trace. Come anonymous and leave nothing behind. Four: Know when to get out. Just thinking about it means it's time. Before you lose your edge, before you become a target."

TRIVIA

The picture was shooting during the Coup d'etat on September 19—filming was halted for only six hours.

THE BANK JOB

The true story of a heist gone wrong…in all the right ways.
—Movie tagline

Box Office: $30 million

Heist films come in several varieties. They can emphasize the process of planning or carrying out a grand-scale robbery, the glamour of getting away with a crime, the philosophical implications of the individual against the establishment, or the gritty consequences of such acts. *The Bank Job,* based on a real theft in London in 1971, tries to balance the first and last of these varieties and throws in an unusual plot development of which the thieves are unaware.

Terry Leather (Jason Statham) runs a garage and lives peacefully with his wife Wendy (Keeley Hawes) and their two young daughters. Then he is approached by Martine Love (Saffron Burrows), the former girlfriend of one of his mates, Kevin Swain (Stephen Campbell Moore). She wants Terry to rob a bank but is not quite honest with him. Martine has been arrested for trying to bring drugs into the country, and to clear herself she must work with British intelligence to steal incriminating photographs of an important personage from a safety deposit box. Princess Margaret, the most reckless member of the royal family, has been photographed having sex in the Caribbean.

Although Terry never quite trusts Martine, he could use the money from the haul and sets about enlisting a gang. In addition to Kevin, a photographer, the members are Dave Shilling (Daniel Mays), an actor, Guy Singer (James Faulkner), a shady character who can pass as a gentleman, and Bambas (Alki David), a professional criminal who knows how to tunnel into the bank vault. *The Bank Job* shifts between Terry and his gang, Tim Everett (Richard Lintern), the MI5 agent giving Martine her orders, Lew Vogel (David Suchet), an operator in prostitution and pornography who has numerous corrupt policemen on his payroll, and Michael X (Peter De Jersey), a black militant involved in drug smuggling and prostitution. Most of these characters and plots overlap at some point, as when Everett has a young agent, Gale Benson (Hattie Morahan), infiltrate Michael X's group.

The Bank Job offers two kinds of dramatic tension. There is the robbery itself, when Terry's friend Eddie (Michael Jibson) keeps watch from a nearby rooftop and talks to the thieves on a walkie-talkie. These conversations are accidentally intercepted by a ham radio operator (Alistair Petrie), who notifies the police. Roy Given (Gerard Horan), seemingly the only honest policeman in London, tries valiantly to find the location of the robbery-in-progress. After Given fails, the vicious Vogel enters the picture to try to force the thieves to turn over their loot. The ensuing violence may be seen by some as disruptive to the film's essentially lighthearted tone.

In *The Bank Job* the well-paced robbery sequence, the frequent humor, and the period details work well. The pubs, shops, and house of prostitution all seem authentic, as do the garish or painfully conservative clothing worn by most of the characters. The film demonstrates the gritty realism of British crime films of the period, for example, *Get Carter* (1971), as well as the groundbreaking television series *The Sweeney* (1975-1978). Screenwriters Dick Clement and Ian La Frenais, whose impressive credits include *The Commitments* (1991) and *Flushed Away* (2006), are ideal for such a subject. The pair wrote the charming heist comedy *The Jokers* (1967) and the violent gangster drama *Villain*

(1971), which has some similarities to *The Bank Job,* especially in the character of Vogel.

Director Ronald Donaldson has a reputation as a craftsman more than an artist, displaying a particular gift for heightening tension in such films as *No Way Out* (1987) and *Thirteen Days* (2000). Donaldson not only knows how to pace a film and cram considerable information into a frame, but he directs actors quite well. Statham, known primarily for his martial arts films, gives his first truly realized performance, suggesting Terry's ambivalence about his actions with small gestures. Suchet, miles away from his famous Hercule Poirot television performances, shows Vogel's conflicting pleasure and disgust at his behavior. If the world is corrupt, Vogel seems to be saying, I would be a fool not to be corrupt, too. Peter Bowles, another actor who has done his best work on television, helps make Everett's mean-spirited boss representative of the hypocrisy of those in power. Mays provides both comic relief and poignancy as the actor-thief who thinks he can use his theatrical skills to get out of any situation.

The Bank Job received generally glowing reviews because it embodies highly professional competence. The filmmakers knew what they wanted to achieve and took their audience along quickly on an exciting ride.

Michael Adams

CREDITS

Terry Leather: Jason Statham
Martine: Saffron Burrows
Dave: Daniel Mays
Lew Vogel: David Suchet
Tim Everett: Richard Lintern
Guy Singer: James Faulkner
Origin: Great Britain, USA
Language: English
Released: 2008
Production: Charles Roven, Steve Chasman; Mosaic Media Group, Relativity Media, Ominilab Media Group; released by Lions Gate Films
Directed by: Roger Donaldson
Written by: Dick Clement, Ian La Frenais
Cinematography by: Michael Coulter
Music by: J. Peter Robinson
Sound: Simon Hayes
Editing: John Gilbert
Art Direction: Phil Harvey, Mark Scruton
Costumes: Odile Dicks-Mireaux
Production Design: Gavin Bocquet
MPAA rating: R
Running time: 111 minutes

REVIEWS

Boston Globe Online. March 7, 2008.
Chicago Sun-Times Online. March 7, 2008.

Entertainment Weekly Online. March 5, 2008.
Hollywood Reporter Online. March 4, 2008.
Los Angeles Times Online. March 7, 2008.
New York Times Online. March 7, 2008.
Rolling Stone Online. March 20, 2008.
San Francisco Chronicle. March 7, 2008, p. E7.
Variety Online. February 28, 2008.
Wall Street Journal. March 7, 2008, p. W1.
Washington Post. March 7, 2008, p. C1.

QUOTES

Lew Vogel: "I think drugs are responsible for the moral decay of this country's young. Smut, smut, and more smut—that's my special area of interest."

TRIVIA

One of the most difficult scenes to film, according to director Roger Donaldson was the one in the brothel. The script called for the women to wear only garters. However, because most of the women had shaved their genitals (which would have been anachronistic for 1971), the actresses had to wear pubic wigs called "merkins" which were hard to secure in place and kept slipping off the actresses.

BATTLE IN SEATTLE

The whole world is watching.
    —Movie tagline

In late November, 1999, the World Trade Organization (WTO) convened at the Washington State Convention and Trade Center in Seattle, Washington to launch its millennial trade negotiations—the first ever conducted in the United States. These negotiations sparked unprecedented anti-economic globalization protests by more than 40,000 people who took to the streets surrounding the Washington State Convention and Trade Center in what is otherwise known as the Battle of Seattle. Irish actor Stuart Townsend's directorial debut, which he also wrote, is a fictional, dramatic account of these protests, which quickly turned from a peaceful demonstration into full-blown riots and widespread chaos.

The narrative echoes that of Paul Haggis's superior *Crash* (2004), another ensemble piece that simultaneously depicts a host of characters whose actions cause controversial and catastrophic events that affect the other characters in unexpected ways. Townsend tells his story through the protesters, police, local government figures, and WTO officials amid the protest, as well as seamlessly blending actual television footage of the events. His flawed but bold account clearly favors the protestors,

and in his attempt to portray these various groups diplomatically, Townsend's film appears to be too smooth and conventional for such an explosive story. Moreover, despite a brief prologue that attempts to demystify the WTO and why it attracted so many protestors, many viewers will need further research to understand the larger picture.

The vastly different protesters include Django (André Benjamin), Lou (Michelle Rodriguez), and Jay (Martin Henderson). The more radical Lou and one of the protest's leaders, Jay, find romance amid their dangerous mission to hang an anti-WTO banner from a crane. Their characters are poorly written clichés straight out of a 1940s romantic comedy; they alternately bicker about what tactics to use and praise each other's idealistic commitment to the cause, while simultaneously falling in love. The standout among the characters is the slick, black animal rights activist Django, played by the band OutKast's André Benjamin, who takes to the streets in a turtle costume.

Others join the cause at a later time: Jean (Connie Nielsen) is a television reporter who boldly eschews her station bosses' demands and joins the cause of the protesters after witnessing widespread police brutality; Sam (Jennifer Carpenter) is a lawyer who fights for the protesters' release from jail; and Dr. Maric (Rade Serbedzija), a member of Doctors Without Borders, scolds the WTO for its money-focused approach.

The windows of the department store where the five-months pregnant Ella (Charlize Theron) works are smashed during the protests, and while making her way home she is hit in the stomach by an errant police baton. Dale (Woody Harrelson), her sensitive policeman husband, is forced to continue to work, his pent-up rage causing him to beat up protester Jay (Martin Henderson) in a church into which Dale has chased him. The over-sentimental screenplay then makes the heinous error of Dale's later seeing the error of his way and tracking down Jay to apologize. Inexplicably, Jay accepts his apology. Like most of the protesters, Ella and Dale do not seem to be three-dimensional characters with actual lives; instead, they merely exist to further the viewpoint of the filmmaker and act as foils to other characters.

The film is less focused on Ray Liotta's peacemaking character Mayor Jim Tobin (a fictional version of Seattle's real-life then mayor Paul Schell), whom the federal government and the governor pressure to regain order. A former Vietnam War protestor, Tobin does not condone police violence but is forced to order mass arrests and eventually call in the National Guard. In reality, there was a tidal wave of negative publicity, and the 600 arrests that were made were later found to violate the protesters' Fourth Amendment rights. Although there was rampant police brutality, among the majority of peaceful protesters there was also a faction of anarchists who were not above using violence to achieve their ends.

Several critics compared Townsend's film with Haskell Wexler's much-preferred *Medium Cool* (1969) about the demonstrations at the 1968 Chicago Democratic National Convention in Chicago. The result of the protests in Seattle was that the November 30, 1999 WTO meeting did not take place as planned, and its free-trade agenda was seriously questioned. Depending on the viewer's opinion, Townsend has either made a movie that calls attention to an important U.S. political demonstration that may once again reinvigorate the debate on the global economy, development, and environmental issues—as he argues the real Battle in Seattle ultimately accomplished—or a film that glorifies anti-capitalist social revolutionaries. In a post-9/11 environment, for most people, it is simply a film that calls attention to the fact that the relatively obscure event took place at all.

Hilary White

CREDITS

Django: André Benjamin
Sam: Jennifer Carpenter
Lou: Michelle Rodriguez
Jay: Martin Henderson
Mayor Jim Tobin: Ray Liotta
Dale: Woody Harrelson
Ella: Charlize Theron
Jean: Connie Nielsen
Johnson: Channing Tatum
Abassi: Isaach de Bankole
Randall: Joshua Jackson
Dr. Maric: Rade Sherbedgia
Origin: USA
Language: English
Released: 2007
Production: Maxime Remillard, Stuart Townsend, Kirk Shaw, Mary Aloe; Remstar, Insight Film Studios, Proud Mary Entertainment; released by ThinkFilm, Redwood Palm Pictures
Directed by: Stuart Townsend
Written by: Stuart Townsend
Cinematography by: Barry Ackroyd
Music by: One Point Six
Sound: John Boyle
Editing: Fernando Villena
Art Direction: Kirston Franson
Costumes: Andres Des Roches
Production Design: Chris August

MPAA rating: R
Running time: 100 minutes

REVIEWS

Hollywood Reporter Online. September 14, 2007.
New York Times Online. September 19, 2008.
San Francisco Chronicle. September 19, 2008, p. E5.
Variety Online. September 11, 2007.
Village Voice Online. September 16, 2008.

BE KIND REWIND

You name it, we shoot it.
—Movie tagline

Box Office: $11.1 million

A paean to the power of filmmaking as a gateway to wonder and a reason to bring people together, *Be Kind Rewind* is well intentioned, but a squandered premise undermines what by all rights should be a delightful, powerful, and possibly hilarious movie. As helmed by Michel Gondry, the director behind the magnificent *Eternal Sunshine of the Spotless Mind* (2004) and the often maddening but fascinating *Science of Sleep* (2006), *Be Kind Rewind* is a fanciful amalgam of everyday people with unusual quirks who discover the power of community through both shared experience and common mythology. Although it exudes a genuine love of filmmaking, storytelling, and a do-it-yourself ethos, *Be Kind Rewind* falters due to its over-indulgence in sentimentality and its inability to find a through-line action capable of unifying (and justifying) its disparate elements.

The film stars Mos Def as Mike, who works at Mr. Fletcher's (Danny Glover) VHS-only video rental store in Passaic, New Jersey, called "Be Kind Rewind" (a reference to a sticker once put on rental videotapes, indicating to the customer that tapes should be rewound before returning them to the store). Mike's friend Jerry (Jack Black) loiters at the store, and both Mike and Jerry are captivated by Mr. Fletcher's story that legendary jazz pianist Fats Waller was born in the building. When the city threatens to demolish the store, Mr. Fletcher leaves on a trip to spy on a successful DVD chain in hopes of turning his business around to save the building. As Mr. Fletcher is leaving, he scrawls a backwards message to Mike on the window of the departing train to "Keep Jerry Out" of the video store, but it takes Mike quite awhile to figure out what Mr. Fletcher's message actually says. Meanwhile, Jerry, a conspiracy theorist, is convinced that the power plant near his trailer is melting his brain, and he tries to enlist Mike in a plan to sabotage the plant. Mike refuses, and when Jerry attempts to wreck the plant himself, Jerry receives a tremendous jolt of electricity and becomes magnetized. The next time Jerry enters the video store, he inadvertently erases all of the tapes, destroying Mr. Fletcher's entire inventory and possibly ruining his livelihood. When the store's best customer and Mr. Fletcher's friend, the eccentric Ms. Falewicz (Mia Farrow), comes in to borrow *Ghostbusters* (1984), Mike, who fears letting Mr. Fletcher down, decides to re-shoot Ghostbusters with Jerry, assuming that Ms. Falewicz is too eccentric to notice any difference. Mike and Jerry create a twenty-minute version of *Ghostbusters* using an old VHS video camera and ultra-cheap special effects. When other patrons come to the store with similar requests, Jerry and Mike do the same for other movies, including *The Lion King* (1994), *RoboCop* (1987), *2001: A Space Odyssey* (1968), and *Driving Miss Daisy* (1989), among others. As the films gain in popularity, Jerry and Mike charge extravagant fees for their rental, claiming that the tapes are from Sweden—soon patrons regularly ask for movies that have been "Sweded."

When Mr. Fletcher returns from his trip and finds out what has been happening, Mike and Jerry convince him that they should keep making the movies and use the money to pay for repairs to the building. Eventually, the entire town becomes involved in the filmmaking process (with everyone in town invested, the videos become more popular than ever), but this is short lived for an attorney (Sigourney Weaver) comes to town and, claiming copyright infringement, destroys all of the tapes. When city officials threaten to destroy the building that houses the store, Mr. Fletcher reveals that the Fats Waller story is a fabrication, one he kept telling because Mike loved it so much. Emboldened by their newfound ability to make movies, the neighbors make a film about the fictional life of Fats Waller and, at the screening, even the wrecking crew sent to destroy the building is moved by the homespun charm of the community's efforts.

Be Kind Rewind falls prey to a potential danger that exists in all of Michel Gondry's films: The quirky elements often threaten to overwhelm an otherwise charming film. In the case of *Be Kind Rewind,* the plot excesses hamper the narrative flow and render much of what should be funny about the film chuckle-worthy at best. The film is, after all, about what happens when all of the videotapes in a VHS rental store are erased and the store's lone employee and his friend decide to remake the movies themselves—the concep and even the term "Sweded" films are funny in their own right—and though some of the super-short remakes are in fact quite funny, they are the unusual bright spots in what is really a plodding film that explores what is lost in the usurpation of the old by the new and the necessity of com-

munity and shared stories. Perhaps the greatest flaw in *Be Kind Rewind* is the promise of its own potential: the movie has a proven director with a singular vision; the very premise of the movie seems tailor-made for laugh-out-loud hilarity (the notion of Jack Black and Mos Def in a film in which their characters must remake *Driving Miss Daisy* is a pitch-meeting image designed to get a project greenlit); and the cast is certainly equal to the film's premise. All of that potential is unfulfilled, however: Gondry is so interested in extolling the virtues of the do-it-yourself ethic that he neglects to make a film equal to his idealism; the premise of the movie itself is more humorous than the execution (it is definitely funnier to think about two guys having to remake *Men in Black* [1997] than actually seeing them do it—the "Sweded" concept is really more geared toward a viral YouTube phenomenon than a premise that would sustain a feature-length film); and the cast, by and large, seems at sea in a film of interesting ideas looking for a unifying force.

Furthermore, the fact that the excesses of *Be Kind Rewind* extend to the performances themselves worsens an already a hard-to-swallow jumble of ideas. The film's two leads, Jack Black and Mos Def, play the entire film as if they were handed an improv situation in a college acting class and were told not to drop the scene no matter what happens or no matter how strange it may be. Actors can occasionally pull off such demands in a way that at the very least makes an attempt to reflect (and in the process deflect) the viewer's potential resistance to the implausible—for instance, if a character in the film suddenly finds his brain magnetized due to an attempt to sabotage a power plant, it would do well for the characters to acknowledge that the incident is unusual and probably worthy of alarm. Yet when the film calls on the characters (and the actors and the audience) to unquestioningly accept the events as they happen, no matter how outrageous, it makes increasingly difficult for the actors and the audience to embrace constant leaps in logic. Black and Mos Def seem cut adrift in the world of *Be Kind Rewind*: Since the characters do not acknowledge the outrageousness of their circumstances, the actors are forced to play all of their scenes with a sort of relentlessness, almost to the point of desperation, to make themselves and the audience suspend disbelief. To their credit, Gondry and all of the actors put in an heroic effort to keep *Be Kind Rewind* focused on the film's central themes of the power of the imagination and the spirit of cooperation to bring communities together, the need for a shared mythology to bind us, and a general love for the filmmaking process (as well as the power of the filmed image to accomplish the exercise of imagination, bringing the community together, and creating shared mythology), but unfortunately the shoddy approach to *Be Kind Rewind*'s storytelling completely undermines these lofty goals, threatening to devalue them to the level of base sentimentality. If Gondry feels that this particular story is the most effective vehicle for his ideas about storytelling, mythology, and community, then the film should effortlessly convey those ideas in a powerful, indisputable way. Instead, the film's off-hand approach to its own oddity while pretending that the events it depicts are somehow grounded in an otherwise normal, everyday world creates a cognitive dissonance between what the audience is being told (filmmaking is a powerful conduit for expression and collective endeavor) and what it experiences (Gondry's ideas about the power of filmmaking appear in a film that fails to convincingly make a case for its own premise). If a film is going to make assertions about the power of filmmaking, then the film itself should be the very embodiment of those assertions.

The world of *Be Kind Rewind* is one that would be lovely to visit, even to strive for, were it not so clear that the film itself cannot entirely believe in the whimsy it espouses. The film is very sentimental and definitely has something of value to say about the power of movies to give expression to the imagination, but *Be Kind Rewind* suffers from incomplete ideas and a premise incapable of being effectively sustained for ninety minutes. Gondry's fancifulness works against him here—this is a story screaming for an anchor, but Gondry trusts his vision to the point of eschewing any prudent impulse to contain himself or his actors. *Be Kind Rewind* is not a bad film, but a "Sweded" version of it would probably make its case more effectively, and would almost certainly be funnier.

John Boaz

CREDITS

Jerry: Jack Black
Mike: Mos Def
Mr. Fletcher: Danny Glover
Miss Falewicz: Mia Farrow
Alma: Melonie Diaz
Manny: Arjay Smith
Ms. Lawson: Sigourney Weaver
Craig: Chandler Parker
Wilson: Irv Gooch
Origin: USA
Language: English
Released: 2008
Production: Michael Gondry, Julie Fong, Georges Bermann; Partizan Films; released by New Line Cinema
Directed by: Michel Gondry

Written by: Michel Gondry
Cinematography by: Ellen Kuras
Music by: Jean-Michel Bernard
Sound: Pavel Wdowczak
Music Supervisor: Linda Cohen
Editing: Jeff Buchanan
Art Direction: James Donahue
Costumes: James Donahue, Rachel Afiley, Kishu Chand
Production Design: Dan Leigh
MPAA rating: PG-13
Running time: 100 minutes

REVIEWS

Boston Globe Online. February 22, 2008.
Chicago Sun-Times Online. February 22, 2008.
Entertainment Weekly Online. February 20, 2008.
Hollywood Reporter Online. January 21, 2008.
Los Angeles Times Online. February 22, 2008.
New York Times Online. February 22, 2008.
New Yorker Online. February 25, 2008.
Rolling Stone Online. March 6, 2008.
San Francisco Chronicle. February 22, 2008, p. E6.
Variety Online. January 20, 2008.
Washington Post. February 22, 2008, p. C1.

QUOTES

Jerry: "That's the lamest excuse I've ever heard! That's totally non-sequitary!"

TRIVIA

The term "Sweded" was created due to the Swedish government's liberal position with regards to electronic file-sharing. While many multi-media corporations have succeeded in having files of their copyrighted works removed from Internet web sites, Sweden has tolerated such sharing as a representation of free speech.

BEAUFORT

Beaufort does not cover new territory, but its anti-war message is well presented. Joseph Cedar's film captures the somber and scary realities of an Israeli unit waiting to leave a mountain outpost called Beaufort Castle on the eve of the 2000 Lebanon withdrawal. Comparable to the films of Amos Gitai, *Beaufort* takes an anti-Occupation position, although it does not preach about it. Rather, Cedar and Gitai consider the complexities of Israel's conflicts with its Arab neighbors, as well as within its own borders. *Beaufort* is not as critical of Israel as Gitai's work, but Zionists and right-wingers may not appreciate that fact.

Cedar's story and screenplay (based on the novel *Im Yesh Gan Eden* by Ron Leshem, who co-wrote the screenplay) follows one particular troop unit a few months before the pullout. Liraz Liberti (Oshri Cohen), the young (too young?) commander, tries to lead his men while protecting them from the bombs dropped by the unseen enemy, Hezbollah, the radical group that would like to hasten the Israeli retreat. Unfortunately, Liberti makes some disastrous decisions, which lead to the death of several of his fellow soldiers. Still, he commands the respect of the survivors, as most of them blame the upper echelons of the military (and the political leaders) for what they come to see as a pointless occupation of Lebanon (dating back to the 1982 war) and a careless withdrawal plan. Ultimately, the Israeli fighters become easy targets, and their final mission becomes almost absurd as it is ironic.

If Joseph Cedar is making a political statement, *Beaufort* demonstrates that war is neither romantic nor noble, but that message is hardly new in the arts. Lewis Milestone's *All Quiet on the Western Front* (1930), Jean Renoir's *The Grand Illusion* (1937), and Stanley Kubrick's *Paths of Glory* (1957) more powerfully demonstrate that war is hell. Yet like the Gitai films (particularly *Kippur* [2000]), *Beaufort* offers a quiet and realistic intensity, showing that much of combat is simply waiting and worrying (Yishai Adar's original score is so quiet as to be almost imperceptible). In addition, like the last section of Kubrick's *Full Metal Jacket* (1987), the mise en scène is almost otherworldly at times—evoking the science fiction genre and owing more to Andrei Tarkovsky's *Solaris* (1972) than to Steven Spielberg's *Saving Private Ryan* (1998).

Appropriately given its theme, *Beaufort* moves glacially, so war movie buffs expecting much action will be disappointed by what they consider to be a flaw. Yet among the several major flaws in the film is the cliché tactic of having characters reveal their back stories, only to be killed shortly thereafter. Whether or not this method was supposed to humanize the soldiers or elicit additional sympathy, the device is tiresome, as is the sentimental song played midway, during which much male bonding, including crying, occurs. This sentimental sequence is regrettable in the midst of an otherwise tough-minded picture.

The performances are solid throughout, though only Oshri Cohen exhibits genuine charisma as the commander in over his head. From Ofer Inov's fluid cinematography to Miguel Markin's muted production design to the minimalist but haunting Yishai Adar score, the technical credits are generally excellent.

The critics responded well to *Beaufort*. A.O. Scott in the *New York Times,* said "*Beaufort* moves slowly,

reflecting perhaps a bit too faithfully the dull, stressful routines of life in this bunker. The architecture of its plot also has some of the blockiness of an old-fashioned combat picture. If a character has a big, personality-revealing scene—talking about his girlfriend back home, or showing what an irrepressible cutup he is—you can bet that a missile is heading his way before too long." Leslie Felperin in *Variety* wrote, "Although there's muted criticism here of military strategy, script endeavors to maintain a politically neutral stance, sticking to the ground soldiers' points of view, rendered convincingly here by [the] cast and third-time [director] Joseph Cedar." Conversely, Mick LaSalle in the *San Francisco Chronicle* dissented, writing, "The best that can be said for *Beaufort* is that it's a little like what it must have been like to be there—but it's not. It can't be, because the defining circumstance of ongoing fear and mortal terror is missing. The failure of the filmmaker to dramatically replicate those emotions, at least in some form, prevents *Beaufort* from being anything more than a noble gesture."

Beaufort will become tedious for viewers used to an MTV aesthetic or those who expect more traditional war film tropes. However, patient viewers will be rewarded by an intelligent look at mission creep, that is, the gradual process by which a mission's objectives change over time, and its unholy results. This film provides sad commentary on war in general and, most topically, America's occupation of Iraq.

Eric Monder

CREDITS

Liraz: Oshri Cohen
Ziv: Ohad Knoller
Kimchy: Alon Abutbul
Oshry: Eli Eltonyo
Balis: Gal Friedman
Avishai: Nevo Kimchi
Pavel: Daniel Brook
Shpitzer: Arthur Perzev
Origin: Israel
Language: Hebrew
Released: 2007
Production: David Mandil, David Silber; United King Films, Metro Communications, Movie Plus; released by Kino International
Directed by: Joseph Cedar
Written by: Joseph Cedar
Cinematography by: Ofer Inov
Music by: Ishai Adar
Editing: Zohar M. Sela

Art Direction: Miguel Markin
Production Design: Miguel Markin
MPAA rating: Unrated
Running time: 125 minutes

REVIEWS

Entertainment Weekly. January 28, 2008, p. 57.
New York Times Online. January 18, 2008.
Variety Online. February 14, 2007.
Village Voice Online. January 15, 2008.

QUOTES

Shpitzer: (singing in memore of Zitlawy) "I won't be afraid to fall / Won't be afraid to grow / To sink or swim / To live or die."

TRIVIA

The film became Israel's official submission in the Foreign Language Film category for the 80th Academy Awards® when *The Band's Visit* was disqualified by AMPAS.

AWARDS

Nomination:

Oscars 2007: Foreign Film.

BEDTIME STORIES

> *What if the stories you told came to life?*
> —Movie tagline
> *Whatever they dream up...he has to survive.*
> —Movie tagline
> *Every day is a new adventure.*
> —Movie tagline

Box Office: $109.6 million

A PG-rated Disney family comedy and Adam Sandler make strange bedfellows, as illustrated in the overly complicated, critically panned *Bedtime Stories.* What might have been a charming fantasy about a kindly janitor reading whimsical bedtime stories to his young niece and nephew (à la the *The Princess Bride* [1987]) that magically come true, turns into a badly miscast, big-budget, computer-genrated-imagery-laden nightmare. Perhaps the film's main flaw is that it fails to focus on the children and the fantasies; rather, it revolves around Sandler's character and his bid to achieve career success, rectify his father' errors, and romance the girl. Sandler is more attuned to the R-rated crudity and edgy humor that made him a star, so his charisma in this role is nil. Furthermore, he is surrounded by poorly written

caricatures that are impossible to care about and propelled through a flawed plot to a clichéd conclusion.

Sandler portrays Skeeter Bronson, whose father Marty (Jonathan Pryce) was the proud owner of a quaint Los Angeles motel until he was forced to sign over his failing business to the scheming Barry Nottingham (Richard Griffiths). Although Barry promised a bright future for the young Skeeter, thirty years later he works as the successful hotel's embittered handyman. When Skeeter's sister Wendy (Courtney Cox) leaves to look for a job in Arizona, she entrusts her young daughter and son (Laura Ann Kesling and Jonathan Morgan Heit) to Skeeter, who takes care of them part time, job-sharing with Wendy's best friend, the attractive Jill (Keri Russell). Jill immediately dislikes Skeeter and thus becomes his love interest.

Although Skeeter does not believe in happy endings, the imaginative bedtime stories he crafts for the children—a talent his father passed on to him—compensate for the little else he knows about child rearing. These tales are also the highlight of the film, which showcases a plethora of advanced special effects. Sure to please its target audience of children, these tales range in hero from astronauts and Greek gladiators to medieval knights and cowboys. The children add to the stories, which begin to come true and affect Skeeter's real life. This happening inspires the handyman' attempt to control the stories so that he might become manager of the new hotel Nottingham plans to construct on the site of Jill's elementary school.

Various other distracting plot threads place Skeeter in a rivalry with the creepy hotel manager Kendall (Guy Pearce) for the manager position of the new hotel. The handyman also vies for the affection of Nottingham's daughter Violet (Teresa Palmer) and attempts to save Jill's school. As in many comedies of this type, Skeeter has a humorous animal sidekick—here the children's pet guinea pig, Bugsy, apparently so named for his giant bulging eyes. Nearly as odd is Skeeter's other sidekick, Mickey (Russell Brand), who rescues Skeeter when a bee stings the handyman's tongue right before he must deal with Nottingham.

Equally at home in character roles—playing Andy Warhol in *Factory Girl* (2006)— and leading man roless —*Memento* (2000)—is Guy Pearce, who is outrageously miscast here; thus, his melodramatic performance is difficult to watch. So too, the controversial, tousled British comedian Brand seems out of place in a Disney film; rather, he is much better suited to his role as a womanizing rock star in *Forgetting Sarah Marshall* (2008). Of the supporting actors, only Russell with her naturalistic performance seems at home in *Bedtime Stories.*

Sandler is oddly constrained by his role, which is nonetheless a familiar one for the former *Saturday Night Live* comedian: an underachieving man/child who eventually finds success, his churlishness hiding his ultimate good-heartedness. Although this kinder, gentler, PG-rated Sandler may not have been completely successful, the film grossed some $85 million. At one point, Skeeter tells the kids: "I'm like the stink on your feet—I'll always be there." Skeeter may be correct in his assessment of his character's appeal to viewers and in his real-life counterpart's longevity, yet there is also a heartening message to be taken from this middling children's film. As Skeeter's father Marty once told his young son: "Your fun is only limited by your imagination."

Hilary White

CREDITS

Skeeter Bronson: Adam Sandler
Jill: Keri Russell
Kendall: Guy Pearce
Wendy: Courteney Cox
Violet: Teresa Palmer
Mickey: Russell Brand
Aspen: Lucy Lawless
Barry: Richard Griffiths
Marty Bronson: Jonathan Pryce
Donna Hyde: Aisha Tyler
Patrick: Laura Ann Kesling
Bobbi: Madisen Beaty
Origin: USA
Language: English
Released: 2008
Production: Andrew Gunn, Adam Sandler, Jack Giarraputo; Happy Madison Productions, Offspring Entertainment, Conman and Izzy; released by Walt Disney Pictures
Directed by: Adam Shankman
Written by: Tim Herlihy, Matt Lopez
Cinematography by: Michael Barrett
Music by: Rupert Gregson-Williams
Sound: Thomas Causey
Music Supervisor: Michael Dilbeck, Brooks Arthur
Editing: Tom Costain, Michael Tronick
Art Direction: Chris Burian-Mohr
Costumes: Rita Ryack
Production Design: Linda DeScenna

REVIEWS

Boston Globe Online. December 24, 2008.
Chicago Sun-Times Online. December 24, 2008.
Entertainment Weekly Online. December 24, 2008.
Hollywood Reporter Online. December 22, 2008.
New York Times Online. December 25, 2008.
San Francisco Chronicle. December 29, 2008.
Variety Online. December 22, 2008.
Washington Post. December 29, 2008.

QUOTES

Marty: "Your fun is only limited by your imagination."
Skeeter: " Haven't you heard? Goofy is the new handsome."

TRIVIA

Buzz Lightyear (from the Toy Story films) makes a cameo appearance in the audience during the space story.

BEVERLY HILLS CHIHUAHUA

50% warrior. 50% lover. 100% chihuahua.
—Movie tagline
I, Chihuahua.
—Movie tagline

Box Office: $94.5 million

With its impressive cast of voice talent and its inherent liveliness, *Beverly Hills Chihuahua* is a Disney, live-action, talking-animal comedy that does not reach *Babe* (1995) or *One Hundred and One Dalmatians* (1961) in status but is solid, family-friendly entertainment. The title suggests a canine version along the lines of *Clueless* (1995) or *Legally Blonde* (2001), and while this likeness is partially true, the film takes the Chihuahua heroine Chloe(voice of Drew Barrymore) to some unsavory parts of Mexico. Although her journey of self-discovery is sometimes depicted in a clichéd manner, it is more touching than some may expect. First-time screenwriters Jeff Bushell, who also wrote the story, and Analisa LaBianco received assistance from director Raja Gosnell, who gained a wealth of prior talking-dog experience when helming *Scooby-Doo* (2002) and its sequel *Scooby-Doo 2: Monsters Unleashed* (2004).

Chloe, a Beverly Hills mansion-dwelling Chihuahua living with her owner, cosmetics entrepreneur Vivian (Jamie Lee Curtis), in the lap of luxury, dresses in a diamond collar and designer booties. Chloe's cushy existence is imperiled Viv leaves her in the care of her irresponsible niece, Rachel Ashe Lynn (Piper Perabo). Subsequently Chloe finds herself in the clutches of a ring of dogfighters in Mexico. She manages to avoid risking life and limb in the ring with the help of gruff

German shepherd Delgado (voice of Andy Garcia), a former police dog with a fatal flaw: he has no sense of smell. Chloe and new friend Delgado roam Mexico, pursued by Vasquez (José Maria Yazpik) and his Doberman Pinscher Diablo (voice of Edward James Olmos). While on the run, they meet an assortment of underprivileged, anthropomorphic animals, including a savvy rat (voice of Cheech Marin) and his iguana partner-in-crime (Paul Rodriguez), who have some of the film's best dialogue and feature in a very funny scene, escaping in a piñata from a rabid shop owner.

Chloe confronts her Mexican heritage when she and Delgado encounter a pack of Chihuahas that lives in an Aztec ruin whose members follow the Chihuahua Pride teachings of Montezuma (voice of Plácido Domingo). Although initially appalled by the homeless dogs, Chloe learns that rather than simply being a spoiled heiress, she, and her breed are actually "descended from an ancient line of proud warriors" whose "ancestors went into battle, alongside Aztec soldiers" (at least they are according to some early narration). Chloe proudly adopts their motto: "We are tiny, but we are mighty."

In the lackluster human subplot, Rachel searches for Chloe, reluctantly accepting the help of Viv's handsome Mexican landscaper, Sam Cortez (Manolo Cardona), whose own Chihuahua Papi (George Lopez) is in love with Chloe. Just as Chloe spurned Papi for being a lower-class stray, Rachel originally detested Sam, but theirs ultimately becomes another interracial love story. Perhaps rightly so, the canine characters and their adventures in *Beverly Hills Chihuahua* are far more entertaining than those of their human counterparts, which merely seem to exist in order to further the film's message of class equality and interracial harmony.

While there are a few completely computer-generated animals, including the rat and iguana, *Beverly Hills Chihuahua* primarily employs real dogs and uses special effects to make them "speak." This approach is mostly convincing, despite the fact that some of the dogs' facial expressions look forced. The voice work by some of the entertainment industry's best-known Latino performers, including Garcia, Lopez, Olmos, and Marin, is uniformly excellent, and Barrymore's lilting California-girl accent is perfectly suited to her character as well.

Although this broad comedy satirizes Latino stereotypes, most of it is in good taste, and all of it is in good fun. The message is an uplifting one of taking pride in one's heritage and finding empowerment. In the film, Disney also advocates for real-life dogs down on their luck, advising viewers to adopt shelter dogs instead of buying from breeders. In conclusion, with its combination of memorable characters and humorous yet poignant plot, *Beverly Hills Chihuahua* takes its rightful place alongside other lovable canine films, ranging in time from *Benji* (1974) to *Marley & Me* (2008). Films featuring cute dogs in peril will always find a place in the cinema.

Hilary White

CREDITS

Bryan: Nick Zano
Rachel: Piper Perabo
Sam Cortez: Manolo Cardona
Vasquez: Jose Maria Yazpik
Chloe: Drew Barrymore (Voice)
Foxy: Salma Hayek (Voice)
Papi: George Lopez (Voice)
Delgado: Andy Garcia (Voice)
Aunt Viv: Jamie Lee Curtis (Voice)
Blair: Marguerite Moreau (Voice)
Sebastian: Michael Urie (Voice)
Manuel: Richard "Cheech" Marin (Voice)
Chico: Paul Rodriguez (Voice)
Monte: Placido Domingo (Voice)
Diablo: Edward James Olmos (Voice)
Delta: Loretta Devine (Voice)
Chucho: Luis Guzman (Voice)
Origin: USA
Language: English
Released: 2008
Production: David Hoberman, John Jacobs, Todd Lieberman; Mandeville Films, Smart Entertainment; released by Walt Disney Pictures
Directed by: Raja Gosnell
Written by: Jeffrey Bushell, Analisa LaBianco
Cinematography by: Phil Mereaux
Music by: Hector Pereira
Sound: Santiago Nunez
Music Supervisor: Buck Damon
Editing: Sabrina Plisco
Art Direction: Hania Robledo
Costumes: Maria Estela Fernández
Production Design: Bill Boes
MPAA rating: PG
Running time: 86 minutes

REVIEWS

Boston Globe Online. October 3, 2008.
Entertainment Weekly Online. October 1, 2008.
Hollywood Reporter Online. September 29, 2008.
Los Angeles Times Online. October 3, 2008.
New York Times Online. October 3, 2008.

San Francisco Chronicle. October 3, 2008, p. E1.
Variety Online. September 29, 2008.
Washington Post. October 3, 2008, p. C1.

QUOTES

Rafa: "I've never had my teeth brushed before. It's…minty!"

TRIVIA

According to actor George Lopez, the chihuahua he voices in the movie—Papi—was almost put down before being rescued for the film.

BLINDNESS

In a world gone blind, what if you were the only person who could see?
—Movie tagline
Your vision of the world will change forever.
—Movie tagline

Box Office: $3.3 million

Nobel-Prize-winning Portuguese novelist José Saramago writes frightening and imaginative dystopian books, and in his novel *Blindness* (1995), he concocted a fantastic scenario in which an entire city succumbs to an epidemic contagion of sudden blindness. Although this novel seemed to present insurmountable obstacles to filming, screenwriter Don McKellar and director Fernando Meirelles (*City of God* [2002]) attempted it nevertheless, with intriguing but far from satisfying results.

Hewing closely to the novel, the film opens with a motorist on a busy street during an urban rush hour suddenly losing his sight. He is helped home by a Good Samaritan who turns out to be a thief, who steals his wallet. When his wife arrives home, she takes her husbnad to see an eye doctor (Mark Ruffalo), who cannot explain what has happened. Soon, all the patients who were in the doctor's waiting room—including a young boy and a prostitute—go blind, and so does the doctor and the motorist's wife.

It takes only a few hours for the Big Brother-style government to take action, rounding up and quarantining all those who have been stricken by blindness. The doctor's wife (Julianne Moore), seeing that he is about to be taken away in an armored truck, insists on going with him, pretending that she herself has succumbed to the contagion, though she has not.

The newly blind are carted off to a former mental institution, a horrible spartan place with metal beds, group showers, concrete floors, and no amenities. There they are left to fend for themselves, with authorities dropping off boxes of food in the courtyard while guards in bunkers prevent them from escaping. No one from the outside has contact with them, but the group learns from a report on a man's transistor radio that the contagion has spread everywhere, crippling the country.

Conditions inside the institution become harsh quickly, but the doctor's wife (none of the characters have actual names) struggles to care for everyone. She never loses her sight but pretends she is one of the blind, presumably for fear of the consequences if discovered. Ruffalo's doctor also takes charge and organizes one of the five wards, in which sleep the boy, the prostitute, the motorist and his wife, the thief, and a wise man with an eye patch (Danny Glover).

Thus the stage is set for a series of conflicts that are much like those that occur in other stories in which people are cut off from civilization. In this case, the added twist is that all these people are newly disabled. The guards shoot some of them in the courtyard, various squabbles break out, the doctor and his wife become testy and estranged, and a tyrant appears—the self-pronounced King of Ward Three (Gael García Bernal), who has a gun and an assistant who was born blind and thus knows how to survive better than the others. How he acquired the gun and why the assistant was put into the institution are not explained. Soon the "king" commandeers the food supply and demands first jewelry and then the services from the women in exchange for the food. Events quickly take an ugly turn, and the doctor's wife has to decide to what ends she is willing to go to protect herself and her companions.

Blindness presents a disturbing scenario that is not for the squeamish and is barely redeemed by a hopeful last act. Yet on a metaphorical level, it is a moral tale about the depths of human depravity and the power of persistence and courage in service of the collective good. However, the impact of the moral choices and ethical issues and survival challenges that these characters all face is diminished by their use as one-dimensional props for the morality tale. Try as she might, even Moore cannot escape the confines of a character that is angelic, heroic, and resourceful. Because she has no back-story, viewers cannot understand the depths of or rationale for her courage and perseverance. The conflict between the doctor and his wife seems to be forced, and his unfaithfulness is unexpected. Other one-dimensional positive characters include Glover, who seems sublimely gentle and sweet; the boy, who represents utter vulnerability; and the prostitute, who is the proverbial hooker with a heart of gold. Conversely, The King and his assistant are evil incarnate.

In addition to implausible characters, the methods these characters employ to adapt to their sudden blindness do not ring true. While some stumble a little, and some express occasional bewilderment, most of them seem to adapt too quickly and are rather matter-of-fact about their transformation. In real life people in this quandary would likely fall apart emotionally, at least for awhile, and struggle more physically, but these characters lack intense responses. Thus, it is difficult to believe in the fantastic premise because viewers do not see the impact of blindness portrayed in believable ways.

Meirelles had to decide from what perspective to tell the story. In portraying diminished physical capacities, a comparison can be made to *The Diving Bell and the Butterfly* (2007), in which a magazine editor is felled by a stroke. Originally viewers see his recovery only from his perspective, but then the camera shows the editor as one of the characters he interacts with, that is, from a standard neutral observer's perspective. In *Blindness,* however, it would be difficult to tell the story from the point of view of the sufferers because there would be nothing to see but a blank screen. Meirelles chose to switch back and forth between insider and outsider perspectives, staying mostly in the outsider perspective and occasionally using a white screen (it is a "white" blindness) to indicate someone has gone blind. Yet this solution is unsatisfactory. The director overuses shots set against a white background, especially scenes of dark figures against the white background, a technique that implies that the sufferers experience a sort of shadow world. Instead, perhaps viewers should have been offered extended scenes of what it is like suddenly not to be able to see and to only be able to hear.

In the end, this incomplete attention to the details of the blindness also ends up making the viewer feel like the blindness itself is only a metaphor, a concocted condition set up to prove the writer's points about human nature and human possibility. In the book, this blindness premise succeeded much better than in the movie. A film needs fleshed-out characters and fully realized situations, not pieces moving on a moral chessboard.

Michael Betzold

CREDITS

Doctor's Wife: Julianne Moore
Doctor: Mark Ruffalo
Old man with black eye patch: Danny Glover
King of Ward 3: Gael Garcia Bernal
Girl with dark glasses: Alice Braga
The accountant: Maury Chaykin
The Thief: Don McKellar
Origin: Brazil, Canada

Language: English
Released: 2008
Production: Niv Fichman, Andrea Barata Ribeiro, Sonoko Sakai; Rhombus Media, O2 Filmes, Bee Vine Pictures; released by Miramax Films
Directed by: Fernando Meirelles
Written by: Don McKellar
Cinematography by: Cesar Charlone
Music by: Marcus Antonio Guimaraes
Sound: Guilherme Ayrosa
Editing: Daniel Rezende
Art Direction: Joshu de Cartier, Tiago Marques Teixeira
Costumes: Renee April
Production Design: Tule Peake
MPAA rating: R
Running time: 118 minutes

REVIEWS

Boston Globe Online. October 3, 2008.
Chicago Sun-Times Online. October 2, 2008.
Entertainment Weekly Online. September 24, 2008.
Hollywood Reporter Online. May 14, 2008.
Los Angeles Times Online. October 3, 2008.
New York Times Online. October 3, 2008.
New Yorker Online. October 6, 2008.
San Francisco Chronicle. October 3, 2008, p. E7.
Variety Online. May 14, 2008.
Washington Post. October 3, 2008, p. C4.

QUOTES

Doctor' Wife: "The only thing more terrifying than blindness is being the only one who can see."

TRIVIA

In preparation for the film, actors, extras, and crew were sent to "blind camps" where they were blindfolded, taken to an unknown location, and left in the middle of the street. Despite a handler always on hand to guide the participants, the director claims that someone always brokedown.

BODY OF LIES

Trust no one. Deceive everyone.
—Movie tagline

Box Office: $39.3 million

Body of Lies has much to offer. In addition to featuring stars Leonardo DiCaprio and Russell Crowe, the film was helmed by Ridley Scott, one of the directors most skilled at combining cinematic art with marketplace demands, as demonstrated by *Alien* (1979), *Blade Run-*

ner (1982), and *Gladiator* (2000). The subject, the efforts of intelligence agents to halt terrorism, is certainly timely. Yet the film was not given much of a reception by either reviewers or audiences. Because all previous films dealing directly or indirectly with the Iraq War have been box-office failures, *Body of Lies,* despite its star power, seemed destined for disappointment.

Roger Ferris (Leonardo DiCaprio), a CIA field agent in the Middle East, is constantly risking his life and those of what the agency calls "assets," while his immediate boss, Ed Hoffman (Russell Crowe), calmly carries on his suburban life back in the United States. Scott and screenwriter William Monahan give much of *Body of Lies* an ironic coating by contrasting Ferris's life of constant violence with Hoffman's more mundane world. As Ferris dodges bullets, Hoffman barks orders into his cell phone while watching his daughter play soccer and eating Pepperidge Farms Goldfish crackers.

Ferris and Hoffman's primary goal is to find the terrorist Al-Saleem (Alon Abutbul), whose group is responsible for bombings in England and is expected to spread its activities across Europe and, eventually, the United States. Hoffman has Ferris contact Hani Salaam (Mark Strong), head of Jordanian intelligence, to enlist his aid. The super-confident Hani looks upon American agents with disdain because they are not as well organized as his men and because they think they understand the Arab mind.

Body of Lies consists of Ferris's attempts to do his job and protect his assets despite the lack of full cooperation from Hani and the interference of Hoffman. Ferris is a beleaguered Everyman caught between two massive egos, both of whom see themselves as infallible. Just as in the best novels of John le Carré, the film strikes a balance between Ferris's life-and-death decisions and the jealousies among and infighting within intelligence agencies. A subplot involves Ferris's tentative romance in Jordan with Aisha (Golshifteh Farahani), an Iranian-born nurse. Some reviewers complained that the Ferris-Aisha relationship is extraneous, but toward the end of the film it contributes to a convergence of all the plot elements.

Because of the inability of such films as *Redacted* (2007), *In the Valley of Elah* (2007), *Lions for Lambs* (2007), and *Stop-Loss* (2008) to attract audiences, Iraq War-themed films have come to be seen as box-office jinxes. While the war is mentioned in *Body of Lies,* the larger issues are terrorism and bureaucracies. Ferris embodies the fears felt by many because he must constantly look over his shoulder and does not know whom to trust. As Monahan's screenplay makes obvious, Ferris is merely a pawn being manipulated by Hoffman, Hani, and Al-Saleem.

Although the film, adapted from a 2007 novel by *Washington Post* columnist David Ignatius, never hints at how Ferris came to be the man he is, the spy, no James Bond, is easy to identify with because he is an everyman caught up in an existential crisis. Ferris is subjected to extensive abuse rivaling even the punishment meted out to Marlon Brando in *One-Eyed Jacks* (1961): he is wounded in a bombing, tortured, and attacked by dogs—all while Hoffman watches impassively through drone surveillance. Because Ferris relies upon technology to conduct his operations, the film implies that the CIA is just as impersonal toward its operative as if he were a computer chip. Humans die; technology is forever. The spy's far-from-extraneous relationship with Aisha is a sign of his need for a human connection he can trust.

Scott has not previously made a spy film, yet he covered similar territory in the battle sequences in the Somalia-set *Black Hawk Down* (2001). In both films, the protagonists find themselves charging through streets, with gunfire erupting all about them. *Bodies of Lies,* smoothly edited by Pietro Scalia, displays Scott's penchant for kinetic energy. Like *American Gangster* (2007), the film has a relentless pace and is never boring. Monahan, who wrote Scott's Crusades epic, *Kingdom of Heaven* (2005), and won an Academy Award® for *The Departed* (2006), knows how to balance the action and more thoughtful elements of his screenplays.

DiCaprio and Crowe's performances do justice to Monahan's screenplay. Mistaking the actor for the character, however, some reviewers complained that Crowe gives a lazy performance as Hoffman; yet in his fourth film with Scott, Crowe turns himself into a character actor, reportedly gaining fifty pounds for what is essentially a supporting role. Crowe then employs a minimum of gestures and inflections, using a non-specific Southern accent to create an image of Hoffman as a no-nonsense bureaucrat unaware of any weaknesses. Hoffman treats Ferris as a wayward adolescent, always calling him "buddy." Ironically, Ferris is one of the more adult roles tackled by DiCaprio, who, with his thin voice and boyish looks, sometimes seems to be a child pretending to be a man, as does his *Catch Me If You Can* (2002) character. DiCaprio's combination of likeability, intensity, and vulnerability make Ferris a compelling character.

Early in their careers Crowe and DiCaprio worked together in the underrated Sam Raimi Western *The Quick and the Dead* (1995), and they play off each other effortlessly. The subtlety of Crowe's work is captured when an angry Ferris knocks Hoffman down, and the actor regains his feet, showing no recognition of the violence of his colleague's action. Crowe's matter-of-fact approach perfectly complements the barely harnessed energy of DiCaprio's style.

As good as the two superstars are, they are matched by Strong. Best known for torturing George Clooney in the similar *Syriana* (2005), Strong presents Hani as a smooth operator priding himself on seeing more angles to anti-terrorist operations than his Western colleagues can imagine. Hani is a man of contrasts, quickly shifting from calm resolve to angry impatience, as when he sneers at Ferris's supposed Arab expertise. Scott shoots Ferris and Hoffman from all angles but films Hani to emphasize his resolve. Third World spies are almost always inferior to their Western counterparts in such films, yet Hani is much more clever than Ferris and Hoffman realize. Dressed in Savile Row suits and speaking deliberately, Strong eschews Arab stereotypes, making Hani a charismatic, enigmatic figure. The way Hani calls Ferris "my dear" is deliciously menacing.

Scott is considered overrated by some, and many reviewers judge his films a bit more harshly than they deserve. A. O. Scott of the *New York Times* was distracted by DiCaprio's on-and-off North Carolina accent and Crowe's "body mass index," finding *Body of Lies* a boring hodgepodge of randomly connected ideas. Likewise, Claudia Puig of *USA Today* called it far-fetched, unfocused, and too familiar. While David Denby of the *New Yorker* praised Scott's craftsmanship, he did not feel the film conveys an understanding of terrorism.

Body of Lies suffers, perhaps, from being too much of the moment, both in terms of news events in the Middle East and of similar recent films. Several reviewers compared it unfavorably to the entertaining and complex Jason Bourne series. Nevertheless, *Body of Lies* is a smoothly made, engrossing look at the ambiguities of espionage and terrorism and may one day receive its due.

Michael Adams

CREDITS

Roger Ferris: Leonardo DiCaprio
Ed Hoffman: Russell Crowe
Hani: Mark Strong
Gretchen Ferris: Carice van Houten
Aisha: Golshifteh Farahani
Skip: Vince Colosimo
Holiday: Michael Gaston
Bassam: Oscar Isaac
Garland: Simon McBurney
Al-Saleem: Alon Aboutboul
Origin: USA
Language: English
Released: 2008
Production: Ridley Scott, Donald DeLine; Scott Free; released by Warner Bros.

Directed by: Ridley Scott
Written by: William Monahan
Cinematography by: Alexander Witt
Music by: Marc Streitenfeld
Sound: Richard Van Dyke
Editing: Pietro Scalia
Art Direction: Marco Trentini
Costumes: Janty Yates
Production Design: Arthur Max
MPAA rating: R
Running time: 129 minutes

REVIEWS

Boston Globe Online. October 10, 2008.
Chicago Sun-Times Online. October 8, 2008.
Entertainment Weekly Online. October 7, 2008.
Hollywood Reporter Online. October 2, 2008.
Los Angeles Times Online. October 10, 2008.
New York Times Online. October 10, 2008.
New Yorker Online. October 13, 2008.
Rolling Stone Online. October 16, 2008.
San Francisco Chronicle. October 10, 2008, p. E1.
Variety Online. October 2, 2008.
Wall Street Journal Online. October 10, 2008.
Washington Post. October 10, 2008, p. C1.

QUOTES

Ed Hoffman: "Our world as we know it is much simpler...to put to an end than you might think."

TRIVIA

Although actress Carice van Houten played Roger's wife Gretchen Ferris, all of her scenes were cut and the character is absent from the final cut of the film.

BOLT

Real life's a total adventure!
—Movie tagline

Box Office: $114 million

After the stunning creativity of *Ratatouille* (2007) and *WALL-E* (2008), viewers expect more from American animated films than in the days before Pixar animation made animation more realistic looking. While *Bolt*, from Walt Disney Animation Studios, may not have the originality and genius of some of its computed-created predecessors, it is still considerable fun, a pleasant entertainment rather than a masterpiece.

Bolt (John Travolta), the canine star of a popular action television series, thinks he really has superpowers.

Like the hero of *The Truman Show* (1998), Bolt does not realize he is a television character. The program's director (James Lipton) and crew keep the cameras and sound equipment out of his line of vision to maintain his acceptance of their world of make-believe. As a result, there are no rehearsals and no retakes. Bolt, a white German shepherd, thinks he belongs to Penny (Miley Cyrus), the show's young star, and that he is constantly rescuing her and her scientist father (Ronn Moss) from the clutches of the evil, cat-loving Dr. Calico (Malcolm McDowell). While *Bolt* attempts a limited degree of realism, some viewers may be bothered by the illogic of Bolt's inability to spot the technicians and equipment and by his reluctant acceptance of being abandoned by Penny each weekend. Yet these are minor quibbles only a Grinch would notice.

Circumstances soon lead Bolt away from the safe confines of his set and out into the real world when he is accidentally packaged and shipped from Hollywood to New York. He slowly discovers that his supposed powers are not so super, believing that Styrofoam weakens him, and learns to live with his new limitations, an example of the film's relatively subtle messages. He hooks up with Mittens (Susie Essman), a world-weary Manhattan alley cat, and Rhino (Mark Walton), a hamster who lives in a plastic ball and leaves his Ohio trailer park to seek adventure with the hero he has admired on television.

Much of the considerable humor in *Bolt* comes from Rhino's continued belief in Bolt's extraordinariness, and some poignancy arrives with Mittens' loss of some of her hard-boiled attitude. Animals need love and friendship, says the film. Screenwriters Dan Fogelman and Chris Williams, who also co-directed with Byron Howard, offer some show-business satire to keep the interest of adult viewers familiar with the television series *Entourage* (begun on 2004) and *30 Rock* (begun in 2006). Early in the film is an extended action sequence with Bolt saving Penny amid a series of explosions and menacing black helicopters. While ostensibly spoofing action films, this segment offers more visceral excitement than anything in, say, *Quantum of Solace* (2008). Yet the central story, with only a modicum of sentimentality and not too much cuteness, should satisfy most viewers. In that regard, *Bolt* resembles the films of Hayao Miyazaki, and Penny's sincere, sensitive, but determined image recalls those of the young women who populate the great Japanese animator's works.

All of the lesser-known voice actors are excellent. Especially good is Greg Germann as Penny's oily, hyperactive agent. Travolta might seem an odd choice to portray a young dog, but despite being in his fifties, the actor continues to have a youthful voice, and he wonderfully conveys Bolt's cockiness, innocence, and disappointment. Essman, best known as the foul-mouthed wife of Larry David's agent on the television series *Curb Your Enthusiasm* (begun in 2000), ably demonstrates the softening of Mittens's initially sarcastic personality. Best of all is Walton, a visual development artist for Disney who recorded Rhino's dialogue as an aid to the filmmakers. When Williams and Howard could not find an actor to surpass Walton's rendering of the hamster, Walton's temporary reading became permanent. Based on the pet chinchilla of John Lasseter, the co-founder of Pixar overseeing his first production at Disney, Rhino steals the film with his endless enthusiasm and optimism, for Walton's voice matches the hamster's energy.

Shown in digital 3-D in some theaters, *Bolt* is not as visually luxurious as Brad Bird's *Ratatouille* or Miyazaki's *Howl's Moving Castle* (2004) or as moving as Bird's *The Iron Giant* (1999), but it is still delightful.

Michael Adams

CREDITS

Dr. Calico: Malcolm McDowell (Voice)
The Director: James Lipton (Voice)
The Agent: Greg Germann (Voice)
Bolt: John Travolta (Voice)
Mittens: Susie Essman (Voice)
Rhino: Mark Walton (Voice)
Penny: Miley Cyrus (Voice)
Origin: USA
Language: English
Released: 2008
Production: Clark Spencer; Walt Disney Animation Studios; released by Walt Disney Pictures
Directed by: Chris Williams, Byron Howard
Written by: Chris Williams, Dan Fogelman
Music by: John Powell
Sound: Randy Thom
Music Supervisor: Tom MacDougall
Editing: Tim Mertens
Art Direction: Paul Felix
MPAA rating: PG
Running time: 96 minutes

REVIEWS

Boston Globe Online. November 21, 2008.
Entertainment Weekly Online. November 19, 2008.
Hollywood Reporter Online. November 13, 2008.
Los Angeles Times Online. November 21, 2008.
New York Times Online. November 21, 2008.
San Francisco Chronicle. November 21, 2008, p. E1.

Variety Online. November 13, 2008.
Wall Street Journal Online. November 21, 2008.
Washington Post. November 21, 2008, p. C1.

QUOTES

Mittens (to Bolt): "Nothing you think is real is real."

TRIVIA

The last four digits visible on the copier when Penny is printing "lost dog" flyers are 8423, which is a reference to the number (877) 504-8423 (a number reserved by ABC for movies and television series which, when called, will provide a recorded message about how fake the number is).

AWARDS

Nomination:

Oscars 2008: Animated Film
Golden Globes 2009: Animated Film, Song ("I Thought I Lost You").

BOTTLE SHOCK

Based on a true story of love, victory, and fermentation.
—Movie tagline

Box Office: $4 million

The versatile Alan Rickman gives a standout performance as a snooty British wine connoisseur in *Bottle Shock,* the first feel-good wine comedy since *Sideways* (2004). The film is based on a little-known but fascinating true story that took place in 1976, when America celebrated her Bicentennial, and in a blind taste test held in France, an American wine from California's then-unknown Napa Valley miraculously won over all the French judges. "The Judgment of Paris" as it was called, forever placed Napa as a premier wine-making region. Of the way the competition is portrayed, *San Francisco Chronicle* reviewer Reyhan Harmanci amusingly observed, "The movie plays it as another fist-pumping example of the triumphant American underdog (think *Rocky* with wine)."

Filmmakers Randall Miller, who wrote and directed, and wife Jody Savin, who co-wrote the script along with story author Ross Schwartz, loosely craft their 1970s-era film around this story, while adding a Robert Altman-like cast of characters, conflicts, and locations. At various times, the film also reads like a love letter to the hilly Napa landscape, with overhead shots aplenty gently lingering over grape-filled arbors. *Bottle Shock* uneasily teeters between drama and near-slapstick comedy within

the film's sometimes dangerously rickety structure. Performances are also uneven, with Rickman and his mix of dry humor and gravitas able to sustain most of the film's weight.

In Paris, viewers are introduced to Steven Spurrier (Alan Rickman), the British owner of the pretentiously named "The Academy of Wine." American wine representative Maurice (Dennis Farina), who is nearly as loud as his polyester suits, frequents Spurrier's struggling shop and, in discussions abou wine, mentions that California wines are an up-and-coming product. In an effort to drum up some much-needed publicity, Spurrier decides to sponsor a blind taste-test between the wines of America and France. Spurrier travels to Napa to find the region's best wines for his contest and learns much about the superior quality of and pride taken in making American wines.

It is in the Napa Valley where a beleaguered former lawyer, Jim Barrett (Bill Pullman), bravely struggles to keep afloat his little vineyard, Chateau Montelena, on which three different banks hold liens. Complicating matters is his ne'er-do-well son Bo (Chris Pine), a surfer boy who prefers drinking beer with his friends to wine-making with his father. Miller adequately illustrates the generational struggle between father and son but shows cuts of aerial shots of Napa far too often. Yet another father/son-type dynamic simultaneously plays out at Chateau Montelena with an employee of Jim's, the Latino Gustavo Brambilia (Freddy Rodríguez), secretly a wine expert, and Mr. Garcia (Miguel Sandoval). The final main character is a pretty intern (Rachel Taylor), who completes the love triangle with best friends Bo and the ambitious Gustavo, who is working at becoming a vintner himself.

The film's version of the serendipitous chain of events that led to Montelena's Chardonnay being accepted into the contest is rather dubious, but the dramatic results of the contest no doubt changed the global wine industry, American wineries, Napa Valley vintners, and the Barretts, who are all real-life characters, as is Spurrier.

All of the film's best scenes involve Rickman, who plays the consummate wine snob with pitch perfect aplomb, but Pullman carries his own while in the frame with the illustrious actor as they spar over viniculture prowess. Farina, with his distinct Chicago accent, is the film's other standout, providing a perfect foil for Rickman's upper crust character and the perfect contrast for the Paris locale.

Critics were almost equally divided on *Bottle Shock* and its inspiring but perhaps overly ambitious dramatization of a true story. Despite the film's flaws, it succeeds due to its obvious passion. As the *Washington Post*'s

Stephen Hunter observed: "Everyone in it simply loves wine, as drink, as science, as art, as culture, as civilized delight. I'm guessing that includes the director and the producers and probably the investors and the key grips and the guy who put out the doughnuts each morning. It's just so much fun to be in the presence of so many people obsessed with a gift from God such as the eternal tingle of pleasure that comes in those little green bottles!" For this reason, oenophiles and many others will surely appreciate the pleasures offered by *Bottle Shock*.

Hilary White

CREDITS

Steven Spurrer: Alan Rickman
Jim Barrett: Bill Pullman
Bo Barrett: Chris Pine
Sam: Rachael Taylor
Gustavo Brambilia: Freddy Rodriguez
Joe: Eliza Dushku
Maurice: Dennis Farina
Mr. Garcia: Miguel Sandoval
Prof. Saunders: Bradley Whitford
Bill: Joe Regalbuto
Origin: USA
Language: English
Released: 2008
Production: J. Todd Harris, Randall Miller, Jody Savin, Marc Toberoff, Brenda Lhormer, Marc Lhormer; Unclaimed Freight, Zine Haze Productions; released by Freestyle Releasing
Directed by: Randall Miller
Written by: Randall Miller, Jody Savin, Ross Schwartz
Cinematography by: Michael Ozier
Music by: Mark Adler
Sound: Nelson Stoll
Editing: Randall Miller
Costumes: Jillian Kreiner
Production Design: Craig Stearns
MPAA rating: PG-13
Running time: 110 minutes

REVIEWS

Boston Globe Online. August 6, 2008.
Chicago Sun-Times Online. August 5, 2008.
Entertainment Weekly Online. August 8, 2008.
Hollywood Reporter Online. January 29, 2008.
Los Angeles Times Online. August 6, 2008.
New York Times Online. August 6, 2008.
Rolling Stone Online. August 6, 2008.
San Francisco Chronicle. August 6, 2008, p. E5.
Variety Online. January 18, 2008.
Washington Post. August 6, 2008, p. C1.

QUOTES

Gustavo: "You have to have it in your blood, you have to grow up with the soil underneath your nails, the smell of the grapes in the air that you breathe. The cultivation of the vine was an art form. The refinement of the vine is a religion that requires pain and desire and sacrifice."

TRIVIA

Scenes of the Parisian streets were actually filmed in Sonoma, Californai using cars provided by members of the Arcane Auto Society car club.

THE BOY IN THE STRIPED PAJAMAS

Lines may divide us, but hope will unite us.
—Movie tagline

A timeless story of innocence lost and humanity found.
—Movie tagline

Box Office: $9 million

One of the more blatantly manipulative films of not just 2008 but the entire '00s, *The Boy in the Striped Pajamas* pulled many a heartstring when it played in theaters, but it is an emotionally hollow film, an exercise in audience provocation by putting children in harrowing situations and pushing viewers into feelings instead of letting them come naturally. *The Boy in the Striped Pajamas* is merely an example of a filmmaker's knowledge that children in peril and Holocaust stories have an inherent emotional power, and he uses that power to make viewers cry, whether they like it or not. This is not just another misguided drama; it is manipulation of the highest order. It is reasonable to believe that the source material might have worked on the printed page when it was originally published, but so many poor decisions were made in the filmmaking process that it robbed the narrative of authenticity. *The Boy in the Striped Pajamas* takes a potentially powerful story and deflates it with offensive, manipulative filmmaking devices.

Based on the novel by John Boyne, *The Boy in the Striped Pajamas* is the story of a friendship formed through the fence of a concentration camp between an eight-year-old German boy named Bruno (Asa Butterfield) and a Jewish boy in "striped pajamas" named Shmuel (Jack Scanlon). Bruno's father Ralf (David Thewlis) is a Nazi officer who moves to a new assignment in the countryside with his family, including wife

Elsa (Vera Farmiga) and daughter Gretel (Amber Beattie). Bruno is initially trapped at home and not allowed to leave the premises, but he escapes through a mistakenly left open door and finds Shmuel, whom he believes lives on a farm. Bruno begins to have doubts about his father after listening to Shmuel and even befriending a Jew forced to work in his own home. Meanwhile, Gretel becomes more entranced with the teachings of the Third Reich, and Elsa begins to realize what her husband is doing in the War. Naturally, the friendship between Bruno and Shmuel is going to have a bitter and cruel ending, but it is a far more painful one than anyone imagines.

From the beginning, something about *The Boy in the Striped Pajamas* feels wrong. The film is about Germans in World War II, but, for some unexplainable reason, everyone speaks not only in English but with British accents. Fantastic films about the Holocaust like *Downfall* (2004) and *Fateless* (2005) have been made in recent years with characters speaking the language they would have spoken in real life. It feels like filmmaking has reached a point where David Thewlis playing a German soldier with a crystal clear British accent is unacceptable.

This may seem like nitpicking, but it plays into a much deeper flaw in the storytelling in *The Boy in the Striped Pajamas,* the idea that viewers can only relate to this heartbreaking tale if the people look like them and speak their language. There is a palpable sensation that the decision to have the actors speak English was made to be even more manipulative, making a German Nazi family's experience during the Holocaust that much more emotionally draining. The very concept that a Nazi family had a difficult time mere yards from a concentration is camp is dramatically problematic enough, but it might have felt genuine if the actors had chosen to speak German. It is not far off from the same stomach-churning xenophobia that lead to the never-ending spate of movies about Africa told through the eyes of the pretty white people trying to save the people who live there.

What saves *The Boy in the Striped Pajamas* from being one of the worst films of 2008 is the caliber of the cast. Vera Farmiga is quietly developing into one of the more interesting actresses of her generation (although her work in two other 2008 films, *Nothing But the Truth* and *Quid Pro Quo* is far more interesting), and the two children, Asa Butterfield and Jack Scanlon, are believable, particularly the former (once the issue of accents and language is discarded). Thewlis is always good.

The script and direction of *The Boy in the Striped Pajamas* deserve the blame for this film's failure. Even the focus feels like nothing but manipulation. No one would ever suggest that anyone deserves what happens to the family in *The Boy in the Striped Pajamas,* but the idea that a Nazi family suffered unspeakable pain as they, directly or indirectly, destroyed the lives of millions of Jews and generations to come is a very tough sell dramatically. Moreover, when it comes across like soap opera and exploitation, it can be particularly difficult to swallow.

Brian Tallerico

CREDITS

Father: David Thewlis
Mother: Vera Farmiga
Pavel: David Hayman
Lt. Kotler: Rupert Friend
Bruno: Asa Butterfield
Shmuel: Jack Scanlon
Gretel: Amber Beattie
Grandma: Sheila Hancock
Grandpa: Richard Johnson
Herr Liszt: Jim Norton
Origin: USA, Great Britain
Language: English
Released: 2008
Production: David Heyman; BBC Films, Heyday Films; released by Miramax Films
Directed by: Mark Herman
Written by: Mark Herman
Cinematography by: Benoit Delhomme
Music by: James Horner
Sound: John Casali, Rodney Glenn
Editing: Michael Ellis
Art Direction: Rod McLean
Costumes: Natalie Ward
Production Design: Martin Childs
MPAA rating: PG-13
Running time: 94 minutes

REVIEWS

Chicago Sun-Times Online. November 5, 2008.
Entertainment Weekly Online. November 4, 2008.
Hollywood Reporter Online. September 11, 2008.
Los Angeles Times Online. November 7, 2008.
New York Times Online. November 7, 2008.
Rolling Stone Online. November 13, 2008.
San Francisco Chronicle. November 7, 2008, p. E1.
Variety Online. September 11, 2008.
Village Voice Online. November 4, 2008.
Wall Street Journal Online. November 7, 2008.

BRA BOYS

Blood is thicker than water.
  —Movie tagline

A fascinating surf documentary that combines the strong bonds of brotherhood with social commentary, *Bra Boys* saw a very limited U.S. release but became the highest-grossing, non-IMAX documentary in its native Australia. The film is very much in the same vein as Stacy Peralta's *Dogtown and Z-Boys* documentary from an insider about the insiders' world of surfing and skateboarding in Santa Monica, California but co-writer/co-director and club member Sunny Abberton's down-under *Bra Boys* is much more raw and subjective than Peralta's film.

From a small surf club in the 1960s, Bra Boys has grown into a notorious, self-described "surf tribe" that has spawned such big waver surfers as Sunny's brother Koby Abberton. The gang has famously clashed with police, other gangs, and allegedly other members of the professional surfing community. This film seems like an attempt to raise its profile and position the group more as surf advocates and activists for justice in the community. Amid the wave shredding, carousing, and male bonding, the film shows scenes of the Bra Boys' mediating efforts during Sydney's 2005 race riots. Narrating the film is another rather notorious Aussie, Russell Crowe, who is developing his own, larger-budget version of *Bra Boys*.

The group is named after Maroubra Beach in suburban Sydney where drugs, poverty, and violence are prevalent. Muscled machismo permeates every facet of the film, which opens with home movies of backyard smack-downs and moves into the testosterone-infused, tattooed backs of the tribe's male members. *San Francisco Chronicle*'s Peter Hartlaub observed in his advisory: "This film contains profanity, bloody violence, adult themes, and almost no women. Other than Ma, everyone in this city appears to be a 32-year-old man."

The film opens with a historical look at surfing and surfers as social undesirables, then explores the history of the Bra Boys in particular. Finally, Abberton focuses on his family's personal drama, growing up in a broken home in Sydney's slums. They are taken in by their grandmother, Ma, and turn to surfing to escape their wretched surroundings. (Maroubra Beach is bordered by the world's biggest sewage plant and a prison.) Surfing as salvation is a key theme the film explores and separates the film from those typical of the sports/surf film genre. That said, one of the film's highlights involves a surfing contest between Koby and world renowned surfer Kelly Slater. Surf world legend Laird Hamilton also cameos.

Much of the second half of the film is a biased, intentionally vague look at the 2003 homicide trial of brother Jai Abberton, who was eventually acquitted, that later involved brother Koby, who was given a suspended nine-month jail sentence for perversion of justice. While it does little to shed new light on the details of the trial, it does underscore one of the film's themes of the Bra Boys' always staying true to one another no matter the circumstances.

The film's reception worldwide was mixed. Most critics agreed that the film was inexpertly directed and hardly an objective look at the gang and especially the Abbertons' trial. Hartlaub noted, "What began as a probing look at this culture feels in the end like pro-surf gang propaganda." Some reviewers also called Crowe's narration monotonous. Yet all agreed that the subject and participants are genuinely engrossing and that *Bra Boys* sheds light on this poverty-stricken area of Australia in particular and on poverty and displacement in urban areas worldwide.

Hilary White

CREDITS

Narrator: Russell Crowe (Voice)
Origin: Australia
Language: English
Released: 2007
Production: Sunny Abberton, Mark Lawrence; Bradahood Prods., Garage Industries; released by Berkela Films
Directed by: Sunny Abberton
Written by: Sunny Abberton
Cinematography by: Macario De Souza, Brooke Silvester
Music by: Jamie Holt
Editing: Macario De Souza
MPAA rating: R
Running time: 86 minutes

REVIEWS

Entertainment Weekly Online. April 11, 2008.
Hollywood Reporter Online. April 9, 2008.
Los Angeles Times Online. April 11, 2008.
New York Times Online. April 11, 2008.

Variety Online. March 16, 2007.
Village Voice Online. April 8, 2008.

BRIDESHEAD REVISITED

Love is not ours to control.
　　—Movie tagline

Every temptation has its price.
　　—Movie tagline

Box Office: $6.4 million

Director Julian Jarrold brings Evelyn Waugh's 1945 classic English novel to the big screen for the first time, but is in no danger of eclipsing the acclaimed 1981 television miniseries that featured an illustrious cast, including Laurence Olivier and Claire Bloom, and that made Jeremy Irons an international star. Both versions explore the relationship of the aristocratic Marchmain family to the narrator, Oxford University student Charles Ryder (Matthew Goode), but Jarrold's more modern version relies on elaborate surroundings and impressive period costumes rather than on delving more seriously into the workings of the characters and the social and religious themes presented in the novel and miniseries.

A drunken night at Oxford University is the catalyst for the friendship between Lord Sebastian Flyte (Ben Wishaw) and commoner Charles Ryder who meet during a pre-WWII fall. Charles is fascinated with the very popular but eccentric youth, who carries around a teddy bear named Sebastian and is surrounded by a colorful group of friends. Whereas the novel and the miniseries tread lightly over Charles's "romantic friendship" with Sebastian, Jarrold's version takes a heavier hand, replacing homosexual overtones with an overt expression of their love: a passionate kiss. When Sebastian takes Charles to his family's palatial country estate, Brideshead, Charles then transfers his schoolboy crush to Sebastian's sister Julia (Hayley Atwell) and is enchanted by the entire family.

Jarrold cast some heavy hitters, notably Emma Thompson, who turns in the film's best performance as Lady Marchmain, whom Jarrold too broadly paints as the villain of the story. Lady Marchmain strenuously upholds the family's Catholicism and Charles is an unrepentant atheist, which puts him squarely outside the family circle. *The New York Times*'s A.O. Scott sums up a dramatic enchange between Charles and Lady Marchmain over dinner: "…the argument, as Mr. Jarrold stages it, carries no sense of intellectual conviction or historical context. It's more like Dr. Seuss than Evelyn Waugh…" This is a typical example of how the filmmakers cause all the scenes involving the main theme of religion to seem artificial and strained.

Lady Marchmain nonetheless dispatches Charles on one last errand: to find Sebastian. Long an alcoholic, he finds his old schoolmate in Morocco, a virtually unrecognizable wretch after a long descent into opium addiction. Wishaw, who brilliantly portrayed an idiosyncratic serial killer in another period film, *Perfume* (2006), is equally adept at playing the jauntier, younger Sebastian as well as conveying remnants of his former aristocratic splendor even in his deeply ruinous state.

Told from Charles's perspective in flashback, he is a captain during World War II stationed at Brideshead, and his memories tell the story of his brief but indelible affiliation with the Marchmains. The role of Charles is the lynchpin of the story and calls for a delicate balance of shy, adrift, awestruck youthfulness and a sensitivity and intelligence that evoke future potential. Jarrold and screenwriters Andrew Davies and Jeremy Brock reimagine the character as alternately more opportunistic and more insipid. The script notwithstanding, Goode struggles to fill Jeremy Irons's shoes, and his bland performance induces more yawns than sympathy.

Unfortunately Jarrold evokes memories of the finer television incarnation of the story by filming on the same estate as the miniseries, which also had the luxury of telling the story over a much more protracted period of time. Even so, Jarrold and the screenwriters go over the same ground without providing anything psychologically or emotionally novel or adding any significant stylistic touches—beyond lush photography and homosexual sensationalism—that would justify its big screen retelling. What made the novel and the miniseries so fascinating were the nuanced layers of British society of the era, in other words, its customs, its religious bigotry, its notorious classism, and most importantly to this story, its repressed sexuality. Jarrold's *Brideshead Revisited* leaves nothing to the imagination and is all the worse for it.

Hilary White

CREDITS

Charles Ryder: Matthew Goode
Sebastian Flyte: Ben Whishaw
Julia Flyte: Hayley Atwell
Lady Marchmain: Emma Thompson
Lord Marchmain: Michael Gambon
Cara: Greta Scacchi
Rex Mottram: Jonathan Cake
Edward Ryder: Patrick Malahide
Origin: USA, Great Britain
Language: English
Released: 2008

Production: Robert Bernstein, Douglas Rae, Kevin Loader;
U.K. Film Council, BBC Films, HanWay Films, Ecosse
Films; released by Miramax Films
Directed by: Julian Jarrold
Written by: Andrew Davies, Jeremy Brock
Cinematography by: Jess Hall
Music by: Adrian Johnston
Sound: Danny Hambrook
Editing: Chris Gill
Art Direction: Lynne Huitson
Costumes: Eimer Ni Mhaoldomhnaigh
Production Design: Alice Normington
MPAA rating: PG-13
Running time: 135 minutes

REVIEWS

Boston Globe Online. July 25, 2008.
Chicago Sun-Times Online. July 23, 2008.
Entertainment Weekly Online. July 24, 2008.
Hollywood Reporter Online. July 18, 2008.
Los Angeles Times Online. July 25, 2008.
New York Times Online. July 25, 2008.
Newsweek Online. July 18, 2008.
San Francisco Chronicle. July 25, 2008, p. E5.
Variety Online. July 18, 2008.
Village Voice Online. July 23, 2008.
Washington Post. July 25, 2008, p. C2.

QUOTES

Sebastian Flyte: "Just the place to bury a crock of gold. I
should like to bury something precious, in every place I've
been happy. And then when I was old, and ugly and
miserable, I could come back, and dig it up, and
remember."

TRIVIA

The Marchmain estate of Brideshead was filmed at Castle
Howard, the same estate used in the 1981 miniseries.

THE BUCKET LIST

When he closed his eyes, his heart was opened.
—Movie tagline

Box Office: $93.4 million

The Bucket List is a poignant film that manages to
be heartwarming, sad, and hilarious at the same time,
thanks to a smart script and excellent performance from
the two leads, Jack Nicholson and Morgan Freeman.
This tale of two very different men stricken with cancer
is not a complex or completely original one, dramatizing

the lessons that each man teaches the other (though one
has an arguably larger influence) and reflecting on some
of the fundamentally important keys to a satisfied life,
but it is an emotionally moving and very memorable
one. The film's success lies in the way that it rather
simply speaks to truths of the human condition that are
frequently and tragically missed.

Nicholson plays Edward Cole, the wealthy, self-
important, somewhat snide owner of the hospital where
he finds himself a patient upon discovering that he has
brain cancer. Morgan Freeman plays Carter Chambers, a
level-headed, very intelligent auto mechanic who has
worked all his life to provide the very best for his family
and who is proud of the accomplished adults his children
have become. Carter likewise finds that he has cancer
and ends up sharing a hospital room with Edward.
Eventually, in a predictable yet uncontrived turn of
events, the two hit it off, as dissimilar as they are, and
become friends. One day, when both men have gone
into remission and are soon to be released from the
hospital, Edward picks up a crumpled piece of paper on
which Carter had been writing but finally meant to
throw away—Carter explains that it is a "bucket list," a
list of things he had always dreamed of doing before he
died ("kicked the bucket"). While Carter dismisses it as
a foolish idea, Edward becomes inspired by the list and
declares that they should both come up with a list and
actually do the things they have put down on paper.
After all, Edward can afford it. Carter protests at first,
but soon the two of them begin an adventure together,
intent on traveling the world to live out their dreams.
The plan angers Carter's wife Virginia (Beverly Todd),
who tries to convince her husband that he should spend
the remainder of his days with his family. Yet Carter
insists that it is something he needs to do.

Their adventure takes them, among other things,
skydiving, car racing, and climbing an Egyptian
pyramid. Along the way, they learn more about each
other—for instance, Carter learns that Edward has a
daughter he has not spoken to in years. Ultimately, the
two men return home before doing everything on their
lists, as Edward finally realizes that it is time for Carter
to return to his family, who needs him. Upon his arrival
back home, Carter has a renewed appreciation for his
family and a refreshed love for his wife, feeling younger
and more "alive" than he has in a long time, but sadly
he very soon succumbs to the cancer and passes away. In
one of the most emotionally powerful scenes in the film,
Edward delivers a eulogy that speaks of how Carter
changed his life and how he loved this friend, who had
accompanied him on one of the most important
journeys he had ever taken.

Interestingly, the movie is bookended with a
voiceover by Carter. The opening voiceover speaks of

Edward and how he had done more in the last months of his life than most men do in a lifetime, and the final voiceover—speaking as if from beyond the grave—also focuses on Edward, explaining how he died and was laid to rest beside his friend high atop a snow-covered mountain. Although the bookends focus on Edward, he is no more important a character than Carter. Indeed, Edward experiences a more dramatic change than Carter, as a result of Carter's influence in his life, but Carter is also equally at the heart of the story, for Edward would have probably died a sad and grumpy man if not for him.

In the hands of less capable actors, *The Bucket List* could have easily come across as silly or maudlin, trying too hard to play to emotions. Yet Nicholson and Freeman achieve a kind of balance between sincerity and playfulness that makes both characters endearing and genuine. The interaction and banter between them displays a camaraderie that includes both open honesty and lighthearted humor. Their developing relationship speaks to a common humanity that can bring people from two very different worlds together and allow them to share a deep bond. The two actors do an excellent job of portraying this bond and conveying a sense that the characters really do like and care about each other.

The screen and the page have hosted many stories with themes about living life to the fullest, but *The Bucket List* touches on that theme in a very heartwarming yet humor-filled way that manages to not seem a retread of similar tales. The film also reinforces the importance of family and the real measures of success in life. Carter Chambers states it well when he tells Edward, "You measure yourself by the people who measure themselves by you." By the end of the movie, the theme applies to both men, and it is very satisfactory to realize that it does. Therein lies the magic of this simple but significant film.

David Flanagin

CREDITS

Edward Cole: Jack Nicholson
Carter Chambers: Morgan Freeman
Thomas: Sean Hayes
Virginia Chambers: Beverly Todd
Roger: Alfonso Freeman
Angelica: Rowena King
Dr. Hollins: Rob Morrow
Origin: USA
Language: English
Released: 2007
Production: Craig Zadan, Neil Meron, Alan Greisman, Rob Reiner; released by Warner Bros.

Directed by: Rob Reiner
Written by: Justin Zackham
Cinematography by: John Schwartzman
Music by: Marc Shaiman
Sound: Robert Eber
Editing: Robert Leighton
Art Direction: Jay Pelissier
Costumes: Molly Maginnis
Production Design: Bill Brzeski
MPAA rating: PG-13
Running time: 97 minutes

REVIEWS

Hollywood Reporter Online. December 12, 2007.
Los Angeles Times Online. December 25, 2007.
New York Times Online. December 25, 2007.
Premiere Online. December 20, 2007.
Variety Online. December 11, 2007.
Village Voice Online. December 18, 2007.

QUOTES

Carter: "You measure yourself by the people who measure themselves by you."

TRIVIA

Prints of the film were shipped to several theaters under the title "Roads to Paradise."

BURN AFTER READING

Intelligence is relative.
—Movie tagline

Box Office: $60.3 million

When Ethan and Joel Coen followed their critical and commercial hit *Fargo* (1996) with the off-beat comedy *The Big Lebowski* (1998), many reviewers and filmgoers were puzzled and disappointed. In the years since, *The Big Lebowski* has grown from cult film to classic status, becoming the Coens' most beloved film. The writing-directing brothers received their greates critical acclaim, as well as Academy Awards®, for *No Country for Old Men* (2007), only to follow it with another dark, slapstick farce, *Burn After Reading*. While this film's reception has not been as harsh as that initially received by *The Big Lebowski,* it has had several naysayers. It is not as completely realized as the earlier film, but it, too, is a marvel of comic craftsmanship.

Burn After Reading has an unusual structure, beginning as if it is a serious look at the mores of Washington,

D.C. Osbourne Cox (John Malkovich), a veteran CIA analyst, is fired because of a drinking problem he denies. His wife, Katie (Tilda Swinton), a pediatrician, is having an affair with Harry Pfarrer (George Clooney), a United States marshal who never seems to go to work. A lover of life, Harry is passionate about Katie, still adores his wife, Sandy (Elizabeth Marvel), a well-known writer of children's books, and arranges for dates with others through an online service, never hiding that he is married.

Because he has to do something with his time, Cox decides to write his memoirs. Through a convoluted, slowly revealed set of circumstances, a computer disk containing his notes falls into the hands of two not very bright workers at Hardbodies gym. Chad Feldheimer (Brad Pitt), the much dimmer of the two, thinks Cox can be blackmailed. Linda Litzke (Frances McDormand) goes along with her friend because she needs money to pay for plastic surgery to make her more appealing to men. A seemingly atypical sentimental element comes into play with the unrequited affection for Linda by her boss, Ted (Richard Jenkins), though the Coens undercut the audience's expectations with a wildly probable absurdity. The various elements of the plot begin converging when Harry and Linda meet online and hit it off in person. He sees none of her supposed defects; she sees a passion and honesty missing from the other men she has encountered.

Alfred Hitchcock famously referred to arbitrary plot devices as McGuffins. They do not matter much in themselves and are important only so far as they propel the plot, as with the microfilm James Mason plans to smuggle out of the country in *North by Northwest* (1959). The Coens cleverly acknowledge their debt to Hitchcock by making Cox's disk completely worthless. It offers no secrets and would almost certainly not be published. That so much turmoil occurs because of it only adds to the absurdity of the proceedings. Chad and Linda think it is valuable because they are so desperate for some excitement in their placid lives. Though many reviewers claim that Chad finds the disk, it is actually discovered by another Hardbodies employee, Manolo (Raul Aranas), whose repeated account of finding it grows more hilarious each time, as the Coens emphasize the ridiculousness of the circumstances.

What is most clever about *Burn After Reading* is the way the various plotlines and characters intersect with something resembling a mathematical logic, often with completely unexpected results. The fluidity of the narrative, making the complex look simple, recalls the novels of P.G. Wodehouse in his prime. As with Wodehouse, the Coens' characters are cartoons, with just enough recognizable humanity.

The shift from drama to light comedy to much darker comedy may be bothersome for some. The Coens have been criticized as misanthropic, trying too hard to be hip and ironic, caring nothing for their characters. With the exception of the soft ending of *Raising Arizona* (1987), there is not an ounce of sentimentality in the brothers' films, and sometimes this approach can be jarring, as with the eruptions of violence in *Fargo*. The violent acts in *Burn After Reading,* however, do not disrupt the tone so much as propel it into another level of humor. As *No Country for Old Men* indicated, the Coens have learned some restraint over the years and do not actually show all the consequences of their characters' actions.

On one level *Burn After Reading* can be seen as a satire of spy films, such as *Spy Game* (2001), with Pitt, and *Syriana* (2005), with Clooney, taking the conventions of the genre, especially paranoia, and twisting them to comic effect. Familiarity with these conventions is not essential for enjoyment of the proceedings, however. The Coens' playfulness can also be seen in the film-within-the-film, a lame romantic comedy Linda attends with two dates. This film, starring Dermot Mulroney and an unseen Claire Danes, is the kind of conventional Hollywood claptrap the Coens strenuously oppose. A clip also pokes fun at Quentin Tarantino's notorious foot fetish. Ethan Coen has reported that the film's poster claims it is based on a novel by Cormac McCarthy, creator of the source of *No Country for Old Men* and is directed by Sam Raimi. Best known as the director of the Spider-Man series (begun in 2002), Raimi also directed the low-budget noir spoof *Crimewave* (1985), from a script by the Coens. While some have claimed *Crimewave* to be a rough draft for *Burn After Reading*, there are only superficial similarities.

One constant in Coen films is the quality of the performances. McDormand has her best comic role since *Fargo* and fearlessly throws herself into the farce. Yet Manohla Dargis of the *New York Times,* a prominent opponent of the film, accused the Coens of cruelty in the way Linda is presented. (McDormand is married to Joel Coen.) There were no such complaints about Pitt's portrayal of an overly excitable man with limited intellectual capacity. Like McDormand, Pitt is not afraid to look foolish, and Chad's wild gyrations to music are priceless. As he has shown with *True Romance* (1993), Pitt has a true gift for dumbness. Chad's elaboration pompadour may be a nod toward his even more excessive hairdo in *Johnny Suede* (1991).

Malkovich also gives an over-the-top performance as the ill-tempered Cox, becoming more farcically extreme as the film progresses. Swinton perfectly captures the cold aloofness of a professional with no time for nonsense, not even from her patients. Clooney offers a subdued version of the comic mannerisms he displays in the Coens' *O Brother, Where Art Thou?* (2000), though some reviewers accused him of simply repeating what he has done before. Clooney, who could get away with coasting on his considerable charm, makes Harry a likable mixture of the smooth and the confused. Harry's happy smile when he first sees Linda is one of the film's many highlights.

Burn After Reading also provides good roles for character actors. As Linda's potential plastic surgeon listening to her elaborate expectations, Jeffrey DeMunn gives an excellent demonstration of the comic effects of the well-timed pause. Even better comic timing occurs in the scenes between David Rasche, as the agent who fires Cox, and the inestimable J. K. Simmons, as his superior. The quick banter between the two is hilarious, especially in the film's final and best scene when Simmons wraps up all the loose ends in a not quite tidy package. *Burn After Reading* may not attract the cult status of *The Big Lebowski* because viewers will not so readily see themselves in these characters, but the film, especially in its final twenty minutes or so, is almost as funny.

Michael Adams

CREDITS

Chad Feldheimer: Brad Pitt
Harry Pfarrer: George Clooney
Osbourne Cox: John Malkovich
Katie Cox: Tilda Swinton
Linda Litzke: Frances McDormand
Ted Treffon: Richard Jenkins
CIA Superior: J.K. Simmons
CIA Officer: David Rasche
Krapotkin: Olek Krupa
Plastic Surgeon: Jeffrey DeMunn
Sandy Pfarrer: Elizabeth Marvel
Origin: USA
Language: English
Released: 2008

Production: Joel Coen, Ethan Coen; Working Title Productions, Relativity Media, StudioCanal; released by Focus Features
Directed by: Joel Coen, Ethan Coen
Written by: Joel Coen, Ethan Coen
Cinematography by: Emmanuel Lubezki
Music by: Carter Burwell
Sound: Peter Kurland
Editing: Joel Coen, Ethan Coen
Art Direction: David Swayze
Costumes: Mary Zophres
Production Design: Jess Gonchor
MPAA rating: R
Running time: 96 minutes

REVIEWS

Boston Globe Online. September 12, 2008.
Chicago Sun-Times Online. September 12, 2008.
Entertainment Weekly Online. September 10, 2008.
Hollywood Reporter Online. August 27, 2008.
Los Angeles Times Online. September 11, 2008.
New York Times Online. September 12, 2008.
San Francisco Chronicle. September 12, 2008.

QUOTES

Osbourne Cox: "No. No, I'm sorry, I don't know the number to, uh, my savings account because believe it or not I don't spend my entire day sitting around trying to memorize the f**king numbers to my f**king bank accounts! Moron!"

TRIVIA

The film was shot mostly in and around New York as the Coens wanted to remain near their families and George Clooney was working on another project in the area.

AWARDS

Nomination:

British Acad. 2008: Orig. Screenplay, Support. Actor (Pitt), Support. Actress (Swinton)
Golden Globes 2009: Actress—Mus./Comedy (McDormand), Film—Mus./Comedy
Writers Guild 2008: Orig. Screenplay.

C

CADILLAC RECORDS

If you take the ride, you must pay the price.
—Movie tagline

Box Office: $8.1 million

American popular music in the 1950s and the evolution of rock and roll have been especially popular topics for filmmakers. as *Ray* (2004), *Beyond the Sea* (2004), *Walk the Line* (2005), and *Dreamgirls* (2006) have approached this era with varying degrees of success. *Cadillac Records* takes a potentially compelling subject, the rise of Chess Records, and gives it the typical biographical film treatment, though the performances make the result interesting nevertheless.

Leonard Chess (Adrien Brody), a Polish immigrant in Chicago in 1941, decides to abandon his scrap-metal business and open a blues club in an African American neighborhood. His fortunes and those of Muddy Waters (Jeffrey Wright) become intertwined when the Mississippi bluesman arrives to become an innovator in electric blues guitar and the evolving Chicago blues style. Chess begins a record label, with Waters's "I Can't Be Satisfied" becoming a big hit in what was then called "race music."

Some of the best moments in writer-director Darnell Martin's film take place during recording sessions when Chess allows his performers to be spontaneous and break the standard rules of making records, as when Little Walter (Columbus Short) leans his harmonica into Waters's microphone, creating a new blues sound. Chess hires Willie Dixon (Cedric the Entertainer), the greatest blues songwriter and also the film's narrator, to write such songs as "Hoochie Coochie Man" for Waters and "My Babe" for Walter. As the success of Chess Records

grows, Chess adds such artists as Howlin' Wolf (Eammon Walker), Chuck Berry (Mos Def), and Etta James (Beyoncé Knowles). Waters is initially suspicious of Berry's music, calling it country rather than blues, but Chess is presented as a visionary who embraces the changes brought on by rock and roll. Even so, the film does not depict many other notable Chess artists, including Bo Diddley, John Lee Hooker, and Koko Taylor.

Cadillac Records is about much more than music, including the racism directed toward the black musicians, including Walter's being brutally beaten by police in front of Chess and Waters. The film's title comes from Chess's practice of paying his artists with new cars rather than the royalties they deserve. Martin's portrait of Chess is rather sketchy in that it never explains what draws him to this music, why he cheats his employees, or why he neglects his wife, Revetta (Emmanuelle Chriqui). Complications ensue. Waters develops a drinking problem and cheats on his faithful wife, Geneva (Gabrielle Union). He also introduces the unstable Walter to alcohol. Waters is jealous of the intense Wolf, and their relationship deteriorates from mistrust to hate. Berry's fondness for young white women gets him into legal trouble, and the daughter of a black prostitute and a white father she has never known, James becomes a drug addict. Naturally, she and the restless Chess are drawn to each other.

All of this should be more fascinating than it is because Martin, best known for her depiction of domestic issues in *I Like It Like That* (1994), treats the material with the standard formula for show business biographical films: chronological order, switching back and forth between songs and discord among the characters, financial and legal woes, trouble on the road, booze, drugs, sex, and other pitfalls of fame. In other words, Martin offers the same predictable structure that weakens the impact of *Ray* and *Walk the Line*. The director has worked extensively in television series and gives Vincent D'Onofrio and Eric Bogosian, two of her *Law and Order: Criminal Intent* (begun in 2001) televison series colleagues, small but pivotal roles as disk jockeys. Like television directors, however, she is too fond of close-ups and provides too little visual flair.

Martin excels, however, at handling her actors. Despite his underwritten role, Brody gives Chess an odd mixture of confidence and insecurity, especially in the scenes with James. Wright, one of the most adaptable American actors, makes Waters the film's moral center, despite the musician's many weaknesses. Martin is especially good at showing the singer's befuddlement when Waters first sees Berry's patented duck walk. Short, reminiscent of the young Richard Pryor, is overpowering as the volatile Walter. Walker matches his intensity as the glowering Wolf, whose every movement and gesture seem threatening. Knowles, the popular singer of lightweight pop, seems a questionable choice to play the earthy James, but she is marvelous at conveying the singer's confusion and disappointment. Gaining fifteen pounds also helps in capturing James's larger-than-life image. Best of all is Mos Def, displaying the anger lurking just beneath Berry's playful surface.

Mos Def resembles his character more than any of the other actors and offers a reasonable proximity of Berry's singing. Walker also captures Wolf's distinctive growl, as Short does Walter's ebullience. Wright tries valiantly to match the strength and anger of Waters' voice but is not quite strong enough to pull it off. Knowles imitates James's style perfectly but lacks the power of the original, arguably one of the most versatile singers ever.

Cadillac Records, unfortunately, follows in the tradition of *Dreamgirls* in paying too little attention to the accuracy of its chronology. The worst of many offenses involves having Berry upset that the Beach Boys's 1963 "Surfin' USA" seems to plagiarize his music and having the Rolling Stones meet Muddy Waters at Chess Records, which occurred in 1964, before the advent of Elvis Presley in 1956. Chess is also shown smoking filter cigarettes in 1947, seven years before the product was easily available in the United States. Just as *Ray* and *Beyond the Sea* eliminate Nesushi Ertegün as his brother Ahmet's partner in Atlantic Records, Phil Chess, cofounder of Chess Records, does not exist in *Cadillac Records*. More confusing is the presentation of the Chess-James relationship. The two are obviously sexually attracted, but Martin is frustratingly vague about whether the relationship is consummated. In real life it was not.

The film's many flaws, which also include Chess and Waters's disappearing for long periods, are nearly overcome by the enthusiasm of Martin and her performers for the vitality of the music. Despite the efforts of educators and documentary filmmakers, blues remains the most neglected American art form. Because of this film, however, people who might not otherwise hear Waters's "I'm a Man," Wolf's "Smokestack Lightnin'," and James's "I'd Rather Go Blind" will have that opportunity.

Michael Adams

CREDITS

Revetta Chess: Emmanuelle Chriqui
Leonard Chess: Adrien Brody
Geneva Wade: Gabrielle Union
Etta James: Beyonce Knowles
Chuck Berry: Mos Def
Muddy Waters: Jeffrey Wright
Howlin' Wolf: Eamonn Walker
Willie Dixon: Cedric the Entertainer
Isabelle Allen: Tammy Blanchard
Little Walter: Columbus Short
Alan Freed: Eric Bogosian
Origin: USA
Language: English
Released: 2008
Production: Sofia Sondervan, Andrew Lack; Parkwood Pictures, Sony Music Film; released by Sony Pictures
Directed by: Darnell Martin
Written by: Darnell Martin
Cinematography by: Anastas Michos
Music by: Terence Blanchard
Sound: Jeff Pullman, Stuart Deutsch
Music Supervisor: Beth Amy Rosenblatt
Editing: Peter C. Frank
Art Direction: Nicholas Locke
Costumes: Johnetta Boone
Production Design: Linda Burton
MPAA rating: R
Running time: 108 minutes

REVIEWS

Boston Globe Online. December 5, 2009.
Chicago Sun-Times Online. December 3, 2009.
Entertainment Weekly Online. December 3, 2009.
Hollywood Reporter Online. November 25, 2009.
Los Angeles Times Online. December 5, 2009.
New York Times Online. December 5, 2009.
Rolling Stone Online. December 18, 2008.

San Francisco Chronicle. December 5, 2009, p. E1.
Variety Online. November 25, 2009.
Wall Street Journal Online. December 5, 2008.
Washington Post. December 5, 2009, p. C1.

QUOTES

Muddy Waters: "You and me not gonna wake up every morning and get everything we want. Mostly we got to take what come."

AWARDS

Nomination:

Golden Globes 2009: Song ("Once in a Lifetime").

CARAMEL
(Sukkar banat)

Box Office: $1 million

At the center of *Caramel,* (also known as *Sukkar banat*) Lebanon's foreign film Oscar® entry for 2007, a scene appears in which the protagonist Layale (writer-director Nadine Labaki) goes to a series of increasingly slummy hotels in her effort to reserve a room to meet her married lover. Previously, the two of them have used her car, driving to a junkyard and also parking beneath a highway overpass. Because it is Beirut, however, Layale must show proof of marriage to get a hotel room. Finally, she settles on a run-down, disappointment of a room in a building where the clerk fails to ask for identification. She cleans and then eagerly decorates the room, even setting out a cake she has brought—only to have the man fail to show. Layale then invites over her female friends, and they cut the cake and relax and commiserate with each other as one of them ruefully admits that "living a lie" is something that wears a person out.

Caramel focuses, in the intertwined, mosaic manner of a Chekhov drama, on the lives of a handful of characters who have befriended each other at Layale's Si Belle Salon, a beauty shop in downtown Beirut where the excited cry "Heat the sugar, please!" refers to the preparation of caramel as a depilatory. All of them cope with the stress of seeking a happier life and a way to diminish the toll of living various lies. All of the plot-lines reveal an honesty and bittersweet flavor that replaces the strife of the war-torn city with a refreshing and winning humanity.

Layale herself is a thirtyish Christian who still lives at home with her parents, as is the unmarried custom. Her affair with her unseen lover loses its clichéd dimension when his wife Christine (Fadia Stella) comes to the beauty salon for a waxing, and Layale experiences a complex rush of emotions, including sympathy over hearing of the extensive preparations her rival has gone through for her anniversary. In another strand of the plot, Nisrine (Yasmine Al Masri) is engaged to Bassam (Ismaïl Antar), a Muslim. As her wedding nears, Nisrine fears Bassam's eventual discovery of her experienced sexual past. Like Layale at the seedy hotel, Nisrine rounds up her friends for support and takes them with her to a clinic where she hopes that a few careful surgical stitches will restore a facsimile of her virginity. A completely different and more sinister tone, however, is added to this plot when Nisrine and Bassam sit and converse in their car and are picked up and questioned by a suspicious policeman. The darker side of life in Beirut seems never very far from the hopeful struggles of the characters.

Another story concerns Jamale (Gisèle Aouad), an aging actress who fears losing jobs in commercials to younger competitors; the lengths to which she goes to suggest her lost youthfulness give the film its broadest comedy. Next door to the beauty shop another story develops with Aunt Rose (Siham Haddad), an old seamstress who faithfully looks after her unstable sister Lili (Aziza Semaan), even though such devotion will probably cost Rose her chance for a relationship with her gentleman caller, Mr. Charles (Dimitri Staneofski). In a plot-line developed with very little dialogue at all, Rima (Joanna Moukarzel) reveals her latent lesbianism through the recurrent, luxurious shampoos and nuanced glances she bestows on one of her new customers.

The film's greatest appeal lies in its consistent ability to find the revealing human detail. The local traffic cop, Youssef (Adel Karam, who is the only professional actor among the cast), loves Layale. She is oblivious to his feelings in spite of the repeated parking tickets with which he has papered her windshield in an attempt to get her to notice him. In one scene, Layale looks out of the window of her salon while talking on the telephone with her lover as her smitten policeman watches her from across the street and talks to him himself in an affectionate imaginary conversation. The Nisrine plot finds its emotional culmination on the night before her wedding and her last night in her parents' house. In a two-shot of her sitting on her bed with her mother, Nisrine obediently receives all her mother's loving advice in one of the film's most touching moments ("That's life—only God knows what's ahead"). The wedding that concludes the film offers an ending in keeping with the off-beat tone of the rest of the story. A flock of doves takes wing over the outdoor celebration, but Layale feels the plop of an unwelcome dropping as the birds fly over. The embarrassment, like so many of the situations in the film, elicits good-natured laughter from the characters rather than scorn, and the wedding concludes with Layale dancing with Youssef, her hopeful policeman-suitor.

Glenn Hopp

CREDITS

Layale: Nadine Labaki
Nisrine: Yasmine Al Masri
Rima: Joanna Moukarzel
Jamale: Gisele Aouad
Rose: Sihame Haddad
Lili: Aziza Semaan
Origin: France
Language: Arabic, French
Released: 2007
Production: Anne-Dominique Toussaint; Les Films des Tournelles, Roissy, Arte France Cinéma, Les Films des Beyrouth, Sunnyland; released by Roadside Attractions
Directed by: Nadine Labaki
Written by: Nadine Labaki, Jihad Hojeily, Rodney Al Haddad
Cinematography by: Yves Schnaoui
Music by: Khaled Mouzanar
Editing: Laure Gardette
Costumes: Caroline Labaki
Production Design: Cynthia Zahar
MPAA rating: PG
Running time: 95 minutes

REVIEWS

Boston Globe Online. February 8, 2008.
Christian Science Monitor Online. February 1, 2008.
Entertainment Weekly Online. January 30, 2008.
Hollywood Reporter Online. September 17, 2007.
Los Angeles Times Online. February 1, 2008.
New York Times Online. February 1, 2008.
San Francisco Chronicle. February 1, 2008, p. E8.
Time Online. February 1, 2008.
Variety Online. May 21, 2007.
Village Voice Online. January 29, 2008.

TRIVIA

The film was Lebanon's official submission in the Best Foreign Language Film Category for the 80th Annual Academy Awards®.

CASSANDRA'S DREAM

> *How far will you go to make your dreams come true?*
> —Movie tagline

> *Family is family. Blood is blood.*
> —Movie tagline

Woody Allen's third British film is much darker than its predecessors. While *Match Point* (2005) is an endlessly surprising murder/morality yarn with occasional jolts of humor, and *Scoop* (2006) is an off-beat comedy about the search for a serial killer, *Cassandra's Dream,* heavily influenced by Greek tragedy, is a bleak look at how ambition turns two brothers into murderers. Relentlessly grim, it has not one second of humor.

Ian (Ewan McGregor) toils at the modest London restaurant owned by his father (John Benfield), and his brother, Terry (Colin Farrell), is a mechanic at a garage specializing in fancy sports cars. The father depends upon Ian's taking over the family business and becomes incensed whenever his son mentions having larger ambitions. (Terry's freedom from family responsibilities is ignored by Allen.) Ian has a chance to invest in a Los Angeles hotel, and when he meets the beautiful young actress Angela Stark (Hayley Atwell), he boasts of being "in hotels," so to impress and keep Angela interested, Ian must find the money to realize his dream.

Ian's chance for success presents itself in the form of Howard (Tom Wilkinson), a wealthy businessman and the brother of the boys' mother (Clare Higgins). Ian convinces the relatively unambitious Terry to try to wheedle the needed funds from Howard, and their uncle is only too happy to oblige—as long they commit a murder for him. It turns out that Howard is a tad unethical and wants to prevent Martin Burns (Philip Davis), a business associate, from testifying about his crimes. The timid Ian does not want to kill anyone, but if that is the only way he can break away from his dismal life in the restaurant and win the luscious Angela, so be it. Terry is appalled by the prospect of murder but finally allows brotherly love to sway him.

The murder, of course, has consequences, and therein lies part of the problem with *Cassandra's Dream.* After the slow buildup to the murder, nothing afterward is particularly surprising, though the writer-director clearly thinks he has provided unexpected twists at the end. The film superficially resembles *Match Point,* both dealing with ordinary men compelled to commit desperate acts, yet while the earlier film continually reinvents itself, *Cassandra's Dream,* lacking any but the easiest of ironies, limps awkwardly toward its telegraphed conclusion. Conversely, *Match Point* is the work of a master filmmaker in complete control of all aspects of his medium. *Cassandra's Dream* is the work of an uninspired artist going through the motions with tired material.

The Allen film *Cassandra's Dream* most closely resembles is *Crimes and Misdemeanors* (1989), and Terry, overwhelmed by guilt, can be seen as a working-class version of the character played by Martin Landau in the earlier film. *Cassandra's Dream* is like *Crimes and Misdemeanors* without the contrasting humorous story focusing on Allen's bumbling filmmaker and Alan Alda's pompous television producer. With the complete absence of comedy, *Cassandra's Dream* becomes perhaps Allen's bleakest film for the brothers are introduced in a state of mild desperation and slowly sink into complete despair.

Contributing greatly to this dark mood is Philip Glass's score, as Allen abandons, for once, his reliance on music from his extensive jazz and classical collection. As he does in *The Hours* (2002), Glass shifts between his distinctively repetitive minimalism and traditional film music, soaring melodramatically here and there, underlining the protagonists' anxieties. Likewise, cinematographer Vilmos Zsigmond, who once shot beautiful films such as *The Hired Hand* (1971), gives the film an underexposed look, to cast a gray pall over the proceedings.

The performances are in keeping with Allen's despairing approach. Benfield is blustery; Higgins is shrill. Wilkinson is initially calm and confident but flusters Howard when the uncle asks Ian and Terry to kill for him, sputtering, breaking off sentences, much like Allen's characters in *Hollywood Ending* (2002). Atwell is appealing, though she fails to demonstrate what Angela sees in the drab, insecure Ian. On the other hand, Sally Hawkins, as Terry's cockney girlfriend, is spunky, and Davis makes Burns sympathetic enough to create pain at his death.

Giving one of his most restrictive performances, McGregor shifts Ian from blandly pleasant to desperate, with little in between. Farrell, however, shows the kind of depth long expected from him. He could easily overact to convey Terry's tormented soul but shows the character's increasing pain following the murder with small gestures, a sinking of the head, tension in the eyes.

The surprisingly smooth dialogue Allen created for *Match Point* abandons him here. Everything seems aimed at maneuvering the characters through the plot points. Allen's irritatingly bad habit of having characters constantly call each other by their names flusters Farrell so much that he calls McGregor "Terry" during a heated exchange.

Cassandra's Dream refers to the sailboat the brothers buy early in the film. They name the vessel for a dog on which Ian has placed a winning bet. The dog, the boat, and the title underscore Allen's chance theme. Just as bettors never win every time, Allen's luck runs out here.

Michael Adams

CREDITS

Ian Blaine: Ewan McGregor
Terry Blaine: Colin Farrell
Angela Stark: Hayley Atwell
Kate: Sally Hawkins
Uncle Howard: Tom Wilkinson
Mr. Blaine: John Benfield
Mrs. Blaine: Clare Higgins
Nigel: Tom Fisher
Origin: France, USA
Language: English
Released: 2007
Production: Letty Aronson, Gareth Wiley, Stephen Tenenbaum; Wild Bunch, Virtual Films, Iberville Prods., Wolverine Prods.; released by Weinstein Co.
Directed by: Woody Allen
Written by: Woody Allen
Cinematography by: Vilmos Zsigmond
Music by: Philip Glass
Sound: Peter Glossop
Editing: Alisa Lepselter
Art Direction: Nick Palmer
Costumes: Jill Taylor
Production Design: Maria Djurkovic
MPAA rating: PG-13
Running time: 108 minutes

REVIEWS

Boston Globe Online. January 17, 2008.
Chicago Sun-Times Online. January 17, 2008.
Entertainment Weekly Online. January 16, 2008.
Los Angeles Times Online. January 18, 2008.
New York Times Online. January 18, 2008.
New Yorker Online. January 21, 2008.
San Francisco Chronicle. January 18, 2008, p. E5.
Variety Online. September 2, 2007.
Village Voice Online. January 15, 2008.
Washington Post. January 18, 2008, p. C5.

TRIVIA

This is the first Woody Allen film to feature a stereo soundtrack.

CHANGELING

To find her son, she did what no one else dared.
—Movie tagline

Box Office: $35.7 million

Imagine waters that gain power and momentum as they are funneled through a gorge, surging, emerging, and then diverging into a host of distributaries that cannot compare to the concentrated thrust of that initial flow. That is what director Clint Eastwood's *Changeling* is like, a film that focuses viewers' attention on a confluence of gripping horrors, only to have that forcefulness significantly dissipate as it broadly diffuses and runs on and on. The story the film tells is based on truth so disquieting and outrageous that audiences are likely to react, as the film's central character does, with shocked disbelief that such things could actually transpire. In his first produced feature film screenplay, former journalist and veteran television writer J. Michael Straczynski saw *Changeling* as a tribute to that protagonist, wanting to elucidate both the travails that befell her and the positive repercussions that resulted from her refusing to stay down. Unfortunately, endeavoring to disseminate all this information by dramatizing the story's every path upon the screen ultimately detracts from what had been the potent conveyance of a truly wrenching, wretched real-life nightmare.

There is something eerie in the air from the start of *Changeling*, a sense of melancholic foreboding. The camera slowly glides through a quiet residential neighborhood of yesteryear, a setting that should fill one with a warm, cozy sense of nostalgia, if the visuals were not unsettlingly desaturated to nearly a cold black and white. This lack of color seems to signal that something is stealthily, incongruously wrong here amidst what should have been a vibrant Los Angeles springtime when the 1920s were still roaring. There and then dwelled Christine Collins (Angelina Jolie, good but falling short of a fascinating fullness equal to that of her lips), the doting mother of nine-year-old Walter (Gattlin Griffith), whom she is raising alone because his father (by pointed contrast) was afraid of responsibility. Viewers see Christine dutifully getting her boy ready for school, riding with him on the city's now extinct red trolley cars before continuing on to her job supervising switchboard operators for Pacific Telephone and Telegraph. They also repeatedly hear her speaking lovingly to Walter, as well as holding his hand protectively before sending him off with a kiss. Of course, such underscoring of this mother's attachment to her only child, the centerpiece of her life and reason to live it, aim to make the subsequent sudden breaking of that bond tug with maximum force at the audience's heartstrings, and rightfully so.

On March 10, 1928, Christine agreed to fill in for someone at work, even though obviously torn because she had promised to take Walter to the movies and hated to disappoint him. After leaving a lunch for him and instructions for neighbors to look in on the self-proclaimed self-sufficient youngster, Christine departs, and as the image of Walter waving goodbye in the window gradually recedes, an anxiety-inducing, haunting moment is created that will make anyone possessing an ounce of parental protectiveness feel like reaching out to grab him before he disappears completely. Running a little late coming home and then just missing her trolley (a lingering, "what if?" moment), Christine arrives to find no sign of Walter, and she searches the vicinity with increasing alarm. When she calls the police to report that something terrible has happened, they pooh-pooh her repeated assertions, a portent of infinitely more heartless treatment to come.

Through words delivered in person to his congregation as well as to his flock of radio listeners, activist Reverend Gustav Briegleb (John Malkovich) conveys how the City of Angels has gone to hell, ruled by a notoriously corrupt no-holds-barred-nor-bullets-spared regime headed by Mayor George E. Cryer (Reed Birney) and Police Chief James E. "Two Guns" Davis (Colm Feore). When a child is finally found in July in DeKalb, Illinois, not only resembling but reportedly identifying himself as Walter Collins, these authorities are thrilled to be able to blunt the criticism of Briegleb and others with some rare positive press resulting from their unification of mother and son amidst much fanfare.

Christine cannot get to her son fast enough, but she is crestfallen to see a pint-sized stranger (Devon Conti) staring back at her. "It's not my son," the shocked woman asserts for the first of countless times. One-note meanie Capt. J.J. Jones (Jeffrey Donovan), sensing a much-needed opportunity slipping away, doggedly tries to remove this unexpected fly from the ointment, but Christine is adamant. Hardly reassured by declarations that elapsed time and dizzying emotions are preventing her from recognizing her own flesh and blood, a rattled and dazed Christine pastes a smile upon her face as the crush of photographers and reporters advances. In this state, she is quietly but outrageously manipulated into agreeing to at least take the boy home for the time being, "on a trial basis." Her bewilderment is heartbreaking to watch, and as the rear window of the vehicle in which Christine and the boy depart visually yokes them together in the back seat, her discomfiture is queasily palpable.

This is when *Changeling* acutely grips viewers with a profoundly disconcerting creepiness. It is as if this apparently faux fils has stepped out of an episode of Rod Serling's *Twilight Zone*, insisting he is Walter, calling Christine "Mommy," reciting their address by heart, and expressing relief to be back. (Many who saw the film seem to have expected a stretch of edgy uncertainty as to whether Christine had become unbalanced and as a result not seeing quite straight.) Once she sees that this boy with the inscrutable gaze is not only inches shorter than Walter but also circumcised, there is a thoroughly chilling, shadowy sequence in which the woman demands to know who he is and what he is aiming to achieve, covering her mouth and slowing backing away, as if in the inexplicable presence of something supernaturally terrifying. (Viewers might not catch that this troublemaking imposter had lied to get to Hollywood in hopes of meeting his idol, cowboy picture star Tom Mix.)

When Straczynski submitted his draft of *Changeling*, he understandably chose to affix numerous newspaper clippings to it that would counter the incredulity he expected would result as the film's story unfolds. Viewers were aghast and outraged to see the shameful persecutory extremes to which the LAPD went in dismissing and then silencing the public assertions of this poor mother, who simply wanted an admission that a mistake had been made and a renewed effort to find her real son before it would be too late. Their unwarranted (in every sense of the word) actions escalate to spiteful character assassination and then to throwing her in a hellish mental ward, where other perfectly sane pests of the police (mainly "uppity" women) were locked away and electroshocked into acquiescence—"until their senses are restored." Cinematographer Tom Stern, who added to *Changeling*'s noirish atmosphere with starkly-contrasting lights and darks throughout, uses horizontal shadows thrown across Christine's face from a venetian blind to visually underscore her entrapment. She unflinchingly refused to gain her freedom by signing a statement that would recant all her claims and criticisms, a document repeatedly presented by Dr. Jonathan Steele (Denis O'Hare, vying with Donovan to create the film's most detestable authority figure.)

It is at this point that the first trickles of *Changeling*'s debilitating divergence begin. While continuing to follow Christine endeavoring to cope in confinement, the film's attention appears to drift away to a juvenile deportation case handled by the film's laudable cop, Detective Lester Ybarra (Michael Kelly, standing out through understatement). This leads to the ghastly discovery of a mass grave full of chopped up children, boys who had been sexually abused, generally tortured, and then axed to death by Gordon Northcott (Jason Butler Harner, showily riveting and off-putting at the same time) with the forced and soul-crippling assistance of his teenaged cousin Sanford Clark (affecting Eddie Alderson). Sanford identifies Walter as one of the youngsters brought to the remote Northcutt farm's chicken coop for slaughter (although he may or may not have been among the precious few who escaped), with horror film-like flashbacks depicting what might have been better left to the audience's imagination. Despite the gradually revealed relevance of what had up to that point seemed like a thematically related but superfluous detour, these scenes unfortunately detract from the primary proceedings upon which they eventually shed light.

"Never start a fight," Christine had admonished Walter early on, but then stressed that, if someone else does, it is important to stand up and "always finish it." Christine follows her own advice once the Northcutt investigation confirms that the real Walter had indeed not reentered her home and she is thus grudgingly released from the hospital with the help of Briegleb and the heroically commanding and high-profile attorney S.S. Hahn (Geoff Pierson). *Changeling* was meant to highlight the steadfast determination with which a cloche-bedecked, boldly lipsticked survivor stood up to and brought down the slew of formidable men who wronged her, or, as *Changeling*'s posters put it, "did what no one else dared." However, as Christine makes sure the other wrongly committed "Code 12" ladies are released (including Amy Ryan's prostitute, Carol Dexter), attends hearings to penalize and prevent official malfeasance as well as Northcutt's trial and drawn-out, excruciatingly disturbing hanging, this protracted parade of comeuppance, while thoroughly deserved, bloats and further slackens the 140 minute, already deliberately paced production. Simply too much ground is traversed here, with *Changeling* finally seeping to an end in 1935 when hopes are raised by news of yet another boy's resurfacing, and while Christine does not get her own son back, she is provided with renewed hope that was unfortunately never fulfilled.

Despite unquestionably compelling source material, strong production values, and CGI work that transformed modern-day L.A. to transport viewers back in time, *Changeling* failed to live up to the expectations of Eastwood's many admirers. Straczynski reportedly felt that the film failed to win the top prize at Cannes due to judges who could not swallow the fact that the story is not fiction. However, they may have merely felt like the *New York Times*'s A. O. Scott, who stated: "The film spoils itself. At around the 90-minute mark, all of the considerable tension and suspense drain away" as *Changeling* "lurches from one stagy set piece and from one genre to another, losing its focus and coherence in the process."

David L. Boxerbaum

CREDITS

Christine Collins: Angelina Jolie
Rev. Gustav Briegleb: John Malkovich
Capt. J.J. Jones: Jeffrey Donovan
Det. Lester Ybarra: Michael Kelly
Chief James E. Davis: Colm Feore
Gordon Northcott: Jason Butler Harner

Sanford Clark: Eddie Alderson
Carol Dexter: Amy Ryan
Dr. Jonathan Steele: Denis O'Hare
Dr. Earl W. Tarr: Peter Gerety
Walter Collins: Gattlin Griffith
Origin: USA
Language: English
Released: 2008
Production: Clint Eastwood, Brian Grazer, Ron Howard, Robert Lorenz; Relativity Media, Malpaso, Image Ent.; released by Universal Pictures
Directed by: Clint Eastwood
Written by: J. Michael Straczynski
Cinematography by: Tom Stern
Music by: Clint Eastwood
Sound: Walt Martin
Editing: Joel Cox, Gary D. Roach
Art Direction: Patrick M. Sullivan Jr.
Costumes: Deborah Hopper
Production Design: James Murakami
MPAA rating: R
Running time: 141 minutes

REVIEWS

Boston Globe Online. October 24, 2008.
Chicago Sun-Times Online. October 23, 2008.
Entertainment Weekly Online. October 22, 2008.
Hollywood Reporter Online. May 20, 2008.
Los Angeles Times Online. October 24, 2008.
New York Times Online. October 24, 2008.
New Yorker Online. October 27, 2008.
Newsweek Online. October 18, 2008.
Rolling Stone Online. October 30, 2008.
San Francisco Chronicle. October 24, 2008, p. E1.
Variety Online. May 20, 2008.
Washington Post. October 24, 2008, p. C1.

QUOTES

Christine Collins: "The boy they brought back is not my son."

TRIVIA

Angelina Jolie's character says "Never start a fight, but always finish it" twice. This is the same quote that Captain John Sheridan says his father always told him in the 1990s sci-fi series *Babylon 5* which writer J. Michael Straczynski also wrote.

AWARDS

Nomination:

Oscars 2008: Actress (Jolie), Art Dir./Set Dec., Cinematog.

British Acad. 2008: Actress (Jolie), Cinematog., Costume Des., Director (Eastwood), Film Editing, Orig. Screenplay, Sound, Production Des.
Golden Globes 2009: Actress—Drama (Jolie), Orig. Score
Screen Actors Guild 2008: Actress (Jolie).

CHAOS THEORY

This man will bring order to the universe...or not.
—Movie tagline
He planned his life like clockwork. Now things are going cuckoo.
—Movie tagline

Chaos Theory, starring Ryan Reynolds, begins as a light teen teaser, sharply shifts into comedy bordering on melodrama, and then veers back again. Reynolds plays Frank Allen, an obsessive best-selling author and lecturer of "The Five Minute Efficiency Trainer," a system that advocates a borderline neurotic obsession with writing tasks on cue cards in an effort toward carpe diem. When Frank's wife Susan (Emily Mortimer) sets a clock forward to play with Frank's schedule, it sets off a chain of events that leads Frank to tangerine martinis and Paula (Sarah Chalke), who has put Frank on her "to-do" list. After narrowly escaping an affair and fleeing back to his wife, Frank ends up in a car accident alongside a pregnant woman and he is mistakenly confused for being the child's father. While attempting to prove his innocence to Susan, he learns shocking news that his best friend may be his child's father. To go further would be to spoil the twists, but Daniel Taplitz's script has most of its holes plugged by Marcos Siega's beautiful storytelling and a compelling performance from Reynolds.

The title itself, "Chaos Theory," speaks of its being a movie of severe changes. As Frank says, "Life is messy." The chaos theory itself studies the behavior of an entity that changes over time. Through quite simple and natural events, Frank is certainly thrown into wildly different behaviors over time, from being the proud family man, to being drunkenly content to scribble lists, to near-suicide and murder, and back again.

For example, there is a brilliant and cleverly short scene between Frank and his doctor. At the beginning of this brief scene Frank has been thrown out of his home, and he is anxiously awaiting the proof that he is not the father of the child he has been accused of fathering. He is told, very simply, that he could not possibly be the father; he has been "sterile since birth." Chanting under his breath that he "has a little girl at home," he is plunged into carousing (albeit still making lists) as a death-defying, devil-may-care idiot. However dashingly dramatic the choices may be, it is a beautiful image of existence: to see everything change in this man's life in only seconds, and then to see him stunned for minutes of film time before moving on.

Both Frank and Susan's reactions are determined largely by chance. Frank has his index cards from which he chooses at random what his next action will be. The two of them meet, with Susan standing on a table, drink in hand, telling a group of New Year's partiers that whoever has the best name for their penis...will be her husband! As such, *Chaos Theory* is not only a flashy film, but also a beautiful commentary on the absurdity and importance of space and time.

The camera work is by no means showy, but it would be easy to miss its unhurried pace and willingness to sit still and let the actors do the work. The color red is prominently used to connect the Allen family: An early shot exclusively of Frank's red socks at his daughter's wedding, his daughter's red sweater illuminated by flashing red police lights, and the dress that Susan wears when she and Frank first met. The design of this film is a series of elegant solutions; simple, yet very clear storytelling.

Those looking for a romantic comedy may be startled by the emotional demands it makes on its audience and the bizarre twists that put the Allens' marriage to the test. The snap realizations of all of the characters come, at the least, as an incredulous surprise, but they are never implausible. Futhermore, because the reactions to these surprises are given such weight in the script and on the screen, the viewer is swept easily along. The film works in its antithesis. The wilder the switches of Frank's fate become, the bigger the laughs. There is a deft balance in switching from black comedy to heartfelt romance, but in this aspect *Chaos Theory* mostly succeeds.

Reynolds gives a refreshing leading-man performance that ranges with the film from comedy to pathos and back again. There is a cynical edge that is strengthened by a deep warmth in his performance, which can make murder funny and love murder.

Richard Baird

CREDITS

Frank Allen: Ryan Reynolds
Susan Allen: Emily Mortimer
Buddy Endrow: Stuart Townsend
Paula Crowe: Sarah Chalke
Ed: Mike Erwin
Peg: Constance Zimmer
Jesse Allen: Elisabeth Harnois
Damon: Chris Martin
Nancy: Jocelyne Loewen
Origin: USA
Language: English
Released: 2008
Production: Frederic Golchan, Erica Westheimer; Castle Rock Entertainment, Lone Star Film Group; released by Warner Bros.
Directed by: Marcos Siega
Written by: Daniel Taplitz
Cinematography by: Ramsay Nickell
Music by: Gilad Benamram
Sound: James Kusan
Editing: Nicholas Erasmus
Art Direction: Margot Ready
Costumes: Tish Monaghan
Production Design: Sandy Cochrane
MPAA rating: PG-13
Running time: 86 minutes

REVIEWS

Boston Globe Online. April 11, 2008.
Chicago Sun-Times Online. April 11, 2008.
Hollywood Reporter Online. April 7, 2008.
New York Times Online. April 11, 2008.
San Francisco Chronicle. April 11, 2008, p. E9.
Variety Online. April 4, 2008.
Village Voice Online. April 8, 2008.
Washington Post. April 11, 2008, p. C5.

QUOTES

Frank Allen: "Do you have any idea how embarrassing it is to show up late to a lecture on the efficiency use of time?"

CHARLIE BARTLETT

Popularity is a state of mind.
—Movie tagline
First come. First cured.
—Movie tagline
When Charlie Bartlett listens, everyone talks.
—Movie tagline

Box Office: $3.9 million

Both a nod to the 1980s "teens against the adult world" films, especially the seminal John Hughes movies *The Breakfast Club* (1985) and *Ferris Bueller's Day Off* (1986), and more recent high-minded comic ventures focused on eccentric and wealthy characters, most notably those Wes Anderson's *Rushmore* (1998) and *The*

Royal Tenenbaums (2001), *Charlie Bartlett* attempts to transcend some of the more stock elements of the teen genre by giving all of the characters (their oddities notwithstanding) fairly real-world problems and exploring the consequences of choices. Directed by Jon Poll and starring Anton Yelchin as Charlie and Kat Dennings of *The 40 Year Old Virgin* (2005) and *Nick and Nora's Infinite Playlist* (2008), as Susan Gardner, Charlie's love interest. This interesting yet disappointing movie also features the slightly unbalanced principal, Nathan Gardner, played by the always solid Robert Downey, Jr.

By and large, the plot of *Charlie Bartlett* is fairly standard teen movie fare, with something of a twist: Charlie Bartlett is, in a way, the standard oddball outsider who unites other teens against the constrictive adult world, but he is also unique in that he is a super-wealthy outsider, sent to public school by virtue of the fact that no private institution would have him after his many expulsions. With the help of the high school bully (whom Charlie is able to tame by using a sort of snake-charmer version of the psycho-babble that Charlie himself has obviously been exposed to for years), Bartlett is able to parlay his unfettered access to psychiatrists into a burgeoning prescription drug trade among his fellow high school students. Charlie also takes up the role of unofficial school psychiatrist and begins to fulfill his own fantasies of becoming popular simply by listening to his peers and providing them with some guidance (and occasionally medication). Events begin to get a bit out of hand, however, when Charlie attracts the attention of Susan Gardner, the principal's daughter. Smarting from his divorce, clearly not enjoying his calling as principal, and struggling with alcohol abuse issues, Nathan Gardner becomes fixated on Charlie not only for the threat Principal Gardner believes Charlie poses to his relationship with his daughter, but also for the clear influence Charlie has over the student body. Charlie and Susan eventually get into an altercation with Mr. Gardner when Mr. Gardner sees Charlie hand Susan a bag—thinking it is drugs, Mr. Gardner grabs Susan's arm and handles her roughly until Charlie punches him. When Susan and Charlie leave, Mr. Gardner looks in the bag and finds nicotine gum (Charlie was trying to help Susan relinquish her smoking habit). The movie ends with a sort of unraveling effect—Charlie and Mr. Gardner come to an understanding when Charlie almost drowns trying to make sure Mr. Gardner doesn't shoot himself while drunkenly shooting at a remote controlled boat and, in the aftermath, Charlie convinces Mr. Gardner to come to the school to see Susan act and sing in the school play, and Mr. Gardner convinces Charlie to visit his dad, who is in prison for tax evasion. (This father is a great source of shame for Charlie throughout the film—his father is a taboo subject and, when taken

to the prison by his mother earlier in the movie, Charlie simply waits in the car).

Charlie Bartlett has a few commonalities with other teen genre films, like *Ferris Bueller's Day Off, Rushmore,* or *Say Anything...* (1989), like the struggle of youth attempting to rise above the mundane grind of high school, and putting forth questions of identity and accepting of one's self. On its surface, the film is about an outsider who comes to a public school and shakes up the established order through prescription pharmaceuticals, sage advice, and a willingness to cross social boundaries. *Charlie Bartlett,* however, is not so much a *Ferris Bueller* for the twenty-first century as a sort of high school, bubble-gum riff on *One Flew Over the Cuckoo's Nest* (1975). Charlie himself is a kind of toned down, young, rich, WASP version of R.P. McMurphy (Jack Nicholson's character in *Cuckoo's Nest*), and the insane asylum has been replaced by a public high school. Through the course of the film, all of the characters, Charlie included, come to learn something about themselves: Charlie learns that popularity comes with responsibility; Principal Gardner learns that by being true to himself, instead of attempting to do that which his roles as a father and educator demand of him, he will be a better father and educator; and the students learn that they are not so different from one another after all, and that by working together they can effect a change in how they are perceived by the adult world. In other words, *Charlie Bartlett* spends a great deal of its time, in the tradition of most teen journey films, exploring how social roles affect self-perception and hinder people from becoming what they might possibly be.

An element of Charlie's character, however, serves to undermine the efficacy of the film either as emblematic of the teen genre or as an attempt to transcend the genre: Charlie is markedly disconnected from the events that take place around him, to the point that there are no stakes for him. Everything about Charlie puts him at a remove from his surroundings, so rather than mirroring either the actual teenage boy journey or that of scores of fictional counterparts (Ferris Bueller, Max Fischer, Lloyd Dobbler), Charlie functions much more like an alien among humans than an outcast among peers. Charlie is anything but an Everyman. He is outrageously wealthy, and that establishes him as existing completely outside the world of public high school. To be sure, high school films usually focus on the journey of an outsider, but Charlie's wealth keeps him safe from the threats and pressures posed to the average student. A change-agent like Charlie may make for a good peripheral character in a film like this, but as a central character, Charlie is so above the influence of school machinations, so obviously insulated by the fact that his family is rich, that he is detached from the specifics of his surroundings. Thus his desire for popularity has little to do with trying to make sense of his public high school existence or trying to transcend it; rather, it is a general fantasy of his to be popular, regardless of venue. Charlie's money provides him both connections to therapeutic resources most health-plan carrying adults cannot dream of as well as distance from the everyday march of school life, and this combination allows him to become the unofficial psychiatrist of his high school. It is no coincidence that his detached nature in combination with his extreme wealth lead him in this direction.

Charlie's distance from his circumstances manifests itself not only in the facts of his wealth and privilege, but also in his character traits. Before he confronts the school bully, Murphy Bivens (Tyler Hilton), in order to hire him essentially as the muscle for his drug/therapy operation, the audience gets to see Charlie practice what he is going to say in order to convince him to join in the endeavor. The ostensible purpose of the scene is to establish Charlie's preternatural ability to read people effectively, but this could have been accomplished simply by showing Charlie's actual confrontation with Murphy alone. By choosing to show Charlie's rehearsal of the face-off, it suggests that Charlie is calculating. Why not make friends with the "slow" kid that no one else will talk to or sit with when there is nothing to lose by doing it? Granted, Charlie seems to be a good guy who would do the right thing anyway, but it is hard to ignore that his money protects him, and separates him from the pressures of high school that dog practically any other student anywhere, real or fictional. The one part of Charlie's biography that seems to hinder him somewhat is his father's imprisonment, but even that is revealed to have no harsher effect on Charlie that a deep-seated shame—not rage or sorrow at his father's absence, just shame at the fact that his father is doing time for tax evasion. In fact, Charlie's problems are in stark contrast to those of principal Gardner, who has everything to lose. He is a man who recognizes his connection to events and what is at risk should things go south. His story has a weight approaching tragedy; for example, by attempting to do what he sees as right and what he genuinely believes to be in the best interest of his daughter, his school, and himself, he stands to lose everything he wants to save (his daughter, his job, his dignity, and perhaps even his sanity). True, Charlie and Principal Gardner need one another in order to change, and each represents the other's extreme opposite in outlook: Charlie needs to see that the people in his life are precious, and Principal Gardner needs to look beyond what he thinks he should do (trying to be a principal) and what he knows he should do (be a great history teacher and father). Because Anton Yelchin and Robert Downey, Jr. are high-caliber actors who bring

lots of depth and dynamism to their roles and their characters' relationships, in the end they give the film whatever weight it has. Conversely, Charlie's total separation from the gravity of his circumstances makes him seem not particularly invested in his world, which makes it difficult for the audience to invest fully in *Charlie Bartlett*. The film suffers, then, from its own high-mindedness, which is unfortunate because the performances are strong overall and *Charlie Bartlett* has some interesting points to make about life choices and the desire to be popular.

John Boaz

CREDITS

Charlie Bartlett: Anton Yelchin
Susan Gardner: Kat Dennings
Principal Gardner: Robert Downey Jr.
Marilyn Bartlett: Hope Davis
Murphy Bivens: Tyler Hilton
Kip Crombwell: Mark Rendall
Dustin Lauderbach: Jake Epstein
Whitney Drummond: Megan Park
Henry Freemont: Ishan Dave
Jordan Sunder: Jonathan Malen
Origin: USA
Language: English
Released: 2007
Production: David Permut, Jay Roach, Sidney Kimmel, Barron Kidd; Everyman Pictures, Texon Entertainment; released by MGM
Directed by: Jon Poll
Written by: Gustin Nash
Cinematography by: Paul Sarossy
Music by: Christophe Beck
Sound: Michael O'Farrell, Michael Haight
Music Supervisor: Dave Jordan, Jojo Vilaneuva
Editing: Alan Baumgarten
Costumes: Luis Sequira
Production Design: Tamara Deverell
MPAA rating: R
Running time: 96 minutes

REVIEWS

Boston Globe Online. February 22, 2008.
Chicago Sun-Times Online. February 22, 2008.
Entertainment Weekly Online. February 20, 2008.
Hollywood Reporter Online. June 26, 2007.
Los Angeles Times Online. February 22, 2008.
New York Times Online. February 22, 2008.
San Francisco Chronicle. February 22, 2008, p. E6.

Variety Online. May 9, 2007.
Wall Street Journal. February 22, 2008, p. W1.

QUOTES

Charlie Bartlett: "Well, see, that's my whole point. I mean you could've been born a single cell organism on the planet Zortex. In fact, given the odds, it's probably more likely, but you weren't. You we're born a human being. And not just any human being in the history of human beings, but a human being that gets to be alive today. That gets to listen to all kinds of music, that gets to eat food from every culture, that gets to download porn off the internet. So really, you have everything to live for."

CHICAGO 10

*The convention was drama. The trial was
   comedy.*
   —Movie tagline

In 1969, the great cinematographer Haskell Wexler made the powerful semi-documentary movie *Medium Cool,* about his involvement in the protests at the 1968 Democratic National Convention. Now a new generation will have an opportunity to understand what took place when anti-war activists clashed with police in the parks and on the streets of Chicago.

Written and directed by Brett Morgen (*The Kid Stays in the Picture* [2002]), this new look at the famous events of August 1968 is sandwiched into a reenactment of the trial of eight activists in a federal courtroom more than a year later. That is more customarily known as the trial of the Chicago Eight, or sometimes the Chicago Seven (as Black Panther activist Bobby Seale's case was eventually separated from the others). Morgen apparently makes the number ten by including the group's two attorneys, including the famous William Kuntsler, because they were eventually slapped with jail sentences on various contempt of court charges. (All of the charges were eventually overturned on appeal.)

The result is what sounds like an unwieldy stew of techniques: The courtroom scenes are portrayed using Rotoscoping animation and professional voice talent (Hank Azaria, Nick Nolte, Mark Ruffalo, Roy Scheider, and Liev Schreiber, among others). These scenes are interspersed with archival footage of the accused as they conduct press conferences and rallies during and after the trial, and the progress of the trial itself is shown between some rare footage of the turmoil over the four days in Chicago. When necessary, animation is used to fill in the gaps: one night's police raid on protesters who hoped to camp out overnight at Lincoln Park is illustrated through live footage, but the next raid is done with animation. In one scene, animated speakers are shown addressing a rally in Grant Park, presumably because there was footage of the entire crowd available but not of the speakers on stage.

At first, the mingling of techniques seems disconcerting, but eventually it becomes quite effective. The viewer sees real images of the real protest leaders—Dave Dellinger and Rennie Davis of the Mobilization to End the War, and Abbie Hoffman and Jerry Rubin of the Youth International Party (Yippies), plus Seale and the other defendants—and cartoon images of them. Yet, as so well illustrated by director Richard Linklater in *Waking Life* (2001), Rotoscoping can bring life and vitality to animation, as well as a sort of surrealism, and the trial itself is perfectly suited to this treatment. As presided over by Judge Julius Hoffman (voice of Roy Scheider), who is drawn with a pink nose, the trail is an extended cartoon anyway, a folly in which the judge continually mispronounces the defendants' names, makes absurd rulings that always favor the prosecution, and shows a weak grasp of the issues at stake. It is also a sort of circus in which the Yippies Hoffman and Rubin play pranks, hide-and-seek, come to court dressed in judge's robes, and generally wreak havoc.

One of the funniest scenes is hippie poet Allen Ginsberg on the witness stand, being ordered by the prosecutor to recite a poem about various bodily fluids; afterwards, he chants "Om," the Buddhist mantra to bring peace, and there is priceless footage of a real news report in which the anchorman says Ginsberg was chanting "um." There are plenty of rarely seen clippings of Hoffman and Rubin prancing around with their followers at what they billed as a "festival of life" in Chicago. Quite quickly, the trial becomes understandable as a continuation of the confrontation in the streets, between inflexible authorities and uncompromising activists who cannot be controlled.

Although *Chicago 10* is clearly sympathetic to the views of the protesters, it is also an unvarnished look at the actual 1960s (as opposed to the nostalgic images that too often substitute for the gritty reality). The protesters are noble and determined, but they are also frightened and confused. They were infiltrated and sometimes provoked by undercover cops, yet they were not shy about characterizing the police as "pigs" and were inconsistent about applying principles of nonviolence. The protesters are as ill equipped to negotiate how to respond to an armed show of force as the authorities are ill equipped to cope with a disorganized, anarchic mass of unruly youth.

In retrospect, what happened in Chicago could accurately be characterized, as a clip shows Walter Cronkite did characterize it, as a police riot, and the trial was little more than a farce, which the defendants used for their own publicity purposes. However, there is genuine horror and tragedy in *Chicago 10* too, when it is seen as a vision of a society on the brink of collapse. When Judge Hoffman orders security guards to bind and gag Seale, as he continually asserts his constitutional right to defend himself (which Hoffman has denied), a hush falls over the proceedings. Morgen brilliantly juxtaposes this scene with one in which Dellinger and the other leaders, trying to march without a permit to the Convention Center, are blocked by a line of police, and then they sit down on the sidewalk in a dramatic plea for their right to assemble.

Most of the film is not so brilliantly balanced, though, and some footage that is used seems egregious or misplaced in the narrative: for example, a scene in which a long-haired activist confronts a matronly woman on the street, and another in which a young black woman expresses no sympathy for the mostly white protesters being clubbed downtown. At several places the narrative breaks down, but given the chaotic nature of the events and the incomplete documentary film record of them, that is understandable. Errors of omission exist too. Viewers might expect that in a film about protests at the 1968 Democratic convention, there would be one mention of Robert Kennedy's assassination or the fact that Hubert Humphrey was nominated with a pledge to continue the Vietnam War. A little more basic background would have improved viewer understanding of historical events; yet overall, with music by Eminem, among others, and the use of modern animation, *Chicago 10* makes this important story of the protests and the resulting trial accessible to new audiences forty years after it took place. What Morgen has done is a fine way of making history come alive again, in all its ugly messiness.

Michael Betzold

CREDITS

Abbie Hoffman/Allen Ginsberg: Hank Azaria (Voice)
David Dellinger/David Stahl: Dylan Baker (Voice)
Thomas Foran: Nick Nolte (Voice)
Jerry Rubin: Mark Ruffalo (Voice)
Judge Julius Hoffman: Roy Scheider (Voice)
William Kinstler: Liev Schreiber (Voice)
Bobby Seale: Jeffrey Wright (Voice)
Anita Hoffman: Amy Ryan (Voice)
Marry Ellen Dahl: Debra Eisenstadt (Voice)
Origin: USA
Language: English
Released: 2007
Production: Brett Morgen, Graydon Carter; River Road Entertainment, Participant Productions, Public Road Prods., Consolidated Documentaries; released by Roadside Attractions

Directed by: Brett Morgen
Written by: Brett Morgen
Music by: Jeff Danna
Editing: Stuart Levy
MPAA rating: R
Running time: 103 minutes

REVIEWS

Boston Globe Online. February 29, 2008.
Chicago Sun-Times Online. February 29, 2008.
Entertainment Weekly Online. February 26, 2008.
Los Angeles Times Online. February 29, 2008.
New York Times Online. February 29, 2008.
San Francisco Chronicle. February 29, 2008, p. E5.
Variety Online. January 19, 2007.
Washington Post. February 29, 2008, p. C1.

AWARDS

Nomination:

Writers Guild 2008: Doc. Screenplay.

CHOKE

Box Office: $2.9 million

Between working at a colonial theme park and attending sexual addiction recovery workshops, the sardonic and detached Victor Mancini (Sam Rockwell) frequents upscale dining establishments. There he feigns choking to allow fellow diners to "rescue" him, eliciting feelings of sympathy, which takes the form of money that he, in turn, uses to pay for his ailing mother's hospital bills. This outlandish premise for the black comedy *Choke* has all the elements required for an interesting, subversive independent production, and then some. While even more caustic and farcical plot elements emerge later in a story already filled with controversial and unique plot elements, *Choke* is not able to bring all the elements together into a fully cohesive and satisfying whole. The low-budget film is the directorial debut of actor Clark Gregg, who also adapted the screenplay from the 2001 novel of the same name by Chuck Palahniuk. Palahniuk is best known for his novel *Fight Club* that was adapted for a film of the same name directed by David Fincher in 1999. As scripted, the damaged characters of *Choke* never seem truly three-dimensional, and when their pain is played for comedy's sake—namely, the sex addiction—the film works best. When it deals with the more sober issue of Victor's childhood trauma that resulted in serious mother issues, it is not as successful, despite his mother being played by the always-fascinating Anjelica Huston. In *Choke* character arc is a virtually nonexistent concept.

Mancini works unhappily in an uncomfortable costume at a colonial-themed park, alongside his friend, Denny (Brian William Henke). Both recovering sex addicts, Victor and Denny attend group therapy meetings, where the more-handsome Victor is easily able to find a willing partner for a brief tryst. In the evenings, Victor runs a regular con at fancy restaurants. His one redeeming quality, it seems, is what he does with the money, which is pay for the expensive psychiatric treatment of his hospitalized, Alzheimer's-afflicted mother Ida (Anjelica Huston).

It is mainly due to his mother, however, that the unhappy Victor chooses to escape reality through having sex as often as possible. As a child, his unstable mother could not take proper care of him and gave him up for adoption, but she frequently kidnapped him from the foster homes he was ultimately placed in. Despite being an emotionally wrecked adult, Victor finds a real connection of some kind with his mother's nurse Paige (Kelly Macdonald).

When Ida no longer recognizes Victor, he sends Denny to pose as him and question his mother about the father he never knew and Ida's Italian-language diary is discovered. Paige volunteers to translate and reveals that Victor may be the product of cloned foreskin that Ida stole and is, then, perhaps the son of Jesus. As Ida's health worsens, the unusual Paige radically suggests an experimental stem cell treatment that would require Victor to have a child and gamely suggests they try to have one together. Victor, however is rendered impotent around her because, as Denny tells him, he is in love with her. The film ends with Victor accidentally, and quite ironically, choking his mother to death while feeding her and revealing, in the process, that Paige is not a nurse at the hospital but herself a patient.

While the film radically shifts tone from wacky sex comedy to bleak relationship drama, it loses momentum and strains believability. Aside from some half-hearted moralizing, much of the dialogue is caustically funny and appropriately sarcastic. "What would Jesus *not* do?" Victor humorously ponders. Just the suggestion that the scruffy sex addict may be the second coming is wonderfully absurd, while, doubtless, also being offensive to many. The film's overly sentimental dramatic scenes are a jarring contrast with the raunchy black comedy.

A master of character studies, Sam Rockwell has shown admirable adaptability in a wide range of films and film genres in roles as varied as the goofy, two-headed space cowboy in the comedy *The Hitchhiker's Guide to the Galaxy* (2005); a killer cowboy's brother in the drama *The Assassination of Jesse James by the Coward Robert Ford* (2007); and a put-upon father of a bad seed in the horror/thriller *Joshua* (2007). His performance here is typically solid, yet flawed by the character's lack of complexity. As Roger Ebert noted in his *Chicago Sun-Times* review, "*Choke* centers on a character who is content to be skanky and despicable and who does not reform, although the plot seems to be pushing him alarmingly in that direction." Anjelica Huston also does her best with the small, undemanding role, while director Gregg gives himself a scene-stealing role as Victor and Denny's boss, Lord High Charlie.

Hilary White

CREDITS

Victor Mancini: Sam Rockwell
Ida Mancini: Anjelica Huston
Dr. Paige Marshall: Kelly Macdonald
Ursula: Bijou Phillips
Denny: Brad William Henke
Lord High Charlie: Clark Gregg
Cherry Daquiri: Gillian Jacobs
Origin: USA
Language: English
Released: 2008
Production: Beau Flynn, Tripp Vinson, Johnathan Dorfman, Temple Fennell; Contrafilm, ATO Pictures; released by Fox Searchlight
Directed by: Clark Gregg
Written by: Clark Gregg
Cinematography by: Tim Orr
Music by: Nathan Larson
Sound: Christof Gebert
Editing: Joe Klotz
Art Direction: Matteo De Cosmo
Costumes: Catherine George
Production Design: Roshelle Berliner
MPAA rating: R
Running time: 89 minutes

REVIEWS

Boston Globe Online. September 26, 2008.
Chicago Sun-Times Online. September 25, 2008.
Entertainment Weekly Online. September 24, 2008.
Hollywood Reporter Online. January 29, 2008.
Los Angeles Times Online. September 26, 2008.
New York Times Online. September 26, 2008.
San Francisco Chronicle. September 26, 2008, p. E7.
Variety Online. January 22, 2008.
Village Voice Online. September 24, 2008.
Washington Post Online. September 26, 2008.

QUOTES

Phil: "A lot of people would say it's a bad idea, on your first day out of prison, to go right back to stalking the tranny hooker that knocked out five of your teeth. But that's how I roll."

TRIVIA

The author of the book on which the movie was based, Chuck Palahniuk, can be seen at the end of the film—he is the man sitting next to Victor on the plane.

A CHRISTMAS TALE
(Un conte de Noël)

Box Office: $1 million

Arnaud Desplechin's *A Christmas Tale* (*Un conte de Noël*) is nearly the exact opposite of what American audiences have come to expect from movies with the holiday in the title (*Four Christmases* [2008], *Christmas with the Kranks* [2004], *Surviving Christmas* [2004], etc.) This is not a standard dysfunctional family drama. There is quite a bit more to what Desplechin is trying to do than the predictable clichés that are usually delivered by the genre. Audiences looking for heartwarming endings or slapstick humor should seek them elsewhere. And yet, there is something easily identifiable in the incredibly twisted and damaged clan of the Vuillards that makes them feel completely three-dimensional. The success of *A Christmas Tale* is slightly deflated by pretentious pacing that leads to an unnecessarily extreme length, but there are incredible performances and much to adore about this complex film.

Catherine Deneuve, still one of the most striking and consistent actresses anywhere in the world, plays matriarch Junon Vuillard in *A Christmas Tale*. Junon is married to the older Abel (Jean-Paul Roussillon), and the two have had a tragic past before the movie even begins. In a mesmerizing prologue full of revelations that most Hollywood writers would have saved for a raucous Christmas dinner family fight, it is revealed that Junon and Abel's oldest child, Joseph, was diagnosed with a rare disease that none of the Vuillards, not even Joseph's sister Elizabeth (Anne Consigny,) had the blood type to save. So, Abel and Junon decided to have another child to save their favorite son. Henri (Mathieu Amalric) was born, but it was too late, and Joseph died.

The Vuillards had yet another child named Ivan (Melvil Poupaud) and everyone tried to move on with their wounds and pain repressed. The pain of the past is brought up again when a grown Elizabeth decides that she wants her younger brother, the one who was born merely to save the life of her beloved lost sibling, banished from her life. She makes a deal to never see Henri again. Elizabeth moves forward with her life and

tries to manage her emotionally and mentally unstable son, while Henri dives deeper into self-loathing and regret over the fact that he has been discarded by nearly every member of his family. The divided Vuillards reunite six years later when Junon is diagnosed with the same disease that killed her son. Of course, only Henri can save her. In the days before Christmas, Henri, Ivan, Elizabeth, and their extended and immediate family return to the house where they grew up to deal with their deeply damaged history.

A simple plot recap of *A Christmas Tale* may make the film sound a bit like a soap opera, but Desplechin is far from melodramatic as a writer or director. In fact, he purposefully avoids melodrama, allowing his characters to breathe instead of over-react. *A Christmas Tale* is a deeply woven, character-driven story. As soon as it feels like Desplechin has settled on a theme or concentrated on a few characters, he goes somewhere unexpected. Madness, lost love, sibling rivalry, and family tragedy are all interwoven into a screenplay that can also be surprisingly funny at times. There are scenes and moments where it almost feels like Desplechin's screenplay goes from complex to unfocused. It is a fine line between letting characters develop and boring the audience. At 150 minutes, *A Christmas Tale* feels a little bloated; a more straightforward and shorter film would have been just as effective.

What truly elevates *A Christmas Tale* into one of the more critically beloved films of the year is the spectacular ensemble that Desplechin assembled to deliver his material. Consigny, Roussillon, Deneuve, and Amalric give some of the best performances of 2008, but they are merely in the forefront of a cast that does not give a single false note. Amalric is particularly riveting. The flawless ensemble makes the pretentious length, a flaw of the direction and writing, much easier to overlook.

Critics adored *A Christmas Tale*, which made several top ten lists, including taking the stellar spot in lists from critics at *Salon*, *Slate*, the *Austin Chronicle*, the *Globe and Mail*, the *Seattle Post-Intelligencer*, and the *Oregonian*. Other major critics, including those at the *Los Angeles Times*, *Chicago Tribune*, *New York Post*, *Variety*, and the *New York Times* put the film on their top ten lists as well. It was easily one of the best reviewed films of the year and one of the most beloved by art house audiences.

Brian Tallerico

CREDITS

Junon: Catherine Deneuve
Abel: Jean-Paul Roussillon

Henri: Mathieu Amalric

Sylvia: Chiara Mastroianni

Claud: Hippolyte Girardot

Elizabeth: Anne Consigny

Ivan: Melvil Poupaud

Faunia: Emmanuelle Devos

Rosaimee: Françoise Bertin

Paul: Emile Berling

Simon: Laurent Capelluto

Origin: France

Language: French

Released: 2008

Production: Why Not Productions, France 2 Cinema, Wild Bunch, BAC Films Ltd.; released by IFC Films

Directed by: Arnaud Desplechin

Written by: Arnaud Desplechin, Emmanuel Bourdieu

Cinematography by: Eric Gautier

Music by: Gregoire Hetzel

Sound: Nicolas Cantin

Editing: Laurence Briaud

Art Direction: Dan Bevan

Costumes: Nathalie Raoul

MPAA rating: Unrated

Running time: 150 minutes

REVIEWS

Entertainment Weekly Online. November 12, 2008.

Hollywood Reporter Online. May 14, 2008.

Los Angeles Times Online. November 14, 2008.

New York Times Online. November 14, 2008.

Rolling Stone Online. November 27, 2008.

Variety Online. May 16, 2008.

Village Voice Online. November 11, 2008.

Wall Street Journal Online. November 14, 2008.

Washington Post. September 21, 2008.

THE CHRONICLES OF NARNIA: PRINCE CASPIAN

A New Age Has Begun.
　　　—Movie tagline

Everything you know is about to change forever.
　　　—Movie tagline

Box Office: $141.6 million

Based on the second book in C.S. Lewis's classic fantasy series *The Chronicles of Narnia*—and a sequel to the blockbuster hit *The Chronicles of Narnia: The Lion, the Witch and the Wardrobe* (2005)—Walden Media's

The Chronicles of Narnia: Prince Caspian is a more mature film than its predecessor, yet it may have suffered from strategic missteps by distributor Walt Disney that led to its meeting a less impressive reception in theaters. The film was generally received well and would be categorized as a moderate success in financial terms, but its differences from the first movie, while in some cases arguably superior, contributed to a weaker performance at the box office. *Prince Caspian* is a darker, more brooding film than *The Lion, the Witch and the Wardrobe,* and as such it seems less like a children's movie, though it still succeeds in remaining family-friendly.

The book *The Chronicles of Narnia: Prince Caspian,* which is widely considered the weakest of the series, is hampered by a less imaginative plot and thinner character development than in the other six books. The four main characters introduced in *The Lion, the Witch and the Wardrobe*—Peter, Susan, Edmund, and Lucy Pevensie—have less to do in the story, and a large portion of the book is a "flashback" section in which prior events are related to the four Pevensies to provide the necessary backstory. Not surprisingly, there is a new main character in the book, and that is Prince Caspian himself, but his story takes precedence over the development of the established characters. In adapting the book to the screen, director Andrew Adamson and his team of screenwriters faced the dilemma of how to best translate this nonlinear story so as not to have the four characters from the previous film take a back seat to the conflict involving Caspian. The filmmakers wisely chose to restructure the plot so that everything unfolds along a linear timeline; they also strove to delve more deeply, where possible, into the character development of the four Pevensie children, so they were not as overshadowed by Caspian.

Unlike the book, the movie begins in the land of Narnia rather than in "our" world, introducing the character of Caspian (Ben Barnes), a Telmarine prince whose life comes under threat when the wife of his wicked uncle Miraz (Sergio Castellitto) gives birth to a son. Caspian's friend and teacher Dr. Cornelius (Vincent Grass) warns him that he must flee the castle at once and head for the woods. Pursued by Miraz's soldiers, the prince rides to the woods and there encounters native Narnians in the form of dwarfs Trumpkin (Peter Dinklage) and Nikabrik (Warwick Davis) and badger Trufflehunter (voice of Ken Stott); in a moment of panic, he blows the ancient horn of Queen Susan, which had been given him by Cornelius and is said to have the power to summon help from the ancient world.

The story shifts to England, where one year has passed since Peter (William Moseley), Susan (Anna Popplewell), Edmund (Skandar Keynes), and Lucy (Georgie

Henley) traveled to the world of Narnia through the wardrobe. All four of them miss their experience in Narnia, where they had ruled as kings and queens for years before returning to their own world (time passes differently between the two worlds). Peter especially has a hard time being a "kid" again when he was High King in Narnia. As the film reintroduces the four Pevensies, they are in a railway station waiting to return to school. Suddenly, unexpectedly, they feel the sensation of being pinched, and then, in front of their eyes, their surroundings began to change and they find themselves on a beach.

High atop the cliffs that rise above them, they see the ruins of an ancient structure. After investigating the ruins, they realize that not only have they returned to Narnia, but they are on the grounds where once stood the great castle of Cair Paravel, their home when they had ruled as the Four Kings and Queens of Narnia. They begin to learn what has happened after coming across a boat manned by two Telmarine soldiers who are about to drown a bound and gagged dwarf—it is in fact Trumpkin, who was captured when Caspian fled into the old Narnian woods. When the children save the grumpy dwarf, he is amazed and obviously initially disappointed to learn that they are the Kings and Queens of old, having been summoned by the blowing of Susan's horn. In time, he realizes that they are not just children and explains to them that Narnia has changed drastically since they disappeared. Thirteen hundred years have passed, and in that time, Narnia was conquered by the Telmarines and is currently ruled by Miraz, who took over when Caspian's father died. The Telmarines tried to exterminate the Narnians, who largely took refuge in the old woods. Trumpkin and the Pevensies then set out on a journey to meet up with the Narnians and devise a plan for saving them from the tyranny of Miraz. Meanwhile, Caspian befriends the Narnians and vows to help them take back their land if they will follow him in the cause of overthrowing Miraz. The Narnians swear their allegiance to him.

During their trek through the woods, Lucy claims that she sees the lion Aslan (voice of Liam Neeson), the lord over all Narnia who appointed them Kings and Queens and defeated the White Witch (Tilda Swinton) in the first film, but no one else sees him. She later encounters the lion while the others are asleep and he tells her to trust in him, but then she awakens to find that she must have been dreaming. Soon thereafter, the Pevensies meet Caspian and the Narnians. Not surprisingly, some tension erupts between Caspian and Peter, who reminds everyone that he is High King. Everyone then travels to the sanctuary of Aslan's How, where they plan what to do next. They soon discover that, unfortunately, Miraz has learned of their existence and their

location and will be sending his army to defeat them as soon as his men finish building a bridge across the Great River at Beruna.

While young Lucy encourages them to wait on Aslan for help, Peter, Caspian, and the others debate whether they should attack Miraz head-on before he comes after them or hold their ground firmly within Aslan's How, treating it as a kind of fortress. Ultimately they decide to follow Peter in an attack on Miraz's castle. Unfortunately, though the assault on the castle does allow them to rescue Dr. Cornelius, the battle turns into a loss as many of the Narnians wind up trapped behind the castle gates, where they are slaughtered. Upon their dejected return to the How, the survivors determine that their only course of action is to ready their defense against Miraz's army. However, they also send Lucy out to search for Aslan. A personal duel between Peter and Miraz buys them a little time while Lucy rides away into the woods, but even though Miraz winds up dead—defeated by Peter but actually killed by one of his own, Lord Sopespian (Damián Alcázar)—the Telmarine army launches an attack on the Narnians. Meanwhile, Lucy does indeed find Aslan, who asks why she did not search for him earlier. He tells her it is time to awaken old friends and lets out a roar that awakens the trees, which then join the war against the Telmarines. When the Telmarine army attempts to retreat and cross the Great River, Aslan calls forth the river-god, who destroys the bridge. The battle ends in victory upon the surrender of the Telmarine army, and in the end Caspian is named King of Narnia.

The film departs from the book in several ways, but the changes serve to tell a more engaging and dramatic on-screen story. In the book, Aslan does appear earlier, and there is only one relatively brief battle against the Telmarines, so that the conflict with Miraz occurs and is resolved rather quickly. In adapting the story for the screen, Adamson and his team chose to develop a theme of faith that is present in the book but not so pronounced and clear. Peter in particular struggles with his role as High King and his responsibility to save Narnia—and to the film's credit, his character is more rounded out by the implication that some of his struggle has to do with pride, not simply saving the world he has come to love. The fact that Aslan does not arrive right away adds tension to the story that would not have existed if the film had closely followed the book. The attack on Miraz's castle, the resulting failure and loss of life, and the temptation to resurrect the White Witch as an ally play out more dramatically and with more complexity, so these changes make sense and might even be considered improvements upon the original story.

Characterization in general is handled effectively among the main characters, though the characters of

Peter, Lucy, Caspian, and Miraz stand out as the most fully developed and the most interesting. One additional departure from the book is a romantic attraction between Susan and Caspian (which some fans of the book decried), and while it makes possible a touching moment at the end when Aslan explains that Peter and Susan will not be returning to Narnia and Susan then gives Caspian a quick kiss, the overall subplot is largely inconsequential and underdeveloped.

Most of the performances are more than adequate, though Popplewell and Keynes occasionally seem to be reading their lines (yet their performances are generally better than in the first film). Moseley, Henley, and Castellitto seem most in tune with their characters and do a good job of bringing them to life and eliciting the right kind of response from the viewer. Dinklage also brings warmth and likeability to the grumpy dwarf Trumpkin, and the realistically rendered computer-generated character of the valiant mouse Reepicheep springs to animated, humorous life with the voice of Eddie Izzard.

Visually, even though fewer locations are visited than in the first film, *Prince Caspian* achieves a more epic feel with a slightly grittier atmosphere than *The Lion, the Witch and the Wardrobe*. The film is literally and figuratively darker—thematically, it is a darker storyline, with more treachery and brutality and in which everything is not always black and white. In keeping with that tone, much of the film is darker in terms of lighting. Up until the end of the film, Miraz's castle is a dark and dreary place, and even the Narnians must take shelter in the darkness of the underground sanctuary of Aslan's How.

Overall, the filmmakers fashioned a film that is emotionally and psychologically richer than the book, and some critics went so far as to hail *Prince Caspian* as a better movie than its predecessor. Ironically, however, audiences did not head to the theaters to see it the way they did with *The Lion, the Witch and the Wardrobe*. Disney did not launch the same kind of marketing campaign that helped promote the first movie, and some observers noted that the film may have performed better in the winter (like *The Lion, the Witch and the Wardrobe*, which opened in December) than in the summer, where it was crowded out by such summer blockbusters as *Iron Man* (2008) and *Indiana Jones and the Kingdom of the Crystal Skull* (2008). Additionally, whereas *The Lion, the Witch and the Wardrobe* was viewed as very family-friendly, initial word-of-mouth pointed to the darker, more intense nature of *Prince Caspian,* which likely kept some families from taking their children to see it in the theater.

David Flanagin

CREDITS

Lucy Pevensie: Georgie Henley
Edmund Pevensie: Skander Keynes
Peter Pevensie: William Moseley
Susan Pevensie: Anna Popplewell
King Miraz: Sergio Castellitto
General Glozelle: Pierfrancesco Farino
Trumpkin: Peter Dinklage
Nikabrik: Warwick Davis
Prince Caspian: Ben Barnes
The White Witch: Tilda Swinton
Aslan: Liam Neeson (Voice)
Reepicheep: Eddie Izzard (Voice)
Origin: USA
Language: English
Released: 2008
Production: Mark Johnson, Philip Steuer, Andrew Adamson; Walden Media, Silverbell Films; released by Walt Disney Studios
Directed by: Andrew Adamson
Written by: Andrew Adamson, Christopher Markus, Stephen McFeely
Cinematography by: Karl Walter Lindenlaub
Music by: Harry Gregson-Williams
Sound: Tony Johnson
Editing: Sim Evan Jones
Art Direction: Frank Walsh
Costumes: Isis Mussenden
Production Design: Roger Ford
MPAA rating: PG
Running time: 140 minutes

REVIEWS

Boston Globe Online. May 16, 2008.
Chicago Sun-Times Online. May 15, 2008.
Entertainment Weekly Online. May 14, 2008.
Hollywood Reporter Online. May 9, 2008.
Los Angeles Times Online. May 16, 2008.
New York Times Online. May 16, 2008.
Newsweek Online. May 14, 2008.
Rolling Stone Online. May 29, 2008.
San Francisco Chronicle. May 15, 2008, p. E1.
Variety Online. May 9, 2008.
Washington Post. May 16, 2008, p. C1.

QUOTES

Prince Caspian: "Two days ago, I didn't believe in the existence of talking animals...of dwarves or...or centaurs. Yet here you are, in strengths and numbers that we Telmarines could never have imagined. Whether this horn is magic or not, it brought us together and together, we have a chance to take back what is ours!"

TRIVIA

Aslan, one of the more prominent characters of Narnia, is missing for almost 95 percent of the film.

CITY OF EMBER

Discover the secret.
—Movie tagline

Escape is the only option.
—Movie tagline

Box Office: $7.8 million

That *City of Ember* features a little girl innocently munching on information that shows the way to a better life seems highly appropriate, as the film aims to give viewers—especially younger ones—a lot to chew on. It is based upon the first in a series of popular science fiction books by Jeanne DuPrau, who grew up in the 1950s and remembers well how the Cold War had made her shiver. Americans at that time found a rather naïve solace in excavating in their backyards bomb shelters, supposedly capable of keeping their families just far enough below the ravages of a Soviet atomic onslaught to remain safe and snug. Afterward, the plan was to emerge again like groundhogs, despite what could have been a nuclear winter lasting a much longer than six weeks. DuPrau wondered what would happen if a massive number of people had to take refuge together beneath the surface of the Earth and stay there for centuries, calling a subterranean city home for two hundred years.

Such has happened to the citizens of Ember, but now their gigantic generator, the sole source of electricity, is failing and about to plunge the populace into terrifying, total darkness. Food supplies are dwindling, as well. The people are unfortunately trusting in a secretly corrupt, self-interested mayor to solve their predicament. Some, especially a Mrs. Murdo (Mary Kay Place), retain blind faith in Ember's legendary creators, "the Builders", who surely would not have set a plan in motion with no exit strategy that would inevitably lead to extinction amidst pitch-blackness. In truth they had not, but the significance of a locked briefcase containing instructions about how to leave has at some point been forgotten, popping open at the bottom of a cluttered closet after two centuries to offer salvation—and no one notices except the aforementioned tot.

However, two bright teenagers come to utilize the partially masticated directions retrieved from the child to confront this impending doomsday with youth's inexhaustible curiosity, hope, and bravery. After watching *City of Ember*, the characters' real-life peers were supposed to be inspired to save their own imperiled world. After seeing adult ineffectualness, complacency,

and folly contrasted with the more admirable example of the film's heroic yet sympathetic young protagonists, viewers are to feel empowered to do a better job than their elders did as stewards of Earth. "In telling this story to…mostly young people, I want to send the message that we have the great responsibility of protecting our environment," DuPrau explained. The best of intentions made for a fine book, but unfortunately only a mediocre—albeit laudably themed—film.

If Ember's ability to exist hinges on its massive generator, the film's ability to generate interest in its plot rests most heavily on the shoulders of its fourteen-year-old lead, Saoirse Ronan, who was riveting in (and Oscar®-nominated for) her role in *Atonement* (2007). Even circumstances grow increasingly dire around Ronan's Lina Mayfleet, the character continues to shine with an appealingly fierce intelligence and bristling determination. Especially in close-ups of her striking face and even tighter shots highlighting an intriguing, intense look of concentration in her eyes, Ronan once again exudes a degree of that impressive magnetism, precociously capable of holding an audience's attention.

There is undoubtedly significance in the fact that Lina winds up with the job of messenger on Assignment Day, as it is she who, by recognizing the importance of the gnawed papers, plays the key role in delivering Ember from peril. As the city's telephone service has been discontinued, red-caped, fleet-footed Miss Mayfleet transmits people's words from place to place in a manner that epitomizes adolescent exuberance and exhibits unmistakable drive. When her boss begins to list the rules she must follow, Lina interrupts to impressively recite them by heart before darting off. The fact that she is an orphan who must look after both her sister (the aforementioned nibbler) and ancient, muddled Granny (Liz Smith) further helps to make viewers embrace the appealing character and hope for the success of her quest. Less engaging by comparison but equally brave and resourceful is Lina's cohort, Doon Harrow (Harry Treadaway), who ends up assigned to the Pipeworks below Ember and becomes convinced that efforts to save the generator are doomed. (It was surprising to many fans of DuPrau's book that twenty-four-year-old Treadaway was cast to play someone who is over a decade younger in the original story.)

Despite the fact that it has always been illegal to attempt exploration of whatever lies beyond the city limits (residents have been told there is merely black nothingness), it is still rather hard to swallow that Lina and Doon are the only two people willing to take dramatic, drastic action as Ember's hopes fade precipitously. Most likely to underscore the story's push for youthful proactiveness, the adults remain especially and amazingly unmotivated. Even the ones who eventually offer some assistance spend most of the film exhibiting a profound, baffling lack of panic. Doon's father (Tim Robbins), who once tried to search for a way out with Lina's father (who perished in the effort), now merely tinkers with self-made contraptions consisting of various odds and ends, alternatively cursing the Builders and imparting great wisdom to his son about how, for example, there is more to a bottle cap than just keeping liquid in. The young man's wizened and profoundly narcoleptic boss, Sul (Martin Landau), simply goes on doing the best he can, patching the generator's pipes in a literal and figurative band-aid approach that fails to satisfy Doon. Worn-out Sul stubbornly clings to a narrow focus on his specific duties, wholly incapable of thinking outside the box about ways to get outside of Ember. Clary (Marianne Jean-Baptiste), despite struggling to produce food under faltering artificial lights, advises that it is best to leave things in the hands of the mayor (Bill Murray). He is actually only interested in serving and saving himself, hunkering down in a secret bunker filled with horded food when not ordering Lina and Doon's arrest between gluttonous chomps on what appear to be turkey legs. Murray's corpulent, corrupt character comes off as sluggish rather than menacing, perhaps due to all that tryptophan.

While reviewers of DuPrau's 2003 book described it as "electric," "compelling," and "suspenseful," such adjectives cannot be leveled at the film. Although Lina and Doon's ultimately triumphant puzzle-solving detective work while evading the authorities is passably interesting, what transpires is less than exhilarating. Their eventual boat ride through a dark tunnel (with Poppy in tow) reminds one more of an amusement park ride than true, nail-biting peril. What does enthrall, however, is production designer Martin Laing's highly imaginative and detailed creation of a rock-encased safe haven that now unsettlingly threatens to become a society's tomb. As *Variety*'s Justin Chang put it, "The visual design is so captivating and unusual that, at a certain point, you wish you could ditch Doon, Lina and her mute-cute sister…and explore Ember on your own for a couple hours." Huge, sprawling sets were constructed in an immense hangar in Northern Ireland that was most famously used by shipbuilders Harland and Wolff to paint the hull of the ill-fated Titanic. While townspeople (portrayed, for some reason, by hundreds of almost exclusively Caucasian actors and extras) bustle about, all the makeshift, make-do outfits, chipped paint, bursting, rusted pipes, and a general shadowy, dank griminess clearly convey the inexorable decline of a dying Ember. Especially as the blackouts increase in frequency and duration, accompanied by disconcerting rumbles and crashes, a nagging sense of claustrophobia-fueled apprehension is successfully created. Along with the

relieved youngsters, viewers will likely find themselves enjoying the propitious finale's views of blue-skied open spaces.

Unlike its source material, *City of Ember* failed to find a receptive audience. Reportedly made on a budget of $38 million, the film struggled to earn back a fraction of that amount. (One wonders now whether Playtone, Tom Hanks' production company, will choose not to move ahead with its option on the second book in DuPrau's series.) Many reviews were like Chang's, praising the visuals (especially) and the talented cast (somewhat less so) but finding the storytelling at best ho-hum. There were some significant alterations made in adapting the book, such as the addition of large, radioactively mutated creatures like the menacing mole-like one that pursues Lina and Doon through the Pipeworks. The most notable change, however, may be that even the film's trailer let moviegoers know right upfront that Ember exists underground, something that is revealed to both readers and the characters themselves at the very end of DuPrau's work. *Ember*'s director, Gil Kenan, was previously responsible for the promising, Oscar®-nominated *Monster House* (2006), which also used place as a principal character. Unfortunately, the set is the only characteristic about *Ember* that received consistently glowing praise.

David L. Boxerbaum

CREDITS

Lina Mayfleet: Saoirse Ronan
Doon Harrow: Harry Treadway
Mayor: Bill Murray
Loris Harrow: Tim Robbins
Sul: Martin Landau
Looper: Mackenzie Crook
Mrs. Murdo: Mary Kay Place
Barton Snode: Toby Jones
Clary: Marianne Jean-Baptiste
Origin: USA
Language: English
Released: 2008
Production: Tom Hanks, Gary Goetzman, Steve Shareshian; Playtone Pictures, Walden Media; released by Fox Walden
Directed by: Gil Kenan
Written by: Caroline Thompson
Cinematography by: Xavier Perez Grobet
Music by: Andrew Lockington
Sound: Peter Lindsay
Music Supervisor: Lindsay Fellows
Editing: Adam P. Scott
Art Direction: Jon Billington

Costumes: Ruth Myers
Production Design: Martin Laing
MPAA rating: PG
Running time: 95 minutes

REVIEWS

Boston Globe Online. October 10, 2008.
Chicago Sun-Times Online. October 10, 2008.
Hollywood Reporter Online. October 9, 2008.
Los Angeles Times Online. October 10, 2008.
New York Times Online. October 10, 2008.
Rolling Stone Online. October 9, 2008.
San Francisco Chronicle. October 10, 2008, p. E7.
Variety Online. October 9, 2008.
Washington Post. October 10, 2008, p. C6.

QUOTES

Loris Harrow: "Pay attention, pay attention to everything, everything you see. Notice what no one else notices, and you'll see what no one else knows. What you get is what you get, what you do with what you get, that's more the point."

TRIVIA

"Ember" is a Hungarian word which translates as "man" and "human."

CITY OF MEN
(Cidade des Homens)

An unforgettable tale of friendship and survival in a city where the greatest challenge is growing up.
—Movie tagline

The lawless slums of Rio de Janeiro are the setting for the disquieting, disjointed *City of Men (Cidade dos Homens),* a somewhat disappointing follow-up to Fernando Meirelles's international hit, *City of God* (2002). *City of Men* is not exactly a sequel to Meirelles's violence-drenched epic of young gangsters; first of all, it is directed by Paulo Morelli, a longtime colleague and collaborator of Meirelles. Also, its two leading actors, Darlan Cunha and Douglas Silva, played eleven-year-old characters in *City of God;* in this film, they are playing characters who are seventeen years old. Some of the other actors also appeared in both films, and the setting is the same. In fact, *City of Men* is the product of a popular Brazilian television series of the same name that was itself a spin-off of *City of God,* so this new film was inspired by characters and situations depicted in the televised version of Meirelles's concept.

This movie is a little more hopeful than Meirelles's daunting epic of crime and poverty that had the feel of an authentic documentary but it is also, unfortunately, much less compelling. As *City of Men* opens, a gang leader named Midnight (Jonathan Haagensen), who has his headquarters in a compound at the very summit of a slum called Dead Man's Hill, decides to go for a swim, and this whimsical spontaneous decision entails the deployment of lookouts, security guards, and others as his entourage makes its way down the bustling, slanted streets to the beach. Either Midnight is paranoid or he has lots of enemies. Along the way, he and his crew draw the attention of hangers-on and pass by the dwellings of other characters, in particular Ace (Douglas Silva). Ace has just been left in charge of his two-year-old son, Clayton, by his wife Cris (Camila Monteiro), who is as responsible and ambitious as he is immature. Ace's friend Wallace (Darlan Cunha) tries to corral him into joining the party at the beach, and Ace wants to come so much that he decides to bring Clayton along. At the beach, however, Ace proves how irresponsible a father he is by leaving the boy with someone else and then forgetting about him altogether. When he finally remembers and returns, the boy has been carted off by members of Midnight's gang. Ace is eventually reunited with his son and earns the wrath of his wife.

Morelli directs this opening sequence in a flowing but hyperactive fashion. The camera and the story seem to follow one character or another in an almost random way, and this pseudo-documentary, herky-jerky narrative style continues as the film lapses into confusingly entwined stories that have the feel of cobbled-together television episodes.

At first the plot mainly follows Wallace's quest to find his own father. His grandmother will not reveal his identity, and his mother is not alive to tell him. So Wallace and Ace launch an investigation and piece together information that leads them to discover Heraldo (Rodrigo dos Santos), who has been serving time in prison for manslaughter. Along the way, Cris decides to take a job in Sao Paulo for a year and leave Clayton in the care of Ace, a job that Ace is clearly not prepared to handle. Thus the film becomes an extended melodrama about the importance of fatherhood and the failings of these characters and their own fathers to fulfill the duties and obligations of paternity. It is not clear to an outsider whether this is meant to be an indictment of the lower-class Brazilian culture portrayed in the movie and why this theme of absent and failed fathers is so powerful and determinative for these two characters. Unfortunately, the deeper motivation of Wallace does not translate well: the characters seem to speak in shallow clichés and it is difficult to understand what compels them.

Interwoven with this melodrama is a feud between Midnight and a rebellious lieutenant, Fasto (Eduardo 'BR' Piranha), over control of Dead Man's Hill. In the initial scene at the beach, Fasto is angry when Midnight asks him to hold his clothing and jewelry while Midnight takes a swim, but other than this, it is not clear why Fasto decides to launch a coup. Fasto's plans are bantered about so much in the wider ghetto that Midnight learns about them and in turn targets Fasto for assassination. Fasto's sister is in love with Wallace, and this provides a hinge for the two otherwise divergent narratives.

It is difficult to follow what's at stake for the characters involved in the turf war, who is on which side and why, and whether this is mostly a reflection of a diminished attitude toward the value of life. With the gritty, raw authenticity of the violence of *City of God* bowdlerized into melodrama, there is an ill fit between these characters and their viewers. Perhaps Brazilians can understand what their motivations are, but international audiences lack empathy for the characters. No character is flashy enough, bizarre enough, or memorable enough—nor even seemingly cruel or mendacious enough—to become the riveting focus of attention. It is difficult to care about these characters and harder still to figure out whom to root for. There are no clear-cut good guys and lots of villians or at least flawed characters, and even the bad guys aren't remarkable enough to arouse continued interest. What is left is sort of a stream-of-action narrative style that circles, backtracks, and visits plenty of cul-de-sacs but never seems to build up the requisite amount of tension and purpose to sustain audience interest.

The two dramas at the center of this confusing mess—the battle over turf and the quest for the missing father—both seem contrived and ultimately meaningless. *City of Men* lacks coherence, and it does not have the potent punch of the hard-hitting *City of God*. It is too stylized and melodramatic to be believable as a slice-of-life vignette, and it is too disjointed and inconsequential to hold attention as a riveting sociological drama or a series of believable character studies. Although it remains colorful, salty, and fascinating in short stretches, as a feature-length movie, it fails to sustain interest.

Michael Betzold

CREDITS

Acerola 'Ace': Douglas Silva
Laranjinha 'Wallace': Darlan Cunha
Madrugadao: Johnathan Haagensen
Chris: Camila Monteiro
Heraldo: Rodrigo dos Santos

Nefasto: Eduardo BR Piranha
Origin: Brazil
Language: Portuguese
Released: 2007
Production: Andrea Barata Ribeiro, Bel Berlinck, Fernando Mirelles, Transfax Productions; O2 Filmes, Fox Film Corporation, Globo Filmes; released by Miramax Films
Directed by: Paulo Morelli
Written by: Elena Soarez
Cinematography by: Adriano Goldman
Music by: Antonio Pinto
Sound: Paulo Ricardo Nunes
Editing: Daniel Rezende
Art Direction: Rafael Ronconi
Costumes: Ines Salgado
MPAA rating: R
Running time: 110 minutes

REVIEWS

Boston Globe Online. February 29, 2008.
Chicago Sun-Times Online. February 29, 2008.
Entertainment Weekly Online. February 26, 2008.
Hollywood Reporter Online. February 29, 2008.
Los Angeles Times Online. February 29, 2008.
New York Times Online. February 29, 2008.
San Francisco Chronicle. February 29, 2008, p. E6.
Variety Online. October 26, 2007.
Washington Post. February 29, 2008, p. C4.

CLOVERFIELD

Some Thing Has Found Us.
—Movie tagline

Box Office: $80 million

Cloverfield is a fascinating update of the giant monster genre in the tradition of the *Godzilla* movies, but one that incorporates the mise-en-scène of amateur footage that has become ubiquitous in the wake of the September 11, 2001, terror attacks (in the process deliberately invoking many familiar 9/11 images) and the advent of YouTube. Executive Producer J.J. Abrams, the creative force behind such successful and occasionally tormenting television ventures as *Alias* (2001–2006)and *Lost* (begun in 2004), and director Matt Reeves take a rather snicker-worthy premise and turn it into a film that both plugs into the fear America felt after the 9/11 attacks and transforms it into a cinematic excursion through visceral panic.

Cloverfield uses the conceit that what the audience sees is actually footage pulled from a "digital SD card recovered from U.S. area 447, formerly known as Central Park—multiple sightings of case designate Cloverfield." This title card is stamped "Department of Defense." The video footage itself begins in the early hours of April 27 (revealed in the recording's date stamp—the year is not given), in the apartment of Beth McIntyre (Odette Yustman), which is being filmed by one of Beth's friends, Rob Hawkins (Michael Stahl-David). In the midst of filming, Rob realizes that Beth has never been to Coney Island and determines to take her. The footage then jumps forward in time to May 22, during preparations for a party for Rob, who has accepted a vice-president position in his company's Japan office. Rob's party introduces the audience to the other characters who will play major roles in the action to come: Rob's brother Jason (Mike Vogel); Lily Ford, Jason's girlfriend (Jessica Lucas); Hudson Platt (T.J. Miller), nicknamed "Hud," who becomes the videographer for most of the story's action; and Marlena Diamond (Lizzie Caplan), a friend of the group, and Hud's crush. Eventually, Rob has a confrontation with Beth that ends with her and her date leaving the party, and it is revealed by Lily to Jason and Hud that Rob and Beth had slept together, a fact unknown to the rest of the group. As Jason and Hud console Rob, a loud crash is heard, and the city experiences a brief blackout. When the power comes back on, the partygoers turn on the local news to hear that there is a disturbance in lower Manhattan. Several of the partygoers go up on the roof to see what is happening, only to see a distant building explode and to be forced back downstairs in the wake of falling debris. In the street downstairs, Hud determines to keep filming as a charred and battered head of the Statue of Liberty careens down the street—he catches images of an enormous something lumbering through Manhattan, just before the Woolworth Building collapses, sending a wall of dust and ash barreling down the street. Hud, Lily, Jason, and Rob take shelter in an abandoned convenience store. When they emerge, they find Marlena covered in dust. The five decide that, whatever is happening, Manhattan is unsafe and they should try to get out by crossing the Brooklyn Bridge. While they are crossing the bridge, Rob receives a distressed cell phone call from Beth saying that she is trapped in her apartment just as something destroys the Brooklyn Bridge, which apparently kills Jason in the process. The remaining survivors scramble back to Manhattan, and Rob, guilt stricken that his bad behavior forced Beth to leave the party, inadvertently putting her in harm's way, determines to make his way to Beth's apartment to rescue her. The remaining action of the movie chronicles the group's travails as they make their way to Beth's place and attempt to leave Manhattan: while scouring an electronics store in search of a fresh

cell phone battery, Hud watches news footage of the U.S. military battling a gigantic creature in lower Manhattan, which shows the soldiers attacked by spider-like parasites that seem to fall from the creature's hide; the friends are forced to take to the subway when they are caught in a fire-fight between the military and the monster; in the subway, they are attacked by the parasites, and Marlena is bitten; they emerge in a department store that the military has established as a command center and triage area, and Marlena is quarantined when she starts bleeding from her eyes (just moments later, Hud films her apparent explosion behind a curtain). The remaining three friends continue to Beth's nearly destroyed building and rescue an impaled Beth. Miraculously, they make it to a military evacuation point. Lily is placed on a helicopter and is airlifted away. Hud, Rob, and Beth are loaded onto a second helicopter a few seconds later. As they fly over Manhattan, the creature is attacked by the military and lunges at the helicopter, forcing it to crash in Central Park. Beth, Rob, and Hud survive the crash, but Hud is killed by the creature when he attempts to retrieve the camera. Rob and Beth grab the camera and take cover under a bridge in Central Park. A massive bombing campaign can be heard outside the bridge while Rob and Beth profess their love for one another and they are seemingly buried in falling debris. The film jumps to footage of Rob and Beth at Coney Island in April and just before the video abruptly ends, something can be seen falling into the ocean in the distance, accompanied by a muffled sound similar to the creature's roar implying, perhaps, that the creature is of extraterrestrial origin.

The content of Cloverfield, while to some degree the product of standard giant-monster genre tropes, manages to be terrifying. The characters spend most of their time running helplessly from an enemy whose motives and very nature they neither know nor have any hope of truly understanding (if indeed there is a motive). The creature might as well be a giant hurricane; it is such an uncontrollable force of nature—but at least a hurricane is a recognizable phenomenon that has some sort of frame of reference in the real world. A giant monster barreling down Manhattan's streets is terrifying not only because it is deadly, but because its origins, its wants, its goals are not only unknown, they are unknowable. This, along with the very human ties the characters share (they are all friends, many of them romantic couples) evokes audience empathy for the characters in the face of the potential loss of loved ones, while simultaneously raising the stakes the characters face. The characters not only must escape, but they must try to save a trapped friend while not losing others along the way. This makes *Cloverfield* a unique experience, at once both familiar and terrifying.

The content of the film alone, however, would not make the film nearly as successful a piece of evocative cinema had it also been filmed as most traditional monster and disaster movies are—from an objective, third-person perspective. The use of the first-person/amateur videographer perspective has a twofold effect: It not only allows for immersion in the world of the characters (to an exceedingly visceral point), but it also adds a sense of naturalism to the experience by mimicking the now-ubiquitous style of YouTube, allowing for an amazing degree of viewer suspension of disbelief, while plugging into the collective unconscious of an audience that has seen amateur images of the Twin Towers collapsing an uncountable number of times. In *Cloverfield,* the audience is stripped of its voyeur status and is forced to experience what the characters face—viewers are not part of the camera crew, safe behind the curtain that separates the real world from the fictional. *Cloverfield* says to the viewer, "This is really happening." The effect achieved is very similar to that of *The Blair Witch Project* (1999) in which "found" video footage recounts the trip of a group of student filmmakers through a Maryland forest in an attempt to trace the legend of the Blair Witch, but instead winds up documenting what appears to be their one-by-one slayings at the hands of an unseen assailant. Interestingly, some audience members in both *Cloverfield* and *Blair Witch* complained of motion sickness due to the shaky, ultra-amateur, documentary-style camerawork used in both movies.

The combination of the film's content in concert with its chosen mode of execution (shaky, first-person camerawork) makes the movie immersive, visceral, and absolutely nerve-wracking. *Cloverfield* does for post-9/11 America what *Godzilla* (1954) did for post-World War II/Hiroshima Japan: It explores the nation's shock and horror in a safe, yet powerful way. What makes *Cloverfield* daring and not simply well made or innovative is its willingness to trash New York City, a touchy subject for Hollywood following 9/11. For instance, the teaser trailer for the first *Spider-Man* (2002) film that prominently featured the Twin Towers was pulled from theatres, and the ending of *Men in Black II* (2002) had to be rewritten because it was set at the World Trade Center. Moreover, the terror attacks of September 11, 2001, themselves did not receive direct, serious cinematic treatment until the release of director Paul Greengrass's *United 93* (2006), and it, of course, is concerned with the flight that crashed in a Pennsylvania field. In *Cloverfield,* however, the battered head of the Statue of Liberty is tossed haphazardly down a New York City street and lands on its side in an homage to the poster for another sort of New York disaster film, John Carpenter's classic *Escape from New York* (1981), a movie that also attempted, through an allegorical future, to capture

America's sentiment of the day. The Woolworth Building is completely demolished, sending a massive wall of dust and ash raining down on fleeing bystanders (a scene that directly references images from 9/11 amateur video and news footage). The movie invokes the terror of 9/11 and provides the audience with a safe forum to confront these familiar, shocking images and, in doing so, strip them of some of their power.

Cloverfield has one major failure, though a possibly inadvert one—by so successfully invoking the imagery and emotion of 9/11, the film becomes a sort of uneasy allegory of those tragic events and, by indirectly comparing the events of 9/11 themselves to the destruction wrought by a rampaging monster, taking the mode of thought to its logical conclusion: The motives behind the horrifying events of 9/11 cannot be known, and the horrible events that happen to people caught in the path of an unknowable force (a rampaging monster or a group of fanatics) are tragic in their random, seeming disconnectedness from any sort of context that might illuminate why the events themselves have happened (or are happening). By being so rooted in the now and by keeping the perspective of the film entirely with a group of people who have no frame of reference for what is happening to them, the filmmakers seem to suggest that this horrible occurrence has no discernible cause; it is simply the result of the whims of something that is out of our control. By so carefully and effectively using 9/11 images to further their emotional storytelling, the filmmakers also potentially invoke some cognitive dissonance in viewers who choose to follow the film's allegorical components to their logical conclusions. The images of destroyed buildings and people running for their lives look eerily familiar, with the terror and helplessness of the actual events of 9/11 lending a certain power to the fictional events of *Cloverfield,* but terrorists have an agenda, no matter how shocking or seemingly unrelated to anything else their actions may appear at the time. By contrast, a giant monster cannot be similarly subjected to analysis because no context exists for such a creature or its rampage. To deny the possibility that the 9/11 terror attacks were a horrible event that occurred outside any sort of comprehensible real-world context is in all probability not the intention of the filmmakers; however, by making such effective use of 9/11 imagery, and by stoking the emotions associated with those images, Abrams and crew run the risk of inferring a one-to-one correspondence between the creature and the terrorists. Perhaps, if they ever make a sequel, Reeves and Abrams will attempt to explore as intellectually satisfying a portrait of the monster's origins and motivations (though it may not be possible to do this without ruining the very quality that makes the movie so effective—the dread of the unknown) as the emotional roller coaster created by its unexplained rampage through Manhattan.

John Boaz

CREDITS

Marlena: Lizzy Caplan
Lily: Jessica Lucas
Rob: Michael Stahl-David
Jason: Mike Vogel
Hud: T.J. Miller
Beth: Odette Yustman
Origin: USA
Language: English
Released: 2008
Production: J.J. Abrams, Bryan Burk; Bad Robot; released by Paramount
Directed by: Matt Reeves
Written by: Drew Goddard
Cinematography by: Michael Bonvillain
Sound: Ed White
Editing: Kevin Stitt
Art Direction: Doug Meerdink, John Pollard
Costumes: Ellen Mirojnick
Production Design: Martin Whist
MPAA rating: PG-13
Running time: 90 minutes

REVIEWS

Boston Globe Online. January 18, 2008.
Chicago Sun-Times Online. January 17, 2008.
Entertainment Weekly Online. January 16, 2008.
Hollywood Reporter Online. January 17, 2008.
Los Angeles Times Online. January 18, 2008.
New York Times Online. January 18, 2008.
Rolling Stone Online. January 17, 2008.
San Francisco Chronicle. January 17, 2008, p. E1.
Variety Online. January 16, 2008.
Washington Post. January 18, 2008, p. C1.

QUOTES

Hud (to Rob): "Maybe you should've left town a little bit earlier, right?"

TRIVIA

Prints of the film were shipped to theaters with the title "Bertha."

COLLEGE ROAD TRIP

They just can't get there fast enough.
—Movie tagline

Box Office: $45.6 million

The Martin Lawrence who stirred up controversy with his opening monologue on *Saturday Night Live* and released the NC-17 concert film *You So Crazy* (1994) would barely even recognize the Lawrence who stars in the G-rated *College Road Trip* for Disney. Like Eddie Murphy before him, Lawrence has gone from edgy provocateur to slapstick-driven family man. Considering his success in the film *Wild Hogs* (2007) and the relative failure of his more adult-driven films before this recent switch, the "new Martin" makes a little bit of sense, but the directorial choice for *College Road Trip* is even more bizarre. Roger Kumble wrote and directed two *Cruel Intentions* (1999-2000) movies and shot the Ryan Reynolds comedy *Just Friends* (2005). How he became attached to a script that could not be farther from the legendary all-female kiss of *Cruel Intentions* remains a mystery. What is far less mysterious is the involvement of former *Cosby* kid Raven-Symoné, who has made a fortune as the star of *That's So Raven* (2003-2007). Perhaps nobody's involvement but hers really mattered to the final product. The young Disney Channel icon executive-produced *College Road Trip,* probably hoping that it could serve as a transition piece for her move from television star to movie actress. Martin Lawrence, Donny Osmond, and a super-intelligent pig may get a lot of screen time and *somebody* had to direct it, but *College Road Trip* is a Raven-Symoné vehicle in every way. With its target audience in mind, *College Road Trip* is a modest success, but viewers familiar with Kumble and Lawrence's previous work more than Raven-Symoné's accomplishments are unlikely to enjoy the ride.

Raven-Symoné stars as Melanie Porter, a high school senior who has an opportunity to go to Georgetown University, but her overprotective father James (Martin Lawrence), who also happens to be the police chief, is having difficulty giving up control of his baby girl. James wants Melanie to go to Northwestern University, which is less than an hour from the Porter home, but his daughter insists on checking out what Georgetown has to offer. Melanie is all set to go with her two friends Nancy and Katie, but her father surprises her by offering to take the college-bound girl on a different kind of road trip. Of course, James has an ulterior motive and starts his highway journey with a stop at Northwestern, where he has convinced a deputy to portray a cute male student to try and convince Melanie to go to school closer to home. Of course, the faux beau is just the beginning. Along the way, the Porters repeatedly run into the creepily gleeful father-daughter team of Doug (Donny Osmond) and Wendy (Molly Ephraim) and learn that the youngest Porter, Trey (Eshaya Draper), has hitched along for a ride with his trained superpig. Trey is a scientist-in-training, a young man who believes he can train pigs to be superspies. It IS a kid's movie, after all.

Despite some of the flaws of its screenplay and some significant mugging to the camera by Lawrence, *College Road Trip* is a completely inoffensive family movie with its heart very much in the right place. So many of these kids/family movies place the emphasis on physical humor and there is certainly some of that in *College Road Trip,* but the film is surprisingly genuine and heartfelt. Lawrence and Raven-Symoné have an easygoing, believable dynamic, making the idea that they are father and daughter that much more plausible, which makes the film's shortcomings much easier to overlook. When *College Road Trip* gets overtly silly, like with a musical number sung by Raven-Symoné on a bus and basically every interaction with Lawrence and his son's swine, the film starts to feel like a waste of time for children and their parents, but those scenes are usually followed by something that grounds the characters in a reality that is often missing from this kind of material.

Raven-Symoné has made herself a massive star with the pre-teen set because of her show *That's So Raven,* and what is interesting about *College Road Trip* is watching a young woman who is so keenly aware of what works for her audience as an actress and executive producer. It is hard to believe that fans of her show or her celebrity persona in general would not enjoy taking the *College Road Trip* with her. A film that appeals directly to one audience and completely satisfies it could be accused of having too much tunnel vision to make it a breakout hit beyond its demographic, but it should also receive credit for giving its most ardent fans exactly what they are hoping to find.

Brian Tallerico

CREDITS

Chief James Porter: Martin Lawrence
Melanie Porter: Raven-Symoné
Doug: Donny Osmond
Nancy: Brenda Song
Deputy O'Malley: Will Sasso
Michelle Porter: Kym E. Whitley
Katie: Margo Harshman
Trey Porter: Eshaya Draper
Freddy: Vincent Pastore
Scooter: Lucas Grabeel
Origin: USA
Language: English
Released: 2008
Production: Andrew Gunn; GUNNFilms; released by Walt Disney Pictures

Directed by: Roger Kumble
Written by: Ken Daurio
Cinematography by: Theo van de Sande
Music by: Ed Shearmur, Lisa Brown
Sound: Tom Nelson
Editing: Roger Bondelli
Art Direction: Douglas Huszti
Costumes: Francine Jamison-Tanchuck
Production Design: Ben Barraud
MPAA rating: G
Running time: 83 minutes

REVIEWS

Boston Globe Online. March 8, 2008.
Chicago Sun-Times Online. March 7, 2008.
Entertainment Weekly Online. March 5, 2008.
Hollywood Reporter Online. March 7, 2008.
Los Angeles Times Online. March 7, 2008.
New York Times Online. March 7, 2008.
San Francisco Chronicle. March 7, 2008, p. E7.
Variety Online. March 6, 2008.
Washington Post. March 7, 2008, p. C5.

QUOTES

Trey Porter: "You know, Sigmund Freud said the best way to understand women is by listening to them."
Chief James Porter: "Did he say anything about understanding ten year-olds?"

TRIVIA

Eleven pigs were used to portray Albert in the movie.

THE COOL SCHOOL

The Cool School is yet another documentary about a group of artists who never quite got their due. In this case, Morgan Neville's film covers the Los Angeles art scene through the years and, although well-produced and informative, it is also a bit self-indulgent.

Using interviews, archival footage, and stills of the artworks, *The Cool School* tells the story of how dormant, laid-back California was the unlikely setting for an evolving art world explosion, starting in the Beat-era 1950s, continuing through the more radical 1960s and 1970s, that seriously challenged New York's superiority in this area. Edward Ruscha, Ed Moses, Kenneth Price, John Altoon, and Robert Irwin were among the artists who emerged from the postwar Los Angeles scene. These "outsiders" were given prominence by the Ferus Gallery, founded by Walter Hopps in 1957, particularly attracting attention for their initially derided low-brow "found object" pieces, in addition to their Abstract-Expressionist paintings and sculptures. Later, a Marcel Duchamp retrospective and Andy Warhol's gallery debut (with his first Campbell Soup cans) helped make L.A. better respected and established for artists. Praise from critics and celebrities (Dennis Hopper, Dean Stockwell) solidified the location as an art Mecca.

Most of the reviews of the film were favorable. Manohla Dargis in the *New York Times* called *The Cool School* "a breezy, lively documentary...often fascinating, visually charming and intelligently edited...." Nathan Lee in the *Village Voice* added, "...this is essential history...." John Anderson in *Variety* stated, "What *The Cool School* does so well, through its color accents and black-and-white photography, through the kinetic music that propels Jeff Bridges' narration by and the unorthodox attitude that reflects the artists themselves, is impart a sense of discovery. As Neville so obviously feels, making a staid, overly respectful movie about a gang of revolutionaries would miss the point." But Kenneth Baker in the *San Francisco Chronicle* was more reserved: "No one emerges very well defined from this historical shuffle, but those who know the artists' works, or names such as Hopps and Blum, but have never heard them speak, will find *The Cool School* absorbing and informative."

What most of these and other critics failed to notice is the way *The Cool School* falls into the same traps as so many documentaries about artists and writers. For one, by trying to shine a spotlight on something he considers underappreciated, Morgan Neville downplays the achievements of artists in other communities and overpraises the work of his documentary's focus. Neville rarely considers the creativity of the West Coast architects, poets, composers, graphic designers, and avant-garde filmmakers (let alone the Hollywood people) during this same period. And of course one would not expect such a film to explore the work of L.A.'s concurrent East Coast rivals, but a few comparisons would have been welcome and instructive. Sadly, the only New York representative is the supercilious gallery owner Ivan Karp, and there is little mention of Jackson Pollack or Barnett Newman or their European counterparts (Willem de Kooning, Mark Rothko, et al.).

More mysteriously, Neville barely mentions the Bay Area pioneers (Clifford Still, Richard Diebenkorn) or any pre-1950s California artists. Few viewers may miss the scant attention to Artforum's founders, John Coplans and Philip Leider, but if Neville was going to tell the whole L.A. story, he should have noted the importance of this magazine's editors (he does mention when Artforum left the West Coast to go East during a later downturn of interest the L.A. art scene).

Next to the recent documentary *Beautiful Losers* (2008) about the Lower Manhattan art scene in the early 1990s, *The Cool School* is better made and more comprehensive. Yet, neither film acknowledges the obvious: that white males are the still the most privileged people in all art worlds. *Beautiful Losers* only showcases one woman amongst the artists profiled, and *The Cool School* does not include any women (expect if you count Ferus Gallery doyenne, Shirley Nielsen Hopps). Race is barely discussed in either film, although Neville manages to include a segment about how the L.A. riots of the 1960s impacted the work of gallery regulars. Two other documentaries about African-American artists emerging late in life as major creative figures—Pearl Fryer in *A Man Named Pearl* (2006) and Albert Wagner in *One Bad Cat: The Reverend Albert Wagner Story* (2008)—make all these art-themed documentaries of late seem like they are practicing their own form of cultural segregation.

As one would expect from a film made in and about the West Coast, the technical credits are excellent. Neville gets deep-voiced Jeff Bridges (no less) to do the traditional, stodgy narration (co-written by Neville and former reporter Kristine McKenna). The archival shots and stills of L.A. in the 1950s include rare material of the artists at work, nicely edited together with the modern-day interviews. Finally, unlike the scrappier *Beautiful Losers,* the interviews are shot in a slick, professional way, which possibly undercuts the thematic but at least makes *The Cool School* easier on the eyes.

Eric Monder

CREDITS

Narrator: Jeff Bridges
Origin: USA
Language: English
Released: 2007
Production: Morgan Neville, Kristine McKenna; Tremolo Prods., Independent Television Service; released by Arthouse Films
Directed by: Morgan Neville
Written by: Morgan Neville, Kristine McKenna
Cinematography by: Morgan Neville, Dylan Robertson, Chris Perkel
Music by: Dan Crane, William Ungerman
Sound: Michael Kowalski
Editing: Dylan Robertson, Chris Perkel
MPAA rating: Unrated
Running time: 86 minutes

REVIEWS

Entertainment Weekly Online. March 26, 2008.
Hollywood Reporter Online. July 12, 2007.
New York Times Online. March 28, 2008.

San Francisco Chronicle. March 21, 2008, p. E4.
Variety Online. January 27, 2007.
Village Voice Online. March 25, 2008.

THE COUNTERFEITERS
(Die Fälscher)

It takes a clever man to make money, it takes a genius to stay alive.
—Movie tagline

Box Office: $5.4 million

"One adapts or dies."

The human ability to adapt to any situation, even some of the most horrific imaginable, is a truly remarkable one. The history of cinema is filled with stories of men and women who were forced to alter themselves—morally, physically, emotionally, or all of the above—to survive, and there may be no more inherently dramatic a backdrop for that kind of story than Germany during World War II. The Oscar® winner for Best Foreign Language Film, Stefan Ruzowitsky's *The Counterfeiters* (*Die Fälscher*) tells the story of men who were forced to adapt until they could no longer bear the corruption of their own moral code, even for their own survival. Hundreds of stories of the Holocaust have been told in literature and film, but Ruzowitsky's stands above many of them because it keeps its focus on the human element of its story. Ruzowitsky is not trying to make an allegory for all concentrations camps or all Jews, just tell the tale of a select few who, by the courage of their convictions, might have changed the course of the war. By keeping his story on a human scale, both in the way it was written and shot, Ruzowitsky has made a film of lasting power, one of the best films about World War II in recent years. There was much controversy over the odd exclusions from the short list of the Academy's Foreign Language Film category for 2007—*4 Months, 3 Weeks, 2 Days*, *Persepolis*, *The Orphanage*—and it may be true that *The Counterfeiters* does not quite stand up to some of the critically acclaimed snubs, but that part of the story overshadowed the quality of Ruzowitsky's very good film, one that certainly deserved to be mentioned in the same breath.

Based on a true story, Salomon 'Sally' Sorowitsch (Karl Markovics, a man with one of the more interesting faces in recent cinema—part old-fashioned movie icon, part defeated pugilist) was a legendary counterfeiter in pre-war Berlin, living a high life of booze, gambling, and women. After being arrested and spending years in a concentration camp, Sorowitsch finds himself becoming a central figure in a huge Nazi conspiracy in the last two years of the war. Superintendent Friedrich Herzog (Devid Striesow) has Sally transferred to Sachsenhausen to head a team of professionals in their attempt to counterfeit the British pound. With a team that also includes Adolf Burger (August Diehl), a more rebellious counterfeiter whose wife is in Auschwitz, Sally figures that if he does good work, he will not only be allowed to live but be rewarded. Adolf sees the harsh truth of the situation—that, by counterfeiting money for the Nazis, the Jews are basically funding the war effort that is keeping them and people like them in the hell on Earth that were the concentration camps. Sabotage is suggested, but Salomon continues to refuse, knowing that if they are discovered, they will certainly all be killed. Salomon must decide whether prolonging the war to save his friends is acceptable or if his small rebellion could end up ultimately saving many more.

Ruzowitsky shoots most of *The Counterfeiters* with handheld, grainy imagery, adding a gritty realism to the film that truly elevates it above the television movie of the week that it could have easily been with a few different directorial decisions. The real Adolf Burger, who wrote the book that served as the source material for *The Counterfeiters,* has said that he and his comrades were "dead men on holiday." The sensation of not only impending doom but a fully realized world of pain and death fills every frame of *The Counterfeiters.* Even when Sally is enjoying the perks of working for the Nazis who are killing his brethren, the sadness exists in every image. Markovics's long, crooked face perfectly suits a man with an inner conflict that is almost impossible to comprehend.

The structure of *The Counterfeiters*—it is presented as a flashback from a postwar, money-spending Markovics—is a little frustrating and an odd decision. Flashback is an overused device in general, and it would have been more interesting to follow Sorowitsch's story after the war in chronological fashion. Perhaps it would have been even more wise to remove the postwar material from the beginning and abrupt end of the film. There is a strong ending to *The Counterfeiters* in the final days of the actual war that is then, very oddly and anti-climactically, followed by a few scenes with very little impact and an unnecessary narrative coda. A story like *The Counterfeiters* is so powerful that it needs to stand on its own without narrative tricks like voiceover or flashback. For the most part, Ruzowitsky recognized that necessity, and his film delivers.

Brian Tallerico

CREDITS

Salomon Sorowitsch: Karl Markovics
Adolf Burger: August Diehl

Dr. Klinger: August Zirner
Aglaia: Marie Baumer
Red-Haired Woman: Dolores Chaplin
Friedrich Herzog: David Striesow
Holst: Martin Zirner
Origin: Austria, Germany
Language: German
Released: 2007
Production: Josef Aichholzer, Nina Bohlmann, Babette Schroeder; Beta Cinema, Magnolia Films, Aichholzer Films; released by Sony Pictures Classics
Directed by: Stefan Ruzowitzky
Written by: Stefan Ruzowitzky
Cinematography by: Benedict Neuenfels
Music by: Marius Ruhland
Sound: Torsten Heineman
Editing: Britta Nahler
Costumes: Nicole Fischnaller
Production Design: Isidor Wimmer
MPAA rating: R
Running time: 98 minutes

REVIEWS

Guardian Online. October 12, 2007.
Los Angeles Times Online. February 22, 2008.
New York Times Online. February 22, 2008.
Variety Online. May 16, 2007.
Village Voice Online. February 19, 2008.
Wall Street Journal. February 22, 2008, p. W1.

QUOTES

Salomon Sorowitsch (translated): "I'm myself. Everyone else is everyone else."

TRIVIA

This is the first Austrian film to win an Oscar® in the Best Foreign Language Film Category.

AWARDS

Oscars 2007: Foreign Film.

THE CURIOUS CASE OF BENJAMIN BUTTON

Life isn't measured in minutes, but in moments.
—Movie tagline

Box Office: $126.1 million

The Curious Case of Benjamin Button is curious indeed—a long movie based on an obscure short story by F. Scott Fitzgerald. The story is built around an odd but promising idea for current cinema, with its love for special effects and makeup that turn actors into different ages: It is about a man who is born old but becomes younger until he dies as a baby. It is not like anything else Fitzgerald ever wrote, and it was smart for movie people to seize on the story, imagining it as a fantastic adventure for the screen.

Casting Brad Pitt as Button was a stroke of genius, in that Pitt has retained his boyish look even as he has grown into an older and more accomplished actor. Yet what really caught viewers' attention was using Pitt to portray Button even at the beginning of his life, then as an old young man, reducing him in stature by using computer effects and using makeup to portray him as wrinkled and wizened.

To say that Eric Roth and Robin Swicord took liberties with Fitzgerald's story is an understatement. Fitzgerald wrote his fantasy in 1921, and his Button was born in 1860, fought in the Spanish American War, ran his father's hardware store and got rich, and lived seventy years. As a newborn, he could already talk and as a child loved to smoke cigars. In this movie version, directed by David Fincher (*Zodiac* [2007] and *Fight Club* [1999]), Button is born in 1918, on the day World War I ends. He is abandoned at birth by his father, who runs a button factory (Button's Buttons), and adopted by a black woman who helps run an old folks' home. He travels the world in a tugboat and ends up fighting a naval battle in World War II, and hits his prime in the 1960s.

In the Fitzgerald story, Button has a son and raises him until he no longer can. In the movie version, Button's story is revealed to his daughter, Caroline (Julia Ormond), when she reads his diaries to her mother, Daisy (Cate Blanchett), who is dying in a nursing home in New Orleans as Hurricane Katrina is about to strike. The revelation that Button is Caroline's father comes as a surprise only to her, not the viewers, who can easily discern that early in the film.

Having the story told this way is smart, and setting the narration in a city about to be flooded by a hurricane is also a fine idea, as it gives the sense of lives and times being washed away. Otherwise, Fincher and his scriptwriters and producers have attempted to make Benjamin Button's story one of those grand epics of a life spanning eras and places and encompassing relationships with all kinds of characters. The problem is that Button's story is really not all that grand; it merely has a quirky premise. This is a movie that promises a sweep that it never quite delivers.

The fact that Benjamin's adoptive mother is of a different race also gives the film a foothold in today's consciousness, though it is doubtful Fitzgerald would ever have conceived such a plot device in the South during the 1920s. But one of the most important of many major deviations from the story is having Button spend his first seventeen years in a home for the aged. There he learns that people he knows and cares about will eventually die while he outlives them all. This is a point driven home again and again by the movie: Benjamin is doomed to watch everyone age and die as he gets younger. Another related theme is that people meet each other by chance and that fate controls our destiny.

Strangely, though, these insights that are meant to appear profound do not derive from any special appreciation of Button's unique circumstances. Everyone who lives to a certain age will see friends and acquaintances grow older and die. Button seems eventually to know his fate better than normal people, as it is clear he is destined to grow younger until he dies a baby at about the physical age he was when he was born, that is, eighty.

The death of Benjamin's mother in childbirth and his abandonment by his father, who then reclaims his son just before dying, adds an extra layer of pathos to a tale that seems to wallow in all the negative aspects of the passage of time. Instead of celebrating the present day, the movie imbues almost every scene with a patina of dread and loss. Benjamin's unusual lifespan gives him an especially sharp perspective on the vagaries of time and the fact that nothing endures, but it could also have given him an exceptional appreciation of the preciousness of any moment. Instead, Button is often a dour, lost, and dismayed personality. Pitt portrays him with a poignancy that seems to border on dullness.

At perhaps an hour shorter than its 167 minutes, *The Curious Case of Benjamin Button* might have been a good yarn; at its ponderous length, it takes itself far too seriously and provides way too few moments of genuine pleasure and memorable entertainment. Even the few happy moments are always tinged with the sense of loss. Those include the protagonist's two notable romances: an affair with an English diplomat's wife (Tilda Swinton) carried out in a hotel in Russia at night and a long and complicated relationship with Blanchett's Daisy.

Button first meets Daisy when they both are young, and she is visiting her grandmother in the old folks' home; they play together as children, even though Button looks like an old man. Then they have a series of cat-and-mouse missed connections during the years when Daisy launches a career as a virtuoso ballerina while Button sails the seas with the tugboat's Captain Mike (Jared Harris). When finally they return together and fall into each other's arms, the film is nearly two hours old, and the audience reaction is "Finally!" Fincher then dispenses with their brief years of near-perfect coupling in a series of sunny tableaux, though even

these are shadowed with the mandated sense of eventual loss. It is as if Fincher cannot wait to get through the good times before he confronts the looming problem of Benjamin getting too young and Daisy getting too old. When Benjamin decides to leave his daughter because he does not believe he can be a proper father, he is still in the prime of life, and the decision seems a rather selfish one. Unfortunately, even logic must not get in the way of the tone of relentlessly incipient tragedy, the cruelness of fate, that hangs over the movie like a mildewing moss.

Pitt is fine throughout, though he clings to a deep old man's voice for far too long and his southern accent sounds a bit forced and thus corny. Blanchett gives another of her virtuoso performances, especially in her incarnation as the dying Daisy; she is almost unrecognizable. As the younger, flamboyant, red-haired Daisy, she is stunningly luminous, though at many points she, too, seems a bit selfish. Ormond's role as the daughter at her dying mother's bedside leaves little space for anything other than weeping at a history cruelly kept from her.

Except for Taraji P. Henson as Queenie, Benjamin's long-suffering and generous adoptive mother, the other characters elicit little viewer interest. When Mike, who fancies himself an artist because he has tattooed himself, dies at sea in an improbable naval battle, Benjamin sees a hummingbird over the water in what is an incredibly contrived moment. Benjamin the narrator often instructs viewers that that they must care about many of these people, including an old woman who taught him the piano but whose name he cannot himself remember. Swinton's talents are largely wasted as a woman who regrets she has done nothing with life. Surely enough, viewers catch a glimpse of her later, returning at an old age to complete her mission of swimming the English Channel in what amounts to one of the few moments in which the film takes on an optimistic, can-do attitude toward life. Thus this episode stands in stark contrast to the film's habitual gloominess about decay and death.

Button does not make much history, and he does not see much of the world, at least not in anything more than what amounts to snippets of travelogues. Apart from the impossible-to-explain backwards track of his existence, there is nothing all that remarkable in his story. In a contrived prologue we are told about a blind man who made a grand clock that ran backwards; he announces it expresses his desire to reverse time so that the soldiers, including his son who died in World War I, might be able to return home alive. Yet none of these elements cohere. By rights, the story of a man who lives life backwards should be one that gives viewers special insights; however, *The Curious Case of Benjamin Button* simply gives viewers long, dull stretches and heavy-handed, pointed moments involving people and events we are supposed to find meaningful and thus memorable, but are neither. It is a badly bungled and overblown tale.

Michael Betzold

CREDITS

Benjamin Button: Brad Pitt
Daisy: Cate Blanchett
Elizabeth Abbott: Tilda Swinton
Caroline: Julia Ormond
Queenie: Taraji P. Henson
Monsieur Gateau: Elias Koteas
Thomas Button: Jason Flemyng
Captain Mike: Jared Harris
Tizzy: Mahershalhashbaz Ali
Grandma Fuller: Phyllis Somerville
Daisy age 7: Elle Fanning
Daisy age 10: Madisen Beaty
Origin: USA
Language: English
Released: 2008
Production: Kathleen Kennedy, Frank Marshall; released by Paramount Pictures
Directed by: David Fincher
Written by: Eric Roth
Cinematography by: Claudio Miranda
Music by: Alexandre Desplat
Sound: Marc Weingarten
Editing: Angus Wall, Kirk Baxter
Art Direction: Tom Reta
Costumes: Jacqueline West
Production Design: Donald Graham Burt
MPAA rating: PG-13

REVIEWS

Boston Globe Online. December 24, 2008.
Chicago Sun-Times Online. December 25, 2008.
Entertainment Weekly Online. December 24, 2008.
Hollywood Reporter Online. November 25, 2008.
Los Angeles Times Online. December 29, 2008.
New York Times Online. December 25, 2008.
San Francisco Chronicle. December 29, 2008.
Variety Online. November 24, 2008.
Washington Post. December 29, 2008.

QUOTES

Benjamin Button: "It's a funny thing about comin' home. Looks the same, smells the same, feels the same. You'll realize what's changed is you."

Benjamin Button: "Some people, were born to sit by a river. Some get struck by lightning. Some have an ear for music. Some are artists. Some swim. Some know buttons. Some know Shakespeare. Some are mothers. And some people, dance."

TRIVIA

At one time, Rachel Weisz was being considered for the role of Daisy, but she had to decline the part due to scheduling conflicts because of the varying filming dates of the film.

AWARDS

Oscars 2008: Art Dir./Set Dec., Makeup, Visual FX
British Acad. 2008: Makeup, Visual FX, Production Des.

Nomination:

Oscars 2008: Actor (Pitt), Adapt. Screenplay, Cinematog., Costume Des., Director (Fincher), Film, Film Editing, Sound, Support. Actress (Henson), Orig. Score
British Acad. 2008: Actor (Pitt), Adapt. Screenplay, Cinematog., Costume Des., Director (Fincher), Film, Film Editing, Orig. Score
Directors Guild 2008: Director (Fincher)
Golden Globes 2009: Actor—Drama (Pitt), Director (Fincher), Film—Drama, Screenplay, Orig. Score
Screen Actors Guild 2008: Actor (Pitt), Support. Actress (Henson), Cast
Writers Guild 2008: Adapt. Screenplay.

D

THE DARK KNIGHT

Welcome to a world without rules.
—Movie tagline

Out of the darkness...there comes the Knight.
—Movie tagline

Box Office: $533.3 million

The history of the comic book movie genre is filled with stories about what it means to be a hero. It is the driving force of the genre, represented in Peter Parker's regret over letting Uncle Ben die, Clark Kent dealing with the responsibility of being Superman, and Wolverine deciphering his own dark past. What sets Christopher Nolan's *The Dark Knight* apart from those films and helps elevate it to the best of its genre is that the award-worthy script by Nolan and his brother Jonathan Nolan takes the concept of heroism a step further and asks what the impact of a world with extreme good and evil does to the people caught in the middle. *The Dark Knight* is a superhero movie about extreme, chaotic evil, embodied in The Joker and what happens to the average men and women when dark meets light. It is one of the best films of 2008.

The Dark Knight is as ambitious as any mainstream movie released in 2008. Christopher Nolan and his technically masterful team took a genre that often spoke to its audience like they were all thirteen-year-old boys and dared to make a complex examination of modern heroes and villains. *The Dark Knight* transcended its genre to become one of the most critically and commercially successful films of the last decade by virtue of the ambitions of its creative team, one that refused to stick to the perceived limitations of the genre and make

something as dark and dense as anything released in 2008.

Nolan opens his sequel with one of the few relatively calm, daylight shots of the skyline of Gotham. A skyscraper window shatters and men in clown masks ride a zip line to the roof across the street. A bank heist is underway. Nolan and his expert cinematographer, Wally Pfister, pan up behind a man with a clown mask in his hand. Instantly, the audience knows that that this is the Joker (Heath Ledger), but he is in a moment of calm that he will not be in again in the entire film. Like the start of a race, a car screeches up and he and the entire movie, is off and running.

The bleak tone of *The Dark Knight* is clear from its opening set-piece, a bank robbery of a mob bank. The Joker's plan is to take what evil men prize most: their money. And he is willing to sacrifice anything that gets in his way, even his co-conspirators. He puts live grenades in the hands of his hostages and instructs his cohorts to kill each person down the food chain once their purpose on the team has been fulfilled. Immediately, *The Dark Knight* is not an average comic book movie. It is violent, chaotic, riveting, and, of course, dark. It will remain so for the next two-and-a-half hours, all the way to one of the darkest endings since *Star Wars: Episode V—The Empire Strikes Back* (1980), another "Part Two" to which *The Dark Knight* was compared upon its release.

After the conclusion of the introductory heist, the Nolans briefly backtrack to wrap up a few plot threads from the previous film, *Batman Begins* (2005). The Scarecrow (Cillian Murphy) makes a brief appearance as he has convinced people to dress up like Batman to destroy the hero's reputation. The resolution of the Scarecrow plotline serves two purposes—it repeats a common trick from comic books in tying up loose ends at the beginning of the next edition, and it starts a theme that will pervade the entire film: duality. Good and evil, the chaos of The Joker and the rigid rule structure of Batman, the character of Two-Face—duality plays a role in nearly every plot thread of *The Dark Knight.*

Gotham is still covered in a blanket of fear after the action of *Batman Begins,* a film made much richer and better by its follow-up. It is unclear to the average citizen who the vigilante dressed as a bat could be or even what his intentions are, and there is a void in the crime syndicate since the death of Tom Wilkinson's character from Nolan's first film. The Joker has no interest in leading the evil forces of Gotham. He merely wants to exploit the vacuum for what he truly loves, chaos.

Order, in contrast to The Joker's chaos, is the city's "White Knight," D.A. Harvey Dent (Aaron Eckhart). Dent is a natural leader, a man unafraid to confront the scum of the Earth in his courtroom and the face of good in the city. He is romantically linked to Rachel Dawes (Maggie Gyllenhaal), Bruce Wayne/Batman's (Christian Bale) ex-love. Rachel is not the only link between the public hero and the private one, as Jim Gordon (Gary Oldman) also links both men and stands by their sides, realizing that keeping order in a modern metropolis takes all kinds of heroes, both legal and vigilante.

The Dark Knight is more of a "Part II" than a direct sequel to *Batman Begins.* It takes what Nolan set up in that first film and makes it deeper and more rewarding. Too many superhero sequels (for example, *Batman Forever* [1995], *Superman Returns* [2006]) are merely bigger and better versions of the films that came before. They are closer to remakes. Conversely, *Batman Begins* sets up the history of this complex character, and *The Dark Knight* develops the character and plot.

Thematically, *The Dark Knight* is fascinating, but it is the execution of the entire piece, even such "non-intellectual" material as the action sequences and special effects, that make it stand out. What is remarkable about *The Dark Knight* is that it bridges the gap and satisfies both drama and action fans at the same time.

Most viewers will remember *The Dark Knight* especially for Heath Ledger's performance. Hyped for months before its release, in large part due to the tragic passing of Ledger early in the year, the performance more than lived up to expectations. Every choice made by Ledger was not just the right decision; it was one that no other actor would have even considered. It is a riveting and mesmerizing turn that will be a source of

admiration for decades. Ledger even seemed to inspire the entire cast. Gary Oldman and Aaron Eckhart, in particular, give two of the best performances of their careers, and Morgan Freeman and Michael Caine make no false moves.

In the end, *The Dark Knight* is more than just the best superhero movie ever made. It is a symphony of good and evil and the poor citizens caught in the middle. It features deep performances and stunning technical accomplishments that have the potential to impact the genre for years to come. The bar has been raised.

Brian Tallerico

CREDITS

Bruce Wayne/Batman: Christian Bale
The Joker: Heath Ledger
Harvey Dent: Aaron Eckhart
Rachel Dawes: Maggie Gyllenhaal
Lt. James Gordon: Gary Oldman
Alfred Pennyworth: Michael Caine
Salvatore Maroni: Eric Roberts
Dr. Jonathan Crane/Scarecrow: Cillian Murphy
Lucius Fox: Morgan Freeman
Mike Engel: Anthony Michael Hall
Detective Ramirez: Monique Gabriela Curnen
Mayor: Nestor Carbonell
Gamble: Michael Jai White
Barbara Gordon: Melinda McGraw
Gotham National Bank manager: William Fichtner
Reese: Joshua Harto
Commissioner Loeb: Colin McFarlane
Det. Weurtz: Ron Dean
The Chechen: Ritchie Coster
James Gordon, Jr.: Nathan Gamble
Tattooed prisoner: Tommy Lister
Lau: Chin Han
Origin: USA
Language: English
Released: 2008
Production: Christopher Nolan, Charles Roven, Emma Thomas; Legendary Pictures, DC Comics; released by Warner Bros.
Directed by: Christopher Nolan
Written by: Christopher Nolan, Jonathan Nolan
Cinematography by: Wally Pfister
Music by: Hans Zimmer, James Newton Howard
Editing: Lee Smith
Production Design: Nathan Crowley
Sound: Ed Novick
Costumes: Lindy Hemming

MPAA rating: PG-13
Running time: 152 minutes

REVIEWS

Boston Globe Online. July 17, 2008.
Chicago Sun-Times Online. July 16, 2008.
Los Angeles Times Online. July 16, 2008.
New York Times Online. July 17, 2008.
USA Today Online. July 16, 2008.

QUOTES

The Joker: "You just couldn't let me go, could you? This is what happens when an unstoppable force meets an immovable object. You are truly incorruptible, aren't you? Huh? You won't kill me out of some misplaced sense of self-righteousness. And I won't kill you because you're just too much fun. I think you and I are destined to do this forever."

Harvey Dent: "You either die a hero or you live long enough to see yourself become the villain."

TRIVIA

When filming began in Chicago in April 2007, the production was code-named "Rory's First Kiss" to dissuade onlookers and trespassers.

AWARDS

Oscars 2008: Sound FX Editing, Support. Actor (Ledger)
British Acad. 2008: Support. Actor (Ledger)
Golden Globes 2009: Support. Actor (Ledger)
Screen Actors Guild 2008: Support. Actor (Ledger), Outstanding Performance by a Stunt Ensemble

Nomination:

Oscars 2008: Art Dir./Set Dec., Cinematog., Film Editing, Makeup, Sound, Visual FX
British Acad. 2008: Cinematog., Costume Des., Film Editing, Makeup, Sound, Visual FX, Orig. Score, Production Des.
Directors Guild 2008: Director (Nolan)
Writers Guild 2008: Adapt. Screenplay.

THE DAY THE EARTH STOOD STILL

12.12.08 is the Day the Earth Stood Still.
  —Movie tagline

Box Office: $79.3 million

In the original version of *The Day the Earth Stood Still* (1951), an alien named Klaatu and his powerful robot comrade Gort come to earth to rid the galaxy of a violent scourge, the human race, whose world wars and nuclear arms dismay the superior beings in outer space. However, after Klaatu comes to know humans better, he is persuaded to let the Earthlings try harder to be peaceful; and the alien, upon his departure, gives a long lecture about the need to be less violent.

Nearly sixty years later, the visitors from outer space still are not happy with human behavior. This time around, when Klaatu takes human form (Keanu Reeves), he arrives to announce he is going to save the planet—but he really means destroying the people who live on it to keep them from destroying it. There are not many planets in any solar system so ideally suited to carbon-based life, Klaatu points out, and damned if his unidentified race is going to let humans waste this one—not even if John Cleese as Professor Barnhardt pronounces humans ready to give it one last try.

Other than changing the problem from general human violence and bad behavior to environmental violence, the screenplay by David Scarpa follows the original 1951 version by Edmund H. North fairly closely. Instead of a spaceship landing on the Mall in Washington D.C., now there is a glowing orb that lands in Central Park (along with scores more elsewhere around the planet). After being shot by a policeman, Klaatu must be "born" in a hospital, and then moved to an interrogation room, from which he escapes by emitting piercing noises in frequencies so shrill that they render the security guards helpless.

Aiding and abetting him is Helen Benson (Jennifer Connelly), an astrophysicist who is among a legion of scientists hastily mustered by the U.S. government to deal with the threat of an alien invasion, but there are mcuh too late to stop the invasion. (In the original, Helen Benson, played by Patricia Neal, was merely a kindly mother; these days, her character must be a genius.) Almost alone among the government's experts, Benson feels Klaatu is peaceful, and she is willing to risk her career by defying the orders of Secretary of State Regina Jackson (Kathy Bates), who wants Benson to drug him. Bates is badly miscast in a role usually played these days by Meryl Streep and she cannot muster the gravitas needed to cope with the greatest crisis humanity has ever faced, an alien invasion. When she is barking out orders, she sounds like she is merely handling an ordinary invasion (the President and Vice-President are bunkered down in undisclosed locations, so she is running the show as a proxy psychopath).

When, early in the film, we are introduced to Benson's son Jacob (Jaden Smith, son of Will Smith) and we learn the boy's father has recently died in war, it is clear there is going to be a reconciliation, but not until after a long fight between mother and child over how to deal with the alien. When Benson drives Klaatu around New

Jersey so he can make an appointment with another glowing orb, there is Jacob in the backseat, bickering and questioning her every move. There is something reassuring and bizarre about how Klaatu, with all his powers, must be chauffeured around by a working single mom and her child.

Meanwhile, Gort, who looks like an industrial lighthouse, allows himself to be taken captive, all the better to start letting loose a swarm of insects that will presumably destroy only human beings and their evil works (such as Giants Stadium in the Meadowland, which crumbles in seconds) while sparing somehow the unthreatening non-human creatures on the planet. (It is not clear how this mode of destruction is going to save the Earth at all.) Also, this dense cloud of voracious insect-bots can eat up stadiums but cannot penetrate an old pedestrian tunnel in Central Park, a development that is key to the final resolution.

Benson, taking the advice of a colleague named Michael (Jon Hamm), drives Klaatu to see Professor Barnhardt (John Cleese), presumably the wisest man on the planet, even though he cannot seem to get his equations right on his home blackboard. (Klaatu sets him straight.) Yet not even Barnhardt's rumpled, low-key genius can quite convince Klaatu that humans will rise to the challenge only when they are on the brink of losing the planet. It will be up to mother and child to sway him, and Connelly does it without even romancing the alien.

Director Scott Derrickson previously had only the obscure film *The Exorcism of Emily Rose* (2005) to his directorial credit, but he demonstrates a sound grasp of what to do with this material, namely, milk the melodrama for all it is worth. Fortunately Connelly and Smith make a credible pair—they are so mismatched it is almost believable. So too, Reeves makes a great ambassador from outer space: he just maintains his usual stiff manner and uninflected monotone, and then affects some sort of vaguely Eastern European accent, which makes him sound more alien to Americans. The whole movie is a prolonged plea to get Klaatu to do something to call off the planned cataclysm, but he does not yield easily, and Reeves manages to make him sympathetic nonetheless because he is so mournful and hangdog in his expressions.

This second *The Day the Earth Stood Still* will not be as beloved as the original, which was a salutary Cold War fable based on the fear that nuclear power had unleashed a destructive genie from the bottle. Now, we are supposed to be cheered somehow by the prospect that human beings will figure out how to save the planet only if all their electricity and machinery is rendered useless. Klaatu's compromise solution is to turn off the power grid and start over from scratch, which seems more like a set-up for a sequel, possibly *The Day Everything on Earth Stopped Working*. Though Derrickson's film is mostly nonsense, it is fun to watch because it moves along madly and implausibly as a sort of road movie featuring a sensible but strange alien, a super-intelligent mom with a heart, and a mouthy kid who learns a lesson about respecting some real diversity—other life forms. Although viewers should not expect to be bowled over by special effects, they can look forward to being generously entertained.

Michael Betzold

CREDITS

Klaatu: Keanu Reeves
Helen: Jennifer Connelly
Dr. Granier: Jon Hamm
Dr. Barnhardt: John Cleese
Jacob: Jaden Smith
Regina Jackson: Kathy Bates
John Driscoll: Kyle Chandler
Colonel: Robert Knepper
Mr. Wu: James Hong
Origin: USA
Language: English
Released: 2008
Production: Gregory Goodman, Paul Harris Boardman; Dune Entertainment III, Three Arts Entertainment; released by 20th Century-Fox
Directed by: Scott Derrickson
Written by: David Scarpa
Cinematography by: David Tattersall
Music by: Tyler Bates
Sound: David Husby
Editing: Wayne Wahrman
Art Direction: Don MacAulay
Costumes: Tish Monaghan
Production Design: David Brisbin

REVIEWS

Boston Globe Online. December 12, 2008.
Chicago Sun-Times Online. December 11, 2008.
Entertainment Weekly Online. December 10, 2008.
Hollywood Reporter Online. December 11, 2008.
Los Angeles Times Online. December 11, 2008.
New York Times Online. December 12, 2008.
San Francisco Chronicle. December 12, 2008.
Variety Online. December 11, 2008.
Washington Post. December 12, 2008.

QUOTES

Klaatu: "If the Earth dies, you die. If the human race dies, the Earth survives."

AWARDS

Nomination:

Golden Raspberries 2008: Worst Sequel/Prequel.

DEATH RACE

Get ready for a killer ride.
—Movie tagline

Box Office: $36.3 million

Paul Bartel's cult classic *Death Race 2000* (1975) is notable for combining political and social satire with action. In remaking the film, writer-director Paul W. S. Anderson, working with a more substantial budget, has envisioned the same material as bigger and louder but with not as much on its mind.

Jensen Ames (Jason Statham), a former race-car driver, is framed for the murder of his wife (Janaya Stephens) and sent to Terminal Island. The prison is, however, far from a typical maximum-security facility. Because of economic turmoil, the United States of 2012 is a cynical, depraved place, so Terminal Island warden Hennessey (Joan Allen) gives the public what it wants. As millions of consumers watch online, Hennessey's inmates stage races to the death in which the only rule is that there are no rules. Driving heavily armored vehicles mounted with machine guns, they tantalize a jaded public. Because his film is aimed at the same sort of viewer, Anderson never shows the folks at home slavering over the violence.

The participating inmates' incentive, beyond mere survival, is Hennessey's promise to release anyone who wins five straight races. Frankenstein, the masked driver who is a favorite of both the public and the warden, dies of injuries after winning his fourth in a row. Hennessey, keeping the driver's demise a secret, puts Frankenstein's mask on Ames and tells him he will be free with a single victory. The warden can walk unguarded through the prison's exercise area because, as one inmate puts it, "She's the baddest ass in the yard." Unfortunately for Ames, this assessment proves to be very true.

Ames quickly establishes rivalries with two other drivers, the vicious thug Pachenko (Max Ryan) and Machine Gun Joe (Tyrese Gibson), a gay African American who has won three races and will do anything to achieve his freedom. Joe's intensity is exemplified by his using a razor blade to cut notches into his face for each driver he has killed. On Ames's side are Coach (Ian McShane), who prepares the driver's car for races, and Case (Natalie Martinez), a navigator on loan from the nearby women's prison. Information about the convicts' crimes and previous lives is kept to a minimum in Anderson's streamlined screenplay.

The best parts of *Death Race* are the races, well staged by Anderson and smoothly edited by Niven Howie. It is always possible to tell the cars apart and distinguish where they are in relation to each other, without any of those annoying fluctuations in distances between cars from shot to shot so common in chase footage. Because of such films as *Mortal Kombat* (1995) and *Resident Evil* (2002), Anderson is often attacked by reviewers for excessive violence. While *Death Race* is comparatively benign compared to his previous films, there are a few repugnant instances of gruesomeness in which a character's pain or death is meant to be humorous. Bartel's film has several comic moments, but the only true humor in *Death Race* comes from Coach's tough-guy witticisms, one of which is addressed directly to the audience.

McShane seems to be enjoying his role, never condescending to the film's disreputable genre. Neither does Allen, who gives Hennessey a measured intensity. Anderson fills his films with tough female characters: Martinez presents Case as confident on the surface yet vulnerable underneath. Statham is a limited actor occasionally capable of showing complex emotions, as in *The Bank Job* (2008), but he retreats into taciturnity as Ames. In contrast, Gibson gives Joe a charismatic volatility. A pre-*Rocky* (1976) Sylvester Stallone plays Joe in *Death Race 2000,* and Statham's role is filled by David Carradine, who reportedly appears somewhere in the remake, perhaps as the unidentified actor playing Frankenstein at the beginning of the film.

In reviewing *Death Race* in the *New York Times,* Nathan Lee described it as "simple, sick and satisfying." Anderson knows how to present the action effectively without being sidetracked by sociology or psychology. Except for some sadistic violence, the result is moderately entertaining.

Michael Adams

CREDITS

Jensen Ames: Jason Statham
Machine Gun Joe: Tyrese Gibson
Coach: Ian McShane

Warden Hennessey: Joan Allen
Case: Nathalia Martinez
Pachenko: Max Ryan
Ulrich: Jason Clarke
Listsr: Frederick Koehler
Gunner: Jacob Vargas
Travis Colt: Justin Mader
Grimm: Robert LaSardo
Origin: USA
Language: English
Released: 2008
Production: Paul Wagner, Jeremy Bolt, Paul W.S. Anderson, Roger Corman; Impact Pictures, Relativity Media; released by Universal
Directed by: Paul W.S. Anderson
Written by: Paul W.S. Anderson
Cinematography by: Scott Kevan
Sound: Don Cohen
MPAA rating: R
Running time: 105 minutes

REVIEWS

Boston Globe Online. August 22, 2008.
Chicago Sun-Times Online. August 21, 2008.
Hollywood Reporter Online. August 21, 2008.
Los Angeles Times Online. August 22, 2008.
New York Times Online. August 22, 2008.
San Francisco Chronicle. August 22, 2008, p. E5.
Variety Online. August 21, 2008.
Washington Post. August 22, 2008, p. C1.

QUOTES

Hennessey: "This prison is the home to murderers, rapists, and violent offenders of every kind. The United States Penal System sends me the worst of the worst. But the men you've provoked, well, let's just say Mr. Ames that the life term you've joined us for may be a lot shorter than you think."

TRIVIA

Thirty-five cars were utilized throughout the shoot and were maintained by an army of 85 mechanics.

DECEPTION

When you're in this world, no one is who they
seem, and everyone is playing the game.
—Movie tagline

Box Office: $4.5 million

Under certain circumstances, the combination of high-profile stars, including Ewan McGregor, Hugh Jack-man, and Michelle Williams, appearing in a film helmed by a first-time feature director, Marcel Langenegger, might seem to indicate commitment to a fantastic project with a singular vision (see *Reservoir Dogs* [1992] directed by Quentin Tarantino, or *American Beauty* [1999] directed by Sam Mendes for projects in this vein). Add to the mix the fact that said film is being bankrolled in part by the lead actor's production company (Hugh Jackman's "Seed Productions"), and the casual observer might begin to think that this is some sort of passion project, or at least perceived to be a potential cash cow. The ephemeral and fickle nature of success in the film industry often causes star-produced vehicles to list in either one or the other direction. *Deception* is, however, a bit of a mystery as it could not conceivably be seen as an artistic stretch of the erotic thriller genre and it was a dismal flop at the box office, unable to recoup its relatively modest budget of about twenty million dollars. In the final analysis, the greatest mystery of *Deception* is what any of the key players saw in it in the first place.

The film opens with accountant Jonathan Mc-Quarry (Ewan McGregor) performing an audit late into the night in some corporate conference room (the fact that he appears to be alone except for the cleaning staff indicates the hour), when he is interrupted in his task by Wyatt Bose (Hugh Jackman), apparently a lawyer at the firm. Wyatt offers Jonathan a joint and they smoke and chat—Jonathan bemoans his buttoned-up life and Wyatt jokingly concurs. Jonathan takes the subway home and sees an intriguing blond woman on the platform—a keychain dangles out of her purse and bears a large letter "S." Jonathan is clearly taken with her. The next day, Jonathan contacts Wyatt and they play tennis—at a club that night, Jonathan complains that his life and job allow no time for relationships, that he is always at companies briefly and is always hated because he is there to conduct audits. The two men have lunch the following day, set their cell phones down on the same table and accidentally switch phones. Later, when Jonathan realizes what has happened, he tries to contact Wyatt, but Wyatt is in London. Eventually, Jonathan receives a call on Wyatt's phone—a woman who asks cryptically, "Are you free tonight?" He says yes, agrees to meet the woman at a hotel, and she seduces him upon arrival. Later, Jonathan gets a call from Wyatt, who realizes what has happened, and encourages Jonathan to enjoy himself. The callers are part of something called the "List": They are all high-ranking, extremely busy executives, and the List is their means of having "intimacy without intricacy." Using names is forbidden. Over the next several weeks, Jonathan has many trysts using the List, but one night one of his calls turns out to the mysterious "S" (Michelle Williams). Infatuated, Jonathan takes her to dinner instead of settling for the usual anonymous sex. Jonathan meets her again the following night in a Chinatown hotel room, leaves for a moment to get ice, and returns to find blood on the bed. "S" appears to be gone and Jonathan is immediately clubbed and knocked unconscious. He wakes to find the television on tuned to static, and the room has been cleaned.

Ultimately, it is revealed that Wyatt has orchestrated these events and claims to have abducted "S." To see her alive again, Jonathan must use his access to the accounts of the firm of Clute-Nichols (whom Jonathan will be auditing) to steal twenty million dollars for Wyatt and transfer it to an account in Madrid, Spain in Jonathan's name. Jonathan does the job, and discovers later that his apartment has blown up (his superintendent let himself in to check a leaky pipe). The film cuts to Madrid where Wyatt, believing Jonathan to be dead, is posing as Jonathan to claim the twenty million—"S" is with him there, but she is furious when she discovers that Wyatt killed Jonathan. When Wyatt, posing as Jonathan, goes to the bank to make the withdrawal, he discovers that he needs a co-signer—Wyatt Bose. Wyatt gets a call from Jonathan, who was not killed in the explosion, proposing that they simply split the money. So Wyatt and Jonathan make the withdrawal, each posing as the other, and they leave the bank each carrying a suitcase containing ten million dollars. When Wyatt meets "S" in a park later, she shoots Wyatt in retaliation for killing Jonathan and abandons the money. Jonathan ultimately manages to track "S" down and the film ends.

Deception's greatest fault, aside from some of the more implausible aspects of the story (many of which are to be expected in this type of film), is the fact that it is filmed in a way that undercuts any hope of suspense or thrills. Early on in the picture, for instance, when Jonathan sees Wyatt talking to lawyers and employees at the firm Jonathan is auditing, it is pretty clear to the viewer that none of them know Wyatt, that Wyatt is using his prodigious charm to make it appear that he is having a familiar conversation with colleagues. That this is so obvious to the audience, one wonders if perhaps it is meant to be dramatic irony—that the viewer is supposed to be in on something that remains unknown to the character—but the form of the erotic thriller genre demands that the audience discover things as the characters discover them, or the surprise/thrilling aspect of the thriller is rendered moot. This particular problem occurs throughout the film: It is obvious that Jonathan and Wyatt will switch phones long before it happens; it is clear that Michelle Williams' "S" is part of Wyatt's conspiracy long before that information is revealed; and when the superintendent of Jonathan's building makes an appointment to come by to fix a leak, it is clear that he will meet with whatever fate Wyatt intends for

Jonathan. Audiences may not be sophisticated, but the clues left lying around by director Langenegger are so blatant that is it almost impossible not to be one step ahead of the action. Granted, the last half hour of the film boasts a bit more unpredictability for although it is pretty clear that some sort of showdown is in store for Jonathan and Wyatt, exactly how it will play out cannot necessarily be guess. After enduring an hour or so of unsatisfactorily staged and telegraphed revelations that hardly qualify as genuinely surprising, viewers will find it difficult to care about what happens to these characters. Attempting to generate intrigue in the final act of the movie is far too little and much too late.

In fact, the film is so disingenuous, so painfully self-aware of its aspirations (and perhaps even the knowledge of its inability to fulfill them), that viewers simply wish that the film would have the decency to skip to the end and spare the audience from having to slog through encounters and pseudo-revelations that are supposed to pass for details. Even small details that provide a modicum of pleasure for film trivia buffs, such as the naming of the firm that Jonathan must rob "Clute-Nichols"—"Clute" could be a reference to the 1971 film *Klute* about a prostitute who helps a detective solve a crime, and "Nichols" could possibly be a reference to director Mike Nichols, who directed the sexually charged drama *Carnal Knowledge,* about the complicated sex lives of two male friends, also released in 1971—cannot salvage the bad faith generated by the rest of Mark Bomback's pedestrian writing and Marcel Langenegger's shoddy execution. The ambitions of *Deception* (to tell superbly the story of the conning of a working man into the social high life) were last realized most satisfyingly in David Mamet's *The Spanish Prisoner* (1997), though minus the overt eroticism. The only deception perpetrated effectively in *Deception* is getting moviegoers to part with their hard-earned money for the false promise of a well-made, star-studded thrill ride.

John Boaz

CREDITS

Jonathan McQuarry: Ewan McGregor
Wyatt Bose: Hugh Jackman
S: Michelle Williams
Tina: Maggie Q
List Member #5: Rachael Taylor
Wall Street Analyst: Natasha Henstridge
Detective Russo: Lisa Gay Hamilton
Wall Street Belle: Charlotte Rampling
Ms. Pomerantz: Margaret Colin
List Member #1: Paz de la Huerta

Origin: USA

Language: English

Released: 2008

Production: Arnold Rifkin, Robbie Brenner, David L. Bushell, John Palermo, Hugh Jackman; Seed Prods.; released by 20th Century-Fox

Directed by: Marcel Langenegger

Written by: Mark Bomback

Cinematography by: Dante Spinotti

Music by: Ramin Djawadi

Sound: Allan Byer

Editing: Christian Wagner, Douglas Crise

Art Direction: John J. Kasarda

Costumes: Sue Gandy

Production Design: Patrizia Von Brandenstein

MPAA rating: R

Running time: 108 minutes

REVIEWS

Boston Globe Online. April 25, 2008.
Chicago Sun-Times Online. April 25, 2008.
Hollywood Reporter Online. April 25, 2008.
Los Angeles Times Online. April 25, 2008.
New York Times Online. April 25, 2008.
San Francisco Chronicle. April 25, 2008, p. E5.
Variety Online. April 24, 2008.
Washington Post Online. April 25, 2008.

QUOTES

Signature text message: "Are you free tonight?"

TRIVIA

Alternate early titles of the film included *The List* and *The Tourist.*

DEFIANCE

Freedom begins with an act of defiance.
—Movie tagline

Box Office: $28 million

The true story depicted in *Defiance* is so compelling that it is difficult to believe that it has never been filmed before. While most Holocaust dramas focus on the persecution of the Jews and others imprisoned and murdered by the Nazis, *Defiance* presents a small group of Belorussian Jews who resisted the invading Germany army and its collaborators, killing many of them. This fascinating historical event should make for both compelling drama and exciting adventure, but unfortu-

nately Clayton Frohman's screenplay and Edward Zwick's direction leave this potential untapped.

After their parents are murdered by Belorussian police, the Bielski brothers, Tuvia (Daniel Craig), Zus (Liev Schreiber), Asael (Jamie Bell), and young Aron (George MacKay), seek refuge in a forest, where they are gradually joined by dozens of other Jews who have managed to escape from the ghettoes. Much of *Defiance* deals with the differences between the two older Bielskis. Zus is a hothead longing to kill as many of the enemy as possible, while the more philosophical Tuvia agonizes over moral choices. The film alternates between battle scenes, efforts to organize the growing group of refugees, the romantic interests of the three oldest brothers, and bickering between Tuvia and Zus, which eventually leads to Zus's leaving his brothers to join Soviet partisans.

The formulaic structure of the film, based on the book *Defiance: The Bielski Partisans* (1993) by Nechama Tec, makes it seem almost like a made-for-television film. Although *Valkyrie* (2008), another World War II action drama released around the same time, also has a conventional, chronological narrative, its director, Bryan Singer, has a surer hand at pacing, building up suspense better than does Zwick. Because he thinks his story is so powerful it does not need embellishment, Zwick simply plods from one point to the next, leaving viewers thinking they have seen all this before, even if they have not. In comparison, *The Wall* (1982), a television dramatization of the Jewish uprising in the Warsaw Ghetto, is a much livelier, more emotionally engaging treatment of similar material.

With James Newton Howard's occasionally maudlin score underlining every thematic point, *Defiance* almost seems to be shouting such words as "suffering," "compassion," and "nobility" to make sure the audience understands the significance of each scene. The film shares similar flaws with Zwick's earlier unsubtle efforts *Glory* (1989), *The Last Samurai* (2003), and *Blood Diamond* (2006), which alternate violent scenes with ones grappling with prejudice and the lessons to be learned from conflict. Though he has a somewhat better visual sense, Zwick is a throwback to old-fashioned liberal filmmakers, like Stanley Kramer, who directed with their hearts rather than their heads.

Zwick was roundly ridiculed for the big battle scene in *The Last Samurai* in which hundreds of bullets are fired but miss the title character, played by Tom Cruise. The Bielskis suffer minor wounds but likewise magically avoid hundreds, perhaps thousands of deadly bullets. In the big battle scene in *Defiance*, Tuvia fires a machine gun at Nazis only a few yards away only for the shots to kick up dust in front of the enemy, though the gun's angle suggests the bullets should either be hitting their targets or going over the heads of the Nazis.

The acting is less than enthralling as well. After reaching an apex of sorts with *Layer Cake* (2004) and *Casino Royale* (2006), Craig is beginning to show his limitations. For example, to demonstrate that Tuvia is thinking, all he can do is stare blankly or squint. Schreiber does better with an underwritten part, though both actors might have been better served by switching roles. Schreiber generally has a humanity and sense of humor Craig is missing in this film. The women in the brothers' lives, Bella (Iben Hjejle), Zus's lover, and Lilka (Alexa Davalos), Tuvia's, make short but vivid impressions. Davalos is especially good at conveying conflicted emotions. Since playing Sir Arthur Sullivan in *Topsy-Turvy* (1999), Alan Corduner has become one of the most reliable character actors, and in *Defiance* he breathes life into what could have become a clichéd, sentimental role, that of the moral center of the refugees, a teacher who maintains his humor despite the chaos raging around him.

The best aspect of *Defiance* is the cinematography of the great Eduardo Serra. As he did with *The Wings of the Dove* (1997) and *The Widow of Saint-Pierre* (2000), Serra uses a dark palette to emphasize the psychological state of the characters, with softer, seemingly natural light for the more tender moments. The film's most memorable scene comes when Lilka, alone in a snowy wood, is attacked by a wolf. The scene demonstrates the protagonists' resolve to survive, while Serra's beautiful lighting shows that danger can lurk even within the most beautiful, seemingly peaceful of settings. Unfortunately, *Defiance* has too few such poetic moments.

Michael Adams

CREDITS

Tuvia Bielski: Daniel Craig
Zus Bielski: Liev Schreiber
Asael Bielski: Jamie Bell
Chaya: Mia Wasikowska
Lilka: Alexa Davalos
Tamara: Jodhi May
Malbin: Mark Feuerstein
Ben Zion: Tomas Arana
Shamon: Allan Corduner
Bella: Iben Hjejle
Origin: USA
Language: English
Released: 2008
Production: Pieter Jan Brugge, Edward Zwick; Grosvenor Park, Bedford Falls; released by Paramount Vantage

Directed by: Edward Zwick
Written by: Edward Zwick, Clayton Frohman
Cinematography by: Eduardo Serra
Music by: James Newton Howard
Sound: Peter Hliddal
Editing: Steven Rosenblum
Art Direction: Daran Fulham
Costumes: Jenny Beavan
Production Design: Dan Weil
MPAA rating: R
Running time: 136 minutes

REVIEWS

Hollywood Reporter Online. November 10, 2008.
Los Angeles Times Online. December 31, 2008.
New York Times Online. December 31, 2008.
San Francisco Chronicle. January 16, 2009.
Variety Online. November 10, 2008.
Village Voice Online. December 30, 2008.
Washington Post. January 15, 2009.

QUOTES

Asael Bielski: "Nothing is impossible, what we all have done is impossible!"

TRIVIA

The film was shot in Lithuania, about 100 miles away from the location of the actual Bielski brothers camp.

AWARDS

Nomination:

Oscars 2008: Orig. Score
Golden Globes 2009: Orig. Score.

DEFINITELY, MAYBE

Three relationships. Three disasters. One last chance.
—Movie tagline

Box Office: $32.2 million

Definitely, Maybe is a smart and pleasing romantic comedy. Much of its appeal rests in the number of relationships and the number of years spanned by the plot. Will Hayes (Ryan Reynolds) is a father about to be divorced. The signing of the papers and the time he spends with his young daughter Maya (Abigail Breslin) combine to make him reflective enough to respond to Maya's question about how he and her mother met. Will's story, shown in a long flashback as he tells it to

Maya, is really the account of his intermittent involvement with three girlfriends from 1992 until the present. He changes their names to make Maya wonder which one he married.

Writer-director Adam Brooks effectively uses politics as a backdrop for the film. Will begins his story with his younger self living in Wisconsin and in a relationship with Emily (Elizabeth Banks). Will plans a move to New York in order to work for the Clinton presidential campaign, and Emily intends eventually to follow. In New York Will soon meets April (Isla Fischer), who works the copy machine at the Clinton offices, and they become friends with a conversational friction over politics. Will also meets Summer (Rachel Weisz), one of Emily's college friends. Emotionally and romantically, these three women move in and out of Will's life over the next fifteen years. Maya eventually guesses correctly which one is her mother. After the divorce papers are signed, Maya also senses which one of the three girlfriends Will really loves and offers to help her father to try to regain her love. The final scene shows a late-night ride to the apartment of the girlfriend with whom Will wants to reconcile.

The jigsaw plotting of the movie, combining strands of narrative that involve both romantic and political matters, is clarified by Adam Brooks's effective use of books as a plot device. Before he leaves for New York, Emily entrusts Will with returning Summer's journal to her. This journal becomes the way Will meets both Summer and her current lover, Hampton Roth (Kevin Kline), a professor who is also her thesis director. Before returning the journal, Will indulges his immature whim to read it, and then when returning it and meeting the cynical Hampton, Will endures a grilling that calls attention to some of his immature assumptions about the political process. In short, the journal does more than simply advance the story: It reveals Will's emotional and political inexperience, it enriches the first scene with Summer by setting up expectations about her personality that the script can build on, and it also marks the point of innocence that Will later moves beyond as gains experience with the passing years.

The script, however, makes even better use of another book. When Will first visits April's apartment, he is struck by the many different copies she has of the classic novel *Jane Eyre*. April explains that years ago her father, shortly before his unexpected, sudden death, gave her a special birthday copy of the novel that he inscribed. That copy somehow got lost in April's various moves, and now she makes a point to stop at second-hand booksellers to check and sometimes even to buy other inscribed copies in a vain effort to recapture the feeling of the one from her father. The search for the missing *Jane Eyre* thus becomes an effective way of personalizing

April and of organizing her part of the plot. Will's first conversations with April established her as politically and emotionally apathetic, someone who had not yet come into her own as a person, and the book motif foreshadows April's maturation. After his long story to Maya concludes, Will reconnects with April years later and finds her working for Amnesty International. She is a different person from the girl running the copier at Clinton headquarters in 1992. A key scene in the center of the film features a conversation between April and Will when April teaches Will something about finding the right person by saying that "the real deal finds you" when the recipient is ready, that the serendipity of love is more about when than about who. April's growth in the film is clarified, directly or indirectly, by the plot device of the missing (and later found) copy of *Jane Eyre*.

Adam Brooks shows as much care in his direction as in his writing. He has fashioned a refreshing, low-keyed visual style with many waist and wide shots that give the audience viewing options. Brooks rejects the contemporary emphasis on the very tight close-up and often pulls the camera back to show a wider proximity of space and to emphasize mise en scène or the arrangement of materials in the frame. Some of the humor in the film even employs visual punch lines. When, for example, Will talks with Emily in Wisconsin about his impending move to New York, the camera shoots them both from the opposite side of the small apartment. Will's friend Charlie (Daniel Eric Gold) steps into the shot and fills the space in the open door as the conversation turns to how Emily will fill her time with Will gone. After Charlie blurts out a few silly remarks, Will casually closes the door in Charlie's face as a way of trying to close him out of Emily's future as well. Later, as Will is granted a desk from which to work at Clinton headquarters, Brooks shoots him sitting at it behind a pyramid of toilet-paper rolls, his co-workers' prankish way of reminding him of his first office task. The wide shot works nicely because it includes Will's sheepish grin, his smiling co-workers filling the perimeter of the shot, and the visual focal point of the stack of toilet paper. These wider camera distances allow the audience to observe both comic action and reaction in the same unbroken shot. They are the cinematic equivalent of the verbal finesse that Brooks puts into his script.

The wider shots also emphasize the contributions of the excellent cast. Holding two actors in the same waist shot preserves both their facial expressions and the proximity of their body language. Their acting thus springs from a richer visual context. When, for example, Summer serenades Will with her favorite song, "I've Got a Crush on You," her heartfelt but amateur singing is redeemed by a series of medium shots of the two of them in various New York settings. This visual montage of togetherness makes for a pleasing, lyrical moment. Brooks also photographs both Will and Summer scrunched together on the sofa in the same wide shot, each writing intently on a laptop as a visual sign that their emotional closeness is based on their shared political seriousness. The best example is probably the matching scenes of Will's rehearsing his marriage proposal, followed in the next scene by his real proposal. The first plays out at night on a rooftop with the actors framed by sky and stars. The second occurs at a park with the performers surrounded by trees and a lake. That both scenes are undercut by some unexpected obstacles arising does not offset the effectiveness of the frame design.

Most of all, the script is rich in ideas. The premise of the father telling his young daughter about his involvements with his serious girlfriends calls attention at times to some of the double standards of adulthood. For example, Maya pounces on a passing moment in Will's story that shows him smoking, which leads the father to some awkward evasions. The topic of sex is also treated in a way that calls attention to some double standards of adulthood. However, the principal idea that the script explores is that of maturity and how personal integrity is ultimately indissoluble from professional integrity. Will's idealism and desire to work in the Clinton campaign lead both April and Hampton Roth to probe the genuineness of his motives and to wonder whether his idealism strengthens or cripples him. "Be a real man instead of a boy man," Roth admonishes him. Even young Maya occasionally voices some cynicism.

This interplay of sentiment and cynicism fuels most of the developing story. When, for example, Summer writes an overly soft magazine article about Will's new boss, a gubernatorial candidate, Hampton scolds her: "Do your job." She realizes that her affection for Will had somewhat compromised her integrity as a reporter. Later, as she exposes the candidate's darker side in a subsequent article, her professional rigor marks the end of her relationship with Will. One of the strengths of the script, as illustrated also by April's development, is the implication that a person's emotional maturation reverberates meaningfully in his or her vocational life. Many characters struggle with this challenge, and the film uses public events like the Monica Lewinsky scandal as a tool for showing the clash between idealism and realism and for charting the characters' developing awareness. Thus Will's protracted boyishness becomes a way for the film to explore the interplay between sentiment and cynicism. A turning point of sorts occurs at Will's birthday party in the late 1990s when he sits in a bar with his former campaign co-workers from 1992 and speculates, "Maybe [Clinton] should be impeached." In *Definitely, Maybe* the audience sees a handful of

characters who seem to fear too much of either sentiment or cynicism and who struggle with finding the right balance. Exploring the poles of these complex mental states is the film's most stimulating dimension.

Glenn Hopp

CREDITS

Will Hayes: Ryan Reynolds
Maya Hayes: Abigail Breslin
April: Isla Fisher
Emily: Elizabeth Banks
Summer: Rachel Weisz
Russell: Derek Luke
Hampton Roth: Kevin Kline
Arthur: Nestor Serrano
Anne: Annie Parisse
Kelly: Liane Balaban
Rafael: Kevin Corrigan
Gareth: Adam Ferrara
Origin: Great Britain, USA
Language: English
Released: 2008
Production: Tim Bevan, Eric Fellner; Working Title Productions, Studio Canal Plus; released by Universal
Directed by: Adam Brooks
Written by: Adam Brooks
Cinematography by: Florian Ballhaus
Music by: Clint Mansell
Sound: Michael Barosky
Music Supervisor: Nick Angel
Editing: Peter Teschner
Art Direction: Peter Rogness
Costumes: Gary Jones
Production Design: Stephanie Carroll
MPAA rating: PG-13
Running time: 111 minutes

REVIEWS

Boston Globe Online. February 14, 2008.
Chicago Sun-Times Online. February 14, 2008.
Entertainment Weekly Online. February 13, 2008.
Hollywood Reporter Online. February 11, 2008.
Los Angeles Times Online. February 14, 2008.
New York Times Online. February 14, 2008.
San Francisco Chronicle Online. February 14, 2008.
Variety Online. January 24, 2008.
Village Voice Online. February 12, 2008.

QUOTES

Maya (to dad Will): "I can't believe you smoked and drank and were such a slut. But I still love you."
Will: "This song is an excellent cure for the will to live."

TRIVIA

Director Adam Brooks makes a cameo appearance as a used book store owner in the film.

DIARY OF THE DEAD
(George A. Romero's Diary of the Dead)

Where will you be when the end begins?
—Movie tagline

George A. Romero returns to the franchise that has made him a household legend and international horror icon with *Diary of the Dead*, his best film in years and proof that no one does the undead like the master. Each film in the *Dead* franchise—*Night of the Living Dead* (1968), *Dawn of the Dead* (1978), *Day of the Dead* (1985), and *Land of the Dead* (2005)—was a commentary on the world it was released into, and *Diary of the Dead* finds the master reinvigorated by the new generation of technology and the government corruption and mistrust that has been such a part of the first decade of the new millenium. *Diary of the Dead* is Romero's most vibrantly alive film since *Day of the Dead* and proves that this masterful storyteller still has much to say.

Like several other recent releases, including *Cloverfield* (2008) and *Redacted* (2007), *Diary of the Dead* is a movie within a movie. The film is set up as a documentary about the day, to quote the best tagline ever from *Dawn of the Dead*, "Hell got too crowded and the dead were forced to walk the Earth," and shot by a filmmaking crew within the movie. The documentary-within-a-film is entitled "Jason Creed's The Death of Death." Creed is a film student at The University of Pittsburgh and he happens to be making a horror movie when his cast and crew hear the reports of the walking dead. Like a similar device in *Cloverfield*, Jason decides that, while he and his friends run for safety, the events should be documented. As his girlfriend says, "If it didn't happen on camera, it's like it didn't happen, right?"

The filmmaker and his friends set off in a Winnebago to find his girlfriend's unreachable family, and Romero sets up a nightmare cross-country journey. Much more than he did in *Land of the Dead* and *Day of the Dead*, Romero feels like he is actually trying to scare viewers, presenting them with a more traditional horror movie than the more action-driven zombie movies of late. *Diary of the Dead* contains action scenes, but Romero tries harder to get under the viewer's skin than he has in a long time, not driving home the social commentary as much as the other films in the franchise. Definitely scarier than *Land of the Dead* or *Day of the Dead*, Romero proves that he can achieve pure horror and treat deeper themes in his work. Watching a girl who has committed suicide slowly turn into a member of the undead is one of the more powerful images to appear in the genre in a long time.

More importantly, Romero has found his creativity again when it comes to the often-tired world of zombies and human's futile attempts to stop them. Using a heart defibrillator on the head of the undead provokes a pretty interesting response. Going back to "Day One," telling a story of when the zombie infestation began, is something that Romero has not been able to do in four decades. After *Night of the Living Dead*'s infamous start ("They're coming to get you, Barbara!"), the next three *Dead* films all took place in a world where the awareness that Hell was so crowded that the dead were forced to walk the Earth was a fact of life. Essentially rebooting his own franchise gives Romero a spark of energy that has been missing in his work recently. *Diary of the Dead* is more alive than any of the films of the *Resident Evil* or "*28*" franchises.

Although the focus may be more on horror than social commentary, the latter is still there because Romero always has something more on his mind. As with most Romero films, *Diary of the Dead* is not just a straight-up shocker. This fifth zombie film tackles a common subject in cinema nowadays, the information age. Lines like "The camera's the whole thing" help define an interesting world where the recording is paramount. Like *Cloverfield* or *Redacted* (but much smarter than either of those films), Romero uses new media to not only make the horror more powerful but comment on its prevalence in society. When a government controls what its citizens see and hear, there is more honestly on the information superhighway via websites, MySpace pages, and message boards that grow daily more prominent. Romero plays with handheld recordings, web pages, and other products of the new age of information better than any of the recent movies that have attempted the exact same tactic. (However, unlike *Cloverfield*, he refuses to go for nausea with his handheld camera approach.)

George A. Romero is to zombie films as Martin Scorsese is to mob movies or Alfred Hitchcock is to thrillers—there is simply no better director. Romero is so consistently fascinating because he refuses to get stale. He wants his films to be bloody reflections of the time they were made. Forty years after unleashing one of the most influential horror films of all time with *Night of the Living Dead* and thirty years after creating his masterful *Dawn of the Dead*, Romero is still finding new ways to scare an audience. With *Diary of the Dead*, he has done so more confidently and interestingly than he has in years.

Brian Tallerico

CREDITS

Jason Creed: Joshua Close
Eliot: Joe Dinicol
Ridley: Philip Riccio
Debra: Michelle Morgan
Tony: Shawn Roberts
Tracy: Amy Lalonde
Andrew Maxwell: Scott Wentworth
Origin: USA
Language: English
Released: 2007
Production: Peter Grunwald, Artur Spigel, Sam Englebardt, Ara Katz; Artfine Films; released by Weinstein Company
Directed by: George A. Romero
Written by: George A. Romero
Cinematography by: Adam Swica
Music by: Norman Orenstein
Sound: Zenon Waschuk
Editing: Michael Doherty
Costumes: Alex Kavanagh
Production Design: Rupert Lazarus
MPAA rating: R
Running time: 95 minutes

REVIEWS

Boston Globe Online. February 15, 2008.
Chicago Sun-Times Online. February 15, 2008.
Entertainment Weekly. February 22, 2008, p. 76.
Hollywood Reporter Online. September 13, 2007.
Los Angeles Times Online. February 15, 2008.
New York Times Online. February 15, 2008.
Premiere Online. February 13, 2008.
Rolling Stone Online. February 14, 2008.
Variety Online. September 11, 2007.

QUOTES

Debra: "Jason always wanted to be a documentary filmmaker. But for his senior class project, he decided to try to make a horror film. That's what he was shooting on that first night, the night when…everything changed."

Andrew: "The problem doesn't seem to be that people are waking up dead, but that dead people are waking up."

TRIVIA

Several celebrities have voiceover cameos in the film, among them are: Stephen King, Simon Pegg, Quentin Tarantino, Guillermo del Toro, and Wes Craven.

DIMINISHED CAPACITY

*Sometimes what you lose is not as important as
what you find.*
—Movie tagline

Terry Kinney's gentle exploration of loss features a family of lovable losers anchored by a quirky Alzheimer's-afflicted paterfamilias in small-town Missouri. The narrative takes no chances, with its blatant emotional manipulation and contrived eccentricity that proceeds to a Chicago-set denouement without much surprise. Kinney also hails from Chicago, a founder of the renowned Steppenwolf Theatre, and his directorial debut comedy/drama, featuring an exceptional ensemble cast, is able but hardly groundbreaking.

Sherwood Kiraly, along with co-screenwriter Doug Bost, adapted his novel about a Chicago newspaper editor and his retired uncle, both afflicted with the titular mental affliction. In the case of Cooper (Matthew Broderick) it is a concussion resulting in short-term memory loss—the unfortunate result of getting in the way of a bar fight, while Uncle Rollie's (Alan Alda) diminished mental capacity is due to advancing Alzheimer's Disease. Cooper heads back to his Missouri hometown at his mother Belle's (Lois Smith) behest when he is given a leave of absence from his editorial duties at an unnamed Chicago-based newspaper where his reduced short-term memory resulted in a demotion to editor of the comics page.

The character of Rollie as written is quirky in quotation marks. He has a William S. Burroughs-esque way of creating poetry by means of rigging a typewriter with fishing lines so that every time he gets a bite, it types a letter—the literal representation of a technique also known as the cut-up technique or "fishbowling." But Rollie is also a sports fan and constantly brags to the whole town about a valuable 1908 baseball card of the World Series-winning Chicago Cubs right fielder Frank Schulte. Alda makes the role convincing but Kinney's tone is too often wrong for a man struggling with losing his mind and makes it difficult for the character to leave a lasting impression.

Cooper has agreed to help Belle convince Rollie that he needs the professional care offered by a mental health facility. He is sidetracked by a subplot romance with his former flame Charlotte (Virginia Madsen), a mother and artist who is newly divorced. A lackluster Broderick flounders in his surprisingly thin lead role as a delightfully dim journalist dealing with an unruly uncle. Madsen, given the task of caretaker, is allowed a more fully rounded, believable character and turns in a capable, likable performance.

Plot threads neatly converge as one has Charlotte with an appointment in Chicago to try and sell her paintings to a vegan food chain, and another hinges on the baseball card, which takes the family to a Chicago sports memorabilia convention and sets up the film's more exciting scenes. Two extraneous "villains" are injected in the form of the drunken, gun-wielding local rednecks Wendell Kendall (Tom Aldredge) and Donny Prine (Jim True-Frost), the latter following them to Chicago to steal the card.

In Chicago, the family meets the honest baseball card dealer Mad Dog McClure played by Dylan Baker, a scene-stealer who enlivens the film, which has beeen drooping somewhat until this third reel. Aiding and abetting Baker is Lee Vivyan (Bobby Cannavale), a crooked memorabilia trader, who adds authenticity and humor to the convention scenes, which are the film's highlights. There is much ado over the coveted Cubs card, which goes on its own journey as it changes numerous hands.

Kinney, Kiraly, and Bost accurately depict the rabid fans of the Chicago Cubs—Cubs legend Ernie Banks has a cameo—as well as the morbidly fascinating subculture of sports memorabilia dealers and traders. The filmmakers seem to equate the fanaticism of sports fans and dementia, but they miscalculate with a monologue denouncing the whole trade as trying to put a price on precious sports memories. Otherwise, the convention scenes are the bright spots in an otherwise ho-hum, overly calculating family comedy/drama that may have the most to offer Cubs fans.

Hilary White

CREDITS

Cooper: Matthew Broderick
Rollie: Alan Alda
Charlotte: Virginia Madsen
Stan: Louis CK
Dillon: Jimmy Bennett
Mad Dog McClure: Dylan Baker
Lee Vivyan: Bobby Cannavale
Donny Prine: Jim True-Frost
Casey Dean: Jeff Perry
Belle: Lois Smith
Origin: USA
Language: English
Released: 2008
Production: Celine Rattray, Galt Niederhoffer, Daniela Taplin Lundberg; Plum Pictures, Hart Lunsford Films, Benedek Films, Steppenwolf Films; released by IFC Films
Directed by: Terry Kinney
Written by: Sherwood Kiraly and Doug Bost
Cinematography by: Vanja Cernjul
Music by: Robert Berger, Griffin Richardson
Music Supervisor: Tracy McKnight
Editing: Tim Streeto
Art Direction: Matthew Munn

Costumes: Sarah J. Holden
Production Design: Dan Davis
MPAA rating: Unrated
Running time: 92 minutes

REVIEWS

Chicago Sun-Times Online. July 3, 2008.
Entertainment Weekly Online. July 11, 2008.
Hollywood Reporter Online. January 23, 2008.
Los Angeles Times Online. July 4, 2008.
New York Times Online. July 4, 2008.
Variety Online. January 25, 2008.
Village Voice Online. July 2, 2008.

TRIVIA

The part of Wildfire, is played by sound department intern David Martin Rose.

DISASTER MOVIE

Your favorite Hollywood movies are going to be destroyed.
—Movie tagline

Box Office: $14.1 million

The bloated, insipid parody *Disaster Movie* was not only one of the worst-reviewed films of 2008 but also the worst-reviewed of Jason Friedberg and Aaron Seltzer's *Movie* movies—not a very highly placed bar—which includes *Date Movie* (2006), *Epic Movie* (2007), and the *Scary Movie* franchise. While the majority of these films have gone on to attract sizable audiences looking for mindless escapism, *Disaster Movie* debuted only months after writer-director Friedberg and Seltzer's January 2008 release, *Meet the Spartans,* which could explain the severe dip in box office, for *Disaster Movie* recouped a mere $14 million of its $25 million budget.

Taking crass and mindless lobs at a variety of easy pop-culture targets, *Disaster Movie* begins its mind-numbing journey through recent films with a parody of *10,000 B.C.* (2008), featuring the troubled pop star Amy Winehouse (Nicole Parker) as a saber-toothed tiger. One of the various items she extracts from her sky-high beehive hairdo is an enchanted crystal skull, which sets in motion the film's Nicole Richie-thin plot involving the handsome but bland hero, Will (Matt Lanter), saving his pretty but bland girlfriend Amy (Vanessa Minnillo) and the rest of mankind from extinction within a *Cloverfield* (2008) framework of unidentified monsters destroying the world.

Disaster Movie cannot be accused of discriminating against lesser films, spoofing hits and flops alike, with bombs *Jumper* (2008) and *Speed Racer* (2008) alongside *Juno* (2007), *No Country for Old Men* (2007), *Kung Fu Panda* (2008), and *Enchanted* (2007). The title characters from *Iron Man* (2008), *The Incredible Hulk* (2008), and *Hellboy* (2004) dutifully show up, but to call it satire would be a stretch. They stand still while getting beaned by cows flying though the air. Although the film does focus on more relevant celebrities as targets of the makers' misguided anger—Sarah Jessica Parker gets particularly rough treatment, played by a large man in drag and getting roundhouse kicked by *Juno*-inspired character Juney (Crista Flanagan)—it also trots out alarmingly dated, well-worn Michael Jackson for no particular reason other than it required little effort and even less joke writing.

After an extended *High School Musical 3: Senior Year* (2008) spoof and an erotic wrestling scene between the film's requisite sexpots, Lisa (Kimberly Kardashian) and a beautiful assassin (Carmen Electra) in the vein of *Wanted* (2008), Will begins his journey through the beleaguered city to the natural history museum where his girlfriend Amy is trapped. He is accompanied by his friend Gary (Gary 'G Thang' Johnson), Lisa, the wisecracking Juney, and an Enchanted Princess (Nicole Parker), who is actually a happily drug-crazed prostitute picked up from a sewer en route. Arriving at the natural history museum, Will must put the crystal skull back in its rightful place on the altar, à la *Indiana Jones and the Kingdom of the Crystal Skull* (2008) in order to save the world, but not before a belabored, homoerotic wrestling match with a naked warrior calling himself Beowulf (repeatedly yelling, "I am Beowulf!"), while characters from *Night at the Museum* (2006) roam the building.

Among the many wisecracks in this a-joke-a-second film, some are bound to please, as are several standout performances: Crista Flanagan's Ellen Page is dead on and Nicole Parker's cheerfully demented princess is amusing. By far the best and most inspired scene involves giant Alvin and the Chipmunks puppets, which transform from cute and jolly to unexpectedly evil and rabid, attacking and chewing out the still-quipping Juney's spinal cord.

At best, *Disaster Movie* serves as a dumbed-down, pop culture *Jeopardy* whose audiences will enjoy quickly identifying and shouting out the multitude of recent films and news-making celebrities it references. At its worst, however, audiences must suffer through such segments as the unrated version's end credits musical number, which features a seemingly endless send-up of Sarah Silverman's recent sensation, "I'm F***ing Matt

Damon," where all the characters in the film sing about "F***ing" all the other characters. The film is gratefully over at this point.

Hilary White

CREDITS

Will: Matt Lanter
Prince: Tad Hilgenbrink
Beautiful Assassin: Carmen Electra
Amy: Vanessa Minnillo
Calvin: Gary 'G-Thang' Johnson
Enchanted Princess: Nicole Parker
Juney: Crista Flanagan
Lisa: Kim Kardashian
Wolf: Ike Barinholtz
Origin: USA
Language: English
Released: 2008
Production: Peter Safran, Jason Friedberg, Aaron Seltzer; Grosvenor Park, Three in the Box; released by Lionsgate
Directed by: Jason Friedberg, Aaron Seltzer
Written by: Jason Friedberg, Aaron Seltzer
Cinematography by: Shawn Maurer
Music by: Christopher Lennertz
Music Supervisor: Dave Jordan, JoJo Villanueva
Editing: Peck Prior
Costumes: Frank Helmer
Production Design: William A. "Bill" Elliott
MPAA rating: PG-13
Running time: 90 minutes

REVIEWS

Boston Globe Online. August 30, 2008.
Entertainment Weekly Online. August 29, 2008.
Hollywood Reporter Online. August 29, 2008.
New York Times Online. August 30, 2008.
Variety Online. August 29, 2008.

QUOTES

Wolf: "You just got Wolfed! That is my official trademark catchphrase that I got from the web! Let me tell you, there's still a lot of stuff to do out there. Lot of loops you gotta jump through. You gotta go on the internet! You gotta go to some stupid ass website where you can register your catchphrase. I wanted 'bam,' but Emeril already took it."

TRIVIA

Many of the films parodied in this movie were not released prior to thwe script being completed.

Nomination:

Golden Raspberries 2008: Director (Friedberg/Seltzer), Worst Picture, Worst Screenplay, Worst Support. Actress (Electra, Kardashian), Worst Sequel/Prequel.

DR. SEUSS' HORTON HEARS A WHO!

(Horton Hears a Who!)

One Elephant. One World. One Story.
—Movie tagline

Box Office: $154.5 million

Looking to replicate the success of the studio's massively profitable *Ice Age* movies (2002-2006) and tap into the fan base of Dr. Seuss books, Twentieth Century Fox Animation tries to keep pace with Disney/Pixar and DreamWorks with this computer-generated-imagery blockbuster *Horton Hears a Who!* The result may not live up to the standards set by the modern leaders in the form, but is a surprisingly enjoyable and mostly effective children's movie with a sometimes surreal sense of humor to please the parents. Great voice work by a talented ensemble and a successful screenplay helps *Horton Hears a Who!* overcome a visual aesthetic that is never as interesting as it should be and become a clever diversion for children of all ages.

Horton (voice of Jim Carrey) is a gentle giant, a playful pachyderm whose best friend in the Jungle of Nool is Morton the Mouse (voice of Seth Rogen), the little fellow who keeps the big guy grounded down to Earth and his only true friend. One day, Horton thinks he hears a sound on a passing clover flower and convinces himself that there is an entire world on the tiny floating orb. It turns out that Horton's hunch is right, but convincing the rest of the jungle residents that there is intelligent life outside of the one they know will be much more difficult than Horton first thinks. The miniature community in question is known as Whoville and is awkwardly run by the Mayor (voice of Steve Carell), a Who with a loving wife named Sally (voice of Amy Poehler), ninety-six daughters, and one depressed son named JoJo (voice of Jesse McCartney).

When the Mayor and Horton realize the existence of one another, they enter into a co-dependent relationship where the elephant tries to keep Whoville safe and the Mayor tries to convince his constituents that they are not alone in their universe. The Mayor learns that all Who-manity will be destroyed if Horton cannot find it a safer home in the jungle, but Horton can convince no one in Nool (except for Morton), especially the bitter

Sour Kangaroo (voice of Carol Burnett), who turns to the vicious eagle Vlad Vladikoff (voice of Will Arnett) to sabotage the safety of the speck when she becomes concerned that Horton's ramblings may adversely influence the young animals in her jungle. After several near-disasters, the residents of Whoville have to do whatever they can to prove to the other animals in the Jungle of Nool that they exist or face destruction at the hands of the Sour Kangaroo.

Dr. Seuss has always had a surreal, twisted sense of humor. It is this quality to which most children are attracted in stories like *Cat in the Hat* and *The Lorax*, and it is what is most often lacking in the least successful adaptations of his work. *Horton Hears a Who!*, directed by Jimmy Hayward and Steve Martino and written by Ken Daurio and Cinco Paul, captures enough of that left-of-center charm that made Seuss a household name to be ultimately effective, even if the film lacks some of the wit and whimsy of the masterful author's books. When the film finds a way to be unpredictable in the often predictable genre of G-rated animation, most notably in an anime-influenced interlude and the singing of REO Speedwagon's "Can't Fight This Feeling" during the climax, it is a surprisingly refreshing. Most children's films are shockingly predictable, and while the end result of *Horton Hears a Who!* is certainly that (no one expects Whoville to be destroyed), the path chosen to get to that predictable end has its refreshingly unique moments. The directors and writers accomplish the difficult task of not being slavishly faithful to the material, but without straying too far from it at the same time, they maintain a tone that Theodor Seuss Geisel would have appreciated. Perhaps most importantly, they keep the proceedings briskly paced, never allowing the film to lag, like so many modern computer-animated films do.

Visually, *Horton Hears a Who!* is not as stunning as it could have or arguably should have been. If there had been a bit more detail to the characters, the other elements of the film that do work would have been even more successful. The voice cast, especially the always excellent Jim Carrey and Steve Carell, is very good, but the character design is not as memorable as the people behind it. Carrey and Carell are far from alone in excelling behind the microphone. Carol Burnett, Will Arnett, Seth Rogen, Amy Poehler, and the rest of the cast work together seamlessly and creatively to find some excellent and expressive notes that a less skilled voice cast would probably have missed. Unlike those of many recent Seuss adaptations, the cast of *Horton Hears a Who!* works together in a way that befits the legendary legacy of one of the most popular authors of the twentieth century.

Brian Tallerico

CREDITS

Horton: Jim Carrey (Voice)
Mayor: Steven Carell (Voice)
Kangaroo: Carol Burnett (Voice)
Vlad: Will Arnett (Voice)
Morton: Seth Rogen (Voice)
Mary Lou Larue: Isla Fisher (Voice)
Tommy: Jonah Hill (Voice)
Councilmam/Yummo Wickersham: Dan Fogler (Voice)
Sally O'Malley: Amy Poehler (Voice)
Mrs. Quilligan: Jaime Pressly (Voice)
Rudy: Josh Flitter (Voice)
JoJo: Jesse McCartney (Voice)
Who Mom: Debi Derryberry (Voice)
Glummox Mom: Laraine Newman (Voice)
Katie: Joey King (Voice)
Narrator: Charles Osgood
Origin: USA
Language: English
Released: 2008
Production: Bob Gordon, Bruce Anderson; Blue Sky Studios, 20th Century Fox Animation; released by Twentieth Century-Fox
Directed by: Steve Martino, Jimmy Hayward
Written by: Cinco Paul, Ken Daurio
Music by: John Powell
Sound: Randy Thom
Editing: Ken Daurio, Tim Nordquist
Art Direction: Thomas Cardone
MPAA rating: G
Running time: 88 minutes

REVIEWS

Boston Globe Online. March 14, 2008.
Chicago Sun-Times Online. March 14, 2008.
Entertainment Weekly Online. March 12, 2008.
Hollywood Reporter Online. March 10, 2008.
Los Angeles Times Online. March 14, 2008.
New York Times Online. March 14, 2008.
San Francisco Chronicle. March 14, 2008, p. E6.
Time Online. March 13, 2008.
Variety Online. March 9, 2008.
Washington Post. March 14, 2008, p. C1.

QUOTES

Horton: "A person's a person, no matter how small."

TRIVIA

The film was shipped to theaters with the alternate title "88 Keys."

DOOMSDAY

Mankind has an expiration date.
—Movie tagline

Box Office: $11 million

With a set-up reminiscent of John Carpenter's influential *Escape from New York* (1981) and a tone not far removed from George A. Romero's *Land of the Dead* (2005) or George Miller's *Mad Max 2: Beyond Thunderdome* (1985), Neil Marshall's *Doomsday* wants to be a modern post-apocalyptic nightmare, but it is ultimately just a limp, cover version of the films that inspired it. The opening act of *Doomsday* details a plague that attacks Glasgow, Scotland in 2008. To control it, the government quarantines all of Scotland. Years later, in 2033, the Reaper virus is threatening to take over the rest of Great Britain, but the powers that be have discovered life in the thought-desolate Scotland, meaning that there must be a cure on the other side of the wall.

Knowing that this is their last chance to save the rest of the country or be forced to quarantine it as well, Prime Minister Hatcher (Alexander Siddig) and his nefarious right-hand man Canaris (David O'Hara) turn to Captain Nelson (Bob Hoskins) to form a team willing to go over the wall and find medical researcher Dr. Kane (Malcolm McDowell), the man who could be the key to the survival of all humanity. Nelson turns to Major Eden Sinclair (Rhona Mitra), a warrior who was actually born in Glasgow and saved at the last minute of the original quarantine. After insertion, the team is almost immediately ambushed by the Scottish survivors, most of who appear to have seen *The Road Warrior* (1981), because with their Mohawks, tattoos, piercings, and affinity for leather they look like extras from those earlier films. (It appears that being left for dead by a government that has stopped caring makes one become a punk rocker.)

The survivors are smart enough to deduce that if the team of cure-finders came over the wall that not only does that mean there is life beyond it—they have been told for years by Dr. Kane that there was not—but that the soldiers probably have a plan to return. They take Sinclair hostage and even kill and eat one of her men in an over-staged circus of a scene that feels straight out of *Thunderdome*. Sinclair and a small group escape for the hills and try to find Kane before it is too late.

Dialogue in a movie like *Doomsday* is often a secondary concern, but when it is so stubbornly and repeatedly awful that it calls to mind the work of Uwe Boll and Ed Wood, it becomes distracting. The fact is that there is a fine line between B-movie banter and material that a second grader would refuse to turn in for an English class project. *Doomsday* loses that battle before it even arrives at the critical fight because writer-director Neil Marshall makes the egotistical mistake of including a whopping twenty minutes of set-up and exposition, not one line of which rings true. *Doomsday* could have only worked as a straight action movie, but Marshall places way too much emphasis on expository dialogue that still leaves gigantic plot holes. At best, Marshall could have tried to insert themes about corruption or poor city planning into later acts of the film, but by opening with what feels like an interminable amount of set-up, he loses his audience permanently.

Even after Marshall slogs through his set-up, kills off most of the original team, and lets the motorcycle-riding, mace-wielding Johnny Rotten fans loose, he misses what makes movies like these work—a sense of fun. Everything in *Doomsday* is so deadly serious: he mistakes volume and choppy editing for tension and action, respectively. *Doomsday* is so ugly and so loud that it becomes miserable for everyone but the viewer who revels in a woman's being repeatedly punched in the stomach or seeing another get her head chopped off. What Carpenter, Romero, and Miller always infused their work with that Marshall misses completely is a sense of joy in their filmmaking. They allowed their social commentaries to be subtle elements of their films instead of pounding their audience over the head with them, and they focused on the thrill ride, not the horror.

Marshall made waves with two excellent, small films—*Dog Soldiers* (2002) and *The Descent* (2005) (he seems to have a penchant for titles that start with 'D'). In those horror movies, Marshall displayed a keen awareness of space and tension—two qualities that he completely loses in *Doomsday*. Going from a claustrophobic film like *The Descent* to a vast canvas like *Doomsday*, which features tanks, trains, and even a castle complete with armor-clad knights, proves too much of a transition for Marshall. His love for the films that inspired *Doomsday* is clear, but wanting to make a film like those of an idol is one thing; being able to pull off what an undeniable master of the form has accomplished is something completely different.

Brian Tallerico

CREDITS

Eden Sinclair: Rhona Mitra
Kane: Malcolm McDowell
Bill Nelson: Bob Hoskins
Norton: Adrian Lester
John Hatcher: Alexander Siddig
Canaris: David O'Hara
Cally: MyAnna Buring
Sol: Craig Conway
Origin: USA
Language: English
Released: 2008
Production: Steven Paul, Benedict Carver; Crystal Sky Pictures, Intrepid Pictures, Rogue Pictures; released by Universal Pictures

Directed by: Neil Marshall
Written by: Neil Marshall
Cinematography by: Sam McCurdy
Music by: Tyler Bates
Sound: Derek Mansvelt
Editing: Andrew MacRitchie
Art Direction: Simon Bowles, Stephen Carter
Costumes: John Norster
MPAA rating: R
Running time: 109 minutes

REVIEWS

Boston Globe Online. March 15, 2008.
New York Times Online. March 15, 2008.
Variety Online. March 14, 2008.

QUOTES

Kane: "Like so many epidemics before, the loss of so many lives began with a single microscopic organism. It's human nature to seek even the smallest comfort in reason, or logic for events as catastrophic as these. But a virus doesn't choose a time or place. It doesn't hate or even care. It just happens."

TRIVIA

Although much of the film takes place in London and Scotland, most of it was shot in South Africa.

DOUBT

There is no evidence. There are no witnesses. But for one, there is no doubt.
—Movie tagline

Box Office: $32.4 million

Doubt is John Patrick Shanley's powerful, thought-provoking directorial debut film adapted from his 2005 play of the same name that will certainly garner as many prestigious awards as the theatrical version, which earned the Pulitzer Prize for drama, four Tony® Awards, and a Drama Desk Award. Particularly in the arena of acting, *Doubt* is a standout among the films of 2008. Meryl Streep's tour-de-force performance as the ill-tempered, war-waging Sister Aloysius Beauvier is nearly matched by Philip Seymour Hoffman's charismatic and progressive Father Brendan Flynn. Amy Adams's natural vulnerability and innocence as Sister James nicely offsets her senior co-stars' dramatic whirlwind and, in her single ten-minute scene, Viola Davis as Mrs. Muller matches Oscar®-winning Streep's intensity.

Set in 1964 at St. Nicholas Catholic school and parish in the Bronx, the central plot concerns the school's sole black student, twelve-year-old Donald Miller (Joseph Foster II) and Sister Aloysius's suspicions of an inappropriate relationship with the boy initiated by Father Flynn. Although she has no actual proof, she has the certainty of her beliefs, which is enough for her but not enough for the young novice, Sister James (Amy Adams), who, naively, would rather believe such evil does not exist in their midst, and it is certainly not enough for Father Flynn, who, near the film's end, demands she tell him exactly what she saw. That, it turns out, was hardly anything—a boy pulling his wrist back from Flynn's grasp—but it is Aloysius recounting of what she saw out her window that terrifies Flynn nonetheless.

Shanley intrigues his audience with characters who may not be what they seem. Sister Aloysius, the unyielding school Principal, is immediately unsympathetic for she is a humorless, severe disciplinarian who opposes any suggestion of change and deplores human weakness and vice. The children are uniformly terrified of being sent to her office. Her reaction to finding a ballpoint pen on the classroom floor is only matched by reaction to Father Flynn's request for three lumps of sugar in his tea—utter revulsion. Conversely, Father Flynn is portrayed as sympathetic and progressive. He coaches the boys' basketball team and talks to them as equals. He is beloved by Donald Miller, whom he protects from the other children and his physically abusive father. He dares to suggest that secular songs be used in the Christmas pageant, wears his fingernails long, and issues a sermon on tolerance inspired by the disapproving Sister Aloysius. They are natural enemies, as are the cat and mouse that Shanley too obviously injects into not one, but two scenes. Despite appearances, however, it may be that Sister Aloysius is actually the one with the children's best interest in mind, for she wages her unflagging campaign to oust the offending priest, while a wide-eyed Sister James doubts and frets before serenely concluding that Flynn must be innocent.

The film's dramatic high point is the scene between Streep's Aloysius and Davis's Mrs. Miller, Donald's put-upon working mother. She comes to the school at Aloysius's request and is relieved to learn that Donald is passing his classes and that although he was caught with communal wine on his breath, he will not be expelled; instead, he will be allowed to graduate in a few months with the rest of the class. Aloysius is not through probing, however, and while walking Mrs. Miller back to work, she inquires how Donald is doing at home and reveals her suspicions about her son's relationship with Flynn. Mrs. Miller's surprising reaction casts even further doubt upon Aloysius's damnation of Flynn. Donald is different from other boys, she explains, a fact not lost on Donald's father, who beats him for it. In her mind,

any positive attention from a sympathetic father figure like Flynn, no matter what the brand, is better than none at all. It is a gray area that Aloysius has little patience with, who, like her uniform, prefers everything to be cast in black and white.

Doubt thoroughly explores the titular theme, including the obvious religious implications as well as more secular ones. In the opening scene, Father Flynn's sermon speaks of the assassination of President Kennedy, which certainly caused a lack of certainty about the world to millions, and equates doubt as a binding human condition. Doubts constantly arise in the film, not only about the Donald Miller situation, but about the motivations of all the characters, as well. Shanley also explores the pursuit of truth and justice, no matter the consequences, as well as the injustices motivated by fear perpetrated by the Catholic Church that are all too well-known today.

Shanley's first-grade teacher, Sister Margaret McEntee (who started with the name Sister James and on whom the character is based) served as a consultant on the film, which is dedicated to her, and the scenes depicting the contrast of life in the parish are some of the film's best. The black-clad, bonnet-wearing nuns quietly sitting down to a meatless meal with a pitcher of milk is contrasted by the decadence of the cigar-puffing, alcohol-swilling, loudly conversing priests feasting on bloody meat. Shanley has a tendency to go overboard with heavy-handed metaphors, the worst being not one but two scenes where a cat is overtly paraded in to kill a mouse. Diagonally angled camera shots during several key moments are also somewhat manipulative, as are the not-so-subtle use of weather blowing in a bit too conveniently and far too often to punctuate particularly dramatic scenes. The story is engaging enough without such contrivances.

Doubt is a tightly constructed and impeccably written character-driven drama that will emotionally and intellectually engage audiences throughout.

Hilary White

CREDITS
Sister Aloysius Beauvier: Meryl Streep
Father Brendan Flynn: Philip Seymour Hoffman
Sister James: Amy Adams
Mrs. Muller: Viola Davis
Jimmy Hurley: Lloyd Clay Brown
Donald Miller: Joseph Foster II
Sister Veronica: Alice Drummond
Christine Hurley: Carrie Preston
Warren Hurley: John A. Costelloe

Sister Raymond: Audrie Neenan
Origin: USA
Language: English
Released: 2008
Production: Scott Rudin, Mark Roybal; released by Miramax Films
Directed by: John Patrick Shanley
Written by: John Patrick Shanley
Cinematography by: Roger Deakins
Music by: Howard Shore
Sound: Danny Michael
Editing: Dylan Tichenor
Art Direction: Peter Rogness
Costumes: Ann Roth
Production Design: David Gropman

REVIEWS

Boston Globe Online. December 12, 2008.
Chicago Sun-Times Online. December 11, 2008.
Entertainment Weekly Online. December 3, 2008.
Los Angeles Times Online. December 11, 2008.
New York Times Online. December 12, 2008.
San Francisco Chronicle. December 12, 2008.
Washington Post. December 12, 2008.

QUOTES

Father Flynn: "Doubt can be a bond as powerful and sustaining as certainty. When you are lost, you are not alone."

TRIVIA

The play the film was adapted from won the 2005 Pulitzer Prize for Drama and ran for over a year (and approximately 525 performances).

AWARDS

Screen Actors Guild 2008: Actress (Streep)
Nomination:
Oscars 2008: Actress (Streep), Adapt. Screenplay, Support. Actor (Hoffman), Support. Actress (Adams, Davis)
British Acad. 2008: Actress (Streep), Support. Actor (Hoffman), Support. Actress (Adams)
Golden Globes 2009: Actress—Drama (Streep), Screenplay, Support. Actor (Hoffman), Support. Actress (Adams, Davis)
Screen Actors Guild 2008: Support. Actor (Hoffman), Support. Actress (Adams, Davis), Cast
Writers Guild 2008: Adapt. Screenplay.

DREAMS WITH SHARP TEETH

Does sci-fi writer Harlan Ellison deserve a movie made about him? No doubt, Ellison would answer yes, and *Dreams with Sharp Teeth* is a movie the sci-fi author would love—as much the egotistic curmudgeon could love anything. However, viewers unfamiliar with Ellison's writings might not be so awestruck.

Director-producer Erik Nelson pays tribute to Harlan Ellison in *Dreams with Sharp Teeth* by letting Ellison pay tribute to himself. In a series of different interviews (filmed over many years), the irascible writer talks at length about his life and work—mainly in jocular, anecdotal form. There are others interviewed, including his agent, fellow writers, and a few friends (Neil Gaiman, Carol Cooper, and a typically hammy Robin Williams), but Ellison is front, right, and center for most of the ninety-six minutes, delivering epigrammatic pronouncements on the world.

Fortunately, even at seventy-four years old, Ellison is a vigorous and sage raconteur. He tells his stories with equal amounts of rage and intelligence, which is refreshing in contrast to the cautious, parsed, politically correct statements made by most celebrities and politicians these days. Ellison fits into the Bill Maher/Lewis Black mode, even though he is quite a bit older and more set in his ways (he has lived in a house he calls "The Lost Aztec Temple of Mars" since 1966).

Ellison's angry aphorisms are memorable. The self-described "little Jew from Ohio," calls his own fans, "wimps, twinks, flakes, and oddballs," insults and belittles Warner Bros. for asking him to do gratis a DVD extra interview, and takes to task the amateurs of his own profession ("Anybody who doesn't write to get paid is a dunderhead!"). In earlier interviews (e.g., clips from *The Tomorrow Show* with the late Tom Snyder and a separate NBC sit-down chat with Tom Brokaw), Ellison proves he was always acid-tongued and pessimistic, even at a much younger age.

So what is missing from this portrait? Mainly, the work itself. Granted it is difficult to convey a writing style on-screen, but Nelson does not do justice to Ellison's prodigious output. There are mentions of some of Ellison's nearly 2,000 published stories, but the true analysis and/or appreciation is scarce—how he differs from others of his generation (Ray Bradbury, Aldous Huxley, Kurt Vonnegut, Arthur C. Clarke, et al.), how he has influenced contemporary sci-fi writers and filmmakers, or how he feels about his obscured place in the pantheon of a genre he basically dislikes and dismisses.

Dreams with Sharp Teeth would also have benefited from clips from the many film and television shows on which Ellison worked. Instead of hearing Ellison describe the cult episode he wrote for *Star Trek,*, an excerpt might have been more entertaining (maybe this is where Ellison's putdown of Warner Bros. and other Hollywood companies played a damaging role in his career and the choices Nelson was forced to make vis-à-vis archival footage). There is also nothing about Ellison's other cult classic, *A Boy and His Dog* (1975), perhaps the best film adaptation of his work. One would not expect a detailed discussion of the short story, "The Function of Dream Sleep," but why so little about "The City on the Edge of Forever" (the beloved *Star Trek* episode), *A Boy and His Dog, The Outer Limits* (particularly "Demon with a Glass Hand"), or even the laughably over-the-top feature film, *The Oscar* (1966), all but the last of which could provide decent visual examples of Ellison's originality?

Reviews of *Dreams with Sharp Teeth* were mixed. Nick Pinkerton, in the *Village Voice* wrote, "Prose doesn't film—Ellison recites animatedly from his corpus, backed by some hideous CG screensaver graphics, but this hardly reproduces the experience of reading." *The New York Times'* Nathan Lee similarly stated: "Mr. Ellison's written achievement largely takes second stage to his volcanic verbal attitude, of which there's more than enough to overflow an entire outlandish mini-series." *The New York Sun's* Steve Dollar called the film "great entertainment," but also identified its main problem: "What's also curious, given Mr. Ellison's many legal entanglements and five marriages, is that Mr. Nelson never summons anyone who might offer something more than a sympathetic anecdote. There's lots of footage of Mr. Ellison screaming at (or about) other people, some of whom have become close friends after surviving the crucible of his scrutiny. But there's not an instance of anyone screaming back." Nelson (the producer of several Werner Herzog films) and Ellison might have recognized the dramatic value of including opposing points of view; yet, maybe they just wanted to make the Harlan Ellison Show and nothing more.

Eric Monder

CREDITS

Origin: USA
Language: English
Released: 2007
Production: Erik Nelson; Kilimanjaro Corporation; released by Creative Differences
Directed by: Erik Nelson
Cinematography by: Wes Dorman
Music by: Richard Thompson
Editing: Randall Boyd
MPAA rating: Unrated
Running time: 96 minutes

REVIEWS

The New York Sun Online. June 3, 2008.
New York Times Online. June 4, 2008.
Village Voice Online. June 3, 2008.

Director Erik Nelson first recorded Harlan Ellison writing for a PBS documentary in 1981 and later incorporated that footage in this film.

DRILLBIT TAYLOR

You get what you pay for.
   —Movie tagline
The best bodyguard pocket money can buy.
   —Movie tagline

Box Office: $32.8 million

Actual teen comedies of the kind that John Hughes and his peers used to make in the 1980s are rare in the era of *High School Musical* (2006) and superhero movies. Most filmmakers and studios presume that the teen comedy has run its course as teenagers are far more interested in films like *Iron Man* (2008) and are more likely to sneak into *Superbad* (2007) than see a film about their peers. *Drillbit Taylor* is a movie that has its heart in a sweet enough place that it would probably have made prime era John Hughes proud. Based on an idea by Hughes himself, the final product may be more hit-and-miss than works by of the master of 1980s teen comedies, but it just barely misses its mark. *Drillbit Taylor* is surprisingly nostalgic for the days when bullies stuffed kids in lockers and the nerd dreamed about beating up the jock.

The title character in *Drillbit Taylor* is one cut from a mold too commonly used by comedy star Owen Wilson—the lovable loser. In this case, screenwriters Kristofor Brown and Seth Rogen (of *Superbad* and *Knocked Up* [2007] fame) feature more than one loser. The headliner, Drillbit Taylor, is a homeless man who answers an ad on the internet from a pair of freaks and geeks, Ryan (Troy Gentile) and Wade (Nate Hartley). The poor boys have had a lot of trouble in their initial few days of high school. First, they end up wearing the same shirt and learn that first impressions are paramount in the teenage social world. Then, Wade comes to the defense of a pint-sized geek tragically named Emmit Oosterhaus (David Dorfman), and sides are drawn— two and a half nerds on one side and bullies played by Alex Frost and Josh Peck on the other. Even the principal (Stephen Root) sides with the popular kids. The dorks take the only logical course of action—hire some help.

The problem is that Drillbit Taylor is not the professional bodyguard that he makes himself out to be to the freshman heroes. In actuality, Taylor is a homeless man posing as a physical threat, but rarely able to hold his own in a fight, much less teach others how to do so. When the students are in class, Drillbit is busy begging for money and showering on a public beach. Taylor's plan is to gain the confidence of Ryan and Wade and then rob them blind with the aid of his homeless friends. Of course, Drillbit starts to fall for not only the teens but one of their cute teachers (Leslie Mann) after he poses as a substitute at their school. Taylor sides with the lovable dorks and decides to take his job seriously and teach them how to stand up for themselves socially and even physically. One outcast helps others to overcome their awkward social standing—a classic formula of the comedy genre rears its head again.

Most modern teen comedies focus on the gross-out factor or aim at too young of viewers in an effort to gain even a fraction of the audience that has made television movies like *High School Musical* (2006) and series like *Hannah Montana* (begun in 2006) phenomenally popular. *Drillbit Taylor* may be a flawed screenplay, but it almost works because it never quite lets its star completely overtake the vehicle. Young actors Troy Gentile and Nate Hartley are always the central focus of the piece. In fact, it seems likely that the character of Drillbit may have even been a smaller role in the initial conception of the screenplay and was probably expanded when a star of Wilson's caliber signed on. Considering that Rogen co-wrote *Superbad,* another film about a trio of lovable losers, it is not surprising that this near-prequel to that film puts the awkward teens front and center.

Just as *Superbad* would have fallen apart if the writers had left the leads to focus on a scene-stealer played by Owen Wilson, the title character in *Drillbit Taylor* nearly destroys the entire film. Drillbit is both the kind of role that made Wilson a star and also one he can clearly do in his sleep. If this role were played by an unknown actor, the typical tics and shrugs that Wilson employs in his performance might be tolerable, but he has done this routine many times before in such films as *You, Me and Dupree* (2006), *The Big Bounce* (2004), *Shanghai Knights* (2003), among others. Most of what Wilson does in *Drillbit Taylor* feels like a joke that has been told before, and, unfortunately, it was only slightly funny the first time; thus viewers may experience a sensation of déjà vu. The fact that this film is of a genre that has largely disappeared in recent years—heartfelt teen comedy—helps ease the pain somewhat because the film's heart is in the right place, but the near-miss that is *Drillbit Taylor* could be one of the reasons John Hughes stopped making movies years ago.

Brian Tallerico

CREDITS

Drillbit Taylor: Owen Wilson
Lisa: Leslie Mann
Ryan: Troy Gentile

Emmit: David Dorfman
Filkins: Alex Frost
Ronnie: Josh Peck
Wes: Nate Hartley
Origin: USA
Language: English
Released: 2008
Production: Judd Apatow, Susan Arnold, Donna Roth; released by Paramount
Directed by: Steven Brill
Written by: Seth Rogen, Kristofor Brown
Cinematography by: Fred Murphy
Music by: Christophe Beck
Sound: David M. Kelson
Music Supervisor: Manish Raval, Tom Wolfe
Editing: Tom Nordberg
Art Direction: Scott A. Meehan
Costumes: Karen Patch
Production Design: Jackson DeGovia
MPAA rating: PG-13
Running time: 102 minutes

REVIEWS

Boston Globe Online. March 21, 2008.
Chicago Sun-Times Online. March 21, 2008.
Entertainment Weekly Online. March 19, 2008.
Hollywood Reporter Online. March 20, 2008.
Los Angeles Times Online. March 21, 2008.
New York Times Online. March 21, 2008.
San Francisco Chronicle. March 21, 2008, p. E1.
Variety Online. March 19, 2008.
Washington Post Online. March 21, 2008.

QUOTES

Drillbit Taylor: "I'm Drillbit Taylor…US Army ranger, black-ops operative, decorated marksman, improvised weapons expert."

TRIVIA

Former UFC light heavyweight champion Chuck Liddel has a cameo as a potential bodyguard for the boys.

THE DUCHESS

There were three people in her marriage.
—Movie tagline
The scandal that shocked a nation. The courage that defined a woman.
—Movie tagline

Box Office: $13.8 million

If the life of Georgiana Spencer, the Duchess of Devonshire, had not had so many late-eighteenth-century parallels to that of Lady Diana Spencer, her twentieth-century relative, *The Duchess* would probably not have been made. Curiosity about such similarities, however, can carry a film only so far, so, fortunately, *The Duchess* finds plenty of other reasons to justify its existence.

When she is seventeen, Georgiana (Keira Knightley) is betrothed to the much older William Cavendish, Duke of Devonshire (Ralph Fiennes), though she is already attracted to Charles Grey (Dominic Cooper). Georgiana quickly learns that the Duke is interested in her only as a breeder and is a dull, sullen chap to boot. He does, however, have inroads into British politics, and his wife tries to make the best she can of a bad marriage by befriending politicians, among them the radical Whig Charles Fox (Simon McBurney).

The Duchess becomes nationally famous as a fashion icon and exploits her celebrity to draw crowds to Whig rallies. Her campaigning is fine with the Duke as long as she continues to have children. When the mother of his illegitimate daughter (played by both Eva Hrela and Poppy Wigglesworth) dies, he has the three-year-old girl brought to his estate, and after some initial hesitation, Georgiana raises the child as an equal to her own children.

Problems arise when she encounters Grey, a rising Whig and future prime minister, and they begin an affair. When her close friend Bess Foster (Hayley Atwell) is thrown out by her aristocratic husband because of infidelity, Bess comes to live with the Devonshires, only to have a long-term relationship with the Duke. Richard Brinsley Sheridan (Aidan McArdle), a close friend of Georgiana and Fox, is inspired by these events to write his classic comedy of manners, *The School for Scandal* (1877). The enlightened attitudes of the various lovers do not, however, last forever, and the Duke ends his wife's affair with a despicable act. Because there is no clear explanation of what attracts Bess to her host and why the two women remain friends, *The Duchess* can be accused of skimming along the surface of a story that could have been more fascinating.

The Duchess is adapted by Jeffrey Hatcher, Anders Thomas Jensen, and director Saul Dibb from historian Amanda Foreman's biography *Georgiana, Duchess of Devonshire* (1998). Foreman, daughter of screenwriter Carl Foreman, and the filmmakers clearly intend Georgiana to be seen as a would-be feminist, a woman who simply wants to live her life the way she wants but is constrained by the hypocritical conventions of her society. This theme, much more than the similarities with the sad life of Princess Diana, gives the film its narrative impetus.

Dibb keeps the proceedings flowing smoothly. The writer-director attempts a balance between the intimate scenes, the constant parties attended by the protagonists, and their larger public lives. Dibb alternates between close-ups and two-shots, wider shots, and more panoramic views, especially during visits to Bath, where aristocrats flock to heal their wounds at the spa. Cinematographer Gyula Pados creates memorable images through his use of sunlight, clouds, shadows, and candlelight, and Rachel Portman offers a suitably sweeping score, that echoes the lush music of John Barry and Gabriel Yared.

Knightley, a specialist in period drama, gives her most layered performance since *Pride & Prejudice* (2005), presenting Georgiana less as a martyr than as a passionate woman living at the wrong time. Fiennes gives a subtle performance, resisting turning the character into a clichéd monster. For instance, holding his usual actorish tics in check, Fiennes stands out when the Duke, after many years with his Duchess, makes a tentative, uncertain gesture toward understanding.

Atwell and Cooper are serviceable in underdeveloped roles, though Cooper seems more impish than dashing. Charlotte Rampling is sublimely haughty as Georgiana's mother, who always takes the Duke's side. In his few scenes, the prominent stage director McBurney stands out for showing Fox's sincere fondness for the Duchess. Without Fox's assurance that Georgiana is a woman of substance, *The Duchess* might have treaded too closely to being a mere pageant of celebrity.

Michael Adams

CREDITS

Georgiana Spencer, Duchess of Devonshire: Keira Knightley
William Cavendish, Duke of Devonshire: Ralph Fiennes
Charles Grey: Dominic Cooper
Lady Elizabeth 'Bess' Spencer: Hayley Atwell
Lady Spencer: Charlotte Rampling
Fox: Simon McBurney
Richard Brinsley Sheridan: Aidan McArdle
Lady Teazle: Georgia King
Language: English
Released: 2008
Production: Michael Kuhn, Gabrielle Tana; Qwerty Films, Pathe Renn, Bim Distribuzione, Magnolia Mae Films; released by Paramount Vantage
Directed by: Saul Dibb
Written by: Saul Dibb, Jeffrey Hatcher, Anders Thomas Jensen
Cinematography by: Gyula Pados
Music by: Rachel Portman
Sound: Simon Fraser
Editing: Masahiro Hirakubo

Art Direction: Karen Wakefield
Costumes: Michael O'Connor
Production Design: Michael Carlin
MPAA rating: PG-13
Running time: 110 minutes

REVIEWS

Christian Science Monitor Online. September 19, 2008.
Entertainment Weekly Online. September 16, 2008.
Hollywood Reporter Online. September 1, 2008.
Los Angeles Times Online. September 19, 2008.
New York Times Online. September 19, 2008.
Rolling Stone Online. September 18, 2008.
Time Online. September 18, 2008.
Variety Online. September 1, 2008.
Wall Street Journal Online. September 19, 2008.

QUOTES

Georgiana Spencer, Duchess of Devonshire: "You can't ask me to battle nature in my own heart."

TRIVIA

The film's marketing campaign alluded to a connection to the late Princess Diana (who is a descendant of Georgiana's family, The Spencers). Keira Knightley later asserted that there were no connections between her character and the late Royal.

AWARDS

Oscars 2008: Costume Des.
British Acad. 2008: Costume Des
Nomination:
Oscars 2008: Art Dir./Set Dec.
British Acad. 2008: Makeup
Golden Globes 2009: Support. Actor (Fiennes).

THE DUCHESS OF LANGEAIS
(Ne touchez pas la hache)
(Don't Touch the Axe)

Like his fellow New Wave directors, Claude Chabrol, Jean-Luc Godard, Eric Rohmer, and François Truffaut, Jacques Rivette began as a critic for *Cahiers du cinèma,* but his international reputation as a filmmaker has always trailed those of his colleagues. While the other New Wave directors strived to break with the formalized styles of the past while embracing, except for Rohmer, the grubby energy of American genre films,

Rivette has approached film at a more stately, controlled, less commercial pace. Rivette, who turned eighty in March of 2008, has also remained the most literary of the group. Like the novelist Henry James, the inspiration for his most acclaimed film, *Celine and Julie Go Boating* (1974), Rivette thrives on taking a slight subject and mulling over it at length. Even when his films are not taken from literary sources, they emulate literature, especially nineteenth-century novels, in their attention to detail, mood, and character.

The Duchess of Langeais, adapted by Pascal Bonitzer, Christine Laurent, and Rivette from an 1834 novel by Honoré de Balzac, also the source of Rivette's *La Belle noiseuse* (1991), is typical of the director's subdued cinematic style. The film is told as a flashback, beginning with General Armand de Montriveau (Guillaume Depardieu), a hero of the Napoleonic Wars, arriving at a Carmelite convent in Majorca in 1823 to speak with Sister Thérèse, formerly known as the Duchess Antoinette le Langeais (Jeanne Balibar). Antoinette tells the mother superior (Victoria Zinny) that her visitor is her brother, but their true relationship is slowly unveiled.

Five years earlier in Paris, Antoinette is a bored socialite slowly enamored by the dashing figure of the wounded general. Despite being married to an always absent husband, Antoinette slowly falls in love with Armand, who sees her more as a possible conquest. Most of *The Duchess of Langeais* consists of conversations between the two, with Armand remaining rather obtuse about Antoinette's true feelings, which she takes time in recognizing herself. Despite seeming to have much more in common thematically and stylistically with works by later French writers (for example, Gustave Flaubert), Henry James always regarded Balzac as the greatest French writers. What he saw in Balzac is on display in Rivette's film. Armand is a true Jamesian hero who misinterprets the circumstances he finds himself in, impulsively vows revenge for what he perceives as mere coquettishness on Antoinette's part, and realizes his error too late.

The hesitant, inconclusive nature of the Antoinette-Armand relationship is captured by Rivette's visual style. Most of the scenes occur in rooms in which cinematographer William Lubtchansky, the director's usual collaborator, seems to be using natural light. The darkness creeping into the edges of the frames isolates the protagonists, who are often seen in two-shots as if trapped in their small world of miscommunication, and this darkness underscores the isolated, claustrophobic universe they inhabit. Enclosure and escape are prominent Rivette themes, represented most overtly here by the bars separating the protagonists at the convent. Rivette is famous as the first critic, in 1954, to recognize the genius of Otto Preminger, and he emulates that master's fluid style with few cuts within a scene, subtly moving the camera to concentrate on what is most important within a milieu where little seems to happen and thus achieving a marriage of form and content.

As always, Rivette accentuates his effects through his casting. Fortunately, Balibar, a star of Rivette's *Va savoir* (2001), is not conventionally beautiful, making it easier for Armand to misconstrue Antoinette's passion. Balibar dominates the film with both subtle gestures suggesting the tentativeness of the quiet drama in which Antoinette is caught up and a more mannered style fitting for a woman who perceives herself almost as an actress in a melodrama. Rivette relishes having the camera watch Antoinette's hesitant responses to Armand's clumsy advances as she teeters between lust and exasperation. Unlike the blustery performances of his father, Gérard Depardieu, Guillaume Depardieu adopts a subdued approach to convey Armand's confusion and, eventually, despair. Armand gives the appearance of strength; yet he is a flawed hero, both physically and emotionally, with his stiff-legged gait, the result of his war wound, making him more vulnerable and sympathetic. (Depardieu actually has an artificial leg as the result of a motorcycle accident.) Rivette regulars Bulle Ogier and Michel Piccoli also stand out as Antoinette's confidantes with whom she examines Armand's behavior.

The Duchess of Langeais is typical of Rivette's minimalist style. Not afraid to risk boring his audiences, the director offers an introverted chamber piece composed of minor notes laced with a violent undertone, which accumulate to create a melancholy, surprisingly moving effect. What begins as almost a comedy of manners becomes a tragedy instead.

Michael Adams

CREDITS

Antoinette de Langeais: Jeanne Balibar
Armand de Montriveau: Guillaume Depardieu
Princesse de Blamont-Chauvry: Bulle Ogier
Vidame de Pamiers: Michel Piccoli
Le Duc De Grandieu: Barbet Schroeder
Origin: France, Italy
Language: French
Released: 2007
Production: Martine Marignac, Maurice Tinchant; Pierre Grise Productions, Arte France Cinema, Cinemaundici; released by IFC Films
Directed by: Jacques Rivette
Written by: Jacques Rivette, Pascal Bonitzer, Christine Laurent
Cinematography by: William Lubtchansky
Music by: Pierre Allio
Sound: Florian Eidenbenz
Editing: Nicole Lubtchansky
Costumes: Maira Ramedhan-Levi
Production Design: Manu du Chauvigny, Giuseppe Pirrotta
MPAA rating: Unrated
Running time: 137 minutes

REVIEWS

Entertainment Weekly Online. February 20, 2008.
Guardian Online. December 21, 2007.
New York Times Online. February 22, 2008.
Observer Online. December 30, 2007.
Premiere Online. February 20, 2008.
Variety Online. February 15, 2008.
Village Voice Online. February 19, 2008.

E

EAGLE EYE

If you want to live you will obey.
—Movie tagline

Box Office: $101.4 million

Does the first initial of director D.J. Caruso's name stand for derivative? His recent output has certainly made one wonder. Almost every review of his last film, the surprise hit *Disturbia* (2007), noted its obvious resemblance to Alfred Hitchcock's *Rear Window* (1954). Both feature a male confined to his home who peers at neighbors and becomes convinced he has spotted a murderer, voyeuristic time-killing that in the end threatens to kill him, too. Some kindly called it homage, while others referred to Caruso's film as an amazingly brazen ripping-off of someone else's material with neither acknowledgement nor attribution. The estate of Sheldon Abend, which holds all rights to the Cornell Woolrich short story upon which the James Stewart-Grace Kelly classic was based, certainly saw it as illegal duplication, filing a copyright infringement lawsuit in federal court on September 8, 2008. Any lawyers for the defense who went to see Caruso's *Eagle Eye* when it opened less than three weeks later likely cringed, as the film not only seems to once again filch from Hitchcock but also too-closely recalls the best-known work of Stanley Kubrick (among other filmmakers). As a result, many critics and viewers of Caruso's latest work expressed a distinct feeling of déà vu.

Since the heinous attacks of September 11, 2001, Americans have not only been unnerved by talk of terrorists clandestinely plotting in our midst but also about Big brother-type overreach by our own government that could bury cherished ideals and civil liberties in the process of rooting out the evildoers. *Eagle Eye* begins with such legitimate fears about insufficiently bridled surveillance but then wildly extrapolates, wondering what would happen if the ubiquitous technology our society finds so handy was instead used to strong-arm innocents. What if every cell phone, BlackBerry, GPS, ATM, security camera and the like could be accessed and manipulated at will as tools for coercion by a peeved, too-smart-for-our-own-good secret supercomputer run amok?

The original idea came from Steven Spielberg (once again Caruso's executive producer), who had envisioned a disturbingly convincing scenario that would make moviegoers feel as much lingering trepidation about approaching their electronic conveniences as they did about going back into the ocean after seeing his *Jaws* (1975). However, whatever the resulting film lacks in originality, it makes up for in implausibility, repeated in a cacophonous, convoluted, frenzied, and often fiery fashion that moviegoers became sufficiently caught up in. Made on a budget of $80 million, *Eagle Eye* grossed around $100 million in domestic box office.

As National Public Radio's Bob Mondello pointed out, what transpires before the film's title appears on-screen likely made some viewers wonder briefly if they had accidentally entered the wrong door at the multiplex. This prologue shows children romping playfully in a village where a foreign tongue is being spoken. Then, amidst dramatic music (of which *Eagle Eye* has a lot) that signals something highly consequential is about to take place, U.S. Secretary of Defense Callister (Michael Chiklis) arrives at the Pentagon via helicopter to learn that a highly sought-after terrorist target has been spotted at a funeral in said Afghan hamlet. Or has he? All sorts of sophisticated spy equipment analyzes data and spits out less-than-reassuring probabilities as to whether the right man is about to be killed along with, perhaps, the giggling, young collateral. Callister, a steadfast voice of reason who wants to remain in the right while protecting his country, orders the attack aborted. However, he is subsequently overridden by a President who feels less fettered by pesky international agreements like the Geneva Convention, and everyone in the vicinity of the interment is killed. It is a serious-minded and timely introduction that gives viewers pause, but then *Eagle Eye* quickly leaves believability behind and hurtles toward preposterousness, featuring Dramamine-necessitating chase sequences during perplexing plot threads.

Once again Caruso utilizes Shia LaBeouf, just adequate here playing Jerry Shaw, a charming slacker who has dropped out of Stanford, traveled some, and now is barely getting by and bored out of his mind working at a copy store. It is ironic employment, as Jerry is certainly no duplicate of his much-heralded, overachieving Air Force officer twin, Ethan (also LaBeouf), and the latter's death in a car accident shortly into the film seems to give the son who shone less brightly a degree of survivor's guilt. "I'm not him," he quietly reassures mourners initially thrown by his resemblance to the once-promising young man in the casket, a comment that also seems like something of an embarrassed confession. Soon afterward, Jerry is mystified to find his near-empty bank account now holds over $750,000 and, even more shocking, his apartment now looks like a showroom for Terrorists R Us. Suddenly his cell phone rings, and an unidentified woman's voice calmly informs him that the FBI will nab him in seconds if he fails to flee. Immobilized by overwhelming incredulity, Jerry lands in custody and is grilled by curt, no-nonsense Agent Thomas Morgan (Billy Bob Thornton, laying it on thick), who has little interest in Jerry's protestations of innocence.

Across town is paralegal Rachel Holloman (an indistinctive Michelle Monaghan), who has a thoughtless ex-husband and a freckled young son, Sam (Cameron Boyce), who looks like he might be on vacation from a Norman Rockwell painting. The loving mom reluctantly parts with the boy as he and the rest of his school band head off to Washington, D.C., where they will have the honor of performing at the Kennedy Center. Shortly thereafter, she receives a mystifying call from the same voice, ordering the terrified woman to do as she is told or her son will be killed.

Once *Eagle Eye* has introduced and ensnared its Everyman and Anywoman pawns, the demanding anonymous phone caller proceeds to reveal powers that have a mind-boggling lack of limits. She can make a crane crash into the building where Jerry is being held, enabling him to escape with a leap that should rightly have killed him. If he stubbornly refuses to answer his phone, every phone around him rings insistently. She can stop Jerry's train in its tracks and make it back up. She can make high-tension wires fall on and electrocute an Iranian-American who disobeys. Then, once Jerry is thrown together with Rachel in this carefully choreographed (and, it certainly seems, unnecessarily elaborate) plan, the voice comes over the GPS with minute instructions that enable them to outmaneuver the flabbergasted and repeatedly frustrated authorities in hot pursuit. (Rosario Dawson, who joins the hunt as Air Force smart-cookie Zoë Perez, is rather good throughout.) The two protagonists go from Porsche to barge to SUV to Japanese tour bus to military plane cargo hold, racing from city to city at the behest of someone who can alter everything from traffic lights and sprinkler systems to airport X-ray screens and baggage conveyor belts in what becomes implausible and repetitive absurdity. Suspense about Jerry and Rachel's ability to meet the unseen manipulator's requirements is minimized due to the fact that they are facilitated by someone of increasingly apparent omnipotence.

It is eventually revealed that the female voice is a massive government computer named ARIA, parts of which looks like a glowing, golden honeycomb. Because her recommendation to abort the missile attack in the first scene was overruled, she has initiated a tortuous retaliatory plot that has killed Ethan, now needs Jerry's likeness, and will ultimately eliminate the President and a host of others who would succeed him. Listening to ARIA's calmly intoned decrees, viewers will surely think of a female version of HAL from Kubrick's *2001: A Space Odyssey* (1968).

Particularly with Caruso's *Disturbia* as a precedent, those familiar with the works of Hitchcock will undoubtedly note similarities to what transpires in *Eagle Eye*. The legendary British director's preoccupation with the harrowing concept of being falsely accused, most blatantly dealt with in his *The Wrong Man* (1956), is obviously present in Caruso's film. When Jerry and Rachel find themselves walking through a wide-open, flat, and desolate landscape with an unsettling lack of places to hide, and then in a subsequent scene when a plane swoops down to attack the protagonist, one cannot help but think of the famous Cary Grant/crop duster scene in *North by Northwest* (1959). The same motion picture comes to mind as the male and female leads travel across the map, ending up at a national U.S. landmark. Most of all, however, *Eagle Eye*'s climactic scene, in which Jerry proves his worth by selflessly creating a diversion during a State of the Union Address that leaves him wounded but everyone else unharmed, has to have been inspired by the great Albert Hall finale of *The Man Who Knew Too Much* (1956). That film also involves an anguished mother who fears she has seen her son alive for the last time unless the villains' instructions are followed to the letter. Both climaxes take place at important events in August and in cavernous rooms filled with onlookers, and both feature a head of state who is unaware that an assassination attempt is imminent. Music is being played in both scenes, leading suspensefully to an all-important moment marked by a single cymbal crash in *Man* and one particular trumpet note played by Rachel's son that will detonate a highly explosive crystal she unwittingly wears around her neck in *Eagle Eye*. Cross-cutting is utilized in both to create tension as events approach the climax. Finally, there is a loud distraction in both scenes that prevents disaster at the very last moment. Thus, all things considered, surely no one can be blamed for agreeing with the *Boston Globe*'s Ty Burr when he termed *Eagle Eye* "a movie only a copyright lawyer could love."

David L. Boxerbaum

CREDITS

Jerry: Shia LaBeouf
Rachel: Michelle Monaghan
Morgan: Billy Bob Thornton
Zoe Perez: Rosario Dawson
Defense Secretary Callister: Michael Chiklis
Sam: Cameron Boyce
Adm. Thompson: Bill Smitrovich
Maj. William Bowman: Anthony Mackie
Explosives Developer: Marc Singer
David Johnson: Nick Searcy
Mrs. Wierbowski: Lynn Cohen
Ranim: Anthony Azizi
Origin: USA
Language: English
Released: 2008
Production: Alex Kurtzman, Roberto Orci, Patrick Crowley; released by Dreamworks Pictures
Directed by: D.J. Caruso
Written by: Hillary Seitz, Dan McDermott, John Glenn, Travis Adam Wright
Cinematography by: Dariusz Wolsi
Music by: Brian Tyler
Sound: Kirk Francis
Editing: Jim Page
Art Direction: Kevin Kavanaugh, Naaman Marshall, Sean Haworth
Costumes: Marie-Sylvie Deveau

Production Design: Tom Sanders
MPAA rating: PG-13
Running time: 117 minutes

REVIEWS

Boston Globe Online. September 26, 2008.
Chicago Sun-Times Online. September 25, 2008.
Entertainment Weekly Online. September 24, 2008.
Hollywood Reporter Online. September 25, 2008.
Los Angeles Times Online. September 26, 2008.
San Francisco Chronicle. September 26, 2008, p. E7.
Variety Online. September 25, 2008.
Washington Post. September 26, 2008, p. C6.

QUOTES

Jerry: "They changed every traffic light to get us here. The woman, she called me on a stranger's cell phone who happened to be sitting next to me—never met the guy in my life. And then they broke me out of maximum security custody in a way I'm not even going to describe to you because it sounds crazy, and then they lift us off the face of the earth and drop us into this s**tpile. She could probably derail a train, she could probably turn a train into a talking duck."

TRIVIA

A.R.I.A. is voiced by Julianne Moore in an uncredited role.

THE EDGE OF HEAVEN
(Auf der anderen Seite)
(On the Other Side)

The Edge of Heaven (*Auf der anderen Seite*) requires a very large canvas as it dramatizes the extremes of youth and age, dissent and rebellion, terrorism and betrayal, nationality and identity. It has a rich, multinational cast that includes the great German actress Hanna Schygulla, a luminary of the New German Cinema, as a hard "Hausfrau" named Susanne, who becomes more interesting later in the film as a result of grieving for her daughter, Lotte (Patrycia Ziolkowska), who is killed, accidentally and stupidly, by backstreet urchins in Istanbul. Lotte is a lively student who offers aid and assistance to a young Turkish woman named Ayten (Nurgül Yeşilçay), who is seeking political asylum in Germany because at home, in Turkey, she is considered a terrorist (there seem to be echoes of the PKK and the Kurdish separatists lurking in the background here). Although the film is mainly "about" Ayten, to whom Lotte becomes emotionally attached, we do not meet her until about thirty minutes into the story, which begins with a car stopping for gas in an apparently godforsaken rural village in the north of Turkey, followed by a seemingly comic episode involving an older Turk visiting the red-light district of the town of Bremen, in the north of Germany, and meeting a whore named "Jessy" (though her real name is Yeter, and she is played with commanding dignity by Nursel Köse). Yeter has a daughter (who turns out to be Ayten, who was befriended by Lotte) whom she wants desperately to see, since the mother and daughter have been long separated; the daughter thinks the mother works in a shoe store in Bremen. Little does she know.

The story turns political when two Muslim men who visit Yeter, whom they know to be Turkish because they have heard her speaking Turkish, warn her to "repent," as indeed she does when her older Turkish client proposes that she stop being a call girl and live with him. She befriends his son, Nejat (Baki Davrak), who is an educated Turk who teaches German literature at a university in Germany. People die in this movie, awkwardly, stupidly, incomprehensibly, and unnecessarily; and Yeter, who first seems to be a very central character, is the first victim. After her death, Nejat decides to pursue her mission of locating her daughter, Ayten. As the characters come and go through this film, they pass one another in transit without even knowing it. While Yeter is looking for her daughter, Ayten, for example, Ayten is also looking for her mother. Their paths almost cross in Bremen, once on a highway, and again, very nearly, when Ayten sleeps in a lecture hall while Nejat lectures. The audience sees her sleeping with her head down on the desk, but in a flash forward, before being able to recognize who she is. Nejat later gives up his teaching career and returns to Istanbul, where he purchases and then operates a German-Turkish bookstore. When Lotte comes to Istanbul to help her friend Ayten, Nejat rents her an apartment. Later on, after Ayten has been released from a Turkish prison (after having "repented," a key word in the plot), she, too, is taken to that room by Lotte's mother. Thus Nejat may ultimately be destined to "find" Yeter's daughter, but there is no indication that he will, even then, know who she is. Coincidences are constantly frustrating in this motion picture, a quality that partly explains its brilliance.

In *The Edge of Heaven* identity (national, personal, and political) is a major theme, along with a strong yearning for "home" and family. The bookstore Nejat buys in Istanbul is owned by a young German who wants to return to the Heimat because he is homesick. He appreciates the irony of selling a German bookstore in Istanbul to a young Turk who has mastered German literature and was able to build a life in Germany, but ultimately prefers to return to Turkey. Nejat's father has

accidentally killed Yeter by striking her in a drunken rage and is sentenced to a German prison term, but he is finally released and deported to his native Turkey, where he returns to his fishing village on the Black Sea coast. The sequence that opens the film shows Nejat driving to that village to bring about a reconciliation between father and son, since he has never forgiven the father for having murdered Yeter. Little does he know at that point that Yeter's daughter is living with Lotte's mother in the Istanbul apartment that he owns. As Stephen Holden wrote in the *New York Times*, "As the paths of these fascinating, complicated people cross (two go to jail), Mr. Akin regards them with unwavering compassion." Indeed, the entire, masterfully constructed plot is encircled by elegant ironies, and the jurors at the Cannes Film Festival recognized the sophistication of Fatih Akin's screenplay when they awarded it the Ecumenical Jury Prize for Best Screenplay at the Cannes Film Festival.

The Edge of Heaven is the director's fifth feature film, but it was only the third to be released in the United States, when it premiered at Filmfest in Washington, D.C. on May 2, 2008, before its general release on June 20. Although the film may appear to some American viewers as intercultural and perhaps more than a little exotic, *New Yorker* critic Anthony Lane wrote that *The Edge of Heaven* is, in fact, "in the best sense, mainstream cinema. It dives into the current that sweeps all of us along: fathers and sons, mothers and daughters, anyone leaving home and aching to return. The story, though intricate, is never obscure, and it could be set anywhere..." But it does not feel like mainstream cinema. Though some of the characters are flawed, they are all the more human and interesting for all that.

The Edge of Heaven was immediately recognized as a marvel of construction by the "enormously gifted" writer-director Fatih Akin. It also fared quite well with American critics. *Washington Post* film critic Ann Hornaday remarked that the "sheer poetry" of Akin's narrative, is an "intercontinental, interlocking roundelay of six people, some German, some of Turkish descent living in Germany, [that] possesses the searing ironies of an O. Henry story," perhaps without quite grasping that the dramatic ironies of this film are "searing" in ways that surpass the O. Henry model. Even *Entertainment Weekly*, a magazine that usually specializes in glibness and often shows excitement for the most trivial Hollywood products, praised *Edge of Heaven* for managing to be the sort of film that *Babel* (2006) aspired to be, a claim that was also expressed by Ann Hornaday in the *Washington Post* and even by Anthony Lane in the *New Yorker*, who added that, though Akin's film shares such details as language barriers, time shifts, and multiple locations,

"Akin's film doesn't force its characters, as if at gunpoint, to sell us a communal vision of horror."

The geographical, political, and human scope of *Edge of Heaven* is impressive. The characters are freshly imagined and distinctively unpredictable, yet still believable. Europe and "The Orient" are joined, as Turks travel westward to Germany to find work and as Germans travel to Turkey to find relationships or meaning in their lives, or to achieve closure. The German-Turkish director, told the *New York Times* that he thought too much attention had been given to his Turkish-German identity: "Imagine I'm a painter and we speak more about the background of the paintings, or we speak about the framing, but not about the painting." Even though his work is obviously intercultural, the thirty-four-year-old Fatih Akin continues to work from Hamburg, where he was born. *Edge of Heaven* in fact appeared to be one of the first great films of the twenty-first century, but, even so, the picture was ignored by the Academy Award® selection committee in the Best Foreign Film category, a serious and even outrageous oversight of one of the very best feature films of the year and, arguably, of the decade.

James M. Welsh

CREDITS

Suzanne Staub: Hanna Schygulla
Nejat Aksu: Baki Davrak
Ali Aksu: Tuncel Kurtiz
Yeter Ozturk: Nursel Kose
Ayten Ozturk: Nurgul Yesilcay
Lotte Staub: Patrycia Ziolkowska
Origin: Germany, Turkey
Language: German, Turkish
Released: 2007
Production: Andreas Thiel, Klaus Maeck, Faith Akin; Corazon International, Anka Film; released by Strand Releasing
Directed by: Fatih Akin
Written by: Fatih Akin
Cinematography by: Rainer Klausmann
Music by: Shantel
Sound: Kai Luede, Richard Borowski
Editing: Andrew Bird
Art Direction: Tamo Kunz, Sirma Bradley
Costumes: Katrin Aschendorf
MPAA rating: Unrated
Running time: 122 minutes

REVIEWS

Entertainment Weekly Online. May 22, 2008.
The Guardian Online. February 22, 2008.

Hollywood Reporter Online. May 24, 2007.
New York Online. May 26, 2008.
New York Times Online. May 21, 2008.
Newsweek Online. May 20, 2008.
Variety Online. May 23, 2007.
Village Voice Online. May 20, 2008.

TRIVIA

Director Akin likened the film to part *Frantic* and part *Missing.*

88 MINUTES

He has 88 minutes to solve a murder. His own.
    —Movie tagline

Box Office: $17.2 million

The advertising tagline pretty much summarizes the plot of this film: "Jack Gramm has eighty-eight minutes to solve a murder. His own." A better tagline might have been, "This is the movie in which Al Pacino gets ticked off." An incarcerated psychopathic serial killer, Jon Forster (Neal McDonough), holds a grudge against Dr. Jack Gramm (Pacino), forensic psychologist and successful college professor, for having testified against him in court. On the day the serial killer is to be executed, women with whom Jack has been involved are brutalized or sadistically murdered, and the modus operandi seems to match that of the convicted killer in the penitentiary in Walla Walla. The action, which is framed by the year 1997, takes place nine years later in Seattle, Washington. The picture was written by Gary Scott Thompson and directed by Jon Avnet. Jack (who drives a Porsche that is far beyond the pale of ordinary mortals and certainly ordinary academicians) receives a threatening phone call from Forster, who whispers, "Tick, tock, Doc." And that sets the tone for this "classic" suspense.

Why might this silly movie be considered "classic"? Only for one possible reason: because it conforms to Aristotle's classic "unity of time" (after twenty minutes or so of gruesome and nearly unwatchable exposition). It goes by the clock. Like *High Noon* (1952) on speed, except for the clock device, it has nothing in common with Fred Zinnemann's classic Western. You know how many minutes are remaining because you are constantly reminded ("82 minutes, tick, tock, Doc"). Check your pacemaker. But there is a problem: "Movies that make a ticking clock part of the story run the risk the viewers may start checking their watches, and so it is with this one," Manohla Dargis noted in the *New York Times*. Problem is, the running time is 105 minutes, not eighty-eight, in case anyone is really counting (as some surely will be, as they hope for a conclusion). *New Yorker* critic

Anthony Lane was amused to think that movies might be named for their running time, asking: "Would Peter Jackson have dared to put through a Tolkien trilogy called 'Nine and a Quarter Hours of Elves'?" Movie reviewers will crack wise when there is nothing interesting to be said about the movie under review.

USA Today reviewer Claudia Puig found the movie remarkable because it could be "the most preposterous movie of the year," but, if not, it is "certainly the most ridiculous movie starring an Oscar-winning actor." *Washington Post* reviewer Stephen Hunter wondered: "Whatever happened to Al Pacino?" Hunter argues that about the time Pacino made *Heat* (1995), he changed his approach to moviemaking: "He got big, and the pictures got small." Hunter wonders about a scene in which Pacino runs through a parking garage "waving his badge and screaming 'Halt! I'm a forensic psychologist for the FBI!' And if they don't halt, what's he going to do? Psychoanalyze them?" *New York Times* reviewer Manohla Dargis called the movie "mostly a slog," even though "it's often laugh-out-loud laughably bad." Director Jon Avnet, according to *Chicago Tribune* critic Michael Phillips, "hacks his way through a script that barely hangs together." As one headline complained, these "'Minutes' you'll never get back." The reviews were consistently miserable.

It might be amusing to provide a really detailed plot summary, but only because the plot is so complicated (in other words, implausible), and, finally, there is nothing amusing about this film. The exposition is utterly repulsive because of "repeated, sadistic viewings of women strung up and sliced with fetishistic complexity of procedure," in the words of *Entertainment Weekly*'s Lisa Schwarzbaum. At the beginning of the film (after Avnet has spend rather too much time to show how the killer worked in 1997), the FBI comes calling on Dr. Gramm to ask him if the convicted serial killer might be the wrong man. Dr. Gramm literally puts all his cookies on the table as he defends his own infallibility. One might think there would be some pleasure to be had from watching Pacino overact in a really bad role, but one would be wrong, wrong, wrong. Dr. Gramm is a vain, self-dramatizing, hedonistic, egotistical nutcase who would never admit to being wrong. Before all those eighty-eight minutes expire, he has nearly been run down by a motorcycle as he chases through the city and the campus slipping over red herrings, and at one point his Porsche is blown up, but if he had been in it, he would have been killed about twenty minutes early, so that plot point really does not make sense. One of his lady friends, a dean at "Northwest Washington University," gets a major hang-up at the end, but Dr. Jack is there for her. It may occur to some viewers that Al Pacino might be getting too old for this kind of nonsense. But his hair looks great! And the gravelly voice, well you have heard it all before, speaking better scripted lines. One feels embarrassment for Pacino, just as one feels embarrassment for anyone connected with this film. One reviewer was determined to spoil the plot for everyone by giving away the identity of the killer, but then pretended not to remember who it was because the movie was so forgettable. But there is no point being a spoiler by even listing all the men and women suspects; this witless movie spoils itself. And that is as bad as it gets. Viewers desperate for entertainment would do better to stay at home and watch television. There is nothing to like here.

James M. Welsh

CREDITS

Jack Gramm: Al Pacino
Kim Cummings: Alicia Witt
Lauren Douglas: Leelee Sobieski
Shelly Barnes: Amy Brenneman
Jon Foster: Neal McDonough
Frank Parks: William Forsythe
Carol Lynn Johnson: Deborah Kara Unger
Mike Stempt: Ben McKenzie
Guy LaForge: Stephen Moyer
Origin: USA, Germany
Language: English
Released: 2008
Production: Jon Avnet, Randall Emmett, Avi Lerner, Gary Scott Thompson; TriStar Pictures, Millennium Films, Equity Pictures Medienfonds GmbH & Co. KG II, Nu Image Films; released by Sony Pictures
Directed by: Jon Avnet
Written by: Gary Scott Thompson
Cinematography by: Denis Lenoir
Music by: Ed Shearmur
Sound: Darren Brisker
Editing: Peter E. Berger
Art Direction: Jeremy Stanbridge
Costumes: Mary McLeod
Production Design: Tracey Gallacher
MPAA rating: R
Running time: 108 minutes

REVIEWS

Boston Globe Online. April 18, 2008.
Chicago Sun-Times Online. April 18, 2008.
Entertainment Weekly Online. April 16, 2008.
Hollywood Reporter Online. April 14, 2008.
Los Angeles Times Online. April 18, 2008.
New York Times Online. April 18, 2008.

San Francisco Chronicle. April 18, 2008, p. E5.
Variety Online. April 9, 2008.
Washington Post. April 18, 2008, p. C6.

QUOTES

Dr. Jack Gramm (to Kim): "Justice and truth—where do they intersect?"

TRIVIA

The credits list a total of nineteen producers and executive producers.

AWARDS

Nomination:

Golden Raspberries 2008: Worst Actor (Pacino), Worst Support. Actress (Sobieski).

ELEGY

Love has no boundries.
—Movie tagline

Box Office: $3.5 million

Philip Roth may be one of America's most acclaimed novelists, but his works have fared poorly on the big screen. *Goodbye, Columbus* (1969) was a popular success but simplifies Roth's characters and themes and has aged poorly. *Portnoy's Complaint* (1972) reduces the writer's best-known novel to a shrill, unfunny comedy. *The Human Stain* (2003) likewise fails to capture the essence of its source. Ironically, it took a Spanish female filmmaker, Isabel Coixet, to make an outstanding film from a work by an American writer often attacked for being insensitive to women.

Based on Roth's *The Dying Animal* (2001), *Elegy* is the story of an unlikely relationship between David Kepesh (Ben Kingsley), an aging literature professor at an unnamed New York City university, and Consuela Castillo (Penélope Cruz), a Cuban-American graduate student. An intellectual celebrity who appears on *Charlie Rose* and National Public Radio, David has been divorced twice and has had numerous short-term affairs with his students. An exception is his twenty-year relationship with Carolyn (Patricia Clarkson) that began while she was his student and has evolved into a physical and emotional anchor upon which both depend.

David's only other lasting friendship is with George O'Hearn (Dennis Hopper), a Pulitzer Prize–winning poet. The two meet regularly over coffee to talk about their lives and loves. David's most painful relationship is with his son, Kenny (Peter Sarsgaard), a seemingly hap-

pily married, successful thirty-five-year-old physician who has never gotten over his father's walking out on his family years earlier. Kenny punishes David by calling him in the middle of the night seeking counsel the elder Kepesh is reluctant to provide.

More than thirty years David's junior, Consuela offers more than sex. Obsessed with aging, with the inadequacies of his life, David does not immediately embrace Consuela's vitality. He tells himself he wants an uncomplicated affair like all his earlier ones, but he needs more. Consuela sees this need even before he does and in many ways is the more mature of the two. Content with the surface of life and angry at himself for this contentment, David is thrilled by Consuela as well as a bit frightened. His reticence leads to what seems to be an abrupt end to the affair, but life has some surprises in store for David and the other characters.

As the film's title suggests, *Elegy* can be seen as a meditation upon mortality, and it is one of a handful of films to introduce serious illness as a major plot development without using the disease as a cheap emotional shortcut. Yet David suffers from fear of life as much as fear of death, as shown by his distance from Kenny. Even though George is his closest friend, David does not allow himself to acknowledge how much they depend upon each other. *Elegy* is essentially about David's realization that he is foolish to keep Consuela at arm's length.

Death and illness are central concerns of Coixet, as demonstrated by the terminal cancer of the protagonist of *My Life without Me* (2003), the burn victim in *The Secret Life of Words* (2005), and the unfaithful husband falling in love with his dying wife in the "Bastille" segment of *Paris, je t'aime* (2006). But the director, working with a script by Nicholas Meyer, who also adapted *The Human Stain,* treats her themes with a less somber, more cinematic approach than in her earlier films. In one scene David is waiting for Consuela on the steps of some imposing building and imagines seeing her in the arms of another man. This scene, one of many reminiscent of the styles of American and European films of the 1970s, visually underscores David's expectation of losing Consuela, as does a superb sequence of shots showing David at his loneliest.

As with her previous films, Coixet, also the film's camera operator, excels in using her actors, training her camera on them for long, silent stretches to reveal the characters' complex emotions. After being adrift in the world of direct-to-video for years, Hopper gives his best performance since *True Romance* (1993), as George progresses from mere sounding board to fully developed character. Likewise, Clarkson's Carolyn seems initially to be a mere plot device before establishing a substantial identity. As with her outstanding performance in *Married Life* (2008), Clarkson excels in portraying an unfulfilled life.

Elegy reportedly originated from Cruz's interest in making the film, and it is easy to see why the material appealed to her. With the notable exception of *Volver* (2006), Consuela is Cruz's most complex role, shifting from one emotional extreme to another from scene to scene and even within scenes. Getting even more accomplished with each film, Cruz makes Consuela both exhilarating and sadly vulnerable. While there have been many, some would say too many, films about older men and younger women, these May-December relationships often seem contrived, yet Cruz makes the audience believe that Consuela truly loves David.

Sometimes unnecessarily flamboyant, Kingsley portrays David with small gestures and subdued emotionality, giving the professor a quiet dignity. Eschewing his usual mannerisms, the quickly rising voice, the nervous laugh, Kingsley offers one of the most believable and sympathetic intellectuals ever portrayed on film. Such characters are too often caricatures the viewers are meant to ridicule. As with Anthony Hopkins at his best, in *The Remains of the Day* (1993), Kingsley takes a character who thinks he knows himself and slowly peels away his protective surface to expose the pain beneath. Few actors have created such contrasts, as David Kepesh and the vicious Don Logan of *Sexy Beast* (2000). Few actors are capable of vivid diversity.

Michael Adams

CREDITS

David Kepesh: Ben Kingsley
Consuela Castillo: Penélope Cruz
George: Dennis Hopper
Carolyn: Patricia Clarkson
Kenny Kepesh: Peter Sarsgaard
Amy: Deborah Harry
Beth: Sonja Bennett
Susan Reese: Chelah Horsdal
Origin: USA
Language: English
Released: 2008
Production: Tom Rosenberg, Gary Lucchesi, Andre Lamal; Lakeshore Entertainment; released by Samuel Goldwyn Company
Directed by: Isabel Coixet
Written by: Nicholas Meyer
Cinematography by: Jean-Claude Larrieu
Sound: Rob Young
Music Supervisor: Isabel Coixet

Editing: Amy Duddleston
Art Direction: Helen Jarvis
Costumes: Katia Stano
Production Design: Claude Pare
MPAA rating: R
Running time: 108 minutes

REVIEWS

Entertainment Weekly Online. August 8, 2008.
Hollywood Reporter Online. February 11, 2008.
Los Angeles Times Online. August 8, 2008.
New York Times Online. August 8, 2008.
New Yorker Online. August 11, 2008.
San Francisco Chronicle. August 8, 2008, p. E5.
Variety Online. February 10, 2008.
Village Voice Online. August 5, 2008.

QUOTES

George (to David): "Stop worrying about growing old and think about growing up."

THE EXILES

A mesmerizing curiosity and true time capsule, *The Exiles,* a film from 1961, finally received an official theatrical release in 2008. Kent MacKenzie's mixture of narrative and documentary forms was ahead of its time and a fitting way to depict and explore modern Native American life.

The Exiles goes a long way in dispelling myths and stereotypes so common to Hollywood films (even in today's cinema). The unglamorized, unexotic real-life "American Indians" are much more complex and dimensional, though the kitchen-sink urban milieu of their lifestyles are also quite depressing, even heartbreaking.

Over a twelve-hour period during one weekend, we follow only a handful of Los Angeles denizens: there is Yvonne (Yvonne Williams), a pregnant young Apache bride, and her wayward, unemployed husband, Homer (Homer Nish), a Hualapai who drinks and gambles all night at the local clip joints. Then there is Tommy (Tom Reynolds), who is half Mexican, half Native American and who also carouses through the bars at night looking for a good time. A few other people take center stage before morning, as we come learn about the way these "exiles" from Indian reservations try to eke out a living in the big city while trying to maintain their freedom and dignity (though some never succeed).

What makes this portrait particularly special is the way Kent MacKenzie and his crew (notably, the cinematographers Erik Daarstad, Robert Kaufman, and John Morrill) confer dignity to the main characters. Apparently, nothing in the film was included if the cast disapproved. Also, the young director (a British-born USC student at the time) shows a flair for evocative imagery, an unobtrusive yet compelling form of noirish expressionism (all the more extraordinary given that the original budget was only a few hundred dollars!). It is thus sad to know that not only did MacKenzie die young (never to hear any acclaim about his work), but that he also made only one other feature in his life.

While the black-and-white photography is better than the most expensively made Hollywood films, what is disconcerting technically, at least at first, is the use of the actors' voice-overs. Whenever someone speaks, the words do not match up with the post-dubbed dialogue. Obviously, this was intentional, either because shooting "live" with a sound camera proved inconvenient or because the disjunction was an aesthetic choice. The results are not unlike Roberto Rossellini's *Rome, Open City* (1945), which was also post-dubbed throughout, and while this stylistic strategy does not diminish the power or impact of either film, the best, most affecting scenes in *The Exiles* are those featuring the married couple, Homer and Yvonne, because they are frequently accorded voice-overs that represent their thoughts, not their (mismatched) spoken words.

Like John Cassavete's first feature and contemporary release, *Shadows* (1960), also about a group of down-and-out urbanites, *The Exiles* echoes the era of Neo-Realism, and proves a worthy successor. The pioneers of mixing cinéma vérité and traditional storytelling, Robert Flaherty (*Nanook of the North* [1922]) and Humphrey Jennings (*Fires Were Started* [1943]), would have approved, and in some ways, these two films achieve a more resonant feeling of truth and honesty than the unintentionally condescending and ethnocentric work of "the masters." Thematically, the film presages the image of the modern Native American in films like *Smoke Signals* (1995), which is probably why that film's writer, Sherman Alexie (along with acclaimed indie filmmaker Charles Burnett), got involved in producing this restoration (nicely executed by UCLA labs and Milestone Film & Video). But perhaps the best comparison to make is Bruce Baillie's experimental short, *Mass for the Dakota Sioux* (1964), which was one of the only other works in that period to touch on the plight of the Native American in a postindustrial, predominantly Caucasian culture.

Critics enthusiastically greeted the return of this neglected effort. *New York Times* Manohla Dargis wrote, the "upshot of their singular collaborative effort is a beautifully photographed slice of down-and-almost-out life, a near-heavenly vision of a near-hell that Mr. MacK-

enzie situated at the juncture of nonfiction and fiction. He tapped into the despair of this obscured world while also making room for the poetry and derelict beauty of its dilapidated buildings, neon signs, peeling walls and downcast faces." While in the *Village Voice* Jim Ridley wrote, "MacKenzie (who died in 1980 at age 50 after making just one other feature) had an ear for the poetry of ritualized interaction, and an eye for the glint of hard light on city streets. The movie walks a nightworld so crackling with unfocused energy—so alive with threat, promise, and raw honking rock 'n' roll, yet so limited in any sense of a future—that to enter it is to feel your blood surge."

In the *New York Sun*, Nicolas Rapold remarked about the film's only real flaw, but still liked it: "The dialogue in *The Exiles* is looped in, giving the speech a chatty, floating quality that can be distracting at first. But actually, MacKenzie's rich and detailed sound design is one of the finest things about the movie. Pop hits from the period by the Revels, Jerry Lee Lewis, and others flow freely within scenes from jukeboxes, the sonic match to Homer and Tommy's greased-back hair. Bar chatter, cop radio calls, television dialogue ("… no-good Injun!") fill the night; a train bell announces the dawn."

We should all be thankful, even grateful, for the rediscovery of *The Exiles*—not only brave aesthetic achievement by a forgotten filmmaker but a memorable view of the lives of a people and a city also forgotten.

Eric Monder

CREDITS

Yvonne: Yvonne Williams
Homer: Homer Nish
Tommy: Tom Reynolds
Origin: USA
Language: English
Released: 1961
Production: Released by Milestone Films
Directed by: Kent Mackenzie
Written by: Kent Mackenzie
Cinematography by: Erik Daarstad, Robert Kaufman, John Morrill
Music by: Anthony Hilder, Robert Hafner, Eddie Sunrise
Editing: Erik Daarstad, Kent Mackenzie
MPAA rating: Unrated
Running time: 72 minutes

REVIEWS

Chicago Sun-Times Online. July 17, 2008.
Los Angeles Times Online. August 15, 2008.

New York Times Online. July 11, 2008.
Village Voice Online. July 8, 2008.

THE EXPRESS

He changed our country...one yard at a time.
—Movie tagline

Box Office: $9.7 million

The Express is director Gary Fleder's adaptation of the Carl Leavitt book *Ernie Davis: The Elmira Express.* It is the story of Ernie Davis, college football's first African American Heisman Trophy winner in 1961. The story chronicles Davis's and Syracuse University's undefeated 1959 season, and the era's inherent racism that the integrated team encountered as they played throughout the south and ultimately in the Cotton Bowl. The film shows not only Davis's growth and social awareness but that of his coach, Ben Schwartzwalder—a man who "likes winning more than he dislikes Negroes" as one of Davis's teammates points out.

Ernie Davis, played by Rob Brown (a former wide receiver at Amherst College) grew up in Pennsylvania coal country with his grandfather (Charles S. Dutton) until he was reunited with his recently remarried mother and moved to Elmira, New York. The young Davis learns of racism early as the film opens with the youth using his legs to escape a group of local thugs he encounters on some railroad tracks. Railroad tracks are a recurring theme during the first half of the movie as we see Davis running along the tracks many times over as he trains with his teammates and roommate JB (Omar Benson Miller). In Elmira, he encounters a more subtle form of racism as his youth team runs out of team jerseys just as Davis and his fellow African American teammates come to the front of the line.

By the time Davis graduates from high school, he is one of the finest high school players in the country, an accomplished three sport stand-out recruited by over fifty universities, including Notre Dame. Coach Schwartzwalder knows a thoroughbred when he sees one and employs the recently graduated future NFL superstar Jim Brown to coerce Davis into signing with Syracuse. Davis is even given Brown's old number, forty-four. Davis quickly learns that the era's racism has followed him from the classroom to the gridiron and is prevalent even within his own football team. He quietly endures this throughout the first hour of the film like his hero and fellow trailblazer, Jackie Robinson, had ten years before. Early in the movie, the young Davis says of Robinson, "There is a man who is doing a lot without saying nothing." This is Davis's mantra throughout the first half of the story. He is constantly "yes, sir"-ing to

everyone, even as they do him wrong. It is during the team's trip to the bigoted "backwoods" of West Virginia that Ernie takes a stand against the indignities and bottles hurled his way by the opposing fans, and even his own coach, who attempts to remove his star player from the game during a crucial sequence. Schwartzwalder is concerned about showing up the West Virginia team with his black star. From this point forward, we see an Ernie Davis who realizes he is more than just a player on the team and he becomes a most unlikely leader and social trailblazer. He shows strength of character that equals his on-the-field prowess throughout the film, the true embodiment of the strong, silent type.

Dennis Quaid shines as Syracuse coach Ben Schwartzwalder, the gruff old salt who spouts such lines as "It's not about winning trophies Davis, it's about winning games," with such conviction. Just as Davis stands out on the football field, Quaid is in his element here, with his character showing a fine arc. Early in the film, Schwartzwalder views the black athlete as some sort of trend in college football. His unease is apparent in his awkward approach to his "white girl speech," as the players call it. By the end of the film, Quaid's character has embraced the situation telling his players "Don't you let anyone steal history away from you," during his Cotton Bowl halftime speech. By the end of the movie, we see a different Schwartzwalder who sees Davis as more than just another player. Gone is the tension and unease that filled his interaction with the young Jim Brown.

Fleder uses a wide variety of cinematic techniques throughout the game sequences in *The Express*, running the gamut from grainy, black-and-white to bleached-out color. The football sequences are so well done it seems as though we are looking back at genuine game film. This serves as a constant reminder that this is a different era, perhaps a bit too much, though. For the majority of the film he avoids the sports drama clichés but he cannot resist a shot of the victorious Orangemen hoisting their star after the Cotton Bowl victory shot against the red, white, and blue bunting and cheering fans in the grandstand. When Davis is not high stepping in dynamic living sepia-tone, he is forced into dark, murky interior shot after dark murky interior shot, which becomes tiresome and loses much of the intended dramatic effect. It seems that there is no sunlight for Davis and *The Express* except for his Cotton Bowl triumph, and perhaps this is Fleder's point. Davis's brightness and moment in the sun was oh-so-sweet but far too short.

Davis was drafted as the number one pick in the NFL draft and was destined to play alongside his idol Jim Brown for the Cleveland Browns. Tragically, he was diagnosed with acute monocystic leukemia before he could play a single down for Cleveland and passed away at age twenty-three. Upon his passing, the late President

John F. Kennedy sent a telegram that read: "Seldom has an athlete been more deserving of such a tribute. Your high standards of performance on the field and off the field reflect the finest qualities of competition, sportsmanship, and citizenship. The nation has bestowed upon you its highest awards for your athletic achievements. It's a privilege for me to address you tonight as an outstanding American and a worthy example of our youth. I salute you."

The story is similar in theme to other tragic sports biographies like *Brian's Song* (1971) and *The Pride of the Yankees* (1942) in which the star is cut down in the prime of their life. But it is the moving social undercurrent and the strong character dynamic that set this film above the others. Davis's story is such a poignant and moving drama and it is a shame that audiences had to wait almost fifty years after the fact to see it. However, considering the current political climate in the United States and the rise of Barack Obama as the nation's president, the timing of the release is right on the money.

Michael S. White

CREDITS

Ernie Davis: Rob Brown
Ben Schwartzwalder: Dennis Quaid
Ray Simmons Jr.: Clancy Brown
Grandfather Davis: Charles S. Dutton
Jim Brown: Darrin Dewitt Henson
Will Davis: Nelsan Ellis
Jack Buckley: Omar Benson Miller
Bob Lundy: Geoff Stults
Dr. Jim Hewlette: Frank Grillo
Origin: USA
Language: English
Released: 2008
Production: John Davis; Relativity Media, Davis Entertainment Company; released by Universal Pictures
Directed by: Gary Fleder
Written by: Charles Leavitt
Cinematography by: Kramer Morgenthau
Music by: Mark Isham
Sound: David Obermeyer
Music Supervisor: Peter Afterman, Margaret Yen
Editing: William Steinkamp, Padraic McKinley
Art Direction: Seth Reed
Costumes: Abigail Murray
Production Design: Nelson Coates
MPAA rating: PG
Running time: 129 minutes

REVIEWS

Boston Globe Online. October 10, 2008.
Chicago Sun-Times Online. October 8, 2008.
Entertainment Weekly Online. October 7, 2008.
Hollywood Reporter Online. September 26, 2008.
Los Angeles Times Online. October 10, 2008.
New York Times Online. October 10, 2008.
San Francisco Chronicle. October 10, 2008, p. E7.
Variety Online. September 28, 2008.
Washington Post. October 10, 2008, p. C6.

QUOTES

Ben Schwartzwalder: "I won't tell him he'll be the next Ernie Davis, because there'll never be another Ernie Davis."

THE EYE

How can you believe your eyes when they're not your own?
—Movie tagline
You won't believe her eyes
—Movie tagline

Box Office: $31.4 million

Danny and Oxide Pang's *The Eye* (also known as *Gin gwai,* 2002) was a riveting modern ghost story with a twist that hit viewers with as much of an impact as the notorious twist in *The Sixth Sense* (1999). Even more importantly, *The Eye* was actually scary, something most horror movies made this decade have tragically failed to be. With the international success of the English-language versions of *The Ring* (2002) and *The Grudge* (2004), fans of *The Eye* knew it was inevitable that the remake machine would get to their favorite chiller. It took long enough for *The Eye* to be remade that the trend is now in its awful waning days with films like *One Missed Call* (2008) and *Shutter* (2008) producing critical scorn worldwide in early 2008. Neither of those films produced even one scare equivalent to their Asian originals and *The Eye* stands confidently next to them as yet another horror remake that completely misses what worked about its source. The only thing notable about the film is that it will hopefully be a part of the Asian horror remake hat trick that ended the trend once and for all.

Directed by the French team of David Moreau and Xavier Palud (who made the vastly superior *Them* [also known as *Ils,* 2006] but have clearly had all of their skills neutered by the Asian remake machine), *The Eye* stars movie poison Jessica Alba as Sydney Wells, a blind violinist. Twenty years after losing her sight, Sydney has a cornea transplant, allowing her not just to see her sheet music but things that remain invisible to most: people from the other side. Some of the ghosts seem to be trying to communicate with Sydney, but others are oblivious to the fact that she can even see them. At the same time, Sydney is having nightmares of screaming children and foreseen disaster. Alessandro Nivola co-stars as Sydney's therapist and Parker Posey is horribly miscast as Sydney's sister Helen. Neither of her two-dimensional supporters believes poor Sydney, but soon the coincidences pile up to the point that they have to trust that her prophetic visions of fire and death might come true.

Nearly everything that worked about the Pang Brothers' *The Eye* has been tragically altered in the American version. The overall effect has been to turn an atmospheric story into merely a loud one. The biggest failure of the Asian remake trend has been the American desire to "turn it up," which is exactly the wrong instinct when it comes to remaking a moody ghost story. For just one example, instead of just letting us feel Sydney's fear as she encounters something she knows is hard to believe, Moreau and Palud direct Alba to mutter "It's not real" over and over again. Silence is scarier. The decision is only one of many that keep *The Eye* at arm's length, never letting the chills sink below the viewer's skin. Of course, making a ghost story that feels realistic is a tough task, but the remake of *The Eye* always feels like a movie, piling music and dialogue where the original focused on atmosphere over everything else. Even the shocking revelation about Sydney's appearance has completely lost its dramatic impact.

The commercial response to *The Eye* was reasonably strong when considering its worldwide gross (over $50 million), but most critics saw through the horror to the ineffective mess underneath. The *New York Times* noted, "*The Eye* is the latest Western deconstruction of a successful Asian horror movie and it is louder and more literal than its inspiration." The *Hollywood Reporter* summed it up succinctly by calling *The Eye* "Yet another inferior remake of an Asian horror film."

Directors Moreau and Palud are not the only ones to blame for the latest Asian horror remake gone horribly wrong. Jessica Alba gives yet another dull, wooden performance that fails to capture any of the actual fear a character must express to an audience to make a ghost story effective. Alba is ineffective in every single way. Nivola and Posey fail to make out much better, both falling victim to Sebastian Gutierrez's dull screenplay, one that turns them into mere plot devices. Both are talented enough actors that they deserved better.

Ultimately, the scariest thing about *The Eye* is that such highly paid people failed to improve on their source material in any single arena. Every element—performance, direction, even the score—is a step down. Critics often recommend the original over the remake, but rarely has it been easier to understand why.

Brian Tallerico

CREDITS

Sydney Wells: Jessica Alba
Dr. Paul Faulkner: Alessandro Nivola
Helen Wells: Parker Posey
Simon McCullough: Rade Serbedzija
Rosa Martinez: Rachel Ticotin
Alicia Millstone: Chloe Grace Moretz
Anna Christina Martinez: Fernanda Romero
Dr. Haskins: Obba Babatunde
Miguel: Danny Mora
Origin: USA
Language: English
Released: 2008
Production: Paula Wagner, Don Granger, Michelle Manning; Paramount Vantage, C/W Productions, Vertigo Entertainment; released by Lionsgate
Directed by: David Moreau, Xavier Palud
Written by: Sebastian Gutierrez
Cinematography by: Jeffrey Jur
Music by: Marco Beltrami
Sound: Bayard Carey
Music Supervisor: Jay Faires
Editing: Patrick Lussier
Art Direction: Brenda Meyers-Ballard
Costumes: Michael Dennison
Production Design: James Lawrence Spencer
MPAA rating: PG-13
Running time: 97 minutes

REVIEWS

Boston Globe Online. February 2, 2008.
Entertainment Weekly Online. February 6, 2008.
Hollywood Reporter Online. February 4, 2008.
Los Angeles Times Online. February 4, 2008.
New York Times Online. February 2, 2008.
Premiere Online. February 1, 2008.
Variety Online. February 1, 2008.

QUOTES

Sydney Wells: "I'm seeing things I shouldn't see!"

TRIVIA

To prepare for her role, Jessica Alba took violin lessons for six months. She also learned basic Braille.

AWARDS

Nomination:

Golden Raspberries 2008: Worst Actress (Alba).

F

FIREPROOF

Never leave your partner behind.
—Movie tagline

Box Office: $33.4 million

Fireproof, a Christian film produced for $500,000 by a Baptist church in Georgia, written by two associate pastors, and starring a cast of mostly non-actors, debuted at number four when it opened and went on to gross an impressive $33 million. Tapping into the same audience that propelled Mel Gibson's *The Passion of the Christ* (2004) to a dizzying $370 million at the box office, *Fireproof*—starring former teenage heartthrob Kirk Cameron in a simple tale about how a firefighter saves his marriage as well as his soul—is far from the caliber of Gibson's critically acclaimed and controversial religious epic. *Fireproof* does succeed in presenting an overtly religious-themed film that also sufficiently entertains.

The filmmakers, brothers Alex Kendrick (who directed) and Stephen Kendrick, have also made an exponential leap in quality from their previous effort, *Facing the Giants* (2006), a sports drama embraced by the evangelical community for its message but derided by critics and more discerning Christians for the poor quality of nearly everything else. While the script and pacing are uneven at times and the straightforward narrative contains little nuance or surprise, *Fireproof* is a definite improvement.

The simple story concerns a firefighter Caleb Holt (Kirk Cameron) whose marriage to his wife of seven years, Catherine (Erin Bethea), is crumbling. Catherine wants a divorce and Caleb is also willing to call it quits. He goes to his newly Christian father John (Harris Mal-

com) and mother (Phyllis Malcom) for help. John gives him a book called *The Love Dare* and challenges him to follow the forty-day program before forever severing the union. It is through this process that the angry, misguided firefighter learns the mistakes he made in his marriage and how to properly love his wife.

The filmmakers flounder with the story's set-up and the scenes where Caleb and Catherine fight feel rote and perfunctory. The filmmakers use a lazy shortcut in a confrontation where the tension too quickly escalates to the breaking point for Catherine, and Caleb's rage seems unprecedented and unmotivated. The pace improves in the second reel where the couple goes about following the steps, mixing morality lessons with both touching and comedic moments. The Kendricks confide in their friends and the script successfully wrings humor out of the inevitable psychobabble. Slowly the fireman with the short fuse learns to treat Catherine with tenderness and respect that readies him for the more flamboyant gestures later in the program that soften his distant wife's heart.

There are lighthearted, contrasting scenes showing life at the firehouse, Caleb's other family. A solid relationship drama, *Fireproof* is hardly an action film about firefighting in the vein of *Backdraft* (1991), but does include a few, harrowing firefighting action sequences. Caleb rescues a child from a burning house while a scene where a car is trapped on the railroad tracks is unexpectedly imaginative.

The title refers to the character of Caleb's profession as a firefighter as well as his attitude toward life and marriage. He is an unsympathetic character at the start of the film who feels that nothing can touch him. He learns that "Fireproof doesn't mean the fire will never come. It means when the fire comes that you will be able to withstand it." During the time Caleb repairs his marriage, the agnostic fireman resists the clear call to also embrace God that is gently but effectively voiced by not only his father but fellow Christian firefighter Michael Simmons (Ken Bevel). Midway through the film he indeed becomes a full-fledged believer, something this earnestly Christian film obviously feels is a necessity for a successful marriage.

The script treats the character of Catherine with due respect, not as the stereotypical housewife she might have been. She is a successful professional with a life of her own as a publicist at a hospital. Rather than helplessly fret about her husband's bad behavior and implied addiction to Internet pornography, Catherine, who attracts the attention of one of the doctors, faces her own moral dilemma about whether or not to pursue a relationship outside the unhappy marriage.

Kirk Cameron, a former child and teen star best known for his role on television's *Growing Pains,* has since starred in a number of Christian films and video productions, including the *Left Behind* series. Other than Cameron, most of the cast are amateur actors or regular, churchgoing Christians. Despite some of the action scenes where the victims' lack of acting experience is obvious, the performances are surprisingly smooth. And despite rather thin characterizations, the writing is solid.

Critics were evenly split on the film's merits beyond its uplifting Christian message. The *New York Times* critic Neil Genzingler rightly summarized: "This is a decent attempt to combine faith and storytelling that will certainly register with its target audience."

Hilary White

CREDITS

Caleb Holt: Kirk Cameron
Catherine Holt: Erin Bethea
John Holt: Harris Malcom
Michael Simmons: Ken Bevel
Cheryl Holt: Phyllis Malcom
Eric Harmon: James McLeod
Origin: USA
Language: English
Released: 2008
Production: Alex Kendrick, Stephen Kendrick, David Nixon; Sherwood Pictures, Provident Films, Carmel Entertainment; released by Samuel Goldwyn Films
Directed by: Alex Kendrick
Written by: Alex Kendrick, Stephen Kendrick
Cinematography by: Bob Scott

Music by: Mark Willard
Sound: Rob Whitehurst
Editing: Bill Ebel
Production Design: Sheila McBride
MPAA rating: PG
Running time: 122 minutes

REVIEWS

Austin Chronicle Online. October 3, 2008.
Entertainment Weekly Online. September 30, 2008.
Hollywood Reporter Online. September 30, 2008.
Variety Online. September 26, 2008.
Village Voice Online. October 1, 2008.

QUOTES

Caleb Holt: "Marriage isn't fireproof."
Michael Simmons: "Fireproof doesn't mean the fire will never come. It means when the fire comes that you will be able to withstand it."

TRIVIA

Kirk Cameron, a Christian evangelist, refuses to kiss any woman other than his wife. To film a scene in which his character in this movie kisses his wife, the filmmakers had to dress Cameron's real-life wife, Chelsea Noble, as the wife character (played throughout the rest of the movie by Erin Bethea) and shoot the kissing scene in shadow so the difference between Noble and Bethea would not be as evident on screen.

THE FIRST SATURDAY IN MAY

The brothers Brad and John Hennegan cowrote, produced, and directed the documentary *The First Saturday in May,* which follows six trainers of thoroughbreds who hope to get their horses in the field of twenty for the 2006 Kentucky Derby. Five of them do. One of them wins. The film is an interesting celebration of racing and the passion that these trainers and race enthusiasts have. Its strengths lie in its ability to capture much of the pageantry and excitement of racing as well as in clearly setting forth the lengthy process of winning the qualifying races that precede the Derby. Its weakness lies in its superficiality. *The First Saturday in May* is more of a bouquet to the world of racing than an analysis of why winners win or what makes a good trainer or even why racing as a sport inspires such passions. Spending so many months and shooting so much footage following the working lives of so many people should call for greater depth and scrutiny than this colorful and informative but somewhat shallow valentine affords.

At the outset the film introduces the six trainers. (One of them, Frank Amonte, at the start is an assistant trainer who receives a promotion during the racing season.) The audience sees them trackside, briefly meets some of their families, hears from some jockeys and at least one groom, and above all watches their horses. The top twenty horses in a season of stakes races qualify to run in the Derby, and each trainer, presumably, decides how many and which races to enter, though all such strategy is omitted from the film. As the qualifying process progresses, subtitles inform the audience where a particular horse must finish in an upcoming race to stay in consideration for the big race on the first Saturday in May—that at one point, for example, the horse Sharp Humor must win or place at the Florida Derby to qualify as one of the twenty running at Churchill Downs; Sharp Humor comes in second in Florida.

Opportunities arise, but are mostly missed, for taking a deeper look at the subject. At one point trainer Michael Matz walks through a stable talking on his cell and abruptly stops when he passes a horse that snorts. After an abrupt edit, Matz is shown petting the horse reassuringly and resuming his walk. What his trainer's ear noticed or what problem he felt needed addressing is never explained. The film provides very little information on how to train a horse for this race of a lifetime or about what these expert trainers have learned through their many years of working with horses. Two of the trainers have serious disabilities—one being wheelchair bound from a cycling accident, the other having early multiple sclerosis—but beyond a brief comment from one of them about his gratefulness for each new day, there is no explanation of how their love of racing and horses may deepen their lives or enable them to cope with their health challenges. The best moment in the film comes when Michael Matz talks his young son into walking over and petting a skittish thoroughbred. The father explains how doing so lets the horse get to know the boy. Another trainer, Kiaran McLaughlin, decides to change jockeys on his horse, Jazil, in a qualifying race so that a more patient rider might better suit the personality of Jazil, but this strategy is conveyed in a flash to the audience through a subtitle almost as an afterthought rather than through McLaughlin's own words. Consistently, the film is content to present the subject of racing from the outside rather than from the inside.

Every scene offers a good bit of trackside small talk and anecdotes. Many shots show congratulations being offered to winners of qualifying races and snippets of interviews with the press. One trainer shares a snack with his horse, each chomping down on opposite ends of the same carrot. Another lets his horse rub an upper lip on the smoothness of his gold watch. Frank Amonte argues with his son over the boy's reluctance to soil his expensive sneakers in the stables. The audience sees trainers perusing the Derby list of guest passes like the social register, shopping for a good suit at Brooks Brothers, playing golf at a Lexington country club, and smuggling cases of Coors Light into the trainers' area. All of these moments are mostly interesting, especially hearing Kiaran McLaughlin talk about the wisdom of not becoming too attached to the horses he trains and about how Jazil is so kind that it is hard for McLaughlin to follow his own advice. The audience can easily sense and appreciate that the road to the Derby is the summit in these trainers' lives.

Probably the biggest subject that the film fails to address is money and the part it plays in big-time racing. As the horses win qualifying races and solidify their places in field at the 2006 Kentucky Derby, the viewer may naturally wonder how big are the purses of these preliminary races, how much of the winnings go to the owners, and how much to the trainers? Is running at the Derby an end in itself as far as job security for a trainer of thoroughbreds is concerned, or has that point already been passed earlier in their careers by these experts? And, though it is the culmination of months of hard work, how devastating is losing the Derby? As one of the five horses followed by the documentary finishes the Derby tied for fourth but a few weeks later wins the Belmont Stakes and its million-dollar purse, viewers may understandably revise their earlier disappointment over the Derby outcome to something less than crushing. At times viewers may struggle at finding the right way to respond to some of the events in the film. Ultimately, *The First Saturday in May* celebrates horse racing more than it explores it; consequently, it is a film seemingly intent more on pleasing existing racing enthusiasts than on conveying what makes the sport great or on recruiting new fans.

Glenn Hopp

CREDITS

Origin: USA
Language: English
Released: 2008
Production: Brad Hennegan, John Hennegan, Ellen Dux; Churchill Downs; released by Truly Indie
Directed by: Brad Hennegan, John Hennegan
Written by: Brad Hennegan, John Hennegan
Cinematography by: Brad Hennegan, John Hennegan
Music by: Mark Krewatch, Ryan Brothers
Sound: Elmo Weber, Clayton Weber
Editing: Brad Hennegan, John Hennegan, Tamara McDonough

MPAA rating: PG-13
Running time: 100 minutes

REVIEWS

Boston Globe Online. April 18, 2008.
Entertainment Weekly Online. April 17, 2008.
Los Angeles Times Online. April 18, 2008.
New York Times Online. April 18, 2008.
San Francisco Chronicle. April 18, 2008, p. E4.
Variety Online. April 18, 2008.
Village Voice Online. April 15, 2008.
Washington Post Online. April 18, 2008.

FIRST SUNDAY

Keep the faith. Steal the rest.
—Movie tagline

Box Office: $37.9 million

David E. Talbert's *First Sunday* is so disposable and forgettable that it becomes difficult to even write about. The writer/director has put together a comedy that never becomes offensively bad enough to be memorable in its awfulness, but is so dead on arrival that it dissipates from memory before the credits have even finished rolling. *First Sunday* feels like a television movie on every level, from the low production values to the awkward direction, but most TV movies can at least provide a laugh or two to get viewers to the evening news. Talbert's movie is so listless and predictable that it becomes sleep-inducing more often than it provokes laughter. Except for perhaps a few decent supporting performances by some talented actors who deserved better material, *First Sunday* features nothing worth recommending, other than to marvel at why so many interesting actors signed on to a screenplay with so little going on.

First Sunday was clearly conceived as a play, as almost all the action takes place in one location, a church. And only in that location does the movie work at all, with the set-up scenes of the first act that take place outside it falling the flattest in the two-dimensional film. Durell (Ice Cube) and LeeJohn (Tracy Morgan) are a pair of bumbling thieves caught between a rock and a hard place. After a caper involving stolen wheelchairs goes horribly awry, the two find themselves in debt to some very bad men. Meanwhile, Durell is about to watch his wife (Regina Hall) leave the city with his beloved son because she does not have the money to keep her beauty salon open. The poor guy needs some cash. Durell and LeeJohn spot a church in the middle of a donation drive. The congregation wants to move to a

bigger, better church and has been raising money to do so. Durell and LeeJohn break in after hours, only to find members of the congregation there and that someone has beaten them to the safe.

Our "heroes" take over the church and hold its members hostage to try to sweat out the thief. Michael Beach plays the clearly corrupt deacon of the church while Chi McBride plays the pastor. Katt Williams overplays the choir director (but at least he has some life in his performance) and the always-great Loretta Devine plays a sister. Of course, everything is wrapped up in a neat little bow by the final act with the guys not really being "that bad" and the true villains getting everything they deserve. *First Sunday* is never remotely unpredictable or subtle, which is not a problem in broad heart-and-humor comedies like this one, but Talbert seems to have forgotten the laughs and only barely remembered the heart.

The script and its leaden, sitcom-esque direction must take most of the blame for the failure of *First Sunday,* but the two leads need to accept some responsibility as well. Ice Cube was once such a vital, interesting actor in films like *Boyz n the Hood* (1991) and even the *Friday* movies, but it would be an understatement to say that he has been phoning in his performances over the past few years in horrible family comedies like *Are We Done Yet?* (2007) and *First Sunday.* An actor who once showed dramatic and comedic potential now seems bored by his own performance. On the other end of the spectrum is Tracy Morgan, so great on the television sitcom *30 Rock,* but set to only one speed in *First Sunday*—shrill. Even the typically fun Katt Williams is mostly dull and used poorly. Only Loretta Devine and Chi McBride make it through this comedy dud with any respectability.

Critics were unimpressed with *First Sunday* when it played in theaters, recognizing it as a forgettable misfire. Stephanie Zacharek of *Salon* said, "The movie is designed to be uplifting and inspirational, but everything about it is tired and listless. It doesn't so much make you feel the spirit as drain it out of you." Claudia Puig of *USA Today* added, "With plot holes the size of boulders, it's a bad effort at wacky humor and schmaltzy redemption that plods and preaches gratingly." Finally, Brian Lowry of *Variety* correctly summarized the film in one sentence—"A near-claustrophobic comedy that manages to be both predictable and preachy."

Much has been made of horrible comedies like *Epic Movie* (2007) and *Norbit* (2007) and how they were offensive in their awfulness. *First Sunday* is never memorable enough to join them. When critics are making their "Worst of the Year" lists at the end of 2008, it is unlikely that *First Sunday* will find a place on many of them. Like audiences, critics are unlikely to remember that it even exists.

Brian Tallerico

CREDITS

Durell: Ice Cube
Rickey: Katt Williams
LeeJohn: Tracy Morgan
Sister Doris: Loretta Devine
Deacon: Michael Beach
Pastor Arthur Mitchell: Chi McBride
Judge B. Bennet Galloway: Keith David
Omunique: Regina Hall
Tianna: Malinda Williams
Origin: USA
Language: English
Released: 2008
Production: Ice Cube, Matt Alvarez, David E. Talbert, David McIlvain, Tim Story; Cube Vision, Firm Films, Screen Gems, Story Company; released by Sony Pictures Entertainment
Directed by: David E. Talbert
Written by: David E. Talbert
Cinematography by: Alan Caso
Music by: Stanley Clarke
Sound: Walter Anderson
Editing: Jeffrey Wolf
Art Direction: Robert Stohmaier
Costumes: Gersha Phillips
Production Design: Dina Lipton
MPAA rating: PG-13
Running time: 98 minutes

REVIEWS

Baltimore Sun Online. January 11, 2008.
Boston Globe Online. January 11, 2008.
Entertainment Weekly Online. January 16, 2008.
Hollywood Reporter Online. January 7, 2008.
Los Angeles Times Online. January 11, 2008.
New York Times Online. January 11, 2008.
San Francisco Chronicle. January 11, 2008, p. E4.
Variety Online. January 6, 2008.
Washington Post. January 11, 2008, p. C6.

QUOTES

LeeJohn (after he and Durell find the church safe empty): "Who robs a church?"

TRIVIA

Film prints were delivered to theaters under the codename "Bad to Worse."

FLASH OF GENIUS

Corporations have time, money, and power on their side. All Bob Kearns had was the truth.
—Movie tagline

Box Office: $4.4 million

Producer Marc Abraham makes his directorial debut with *Flash of Genius* that attempts to spin a David and Goliath tale of a little guy taking on the big corporate machine. Based on the true story chronicled in John Seabrook's 1993 *New Yorker* article, the film is a biographical exploration of Robert Kearns and his fight to receive credit and compensation for inventing the intermittent windshield wiper, stolen by Ford Motor Company and Chrysler. Although his fight with the Detroit automakers became an all-consuming, lifelong endeavor, the subject matter and lackluster antihero hardly excite the imagination, and this seems an unlikely tale to bring to the big screen.

Unlike Hollywood favorite *Erin Brockovich* (2000), which exudes a noble, justice-for-all quality and an immediately relatable heroine, Kearns's epic underdog tale features a cold, unsympathetic character whose struggle is truly his own and a questionable one at that. Abraham and writer Philip Railsback posit that his relentless fight—that ultimately cost him his career, his marriage, his relationship with his children and, at times, his sanity—was worthwhile. Seabrook's article is a richer, more detailed account of the fight and the personal toll that it took on Kearns, who ultimately won a $30 million patent infringement suit in 1995, more than three decades after patenting his invention.

The film's title refers to a legal patenting term, which defines the work of an inventor and his moment of inspiration. In 1963, Detroit professor of engineering Robert Kearns (Greg Kinnear) is inspired to invent the intermittent windshield wiper in his basement, an invention that he and his business partner Gil (Dermot Mulroney) dream will make them rich and famous. Kearns patents his invention and shops it around to the Big Three automakers. He makes a deal with Ford; they ask for a prototype, then produce it and install it in their vehicles, without compensating him, a few years later.

These events are told in flashback, with the majority of the film outlining Kearns's resolute fight, both in and out of the courtroom, for justice and for the credit and compensation that is due him. His faithful wife Phyllis (Lauren Graham), a schoolteacher, and six children, played by a succession of actors as they age, suffer the brunt of Kearns's decades-long obsession. Acting as his own lawyer, Kearns even recruits his children to aid in his defense.

The film's best scenes are those in the Washington, D.C., courtroom where Kearns fought his case and features a wonderful performance by Alan Alda in a small but memorable role as the savvy, high-priced lawyer Gregory Lawson. The automakers' case is based on the "doctrine of nonobviousness" which counters the "flash of genius" inventor's claim by positing that others might have reached the same conclusion with the same set of tools.

After many years and countless court battles, Kearns's hard-won fight yields a large monetary settlement, but no admission of theft on the part of the automakers.

The role of Robert Kearns is a departure for Greg Kinnear, who, with his boyish good looks, is better known for the charming, smarmy characters he often embodies in films, including *Sabrina* (1995). With this film, he proves he can still play the suave rake, as in 2008's *Ghost Town,* but that he is also capable of playing more complex character roles. Kinnear is thoroughly convincing as the rather unlikable lone wolf who alienates his family and colleagues with his infuriating single-mindedness.

The filmmakers omit the exact dates that these historical events took place and fail to adequately chronicle the passage of time, which lends a lackadaisical, made-for-television air to the proceedings. While an underdog-makes-good story, especially a true one, is always inspiring, *Flash of Genius* does not focus sufficiently on the details that would separate this story from countless others with more sympathetic heroes and juicier premises that have far more at stake. One nice detail is also a subtle one—that Kearns drives a Ford throughout his litigation with the company.

The film does have a catchy tagline that rang especially true in the waning months of 2008, when billion dollar bailouts to big businesses with no strings attached enraged millions of financially strapped taxpayers: "Corporations have time, money, and power on their side. All Bob Kearns had was the truth." Despite its all-American "underdog fights the good fight and finally makes good" appeal, *Flash of Genius* failed to spark the imagination of the moviegoing public, recouping a mere $3.7 million of its $20 million budget.

Hilary White

CREDITS

Robert Kearns: Greg Kinnear
Phyllis Kearns: Lauren Graham
Gil Privick: Dermot Mulroney
Frank Sertin: Daniel Roebuck
Dennis Kearns: Jake Abel
Charles Defao: Tim Kelleher
Gregory Lawson: Alan Alda
Judge Michael Franks: Bill Smitrovich
Origin: USA
Language: English
Released: 2008
Production: Roger Birnbaum, Gary Barber, Michael Lieber; Spyglass Entertainment; released by Universal Pictures
Directed by: Marc Abraham
Written by: Philip Railsback
Cinematography by: Dante Spinotti
Music by: Aaron Zigman
Sound: Glen Gauthier
Editing: Jill Savitt
Art Direction: Patrick Banister
Costumes: Luis Sequira
Production Design: Hugo Luczyc-Wyhowski
MPAA rating: PG-13
Running time: 120 minutes

REVIEWS

Boston Globe Online. October 3, 2008.
Chicago Sun-Times Online. October 2, 2008.
Entertainment Weekly Online. October 1, 2008.
Hollywood Reporter Online. September 6, 2008.
Los Angeles Times Online. October 3, 2008.
New York Times Online. October 3, 2008.
Rolling Stone Online. October 16, 2008.
San Francisco Chronicle. October 3, 2008, p. E1.
Variety Online. September 1, 2008.
Washington Post. October 3, 2008, p. C4.

FLAWLESS

> *He had a scheme. She had a motive.*
> —Movie tagline
> *It took the heist of the century to settle the score.*
> —Movie tagline

Box Office: $1.2 million

Too old-fashioned for its own good, Michael Radford's *Flawless* is a hard-to-pin-down crime film that features at least one strong performance and some eye-opening twists and turns but is ultimately too dry to be the crowd-pleaser that it could have been and too concerned with the predictable beats of the caper genre to be a character study either. Radford (*Il Postino* [1994]) brings a professionalism and snappy pace to his period heist picture but the midsection of the film is too slow for its own good, never developing characters interesting enough to truly care about and yet not providing enough snap and sizzle to the crime itself to satisfy audiences used to the twist-a-minute pace of the modern thriller. Far worse crime films than *Flawless* were released in 2008 and the movie does not do anything drastically wrong, but it also fails to do enough right to make it at all memorable after the credits have rolled.

Flawless opens in modern times, where a makeup-laden Demi Moore plays Laura Quinn, an elderly woman being interviewed for a magazine article entitled "Women Who Led." In this entirely fictional tale, Quinn was the only woman to have been a manager at the London Diamond Corporation. The interviewer is hoping to get a piece about being the only girl in a boy's club but Quinn has another story to tell. She pulls a gigantic diamond out of a box, puts it on the table, and confesses to having stolen it from her employers.

The film flashes back to 1960 and to the world of the London Diamond Corporation, where a younger Quinn is repeatedly passed over for promotion. She finds solace in the kindly janitor, Mr. Hobbs (Michael Caine), who discovers that Quinn is going to be terminated and comes to her with a plan—help him steal just a little bit of diamonds from the safe. The management will barely notice they are gone, the janitor can change his life, and the overlooked female employee can get a modicum of revenge. Quinn chooses to help Hobbs with the understanding that he will steal an almost immeasurably small amount from the safe, just enough that he can fit in his thermos and sneak out with her help, but when she arrives the next morning she finds the giant safe completely empty. Hobbs has found a way to empty the London Diamond Corporation of nearly two tons of product and he now holds them for ransom, telling the owners of the company that they will be returned for one hundred million pounds. An investigator is brought in and he starts to put the pieces of this complex puzzle together. Quinn is trapped, having helped Hobbs with his plan but also working with her bosses to try to stop the diamond market from crashing. It turns out that Hobbs had a very different motivation from greed and that the actual money means very little to him.

Michael Caine is one of the most consistent actors of all time and he is clearly having a great time in *Flawless* but he is truly the only real reason to see it. Moore gives it her best shot but she seems miscast and the screenplay does her no favors, giving her a two-dimensional plot device of a character. Most damagingly, the entire film is too dry for its own good. When the movie should be crackling to life, as Quinn is trapped between the man she knows is responsible for the crime of the century and the company that has consistently ignored her, it really starts to drag. Caine elevates *Flaw-less* above the average heist movie but he is not quite enough to keep it from never becoming what it could have and should have been. The script needed what is often referred to as a "punch up," something to make it not only more memorable but not as dry. Ultimately, *Flawless* is mildly entertaining at best, but with as crowded a marketplace as 2008 has produced, that seems like faint praise.

Even critics who praised *Flawless* echoed the faint praise and recognized the film's serious limitations. Stephen Holden of the *New York Times* called it "a mildly diverting period heist movie" in his positive review and Desson Thompson of the *Washington Post* dubbed the film "an entertainingly nostalgic journey to old Britain." Other reviewers called it "good disposable entertainment"; "a reasonably good time"; "a nicely made if slightly stodgy jewel heist flick." *Flawless* is not a film that got anyone particularly excited. It is old-fashioned in the worst sense of the word, a missed opportunity to build something interesting around Caine's great performance that is far too banal and flat to truly recommend.

Brian Tallerico

CREDITS

Laura Quinn: Demi Moore
Hobbs: Michael Caine
Sir Milton Ashtoncroft: Joss Ackland
Finch: Lambert Wilson
Origin: Luxembourg, Great Britain, USA
Language: English
Released: 2007
Production: Michael Pierce, Mark Williams; Delux Productions, Future Films; released by Magnolia Pictures
Directed by: Michael Radford
Written by: Edward A. Anderson
Cinematography by: Richard Greatrex
Music by: Stephen Warbeck
Sound: Carlo Thoss
Editing: Peter Boyle
Costumes: Dinah Collin
Production Design: Sophie Becher
MPAA rating: PG-13
Running time: 108 minutes

REVIEWS

Boston Globe Online. March 28, 2008.
Chicago Sun-Times Online. March 28, 2008.
Entertainment Weekly Online. March 26, 2008.
Hollywood Reporter Online. October 5, 2007.

Los Angeles Times Online. March 28, 2008.
New York Times Online. March 28, 2008.
San Francisco Chronicle Online. March 28, 2008.
Variety Online. October 2, 2007.
Washington Post. March 28, 2008, p. C1.

FLIGHT OF THE RED BALLOON
(Le voyage du ballon rouge)

Directed by Taiwanese filmmaker Hou Hsiao-Hsien, the sumptuous *Flight of the Red Balloon* (*Le voyage du ballon rouge*) was commissioned by the Musée d'Orsay in Paris and is an homage to Albert Lamorisse's 1956 fable *The Red Balloon.* In Lamorisse's fairy tale, a solitary but resourceful boy is befriended by a red balloon that follows him doggedly through Paris. The balloon is mischievous but devoted, and the boy protects it from harm. Their mutual spell is broken by a group of vicious schoolboys who fell the balloon with rocks. Afterward, all the other balloons in the city come to the boy's aid, and he tethers their strings together, soaring over the rooftops of Paris. Though Hou's film borrows several elements from the original, such as the Parisian setting and the characters of the young boy and the balloon, his is "a flight of fancy grounded in real life," as Salon.com's Stephanie Zacharek has described.

The loosely drawn story begins when Song (Fang Song), in Paris from Beijing to study film, is hired by single mother Suzanne (Juliette Binoche) to care for her young son, Simon (Simon Iteanu). Like Hou, Song is fashioning an homage to *The Red Balloon,* hers a digital video in which Simon appears. As Simon and Song become acquainted, a mysterious red balloon sporadically observes the action from outside an apartment window. The messy details of Suzanne's life interrupt the new nanny and child's quiet rapport. A voice performer for a puppet troupe, Suzanne has fallen on hard times. Simon's father, Pierre, is in Montréal working on a book and fails to provide emotional or financial support in his absence. Exacerbating Suzanne's money woes, her downstairs tenant, Marc (Hippolyte Girardot), has stopped paying rent. Hoping her college-bound daughter, Juliette, will return from Brussels to live in Paris, Suzanne decides to evict the deadbeat Marc. The story closes at the Musée d'Orsay, where Simon and his classmates ponder the painting *Le Ballon* by Félix Vallotton. During the discussion, Simon notices a red balloon hovering above the museum's glass ceiling before it takes flight through the Parisian skyline, the boy's imagination in tow.

As the *Onion A.V. Club*'s Scott Tobias has commented, "Nothing much happens in *Flight of the Red Balloon,* and that's all by design: Hou means to evoke a city and a few of the lonely characters within it, and he does so with consummate grace, affection, and a subtle touch of magic." Most of the magic, of course, is in that red balloon. In Lamorisse's film, the perfectly formed red sphere looked like a modernist punctuation mark on the ancient, granite-hued streets of Paris. Hou's version is just as visually striking—"sailing through [the film] like an airborne cherry," as Manohla Dargis of the *New York Times* so evocatively put it. For a few seconds at the start of the film, the balloon floats so close to the camera, it nearly dominates the entire frame, and the simple elegance of its shape and color is breathtaking.

Song at one point explains to Suzanne how she will use the technique of green-screening to manipulate the balloon in her piece. As a result, the audience of *Flight of Red Balloon* learns how Hou is maintaining the illusion of a sentient balloon in his film. This self-reflexive moment is a departure from Lamorisse's project, which does not call attention to its illusory techniques. Though Hou acknowledges the artificiality behind chroma key, he destroys none of his film's magic. As André Bazin once argued about *The Red Balloon* in *What Is Cinema?* we can "believe in the reality of what is happening while knowing it to be tricked." The audience can achieve that seemingly dissonant position only through the care of a consummate filmmaker who shows "that the basic material of the film is authentic while the film is also truly cinema."

With its long, fluid takes, *Flight of the Red Balloon* certainly seems like a film Bazin would have loved. Though the story follows the everyday troubles of an "ordinary" family, Hou's observant camera shows the dignity of their struggle and in a sense argues that it deserves to be witnessed and recognized. Plus, the film's settings, costumes, and dialogue amount to the authentic material that Bazin valued. The harried Suzanne's apartment is appropriately cluttered—the dining table is covered with papers and various tchotchkes, and walls are lined with books, rolled-up posters, and old VHS tapes. Suzanne's outfits look thrown together, and dark roots peek through her bleached blonde hair. According to the *Village Voice,* the actors were charged with coming up with their own dialogue after Hou sketched the scenes for them; Binoche does most of the talking. As Suzanne, she is by turns distracted, edgy, and passionate—but always natural and always riveting. And though Suzanne may not have enough time to devote to Simon, Hou does not demonize her. In one of the film's most moving scenes, she tries to engage Simon in a conversation as a piano tuner works in their living room. As the tuner adjusts each key, Suzanne gradually becomes more attuned to her son, slowing down enough to listen.

Lamorisse directed his son, Pascal, in *The Red Balloon,* and one must wonder if the story reflected his own parental anxieties about Pascal making his way alone in the world. The balloon may have symbolized his wish, as a parent, to be there for his son, to guide him, to protect him, or to merely keep him company. As J. Hoberman wrote in the *Village Voice,* "*Flight of the Red Balloon* is a movie that encourages the spectator to rummage," and since viewers have time to pore over each frame, they cannot help noticing the various red orbs that appear throughout the landscape: the red reflector on a bicycle in the street, the series of round red decals that appear on the side of a bus, the illuminated red signal on a traffic light, the red bubble-shaped brooch pinned to Suzanne's dress. It is as if Paris is filled with myriad surrogates of that protective red balloon. So in his own subtle way, Hou makes the city seem like a less lonely place as well.

Marisa Carroll

CREDITS

Suzanne: Juliette Binoche
Marc: Hippolyte Girardot
Simon: Simon Iteanu
Song: Fang Song
Louise: Louise Margolin
Anna: Anna Sigalevitch
Origin: France, Taiwan
Language: French
Released: 2008
Production: Francois Margolin, Kristina Larsen; 3H Productions, Margo Films, Les Films du Lendemain; released by IFC First Take
Directed by: Hou Hsiao-Hsien
Written by: Hou Hsiao-Hsien, Francois Margolin
Cinematography by: Mark Lee Ping-Bin
Music by: Constance Lee
Sound: Chu Shih Yi
Editing: Jean-Christophe Hym, Liao Ching Sung
Costumes: Jean-Charline Tomlinson
Production Design: Paul Fayard, Hwarng Wern Ying
MPAA rating: Unrated
Running time: 113 minutes

REVIEWS

Boston Globe Online. April 18, 2008.
Christian Science Monitor Online. April 4, 2008.
Entertainment Weekly Online. April 2, 2008.
Los Angeles Times Online. April 18, 2008.
New York Times Online. April 4, 2008.

Variety Online. April 2, 2008.
Village Voice Online. April 1, 2008.
Wall Street Journal. April 18, 2008, p. W1.
Washington Post. April 18, 2008, p. C6.

TRIVIA

This is the director's first film to be shot outside of Asia.

FLY ME TO THE MOON

Box Office: $13.1 million

The makers of *Fly Me to the Moon* evidently had some good intentions with this animated film, hoping to inspire viewers with a renewed interest in space exploration by crafting a story around the 1969 Apollo 11 moon landing, but unfortunately the movie fails on almost all counts as both an inspiring story or a well-made film. In a year when a superb film like *WALL-E* demonstrates how powerful, artistic, and dramatic an animated feature can be, *Fly Me to the Moon* demonstrates the other end of the spectrum—how bad an animated film can be. Actually, it does not merely demonstrate poor animated filmmaking; it exemplifies flaws that can ruin any film. *Fly Me to the Moon* is an uninteresting, agonizingly slow film that is likely to put both adults and children to sleep. Good intentions do not a good movie make.

The story is about a trio of young flies who hitch a ride on the Apollo 11 and experience an adventure in the process. "Adventure" appears to be the operative word in the film, as the main character, young Nat (voice of Trevor Gagnon), longs to travel somewhere exotic and is sold on the mantra of his Grandpa (voice of Christopher Lloyd): "If it ain't an adventure, it ain't worth doing." So Nat, who happens to live next door to Cape Canaveral, persuades his two friends I.Q. (voice of Philip Bolden) and Scooter (voice of David Gore) to join him as he stows away on the historic flight to the moon. The story follows the flight of the Apollo 11 and its crew (including the three flies) interspersed with scenes back on Earth of Nat's mother (voice of Kelly Ripa) and Grandpa keeping tabs on the flight—the former nervously, with frequent fainting, and the latter proudly, with a touch of regret that he was too old to go along.

There are a couple of villains, too, as apparently villains are required, but these are some of the most forgettable and weakest villains ever devised. The main villain is a Russian fly, Poopchev (voice of Ed Begley Jr.), who somehow has the rank of general and who cannot stand it that a group of American flies are going to be the first flies to the moon. He dispatches a nasty agent named

Yegor (voice of Tim Curry) to sabotage the mission. Strangely, though, Yegor does not appear until late in the story, and when he does, he is fairly easily stopped by Grandpa. Even Poopchev himself only appears in the movie a couple of times, making it painfully obvious he was only included to provide some kind of conflict.

Without exception, the characters are all bland, one-dimensional or two-dimensional characters, many of whom are pale copies of characters that have appeared in numerous other films. From the single-minded (and nice but not interesting) Nat to the mother who faints all the time, from the grandfather who likes to retell the same story over and over to the naïve overweight child (Scooter) who likes to eat all the time, these flies have none of the appeal, vibrancy, or roundness of memorable animated insects like, for example, the ants of *A Bug's Life* (1998). One wonders why the filmmakers thought flies would make interesting characters anyway, and even if it is an animated film, it is difficult to watch the movie and hear Grandpa talking about flying with Amelia Earhart without thinking, "But flies only live at most a couple of months if they are lucky not to get swatted first." Aside from the flat characters, one of the more surprising things about the movie is that the villains are nothing but outdated stereotypes. Even if the setting is in 1969, making villains out of unintelligent Soviets who speak in broken English seems a bit irresponsible.

While the film includes some nicely crafted vistas that convey a sense of realism, most of the animation seems amateurish and almost incomplete or unfinished, betraying its computer-generated origins. Visual movement is slow and uninteresting—for example, in one painfully long sequence, the three young flies spin around in the zero-gravity of the Apollo 11 command module. All they literally do is spin around in basically one spot, and it seems to last so long one might wish it were done in fast-motion. The movie is full of sequences like this, to the extent that one cannot help but wonder why the filmmakers thought this would be interesting or appealing, given all the superior animation that has been produced in recent years.

The story itself moves just as slowly. At almost ninety minutes, the film drags as much as possible. The first section of the film is apparently meant to be character development for Nat and his family, very slowly leading up to his adventure on the space mission, but the characters are so flat that there is almost nothing to develop, and as a result the movie just inches along. One of the most grievous flaws of the story is that the flies do not propel the action—for the most part, they simply participate or stand by and watch as events happen around them. They literally just tag along for the ride. Nat and his friends take action only by sneaking onto the spacecraft and, in one single instance, actually

help the astronauts by fixing a short in the circuitry. Other than that, they are simply there. In that sense, it is hardly an adventure, and the characters experience no growth whatsoever. Likewise, there is no real, genuine conflict propelling the story; the only conflict appears in the very contrived inclusion of the Russian bad guys.

Early on, one of the neighborhood flies makes a comment about acting as if they have eyes in the back of their heads. I.Q. then replies, "But we do have eyes in the back of our heads." Beyond the fact that this is not as amusing as it is intended to be, the odd thing about the comment is that these flies in fact do not have eyes in the back of their heads. They have two eyes and that is all that is visible. This is a perfect example of what is wrong with the film. *Fly Me to the Moon* is a clumsy mess that seems hastily put together without careful attention to story, character, or believability (in the context of the story, even when "suspension of disbelief" is necessary). Even animated films need to provide us with those basic elements of storytelling. This film might as well have been a documentary about the Apollo 11 flight—without all the nonsense about the flies.

David Flanagin

CREDITS

IQ: Philip Daniel Bolden (Voice)
Grandpa: Christopher Lloyd (Voice)
Nat: Trevor Gagnon (Voice)
Nat's Mom: Kelly Ripa (Voice)
Scooter: David Gore (Voice)
Nadia: Nicolette Sheridan (Voice)
Yegor: Tim Curry (Voice)
Himself: Buzz Aldrin (Voice)
Origin: USA
Language: English
Released: 2008
Production: Charlotte Clay Huggins, Caroline Van Iseghem, Gina Gallo, Mimi Maynard; nWave Pictures, Illuminata Pictures; released by Summit Entertainment
Directed by: Ben Stassen
Written by: Domonic Paris
Music by: Ramin Djawadi
Sound: Luc Thomas, Philippe Baudhuin
Art Direction: Jeremie Degruson
MPAA rating: G
Running time: 84 minutes

REVIEWS

Boston Globe Online. August 15, 2008.
Entertainment Weekly Online. August 15, 2008.

Hollywood Reporter Online. August 9, 2008.
Los Angeles Times Online. August 15, 2008.
New York Times Online. August 15, 2008.
San Francisco Chronicle. August 15, 2008, p. E5.
Variety Online. August 8, 2008.
Washington Post. August 15, 2008, p. C5.

FOOL'S GOLD

This February true love takes a dive.
—Movie tagline

Box Office: $70.2 million

About halfway through *Fool's Gold*, it becomes clear that the main dramatic impetus for the film was to see how much of a movie's running time could be filled with a shirtless Matthew McConaughey. Showing more skin than the cast of *10,000 BC* (2008), McConaughey pushes the goodwill occasionally garnered by his lackadaisical surfer dude persona far past the breaking point in *Fool's Gold* and gives one of the more grating and clichéd performances of the year. McConaughey's naked, bongo-playing, borderline stoner public reputation has often been ridiculed, but *Fool's Gold* feels like it was written almost entirely to confirm it, instead of proving that this sometimes interesting actor is capable of anything else. Critics often deride actors for falling back on crutches, playing the same physical tics, speech patterns, and easy character choices again and again, but there are very few examples of that as blatant as *Fool's Gold*, which could just as easily have been called "Matthew McConaughey's Greatest (or Worst) Hits."

To be fair, McConaughey does not deserve all the blame for the complete failure of *Fool's Gold*. Director Andy Tennant does the bare minimum as a director to awkwardly push forward this sometimes unbearable romantic comedy that is neither romantic nor funny. Someone once said that no one ever lost money underestimating the intelligence of the American public, but the shocking laziness of the screenplay and entire production of *Fool's Gold* calls that theory into question. The film feels as if Tennant and his producers determined the bare minimum that needed to be done to get fans of *How to Lose a Guy in 10 Days* (2003) into a theater and refused to go any further. After getting McConaughey shirtless and Hudson in a bikini, the screenwriting appears to have stopped.

The current market's pale excuse for a popular romantic comedy couple costar in *Fool's Gold* as a pair of about-to-divorce treasure hunters named Tess and Ben "Finn" Finnegan. Trying to crib from the *Romancing the Stone* (1984) playbook is not a bad idea for a modern romantic comedy, but the actual treasure hunt at the center of *Fool's Gold* is so poorly conceived as to be both overly complex and incredibly forgettable at the same time. It has something to do with a massive shipwreck that Finn is still convinced that he can find, even if Tess has given up on him. Finn is one of those only-in-the-movies characters who always turn up at the most inopportune times and, after his boat burns and sinks, he works his way onto a vessel chartered by the man Tess works for, a millionaire named Nigel Honeycutt (Donald Sutherland). Tess and Finn have long been looking for the notorious shipwreck of the Queens Dowry, which featured dozens of treasure chests lost at sea in the 18th century, and they convince Nigel to help them out. Tagging along is the tycoon's spoiled daughter Gemma (Alexis Dziena) and Finn's treasure-hunting partner Alfonz (a very annoying Ewen Bremner). Our hero and heroine start to reunite as they get closer and closer to the fortune—if there is anything that Hollywood has taught us, it is that wealth can solve all marital problems.

Any good treasure hunt needs a villain or two, and here is where writers John Claflin, Daniel Zelman, and Andy Tennant really drop the ball. Hot on the heels of the Finnegans are fellow treasure-hunter Moe Fitch (Ray Winstone) and notorious criminal Bigg Bunny (Kevin Hart) and his thugs (including Malcolm-Jamal Warner). Even with more than one bad guy, *Fool's Gold* features no dramatic tension at all. Even after the poor former Huxtable gets shot in the foot, Bigg Bunny adds nothing to the action, almost as if his character was an afterthought. He is representative of the biggest problem with *Fool's Gold*—anyone who has ever seen a mediocre romantic comedy could close their eyes and imagine the entire film. That may have been how it was conceived. There are literally no surprises and nothing that will stand out after viewing it. To call it forgettable would be incorrect because that implies a viewer would have anything to forget. There is nothing there.

The only thing that saves *Fool's Gold* from falling into the category of the worst romantic comedies of the last few years like *License to Wed* (2007) or *Over Her Dead Body* (2008) is the copious charms of Kate Hudson. The once Oscar®-nominated actress can still hold the screen better than most actresses of her generation and she is the only one who survives this treasure hunt completely unscathed. *Fool's Gold* is merely proof that, like a lot of romantic comedy heroines stuck with the slacker boyfriend, she deserves better.

Brian Tallerico

CREDITS

Ben "Finn" Finnegan: Matthew McConaughey
Tess: Kate Hudson

Nigel Honeycutt: Donald Sutherland
Gemma Honeycutt: Alexis Dziena
Alfonz: Ewen Bremner
Moe Fitch: Ray Winstone
Bigg Bunny: Kevin Hart
Cordell: Malcolm-Jamal Warner
Curtis: Brian Hooks
Cyrus: David Roberts
Origin: USA
Language: English
Released: 2008
Production: Donald De Line, Bernie Goldmann, Jon Klane; released by Warner Bros.
Directed by: Andy Tennant
Written by: Andy Tennant, John Claflin, Daniel Zelman
Cinematography by: Don Burgess
Music by: George Fenton
Sound: Paul Brincat
Music Supervisor: Julianne Jordan
Editing: Troy Takaki, Tracey Wadmore-Smith
Art Direction: Raymond Chan
Costumes: Ngila Dickson
Production Design: Charles Wood
MPAA rating: PG-13
Running time: 112 minutes

REVIEWS

Boston Globe Online. February 8, 2008.
Entertainment Weekly Online. February 6, 2008.
Hollywood Reporter Online. February 4, 2008.
Los Angeles Times Online. February 8, 2008.
New York Times Online. February 8, 2008.
San Francisco Chronicle. February 8, 2008, p. E7.
Variety Online. February 3, 2008.
Washington Post. February 8, 2008, p. C1.

QUOTES

Tess Finnegan: "Your uselessness is epic."

TRIVIA

Production of the film was delayed due to a deadly form of jellyfish that prevented actors Matthew McConaughey and Kate Hudson from going into the water.

AWARDS

Nomination:

Golden Raspberries 2008: Worst Actress (Hudson).

THE FORBIDDEN KINGDOM

The path is unsafe. The place is unknown. The journey is unbelievable.
—Movie tagline

Box Office: $52 million

Martial arts fans have waited for years to see the teaming of Jackie Chan and Jet Li on the big screen but the inevitable union in Rob Minkoff's *The Forbidden Kingdom* brings mixed results at best. One of many problems with *The Forbidden Kingdom* arises from a nagging sensation that the pairing of Chan and Li, two of the best martial arts actors of all time, is coming at least a decade later than it should have. In particular, Chan looks too long in the tooth for some of the action and the film fails to play to this once-charismatic actor's strengths. Li is still a versatile physical presence but if *Forbidden Kingdom* had been made in the '90s, the film would have had significantly more power. But that is far from the only problem with *Kingdom,* a film that constantly misses the mark, failing to satisfy either fans of the genre or the teenage boy audience at which it is so clearly aimed. Miscast, slow, and generally misguided, *Forbidden Kingdom* was a project many years in the making that probably never should have seen its way to completion.

The horribly awkward and miscast Michael Angarano plays the lead in *Forbidden Kingdom,* a South Boston teenager named Jason Tripitikas, a young man who collects rare kung fu movies and dreams of a characters like "the Monkey King" (Jet Li). Jason is a regular at a pawnshop owned and operated by the kindly Hop (Jackie Chan). At the store, Jason stumbles across a golden staff in the back corner of the shop and is told by Hop that it needs to be delivered to its rightful owner. On his way home, the gawky boy runs afoul of the local bully named Lupo (Morgan Benoit) who want to rob Hop and need Jason's help to do so. Hop fights back and tries to defend his store with the staff itself but he ends up getting shot by the bully. Wounded, the elderly storeowner tells our young hero that he must deliver the staff himself. As he flees the scene, Jason runs into Lupo again, a scuffle ensues, and he falls from a great height. When he wakes up, he finds himself in another land.

The alternate universe that Jason travels to with his staff is kind of like ancient China viewed through the prism of kung fu movies and a child's imagination of a magical world. Almost immediately, Jason is attacked and the staff is nearly stolen, but he is rescued by the drunken fighter Lu Yan (Jackie Chan). Lu Yan tells Jason of the story of the Monkey King (Jet Li), a rapscallion who found himself on the bad side of the nefarious Jade Warlord (Collin Chou). It turns out that the staff belonged to the King, who was tricked by the Warlord and cast it into the other world just before being turned into stone. There was a prophecy that a "Seeker" would return the staff and free the Monkey King from his imprisonment. Soon, Lu Yan and Jason are rescued from another wave of attackers by the Golden Sparrow (Yifei

Liu), a young woman who saw her family murdered by the Jade Warlord and who seeks revenge.

Meanwhile, the Jade Warlord finds some assistance in his quest for evil from the white-haired witch Ni Chang (Bingbing Li), a fighter who can use her long locks in battle. She promises to get the staff in return for immortality. Rounding out the foursome that seeks to protect the staff is the Silent Monk (Jet Li), a man who first tries to take the magical object with force but soon learns that Jason is the "Seeker" who has been prophesized.

The Forbidden Kingdom has echoes of dozens of movies that came before it, including everything from *Crouching Tiger, Hidden Dragon* (2000) to *The Never-ending Story* (1984), but it never develops an intriguing rhythm of its own. Angarano, so good in *Snow Angels* (2007), is horrendously miscast here, looking more lost than heroic, and the screenplay by John Fusco just piles myth upon legend upon prophecy without ever giving the audience anything relatable with which to hold on. *Forbidden Kingdom* only comes alive in the fight scenes, particularly a good central one between Li and Chan, but even that is marred by the passing of time and the fact that Chan has never been that strong at wire work. (His appeal was always largely based on his genuine stunt work, not harnesses and wires.) The fight choreography, designed by the legendary Yuen Woo-Ping, is all impressively rendered, but somewhat cold, as is the cinematography by the always-good Peter Pau (*Crouching Tiger, Hidden Dragon*). *Forbidden Kingdom* is never poorly visualized or hard to look at, but Minkoff, Li, and Chan feel like they are going through the motions, giving audiences just enough to keep fans of the genre happy but not enough to make what could have been a martial arts classic.

Brian Tallerico

CREDITS

Jason: Michael Angarano
Old Hop/Lu Yan: Jackie Chan
Monkey King/The Silent Monk: Jet Li
Jade Warlord: Collin Chou
Ni Chang: Bingbing Li
Golden Sparrow: Yifei Liu
Lupo: Morgan Benoit
Origin: USA
Language: English
Released: 2008
Production: Casey Silver; Relativity Media, Huayi Brothers Media Group, Weinstein Co.; released by Lionsgate
Directed by: Rob Minkoff

Written by: John Fusco
Cinematography by: Peter Pau
Music by: David Buckley
Sound: David Wyman
Music Supervisor: Adam Smalley
Editing: Eric Strand
Art Direction: Eric Lam
Costumes: Shirley Chan
Production Design: Bill Brzeski
MPAA rating: PG-13
Running time: 105 minutes

REVIEWS

Boston Globe Online. April 18, 2008.
Chicago Sun-Times Online. April 18, 2008.
Entertainment Weekly Online. April 16, 2008.
Hollywood Reporter Online. April 14, 2008.
Los Angeles Times Online. April 18, 2008.
New York Times Online. April 18, 2008.
San Francisco Chronicle. April 18, 2008, p. E5.
Variety Online. April 10, 2008.
Washington Post Online. April 18, 2008.

QUOTES

Jason Tripitikas: " He needs wine. It's his elixir."
Medicine Monk: " We will send a walking monk."
Lu Yan: " Don't you have a running monk?"

TRIVIA

This movie marks the very first collaboration between martial arts masters Jet Li and Jackie Chan.

FORGETTING SARAH MARSHALL

The ultimate romantic disaster movie.
—Movie tagline

Box Office: $63.1 million

A preview of Peter Bretter's adolescence (the main character of *Forgetting Sarah Marshall*) could best be exemplified in NBC's 1999 comedy series, *Freaks and Geeks*. Set in 1980, one of the "freaks" in the cast was a lost and often dispirited stoner-slacker. Nick Andopolis was prone to both dejection and self-deprecating behavior. His charm was often overshadowed by his passionate intensity that smothered the show's lead, Lindsay (Linda Cardellini) who began a budding romance with Nick more out of solace than genuine magnetism. Nick however, prevails. When his father sells his coveted drum set and Lindsay eventually dumps him, he finds a new love interest and finds Disco Night once a week with her at a bowling alley in suburban Detroit, Michigan, where the series took place. Sadly, good television staging teen angst rarely sells beyond one season, as was also seen in ABC's short-lived *My So-Called Life.*

Actor Jason Segel, who played both Nick and Peter respectively, wrote this new installment in the relatively new genre of romantic comedy for men. Produced by Judd Apatow, *Forgetting Sarah Marshall* embraces the format advanced by Apatow in NBC's aforementioned *Freaks and Geeks*, in addition to his show on the Fox network, *Undeclared*. Recent big screen projects include: *The Forty-Year-Old Virgin* (2005), *Superbad,* and *Knocked up* (the latter box office hits released in 2007).

Peter seems to have it all. He is a talented musician who composes foreboding musical notes to a CSI-inspired television show, *Crime Scene: Scene of the Crime.* He is living with the show's female lead, Sarah Marshall (Kristen Bell), and life has an idyllic quality as he dallies around their apartment in his sweatpants while shoveling mouthfuls of sugar-loaded cold cereal from a bowl resembling a moat. Peter is treading in place, living in a dreamlike complacency. He occasionally dabbles in a former dream of writing and composing a puppet-performed rock musical based on *Dracula*. It is this contentment and ebbing aspiration that estranges Sarah and she breaks up with him as he allows his bath towel to drop in the film's humorous clip of a nude Segel that adds to the cinematic trend showing full frontal male nudity. In this case, it is used to represent Peter's vulnerability.

Sarah has left Peter for the impish British rock star du jour, Aldous Snow (Russell Brand). Aldous is seemingly everything Peter is not. He is wealthy, articulate, oversexed and celebrated; a self-made rocker the world fawns over. Devastated, Peter wallows in abject melancholia and hits L.A.'s singles bar scene where he embarks upon a reckless chain of loveless hookups. One anonymous companion-for-a-night continuously murmurs "Hi!" during several linked shots taking them from the night club to the bedroom. Peter's success in the arena of casual sex shows an irony: despite being pathetically self-absorbed, as a successful professional in the entertainment industry, he has already accomplished what other men on a lower playing field would envy. Peter, in the midst of a quarter-life meltdown, decides to take a vacation to a Hawaiian resort he remembers Sarah raving about. To his horror, she is renting a room adjacent to his.

In this addition to the Apatow universe, the characters are not what they initially present. Snow comes across as a shady, overbearing English louche; full

of pomposity, he regards the world as a drab afterthought as he smugly glides around the resort in flip flops and leather pants. But he becomes much more than he seems when he shows sensitivity to Peter. In another overdone scene Snow attempts to "educate" another vacationer, Darald (Jack McBrayer) on the intricacies of pleasing a woman. Darald is a clueless religious caricature who is completely unprepared for honeymoon pleasures. Sarah herself is not as one-dimensional as originally sketched. When she is unceremoniously dumped by Snow and simultaneously receives the news that her show has been canceled, she attempts to reconnect with Peter. Sarah, in a poignant moment, describes to Peter that he became a clingy, pathetic mopey-eyed puppy who gave up his musical ambitions once their relationship deepened. She missed the guy who was still hungry.

Peter's brief "relapse" with Sarah seems to end his budding romance with the resort's cute customer service employee, Rachel (Mila Kunis). Having evolved, Peter returns to the L.A. basin, now without a job, and cultivates his pre-Sarah dream with the completion of his vampiric puppet musical, *A Taste for Love*. He is reunited with Rachel while the audience is exposed once again to full-frontal Segel, providing a humorous bookend to a hilarious romantic comedy.

A.O. Scott of the *New York Times* provides a penetrating observation regarding a staple component of this genre: "...the schlub-hottie pairings that have become ubiquitous on screen lately also reinforce a dreary double standard. Guys are permitted to be flabby, lazy emotional wrecks, but as long as they crack jokes, some action will come their way. Girls, ideally, should have a sense of humor—mainly so they can laugh at those jokes—but for the most part they should look good in a bikini and like sex (though not too much and not anything too weird). Maybe someday, though probably not under Mr. Apatow's aegis, a relatively ordinary-looking woman will have a sex comedy of her own."

David Metz Roberts

CREDITS

Peter Bretter: Jason Segel
Sarah Marshall: Kristen Bell
Rachel Jansen: Mila Kunis
Brian Bretter: Bill Hader
Aldous Snow: Russell Brand
Matthew: Jonah Hill
Chuck, the surfing instructor: Paul Rudd
Det. Hunter Rush: William Baldwin
Animal Instincts detective: Jason Bateman
Wyoma: Maria Thayer
Dr. Rosenbaum: Steve Landesberg
Darald: Jack McBrayer

Liz Bretter: Liz Cackowski
Hotel manager: Gedde Watanabe
Origin: USA
Language: English
Released: 2008
Production: Judd Apatow, Shauna Robertson; released by Universal
Directed by: Nicholas Stoller
Written by: Jason Segel
Cinematography by: Russ T. Alsobrook
Music by: Lyle Workman
Sound: Richard Van Dyke
Music Supervisor: Jonathan Karp
Editing: William Kerr
Costumes: Leesa Evans
Production Design: Jackson De Govia
MPAA rating: R
Running time: 112 minutes

REVIEWS

Boston Globe Online. April 18, 2008.
Chicago Sun-Times Online. April 18, 2008.
Entertainment Weekly Online. April 16, 2008.
Hollywood Reporter Online. March 12, 2008.
Los Angeles Times Online. April 18, 2008.
New York Times Online. April 18, 2008.
New Yorker Online. April 21, 2008.
San Francisco Chronicle. April 18, 2008, p. E1.
Variety Online. March 11, 2008.
Wall Street Journal. April 18. 2008, p. W1.
Washington Post. April 18, 2008, p. C1.

QUOTES

Surfing Instructor: "If you get bitten by a shark, you're not just gonna give up surfing, are you?"
Peter Bretter: "Yeah, probably."

TRIVIA

Screenwriter and star Jason Segel told *New York Times* interviewer Dave Itzkoff that both the naked breakup and Dracula puppet musical scenes were drawn from his real life experiences. In the article, Segel admitted that he really did once have a girlfriend who broke up with him while he was completely naked (although rather than being devastated during it, he thought to himself, "This is hilarious. I cannot wait for her to leave so I can write this down.") And before he was a successful actor, Segel tried to write a musical adaptation of *Dracula* for puppets.

FOUR CHRISTMASES

His father, her mother, his mother and her father all in one day.
—Movie tagline

Box Office: $120.1 million

Seth Gordon's *Four Christmases* continues the head-scratching and intolerable pattern of at least one annual misanthropic holiday movie from a Hollywood machine that mistakenly thinks obnoxious, Scrooge-like characters are endearing or humorous. They are not. Shockingly unfunny and insulting to what its creators clearly consider the "flyover states," *Four Christmases* is a brutally bad movie, one of the worst holiday flicks that anyone has ever made and a career-low for many of the participants.

Orlando "Brad" McVie (Vince Vaughn) and girlfriend Kate (Reese Witherspoon) lie to their families every Christmas season and take a warm-weather vacation instead of spending times with their loved ones. One year, Kate and Brad get stuck at the San Francisco airport after bad weather cancels every outbound flight and find themselves suddenly committing to visiting all four of their crazy families in one day. Bouncing from Brad's father (Robert Duvall) to Kate's mother (Mary Steenburgen) to Brad's mother (Sissy Spacek) to Kate's father (Jon Voight), the couple is forced to celebrate four Christmases. Kristin Chenoweth, Tim McGraw, and Jon Favreau get sucked in to play small roles, and Seth Gordon makes his narrative directorial debut following the excellent *The King of Kong: A Fistful of Quarters* (2007), after reportedly being handpicked by Vaughn himself. What Gordon ever did to Vaughn to deserve such an awful job is still unclear.

By now, the once-promising Vince Vaughn shtick has become as tired as the recent career decisions by Eddie Murphy or the easily impersonated post-Oscar® work of Robin Williams. It is tired, old, and grating to see Vaughn do the same routine over and over again and mind-boggling that he did not take the criticisms of *Fred Claus* (2007) to heart. Very few actors can lay claim to the worst holiday movie of the year two years in a row. Not only could Vaughn do this material in his sleep, it looks like he was directed to do so by Gordon. Reese Witherspoon fares a little better and it is slightly interesting to see one of America's movie sweethearts play such an unlikable character, but the Oscar® winner deserved better than this horrendous script.

Filmmakers continue to misunderstand the natural human reaction of getting frustrated with their ridiculous families around the holidays by turning it into straight-up misanthropy. Critically reviled films like *Surviving Christmas* (2004), *Christmas with the Kranks* (2004), *Fred Claus* (2007), and, now, *Four Christmases* litter the marketplace and make a critic's job that much harder around the holidays. With every passing year, even a relatively average movie like *National Lampoon's Christmas Vacation* (1989) looks like a classic.

What the modern Christmas movie misses is that the love for its characters cannot be faked. The script for *Four Christmases* by Matt Allen, Caleb Wilson, Scott Moore, and Jon Lucas is incredibly disingenuous in the way it points and laughs at the purportedly average people of this country and then manipulatively tries to pull heartstrings in the final act. The writer's strike reportedly made rewrites during production impossible. It shows.

Four Christmases is a cavalcade of embarrassing and insulting behavior. Everyone is loudly screaming, fighting, or excreting bodily fluids through the entire film. This is no one's family. There is nothing to identify with. It is a fake Hollywood idea of what families are like around the holidays and people should be offended that this is what the writers think of you—that the average holiday is nothing but constant arguing, top-of-the-lungs yelling, streaking, breast-feeding jokes, puking babies, name-calling, and spray cheese.

Critics were appropriately vicious to *Four Christmases* when it was in theaters. *The Hollywood Reporter* called it "one of the most joyless Christmas movies ever." *Variety* noted the film's misanthropy and said that it was an "occasionally amusing but thoroughly cheerless holiday attraction that is in no way a family film."

Four Christmases is never funny, but always insulting. It is the kind of juvenile, stupid humor where someone falling of the roof is inevitable and a puking baby is almost a necessity. A kid puts a used pregnancy test in her mouth. What anyone possibly thought was funny about that is beyond explanation. There is no point in even discussing the oral sex jokes with the elderly. Perhaps worst of all, *Four Christmases* is tragically paced. Running only eighty minutes, *Four Christmases* feels at least double its running time. It may be the one thing that the filmmakers got right about the average holiday experience—that the season usually feels longer than most other times of the year.

Brian Tallerico

CREDITS

Kate: Reese Witherspoon
Brad: Vince Vaughn
Howard: Robert Duvall
Courtney: Kristin Chenoweth
Denver: Jon Favreau
Pastor Phil: Dwight Yoakam
Dallas: Tim McGraw
Paula: Sissy Spacek
Creighton: Jon Voight

Marilyn: Mary Steenburgen
Susan: Katy Mixon
Aunt Donna: Colleen Camp
Origin: USA
Language: English
Released: 2008
Production: Roger Birnbaum, Gary Barber, Jonathan Glickman; New Line Cinema, Spyglass Entertainment, Wild West Picture Show, Type A Films; released by Warner Bros.
Directed by: Seth Gordon
Written by: Jon Lucas, Scott Moore, Matt R. Allen, Caleb Wilson
Cinematography by: Jeffrey L. Kimball
Music by: Alex Wurman
Sound: Jeff Wexler
Music Supervisor: Bob Bowen
Editing: Mark Helfrich, Melissa Kent
Art Direction: Michael Atwell, Oana Bogdan
Costumes: Sophie de Rakoff Carbonell
Production Design: Shepherd Frankel
MPAA rating: PG-13
Running time: 88 minutes

REVIEWS

Boston Globe Online. November 26, 2008.
Chicago Sun-Times Online. November 25, 2008.
Entertainment Weekly Online. November 25, 2008.
Hollywood Reporter Online. November 22, 2008.
Los Angeles Times Online. November 26, 2008.
New York Times Online. November 26, 2008.
San Francisco Chronicle. November 26, 2008, p. E1.
Variety Online. November 23, 2008.
Washington Post. November 26, 2008, p. C10.

QUOTES

Howard: "Boys, I don't want to speak ill of your mother on Christmas, but she's nothing but a common street whore."

TRIVIA

All four actors portraying the parents are Oscar® winners for acting. Robert Duvall (*Tender Mercies* (1983)), Sissy Spacek (*Coal Miner's Daughter* (1980)), Jon Voight (*Coming Home* (1978)), and Mary Steenburgen (*Melvin and Howard* (1980)).

Cast includes two Country-Western singers (Dwight Yoakam and Tim McGraw) and three people who have won Oscars® for playing Country-Western singers (Reese Witherspoon in *Walk the Line* (2005), Robert Duvall in

Tender Mercies (1983) and Sissy Spacek in *Coal Miner's Daughter* (1980)).

4 MONTHS, 3 WEEKS AND 2 DAYS

(4 luni, 3 saptâmani si 2 zile)

How far would you go for a friend?
—Movie tagline

Box Office: $1.1 million

It is 1987 in Romania, still under the rule of Nicolai Ceaucescu. American critics assumed the setting was Bucharest, but interior evidence suggests another city, in Moldavia, not Wallachia. Because Gabita (Laura Vasiliu), a student apparently at the Cuza University in the Moldavian city of Iasi (where director Cristian Mungiu grew up, with his family, on the Strada Sararie—the Salt Road—and where much of the film seemed to be located) is several months pregnant (the title identifies the pregnancy's term), she and her roommate Otilia (Anamaria Marinca) have arranged to meet an abortionist (Vlad Ivanov), Mr. Bebe (named with hideous irony). This decision is not to be taken lightly. Beyond the obvious emotional trauma of the procedure, abortion is illegal, and if discovered by the authorities, prison sentences would be virtually automatic, though the penalty could be even worse, since, as Mr. Bebe explains, after the fourth month the crime is not abortion, but murder. In point of fact, both abortions and birth control were banned in Ceaucescu's Romania from 1966 to 1989, during which time over a half million women died as a result of illegal abortions. So, when the abortionist, Bebe, arrives on the scene, the audience is given a series of warnings about the illegality as well as the pain, bleeding, and other complications Gabita may have to face. "Don't move," Bebe keeps saying, "as long as the probe is inside you. There may be a lot of bleeding...and when it begins to come out, go to the toilet." And he advises Otilia not to dispose of the fetus in the immediate vicinity, but to take it to a high-rise apartment building and drop it down a rubbish chute. There is a great deal of bargaining about money. Since Gabita has been pregnant at least a month more than she had initially indicated (the first of many lies we realize she has been telling everyone), the price has gone up. There is not enough money. But then Bebe looks at Otilia meaningfully. So, while Gabita retires discreetly to the bathroom, Otilia remains in the room with Bebe...and after that "business" is done, Otilia comes into the bathroom while Gabita goes back to the bed.

At length, the procedure begins. Gabita lies prone while Bebe inserts a rubber tubing device (from our side view, we do not see anything more graphic). Time passes while she lies back motionless, Bebe leaves, and Otilia sits quietly. She and Gabita exchange only a few words, but they say a lot about Gabita's confusion, her lies, her disorientation. But now it is time for Otilia to leave briefly to attend her boyfriend's mother's birthday dinner. The dinner party is nightmarishly absurd. Otilia sits there, mute, while the drinks and the banal conversation flow ceaselessly around her, but she is only marking time. After a brief conversation with Adi (Alexandru Potocean), her selfish, inconsiderate boyfriend, during which time she confesses to her role in the abortion and demands to know what he would do if she were to get pregnant; she then places a call back to Gabita, but there is no answer. In a panic, she flees the apartment and rushes through the dingy night streets back to Gabita and the hotel room where the illegal procedure was performed.

Gabita says the fetus has been delivered and is in the bathroom. Otilia gathers up the sodden lump (after leaving it on display for what seem several minutes on the floor for the camera), wraps it up, and after promising Gabita she will bury it, she leaves the apartment building. After another odyssey through the darkened streets, she enters a darkened building (at that time all buildings in Romania were dark at night, and even after 1989 people needed flashlights to negotiate unlighted halls in apartment buildings), climbs several flights of stairs, and tosses the bundle into the trash chute. By the time Otilia returns back to Gabita's hotel room, her friend has gone downstairs and, to Otilia's astonishment, is preparing to down a meal. "Let's never talk of this again," demands Otilia. They sit in a long silence. Otilia turns toward the camera. After the camera pauses significantly to capture the effect, it fades to black. Although Gabita needs the abortion, the film really belongs to Otilia. She is indomitable, and, in the instance of succumbing to the rape by Bebe, self-sacrificing, too.

Interviewed by "All Things Considered" in America on National Public Radio, writer-director Cristian Mungiu explained that this "period film" was based on the experience of someone he had known. Mungiu was introduced to filmmaking by the French director Bernard Tavernier, who shot a film in Romania in 1995 and allowed Mungiu to work with him. Mungiu's notion of a "period film" he got from Tavernier, signifying a film that "looks like yesterday but feels like today."

Cristian Mungiu explained to Terry Gross, for her National Public Radio program "Fresh Air," his motive for shooting the film in a series of long takes, captured by cinematographer Oleg Mutu: "Something about the long take signals to the viewers that what they see is true." Hence, "No editing. No tricks. Nothing to hide. A close-up signals [that] you as a filmmaker are manipulating the viewer's attention." This explains the long shot of the aborted fetus on the floor of the hotel room before Otilia disposes of it; it also explains the long shot of Otilia and Gabita sitting silently at dinner in the hotel at the end. Though there may be much to explain, the purposeful silence is beyond words. There is also no music, except for an upbeat duet over the credits. The lyrics suggest that this woman will think back over what she has seen as the lyrics reflect back to what was seen. The final shot signals that it is up to the viewer to form an opinion. The film shows what an abortion is and forces viewers to draw their own moral conclusions.

Romanians in the city where the action was filmed who knew the director and his family found the film certainly effective and authentic, but nonetheless very difficult to watch, for it reminded them of the way things were under Communism, and among educated Romanians, there was very little nostalgia for Communism. Arranging the hotel for the abortion is beyond Gabita's competence. Mr. Bebe has made some very specific demands about which hotel would be "safe," preferring the Hotel Moldva, though Otilia is seen negotiating at what looks very like the registration desk of the Hotel Unirii on the Piata Unirii (Union Plaza) in Iasi, even though many American reviewers assumed the action was set in Bucharest.

They also assumed the film was about abortion, though Cristian Mungiu told Terry Gross that the film was in fact about decision making, freedom, and responsibility more than about abortion as such. Mungiu also wanted to create an atmosphere, both actual and spiritual, suggesting the lack of enthusiasm people had for living during the Ceausescu regime: "I wanted to tell the story from the perspective of somebody living then," Mungiu said. Color was desaturated in an attempt to render that atmosphere. "There is no sun in this film," Mungiu explained: "We had no light outside after dark. You feel the fear that this girl [Otilia] experiences."

The San Francisco Chronicle reviewer thought this was "the best foreign film to play in the Bay Area since *After the Wedding*," and wondered why "for some reason it wasn't nominated for best foreign film at this year's Oscars®." It was judged to be "suspenseful, eerie, nerve-jangling and innovatively executed," and, indeed, the director takes his time, giving the audience time to think about the story and characters they are witnessing. Although perhaps the most grim film of the year, Mungiu's picture provided *Newsweek* film critic David Ansen with further evidence "that the Academy's system for

selecting foreign films is a long-standing joke." It was not nominated, even though it had won the Palme d'Or at the Cannes Film Festival and the European Film Award, and even though "it was voted best foreign film by both the National Society of Film Critics and the Los Angeles Film Critics Association." Joe Morgenstern of the *Wall Street Journal* seconded this opinion: "Last week an Oscar® committee disgraced itself, and once again discredited the foreign-film selection process, by eliminating this Romanian entry from the short list for an Academy Award®." In filming this grimly unsentimental abortion story, the director took a decidedly uncommercial approach. The ten-minute takes are intended to allow the emotions of the actors to intensify, which is generally the case. No doubt the film was too experimental and too daring for the Motion Picture Academy. Or perhaps the film was simply too intelligent for the Academy, which also declined to nominate the German-Turkish production *The Edge of Heaven*. Both pictures were shamefully neglected, and both represented the year's best work.

James M. Welsh

CREDITS

Gabita: Laura Vasiliu
Otilia: Anamaria Marinca
Adi: Alex Potocean
Mr. Bebe: Vlad Ivanov
Origin: Romania
Language: English
Released: 2007
Production: Oleg Mutu, Cristian Mungiu; Mobra Films, Saga Films; released by IFC First Take
Directed by: Cristian Mungiu
Written by: Cristian Mungiu
Cinematography by: Oleg Mutu
Sound: Titi Fleancu
Editing: Dana Bunescu
Costumes: Dana Istrate
Production Design: Mihaela Poenaru
MPAA rating: Unrated
Running time: 113 minutes

REVIEWS

Boston Globe Online. February 1, 2008.
Chicago Sun-Times Online. February 7, 2008.
Entertainment Weekly Online. January 25, 2008.
Guardian Online. January 11, 2008.
Los Angeles Times Online. December 21, 2007.
New York Times Online. December 25, 2007.
Observer Online. January 13, 2008.

Rolling Stone Online. January 23, 2008.

San Francisco Chronicle. February 1, 2008, p. E1.

Variety Online. June 6, 2007.

Village Voice Online. January 22, 2008.

Wall Street Journal. January 25, 2008, p. W1.

TRIVIA

Originally titled "Tales from the Golden Age" and envisioned as a satire.

AWARDS

Nomination:

Golden Globes 2008: Best Foreign Language Film.

FROST/NIXON

400 million people were waiting for the truth.
—Movie tagline

Box Office: $18.4 million

Richard M. Nixon is arguably the most fascinating American political figure of the twentieth century. How could a man so ordinary, so uncomfortable in public, become a United States senator, the vice president of the United States, and, after losing presidential and gubernatorial (California) elections, resurrect himself and win two presidential elections? Some might also ask how, after failing to win the war in Vietnam and resigning from office because of the Watergate scandal, could he go on living with himself? It is the latter to which *Frost/Nixon,* to a degree, devotes itself.

Ron Howard's film, adapted by Peter Morgan from his 2006 play, alternates between Nixon (Frank Langella), following his 1974 resignation, and British television personality David Frost (Michael Sheen), whose fortunes are also in decline. Frost has lost his daily American talk show and has to commute between England and Australia for his weekly programs, one of which he also loses in the course of the film. Desperate to revive his sagging career, Frost decides to entice Nixon into a series of interviews covering a variety of topics, including Vietnam and Watergate. At the urging of his agent, the legendary Irving "Swifty" Lazar (Toby Jones), the former president agrees to the interviews for $600,000. Frost is considered a lightweight posing no threat to Nixon, who also sees the interviews as the first step toward rehabilitating his reputation.

Most of *Frost/Nixon* is devoted not to the interviews themselves but to the negotiations surrounding them, especially Frost's preparations. Until the Watergate segment, however, Frost does not do much preparation,

leaving that to his British producer, John Birt (Matthew Macfadyen); an American television journalist, Bob Zelnick (Oliver Platt); and an American historian, James Reston Jr. (Sam Rockwell), son of a famous *New York Times* journalist. Birt, a close friend of Frost, wants the interviews to go smoothly. Zelnick wants them to have some journalistic integrity. The combative Reston, highly dubious about Frost's skills as an interviewer, wants to nail Nixon for his Vietnam and Watergate sins.

As the film progresses, the three become increasingly peeved at Frost's inability to live up to their expectations. During the early interviews, Frost repeatedly flubs chances to gain an advantage over the comparatively wily politician. After a rare moment of self-reflection, Frost decides he can get Nixon to admit some culpability about the Watergate cover-up and enlists Reston's help in making sure he is finally prepared. Because the major television networks rejected Frost's project, claiming to be appalled at his paying for Nixon's cooperation, the talk-show host had to sell the project to advertisers and television stations himself. With twenty-eight hours of interviews distilled into four ninety-minute segments, the 1977 programs drew forty-five million viewers, a record for the time.

Frost/Nixon takes several liberties with history, with Morgan inventing a late-night telephone conversation between Frost and an intoxicated, maudlin Nixon. The historical accuracy of the film has been criticized by some, including veteran journal Elizabeth Drew, author of two Watergate books, who calls it fundamentally dishonest, primarily because the admission of the film's Nixon about Watergate is more explicit than what the former president actually said. Morgan can be defended for following the tradition of historical playwrights from William Shakespeare forward by distorting the truth for dramatic effect. *Frost/Nixon* is less a docudrama than a character study and an examination of how the media both capture and manipulate history.

All the President's Men (1976), still the best Watergate film, is less about politics and history than the journalistic process, and *Frost/Nixon* is primarily about the thin line between television as a medium for recording history and as a means of entertainment. Frost's staff regrets his image of himself as an entertainer, who began his career as a comedian, yet his sense of showmanship is what finally saves him during his battle with Nixon. Howard begins the film with a montage of television news clips about Watergate, completely ignoring that newspaper reporters did most of the significant work in uncovering the scandal, because of the perception that anything televised has greater immediacy than its print counterpart, regardless of whether the latter has more depth and validity.

Just as Frost uses the Nixon interviews to salvage his career, so does Howard with *Frost/Nixon*. After winning an Academy Award® for *A Beautiful Mind* (2001), the director stumbled with *The Missing* (2003), *Cinderella Man* (2005), and, especially, the universally reviled *The Da Vinci Code* (2006). Howard resembles Frost in being dismissed by many as a lightweight, a filmmaker whose main goal is to make material palatable for a mass audience, thereby robbing his films of any individuality or style. As someone who grew up on television, acting on *The Andy Griffith Show* (1960–1968) and *Happy Days* (1974–1984), Howard seems made for a look at how television works. His work on *Frost/Nixon* also seems more focused, more self-assured than his earlier films. Giving it a documentary feel, much like the best films of Costa-Gavras, Howard paces the film expertly, carefully building up to the final interview, and for once he knows how to use the camera, alternating between close-ups, two shots, and group shots, even dramatically employing a handheld camera at one point to emphasize Frost's desperation.

Morgan's screenplay, which resembles the interplay between British Prime Minister Tony Blair and Elizabeth II in his *The Queen* (2006), also improves upon his entertaining but somewhat glib play. More than just opening up the play with shorter scenes and exterior locations, this *Frost/Nixon* probes deeper into the characters, with supporting figures who verge on caricature in the play becoming more vivid. While the play is reasonably fast paced, the film stops frequently for reflection, watching the characters agonize over their failings. One of the most effective moments comes when Frost becomes distraught at disappointing his colleagues and is unable to escape their belittling gazes, followed soon thereafter with Nixon experiencing similar turmoil. Howard knows when to use close-ups for dramatic effect in such scenes and when to let such shots linger to force the audience to identify with the characters' uncertainty.

Best known for his incisive portrayals of Blair in *The Queen* and the earlier, much better television film *The Deal* (2003), Sheen has the difficult task of portraying a man who thinks too little. In addition to capturing Frost's mannered way of speaking and awkward body language while on air, Sheen ably conveys the man's struggle off camera to be something better.

No interpretation of Nixon can avoid the man's neuroses and self-caricature, as demonstrated by Philip Baker Hall in Robert Altman's *Secret Honor* (1984) and Anthony Hopkins in Oliver Stone's *Nixon* (1995). Like those fine actors, Langella does not much resemble the disgraced president, including being much larger, but a receding-hairline wig helps, and Langella wonderfully represents the clumsy cadences of Nixon's voice. On stage Langella came close to making Nixon a caricature, adopting a shambling walk like a cartoon bear. In the film Langella is best during the former president's quieter moments. When Langella's Nixon grows introspective, he clearly does not like what he sees.

The approach of Howard, who admits voting for Nixon in 1972, recalls Stone's. Neither filmmaker may have set out to offer a sympathetic look at the man who dragged his nation through two years of controversy and uncertainty, but the cinematic Nixon is strangely likable, a man of intelligence and some humor who somehow just cannot keep from doing the wrong thing. One of the film's (and Langella's) most moving moments comes when Nixon tells Frost he admires his ability to socialize. Nixon looks so ill at ease in public because he is so uncomfortable inside his own skin.

Michael Adams

CREDITS

David Frost: Michael Sheen
Richard Nixon: Frank Langella
James Reston Jr.: Sam Rockwell
Jack Brennan: Kevin Bacon
Caroline Cushing: Rebecca Hall
John Burt: Matthew Macfayden
Bob Zelnick: Oliver Platt
Swifty Lazar: Toby Jones
Pat Nixon: Pat McCormick
Tricia Nixon: Jenn Gotzon
Origin: USA
Language: English
Released: 2008
Production: Brian Grazer, Ron Howard, Tim Bevan, Eric Fellner; Imagine Entertainment, StudioCanal, Relativity Media, Working Title Films; released by Universal Pictures
Directed by: Ron Howard
Written by: Peter Morgan
Cinematography by: Salvatore Totino
Music by: Hans Zimmer
Sound: Peter J. Devlin
Editing: Mike Hill, Dan Hanley
Art Direction: Brian O'Hara, Gregory Van Horn
Costumes: Daniel Orlandi
Production Design: Michael Corenblith
MPAA rating: R
Running time: 122 minutes

REVIEWS

Entertainment Weekly Online. December 3, 2008.
Hollywood Reporter Online. October 15, 2008.
Los Angeles Times Online. December 5, 2008.

New York Times Online. December 5, 2008.
New Yorker Online. December 8, 2008.
Rolling Stone Online. December 11, 2008.
Variety Online. October 15, 2008.
Village Voice Online. December 2, 2008.
Wall Street Journal Online. December 5, 2008.

QUOTES

David Frost: "Are you really saying the President can do something illegal?"
Richard Nixon: "I'm saying that when the President does it, that means it's not illegal!"

TRIVIA

Even while off-camera, all of the actors would remain in character and continue the Frost/Nixon rivalry by bickering and making fun of each other.

AWARDS

Nomination:

Oscars 2008: Actor (Langella), Adapt. Screenplay, Director (Howard), Film, Film Editing
British Acad. 2008: Actor (Langella), Adapt. Screenplay, Director (Howard), Film, Film Editing, Makeup
Directors Guild 2008: Director (Howard)
Golden Globes 2009: Actor—Drama (Langella), Director (Howard), Film—Drama, Screenplay, Orig. Score
Screen Actors Guild 2008: Actor (Langella), Cast
Writers Guild 2008: Adapt. Screenplay.

FROZEN RIVER

Box Office: $2.4 million

The independent triumph *Frozen River* is a gritty and realistic look at poverty, racism, desperation, and the struggle to survive in an America on the brink of a depression. Writer/director Courtney Hunt's thoughtful and singular debut explores all this while looking at the bonds of two women in upstate New York who become unlikely partners in smuggling illegal immigrants over the Canadian border. The scantily released, low-budget *Frozen River* won over critics with its fresh and unique voice, taking the Grand Jury Prize at the Sundance Film Festival and winning Oscar® nominations for Hunt's original screenplay and lead actress Melissa Leo.

As wintry and bleak as its title suggests, the story is set a few days before Christmas in the upstate New York town of Massena, across the St. Lawrence River from Canada and near the Mohawk Indian reservation. In a broken-down trailer, Ray Eddy (Melissa Leo) is left to raise her children, fifteen-year-old T.J. (Charlie McDermott) and five-year-old Ricky (James Reilly) alone after her gambling addict husband lost their down payment for a new trailer at the reservation's bingo parlor and then slunk away without a word.

She meets another single mother, bingo parlor employee Lila Littlewolf (Misty Upham), while attempting to track down her husband and instead finds the Mohawk woman driving home in the car he abandoned. Lila offers Ray a lucrative deal to sell the car to a smuggler she knows. Ray learns that Lila is as desperate as she is, trying to regain custody of her one-year-old child who was taken by her mother-in-law at birth to raise.

Lila, who also lives in a trailer on the reservation, has experience trafficking illegal immigrants across the frozen river to the border town and eventually the desperate Ray becomes involved, at first unwittingly. Ray's part-time job at a dollar store is not enough to make ends meet and she is unable to secure full-time work but she will not agree to her son T.J.'s offer to drop out of school to get a job to help out. The outlook is grim and they are literally surviving on popcorn and Tang. Since the smuggling business is a lucrative one, Ray goes about the extremely dangerous business, rendezvousing with a menacing Quebecois Jacques (Mark Boone Jr.) and leaving with the Pakistani and Chinese aliens hidden in the trunk for the treacherous ride across the frozen river.

Although Ray, weathered and worn-looking, is extremely pragmatic in her approach to life and her illegal activities, she does harbor some very real fears. She carries a gun in case of trouble and wonders if she may be unwittingly aiding Pakistani terrorists. Her family's survival is nonetheless her primary concern, something that she and Lila have in common, and bravely, she will not stop until she earns enough to save her home.

Hunt builds tension as the possibilities for disaster grows exponentially. They may be smuggling terrorists. They may get pulled over by the police. And perhaps the most immediate fear is that the ice they must navigate their vehicle over—heavy with the weight of their stowaways—may break at any time.

Through the two women's laconic connection, Hunt explores the relationship of the Mohawks to the city's white inhabitants. Lila is valuable to Ray in introducing her to this dangerous but lucrative underworld. Ray is valuable to the smugglers because she is white and therefore less likely to be stopped by the state troopers. The Mohawk reservation is sympathetic to the smugglers, who are allowed to use it as a stopover, as they stake claim to both Canadian and U.S. territories and are not bound by conventional border laws. While there is no dialogue to overtly state the women's attachment

Funny Games

to one another, which was initially based on necessity, there is an implied but deep emotional connection silently conveyed by the eminently skilled actresses. Michael O'Keefe is low-key but effective as State Trooper Finnerty who encounters the women on their final run and brings their trafficking to an end. It is not a happy ending, but a realistic one.

Taking her short film and expanding it to feature length, Hunt's story is unsentimental, taut, and extremely well crafted aided by Reed Morano's expert cinematography, which brings a beauty to the bleak northern surroundings. The film's female leads, Leo and Upham, skillfully provide the chemistry and emotionality necessary to carry the weight of this auspicious film's powerful narrative.

Hilary White

CREDITS

Ray Eddy: Melissa Leo
T.J.: Charlie McDermott
Trooper Finnerty: Michael O'Keefe
Jacques Bruno: Mark Boone Jr.
Lila Littlewolf: Misty Upham
Ricky: James Reilly
Guy Versailles: Jay Klaitz
Bernie Littlewolf: John Canoe
Origin: USA
Language: English
Released: 2008
Production: Heather Rae, Chip Hourihan; Harwood Hunt Prods., The Cohen Media Group, Off Hollywood Pictures; released by Sony Pictures Classics
Directed by: Courtney Hunt
Written by: Courtney Hunt
Cinematography by: Reed Dawson Morano
Music by: Peter Golub, Shahzad Ali Ismaily
Sound: Micah Bloomberg
Editing: Kate Williams
Art Direction: Brian Rzepka
Costumes: Abby O'Sullivan
Production Design: Inbal Weinberg
MPAA rating: R
Running time: 97 minutes

REVIEWS

Boston Globe Online. August 22, 2008.
Chicago Sun-Times Online. August 14, 2008.
Entertainment Weekly Online. July 30, 2008.
Los Angeles Times Online. August 1, 2008.
New York Times Online. August 1, 2008.

San Francisco Chronicle. August 15, 2008, p. E8.
Time Online. July 31, 2008.
Variety Online. January 20, 2008.
Wall Street Journal. August 1, 2008, p. W1.

QUOTES

Ray Eddy: "I think we need to talk about this Troy...come on out. Troy? (shoots gun)"
Ray Eddy: "I mean it, honey."

AWARDS

Ind. Spirit 2009: Actress (Leo)
Nomination:
Oscars 2008: Actress (Leo), Orig. Screenplay
Ind. Spirit 2009: Director (Hunt), Film, Support. Actor (McDermott), Support. Actress (Upham), First Screenplay
Screen Actors Guild 2008: Actress (Leo).

FUNNY GAMES

Shall we begin?
—Movie tagline

Box Office: $1.2 million

Constructed more as a dose of foul-tasting medicine to be endured than a piece of entertainment, Michael Haneke's remake of his own 1997 film is designed to push both buttons and limits. A full-force tidal wave of unmitigated bile, the original film was made as a response to the Austrian director's distaste toward casual violence in American cinema. Citing the works of Quentin Tarantino as an example of popular films in which violence was handled in such a way as to have almost no consequence, the original *Funny Games* is a brutal and searing story in which ugly violence is the point of the film, confronting viewers and daring them to find entertainment in it. Unfortunately, being a radically uncommercial German-language film, it was barely screened in America. Over ten years later, Haneke has created a nearly shot-for-shot remake, this time in English, and with recognizable stars—but his vision remains as punishing and uncompromising as it was at its inception.

As the film opens, a family is driving en route to their weekend home on Long Island. As wife Ann (Naomi Watts), husband George (Tim Roth), and preteen son Georgie (Devon Gearhart) listen to classical music, they drive past the home of a neighbor with whom they are to play a golf game the following day and wave to him as he speaks to a pair of young men in tennis whites. Minutes later, Ann is in the kitchen when there is a knock at the door. It is Peter (Brady Corbet), one of the mysterious young men, asking to borrow some eggs on behalf of the neighbors. Ann complies, but Peter drops them on the way out and demands more. Perturbed, Ann gives him more eggs and, suspecting that he is playing some sort of mind game with her, demands that he leave the house. Soon, Paul (Michael Pitt), Peter's cohort, arrives and an argument escalates, resulting in George slapping Paul across the face. Paul, keeping an eerily cool demeanor, strikes George in the leg with a golf club, badly injuring him, and it becomes apparent that Peter and Paul have engineered the situation from the start. They proceed to keep the family as hostages in their own home with no apparent motive, brutalizing them both psychologically and physically and proposing a bet that the family will not survive to see the next morning.

The most easily summarizable portion of *Funny Games* is the first thirty minutes. Everything that follows is a cruel and extended game of cat and mouse that follows no rules in an attempt to enervate and infuriate the audience. Following on the heels of the worldwide success of *Caché* (2005), Haneke is making a very clear statement about his lack of need for approval. The urgency with which he feels the need to disseminate *Funny Games*'s message can be inferred by his desire to painstakingly recreate his own film (the same plans were even used to recreate the house) for English-speaking viewers who may have been put off by the idea of reading subtitles. But does that make this the least important or most vital film in his canon? As Derek Elley deduces in *Variety*, "…as the film progresses, it becomes painfully clear there's no real point to the story; what we're witnessing is a cool, intellectual exercise, as devoid of character and motivation as the two psychos themselves."

As Ann, Watts—who is also a producer—starts the film as snooty and indignant, but her treatment at the hands of Peter and Paul reduces her to an emotional wreck struggling to retain her sanity. It is a strong performance in a physically and emotionally wrenching role that also bravely requires her to spend a good portion of the film in her underwear (a requirement that Susanne Lothar incidentally did not have to meet in the original version). Roth, who starred in Quentin Tarantino's *Reservoir Dogs* (1992) and *Pulp Fiction* (1992)—two of the works that Haneke was reputedly responding to with the original *Funny Games,* amusingly enough—seems underused. George is seriously injured early in the script, and the usually commanding Roth seems relegated to the sidelines, often gasping in pain. Pitt and Corbet's preppy tormentors are both effectively despicable. The commander in chief to Corbet's sniveling minion, Pitt (*Hedwig and the Angry Inch* [2001], *The Dreamers* [2003]) once again proves himself to be a

fearless actor interested in appearing in films that break more rules than box office records.

Though violence is a common presence in Haneke's works, it is the sustained level of cruelty and tension that viewers may find problematic in *Funny Games*. The film unfortunately strides a line that puts it in a commercial hinterland——not gory enough for horror fans, too blisteringly harsh for most everyday film fans. In addition, there is a moment when Peter addresses the audience, along with another postmodern third act gag that is so frustrating that it may cause even those who are not turned off by the violence to turn against the film. Not that Haneke would care. As noted by Scott Tobias in *The Onion*, "*Funny Games* feeds off hatred like a monster, and as it storms into American theaters, it stands to generate enough ill will to light up the Las Vegas strip."

Unfortunately, after the superb *Caché,* this *Funny Games*—despite being exceptionally well-made—seems like a step backward for an artist at the height of his powers. From the blasts of John Zorn's avant-metal that punctuate the soundtrack and give the film a crass, jocular tone, to the lingering shot of a blood-spattered television broadcasting a NASCAR race, some of Haneke's touches here are ham-fisted by any measure. And while he gets his point across loud and clear, at the root, it is a very fine line between violence with a message and violence for titillation. In the end *Funny Games* will probably just gather a video store reputation as a scary endurance test—just another log on the fire for those who were supposed to learn something from it.

David Hodgson

CREDITS

Anna Farber: Naomi Watts
George Farber: Tim Roth
Paul: Michael Pitt
Peter: Brady Corbet
Georgie: Devon Gearhart
Origin: Italy, Germany, France, Great Britain, USA
Language: English
Released: 2007
Production: Chris Coen, Hamish McAlpine; Celluloid, Halcyon Productions, Tartan Films, X Filme, Lucky Red; released by Warner Independent
Directed by: Michael Haneke
Written by: Michael Haneke
Cinematography by: Darius Khondji
Sound: Thomas J. Varga
Editing: Monika Willi
Art Direction: Hinju Kim

Funny Games

Costumes: David C. Robinson
Production Design: Kevin Thompson
MPAA rating: R
Running time: 112 minutes

REVIEWS

Boston Globe Online. March 14, 2008.
Chicago Sun-Times Online. March 14, 2008.
Entertainment Weekly Online. March 12, 2008.
Los Angeles Times Online. March 14, 2008.
New York Times Online. March 14, 2008.
New Yorker Online. March 17, 2008.
San Francisco Chronicle. March 14, 2008, p. E7.
Variety Online. October 20, 2007.
Washington Post. March 14, 2008, p. C5.

QUOTES

Anna: "Why don't you just kill us?"
Peter (smiling): "You shouldn't forget the importance of entertainment."

TRIVIA

The production crew used the blueprints from the 1997 original. The set of the house in the 2007 American remake has the same proportions as that of the 1997 set.

G

GET SMART

Saving the world...and loving it.
—Movie tagline

Box Office: $130.3 million

As penned by Mel Brooks and Buck Henry, the 1960s television comedy *Get Smart* was many things—a deft satire of the federal government's shadowy obsession with secrecy during the Cold War (and of the Cold War mentality in general), an excellent send-up of mid-twentieth-century cinematic spy thrillers (especially spy *par excellence* James Bond)—but most of all, it was funny. From the brilliant dialogue to the over-the-top subject matter, the excessive and ridiculous gadgetry to the lampooning of twentieth-century bureaucratic life, and the combination of Barbara Feldon's competent Agent 99 with Don Adams's bungling and inept (yet well-meaning and exceedingly lucky) Agent 86, Maxwell Smart, the show served as an excellent barometer of the undercurrent of the times by tapping into America's collective Cold War anxiety and exposing its inherent ridiculousness. The TV version of *Get Smart* took America's greatest Cold War anxieties and made them the subject of prime time laughs. The film adaptation of *Get Smart* seeks to do something similar by taking the tropes of the TV show (the gadgets, a bungling spy and his much more competent partner, pitting two global organizations against one another—one, CONTROL, committed to maintaining order, and the other, KAOS, bent on global domination) and grafting them onto a twenty-first-century mentality, a world more informed by the War on Terror and Jason Bourne than the Cold War and James Bond, with mixed results. Though the

Get Smart of 2008 makes a good faith effort to be true to the spirit of the original series, the fact is that director Peter Segal's update simply fails to be funny.

Geopolitical events since the 1960s notwithstanding, the plot of *Get Smart* would be right at home in the television series, including the classic scheme of using a nuclear threat for the purpose of large-scale extortion. The film opens with a montage of Maxwell Smart (Steve Carell) preparing for his day at the ultra-secret American spy agency, CONTROL (an acronym for nothing, this is simply the agency's name), and the sequence attempts to bridge the gap between the series and the world of the film not only by including an updated version of Smart's walk past several preposterously complex security doors, but also by having the entrance to CONTROL headquarters concealed in plain sight within a museum (loaded with cars, suits, and gadgets from the original series) dedicated to the CONTROL of the Cold War, circa the late 1960s, now supposedly defunct. It is revealed that Smart is an analyst who aspires to be a field agent in the mold of his idol, Agent 23 (played by Dwayne Johnson, a.k.a. The Rock). Despite Smart's excellent scores on the field agent exam, he is initially thwarted in this by the Chief (Alan Arkin), who says that Smart is too valuable as an analyst, but Smart is made an acting agent when CONTROL headquarters is infiltrated and trashed, hinting darkly that there is a double agent in the ranks. Thinking the attack to be the work of the nefarious world-domination outfit KAOS, Max is promoted to field agent and paired with Agent 99 (Anne Hathaway), who has recently undergone extensive plastic surgery to conceal her identity (and which conveniently helps explain that Max and 99 are about the same age, despite the clear age difference in the actors), to find out what KAOS is up to. The pair fly to Russia to find that KAOS is stockpiling nuclear weapons in a facility disguised as a bakery, run by Siegfried (Terence Stamp), a high-ranking KAOS operative. Smart and 99 destroy the facility, and Agent 23 is dispatched to investigate the site. When he says he can find no evidence of nuclear material, Max is believed to be the double agent (since he is the one who actually sees the portion of the building that houses the nukes while 99 is elsewhere) and is taken into custody. In prison, Max figures out that Siegfried will detonate a nuclear bomb in Los Angeles (later found to be Walt Disney Concert Hall, during the end of Beethoven's Ninth Symphony, specifically). He manages to escape prison, equipping himself with vintage CONTROL gear from the museum. He arrives in Los Angeles and explains the plot to the Chief and Agent 99 who do not initially believe him, but ultimately Agent 23 is found to be emitting trace radioactivity, proving that he covered up the presence of the nuclear material at the KAOS facility and revealing him as the double agent. After a chase in which Agent 23 attempts to flee with 99 as a hostage (he fails and is killed), Max returns to the concert hall and prevents the bomb from exploding, and a brief wrap-up shows that Siegfried escapes, and Max and 99 start a romantic relationship.

The major problem with this reimagined *Get Smart* is that it does not negotiate the tricky balance of the action-comedy genre well and, despite the gags, tends to lean a bit too heavily on the side of action. This sort of "Lone Superpower/War on Terror" iteration of *Get Smart* is at least partly in the mold of *True Lies,* the 1994 James Cameron action-comedy (and the one that set the standard for the action and effects-heavy comedy film), and is definitely informed by the Jason Bourne movies. The upshot of these influences is that *Get Smart* tends to be at its worst when it is trying to be funny—given the high-energy action and the scale of the effects sequences (stunts, explosions, lots of extras), the slapstick laid on top of these moments feels out of place when it should be integral and organic. Occasionally, a small-scale visual joke pays off, such as when Max throws a phone receiver with a short cord at a KAOS henchman and the throw comes up several feet too short as a result. By and large, however, the comedy bits should be at the same level as the action, and often they are not: a dance sequence featuring Smart and a large woman dancing competitively with 99 and a KAOS villain falls flat not only because of its own ridiculousness, but also because it has no function in the context of the plot (it isn't a diversion of any sort, or a means of acquiring information, so why would field operatives in enemy territory

call attention to themselves in this way?); a scene in which Max must navigate a laser-triggered alarm maze (an obligatory scene for an espionage film) is rendered completely silly, but not funny, by a rat that stows away in Max's suit; Max walks through a beaded curtain, and the beads fall to the floor for no reason—no struggle causes it, nothing is shown catching on the curtain, the beads simply fall and the joke falls flat (luckily, this scene actually has a function in that a bunch of KAOS lackeys later trip on the beads, allowing Max and 99 to escape, which helps excuse the bit's presence in the movie). If the jokes were as powerful as the explosions, or as well wrought as the action sequences are designed, *Get Smart* could be so much more than it is.

This is not to say, however, that *Get Smart* is not enjoyable, or that the filmmakers have not gone to great lengths to pay homage to the original series. The film does boast some noteworthy positives. For instance, Steve Carell and Anne Hathaway have genuine chemistry, which is no small feat given the significant age difference between them. Also, much to the film's credit, *Get Smart* does not use Hollywood's standard Arab Muslim extremist punching bags as villains. Dwayne Johnson proves yet again to be a fine comedic actor, able to summon his considerable charm, swagger, and machismo for maximum effect—he can certainly hold his own with comedic heavyweights—and Alan Arkin seems born to play the Chief (he has the funniest line in the film, made all the more hilarious by his well-timed, deadpan delivery).

Get Smart contains many references to the original series, a sign not only of the desire to please the show's fan base but also of the care with which the project has been approached. Many of Max's catchphrases pop up, including, "Would you believe …?", "…and loving it!", and, "Missed it by that much." The CONTROL museum, filled with props and costumes from the series, as well as the security door sequence, also trumpet the filmmakers' awareness of and indebtedness to the source material. The film is laden with other carefully constructed tributes as well: Bernie Kopell, who played Siegfried in the series, has a cameo (sporting his German accent, no less); Max's research materials in the opening credits contain references to Mr. Big and the Claw, villains from the show who do not appear in the film; the malfunctioning privacy device, the "Cone of Silence," is used once; and even the robotic agent Hymie (Patrick Warburton) makes an appearance at film's end. Though these references add a sense of warmth and respect to the proceedings, they do not enhance the film enough to the level of heir-apparent to the series. Alas, in the final analysis, *Get Smart* as directed by Segal, though obviously a remake with good intentions, has simply "missed it by that much."

John Boaz

CREDITS

Maxwell Smart: Steven Carell
Agent 99: Anne Hathaway
Agent 23: Dwayne "The Rock" Johnson
Chief: Alan Arkin
Siegfried: Terence Stamp
Agent 91: Terry Crews
Larabee: David Koechner
Shtarker: Ken Davitian
Agent 13: Bill Murray
Bruce: Masi Oka
Opel Driver: Bernie Kopell
Lloyd: Nate Torrence
Hymie: Patrick Warburton
The President: James Caan
Origin: USA
Language: English
Released: 2008
Production: Andrew Lazar, Charles Roven, Alex Gartner, Michael Ewing; Village Roadshow Pictures, Mosaic Media Group, Mad Chance, Callahan Filmworks; released by Warner Bros.
Directed by: Peter Segal
Written by: Tom J. Astle, Matt Ember
Cinematography by: Dean Semler
Music by: Trevor Rabin
Sound: Jose Antonio Garcia
Editing: Richard Pearson
Art Direction: James Hegedus
Costumes: Deborah L. Scott
Production Design: Wynn Thomas
MPAA rating: PG-13
Running time: 110 minutes

REVIEWS

Boston Globe Online. June 20, 2008.
Chicago Sun-Times Online. June 19, 2008.
Hollywood Reporter Online. June 13, 2008.
Los Angeles Times Online. June 20, 2008.
New York Times Online. June 20, 2008.
San Francisco Chronicle. June 20, 2008, p. E1.
Variety Online. June 10, 2008.
Wall Street Journal. June 20, 2008, p. W1.
Washington Post. June 20, 2008, p. C1.

QUOTES

Maxwell Smart: "I think it's only fair to warn you, this facility is surrounded by a highly trained team of 130 black op snipers."

Siegfried: "I don't believe you."
Maxwell Smart: "Would you believe two dozen Delta Force commandos?"
Siegfried: "No."
Maxwell Smart: "How about Chuck Norris with a BB gun."

TRIVIA

Don Adams, the original Maxwell Smart, was born Donald Yarmy. The airline that took Max and 99 to Russia was called Yarmy International as a tribute to him.

GHOST TOWN

He sees dead people...and they annoy him.
—Movie tagline

Box Office: $13.3 million

From *What's Up, Doc?* (1972) to *13 Going on 30* (2004), there have been many unsuccessful attempts to replicate the humor and romance of the screwball comedies of the 1930s and early 1940s. Films such as *Midnight* (1939) and *The Lady Eve* (1941) threw together unlikely couples, enlivening their rocky path to true love with slapstick and verbal wit, two qualities over which contemporary filmmakers often stumble. While *Ghost Town* may not be a perfect example of the genre, it succeeds better in combining comedy and romance than most of its predecessors.

Frank Herlihy (Greg Kinnear) lives for pleasure, loving both his faithful wife, Gwen (Téa Leoni), and his unseen mistress. Frank is the kind of guy who strolls casually through Manhattan in a tuxedo at a time when all the passersby are on their way to work. Chattering away on his cell phone, Frank is hit by a bus and becomes a ghost destined to continue aimlessly walking the streets until he can solve a problem related to a loved one. He wants to prevent Gwen from marrying Richard (Billy Campbell), a do-gooder who is everything Frank was not, so the jealous deceased sees Richard as smug and insufferable.

But how is Frank to achieve his goal? Then Bertram Pincus (Ricky Gervais), a misanthropic dentist, dies for seven minutes during a colonoscopy and can suddenly see ghosts, all of whom pester him about solving problems. Eventually, Frank wears down Bertram who reluctantly agrees to try to foil the coming nuptials by wooing Gwen, and this is where the screwball comedy comes in. With a nod toward the film's debt to *Bringing Up Baby* (1938), Gwen is an archaeologist. While she is tall, beautiful, smart, outgoing, and caring, Bertram is her opposite: short, fat, homely, and grumpy. And for a dentist he has shockingly bad teeth. Matters are further complicated because the two live in the same apartment building, with the rude Bertram closing an elevator in her face and taking her taxi. As a result, whenever he approaches, she shrinks away.

Ghost Town varies from the traditional screwball comedy because Bertram is hardly a catch, unlike the characters traditionally played by Gary Cooper, Cary Grant, and Henry Fonda. It is no surprise when the heroines choose Grant over the comparatively awkward characters played by Ralph Bellamy in *The Awful Truth* (1937) and *His Girl Friday* (1940), but Richard is another matter: much, much better looking than Bertram and a heroic humanitarian to boot. This being a comedy, though, the outcome is inevitable, though director David Koepp, who co-wrote the screenplay with John Kamps, takes the story on some unpredictable detours.

The biggest weakness of *Ghost Town* is that as a director, Koepp is a good screenwriter. Best known for writing or co-writing *Jurassic Park* (1993), *Mission Impossible* (1996), and *War of the Worlds* (2005), hardly romantic comedies, Koepp is a point-and-shoot filmmaker, positioning the actors in the center of the frame and letting scenes drag on too long. A scene in which Bertram sneaks out of and back into his office to elude a waiting room full of ghosts is clumsily executed and completely extraneous. A cut from Gwen's telling Bertram she has a dog to a shot of the dentist sitting uncomfortably next to a huge mastiff is about as cinematic as Koepp gets.

As with most recent romantic comedies, *Ghost Town* has nondescript cinematography, by Fred Murphy, as if beautiful images, shadowy lighting, or an unusual color scheme would be off-putting. While the film is not as ugly and grainy as many comedies, the use of attractive Manhattan settings would be heightened with a more artistic approach.

Ghost Town works as well as it does primarily because of the cast. The screwball comedy it most closely resembles is *Topper* (1937), in which the ghosts of carefree socialites played by Grant and Constance Bennett try to help a stuffy banker, played by Roland Young, enjoy life. While reviewers compared Kinnear to Grant because of the similarities of their characters, Kinnear's style is more wise guy than suave playboy. Kinnear's arch, slightly cynical approach to Frank resembles characters portrayed by William Holden, not surprising since Kinnear has the Holden role in the unfortunate 1995 remake of *Sabrina* (1954). Kinnear makes Frank likable by showing the character recognizes his smarminess yet is unrepentant about his bad behavior.

As she has shown in such films as *Flirting with Disaster* (1996), Leoni has considerable comedic skills,

yet *Ghost Town* requires her primarily to respond to the wackiness of others, principally Bertram. Leoni and Gervais, after some initial tension between their characters, gradually develop a smooth comic rhythm, with the actors playing well off each other. The charming Leoni is convincing as the love interest of Ben Kingsley's alcoholic hit man in *You Kill Me* (2007) and makes Gwen's even more unlikely affection for Bertram believable.

In his first starring film role, Gervais finds a set of neuroses different from those which made him famous in television's *The Office* (2001–2003) and *Extras* (2005–2007). Gervais makes Bertram's progress from sad, lonely man to one who embraces life credible, though the screenplay threatens to become too mushy toward the end of the film. Though Koepp strangely expressed doubts, just before *Ghost Town* opened, about the casting of a British comedian unknown to the majority of American filmgoers, Gervais delivers the dialogue with his usual nervous, fast-talking manner as if he has adapted it to his distinctive style.

Giving *Ghost Town* a mostly enthusiastic review in the *New York Times,* Stephen Holden acknowledged that it is a modest achievement as a screwball comedy but lacks the messy contrivances of recent attempts at the genre. *Ghost Town* is a minor romantic comedy but offers just enough chuckles and charm.

Michael Adams

CREDITS

Bertram Pincus: Ricky Gervais
Frank Herlihy: Greg Kinnear
Gwen: Téa Leoni
Mrs. Pickthall: Dana Ivey
Richard: Billy Campbell
Surgeon: Kristen Wiig
Ghost Dad: Alan Ruck
Origin: USA
Language: English
Released: 2008
Production: Gavin Polone; Spyglass Entertainment, Pariah Films, Dreamworks Pictures; released by Paramount
Directed by: David Koepp
Written by: David Koepp, John Kamps
Cinematography by: Fred Murphy
Music by: Geoff Zanelli
Sound: Bob Hein
Editing: Sam Seig
Art Direction: Nicholas Lundy
Costumes: Sarah Edwards
Production Design: Howard Cummings

MPAA rating: PG-13
Running time: 102 minutes

REVIEWS

Boston Globe Online. September 19, 2008.
Chicago Sun-Times Online. September 18, 2008.
Entertainment Weekly Online. September 16, 2008.
Hollywood Reporter Online. September 8, 2008.
Los Angeles Times Online. September 19, 2008.
New York Times Online. September 19, 2008.
Rolling Stone Online. October 2, 2008.
San Francisco Chronicle. September 19, 2008, p. E1.
Variety Online. September 8, 2008.
Wall Street Journal Online. September 19, 2008.
Washington Post. September 19, 2008, p. C1.

QUOTES

Hospital Nurse (after Bertram's colonoscopy): "Come back soon."

Bertram Pincus: "What a terrible thing to say in a hospital."

TRIVIA

The Beatles' "I'm Looking Through You" is used in the movie, one of the very few occasions where the original version of a Beatles song has been used in a film.

A GIRL CUT IN TWO
(La Fille coupée en deux)

One man's love is another man's lust.
—Movie tagline

Legendary French director Claude Chabrol and cowriter Cécile Maistre based their screenplay for *A Girl Cut in Two* on a real-life American tragedy that occurred in 1906 involving prominent architect Stanford White, his teenage actress paramour Evelyn Nesbit, and her millionaire husband Harry K. Thaw. Chabrol, one of the French New Wave's most prolific directors with more than fifty films to his credit, is known as the French Alfred Hitchcock and he has imbued his latest film, essentially a love triangle, with all the aspects of his signature suspenseful psychological thrillers mixed with wicked black comedy. As the violence of the title suggests, the consequences suffered by the characters of Chabrol's *A Girl Cut in Two* are far more dramatic than those of a typical French romantic comedy and in keeping with the director's sense of elevated reality.

Like the majority of Chabrol's films, *A Girl Cut in Two* takes place in a pleasant, bourgeois environment, and establishes his usual victim/predator relationship.

The ambitious Lyon television weathergirl Gabrielle Deneige (Ludivine Sagnier), a beautiful, naïve young blonde whose last name translates as "snow," perfectly fits the bill of innocent victim in the Hitchcockian vein. In France, Sagnier is well known, and has worked with a number of high-profile French directors in her thirty-plus films, including François Ozon's *8 Femmes* (2002), alongside the likes of Catherine Deneuve and Isabelle Huppert. She is known in the United States for *Swimming Pool* (2003), in which she appeared topless, as well as playing Tinkerbell in *Peter Pan* (2003), which is the role that Chabrol claimed won her the role of Gabrielle, who embodied the same radiance and seduction mixed with mischievousness and a touch of perversion.

Gabrielle meets the celebrated and brilliant novelist Charles Saint-Denis (François Berléand) after an interview at her TV station and immediately falls in love with the much-older, married writer. She is also pursued by the determined young Paul Gaudens (Benoît Magimel), who is not only handsome and wealthy but poised to inherit his family's pharmaceutical fortune. Both these men are the predators, whose power and means render Gabrielle little more than a pawn in their quest to get what they want.

Charles exploits Gabrielle's utter devotion, taking her to a private club where he instructs her to perform sexual acts with his friends to prove her love. Afterward, he ends his relationship with the love-struck Gabrielle. In retaliation, Gabrielle begins seeing Paul, although she is not in love with the spoiled, self-indulgent heir and his fiercely protective mother Geneviève (Caroline Silhol) openly despises her. Paul, fueled by his jealousy over Gabrielle's prior relationship with Saint-Denis, seeks to dominate her completely and will not rest until she agrees to marry him.

Reading about Gabrielle's impending nuptials in the paper fuels Charles to try to reignite their relationship. Gabrielle is again willing to sacrifice Paul and marriage to be with him if only he will leave his wife (Valeria Cavalli). Although Charles claims to love her, he refuses and the wedding proceeds. The scene is now set for the final act, which contains the tragic consequences of all that has come before.

During a trip to Lisbon, the mentally unbalanced Paul learns of the sex club incident involving his wife and Saint-Denis. A foreshadowing scene shows him threatening Gabrielle with a gun, pulling the trigger to his own head to reveal it is not loaded. Later, Paul and his mother, along with Gabrielle, attend a benefit dinner with Saint-Denis as the keynote speaker. Paul walks onstage, pulling out the same gun, and shoots Saint-Denis for "perverting" his wife, using the same words as the unstable Thaw after he shot White.

With Charles dead and Paul in prison, Geneviève delivers the trifecta of manipulation of the poor Gabrielle by getting her to testify to Charles's perversions to aid Paul's case. In the end, she learns that Geneviève, too, has used her and she will get no money from a divorce that Paul has instigated.

Sagnier's seasoned performance gives Gabrielle suitable dimension—with intelligence and sensitivity—to make her sympathetic and realistic instead of a mere mindless plaything tossed around by two powerful men. Silhol delivers a withering monologue that makes her performance as the disdainful Geneviève one of the film's best, along with standouts Mathilda May, as Charles's agent, and Valeria Cavalli.

Chabrol has said of *A Girl Cut in Two* that it is a chaste film about sexual perversity. None of the sex acts that feature so prominently in the plot are seen but are merely implied, and there is no nudity. The audience is left to freely imagine what has gone on behind closed doors, which is much more powerful that any onscreen image. Further, Saint-Denis is revealed to be impotent, which is why he took Gabrielle to the club to be with his friends, recalling Lars von Trier's *Breaking the Waves* (1996), whose physically paralyzed husband asks his wife to be with other men. It is a sex story absent of sex.

The final shots of *A Girl Cut in Two* end with the once promising career woman Gabrielle—now an assistant in a magic show—literally being cut in two, turning her head so the audience cannot see her tears but finishing the trick with a smile: Chabrol's nod to cinematic illusion.

Hilary White

CREDITS

Gabrelle Deneige: Ludivine Sagnier
Paul Gaudens: Benoit Magimel
Charles Saint-Denis: François Berléand
Capucine Jamet: Mathilda May
Marie Deneige: Marie Bunel
Dora Saint-denis: Valeria Cavalli
Genevieve Gaudens: Caroline Sihol
Origin: France, Germany
Language: French
Released: 2007
Production: Patrick Godeau; Aliceleo Cinema, France 2 Cinema, Integral Film; released by IFC Films
Directed by: Claude Chabrol
Written by: Claude Chabrol, Cecile Maistre
Cinematography by: Eduardo Serra
Music by: Matthieu Chabrol
Sound: Thierry Lebon

Editing: Monique Fardoulis
Costumes: Mic Cheminal
Production Design: Francoise Benoit-Fresco
MPAA rating: Unrated
Running time: 115 minutes

REVIEWS

Hollywood Reporter Online. August 10, 2007.
New York Times Online. August 15, 2008.
Variety Online. August 7, 2007.
Village Voice Online. August 12, 2008.

QUOTES

Gabrielle Aurore Deneige: " What do you do for a living?"
Paul André Claude Gaudens: "I live."

TRIVIA

Four Chabrols worked on the film: Director and co-writer Claude Chabrol; his screenplay-supervisor wife Aurore Chabrol; and his two sons, composer Matthieu Chabrol and actor Thomas Chabrol.

GRAN TORINO

Box Office: $142.1 million

Clint Eastwood rides again after a four year hiatus from acting, as Walt Kowalski, an Archie Bunker meets Dirty Harry retired auto worker who angrily confronts his changing neighborhood. *Gran Torino* is an urban Western with the traditional Wild West locales traded in for the gritty urban landscape of Detroit; the outmoded American working class dream comes face-to-face with white flight and an influx of Asian pioneers. The marauding banditos are replaced by semiautomatic weapon-toting gangbangers who terrorize the local citizenry. There is lots of steely-eyed staring, toe-to-toe confrontations, drinking, tobacco-chewing and spitting, and gun play, set against a lawless backdrop.

Gran Torino opens with the opposing themes of life and death. First the audience is introduced to Walt Kowalski at his wife's funeral. Anger oozing from every pore, Walt can do little but growl at the family around him as they come to pay their last respects. The seething continues during the wake held at the Kowalski family home, where Walt barely speaks. The house is an oasis in the middle of a rundown neighborhood. Next door, the Vang Lors, a Hmong family, is having a celebration for a family newborn. As the Kowalskis dine on ham and mashed potatoes, the family next door is slaughtering a chicken in the backyard. Later, when Thao, the young boy from next door, comes by to borrow some jumper cables, Walt unloads on the youth: "Have some respect zipper head! We're in mourning here." It is quite obvious that political correctness or basic manners do not exist in Walt's world. He is a man who demands respect but has little desire to show any to anyone else.

Thao, played by Bee Vang, is a smart boy who lacks a strong male role model in his life and, as a consequence, is quite shy and reserved—so much so that at one point Walt asks if Thao is mentally handicapped. Walt has no use for these people and even less for a boy like Thao, who is being pressured by his cousin Spider (Doua Moua), a Hmong gangbanger, to join his crew. The two worlds are thrust together when Thao's sister Sue (Ahney Her) is aided by the gun-toting Eastwood when she is harassed by some black youths. Walt is a Korean War veteran who has seen the horror of war and looked death in the face. He is not about to take any guff from some gangster wanna-bes; backing down is not in his vocabulary. Contrasting Walt is the young idealistic priest, Father Janovich (Christopher Carley), who promised Walt's deceased wife that he would watch over him. Like everyone else, Walt has only disdain for the baby-faced Padre.

When Thao attempts to steal Kowalski's trusty steed—a 1972 Gran Torino—as a gang initiation, the two come face to face, with Walt nearly shooting the would-be thief. Thao's embarrassed family forces Thao make good by Walt and pay off his debt by working for Walt, repairing the dilapidated houses on their block. Slowly, the two grow closer with the old man eventually taking Thao, whom Walt calls Toad, under his wing and becoming the boy's most unlikely father figure, teaching him to cuss and deliver Kowalski-style racial epithets. When Thao is jumped by Spider's thugs who burn his cheek with a cigarette, Walt realizes the boy does not stand a chance in a world filled with a gang on every corner and attempts to intervene. He administers some frontier justice in the form of a beating to one of the Hmong gang members. The gang members' retaliation is swift and brutal. They shoot up the Vang Lor's home in a drive-by attack, wounding Thao in the process. But the worst is yet to come. The family thinks that Sue is with the family only to find she has been brutally beaten and raped. True to the Hmong code of silence, the family does not press charges.

The attack sets the table for a heavy helping of revenge served up Dirty Harry–style, and Thao, blinded by rage, is eager to help Walt craft a plot to settle the score. He urges the boy to return later because these things must be carefully planned. Walt finally goes to Father Janovich for confession, fulfilling his late wife's wishes. When Thao returns, Walt tells the boy killing is not to be taken lightly and locks him in the basement so Walt can do the deed, taking on the bandits by himself. In a classic Old West showdown, Walt rides into town alone to confront the gang. Standing tall, armed with little more than a cigarette, Walt stands in front of the gangster's duplex with guns pointing at him from every doorway and window, and in full view of the neighbors, the gang unloads their weapons into him as he reaches into his coat pocket to pull out his lighter—a cold-blooded murder of an unarmed man. The scene ends with Walt lying face up on the lawn like the crucified Jesus. The gangsters go to prison and no longer pose a threat to Thao or the neighborhood.

The *Gran Torino* screenplay, written by Nick Schenk, was adapted from a story by Schenk and Dave Johannson originally set in the inner ring of Minneapolis but later changed to Detroit. The script, with its excessive racial and ethnic slurs hurled about by Eastwood's character, gives the actor a narrow range to work within. Even as he grows to accept the Vang Lors, claiming at one point that he has more in common with these people than his own family, he continues to fire every imaginable racial insult their way. The script has its moments, but too often the dialogue seems out of place and overwritten for the characters.

As expected, Clint Eastwood carries the film and rises above the writing to deliver some memorable moments. Who else could point his finger like a gun at a bunch of thugs and get away with it, not once but multiple times? Ahney has some fine banter with Eastwood and seems quite at ease, whether trading barbs or acting as a cultural tour guide. Bee Vang as Thao is punching above his weight here, having to share so much screen time with Eastwood. He occasionally calls to mind a Hmong version of *Amerian Idol* teddy bear David Archuleta who just cannot be mean enough for the situation.

Gran Torino manages to take on the changing face of America and the problems the changing social fabric has on society and those who cannot accept that change. Walt, like the city of Detroit and much of the industrial, working middle class, are now the grizzled old hold-outs facing the realities of a new society and a fresh set of pioneers.

Michael S. White

CREDITS
Walt Kowalski: Clint Eastwood
Mitch Kowalski: Brian Haley
Steve Kowalski: Brian Howe
Ashley Kowalski: Dreama Walker
Karen Kowalski: Geraldine Hughes

Barber: John Carroll Lynch
Father Janovich: Christopher Carley
Thao: Bee Vang
Sue: Ahney Her
Origin: USA
Language: English
Released: 2008
Production: Robert Lorenz, Bill Gerber, Clint Eastwood; Malpaso Productions, Village Roadshow Pictures, Double Nickel Ent.; released by Warner Bros.
Directed by: Clint Eastwood
Written by: Nick Schenk
Cinematography by: Tom Stern
Music by: Kyle Eastwood, Michael Stevens
Sound: Walt Martin
Editing: Joel Cox, Gary D. Roach
Art Direction: John Warnke
Costumes: Deborah Hopper
Production Design: James Murakami
MPAA rating: R
Running time: 116 minutes

REVIEWS

Boston Globe Online. December 24, 2008.
Chicago Sun-Times Online. December 18, 2008.
Entertainment Weekly Online. December 10, 2008.
Hollywood Reporter Online. December 5, 2008.
Los Angeles Times Online. January 16, 2009.
New York Times Online. December 12, 2008.
San Francisco Chronicle. December 19, 2008.
Variety Online. December 5, 2008.
Washington Post. December 29, 2008.

QUOTES

Duke: "What you lookin' at, old man?"
Walt Kowalski: "Ever notice how you come across somebody once in a while you shouldn't have f**ked with? That's me."

TRIVIA

This was one of the first films to take advantage of the state of Michigan's new law that provided tax incentive packages to film productions.

Open casting calls for Hmong actors were held in Hmong communities in Detroit, Michigan; Saint Paul, Minnesota; and Fresno, California. None of the Hmong actors in the cast had acted in a film before except Doua Moua.

AWARDS

Nomination:

Golden Globes 2009: Song ("Gran Torino").

H

HAMLET 2

*One high school drama teacher is about to make
a huge number 2.*
—Movie tagline

Box Office: $4.8 million

The uproariously funny satire *Hamlet 2,* starring
British comedian Steve Coogan, takes a page from
another hilarious British comedian, Christopher Guest,
and his amateur-thespian comedy *Waiting for Guffman*
(1996). Both feature stunningly untalented, failed actors-
turned-drama teachers in small towns who, with an
abundance of heart, backwardly stumble into making
their mark in the theater world. Both portray the world
of amateur dramatics to a tee—Guest's film detailed
community theater; here it is high school musicals and
their associated backstage drama—in all their cheesy
glory. Coogan's character stages an almost inconceivable
musical sequel to William's Shakespeare's *Hamlet,* using
a novel "device"—a time machine—to remedy the pesky
fact that everyone dies at the end of that play while
incorporating such unlikely characters as Jesus and Hillary Clinton. *Hamlet 2,* directed by Andrew Fleming and
written by Fleming and Pam Brady, also has a heart,
taking on one of the themes of *Hamlet* in its exploration
of the father-son relationship.

Steve Coogan plays Dana Marschz (his unpronounceable last name is a running joke), an offbeat but
optimistic high school drama teacher who lives with his
wife Brie (Catherine Keener) and a moronic, monosyllabic boarder Gary (David Arquette) in Tucson, Arizona.
The influx of a group of tough-talking Latino students
more interested in seeking an easy elective than learning
the craft of acting upsets the balance of Dana's class, to
the dismay of eager thespians Rand Posin (Skylar Astin),
the teacher's pet, and the outspokenly racist Epiphany
Sellars (Phoebe Strole). Having failed as a commercial
actor, Dana is determinedly upbeat and inspiring his
difficult new students becomes his new mission in life,
often referencing his favorite films *Mr. Holland's Opus*
(1995) and *Dead Poets Society* (1989), which none of his
new students have even heard of.

While Coogan, who also had a small but excellent
supporting role in 2008's *Tropic Thunder,* has consistently
shown off strong comedic chops in such recent classics
as Michael Winterbottom's *24 Hour Party People* (2002)
and *A Cock and Bull Story* (2005), one of the best
surprises in the film is the debut performance of Shea
Pepe. In a small but pivotal part, Pepe plays the precocious freshman film critic, Noah Sapperstein, whose
highly insightful and expertly written, lambasting
critiques of Dana's shows, which are based on big-budget
Hollywood films such as *Erin Brockovich* (2000), have
brought him under the scrutiny of the budget-cutting
Principal Rocker (Marshall Bell). With his low-key
demeanor and lisping, deadpan delivery, Pepe's scene-
stealing turn is reminiscent of Christopher Mintz-Plasse's
breakthrough debut in 2007's *Superbad.*

Rocker informs Dana that the school is cutting the
drama department altogether and his next show will also
be his last. Heeding Sapperstein's advice, Dana writes
something original, a musical sequel to *Hamlet* called
Hamlet 2 that introduces Shakespeare's characters to
Jesus, Einstein, and Hillary Clinton with such outrageous numbers as "Rock Me Sexy Jesus" and the Tucson
Gay Men's Chorus providing the music. One of Dana's

more difficult students, Octavio (Joseph Julian Soria), turns out to be a gifted actor and scores the lead role. The film throws the Latino stereotypes out the window when Octavio's parents object to him being in the play not because of the risqué material but because his intellectual, upper-class mom and dad find the whole premise ridiculous and beneath their Brown University–bound son.

Keener has been cast twice in 2008 as an unhappy, philandering, and abandoning wife (*Synecdoche, New York* [2008]) and her bored, restless Brie runs off with Gary after unsuccessfully trying to conceive with Dana. Already strained from trying to mount his production offsite after the school has ousted his controversial show, Dana's seven years of sobriety have come to a spectacular end. His students, now heavily invested in the production after finding a warehouse site to mount it and providing technical support, are now called upon to rally their teacher. Dana also finds unlikely support from Elisabeth Shue (playing herself), whom he met at the fertility clinic with Brie, and a spunky lawyer Cricket Feldstein (Amy Poehler) who breezily fends off injunctions to shut down the much-talked-about show now swarmed with media and angry mobs.

The actual play is beyond description, but the touching highlight, which has Hamlet traveling back in time in his shop-class constructed time machine to save Laertes, Gertrude, Ophelia, and finally facing his father while the Tucson Gay Men's Chorus sings Elton John's "Someone Saved My Life Tonight" is priceless. Coogan plays Jesus, naturally, and, in a touching segment, forgives his own father onstage. It is hard not to root for this bumbling, well-meaning teacher beset by so many troubles that finally, spectacularly triumphs, so few will begrudge the rather unbelievable Broadway success that is finally bestowed upon him at the film's end.

Hilary White

CREDITS

Dana Marschz: Steve Coogan
Brie Marschz: Catherine Keener
Principal Rocker: Marshall Bell
Cricket Feldstein: Amy Poehler
Rand Posin: Skylar Astin
Epiphany Sellars: Phoebe Strole
Octavio: Joseph Julian Soria
Gary: David Arquette
Herself: Elisabeth Shue
Ivonne: Melonie Diaz
Mr. Marquez: Marco Rodriguez
Origin: USA

Language: English
Released: 2008
Production: Eric Eisner, Aaron Ryder, Leonid Rozhetskin; L & E Pictures; released by Focus Features
Directed by: Andrew Fleming
Written by: Andrew Fleming, Pam Brady
Cinematography by: Alexander Grusynski
Music by: Ralph Sall
Sound: Paul Cusack
Editing: Jeff Freeman
Art Direction: Guy Barnes
Costumes: Jill Newell
Production Design: Tony Fanning
MPAA rating: R
Running time: 92 minutes

REVIEWS

Boston Globe Online. August 22, 2008.
Chicago Sun-Times Online. August 21, 2008.
Hollywood Reporter Online. January 23, 2008.
Los Angeles Times Online. August 22, 2008.
New York Times Online. August 22, 2008.
Rolling Stone Online. August 21, 2008.
San Francisco Chronicle. August 22, 2008, p. E1.
Time Online. August 21, 2008.
Variety Online. January 25, 2008.
Washington Post. August 22, 2008, p. C1.

QUOTES

Dana Marschz: "Chuy, you're going to have a magical life. Because no matter where you go, it's always going to be better than Tucson."

HANCOCK

Meet the superhero everybody loves to hate.
—Movie tagline
He's saving the world whether we like it or not.
—Movie tagline

Box Office: $227.9 million

A veteran of such big-budget hero-genre films such as *Men in Black* (1997) and *Independence Day* (1996), Will Smith has built an extremely successful career out of playing likable and capable Everymen who rise to meet extraordinary challenges and, in the process, he manages to conquer mid-summer box office totals in the process. The most interesting feature of *Hancock*, as directed by Peter Berg (who helmed 2007's *The Kingdom*, which similarly was a box office success but received mixed critical notices), is how the film not only utilizes

Mr. Smith's associations with a particular heroic cinematic image in order to subvert that image to some degree, but also how well the film does the same with the superhero genre in general, largely through the elements of the technical filmmaking. The film requires the audience's considerable investment in Will Smith as a kind of lovable, smart-alecky yet reliable protector to allow the filmmakers to paint Hancock as a loathsome misanthrope. For all of the positives that can be enumerated about the film's deconstruction of the superhero genre and mystique, however, just as much can be said about *Hancock's* failure to sustain itself. Although the film offers some interesting perspective on the nature of the superhero (must a superhero necessarily be alone, separate, disconnected?) it does so at the expense of maintaining *Hancock* as a unified whole. Though a box office success, the film is ultimately marred by an unnecessary plot development and a jarring tonal shift (both of which can be rationalized within the context of the story but which do not fit organically with what is established in the first two-thirds), which serve to undermine what is an otherwise clever attempt at reframing the flawed superhero.

Hancock opens strong with a fairly nondescript police chase on an L.A. freeway. What appears to be a derelict sleeps on a bench as a young boy prods him to wake up, saying, "Hancock!" When the bum, obviously Hancock (Will Smith), awakes, he angrily and drunkenly asks the kid what he wants. The kid points at a TV set that is playing live footage of the chase, and Hancock grudgingly takes flight, bottle in hand, to stop the apparent criminals, which he does but in the process causes quite significant property damage, apparently a recurring theme with Hancock and the source of much public animosity against him. When Hancock rescues idealistic PR man Ray Embrey (Jason Bateman) after Ray gets stuck on the train tracks following a failed pitch for his all-heart logo (for companies interested in promoting a positive corporate image), he manages to derail the train, destroy cars, and injure lots of people in the process, causing many involved in the accident to ask, "Why didn't you just fly the car out of the way?" Ray alone, despite his injuries and destroyed car, thanks Hancock for saving his life and suggests that Hancock come home with him for dinner. Hancock meets Ray's family, his wife Mary (Charlize Theron), who seems to eye Hancock with suspicion, and Ray's son Aaron (Jae Head), who views Hancock with awe and treats him kindly. Inspired by his rescue, Ray seeks to rehabilitate Hancock's reputation and make over his image. Ray suggests that Hancock call a press conference and announce that he will in fact do jail time for all of the damage that he has caused, and in his time away, Ray suspects, crime will go up and the people will clamor for Hancock's

return. Sure enough, after some jailhouse escapades (including less-than-productive therapy sessions, some etiquette lessons from Ray—Ray's insistence that Hancock tell people "good job" for their assistance is actually quite funny—and some encounters with people on the inside who have been incarcerated by Hancock), Hancock is called upon by the mayor to deal with a sticky bank robbery turned hostage situation. Hancock defeats the bank robbers and frees the hostages, in the process cutting off the lead bank robber's hand. Hancock, Ray, and Mary go out that night for a celebratory dinner, Ray has a little too much to drink, and Hancock puts Ray to bed. In the kitchen, he makes a pass at Mary and discovers that she is superhuman too when she throws him through a wall. Hancock threatens to give her away to Ray unless she tells him everything. It turns out that they have been around for about three thousand years and that they were married once. Their race was built in pairs, and when they get close to each other they become mortal. This begins to happen to Hancock and he is shot and wounded while stopping a liquor store robbery. Meanwhile, the bank robber whose hand Hancock severed orchestrates a jailbreak and with other like-minded prisoners in tow, heads to the hospital where the wounded Hancock has been taken. Mary is wounded in the battle that follows, but Hancock and Ray manage to subdue the criminals, and Hancock leaves the city afterward so that he and Mary can recover from their wounds, regain their powers, and become immortal again. Hancock relocates to New York City and begins to work as a superhero there.

The structure and content of *Hancock* present the viewer with some real dissonance, cognitive and otherwise, and the problem is rooted in something far deeper than the fact that the film takes a jarring turn for its final third. Perhaps what is most upsetting about *Hancock* is not its many quantifiable inconsistencies, but the disappointment at what the film could have been. *Hancock* begins strong as a film about the earthly concerns of an unearthly figure—the rehabilitation of a derelict superhero and the salvaging of his public image. This is the portion of the film that is most successful. Berg uses the camera and visual effects to create an extremely photorealistic world for Hancock and manages to use these elements combined with the over-the-top ridiculousness of a drunken superhero who hates the people he saves, along with Will Smith's natural charm and charisma, to find the humorous moments in between all of the fast-paced, jerky, and highly destructive superhero action. The very idea of a superhero in need of a PR makeover in the wake of all of the collateral damage he has caused is a novel one, and Hancock's public image problem and his journey back into the good graces of the people is sufficient in itself—that alone is a complete film, and this is ably explored in *Hancock*'s first hour. But in the final third of *Hancock*, Berg and company shift focus to Ray's wife, the mysterious Mary, Hancock's shadowy past, and the threat from a completely superfluous villain. The film veers off into what seems to be meant as an exploration of the truly separate and lonely nature of the superhero's existence: Hancock and Mary are from an ancient supernatural race that was built in pairs and they become mortal if they connect with their other. As a blank-slate character, with no memory or origin story, it is true that the door is open for just about any history for Hancock—Mary's emergence as one of his lost kind, and the fact that if they get close to one another they become mortal are not in themselves violations of the story per se. Hancock had to come from somewhere after all, and just because he thinks he is the only one of his kind does not make it so—but this is certainly a violation of the tone established in the first two-thirds of the film. To make Hancock's inability to connect with others so overtly metaphysical and spiritual removes the film from the earthly concerns the movie so effectively establishes and develops until its final act.

It must be stated that there are elements of excellence in *Hancock:* Will Smith and Jason Bateman turn in fine performances (though Bateman is underused); Peter Berg and his special effects crew give a wonderfully raw feel to Hancock's superpowers—every time Hancock takes flight the camera communicates the uneasy nature of a human form airborne, and every landing carries the devastating force of a tornado and an earthquake combined. But watching *Hancock* is like watching the problems that bedeviled the *Matrix* trilogy unfold in a single movie instead of over three films: The initial joy and exhilaration of discovering the main character and his world is ultimately destroyed by the introduction of related yet not integral elements and ideas, and all of this is mixed together in such a way that the whole product becomes tainted. The film might have been able to integrate its more mythical themes had it sought to be another kind of superhero movie, a more conventional one—one in which Hancock perhaps leaves humanity behind for a time while he goes off to discover his true past after encountering Mary (vis-à-vis Clark Kent/Kal El's journey of self-discovery in the *Superman* saga). In short, had the backstory been more developed or presented differently, the abrupt shift in tone might make more sense and not weaken the film so drastically. The fact is, however, that the filmmakers spend an hour exploring a particular kind of hero journey for *Hancock* and then pull the rug out from under both him and the audience in the final half hour. The result is a film that shows great promise and then manages to squander that promise in a flurry of jumbled,

half-realized concepts that make for a somewhat interesting but ultimately unfulfilling wreck of a film.

John Boaz

CREDITS

John Hancock: Will Smith
Ray Embrey: Jason Bateman
Mary Embrey: Charlize Theron
Red: Eddie Marsan
Jeremy: Johnny Galecki
Mike: Thomas Lennon
Aaron: Jae Head
Origin: USA
Language: English
Released: 2008
Production: Akiva Goldsman, Michael Mann, Will Smith, James Lassiter; Relativity Media, Weed Road Pictures, Overbrook Entertainment, Columbia Pictures, Blue Light; released by Sony Pictures Entertainment
Directed by: Peter Berg
Written by: Vince Gilligan, Vy Vincent Ngo
Cinematography by: Tobias Schliessler
Music by: John Powell
Sound: David MacMillan
Music Supervisor: George Drakoulias
Editing: Paul Rubell, Colby Parker Jr.
Art Direction: William Hawkins, Dawn Swiderski
Costumes: Louise Mingenbach
Production Design: Neil Spisak
MPAA rating: PG-13
Running time: 92 minutes

REVIEWS

Boston Globe Online. July 1, 2008.
Chicago Sun-Times Online. June 30, 008.
Entertainment Weekly Online. July 1, 2008.
Hollywood Reporter Online. June 24, 2008.
Los Angeles Times Online. July 1, 2008.
New York Times Online. July 2, 2008.
New Yorker Online. July 7, 2008.
Rolling Stone Online. July 1, 2008.
San Francisco Chronicle. July 2, 2008, p. E1.
Variety Online. June 24, 2008.
Washington Post. July 2, 2008, p. C1.

QUOTES

Hancock (comes flying in a leather suit and the police men are looking at him): "What? It's a little tight."

TRIVIA

The script, originally titled 'Tonight, He Comes,' floated around in Hollywood for more than a decade.

THE HAPPENING

We've sensed it. We've seen the signs. Now… it's happening.
—Movie tagline

Box Office: $64.5 million

The once-promising career of M. Night Shyamalan has come a long way since *Time Magazine* put the talented writer/director on their cover and dubbed the young man "The Next Steven Spielberg." After *The Sixth Sense* (1999), *Unbreakable* (2000), and *Signs* (2002), no one blamed a major magazine for thinking that Shyamalan might take the mantle of storytelling genius from the man who successfully turned genre-based product into mainstream phenomena. Shyamalan had already transformed subjects like ghosts, superheroes, and aliens into critical and commercial gold. It appeared that he could do no wrong. Times have changed for Night, who has watched each of his last three films put a bigger hole in the theory that he would be the next Spielberg. *The Village* (2004) was a step down and then *The Lady in the Water* (2006) sunk Shyamalan in the eyes of even some of his most ardent fans. The few people left on Shyamalan's side anxiously anticipated *The Happening,* Night's first R-rated horror film, and predicted a return to form for the controversial director. What they got instead was a film that bears almost no resemblance to *The Sixth Sense, Unbreakable,* or *Signs,* a disaster on nearly every level that failed to satisfy moviegoers or critics and may have been strike three for this once-promising auteur.

The Happening opens with the most effective and disturbing scenes in the film. People in New York City suddenly stop moving and then choose the closest implement to end their lives. A woman on a Central Park bench pulls a hairpin from her head and jabs it into her jugular. Construction workers in the city throw themselves from the roof of their job site. A police officer shoots himself with his own weapon. Shyamalan films these early scenes with an apocalyptic sense of mystery that keeps them riveting and the audience wondering what could possibly be happening. At first, the populace assumes that the widespread panic has been caused by a bioterrorist attack, but the scope of the disaster—the mass suicide quickly spreads to the entire northeastern United States—makes it clear that something much darker is going on.

Against this background, Shyamalan introduces the audience to Elliot Moore (Mark Wahlberg), a high school science teacher in Philadelphia. Caught mid-class when news of the mass suicides spreads, Elliot makes the wise move of leaving town by train with his friend Julian (John Leguizamo) and wife Alma (Zooey

Deschanel). The train abruptly stops in the small town of Filbert after the conductor loses contact with "everyone." Julian learns that the panic has hit the town where his wife is located and he leaves his daughter Jess (Ashlyn Sanchez) with Elliot and Alma to hitch a ride and find her. The newly formed trio just happens to encounter a botanist and his wife, who think that the attacks may be nature-related, Mother Earth fighting back against the virus (humanity) that has been destroying it. As they struggle for survival, Elliot and Alma figure out that there is safety in small numbers, as the larger groups of people, like the city centers, are being wiped out first by nature's fury. They hope that if they can stay alive long enough, Mother Nature will let them live.

Many critics and audiences ridiculed Shyamalan for the rather ridiculous killer plants concept of *The Happening,* but "man versus nature" is as old a theme as the thriller genre. It was the execution of *The Happening* that made it fall as flat as a scary version of *Little Shop of Horrors* (1986). Shyamalan's ear for dialogue was never his strong suit, but nothing he had written before compares to the awkward, unbelievable exchanges heard in *The Happening.* Good actors like Mark Wahlberg and Zooey Deschanel sound ridiculous saying things like "Just when you thought there couldn't be any more evil that can be invented" and "Can this really be happening?" The dialogue is obvious and awkward, making none of the characters remotely believable. When the concept of a script is as far-fetched as *The Happening,* making sure that the people in such an out-there situation feel relatable and realistic becomes even more essential, and Shyamalan never once gives his audience something that rings true.

Stilted dialogue and unbelievable characters are bad enough, but what truly sinks *The Happening* is the complete lack of confidence displayed by a filmmaker who used to be so assured. As a writer, Shyamalan has no idea what to do after his set-up. The film almost feels half-written, as if Night had what he thought was a great idea and forgot that he would have to write two more acts for a complete film. Roughly halfway through the film, Elliot and Alma are in the middle of a field, completely unaware of where to go next and it becomes difficult to shake the sensation that Shyamalan is just as lost in that open space, not completely positive how to segue into the second half. As a director, *Signs* and *The Sixth Sense* exuded confidence, a director leading his audience by the nose to precisely where he wanted to take them. In *The Happening,* the same writer/director has no idea where to go next and he loses his audience right there in that field, and after increasingly less-accomplished films since *Signs,* he may have lost them forever.

Brian Tallerico

CREDITS

Elliot Moore: Mark Wahlberg
Alma Moore: Zooey Deschanel
Julian: John Leguizamo
Josh: Spencer Breslin
Mrs. Jones: Betty Buckley
Realtor: Joel de la Fuente
Nursery Owner: Frank Collison
Jess: Ashlyn Sanchez
Jared: Robert Bailey Jr.
Origin: USA
Language: English
Released: 2008
Production: M. Night Shyamalan, Sam Mercer, Barry Mendel; UTV Motion Pictures, Spyglass Entertainment, Blinding Edge Pictures; released by 20th Century-Fox
Directed by: M. Night Shyamalan
Written by: M. Night Shyamalan
Cinematography by: Tak Fujimoto
Music by: James Newton Howard
Sound: Tod A. Maitland
Editing: Conrad Buff
Art Direction: Tony Dunne
Costumes: Betsy Heimann
Production Design: Jeannine Oppewall
MPAA rating: R
Running time: 91 minutes

REVIEWS

Boston Globe Online. June 13, 2008.
Chicago Sun-Times Online. June 12, 2008.
Entertainment Weekly Online. June 11, 2008.
Hollywood Reporter Online. June 10, 2008.
Los Angeles Times Online. June 13, 2008.
New York Times Online. June 13, 2008.
San Francisco Chronicle. June 13, 2008, p. E1.
Variety Online. June 10, 2008.
Wall Street Journal. June 13, 2008, p. W1.
Washington Post. June 13, 2008, p. C1.

QUOTES

Train conductor: "The train service has been discountinued. This will be the last stop for all passengers."
Elliot Moore: "Hey, what do you mean? Where are we?"
Train conductor: "Filbert, Pennsylvania."

Elliot Moore: " Filbert? Does anybody know where that is? Why are you giving me one useless piece of information at a time? What's going on? Hey, why would you just stop? You can't just leave us here!"
Train conductor: "Sir, we lost contact."
Elliot Moore: "With whom?"
Train conductor: " Everyone."

TRIVIA

M. Night Shyamalan wrote the screenplay with Mark Wahlberg specifically in mind for the lead role.

AWARDS

Nomination:

Golden Raspberries 2008: Worst Picture, Worst Actor (Wahlberg), Worst Director (Shyamalan), Worst Screenplay.

HAPPY-GO-LUCKY

Box Office: $3.5 million

The title of Mike Leigh's widely acclaimed comedy/drama *Happy-Go-Lucky* refers to the film's sunny heroine, Poppy, who responds to life's many challenges with a smile and a joke and a giggle that is infectious. With this waifish, relentlessly upbeat North London elementary school teacher, the British writer/director shows us a side of human nature not often delved into in films—happiness, and how it often seems at odds with the rest of the world.

Perhaps even more interesting than the subject of the film is its creator. Mike Leigh is a veteran filmmaker whose previous slice-of-life dramas have tended to illuminate the dark side of humanity. His previous multi-Oscar® nominated film, *Vera Drake* (2004), was a tragedy about a well-meaning abortionist. The fact that multi-award winning *Happy-Go-Lucky* walks on the lighter side of life, however, does not make it any less profound. As always, Leigh's exhaustive rehearsal process with actors he has worked with in the past involves delving deeply into each of the film's characters, their backstory, character arc, and motivation. This in turns shapes the dialogue and the story. The result is a rich story with multilayered characters that resonates deeply with audiences.

Poppy Montgomery (Sally Hawkins) is an elementary school teacher who looks and acts much younger than her thirty years, often spending evenings drinking and clubbing with her flat-mate of ten years Zoe (Alexis Zegerman) and younger sister Suzy (Kate O'Flynn). The opening credits show Poppy riding her bike through the London streets, smiling and waving to strangers with her typical childlike enthusiasm and colorful, bohemian-chic attire. Her constant chirpy chattering and jokey asides annoy some, like the grumpy bookseller (Elliot Cowan) who completely ignores her as she pulls out the title "Road to Reality," and smilingly says she does not want to go there. Although her friends love her, sometimes even they suggest she adopt a more realistic attitude toward life. The film's drama stems from her interactions with others—mainly other teachers—both meaningful and brief. It is how she deals with those around her that fascinates, and tension arises as the film progresses and we look for cracks in her façade and wonder when the other shoe will drop. The fact that it really never does is also what makes *Happy-Go-Lucky* even more interesting, as it breaks from film conventions we have come to expect.

Poppy enjoys going to a trampoline gym where she happily bounces away—until a sore back stops her. No worries, Poppy heads to a chiropractor where she giggles through the pain and the spinal adjustment. When a coworker invites her to her Flamenco dancing class, she gamely accepts. The scene is one of the film's funniest because of contrast between the deeply passionate Spanish Flamenco teacher (Karina Fernandez), who works herself up so emotionally that she runs out of the class, and Poppy, treating all the dramatic stomping, clapping, and the dance's heart-wrenching history as just a lark.

The main drama, however, comes unexpectedly when Poppy's bike is stolen and she enrolls in driving classes. She encounters yet another teacher, Scott (Eddie Marsan), an angry, misanthropic, racist whose teaching methods are structured, methodical, and inflexible. Despite his constants complaints and objections to everything from her high-heeled boots (unsuitable, he says, for driving) to her freewheeling, single lifestyle, Poppy continues merrily with lessons that would be unbearable to most.

She persists with her lessons, it becomes clear, because she is trying to help Scott, like everyone else she encounters whom she feels is in need. As angry as he is, Scott is not nearly as frightening as the bearlike, deranged homeless man (Stanley Townsend) Poppy courageously tries to connect with. She tries to converse with him in his unintelligible language and follows him around a deserted building long after it becomes comfortable to do so, just so he can feel a human connection. When a boy at school becomes abusive toward the other children, Poppy pulls him aside and tries to find out what is the root cause of his disruptive behavior. This leads to a fateful meeting with a handsome and friendly social worker, Tim (Samuel Roukin), who is immediately attracted to her uplifting and obliging spirit.

The dénouement is a head-on collision of sorts between Scott and Poppy. Poppy has seen Scott secretively lurking outside her apartment building, something he would never admit to. His growing fascination with his pupil leads to a heated physical confrontation that shows a more contemplative side of Poppy, clearly upset by Scott's attack on her, as she tries (just like with her troubled student) calmly and rationally to find out what is bothering him so much. Although getting to the root of such a troubled soul proves impossible, Poppy never stops trying.

The film works as well as it does due to its fine ensemble of actors, especially the two leads. Hawkins, trained in the theater, deftly plays Poppy without ever making her seem shallow, flighty or even worse, annoying, all of which are easily imagined upon hearing a description of her character. Marsan never loses his eerie intensity yet amazingly also manages to convey a barely perceptible softening for his student with just a look or well-placed pause.

It may be a stretch to describe the film as a distaff, art house version of another 2008 release, *Yes Man,* but it does have much the same sort of refreshing positivity. *Happy-Go-Lucky* meanders happily along with Poppy, but far from purposelessly.

Hilary White

CREDITS

Poppy: Sally Hawkins
Scott: Eddie Marsan
Heather: Sylvestria Le Touzel
Zoe: Alexis Zegerman
Tim: Samuel Roukin
Alice: Sinead Matthews
Suzy: Kate O'Flynn
Tash: Sarah Niles
Flamenco instructor: Karina Fernandez
Origin: Great Britain
Language: English
Released: 2008
Production: Simon Channing Williams; Summit Entertainment, Ingenious Film Partners, Thin Man, Film 4; released by Miramax Films
Directed by: Mike Leigh
Written by: Mike Leigh
Cinematography by: Dick Pope
Music by: Gary Yershon
Sound: Tim Fraser, Nigel Stone
Editing: Jim Clark
Art Direction: Patrick Rolfe, Denis Schnegg
Costumes: David Crossman

Production Design: Mark Tidesley
MPAA rating: R
Running time: 118 minutes

REVIEWS

Entertainment Weekly Online. October 7, 2008.
Hollywood Reporter Online. February 13, 2008.
Los Angeles Times Online. October 10, 2008.
New York Times Online. October 10, 2008.
New Yorker Online. October 13, 2008.
Rolling Stone Online. October 16, 2008.
San Francisco Chronicle. October 10, 2008, p. E13.
Variety Online. February 12, 2008.
Wall Street Journal Online. October 10, 2008.

QUOTES

Scott: "Bear with me."
Poppy: "Is there? Where is he?"

AWARDS

Golden Globes 2009: Actress—Mus./Comedy (Hawkins)
Nomination:
Oscars 2008: Orig. Screenplay
Golden Globes 2009: Film—Mus./Comedy.

HAROLD & KUMAR ESCAPE FROM GUANTANAMO BAY

This time they're running from the joint.
—Movie tagline

Box Office: $38.1 million

Juvenile gross-out humor and sexism aside, *Harold & Kumar Escape from Guantanamo Bay* is a funny and well-crafted commentary on contemporary American society. The follow up to *Harold & Kumar Go to White Castle* (2004)—the acclaimed stoner tale of two friends on an all night, marijuana-inspired quest for burgers—*Escape from Guantanamo Bay* picks up immediately where the first biracial buddy flick left off, but with a bigger budget, better production value, and newly acquired social and political consciousness. Fast-paced and quick-witted, it sticks to the classic screwball adventure comedy genre and remains true to the spirit and format of *White Castle*. Cowriter/directors Jon Hurwitz and Hayden Schlossberg tied together the sequel and the original with numerous back references in the form of continuing plotlines, inside jokes, and returning minor characters. Former child actor Neil Patrick Harris

also makes an encore appearance, playing another twisted, drunk and drugged-out version of himself in a hitchhiking scenario modeled closely after his first extended cameo role.

Despite the boldly worded title, Harold Lee (John Cho) and Kumar Patel (Kal Penn) spend little time actually incarcerated in or escaping from Guantanamo Bay, the notorious U.S. detention center for suspected terrorists. Rather, the two best friends pass most of the movie traveling a frustrating, indirect route from New Jersey to Amsterdam by way of Washington D.C., Cuba, Miami, Texas, and the Deep South. Once in Amsterdam, Harold hopes to have the "most romantic week of (his) life" by surprising Maria (Paula Garcés), his neighbor and budding love-interest from the conclusion of the previous movie. Kumar's romantic target is Vanessa (Danneel Harris), his ex-girlfriend who is about to marry the rich and good-looking Colton (Eric Winter), a smug Brook Brothers–wearing type whom the characters knew in college. Harold and Kumar run into the couple at the airport, right before taking off on their ill-fated flight to Amsterdam. To Kumar's chagrin, the fiancés are on their way to Colton's family home in Texas to get married.

After being mistakenly apprehended on the plane for having a smokeless bong resembling a real bomb, Harold and Kumar are sent to Guantanamo Bay by Ron Fox (Rob Corddry), the paranoid, overzealous and incompetent agent filling in for the vacationing head of an unnamed federal security agency assumed to be the Department of Homeland Security. Managing to escape the horrific prison, the fugitives decide to travel to Texas to search for Colton, who they hope will help clear their names through his father's political connections; his pals include the president of the United States himself, who is expected to be in attendance at the wedding. Kumar, of course, has an ulterior motive for going to Texas: to win back Vanessa.

The movie begins with the first of several fantasy sequences predictably interrupted by some comically rude or otherwise unpleasant event. Sex, drugs, and racism are recurring themes as Harold and Kumar find themselves in a series of quirky scenarios based around their ethnically diverse friends and other eccentric people they encounter by chance along the way. The relationship between the serious Harold and the slacker Kumar becomes strained due to their differences, but their common feelings for their respective objects of affection eventually repair the bond and bring the long-time friends back together. Needless to say, they endure many madcap adventures and mishaps before either can be united with their lady loves and enjoy all that Amsterdam has to offer.

The differences between *White Castle* and its sequel are notable. Slightly more mature than the entertaining and relatively uncontroversial first movie, *Escape from Guantanamo Bay* distinguishes itself with a degree of political outrage, boldly using satire to criticize the United States government and the Department of Homeland Security for their handling of the War on Terror. Despite the stupidly outrageous circumstances leading up to the imprisonment of the American-born Harold and Kumar, the plot's basic premise regarding innocent minorities mistaken for terrorists and stripped of their rights is not an uncommon occurrence or hard-to-believe scenario in post-9/11 America. Unfortunately, what appears to have been the sincere intent on the part of the filmmakers to express dissent over certain government policies and practices was evidently lost on activist groups such as Amnesty International; the group called for a boycott upon the film's release, insisting that the real Guantanamo Bay is not a laughing matter.

In fact, *Escape from Guantanamo Bay* is far from a typical "white bread" road movie for teens and young adults. In addition to having a strong political message, it proves that America has become a fully multicultural society. The returning costars—a Korean American and an American of East Indian descent—are joined this time by a much greater number of multiethnic supporting actors than were featured in the original. Although the jokes are typically crass, the racial humor is based in irony, and common stereotypes are exploited to make fun of racism and ignorance. Serious points about politics and race are heavily sugar-coated with irreverent and hedonistic hilarity, however, which unfortunately may cause the intended sentiment to be lost on the average adolescent or on other intellectually unenlightened audience members. Correspondingly, more sophisticated and discerning movie viewers will probably be turned off from watching *Harold & Kumar Escape from Guantanamo Bay* altogether, based on its surface immaturity and inherent silliness, missing out on its unexpected but cleverly subversive insights.

Jaye Furlonger

CREDITS

Harold: John Cho
Kumar: Kal Penn
Ron Fox: Rob Corddry
Deputy Frye: Jack Conley
Dr. Beecher: Roger Bart
Himself: Neil Patrick Harris
Raylene: Missi Pyle
Vanessa: Danneel Harris
Colton: Eric Winter
George W. Bush: James Adomian
Sally: Beverly D'Angelo
Goldstein: David Krumholtz
Rosenberg: Eddie Kaye Thomas
Interpreter: Ed Helms
Mr. Lee: Clyde Kusatsu
Grand Wizard: Christopher Meloni
Maria: Paula Garcés
Origin: USA
Language: English
Released: 2008
Production: Greg Shapiro, Nathan Kahane; Mandate Pictures, Kingsgate Films; released by New Line Cinema
Directed by: Jon Hurwitz, Hayden Schlossberg
Written by: Jon Hurwitz, Hayden Schlossberg
Cinematography by: Daryn Okada
Music by: George S. Clinton
Sound: Richard Schexnayder
Music Supervisor: Season Kent
Editing: Jeff Freeman
Art Direction: Kevin Hardison
Costumes: Shawn-Holly Cookson
Production Design: Tony Fanning
MPAA rating: R
Running time: 102 minutes

REVIEWS

Boston Globe Online. April 25, 2008.
Chicago Sun-Times Online. April 25, 2008.
Entertainment Weekly Online. April 25, 2008.
Hollywood Reporter Online. March 10, 2008.
Los Angeles Times Online. April 25, 2008.
New York Times Online. April 25, 2008.
Premiere Online. April 24, 2008.
San Francisco Chronicle. April 25, 2008, p. E5.
Variety Online. March 9, 2008.

QUOTES

Vanessa: "Did you take calculus in high school or something?"
Kumar Patel: "No, actually my dad taught me in sixth grade."
Vanessa (laughing): "What are you, like Doogie Howser?"
Kumar Patel: "No. Although that would be incredible. He's my hero. I love that show."

TRIVIA

Neil Patrick Harris worked four days on this movie.

HELL RIDE

The rebellion against all there is.
—Movie tagline

Quentin Tarantino first indulged his love of 1960s and 1970s fuel-injected, exploitation films in his half of

Grindhouse's (2007) double feature, "Death Proof." Despite the fact that *Grindhouse* was both a critical and box office disappointment, the bumpy ride continues with *Hell Ride,* another B-movie homage, which Tarantino produced with biker movie veteran actor Larry Bishop, who also wrote, directed, and starred. The result is a confusing, testosterone-fueled biker action movie with revenge driving the plot.

Pistolero (Larry Bishop) heads the desert-dwelling, middle-aged motorcycle gang, the Victors. Rounding out the trio of main characters is Comanche (Eric Balfour) and the Gent, played by Tarantino regular Michael Madsen, so called because he eschews leather for a tuxedo jacket and ruffled shirt. It is essentially a case of apparel trying to pass for character in a script that fails to flesh out any of the characters beyond quirky "characteristics" such as this. Madsen fares better than most of the actors, however, and is the most convincing, not to mention youngest, of the grimacing gangbangers.

The muddled story and convoluted storytelling—with much Tarantino-esque flashback and flash-forward time jumping—is centered around a simple plot of revenge. It is nearly halfway through the film before it is finally revealed that a Comanche woman was killed some thirty years ago and that is somehow the reason for the revenge that is currently being exacted. The maniacal Billy Wings (Vinnie Jones), the crossbow toting leader of the rival gang the 666ers, has also killed one of Pistolero's best men, leading the Victors on a fiery, bloody rampage that makes up the majority of the film.

As the Victors seek a showdown with their rivals, there is nearly as much in-fighting within the gang, which is never fully explained, and a string of barely clad, broken-hearted women who pose nearly as much of a threat to Pistolero as the 666ers.

All the time, worn biker film conventions are honored, including a plethora of gunplay, ample gory violence, and loads of seminude, nubile young women inexplicably draped all over the grungy Pistolero. The sheer amount of female rear nudity may qualify as a fetish of Bishop's nearly equal to that of Russ Meyer's breast obsession. Amid the graphic sex romps with numerous women all less than half his age, the revenge premise seems like an afterthought to justify Bishop's ego gratification. Even allowing that gratuitous nudity is doubtless a vital part of the genre, that aside, Bishop is not afraid to also weave in a healthy dose of self-congratulatory dialogue in the already verbose, overly-stylized script that lauds the greatness of his antihero, Pistolero.

Starring in such cult classics as *Chrome and Hot Leather* (1971) and *Angel Unchained* (1970), modern audiences will recognize Bishop as the unsympathetic

strip-club boss in Quentin Tarantino's *Kill Bill: Vol. 2* (2004), apparently sparking their collaboration. Bishop appropriates many of Tarantino's signature stylistic elements but without the *Pulp Fiction* (1994) director's far more tasteful aesthetics. Bishop's script in particular, rife with long-winded, pseudo-poetic monologues, exude a distinct Tarantino vibe but are filled with the most vulgar and crass imaginings and completely devoid of either finesse or believability. At other times, the dialogue is oversimplified, requiring Madsen to blow into a beer bottle and then utter such first-grade observations as, "I'm an owl."

With cameos in more than one of the most abysmal films of 2008 (see *An American Carol*) Dennis Hopper is in danger of becoming a self-parody, although his appearance in *Hell Ride* at least makes sense, playing on his *Easy Rider* (1969) image. And Hopper fans will heartily enjoy watching their still relevant hero mount an iron steed once again. *Kill Bill*'s David Carradine also cameos as a 666er, the Deuce.

Hard-core biker films were largely forgotten after Marlon Brando's *The Wild One* (1953) spurred copycat films through the 1950s and 1960s. With its band of middle-aged marauders, *Hell Ride* is hot on the heels of the unexpectedly successful *Wild Hogs* (2007), another over-the-hill biker, male fantasy that proves there may still be a market for the genre. *Hell Ride*, with a mere $195,000 in tickets sales, can hardly complete with the more commercial *Wild Hogs,* which grossed an impressive $140 million box office and boasts a sequel in the works. The best *Hell Ride* can hope for is parlaying its grungy appeal into a cult following on DVD.

Hilary White

CREDITS

Pistolero: Larry Bishop
The Gent: Michael Madsen
Comanche: Eric Balfour
Billy Wings: Vinnie Jones
The Deuce: David Carradine
Eddie 'Scratch' Zero: Dennis Hopper
Nada: Leonor Varela
Origin: USA
Language: English
Released: 2008
Production: Larry Bishop; Michael Steinberg, Shana Stein; released by Dimension Films
Directed by: Larry Bishop
Written by: Larry Bishop
Cinematography by: Scott Kevan
Music by: Daniele Luppi

Sound: Matthew Nicolay
Music Supervisor: Mary Ramos
Editing: William Yeh, Blake West
Costumes: Ariyela Wald-Cohain
Production Design: Tim Grimes
MPAA rating: R
Running time: 84 minutes

REVIEWS

Boston Globe Online. August 8, 2008.
Chicago Sun-Times Online. August 8, 2008.
Entertainment Weekly Online. August 11, 2008.
Hollywood Reporter Online. February 26, 2008.
Los Angeles Times Online. August 8, 2008.
New York Times Online. August 8, 2008.
Variety Online. August 6, 008.

TRIVIA

The film had a DVD release date before a theatrical release date.

HELLBOY II: THE GOLDEN ARMY

Saving the world is a hell of a job.
—Movie tagline
Believe it or not—he's the good guy.
—Movie tagline

Box Office: $75.9 million

Bearing the construct of a romantic comedy mixed with an H. P. Lovecraft short story, Guillermo del Toro directs this sequel of the stogie-chomping, pancake-eating, wisecracking demon, Hellboy (Ron Perlman). Based on the successful Dark Horse Comics character, Hellboy works for a clandestine government organization, the Bureau for Paranormal Research and Defense (B.P.R.D.). The agency investigates and battles preternatural entities that threaten human civilization. Although demon spawned, Hellboy is trying to fit in with the rest of humanity. He even has a daily regimen similar to a man shaving of sanding down his horns to stumps, which make it look like he has a pair of goggles resting high on his forehead. Although extracted from an infernal dimension by a Nazi specializing in the occult for the Third Reich in 1944, Hellboy's demeanor is that of an adolescent in many respects, as his maturation process is significantly slower than humans. He is prone to mood swings, loves candy, and has an affinity for cats. In *Hellboy II: The Golden Army*, del Toro is able to continue his passion for magical fantasy as seen in his signature highpoint, *Pan's Labyrinth* (2006).

This tale begins on a U.S. Army base in 1954. Hellboy is being told a bedtime story by Professor Trevor 'Broom' Bruttenholm (John Hurt), who adopted the diabolical-appearing youth. Earth was coinhabited by another, far more superior race of beings who ruled it. During a brutal war, the ruler of the elfish creatures, King Balor (Roy Dotrice), had a mechanical legion constructed (the inappropriately named Golden Army). This immortal robotic force brutally massacred a large segment of their human adversaries. Balor decided to make a treaty with the humans: Elfland would endure in the forests and man could dwell in the cities. Balor's son, Prince Nuada Silverlance (Luke Goss), disagreed with the monarch's decision and left the kingdom. This Golden Army is placed in a state of limbo and can only be reactivated by three pieces of a crown being placed back together. The elfin race possessed two pieces, while humanity was the custodian of the third.

Flash-forward to the present day, where in the underground kingdom of the elves, Prince Nuada overthrows his father by murdering him and attains the first piece of the crown. He procures the piece from an auction in New York City by a museum. The piece's origin has been relegated to the way of ancient folklore. Nuada's challenge is to get the third piece from his twin sister Princess Nuala (Anna Walton), who fled the kingdom.

At the B.P.R.D., Hellboy is in the midst of personal drama. He is having problems with his girlfriend Liz Sherman (Selma Blair). (Liz is a paranormal who has pyrokinetic abilities and lives outside the agency's headquarters). He also is conflicted about the agency's stance to remain an undercover organization. Following a battle in which he and other field agents suppress a league of sharp-toothed, carnivorous, regenerating insect-like creatures that have committed a massacre at the auction for the crown piece. Unleashed by Prince Nuada, Hellboy and his teammates subdue the horde. Hellboy, feeling underappreciated for his humanitarian exploits, strives against administrative policy and goes public.

The agency has a mysterious new addition to their team, a gaseous German entity Johann Krauss (James Dodd with voice of Seth MacFarlane). Krauss is composed of ectoplasm and serves as the group's new leader as well as its resident medium. Due to his ethereal form, he must wear a containment suit to avert death by dissipation. Krauss, head of the B.P.R.D.'s Ectoplasmic Research Branch in Washington, D.C., immediately finds the team's amphibious psychic, Abe Sapien (Doug Jones) and the outfit's stuffy bureaucratic caretaker Tom Manning (Jeffrey Tambor) to be competent. He has reservations about Hellboy, though.

Following Nuala's capture (she was being protected by the B.P.R.D.), the contingent arrives in Northern Ireland for a final battle with Nuada. Despite being opposed to the gothic-looking elf prince, Hellboy empathizes with his position on humanity as an ungrateful bunch who consider them monsters. The ensuing climatic battle is something of a letdown when contrasted with the rest of the script.

The film's humor is its strongest aspect; it only enhances the macabre supernatural elements pervasive in the work. Del Toro utilizes slapstick comedy as well as ironic one-liners to give the premise levity throughout the story's progression. The movie's most hilarious bit involves the Barry Manilow song, "'Can't Smile Without You." The first time it is played, Hellboy is getting drunk with Abe and the two are acting like spurned teens as they listen to Manilow croon. The film ends with Liz informing Hellboy that they are about to have twins. Hellboy's shocked expression is frozen in a still shot with the same Manilow song playing. It could easily serve as a prologue for the next installment's global threat.

David Metz Roberts

CREDITS

Hellboy: Ron Perlman
Liz: Selma Blair
Abe Sapien: Doug Jones
Prince Nuada: Luke Goss
King Balor: Roy Dotrice
Professor Broom: John Hurt
Tom Mannign: Jeffrey Tambor
Mr. Wink/Cronie Troll/Cathedral Head/Fragglewump: Brian Steele
Princess Nuala: Anna Walton
Johann Krauss: Seth MacFarlane (Voice)
Origin: USA
Language: English
Released: 2008
Production: Lawrence Gordon, Lloyd Levin, Michael Richardson; Relativity Media, Dark Horse Entertainment; released by Universal Pictures
Directed by: Guillermo del Toro
Written by: Guillermo del Toro, Mike Mignola
Cinematography by: Guillermo Navarro
Music by: Danny Elfman
Sound: Mac Ruth
Music Supervisor: Kathy Nelson
Editing: Bernat Vilaplana
Art Direction: Peter Francis
Costumes: Sammy Sheldon
Production Design: Stephen Scott

MPAA rating: PG-13
Running time: 110 minutes

REVIEWS

Boston Globe Online. July 11, 2008.
Chicago Sun-Times Online. July 10, 2008.
Entertainment Weekly Online. July 9, 2008.
Hollywood Reporter Online. June 29, 2008.
Los Angeles Times Online. July 11, 2008.
New York Times Online. July 11, 2008.
Rolling Stone Online. July 10, 2008.
San Francisco Chronicle. July 10, 2008, p. E1.
Variety Online. June 29, 008.
Wall Street Journal Online. July 11, 2008.
Washington Post. July 11, 2008, p. C1.

QUOTES

Johann Krauss: "You have one fatal flaw."
Hellboy: "Oh, I wanna hear this."
Johann Krauss: "No, you don't. You can't take criticism."
Hellboy: "Try me."
Johann Krauss (pokes Hellboy): "Can't...take it."
Hellboy (yells): "What's my flaw?"
Johann Krauss: "Your temper! It gets the best of you. Makes you weak, makes you vulnera..." (Hellboy punches him)

TRIVIA

Just like the first film, none of the cast member's names are written on the posters, mentioned in the trailers or shown in the opening credits.

AWARDS

Nomination:

Oscars 2008: Makeup
Screen Actors Guild 2008: Outstanding Performance by a Stunt Ensemble.

HENRY POOLE IS HERE

Changing his attitude will take a miracle.
    —Movie tagline

Box Office: $1.8 million

Writing and directing a drama about the conflict of faith and hope that must happen in the average man who finds himself handed a death sentence by a doctor with bad news is a tightrope from day one, but *Henry Poole is Here* only went downhill from its awkward set-up. Instead of trying to inject a tale that might come off as preachy with believability and subtlety, director Mark

Pellington (*Arlington Road* [1999], *The Mothman Prophecies* [2002]) went in the other direction, hammering the ham-fisted themes of the screenplay like a preacher pounding on the pulpit instead of presenting anything to which audiences could actually relate. *Henry Poole Is Here* offers so little but poorly conceived lessons about faith that, were it not for the involvement of major actors, one might mistake it for a church-produced film to be watched in parochial school. Only a pair of talented actresses makes it out of this cinematic sermon unscathed. Everyone else will have to atone.

Henry Poole (Luke Wilson) is a man with an unspecified, but clearly short, amount of time left to live. He first offers any amount of money to buy the home where he spent his formative years to spend his last, but he ends up moving in just down the street. Lucky for the understandably depressed Poole, he happens to move into a house between a kind, faithful woman named Esperanza (Adriana Barraza) and a gorgeous single mother named Dawn (Radha Mitchell). Dawn's redheaded daughter Millie (Morgan Lily) likes to audio tape the people in her neighborhood, including Henry, and has not spoken a word since her father abandoned them a year ago. After one of her visits, Esperanza spots a water stain in the new stucco job on the side of Henry's house and she is immediately struck by its resemblance to Jesus Christ. When a spot of blood forms on the vague image and nothing will wash it away, Esperanza and her friends become convinced that they are in the middle of a full-blown miracle. As Henry spends his last days in a haze of junk food and cheap booze, he is forced to come to terms with his own atheism, as more and more unexplainable events happen in the vicinity of his backyard.

"Dawn" on one side and "Hope" (which is what "Esperanza" means in Spanish) on the other. Writer Albert Torres even has the nerve to include a pivotal supporting character named "Patience." Overt symbolism is one thing, but a writer with the impudence to do so in the very names of his characters is inexcusable—the kind of device usually reserved for bad theater. There was a point in the development of *Henry Poole Is Here* at which the screenplay, even with its ridiculous appellations, could have been saved with an ounce of subtlety, but Torres and Pellington go in the exact opposite direction with the actual production. In case there might be one person who does not get the allegory, characters literally start to question each other's faith, while others become some of the most blatant plot devices in the history of drama. It has been a long time since a child has been used in such a manipulative manner to drive the plot forward as poor Millie in *Henry Poole Is Here*. The talented Barraza (*Babel* [2006]) and the always-intriguing Mitchell do their best to add shades of depth to their two-dimensional characters, but the movie is called *Henry Poole Is Here* and there clearly was not room for anyone else.

Luke Wilson has struggled with awkward comedy in recent years, so taking a risk on a religious drama is certainly an admirable move, but Pellington leaves this poor actor out to dry. Extreme close-ups, panning shots up the street to a reflexive Henry, choppy editing—Poole looks more like the lead singer in a music video than a three-dimensional character and it makes Wilson looks physically uncomfortable at times. *Henry Poole Is Here* had some possibly insurmountable screenplay problems, but there may have never been a worse fit for a movie about finding faith in one's own backyard than Mark Pellington. His amped-up style, one that he learned making some excellent music videos, only amplifies the preachy nature of the script and sinks the project. Pellington employs the same in-your-face dynamic that he did in the action of *Arlington Road* and the sci-fi horror of *The Mothman Prophecies*. He made an unending stream of bad decisions with *Henry Poole Is Here*, and this story about a search for redemption ends up worth nothing more than critical damnation.

Brian Tallerico

CREDITS

Henry Poole: Luke Wilson
Dawn: Radha Mitchell
Father Salazar: George Lopez
Meg: Cheryl Hines
Esparanza: Adriana Barraza
Dr. Fancher: Richard Benjamin
Josie: Beth Grant
Millie: Morgan Lily
Patience: Rachel Seiferth
Origin: USA
Language: English
Released: 2008
Production: Tom Rosenberg, Gary Lucchesi, Richard Wright, Gary Gilbert, Tom Lassally; Lakeshore Entertainment, Camelot; released by Overture Films
Directed by: Mark Pellington
Written by: Albert Torres
Cinematography by: Eric Schmidt
Music by: John Frizzell
Sound: Steve Morrow
Editing: Lisa Zeno Churgin
Art Direction: Karen Steward
Costumes: Wendy Chuck
Production Design: Richard Hoover
MPAA rating: PG
Running time: 100 minutes

REVIEWS

Boston Globe Online. August 15, 2008.

Chicago Sun-Times Online. August 14, 2008.

Entertainment Weekly Online. August 15, 2008.

Hollywood Reporter Online. January 23, 2008.

Los Angeles Times Online. August 15, 2008.

New York Times Online. August 15, 2008.

San Francisco Chronicle. August 15, 2008, p. E5.

Variety Online. January 23, 2008.

Washington Post. August 15, 2008, p. C5.

HIGH SCHOOL MUSICAL 3: SENIOR YEAR

Box Office: $90.5 million

In bringing their wildly popular, Emmy® Award-winning *High School Musical* television movies to the big screen, Disney has created a sanitized *Grease* (1978) for a new generation. The film prudently utilizes the same actors, director/choreographer Kenny Ortega, and screenwriter Peter Barsocchini as the made-for-cable *High School Musical* (2006) and *High School Musical 2* (2007). *High School Musical 3: Senior Year* delivers the same high-quality emoting, singing, and dancing from characters that are familiar to the already devoted audience of the franchise. The film likely met the high expectations set for it, recouping more than $90 million of its significantly increased $30 million budget.

High School Musical 3 eschews such controversial topics as teen pregnancy and smoking that the far-campier *Grease* tackled, but features the same type of high school romance and friendships and the problems associated with graduation and life afterward, mixed with catchy, high-energy musical numbers. Unlike the 1950s-depicted world of *Grease,* a film where little emphasis was placed on either education or sports and one of the girls was a dropout with dreams of attending beauty school, the modern, upper-middle class kids of the more earnest *High School Musical 3* encounter such dilemmas as jealousy over friends' Julliard scholarships and mulling over which Ivy League college to attend. Despite its superior choreography—Ortega served as the choreographer of the likes of *Dirty Dancing* (1987) and *Ferris Bueller's Day Off* (1986)—it is also unlikely that the songs of this film—which also rehash songs from its earlier incarnations—will surpass those in *Grease* or will be as long-lasting.

Audiences of *High School Musical* will already be familiar with the lead characters, and the film wastes no time introducing Troy (Zac Efron) and the rest of the high school seniors at halftime of their Wildcats last championship basketball game. After a rousing speech by Coach Bolton (Bart Johnson), the kids realize that high school life as they know it is almost over and they must cherish the last days with their treasured friends while they still can. One of the film's set-pieces is the ensuing musical number, "Now or Never," sung by Troy with the whole team and fans joining in the skillfully choreographed dance.

The lightweight plot revolves around Troy, played by a far more filled-out Zac Efron, and his girlfriend Gabriella (Vanessa Hudgens) who face going to separate colleges after graduation. Gabriella is set to attend Stanford but Troy's basketball scholarship is to the University of Albuquerque. One of the film's themes is the difficult decisions associated with the kids' budding adulthood, and correspondingly, Troy is torn. He wants to please his father who, naturally, wants him to take the scholarship but he also wants to be with Vanessa as well as satisfy his desire to explore his interest in theater. A subplot involves Sharpay (Ashley Tisdale), Ryan (Lucas Grabeel), and Kelsi (Olesya Rulin) nervously awaiting scholarships from Julliard.

In between such grown-up concerns as college and career considerations, there are the requisite scenes involving the all-important prom and who to go with and what to wear, all punctuated by the plethora of song-and-dance that ably propel the story. The film's themes are echoed in a musical-within-a-musical device, as drama teacher Mr. Darbus (Alyson Reed) tasks the students with creating a musical about their final weeks of high school, entitled "Senior Year." This also furthers the prior *High School Musical* films' themes that members of disparate cliques can put their differences aside, find their similarities, and come together—in this case through art—in a similar vein as John Hughes's teen classic *The Breakfast Club* (1985).

The filmmakers took no chances in the making of the G-rated *High School Musical 3,* and the theatrical version is as squeaky clean and bloodless as the earlier television movies. It is genuinely a wholesome family movie, depicting no violence, no profane language, and other than a single kiss between Troy and Gabriella, no obvious sexuality. Of the cast, Efron is the clear-cut standout, his teen heartthrob status unable to overshadow his well-executed singing and dancing.

Critics were nearly as pleased as audiences with *High School Musical 3.* While most thought it was quality family fare, even its detractors, including *The Onion A.V. Club*'s Scott Tobias, allowed, "*HSM 3* has the bubbly brio to carry its hermetic emotions across." The bigger budget was obvious in the quality of the sets and overall production design by Mark Hofeling, able editing of Don Brochu, cinematography by *High School Musical 2*'s Daniel Aranyó, and the music and sound departments. The filmmakers also did the near impossible task of nicely wrapping up the series, at least with its current cast, in this overly earnest, but big-hearted, big-screen extravaganza.

Hilary White

CREDITS

Troy Bolton: Zac Efron
Gabriella Montez: Vanessa Anne Hudgens
Sharpay Evans: Ashley Tisdale
Ryan Evans: Lucas Grabeel
Chad Danforth: Corbin Bleu
Taylor Mckessie: Monique Coleman
Coach Jack Bolton: Bart Johnson
Kelsi Nielsen: Olesya Rulin
Origin: USA
Language: English
Released: 2008
Production: Bill Borden, Barry Rosenbush; released by Walt Disney Pictures
Directed by: Kenny Ortega
Written by: Peter Barsocchini
Cinematography by: Daniel Aranyo
Music by: David Lawrence
Sound: Douglas Cameron
Editing: Don Brochu
Art Direction: Wing Lee
Costumes: Caroline Marx
Production Design: Mark Hofeling
MPAA rating: G
Running time: 100 minutes

REVIEWS

Boston Globe Online. October 24, 2008.
Entertainment Weekly Online. October 22, 2008.
Hollywood Reporter Online. October 17, 2008.
Los Angeles Times Online. October 24, 2008.
New York Times Online. October 24, 2008.
Rolling Stone Online. November 13, 2008.
San Francisco Chronicle. October 24, 2008, p. E1.
Variety Online. October 17, 2008.
Washington Post. October 24, 2008, p. C1.

QUOTES

Sharpay Evans: "Hey, Troy, when's the big game?"
Troy Bolton: "Yesterday."
Sharpay Evans: "Well, good luck. Toodles!"

TRIVIA

More than 1,000 extras were used for the graduation scene.

THE HOUSE BUNNY

Bodaciously going where no bunny has gone before…college
—Movie tagline

Box Office: $48.2 million

The House Bunny was executive produced by Anna Faris, who sought to create a vehicle that would provide her with her long awaited and well-deserved breakout role, along the lines of Reese Witherspoon in *Legally Blonde* (2001). Faris, every bit as talented a comedian as Witherspoon if not moreso, is nicely showcased—watchable and funny with a Marilyn Monroe-esque innocence in her role as bubbly Playboy bunny Shelley Darlington—but the lazy, rehashed *Revenge of the Nerds* (1984) plot, clichéd and thinly drawn supporting characters, and faux-inspirational "it's what's on the inside that counts" message are her ultimate undoing.

The premise is at least original if not promising: a Playboy model gets kicked out of the mansion for turning twenty-seven ("that's fifty-nine in Bunny years") and becomes a house mother who gives a Bunny-style makeover to a struggling sorority. Some interesting ideas are touched upon: aging in a youth-obsessed culture, feminine ideals of beauty versus unretouched reality, and the link between success and attractiveness. The film at least pretends to acknowledge this when one of the girls, resisting her makeover, is convinced to do it as an intellectual experiment involving "conventional archetypes of beauty and their effect on the opposite sex." Some of the raunchy humor works, especially several one-liners, courtesy of writers Karen McCullah Lutz and Kirsten Smith ("the eyes are the nipples of the face," Shelley helpfully tells the girls). Overall, though, director Fred Wolf's film is far too uneven, with Faris providing most of the film's comedy and charisma against a dreary and well-worn campus background.

The day after her twenty-seventh birthday bash, Shelley Darlington (Anna Faris) is blissfully happy, living life at the Playboy Mansion with her beloved cat Pooter and awaiting her inevitable centerfold spread until she receives a note from Hef (Hugh Hefner, playing himself) saying that it is time for her to leave. She is informed by Marvin (Owen Benjamin), the mansion's resident mixologist, that it is because twenty-seven is fifty-nine in Bunny years. It is unlikely the amiable Hefner would agree to be portrayed on film as ageist (one of his girlfriends is indeed over thirty), so it is later revealed that the note was actually written by Marvin and an evil Bunny who wants the centerfold spot for herself.

Sans Pooter, who would rather continue his life of luxury at the mansion, Shelley goes blindly into the real world for which she is stunningly ill-prepared. After spending a night in jail for mistaking an officer's command to take a Breathalyzer test as a sexual proposition, the hapless Bunny lands on the campus, the house mother of the Zeta Alpha Zeta sorority. The sorority is populated by an embarrassingly clichéd cast of misfit characters, including a girl in a full body brace (Rumer Willis), one with a nearly full-term pregnancy (Katharine McPhee), and one that has never spoken (Kiely Williams), led by the bespectacled, brainy Natalie (an appealingly natural Emma Stone).

The simple plot has the sorority in danger of losing its license as it cannot attract any pledges, something Shelley easily remedies with a makeover for the wallflower sisters and a huge bash that wins over the rest of the kids on campus. The cardboard villains are the evil sisters of the rival Phi Beta Mu sorority, who put a cramp in the Zeta's plan by stealing their invitations to a subsequent party, thereby spoiling their plans to win the required thirty pledges. The romantic subplots have Shelley falling for the clean-cut manager of a nursing home, Oliver (Colin Hanks), and Natalie's bombshell makeover netting her Colby (Tyson Ritter), her crush. Beverly D'Angelo plays a badly written, dishearteningly cardboard Cruella DeVille-like rival sorority house mother to contrast Shelley's puppylike innocence.

The girls' makeovers briefly turn them into the kind of mean, superficial coeds they abhor, while Shelley's make-under—with clunky glasses and bookish demeanor—that the Zetas give her to try to appeal to the low-key, serious-minded Oliver, is also a bust. When the Zetas return to their former selves—albeit still noticeably improved—and Shelley once again acts like the lovable ditz that she naturally is, everything turns out all right in the end, while all the mean people neatly get their comeuppance. "Be yourself; only a little better," the film helpfully suggests.

Faris's gamble may not have paid off as handsomely as she would have liked but it may have been a worthwhile one. She certainly comes across well and is by far the best thing in a flawed and hardly groundbreaking romantic comedy that is best described as formulaic. While the majority of critics disliked the film, it was not universally panned by any means and it earned a respectable $48 million at the box office.

Hilary White

CREDITS

Shelley: Anna Faris
Oliver: Colin Hanks
Natalie: Emma Stone
Mona: Kat Dennings
Harmony: Katharine McPhee
Joanie: Rumer Willis
Colby: Tyson Ritter
Lilly: Kiely Williams
Carrie Mae: Dana Min Goodman
Cassandra: Monet Mazur
Dean Simmons: Christopher McDonald
Tanya: Kimberly Makkouk
Mrs. Hagstrom: Beverly D'Angelo
Francis: Charles Robinson
Tall Prostitute: Jonathan Loughran
Himself: Hugh Hefner (Cameo)
Origin: USA
Language: English
Released: 2008
Production: Adam Sandler, Jack Giarraputo, Allen Covert, Heather Parry; Columbia Pictures, Alta Loma Films, Happy Madison Productions, Relativity Media; released by Sony Pictures Entertainment
Directed by: Fred Wolf
Written by: Karen McCullah Lutz, Kirsten Smith
Cinematography by: Shelly Johnson
Music by: Waddy Wachtel
Sound: Bill W. Benton
Music Supervisor: Michael Dilbeck, Brooks Arthur
Editing: Debra Chiate
Art Direction: John Chichester
Costumes: Mona May
Production Design: Missy Stewart
MPAA rating: PG-13
Running time: 97 minutes

REVIEWS

Boston Globe Online. August 22, 2008.
Hollywood Reporter Online. August 20, 2008.
Los Angeles Times Online. August 22, 2008.
New York Times Online. August 22, 2008.
San Francisco Chronicle. August 22, 2008, p. E5.
Variety Online. August 20, 2008.
Wall Street Journal. August 22, 2008, p. W1.

QUOTES

Shelley: "They're kicking me out?"
Marvin: "Maybe it's because of your age."
Shelley: "But I'm 27."
Marvin: "But that's 59 in bunny years."

The movie idea sparked when Anna Faris wondered what happens to the Playboy Bunnies if they leave the mansion.

HOW SHE MOVE

Set your dreams in motion.
—Movie tagline

Box Office: $7 million

Inspired by the trend of popular dance movies, Ian Iqbal Rashid's *How She Move* focuses on the emerging culture of step dancing but with a grittier sense of realism and unknown actors and dancers than most of its peers. The film falls into many of the same dramatic traps as its higher-budget brethren, but finds enough moments in which it displays a believability that is so often missing from movies about dance to merit a recommendation. Writer Annmarie Morais has a soap opera ear for dialogue—most of the heartfelt exchanges in *How She Move* fail to sound genuine—but she does have a more confident ability for storytelling than most dance movie writers, who usually write their films like action movies with a few big set pieces and barely conceived connective tissue. *How She Move* is the rare dance movie that feels like it started with character instead of nothing more than a few wicked dance moves and, by going in that direction, Rashid and Morais have made a unique film that feels both realistic and energetic at the same time.

Raya (Rutina Wesley) is an aspiring medical student who is forced to return home to a neighborhood that she left years ago to go to private school. Back in public school, Raya struggles with family and identity, while trying to figure out how she could possibly raise the money to get the education she wants and deserves. After looking for a prized possession that her junkie sister pawned in her final days, Raya comes across a very well-organized step show in the streets, as if this kind of thing is happening in urban centers around the world and maybe it is, but probably not this cinematically organized and well-lit. Raya comes home to a lot of aggression from the people that she left three years ago, but antagonism in the world of *How She Move* comes in the form of a "step-off," of course. The idea that young women are more likely to stage a dance-off in a garage to settle their issues feels like something that only happens in a movie, but Rashid wisely focuses on the actual dancing instead of choppy editing, slow motion, and other tricks employed by far inferior films like *Step Up 2 the Streets* (2008) and *Feel the Noise* (2007). Not every movie needs that MTV sheen to be effective and being able to see each step and dance move makes for a far more visceral experience.

Raya gets drawn in by her good friend Bishop (Dwain Murphy) after she learns that the prize for an upcoming step-dancing competition is $50,000, something she needs for college tuition. One of many refreshing things about *How She Move* is its depiction of young women studying hard and reading Tolstoy and Du Maurier to try to get ahead. Not every character in a dance movie needs to be more focused on their fashion than their futures. Morais understands that people often use their passions to get ahead in the real world, not just to win the big show.

The new crew formed by Bishop and Raya falls apart after their steps get stolen before a preliminary competition and Raya panics and does her own moves, getting her kicked off the team. Raya needs to gain back the trust of her good friend and possible love interest to get the crew to Detroit for the big show or form her own team.

Moviegoers largely ignored *How She Move*, with a shocking number of message board postings focusing on the grammar of the title (it is ironic that in a setting where "lol" and other abbreviations have become common usage that people failed to recognize the appropriateness of having a slang-based title) instead of actually giving the movie a chance, but most critics agreed that *How She Move* deserved a wider audience. The *New York Times* noted "the strong acting, spectacular dance routines and culturally specific details in *How She Move* turn clichés into catharsis" and *USA Today* praised the "powerful dance sequences and an emphasis on education."

Finally, not every dance movie needs actors out of central casting to work. The genuine Rutina Wesley has a believable screen presence and a dynamic physicality that hold the movie together whenever it threatens to fall apart and most of the actors feel far more genuine than the model-types who populate a typical MTV movie. *How She Move* contains a few too many movies in one—returning home, dancing flick, girl power tale, sexism in urban communities, city problems, etc.—but it is a very rare and notable thing to be able to criticize a dance movie for too much plot when so many of them do not have enough to justify their existence.

Brian Tallerico

CREDITS
Faye Green: Melanie Nicholls-King
Raya Green: Rutina Wesley
Michelle: Tre Armstrong
Bishop: Dwain Murphy
Quake: Brennan Gademans

Trey: Shawn Desman
E.C.: Kevin Duhaney
Origin: Canada
Language: English
Released: 2008
Production: Jennifer Kawaja, Julia Sereny; Celluloid; released by Paramont Vantage
Directed by: Ian Iqbal Rashid
Written by: Annmarie Morais
Cinematography by: Andre Pienaar
Music by: Andrew Lockington
Sound: Steve Marian
Music Supervisor: Amy Fritz
Editing: Susan Maggi
Costumes: Blair Holder
Production Design: Aidan Leroux
MPAA rating: PG-13
Running time: 94 minutes

REVIEWS

Boston Globe Online. January 25, 2008.
Entertainment Weekly Online. January 23, 2008.
Hollywood Reporter Online. January 25, 2008.
New York Times Online. January 25, 2008.
New Yorker Online. February 4, 2008.
San Francisco Chronicle. January 25, 2008, p. E11.
Variety Online. January 24, 2007.
Village Voice Online. January 22, 2008.
Washington Post. January 25, 2008, p. C1.

QUOTES

Raya Green: "It's funny, isn't it? How one moment can change a million after it."

HOW TO LOSE FRIENDS & ALIENATE PEOPLE

Brace yourselves, America.
—Movie tagline

Box Office: $2.7 million

On the surface *How to Lose Friends & Alienate People* seems to be a male take on the same subjects and themes as *The Devil Wears Prada* (2006). While the earlier film looks at the disillusionment of an idealistic young woman who goes to work for a powerful magazine in Manhattan, *How to Lose Friends & Alienate People* offers a less naïve protagonist, as well as more slapstick and satire.

Sidney Young (Simon Pegg), a brash, young British journalist, comes to New York to work for *Sharps* after

Clayton Harding (Jeff Bridges), the magazine's editor, sees himself ridiculed on the cover of Sidney's irreverent London publication. Harding wants Sidney to start at the bottom of the editorial ladder and work his way up. The impulsive Sidney wants instant gratification, primarily lavish parties with beautiful movie stars. Harding considers Sidney a younger version of his formerly rebellious self, and Sidney learns the hard way that he is mere cog in a corporate machine. He can succeed only by playing by the rules; bending them will lead to chaos.

Sidney's colleagues include Alison Olsen (Kirsten Dunst), a young editor initially repulsed by his crude pushiness, and Lawrence Maddox (Danny Huston), a smug senior editor who steals Sidney's ideas. Sidney becomes obsessed by burgeoning star Sophie Maes (Megan Fox) and slowly becomes part of her circle, watched warily by publicist Eleanor Johnson (Gillian Anderson), who has strict control over *Sharps* articles about her clients. *How to Lose Friends & Alienate People* can be faulted for having a predictable arc: Sidney will learn some bitter truths about publishing, show business, and himself, while discovering that Sophie, while not as unattainable as she first appeared, is not the woman for him. Sultry Sophie is also the source of much of the film's satire, as with her unlikely casting as Mother Theresa.

How to Lose Friends & Alienate People is loosely based upon the 2001 memoir by Toby Young, who came to New York in 1995 as a contributing editor at *Vanity Fair*. Young promptly irritated legendary editor Graydon Carter by pestering celebrities and being drunk at public events. While Young pokes fun at himself in his book, he emerges as a more annoying figure than his cinematic counterpoint. Sidney is less a jerk than a klutzy nebbish. He also has a gap in his heart because of the early death of his mother (Janette Scott), an actress. Sidney discovers his true nature through trial and error, unlike the protagonist of the more pompous *The Devil Wears Prada*, who carries an air of smug superiority.

Robert Weide, the primary director of television's *Curb Your Enthusiasm* (2000–2007), makes his feature debut with *How to Lose Friends & Alienate People* and reportedly complained about compromises he and screenwriter Peter Straughan were forced to make. Rather than the sharp satire they envisioned, they had to inject slapstick. Because Pegg is a gifted physical comedian, much of the crude humor works, though some bits, especially Sidney's pulling a venetian blind down on top of himself, are tired.

How to Lose Friends & Alienate People could have had more edge and more visual style, but it is fairly amusing. Sidney is a benign bungler who uses a cynical veneer to mask an essentially sweet soul. It is easy to root for him as he faces humiliation upon humiliation. Much of the character's appeal comes from the likability of Pegg, adopting a more traditional approach to humor, merging the cockiness of Dean Martin with the infantilism of Jerry Lewis, than he displays with his more inventively original characters in *Shaun of the Dead* (2004) and *Hot Fuzz* (2007).

Dunst's role calls upon her mainly to respond to the foibles of others, but she shows some comic skills during Alison's drunk scene. The always-dependable Bridges economically creates a memorable portrait of a self-loathing man who has sold his soul and knows he cannot get it back. Huston's energy enlivens each of his scenes as the villainous Maddox. Fox displays some unexpected talent for comedy as the less-than-self-aware starlet. Good in small roles are Bill Paterson as Sidney's philosopher father, Miriam Margolyes as his disapproving landlady, and Diana Kent as a faded B-movie actress. Best of all is Anderson as a woman who enjoys manipulating people. Anderson has never had such presence in a film.

How to Lose Friends & Alienate People received remarkably harsh reviews. Manohla Dargis of the *New York Times* found it sloppy and unfunny, while Todd Bowles of *USA Today* termed its humor crude. The film is often predictable and trite at the beginning, when Sidney uses a pig to crash a London party and wangle an interview with a bland Thandie Newton, as herself, or when the naïve writer allows himself to be picked up by a transvestite (Charlotte Devaney) in a New York bar. But once it gets rolling, *How to Lose Friends & Alienate People* is often hilarious. It is a minor, flawed film but not without redeeming charms.

Michael Adams

CREDITS

Sidney Young: Simon Pegg
Alison Olsen: Kirsten Dunst
Sophie Maes: Megan Fox

Clayton Harding: Jeff Bridges
Eleanor Johnson: Gillian Anderson
Lawrence Maddox: Danny Huston
Vincent Lepak: Max Minghella
Mrs. Kowalski: Miriam Margolyes
Origin: Great Britain
Language: English
Released: 2008
Production: Elizabeth Karlsen, Stephen Woolley; Number 9 Films, Audley Films, Aramid Entertainment; released by MGM
Directed by: Robert B. Weide
Written by: Peter Straughan
Cinematography by: Oliver Stapleton
Music by: David Arnold
Sound: Jim Greenhorn
Music Supervisor: Karen Elliott
Editing: David Freeman
Art Direction: Raymond Chan
Costumes: Annie Hardinge
Production Design: John Beard
MPAA rating: R
Running time: 110 minutes

REVIEWS

Boston Globe Online. October 3, 2008.
Chicago Sun-Times Online. October 2, 2008.
Entertainment Weekly Online. October 1, 2008.
Hollywood Reporter Online. September 30, 2008.
Los Angeles Times Online. October 3, 2008.
New York Times Online. October 3, 2008.
San Francisco Chronicle. October 3, 2008, p. E7.
Variety Online. September 30, 2008.
Washington Post Online. October 3, 2008.

TRIVIA

Toby Young, the man around whom the film is based, was banned from the set as he was reportedly annoying actors and interrupting Robert B. Weide as he tried to direct scenes.

I

I SERVED THE KING OF ENGLAND

(Obsluhoval jsem anglického krále)

Oscar®-winning Czechoslovakian writer/director Jirí Menzel's black comedy, *I Served the King of England* (*Obsluhoval jsem anglického krále*) is a sly political satire critiquing Communism, adapted from a novel by countryman Bohumil Hrabal, in which the titular king features only distantly. Deft and subtle, Menzel's insightful film is filled with touching and clever details that make this story of a young waiter, whose fortunes turn on a dime, so special.

The story, in Czechoslovakian with English subtitles, follows the life of Jan Díte—which, translated, means John Child—whose small stature belies his huge ambition to be a successful and wealthy hotel owner. Told in flashback, the old, graying Jan Díte (Oldrich Kaiser) is freshly released into early 1960s Czechoslovakia from a fifteen-year prison sentence, his term, in a detail typical of the film's black humor, reduced to fourteen years and eleven months through amnesty. A metaphorical scene has Jan attempting to repair a ruined house in the bleak town he is sent to live in, as he recalls the bad luck that seemed to follow him in voice-over.

As a young man in the 1930s, the hapless Jan Díte (Ivan Barnev) craves the opulent surroundings and grandeur of hotel dining rooms and the life he observes in upscale brothels and wangles a job as a waiter at Prague's finest hotel. That is where he meets his mentor, the impeccable headwaiter Skrivánek (Martin Huba) who,

when queried about his preternatural skill, replies, "I served the King of England."

Jan is also obsessed with beautiful women and *I Served the King of England* also largely features Jan's active sex life. During the time Jan rises to the position of headwaiter at the hotel, the film follows his romantic but brief encounters with a long string of lovelies that he romantically adorns in bed with flowers and fruit. At the dawn of World War II as Germans occupy Czechoslovakia, Jan finds love with Líza (Julia Jentsch) a staunch Aryan who keeps a portrait of Hitler above their bed always in view, even in flagrante delicto. She is killed after enlisting in the German army, but leaves Jan with the box of priceless stamps she looted from Polish-Jewish homes that she lost her life over. Jan is able to use the stamps to realize his life's dream and buy an ownership share in a hotel.

Jan's character is impressed at an early age about the power of money, delighted to learn that all people, even the richest man, will stoop to pick coins on the floor. As he has risen professionally, his greed has also kept pace and Jan has soon become oblivious to all but his own desires. His dream of playing the wealthy hotelier is short-lived as he fails to recognize the political shift, the Communists taking over from the Nazis, that results in a Communist occupation of his precious hotel and Jan being thrown in prison.

With his physical grace and wonderfully expressive face, the Bulgarian Ivan Barnev is uniquely suited for his role as the oblivious but optimistic Jan, which many reviewers have compared to Forrest Gump. *New York Times* reviewer Stephen Holden imaginatively described Barnev's Jan as "a doll-like hybrid of Mikhail Baryshnikov and Derek Jacobi with a dash of Roan Polanski. Jan will cheerfully do what it takes to survive and flourish without political commitment or moral scruples."

The film is Jirí Menzel's sixth adaptation of the work of author Bohumil Hrabal, who died in 1997, and who wrote the screenplay for Menzel's *Closely Watched Trains* (1966), which won the director an Oscar® for best foreign film. Their disparate sensibilities produce a film that displays an innocent, silent-movie-like charm even as it tackles thorny political and social issues. A much-talked about scene in which the hotel pool, filled with comely blonde Aryan women, is essentially used as a Nazi breeding farm, is successfully played for comedy. And Jan's experience as a high-class server to the wealthy and powerful politicos puts him in a unique position to observe their crass behavior, something to which he wrong-headedly aspires. Stephen Holden observed, "These scenes of marathon gourmandizing offer some of the most pungently satirical observations of unfettered gluttony ever filmed."

Menzel's film is a rare one: an insightful and successfully comedic look at the misfortunes of a fictional character which helps illuminate the unlucky fate of a nation.

Hilary White

CREDITS

Jan Díte, old: Oldrich Kaiser
Líza: Julia Jentsch
Skrivanek: Marin Huba
Hotel Chief: Jiri Labus
Jan Díte, young: Ivan Barnev
Professor: Marian Lasica
Hotelier Brandejs: Josef Abrham
Karel the waiter: Jaromir Dulava
Origin: Czechoslovakia
Language: Czechoslovakian
Released: 2007
Production: Robert Schaffer, Andrea Metcalfe; Barrandov Film Studios, Universal Production Partners, Magic Box Slovakia; released by Sony Pictures Classics
Directed by: Jiri Menzel
Written by: Jiri Menzel
Cinematography by: Jaromir Sofr
Music by: Ales Brezina
Sound: Radim Hladik Jr.
Editing: Renji Ishibashi
Costumes: Milan Corba
Production Design: Milan Bycek
MPAA rating: R
Running time: 120 minutes

REVIEWS

The Guardian Online. May 9, 2008.
Hollywood Reporter Online. February 19, 2007.
The Observer Online. May 11, 2008.
Variety Online. January 20, 2007.

QUOTES

Jan: "A person becomes human almost against his own will."

TRIVIA

The actor who played Tichota, the innkeeper in the wheelchair, is Rudolf Hrusínský. His father, also named Rudolf Hrusínský was a legendary Czech actor and a favorite of director Jirí Menzel's.

IGOR

All men aren't created evil.
   —Movie tagline
He's got a monster of a problem.
   —Movie tagline

Box Office: $19.5 million

Anthony Leondis's animated children's monster film has an appealing premise: the ultimate outsider in a land filled with identical outsiders realizes a dream. *Igor* unfortunately combines too-sophisticated writing with much too dark characters and a surprising amount of violence with the plot simplicity typical of a film aimed primarily at young children. While adults may appreciate more of *Igor*'s dark humor and witty banter, no one will enjoy the darkly uninspired animation.

Set in the bleak Kingdom of Malaria, an evil scientist-created race of disfigured, oppressed hunchbacked assistants, all named Igor, unhappily toil for their evil masters. Malaria was once a happy farmland until climate change killed all the crops and the malevolent new King Malbert (voice of Jay Leno) decrees an economy benefiting the land's evil scientists and enslaving anyone with a disfigurement.

There is one Igor who stands out in a sea of duller, lisping Igors. This Igor (voice John Cusack) holds a Yes Masters Degree and dreams of creating his own disfigured monster, like his negligent master, Dr. Glickenstein (voice of John Cleese). Igor has already created a sarcastic sidekick Scamper (voice of Steve Buscemi), whom he brought back to life after being run over. And he also outfitted a robot with a human brain, dubbed Brain (voice of Sean Hayes).

The annual Evil Scientists Fair is approaching and when Dr. Glickenstein is unexpectedly killed while testing the rocket he planned as his entry, Igor keeps his master's death a secret and enters the fair in his place. His entry is an enormous monster created from human tissue that he has engineered to be especially evil. Upon animation, however, Igor's monster (voice of Molly Shannon) turns out to be a gentle giant who misconstrues the word "evil" as "Eva," her new moniker.

Igor attempts to fix Eva's defect by taking her to the "Brain Wash" where she is forced to watch nonstop violence on television. Eva inadvertently adopts the persona of a Hollywood actress after Brain accidently changes the channel in the midst of the treatment. Igor is only able to convince her to go to the fair by telling her she is auditioning for a role in a stage production of *Annie.*

The deliciously named Dr. Schadenfreude (voice of Eddie Izzard), the most evil scientist in all the land who has won the last seventeen Evil Scientists Fairs, discovers that Dr. Glickenstein is dead and learns about Igor and Eva. After unsuccessfully attempting to kidnap Eva, Schadenfreude then lures Igor into giving her to him willingly by promising to fulfill his dream and make him a rich evil scientist, but Igor is able to see through the ruse.

The night before the Fair, Eva finds Igor kissing Dr. Glickenstein's former assistant Heidi, actually Dr. Schadenfreude's girlfriend, Jaclyn (voice of Jennifer Coolidge), in disguise. Igor is arrested and put into the "Igor Disposal," where Scamper and Brain rescue him. In the process of saving Eva at the fairgrounds, Igor uncovers the weather-controlling machine that has kept Malaria in gloom for years. Igor, Scamper, and Brain shut off the device and Malaria is awash once again in sunshine while Igor becomes the new King and all Igors are now free.

With a screenplay by Chris McKenna, *Igor*'s plot is a variation on *Young Frankenstein* (1974) and deals with several of the same adult themes that will be too much for the PG film's young demographic. Igor has made the reanimated Scamper immortal, and the unhappy roadkill rabbit rails against this unwanted fate through repeated and rather disturbing suicide attempts. When Igors go bad, they are put in the Igor Disposal—a monster woodchipper of sorts. And the brainwashing scene with Eva recalls vaguely recalls *A Clockwork Orange* (1971) in reverse, with Igor trying to teach Eva to become an evil crazed killer by showing her images of violence.

McKenna's dialogue is often clever and funny, as reflected in his work on the adult-themed animated television show *American Dad.* However, most of these references—like the appearance of the oft-satirized, Actors Studio icon James Lipton—will sail over the head's of the film's young audience. However, the simple plot elements and clearly made-for-children message of being yourself and achieving your dreams will not hold the interest of adults for long. It is a shame and virtually wastes the voice talent of Cusack, Shannon, Coolidge, and Izzard, who are eminently appealing.

With its computer animation mimicking a distinct stop-animation look, several reviewers noticed the obvious influence of Tim Burton's *Nightmare Before Christmas* (1993) and *Corpse Bride* (2005) while lacking the brightness, sophistication, and artistry of a Pixar or Disney animated production.

Hilary White

CREDITS

Igor: John Cusack (Voice)
Scamper: Steve Buscemi (Voice)
Dr. Glickenstein: John Cleese (Voice)
Brain: Sean Hayes (Voice)
Eva: Molly Shannon (Voice)
Jaclyn: Jennifer Coolidge (Voice)
Dr. Schadenfreude: Eddie Izzard (Voice)
King Malbert: Jay Leno (Voice)
Carl Cristall: Arsenio Hall (Voice)
Dr. Schadenfreude's Igor: Christian Slater (Voice)
Himself: James Lipton (Voice)
Origin: USA
Language: English
Released: 2008
Production: Max Howard, John D. Eraklis; Exodus Film Group; released by Weinstein Company, MGM
Directed by: Anthony Leondis
Written by: Chris McKenna
Music by: Patrick Doyle
Sound: Jonathan Miller
Editing: Herve Schneid
Art Direction: Olivier Besson
Production Design: Loic Rastout
MPAA rating: PG
Running time: 86 minutes

REVIEWS

Boston Globe Online. September 19, 2008.
Entertainment Weekly Online. September 16, 2008.
Hollywood Reporter Online. September 16, 2008.
Los Angeles Times Online. September 19, 2008.
New York Times Online. September 19, 2008.
San Francisco Chronicle. September 19, 2008, p. E5.
Variety Online. September 15, 2008.
Washington Post Online. September 19, 2008.
Washington Post. 2008.

QUOTES

Brain: " Aw, blind orphans get everything!"

This is the second time the song "I Can See Clearly Now" has been used in a movie starring John Cusack.

IN BRUGES

> *Shoot first. Sightsee later.*
> —Movie tagline

Box Office: $7.8 million

Two quirky hit men are sent on a mysterious mission by their boss. They are an odd pair of brutal but sensitive thugs, prone to fits of violence and strange bouts of remorse. The plot is quite familiar: the normalization of thugs, and the celebration of their charming quirks, has been a favorite movie motif since *Pulp Fiction* (1994). But what looks like a standard bad-guys-with-hearts-of-gold black comedy gets some surprising twists and turns at the hands of Irish playwright Martin McDonagh, the writer and director of *In Bruges*.

The trailers made this movie look like sadly silly crime pulp. The film is much more thoughtful and nasty than that. It slyly slinks out of cliché territory just at the point where you grow tired of the bizarre banter and off-key dialogue, and catches your breath in your throat just when you were ready for another easy laugh. There are many moments when McDonagh seems to be trying too hard to be coy, but they are redeemed by the inventiveness of his overarchingly dark outlook. *In Bruges* starts out to be a foolish comedy and ends up as a tart but tasty tragedy. For it seems that McDonagh the screenwriter has just about as much gumption and absurd pathos, in equal measures, as his forlorn and hopeless characters.

We begin with Ken (Brendan Gleeson) and Ray (Colin Farrell) arriving in Bruges, which in this film is depicted as Belgium's medieval tourist trap of a village. The film's long-running joke is that Bruges is the armpit of Europe, at least according to Ray's unrefined taste, but it ends up being a cinematic version of Red Rock West or Punxsutawney, a place you can never really escape, a sort of Sartrean hell. Once you are sent to Bruges, there is apparently no exit.

If you are a Belgian, you might wince throughout the film. The characters' attitude toward the country is not charitable. In fact, McDonagh displays a keen grasp of commonplace but usually unspoken international resentments. Jimmy (Jordan Prentice), a dwarf who is in the town as an actor in an odd, Fellini-esque film, admits to being an American when asked but begs, "Please don't hold it against me." Ray insults a family of overweight tourists but excuses his behavior as appropriate toward ugly Americans. He mistakenly punches a couple of rude diners thinking they are Americans, but reaps the consequences because they are actually Canadians. A prostitute from Amsterdam explains that she has come to Bruges because there is less supply and thus more favorable economics. The only Belgian natives who figure in the plot are a young woman who pretends to be with the film crew but really is a drug dealer and her boyfriend, who robs tourists with a gun that is loaded with blanks.

The opening act of the film tries to milk laughs out of Ken's genuine interest in visiting the medieval tourist sites, but they bore the action-oriented Ray to death. Ray chases the drug dealer and lands a date with her; she likes him despite of, or perhaps because of, his bad behavior in a restaurant where he decks the Canadian and his girlfriend. As played by Farrell, Ray is a petulant, overgrown child prone to fits of violence so he does not seem to register as being immoral.

It turns out, however, that he is haunted by grief. His first hit job, against a priest, turned into tragedy when one of his bullets accidentally hit and killed a child. Ray is remorseful to the point of being suicidal. Then it is revealed that the two men's boss, Harry (Ralph Fiennes), cannot tolerate Ray's mistake either. He has sent them to Bruges so that Ken can kill Ray in a place that's "like a dream."

A dream it is, and a nightmare too. Ken is torn about the assignment, and the plot cascades into a series of contretemps that illustrate the thugs' peculiar sense of morality and principles. To kill a child is wrong and must be punished; perhaps suicide is an appropriate response; or is suicide in fact the wrong way out? Not just the plot, but the ethical questions, thicken and begin to congeal.

In Bruges never loses its sharp satirical edge even when events turn dark and spin out of control. McDonagh takes huge risks that fell flat with some critics; in the midst of a showdown between Harry and Ray, they discuss the proper etiquette of a chase-and-pursuit scene done right. McDonagh, in the tradition of existentialist playwrights, takes his characters into and out of character, revealing their actions as acts and making a meta-morality play out of their conflicts. When, in the end, a chase ends in bloodshed on the set of the pulp movie being filmed in Bruges, it is a finely staged nightmare indeed.

A lot of critics complained that *In Bruges* was jolly good fun until it turned too serious at the end, and there it lost its way. In fact, a better case can be made that what appears to almost a throwaway piece of light and hackneyed entertainment gains real power when McDonagh sharpens his plot and descends into a moral morass of ethics and violence gone awry. Indeed, *In*

Bruges can be seen as a tense debate on the philosophy of guilt, retribution, and suffering.

Gleeson is terrific as the put-upon, long-suffering hired gun who asserts his independence just in time to lay his life on the line for his long-buried principles. And Farrell makes his sheepish, sad-sack buffoon work well; his very inanity makes his vulnerability all the more credible. But while both these men are also of questionable integrity, Fiennes's Harry is a revelation, a well-spoken, refined brute who nonetheless has his own code of honor. In the end, they are all caught up in a dance of fate in a purgatory of their own making, waiting in Bruges on their way to hell, or perhaps already in hell.

Michael Betzold

CREDITS

Ray: Colin Farrell
Ken: Brendan Gleeson
Harry: Ralph Fiennes
Chloë: Clémence Poésy
Eirik: Jérémie Renier
Marie: Thekla Reuten
Jimmy: Jordan Prentice
Origin: Great Britain
Language: English
Released: 2008
Production: Graham Broadbent, Pete Czernin; FilmFour, Blueprint Films, Scion Films; released by Focus Features
Directed by: Martin McDonagh
Written by: Martin McDonagh
Cinematography by: Eigil Bryld
Music by: Carter Burwell
Sound: Alistair Crocker
Music Supervisor: Karen Elliott
Editing: Jon Gregory
Art Direction: Chris Lowe
Costumes: Jany Temime
Production Design: Michael Carlin
MPAA rating: R
Running time: 107 minutes

REVIEWS

Boston Globe Online. February 8, 2008.
Chicago Sun-Times Online. February 7, 2008.
Entertainment Weekly Online. February 6, 2008.
Hollywood Reporter Online. January 21, 2008.
Los Angeles Times Online. February 8, 2008.
New York Times Online. February 8, 2008.
New Yorker Online. February 11, 2008.
Rolling Stone Online. February 7, 2008.
San Francisco Chronicle. February 8, 2008, p. E7.
Variety Online. January 17, 2008.
Wall Street Journal. February 8, 2008, p. W1.
Washington Post. February 8, 2008, p. C6.

QUOTES

Ray: "You can't be givin' horse tranquilizers to midgets!"

TRIVIA

In order to create the feeling of the holiday season, Christmas decorations were kept in some streets of Bruges until the end of March. The town council made an official communication to the people of Bruges explaining the reason why.

AWARDS

British Acad. 2008: Orig. Screenplay
Golden Globes 2009: Actor—Mus./Comedy (Farrell)
Nomination:
Oscars 2008: Orig. Screenplay
British Acad. 2008: Film Editing, Support. Actor (Gleeson)
Golden Globes 2009: Actor—Mus./Comedy (Gleeson), Film—Mus./Comedy.

IN THE NAME OF THE KING: A DUNGEON SIEGE TALE

Rise and fight.
—Movie tagline

Box Office: $4.7 million

After the release of Uwe Boll's *In the Name of the King: A Dungeon Siege Tale,* the legendary writer/director who once put on boxing gloves to spar with some of his harshest critics suggested that he might quit cinema if a million people signed a petition asking him to do so. Electronic signatures started to form on Petition Online before Boll could even finish the thought with hundreds of thousands of people not-so-politely asking the man who directed *House of the Dead* (2003), *Alone in the Dark* (2005), and *BloodRayne* (2005) to never step behind the camera again. A random sampling of user comments— "Suck!," "Please…for the sake of humanity!," and "I wasn't born with enough names to sign this with"—makes the general opinion of Mr. Boll clear, which leads to the most troubling thing about *In the Name of the King: A Dungeon Siege Tale,* the latest cinematic torture courtesy of Uwe Boll, the odd question of why so many talented actors continue to work with a filmmaker so reviled that average people take the time to try to end his career. Bad directors are as common as Starbucks employees, but it becomes harder and harder to fathom why anyone chooses to work with Uwe Boll with every film showing no signs of artistic progress at all.

Past collaborators of Uwe Boll like Tara Reid, Kristanna Loken, and Michael Madsen were, no insult intended, on the downside of their career trajectory, making their involvement in movies based on video games more understandable. But *In the Name of the King* stars more than one talented actor who should know better, including Jason Statham, Ron Perlman, Leelee Sobieski and Ray Liotta, all of whom have been in major releases in just the last year. Seeing Matthew Lillard chew scenery or Claire Forlani look drowsy is to be expected in a nearly straight-to-DVD disaster like this one, but what possibly drew actors like Perlman and Liotta to this career-low will remain one of cinema's greatest mysteries.

Jason Statham plays a character named "Farmer" (as if writer Doug Taylor sketched characters by their profession and forgot to give his lead a name before Boll grabbed the screenplay) in the mythical land of Ehb. Farmer lives with his wife Solana (Claire Forlani) and his young son and spends time with his friend Norick (Ron Perlman). A demon army of Krugs, clearly modeled after the Orcs from the *Lord of the Rings* movies, invade the idyllic life of Farmer, kill his son, and enslave Solana. The Krugs are led by a wizard named Gallian (Ray Liotta), who himself is being supported by King Konreid's (Burt Reynolds) nefarious nephew Fallow (Matthew Lillard). Farmer hits the road with his buddy Norick to support him and vows to rescue his wife and avenge his son's death. Along the way, the gang encounter a group of tree-hanging wood nymphs led by Kristanna Loken, who barely serve the plot and only remind viewers how clearly Boll is trying to crib from the *LOTR* trilogy.

In the Name of the King: A Dungeon Siege Tale (which, like all English-language Boll films, is based on a video game) was so reviled when it premiered in theaters that it almost feels cruel to pile on the hatred. As of this writing, the film maintains a jaw-dropping fifteen out of one hundred score on MetaCritic, a generous 3.8 out of ten on IMDB, and a five percent on Rotten Tomatoes with top critics giving it a score of zero percent and the *Hollywood Reporter* accurately noting that "The film never achieves a suitable level of camp that would make it at least unintentional fun. It also is terminally boring at its 127-minute running time, making one supremely grateful that a half-hour has been cut for this U.S. release."

The noted lack of camp value that was so much a part of why Boll's *Alone in the Dark* and *BloodRayne* marginally worked (in the same way one admires the work of Ed Wood) is what truly sinks *In the Name of the King*. The film commits the cardinal sin of being too boring to be "so-bad-it's-good." Statham and Sobieski deliver their lines in such a monotone, half-awake fashion that it almost feels like either of them could nod off at any minute and the design of the film is atrocious on every level. Some of the green-screen effects would have been dated a quarter-century ago and the wire work would be laughable if not just embarrassing for everyone involved. With some of the worst dialogue in the history of Boll's oeuvre, there is nothing to tap into that guilty pleasure vein unless a viewer finds guilt from stilted acting, horrible design, and clichéd dialogue. At least *House of the Dead* had zombies.

Brian Tallerico

CREDITS

Farmer: Jason Statham
Merick: John Rhys-Davies
Gallian: Ray Liotta
Muriella: Leelee Sobieski
Duke Fallow: Matthew Lillard
King Konreid: Burt Reynolds
Norick: Ron Perlman
Solana: Claire Forlani
Elora: Kristanna Loken
Bastain: Will Sanderson
Commander Tarish: Brian White
General Backler: Mike Dopud
Origin: Germany, Canada
Language: English
Released: 2008
Production: Shawn Williamson, Daniel Clarke; Boll KG Prods., Herold Prods., Brightlight Pictures; released by Freestyle Releasing
Directed by: Uwe Boll
Written by: Doug Taylor
Cinematography by: Mathias Neumann
Music by: Jessica de Rooij, Henning Lohner
Sound: Michael Bartylak
Editing: David Richardson, Paul Klassen
Art Direction: Roxanne Methot
Costumes: Carla Hetland, Tom Burroughs-Rutter
Production Design: James Steuart
MPAA rating: PG-13
Running time: 124 minutes

REVIEWS

Boston Globe Online. January 12, 2008.
Hollywood Reporter Online. January 14, 2008.

Los Angeles Times Online. January 14, 2008.
New York Times Online. January 11, 2008.
Variety Online. January 11, 2008.

QUOTES

Gallian: "You have no idea…how powerful madness can be."

AWARDS

Golden Raspberries 2008: Worst Director (Boll)

Nomination:

Golden Raspberries 2008: Worst Picture, Worst Support. Actor (Reynolds), Worst Support. Actress (Sobieski), Worst Screenplay, Worst Screen Couple (Boll and any actor, camera, or screenplay).

THE INCREDIBLE HULK

On June 13, get ready to unleash the beast.
    —Movie tagline

This summer, our only hope is something incredible.
    —Movie tagline

This June, a hero shows his true colors.
    —Movie tagline

Box Office: $134.8 million

The Incredible Hulk is not a sequel in the truest sense of the word when compared with its predecessor, Ang Lee's work simply titled *Hulk* (2003). By contrast it is a re-imagining of the jade brute's cinematic incarnation. Although not altogether eschewing Lee's interpretation, which often used multiple split screens as a nod to the use of panels in the comic book medium, *The Incredible Hulk* differs in both style and tone. Whereas Lee focused on the tormented psychological framework of the character, one in which Bruce Banner and his monstrous alter ego live in each other's shadow, Louis Leterrier (director of the *Transporter* films) used more humor and preferred to jump early into the bone-crushing, steel wrenching violence on a cataclysmic scale pervasive in the pages of one of Marvel Comics premier characters. In that distorted alternate universe where Vice President Dick Cheney still refers to global warming as spring, it is also rife with mutants and a resident teenager whose DNA has been spliced with an arachnid's. Since his inception at newsstands with *The Incredible Hulk No. 1* published in May 1962, the monosyllabic Hulk, who has the habit of referring to himself in the third person (complete with a pair of tattered purple slacks and an anger management problem), has been ripping apart the Marvel Universe at its seams often while uttering the battle cry, "Hulk Smash!" (Ironically,

Lou Ferrigno, who was never given the opportunity to provide the guttural growls and roars while embodying the character in the 1970s CBS series, completed both for this version, along with the two sentences this CGI version utters).

At best, *The Incredible Hulk* is a loosely hinged re-boot of Ang Lee's Freudian nightmare. It is the second feature film produced by Marvel Studios (the first being one of the summer's blockbusters, *Iron Man* [2008]). Marvel's studio executives decided early on to develop a script more faithful to the source material in addition to giving numerous tributes to the successful television show that ran for five seasons. It strays from giving a lengthy, onerous retelling of the Hulk's genesis, opting to snap it together in a montage of flashbacks at a laboratory along with newspaper clippings reporting sightings of the creature, which has apparently ascended to the status of urban legend akin to that of Big Foot and the Loch Ness Monster. The end of Lee's version left Dr. Banner in a South American jungle doing humanitarian work. This location is the only plot element shared by both films as Leterrier begins his tale there. Banner (given a rebirth by Edward Norton) is living incognito in a Brazilian favela where he is hiding in the "City of God." Here Leterrier suspends a panoramic aerial view of this ghetto next to Rio de Janeiro that is a shocking statement of sordid human existence. The endless bungalows are crammed and stacked on top of each other along hillsides that seem to resemble the tear drops of a weeping God.

Banner is a global fugitive maintaining a low profile where he works at a soft drink bottling factory while studying a time-worn biofeedback technique under the tutelage of a grappling martial arts master (played by Rickson Gracie from the famous Gracie family Jujitsu school). Banner is attempting to surcease his metamorphosis into his rage fueled persona by keeping his pulse rate under 200 beats per minute when the transformation occurs. He is also searching for a permanent cure to his explosive condition. General Thaddeus 'Thunderbolt' Ross (coldly portrayed by Oscar® winner William Hurt) is obsessively pursuing the frail doctor in order to harness the power of the green goliath for military gain, resembling Inspector Javert in Victor Hugo's *Les Miserable.*

Ross recruits the services of a renowned Special Forces soldier from Britain, Emil Blonsky (Tim Roth), to join his posse in finding Banner. They locate him following a mishap in which a drop of Banner's irradiated blood falls into a beverage bottle at the factory where he works and is ingested by an American citizen (played by Stan Lee, who is ritually given cameos in every Marvel production). In a humorous nod to the television series, Banner tells a belligerent coworker in poor Portuguese:

"Don't make me hungry. You wouldn't like me when I'm hungry." This is a take from the opening credits of the TV show where Bill Bixby informs Jack Colvin, "Mr. McGee, don't make me angry. You wouldn't like me when I'm angry." Once the U.S. Army descends on the Brazilian shanty town and unleashes mayhem, the audience learns why Banner would make such a statement. Although the movie's first "Hulk-out" keeps the character in the shadows, his formidable strength is very engaging as he tosses a forklift easier than most would a Frisbee.

This rendering of the Hulk is a solid, imposing figure, filling a nine-foot frame crammed with bulging, striated muscles. Compared with 2003's Hulk, whose height mirrored his escalating rage, this rendition is darker and harder. Ang Lee's Hulk had soft rubbery features. Despite this, CGI limits the Hulk. There is a disconnect once Banner submerges into the Hulk's psyche. It is difficult to sympathize with this Gollum on steroids. Shrek garners more affinity with viewers with Mike Myer's endearing Scottish brogue, which gives the ogre a human quality. Despite operating on a shoestring budget, Lou Ferrigno was able to provide this human dimension in the series. Both Bixby and Ferrigno evoked compassion; Dr. Banner and the Hulk were simply altered states of the same being. (Bixby was given a posthumous cameo in the film as Banner channel surfs and runs across a rerun of *The Courtship of Eddie's Father*.) This is not conveyed in the movie; there is the man splitting scenes with a computer-generated green behemoth.

Similarly, the chemistry between Banner and his true love, Betty Ross (Liv Tyler), is less than sultry. Although they share a humorous moment (during a stay in a hotel room, Ross and Banner are in the midst of getting intimate, but he has to hold back as his pulse rate is getting dangerously close to the 200 Hulk-out point), their romance lacks the credibility portrayed by Eric Bana and Jennifer Connelly. Ross is the daughter of General Ross, which allows for the gruff military leader to have a personal vendetta against Banner as the Hulk's first appearance put Betty in traction.

A good choice was made for the film's villain. In both the film and the comics, Emil Blonsky transforms into the Abomination, a character more formidable than the Hulk. Being a prematurely aged, seasoned career soldier, Blonsky becomes consumed with obtaining greater power than the Hulk. General Ross gives him a taste of this power by giving him the super soldier serum, a reference to the substance that endowed Captain America with heightened strength, reflexes, and speed. Blonsky is able to maneuver against the Hulk for a short time but it is the Army's sonic emitting cannon that nearly subdues the Hulk. Arrogant despite losing yet another round, Blonsky bitterly shouts in the Hulk's face, "Is that it? Is that all you've got?" Hulk responds with his foot and bunts the cockney soldier like a soccer ball, shattering most of his skeletal frame.

In what stands as the film's greatest comic relief, Tim Blake Nelson plays the eccentric overzealous mad scientist, Dr. Samuel Stern, who is assisting Banner in searching for a cure. His motivation is rooted in a perverse joy rather than benevolence. Stern is known as the Hulk villain, the Leader in the comic series. Following his assisting Blonsky's transformation into the Abomination via injecting him with Banner's blood, Stern himself is exposed to the tainted blood through a cut to his head (a possible setup for the third *Hulk* cinematic installment).

Although favored critically, *The Incredible Hulk* did not fare much better than *Hulk* at the box office, grossing $132.5 million to Lee's $132.1 million. Its sibling film, *Iron Man,* and Warner Brother's *The Dark Knight* (2008) were simply crafted better with complex character development and sophisticated script writing. However, what makes the film fun is the sheer eye candy joy of watching the Hulk explode into a pulverizing force of nature ripping a police squad car in two and using the halves as boxing gloves before dispensing a salvo of heavy blows against his abominable nemesis. If this is a coveted aspect for some viewing a superhero movie, *The Incredible Hulk* is a credible fix.

David Metz Roberts

CREDITS

Bruce Banner: Edward Norton
Emil Blonsky: Tim Roth
Betty Ross: Liv Tyler
Gen. Thaddeus 'Thunderbolt' Ross: William Hurt
Samuel Sterns: Tim Blake Nelson
Leonard: Ty Burrell
Major Kathleen Sparr: Christina Cabot
General Joe Greller: Peter Mensah
Tony Stark: Robert Downey Jr
Origin: USA
Language: English
Released: 2008
Production: Avi Arad, Gale Anne Hurd, Kevin Feige; Marvel Studios, Valhalla Motion Pictures; released by Universal
Directed by: Louis Leterrier
Written by: Zak Penn
Cinematography by: Peter Menzies Jr.
Music by: Craig Armstrong
Sound: Greg Chapman
Music Supervisor: Dave Jordan

Editing: John Wright, Rick Shaine, Vincent Tabaillon
Art Direction: Daniel T. Dorrance
Costumes: Denise Cronenberg, Renee Bravener
Production Design: Kirk M. Petruccelli
MPAA rating: PG-13
Running time: 112 minutes

REVIEWS

Boston Globe Online. June 13, 2008.
Chicago Sun-Times Online. June 12, 2008.
Entertainment Weekly Online. June 11, 2008.
Hollywood Reporter Online. June 11, 2008.
Los Angeles Times Online. June 13, 2008.
New York Times Online. June 13, 2008.
San Francisco Chronicle. June 12, 2008, p. E1.
Variety Online. June 11, 2008.
Wall Street Journal. June 13, 2008, p. W1.
Washington Post. June 13, 2008, p. C1.

QUOTES

Betty Ross (Betty and Bruce need to get across town in New York City): "The subway is probably quickest."

Bruce Banner: "Me in a metal tube, deep underground with hundreds of people in the most aggressive city in the world?"

Betty Ross: "Right. Let's get a cab."

TRIVIA

Stylistically, the filmmakers chose a darker shade of green from *Hulk* (2003), and decided to not make him as large. His size does not increase as he becomes further enraged, staying at a consistent height.

INDIANA JONES AND THE KINGDOM OF THE CRYSTAL SKULL

Box Office: $317.1 million

When it was first announced that Paramount was going ahead with a fourth Indiana Jones film, coming almost twenty years after the last chapter in the popular adventure-serial series, the main question for many Indiana Jones fans was, "Can a sixty-six-year-old Harrison Ford keep up with the Joneses, in terms of playing a convincing action lead at his advanced age?" However, after the finished film was screened, any questions regarding Ford's vitality were immediately dismissed and were replaced with another, infinitely more urgent question—"Who is to blame for this cinematic atrocity?"

The most obvious answer is Indy-creator and series producer George Lucas, a filmmaker who seems determined to prove the truth behind the old adage, "You can't go home again." Lucas's *Star Wars* prequel trilogy was not only a painfully awkward and ill-conceived mess from start to finish, but it was also so exploitative and derivate of Lucas' original *Star Wars* films that the new trilogy's very existence almost lessens the memory of the original movies. One would have hoped that Steven Spielberg—director of the three previous Jones films and a significantly better filmmaker than Lucas—would have been able to rein in his old friend's propensity for pandering and self-indulgent filmmaking, which ran rampant on the prequel trilogy, but, alas, *Indiana Jones and the Kingdom of the Crystal Skull* feels infinitely more like a Lucas film than a Spielberg film. This sense of Lucas as the "Phantom Menace" of *Indiana Jones 4* was backed by several media reports, most notably, a revealing profile in the February 2008 issue of *Vanity Fair* in which Spielberg and Ford speak candidly about their doubts about Lucas's insistence on dictating the film's main plot device, doubts reiterated by the article's author in the final line of the profile—"And if you don't like the key piece at the center of *Indiana Jones and the Kingdom of the Crystal Skull*—the MacGuffin—you'll know who to blame" (i.e., Lucas).

So what exactly should Lucas be blamed for? There is a wide range of problems with *Kingdom of the Crystal Skull*, with perhaps the most obvious one residing in the film's title: the "Crystal Skull," a.k.a. the "macguffin" (a slang term for a plot device popularized by Alfred Hitchcock) that Lucas allegedly insisted on. While the previous Indy movies each focused on one of the world's major religions for their thematic material—*Raiders of the Lost Ark*, Judaism; *Temple of Doom*, Hinduism; *Indiana Jones and the Last Crusade*, Christianity—*Kingdom of the Crystal Skull* instead embraces the B-movie goofiness of UFOs and extraterrestrials, a decision that immediately robs the film of the historical depth and gravitas of the previous chapters. While some may argue that UFO enthusiasts have created their own religion around their beliefs, UFO-ism simply doesn't have the history or depth to work as an engaging backdrop for a world-spanning archaeologist like Dr. Jones. Even if the historical scholarship in the previous Jones movies was shaky, the films were able to borrow enough from the history of world religions to make it sound like they knew what they were talking about. *Kingdom of the Crystal Skull*, on the other hand, never makes that leap toward legitimacy, perpetually sounding like a trashy pulp sci-fi novel that the authors researched one afternoon on Wikipedia.

Indiana Jones and the Kingdom of the Crystal Skull opens *in media res* in 1957 as a band of Russian soldiers, disguised as American GIs, shoot their way into a secret Air Force base in Roswell, New Mexico—a familiar locale for UFO conspiracies—dragging along a beleaguered Dr. Jones (Harrison Ford) and his gruff sidekick Mac (Ray Winstone). The Russians are led by the intimidating Colonel Irina Spalko (Cate Blanchett, in the film's most engaging, scenery-chewing performance), a dominatrix-like Communist with a hint of psychic powers. Spalko brings Indy to a massive government warehouse—which should be familiar to anyone who remembers the closing moments of *Raiders of the Lost Ark*—and insists that he lead her to a mysterious "alien" artifact, the crystal skull, that Jones helped examine years earlier. Jones complies, retrieves the skull, and is barely able to escape, suffering through a betrayal by Mac, a fight on a rocket sled, and a nuclear test blast, which he survives by hiding within a lead-lined refrigerator. (This moment was notoriously unpopular with audiences, with some online pundits petitioning that the popular phrase "Jump the Shark"—pop culture slang for the moment a film or TV show loses its way—should now forever be replaced by the phrase "Nuked the Fridge.")

Returning to the safety of academia, Dr. Jones is surprised to find himself painted as a Communist sympathizer by U.S. government agents and even more surprised by the appearance of a leather-clad greaser named Mutt Williams (Shia LaBeouf), who arrives just in time to help Indy escape from more Russian agents. Mutt informs Indy that his old colleague, Harold Oxley, has disappeared in Peru after discovering another crystal skull, presumably captured by the Russians, who seem to believe that the skulls can be used to tap into limitless psychic power. Mutt's mother, Mary, has also been abducted by the Russians, so Indy begrudgingly agrees to travel with Mutt to South America to investigate the disappearances. After Jones and Mutt follow a trail of clues leading to the crystal skull Oxley had hidden from the Russians, the pair is captured by Colonel Spalko and taken to the Russian camp in the Peruvian jungle, where they discover Mac (working with Spalko), a mentally-addled Oxley (John Hurt), apparently affected by his encounter with the skull, and Mutt's mother, "Mary," otherwise known as Marion Ravenwood (Karen Allen), Jones's love interest from *Raiders of the Lost Ark*. While Spalko uses the skulls to reveal the location of Akator, a lost city in the Amazon rainforest, Indy discovers that Mutt is, in fact, his biological son, a fact that neither Jones nor Mutt was aware of. Indy, Marion, Mutt, and Oxley soon escape from the Russians, starting a massive jungle-spanning race to Akator with each group hoping to be the first to unlock the secret of the crystal skulls.

Given the high pedigree of the cast and the multiple references to *Raiders of the Lost Ark*—arguably the best of the three previous Indiana Jones movies—*Kingdom of the Crystal Skull* had ample potential for greatness. Unfortunately, there's simply nothing in the film to take seriously, which undercuts almost every moment in the narrative. Granted, there is no real expectation that an Indiana Jones movie should be deadly serious at all times, but it is hard to care about a film that is constantly winking and nodding at its audience. The original Indiana Jones movies do an expert job of blending adventure and comedy, constantly placing our hero in impossible situations, raising the stakes again and again, until the scenes are either resolved through pulse-pounding action or defused through knowing humor. Alternately, *Kingdom of the Crystal Skull* never places Indiana Jones in any situation that actually feels real or dangerous. The overall aesthetic is far too cute—a fact backed up by the odd proliferation of adorable CGI animals in the film, ranging from prairie dogs to monkeys—which simply robs the pacing of any urgency or tension. It is hard to understand how the original *Raiders of the Lost Ark*, which featured exploding heads, evil Nazis, and a darkly ambiguous ending, has any relation thematically to *Kingdom of the Crystal Skull,* with its family-friendly tone, easy answers, and Boris-and-Natasha bad guys.

It should be noted that Spielberg is too skilled a filmmaker to make *Kingdom of the Crystal Skull* a complete write-off. The scenery is beautifully filmed, some of the action sequences are expertly executed (particularly a motorcycle chase through a college campus), and there are moments of the original Indiana Jones spark sprinkled throughout. (One of the few moments that effectively places Indy within his new 1950s setting comes when the Communist Spalko asks if Jones has any "defiant last words" and Indy simply replies "I like Ike.") However, those moments of glimpsed potential almost make the rest of the film that much harder to sit through. Ford does a decent job of reviving what is arguably his most charismatic role to date, but everything around him is so cartoonish that his charisma has little to play against. Mutt is a caricature of a '50s greaser, Spalko is a comic book super-villain, and Karen Allen spends the movie effectively neutered, being never given the chance to tap into Marion's defiant independence from *Raiders* and instead being relegated to walking around with a goofy smile on her face that just seems to say, "I'm just happy to be here. This is the best job I've had since *Scrooged*."

And, bringing it back to the macguffin, the alien plot device is so thin, it could barely sustain an episode of *The X-Files*. The whole film is as insubstantial as the contents of the Ark of the Covenant, and there's simply not enough in *Kingdom of the Crystal Skull* to justify the return of a character as iconic as Indiana Jones.

Unfortunately, given the film's box office success—which was almost inevitable due to the generations of goodwill engendered by the previous Jones films—one wonders if George Lucas is even aware of how badly he failed one of his most famous creations. Hopefully, whether he accepts his deserved blame or not, Lucas has finished abusing the legacy of Indiana Jones for now and can go ahead and start ruining the legacy of one of his other cinematic creations. *Howard the Duck*, perhaps?

Tom Burns

CREDITS

Indiana Jones: Harrison Ford
Mutt Williams: Shia LaBeouf
Marion Williams: Karen Allen
Irina Spalko: Cate Blanchett
George 'Mac' McHale: Ray Winstone
Dean Charles Stanforth: Jim Broadbent
Professor Oxley: John Hurt
Russian Soldier No. 3: Andrew Divoff
Colonel Dovchenko: Igor Jijikine
Smith: Neil Flynn
Cemetery Warrior No. 2: Ernie Reyes Jr.
Origin: USA
Language: English
Released: 2008
Production: Frank Marshall; Lucasfilm Ltd.; released by Paramount
Directed by: Steven Spielberg
Written by: David Koepp
Cinematography by: Janusz Kaminski
Music by: John Williams
Sound: Ronald Judkins
Editing: Michael Kahn
Costumes: Mary Zophres
Production Design: Guy Hendrix Dyas
MPAA rating: PG-13
Running time: 122 minutes

REVIEWS

Boston Globe Online. May 19, 2008.
Chicago Sun-Times Online. May 18, 2008.
Entertainment Weekly Online. May 19, 2008.
Hollywood Reporter Online. May 18, 2008.
Los Angeles Times Online. May 19, 2008.
New York Times Online. May 22, 2008.
Rolling Stone Online. June 12, 2008.
San Francisco Chronicle. May 22, 2008, p. E1.
Time Online. May 18, 2008.
Variety Online. May 18, 2008.

Wall Street Journal. May 21, 2008, p. D1.
Washington Post Online. May 22, 2008.

QUOTES

Mac: "This ain't gonna be easy."
Indy replies: "Not as easy as it used to be."

TRIVIA

Sean Connery was approached for a cameo appearance as Henry Jones Sr., Indiana's father, but he turned it down, finding retirement too enjoyable. George Lucas later stated that in retrospect it was good that Jones Sr. did not appear, as it would disappoint the audience when he would not come along for the adventure. Harrison Ford also joked that he was getting old enough to play his own father, so Sean wasn't needed anymore.

AWARDS

Golden Raspberries 2008: Worst Sequel/Prequel
Nomination:
British Acad. 2008: Visual FX
Screen Actors Guild 2008: Outstanding Performance by a Stunt Ensemble.

IRON MAN

Box Office: $318.4 million

In May of 2008, Jon Favreau's *Iron Man* launched the most successful superhero franchise since 2002's *Spider-Man* and proved that the genre was capable of more than just high-budget special effects by incorporating complex issues like war profiteering and personal redemption into summer movie escapism. *Iron Man* succeeds mostly by being more purely enjoyable than most entries that preceded it in the creatively corrupt genre and having a stronger-than-average ensemble. *Iron Man* has more in common with Sam Raimi's *Spider-Man* than just its stellar gross. Both films were perfect summer kick-offs, clever rides that were fun in the moment but something that easily grow deeper with a superior sequel after the entire team has worked out the growing pains of issue number one.

Like a lot of the best superheroes, *Iron Man*'s Tony Stark (Robert Downey Jr.) comes with significant flaws. Stark is a multimillionaire, heavy drinker, womanizer, and all-around playboy in the super-sarcastic style that has practically been patented by the great Downey Jr. Tony forgets the names of the beautiful young female reporters that he beds and would rather play craps than accept awards from his peers. The infamous celebrity has only three real friends—assistant Pepper Potts (Gwyneth

Paltrow), military buddy Rhodey (Terrence Howard), and business partner and semi-mentor Obadiah (Jeff Bridges).

Stark's millions come from being the figurehead of a company that profits from making weapons of mass destruction. While on a trip to sell some of Stark Industries' new Jericho Missiles, the world-renowned figure is blindsided in his convoy, filled with deadly shrapnel, kidnapped by terrorists, and held hostage. Stark's captors demand that the weaponry master create a missile for them, but Tony has another idea. While pretending to build the weapon with his fellow captive Yinsen (Shaun Toub), the man who saved his life, Stark builds an early incarnation of the iconic Iron Man suit and blasts his way out of the caves in which he has been imprisoned.

Tony Stark/Iron Man shoots his way through a few gun-toting terrorists, Yinsen teaches our hero a lesson about sacrifice, and the forever-changed man makes his way back to a United States surprised to see him alive. The new Tony Stark is more than a little conflicted about being a wartime profiteer and tries to dismantle his entire company. The lovely Pepper seems supportive and possibly in the middle of realizing that she loves this more sensitive version of her longtime boss, but Obadiah bristles at his business partner's attempts to destroy everything they have built together. Rhodey basically just fulfills a few necessary plot points, but his character will play a much bigger role in the planned sequel (although Howard has been recast with Don Cheadle taking the role after money disputes with the original film's costar). After his return, Stark has to battle both the war machine headed by Obadiah and stop his original captor Raza's (Faran Tahir) plans for world domination, slowly coming to the realization that his problems may not be as unrelated as he first assumed.

A lot of what works about *Iron Man* can be credited to the great Robert Downey Jr., giving easily one of the best performances in superhero movie history, arguably the best lead turn ever seen in the genre. While so many caped heroes are often deadly dull (even Peter Parker and Bruce Wayne fail a bit in the charisma department in their most successful incarnations), Downey plays Stark like the captivating and fascinating character only he could play. Downey makes the bumpy patches of a pretty deeply flawed screenplay significantly easier to handle and the film is worth seeing and successful largely because of what he does in it. To be fair, Gywneth Paltrow is more charming than she has been in years and Terence Howard is good but very thinly drawn. On the other hand, Bridges is pretty bad, chewing the scenery as much as possible, trying his hardest to turn a weakly written villain into something greater and failing. The lack of a compelling villain in *Iron Man* is the biggest

problem with the film. The proceedings are missing a sense of urgency because the villain is never clearly defined, which does not allow the audience to feel like the hero or anyone for that matter is in any serious danger. A superhero is only as interesting as the villain he is trying to stop or as the world he is trying to save. *Iron Man* is a film about a complex man discovering that he is a hero. By focusing so much on the origin story, which allows Downey to steal the show completely, *Iron Man* feels like chapter one of a longer story, intriguing enough to kick-start a franchise and guarantee the profits of a sequel, but a little dissatisfying as a stand-alone film.

Ultimately, the origin of *Iron Man* works best when it feels like Robert Downey Jr. is going off-book with a line or character choice and inhabiting Tony Stark enough to bring him feel three-dimensionally flawed and human. Too many actors play superhero alter-egos as flawless icons, but Downey makes his Iron Man feel surprisingly real. Downey is perfect, but too much of Favreau's film fails to follow his lead and often looks and feels a little too refined. The chinks in Iron Man's armor are always more interesting than the polished, hot-rod red. When the script by Mark Fergus, Hawk Ostby, Art Marcum, and Matt Holloway is forced, as it too often is, to focus on the tech-speak surrounding the design of the suit or about the weapons and the business of Stark Industries, it is surprisingly dry and dull. And there are really only a few action set-pieces, none of which are that remarkable or memorable and all of which are little over-produced. There is a fine line between CGI effects that look great in a summer movie and ones that look like a video game, and *Iron Man* sometimes crosses that line, making it hard to believe there is a real man under that shiny red suit. Even with a strong ensemble and some clever choices by Jon Favreau, the focus on the origin story and the relatively lackluster action scenes make *Iron Man* feel like the warm-up for a much bigger, better, and inevitable sequel.

Brian Tallerico

CREDITS

Tony Stark/Iron Man: Robert Downey Jr.
Pepper Potts: Gwyneth Paltrow
Col. James 'Rhodey' Rhodes: Terrence Howard
Obadiah Stane/Iron Monger: Jeff Bridges
Nick Fury: Samuel L. Jackson
Yinsen: Shaun Toub
Christine Everhart: Leslie Bibb
Gen. Gabriel: Bill Smitrovich
Agent Phil Coulson: Clark Gregg

Maj. Allen: Tim Guinee
Raza: Faran Tahir
Ahmed: Ahmed Ahmed
CAOC Analyst: Joshua Harto
William: Peter Billingsley
Hogan: Jon Favreau
Abu Bakaar: Sayed Badreya
Jarvis: Paul Bettany (Voice)
Origin: USA
Language: English
Released: 2008
Production: Avi Arad, Kevin Feige; Marvel Studios, Fairview Entertainment, Dark Blades Films, Road Rebel; released by Paramount Pictures
Directed by: Jon Favreau
Written by: Mark Fergus, Art Marcum, Mat Holloway, Hawk Ostby
Cinematography by: Matthew Libatique
Music by: Ramin Djawadi
Editing: Dan Lebental
Art Direction: David Klassen
Costumes: Rebecca Bentjen, Laura Jean Shannon
Production Design: J. Michael Riva
MPAA rating: PG-13
Running time: 126 minutes

REVIEWS

Boston Globe Online. May 2, 2008.
Chicago Sun-Times Online. June 20, 2008.
Entertainment Weekly Online. April 30, 2008.
Hollywood Reporter Online. April 28, 2008.
Los Angeles Times Online. May 1, 2008.
New York Times Online. May 1, 2008.
San Francisco Chronicle. May 2, 2008.
Variety Online. April 25, 2008.
Wall Street Journal Online. May 2, 2008.

QUOTES

Tony Stark: "Is it better to be feared or respected? I say, is it too much to ask for both?"

TRIVIA

Stan Lee plays the man with three blondes, whom Tony Stark mistakes for Hugh Hefner. He later mentioned that it was his most fun cameo.

AWARDS

Nomination:

Oscars 2008: Sound FX Editing, Visual FX
British Acad. 2008: Visual FX

Screen Actors Guild 2008: Outstanding Performance by a Stunt Ensemble.

I'VE LOVED YOU SO LONG

(Il y a longtemps que je t'aime)

Box Office: $3.1 million

I've Loved You So Long (Il y a longtemps que je t'aime) is a thoughtful and deliberate French film starring the Oscar®-nominated British actress Kristin Scott Thomas (*The English Patient* [1996]), whose haunted character drives the emotional narrative. Philippe Claudel's triumphant directorial debut, one of the best-reviewed films of the year, echoes another of 2008's critically acclaimed films, *Rachel Getting Married*. Both involve the death of a child, a guilt-ridden sister's release from an institution, and the ensuing family tensions yet are distinctly different films.

Claudel was a successful novelist in France becoming a screenwriter and director. With a keen eye for character, his screenplay is highly nuanced and engaging, with an organic dramatic tension that leaves the reason that the main character, Juliette (Kristin Scott Thomas), was imprisoned for fifteen years unknown for most of the film. Rather than becoming a gimmick, Claudel allows the revelation to come subtly in its own time and, although it strains logic that slightly diminishes the power and mystery of the character-driven film up until that time, it is not disappointing.

Rather, the film explores the relationship of Juliette to her estranged family and the strange, new world around her. It is a demanding role, with Juliette very much a broken shell of a woman, first seen looking worn while smoking a cigarette at an airport, pensively awaiting her younger sister Léa (Elsa Zylberstein), who volunteers to pick her up after her long incarceration. Thomas is called upon to convey a deep, internal conflict—caused by her unknown crime and attitudes toward it as well as the imprisonment that has made her a social pariah—and to sustain this for the length of the film, causing tension with whomever she encounters. The emotionally frozen French felon is an unfamiliar character for Thomas, usually seen as the epitome of British, upper-class, reserved elegance in such films as *The English Patient*, *Gosford Park* (2001), and *Four Weddings and a Funeral* (1994).

Although there is a tense relationship between the two fueled by issues of guilt and trust, Léa is eager to reconnect with Juliette, whom she invites to live with her in the college town of Nancy where Léa is a literature instructor. Juliette, however, is reluctant to get close to anyone. Rejected by the rest of the family after committing her crime, Juliette can sense the judgment of others, some who know her crime and other who do not. Her brother-in-law, Léa's husband Luc (Serge Hazanavicius), worries about Juliette being around their two Vietnamese adopted daughters. She is forced to undergo uncomfortable questioning at a dinner by a family friend (Olivier Cruvellier). But Luc's father (Jean-Claude Arnaud), who has survived a stroke, also lives with the family, and the fact that he is now unable to speak—busying himself with nonstop reading—is perhaps the reason Juliette chooses him as one of the first she tentatively bonds with as she seeks an escape from the prison of her own making.

Slowly and reluctantly, she connects with others as well in her noble struggle to rejoin society without incurring further pain. As she goes about her new life and looks for a job, she encounters some friendly faces, like the offbeat Capitaine Fauré (Frédéric Pierrot), as well as Léa's compassionate colleague Michel (Laurent Grévill), who has taught in prisons and befriends the beleagured ex-convict. This is where Claudel makes the case of the importance of art in rehabilitation. As A. O. Scott said in the *New York Times,* Juliette's "rehumanization" is "...accomplished through contact with other people...and also through activities like reading, looking at paintings and going to the cinema. In an entirely believable and matter-of-fact way, Mr. Claudel's film makes a case for the psychological and ethical necessity of art."

The lead characters quest for understanding and redemption comes a bit too neatly at the end when the truth about Juliette's crime finally erupts. Jailed for murdering her six-year-old son, Juliette finally reveals what her sister and everyone else who knew of the crime craved to know for fifteen years. The reason she did it was that her son had a terminal illness and Juliette, a doctor, was merely providing much-needed relief from his constant pain in the form of a mercy killing. That she would not have told her family, who apparently did not know that her son was ill, defies logic and caused her to suffer needlessly during those long years in prison.

Nevertheless, the emotional investment is not wasted. The audience is relieved that the mystery of her crime and the motivation behind it is solved and that Juliette, who many may have imagined the worst about, is vindicated in the end. This has as much to do with Thomas's powerful performance as well as Claudel's suc-

cess in crafting a taut, tense drama that is, at heart, a simple story about two sisters mending their relationship that happens to have an explosive revelation in the end.

Hilary White

CREDITS

Lea: Elsa Zylberstein
Michel: Laurent Grevill
Captain Faure: Frederic Pierrot
Juliette: Kristin Scott Thomas
Luc: Serge Hazanavicius
Lys: Lise Segur
Papy Paul: Jean-Claude Arnaud
Samir: Mouss Zouheyri
Origin: France, Germany
Language: French
Released: 2008
Production: Yves Marmion; UGC, Integral Film, France 3 Cinema; released by Sony Pictures Classics
Directed by: Philippe Claudel
Written by: Philippe Claudel
Cinematography by: Jerome Almeras
Music by: Jean-Louis Aubert
Sound: Pierre Lenoir, Stephane Brunclair
Editing: Virginie Bruant
Art Direction: Samuel Deshors
Costumes: Jacqueline Bouchard
MPAA rating: PG-13
Running time: 115 minutes

REVIEWS

Boston Globe Online. October 31, 2008.
Chicago Sun-Times Online. October 29, 2008.
Entertainment Weekly Online. October 29, 2008.
Hollywood Reporter Online. February 19, 2008.
Los Angeles Times Online. October 24, 2008.
New York Times Online. October 24, 2008.
San Francisco Chronicle. October 31, 2008, p. E5.
Variety Online. February 14, 2008.
Wall Street Journal Online. October 24, 2008.

AWARDS

British Acad. 2009: Foreign Film
Nomination:
British Acad. 2008: Actress (Scott Thomas), Orig. Screenplay
Golden Globes 2009: Actress—Drama (Scott Thomas), Foreign Film.

J-K

JOURNEY TO THE CENTER OF THE EARTH

Same planet. Different world.
—Movie tagline

Box Office: $101.7 million

Director Eric Brevig was a visual effects supervisor on major CGI event films like *Men in Black* (1997), *Pearl Harbor* (2001), *The Day after Tomorrow* (2004), and *The Island* (2005) before helming his own picture, a 3-D remake of Jules Verne's classic, *Journey to the Center of the Earth.* A filmmaker's path from behind the scenes to the directorial chair is not always worth mentioning, but Brevig's background in special effects is incredibly relevant to the failure of *Journey to the Center of the Earth,* a film that might serve as a decent reel for an upcoming visual effects supervisor but is shockingly lacking in anything else worth recommending. With such a heavy focus on three-dimensional imagery that feels more dated than usual in its blatant inclusion of devices aimed directly at the audience (for example, when a character starts playing with a yo-yo, there is no doubt that it is there only to eventually be spun "into the crowd" via 3-D), *Journey to the Center of the Earth* is shockingly light on storytelling or character. The "throw at the camera" tricks might be more bearable if they were not the only thing notable about *Journey to the Center of the Earth,* but even the young adult target audience would be dreadfully bored without them. The 3-D nature of the film does not seem like an inherent part of the storytelling as much as it feels like a necessity to keep the audience from dozing off.

Sean (Josh Hutcherson) is a typical thirteen-year-old—he would rather be spending time with his PlayStation than doing anything with the lame adults in his life. But his explorer uncle Trevor (Brendan Fraser) drags the young Sean along for an adventure that will put anything Sony can dream up to shame. The film adaptation, which is more of a sequel to than a loyal retelling of the Jules Verne classic, opens with a shot of a screaming man running across cracking ground as he flees from a Tyrannosaurus Rex. The man who tumbles into the fiery abyss turns out to be Max, the brother of Fraser's Trevor and the now-missing father of Sean. Max disappeared a decade ago and it left both of his loved ones scarred. Sean comes to stay with Trevor at the same time that the explorer notices that seismic readings from around the globe happen to match the ones that were noticed when Max first disappeared. Max was a "Vernian," a rare person who believes that Verne's *Journey to the Center of the Earth* was biography, not fiction. Realizing that Max might have found a way to the Earth's core and could actually still be alive there, Trevor grabs Sean and heads off in his brother's footsteps. Sean and Trevor come across a sexy guide named Hannah (Anita Briem) and before long the odd threesome is miles below the Earth's surface, smashing giant piranha, following birds that glow in the dark, and, of course, running from T-Rex.

The second act of *Journey to the Center of the Earth* features a roller coaster ride through a mine shaft that has a bit of a visceral thrill simply because the storytelling and the three-dimensional device finally seem to serve the same purpose—a thrill for the audience. Except for that sequence, *Journey to the Center of the Earth* is shockingly lifeless. Fraser has a tendency to blandly blend into the background of two-dimensional movies and it is a significant problem when his lifelessness is being amplified by effects aimed directly at the audience. The two actors not named Fraser do better work, but even Hutcherson, who proved he had depth in *The Bridge to Terabithia* (2007), and Briem, who has enough screen presence that she could be an interesting actress to watch, struggle with a script that gives them little depth beyond "Run!"

The lack of interesting characters or performances are even more remarkable when one considers that there is really nothing on screen but actors. Everything else was created after the fact. Of course, only a cynic could truly complain about the lack of believability in a movie about three people crossing the globe the hardest way possible, but the lack of effort put into creating a fully-realized, interesting world under our own is what truly sinks *Journey to the Center of the Earth*. So much of the movie looks like people in front of a green screen on a poorly designed set that it becomes impossible to enjoy the film as anything more than a series of special effects. In that sense, the film is consistent with Brevig's aforementioned filmography—too consistent.

Brian Tallerico

CREDITS

Trevor Anderson: Brendan Fraser
Sean Anderson: Josh Hutcherson
Hannah: Anita Briem
Origin: USA
Language: English
Released: 2008
Production: Beau Flynn, Charlotte Huggins; Walden Media, New Line Cinema; released by Warner Bros.
Directed by: Eric Brevig
Written by: Michael D. Weiss, Jennifer Flackett, Marc Levin
Cinematography by: Chuck Shuman
Music by: Andrew Lockington
Sound: Louis Marion, Pascal Beaudin
Music Supervisor: Lindsay Fellows
Editing: Paul Martin Smith, Dirk Westervelt, Steven Rosenblum
Art Direction: Michele Laliberte
Costumes: Mario Davignon
Production Design: David Sandefur
MPAA rating: PG
Running time: 92 minutes

REVIEWS

Boston Globe Online. July 11, 2008.
Chicago Sun-Times Online. July 11, 2008.
Entertainment Weekly Online. July 9, 2008.
Hollywood Reporter Online. June 29, 2008.
Los Angeles Times Online. July 11, 2008.
New York Times Online. July 11, 2008.
Rolling Stone Online. July 10, 2008.
San Francisco Chronicle. July 10, 2008, p. E1.
Variety Online. June 29, 2008.
Wall Street Journal Online. July 11, 2008.
Washington Post Online. July 11, 2008.

QUOTES

Trevor Anderson: "Ladies and gentlemen, I give you the center of the Earth."

TRIVIA

Director Paul Chart was originally attached to the project but dropped out when the decision was made to shoot the film in 3-D and Chart feared the film would become more "theme park ride" than epic action-adventure. He was ultimately replaced with special effects specialist Eric Brevig and the film was reworked to emphasize the new 3-D format.

JUMPER

Anywhere is possible.
    —Movie tagline
Anywhere. Anything. Instantly.
    —Movie tagline

Box Office: $80.1 million

Jumper is a movie about a young man who has extraordinary powers but does not want to do anything with them but have selfish fun. It is not clear how or why the protagonist, David Rice (Hayden Christiansen), has acquired the ability to transport himself anywhere he wants to in the world—*Jumper* is big on dazzle, short on explanation. But even though the hero lacks the ambition to do much of anything of consequence, good or evil, with his extraordinary power, he still has enemies who want to stop him.

The lead agent of the enemies is Roland Cox (Samuel L. Jackson), whose hair has been painted white. There is no other explanation for why his mustache and goatee are dark with barely a trace of gray. Perhaps he was fried by the electrical volts he uses to zap the "jumpers"—people like David. In fact, after one such fight, Roland displays splotches of white paint on his cheek, just below his hairline, so maybe the bad spray job rubbed off in the thick of the battle.

Jumper establishes instant identification with its target audience—teens who dream of escaping their humdrum home town—in an opening sequence in which fifteen-year-old David (Max Thieriot) gives a hand-made snow globe to Millie (AnnaSophia Robb), a classmate he has a crush on. A bully grabs the gift and throws it across the schoolyard and onto a frozen river. David runs after it, falls through the ice and, instead of drowning, finds himself in the stacks of the Ann Arbor Public Library. Later, after he comes home, he locks himself in his room and, when his father demands entrance, transports himself to New York City. There, one of the first things he does is rob a bank by "jumping" into the vault. He is not a paragon of moral virtue.

After spending eight inexplicable and hedonistic years popping up all over the world, lounging one minute on the top of a pyramid and the next minute flying himself to London or Paris to bed another girl, David returns home to Ann Arbor and discovers the grown-up Millie (Rachel Bilson) is not only one hot number, but still available. Right from the start, none of this makes any sense: Everyone thinks David has died, but of course if he had drowned his body would have been found in the river, and it was not. Millie is not surprised he is alive because he left the snow globe on her backyard swing before he took off. His father believes David is alive, on faith, and also because David occasionally jumps back in his bedroom and speaks to him through the latched door. His mother (Diane Lane) abandoned him at age five but pops up occasionally to warn her son that he is in danger.

David takes Millie to Rome, on a plane, and inside the Coliseum, where they are prowling after hours, David has a second encounter with Roland's people and also meets Griffin (Jamie Bell), another jumper. Griffin tells David the people who are after them are Paladins, a fanatic religious cult, whose members have been killing jumpers since medieval times. Oh, and they are also responsible for witch-hunts and the Inquisition. Griffin and David both discover they lost their moms at age five, and Griffin tells David there is no hope for any of his loved ones, because the Paladins will get them. David convinces Griffin to make a pact to join forces to save Millie and kill Roland.

In his next encounter with Roland, David complains: "I'm not hurting anybody." Roland replies: "Not yet, but you will. Sooner or later you all go bad." And Roland later explains: " Only gods should have this power. Not you, David." And that is all the explanation you are going to get for why Roland and his cohort are fighting David and Griffin.

Jumper, directed by Doug Liman and cowritten by David S. Goyer and Jim Uhls, is uninterested in deeper meanings. It posits that there are people born with powers to transport themselves anywhere they want on the world, but there is no particular reason they have these powers. They do not want to save humanity or individual human beings from difficult straits, they only want to use their powers to have a good time—yet they are still persecuted. The people who made this film must have thought this would appeal to a wide section of mildly disaffected youth who just want to be left alone to party but are not because adults will not let them.

Most of the film transpires as a series of battles between Roland and David, eventually also involving Millie and Griffin. Roland tries to zap the jumpers with his special gun and snare them with its projectile wires, and David eludes him by jumping to exotic locations all over the world. Eventually David stupidly leads Roland to Griffin's hideout, which is on Mount Everest. At one point David and Griffin have their own brawl, and they jump from one place to another while their fight continues.

The filmmakers believe you will be dazzled by the idea that jumpers can go anyplace they like, but there are a couple problems with their execution of this concept. One is that David lazily uses his powers to get across a room rather than just take a few steps; unlike most characters with special powers, he does not reserve his energies for big showdowns. Another is that the movie keeps using the same locations over and over—the Pyramids and Manhattan are favorite spots. It is like David lives in a philistine's version of the actual world, and the filmmakers do not want to challenge viewers with locations that might be unfamiliar—like, say, the Brazilian rain forest or the Russian steppes.

But the biggest problem is that we do not care about David. His use of his powers is entirely self-serving, and his quest to defeat Roland and escape the Paladins is equally selfish: he merely wants to get and keep the girl. What is the rooting interest in David's plight? It does not help that Christiansen is now proving what too many critics said when he first got a starring role as Anakin Skywalker in the *Star Wars* prequels: his acting range is extremely limited. Christiansen gives us an incurious slacker who communicates by raising his eyebrows or tilting his head. He is the kind of shallow guy you would meet in a bar: smug in his own spare good looks, annoyingly in love with himself. Christiansen has no depth. Bilson matches him in shallowness; she, too, plays a character with no marked ambitions or strong personality. All they want to do is to be left alone to have a good time.

In love with its own concept, *Jumper* displays a surprising lack of ingenuity or ideas. All the writers can do with the story of a young man who can jump anywhere is to stage endless hide-and-seek games with religious warriors whose own purpose is vague and shadowy. It is a half-baked movie looking for a reason to use its own energies, and finding few. And it is doubtful that, in this age of sophisticated computer graphics, anyone is going to be much impressed by the jump techniques—which consist simply of making David and Griffin appear and disappear abruptly, accompanied by loud whooshing noises. Nothing special about those effects. Peter Pan could do better.

Michael Betzold

CREDITS

David: Hayden Christensen
Griffin: Jamie Bell
Roland: Samuel L. Jackson
Millie: Rachel Bilson
Mary: Diane Lane
William: Michael Rooker
Young Millie: AnnaSophia Robb
Young David: Max Thieriot
Origin: USA
Language: English
Released: 2008
Production: Arnon Milchan, Lucas Foster, Jay Sanders, Simon Kinberg; Regency Enterprises, New Regency, Hypnotic, Dune Entertainment; released by 20th Century-Fox
Directed by: Doug Liman
Written by: David S. Goyer, Simon Kinberg, Jim Uhls
Cinematography by: Barry Peterson
Music by: John Powell
Sound: John J. Thomson
Music Supervisor: Julianne Jordan
Editing: Saar Klein, Dean Zimmerman, Don Zimmerman
Art Direction: Peter Grundy
Costumes: Magall Guidasci
Production Design: Oliver Scholl
MPAA rating: PG-13
Running time: 88 minutes

REVIEWS

Chicago Sun-Times Online. February 14, 2008.
Entertainment Weekly Online. February 13, 2008.
Hollywood Reporter Online. February 13, 2008.
Los Angeles Times Online. February 14, 2008.
New York Times Online. February 14, 2008.
San Francisco Chronicle. February 14, 2008, p. E1.
Variety Online. February 12, 2008.
Washington Post. February 14, 2008, p. C9.

QUOTES

Roland: "Only God should have this power."

TRIVIA

The high school depicted in the film is Huron High School in Ann Arbor, Michigan (the school which writer David S. Goyer attended).

THE KILLING OF JOHN LENNON

I was nobody until I killed the biggest somebody on Earth.
—Movie tagline

At the start of writer/director Andrew Piddington's docudrama *The Killing of John Lennon,* there is a title that proclaims that all the words spoken by Mark David Chapman (Jonas Ball) in the film come from his actual journals. Thus, this is a movie narrated by an actor using the assassin's own words. It is an interesting and promising approach to an iconic moment in recent history—but, unfortunately, *The Killing of John Lennon* fails to produce any new important insights into one of the seminal acts of violence of the late twentieth century.

What we do get instead is fascinating and frustrating—a thorough if somewhat mystifying portrait of Chapman and his murky motivations. The movie opens with Chapman in Honolulu, where he has married a local woman. But the movie does not say much about this union, which does not seem to have solved Chapman's feeling of being a purposeless misfit in society. We do not really get much information about the woman or the relationship. This is one big problem with the film's reliance on Chapman's own words alone: there are significant gaps in his story. We do not understand the life experiences that have led him, at this point in his life, to feel so thwarted and disconnected. He has a couple of brief encounters with his mother (Krisha Fairchild), in which it is clear she is selfish and more concerned about her latest man than about her son. But despite these passing encounters, Chapman is presented as a stew of inexplicable rage.

His free-floating animus toward a culture from which he feels estranged finds a focus when he checks a book out of the Honolulu public library: *The Catcher in the Rye.* In the J. D. Salinger classic about young Holden Caulfield's intense rage and alienation, Chapman finds not just strong inspiration but a direct coded message, and he settles on a purpose to give meaning to his life: to kill John Lennon. But why? How does Salinger's book define that as his mission? It is never made completely clear, and so the puzzle of Chapman remains largely unsolved.

Chapman takes a first abortive trip to New York City, where he is temporarily shaken out of his plan.

But he soon returns, and starts hanging around the Dakota Apartments, casing out the stately residence where Lennon and Yoko Ono live with their young son, Sean. On the sidewalk, he talks to a couple of female Lennon groupies who turn down his awkward invitation to dinner. Later, he rages in his hotel room when he hears two men having sex in the next room and he fantasizes about shooting gays. The connection between his homophobia and his plot against Lennon is unclear, and so is his often-repeated idea that Lennon is somehow a "phony"—it is never explained what Chapman means by this characterization.

Ball does a cleverly frightening interpretation of Chapman, looking like a real odd duck in his winter hat with ear flaps, yet capable of appearing close to normal in his encounters with others on the street, and then having almost epileptic fits of rage while alone. Ball makes Chapman credible as a man who can hide and manage to control his insanity at most times. What is most frightening is that Chapman does not understand himself why he is driven to act against Lennon.

When he finally shoots Lennon, about two-thirds of the way through the film, the event is portrayed as bizarrely as it was—without Hollywood histrionics or superfluous dramatics. Chapman is in a shadow world, and the killing thrusts him into another reality, one of being in the glare of the public spotlight. As a bone to conspiracy theorists, just after the shooting we hear a voice telling him to throw away his gun and run for safety, but it is not connected to even a thread of other information. Piddington apparently did not want to explore the entire issue of whether Chapman acted alone or had help and many key questions are left unanswered: for instance, where did Chapman, who was unemployed, get the money for his flights and hotel rooms?

After the killing, the film spends a bit of time walking audiences through the crush surrounding Chapman's immediate arrest and treatment by authorities: how the officer in charge is determined not to have "another Jack Ruby" take out the assassin; how the press creates a circus; how an initial interview with a prison psychologist is conducted; and how mourners worldwide react to the killing, as shown on television clips. Now Chapman seems both more lost and more purposeful; he eventually adapts to his new celebrity status and decides to use his trial to advance his goal of getting the whole world to read *The Catcher in the Rye*—and understand it as he does, as work of transcendent illumination.

While much of this part of the film is fascinating, Piddington eventually tires of the details of Chapman's legal fight and rushes forward to the verdict. At the end, we are left with a frightening portrait of a killer who has thrust himself into notoriety with an act of boldness

that does define him and give him the identity he has so long sought. Ball creates a memorable character, all the more chilling for being true to the thoughts, behavior, and manner of the assassin.

Yet this insider approach to the subject matter, focusing solely on Chapman's own interior monologue, does not provide any important new insights into his motivation. It does not explain exactly what about Salinger's book inspires him to kill Lennon, and why he targets this Beatle precisely. We do not know why he considers Lennon a "phony" even though he professes to love the Beatles' music. It does not give us a new window into Lennon's bubble of celebrity and how he was left so vulnerable. And it does not expend much effort in setting Chapman's act in the context of the cultural and emotional cataclysm it induced.

The trouble with a killer's own words is that they explain everything in the way the killer wants things explained. In Chapman's case, however, his motivations seem opaque even to himself, so we learn nothing really clear or satisfying. *The Killing of John Lennon* is really focused on the interior thoughts of Mark David Chapman and does not deliver the broader view the title promises. We are left with a frustratingly narrow window on this important event and the overwhelming feeling of being cheated out of a satisfying explanation. Perhaps, however, that is the most realistic thing we can expect—because this assassination seems doomed, unless you believe the conspiracy theorists, to be forever muddled and opaque.

Michael Betzold

CREDITS

Detective John Sullivan: Robert Kirk
Mark David Chapman: Jonas Ball
Gloria Chapman: Mie Omori
Chapman's mother: Krisha Fairchild
Origin: Great Britain
Language: English
Released: 2007
Production: Rakha Singh; Picture Players; released by IFC Films
Directed by: Andrew Piddington
Written by: Andrew Piddington
Cinematography by: Roger Eaton
Music by: Makana
Sound: Duane Thomsen
Editing: Tony Palmer
Art Direction: Anu Schwartz, Skeeter Stanback
Costumes: Michael Bevins
Production Design: Tora Peterson

MPAA rating: Unrated
Running time: 114 minutes

REVIEWS

Guardian Online. December 7, 2007.
Hollywood Reporter Online. January 1, 2008.
New York Times Online. January 2, 2008.
Variety Online. February 15, 2007.
Village Voice Online. January 2, 2008.

KIT KITTREDGE: AN AMERICAN GIRL

Box Office: $17.6 million

Margaret Mildred "Kit" Kittredge (Abigail Breslin) is a ten-year-old budding reporter at the onset of the Great Depression, who solves a crime and learns valuable lessons about the challenges of life during that era. Kit's father loses his business and her family faces losing their home, as have several of Kit's close friends and neighbors. Although Kit's mother frets, "you should be playing, not worrying about boarders and mortgages," by the film's end, Kit offers these words of wisdom: "The Depression had changed each one of our lives. And while it made us struggle, it also made us strong. Now no matter what life had in store…I was ready." As the year 2008 progressed and the recession worsened in the United States, unemployment rose to nearly unprecedented levels, and more and more families were forced into foreclosure, this family comedy/drama takes on a new, unforeseen importance and makes the film's lessons all the more poignant and relevant.

That *Kit Kittredge: An American Girl* is also amazingly appealing for audiences of all ages and phenomenally cast is all the more surprising since American Girl began as a line of pre-teen dolls from important periods in American history. The popular books chronicling their adventures, including Valerie Tripp's *Kit Kittredge: An American Girl,* have sold more than 120 million copies. *Kit Kittredge: An American Girl* is the first theatrical version of the series, while three earlier television movies exist. The first, *Samantha: An American Girl Holiday,* starring AnnaSophia Robb, was famously produced by fan Julia Roberts.

Oscar®-nominated Abigail Breslin stars as the title character, Kit, a precocious but likable ten-year-old who chirpily storms into the local *Cincinnati Register* offices with a story about the Depression from a kid's perspective with every expectation of being published. When the paper's curmudgeonly editor Mr. Gibson (Wallace Shawn) quickly divorces her of that notion, Kit is un-

phased, and ingeniously looks for her next story by "shadowing" two hobos her mother Margaret (Julia Ormond) has hired, teenage Will (Max Theiriot) and his friend Countee (Willow Smith), a very young boy. Kit and her friends Stirling Howard IV (Zach Mills) and Ruthie Smithens (Madison Davenport) learn to read "hobo signs" and visit the hobo jungle, a tent village where men and women who once had homes and jobs now huddle together in the woods, sharing food and riding the rails to find work. Gibson, once again, rejects her story on the kindness and goodness of hobos, citing the spate of robberies in which hobos were suspected that was plaguing the entire country.

Kit realizes how close she and her family may be to the down-on-their-luck hobos when she finds out her father Jack (Chris O'Donnell) has lost his business and must go to Chicago to find a job, promising to write weekly. In order to make ends meet and keep up with the mortgage, the Kittredge's decide to rent out rooms, including Kit's, and Kit gladly moves into the attic. Soon the house is bustling with a host of colorful boarders as "A'int We Got Fun" plays. There is the suave magician Jefferson Jasper Berk (Stanley Tucci), who catches the eye of the single-but-looking dancer Miss May Dooley (Jane Krakowski); the kooky bookmobile librarian Miss Lucinda Bond (Joan Cusack); Mrs. Louise Howard (Glenne Headly), Stirling's disapproving mother, who has been cruelly abandoned by her husband. A mystery unfolds when Margaret's lock-box is stolen containing all their money and many of the boarders' valuables.

The police suspect hobo Will, which is confirmed by Mr. Berk who saw him flee into the night with the box. Kit will not believe her friend could do such a thing and has documented evidence from earlier crimes that the real perpetrator has a large colorful tattoo on his arm, which Will does not. She and her friends investigate and find that the robberies were actually perpetrated by Mr. Berk along with his newly arrived cousin, Freidreich (Dylan Smith), who has the offending tattoo, and in a nicely done plot twist, the bungling Miss Bond. Another interesting and unforeseen twist is that Countee, dressed by Will as a girl to "hide her in plain sight," actually turns out to be a girl posing as a boy in order to ride the rails more safely with Will. The film's heartwarming ending has the stolen goods duly returned by a reformed Miss Bond, Kit's story published in the paper, and Jack returning home to his adoring family.

The film presents a thoughtful portrayal of the hobos, hobo life, and the poverty suffered by children and adults alike during the Depression and successfully incorporates that into a highly entertaining family mystery. While it is certainly a sanitized version of the time, it is after all a children's film, and director Patricia Rozema and screenwriter Ann Peacock do an admirable job of balancing the cold hard realities with softer edges and a rosier hue to make it palatable for children without straying too far into fantasy.

Hilary White

CREDITS

Kit Kittredge: Abigail Breslin
Margaret Kittredge: Julia Ormond
Jack Kittredge: Chris O'Donnell
Miss Bond: Joan Cusack
Ruthie Smithens: Madison Davenport
Miss Dooley: Jane Krakowski
Stirling Howard: Zach Mills
Will Shepherd: Max Thieriot
Mr. Berk: Stanley Tucci
Mr. Gibson: Wallace Shawn
Countee: Willow Smith
Mr. Pennington: Colin Mochrie
Mrs. Howard: Glenne Headley
Origin: USA
Language: English
Released: 2008
Production: Elaine Goldsmith-Thomas, Julie Goldstein, Lisa Gillan, Ellen L. Brothers; New Line Cinema, HBO Films, Red Om Films; released by Picturehouse
Directed by: Patricia Rozema
Written by: Ann Peacock
Cinematography by: David Boyd, Julie Rogers
Music by: Joseph Vitarelli
Sound: Glen Gauthier
Music Supervisor: Evyen Klean
Art Direction: Michele Brady
Costumes: Trysha Bakker
Production Design: Peter Cosco
MPAA rating: G
Running time: 100 minutes

REVIEWS

Chicago Sun-Times Online. June 20, 2008.
Entertainment Weekly. July 11, 2008, p. 55.
Hollywood Reporter Online. June 19, 2008.
Los Angeles Times Online. June 20, 2008.
New York Times Online. June 20, 2008.
San Francisco Chronicle. July 2, 2008, p. E10.
Variety Online. June 18, 2008.
Washington Post. July 2, 2008, p. C1.

QUOTES

Miss Bond: "I'm sorry…we were trying to be like Robin Hood. You know, steal from the rich to give to the poor.

But…really, all we were doing was stealing from the rich…and the poor…and keeping it for ourselves. That's what we did, really."

TRIVIA

The film was shot in 27 days.

KUNG FU PANDA

Prepare for awesomeness.
—Movie tagline

Box Office: $215.4 million

Jack Black has a unique ability to play affable losers with big ambitions who make good (to varying degrees)—*School of Rock* (2003) and *Nacho Libre* (2006) are prime examples in this vein. Though not his first foray into animation, *Kung Fu Panda* was written with Jack Black in mind, and it is a nearly perfect animated rendition of his well-established idiom—the film even manages to translate Black's own prodigious physicality to lovable Po the panda. Black's characters often comment on their weight in his films, and whereas Black fully throws himself into the physical aspects of his roles for comedic effect, the animators have managed to capture that essence as well. Backed by a phenomenal supporting cast, a good story, wonderful visuals, and all-around excellent execution, *Kung Fu Panda* is a strong animated film, which has just as much in it for adults to enjoy as it does for children (the movie's obvious demographic).

Kung Fu Panda opens with what turns out to be a dream sequence in which Po the panda (Jack Black) imagines himself to be a great Kung Fu master, fighting alongside China's greatest heroes, the Furious Five: Tigress (voice of Angelina Jolie), Monkey (voice of Jackie Chan), Viper (voice of Lucy Liu), Crane (voice of David Cross), and Mantis (voice of Seth Rogen). About to take on the ten thousand demons of Demon Mountain, Po awakes from his dream into his real life as a noodle house employee in his father's restaurant (that his father, voiced by the venerable character actor James Hong, is a goose is never addressed as unusual), forlorn to be trapped in his apparent noodle-filled destiny. The film cuts to a nearby mountaintop where the Furious Five are training with their master, Shifu, a rare red panda (voice of Dustin Hoffman). Shifu is summoned by his master Oogway, a turtle (voice of Randall Duk Kim), who tells him that he has had a premonition that Shifu's former pupil, Tai Lung (a snow leopard, voiced by the ever-sinister Ian McShane), who was imprisoned after attempting to steal the Dragon Scroll—a document that is supposed to grant the reader the secret to limitless power, that of the Dragon Warrior—will return to the Valley of Peace. Shifu and Oogway immediately call for a tournament and ceremony for selection of the Dragon Warrior.

Po hears of the tournament and tries to attend, but is forced to drag the noodle cart up the mountainside to the site of the tournament, the Jade Palace. The effort makes him late, and the gates are closed before he can enter. In a last-ditch effort to see the action, Po straps several fireworks to a chair and rockets himself into the courtyard, only to fall right in front of Oogway, who points at Po, indicating that Po has been selected as the Dragon Warrior. Horrified that a flabby panda has obviously been mistakenly chosen to be the most powerful warrior of all time, Shifu vows to work Po so hard that Po will want to quit, allowing one of the Furious Five to become the Dragon Warrior. Meanwhile, Tai Lung makes a dramatic escape from the prison and immediately heads to the Valley, bent on acquiring the Dragon Scroll. When Shifu delivers the news to Oogway, the old turtle insists that Po is their only hope, and that Shifu must believe in him—with that, Oogway passes away in a whirl of leaves and departs to the spirit world. Shifu decides to accept Oogway's assessment and vows to train the Panda in good faith. Shifu inadvertently discovers that Po has natural Kung Fu talent that emerges when food is used as a reward. The Furious Five, in the interim, decide to try to stop Tai Lung from reaching the Valley and, despite a valiant effort, are defeated. Upon returning, they report that Tai Lung is near. Shifu gives Po the Dragon Scroll as the final stage of his training in order to be given its power in order to defeat the approaching Tai Lung, but the scroll is revealed to be blank.

Shifu tells Po and the Five to evacuate the Valley while Shifu remains in the temple to face his former student. A despondent Po helps his father flee and his father tries to console Po by confiding that the secret ingredient in his secret ingredient soup is…nothing. The belief that something about the soup is special is what makes it special. Po understands this to be the secret of the Dragon Scroll—it is within one's self to be the Dragon Warrior, there is no secret ingredient. Po returns to the Jade Palace and has an epic battle with Tai Lung, but Po's skills combined with his panda's physiology allow him to effectively fight Tai Lung and also make him immune to several of the Snow Leopard's nerve attacks (which would paralyze another opponent, but which only tickle Po). With Tai Lung defeated, peace is restored to the valley and to Shifu (who felt guilty about training Tai Lung as a youngster), and Po takes his place alongside the Furious Five as one of Kung Fu's greatest masters.

The inspiration for much of the design and overall look of *Kung Fu Panda* comes from ancient Chinese paintings, recent Kung Fu films such as *Crouching Tiger, Hidden Dragon* (2000) and *Hero* (2004, also known as *Jet Li's Hero*), and even a slight bit of influence from Genndy Tartakovsky's groundbreaking animated Kung Fu fantasy action series *Samurai Jack*. In fact, the dream sequence that opens *Kung Fu Panda* not only is the perfect melding of these influences, but also by virtue of being chosen as the scene that introduces the audience to the world of *Kung Fu Panda,* seems to serve as the directors'/designers' opening thesis for the look of the film—it states concisely, "These are the sources we have pulled from, the references we have chosen to evoke, in order to depict the nature of this animated world." These choices serve to provide both a strong foundation in the world of Chinese-inspired action cinema for the novice viewer and to act as touchstones for those already initiated in the visual and stylistic elements of the Kung Fu genre (both live and animated)—a viewer (especially a child) need not know that the restaurant battle scene depicted in the opening dream sequence of *Kung Fu Panda* is almost certainly a direct reference to a similar (and famous) scene from *Crouching Tiger, Hidden Dragon* to appreciate the design of Po's fight against a horde of foes or to understand that Po has an (over)active imagination, but for those who know the reference and can see the connection, the message communicated to the audience by the filmmakers is one of competence, a love of the genre, and a desire to invoke not only the style of Kung Fu cinema but also its values (belief in one's self and others, acceptance, and the imperative to use power and knowledge wisely). Once the film shifts into the everyday reality of Po's world, these elements are dialed back a bit, but their essence remains and resonates through the course of the entire movie.

Furthermore, the details that make *Kung Fu Panda* so delightful reside not only in the filmmakers' obvious love and respect for the Kung Fu genre, but also for the animated feature. For example, the design of the Furious Five—Tigress, Monkey, Viper, Crane, and Mantis, all of which were chosen because they represent actual Kung Fu fighting styles and techniques—allows them to move with a stylized precision and grace that captures not only the motion of animals, but in the execution of the moves themselves manages to be an effective amalgam of human and animal movement. This is nothing short of phenomenal considering all of the high-intensity action that must be depicted by the on-screen animation. Also, the themes explored in *Kung Fu Panda*—belief in one's self and in others, the idea that there are no coincidences in life, and an implied imperative of acceptance, the willingness to let go of preconceptions and prejudices in order to change, to become, or simply to move on—are in line not only with the tenets of the martial arts genre, but they are also congruous with the positive messages often communicated by animated features (see any number of Pixar films for examples). That the filmmakers have managed to blend the messages of Eastern philosophy into a form fit for the cartoon crowd shows how well the directors, writers, and animators have translated the world of martial arts to the world of animation. And, finally, it must be noted that every possible opportunity is taken to make *Kung Fu Panda* as heartwarmingly funny as possible. From the use of various slow-motion shots, to the well-orchestrated fight sequences, every ounce of the ponderous girth of lovable Po is utilized for full comedic effect. Whether Po is falling on Tai Lung's head in slow-motion, or rocketing over a crowd to catch a glimpse of the Dragon Warrior, *Kung Fu Panda* makes excellent use of its chief protagonist to provide a sympathetic anchor for the story and a source for considerable, genuine laughs.

For all of the masterful storytelling in *Kung Fu Panda*, visual and otherwise, the true joy of the film is how fun and funny it is. Not only does the film pay homage to some of the best Kung Fu movies of the recent past, but it also manages to squeeze in a delightful rendition of the 1970s hit "Kung Fu Fighting," sung by Black and Gnarls Barkley front man Cee-Lo. *Kung Fu Panda* can certainly claim its place as one of the great masters of the genre.

John Boaz

CREDITS

Po Panda: Jack Black (Voice)
Master Shifu: Dustin Hoffman (Voice)
Monkey: Jackie Chan (Voice)
Tigress: Angelina Jolie (Voice)
Viper: Lucy Liu (Voice)
Tai Lung: Ian McShane (Voice)
Mantis: Seth Rogen (Voice)
Crane: David Cross (Voice)
Commander Vachir: Michael Clarke Duncan (Voice)
Mr. Ping: James Hong (Voice)

Zeng: Dan Fogler (Voice)
Master Oogway: Randall Duk Kim (Voice)
Origin: USA
Language: English
Released: 2008
Production: Melissa Cobb; DreamWorks Animation; released by Paramount
Directed by: John Stevenson, Mark Osborne
Written by: Jonathan Aibel, Glenn Berger
Cinematography by: Yong Duk Jhun
Music by: Hans Zimmer, John Powell
Editing: Claire Knight
Art Direction: Tang K. Heng
Production Design: Raymond Zibach
MPAA rating: PG
Running time: 90 minutes

REVIEWS

Boston Globe Online. June 6, 2008.
Chicago Sun-Times Online. June 5, 2008.
Entertainment Weekly Online. June 4, 2008.
Hollywood Reporter Online. May 28, 2008.
Los Angeles Times Online. June 6, 2008.
New York Times Online. June 6, 2008.
San Francisco Chronicle. June 6, 2008, p. E1.
Variety Online. May 15, 2008.
Wall Street Journal Online. June 6, 2008.
Washington Post. June 6, 2008, p. C1.

QUOTES

Po: "Skadoosh!"

TRIVIA

The code title used during production of the film was "Daydreamer."

AWARDS

Nomination:

Oscars 2008: Animated Film
Golden Globes 2009: Animated Film.

L

LAKEVIEW TERRACE

What could be safer than living next to a cop?
—Movie tagline

Box Office: $39.2 million

Writer-director Neil LaBute (*Your Friends & Neighbors* [1998], *The Wicker Man* [2006], *In the Company of Men* [1997]) usually focuses on the strange twists and turns that male-female relationships can take under duress. In *Lakeview Terrace*, he directs a story written by others (David Loughery and Howard Korder) that adds a racial dimension to his favorite template.

By centering his story around a black cop, Abel Turner (Samuel L. Jackson), who is a hypocrite and a racist, LaBute takes a bit of a risk. But he has created such a fully realized and well-motivated character full of hate—and Jackson does such an excellent job of making Turner a complex and believable monster—that any objections of unfairness should be quelled. This is a story that takes pains to delve deeply and even-handedly into the many forms that racial prejudice can take, and its characters have plenty of credibility.

Lakeview Terrace breaks fairly new ground only in the racial overtones of its plot. On the face of it, this is simply a bad-neighbor movie, a genre that is a staple of Hollywood horror and comedy. And many parts of the plot seem belabored, hackneyed, and silly, as when Abel's security floodlights interrupt the sleep of his new neighbors.

The neighbors are a racially mixed young couple, Chris (Patrick Wilson) and Lisa (Kerry Washington), who have moved into suburban Los Angeles because

Chris has been transferred to a new job managing a store in a supermarket chain. Lisa is a freelance clothes designer who works out of the home, or so we gather from one small scene; the movie pays scant attention to either of their jobs. More important to the plot is Abel's occupation: he is a cop with twenty-eight years on the force, who works the streets with a young partner. Abel is a mess of contradictions, and the biggest one is this: At home, as a single parent, he takes pains to set down strict rules for his teenage daughter and preteen son, including the use of proper English. At work, he is a tough, streetwise cop who cuts deals with drug dealers for information and speaks the crude language of the streets.

Abel throws his weight around on the suburban cul-de-sac where he lives, making a big show of going on neighborhood patrols and warning his new neighbors about the dangers of young punks who prowl the arroyo behind their homes at night and might come up to the ridge of suburbia to steal and plunder. But from the minute Chris and Lisa move in, he is also spying on them suspiciously, and it is soon clear he has another agenda. He is angry at Chris for having a black woman for a wife.

For most of the film, Abel's prejudice seems not only foolish and unfounded but despicable. Late in the movie, however, we find out the motivation for his anger—his own wife died in a car crash three years earlier while riding during the middle of a workday with her white supervisor, presumably to or from a tryst. Perhaps that revelation should have come earlier, because by that point no one is in the audience feels much sympathy for Abel.

Besides refusing to turn off the floodlights that are robbing his new neighbors of sleep, Abel also breaks into their house and messes up their air conditioning, mangles Chris's hand with a wrench when Chris offers to help him fix something in his car engine, reveals to Lisa at a party that Chris secretly has not given up his habit of smoking, breaks into the garage and slashes the tires of their Prius, throws a bachelor party and makes a videotape of Chris being forced to be intimate with an exotic dancer, and does so many other barely plausible things that the film constantly teeters on the edge of satire, unintentionally. All these things Abel gets away with because he is a cop, an expert at humiliation, and a devious and immoral man. And every chance he gets, he plays the race card to try to belittle Chris or force him into retaliation. The movie is at its silliest when Chris decides to join the battle by installing his own floodlights, planting trees along their property line, and trying to go "mano a mano" with Abel.

Of course, in the process of harassing his neighbors, Abel drives a wedge between them. Lisa, who wants to have a baby, skips taking birth-control pills and gets pregnant, infuriating Chris. And that escalates the stakes: a couple on shaky ground has to uncover the strength of their love in order to defeat a self-proclaimed family man who believes only in his own righteous wrath. With the battle defined that way, there is not much doubt who is going to triumph in the end.

Throughout the film, there is a looming threat of wildfires raging in the hills nearby. You expect they will eventually play a role in the climax, but they do so only tangentially. Apparently they are meant to be a metaphor for the hellish evil Abel continually cooks up for his neighbors. In the end, there is an image of Abel, hose in hand, spraying his roof and eaves, while an inferno rages behind him—just in case you do not know by then that he is the devil incarnate.

Though often heavy-handed, *Lakeview Terrace* is redeemed by good performance from its three stars. Washington is by turns delightfully adorable, spunky, and combustible. Wilson piles up his frustrations into a seething stew. But Jackson carries the weight of the movie by making Abel into an iconic embodiment of rage gone terribly wrong, a man of deep hypocrisy who nonetheless clings to his slippery hold on morality, who deeply believes in his family but is so wounded by his grief that he cannot abide the happiness of another family. His is the best kind of monster, a man not born evil or by nature villainous, but a complicated mess of simmering resentment brought down by his own weaknesses. Jackson combines his trademark bad-ass persona with a stubborn prickliness, and he transcends his own standard screen image by doing the hard work

of fully inhabiting a broken man who thinks he is still functioning.

Michael Betzold

CREDITS

Abel Turner: Samuel L. Jackson
Chris Mattson: Patrick Wilson
Lisa Mattson: Kerry Washington
Celia Turner: Regine Nehy
Javier Villareal: Jay Hernandez
Clarence Darlington: Keith Loneker
Lt. Morgada: Eva LaRue
Julio Pacheco: Mel Rodriguez
Marcus Turner: Jaishon Fisher
Harold Perreau: Ron Glass
Origin: USA
Language: English
Released: 2008
Production: James Lassiter, Will Smith; Overbrook Entertainment, Screen Gems; released by Sony Pictures Entertainment
Directed by: Neil LaBute
Written by: David Loughery, Howard Korder
Cinematography by: Rogier Stoffers
Music by: Jeff Danna, Mychael Danna
Sound: Lee Orloff
Editing: Joel Plotch
Art Direction: Tom Taylor, Paul Sonski
Costumes: Lynette Meyer
Production Design: Bruton Jones
MPAA rating: PG-13
Running time: 110 minutes

REVIEWS

Boston Globe Online. September 19, 2008.
Chicago Sun-Times Online. September 18, 2008.
Entertainment Weekly Online. September 16, 2008.
Hollywood Reporter Online. September 7, 2008.
Los Angeles Times Online. September 19, 2008.
New York Times Online. September 19, 2008.
San Francisco Chronicle. September 19, 2008, p. E5.
Variety Online. September 7, 2008.
Wall Street Journal Online. September 19, 2008.

LEATHERHEADS

> *In the beginning, the rules were simple. There weren't any.*
> —Movie tagline

Box Office: $31.3 million

There have been dozens of American sports films, several of them comedies, but romantic sports comedies are unusual. *Bull Durham* (1988) represents the epitome of this genre, and George Clooney's *Leatherheads* could be seen as a football version of Ron Shelton's baseball film. Both center around over-the-hill athletes who find themselves competing against younger men not only the playing fields but in the arena of romance.

Leatherheads presents professional football as it was practiced in 1925, years before the National Football League surpassed baseball as America's favorite spectator sport. Dodge Connolly (George Clooney), the aging star of the Duluth Bulldogs, finds himself in a dilemma when his team's sponsor withdraws its support. At a time when college football regularly filled stadiums with 40,000 or more spectators, the professionals played before hundreds on barely adequate fields. As the film opens, the Bulldogs forfeit a game they are winning when the opposition steals the team's only football.

Hearing of the crowds drawn by Princeton star Carter Rutherford (John Krasinski), Connelly decides to save the Bulldogs and himself by enticing Rutherford to join the team. His obstacle is Rutherford's agent, C. C. Frazier (Jonathan Pryce), also a former adversary, though the prior Connelly-Frazier relationship is never explained. When Frazier finally sees that it is better to make money from Rutherford's exploits immediately rather than later, the college sensation joins the Bulldogs.

A new problem arises in the form of *Chicago Tribune* reporter Lexie Littleton (Renée Zellweger). In addition to being a football star, Rutherford is also a hero of the Great War, but Littleton's boss (Jack Thompson) has evidence that his bravery is a fraud and wants her to expose Rutherford. If she does so, of course, Connelly is back where he started.

Littleton becomes reluctant to tarnish Rutherford's fame as she slowly grows fond of him. At the same time, Connelly begins liking her. The resulting romantic triangle, with an older and a younger man attracted to the same woman, again recalls *Bull Durham*.

Clooney has said that *Leatherheads* was inspired by the Hollywood romantic comedies of the 1930s and 1940s, specifically such films as *The Philadelphia Story* (1940), *His Girl Friday* (1940), and *The More the Merrier* (1943). In each a man and woman have an antagonistic relationship that gradually develops into love. Clooney has often been called the modern Cary Grant, star of the first two of these films. Krasinski gives Rutherford a sincere innocence reminiscent of characters played by James Stewart, also a star of *The Philadelphia Story*. Littleton is clearly based on the reporter played by Rosalind Russell in *His Girl Friday*.

Leatherheads occasionally tries to emulate the fast-talking comedy dialogue of screwball comedies, most famously in *His Girl Friday*, but the film finally disappoints because it can never settle on a single style or tone. The scenes between Connolly and Littleton have some spark, but those with Littleton and Rutherford are much flatter. Half the film has a fast pace, while the remainder just lumbers along. Clooney and his screenwriters never seem certain about whether their real interest is romance or football, which essentially disappears for a half hour midway through. What is left is too much football for fans of romantic comedies and too little for sports fans.

Leatherheads was originally developed for director Steven Soderbergh in 1993 by screenwriters Duncan Brantley, then Soderbergh's brother-in-law, and Rick Reilly of *Sports Illustrated*. The screenwriters, inspired by their fondness for tales of the struggles of professional football in its early days, drew upon the story of Red Grange, the Illinois star considered the best college player of his time. The day after playing his final college game in 1925, Grange, at the urging of his agent, C. C. Pyle, signed with the Chicago Bears for a nineteen-game barnstorming tour that helped legitimize the National Football League.

Leatherheads attracted the attention of Casey Silver, head of production at Universal Studios, but when Silver left Universal, the project when into limbo until rescued by Clooney. The star-director reworked the script and appealed unsuccessfully to the Writers Guild of America to receive screenplay credit.

Leatherheads, whose title refers to the leather helmets worn by the players, is pleasant enough, the football scenes are generally believable, though Krasinski does not run like an athlete, and Clooney gives Connolly considerable charm, but the film is instantly forgettable. Cinematographer Newton Thomas Sigel shoots the football scenes in an orange, almost sepia, glow meant to evoke the period, but these images eventually become tiresome. Randy Newman's score recalls the 1920s less than it does the work of his uncles Alfred, Emil, and Lionel Newman, especially the thunderous film music they composed in the 1950s. The unsubtle score seems determined to overwhelm the slight story into submission.

Leatherheads is also full of factual errors and anachronisms. Rutherford is described as having left Princeton to fight in World War I, but the war ended in 1918 and he is still a student in 1925. The film's sluggish pace, unfortunately, gives many opportunities to notice such mistakes. *Leatherheads* was originally scheduled to be released in the fall of 2007 only to be delayed until the spring of 2008, an odd time for a football film. When its opening-weekend business was disappointing, a Universal executive blamed the NCAA basketball finals for keeping sports fans away. For those who question the judgment and wisdom of the people operating the major studios, here is an excellent example.

Michael Adams

CREDITS

Dodge Connolly: George Clooney
Lexie Littleton: Renee Zellweger
Carter Rutherford: John Krasinski
CC Frazier: Jonathan Pryce
Commissioner: Peter Gerety
Harvey: Jack Thompson
Suds: Stephen Root
Coach Ferguson: Wayne Duvall
Big Gus: Keith Loneker
Origin: USA
Language: English
Released: 2008
Production: Casey Silver, Grant Heslov; Smokehouse Pictures; released by Universal
Written by: Duncan Brantley, Rick Reilly
Cinematography by: Newton Thomas Sigel
Music by: Randy Newman
Sound: Edward Tise
Editing: Stephen Mirrione
Art Direction: Christa Munro, Scott Ritenour
Costumes: Louise Frogley
Production Design: James Bissell
MPAA rating: PG-13
Running time: 113 minutes

REVIEWS

Boston Globe Online. April 4, 2008.
Chicago Sun-Times Online. April 4, 2008.
Entertainment Weekly Online. April 1, 2008.
Hollywood Reporter Online. March 28, 2008.
Los Angeles Times Online. April 4, 2008.
New York Times Online. April 4, 2008.
Rolling Stone Online. April 17, 2008.
San Francisco Chronicle. April 4, 2008, p. E1.
Variety Online. March 28, 2008.
Washington Post. April 4, 2008, p. C1.

QUOTES

Lexie Littleton: "Being the slickest operator in Duluth is sort of like being the world's tallest midget, if you ask me!"

TRIVIA

Star/director George Clooney and Renee Zellweger premiered the film in Clooney's hometown of Maysville, Kentucky on March 24, 2008.

THE LIFE BEFORE HER EYES

(In Bloom)

Your life can change in an instant. That instant can last forever.
—Movie tagline

Laura Kasischke is too tough for Hollywood. The low-profile Michigan poet-novelist writes bracingly beautiful books full of gruesome cruelty and tragedy. Her 2002 novel *The Life Before Her Eyes* was not only richly cinematic but challenging. How do you pull off a story with this explosive premise: A Columbine-style killer confronts two girls, best friends, in a high-school bathroom and asks them to tell him which one of them he should shoot and which he should let survive? That is the set-up, and then the story fast-forwards fifteen years into the life of one of the girls, with a husband, a career, and haunting memories, and pulls off a mesmerizing feat of storytelling centered around the role of conscience, will, and imagination in the fate of an individual's life.

It is a surprisingly tender story about the potential cruelties of the springtime of life: the quick rushing bloom of possibility. Kasischke says she wrote it imagining that female adolescence is like a Midwestern spring: quick, bracing, and messy. Director Vadim Perelman, whom some critics lauded for his sensitive handling of a previous challenging novel in *House of Sand and Fog* (2003), gets the lush setting and the cruelty of fate right, but manhandles the delicate balance of tenderness and toughness the story requires. Judging by Perelman's ardent but misguided effort, and the overly sincere but clumsy script by first-timer Emil Stern, *The Life Before Her Eyes* might be just too difficult a feat of storytelling for all but the most masterful filmmakers, since it requires a painstaking building of supposition and expectation.

Perelman is in too much of a hurry, too enamored of the violence, and too fascinated by the adolescent sexuality of Evan Rachel Wood, but in the end his key failure is one of courage. For all the times the script repeats an anatomy teacher's catchphrase about the heart being the body's strongest muscle—about four or five times too many—in the end Perelman does not have the heart to follow through on the central mystery of the story. Instead, he chickens out and tries to redeem an unredeemable character. This leaves the audience gasping and grasping for a plausible explanation.

Not even a valiant effort by Uma Thurman to inhabit the challenging role of the adult Diana, the grown-up bad girl whose life seems to be unraveling, can salvage the way Perelman has directed her performance. Kasischke is careful to convince her readers that Diana has a perfectly happy life before it starts to unravel, but Thurman from the very start displays a guilt-wrenched expression and a hunch-shouldered burden, with not a hint of contentment. She is haunted like a victim in a B-grade horror movie, and while her performance captures the nightmarish quality of her character, it is all of a single note.

Perelman does get the seasonal, naturalistic subtext of the Kasischke novel (at one point the working title for the film was the much inferior *In Bloom*), but images of rotting dead birds lying in the lush grass of a spring in full flower are not very subtle either. And he keeps hitting audiences over the head with repetitions of the scene with the killer and the two girls in the bathroom—and all manner of gratuitous shots of the mayhem outside that room, none of which matters to the story. He rubs our noses in the gore as if he mistrusts the story to carry its own water, and he hits way too hard and too often on the themes he has teased out—the power of conscience and the threat of eternal regret. Too many scenes are repeated to try to hammer home the point.

It is still a powerfully chilling story, but the tone is wrongheaded. This is not a story about mayhem and martyrdom but about the power of choice. And what it really means to "choose life" fully, in the present—to grab on to what is here and now and the richness and vitality of everything around you. We get glimpses of that, mixed with the anguished tentativeness of adolescence, in the performances of Wood as the young Diana and that of Eva Amurri as her best friend but moral polar opposite, Maureen. They are well-drawn characterizations and rise well above the teenager stereotypes so rampant in most current films. And they are given an extra layer of poignancy because the viewer knows from the start that their reckless, searching adventures are headed for tragedy.

The young Diana is shacking up with an older, on-the-edge kind of man, and she is not above flirting with professors either. Wood is in danger of becoming defined by this type of role, that of the free-spirited nymph with an angelic face. She knows how to play this character almost by heart, but she is a fine young actress who has the balance between adventurousness and self-awareness teetering just exactly right. It is not her fault that directors like Perelman tend to linger too long on her beautiful, smirking face with its pretense of innocence barely concealing licentiousness. When Diana tells her boyfriend that he must like her especially much "because I'm seventeen," there is a palpable and icky leering quality to the scene.

By contrast, Perelman seems to skimp on Maureen. She is supposedly enamored of a boy named Nate, but he is barely in the movie, so her desires are not given flesh. Compared to Diana, she is a straight arrow; she has seen Jesus and drives a car with a "Choose Life" bumper sticker (why there is no furious fight over Diana's abortion is hard to figure). Nevertheless, Amurri, Susan Sarandon's daughter, steals every scene she is in and seems to do so effortlessly. She has her mother's easy, commanding self-confidence and screen presence and her own surfeit of open, believable affability and contentment. Small smirks and knowing smiles redeem her character from being a clichéd good girl. She is sunny but sly.

As an unconventionally plotted story that depends highly on inducing belief and then suspending it, *The Life Before Her Eyes* is no easy ride, for director, actors, or viewers. Critics divided viciously on it, with some even deriding the story's central twist as cheap and unforeseen. That is a measure of how badly you can ruin a delicate piece of storytelling by trying to make a Hollywood-style ending out of a decidedly un-Hollywoodish tale.

Michael Betzold

CREDITS

Diana McFee: Uma Thurman
Young Diana: Evan Rachel Wood
Maureen: Eva Amurri
Mr. McClood: Jack Gilpin
Marcus: Oscar Marcus
Emma McFee: Gabrielle Brennan
Paul McFee: Brett Cullen
Origin: USA
Language: English
Released: 2007
Production: Vadim Perelman, Anthony G. Katagas, Aimee Peyronnet; 2929 Productions; released by Magnolia Pictures
Directed by: Vadim Perelman
Written by: Emil Stern
Cinematography by: Pawel Edelman
Music by: James Horner
Editing: David Baxter
Costumes: Hala Bahmet
Production Design: Maia Javan
MPAA rating: R
Running time: 90 minutes

REVIEWS

Entertainment Weekly. April 25, 2008, p. 102.
Hollywood Reporter Online. September 9, 2007.
Los Angeles Times Online. April 18, 2008.
New York Times Online. April 18, 2008.
San Francisco Chronicle. April 25, 2008, p. E5.
Variety Online. September 9, 2007.
Village Voice Online. April 15, 2008.
Washington Post. April 25, 2008, p. C1.

QUOTES

Mr. McClood: "And if there's anything I want you guys to take with you from this class, as you're abusing your bodies over break, is three things: the heart is the body's strongest muscle, that the brain has more cells in it than our galaxy has stars, and that the body is 72 percent water. So wherever you go over vacation, don't get too dehydrated."

THE LONGSHOTS

The new coach has a secret weapon.
—Movie tagline

Box Office: $11.5 million

The Longshots is a simple, uplifting film based on the true story of Jasmine Plummer, who at eleven years old became the first female quarterback to play in a Pop Warner football tournament. The film, by first-time director Fred Durst (of Limp Bizkit fame) is a fresh take on the tired, inspiration youth sports genre. He pares down the film to a simple, accessible character study and downplays the sports aspect, the football, never overshadow the human aspect.

The shy bookish character Jasmine is played by Keke Palmer, who starred in the true story-inspired *Akeelah and the Bee* (2006). Jasmine seems the most unlikely of football heroes; she is a melancholy youth who longs for her absentee father and dreams of being a model. Her shyness even prevents her from signing up for after school activities like fashion. Palmer has a natural and easy style of acting that never seems like acting, she even manages to pull off the football scenes with a fair amount of believability. Palmer and costar Ice Cube share great chemistry that comes across time and time again as they grow together throughout the journey.

The story takes place in the small town of Minton, Illinois—a town that has lost its main employer, a packaging plant. An opening sequence shows that the city has become a ghost town with boarded-up buildings, a rundown Main Street, and a makeshift hovel. Director Fred Durst then takes us to the local church service where the pastor, Reverend Pratt (Garrett Mor-

ris), is delivering as uplifting a sermon as his tired bones can muster, imploring his congregation to look inside themselves. He says, "If you concentrate on what you don't have, you forget what you do have." Simple words that he comes back to again later in the film that also serves as one of the film's underlying themes. *The Longshots* is a simple story that presents the usual youth film themes of belief in one's self, perseverance, and finding one's hidden talent but plays them in a fresh, down-to-earth manner.

The Longshots producer and costar Ice Cube is quite genuine with his portrayal of Jasmine's Uncle Curtis, the out of work Budweiser drinking, football-toting, teddy bear. Curtis and Jasmine are thrust together when Jasmine's mother (Tasha Smith) is forced to pick up extra hours at the local diner. She approaches the unemployed Curtis, who reluctantly agrees to look after Jasmine. When Curtis discovers his niece has a natural gift for throwing a football, he pours himself into this relationship. He even manages to find creative ways to encourage Jasmine by having her throw footballs to "targets" consisting of posters of Beyoncé, Foxy Brown, and Tyra Banks placed on the field. The afterschool activity takes on another dimension when Curtis has Jasmine try a few plays with the local Pop Warner team that is as hapless and down and out as the town itself. She is a natural and this propels them to a championship tournament in Miami. But first, the team must overcome the economic hurdle of finding the funds to get to Miami and the town is inspired by Reverend Pratt's words to look within for what you do have. The town pitches in with the few dollars they do have and Curtis even comes through, donating his "get out of Minton fund" to the cause. The town goes one step further and, in an inspired act of civic pride, spruces up Main Street. After the Big Game with its non-Hollywood ending, Jasmine's father reappears, hoping to reunite with her, after being away for five years. Now it is Jasmine's turn to walk away.

Conrad W. Hall's fine cinematography captures the gritty, down-and-out feel of the town and its people. Durst often chooses a longer shot allowing the action to develop in a scene and relying less on clever editing that would belie the film's simply style.

Nick Santura and Doug Atchison, who also wrote *Akeelah and the Bee,* have rewritten some of the facts for the movie, changing the location from the Chicago suburb of Harvey (ironically, this is Keke Palmer's hometown as well) to Minton and downplaying the real Jasmine Plummer's athletic talents. She was not only a groundbreaking quarterback but also a star wrestler and honor student. The filmmakers haven chosen a subtle, accessible portrayal of character growth. When Jasmine discovers Curtis reading her precious book, the one she always hid behind, she reacts by telling him that he can have it. She also encourages Curtis to clean up his act and wash his clothes. This is not the usual, over-the-top epiphany usually seen in these kinds of movies.

Michael S. White

CREDITS

Curtis Plummer: Ice Cube
Claire Plummer: Tasha Smith
Jasmine Plummer: Keke Palmer
Coach Fisher: Matt Craven
Ronnie: Jill Marie Jones
Winston: Glenn Plummer
Roy: Malcolm Goodwin
Cyrus: Dash Mihok
Damon: Miles Chandler
Origin: USA
Language: English
Released: 2008
Production: Ice Cube, Matt Alvarez, Nick Santora; Cube Vision, Dimension Films, Blackjack Films; released by MGM
Directed by: Fred Durst
Written by: Doug Atchison, Nick Santora
Cinematography by: Conrad W. Hall
Music by: John Swihart, Teddy Castellucci
Sound: Walter Anderson
Music Supervisor: Spring Aspers
Editing: Jeffrey Wolf
Costumes: Mary McLeod
Production Design: Charles Breen
MPAA rating: PG
Running time: 94 minutes

REVIEWS

Austin Chronicle Online. August 22, 2008.
Chicago Sun-Times Online. August 21, 2008.
Hollywood Reporter Online. August 19, 2008.
Los Angeles Times Online. August 22, 2008.
New York Times Online. August 22, 2008.
San Francisco Chronicle. August 22, 2008, p. E5.
Variety Online. August 20, 2008.
Washington Post Online. August 22, 2008.

TRIVIA

Actress Keke Palmer trained for six weeks to learn how to correctly throw a football and to call plays authentically.

THE LOVE GURU

His karma is huge.
  —Movie tagline

Get ready for the summer of love.
  —Movie tagline

Box Office: $32.2 million

In creating *The Love Guru,* Mike Myers seemed intent on combining his interests in Eastern philosophy, hockey, and slapstick comedy. It is rather intriguing and certainly a novel concept that, in the hands of someone as talented and intuitive as Myers, could work. But Myers's final product, involving a giggling, waxed-mustachioed guru hired to help the losing Toronto Maple Leafs hockey team win the Stanley Cup, utilizes such tired, old jokes and clichéd, scatological, and sophomoric humor that it loses all of its surprise.

Myers previous, more successful *Austin Powers* and *Wayne's World* films certainly were also built on lowbrow humor but both franchises were far more sophisticated and subtle in comparison. In this film, Myers reuses his Austin Powers–style, big musical number opening credits and while it depicts nearly every Eastern Indian stereotype, it nonetheless shows comedic promise. The highly amusing closing credits are even better, with Myers jamming on a double-neck sitar to Steve Miller's "The Joker." It is everything in between that poses a problem.

Mike Myers plays the perpetually pleased with himself "neo-Eastern, self-help spiritualist" with an off-the-wall sense of humor who desires more than anything to be on Oprah so he can surpass Deepak Chopra to become the number one guru in the world. An inordinately talented mimic, Myers is not entirely convincing here as the hapless Westerner Maurice who eventually morphs into the ever-smiling Indian Guru Pitka. Clever special effects show a flashback to a young guru-in-training with Mike Myers adult head humorously grafted onto a child's body.

Myers befriended real-life guru Chopra, who is prominently featured in the film. Jessica Alba cast as the Toronto Maple Leafs owner and Pitka's love interest Jane is no surprise but watching Ben Kingsley, riffing on his Oscar®-winning role as Ghandi, play Maurice's cross-eyed, bad joke-cracking mentor, Tugginmypudha, is particularly painful. As in the Austin Powers's films, countless big-name celebrities are either mentioned or make cameos, including Jessica Simpson, Val Kilmer, the aforementioned Oprah Winfrey, Tom Cruise, Mariska Hargitay (her name is an amusing running joke), and Brad and Angelina. In fact, the entire film is about quantity more than quality, humor-wise. Myers proves he is a pop culture-vulture but he throws so many celebrity cameos, jokes, sight gags, and sound gags up on the screen so fast, that while a few stick, more often than not, they fall flat.

The basic plotline follows Pitka helping the Maple Leafs's star player Darren Roanoke ("Ro-an-choke," fans chant), played by Romany Malco, win his love Prudence (Meagan Good) back from rival Los Angeles King's player Jacques "Le Coq" Grande (Justin Timberlake), so that the Leafs can win the Stanley Cup. Pitka's utilizes the D.R.A.M.A. approach (Distraction, Regression, Adjustment, Maturity, and Action) but reluctantly takes a shortcut and skips a few letters in order to quickly reunite the couple in time for the big game and make his Oprah booking. During the Stanley Cup winning playoff game seven between the L.A. Kings and the Leafs, Darren regresses when his mother unexpectedly shows up and he is unable to play. Pitka cancels his Oprah appearance and returns to Toronto to make things right. The last ditch effort to win involves the Leafs's Coach Cherkov (Verne Troyer) becoming a human hockey puck and two elephants copulating on the ice to Chris Isaak's "Baby Did a Bad Bad Thing,"—the "ultimate distraction"—complete with sportscaster play-by-play commentary. It is over-the-top funny, but comes far too late.

The film is a framework for countless penis jokes beginning with the Tugginmypudha Ashram where he trained, British manager Dick Pants (John Oliver), French Canadian "Le Coq," Coach Cherkov, a capital of Thailand joke (Bangkok), Pitka's oft-clanging chastity belt, and an extended visual in a forced, set-piece dinner scene with Jane. The joke Pitka quotes that was written on a bathroom wall in Barstow is about as good as it gets. Of the umpteen sight gags, including the giant rooster adorning the hood of Le Coq's Iroq-Z and at the bottom of his pool, some resonate. Most were done better in other Myers films or elsewhere. For example, the innocent-looking guard rooster attaching Pitka was much better when done by Monty Python with a rabbit. And the half-size room with the low ceiling for Coach Cherkov was more original and funnier in *Being John Malkovich* (1999). Pitka's repeated definition of intimacy as "into me I see" has been done before (notably, television's *Sex and The City*), as well. Everything in the film is recycled and rehashed from somewhere else.

The Love Guru's best moments conjure images of what the film could have been. Pitka playing pop songs, such as "More than Words" on his sitar as a duet with his sidekick Rajneesh (Manu Narayan) is such a moment. Another involves the love-at-first-sight scene cum Bollywood outtake that nicely showcases a belly-dancing Alba. A similar scene occurs at the end credits.

Myers and first-time director Marco Schnabel (he was the second unit director on *Austin Powers in Goldmember* [2002]) used actual footage from the Stanley Cup playoffs and they provide a nice level of realism to the hockey scenes. The well-cast sportscasters (Stephen Colbert and Jim Gaffigan) add oddball humor but sports fans will need much more to endure *The Love Guru*.

It is obvious Myers and cowriter Graham Gordy have a firm grasp on Eastern spiritualism but it has no place in a slapstick, slap shot hockey sex comedy.

Hilary White

CREDITS

Guru Pitka: Mike Myers
Jane Bullard: Jessica Alba
Darren Roanoke: Romany Malco
Jacques Grande: Justin Timberlake
Prudence Roanoke: Meagan Good
Coach Punch Cherkov: Verne Troyer
Guru Tugginmypudha: Ben Kingsley
Lillian Roanoke: Telma Hopkins
Guru Satchabigknoba: Omid Djalili
Jay Kell: Stephen Colbert
Trent Lueders: Jim Gaffigan
Rajneesh: Manu Narayan
Dick Pants: John Oliver
Himself: Deepak Chopra (Cameo)
Origin: USA
Language: English
Released: 2008
Production: Michael De Luca, Mike Myers; Spyglass Entertainment, Nomoneyfun Films; released by Paramount
Directed by: Marco Schnabel
Written by: Mike Myers, Graham Gordy
Cinematography by: Peter Deming
Music by: George S. Clinton
Sound: Bruce Carwardine
Music Supervisor: John Houlihan
Editing: Lee Haxall, Gregory Perler, Billy Weber
Art Direction: Dennis Davenport
Costumes: Karen Patch
Production Design: Charles Wood
MPAA rating: PG-13
Running time: 88 minutes

REVIEWS

Boston Globe Online. June 20, 2008.
Chicago Sun-Times Online. June 19, 2008.
Hollywood Reporter Online. June 17, 2008.
Los Angeles Times Online. June 20, 2008.
New York Times Online. June 20, 2008.
San Francisco Chronicle. June 20, 2008, p. E5.
Variety Online. June 17, 2008.
Wall Street Journal. June 20, 2008, p. W1.
Washington Post. June 20, 2008, p. C1.

Guru Pitka: "Marishka Hargitay."

TRIVIA

Mike Myers originally planned to debut the Guru Pitka character in *Austin Powers: The Spy Who Shagged Me,* but ultimately opted to fashion an entire movie around the character.

AWARDS

Golden Raspberries 2008: Worst Picture, Worst Actor (Myers), Worst Screenplay

Nomination:

Golden Raspberries 2008: Worst Actress (Alba), Worst Support. Actor (Kingsley, Troyer), Worst Director (Schnabel).

LOVE SONGS
(Les Chansons d'amour)

The French obsession with American musical comedy continues with *Loves Songs* (also known as *Les Chansons d'Amour*), and Francophiles should love it. Everyone else should be wary of this dreary romance with forgettable songs.

Director Christophe Honoré pays tribute to the musical form throughout his film by having his characters sing at the drop of a chapeau. Unfortunately, Honoré has employed actors who are talented at everything but singing, and a composer, Alex Beaupain, who somehow has created thirteen undistinguished French pop tunes that all sound alike.

Honoré's original story starts out as a modern-day, musicalized *Design for Living* (1933) with Ismaël (Louis Garrel) in love and living with two women, Julie (Ludivine Sagnier) and Alice (Clotilde Hesme), the latter a coworker. The ménage-a-trios creates tension, especially for Julie, but before she and Ismaël are able to sort out their feelings, Julie dies suddenly of an embolism. Honoré's narrative then takes on a tragic tone.

Heartbroken, Ismaël mourns Julie, wanders the streets, and tries to seek solace from a high-school student (Grégoire Leprince-Ringuet), who has a crush on Ismaël. Meanwhile, Ismaël ends his relationship with Alice (who starts a romance with Gwendal, played by Yannick Renier) and resists the entreaties of Julie's older sister (Chiara Mastroianni), who, in her grief, seeks answers to her sibling's unexpected death.

Like many nouvelle vague films since Jean-Luc Godard's *A Woman Is a Woman* (1961), *Love Songs* lends a contemporary European edge to the inherently American genre—the musical. Unlike Godard's feature and Alain Resnais's *Same Old Song* (1997), *Love Songs* is rarely (if ever) self-reflexive or auto-critical. Godard, in particular, enjoyed revealing the absurd artificiality of the form by his deliberately frustrating stop-start editing. Meanwhile, Resnais created a much more traditionally entertaining film, but challenged generic expectations with his way of having his contemporary cast dubbed by the original vocalists of the popular songs on the program.

Love Songs is closer in style to two celebrated Jacques Demy musicals, *The Umbrellas of Cherbourg* (1964) and *The Young Girls of Rochefort* (1967). In all these films, the songs emerge "naturally" from the characters and express emotions otherwise difficult to relate in dialogue. Also, the performances are secondary to the music (many forget that Catherine Deneuve was voice-dubbed in both Demy films). In *Love Songs,* Deneuve's daughter, Chiara Mastroianni, at least sings for herself, as do the others in the cast, but Alex Beaupain's score is even less distinguished than Michel Legrand's efforts in terms of creating memorable melodies or evoking deep emotions. At least Mastroianni's solo, "Parc de la Pepiniere," gets effective treatment by Honoré (she sings in direct-address), but most of his staging of the songs barely differs from the dialogue scenes (most of them take place at night on side streets).

Apart from their singing, the cast members perform well. Louis Garrel makes Ismaël more than an immature sad-sack and Ludivine Sagnier shines in the early scenes (before her character's demise) as the confused Julie. The others in the cast provide more than adequate support, particularly Grégoire Leprince-Ringuet as Ismaël's young male lover. Though shot on a limited budget, *Love Songs* is technically proficient and the dark lighting and chilly blue hues underscore the story's sorrowful mood (only the opening shots exploit the more traditionally romantic view of Paris).

Critics were divided about *Love Songs.* In *Variety,* Jay Weissberg wrote, "Honoré's love of musicals is apparent, and he thankfully plays it straight. Avoiding even a hint of tongue-in-cheek irony, he relies on the effectiveness of songs conveying pure, genuine emotions in ways often more difficult to achieve when simply spoken." Yet, A. O. Scott of the *New York Times* disagreed: "... even though Mr. Honoré is trying something very interesting—and even though his nimble cast executes it with grace and more or less in tune—the execution doesn't quite live up to the concept. No single element (apart from those song-lyric subtitles) is bad, exactly, but an element of coherence is missing." Finally, Scott Foundas, in the *Village Voice,* dismissed the entire production with, "That Honoré knows a lot about movies is beyond question—but from first frame to last, *Love Songs* stays as icy to the touch as Julie's premature corpse."

The film is not that ignominious, but as neither a classical musical nor a revisionist postmodern one, *Love Songs* represents a lost and lonely hybrid.

Eric Monder

CREDITS

Julie: Ludivine Sagnier
Jeanne: Chiara Mastroianni
Erwann: Gregoire Leprince-Ringuet
Gwendall: Yannick Renier
Ismaël: Louis Garrel
Julie's mother: Brigitte Rouan
Origin: France
Language: French
Released: 2007
Production: Paulo Branco; Alma Films; released by IFC First Take
Directed by: Christophe Honoré
Written by: Christophe Honoré
Cinematography by: Remy Chevrin
Music by: Alexandre Beaupain
Sound: Guillaume Le Bras
Editing: Chantal Hymans
Art Direction: Emmanuelle Cuillery
Costumes: Pierre Canitrot
Production Design: Samuel Deshors
MPAA rating: Unrated
Running time: 95 minutes

REVIEWS

Entertainment Weekly Online. March 19, 2008.
Los Angeles Times Online. April 4, 2008.
New York Times Online. March 19, 2008.
Variety Online. May 18, 2007.
Village Voice Online. March 18, 2008.

TRIVIA

Director Christophe Honoré makes a brief cameo during the funeral scene.

THE LUCKY ONES

Three strangers with nothing to lose. And everything to find.
—Movie tagline

Sometimes losing your way home means finding yourself.
—Movie tagline

Cowriter/director Neil Burger and the talented cast of *The Lucky Ones* may have their hearts in the right place, but the resulting film is a complete disaster, a deeply flawed drama about three Iraq War soldiers on a bizarre road trip across America's heartland that misses the mark in nearly every way. Tim Robbins, Rachel McAdams, and Michael Peña do their best to salvage a disastrously conceived screenplay, but the film will be as forgotten as so many of the recent Iraq War movies like *Lions For Lambs* (2007), *In the Valley of Elah* (2007), *Stop-Loss* (2008), *Redacted* (2007), and *Rendition* (2007). *The Lucky Ones* may be different in that its setting is solely in the United States, but it falls victim to the same heartstring pulling that usually sinks so many movies about the conflict that will define the George W. Bush presidency. Writers Neil Burger and Dirk Wittenborn have crafted such an overwritten, on-the-nose film that even actors as genuinely talented as the trio that star in *The Lucky Ones* can do nothing with it.

The only scene in *The Lucky Ones* to take place in Iraq is the opening scene with a cocky young soldier named T.K. (Michael Peña) riding in a convoy. They get hit and T.K. takes a piece of shrapnel in his groin, rendering him impotent. T.K. is too embarrassed by his painful injury to tell his fiancée about the problem, so he decides to go to Las Vegas instead of home when he lands in New York City on leave. T.K. thinks that a sex worker will help him work out his problem, so to speak.

When T.K. gets to the Big Apple, he runs into a problem with his layover after all flights are delayed due to a blackout. Naturally, there are a lot of soldiers there on leave looking for a way to get to their final destinations, and T.K. hooks up with two —Cheever (Tim Robbins) and Colee (Rachel McAdams). The former is a gentle man who has finished his tour of duty and cannot wait to see his wife and family again, while the latter is a sweet young woman home on leave and trying to deliver a guitar to her deceased boyfriend's family. Cheever plans to surprise his wife with his arrival at home in St. Louis—something that has predictable results—and the three pile into a rental car and head off across the country.

The Lucky Ones is so overcrowded with clichés that none of the emotional beats of the characters are ever allowed the believability needed to become effective. Burger and Wittenborn made no effort to write a script that felt believable, giving Robbins, McAdams, and Peña nothing more than two-dimensional to play. A confluence of coincidences and clichés would be bad enough, but to get out of the narrative mess that they find themselves in, Burger and Wittenborn need a legendary casino robbery, a Winnebago full of sex workers, and a full-blown tornado to resolve their story. The mildly far-fetched set-up turns downright surreal in a final act that could be used in screenwriting classes as an example of what not to do in order to tie up the loose ends of your story.

To tell a story with the emotional resonance that Burger believes is in his cowritten screenplay for *The Lucky Ones,* the writers needed to focus, first and foremost, on believability. They could have made a modern fairy tale, a fable about lost soldiers coming back to a home that they no longer recognize as their own, but Burger wants to have it both ways. He wants the ridiculous and the emotional, two things that he is not a capable enough screenwriter to wedge into one film. Robbins, typically such a confident actor, looks absolutely lost with his poorly defined character and Peña rarely strikes an interesting beat with his two dimensions. They are both typically strong actors who can find no way to break through the pablum. Rachel McAdams fares slightly better, just barely making Colee the most interesting character in the film.

Unlike a lot of screenwriting disasters, one positive thing that can be said about *The Lucky Ones* is that Burger, Wittenborn, and the entire team clearly had only the best of intentions. *The Lucky Ones* never feels like exploitation, which some lesser Iraq War movies of the several years certainly have. It is merely another piece of bad fiction about a tragically real situation.

Brian Tallerico

CREDITS

Colee Dunn: Rachel McAdams
Fred Cheaver: Tim Robbins
T.K. Poole: Michael Peña
Pat Cheaver: Molly Hagan

Scott Cheever: Mark L. Young
Jeanie Klinger: Annie Corley
Tom Klinger: John Diehl
Pat Cheaver: John Heard
Origin: USA
Language: English
Released: 2008
Production: Brian Koppelman, David Levien, Rick Schwartz, Neil Burger; Roadside Attractions, Sherazade Film Development, Visitor Pictures, QED International; released by Lionsgate
Directed by: Neil Burger
Written by: Neil Burger, Dirk Wittenborn
Cinematography by: Declan Quinn
Music by: Rolfe Kent
Sound: Stacy Brownrigg
Editing: Naomi Geraghty
Costumes: Jenny Gering
Production Design: Leslie A. Pope, Jan Roelfs
MPAA rating: R
Running time: 115 minutes

REVIEWS

Boston Globe Online. September 26, 2008.
Chicago Sun-Times Online. September 25, 2008.
Entertainment Weekly Online. September 24, 2008.
Hollywood Reporter Online. September 8, 2008.
Los Angeles Times Online. September 26, 2008.
New York Times Online. September 26, 2008.
San Francisco Chronicle. September 26, 2008, p. E12.
Variety Online. September 15, 2008.
Washington Post Online. September 26, 2008.

QUOTES

T.K. Poole: "You don't talk about plane crashes while on a plane!"
Colee Dunn: "Why not?"
Fred Cheaver: "For the same reason that when you're on a cruise ship they don't play *Titanic*. It scares people."

M

MAD MONEY

They're having the crime of their lives...
—Movie tagline

Taking the money was easy. Getting away with it would be harder than they ever imagined.
—Movie tagline

Box Office: $20.6 million

The workplace comedy has long history that includes popular mainstream fare like *9 to 5* (1980) and *Office Space* (1999), alongside more independently produced work like *Clockwatchers* (1997) and *The Promotion* (2008). Writers have for years and will continue to go back to the well of humor that tries to find the hilarity in moments to which the everyday worker can easily relate. It is not uncommon for people to assume that their workplace is funnier than most sitcoms or mainstream comedies about the struggles of living paycheck to paycheck and they like to test that theory by going to the movies. The latest workplace comedy is a little different in that it involves extreme behavior that most average workers will not be able to recognize as a part of their daily life—the theft of thousands of dollars—but the basic theme of Callie Khouri's *Mad Money* is one that has been clearly designed to appeal to the everyman—the eternal allure of the almighty dollar.

Bridget (Diane Keaton) has lived an upper class life with her husband Don (Ted Danson) for years, but has started to see it slip away as the recession has forced her family into debt. Bridget has to go back to work and finds a job as a janitor at the Federal Reserve Bank of Kansas City. Not long into Bridget's introduction to the working world, she finds a more convenient way to help

her sliding back account than working from nine to five. Like a lot of federal institutions, the bank destroys damaged dollar bills every day. Bridget hatches a scheme to save those greenbacks from being recycled and she needs the help of Nina (Queen Latifah), the woman who works the shredder, and Jackie (Katie Holmes), the worker who transports the carts of bills through the bank to be destroyed. Like all great plans, the money-stealing scheme is simple and, at first, foolproof. The women are essentially pilfering the same money over and over again, as damaged bills they take once are only going to return to the bank to be taken by them again. The simplicity of it would be tempting to any employee. Of course, once Bridget has paid off her debt with the stolen funds, the natural inclination would be to stop, but the theft is working too well and the desire for more than she needs gets Bridget and her two accomplices into some serious trouble.

The screenplay for *Mad Money* feels so derivative from superior workplace comedies that the familiarity of the entire piece borders on ridiculous. There is nothing here that has not been done before by different writers, which leads judgment of the final product to rest heavily on the three women cast in the lead roles. The casting agency for *Mad Money* deserves most of the credit for any of the film's success. Not only are the three women charismatic enough to elevate the material, but the supporting cast is universally strong, including Danson, *24*'s Roger Cross, and Stephen Root in very well-cast roles. *Mad Money* was pitched in commercials as a "wild comedy" and that misleading pitch probably led to the film's box office failure (it only made $24 million worldwide). The advertisements never made clear that

Mad Money actually wisely avoids too much slapstick comedy that often makes movies like this so unbearable. Director Callie Khouri (most famous for writing *Thelma & Louise* [1991]) focuses on the humanity of the women and gets charming performances from Queen Latifah and the rest of the surprisingly believable cast.

The problem is that *Mad Money* is not funny enough to be a memorable comedy and too derivative to be a memorable drama. Writers Khouri and Glenn Gers never settle on a tone, which leaves *Mad Money* more forgettable than anything else. Most critics felt the same way, as if they could barely remember the movie long enough to review it. Moira MacDonald of the *Seattle Times* correctly noted, "This is an odd, disposable movie; it melts away as you leave the theater, leaving nothing but vague dissatisfaction behind." *Mad Money* feels like the kind of comedy they made much more often in the 1980s, a softer film than usually gets the green light in this era of the gross-out movie. It is a back-handed compliment at best to say that *Mad Money* is never painful, like some of the horrible physical comedies of the year, but it is also simply never that funny. In a common subgenre like the workplace comedy, *Mad Money* never does enough to stand out from the crowded pack.

Brian Tallerico

CREDITS

Bridget Cardigan: Diane Keaton
Nina Brewster: Queen Latifah
Jackie Truman: Katie Holmes
Don Cardigan: Ted Danson
Glover: Stephen Root
Bryce Arbogast: Christopher McDonald
Bob Truman: Adam Rothenberg
Barry: Roger Cross
Origin: USA, Great Britain
Language: English
Released: 2008
Production: Jay Cohen, James Acheson, Frank De Martini, Michael P. Flannigan; Granada, Millennium Films, Lightspeed Media, Swingin' Prods., Big City Pictures; released by Overture Films
Directed by: Callie Khouri
Written by: Glen Gers
Cinematography by: John Bailey
Music by: Martin Davich, James Newton Howard
Sound: Steve Aaron
Music Supervisor: Budd Carr, Nora Felder
Editing: Wendy Greene Bricmont
Art Direction: Kevin Hardison

Costumes: Susie De Santo
Production Design: Brent Thomas
MPAA rating: PG-13
Running time: 104 minutes

REVIEWS

Boston Globe Online. January 18, 2008.
Chicago Sun-Times Online. January 17, 2008.
Entertainment Weekly Online. January 16, 2008.
Hollywood Reporter Online. January 15, 2008.
Los Angeles Times Online. January 18, 2008.
New York Times Online. January 18, 2008.
San Francisco Chronicle. January 18, 2008, p. E5.
Variety Online. January 14, 2008.
Washington Post. January 18, 2008, p. C5.

QUOTES

Nina Brewster: "Do you know what it is when you trade sex for money?"
Jackie Truman: "Advertising!"

MADAGASCAR: ESCAPE 2 AFRICA

Still together. Still lost.
—Movie tagline
The crate escape.
—Movie tagline

Box Office: $180 million

Directors Eric Darnell and Tom McGrath and writer Etan Cohen continue to prove the rule that titles with a "2" in the name that is intended to replace either "to" or "too" should never be trusted: the loud and repetitive *Madagascar: Escape 2 Africa*, is a sequel that works only for the smallest member of the family and squanders most of the goodwill that adults might still have from the first film. Anyone old enough to remember the other awful "2 homonym" sequels like *2 Fast 2 Furious* (2003) or even *Step Up 2: The Streets* (2008) will be aggravated, annoyed, or both by the majority of *Madagascar: Escape 2 Africa*, a film that plays down the strengths of the slightly underrated and enjoyable original film and mistakes quantity for quality in its attempt to be bigger, louder, and generally more hyperactive than its predecessor.

The intention of the creative team behind *Madagascar: Escape 2 Africa* is clear from the very first reel—take everything that audiences liked about the original and turn up the volume like a small child hitting a toy with a rubber mallet ad nauseum. So, after a prologue that sets up that baby Alex the lion (voice of Ben Stiller) was separated from his parents (voice of Bernie Mac and Sherri Shepherd) in Africa, nearly every animal with a speaking part in the original is back to the forefront for the new film. It is not just the main four characters—Alex the Lion, Marty the Zebra (voice of Chris Rock), Melman the Giraffe (voice of David Schwimmer), and Gloria the Hippo (voice of Jada Pinkett Smith)—although it would have been much wiser to stick with that quartet instead of shuffling on every single role from the first film. Returning to support the foursome is King Julien (voice of Sacha Baron Cohen), his sidekick Maurice (voice of Cedric the Entertainer), the monkeys (including voice of Andy Richter), and even the penguins who stole the first movie. And they are all singing and dancing to the numbingly awful dance song from the original, "I Like to Move It" in the opening scene. The antic, eager-to-please tone of the entire film is cemented mere moments into *Madagascar: Escape 2 Africa*. The idea is to present everything an audience member may have liked about the first *Madagascar*, only louder and repeatedly.

The entire menagerie of animal characters, including the penguins, King Julien, and Maurice, take off in a rickety plane and crash land in Africa, where they just happen to run into Alex's parents and his dad's nefarious rival lion, Makunga (voice of Alec Baldwin). After a fight goes very wrong—Alex makes the embarrassing mistake of thinking the combat is a dance-off instead of a battle to the death —the lion who would rather move his feet than bare his teeth is kicked off the reserve and forced to take drastic action to prove he is an adult and return to the comfort of his family and friends. Meanwhile, Marty learns a lesson about individuality after meeting a herd of zebras who look a lot like him, and Melman, who has become the hypochondriac doctor for the African animals, and Gloria, who has finally been reunited with her own kind of animal, enter an unusual love triangle with the alpha male hippo on the prairie.

A giraffe's unrequited love for a hippopotamus, a lion's reconciliation with his family, and a zebra's search for individuality would be enough for one movie, but this is a "2" movie, so the King needs a plotline about a sacrifice to the volcano Gods, the penguins needs to torment tourists, including the old lady from the first movie, and everyone needs to learn a serious lesson about themselves by about minute eighty. To call the overdone screenplay for *Escape 2 Africa* cluttered would be an understatement. And yet, the quantity over quality aesthetic backfires, making none of the myriad of characters or plotlines as interesting or involving as the first film.

As for the voice cast, they all do good work but suffer from the overall battle for screen time. Chris Rock's prodigious talent as a voice actor is particularly wasted without nearly enough dialogue. Stiller, Mac, and Baldwin do the best voice work. One of the saving graces of the film is that the animation is an improvement over the original, given the developments in CGI technology since that film was made. The film looks very good, especially the always-complicated computer-animated hair of Alex's mane. The cast and the upgraded animation go a long way in saving *Escape 2 Africa* from being a complete disaster, even if the screenplay is a total mess. The best voice actors in the world and breakthrough animation cannot disguise a story and dialogue that is all shtick and repetition, something to distract the little ones but more likely to give their parents a headache.

Brian Tallerico

CREDITS

Alex: Ben Stiller (Voice)
Melman: David Schwimmer (Voice)
Marty: Chris Rock (Voice)
Gloria: Jada Pinkett Smith (Voice)
King Julien: Sacha Baron Cohen (Voice)
Maurice: Cedric the Entertainer (Voice)
Zuba: Bernie Mac (Voice)
Mort: Andy Richter (Voice)
Makunga: Alec Baldwin (Voice)
Alex's Mom: Sherri Shepherd (Voice)
Skipper: Tom McGrath (Voice)
Private: Christopher Knight (Voice)
Mason: Conrad Vernon (Voice)
Moto Moto: will.i.am (Voice)
Kowalski: Chris Miller (Voice)
Nana: Elisa Gabrielli (Voice)
Origin: USA
Language: English
Released: 2008
Production: Mireille Soria, Mark Swift; DreamWorks Animation; released by Paramount
Directed by: Eric Darnell, Tom McGrath
Written by: Eric Darnell, Tom McGrath
Music by: Hans Zimmer, will.i.am
Sound: Andy Nelson, Jim Bolt
Editing: H. Lee Peterson
Art Direction: Shannon Jeffries
Production Design: Kendal Cronkhite-Shaindlin
MPAA rating: PG
Running time: 89 minutes

REVIEWS

Boston Globe Online. November 7, 2008.
Chicago Sun-Times Online. November 5, 2008.

Entertainment Weekly Online. November 4, 2008.
Hollywood Reporter Online. November 2, 2008.
Los Angeles Times Online. November 7, 2008.
New York Times Online. November 7, 2008.
San Francisco Chronicle. November 7, 2008, p. E5.
Variety Online. November 2, 2008.
Wall Street Journal Online. November 7, 2008.

QUOTES

Alex: "I wanna prove to my dad that I'm a 'real' lion."
Marty: "As opposed to what, a 'chocolate' lion?"

TRIVIA

A third film in the series was confirmed months before the second entry was even released.

MADE OF HONOR

It takes a real man to become a maid of honor.
—Movie tagline

An unbridaled comedy.
—Movie tagline

Box Office: $46 million

There is nothing truly objectionable about *Made of Honor,* unless you object to unrelenting blandness. Every scene has the limpness of an idea that has been played out before—and better—in countless romantic comedies. Tom (Patrick Dempsey) is a slick, bed-hopping Manhattan bachelor whose set of rules when it comes to women includes "no back to backs." His unlikely best friend is Hannah (Michelle Monaghan), a pretty art restorer who teases Tom about his womanizing ways but would never try to change him. These two are so in sync that Hannah is able to guess what kind of dessert Tom is in the mood for. They even eat off each other's plates, a sure sign that theirs is a union meant to be.

However, a smooth path to true love has rarely sustained a ninety-minute movie. Tom must come to the realization that Hannah is the woman for him only after she has returned from an assignment in Scotland—with a strapping fiancé, Colin McMurray (Kevin McKidd), in tow. When Hannah asks him to be her maid of honor, Tom agrees, and then sets out to sabotage the wedding in order to "steal the bride." And yes, by being the maid of honor, Tom discovers how to be a better man—the best man.

Made of Honor is essentially a vehicle for Dempsey, whose charm is perhaps best suited to the small screen, where his smirks pass for charm. Monaghan has a pert-nosed prettiness that is pleasantly at odds with her slightly husky voice, and she is clearly game to play, but she is hobbled by a script that requires her to realize that she is marrying the wrong man when her betrothed is unwilling to share his chocolate cake with her. McKidd, who has been a compellingly masculine presence in such films as *Dog Soldiers* (2002), is wasted in the role of the wealthy Scottish suitor. Reduced to a low burr and a brawny, kilt-clad form, he spends most of his scenes looking abashed.

Director Paul Weiland shows little feel for the sort of snappy pacing that might have livened up the script. The opening montage of shots includes one of Dean & Deluca, which Weiland apparently believes to be sufficient for establishing locale. Perhaps Starbucks was unavailable—but no, Starbucks makes an extended appearance shortly thereafter.

It is difficult to tell what audience would connect with *Made of Honor.* Yes, it is clearly meant for women—and maybe the occasional romantic-comedy-loving man—but what woman would watch the movie and recognize herself in its female characters? Hannah is more a sketch than a fleshed-out character; she is a vague outline of what the screenwriters—Adam Sztykiel, Deborah Kaplan, and Harry Elfont—seem to have believed would appeal to female viewers—attractive, smart, savvy yet not cynical, still a believer in romance and true love—but also what would best showcase Tom's growth from callow, shallow womanizer to romantic, monogamous hero.

One of the movie's all-too-few comic moments that do not feel recycled comes toward the beginning, when Tom's oft-married father (Sydney Pollack, in his last role) is tying the knot yet again. As the wedding party waits for the bride to arrive at the church, last-minute negotiations are ensuing between the groom and the bride. The cuts between the giddy bridesmaids on the sidewalk and the gold-digging bride and her lawyer within the limo offer a flinty take on marriage as a cold business proposition. It is not so dissimilar to the calculations that must ensue in order to get movies such as *Made of Honor* made. In both cases, romance is viewed as a commodity.

Heather L. Hughes

CREDITS

Tom: Patrick Dempsey
Hannah: Michelle Monaghan
Colin: Kevin McKidd
Joan: Kathleen Quinlan
Thomas Sr.: Sydney Pollack
Felix: Kadeem Hardison

Dennis: Chris Messina
Melissa: Busy Philipps
Christie: Kelly Carlson
Reverend Foote: James B. Sikking
Gary: Richmond Arquette
Gloria: Beau Garrett
Stephanie: Whitney Cummings
Hilary: Emily Nelson
Tiny Shorts Guy: Kevin Sussman
Grandma Pearl: Selma Stern
Origin: USA
Language: English
Released: 2008
Production: Neal H. Moritz; Original Film, Relativity Media, Columbia Pictures; released by Sony Pictures Entertainment
Directed by: Paul Weiland
Written by: Deborah Kaplan, Adam Sztykiel, Harry Elfont
Cinematography by: Tony Pierce-Roberts
Music by: Rupert Gregson-Williams
Sound: Jeffrey J. Haboush, Greg P. Russell
Music Supervisor: Nick Angel
Editing: Richard Marks
Art Direction: Sue Chan
Costumes: Penny Rose
Production Design: Kalina Ivanov
MPAA rating: PG-13
Running time: 101 minutes

REVIEWS

Boston Globe Online. May 2, 2008.
Chicago Sun-Times Online. May 2, 2008.
Entertainment Weekly Online. April 30, 2008.
Hollywood Reporter Online. May 1, 2008.
Los Angeles Times Online. May 2, 2008.
New York Times Online. May 2, 2008.
San Francisco Chronicle. May 2, 2008, p. E5.
Variety Online. April 30, 2008.
Washington Post. May 2, 2008, p. C1.

QUOTES

Dennis: "I can feel my sperm dying inside of me, one at a time."

MAMMA MIA!

A mother. A daughter. Three possible fathers.
Take a trip down the aisle you'll never forget.
—Movie tagline

Box Office: $144.1 million

What is most important in a film musical? The score? The lyrics? The singing? The plot and characters? Should the film version of a Broadway musical be held to the same standards as the stage version? Such questions are only some arising while watching *Mamma Mia!*. For example, how can a film that received some of the worst reviews ever for an adaptation of a stage musical break the record for the most money earned at the American box office by a musical in its first weekend, with its $27.8 million beating the $27.5 million of *Hairspray* (2007)? Understanding and appreciating *Mamma Mia!* involves much more than what appears on the screen.

Mamma Mia! came into being when British theatrical producer Judy Craymer decided the music of the 1970s Swedish pop group ABBA could form the basis for a musical and hired playwright Catherine Johnson to build a plot around the songs. Most musicals come from the opposite direction, taking a play, novel, or film, as in the case of *Hairspray,* from the 1988 John Waters film, and adding the music. Under the direction of Phyllida Lloyd, *Mamma Mia!* opened on London's West End in 1999, and on Broadway in 2001, with several more productions around the world. Its success inspired considerably less-successful musicals drawn from the songs of Johnny Cash, John Lennon, and Elvis Presley. The Broadway production of *Mamma Mia!* was still running when the film premiered.

Mamma Mia! centers around the wedding plans of Sophie (Amanda Seyfried) and Sky (Dominic Cooper) on a Greek island where Sophie's free-spirited mother, Donna (Meryl Streep), runs a modest but picturesque hotel. Twenty-year-old Sophie does not know the identity of her father because Donna had sex with three men around the time she was conceived, so she sends letters to each asking them to attend her wedding. Sophie is pleasantly surprised when all three, Bill (Stellan Skarsgård), Harry (Colin Firth), and Sam (Pierce Brosnan), show up. While each of the possible fathers of the bride is pleased that he may be Sophie's dad, Donna is not happy with the sudden appearance of her former lovers because, well, because the skimpy plot, inspired by *Buona Sera, Mrs. Campbell* (1968), needs some sort of conflict to keep afloat.

Adding flavor to this mixture are Donna's old friends Rosie (Julie Walters), a cookbook writer, and Tanya (Christine Baranski), recovering from her third divorce. Rosie and Tanya were once backup singers in Donna and the Dynamos, apparently in the 1970s, given the platform shoes they wear when they restage their old act. Photographs of the young Bill, Harry, and Sam, as well as several other references, indicate Sophie was conceived at least a decade earlier than is possible. Many reviewers cited this quandary as one of many examples of the sloppiness of the film, once again written by Johnson and directed by Lloyd, yet *Mamma Mia!* exists in a fairyland where such logical concerns are irrelevant.

Though its critics have been a bit too harsh, *Mamma Mia!* has its flaws. Perhaps because the film was shot in three locations, Lloyd never clearly conveys the island's geography and topography. Where the dozens of natives and visitors who pop up now and then to sing and dance in the background come from is puzzling. Some of the harshest critics, especially those commenting online, attacked Lloyd, directing her first film, for having no idea of what to do with the camera. Except for cutting off the top of Sam's head during a conversation with Donna, Lloyd's visual style is serviceable if not exactly stylish. Cinematographer Haris Zambarloukos captures the sparkling glow of the Mediterranean sunlight and gives the nighttime scenes a bluish tinge much softer than his metallic blue-gray lighting in *Sleuth* (2007).

The best that can be said for ABBA's music, written by Benny Andersson, Björn Ulvaeus, and Stig Anderson, is that it was inexplicably popular in its time and continues to be popular around the world. A week following the film's release, Hong Kong director Wong Kar Wai, in planning the Bhutan wedding of actors Carina Lau and Tony Leung, included ABBA music in the ceremony. The songs have appeared in dozens of films and television programs, most significantly *Muriel's Wedding* (1994), about a lonely young woman obsessed by ABBA.

The lyrics are banal, even for pop music: "If you change your mind/I'm the first in line/Honey, I'm still free/Take a chance on me." The tunes have an impersonal, almost robotic quality, as if they were performed by machines and not humans. Yet the music's monotonous rhythms create a hypnotic effect, making it difficult to forget. Another unfair criticism of the film is the accusation that the songs come out of nowhere and have nothing to do with the plot. Since the plot follows the music, this is hardly the case. Donna's despair over her financial straits leads to her singing "Money, Money, Money," the only song in *Mamma Mia!* that sounds like it might actually have come from a traditional musical.

The major difference between the stage and film versions is that most of the performers in the theatrical productions have had some background in singing. This is not the case for the film, and therein lies much of its charm. With more polished performers, *Mamma Mia!* might seem mechanical and empty. As it is, with actors pretending to be singers, the film suggests that it knows the music is mediocre, but these are just ordinary folks having a good time with these innocuous tunes. As an almost amateur effort, *Mamma Mia!* projects some sincerity and a large sense of fun that would be missing from a slicker production.

Of the performers Seyfried has the best voice, singing as well as many popular young women singers but lacking any urgency. Streep has actually sung in four previous films, most notably performing country tunes in *Postcards from the Edge* (1990) and *A Prairie Home Companion* (2006), as well as singing in a 2006 New York Shakespeare Festival production of Bertolt Brecht's *Mother Courage and Her Children,* a world away from the apolitical, simplistic ABBA. In *Mamma Mia!* she sings twelve songs, most with others, bringing a different vocal style to each. In Donna's big number, Streep grabs "The Winner Takes It All" and wrestles it into submission with great intensity.

Baranski and Cooper do ably with their solos. Firth has a modest but pleasant singing voice, while Brosnan's gruff bluster earned comparisons with the bellowing of Clint Eastwood and Lee Marvin in *Paint Your Wagon* (1969). Skarsgård, ironically the sole Swede in the cast, is limited to a few lines in two songs. One of these, however, is the film's musical highlight. Because Rosie wants to make romantic overtures to Bill but is unsure of herself, Walters begins "Take a Chance on Me" in a timid, halting whisper, gradually progressing, as Rosie gains courage, to belting it out.

Mamma Mia! has an odd structure. Most musicals take a breather after each song to set up the next number through dialogue and character interaction. *Mamma Mia!* sometimes pauses only seconds between songs, as if it is desperately trying to cram in as much music as possible. As a result the film sometimes seems to be trying too hard to make its audience have a good time. Despite such shortcomings, *Mamma Mia!* can be enjoyable for those in the right mood. Something like this must be approached with lower expectations than a film with artistic pretensions such as *Sweeney Todd* (2007). The two deliberately bad production numbers in the closing credits signal Lloyd's awareness that this is a minor diversion, nothing more.

Michael Adams

CREDITS

Donna Sheridan: Meryl Streep
Sam Carmichael: Pierce Brosnan
Harry Bright: Colin Firth
Sophie Sheridan: Amanda Seyfried
Bill Anderson: Stellan Skarsgard
Rosie: Julie Walters
Tanya: Christine Baranski
Sky: Dominic Cooper

Origin: USA, Great Britain
Language: English
Released: 2008
Production: Gary Goetzman, Judy Craymer; Playtone Pictures, Littlestar; released by Universal
Directed by: Phyllida Lloyd
Written by: Catherine Johnson
Cinematography by: Haris Zambarloukos
Music by: Benny Andersson, Bjorn Ulvaes, Stig Anderson
Sound: Simon Hayes
Music Supervisor: Becky Bentham
Editing: Lesley Walker
Art Direction: Nick Palmer
Costumes: Ann Roth
Production Design: Maria Djurkovic
MPAA rating: PG-13
Running time: 108 minutes

REVIEWS

Boston Globe Online. July 18, 2008.
Chicago Sun-Times Online. July 17, 2008.
Entertainment Weekly Online. July 16, 2008.
Hollywood Reporter Online. June 29, 2008.
Los Angeles Times Online. July 18, 2008.
New York Times Online. July 18, 2008.
Rolling Stone Online. July 17, 2008.
San Francisco Chronicle. July 18, 2008, p. E1.
Variety Online. July 5, 2008.
Wall Street Journal Online. July 18, 2008.
Washington Post. July 18, 2008, p. C1.

QUOTES

Sky: "It's my last night of freedom…which is what some might see it, but for me it's the last night before the greatest adventure of my life."

TRIVIA

All cast members performed their own singing.

AWARDS

Golden Raspberries 2008: Worst Support. Actor (Brosnan)
Nomination:
British Acad. 2008: Orig. Score
Golden Globes 2009: Actress—Mus./Comedy (Streep), Film—Mus./Comedy.

MARLEY & ME

Heel the love.
—Movie tagline

Box Office: $142.4 million

Marley & Me is an old-fashioned crowd pleaser, the kind of movie that critics usually deride but audiences eat up like candy canes during the holiday season. And that is exactly what happened when *Marley & Me* hit theaters in 2008. Most critics were so-so on the film, but it opened with the highest Christmas day gross of all time (and the highest, non-animated opening ever for star Owen Wilson as a lead) and the film stayed at number one into 2009. It is very easy to see why. The underrated dramedy by director David Frankel (*The Devil Wears Prada* [2006]), adapted by Scott Frank and Don Roos from the autobiographical book by John Grogan, is moving without being manipulative and the kind of heartwarming story of average people that a Hollywood obsessed with sequels and superheroes has not been making that often any more. Frankel's film is far from perfect, but it has an easy charm and honest emotion that is a lot harder to pull off than it looks.

John (Owen Wilson) and Jenny Grogan (Jennifer Aniston) move from Michigan to southern Florida after John gets a job at the *Palm Beach Post*. John has a friend there at the paper, Sebastian (Eric Dane), who is also a reporter, but his buddy lands the more high-profile assignments while John gets stuck with a column he does not particularly enjoy writing. Sebastian suggests to his friend that they get a dog before starting their family and the two adopt a newborn yellow Labrador retriever that they name Marley.

From the first night they have him, Marley is a handful. John tries to have him sleep in the garage while he is being house trained, but Marley needs constant companionship. He destroys and/or eats nearly everything he comes in contact with and John quickly learns that there are enough funny stories about his lovable pooch to make his column a popular hit.

The rest of *Marley & Me* is really just a chronicle of highlights from a young couple's thirties with Marley always in the family picture. Surprisingly, the dog often takes a back seat to the other developments of the Grogan family. Jenny and John struggle to start a family, suffering through a miscarriage before having three kids of their own. The couple fights after Jenny quits her job and John becomes frustrated watching Sebastian do more intense journalism at the *New York Times*. The Grogans eventually move to Philadelphia and age does the inevitable to the now-beloved Marley. The screenplay by excellent writers Scott Frank (*The Lookout* [2007], *Out of Sight* [1998]); and Don Roos (*Happy Endings* [2005], *The Opposite of Sex* [1998]) does a very good job of making Marley a believable part of this average family without focusing all of the attention on him, as a lot of lesser writers would have done.

Frank and Roos deserve the most credit for why *Marley & Me* is sweet and heartwarming without feeling manipulative or overdone, but it certainly helps to have the most charming and affable lead performance from Owen Wilson in years. Downplaying the shtick that sunk movies like *You, Me and Dupree* (2006) and *Drillbit Taylor* (2008), Wilson plays the everyman surprisingly well, making John a likable, three-dimensional character. Aniston takes a back seat to Wilson, but she also comes across more believably than in a lot of her recent work. Director Frankel deserves credit for only occasionally overplaying the drama in *Marley & Me*, making John, Jenny, and the titular canine feel like more than just manipulative devices, which they easily could have become.

Like most dogs, *Marley & Me* is not perfect. The nearly two-hour film could have been at least twenty minutes shorter. By the time John yells "Marley, no!" for the hundredth time it has lost its impact and the role of Sebastian could practically have been cut entirely. Wilson successfully displays John's concern about letting his dream of tough journalism go without having it personified in a superfluous character.

Ultimately, *Marley & Me* is far more effective and charming than most critics were willing to admit. With charismatic leads of the two and four-legged variety, the adaptation of John Grogan's massively successful book is about issues with which everyone can relate— family, love, and, most of all, the funny way life has a way of changing your plans and the human ability to adapt to those changes. Far more effective than it would have been with less talented writers or less charming leads, *Marley & Me* is an effective dramedy for dog lovers and even those without an affinity for man's best friend.

Brian Tallerico

CREDITS

John Grogan: Owen Wilson
Jennifer Grogan: Jennifer Aniston
Lisa: Haley Bennett
Sebastian: Eric Dane
Arnie Klein: Alan Arkin
Mrs. Kornblut: Kathleen Turner
Patrick: Nathan Gamble
Dr. Platt: Ann Dowd
Origin: USA
Language: English
Released: 2008
Production: Gil Netter, Karen Rosenfelt; Regency Enterprises, Fox 2000 Pictures, Sunswept Entertainment; released by 20th Century-Fox

Directed by: David Frankel
Written by: Scott Frank, Don Roos
Cinematography by: Florian Ballhaus
Music by: Theodore Shapiro
Sound: Joe Foglia
Music Supervisor: Julia Michels
Editing: Mark Livolsi
Art Direction: W. Steven Graham
Costumes: Cindy Evans
Production Design: Stuart Wurtzel

REVIEWS

Boston Globe Online. December 24, 2008.
Chicago Sun-Times Online. December 24, 2008.
Entertainment Weekly Online. December 24, 2008.
Hollywood Reporter Online. December 22, 2008.
Los Angeles Times Online. December 29, 2008.
New York Times Online. December 25, 2008.
San Francisco Chronicle. December 29, 2008.
Variety Online. December 22, 2008.
Washington Post. December 29, 2008.

QUOTES

John Grogan: "A dog doesn't care if you're rich or poor, educated or illiterate, clever or dull. Give him your heart and he will give you his."

TRIVIA

Twenty-two different dogs were used to portray Marley.

MARRIED LIFE

Do you know what really goes on in the mind of the person with whom you sleep?
—Movie tagline

Box Office: $1.5 million

In *Married Life*, writer/director Ira Sachs had a dastardly idea: Peer behind the curtain of public manners and domestic civility in a circa-1950s story to reveal conniving characters with the morals of rutting dogs. The sunny veneer of courteous language and decorous interaction that provides his film with a warm period glow masks cruel intentions and diabolical motives.

His characters, however, are too easy targets if the point is to expose the hypocrisy of mid-twentieth-century America (though the setting could just as easily be England, so formal and proper are the speech and habits of the principals). Sachs is not interested in the moral fall of his protagonist, Harry Allen (Chris

Cooper)—at least not in the part of that fall that has led him into an extramarital affair with a bombshell named Kay Nesbitt (Rachel McAdams). The affair is revealed immediately as the film opens, as Harry confides it over lunch to his friend Richard Langley (Pierce Brosnan). So head over heels has Harry fallen that he is already planning to discard his wife Pat (Patricia Clarkson), but since Harry is a sensitive soul and cares for Pat, even if he no longer loves her, he does not want to see her suffer the indignities of a betrayal and divorce. It is more humane, he believes, to kill her softly, with poison, as if he were putting a pet animal to sleep.

Cooper presents Harry as a practical, if somewhat befuddled, man who is trying his best to deal with the hand that has been dealt him. His attitude is only a slight satirical step beyond the prevailing gender mores of the era, and there is a slight satire in Harry's plan. He does not seem to believe he has the option of spurning Kay; he is helpless in her clutches (one look at her and it is clear why—she is stunning). Poor little boy Harry wears a hangdog expression as he plots to kindly dispense of his wife—since he treats her like a pet, he believes that he is engaging in merciful euthanasia to spare her the pain of being left for a younger, prettier woman. It is the least he can do, gentleman that he is.

It is hard even for Cooper, a consummate portrayer of earnest men, to make us believe his character is not either borderline delusional or absolutely bereft of humanity. Harry is not really the villainous type, yet he has decided his happiness is more important than his marriage. It is a puzzle, of course, why Kay, who is not only sexy but also sweet, would fall for an old fool like Harry, and not even these two fine actors can infuse their scenes together with believable chemistry. So you suspect Kay is up to no good from the start.

As Richard, however, Brosnan is typecast. Could any actor of this present era look more like a stereotypical playboy bachelor of the 1950s? From the minute Richard hears Harry's tale, you can almost glimpse the wolf ears sprouting from Brosnan's head. He and Kay are a sure match, and they will undoubtedly play Harry like a fiddle. But for what? Since all these characters are upper-class, money cannot really be the motive.

Sachs unfurls his plot proudly, and it does appear for a while as if he has something oddly compelling underway. Many reviewers compared this film to Hitchcock's work (most of them agreed it did not measure up to the master), but Sachs gives so much away at the start that it is hard to believe there is a real menace lurking. Instead of crackling, sinister details, we get way too much talk here. The central idea is delicious and the turn-the-tables plot twist is ensnaring too, but the climax is disappointing. The problem with starting the film

with the murder plot is that the story has nowhere more interesting to go from there, so it drags on, counting on its borderline-kitschy style and borderline-comic dialogue to see it through. But the kitsch is not deep enough and the comic is not black enough to keep audiences engaged.

By the end of the film you are almost hoping for the promised tragedy just to liven things up, but instead you get a tease and a too-neat climax. For all its considerable period charms—the language, the clothes, the well-appointed interior sets, the very authentic looks of the characters—*Married Life* succumbs to its own mannered approach to its plot. It is hard also to root for any of these characters—they are all shallow and unlikeable, but the problem is we do not know why. Because we are introduced to Harry after he has become a full-blown adulterer, we cannot figure out whether he has any justifiable gripe driving him to destroy his wife (though nothing would justify homicide). So little is revealed about Pat, or about the problems in their marriage, that there is no clue about what has made her husband stray, beyond ennui. It is true that Sachs is trying for a film with true-to-the-era characters who do not readily reveal their emotions, but these four are too much like blank slates.

A lot of reviewers considered this film to be a modernized form of noir, but it is not black enough to so qualify, and its characters are not buffeted by fate so much as by boredom or indifference to the consequences of their actions. Is it really possible to believe a man would think his wife would be better off dead than humiliated by a divorce, or that such a man would feel less guilty and troubled by employing such a solution to his problem? And why cannot Harry be happy having his cake and eating it too? And what is Kay's real motivation? The problem is that we know so little about what makes these characters tick that these key questions are almost impossible to answer.

In the end, *Married Life* is almost as conventional as the period manners and mores that it starts off mocking—or at least holding up to a strong, unforgiving light. It trifles with explosive satire but then shrinks back, and it seems that Sachs does not really have a satisfactory solution to the setup he has concocted—not for any of his characters, and certainly not for his audience.

Michael Betzold

CREDITS

Harry Allen: Chris Cooper
Pat Allen: Patricia Clarkson

Kay Nesbitt: Rachel McAdams
Richard Langley: Pierce Brosnan
John O'Brien: David Wenham
Origin: USA
Language: English
Released: 2007
Production: Sidney Kimmel, Jawal Nga, Steve Golin, Ira Sachs; Metro-Goldwyn-Mayer Pictures, Anonymous Content; released by Sony Pictures Classics
Directed by: Ira Sachs
Written by: Ira Sachs, Oren Moverman
Cinematography by: Peter Deming
Music by: Dickon Hinchliffe
Sound: Lindsay Bucknell
Music Supervisor: Sue Jacobs
Editing: Affonso Goncalves
Art Direction: Gwen Margetson
Costumes: Michael Dennison
Production Design: Hugo Luczyc-Wyhowski
MPAA rating: PG-13
Running time: 90 minutes

REVIEWS

Entertainment Weekly Online. March 5, 2008.
Los Angeles Times Online. March 7, 2008.
New York Times Online. March 7, 2008.
Variety Online. September 25, 2007.
Village Voice Online. March 4, 2008.

MAX PAYNE

Box Office: $40.6 million

Max Payne is the eponymous hero of a video game that was popular, challenging, and innovative in its day. The game featured plenty of slow-motion fight scenes and over-the-top action sequences—some of which were stylistically echoed in the *Matrix* films. Belatedly, it has been made into a film starring Mark Wahlberg. While one would expect such a movie to be cheesy and superficial, *Max Payne* is surprisingly appealing for its genre.

Directed by Irishman John Moore (*The Omen* [2006], *Flight of the Phoenix* [2004]), *Max Payne* is closer to the look and feel of a graphic-comic adaptation such as *Sin City* (2005) than a video-game knockoff like the *Lara Croft* series. It is cheap B-movie noir, set in a New York City where all the scenes are in grimy industrial buildings entered off forbidding alleys. The tones of the film range from dark blue to pitch black, and it's always snowing—a clearly fake kind of movie snow—except

when it's pouring rain on top of dirty piles of snow. Rarely has any film been so frank about the nadir of winter weather in the northern United States.

This dark world is inhabited by a ghost of a man, Max Payne (Mark Wahlberg), who is still reeling from the gruesome murder of his wife and baby. The killer is still on the loose, the case unsolved, and Payne has shriveled in career stature from a streetwise police detective to a desk job in the "cold cases" section. And no case is colder than the murder that took his family and changed his life.

Of course, being the kind of hero that he is, Max Payne will never give up until he unravels the mystery behind the murders. Wahlberg approaches the job in his typical closely guarded fashion. He has done this bit before: a cauldron of hurt and anger concealed behind a matter-of-fact, workman-like resolve. Wahlberg's face, always soft as a baby's even when it is chiseled into the manliest resolve, is perfect for this kind of role—he portrays the hard-bitten, ruthless seeker of vengeance for the injustices visited on the little guy.

Payne, in fact, is a very appealing character, a cross between the kind of role Humphrey Bogart often played and a modern action hero. He is not only haunted, but also wrongly accused of being the perpetrator as the trail gets bloodier and acquaintances are struck down by the same evildoers who murdered his wife and kid. He is a man totally bereft of succor and comfort, and completely without friends, who turn out to be enemies.

The film unfolds as an endless nightmare, and it has the claustrophobic, elusive feeling of a dream that will not end. It is true to its genre, with a sometimes clumsy plot that feels cobbled together and episodic at times, and derivative almost throughout. It was written by Sam Lake, who wrote the original May Payne video games in 2001 and 2003, and Beau Thorne, and the dialogue is as corny and on-the-nose as you would expect. But there are moments of unexpected crispness, and if you take the story for what it is, it is a fairly potent concoction of horror, conspiracy, thriller, action, and police procedural.

Director Moore is not subtle, but he is often surefooted. It is hard to know what to make of him when, right after the prologue, he puts the title screen "One Week Earlier" in big red letters on the front of the police building, but it is a bold stroke, merging the movie narrative with the movie setting. A little more of that would have put the film squarely into comic-book territory, but Moore does not want to go completely over the top. Fans of the video game, in fact, were mostly disappointed that the movie was not quite as outrageous as the game on which it was based. But this work follows the rules of cinema, as it should.

The messy pileup of Valkyries, experimental drugs, and superhuman killers makes the plot far from subtle and far from original, and too much of the acting seems by-the-book, including Beau Bridges in a thankless role. The film's women are darkly menacing and seductive and played by two Eastern European actresses—Mila Kunis and the new Bond girl, Olga Kurylenko. They are employed mainly as eye candy. Wahlberg gives the film an attractive center, but many critics felt he had taken a step down after scoring so many critical points in *The Departed* (2006). But Wahlberg's always been an actor who has done both weighty and action roles. He is not being stretched here, to be sure, and neither is the audience. After all, it is a movie based on a video game. But taken in that context, it is both visually fascinating and fairly innovative.

Moore wisely eschews drenching the film in the slow-motion fighting sequences that the video game is known for, though he provides plenty of gruesomely slow flying bullets near the film's climax. It is almost as if he is daring the core audience to be patient before they get their payoff in cheesy violence. And some will find the director's gold-drenched flashback scenes to Payne's domestic bliss, and the violence that shattered it, to be excessive, but what is the point of being subtle in a film like this? Moore uses the tools of cinema, as he rightfully should, to make the story fit this screen size.

In the end, *Max Payne* will soon be forgotten by critics, and fans of the video game may hate it, but it promises to have renewed life in rentals, and it is good enough to attract a new cult audience, if only they can find a way into it. Moore has actually elevated this story in a way that should make it attractive to fans of B-movie tableaux. It is a visual standout, thanks to the cinematography of Jonathan Sela. There is a nice sense of sweep and scope to its urban exteriors, and the climactic scene acknowledges the power of nature in a film about the forces that can alter human nature. To get this far is no small feat, given where the concept began.

Michael Betzold

CREDITS

Max Payne: Mark Wahlberg
Mona Sax: Mila Kunis
BB Hensley: Beau Bridges
Jim Bravura: Chris Ludacris Bridges
Alex Balder: Donal Logue
Jason Colvin: Chris O'Donnell
Nicole Horne: Kate Burton
Det. Shipman: Ted Atherton

Owen Green: Joel Gordon
Det. Amerini: Rico Simonini
Jack Lupino: Amaury Nolasco
Natasha: Olga Kurylenko
Lincoln: Jamie Hector
Origin: USA
Language: English
Released: 2008
Production: Julie Yorn, Scott Faye, John Moore; Firm Films, Depth Entertainment; released by 20th Century-Fox
Directed by: John Moore
Written by: Beau Thorne
Cinematography by: Jonathan Sela
Music by: Marco Beltrami, Buck Sanders
Sound: Glen Gauthier
Editing: Dan Zimmerman
Art Direction: Andrew Stearn
Costumes: George L. Little
Production Design: Daniel T. Dorrance
MPAA rating: PG-13
Running time: 99 minutes

REVIEWS

Boston Globe Online. October 17, 2008.
Entertainment Weekly Online. October 16, 2008.
Hollywood Reporter Online. October 16, 2008.
Los Angeles Times Online. October 17, 2008.
New York Times Online. October 17, 2008.
San Francisco Chronicle. October 17, 2008, p. E3.
Variety Online. October 16, 2008.
Washington Post. October 17, 2008.

QUOTES

Lincoln: "The Devil is building his army. Max Payne is looking for something that God wants to stay hidden. That is what makes him more dangerous."

TRIVIA

Mark Wahlberg claims to have never played the video game on which the film was based and chose instead to connect to the story through the script.

AWARDS

Nomination:

Golden Raspberries 2008: Worst Actor (Wahlberg).

MEET DAVE

He's a spaceship...and out of this world!
—Movie tagline

Eddie Murphy in Eddie Murphy in "Meet Dave."
—Movie tagline

Box Office: $11.8 million

Eddie Murphy's performance in *Meet Dave* is one of the laziest of this hit-and-miss actor's career, but it is merely part of the fabric of a film that is too weird, forgettable, and half-asleep to be truly horrible. The faintest praise that anyone can pay *Meet Dave* is that it is never so bad that it provokes anger or frustration at having wasted your time watching it. It is merely one of the most oddly forgettable movies ever made, to the point that it becomes hard even to follow the action because the movie dissipates as it unspools. Eddie Murphy recently made comments that hinted at an early retirement for one of the more successful actors of the last quarter-century. It is understandable why he would consider that after watching *Meet Dave*; indeed, it is almost possible to see him doing so while he was making the movie.

Meet Dave opens with a tiny meteor crashing into the bedroom of a young boy (Austin Lynd Myers). The meteor becomes the child's plaything, but it is actually a lot more serious than that—the space rock was sent by an alien race to drain the planet's oceans of their water. The beings that mis-aimed their device come to =retrieve it in the form of a ship that looks like a man, played by Eddie Murphy, who quickly finds the young boy and his single mother (Elizabeth Banks). The robot/ship, "Dave," is filled with tiny people, including one that looks like Eddie Murphy (the captain designed a ship that looked exactly like himself). Apparently, this alien race can create machines that look and sound exactly like them and rocks that drain oceans, but have not yet studied humanity long enough to convincingly mimic a real person. So, Dave sounds kind of like an upper-crust teacher and gets into a string of awkward interactions with everyone around him while the little people inside the man-ship try to figure out the human race. Comedy allegedly ensues.

Meet Dave is a family movie aimed squarely at eight-year-old boys who might chuckle at a grown man unable to understand "Walk/Don't Walk" signs who uses goofy accents to mimic the speech patterns of the people around him, but even that age group is unlikely to laugh at a string of nonsensical physical jokes and a completely inert screenplay.

What is so ironic about *Meet Dave* is that Murphy plays a shell, a spaceship occupied by alien beings, because his fans are pretty sure something similar might have happened in real life around a decade ago. The comedian was once one of the most vibrant and entertaining actors alive in movies like *Raw* (1987), *Bev-*erly Hills Cop* (1984), *Trading Places* (1983), and *48 Hours* (1982), but recent choices like *The Adventures of Pluto Nash* (2002), *Daddy Day Care* (2003), *The Haunted Mansion* (2003), *Norbit* (2007), and now *Meet Dave* have been derided almost universally. Some are better than others, but they all have the same thing in common—a lazy performance from Eddie Murphy. With brief breaks for the *Shrek* movies and *Dreamgirls* (2006), Murphy simply has not put his heart into his material like he used to, and that has never been more apparent than in *Meet Dave*.

Critics were correctly brutal to *Meet Dave*, with Manohla Dargis of the *New York Times* writing, "*Meet Dave,* the latest in a long line of disposable Eddie Murphy vehicles, plays like a half-hour sitcom episode that has been stretched to feature-length running time." Peter Travers of *Rolling Stone* wrote, "Eddie Murphy continues to trash his very real talent with bottomfeeding material." James Berardinelli wrote, "This is made-for-TV material dressed up by Eddie Murphy's participation into a theatrical release."

One has to wonder if *Meet Dave* might have worked with a more committed actor and a talented director— Brian Robbins, the man who made *The Perfect Score* (2004) and the aforementioned *Norbit,* is not a talented director. The concept is not half-bad and there is a strong pair of actresses in supporting roles in Gabrielle Union and Elizabeth Banks. The latter does her absolute best to elevate the material with her single mother role, but even her copious on-screen charisma is dulled by the entirety of the film. The fact is that Eddie Murphy seems bored with his own material in *Meet Dave,* as if he can no longer hide the fact that even he has grown tired of the same old routine.

Brian Tallerico

CREDITS

Dave Ming Cheng/Captain: Eddie Murphy
Gina Morrison: Elizabeth Banks
No. 3: Gabrielle Union
No. 2: Ed Helms
Engineer: Judah Friedlander
Lieutenant Left Arm: Shawn Christian
Dooley: Scott Caan
Mark: Marc Blucas
No. 4: Pat Kilbane
Knox: Michael O'Malley
No. 17: Kevin Hart
Josh Morrison: Austin Lind Myers
Origin: USA
Language: English

Released: 2008

Production: Jon Berg, Todd Komarnicki, David T. Friendly; Regency Enterprises, Guy Walks Into a Bar, Friendly Films; released by 20th Century-Fox

Directed by: Brian Robbins

Written by: Bill Corbett, Rob Greenberg

Cinematography by: J. Clark Mathis

Music by: John Debney

Sound: Richard Goodman

Editing: Ned Bastille

Art Direction: Beat Frutiger

Costumes: Ruth E. Carter

Production Design: Clay A. Griffith

MPAA rating: PG

Running time: 90 minutes

REVIEWS

Boston Globe Online. July 11, 2008.
Chicago Sun-Times Online. July 11, 2008.
Hollywood Reporter Online. July 10, 2008.
Los Angeles Times Online. July 11, 2008.
New York Times Online. July 11, 2008.
San Francisco Chronicle. July 11, 2008, p. E7.
Variety Online. July 10, 2008.
Wall Street Journal Online. July 11, 2008.
Washington Post. July 11, 2008, p. C2.

QUOTES

Knox: "Do me a favor, OK? Act like a cop and stop caring."

AWARDS

Nomination:

Golden Raspberries 2008: Worst Actor (Murphy), Worst Screen Couple (Murphy in Murphy).

MEET THE SPARTANS

The bigger the hit, the harder they fall.
—Movie tagline

Box Office: $38.2 million

If the horrible *Date Movie* (2006) and the even worse *Epic Movie* (2007) were the bottom of the comedy barrel, *Meet the Spartans* proves that filmmakers can make a lateral move along the base and that there actually *are* other ways to go but up. Writer/directors Jason Friedberg and Aaron Seltzer continue to be the two most overpaid comedy filmmakers in Hollywood, assuming that they have must been paid something, and anything is too much for the nonexistent writing going

on in what has become an annual humorless disaster at the multiplex. Friedberg and Seltzer have practically cornered the market on an offensively lazy style of comedy writing—one that thinks merely reminding a viewer that a movie or a celebrity exists is the same thing as actually writing a joke. The team wrote and directed *Date Movie, Epic Movie,* and now *Meet the Spartans,* with *Disaster Movie* on the way in 2009. The continuation of their career into 2009 and beyond sounds more like a threat than an in-production resumé.

The everything-and-the-kitchen-sink style that Friedberg and Seltzer employed in *Date Movie* and *Epic Movie* actually gains a little focus in *Meet the Spartans,* as the two settle on one film to take most of the satirical jabs. The screenplay fluctuates wildly between movie and pop culture jokes but always comes back to a general send-up of Zack Snyder's *300* (2007), a movie that felt a bit like a parody already. Naturally, the shirtless men with shiny swords become the brunt of a never-ending barrage of homophobic jokes that are only loosely structured around an actual plot. A hit movie like *300* is nothing more than comedy fish in a barrel for writers like these, who clearly scour the box office charts looking for the "jokes" for their next movie.

The main Spartan to meet is King Leonidas (Sean Maguire), and Margo (Carmen Electra) is his queen. The two have a child and live a happy life until Captain (Kevin Sorbo) comes to tell him that a messenger has arrived in the name of Xerxes (Ken Davitian) to demand the submission of Sparta. One of many ridiculously extended bits follows, this one surrounding the "Pit of Death" from *300.* To parody the "pit," *Spartans'* Leonidas kicks in a stream of pop culture icons including Britney Spears (Nicole Parker), a Sanjaya Malakar impersonator (Tony Yalda), and three awkwardly parodied *American Idol* judges. Leonidas visits the Oracle who, for some unexplained reason, is an Ugly Betty lookalike (Crista Flanagan), who tells him that he will go to war and die. Sadly, his death does not come quickly.

Leonidas leads thirteen men (they tried for 300 but fell a little short), including Captain, his son Sonio (Travis Van Winkle), and an overweight Spartan named Dilio (Jareb Dauplaise). The thirteen soldiers skip their way to a meeting place with Xerxes, who throws a number of pop culture clichés and references at the heroes, including a dance contest like the ones seen in the *Step Up* movies (2006 and 2008) and *Stomp the Yard* (2007), and a *Deal or No Deal* parody. The first round of battle ends in a "Yo Momma" fight. Through all of the *300* action, a hunchbacked Paris Hilton (Nicole Parker), Lindsay Lohan (Emily Wilson), the "Leave Britney Alone" video, and even Allspark from *Transformers* (2007) find their way into the "story". Nothing from the pop culture fabric of the last twelve months is off limits.

Like their other movies, *Meet the Spartans* fails because Friedberg and Seltzer mistake reference for writing. To them, just the fact that Britney Spears shaves her head or the fact that there was a torture scene in *Casino Royale* (2006) serves as a joke. *Meet the Spartans* was a hit, making almost $80 million worldwide even though only 2 percent of critics gave it a "fresh" rating on *Rotten Tomatoes*, and yet it still ranks in the bottom 100 for user ratings on *IMDB*. People saw it, but both critics and viewers hated it, and it looks even worse just a few months since its release, because the references are already dated and even more clichéd. Pop culture parodies this clever can be found online in a matter of seconds, but good comedies have a shelf life. In some ways, Friedberg and Seltzer are the comedy writers for the YouTube generation of viewers interested in a quick fix before they move on to the next link. Like a lot of the clips on that site seeking fifteen seconds of fame, *Meet the Spartans* was lazy and out-of-date before it even hit theaters.

Brian Tallerico

CREDITS

Queen Margo: Carmen Electra
Xerxes: Ken Davitian
Captain: Kevin Sorbo
Traitoro: Diedrich Bader
Leonidas: Sean Maguire
Persian Emissary: Method Man
Messenger: Phil Morris
Sonio: Travis Van Winkle
Dilio: Jareb Dauplaise
Origin: USA
Language: English
Released: 2008
Production: Aaron Seltzer, Jason Friedberg, Peter Safran; Regency Enterprises, New Regency Pictures; released by 20th Century-Fox
Directed by: Aaron Seltzer, Jason Friedberg
Written by: Aaron Seltzer, Jason Friedberg
Cinematography by: Shawn Maurer
Music by: Christopher Lennertz
Sound: Jeffrey Haupt
Editing: Peck Prior
Art Direction: William Ladd Skinner
Costumes: Frank Helmer
Production Design: William A. Elliot
MPAA rating: PG-13
Running time: 83 minutes

REVIEWS

Boston Globe Online. January 26, 2008.
Entertainment Weekly Online. January 30, 2008.
Hollywood Reporter Online. January 28, 2008.
New York Times Online. January 26, 2008.
Variety Online. January 25, 2008.
Village Voice Online. January 29, 2008.

QUOTES

Leonidas: "The Oracle also said our painted on abs look fake!"

AWARDS

Nomination:

Golden Raspberries 2008: Worst Picture, Worst Support. Actress (Electra), Worst Director (Friedberg, Seltzer), Worst Screenplay, Worst Sequel/Prequel.

MILK

Never blend in.
—Movie tagline

Box Office: $31.1 million

As 1970s gay rights activist Harvey Milk, Sean Penn may be one of the most likeable characters ever to appear in a movie. His eyes dancing with humor and affection, his heart full of hope and dreams, and his voice calm and patient even under pressure, Penn makes Milk into something as pleasurable and soothing as the man's last name. Even when he is sounding most strident in his denunciations of the bigots who have targeted gay people for persecution, you just want to give Penn a hug. He is gorgeous, kind, forgiving, principled, and visionary.

Director Gus Van Sant is known for biting satire featuring amoral people—witness Nicole Kidman's self-aggrandizing charlatan in *To Die For* (1995)—and also for brutally frank depictions of human depravity, such as *Elephant* (2003), his version of the Columbine high school shooting. But in *Milk* Van Sant goes all soft and gooey, employing swelling melodramatic music and a reverential approach to his worthy subject.

Perhaps Harvey Milk really was a saint, but if so he would have made an inept revolutionary. Van Sant's movie gives us a man of pure heart and generous intent, with barely a trace of ego, who became the nation's first openly gay politician and a transformative figure in one of the most forgotten yet most important movements for civil rights in the later twentieth century. This is a man who could be both soft and powerful, and we want to believe in him utterly. Certainly Milk's accomplishments are heroic and attention to the movement is overdue. *Milk* is in fact a landmark film in giving full voice and scope to the events in San Francisco that became central to the gay rights movement.

Relying heavily on Rob Epstein's 1984 documentary *The Times of Harvey Milk* and using a script by Dustin Lance Black, Van Sant resurrects the story of a barrier-smashing politician who was central to the awakening gay power movement of the 1970s. Before the scourge of AIDS ravaged the gay community, Milk, known as the "Mayor of Castro Street", was the unofficial leader of San Francisco's gay district, and after several unsuccessful tries at citywide offices, he was elected to the city's Board of Supervisors in 1977. A year later, he and Mayor George Moscone (Victor Garber) were shot to death by a rival supervisor, Dan White (Josh Brolin). But Milk's year in office coincided with the defeat of a Christian Right ballot proposal, backed by antigay spokeswoman Anita Bryant, to ban homosexuals from teaching in California public schools, and he transformed the political landscape in San Francisco by openly espousing and cementing gay power.

Puzzlingly, Van Sant lets audiences know Milk's fate right from the start. Many older viewers, of course, already would be aware of the murder. But others would have been shocked by what happens if they had not been forewarned. The film is narrated by Milk, using a tape recording of observations of his political journey that he dictated just before his death; it is not so much that he foresaw his assassination but that the threat of it was a constant companion. This itself gives his story tremendous tension, but Van Sant defuses it with his revelation at the film's beginning.

We pick up the story of Milk on his fortieth birthday as he picks up a young lover, Scott (James Franco), in a New York City subway. Milk announces he has accomplished nothing in his life yet; he is a businessman who has worked for an insurance company. Scott suggests he needs a "new scene," and Milk persuades him to move with him to San Francisco. There, they open a camera shop on Castro Street in a longtime Irish American neighborhood named Eureka Valley that is rapidly changing. When the bar owner across the street threatens to close down his shop, Milk is spurred to start his own gay merchants' association.

Lounging in bed, Scott asks Milk why he's suddenly an activist. Milk replies he is just being a smart businessman. But it is more than that, and Scotty's question is never fully answered. It is a key omission: All we know about Milk's first forty years is that they were uneventful and he was in the closet, but overnight he becomes a politically savvy gay activist. We do not see clearly enough the motivation for the transformation.

More's the pity, because in many other respects *Milk* is tremendously observant. It gets the flavor of the era exactly right: the brutal and egregious raids by police, the tentative steps to move out of the closet and into activism by gay men, the joining of flower power to political awareness to consciousness-raising. Yet the birth pangs of the movement still seem truncated. Suddenly Milk has an entire staff of political operatives at his side, running his campaigns. Was it the heady times or something in his character that propelled him forward?

Van Sant, to his credit, is highly interested in the way Milk's political career affects his personal life. He details the toll that Milk's almost yearly political races take on his relationship with Scott, and what happens when Milk discards Scotty for a jealous, paranoid Latin lover named Jack (Diego Luna). When Milk admits that Jack is easy to handle because he does not have to talk about politics with him—or much of anything else—we see the personal cost of Milk's political career. And by then it is too late. Milk's personal tragedies are at the core of this film's huge and embracing heart.

Just as with Milk himself, the political transformation of his campaign manager Cleve Jones (Emile Hirsch) is underexplained. One minute Jones is just a young kid from Phoenix turning tricks, and Harvey is attracted to him physically but wants to lecture him. A few scenes later the rampant flirting between them has suddenly been replaced by deep political kinship. Jones explains how he was radicalized in Barcelona when drag queens refused to tolerate police harassment at a protest march. It may be true, but it comes off as rather pat.

Audiences sympathetic to Milk's cause will find themselves buoyed and uplifted by the principled and aggressive response Milk musters to all challenges; other audiences may be mystified. *Milk* has all the earmarks of a biography smug in its belief that its subject is not just worthy but a shining beacon. It is a lot like the movie *Gandhi* (1982) in that respect, though not on as grand a scale. We see Milk grow before our eyes in leaps and bounds as a political visionary. Still, Penn gives Milk's speeches a voice consistent with his personal interactions; he seems the same person off and on the stump, and it is hard to believe from the rally scenes that this man could lead thousands. He seems too unassuming.

Yes, Van Sant allows his hero some foibles: We see Milk preen before a mirror before he steps out of City Hall to engineer a preplanned ploy to head off a potential riot among his supporters. We seem him lecture and threaten the mayor, and he is called to reckoning for that, but replies that he is merely behaving like straight men in office have always done. We also see he has a fondness for younger men, and that he shares in the unrelenting fear that comes with being gay in America, running for safety one night from an unknown pursuer.

Milk is never all that threatening though. He is a "good" gay man, able to speak with Teamsters, ready to don a suit and tie and look and act respectable. So when he characterizes himself as a genuine menace to society, he does not come off as plausible. Yet Penn manages to portray how a burning desire for justice can make a man larger than he seems, and Milk's genuine desire to see himself as just a tool of a larger movement puts him squarely in the tradition of other American activists. In this respect, *Milk* is much like other portrayals of American heroes, and it has the advantage of pathos that comes from a hero cut down too young, a very familiar motif for those who grew up in the 1960s.

We hear the rhetoric of bigotry in the mouth of State Senator John Briggs (Denis O'Hare), the leader of the antigay petition drive. And we see the fear in the eyes of White. But just as *Milk* falls short of sufficiently explaining what made Harvey Milk tick, it does not quite explain what drove White to murder, though Brolin does his best to make White a haunted man. In this film, so charitable as it is, even the enemies are not monstrous, and Milk thinks the best of them; about Dan White, he says he is not bigoted but just uneducated. And Milk believes prejudice against homosexuals would cease if only everyone recognized as gay one person they knew. His tactic is to overcome by honesty and openness, and that is part of what makes him so likeable.

The film depicts White's actions as the result of a long pileup of pretty grievances, and White is portrayed as a man who is jealous of Milk's success and feels diminished and humiliated by comparison. Milk's ascendancy renders White impotent to deliver to his conservative constituents. The last straw is that White, resigning from the board, is not even allowed to change his mind and return. He has become, in his mind, the outcast that Milk was originally. This is indeed a tragedy, but a half-baked one; one longs for a deeper and fuller explanation of White's famous, supposedly junk-food-induced insanity.

Instead, Van Sant lays the maudlin melodrama on a bit too thickly, with an operatic ending. He almost makes the mistake of oversanctifying Milk, but Penn continually pulls us back to the human warmth of the man, whose goodness and joy in life and righteous fervor is impossible to disdain. And thus, for once, Van Sant has made a film without irony or black humor. It is a movie that is difficult not to like. Surely, it is time that long-suffering and victimized American gays finally have a genuine hero on the screen, after so many decades of being belittled and made to be buffoons in all kinds of movies and in all kinds of real-life situations. In Penn's *Milk*, all Americans will recognize a new and deserving prince of justice.

Michael Betzold

CREDITS

Harvey Milk: Sean Penn
Dan White: Josh Brolin
Cleve Jones: Emile Hirsch
Scott Smith: James Franco
Jack Lira: Diego Luna
Jim Rivaldo: Brandon Boyce
Danny Nicoletta: Lucas Grabeel
Mayor George Moscone: Victor Garber
Anne Kronenberg: Alison Pill
State Senator John Briggs: Denis O'Hare
Rick Stokes: Stephen Spinella
Michael Wong: Kelvin Yu
Dick Pabich: Joseph Cross
David Goodstein: Howard Rosenman
Art Agnos: Jeff Koons
Origin: USA
Language: English
Released: 2008
Production: Dan Jinks, Bruce Cohen, Michael London; Axon Films, Groundswell Productions; released by Focus Features
Directed by: Gus Van Sant
Written by: Dustin Lance Black
Cinematography by: Harris Savides
Music by: Danny Elfman
Sound: Felix Andrew, Neil Riha
Editing: Elliot Graham
Art Direction: Charley Beal
Costumes: Danny Glicker
Production Design: Bill Groom
MPAA rating: R
Running time: 127 minutes

REVIEWS

Boston Globe Online. November 26, 2008.
Chicago Sun-Times Online. November 24, 2008.
Entertainment Weekly Online. November 25, 2008.
Hollywood Reporter Online. November 2, 2008.
Los Angeles Times Online. November 26, 2008.
New York Times Online. November 26, 2008.
New Yorker Online. December 1, 2008.
Rolling Stone Online. November 27, 2008.
San Francisco Chronicle. November 25, 2008, p. E1.
Variety Online. November 2, 2008.
Washington Post. November 26, 2008, p. C1.

QUOTES

Harvey Milk: "My name is Harvey Milk and I'm here to recruit you!"

TRIVIA

Sean Penn's uncanny physical transformation into Harvey Milk was achieved using a prosthetic nose and teeth, contact lenses, and a redesigned hairline.

Oscars 2008: Actor (Penn), Orig. Screenplay

Ind. Spirit 2009: Support. Actor (Franco), First Screenplay

Screen Actors Guild 2008: Actor (Penn)

Writers Guild 2008: Orig. Screenplay

Nomination:

Oscars 2008: Costume Des., Director (Van Sant), Film, Film Editing, Support. Actor (Brolin), Orig. Score

British Acad. 2008: Actor (Penn), Film, Makeup, Orig. Screenplay

Directors Guild 2008: Director (Van Sant)

Golden Globes 2009: Actor—Drama (Penn)

Ind. Spirit 2009: Actor (Penn), Cinematog.

Screen Actors Guild 2008: Support. Actor (Brolin), Cast.

MIRACLE AT ST. ANNA

World War II has its heroes and its miracles.
—Movie tagline

Box Office: $7.9 million

Films about World War II traditionally have neglected the roles played by African American soldiers. While individual black soldiers have appeared here and there beginning with films such as *Red Ball Express* (1952) and *Pork Chop Hill* (1959), the African American regiments known as "Buffalo Soldiers," a name originally given to the troops who fought Native Americans following the Civil War, have been ignored. Spike Lee attempts to tell their story in *Miracle at St. Anna*, with decidedly mixed results.

The film opens in New York City in 1983 when post office clerk Hector Negron (Laz Alonso) suddenly pulls out a Luger and shoots a customer (Sergio Albelli). *New York Daily News* reporter Tim Boyle (Joseph Gordon-Levitt) accompanies the police to Hector's apartment, where a valuable sculpted head is discovered. *Miracle at St. Anna* flashes back to Italy in 1944 to reveal slowly the significance of the head and Hector's motive for the shooting.

Because of the racism and incompetence of their white commanding officer, Captain Nokes (Walton Goggins), four soldiers find themselves trapped behind enemy lines in a small village near the legendary Mountain of the Sleeping Man. Staff Sergeant Aubrey Stamps (Derek Luke) is the no-nonsense leader of the four, dedicated to fulfilling his duties. Sergeant Bishop Cummings (Michael Ealy), a former minister, is out only for himself. Private Sam Train (Omar Benson Miller) is a gentle giant terrified of death. Train has recovered the head after the fleeing Nazis blew up a medieval bridge in Florence, and he sees it as a good-luck talisman. (The destruction of this bridge is one of many Nazi crimes against art depicted in the compelling 2006 documentary *The Rape of Europa*.) Train also acquires a young Italian orphan, Angelo (Matteo Sciabordi), injured during a German shelling. The Puerto Rico-born Hector, a corporal, becomes valuable when the soldiers reach the village because he can speak some Italian.

Strangely, though it seems at the beginning that Hector is going to be the main character, he has less to do than his fellow soldiers. He tries to maintain peace once the soldiers reach the villagers, who are led by the fascist Ludovico (Omero Antonutti) as arguments erupt between the African Americans and the Italians and within each group. Both the noble Stamps and the lustful Cummings are drawn to Ludovico's luscious daughter, Renata (Valentina Cervi). Tensions increase further with the arrival of the partisans, led by Peppi (Pierfrancesco Favino). Some of *Miracle at St. Anna* is based on fact, like the Nazi slaughter of 560 villagers, all women, children, and old men, at Sant'Anna di Stazzema. Angelo has witnessed this horror and the death of his beloved brother, Arturo (Leonardo Borzonaca), and he also knows the identity of the traitor among Peppi's men.

Screenwriter James McBride, adapting his 2002 novel, tries to include too many plotlines, making the film seem bloated. Although the film is ostensibly a tribute to the Buffalo Soldiers, the four protagonists disappear for long stretches as the film shifts focus to subtitled scenes with the partisans and the Nazis. Though reviewers complained about the 160-minute running time, this should not be an obstacle for a film as long as the proceedings and the cinematic style are interesting. Unfortunately, neither is the case with *Miracle at St. Anna*.

During the prologue Lee uses, unnecessarily, a swirling camera for a scene between Boyle and a police detective (John Turturro), floats the camera down a hallway soon afterward, and employs quick cutting during the first battle scene to convey the chaos of war. After that his style grows more conventional, with too many scenes with the characters in the center of the frame. It is as if the often didactic director chose to be more conservative visually so that viewers could concentrate on his themes. And what are these exactly? There was extensive racial prejudice in the 1940s? Italians hated foreigners? Nazis were monsters?

Buried somewhere within *Miracle at St. Anna* may be a good, small film struggling to find its way out of the narrative morass. While individual scenes and moments within scenes work, especially the knowing glances between Stamps and Renata, many other scenes go on and on as if Lee is trying to talk the audience into submission. Then there is sloppiness, such as not explaining why Hector has taken his gun to work and how it could go undetected. Add the inescapable sentimentality of the Angelo character, and what is left is a gooey, boring mess. The score by Terence Blanchard, Lee's usually reliable composer, does not help matters, relentlessly emphasizing the desired emotional response. Lee has claimed the film was influenced by Italian neorealist cinema, but it is hard to spot similarities with films such as Vittorio De Sica's *Miracle in Milan* (1951) and Roberto Rossellini's *Paisan* (1946), which features African American soldiers.

Miracle at St. Anna was greeted angrily following a pre-release screening in Rome because it depicts an Italian traitor as responsible for the Sant'Anna di Stazzema massacre. McBride defended his story as a fictional interpretation of historical events. More problematic is resorting to clichés, as with the three hysterical examples of white bigots, though Lee is not known for his subtlety. At another extreme, Cummings, Train, and some minor characters tread closely to racial stereotypes. About the only thing salvageable in *Miracle at St. Anna* are the performances, especially those of Luke, Cervi, Favino, and Sciabordi.

Hector is shown watching John Wayne in *The Longest Day* (1962) and bitterly objecting to the absence of black soldiers. Lee has strongly criticized Clint Eastwood for failing to include African Americans in *Flags of Our Fathers* (2006) and *Letter from Iwo Jima* (2006), and while *Miracle at St. Anna* redresses this wrong, it is not the film the Buffalo Soldiers deserve. Lee has ably handled large-scale subjects before, as with *Malcolm X* (1992), and his film *Inside Man* (2006) arguably demonstrates his most adept filmmaking. The failure then of *Miracle at St. Anna* is especially puzzling.

Michael Adams

CREDITS

Staff Sgt. Aubrey Stamps: Derek Luke
Sgt. Bishop Cummings: Michael Ealy
Cpl. Hector Negron: Laz Alonso
Pvt. Sam Train: Omar Benson Miller
Peppi Grotta: Pierfrancesco Favino
Renata: Valentina Cervi
Antonio Ricci: John Turturro
Tim Boyle: Joseph Gordon-Levitt
Angelo Torancelli: Matteo Sciabordi
Enrico: John Leguizamo
Zana Wilder: Kerry Washington
Col. Driscoll: D.B. Sweeney

Gen. Ned Almond: Robert John Burke
Higgins: Malcolm Goodwin
Nokes: Walton Goggins
Platoon Commander Huggs: Omari Hardwick
Origin: USA, Italy
Language: English
Released: 2008
Production: Spike Lee, Robert Cicutto, Luigi Musini; 40 Acres and a Mule Filmworks, RAI Cinema, On My Own, Produzioni Cinematografiche; released by Touchstone Pictures
Directed by: Spike Lee
Written by: James McBride
Cinematography by: Matthew Libatique
Music by: Terence Blanchard
Sound: Maurizio Argentieri
Editing: Barry Alexander Brown
Art Direction: Donato Tieppo
Costumes: Carlo Poggioli
Production Design: Sarah Frank, Tonino Zera
MPAA rating: R
Running time: 160 minutes

REVIEWS

Boston Globe Online. September 26, 2008.
Chicago Sun-Times Online. September 25, 2008.
Entertainment Weekly Online. September 24, 2008.
Hollywood Reporter Online. September 8, 2008.
Los Angeles Times Online. September 26, 2008.
New York Times Online. September 26, 2008.
San Francisco Chronicle. September 26, 2008, p. E1.
Variety Online. September 7, 2008.
Washington Post. September 26, 2008, p. C1.

QUOTES

Pvt. Sam Train: "God don't like ugly."
Sgt. Bishop Cummings: "Well, he don't seem to like pretty a whole helluva lot either."

TRIVIA

Wesley Snipes and Naomi Campbell were originally cast in the film but had to drop out due to scheduling conflicts.

MIRRORS

There is evil…on the other side.
—Movie tagline

Box Office: $30.6 million

Mirrors, a remake of the 2003 Korean thriller *Geoul Sokeuro* (*Into the Mirror*), was directed by emerging horror master Alexandre Aja, who cowrote the screenplay with Grégory Levasseur. Set in present-day New York City, the creepy thriller possesses all the hallmarks of its genre, from a tragically flawed hero to a foreboding setting, disturbing back story, dramatic score, and blood-chilling special effects.

The opening sequence of *Mirrors* sets a dark, menacing tone in establishing common, everyday mirrors as a source of unexplained evil. A terrorized man (Josh Cole) runs from an unknown assailant through the Lenox Avenue subway station, ending up trapped inside an employee locker room. As the lights flash on and off, the locker doors open to reveal mirrors inside, and the man realizes that he has failed to elude his hunter. Pleading "I wasn't trying to escape," he approaches a large wall mirror as it cracks in implied dissatisfaction. He picks up a fallen shard and watches in horror as his stern-looking reflection uses it to slash its own throat, causing him mortal injury. His gruesome death is later presumed to have been a suicide.

The film's psychologically stressed protagonist, Ben Carson (Kiefer Sutherland), is a disgraced ex-NYPD cop trying to get his life back together three years after accidentally shooting and killing another officer. Estranged from his wife Amy (Paula Patton), a coroner, and their children Michael (Cameron Boyce) and Daisy (Erica Gluck), he lives with his younger sister Angie (Amy Smart) and hopes that his new job and three-month-old sobriety soon will allow him to return to his family in the suburbs. Ben's new place of employment is the fictitious old Mayflower Department Store, the former St. Matthews Hospital that was purchased by the Mayflower family in the 1950s after a brutal massacre involving mental patients forced its closure. Once the most beautiful and luxurious department store in the city, the monumental edifice now sits looming and abandoned, having been devastated by fire five years previously. The inferno, set by a security guard, ripped through the store's interior, killing and injuring many people while leaving most of its furnishings damaged but intact. As the new night watchman, Ben's job is to patrol the burned-out building, frozen in time due to ongoing legal battles that have prevented any repairs. On his initial tour, Ben remarks that the store's gigantic mirrors are surprisingly immaculately clean, to which veteran day watchman Lorenzo (John Shrapnel) nonchalantly explains that the previous night-time security guard had been obsessed with polishing the mirrors.

Ben's first night alone on the job rattles his nerves sufficiently. Exploring the empty building by flashlight, he discovers strange handprints on the mirrors as well as a flooded basement. He also witnesses his first paranormal vision in the mirror—an open door that he confirms is actually shut. The next morning, he tries to disregard the events of the previous night, even though he is further shaken by a hideously distorted reflection of his face in the bathroom mirror of his sister's apartment. Still feeling optimistic about being newly employed, he visits his kids at home unannounced, angering his long-suffering wife who is convinced that he will never change. Back at the Mayflower later that night, Ben has a far more chilling experience than the previous evening'. Guided by the tortured screams of a woman, he ends up in the ladies dressing room where, in the mirrors only, he catches elusive glimpses of her badly burned body lying on the floor of a changing stall. He realizes that he is not hallucinating, that there is indeed something strange and horrible going on inside the old building. On his frantic way out, he finds the lost wallet belonging to the last night watchman, Gary Lewis, whose drivers' license photograph reveals to the audience that he was the man killed in the subway at the opening of the film. Inside the wallet is a piece of paper containing the word "ESSEKER." That same night at home, Ben's son Michael sees a burnt woman in the mirror of his bedroom closet door. Although Amy passes it off as a simple nightmare, clearly some sort of dubious connection has been forged between Ben, his family, and the odd goings-on at the Mayflower.

As Ben struggles to get to the bottom of what is occurring, both his sister and wife express concern over his mental health, blaming his delusions on the potent pills he is taking for his alcohol addiction. Nevertheless, he perseveres in unraveling the mystery with the help of a box containing newspaper clippings about the Mayflower's dark past, perplexingly sent to him by Lewis only days before the former night watchman died. Ben learns through one of the articles that the security guard who set the fire not only was obsessed with the store's mirrors, but also was charged with killing his own family. With the reluctant assistance of Amy, Ben examines the body of Lewis in the city's morgue and reviews his case file, noticing in a photograph that the mirror shard in his hand is not covered in blood like the one held in his reflection. Meanwhile, the entire Carson family unwittingly has become prey to the unknown evil force lurking inside the mirrors. Angie, after looking at herself in the bathroom mirror, is viciously killed by her reflection while taking a bath. Young Michael becomes quietly fixated by mirrors and appears to be communicating with someone or something on the other side.

After much marital strife between Ben and Amy, who thinks Ben is losing his mind, she sees Michael get up and walk away from his own seated reflection. Finally believing her husband that their family is in some kind of danger, she helps Ben paint over all the mirrors in the house, and she and the children hunker down while he goes to Pennsylvania in search of Anna Esseker, the woman whose last name was found in Lewis' wallet and then later scratched into a mirror at the Mayflower. As a young girl, Esseker was prone to violent outbursts and was suspected of being demonically possessed by her family. She was eventually committed to St. Matthew's Hospital for schizophrenia. Released only days before the infamous massacre, she was allegedly cured of her mental illness by a doctor's experimental treatment that forced her to sit in a room of mirrors and confront her own image. Although her personality was completely changed afterwards, Esseker still had "trouble" with mirrors, and therefore was sent by her superstitious rural kin to a place without mirrors — the monastery where Ben now finds her decades later. Now a nun, Esseker reveals to him that she did not have schizophrenia, but that a demon had left her body and entered the hospital mirrors during her treatment. After she refuses to return to the old hospital to confront the demon, Ben abducts her and takes her back to the long-forgotten psychiatric lab entombed in the Mayflower's basement.

As *Mirrors* draws to a close, three climactic showdowns take place, between Esseker and the demon, the demon and Ben, and the demon and Ben's wife and kids. At the Mayflower, mirrors shatter as the demonic force reenters Anna Esseker's convulsing body. Meanwhile, despite Ben's efforts to protect his family, Michael is convinced that the demon is friendly, and he has allowed the dark force to penetrate their home by scraping off the paint covering the mirrors and by flooding the house with reflective water. While Amy and the children fight for their lives across town, Ben engages the demon in hand-to-hand combat through the flooded halls of the old hospital. He finally manages to kill it and release his family from its grip by impaling Esseker's possessed body on a broken steam pipe. As the three Carsons rejoice at home, Ben emerges triumphantly from the dark old department store into welcoming daylight. However, he quickly realizes that all the signs and words are written backwards. Apparently killed during the struggle, Ben is now horrified to discover that he himself has become trapped in a reverse world.

Jaye Furlonger

CREDITS

Ben Carson: Kiefer Sutherland
Amy Carson: Paula Patton
Angela Carson: Amy Smart
Michael Carson: Cameron Boyce
Anna Esseker: Mary Beth Peil
Robert Esseker: Julian Glover
Lorenzo Sapelli: John Shrapnel
Daisy Carson: Erica Gluck

Origin: USA
Language: English
Released: 2008
Production: Alexandra Milchan, Gregory Lévasseur, Marc Sternberg; Regency Enterprises, New Regency; released by 20th Century-Fox
Directed by: Alexandre Aja
Written by: Alexandre Aja, Gregory Lévasseur
Cinematography by: Maxime Alexandre
Music by: Javier Navarrete
Sound: Albert Bailey
Editing: Baxter
Art Direction: Stephen Bream
Costumes: Ellen Mirojnick, Michael Dennison
Production Design: Joseph C. Nemec III
MPAA rating: R
Running time: 110 minutes

REVIEWS

Boston Globe Online. August 16, 2008.
Hollywood Reporter Online. August 15, 2008.
Los Angeles Times Online. August 18, 2008.
New York Times Online. August 16, 2008.
Variety Online. August 15, 2008.

QUOTES

Angela Carson: "Mirrors are just glass and silver, Ben. That's it. There's nothing behind them."

MISS PETTIGREW LIVES FOR A DAY

Every woman will have her day.
—Movie tagline

Box Office: $12.3 million

Based on the 1938 novel by Winifred Watson, Bharat Nalluri's *Miss Pettigrew Lives for a Day* is an effective comedy anchored by two pitch-perfect, old-fashioned performances that consistently keep the bubbly film light and airy. Oscar® winner Frances McDormand plays the title character, Guinevere Pettigrew, a woman who is struggling to make ends meet in the late 1930s. She is let go from her employment agency and grabs one more client's number on the way out, trying to get at least a final assignment. Pettigrew stumbles into the life of Delysia Lafosse (the perfectly cast Amy Adams), a nightclub singer and aspiring actress, and neither woman will ever be the same.

When Pettigrew arrives at the lavish apartment of Lafosse, she finds that the ingénue has a few bad habits, including awkwardly juggling men. When Pettigrew saves the day by hiding Lafosse's infidelity, she gets hired and is downright adored by the young lady. It turns out that the actress is dealing with three men, a penniless but lovable musician named Michael Pardue (Lee Pace), a controlling nightclub owner, Nick Calderelli (Mark Strong), and a young theater producer named Phil Goldman (Tom Payne). Quickly, Miss Pettigrew is swept up into high society life, accompanying Delysia on shopping trips, receiving a full makeover, and falling for a lingerie designer named Joe Blomfeld (Ciarán Hinds), who happens to be attached to a manipulative woman named Edythe Dubarry (Shirley Henderson). A series of events and misunderstandings that were the hallmark of screwball comedies in the 1930s and 1940s make the next twenty-four hours of Miss Pettigrew's life a whirlwind that includes love, friendship, and more glamour than she ever imagined.

Renée Zellweger and Keira Knightley may be the reigning queens of period pieces, but Amy Adams makes the case that there is no actress who looks more like she stepped out of a bygone era of cinema than the Oscar® nominee does in *Miss Pettigrew Lives for a Day*. Adams plays this comedy in a broad, wide-eyed way that would be right at home in the comedies of the '40s and '50s. It is almost as if she embodies Delysia not as a real woman from the late '30s but as an actress of that period would play her. She pops off the screen in a way that so many of her peers do not, and would be right at home in any of the starring roles of Rita Hayworth or Katharine Hepburn from the '40s. Her screen presence is radiant, and she goes a step further and brings a depth to the role that a lot of actresses would have missed entirely. The always great McDormand matches her in every way, perfectly executing the transformation of this great character from homeless to social secretary to the stars without overselling the transformation like a lot of actresses would. *Miss Pettigrew Lives for a Day* reportedly was in some state of development for decades—it nearly became a movie shortly after the book was released, and then the ownership of the rights sat in limbo for generations—but it seems like a touch of good fortune that the book was never filmed until Adams and McDormand were the right age to star in it. They are both flawless.

McDormand and Adams are favored by a detailed design aesthetic that vividly recreates both the drab poverty of Miss Pettigrew's first life and the flash and glamour of the new one she takes on after meeting Delysia. Some of the production design choices border on too staged, making the proceedings often feel more like a play than a film, but *Miss Pettigrew Lives for a Day* is certainly a movie that is always easy on the eyes. As for the supporting cast, Hinds brings some unexpected

gravity to his role, but Pace seems a little miscast and some of the high society patois in the second act gets a little dry and repetitive. Most damagingly, the emotional chords of the third act, when the war looms heavy on the horizon, feel a little forced, and take some of the air out of the final product. When Adams and McDormand (and, to a lesser extent, Hinds) are allowed to shine like the stars of yesteryear, *Miss Pettigrew Lives for a Day* truly sparkles with a charm and wit rarely seen in modern comedies. It may have taken seven decades to go from page to screen, but the final product was worth the wait.

Brian Tallerico

CREDITS

Guinevere Pettigrew: Frances McDormand
Delysia Lafosse: Amy Adams
Michael: Lee Pace
Joe: Ciaran Hinds
Nick: Mark Strong
Edythe: Shirley Henderson
Charlotte: Christina Cole
Phil: Tom Payne
Origin: Great Britain, USA
Language: English
Released: 2008
Production: Nellie Bellflower, Stephen Garrett; Kudos Productions, Keylight Productions; released by Focus Features
Directed by: Bharat Nalluri
Written by: David Magee, Simon Beaufoy
Cinematography by: John de Borman
Music by: Paul Englishby
Sound: Chris Munro
Music Supervisor: Karen Elliott
Editing: Barney Pilling
Art Direction: Nick Gottschalk
Costumes: Michael O'Connor
Production Design: Sarah Greenwood
MPAA rating: PG-13
Running time: 92 minutes

REVIEWS

Boston Globe Online. March 7, 2008.
Chicago Sun-Times Online. March 7, 2008.
Entertainment Weekly Online. March 5, 2008.
Hollywood Reporter Online. March 3, 2008.
Los Angeles Times Online. March 7, 2008.
New York Times Online. March 7, 2008.
San Francisco Chronicle. March 7, 2008, p. E7.

Variety Online. February 29, 2008.
Wall Street Journal. March 7, 2008, p. W1.
Washington Post. March 7, 2008, p. C1.

QUOTES

Miss Pettigrew: "I am an expert on the lack of love."

MONGOL

Greatness comes to those who take it.
—Movie tagline

Box Office: $5.7 million

Was it historical, or was it entertainment? In fact, though suspiciously made up of the stuff of legends, this Russian film was considered both, an historical entertainment, but the title might have been *Mongols & Tartars, Yaks & Yurts. Mongol* is only the beginning of an epic story of the Mongol empire and the military genius who rose to power and then conquered the civilized world during the early 13th century, Genghis Khan, born Temudjin, the son of a tribal Khan, in the year 1162. The film might more accurately have been titled *Young Genghis Khan*, or perhaps *Young Genghis Khan in Love and War*. The original subtitle calls it the "Untold Story of the Rise of Genghis Khan," but if this story were truly untold, how did the filmmakers discover and know how to tell it? It is a safe bet that the film is a fantasy and a fabrication inspired by the legend of Genghis Khan, and it would be foolish to embrace it too readily as history. On the other hand, the film offers vivid impressions of how the Mongol clans might have lived (and perhaps still live today) in yurts as nomads, and of their amazing skills and prowess as horsemen and warriors.

Regardless, these Russian filmmakers certainly know how to spin a yarn. The trick here is to humanize the legendary, and to wrap the film's history lesson in the guise of family drama. The boy Temudjin's (Odnyam Odsuren) father, a local Khan, is deceived and murdered by his enemies. The father and son meet a war party and exchange ceremonial bowls of fermented mare's milk. Temudjin's father is poisoned by the drink, and after he dies, his title is usurped by a nasty clansman who vows to kill Temudjin before he can avenge his father's death, but custom forbids the new Khan from killing Temudjin while he is still a child, so the boy escapes his captor and lives to fight another day. Before this tragedy occurs, however, Temudjin has been taken by his father to find and choose a wife, though he is barely ten years old. He meets a compellingly cheeky young girl named Börte (Bayertsetseg Erdenebat), who advises him to choose her, and since it is love at first

sight, he does just that. In this way, sweet and tender young romance triumphs before the horizon is made murky by the dark clouds of tragedy.

A few words may be in order here concerning the film's historical context. There are few Western accounts of the Mongols, "who by us are called the Tartars," as Friar John of Plano Carpini, envoy of the Apostolic See to the Tartars, wrote at the conclusion of his *History of the Mongols* (1245-1247), the most widely known early narrative by one who had travelled to the court of the Great Khan, Chingis (Temuchin). *The Mongol Mission,* edited by Christopher Dawson (New York: Sheed & Ward, 1955), reprints the narratives of John of Plano Carpini, Brother Benedict the Pole, William of Rubrick, and letters of John of Monte Corvino and others, as well as two bulls of Pope Innocent IV addressed to the emperor of the Tartars. Biography is less than precise here, but Dawson writes that "Temuchin, as Chingus was originally called, was born, probably in 1167 [according to Christopher Dawson; the film dates his birth confidently to 1162, presuming the Russians now know better], the son of a Mongol chief of royal descent but of little power, who was killed by the Tartars when his son was still a child." That roughly approximates what the first hour of the film dramatizes.

The screenplay was written by Arif Aliyev in collaboration with director Sergei Bodrov. The film apparently invents specifics of Temudjin's life: how the boy escapes from his father's usurper; how Temudjin, strongly played by young Odsuren, comes to meet the boy Jamukha (Amarbold Tuvshinbayar) and how the two of them bond as blood brothers; how the boy chooses charming young Börte to be his wife; and how Temudjin and Jamukha grow into rivals after Jamukha and his warriors help Temudjin rescue Börte from captivity (though it would have been highly unusual for Mongols to go to war over a woman). Khulan Chuluun as the grown-up Börte makes a fine visual match for the well-known Japanese actor Tadanobu Asano, who stars as the grown Temudjin. Honglei Sun, who plays the grown Jamukha, won the 2008 Asian Film Award for Best Supporting Actor for his gritty performance as Temudjin's rival Khan.

The film, then, is a sort of cinematic Bildungsroman about a warrior in the making as Temudjin makes his way in the world, provides solace to his mother, rescues himself and then his pregnant wife, fights and defeats his enemies, and becomes the mighty conqueror whose kingdom will stretch from Cathay in the East to Russia, Hungary, and Bulgaria in the West. The film of course claims to be based on scholarly accounts, but it plays like legend and captures a majestic sense of atmosphere and scope. If the historical and biographical details prove to be sparse, what value might this film have to historians in the classroom? Probably just as much as any Hollywood spectacle pretending to show the glory or the decadence of Rome or the miracles of Joan of Arc or the questionable triumphs of the Crusades. But if one comes to expect silly, bloated fantasies, then *Mongol* may seem less disappointing than many Hollywood products. If the Russian crew is pushing a contemporary agenda, that will be less apparent to American viewers who know next to nothing about the Tartar invasions of the 13th and 14th centuries. At the same time, the film will give a vivid impression of how the tribal Mongols might have lived and ruled themselves on the steppes of Central Asia, and how they might have fought on those tough little ponies that enabled them to sweep across a continent or two. As John of Plano Carpini wrote, after the Tartars had conquered the Turks, "they attacked Russia, where they made great havoc, destroying cities and fortresses and slaughtering men; and they laid siege to Kiev, the capital of Russia; after they had besieged the city for a long time, they took it and put the inhabitants to death. When we were journeying through that land we came across countless skulls and bones of dead men lying about the ground. Kiev had been a very large and thickly populated town, but now it has been reduced almost to nothing, for there are at the present time scarce two hundred houses there and the inhabitants are kept in complete slavery. Going on from there, fighting as they went, the Tartars destroyed the whole of Russia." Such devastation is beyond the time frame of the film, so the viewers are spared these awful details, but without such accounts, could anyone understand the utter ruthlessness of these invaders? And without that, can the film have any claims to authenticity?

Mongol was highly acclaimed in Russia, where it won the Golden Nika Award for Best Film in Moscow in March 2008. In fact, Sergei Bodrov's film won in six categories: Best Film, Best Director, Best Cinematography, Best Sound, Best Production Design, and Best Costumes. Beyond its awards in Russia, the film was such an international success that Sergei Bodrov is currently planning a sequel to be filmed in Kazakhstan. And since the film concludes at just the point where Genghis Khan is about to extend his conquest, a sequel would seem to be the next logical step, a much stronger motive than most sequels have enjoyed. The film certainly deserved to win the Golden Nika award for Best Cinematography by Sergei Trofimov and Rogier Stoffers. The film is magnificently visual without having to resort to or rely on digital effects. Michael Sragow, the *Baltimore Sun* film critic, praised the film for the "arid beauty of the Great Steppes and the sweep of the battles, rendered with splatters of gore that lend a Jackson Pollock-like excitement to the clear, strong

staging." He disliked the way the film "dabbles in mysticism," however, involving the hero's pilgrimages to the "Sacred Mountain" (probably a movie invention, or maybe the stuff of legend), but found value in its "magnificent stagecraft" and considered it "suitably roiling and touching as a martial-marital epic." Bodrov mines nostalgia in the way he recaptures really large-scale, multinational epic filmmaking of the sort that Hollywood has all but forgotten.

Mongol was distributed in the United States as an Academy Award® nominee for Best Foreign-language Film. Critical reception of Sergei Bodrov's epic film was favorable, to the point of being nostalgic. *New York Times* reviewer A. O. Scott praised Bodrov's "grand-scale moviemaking," for example. *Baltimore Sun* movie critic Michael Sragow described it as a "Birth-of-a-Nation epic" about the "man who united all the Mongols and made them follow a handful of common laws instead of customs that they broke at will," but the reference to D.W. Griffith seemed more convenient or even clichéd than meaningful. *Washington Post* reviewer Stephen Hunter was so befuddled and stumped by the film's historical background that he confessed running to Wikipedia for help, until, with a blast of perception and insight, he settled his wits and imagined the film to be a sort of "Eastern Western," in which the Mongols were like Indians, chasing after yaks rather than buffalo, and riding their ponies halfway around the world from China to Bulgaria. Hunter imagined the film's title might better have been *Genghis Khan: A Love Story,* so strongly was Hunter's reaction shaped by powerful movie clichés. But how much can readers expect from movie reviewers who write novels on the side and for whom clichés may be primarily important? *Washington Post* reader Jonathan Keiler of Bowie, Maryland, wrote (on July 5) to voice his disdain for Hunter's review for describing the Mongol tribes as "living a 'hunter gatherer' existence and following 'the yak.'" Keiler pointed out that the Mongols were "nomadic pastoralists," who "kept large herds of ordinary livestock that traveled with them across the steppes. That livestock satisfied most" of their needs. The American Plains Indians, on the other hand, *were* indeed hunter-gatherers, and therefore not "capable of forming large and sophisticated armies," like the Mongols and the Huns of Central Asia.

Even though the film challenged disadvantaged reviewers, *Mongol* did respectable business at the U.S. box office for a foreign film in a typically wretched and trivial summer market. *Variety* ranked it 24th in its first week out, but it was playing on only five screens. During its second week of business in the United States its distribution had widened to ninety-four screens and improved its ranking to 13th place, earning nearly $780,000. And whatever its box-office life span, it will no doubt be destined to live on forever in the World Civilization classrooms of America. Count on that.

James M. Welsh

CREDITS

Temudjin: Tadanobu Asano
Jamukha: Honglei Sun
Börte: Khulan Chuluun
Young Temudjin: Odnyam Odsuren
Young Jamukha: Amarbold Tuvshinbayar
Young Börte: Bayartsetseg Erdenebat
Esugei: Ba Sen
Origin: Kazakhstan
Released: 2007
Production: Sergei Bodrov, Sergei Selyanov, Anton Melnik; CTB Film Co., Andreevskiy Flag Co.; released by Picturehouse
Directed by: Sergei Bodrov
Written by: Sergei Bodrov, Arif Aliyev
Cinematography by: Sergei Trofimov, Rogier Stoffers
Music by: Tuomas Kantelinen
Sound: Bruno Tarrière, Maxim Belovolov
Editing: Zach Staenberg, Valdís Óskarsdóttir
Costumes: Karin Lohr
Production Design: Dashi Namdakov
MPAA rating: R
Running time: 120 minutes

REVIEWS

Boston Globe Online. June 20, 2008.
Chicago Sun-Times Online. June 20, 2008.
Entertainment Weekly Online. June 6, 2008.
Hollywood Reporter Online. June 9, 2008.
New York Times Online. June 6, 2008.
San Francisco Chronicle. June 20, 2008, p. E5.
Variety Online. September 17, 2007.
Washington Post. June 20, 2008, p. C1.

QUOTES

Jamukha: "Don't tell anyone we went to war over a woman."

TRIVIA

Some locations were so remote that roads had to be built to access them.

THE MUMMY: TOMB OF THE DRAGON EMPEROR

A new evil awakens.
—Movie tagline

Box Office: $102.4 million

Stephen Sommers's *The Mummy* (1999) and *The Mummy Returns* (2001) could be called derivative, lesser versions of what Steven Spielberg and George Lucas accomplished with the original *Indiana Jones* trilogy. Like Harrison Ford's iconic creation, Brendan Fraser's Rick O'Connell solves history's mysteries with a wisecracking, adventurous attitude. With his partner in action and love, Evey (Rachel Weisz), by his side, O'Connell defeated the legendary High Priest Imhotep not once, but twice. The O'Connells may have failed to live up to the legendary creations that inspired them—including dozens of heroes from movie serials that gave creative birth to Indy himself—but they were affable centerpieces for escapist fare that it now appears will play in perpetuity on basic cable. After winning an Oscar® for *The Constant Gardener* (2005), Weisz left the *Mummy* franchise behind and Stephen Sommers decided not to come back for a third film. Even Imhotep decided to sit this one out. The very talented Maria Bello stepped into Weisz's undead-killing shoes and Rob Cohen (*xXx* [2002], *Stealth* [2005]) took over directorial duties. The major changes should have worried fans of the franchise, but even the most vitriolic *Mummy* critic could not have been prepared for the complete disaster that is *The Mummy: Tomb of the Dragon Emperor,* a film that will be remembered for being one of the worst sequels of all time, assuming that it is remembered at all.

Tomb of the Dragon Emperor opens with one of the longest prologues in movie history, as narrator Michelle Yeoh sets up the legendary character of the forgettable title. The great and underutilized Yeoh plays Zi Yuan, a witch whom the notorious Han Emperor (Jet Li) turned to in a quest for immortality. The Emperor's lust for power was too much for one lifetime, so he instructed Zi Yuan to cast a spell that would allow him to live forever. A pesky love triangle between the Emperor, Zi Yuan, and the Emperor's general led to dissension and death, forcing the witch to curse the Emperor with a spell that froze him and his army in stone forever.

Two thousand years later the notorious, adventure-seeking O'Connells (Brendan Fraser and Maria Bello) have retired, leaving their son Alex (Luke Ford) to do the digging on his own. Alex happens to be looking for the tomb of the Han Emperor in China, while Rick and Evey are asked to transport a legendary jewel called the Eye of Shangri-La to Shanghai. Of course, the jewel plays a major role in the awakening of the Han Emperor, who knows that if he can lead his awakened army across the Great Wall of China then they will live forever. After the Eye brings the Dragon Emperor back to fire-shooting life, the reunited O'Connells—along with, from the first two films, John Hannah as Evey's brother, and a love interest for young Alex in the spunky young warrior Lin (Isabella Leong)—must search for the mysterious

Shangri-La, where only the woman who once brought the murderous leader to his knees could possibly do so again.

Fraser slides back into his role with ease, but everyone around him looks uncomfortable at best. Ford is laughably bad, and his romantic subplot with Leong features some of the least interesting romantic chemistry in the history of the genre. The fact that Ford appears to be playing a game of pick-the-accent, going with Boston one day and British the next, does not help his stilted, horrible performance. And the lovely and talented Maria Bello nearly matches him. Weisz and Bello may be equally talented actresses, but the idea that they could play the exact same character was naive. There is a spunky adventurer quality that Weisz brought to the first two *Mummy* films that Bello simply looks awkward trying to recreate. And her British accent is one for acting classes to examine as a cautionary tale.

The laughable acting and the borderline incoherent storyline in *Tomb of the Dragon Emperor* (at one point, Yetis appear out of nowhere, and at another, the Emperor starts shape-shifting merely to show off the film's special effects budget) would be more tolerable if the action sequences—the true bread and butter of a slice of summer escapism like this—were even halfway decent. Cohen fails to deliver a single memorable special effect or action scene with any visceral impact. The waste of money on display is more remarkable than any of the poorly edited fight scenes or armies of the undead. When Rick and the Emperor finally go mano-à-mano, what is truly stunning is the lack of dramatic weight or even moviemaking glee usually found in a summer action movie. Even in pure escapism, the audience needs some reason to care who live, who dies, and who stays undead.

Brian Tallerico

CREDITS

Rick O'Connell: Brendan Fraser
The Emperor: Jet Li
Evelyn O'Connell: Maria Bello
Alex O'Connell: Luke Ford
Jonathan Carnahan: John Hannah
Zi Yuan: Michelle Yeoh
Lin: Isabella Leong
General Yang: Chau Sang Anthony Wong
Maguire: Liam Cunningham
Ming Guo: Russell Wong
Origin: USA
Language: English
Released: 2008

Production: Sean Daniel, James Jacks, Stephen Sommers, Bob Ducsay; Relativity Media, Alphaville; released by Universal
Directed by: Rob Cohen
Written by: Alfred Gough, Miles Millar
Cinematography by: Simon Duggan
Music by: Randy Edelman
Sound: Louis Marion
Editing: Joel Negron, Kelly Matsumoto
Art Direction: Isabelle Guay
Costumes: Sanja Milkovic Hays
Production Design: Nigel Phelps
MPAA rating: PG-13
Running time: 114 minutes

REVIEWS

Boston Globe Online. August 1, 2008.
Chicago Sun-Times Online. July 31, 2008.
Entertainment Weekly Online. July 30, 2008.
Hollywood Reporter Online. July 30, 2008.
Los Angeles Times Online. August 1, 2008.
New York Times Online. August 1, 2008.
San Francisco Chronicle. July 31, 2008, p. E1.
Time Online. August 1, 2008.
Variety Online. July 30, 2008.
Washington Post Online. August 1, 2008.

QUOTES

Jonathan Carnahan: "I hate mummies. They never play fair."

TRIVIA

Brendan Fraser and John Hannah are the only two actors to appear in all three films in the Mummy series.

MY BEST FRIEND'S GIRL

It's funny what love can make you do.
  —Movie tagline

Box Office: $19.2 million

My Best Friend's Girl is a typical chick flick of the romantic comedy variety, but doused with an extra added portion of crudeness to appeal to the guy set. Directed by Howard Deutch and written by Jordan Cahan, the unlikely but somewhat endearing story is centered on a love triangle consisting of Sherman "Tank" Turner (Dane Cook)—an outward lout with a suppressed soft-hearted inner nature—nice guy Dustin (Jason Biggs)—Tank's best friend and roommate—and the smart, beautiful, and classy Alexis (Kate Hudson), who Dustin works with and adores. Presenting a twist on the old adage "the good guy always gets the girl," *My*

Best Friend's Girl keeps the audience guessing as to which good guy—if either—will eventually win. Although a little on the long side at nearly two hours, the film is nevertheless entertaining so long as a person is not bothered by explicit sexual humor or the oversimplification of plot and character that comes with a happy and convenient Hollywood ending.

Pining over the same girl are twenty-somethings Tank and Dustin. Their parents were friends since before the two were born, but though they grew up like cousins, they could not be more different. Hard-working Dustin is sweet and serious, while the slacker, foul-mouthed Tank shows no ambition but to kick back at an easy call-center job by day and make extra money at night through his dubious side profession: Jilted boyfriends hire him to get their ex-girlfriends to come back to them by taking the unsuspecting women out on what is guaranteed to be the worst dates of their lives. First, he arranges a chance encounter so that he can act charming and ask the female victim out on a date. After picking her up hours late, he suddenly acts like the biggest, most unrelenting and uncouth jerk on the planet. By the time the dreadful evening is finally over, the woman is so traumatized that she is ready to go running back to the safety of her old boyfriend—a saint in comparison.

The movie opens with a heated argument between Tank and his date, Rachel (Diora Baird), at her doorstep. Furious at his continuing sexual advances, she recounts for him in flashback the ten most amusingly awful moments of the night, everything from Tank choosing a disgustingly dirty restaurant with a menacingly rude waiter, to getting drunk, speaking lewdly, urinating in a potted plant, and more. This behavior establishes his character as a women's worst nightmare and a moron of the highest order, but glimmers of his real self eventually shine through in his battle of conscience over preserving his friendship with Dustin and dealing with irrepressible feelings for his best friend's girl.

Dustin, who is cute and harmless, lacks all of Tank's confidence and swagger. Against Tank's advice, he clumsily tells Alexis that he loves her after only five weeks of casually seeing each other outside of work. To his dismay, she rebuffs his affection and insists that she just wants to be friends and to get more life experience dating other people. An earlier sequence between Alexis and her roommate and confidant Ami (Lizzy Caplan) reveals that the precocious beauty has slept with only two men. Although heartbroken, Dustin tries to take the setback in stride and refuses Tank's initial offer to take out Alexis and give her some of his infamous ill treatment. After seeing her flirt with another coworker, however, he changes his mind and hires the anti-Romeo to work his dark magic. Of course, nothing goes accord-

ing to plan, and Alexis proves to be a feisty and formidable match for the master manipulator. Although Tank is in fine form, Alexis is drunk and determined to ignore his bad behavior in order to experience a raunchy and impersonal fling for the first time in her life. To her frustration, however, he drops her off at home and drives away, already feeling conflicted over his attraction to her and his loyalty to Dustin.

Still desperate to win over Alexis, Dustin sends her a bouquet of roses and a poem in Tank's name, hoping to trick him into going out on second date with her. A hilarious scene ensues in which she calls Tank at work to chastise him for not having sex with her. Only, she is mistaken for a dissatisfied air filtration customer and put on speakerphone to air her grievances in front of an entire training class that Tank is leading. Soon enough, the two are unable to fight the obvious chemistry between them, and their disastrous first date ends up morphing into a relationship based on regular casual sex. The deception puts the lifelong friendship of Dustin and Tank to the ultimate test, and once Dustin discovers what is going on, he sends Tank packing. Distraught and torn, our tragic hero is forced to move in with his womanizing father, Professor Turner (Alec Baldwin), a lecherous feminist studies college instructor who waxes sentimental over his ex-wife, Tank's mother, while also apparently unable to control his most vile thoughts and urges.

The predictable resolution of *My Best Friend's Girl* comes several months after an uncomfortably raucous but funny sequence in which Tank, fueled by the belief that Dustin is the one who truly deserves Alexis, intentionally disrupts and ruins her sister's wedding. In a stroke of comedic coincidence, the bride turns out to be the same outraged woman that Tank was hired to take out at the start of the film. Uninvited, Dustin, who has dutifully remained friends with Alexis, also shows up drunk to the wedding. Several more twists and turns add amusing but unnecessary length to the light-hearted fare before Tank can finally win back the object of his affection. Having spent an extended amount of time with his dirty-dog father, he has come to realize that he might not be the impenetrable lady-killer he once thought he was. Meanwhile, the friends have reconciled and Dustin has benefited from the mentoring of Professor Turner, managing to find love with Ami, Alexis's roommate, whose penchant for sex toys is worthily matched by his own collection of pornographic DVDs.

Jaye Furlonger

CREDITS
Alexis: Kate Hudson
Tank: Dane Cook

Dustin: Jason Biggs
Ami: Lizzy Caplan
Professor Turner: Alec Baldwin
Craig: Nate Torrence
Rachel: Diora Baird
Colleen: Jenny Mollen
Hilary: Riki Lindhome
Josh: Taran Killam
Laney: Kate Albrecht
Carly: Amanda Brooks
Lizzy: Mini Anden
Merrilee: Faye Grant
Origin: USA
Language: English
Released: 2008
Production: Adam Herz, Greg Lessans, Josh Shader; New Wave Entertainment, Superfinger Entertainment, Terra Firma Films, Management 360; released by Lionsgate
Directed by: Howard Deutch
Written by: Jordan Cahan
Cinematography by: Jack N. Green
Music by: John Debney
Sound: Edward Tise
Music Supervisor: Jay Faires
Editing: Seth Flaum
Production Design: Jane Ann Stewart
Art Direction: T. K. Kirkpatrick
Costumes: Marilyn Vance
MPAA rating: R
Running time: 101 minutes

REVIEWS

Boston Globe Online. September 20, 2008.
Entertainment Weekly Online. September 19, 2008.
Hollywood Reporter Online. September 19, 2008.
New York Times Online. September 20, 2008.
Variety Online. September 19, 2008.

QUOTES

Professor Turner: "The truth will set you free but before it does, itcss gonna piss you off!"

AWARDS

Nomination:

Golden Raspberries 2008: Worst Actress (Hudson).

MY BLUEBERRY NIGHTS

How do you say goodbye to someone you can't imagine living without?
—Movie tagline

With such films as *In the Mood for Love* (2000) and *2046* (2004), Hong Kong director Wong Kar-wai has established himself as one of the world's most acclaimed and popular filmmakers. Fans of his sultry, stylized romances and crime films have looked forward to his expanding his horizons. *My Blueberry Nights,* his first English-language film, unfortunately does little to advance his reputation.

Elizabeth (Norah Jones) and Jeremy (Jude Law) meet when she comes to his Brooklyn café looking for the man who has jilted her. She leaves the keys to her former lover's apartment in case he returns to the café. Elizabeth returns each night to see if the keys are still there, and discovers that Jeremy has a collection of such keys and that he is also nursing a broken heart. They commiserate with each other until she decides to seek solace by heading west.

Working in a Memphis bar, Elizabeth meets someone even more miserable than she is. Arnie (David Strathairn) has become an alcoholic since he was dumped by his much younger wife, Sue Lynne (Rachel Weisz). Arnie, a policeman, has given up drinking several times, only to be overwhelmed by self-pity. When Sue Lynne appears in the bar with a new lover, melodrama ensues.

Elizabeth then makes her way to a Reno casino and becomes friends with professional poker player Leslie (Natalie Portman). Quickly spotting Elizabeth's gullible goodness, Leslie manipulates the waitress into staking her. Leslie's secret turns out to be her love-hate relationship with the man who made her a gambler, her father. After seeing how Arnie, Sue Lynne, and Leslie have punished themselves in the name of love, Elizabeth returns to Jeremy's café.

The Brooklyn portions of *My Blueberry Nights* are most like Wong's earlier films, owing a considerable debt to the relationship between the lovelorn policeman and the waitress in *Chungking Express* (1994). These scenes also recall the tentative development of intimacy between the protagonists of *In the Mood for Love* and demonstrate Wong's indirect approach to romance. Elizabeth and Jeremy are not sure who they are and what they want until they begin sharing their disappointments. In contrast, the Memphis sequence is tedious and painful, its characters slurring clichés out of a bad country-and-western song. The Nevada portion of *My Blueberry Nights* is at least not depressing, though it seems rather pointless.

One of the many problems with *My Blueberry Nights* is the odd selection of Lawrence Block as Wong's cowriter. Block is one of America's best crime writers, the creator of the comic burglar-turned-bookseller series featuring Bernie Rhodenbarr and the far grittier Matt

Scudder series about a reformed-alcoholic ex-police detective. Block knows the New York crime scene thoroughly, but romantic entanglements are not prominent in his fiction. He can write hardboiled or funny dialogue, but he does not handle aching sincerity as well.

The dialogue in *My Blueberry Nights* is too often forced and stilted, like a bad translation, placing an undue burden on the actors, especially the novice Jones, the young jazz singer making her acting debut. Jones, whose singing can be heard on the soundtrack along with well chosen songs by Ruth Brown, Otis Redding, Amos Lee, Cassandra Wilson, and Cat Power (who appears briefly as Jeremy's lost love under her real name, Chan Marshall), fares much better when called upon to respond to the actions of others than when Elizabeth is at the center of a scene. Strathairn has made a career of playing weak, flawed men, yet his Arnie is too maudlin, the actor seeming almost embarrassed by the character's desperate behavior. Weisz overacts as the blowsy Southern belle. It is difficult to determine if the resemblance between Jones and Weisz is deliberate on Wong's part or merely chance. If deliberate, Sue Lynne is what Elizabeth is in danger of becoming. Portman gives Leslie an appealing cockiness while playing cards but suffers from the bad writing in her scenes with Jones. Only Law acquits himself well, realizing that Jones needs all the help she can get and generously coaxing an almost good performance from the singer, effacing himself to make her look good. The film's energy perks up whenever Jeremy is on the screen.

As flawed as it is, *My Blueberry Nights* at least looks like a Wong film, despite the director's estrangement from Christopher Doyle, his longtime cinematographer. Like Doyle, Darius Khondji bathes the film in a mixture of neon colors and more somber greens and reds. The palette of Khondji, best known for *Seven* (1995), changes from the cold nighttime colors of Brooklyn to the more gaudy hues of the Memphis bars to the subdued daylight of Nevada. Wong also repeats some of his favorite visual tropes, as with a poetically framed shot of a rooftop out of *2046*.

As an acclaimed director's venture into a new language and environment, *My Blueberry Nights* is not an embarrassment comparable with Ingmar Bergman's *The Touch* (1971) or Michelangelo Antonioni's *Zabriskie Point* (1970). It has sufficient visual flair and moves along fairly smoothly—with the notable exception of the Memphis segment—but it remains a major disap-

pointment because of the high quality of Wong's previous films.

Michael Adams

CREDITS

Jeremy: Jude Law
Arnie: David Strathairn
Sue Lynne: Rachel Weisz
Leslie: Natalie Portman
Elizabeth: Norah Jones
Katya: Chan Marshall
Origin: France, Hong Kong
Language: English
Released: 2007
Production: Wang Wei, Wong Kar-wai, Jean-Louis Piel, Stéphane Kooshmanian, Jack Pan Yee Wah; Block 2 Pictures Inc., Jet Tone Films, StudioCanal; released by Weinstein Company
Directed by: Wong Kar-wai
Written by: Lawrence Block, Wong Kar-wai
Cinematography by: Darius Khondji
Music by: Ry Cooder
Sound: Drew Kunin, Lee Orloff
Editing: William Chang
Costumes: Sharon Globerson
Production Design: William Chang
MPAA rating: PG-13
Running time: 90 minutes

REVIEWS

Entertainment Weekly Online. April 2, 2008.
Hollywood Reporter Online. May 17, 2007.
Los Angeles Times Online. April 4, 2008.
New York Times Online. April 4, 2008.
Premiere Online. March 31, 2008.
Variety Online. May 16, 2007.
Village Voice Online. April 1, 2008.
Wall Street Journal Online. April 4, 2008.

QUOTES

Jeremy: "There's nothing wrong with the Blueberry Pie, just people make other choices. You can't blame the Blueberry Pie, it's just...no one wants it."

TRIVIA

Neither Norah Jones or the director are fans of blueberry pie.

N

NEVER BACK DOWN

Box Office: $24.8 million

Never Back Down has more of an air of inevitability than any other film released in 2008. With the growing popularity of MMA (Mixed Martial Arts) and teen series like *Gossip Girl* and *The Hills,* it was merely a matter of time before a film blended the world of *The O.C.* and with the latest trend in competitive fighting. If director Jeff Wadlow and writer Chris Hauty had not made *Never Back Down,* it is very likely that someone else would have. The derivative nature of *Never Back Down* drags the entire project into a realm of familiarity that never quite allows the film to justify its existence as art, entertainment, or after-school special. It feels more like an obligation for everyone involved than a passion project and, even with that in mind, Wadlow and Hauty still make several crucial mistakes that result in them losing the movie match.

The charismatic Sean Faris stars in *Never Back Down* as the rebellious Jake Tyler, a kid who takes out too much of his aggression on the football field. Jake's anger management issues come at least partially from the fact that his father died in a drunk-driving accident while the poor young man was in the passenger seat. Tyler blames himself for not taking the keys from his intoxicated loved one, and feels partially responsible for the well-being of his loving mother Margot (Leslie Hope) and tennis prodigy younger brother Charlie (Wyatt Smith). In the opening scenes, Jake gets into an all-out brawl with most of the players on a football field and the family moves to Florida to give him a change of scenery and to allow his kid brother to compete on the junior tennis circuit. In the YouTube era, mistakes from the Midwest have a way of finding their way to the South, and a viral video of Jake's on-field antics follows the Tyler family. Jake gets essentially forced into the world of street fighting after the modern version of the high school bullies realize that to maintain their street credibility they will have to take down the new toughest kid in town.

Jake starts to fall for the prettiest girl at school, the hilariously named Baja Miller (Amber Heard), so he naturally jumps at the opportunity to go to a house party that he knows she will attend. When he gets there, poor Jake discovers that the whole affair has essentially been set up to introduce Tyler to the world of MMA by way of a public beating by the big star in town, Ryan McCarthy (Cam Gigandet), who also happens to be Baja's beau. To pick himself up off the mat both socially and physically, Jake turns to the MMA fighting school run by Jean Roqua (Djimon Hounsou), a legendary fighter who trains the young athlete how to use his fists and feet to fight and, more importantly, when to walk away. Roqua teaches that a fighter should offer a killer roundhouse kick only in the protection of loved ones or for his own safety, which, as in any inspirational sports movie, becomes a part of the inevitable climax of *Never Back Down.*

Like a lot of hardcore fighting fans, *Never Back Down* takes itself so seriously that it quickly borders on laughable. The ensemble, especially Oscar® nominee Hounsou and gorgeous newcomer Heard, are always interesting, but writer Hauty and director Wadlow make the mistake of treating every single scene of their film like it is a matter of life and death for everyone involved.

Faris has an easy-going screen presence that could help make him a star someday, but *Never Back Down* is very unlikely to offer much to anyone outside of the hard-core fighting audience. The intensity of the proceedings might have worked in a realistic film, but the music video sheen supplied by Wadlow drains the film of any element of realism, which makes the unceasing urgency of Hounsou, Faris, and the screenplay as a whole feel overblown. While the cast is playing the piece like every action is the most important of these character's lives, the quick-cut editing and music montages make emotional connection an impossibility. *Never Back Down* had a chance to work as *Karate Kid*-esque escapism with a little motivational message thrown in for good measure, but instead it is all message, as if MMA is the only way to save a troubled teen. The whole affair is about as subtle as a swift kick to the head.

Brian Tallerico

CREDITS

Jake Tyler: Sean Faris
Baja Miller: Amber Heard
Jean Roqua: Djimon Hounsou
Margot Tyler: Leslie Hope
Ryan McCarthy: Cam Gigandet
Max Cooperman: Evan Peters
Charlie Tyler: Wyatt Smith
Origin: USA
Language: English
Released: 2008
Production: Craig Baumgarten, David A. Zelon; Mandalay Independent Pictures, BMP; released by Summit Entertainment
Directed by: Jeff Wadlow
Written by: Chris Hauty
Cinematography by: Lukas Ettlin
Music by: Michael Wandmacher
Sound: Thomas Allen
Music Supervisor: Julianne Jordan
Editing: Victor Dubois, Debra Weinfeld
Art Direction: Andrew White
Costumes: Judy Ruskin Howell
Production Design: Ida Random
MPAA rating: PG-13
Running time: 110 minutes

REVIEWS

Boston Globe Online. March 14, 2008.
Hollywood Reporter Online. March 14, 2008.
Los Angeles Times Online. March 14, 2008.
New York Times Online. March 14, 2008.
San Francisco Chronicle. March 14, 2008, p. E6.
Variety Online. March 13, 2008.
Village Voice Online. March 11, 2008.
Washington Post Online. March 14, 2008.

QUOTES

Baja Miller: "The only time you're happy is when you're hurting people."

NICK & NORAH'S INFINITE PLAYLIST

Box Office: $31.4 million

Michael Cera and Kat Dennings, two of the best young actors of their generation, add a dimensionality to the mostly charming *Nick & Norah's Infinite Playlist* that is almost always missing from the genre of the teen comedy, bringing a little magic to a romantic night on the town that can barely keep up with their vibrant, excellent performances. Cribbing heavily from the playbook of John Hughes and early Cameron Crowe, Peter Sollet's sweet film succeeds by refusing to talk down to its audience or portray its young characters as idiots. Despite what Hollywood would have you believe, not every young person is obsessed with the pursuit of sex and booze, and *Nick & Norah's Infinite Playlist* works because it treats its cast and audience with respect, (mostly) eschewing gross-out humor in favor of jokes based on relatable, human behavior. Despite a few weakly written roles in the supporting cast, the title characters in *Nick & Norah's Infinite Playlist* develop in a way almost unheard of in the teen movie genre—they feel genuine.

Nick O'Leary (Michael Cera) is a romantic bass player who has recently been dumped by his over-the-top, slutty ex-girlfriend Tris (Alexis Dziena) on his "b-day," and is dragged out of his lovelorn doldrums for a performance by his bandmates in the Jerk-Offs, Thom (Aaron Yoo) and Dev (Rafi Gavron). Into the club that the Jerk-Offs is playing come Norah Silverberg (Kat Dennings) and her best friend Caroline (Ari Graynor). The two girls go to school with and loathe the materialistic Tris, and every time the stuck-up princess throws out one of Nick's mix CDs Norah saves it from the trashcan. She has secretly formed a connection with the music-loving young man without the two ever having met. It is only a matter of time before they fall in love.

Nick and Norah turn out to have more than just their taste in music in common. They are both incredibly sweet people, both dealing with obnoxious exes

(Norah's is played by the great Jay Baruchel), both have codependent friends, and both adore the band Where's Fluffy, who happen to be playing a secret show somewhere in New York City that very night, the location of which is communicated through text messages and scribbling on bathroom walls. Nick and his bandmate friends and Norah and her dangerously drunk gal pal head out for a night in Manhattan in search of their favorite band, closure with their exes, and maybe even true love.

Nick & Norah's Infinite Playlist plays like a good pop song. It may be catchy and sweet, but if you look too closely, it threatens to fall apart before your eyes. There is so little to Lorene Scafaria's screenplay of *Nick & Norah's Infinite Playlist* (based on the book by David Levithan and Rachel Cohn) that almost all of the success or failure of the film falls on the shoulders of the young cast. If there had been one more interesting supporting character instead of just a string of distracting cameos (odd choices like Andy Samberg, John Cho, and Kevin Corrigan pop up in one-scene roles) and some pretty two-dimensional best friend and evil ex characters, *Nick & Norah's Infinite Playlist* might have become an instant classic in the romantic comedy genre. It nearly makes it solely because of the great Cera and Dennings, but the overall product feels more disposable than the best work of John Hughes and Cameron Crowe, two clear inspirations for the film, kind of like a catchy pop tune—enjoyable while it plays, but missing a little weight or gravity to make it truly linger.

What Cera and Dennings bring to *Nick & Norah's Infinite Playlist* is something inarguably essential to the romantic comedy and something that was missing from the vast majority of the genre in 2008—the sensation that these two people are truly falling in love. The film contains the most genuine scene of intimacy that has graced the big screen in years, a moment so heartfelt and genuine that it verges on feeling like a private moment between these two lovely people that we the audience should not even be there to witness. Just having one scene like that in a genre as manipulative and typically fake as the romantic comedy is remarkable enough to recommend *Nick & Norah's Infinite Playlist,* a film that finds magic in two excellent performances from a pair of young stars who bring depth and believability to everything they touch.

Brian Tallerico

CREDITS

Nick: Michael Cera
Norah: Kat Dennings
Tris: Alexis Dziena

Thom: Aaron Yoo
Dev: Rafi Gavron
Caroline: Ari Graynor
Tal: Jay Baruchel
Gary: Zachary Booth
Origin: USA
Language: English
Released: 2008
Production: Chris Weitz, Paul Weitz, Andrew Miano, Kerry Kohansky; Depth of Field, Mandate Pictures, Columbia Pictures; released by Sony Pictures
Directed by: Peter Sollett
Written by: Lorene Scafaria
Cinematography by: Tom Richmond
Music by: Mark Mothersbaugh
Sound: Damian Canelos
Music Supervisor: Linda Cohen
Editing: Myron Kerstein
Art Direction: Chuck Renaud
Costumes: Sandra Hernandez
Production Design: David Doernberg
MPAA rating: PG-13
Running time: 90 minutes

REVIEWS

Boston Globe Online. October 3, 2008.
Chicago Sun-Times Online. October 2, 2008.
Entertainment Weekly Online. October 1, 2008.
Los Angeles Times Online. October 3, 2008.
New York Times Online. October 3, 2008.
Rolling Stone Online. October 16, 2008.
San Francisco Chronicle. October 3, 2008, p. E1.
Variety Online. September 5, 2008.
Wall Street Journal Online. October 3, 2008.
Washington Post. October 3, 2008, p. C5.

QUOTES

Norah (on Nick's ex-girlfriend): "I could floss with that girl."

TRIVIA

Ari Graynor had to improvise her speech at the Port Authority after Kevin Corrigan decided to not speak during his scene.

NIGHTS IN RODANTHE

It's never too late for a second chance.
—Movie tagline

Box Office: $41.8 million

If saltwater is gushing forth in uncontrollable torrents and the setting is coastal North Carolina, either a storm surge is once again buffeting the Outer Banks or weeping Nicholas Sparks fans are being swept away by yet another of his Tar Heel tearjerkers. *Nights in Rodanthe*, the third feature film to spring from the author's string of bestselling novels, aims to provide viewers with both experiences, but neither its hurricane nor its ill-fated whirlwind romance pack a remarkable punch. As usual, full enjoyment of the Sparks experience likely requires a preponderance of estrogen and a purse full of tissues, and husbands or boyfriends may feel increasingly stuck while watching this "chick flick" as the syrupy dialogue really starts to flow forth. The film aims to make moviegoers nod in lachrymose agreement that it is better to have loved and lost in an especially tragic way than never to have loved at all, but many of both sexes who did find enjoyment here still admitted that all the swoony, clunky-sounding dialogue, contrivances, clichés, and impossible-to-miss foreshadowing had piled up more than the post-hurricane driftwood. Most critics agreed.

This adaptation of Sparks's 2002 unabashedly soggy melodrama, the big screen directorial debut of respected Broadway producer/writer/director George C. Wolfe, does boast some exquisite shots of natural beauty and a degree of spark provided by the latest pairing of Richard Gere and Diane Lane. Here, they adequately but not memorably play wounded characters thrown together by Lady Luck and Mother Nature to share one brief, shining moment of revivifying true love, fortunately without any enticing Frenchmen to cause considerable complications as in their far superior *Unfaithful* (2002). Even before Dr. Paul Flanner (Richard Gere) and Adrienne Willis (Diane Lane) arrive separately at water's edge, they are both clearly and quite appropriately at sea. Adrienne is shown to be a harried but devoted and loving mother of an asthmatic son and a daughter (a lacking Mae Whitman) with a tattooed stomach and a tart mouth. Adrienne races around snatching up unhelpfully strewn clothes while trying to be heard over blaring music and the bickering siblings. Her husband, Jack (Christopher Meloni), who strayed from their marriage with a more youthful alternative, picks up the kids while simultaneously dropping the bombshell that he wants Adrienne to take him back. Her beloved father (about whom she is dreaming in the film's first—and last uncomplicated—moments) has recently died, and so the poor woman is suddenly faced with a pivotal decision about how to proceed while just about running on empty.

Adrienne decides to decompress and digest what Jack has asked of her while running an inn overlooking the Atlantic as a favor to its proprietor, Jean (Viola Davis), her old and close friend. The character of breezy, saucy, single Jean, her words unfiltered and actions unfettered, exists to provide a stark contrast to Adrienne's

conflicted angst, careful deliberation, knotty marital entanglements, and maternal responsibilities that can sometimes weigh and wear one down. Only one of the women has been free to pursue the artistic aspirations of younger days, and a pained (and, one assumes, envious) Adrienne cannot help but wistfully wonder about self-expression and success aborted by a marriage that, depending upon what she decides, may also not live on.

At least equally troubled and adrift is Paul, once an infinitely self-assured, career-obsessed surgical god who has now lost his own marriage, a connection to his doctor son, Mark (James Franco in an unbilled cameo), and a patient whose husband is currently suing him for malpractice. The impressive, chandeliered residence that was once his now belongs to someone else, and he drives off to Rodanthe to speak to the grieving widower whom, out of thoughtlessness and selfish, wounded pride, Paul had failed to meet with after a tragedy that apparently was no one's fault. How fortuitous that, as the film's many contrivances begin, not only has Paul booked a room at Jean's inn while Adrienne is there, but also he just happens to be her only guest.

At least twice it is noted that the hot water takes a little time to burble up through the establishment's pipes, apparently a reassuring signal to viewers to patiently wait for something steamy ahead between the principals. However, as with the inn's plumbing, those anticipating any torrid torrents will be disappointed by *Nights in Rodanthe*. As expected, Paul's initial curt reserve relaxes, frostiness giving way to familiarity as the two talk and relate to each other's tales of marital woe, regrettable communication gaps with offspring, and life's insistence on unexpected and often trying turns. A two shot purposefully unites them during a candlelit dinner. A long shot of the inn at dusk, in which Adrienne and Paul strike similar poses as they stare thoughtfully out at the waves while standing on separate balconies, also visually underscores how mutual understanding, some parallel, concurrent pain, and proximity are leading to the coalescing of this couple.

It is when the strong storm comes that the film truly begins to show its weaknesses. Predictably, Paul, much as he wants to head out of town after a thoroughly unproductive and highly charged encounter with the dead patient's bitter son (Pablo Schreiber), cannot get a flight out before the storm, and responsible Adrienne valiantly stays put, too. Of course, the tumult literally tosses the two into each other's arms for a clinch that leads to a kiss that will lead to more. As expected, meeting Paul has opened Adrienne's eyes wide in astonishment to the possibility of a much happier second act to her life. Not surprisingly, she in turn forces him to realize that crushed widower Torrelson (Scott Glenn) would likely be less litigious if the defensive doctor would drop all his bloodless justifications and finally allow his rigidly concealed but nonetheless sincere sorrow over what happened to show through. As wholly anticipated, the healed duo's relationships with their respective estranged children are eventually repaired. (Adrienne's daughter turns from seething, potent handful to dewy-eyed, repentant helper with unconvincing rapidity.)

In *Nights in Rodanthe*'s march of obvious metaphors, the onslaught is supposed to represent the release of their powerful, pent-up emotions, as well as a cathartic, washing-away of distress. As Adrienne and Paul prepare for the hurricane, giddily lobbing past-date canned goods into the garbage, it is a literal manifestation of the emotional unburdening that has begun, the discarding of what will do no one any good to hang onto any longer. Surely no one will miss the significance of an old inn that, like Adrienne and Paul, has been through a lot but possesses the strength to weather the storm. Also blatantly included is Adrienne's crafting of lovely treasure boxes out of gnarled, highly distressed pieces of driftwood, symbolizing the beautiful metamorphosis each has triggered in the other.

Especially after the rain has subsided, the corny and awkward romantic dialogue begins to fall from the protagonists' lips in earnest. Most trite and cringeworthy in their sentimentality are the letters, read in voiceover, that the two exchange once Paul heads off to remote Ecuador and successfully reconnects with Mark. When he nostalgically recalls from that mountainous region the "peaks and valleys" he had traced along Adrienne's body, and moons (or is it moans?) that "when I write to you, I feel your breath," some will sigh ecstatically and others with eye-rolling exasperation.

Once Adrienne and Paul are overjoyed with each other, it would certainly seem prudent, this being a typically bittersweet Sparks tale, to have an undertaker standing by. However, even those unfamiliar with the author's modus operandi will be fully expecting Paul's demise (this time swept away less happily by an Ecuadorian mudslide) thanks to foreshadowing of the flashing neon light variety. (Also heavy-handed is Jeanine Tesori's score, pumping up emotional moments with swells of overwrought orchestration.) When the doctor parts with his lady love to head off to South America but then suddenly stops his car to dash back for one more lingering embrace, everyone watching will get ready to cross Paul off the list of the living. Earlier on, when Adrienne had told him that the area's wild horses never appear right nearby, he somewhat eerily intones that one day they will. So is anyone's mouth agape along with an overjoyed Adrienne's when a whole herd of them stampede by her on the beach like assuaging equine emissaries from beyond? More than a few viewers might be tempted to

leap atop one of the steeds and head off from *Night in Rodanthe* in search of films with better scripts.

David L. Boxerbaum

CREDITS

Adrienne Willis: Diane Lane
Dr. Paul Flanner: Richard Gere
Mark Flanner: James Franco
Robert Torrelson: Scott Glenn
Jack Willis: Christopher Meloni
Amanda Willis: Mae Whitman
Jean: Viola Davis
Charlie Torrelson: Pablo Schreiber
Danny Willis: Charlie Tahan
Dot: Becky Ann Baker
Origin: USA
Language: English
Released: 2008
Production: Denise Di Novi; Village Roadshow Pictures; released by Warner Bros.
Directed by: George C. Wolfe
Written by: Ann Peacock, John Romano
Cinematography by: Affonso Beato
Music by: Jeanine Tesori
Sound: Susumu Tokunow
Editing: Brian A. Kates
Art Direction: William G. Davis
Costumes: Victoria Farrell
Production Design: Patrizia von Brandenstein
MPAA rating: PG-13
Running time: 96 minutes

REVIEWS

Boston Globe Online. September 26, 2008.
Chicago Sun-Times Online. September 25, 2008.
Entertainment Weekly Online. September 24, 2008.
Hollywood Reporter Online. September 21, 2008.
Los Angeles Times Online. September 26, 2008.
New York Times Online. September 26, 2008.
San Francisco Chronicle. September 26, 2008, p. E7.
Variety Online. September 21, 2008.
Washington Post Online. September 26, 2008.

QUOTES

Adrienne Willis: "Well, you fall in love with someone, you know…and you make a family…and you become what you think you're supposed to be. And you change and you give up certain things. Then they look at what you've got left and you wish you'I don't know, you just think maybe you shouldn't have."

NIM'S ISLAND

Be the hero of your own story.
—Movie tagline

Box Office: $48 million

Nim's Island may have only taken one woman to bring it to the page (author Wendy Orr) but it took four screenwriters, two of whom also directed, and considerable star power to turn it into a feature film. The result is almost the kind of story that an actual preteen girl would write, probably due to the involvement of so many people in the writing process. The end product is a little inconsistent in tone and cluttered with subplots, but its two powerfully talented female stars and genuinely heartfelt themes save it from the crowded bargain bin of kids movies that fall flat. With some editing and more directorial consistency, *Nim's Island* could have been a stronger film, but its failures are not significant enough to take away from what co-writer/directors Mark Levin and Jennifer Flackett do right with their charismatic leads.

Abigail Breslin (*Little Miss Sunshine* [2006], *Definitely Maybe* [2008]) stars as the titular Nim Rusoe (a name that is clearly meant to bring to mind the name of the famous Robinson Crusoe), an intrepid young woman who lives with her scientist father Jack (Gerard Butler) on a gorgeous deserted island. Jack Rusoe searches for new species while Nim dances with her friends that include a sea lion, seagull, and bearded dragon. Luckily, none of the animals talk, although they do dance to the Talking Heads. Nim loves living off the grid and fears very little in her island paradise. She spends her nights reading the adventures of Alex Rover, an intrepid, Indiana Jones-esque hero (also played by Gerard Butler, who proves that he should get an action/adventure role like this soon). But Alex is actually short for Alexandra (Jodie Foster), and the author of these magical tales is an agoraphobic who is often too scared of the world outside of her front door to even get her mail.

One morning, Jack heads out on a seafaring, scientific trip and leaves the increasingly-adult Nim to care for herself. Of course, Jack picks the wrong day to let his daughter be independent, and he gets stranded in the middle of the ocean. After a near-death experience of her own Nim realizes that she might be in some actual mortal danger, and she reaches out via email to the one "man" she thinks can save her, Alex Rover. Nim tries to survive on the island while Jack tries to get home to her and Alexandra conquers her own fears to come to her rescue. Meanwhile, in a subplot that never should have happened, a group of tourists arrive on the island by cruise ship and Nim, thinking that they are pirates meant to take over her land, tries to turn them off the island by hurling lizards at them and getting her sea lion to expel gas nearby. The tourist/pirate subplot feels pulled from another, far inferior movie, and should never have been included in what could have been a far more consistent heartwarmer without it.

The "A plot" of *Nim's Island*—the one that parallels Nim and Alexandra's lessons learned about the risks and rewards of adventure—is heartfelt and completely effective. Foster shows a lighter side that we have not seen in years (since at least 1999's *Anna and the King*, and arguably since 1994's *Maverick*) and Abigail Breslin continues to establish herself as one of the most talented actresses of her generation. It does not feel like a coincidence that Breslin reminds viewers of Foster's work in similar, girl-power-driven films for Disney when she was Abigail's age, and this film almost plays like a passing of the torch from one star to the younger version of herself. *Nim's Island* has a sweet and underplayed girl-power message that blends well with the idea that there is more reward had from leaving the house than from sitting in front of a computer. Foster, Breslin, and Butler bring a humanity and screen presence to their characters that is often missing from movies aimed at kids. All *Nim's Island* needed to become one of the better recent films of its genre would have been a little thematic tightening in the screenplay—the tourist subplot is not only poorly executed but also fails on a continuity level if one considers that it drains the film of tension regarding Nim's survival when dozens of poorly dressed travelers are right there on the beach. But the consistently believable and fun work by Foster and Breslin make all of the flaws of the preproduction of *Nim's Island* much easier to forgive. It may have taken one woman to bring *Nim's Island* to the page and four writers to bring it to the screen, but its success must be credited to its two female stars.

Brian Tallerico

CREDITS

Nim Rusoe: Abigail Breslin
Alexandra Rover: Jodie Foster
Jack Rusoe/Alex Rover: Gerard Butler
Origin: USA
Language: English
Released: 2008
Production: Paula Mazur; Walden Media; released by 20th Century-Fox
Directed by: Marc Levin, Jennifer Flackett
Written by: Marc Levin, Jennifer Flackett, Joseph Kwong, Paula Mazur
Cinematography by: Stuart Dryburgh
Music by: Patrick Doyle
Sound: David Lee
Music Supervisor: Lindsay Fellows
Editing: Stuart Levy
Art Direction: Colin Gibson
Costumes: Jeffrey Kurland

MPAA rating: PG
Running time: 95 minutes

REVIEWS

Boston Globe Online. April 4, 2008.
Chicago Sun-Times Online. April 4, 2008.
Hollywood Reporter Online. April 4, 2008.
Los Angeles Times Online. April 4, 2008.
New York Times Online. April 4, 2008.
San Francisco Chronicle. April 4, 2008, p. E7.

Variety Online. April 3, 2008.
Washington Post Online. April 4, 2008.

QUOTES

Nim Rusoe (to Alexandra): "You came here all the way from San Fransisco and you don't know how to do anything."

TRIVIA

The Australian sea lions who played Selkie in the film are named Spud and Friday and live at Sea World Australia.

O

ONE MISSED CALL

What will it sound like when you die?
—Movie tagline

Box Office: $26.8 million

Much was written in the summer of 2007 about the relative box-office failure of Eli Roth's *Hostel: Part II* putting an end to what had been called the "torture porn" subgenre in the world of horror. The idea that one high-profile flop could put the final nail in the coffin of a critically reviled assembly line of films has led critics to wonder what kind of cinematic disaster audiences will have to endure for the more troublesome and more loathsome type of completely mangled remakes of quality Asian horror films to go the way of Eli Roth's milieu. If the nearly-as-bad *The Eye* (2008) and *Shutter* (2008) had not hit theaters shortly after its release, *One Missed Call* could have been the *Hostel: Part II* of Asian horror remakes. It clearly should have been, as the film fails to work on any single level. With a nonsensical plot, half-asleep performances, and a complete lack of actual scares, *One Missed Call* is so bad it threatens to end not only the Asian horror remake trend, but also the entire genre altogether. Horror fans should be grateful that so few people actually saw the film, much less liked it (it ranked a stunning 0 percent with critics on Rotten Tomatoes), that it failed to register long enough to have an impact.

One Missed Call is debut director Eric Valette's remake of the legendary Takashi Miike's *Chakushin ari* (2003). Like so many horror movie heroines, Bethany Raymond (Shannyn Sossamon) is a very unlucky girl. In *One Missed Call,* she watches as most of her friends

receive cell phone messages of their own voices at the moments of their deaths. The "missed call" messages are date and time-stamped, giving the victims the exact moment that they will be killed in one of those only-in-the-movie ways that is intended to thrill but only serves as a crutch for the writers who think their concept is creepy enough that they need not write any actual scares. Working from a structure similar to that in the *Final Destination* movies, the poor victims of *One Missed Call* are walking time bombs, people who know the times and dates of their deaths but still have no hope of avoiding them.

After each victim of cell-phone horror succumbs to his fate, a red candy is found in his mouth, ostensibly adding to the mystery but actually providing the writers with another plot thread to only vaguely attempt to tie up. Bethany befriends a cop named Jack Andrews (Edward Burns) who also has a family connection to the nightmare holding her friends in its grasp. In the supporting cast, despite being wasted, Ray Wise steals the entire movie just by showing an ounce of life as a television show host trying to profit from the nightmare. There have been a number of bad horror remakes, but very few made with the same general ennui and lack of energy as *One Missed Call.* Sossamon and Burns look half-asleep, and director Valette thinks that all it takes to scare an audience is loud music and a jump-cut. Every action, even one as casual as the handing off an asthma inhaler, is accompanied by pathetic scare tactics that even the most casual horror fan will register as false and manipulative.

One Missed Call joins a festival's worth of American retreads that simply fail to understand that what works in J-horror and its Asian brethren values mood and atmospherics over plot. Films like *Ju-On* (2000), *Ringu* (1998), *Gin gwai* (2002), and the works that were inspired by them emphasize and style over everything else, but the Hollywood machine always tries to turn mood pieces into plot ones and fails. Having said that, the horrible *One Missed Call* is neither a mood piece nor a plot-driven horror film—it has little of either. The screenplay barely tries to explain the ridiculous back story that led to the cell phone messages—something to do with abuse, fire, and some really awful acting—but the movie never gives in to its origins in a genre far more concerned with scares than plots that can be easily recapped. Worst of all, *One Missed Call* is shockingly toothless, barely earning even its PG-13 rating. Even the gore hounds will be bored to tears. *One Missed Call* is the very tail end of a trend, and merely proof as to why it has met its too-late demise.

Brian Tallerico

CREDITS

Beth: Shannyn Sossamon
Jack: Edward Burns
Taylor: Ana Claudia Talancón
Ted: Ray Wise
Leann: Azura Skye
Ray: Jason Beghe
Mickey: Margaret Cho
Shelley: Meagan Good
Origin: Germany, Japan, USA, Great Britain
Language: English
Released: 2008
Production: Broderick Johnson, Andrew A. Kosove, Scott Kroopf, Jennie Lew Tugend, Lauren C. Weissman; Alcon Entertainment, Kadokawa Productions, Equity Pictures Medienfonds GmbH & Co. KG II, Intermedia Films; released by Warner Bros.
Directed by: Eric Valette
Written by: Andrew Klavan
Cinematography by: Glen MacPherson
Music by: Reinhold Heil, Johnny Klimek
Sound: Whit Norris
Music Supervisor: Deva Anderson
Editing: Steve Mirkovich
Art Direction: Christina Wilson
Costumes: Sandra Hernandez
Production Design: Laurence Bennett
MPAA rating: PG-13
Running time: 87 minutes

REVIEWS

Boston Globe Online. January 5, 2008.
Entertainment Weekly Online. January 9, 2008.
Hollywood Reporter Online. January 7, 2008.
New York Times Online. January 5, 2008.
Premiere Online. January 7, 2008.
Variety Online. January 4, 2008.

QUOTES

Leann: "I haven't been sleeping to well."
Beth: "Call me tonight. I'll read you my paper on developmental perspectives in abuse cases. It's better than Ambien."

TRIVIA

Guillermo del Toro was asked to direct the film but declined, choosing to make *Hellboy II: The Golden Army* instead.

THE ORPHANAGE
(El Orfanato)

A tale of love. A story of horror.
—Movie tagline
No secret stays locked away forever.
—Movie tagline

Box Office: $7.1 million

The depths of maternal love—and grief—are at the heart of *The Orphanage* (*El Orfanato*). Though it has moments as eerie, tense, and satisfyingly shiver-inducing as any recent horror movie, goosing or grossing out the audience is clearly not what director Juan Antonio Bayona and writer Sergio Sánchez had in mind. They are more interested in exploring what happens when the horror of the truth is greater than that of the unknown.

Laura Sanchez (Belén Rueda) returns to Shepherd Orphanage, the seaside home where she lived until she was adopted. With her doctor husband, Carlos (Fernando Cayo), she plans to reopen the orphanage, this time as a home for disabled children.

At first, Laura is happy to be back—unlike the childhoods endured by most cinematic orphans, hers was not filled with misery. She and Carlos focus most of their concern on their HIV-positive adopted son, Simón (Roger Príncep). Cherubic-faced and inquisitive, Simón appears comfortable playing with his imaginary friends Watson and Pepé in the large house. But when a trip to the coves near the orphanage leads Simón to begin vociferously claiming that he has gained several new friends, the family's serenity is disturbed. And when Simón disappears during a party held to welcome the children who will be moving in, that serenity is shattered.

Six months later, Simón is still missing, and Laura and Carlos are attending a bereavement group, though

Laura finds no comfort in the other grieving parents. She is convinced that her son is alive, taken by the friends he spoke of, and she will try anything to find him. Despite the skepticism of her husband and Pilar (Mabel Rivera), a police psychologist working on the case, Laura consults a medium, Aurora (Geraldine Chaplin, whose high cheekbones and tightly drawn skin make her look spectral even before she is bathed in ghostly light during one of the movie's most terrifying scenes).

Though Carlos leaves the orphanage, unable to continue living there with the memories of Simón and his former happiness, Laura refuses to depart. After she discovers the skeletons of five children—her former playmates at Shepherd—she requests two more days alone before she will rejoin her husband. Then, she prepares to get back her son by calling the ghosts home.

Rueda has a gorgeous, lived-in face, and she throws herself into the role of Laura with no vanity or self-consciousness. When she smashes at a locked door with hands and feet, Laura's yearning to not merely see her son again, but to hold him and to bury her face deep in his hair, is palpable. Regrettably, Cayo is not Rueda's equal in power and passion, though in his defense, he is saddled with the role of the voice of reason.

Guillermo del Toro produced *The Orphanage,* and the influence of *Pan's Labyrinth* (2006) is clear—in the movie's smooth, enthralling unfolding; in Bayona's handling of the child actors; in the way the viewer's perception of everything that has occurred is suddenly shifted near the end. Bayona establishes and sustains a sense of tightly coiled dread, so when there is a burst of blood, it carries a genuine jolt. American horror-film directors overly enamored of gore would do well to watch and learn from him.

Heather L. Hughes

CREDITS

Laura: Belén Rueda
Aurora: Geraldine Chaplin
Pilar: Mabel Rivera
Carlos: Fernando Cayo
Simón: Roger Príncep
Benigna: Montserrat Carulla
Origin: Spain
Language: Spanish
Released: 2007
Production: Joaquín Padró, Mar Targarona, Álvaro Augustín, Guillermo del Toro; Rodar y Rodar, Telecinco; released by Picturehouse
Directed by: Juan Antonio Bayona
Written by: Sergio G. Sánchez

Cinematography by: Óscar Faura
Music by: Fernando Velázquez
Sound: Xavier Mas, Marc Orts
Editing: Elena Ruiz
Art Direction: Iñigo Navarro
Production Design: Josep Rosell
Costumes: Maria Reyes
MPAA rating: R
Running time: 100 minutes

REVIEWS

Boston Globe Online. January 11, 2008.
Chicago Sun-Times Online. December 28, 2007.
Hollywood Reporter Online. December 28, 2007.
Los Angeles Times Online. December 28, 2007.
New York Times Online. December 28, 2007.
New Yorker Online. January 14, 2008.
Newsweek Online. December 24, 2007.
San Francisco Chronicle. December 28, p. E1.
Variety Online. May 21, 2007.
Washington Post. January 4, 2008, p. C6.

TRIVIA

This was Spain's official submission in the Best Foreign Language Film category for the Academy Awards® in 2008.

THE OTHER BOLEYN GIRL

Two sisters divided for the love of a king.
—Movie tagline
The only thing that could come between these sisters…is a kingdom.
—Movie tagline
They were the closest of sisters, until the most powerful man in the world made them rivals.
—Movie tagline

Box Office: $26.8 million

Following several recent successful television productions about the reigns of Henry VIII and Elizabeth I, as well as one excellent film, *Elizabeth* (1998), there was no reason to suspect that yet another examination of the tempestuous Tudor dynasty would not also succeed. Unfortunately, *The Other Boleyn Girl* is a stilted exercise.

Based on Philippa Gregory's popular 2001 novel, the film ostensibly looks at Mary Boleyn (Scarlett Johansson), who has an affair with Henry VIII (Eric Bana) before he falls in love with her sister, Anne (Natalie Portman). While Anne Boleyn's story is one of the most famous in history because of its religious and political ramifications, particularly England's break with the Catholic Church, which refused to approve the king's divorce from Katherine of Aragon (Ana Torrent), her sister's is less well known. Mary catches Henry's eye at court, and he asks her father, Sir Thomas Boleyn (Mark Rylance), to arrange for her to find her way into his bed, despite her recent marriage to William Carey (Benedict Cumberbatch). Boleyn willingly complies, despite the objections of his wife, Lady Elizabeth (Kristin Scott Thomas), because currying the king's favor will help the family gain power and influence.

Initially horrified at the prospect, Mary finds herself grudgingly falling in love with the king. In fiction a new development would complicate matters further, and this is just what happened in real life. Henry spots Anne and dumps Mary for her slightly younger sister. Anne finds herself as conflicted Mary has been, but she, too, falls in love. Yet Anne refuses to share the king's bed before marriage, launching one of history's most bittersweet love stories.

With such potential for compelling drama, how *The Other Boleyn Girl* fails is due, in part, to the actors. Henry VIII is one of the most notoriously lusty figures of all time, yet the badly cast Bana plays him with purse-lipped petulance. When contemplating the enormous consequences of his break with the church, Henry merely seems constipated. David Morrissey is one of the best English actors when he is on television, yet he rarely fares well in films. As the Duke of Norfolk, Anne's ambitious, treacherous uncle, Morrissey is stiff and uncomfortable, and saddled with a distractingly bad wig. Johansson has done well in period pieces previously, notably the splendid *Girl with a Pearl Earring* (2003), but she seems adrift here, never quite finding the range of emotions the role calls for. Portman displays a greater range without making Anne especially sympathetic or interesting.

Johansson and Portman apparently were cast not despite their quite modern looks but because of them, the better to appeal to contemporary sensibilities. This approach may help account for the peevish impetuousness of their characters, resulting in the film seeming at times like an episode of "Sex in the Renaissance." Anne wears a necklace sporting the letter B. Even in the unlikely event that such is historically accurate, it makes her seem more like Carrie Bradshaw than the queen of England. It is even less likely that she would continue wearing the ugly, distracting necklace after her marriage. The only credible performance in *The Other Boleyn Girl* comes from Scott Thomas, who also plays Johansson's mother in *The Horse Whisperer* (1998). Only her Lady Elizabeth carries any moral authority.

The Other Boleyn Girl is disappointing because of the pedigree of its makers. Justin Chadwick, making his first feature after several television films and miniseries, directed the highly acclaimed *Bleak House* (2004). While Chadwick adeptly captures the intimacy and emotionality of Charles Dickens's novel, in *The Other Boleyn Girl* he appears more interested in spectacle, relishing the splendor of the accoutrements in Henry's court, shooting the pageantry of processions from overhead. The money spent on *The Other Boleyn Girl* is all too visible.

The most disheartening aspect of the film is that it was written by Peter Morgan, screenwriter of *The Last King of Scotland* (2006) and *The Queen* (2006). In his films, television plays such as *The Deal,* and plays such as *Frost/Nixon* (2007), Morgan has shown himself to be a master at exploring the ambiguities of power and politics. With *The Other Boleyn Girl,* however, he seems more concerned with hitting all the main plot points, paying little attention to theme. Henry's conflict with Katherine is gone in the blink of an eye. Despite the title, more attention is paid to Anne, leaving Mary to respond primarily to the ups and downs of her sister's turbulent life. The half-heartedness of the filmmaking is displayed in its emulation of the ending of the boring but better acted *Anne of the Thousand Days* (1969).

The problem is not that Morgan is out of his depth with the Renaissance. He also wrote the television film *Henry VIII* (2003), which conveyed the passion and historical sweep missing from *The Other Boleyn Girl* and offered, in Ray Winstone, arguably the most complex interpretation ever of the monarch. There is nothing particularly wrong with Morgan and Chadwick's "Sex in the Renaissance" approach either. It works in Showtime's over-the-top *The Tudors* (begun in 2007). Despite frequent historical inaccuracies, such as Henry's rippled abdomen, *The Tudors* is at least lively and entertaining.

The film is not even the best version of Gregory's novel. It was adapted for television in 2003 with a much lower budget, requiring writer-director Philippa Lowthorpe to make do with fewer costumes and use shadowy lighting to disguise the modest sets. More importantly, Jodhi May as Anne, Natascha McElhone as Mary, and, especially, Jared Harris as Henry gave much more fully realized performances, capturing the anguish, self-doubt, and self-disgust of the characters—everything missing from this bloated big-screen version.

Michael Adams

CREDITS
King Henry VIII: Eric Bana
Anne Boleyn: Natalie Portman

Mary Boleyn: Scarlett Johansson
Duke of Norfolk: David Morrissey
Sir Thomas Boleyn: Mark Rylance
George Boleyn: Jim Sturgess
William Stafford: Eddie Redmayne
William Carey: Benedict Cumberbatch
Katherine of Aragon: Ana Torrent
Jane Parker: Juno Temple
Henry Percy: Oliver Coleman
Lady Elizabeth Boleyn: Kristin Scott Thomas
Origin: Great Britain, USA
Language: English
Released: 2008
Production: Alison Owen; Ruby Films, Relativity Media, Columbia Pictures, BBC Films; released by Sony Pictures
Directed by: Justin Chadwick
Written by: Peter Morgan
Cinematography by: Kieran McGuigan
Music by: Paul Cantelon
Sound: John Midgley
Editing: Carol Littleton, Paul Knight
Art Direction: David Allday
Costumes: Sandy Powell
Production Design: John Paul Kelly
MPAA rating: PG-13
Running time: 115 minutes

REVIEWS

Boston Globe Online. February 29, 2008.
Chicago Sun-Times Online. February 29, 2008.
Entertainment Weekly Online. February 26, 2008.
Hollywood Reporter Online. February 19, 2008.
Los Angeles Times Online. February 29, 2008.
New York Times Online. February 29, 2008.
Rolling Stone Online. March 20, 2008.
San Francisco Chronicle. February 29, 2008, p. E5.
Variety Online. February 15, 2008.
Wall Street Journal. February 29, 2008, p. W1.
Washington Post. February 29, 2008, p. C1.

QUOTES

Anne Boleyn: "Good Christian people, I am come hither to die, for according to the law, and by the law I am judged to die, and therefore I will speak nothing against it. I am come hither to accuse no man, nor to speak anything of that, whereof I am accused and condemned to die, but I pray God save the king and send him long to reign over you, for a gentler nor a more merciful prince was there never: and to me he was ever a good, a gentle and sovereign lord. And if any person will meddle of my cause, I require them to judge the best. And thus I take my leave of the world and of you all, and I heartily desire you all to pray for me. O Lord have mercy on me, to God I commend my soul."

TRIVIA

The necklace that Anne wears is the same as one worn in the ABC television program *Ugly Betty*.

OVER HER DEAD BODY

Just because she's passed on…doesn't mean she's moving on.
—Movie tagline

Box Office: $7.5 million

Jeff Lowell's *Over Her Dead Body* is a stunningly awful romantic comedy, the kind of film that leaves audiences and critics scratching their heads as to how it ever made it past the preproduction stage, and it should disappear into film history with little fanfare. Films are often torn asunder by an incompetent director, meddling studio, or miscast ensemble. Even some of the most notorious flops in the history of Hollywood have stories of nightmare productions that can somehow excuse the disaster that made it to the big screen. But films like *Over Her Dead Body* are a different kind of awful simply because it is so difficult to figure out how anyone involved ever thought such a mess would come together into a complete film. The script stage, casting, execution, and postproduction must have made clear to at least some of the talent involved that what they had was one of the most shrill, cruel, shockingly unfunny comedies of the last several years. Comedy may be subjective, but movies this bad should have provided some sort of warning sign during the production and it can be only for the almighty dollar that the horrendous final product was even allowed into theaters.

A bizarrely morbid comedy that cannot be called "black" or "dark" because those commonly used terms suggest that a film has some sort of teeth, *Over Her Dead Body* opens with the horrendous death of the about-to-wed Kate (Eva Longoria). In the first of many mistakes made by writer/director Jeff Lowell, the screenplay presents Kate as a shrill, demanding bride, and gives the viewer no reason to care about her passing or any chance to identify with her plight after she is crushed by a giant angel made of ice. Kate's fiancé Henry (Paul Rudd) has difficulty moving on, and his worried sister (Lindsay Sloane) thinks that a psychic named Ashley (Lake Bell) could offer the spiritual reassurance that her sibling needs. Henry's sister even goes so far as to give Ashley the diary that belonged to Kate so she can convince Henry that she can actually communicate with the deceased bride-to-be.

After making clear that no one involved with the film has any idea how real people actually deal with grief, *Over Her Dead Body* turns into an odd combination of romantic comedy, ghost story, and proof that it is really not a "Wonderful Life." Kate returns as the "anti-Clarence," an evil angel on the shoulder of Ashley who is constantly trying to destroy the fake psychic's blooming relationship with her client. Ashley tries to make the supernatural threesome work by thwarting the increasingly embarrassing techniques employed by Kate, including making the poor girl hear voices that send her running half-naked from the gym shower and convincing her that Henry has a flatulence problem. The latter scene may be the most embarrassing for actors involved in any film released in 2008. Kate-created hallucinations continue to pester Ashley, who turns to her friend and business partner Dan (Jason Biggs) for assistance.

Comedies that simply fail to be funny are a certain kind of bad, but ones that go from unfunny to downright unlikable are rare, and *Over Her Dead Body* is undeniably in the latter category. With not a single character, dead or alive, for the audience to root for, the romantic stakes of Lowell's screenplay are nonexistent. Even the sometimes talented cast looks lost in the sea of lackluster jokes and genre clichés. Paul Rudd often excels in this kind of material and he must have jumped at the chance for a major romantic comedy lead, but he has been reduced to an impression of his more annoying techniques as an actor. Lake Bell gets nothing but physical comedy to develop her character and falls victim to the weak screenplay. Even Eva Longoria starts to engender audience sympathy because she is given nothing to work with but ill will and malicious intent in her horrendous character. For a film like this to have a hope of working, the audience needs to be given a reason to care about Kate, Henry, and Ashley, or the writers at least should make the bridezilla from beyond something of an antihero. Lowell never even gave character detail like why Kate would torment an innocent woman, or why Ashley would put it up with it for a schlub of a guy who merits not a second thought. The vicious bride, the emotional guy, the new girl with the pretty smile—everyone in *Over Her Dead Body* is nothing more than a stereotype on paper and grating on the big screen. The title refers to the only way anyone should ever see it.

Brian Tallerico

CREDITS

Kate: Eva Longoria
Henry: Paul Rudd
Ashley: Lake Bell
Dan: Jason Biggs
Chloe: Lindsay Sloane
Sculptor: Stephen Root
Father Marks: William Morgan Sheppard
Origin: USA
Language: English
Released: 2008
Production: Paul Brooks, Peter Safran; Gold Circle Films; released by New Line Cinema
Directed by: Jeff Lowell
Written by: Jeff Lowell
Cinematography by: John Bailey
Music by: David Kitay
Sound: James Tanenbaum
Music Supervisor: Sarah Webster
Editing: Matthew Friedman
Art Direction: Nathan Ogilvie
Costumes: Tracy Tynan
Production Design: Cory Lorenzen
MPAA rating: PG-13
Running time: 95 minutes

REVIEWS

Boston Globe Online. February 1, 2008.
Chicago Sun-Times Online. February 1, 2008.
Hollywood Reporter Online. February 1, 2008.
Los Angeles Times Online. February 1, 2008.
New York Times Online. February 1, 2008.
San Francisco Chronicle. February 1, 2008, p. E5.
Variety Online. January 31, 2008.
Washington Post. February 1, 2008, p. C1.

QUOTES

Ashley: "Sorry, the phone scared me so I killed it."

TRIVIA

Orignal titles for the film included both "How I Met My New Boyfriend's Dead Fiancee" and "Ghost Bitch."

P

PARANOID PARK

Gus Van Sant gets his biggest kudos when his films are most obscure. Such was the case for his breakthrough *Drugstore Cowboy* (1989), a confusing and diffident road trip of a movie that was hailed by some critics as an early indie masterpiece. And certainly that is true for his latest, *Paranoid Park,* a thin movie embroidered by so much art-film pretension that a lot of critics were once again seduced by appearances. But lots of skateboarding footage does not make a movie masterful. If it did, *Paranoid Park* would be a masterpiece.

Adapted by Van Sant from a novel by Blake Nelson, *Paranoid Park* is a slow-moving character study built circuitously around a single bizarre incident of violence. Often there are good reasons for a tale to be told out of chronological order, but here the main reason seems to be that it might fool the viewer into thinking this is a piece of deep art. Much of the film seems like filler, however. We get many scenes of slow-motion skateboarding at the eponymous skate park in Portland, Oregon, sometimes set to murky snippets of soundtracks from the Fellini film *Juliet of the Spirits* (1965).

All this skateboarding represents the culture that the story's protagonist, Alex Tremain (Gabe Nevins), a sixteen-year-old caught in a wrinkle of time, moves through. But he is not really even a skateboarding fanatic, just a wannabe who temporarily has become fascinated by the fact that the park's denizens have worse home lives than he does. His is dominated by the separation and impending divorce of his parents, a situation that is making Alex's thirteen-year-old brother so tense

that he often vomits after his meals. Alex, seemingly, takes it all in stride.

Paranoid Park might be contrasted with the big hit *Juno* (2007). The latter is full of likeable characters, particularly the title girl, who are smart and sassy and whose everyday conversation is ironic, hip, and funny. She triumphs over a major potential disaster in her life, a weird twist of fate, by doing the Right Thing in a big and entertaining way. *Paranoid Park* is populated by mumbling, barely engaged teenagers who can hardly put together a sentence, much less a witty joke. The protagonist stumbles over an equally challenging incident, but fails to do anything right about it except retreat further into his own isolation. Guess which movie is the more true to life?

Van Sant is an expert at sneaking us into this terrifyingly uncommunicative and confusing world of adolescence. He proved how adept he was with the frightening, brave, and extremely credible *Elephant* (2003), an unflinching look at school shootings that did not take sides or drench viewers in moral lessons. In fact, Van Sant has absolutely no interest in morality at all. He is obsessed with a different kind of landscape: what the world looks like from the point of view of the abandoned, obsessed, and unreachable humans who move through it like zombies. And in *Paranoid Park,* he succeeds in that mission largely thanks to the wide-eyed, deer-in-the-headlights, blank-look performance of his lead actor Nevins; it is a rather remarkable performance by an unknown.

With all this skill, Van Sant does not need to show Alex moving in painful slow-motion through school corridors, to drag out the story with experimental-film sequences that look like they were done by sincere amateurs. Van Sant is no amateur (look at his stunning, polished work in *To Die For* (1995) and *Good Will Hunting* (1997) but he mistakenly thinks audiences need his parlor tricks to grasp his point. But they do not: We already know Alex is a lost soul in a lost world, and that he will carry around this secret of a strange night in his youth for his whole life. And that this itself is a fascinating and worthy subject for a small film.

While Van Sant mostly meanders and stumbles around his paranoid, constricted landscape, he does triumph stylistically at times. A shower scene in which the water drips down off Alex's hair while the bathroom wallpaper itself seems to chirp like birds in a rainforest is a remarkable piece of filmmaking. The scene of the tragedy itself is both nauseating and electrifying. And Van Sant's ability to immerse his audience in his protagonist's world, pushing even his parents into shadowy, far-away background figures, is considerable. But the story itself is paltry, and Van Sant confuses economy and directness with art. The characters, and even the central incident of the film, are all underwritten. A key figure in the tragedy simply runs away and disappears not only from the film, but somehow from the calculations of the protagonist. A rescuer appears in the form of a female muse, Macy (Lauren McKinney), and she's a bit too much like an acne-faced Ellen Page—not quite as sassy but preternaturally wise, and too easy a foil for Alex's dumped cheerleader girlfriend, a shallow, grasping sort. With the central tragedy unearthed at last (a security guard is run over and cut in half by a freight train), Van Sant shifts his tone several times, as if experimenting with some form of satire or sex comedy. His refusal to adhere to any conventional arc of storytelling is also not in itself art, and not helpful. His film seems as randomly constructed as the flight of a pinball in a machine (or, and perhaps this is the point, a skateboard), and it is a sure sign of a director who lacks the confidence that the story he is filming has sufficient weight. What results is a character study, compellingly acted and with extremely credible dialogue, that nonetheless lacks character and depth. And that is a pity, because Van Sant is potent when he is not so busy trying to come off as so diffident.

The results are mixed. As a saga of alienated adolescence, *Paranoid Park* is frighteningly real. But the central incident of the story—the answer to Macy's question of what happened to Alex—seems not just random, but completely disconnected from anything else in the movie. Of course, that kind of thing is the center of gravity for a nihilist exercise, and in some circles it proves how weighty the exercise is. But it also could be viewed as mere pretense. Perhaps *Paranoid Park* could most generously be compared to a filmed version of one of

those J.D. Salinger short stories where young protagonists are buffeted by meaningless and incomprehensible events. But that is being way too generous, because Salinger's characters are memorable and complicated, and this film's are mostly blank.

Michael Betzold

CREDITS

Jennifer: Taylor Momsen
Scratch: Scott Green
Alex: Gabe Nevins
Macy: Lauren McKinney
Jared: Jake Miller
Detective Dan Liu: Richard Lu
Origin: USA
Language: English
Released: 2007
Production: Neil Kopp, David Cress, Charles Gillibert, Nathanael Karmitz; MK2; released by IFC Films
Directed by: Gus Van Sant
Written by: Gus Van Sant
Cinematography by: Christopher Doyle, Rain Kathy Li
Sound: Felix Andrew
Editing: Gus Van Sant
Art Direction: John Pearson-Denning
Costumes: Chapin Simpson
MPAA rating: R
Running time: 90 minutes

REVIEWS

Hollywood Reporter Online. March 22, 2007.
New York Times Online. March 7, 2008.
Rolling Stone Online. March 20, 2008.
Variety Online. January 6, 2007.
Village Voice Online. March 4, 2008.

QUOTES

Alex: "I'm writing this a little out of order. Sorry. I didn't do so well in creative writing."

TRIVIA

Director Gus Van Sant can be seen in the coffee shop scene reading a newspaper.

PATHOLOGY

No body is safe.
    —Movie tagline
Every body has a secret.
    —Movie tagline

Writers Mark Neveldine and Brian Taylor bring the hyperkinetic, violent style that they employed in *Crank* (2006) to the world of medicine in the twisted and unique *Pathology*, a movie that may not come completely together and undeniably goes off the rails in the final act, yet certainly stands out from and above the often generic and derivative thriller genre. When Neveldine and Taylor and director Marc Schoelermann delivered *Pathology* to MGM, it clearly took the studio off guard. They had no idea how to market this demented and dark movie, and the film completely floundered at the box office, not even grossing $110,000 domestically after not screening for critics. But *Pathology* is a case of a studio misjudging a film's potential. There is enough original, interesting work in *Pathology* that it could have found an audience and very likely will in the years to come. Movies this unusual usually do.

Reminiscent of Joel Schumacher's *Flatliners* (1990) as well as the work of David Cronenberg, *Pathology* is essentially about a group of young people who have stopped valuing life as they deal with the consistent reminder of death. *Heroes*'s Milo Ventimiglia stars as med school student Ted Grey, who moves to a big city to take part in a prestigious pathology program. Ted is an outcast at first, but soon he is taken in by the popular and beautiful people in the program and allowed into their violent world. Led by Dr. Jake Gallo (Michael Weston), Ted's classmates have devised something truly evil to keep themselves entertained. The job of a forensic pathologist is to determine cause of death, so each member of this clique tries to devise more intriguing and hard-to-determine ways to kill people, and then their colleagues must solve the case in an increasingly dangerous game. They also happen to be drug addicts and into kinky sex. Ted even falls for the truly demented Jake's girlfriend, Dr. Juliette Bath (Lauren Lee Smith). Jake, Juliette, and the others have lost all value for human life and things get truly life-threatening for Ted the more he gets drawn in, even putting his fiancée (Alyssa Milano) at risk.

It is almost impossible for a movie like *Pathology* to not write itself into a corner, and Neveldine and Taylor do struggle with the final act. The problem with set-ups like this one is that they leave no room for rising action. When a movie features violent murder and twisted behavior in the first act, the action that follows becomes harder and harder to top. *Pathology* opens with beautiful people playing "ventriloquist's dummy" with dead bodies. Where do you go from there? Having said that, *Pathology* does not stretch incredulity as much as it easily could have, and it keeps the audience interested more consistently than do most generic thrillers. Neveldine and Taylor find a way to avoid a lot of the screenwriting pitfalls of this kind of film. There are two major twists in the final act, and the big one, the climax, actually works (even if the first one is a little unbelievable). *Pathology* is dark, sometimes riveting, complex cinema with some great cinematography and interesting ideas. It is clearly not for everyone, which is why the studio had no idea what to do with it, but it is likely to find a devoted cult audience on DVD.

For a film that a large majority of critics were not even given the chance to see, the ones who did pay for a seat at *Pathology* actually were much kinder to it than most films held back from scrutiny. Mark Olsen of the *Los Angeles Times* said, "Gleefully brimming with body parts and bad behavior, *Pathology* is a fun piece of flamboyant tastelessness." Sandy MacDonald of the *Boston Globe* echoed the sentiment, saying, "Even squeamish viewers are apt to be captivated by the tight, credible scripting; these 20-somethings talk and behave like today's irony-clad young sophisticates. And whatever your opinion of the subject matter, you can't fault the filmmaking." Perhaps Scott Tobias of *The Onion* summed up *Pathology* best by calling it "the guiltiest of guilty pleasures."

Interestingly, Pete Hammond derided *Pathology* for being "somewhere in a world between *Flatliners, Saw,* and *Last Tango in Paris*" but, to this critic, that is what makes the film more refreshing than the countless thrillers every year that do not aspire to anything remotely different. The thriller genre is one that long ago stopped being actually thrilling, and Schoelermann, Neveldine, and Taylor at least refuse to go through the predictable motions that we have come to expect. There is nothing traditional about *Pathology*, a film that hits its twisted vein of action and dark humor more often than it misses its mark.

Brian Tallerico

CREDITS

Ted Grey: Milo Ventimiglia
Jake Gallo: Michael Weston
Gwen Williamson: Alyssa Milano
Juliette Bath: Lauren Lee Smith
Griffin Cavenaugh: Johnny Whitworth
Dr. Quentin Morris: John de Lancie
Catherine Ivy: Mei Melançon
Ben Stravinsky: Keir O'Donnell
Origin: USA
Language: English
Released: 2008
Production: Mark Neveldine, Brian Taylor, Gary Gilbert, Gary Lucchesi, Tom Rosenberg, Skip Williamson, Richard Wright; Lakeshore Entertainment, Camelot; released by MGM

Directed by: Marc Schoelermann
Cinematography by: Ekkehart Pollack
Music by: Johannes Kobilke, Robert Williamson
Sound: Mary Jo Devenney
Editing: Todd E. Miller
Art Direction: Talon McKenna
Costumes: Frank Helmer
Production Design: Jerry Fleming
MPAA rating: R
Running time: 93 minutes

REVIEWS

Boston Globe Online. April 19, 2008.
Hollywood Reporter Online. April 21, 2008.
Los Angeles Times Online. April 21, 2008.

QUOTES

Jake Gallo: "Really, who needs a reason? We're animals. It's our nature to kill. Remember?"

TRIVIA

In preparation for the film, many cast members observed a number of actual autopsies being performed.

PENELOPE

Sometimes true love is right under your nose.
—Movie tagline

A fairytale like no other.
—Movie tagline

What makes us different makes us beautiful.
—Movie tagline

Box Office: $10 million

Charm, flashes of dry wit, and a lesson about self-esteem go a long way toward making the fanciful *Penelope,* directed by Mark Palansky, a very pleasing, modern-day fairy tale. Christina Ricci stars as Penelope Wilhern, a young woman who suffers from a family curse that has left her with a pig's snout where her human nose should be and made her a virtual prisoner in her parents' mansion since birth. It is believed that only when she finds someone of her own kind (a blueblood) to love her will the curse be lifted. It is an offbeat, original film that largely works because of its sense of humor, eccentric production design, and Ricci's sympathetic performance as a woman longing to find true happiness and lasting love.

Suitors line up to meet Penelope but are so repulsed by her physical deformity that they flee when they lay eyes on her. (Ricci, incidentally, is actually rather cute even with a pig's nose, making everyone's horror at her visage something of an overreaction, albeit one that is necessary to the plot.) One young gentleman, Edward Vanderman (Simon Woods), becomes so unhinged that he reports the experience to the police and is at once dismissed publicly as a crazy man. Determined to prove the veracity of his story, he teams up with a tabloid reporter named Lemon (Peter Dinklage), who many years ago lost an eye at the hands of Penelope's mother, Jessica (Catherine O'Hara), and now wants vindication. Together they hire the patrician but down-on-his-luck Max (James McAvoy) to pose as a would-be suitor and sneak a photo for all the world to see. But Max ends up falling for Penelope and, in what may be the true test of love, does not run away. Despite his newfound affection for her, however, he refuses to marry Penelope, prompting her to escape the confines of her home and experience life for herself.

Penelope's trip through the city (with a scarf covering half of her face) is a small delight as she walks through a carnival and takes in all the glorious sights. Her sense of wonder at seeing a world previously hidden from her is quite touching. But just as Penelope stakes her claim to independence, the plot itself loses some of its focus, shifting suddenly from a beguiling romance to a journey of self-discovery. Moreover, since she is never really in much danger in the big city, the journey itself lacks some dramatic punch. Nonetheless, it derives humor from Penelope not quite knowing how to function in society and interact with strangers—she is initially puzzled by checking into a hotel, fears that joggers are running after her, and does not know how to catch a beer slid down a bar.

Penelope makes friends with a bike messenger named Annie (Reese Witherspoon, who also served as a producer of the film). Although Annie's brash, no-nonsense attitude makes her a nice foil to Penelope's naïf, the character is rather superfluous, and their relationship is not very well developed beyond a cute montage of them roaming the city.

There is, additionally, an arbitrariness in the way the various plot threads ultimately come together, giving the screenplay an unpolished feel. Penelope accidentally becoming a beloved minor celebrity when her face is revealed may be a clever twist on the ostracism we would normally expect, but the commentary on the public's fascination with celebrity feels half-baked. And the reaction from Edward's family that he must now marry Penelope to save face feels like a contrived way to provoke the climax in which Penelope rejects the wedding and affirms her own self-worth. Loving herself turns out to be all that was needed to break the spell, but this lesson in self-esteem begs the question of why her nose should then become normal if the message is ultimately supposed to be about the value of self-acceptance. Add to the mix the revelation that "Max" is really a poor boy named Johnny who was only pretending to be a blue-blood, and we are left with a screenplay that suffers from fuzzy plot transitions and too many needless twists and turns. Indeed, much of the film's middle section feels concocted to keep the would-be couple apart until the end.

What saves the film from its uneven screenplay by Leslie Caveny, however, is the goodwill generated by the actors and the sense of whimsy enlivening the fairy-tale world, punctuated by colorful, playful production design, including a swing in Penelope's playroom, courtesy of Amanda McArthur. Ricci makes an adorable heroine to cheer on and shares a romantic chemistry with McAvoy, who proves himself a worthy light romantic lead, as he did in 2007's *Starter for 10*. Their characters' initial courtship across a one-way mirror is quite sweet, and their ultimate union is very heartfelt. And O'Hara brings a deft combination of humor, poignancy, and a touch of meanness to a mother who, deep down, loves her daughter but does not always show it in the best way.

Despite a thin narrative and some plot machinations that strain to bring the story to a satisfying finish, *Penelope* is nonetheless a small delight that blends humor, fantasy, and two appealing leads into a winning tale of love and the maturation of a young woman. It is too bad that the film sat on the shelf for a long time before finally being given a rather limited release. Despite some flaws, its family-friendly appeal and sheer likeability should have garnered it a wider audience.

Peter N. Chumo II

CREDITS

Penelope Wilhern: Christina Ricci
Johnny/Max: James McAvoy
Jessica Wilhern: Catherine O'Hara
Lemon: Peter Dinklage
Franklin Wilhern: Richard E. Grant
Annie: Reese Witherspoon
Edward Vanderman: Simon Woods
Jake/Witch: Michael Feast
Mr. Vanderman: Nigel Havers
Krull: Lenny Henry
Wanda: Ronni Ancona
Origin: Great Britain
Language: English
Released: 2006
Production: Scott Steindorff, Reese Witherspoon, Jennifer Simpson, Dylan Russell; Type A Films, Grosvenor Park, Tatira Active; released by Summit Entertainment

Directed by: Mark Palansky
Written by: Leslie Caveny
Cinematography by: Michel Amathieu
Music by: Joby Talbot
Sound: Martin Trevis
Editing: Jon Gregory
Art Direction: Gerard Bryan
Costumes: Jill Taylor
Production Design: Amanda McArthur
MPAA rating: PG
Running time: 101 minutes

REVIEWS

Boston Globe Online. February 29, 2008.
Chicago Sun-Times Online. February 29, 2008.
Entertainment Weekly Online. February 26, 2008.
The Guardian Online. February 1, 2008.
Hollywood Reporter Online. September 15, 2006.
Los Angeles Times Online. February 29, 2008.
New York Times Online. February 29, 2008.
San Francisco Chronicle. February 29, 2008, p. E6.
Variety Online. September 10, 2006.
Wall Street Journal. February 29, 2008, p. W1.
Washington Post Online. February 29, 2008.

QUOTES

Penelope: "And we lived happily ever after...well, happily ever after so far at least."

TRIVIA

The bogus title "Scarfy" was given to the film for security purposes when it was delivered to theaters.

PERSEPOLIS

Box Office: $4.4 million

Persepolis is the animated feature film based on two graphic novels by Marjane (Marji) Satrapi, a native Iranian now living in France. The French film tells the autobiographical story of Satrapi's childhood and adolescence set against the last thirty years of Iranian history. Codirector and writer Vincent Paronnaud has shaped the material into something closely resembling the traditional three-act structure of many movies (even using at times the rare fade out). It is probably good that he did, since the purposely episodic plot coheres better by emphasizing the main divisions of Satrapi's life—childhood in Iran, adolescence in Austria, and young adulthood in Iran. In addition, the film has been movingly and painstakingly drawn by hand at twenty-four images per second, partly to avoid the sleekness and perfection of computer-generated pictures, but also, no doubt, as revealed by the predominantly black-and-white images, to emphasize better the starkness of the subject matter.

One of the defining strengths of the film is its rigorous aversion to simplifying the truth about growing up in Iran, at either the governmental or the personal level. The young Marji (voice of Gabrielle Lopes Benites as a child; voice of Chiara Mastroianni as a teen and adult), for example, is not given a falsified picture of Iran under the shah by her progressive parents (voice of Simon Abkarian and Catherine Deneuve). She is told how the shah's father and the shah himself modernized Iran but also how these self-proclaimed emperors yielded to pressure from the West to supply oil and to accept training by the CIA. In one early scene on the playground, a climate of Iranian McCarthyism rises up as one child informs on another. Marji's parents, and later her beloved Uncle Anouche (voiced by François Jerosme), whose activism lands him in and out of Iranian prisons, also do not compromise their candor in telling her about the intellectuals' mistaken assumption that life could not be worse than under the shah. The young girl who thinks of herself as a little prophet turns her back on God when she sees that no divine intervention spares her uncle the deprivations of prison.

Religious fundamentalism and the eight-year war with Iraq make Iran more repressive than before. Young girls who partly embraced the pop culture of the West (Marji's development charts a fondness for Bruce Lee, the Bee Gees, ABBA, and Iron Maiden) now must cover themselves with a veil and a burkha. To wear makeup or a pair of Adidas is to risk being stopped by the police for having "symbols of Western decadence" (in one scene an official stops Marji from running by telling her that "her behind was moving in an obscene way"). Young Iranian boys are given plastic keys that they are told will unlock the gates of heaven and are promised girls in the afterlife if they will fight against Iraq. Guards who are restricted by religious law from killing virgins can with impunity rape their intended victims in order to kill them legally. In one scene, a woman recognizes the director of a hospital as having been a window washer under the old regime. Young Marji's outspoken nature in such a climate alarms her parents, and she is sent for her own safety to Vienna.

The emotional center of the film is given to Marji's indomitable grandmother (voiced by the ninety-something Danielle Darrieux). Before she leaves for Austria, Marji gets straight-from-the-shoulder grandmotherly advice: "Jerks hurt us in their stupidity. Don't react to their cruelty. There is nothing worse than bitterness and revenge. Keep your dignity." The Vienna segment of the story shows Marji making friends with young intellectuals ("Santa Claus wears red and white because he's an invention of Coca-Cola"), learning a student's nonchalance, listening to heavy metal, even claiming to be French, and gradually feeling guilty over her safe life abroad. When she denies her roots, it is her grandmother who anchors her by reminding her to be true to herself, just as later in Iran her grandmother again reawakens Marji's integrity after she has behaved cowardly in public. The adult Marji finds the voice of her younger, outspoken self when in an assembly she points out the double standard concerning the different requirements for female and male attire in Iran. This act of courage her grandmother praises. Like Marji, the entire film is emotionally solidified by the presence of the grandmother.

Perhaps the greatest strength of the film is its amazing scene-by-scene conciseness. An audience must attend very carefully to the developing story as the speed of the plot and the resulting level of interest never seem to slacken. Ruthlessly pruned to the essentials, none of the dozens of scenes lasts too long, and the thought level of the whole film is immensely elevated by this narrative strictness. Watching the film unfold becomes an invigorating experience. At only ninety-five minutes, the film eventually takes on the feel of an epic in the sweeping number of years it covers. The filmmakers distill into each scene the right emotion or touch of drama or telling image or sound.

For example, in one effective transition the camera pushes in close on two swan toys made for Marji by her uncle in prison and then uses a match dissolve to show two swans on a lake in a scene of calm about to be disrupted by the new internal purges of the Iraq war. The link between the common cruelties of both Iranian regimes has thus been suggested with one image. The scenes of Marji in Vienna mark her adolescent development with some emphatic details. Her one-sided relationship with her second boyfriend, for example, is encapsulated in just a few telling before-and-after images. It is shown first as it occurs (with her responding politely to the play he has written) and then as she has come to view the events in retrospect (with the thought of the play literally making her vomit). When Marji finally returns to Iran as a young woman, the conciseness is heard in her father's trenchant summation of the war with Iraq: "A million dead for nothing. Now, they name streets after the martyrs. That's all the families have left—street names." In an age of cinematic bloat and lack of discipline, *Persepolis* is a treasure, a carefully cut jewel that has depth, emotion, pace, and intelligence.

Glenn Hopp

CREDITS

Marjane (teen/adult): Chiara Mastroianni (Voice)
Marji's grandmother: Danielle Darrieux (Voice)
Marji's father: Simon Abkarian (Voice)
Marjane (child): Gabrielle Lopes Benites (Voice)
Marji's mother: Catherine Deneuve (Voice)
Uncle Anouche: François Jerosme (Voice)
Origin: France
Language: French
Released: 2007
Production: Marc-Antoine Robert, Xavier Rigault, 2.4.7 Films; France 3 Cinema, Franche Connection Animations; released by Sony Pictures Classics
Directed by: Marjane Satrapi, Vincent Paronnaud
Written by: Marjane Satrapi, Vincent Paronnaud
Music by: Olivier Bernet
Sound: Samy Bardet
Editing: Stéphane Roche
Art Direction: Marc Jousset
Production Design: Marisa Musy
MPAA rating: PG-13
Running time: 95 minutes

REVIEWS

Boston Globe Online. January 11, 2008.
Chicago Sun-Times Online. January 17, 2008.
Entertainment Weekly. January 18, 2008, p. 66.
Los Angeles Times Online. December 25, 2007.
New York Times Online. December 25, 2007.
New Yorker Online. December 24, 2007.
Newsweek Online. December 17, 2007.
San Francisco Chronicle. January 11, 2008, p. E1.
Variety Online. May 23, 2007.
Village Voice Online. December 18, 2007.

QUOTES

Grandmother: "Listen. I don't like to preach, but here's some advice. You'll meet a lot of jerks in life. If they hurt you, remember it's because they're stupid. Don't react to their cruelty. There's nothing worse than bitterness and revenge. Keep your dignity and be true to yourself."

TRIVIA

The showing of the film was protested at several film festivals by the Iranian government.

AWARDS

Nomination:

Oscars 2007: Animated Film
British Acad. 2008: Animated Film, Foreign Film
Ind. Spirit 2008: Foreign Film.

PINEAPPLE EXPRESS

Put this in your pipe and smoke it.
—Movie tagline
One hit could ruin your whole day.
—Movie tagline

Box Office: $87.3 million

One of five 2008 releases to bear a writing and/or production credit from comedy juggernaut Judd Apatow, *Pineapple Express* sees Apatow once again teaming with Seth Rogen, who became a bona fide box-office star in 2007 with *Knocked Up* and *Superbad*. Written by Rogen and his *Superbad* writing partner Evan Goldberg from a story by Apatow, the film is a loose and clever mash-up of drug comedies and action/buddy films that is tailor-made for fans of Apatow and Rogen's gleefully crass—but ultimately sweet-natured—collaborations. The wild card this time around, however, is gifted young director David Gordon Green, whose body of work to this point has been wholly original and unlikely to appear at the suburban multiplex.

Dale (Seth Rogen), a twenty-six-year-old process server with a fondness for marijuana, contacts his dealer, Saul (James Franco) to buy a new supply. Saul provides Dale with a bag of the titular variety, named for meteorological conditions originating in Hawaii; it is so rare that Saul compares smoking it to killing a unicorn. During their transaction, Saul expresses a desire to become better friends with Dale, but Dale believes that a customer-dealer relationship should remain as such, and happily leaves with his purchase. On his way to serve a subpoena to drug kingpin Ted Jones (Gary Cole), he decides to smoke up before getting out of the car. Shortly after inhaling, he sees Jones shoot and kill a man though a second-floor window with the help of a corrupt policewoman (Rosie Perez). Now a witness to murder, Dale panics and flees, but not before Jones sees him. Fearing that he may be killed as a witness to murder, he returns to Saul's apartment to seek refuge. Saul, realizing that his contact with Dale has put him in danger as well, contacts his supplier, Red (Danny McBride), to see if he knows anything about Jones. In fact, Jones is Red's supplier and has already traced Dale back to Saul with the aid of the partially unsmoked rare Pineapple Express joint that Dale left at the crime scene, and Jones has already sent his henchmen (Kevin Corrigan and Craig Robinson) to Red's house to kill Saul and Dale. Now, inadvertently caught in the middle of a turf war between Jones and an Asian crime syndicate, Dale and Saul must keep running, but they find that their journey plants the seeds of the friendship that Dale had been reluctant to pursue.

Green, probably best known for his acclaimed 1999 debut *George Washington,* surprised many by attaching himself to a project as commercial as this, but he keeps the laughs and action moving along at a brisk clip, always ensuring that the two are intertwined—even when the proceedings turn surprisingly violent. Despite his art-house credibility, he has made no secret about his love for crowd-pleasing relics of the 1980s such as *Tango and Cash* (1989) and *Iron Eagle* (1986), and action comedy/buddy films of the 1970s like Terrence Malick's rarely seen *The Gravy Train* (1974) and *Thunderbolt and Lightfoot* (1974). He has given *Pineapple Express* a freewheeling vibe characteristic of those earlier films, right down to the newly recorded Huey Lewis and the News tune over the closing credits. While a film of this sort does not allow for many of Green's signature flourishes, his style is most evident in a funny, charming, and bucolic montage as Saul and Dale hide out in the forest, passing the time by playing leapfrog and sharing their marijuana with a caterpillar. As Robert Wilonsky noted in the *Village Voice,* "Green and longtime cinematographer Tim Orr don't act like they're making an action movie; as far as they appear to be concerned, this is an idyllic romance occasionally interrupted by fisticuffs, gunplay, or car chases—all of which are rendered with a realist's eye for detail, no matter how violently grim or glazed-eye goofy."

The opening scene is a black and white flashback to a 1940s U.S. army marijuana experiment in an underground facility that leads to the drug being classified as illegal. While there is a loose connection to this scene later in the film (this same location is used for the shootout at the conclusion), its place at the beginning leads one to believe that the script should make more of a statement about marijuana's role in society, but instead is comes off as something of a non sequitur. The balance of action and comedy is slightly uneven, and some viewers may have issues with the film's desire to coax laughter out of bloody injuries and fatalities, even if the majority of them happen to the most deserving characters. But while the plot follows very familiar arcs of friendship/falling-out/reconciliation within a standard "I witnessed a murder" chase scenario, the unusual pacing and frequent laughs give the film its own offbeat charm and energy.

Green makes the most of the film's three primary action sequences. In the first, Saul and Dale arrive at Red's house, only to find that Red has already been strong-armed by Jones's henchman into helping deliver Saul and Dale into their clutches. The ensuing fight scene between Saul, Dale, and Red—which is one of the more absurd to be committed to celluloid—completely tears Red's bathroom apart and ends with his head being put through a wall. Next, while driving a stolen police car, Saul attempts to kick out a Slurpee-covered windshield at high speed only to get his foot caught in the glass. Finally, the concluding shootout at the underground pot grow house is a parody of big action set pieces that manages to be surprisingly gory, off-puttingly casual about the casualties incurred, and rather hilarious. The image of a burly Rogen dropping in slow motion from a balcony onto a bad guy's shoulders is not an easy one to forget.

The appeal of *Pineapple Express* partially depends on one's feelings about Rogen, who, like Jack Black, has a commanding and appealing screen presence but always seems to be playing variations on himself. Like his previous roles, Dale is a self-deprecating schlub who smokes a lot of pot—a character Rogen's existing supporters will be glad to cheer on. Rogen was originally intended to fill the more obvious role of Saul, opposite Franco's Dale. This smart change in casting allows Franco a chance to show his lighter side, proving him to be the perfect choice for the drug dealer who is saving up to put his granny in a better retirement home and who keeps a mental list of his favorite civil engineers. According to Manohla Dargis of the *New York Times,* he gives an "unshowy, generous performance and it greatly humanizes a movie that, as it shifts genre gears and cranks up the noise, becomes disappointingly sober and self-serious." Reunited for the first time since Apatow cast them together on cult television favorite *Freaks and Geeks* a decade ago, Rogen and Franco make an appealing team. But while Franco surprises with his comic timing, *Pineapple's* MVP status must go to Danny McBride, who has quickly proven himself to be the sideman of choice for discriminating comedy fans. This is McBride's third 2008 release (after *The Foot-Fist Way* and *Tropic Thunder*), and his mulleted, white trash punching bag Red is the film's most vivid and consistently hilarious comic creation.

Apatow's productions are definitely cut from the same cloth, and for their millions of admirers, they also have their detractors. *Pineapple Express* is not going to change their minds. As with his other productions, this one is populated by emotionally stunted man-children who would rather keep company with one another than deal with women. (Here, Dale's girlfriend Angie [Amber Heard] is in high school, and even she proves too mature for him....) Ultimately, though, this is a celebration of the platonic love that blooms between guys who endure a difficult experience together. Where "stoner" films in the past have laconically reveled in the way in which their characters do nothing, here Saul and Dale never stop smoking, but they never get to sit down. It is not high-minded entertainment, but it is likely to be a perennial favorite for fifteen-year-old boys, man-children, and the women who love them.

J. David Hodgson

CREDITS

Dale Denton: Seth Rogen
Saul Silver: James Franco
Ted Jones: Gary Cole
Carol: Rosie Perez
Angie Anderson: Amber Heard
Gen. Bratt: James Remar
Pvt. Miller: Bill Hader
Red: Danny McBride
Shannon Anderson: Nora Dunn
Budlofsky: Kevin Corrigan
Robert Anderson: Ed Begley Jr.
Bobby: Bobby Lee
Matheson: Craig Robinson
Walter: Jack Kehler
Ken: Ken Jeong
Origin: USA
Language: English
Released: 2008
Production: Judd Apatow, Shauna Robertson, Nicholas Weinstock; Columbia Pictures, Relativity Media; released by Sony Pictures Entertainment
Directed by: David Gordon Green
Written by: Seth Rogen, Evan Goldberg
Cinematography by: Tim Orr
Music by: Graeme Revell
Sound: Christof Gebert
Music Supervisor: Jonathan Karp
Editing: Craig Alpert
Art Direction: Marc Dabe
Costumes: John Dunn
Production Design: Chris Spellman
MPAA rating: R
Running time: 111 minutes

REVIEWS

Boston Globe Online. August 6, 2008.
Chicago Sun-Times Online. August 5, 2008.
Entertainment Weekly Online. August 5, 2008.
Hollywood Reporter Online. July 19, 2008.
Los Angeles Times Online. August 6, 2008.
New York Times Online. August 6, 2008.
Rolling Stone Online. August 7, 2008.
San Francisco Chronicle. August 6, 2008, p. E1.
Variety Online. July 19, 2008.
Washington Post. August 6, 2008, p. C1.

QUOTES

Dale Denton: "In case you haven't noticed—which you haven't, 'cause from what I can tell, you don't notice anything ever—we are not very functional when we're high."

TRIVIA

The expletive "f**k" and its derivatives are uttered 180 times in the film.

AWARDS

Nomination:

Golden Globes 2009: Actor—Mus./Comedy (Franco).

THE PIRATES WHO DON'T DO ANYTHING: A VEGGIETALES MOVIE

Box Office: $12.9 million

The *VeggieTales* children's video movie franchise used its recurring, vegetable-based characters to retell Bible tales. The brand's first major studio release, *The Pirates Who Don't Do Anything: A VeggieTales Movie,* uses the franchise's usual array of animated produce to craft a pirate story that is actually a well-disguised parable. With its upbeat message and sing-along songs, the innocuous, second *VeggieTales* theatrical release will satisfy the youngest of audiences and those looking for reliable, faith-based family fare.

Director Mike Nawrocki and writer Phil Vischer, who both provide the voices of the main characters, begin their pirate yarn with a battle at sea. Familiar *VeggieTales* characters take on the roles of the pirates: Larry the Cucumber is here as Elliot (voice of Mike Nawrocki), Mr. Lunt is now Sedgewick, and Grandpa Grape is George (both voice of Phil Vischer). These three busboys from a pirate-themed dinner theater are spirited away from their hum-drum lives by a "Help Seeker" machine and suddenly find themselves in the seventeenth century, pitted against the dreaded pirate Robert the Terrible (voice of Cam Clarke), a gourd who sports terrifying mechanical arms and legs. Robert has attacked a ship carrying two young leeks, his nephew Alexander (voice of Yuri Lowenthal), whom he captures, and niece Eloise (voice of Laura Gerow), in his quest to eradicate the heirs to his brother's throne. Eloise has used the Help Seeker her father invented to find a hero to save her brother, and she receives the three lazy busboys.

The extremely reluctant heroes Elliot, Sedgewick, and George lack the necessary confidence and ambition, not to mention energy, for the tough job ahead, and are not sure they can summon whatever they need to succeed—an opinion shared by Eloise's snooty British butler Willory (voice of Phil Vischer). They are, nonetheless, assured by the King (voice of Cam Clarke) that they are, in fact, the men for the job: "The hero is the one who does what's right—no matter how hard it is."

While the material is mostly pat, there are some imaginative segments that brim with song, as when the boys face some cantankerous Cheese Curls and rock monsters. Fans of the franchise will recognize cameos from Madame Blueberry, Archibald Asparagus, and Bob the Tomato. Perhaps the most fun is the campy, energetic parody of the B-52s song "Rock Lobster" that plays during the film's end credits.

The message is that life is a sometimes difficult adventure filled with trials, and though we often feel we are not up to the challenge, even the lowest vegetable can find strength and untapped reserves bestowed by a higher power. The King very much represents God, and the pirates, in fact, are not the true heroes and ultimate saviors who must rely on the God-figure. The more devout fans of the faith-based series may crave the more overt religious message that may be found in the franchise's *Jonah: A VeggieTales Movie* (2002), a humorous Old Testament retelling. *The Pirates Who Don't Do Anything* is an original veggie adventure that the film's young viewers will probably take at face value: a fun pirate story.

Critics opinions of the film were mixed. *New York Times* reviewer Neil Genzlinger thought the filmmakers borrowed a bit too heavily from children' classic *The Wizard of Oz* (1942), as its three bumbling protagonists are transported into a different place and time to rescue a princess and "...like the Scarecrow et al., find their brains, courage and heart along the way. An Oz-like man even gives them awards at the end."

The story suffers from some pacing problems and in between the engaging battles and amusing songs—including the Christian rock band Relient K's popular rendition of the title song—the films drags a bit. The eccentric characters, however, are at their most vividly illustrated in what is certainly the most visually sophisticated of all the *VeggieTales* movies.

Hilary White

CREDITS

Robert the Terrible: Cam Clarke (Voice)
Elliot: Mike Nawrocki (Voice)

George/Sedgewick: Phil Vischer (Voice)
Princess Eloise: Laura Gerow (Voice)
Alexander: Yuri Lowenthal (Voice)
Origin: USA
Language: English
Released: 2008
Production: Phil Vischer, Mike Nawrocki, David Pitts; Big Idea; released by Universal
Music by: Kurt Heinecke
Sound: Ryan Henwood
Editing: John Wahba
Art Direction: Charles Vollmer, Andrew Woodhouse
MPAA rating: G
Running time: 85 minutes

REVIEWS

Boston Globe Online. January 12, 2008.
Hollywood Reporter Online. January 11, 2008.
Los Angeles Times Online. January 11, 2008.
New York Times Online. January 11, 2008.
Variety Online. January 10, 2008.
Washington Post. January 11, 2008, p. C6.

QUOTES

Blind Man: "Help will come from above in the shape of...a donkey."

PRICELESS
(Hors de prix)

She only dated men with money...until she met a man with a heart.
—Movie tagline

Box Office: $2.1 million

Billed as a modern retelling of the 1961 classic *Breakfast at Tiffany's*, *Priceless* (*Hors de prix*) is a breezy bauble of a French film. Director Pierre Salvadori's affection for vintage Hollywood comedies is apparent in this highly entertaining romp through the coastal resort towns of southern France.

French superstar Audrey Tatou stars as Irène, a gold digger who flits about the Côte d'Azur as the paid companion of rich old men. One evening while staying at a swanky Biarritz resort, Irène mistakes hotel bartender Jean (Gad Elmaleh) for a wealthy playboy closer to her own age. The two celebrate Irène's birthday with several drinks and end up spending a blissful night together in the hotel's royal suite. Upon waking, Irène learns that Jean is merely a hotel employee, so she is quickly off again with her aging sugar daddy.

A year later, the protagonists meet up again, and Irène immediately bankrupts Jean with a shopping spree in Nice. Although it is obvious that Jean is completely smitten with Irène, he falls in with a wealthy older woman (Marie-Christine Adam), while Irène tutors him on the art of being a "kept" man. Clearly, Irène and Jean are two of a kind, playing the same game. The scheming duo then engage in a secretive romance while trying to keep up appearances with their older companions. Although the two main characters are both, in effect, prostitutes, the film never gives way to sordidness or vulgarity. The Gallic comedy is so charming, blithe, and gorgeously shot that the audience forgets that the film is, at its core, a story about love for sale.

A highlight of this sophisticated film is the strong performances of the lead actors. The stylishly beautiful and endearing Tatou is pitch-perfect as the bad-girl heroine who wants to live the high life. For his part, Elmaleh displays perfect comic timing and lends the right deadpan touch to his role as the nice guy who falls for the calculating schemer.

Overall, critics were positive in their reviews of *Priceless,* while acknowledging the film's predictable nature and the darker elements of the storyline. Reviewers largely found the movie to be an amusing sex comedy, complete with stunning scenery and a luxury-goods lifestyle. In his review for the *Seattle Post-Intelligencer,* critic William Arnold wrote, "Salvadori loves these characters like his own children, and he has a gift for comic timing, a typical Gallic sense of the absurd, and a flair for the wit, sophistication, and high-gloss luxury backgrounds of Golden Age Hollywood."

In a similar vein, Michael Phillips commented in the *Chicago Tribune,* "the thing about a certain grade of contemporary French comedy, of which *Priceless* is a fine example, is the quality of the playing style. Nobody forces the situations, even the broadest ones. *Priceless* would no doubt suffer the usual crassification if Hollywood ever remade it in English. The film may be a contraption, but it is acted with simplicity and charm."

Ty Burr perhaps summed it up best in his remarks for the *Boston Globe:* "*Priceless* is a bauble—an art-house diamond made of paste that somehow still gives you good glimmer for the money. If you think about the movie for even a minute, you'll realize you've been had. If you sink into it like a hot bath, you may end up sighing with pleasure."

Although this modern French farce is as light as air, *Priceless* is a delicious bonbon, best enjoyed as a guilty pleasure.

Beth A. Fhaner

CREDITS

Irène: Audrey Tautou
Jean: Gad Elmaleh
Jacques: Vernon Dobtcheff
Agnès: Annelise Hesme
Madeleine: Marie-Christine Adam
Gilles: Jacques Spiesser
Origin: France
Language: French
Released: 2006
Production: Philippe Martin; Les Films Pelleas; released by Samuel Goldwyn Films
Directed by: Pierre Salvadori
Written by: Pierre Salvadori, Benoît Graffin
Cinematography by: Gilles Henry
Music by: Camille Bazbaz
Sound: François Morel, Jean-Christophe Winding
Editing: Isabelle Devinck
Costumes: Virginie Montel
Production Design: Yves Fournier
MPAA rating: PG-13
Running time: 106 minutes

REVIEWS

Boston Globe Online. April 11, 2008.
New York Times Online. March 28, 2008.
San Francisco Chronicle Online. April 4, 2008.
Variety Online. December 19, 2006.
Village Voice Online. March 25, 2008.
Wall Street Journal. March 28, 2008, p. W1.
Washington Post Online. April 4, 2008.

QUOTES

Irene: "But charm is more valuable than beauty. You can resist beauty, but you can't resist charm."

PRIDE AND GLORY

The last thing you want to uncover…is the truth.
—Movie tagline
Truth. Honor. Loyalty. Family. What are you willing to sacrifice?

Box Office: $15.7 million

Pride and Glory tries to be a gritty, realistic look at Irish American police officers in New York City. Despite some good moments here and there, however, writer/director Gavin O'Connor's film is too melodramatic and too often falls back on clichés.

Ray Tierney (Edward Norton) is a bitter detective hiding away in Missing Persons after a traumatic experience not explained until late in *Pride and Glory*. His brother, Francis Tierney, Jr. (Noah Emmerich), commands a group of officers that includes their brother-in-law, Jimmy Egan (Colin Farrell). Francis tries to do everything by the book, while Jimmy is a hothead striving to twist situations to his advantage. When four cops are killed in an ambush during a drug raid in Washington Heights, Ray, Francis, and Jimmy find themselves embroiled in a corruption scandal, much to the disgust of Francis Tierney, Sr. (Jon Voight), the family's alcoholic patriarch and also a police officer.

Ray is about to be divorced from Tasha (Carmen Ejogo), although the couple still love each other. Francis's wife, Abby (Jennifer Ehle), has terminal cancer. Married to Ray and Francis's sister Megan (Lake Bell), Jimmy is resentful that he is expected to support his growing family on $65,000 a year. At his father's goading, Ray joins the task force investigating the ambush, and what he uncovers turns him, Francis, and Jimmy against each other.

O'Connor, the son of a New York policeman, and cowriter Joe Carnahan attempt valiantly to explore Irish American mores, the sense of brotherhood felt by police officers, and the complex emotions experienced by brothers and by extended families. Yet, because *Pride and Glory* tries to cover too much ground, it treats its subjects superficially. Except for two shockingly violent scenes, everything about the film is predictable, including an exceedingly maudlin Christmas dinner.

O'Connor, whose films include the mother-daughter road movie *Tumbleweeds* (1999) and the Olympic hockey drama *Miracle* (2004), knows about family relationships and the macho world of male friendship. Carnahan wrote and directed the hard-boiled crime drama *Narc* (2002) and the cartoonish *Smokin' Aces* (2006), and knows violence and machismo. The filmmakers are clearly striving to emulate Sidney Lumet's groundbreaking New York police films such as *Serpico* (1973) and *Prince of the City* (1981). While Lumet looks piercingly at the moral dilemmas faced by honest police officers surrounded by corrupt cops, *Pride and Glory* merely skirts around the issues, using corruption as a mere plot mechanism for a thriller.

Too often *Pride and Glory* is reminiscent of similar, better films. There are the conflicts among two brothers and a father, two of them policemen, as in James Gray's *We Own the Night* (2007); the good cop–corrupt cop dynamics of Martin Scorsese's *The Departed* (2006); and the love-hate between brothers as in Lumet's *Before the Devil Knows You're Dead* (2007). In comparison, *Pride and Glory* is just too formulaic, as it moves back and forth between anguished emotional encounters and acts of violence and back again. The painfully ironic

circumstances leading to the resolution of one character's fate are especially melodramatic. Matters might be different if the film was consistently over-the-top, but it simply sputters from one contrived situation to another.

While the problems with *Pride and Glory* come mostly from the script, the pacing is awkward, with too many scenes running too long. O'Connor does, however, frame shots reasonably well. His staging of the interdepartmental police football game at the beginning is also exceptional. Having the game hinge on a defensive rather than offensive play is one of the few times *Pride and Glory* does not go for the obvious. The lighting of cinematographer Declan Quinn is appropriately moody, making the gloomy city, mostly Harlem and the Bronx, look as dangerous as it does in Lumet's films and *The French Connection* (1971). Mark Isham's score, on the other hand, is monotonously somber and unimaginative.

Farrell gives Jimmy the coiled nervousness he has used too many times, and Voight's Francis, Sr., is a caricature of an Irish American paterfamilias, though the character is the film's most weakly written. Emmerich is good at showing how Francis, Jr., is torn between doing the right thing and being loyal to his family and cohorts, alternating between strength and indecision. The always reliable John Ortiz stands out as a guilt-ridden bad cop. Ortiz's delivery of a monologue explaining the film's title is one of the few moments of genuine pathos. Best of all is Norton's internalizing of Ray's rage. The subtlety of Norton, rarely an unnecessarily demonstrative actor, stands out in a film overloaded with emotion. His two scenes with Ejogo have an economic melancholy missing elsewhere in *Pride and Glory*.

Those involved with *Pride and Glory* should know something about brothers. Carnahan's brother, Matthew Michael Carnahan, is also a screenwriter. O'Connor's brother, Gregory O'Connor, is one of the film's producers and also collaborated on the story on which the film is based. Emmerich's brother, Toby Emmerich, is an executive producer as well as the head of New Line, the film's producer and distributor. *Pride and Glory* was made in 2006 and had to sit on the New Line shelf while the studio remained uncertain about when and whether to release it. After finally announcing a 2008 release date, New Line switched to a 2009 date, only to change its mind again. Perhaps the film's derivative nature contributed to the uncertainty about its fate.

Michael Adams

CREDITS

Ray Tierney: Edward Norton
Jimmy Egan: Colin Farrell

Francis Tierney, Sr.: Jon Voight
Francis Tierney, Jr.: Noah Emmerich
Abby Tierney: Jennifer Ehle
Ruben "Sandy" Santiago: John Ortiz
Kenny Dugan: Shea Whigham
Eddie Carbone: Frank Grillo
Megan Egan: Lake Bell
Eladio Casado: Rick Gonzalez
Bill Avery: Wayne Duvall
Tasha: Carmen Ejogo
Origin: USA
Language: English
Released: 2008
Production: Greg O'Connor; New Line Cinema, O'Connor Brothers, Solaris Entertainment; released by Warner Bros.
Directed by: Gavin O'Connor
Written by: Gavin O'Connor, Joe Carnahan
Cinematography by: Declan Quinn
Music by: Mark Isham
Sound: William Sarokin
Music Supervisor: Nic Harcourt
Editing: Lisa Zeno Churgin, John Gilroy
Art Direction: James Donahue
Costumes: Abigail Murray
Production Design: Dan Leigh
MPAA rating: R
Running time: 129 minutes

REVIEWS

Boston Globe Online. October 24, 2008.
Chicago Sun-Times Online. October 23, 2008.
Entertainment Weekly Online. October 22, 2008.
Hollywood Reporter Online. September 10, 2008.
Los Angeles Times Online. October 24, 2008.
New York Times Online. October 24, 2008.
Rolling Stone Online. October 30, 2008.
San Francisco Chronicle. October 24, 2008, p. E5.
Variety Online. September 9, 2008.
Washington Post Online. October 24, 2008.

QUOTES

Sandy: "Becoming a cop, the pledge we took to uphold something honest. We let it all rot from under us. I was a good man once."

TRIVIA

Althought the movie was completed in 2006, it was left on the shelf at New Line until Warner Bros. picked up New Line's content.

PROM NIGHT

It's midnight. Everyone's ready to go home...but someone has other plans.
—Movie tagline

A party to die for.
—Movie tagline

Box Office: $43.8 million

Only a little over ten years after Kevin Williamson and Wes Craven sent up the clichés of '80s horror in the brilliantly subversive *Scream* (1996) and effectively put an end to slasher-flick mania for at least a few years, Hollywood has fallen back into the same traps, not only repeating the mistakes of that era of filmmaking but amplifying them with a horrendous piece of junk like *Prom Night,* a remake that takes an already mediocre film and makes it look like a genre classic by comparison. The flaws of 1980's *Prom Night* can almost be forgiven in light of nostalgia and the power of Jamie Lee Curtis's presence as the scream queen of her era, but the remake takes everything that was wrong with the original—and the current state of the horror genre in general—and makes it significantly worse. Gaps in logic and stunning patches of boredom follow two-dimensional characters and unbelievable behavior on the list of problems with *Prom Night,* a film that provides not one genuine scare, dramatic moment, satirical jab at the genre, or even a line of dialogue that feels real. The filmmakers refuse to even go for camp, never allowing *Prom Night* to fall into the so-bad-it's-good category that consistently threatens. The characters in *Scream* would have hated it.

Ironically, *Prom Night* opens with a scene not unlike the infamous Drew Barrymore opening from *Scream* (though not scary, subversive, or dramatic in any way). Donna (Brittany Snow, a few years past being able to believably play a high school student) comes home to find a killer in her house. The man (Johnathon Schaech) is one of the girl's teachers and he has become obsessed, violently looking for Donna and murdering her entire family in that search. Three years later, Donna is still dreaming of that horrible night but has pulled herself together enough to go to her senior prom. As her friends Claire (Jessica Stroup) and Lisa (Dana Davis) are introduced there may as well be flashing signs over their heads that say "victim." The only suspense is in wondering in which order they will be killed by the sure-to-return bad guy from three years ago. Donna's date is the equally perfect-looking Bobby (Scott Porter), who picks up the heroine from her guardians and everyone happily heads off to prom on the same night that the dark man from Donna's past returns for more. Carnage ensues.

Critical reaction to *Prom Night* was more vicious than any of the murderous activity in the film itself. Peter Howell of the *Toronto Star* correctly noted that "there's absolutely zippo to fear about this movie, unless you're the kind of person who jumps when formula bogeymen do exactly what you'd expect them to do." Even the Internet community, which often comes to the defense of the horror genre, was in agreement with Scott Weinberg of *Cinematical*, who hilariously commented that "to call *Prom Night* a horror movie is to call chewing gum a cheeseburger." Perhaps Wesley Morris of the *Boston Globe* said it best when he wrote, "There's no suspense or perversity. You don't care who lives or dies—just please make it soon."

Prom Night might conceivably have worked if it had stayed set in the '80s. In that case, the clichés might have felt like a nod to the horror movies of the era instead of just dated and overused. Director Nelson McCormick and writer J.S. Cardone have zero cinematic background of note (McCormick comes from TV and Cardone wrote the loathed *The Covenant* [2006]), which makes it clear that the producers of *Prom Night* were convinced that the remake would write and direct itself. The film is shockingly lifeless. Even the worst horror films of recent years found something, usually gore, to emphasize, but *Prom Night* oddly focuses on nothing at all, unless "jump scares" count. It not only is not scary, it almost feels like McCormick and Cardone were trying to be dull. They imbue the film with no creative energy worth mentioning and bring new meaning to the phrase "by-the-numbers." The lack of a single worthwhile scare in the entire film and the preponderance of jump cuts and choppy editing make it clear that postproduction was relied on far too heavily in the storytelling. Critics have been quick to pan remakes of '80s horror films, but *Prom Night* is a new low, sliding underneath a bar that had practically hit the ground already; it is proof that a remake need not be of an Asian horror movie to be horrendous. McCormick is reportedly finishing postproduction on another '80s remake, *The Stepfather*. The horror world needs a new *Scream* more than ever.

Brian Tallerico

CREDITS

Donna Keppel: Brittany Snow
Richard Fenton: Johnathon Schaech
Detective Winn: Idris Elba
Lisa: Dana Davis
Claire: Jessica Stroup
Bobby: Scott Porter
Ronnie: Collins Pennie
Michael: Kelly Blatz
Crissy Lynn: Brianne Davis
Origin: USA
Language: English
Released: 2008
Production: Neal H. Moritz; Screen Gems, Original Film, Newmarket Films, Alliance Film Productions; released by Sony Pictures Entertainment

Directed by: Nelson McCormick
Written by: J.S. Cardone
Cinematography by: Checco Varese
Music by: Paul Haslinger
Sound: Jeffrey J. Haboush, Greg P. Russell
Music Supervisor: Gerry Cueller
Editing: Jason Ballantine
Art Direction: Chris Cornwell
Costumes: Lyn Elizabeth Paolo
Production Design: Jon Gary Steele
MPAA rating: PG-13
Running time: 88 minutes

REVIEWS

Boston Globe Online. April 12, 2008.
Hollywood Reporter Online. April 14, 2008.
New York Times Online. April 12, 2008.
Variety Online. April 11, 2008.

QUOTES

Crissy Lynn: "If he were any dumber, I'd have to water him."

THE PROMOTION

Two guys. One job. No rules.
—Movie tagline

Set in Chicago, *The Promotion* is a clever and engaging workplace comedy that follows the rivalry of two assistant managers of a Donaldson's grocery store, Doug Stauber (Seann William Scott) and Richard Wehlner (John C. Reilly), in heavy competition for the head manager position of a new, soon-to-be built store. The plot is sympathetic to both characters, focusing on the complex relationship between coworkers forced into conflicting roles as friends and adversaries. Written and directed by Steven Conrad, the movie has a quirky, indie-like quality that manages to avoid many of the clichés often found in more mainstream fare.

Doug Stauber, the thirty-three-year-old narrator and protagonist, is embarrassed by his life and frustrated by the daily humiliations he endures at Donaldson's. He and his wife Jen (Jenna Fischer) still ride public transit and live in a small, thin-walled apartment next door to a noisy and intrusive banjo player. At work, he deals with lackluster employees, customer complaints, and "cutthroughs"—loiterers and troublemakers from the adjacent public housing project who have turned the store's parking lot into a haven for crime. The parking lot becomes Doug's own personal battleground as customer comment cards detailing nightmare experiences become a major issue and potential breaking point with his employer. Jen's good-looking and charming boss Dr. Timm (Bobby Cannavale)—an obnoxiously heroic and successful children's surgeon who never remembers Doug's name—further adds to his sense of hopelessness and inferiority.

New hope arrives for the Staubers, however, with the announced opening of a new Donaldson's store in their own neighborhood. Doug's manager Scott Fargas (Fred Armisen) assures him that he is a "shoo-in" for its manager position. Confident that he will get the promotion, Doug promises Jen that finally they will be able to afford their own home without her having to go back to school in order to land a higher paying job. The outlook appears promising until an unexpected challenger transfers to the store from a sister company in Quebec. Also an assistant manager, Richard Wehlner is a nice guy and older family man with a stronger resumé than Doug's. Forming a bond of trust, he confides that he is a former drug addict and alcoholic, and throughout the movie he struggles with his demons and tries to keep his Scottish wife Laurie (Lili Taylor) and young daughter from leaving him. Despite Richard's checkered past, his Canadian accent, Christian missionary background, and reliance on self-help recordings emphasize his naturally sweet disposition and naiveté. Although his greater experience and sterling reputation appear to give him an initial advantage over Doug, he unwittingly dooms himself with a combination of innocent slips-of-the-tongue, unconsciously inappropriate behavior, and hapless bad-timing. Emerging as an obvious outsider—with a large-scale portrait tattoo of the rock band Kiss on his stomach to prove it—he takes little time in losing the respect of his colleagues and underlings, and eventually the Donaldson's board.

The Promotion relies on hilarious one-upmanship and other situational comedy to move the story along while illustrating Doug's growing maturity and capacity for compassion. Even though he has put himself into a bind by lying to Jen (he calls it a "wish-lie"), telling her that he has already gotten the new job, he cannot help but identify with Richard, despite Richard's deliberate attempt to sink his chances with what comes to be referred to as the "Tater Tot Incident," in which Richard has Doug written up for throwing a frozen potato nugget, accidentally hitting him in the hand and allegedly causing an injury. The men eventually reach a point of mutual respect and acceptance, however, with Richard summing up their shared predicament: "We're all just out here trying to get some food…sometimes, we bump into each other." In the end, he spoils his own chance at the promotion by smoking marijuana, which shows up on his drug test at the final interview. Doug, who experiences a growth in personal maturity through his associa-

tion with Richard, sums up his improved sense of self in the final narration: "Was I the better man?…I just felt like a man."

The emergence of Doug as *The Promotion*'s triumphant hero is a typical conclusion for this type of light comedy, but the overall journey is still less predictable than the norm. A pleasant, underrated surprise, the film stands up as undeniably entertaining. In addition to the two main stars, a diverse cast features several recognizable, competent, and generally well-liked television and movie actors including Jason Bateman in a brief cameo role as a corporate team-building consultant. The movie is hampered by only a few minor flaws including, most notably, Lili Taylor's poorly executed Scottish brogue, and John C. Reilly's sometimes faltering and uneven Canadian accent, not to mention one or two silly and trivial reoccurring gags in an otherwise reasonably concise storyline. Nevertheless, *The Promotion* contains enough inventive plot turns, legitimately funny bits, and good dialogue to keep it interesting through to the end.

Jaye Furlonger

CREDITS

Doug: Seann William Scott
Richard: John C. Reilly
Jen: Jenna Fischer
Laurie: Lili Taylor
Scott: Fred Armisen
Board Exec: Gil Bellows
Dr. Timm: Bobby Cannavale
Ernesto: Rick Gonzalez
Teddy Grahams: Chris Conrad
Origin: USA
Language: English
Released: 2008
Production: Jessika Borsiczky Goyer, Steven A. Jones; released by Dimension Films
Directed by: Steve Conrad
Written by: Steve Conrad
Cinematography by: Lawrence Sher
Music by: Alex Wurman
Sound: Scott D. Smith
Music Supervisor: Tracy McKnight
Editing: Tim Streeto, Myron I. Kerstein
Art Direction: Doug Meerdink
Costumes: Susan Kaufmann
Production Design: Martin Whist
MPAA rating: R
Running time: 85 minutes

REVIEWS

Chicago Sun-Times Online. June 6, 2008.
Hollywood Reporter Online. March 10, 2008.

Los Angeles Times Online. June 6, 2008.
New York Times Online. June 6, 2008.
Variety Online. March 9, 2008.
Village Voice Online. June 3,2008.

QUOTES

Doug: "I'm not a lion…I'm a guy."

Q-R

QUANTUM OF SOLACE

Box Office: $168.3 million

Casino Royale (2006) was acclaimed for returning James Bond to his roots, eschewing the high-tech gadgets and the bad jokes that had made the long-running spy series more cartoonish over the years. *Quantum of Solace* continues this gritty realism, but what seemed refreshing in *Casino Royale* seems a bit tired now, 007 a tad too glum.

Quantum of Solace begins where the previous film left off, with Bond (Daniel Craig) in a high-speed chase in Italy, eluding his pursuers to deliver Mr. White (Jesper Christensen) to his boss, M (Judi Dench). Bond suspects White has something to do with the death of his lover, Vesper Lynd, at the end of *Casino Royale.* There are so many references to Vesper throughout *Quantum of Solace* that those who have not seen the earlier film or remember it clearly may occasionally be puzzled.

After White escapes, Bond is sent to Haiti to look into the activities of Dominic Greene (Mathieu Amalric), a businessman who claims to be an environmentalist but is clearly up to no good. Bond enlists the aid of Camille (Olga Kurylenko), who has infiltrated Greene's organization in hopes of dispatching General Medrano (Joaquín Cosio), the Bolivian strongman responsible for the deaths of her parents. After a detour to Austria, the film lands the protagonists in Bolivia, where Medrano has given Greene water rights.

Although Greene is ostensibly the villain, much of the focus of *Quantum of Solace* is on the quests of Bond and Camille for revenge, and the details of Greene's plan to gain control of the world's water supply are left fuzzy by screenwriters Paul Haggis, Neal Purvis, and Robert Wade, who also collaborated on *Casino Royale.* Greene's function seems to be primarily to lead the avengers to White and Medrano. The understated realism that works in the earlier film appears too understated here. There is just not enough at stake to make the proceedings that interesting. The screenwriters make M suspicious of Bond to try to inject a sense of urgency.

After *Casino Royale* director Martin Campbell turned down the film, Marc Forster seemed an odd choice to take on a big-budget action assignment. The strengths of the director of *Monster's Ball* (2001), *Finding Neverland* (2004), and *The Kite Runner* (2007) are storytelling and nuances of character, not gunplay and explosions. While Forster has been criticized for the plodding nature of *Quantum of Solace,* he does as well as he can with the material he was given. Forster handles the actors well, but there is vagueness about what is going on, both in the opening scene—a rather pedestrian boat chase—and near the conclusion—a showdown at a desert resort inexplicably without any guests other than the bad guys. Much better is the way Bond exposes Greene's fellow conspirators during a performance of Puccini's *Tosca* (1900), and a foot chase in Siena ending with Bond and his prey crashing through a roof.

Called by some the best Bond ever, even surpassing Sean Connery, the original 007, Craig is likewise handcuffed by the script. The tough, cool Bond of *Casino Royale* comes off as merely morose. The diminutive, owl-eyed Amalric is an odd choice to oppose Bond, though his casting fits with the desire for realism. As he has shown in numerous French films, especially *The Diving Bell and the Butterfly* (2007), Amalric is an outstanding actor, but he is given too little to work with here and simply alternates between evil smugness and evil intensity. Former model Kurylenko ably conveys Camille's pathos, and she is suitably athletic in the action scenes. Even better is Gemma Arterton as a young but quick-thinking agent sent to keep watch on Bond in Bolivia. The charming Arterton's liveliness is a strong contrast to what is required of the rest of the performers.

Despite mixed reviews, including complaints about its being too brutal and dark, and unflattering comparisons to the Jason Bourne series, *Quantum of Solace* set a record for the Bond franchise with an opening weekend take of $67.5 million, but went on to make less than half that the following weekend. Audiences may have been expecting the film to try to top *Casino Royale,* but while it is not bad, it seems less a continuation than an afterthought, just like the title, which was taken from a short story by Bond creator Ian Fleming that has nothing else to do with the film. A reference is made in passing to Quantum as the name of Greene's organization, yet the title still has no discernable meaning.

In addition to paling beside the rousingly entertaining *Casino Royale, Quantum of Solace* evokes memories of Bond's prime with a visual allusion to *Goldfinger* (1964), though this time the gold of the original is replaced by oil, the planet's new most valuable resource. *Goldfinger,* despite some flaws, is one of the more entertaining Bonds, a quality the wrongheaded makers of *Quantum of Solace* strangely chose to ignore. There just is not enough inventiveness, nothing much memorable.

Michael Adams

CREDITS

James Bond: Daniel Craig
M: Judi Dench
Dominic Greene: Mathieu Amalric
Camille: Olga Kurylenko
Felix Leiter: Jeffrey Wright
René Mathis: Giancarlo Giannini
Mr. White: Jesper Christensen
Corinne Veneau: Stana Katic
Agent Fields: Gemma Arterton
General Medrano: Joaquín Cosio
Gregg Beam: David Harbour
Origin: USA
Language: English
Released: 2008
Production: Michael G. Wilson, Barbara Broccoli; Eon Productions; released by Columbia Pictures
Directed by: Marc Foster

Written by: Paul Haggis, Neal Purvis, Robert Wade
Cinematography by: Roberto Schaefer
Music by: David Arnold
Sound: Eddy Joseph
Editing: Matt Chesse, Richard Pearson
Art Direction: Chris Lowe
Costumes: Louise Frogley
Production Design: Dennis Gassner
MPAA rating: PG-13
Running time: 105 minutes

REVIEWS

Boston Globe Online. November 14, 2008.
Chicago Sun-Times Online. November 12, 2008.
Entertainment Weekly Online. November 4, 2008.
Hollywood Reporter Online. October 24, 2008.
Los Angeles Times Online. November 13, 2008.
New York Times Online. November 14, 2008.
New Yorker Online. November 17, 2008.
Rolling Stone Online. November 27, 2008.
San Francisco Chronicle. November 14, 2008, p. E1.
Time Online. October 31, 2008.
Variety Online. October 24, 2008.
Wall Street Journal Online. November 14, 2008.
Washington Post. November 14, 2008, p. C1.

QUOTES

M (to Bond): "If you could avoid killing every possible lead it would be appreciated."

TRIVIA

Daniel Craig felt *Casino Royale* was physically less demanding than this film. He was injured about three times during production due to the intense stunt work he was required to perform.

AWARDS

Nomination:

British Acad. 2008: Sound, Visual FX.

QUARANTINE

On March 11, 2008 the government sealed off an apartment complex in Los Angeles. The residents were never seen again. No details. No witnesses. No evidence. Until now.
—Movie tagline

Box Office: $31.6 million

Remaking horror movies has become a hackneyed cliché. The 1970s seems to be the decade of choice for studio moguls to cannibalize. Similar to a rotting, maggot-infested corpse cast along a desolate highway, the horror film industry is enduring a kind of infinite density, forever collapsing upon itself. During the 2000s this genre has experienced a peak of unoriginality along with a dearth of artistry, with "reconceived" works such as *The Amityville Horror* (2005), *Day of the Dead* (2008), *The Texas Chainsaw Massacre* (2003), *The Fog* (2005), *The Hills Have Eyes* (2006), *House of Wax* (2005), and *Halloween* (2007), to name a few. Director John Erick Dowdle decided it was not necessary to excavate so deeply, believing that this remake of the 2007 Spanish film *[Rec]* was long overdue.

While many scenes are carbon copies of scenes in Jaume Balagueró's film, complete with dialogue differing only in translation, Dowdle gains inspiration from a horrific muse by naming his work *Quarantine*, which serves both as title and a warning to viewers. The film incorporates an overused technique, managing to bring it to a higher threshold of annoyance (if not nausea): the use of the shaky cam under the conceit of making a documentary. During the film's extended prologue, this faux documentation works fine as the story introduces a nubile Los Angeles telecaster, Angela Vidal (Jennifer Carpenter), and her cameraman, Scott (Steve Harris). The duo is endeavoring to shadow and ride along with an L.A. fire station's crew for an evening. Scott's camera is steady throughout this introductory period wherein the relationships between the characters are established. The film is successful at piquing the viewer's interest. From this point, the story plummets into a frustrating spool of mayhem.

The firehouse responds to a 911 call and arrives in full emergency gear to a rundown apartment building where one of the tenants has been screaming. The crew comes across a raspy, unresponsive elderly woman who is foaming at the mouth. She suddenly explodes into action, taking a bite out of the neck of one of the firefighters before being restrained. The tension escalates into bedlam as the rescue crew, two cops, and the remaining residents discover that the entire complex has been locked and sealed from the outside. The movie quickly devolves into a third-rate zombie flick. While treating the mounting number of victims, a veterinarian, Lawrence (Greg Germann), explains that the bitten are exhibiting symptoms of rabies, yet he cannot determine why their condition is so accelerated. The captives learn that the Center for Disease Control has ordered their containment, which is enforced with deadly force when a resident attempts to exit the doomed complex from an upper-story window. The zombies grow in number as the number of people unexposed to the virulent mutated virus dwindles. Amid the chaos, Scott finds that his camera serves not only as a recorder of events but also as an effective lethal weapon, as he bludgeons a full-blown rabid zombie to death, splattering the camera lens with infected blood in the process. He carefully wipes it clean and continues recording. With that kind of composure, Scott would have been an asset as a cameraman for George A. Romero. It is only during the film's climax that there is a morsel of intrigue: Angela and Scott, the only two people still unaffected, find themselves in the attic unit where they uncover yellowing newspaper clippings reporting on a "doomsday cult" that has been harvesting the virus in order to unleash a lethal pandemic. The last scene is viewed in the camera's night vision feature, casting everything in an eerie green glow. Following Scott's grisly murder by a decrepit old man, Angela is seen being pulled into darkness as she frantically claws the wooden floor. (Unfortunately this shot, the film's spoiler, was used in both its trailers and in the promotional poster.)

The frenetic camera work exacerbates the weakness of *Quarantine*'s script. Any empathy for the characters cultivated the film's beginning is quickly lost as the jumbling makes it virtually impossible to decipher what is happening. Coupled with Jennifer Carpenter's incessant whimpering and hyperventilating, the film is a grating experience. Her screaming banshee act is best laid to rest with *The Exorcism of Emily Rose* (2005); it is a trend that was seen in *The Blair Witch Project* (1999) as well as this year's *Cloverfield*. If clichés have a lifespan, it is time to bury the first-person shaky-cam technique.

David Metz Roberts

CREDITS

Angela Vidal: Jennifer Carpenter
Sadie: Dania Ramirez
George Fletcher: Johnathon Schaech
Jake: Jay Hernandez
Danny Wilensky: Columbus Short
Kathy: Marin Hinkle
Yuri Ivanov: Rade Serbedzija
Randy: Denis O'Hare
Lawrence: Greg Germann
Scott Percival: Steve Harris
Origin: USA
Language: English
Released: 2008
Production: Doug Davison, Roy Lee, Sergio Aguero, Clint Culpepper, Julio Fernández; Vertigo Entertainment, Screen Gems, Andale Pictures; released by Sony Pictures
Directed by: John Erick Dowdle

Written by: John Erick Dowdle, Drew Dowdle
Cinematography by: Ken Seng
Sound: Shawn Holden
Editing: Elliot Greenberg
Art Direction: Chris Cornwell
Costumes: Maya Lieberman
Production Design: Jon Gary Steele
MPAA rating: R
Running time: 89 minutes

REVIEWS

Boston Globe Online. October 11, 2008.
Entertainment Weekly Online. October 10, 2008.
Hollywood Reporter Online. October 10, 2008.
Los Angeles Times Online. October 11, 2008.
New York Times Online. October 11, 2008.
Variety Online. October 10, 2008.
Wall Street Journal Online. October 3, 2008.

QUOTES

Yuri Ivanov: "They won't let us out."

TRIVIA

Unlike most Hollywood films, this movie features no musical
   score.

RACHEL GETTING MARRIED

Box Office: $12.6 million

In a December 2008 interview with PBS talk-show
host Tavis Smiley, *Rachel Getting Married*'s director,
Jonathan Demme, explained his decision to make
Rachel's groom, Sidney (Tunde Adebimpe), a musician
from New Orleans, and to include a serviceman on
leave from Iraq among the wedding guests. "I felt funny
making a film in this day and age without acknowledging New Orleans...We mustn't ever forget New Orleans
until things are made right...we also can't forget that
we're in this war and the people over there." Because of
his demonstrable decency and compassion, it's not hard
to surmise why Demme is so often referred to by critics
as our most "humane" filmmaker. He is the perfect director to helm *Rachel Getting Married,* a film filled with
complex people on the tortuous path to redemption. He
sees his characters for who they are, flaws and all, while
always giving them the benefit of the doubt.

When the film begins, recovering addict Kym Buchman (Anne Hathaway) is leaving rehab for the weekend
to attend her sister Rachel's (Rosemarie DeWitt)
wedding. Her childhood home is bustling with activity
and music, as friends and family prepare for the upcoming festivities. Although the sisters are close enough to
finish each other's sentences, long-held grievances repeatedly bubble to the surface. Kym's relationship with her
divorced parents is also strained, and she seeks relief
from the smothering attention of her father, the effusive
Paul (Bill Irwin), and a closer connection with her
mother, the remote Abby (Debra Winger). A frantic trip
to an Alcoholics Anonymous meeting seems to offer
solace, but Kym remains on the defensive, anticipating
criticism at every turn and launching biting pre-emptive
strikes against the other house guests, including the
maid of honor and the bride herself. (Noting Rachel's
slim physique, Kym comments, "I would swear to God
you're puking again.") Her self-absorbed yet self-loathing
toast at Rachel and Sidney's rehearsal dinner serves only
to ratchet up the tension.

Eventually it is revealed that ten years earlier, a
stoned Kym was responsible for the accidental drowning
death of Ethan, the youngest Buchman sibling. Kym
believes Abby was also culpable (because she allowed the
drug-addicted Kym to babysit her little brother), and
when she confronts her mother, their fight becomes
shockingly physical. As a distraught Kym drives wildly
from Abby's house, she winds up crashing the car and
arrives for the wedding with a black eye. When Rachel
sees her injured sister, she quietly nurses her, and the
two reconcile. The highly personal, ebullient wedding
(which features professional performers of all stripes) is a
genuine celebration, and though Rachel attempts to
reunite her mother and sister, Abby does not seem ready,
willing, or able.

Hathaway's raw, daring performance as Kym has
been rightly hailed by critics. By turns self-pitying,
manipulative, and antagonistic, Kym is not an easy
character to like, but Hathaway helps viewers realize
that Kym's passive-aggressive tactics are a means of self-
defense. (The audience will likely feel more sympathetic
to her almost biblically tragic plight than do the
characters closest to her.) For most of her visit, Kym
talks nonstop, and Hathaway's agitated performance
suggests that the character's thoughts come lightning-
quick, too fast for her to filter. Once Rachel shows her
compassion, however, Kym visibly winds down; during
the wedding, she is quiet and reflective, and her reactive
behavior subsides. It is a testament to Hathaway's
performance that this change seems organic.

The work of the other leads is equally strong. As
DeWitt plays her, Rachel, "the good daughter," is no
saint. In her attempts to pit Paul and Abby against Kym
during the wedding preparations, she comes across as
needy, immature, and bitter. And though Rachel is

understandably angry with Kym for her role in Ethan's death, it is clear she just as deeply resents her sister for historically monopolizing their parents' attention. Here DeWitt and screenwriter Jenny Lumet keenly illustrate how familial ruptures both profound and "petty" can leave lasting scars. At the wedding—that seems utopian in its joy, optimism, and inclusiveness—Rachel strives to be the best version of herself, but the memory of Ethan's death is always lurking, ready to lure the entire family back to despair. The Buchmans yearn to believe they would have been so good, so happy, if only Ethan had not died. It is a misguided fantasy, but a heartbreakingly human one.

Kym and Rachel clearly had problems before Ethan's death—Kym was already using, and it is hinted that Rachel was coping with an eating disorder before that point. Like the Whitman brothers in Wes Anderson's 2007 film *Darjeeling Limited,* the Buchman sisters have spent their lives struggling to capture the love of a distant and elusive mother. The character of Abby could have come across merely as an enigma, as Patricia does in *Darjeeling Limited* (or as a monster, à la Beth in *Ordinary People* [1980]), but through Demme's sympathetic direction and Winger's shaded portrayal, a more complicated portrait emerges. Visibly moved by the sweet, stirring vows at Rachel's wedding, Abby seems pained by the experience. It is as if she is too wounded to withstand deep emotion of any kind, be it anger, sadness, or joy.

Though *Rachel Getting Married* shares themes with *Darjeeling Limited,* Demme's loose aesthetic approach could not be more different than Anderson's meticulous one. Shot with a handheld digital camera in natural light, the movie has an intimate, improvised feel. In a director's statement, Demme said he was inspired by the films of Robert Altman, and hoped that he and cinematographer Declan Quinn could make the film seem like "the most beautiful home movie ever made, as though every scene was captured on digital by a friend with a camera, or even by the ghost of a character whose death haunts this family." While some viewers may lose patience with the film's pacing—especially during the rehearsal dinner and wedding sequences, which Demme does not rush—the director's decisions make the story seem as if it is authentically unfolding, with all the messiness of an actual family gathering. The diagetic music played throughout further enriches the unique landscape of this film.

Because most of the film is so well-observed, the few contrived moments ring especially false, as when Kym, during a playful family competition, inadvertently unearths a reminder of Ethan. As Cyndi Fuchs of popmatters.com has observed, "In using [this dramatic mechanism], the plot turns explicitly manipulative." It is the single misstep in an otherwise sure-footed and remarkable movie.

Marisa Carroll

CREDITS

Kym: Anne Hathaway
Rachel: Rosemarie DeWitt
Paul: Bill Irwin
Abby: Debra Winger
Sidney: Tunde Adebimpe
Kieran: Mather Zickel
Emma: Anisa George
Carol: Anna Deavere Smith
Origin: USA
Language: English
Released: 2008
Production: Jonathan Demme, Marc Platt, Neda Armian; Clinica Estetico; released by Sony Pictures Classics
Directed by: Jonathan Demme
Written by: Jenny Lumet
Cinematography by: Declan Quinn
Music by: Zafer Tawil, Donald Harrison Jr.
Sound: Jeff Pullman
Editing: Tim Squyres
Costumes: Susan Lyall
Production Design: Ford Wheeler
MPAA rating: R
Running time: 111 minutes

REVIEWS

Entertainment Weekly Online. October 1, 2008.
Hollywood Reporter Online. September 3, 2008.
Los Angeles Times Online. October 3, 2008.
New York Times Online. October 3, 2008.
New Yorker Online. October 6, 2008.
Rolling Stone Online. October 2, 2008.
Variety Online. September 3, 2008.
Wall Street Journal Online. October 3, 2008.
Washington Post. October 17, 2008.

QUOTES

Rachel's wedding rehearsal toast: "I am Shiva the Destroyer and your harbinger of doom for this evening."

TRIVIA

The dishwashing scene was based on an actual event involving Sidney Lumet (the screenwriter's father) and Bob Fosse.

AWARDS

Nomination:

Oscars 2008: Actress (Hathaway)

RAMBO

Heroes never die...they just reload.
—Movie tagline

Box Office: $42.7 million

The last time John Rambo (Sylvester Stallone) graced the silver screen, he was in Soviet-occupied Afghanistan in a rescue effort to save his old war commanding officer, Colonel Trautman (the late Richard Crenna). The aptly titled *Rambo III* (1988) presumably left Rambo in Thailand, where this fourth installment begins. It is there that the ex-patriot, former renegade Special Forces veteran of the Vietnam War is quietly eking out a living along the banks of the Salween River by capturing and selling snakes and by transporting tourists in the boat he owns. He also spends his time spearfishing and delving into blacksmith work.

Rambo begins by showing actual footage of fairly recent events in the world's longest ongoing civil war, occurring in Burma (officially recognized by the United Nations as the Union of Myanmar) under the regime of Than Shwe. The country's military junta sweeps through the jungle villages of the ethnic minority, the Karen, who are brutally murdered, tortured or conscripted into the state's military.

Rambo is approached by a group of American missionaries who wish to provide humanitarian aid for a Karen village. They are a group composed of a few doctors who, in addition to conducting bible studies, intend to provide much-needed medical attention to deprived villagers. Rambo initially declines because he considers Burma a war zone and cynically states that anything aside from the provision of weapons is for naught. It takes the friendly feminine grace of Sarah Miller (Julie Benz), the sole woman of the group, to convince Rambo to agree to provide passage for them into Burma. Despite Rambo's dearth of facial and vocal expressions, save a dour look etched in a face resembling granite, he is charmed into complying with the idealistic woman's wishes.

Along the way, they are stopped by a boat of Burmese pirates who demand Sarah as the price of passage upriver. Exploding into action, Rambo kills the armed crew with a quick sweep of the gun concealed in his waistband. Although he saved them from a brutal demise, the pacifist missionaries are opposed to Rambo's method of kill or be killed. Once they reach their destination, the leader of the group, Burnett (Paul Schulze), informs Rambo his services are no longer be required as he himself intends to lead the group out of Myanmar by road upon the completion of their mission.

After an interlude during which the church group successfully aids the Karen people, the village is besieged by a Burmese army unit under the command of the sadistic, chain-smoking Major Tint (played by a bona fide Karen freedom fighter, Maung Maung Khin), who, for enjoyment, violently forces Karen prisoners to walk through minefields. The Burmese agenda appears to be small-scale genocide. Tint's unit slaughters the villagers: Murdering men, women, and children of the Karen is an implacable undertaking he enjoys. He kidnaps the survivors, including the American missionaries.

Rambo is approached by the group's pastor, who has traveled to Thailand after his parishioners missed their return date. Fearing the worst and seemingly not as irenic as his congregants, Reverend Arthur Marsh (Ken Howard) has hired a team of diverse mercenaries and requests that Rambo transport them upriver as well. Humility has its limits. Rambo experiences a moment of clarity as he forges a machete: He realizes that he is a warrior and that when needed, killing is the easy part for him. Joining the motley squad, Rambo quickly assumes the role of leader and implements his strategic skills to formulate a rescue operation. The band is temporarily split up, with Rambo alongside Sarah and the team's marksman. During the climactic battle, Rambo commandeers a truck with a .50 caliber gun mount and proceeds to mow down the Burmese army unit. With the assistance of the Karen freedom fighters, Rambo's group prevails, sustaining few casualties.

The plot of the film is simple, with very few twists and turns. Most of the short film (93 minutes) is a plume of carnage. Due to contemporary special effects, *Rambo* is able to join the ranks of the recent war movies that vividly detail a man exploding or being strafed by machine gunfire, or bodies in motion literally ripped in half. The gore-infused action is so visually intense in *Rambo,* it makes the first 24 shaky-camera minutes of *Saving Private Ryan* (1998) look like a patriotic *Tom and Jerry* cartoon.

Gloomy, laconic, and prone to casting cold, woebegone stares, Stallone (who directed the film and cowrote the script), stacked with bulging muscles via human growth hormone, remains one-dimensional in this addition to the Ramboverse. Stallone's other iconic cinematic figure, Rocky Balboa, is an ebullient puppy by comparison. The missionaries are unconvincing in their purpose, dull in delivery, and flat in their Christian conviction. The cadre of mercenaries Rambo ends up leading are as cartoonish as the Keystone Cops in that they ooze clichéd 1980s machismo. Although Stallone wanted to drive the film with humanitarian purpose, it scarcely deviates from its predecessors in battlefield carnage and, in fact, raises the bar significantly with 236 kills, surpassing the combined death toll of the all previous films in the series.

Regarding his choice of setting for *Rambo,* Stallone said in an interview with *MoviesOnline,* "I thought the Burmese setting would be ideal because it's a story that's not just about Rambo. It's actually happening. It's true.... From the time I heard about it and began researching it, I thought, 'if I could just combine the two—raising awareness of the Karen-Burmese civil war and giving the audience a good adventure story—that would be perfect.'"

In the film's last scene we see Rambo, who, in a personal reckoning, has decided to see his full-blooded Native American father, walking along a rural highway in the Arizona desert. A dilapidated mailbox stands in front of a sprawling ranch. It does not bear a number, but reads "R. Rambo." Unfortunately, the reunion scene between father and son could have provided the film with much-needed depth.

Stallone explained his character's moment of clarity: "I kill for myself. I don't kill for my country. Stop using this excuse that I'm a hero. I'm not. I've just got this penchant for violence inside of me that has to come out." Come out it did. That is the true purpose of *Rambo.*

David Metz Roberts

CREDITS

John Rambo: Sylvester Stallone
Sarah: Julie Benz
Burnett: Paul Schulze
Arthur Marsh: Ken Howard
En-Joo: Tim Kang
Lewis: Graham McTavish
Diaz: Rey Gallegos
Reese: Jake La Botz
Tint: Maung Maung Khin
Origin: USA
Language: English
Released: 2008
Production: Avi Lerner, John Thompson, Kevin King-Templeton; Equity Pictures Medienfonds GmbH & Co. KG II, Nu Image Films, Millennium Films; released by Lionsgate
Directed by: Sylvester Stallone
Written by: Sylvester Stallone, Art Monterastelli
Cinematography by: Glen MacPherson
Music by: Brian Tyler, Ashley Miller
Sound: Greg Chapman
Editing: Sean Albertson
Art Direction: Suchartanun Kuladee
Costumes: Lizz Wolf
Production Design: Franco-Giacomo Carbone
MPAA rating: R
Running time: 93 minutes

REVIEWS

Boston Globe Online. January 15, 2008.
Chicago Sun-Times Online. January 25, 2008.
Hollywood Reporter Online. January 25, 2008.
Los Angeles Times Online. January 25, 2008.
New York Times Online. January 25, 2008.
Premiere Online. January 24, 2008.
San Francisco Chronicle. January 25, 2008, p. E10.
Variety Online. January 24, 2008.
Washington Post. January 25, 2008, p. C6.

QUOTES

John Rambo: "You know what you are. What you're made of. War is in your blood. Don't fight it. You didn't kill for your country. You killed for yourself. God's never gonna make that go away. When you're pushed, killin' is as easy as breathin'."

TRIVIA

Although James Brolin was attached to assume the role of Col. Samuel Trautman after Richard Crenna died, the character was eventually written out of the script.

THE READER

How far would you go to protect a secret?
—Movie tagline
Behind the mystery lies a truth that will make you question everything you know.
—Movie tagline

Box Office: $30 million

In addition to being a thought-provoking look at guilt, responsibility, sex, and love, *The Reader* is an unusual, controversial treatment of the Holocaust. By focusing nonjudgmentally on a perpetrator of the evils of Nazi Germany, the film takes great risks, especially by potentially alienating some viewers who may see it as a sympathetic treatment of someone guilty of a horrendous crime. As a work of art, *The Reader* succeeds mainly because of two powerful performances.

Based on the 1995 novel by Bernhard Schlink, *The Reader* tells the stories of Michael Berg (David Kross and Ralph Fiennes) and Hanna Schmitz (Kate Winslet) from 1958 to 1995. They meet in Heidelberg when Michael (David Kross) is fifteen and Hanna, a streetcar conductor, is thirty-six. She comes to his aid when he falls ill outside her apartment, and when he returns to thank her, they quickly become lovers. Their lovemaking alternates with his reading to her from works by Homer, Mark Twain, Anton Chekov, Leo Tolstoy, and D. H. Lawrence, whose *Lady Chatterley's Lover* (1928) she finds shocking for its sexual content. If Hanna initially seduces him, Michael is made to seduce her over and over through literature.

After several months of passion, Hanna suddenly vanishes from Michael's life, then unexpectedly reappears in 1966 when he is a law student at Heidelberg University. Michael is one of a small group of students Professor Rohl (Bruno Ganz) assigns to attend the trial of six women who guarded Jewish prisoners in a concentration camp during World War II. He is shocked to see that Hanna is one of the accused and dismayed to hear of her crimes. Michael also discovers that another of Hanna's secrets is her illiteracy, but he does not have the courage to do anything about it, though the revelation would help her defense.

Ten years later the adult Michael (Ralph Fiennes), now a lawyer, begins sending the imprisoned Hanna tape recordings of the books he had read to her years before. This act has poignant and surprising consequences when the two finally meet again in 1988. All these years Michael has kept his relationship with Hanna a secret before divulging it first to Ilana Mather (Lena Olin), a survivor of Hanna's most horrific atrocity, and to Julia (Hannah Herzsprung), his daughter.

As far as offbeat love stories go, *The Reader* is most unusual. The romantic/sexual element helped make Schlink's novel a best seller as well as a selection of Oprah's Book Club. Yet the novel is most notable for the economic way Schlink interweaves his themes, making the German sense of guilt following the Nazi era a compelling subject for non-German readers. Both the novel and the film contrast the opposing views of guilt held by Hanna and Michael. While she never quite comes to grips with her sins, Michael is fated to be an observer, unable to act when necessary, agonizing over his guilt about Hanna, as well as his country's legacy to his generation.

Just as Schlink presents his tortured characters rather objectively, the film directed by Stephen Daldry and written by David Hare also withholds judgment, allowing viewers to draw their own conclusions. Central to this approach is a scene during the trial when Hanna challenges the judge (Burghart Klaussner) to explain what he would have done in her circumstances. The

objectivity of the film is somewhat surprising given that Hare, an acclaimed playwright, has a tendency to scold his characters and audiences, an approach that weakens *The Hours* (2002), the screenwriter's previous collaboration with Daldry. The director, who also made *Billy Elliot* (2000), another film about a difficult adolescence, displays a more assured visual style than in his earlier work, handling well the physical and psychological space between the characters, especially in Hanna's seduction of Michael and Michael's tentative relationships toward two other women in his life, Sophie (Vijessna Ferkic), a fellow high school student, and Marthe (Karoline Herfurth), the law student who becomes his wife.

Many reviewers of *The Reader* were annoyed by the film's nonjudgmental tone. The film and its makers have been accused of trivializing the Holocaust, of making a monster sympathetic, of endorsing sexual contact between an adult and an adolescent, and of poorly explaining the characters' motivations. While *The Reader* is subtle—perhaps too subtle for some—an exception is the score by Nico Muhly, a former assistant to Philip Glass, the composer for *The Hours*. Muhly alternates between echoing Glass's repetitive rhythms and trying too hard to underscore the characters' emotions. An overly insistent piece during a trial scene is especially obtrusive.

While Kross, who turned eighteen during the making of *The Reader*, handles the Michael-Hanna scenes well, he is unable to express fully the turmoil of Michael the law student. His scenes with Ganz, who underplays his part wonderfully, demonstrate his inadequacies. Olin offers a movingly quiet interpretation in a pivotal scene that could easily have become overwrought. Though some reviewers complained that Fiennes is predictably morose as the adult Michael, few actors convey the pains of guilt as well. Compare Fiennes's interior performance here with his flamboyant *In Bruges* (2008) gangster and his emotionally stunted aristocrat in *The Duchess* (2008) to see what remarkable range he displayed in 2008.

The main virtue of *The Reader* is Winslet's performance. Like Cate Blanchett, Winslet has a different look and acting style in almost every film. Her Hanna is unlike any of her other roles, a fascinating mixture of strengths and weaknesses. That Hanna turns out to be a concentration camp guard is not surprising given the authoritative way she takes control from her first scene, washing away the vomit after Michael has thrown up in front of her building, and ushering the boy into her room to make him presentable. Hanna maintains control of her relationship with Michael not because of the age difference, but through the power she must exert to balance the deficiencies in her life.

266

Winslet holds her body commandingly erect except when relaxing a bit during the sex scenes and on a bicycle trip to the country. Hanna's body assumes a different type of rigidity, that of fear, whenever the discovery of her illiteracy is threatened. As Hanna ages, her body language changes accordingly, becoming slightly huddled to protect her true self. When Michael silently comes aboard Hanna's empty streetcar late at night, Winslet displays a wide range of emotions in seconds, encapsulating the life of a limited woman incapable of understanding the complexities bombarding her. An ironically golden glow emanates from the trolley, one of several striking images created by two of the world's greatest cinematographers, Roger Deakins, who shot *No Country for Old Men* (2007), and Chris Menges, whose credits include *Local Hero* (1983).

Winslet refuses to sentimentalize Hanna, displaying in the trial scenes no awareness of the horrors the character has committed, and softening her only marginally during her twenty years of incarceration. Along with Schlink, Hare, Daldry, and Fiennes, Winslet understands that viewers must evaluate the moral consequences of Hanna's acts for themselves.

Michael Adams

CREDITS

Michael Berg (older): Ralph Fiennes
Hanna Schmitz: Kate Winslet
Rohl: Bruno Ganz
Ilana (young): Alexandra Maria Lara
Rose Mather/Ilana Mather (older): Lena Olin
Marthe: Karoline Herforth
Michael Berg (young): David Kross
Peter Berg: Matthias Habich
Carla Berg: Susanne Lothar
Origin: USA, Germany
Language: English
Released: 2008
Production: Anthony Minghella, Sydney Pollack, Donna Gigliotti, Redmond Morris; Mirage Enterprises, Neunte Babelsberg Film; released by Weinstein Company
Directed by: Stephen Daldry
Written by: David Hare
Cinematography by: Chris Menges, Roger Deakins
Music by: Nico Muhly
Sound: Manfred Banach
Editing: Claire Simpson
Art Direction: Christian M. Goldbeck
Costumes: Ann Roth, Donna Maloney
Production Design: Brigitte Broch
MPAA rating: R
Running time: 123 minutes

REVIEWS

Entertainment Weekly Online. December 10, 2008.
Hollywood Reporter Online. November 30, 2008.
Los Angeles Times Online. December 11, 2008.
New York Times Online. December 10, 2008.
New Yorker Online. December 15, 2008.
Newsweek Online. November 28, 2008.
Rolling Stone Online. December 25, 2008.
San Francisco Chronicle. December 12, 2008, p. E5.
Variety Online. November 30, 2008.
Village Voice Online. November 30, 2008.
Wall Street Journal Online. December 12, 2008.

QUOTES

Hanna: "It doesn't matter what I feel, it doesn't matter what I think. The dead are still dead."

TRIVIA

The production had to wait to film the sex scenes between Kate Winslet and David Kross until the actor turned eighteen.

AWARDS

Oscars 2008: Support. Actress (Winslet)
British Acad. 2008: Actress (Winslet)
Golden Globes 2009: Support. Actress (Winslet)
Screen Actors Guild 2008: Support. Actress (Winslet)
Nomination:
Oscars 2008: Adapt. Screenplay, Cinematog., Director (Daldry), Film
British Acad. 2008: Adapt. Screenplay, Cinematog., Director (Daldry), Film
Golden Globes 2009: Director (Daldry), Film—Drama, Screenplay.

REDBELT

There's always a way out. You just have to find it.
   —Movie tagline

Box Office: $2.3 million

In *Redbelt,* writer/director David Mamet employs the venerable art of jiu-jitsu (he has been an avid student for over five years, earning the rank of purple belt) as a metaphor for life's mystery, which is often rife with betrayal and compromise. Mamet's martial arts drama is glutted with the Oscar®-nominated screenwriter's signature brusque, repetitive dialogue. Mike Terry (Chiwetel Ejiofor) is an old-school jiu-jitsu instructor operating a run-down academy in a sordid section of Los Angeles. Terry abides by the code of the samurai and instills in his students a confident objectiveness when it comes to fighting. "Commit to the move," he instructs a rising student during a sparring match. Police officer Joe Collins (Max Martini) has both his hands bound. "You know the escape. You know the escape," Terry emphasizes to Collins. This last bit of dialogue is a clear example of Mamet's penchant for having his characters repeat themselves ad nauseum. Ejiofor, however, delivers his lines with a naturalness and sincerity, infusing them with a tranquil self-possession that creates an atmosphere of serenity for those around him. He is an urban Kwai Chang Caine. A possible DVD featurette could be: "The *je ne sais quoi* of Michael Terry: bodhisattva of the Martial Way."

Problems stem from an incident at the beginning of the story when a distraught, psychologically damaged attorney (Emily Mortimer) stumbles into Terry's studio after sideswiping his car. High-strung and jittery (rooted in having being raped), she seizes and discharges Collins's weapon when she misinterprets his attempts at calming her. The stray bullet shatters the studio's storefront window. From this plot element, it quickly becomes very clear that few people of integrity inhabit Terry's world, which is awash with venal opportunists.

Mike's wife Sondra (Alice Braga) is at her wits' end with her husband's nonchalant attitude about the flagging academy's financial state. Succumbing to Sondra's woes, Mike agrees to meet up with his brother-in-law Bruno (Rodrigo Santoro), who runs a seedy bar in addition to promoting open martial arts competitions in the UFC tradition. While at the bar, Mike learns that Joe Collins, who moonlighted as a bouncer for the club, has not been paid for his services. Bruno is perplexed by Mike's lack of interest in using his talent to ride the gravy train. Mike believes that the orchestrated construction of competition interferes with training for the real thing. "Competition weakens the fighter," he says. In Bruno's world, Mike's humility is akin to a foolishness bound to a destitute, marginal existence; two states he finds utterly repulsive.

When a fight breaks out in the bar between television celebrity Chet Frank (played with amicable charm by Tim Allen) and some bar thugs, Mike disarms and subdues them. Grateful, Chet sends a dinner invitation to Mike, along with a $20,000 gold Rolex. Ever true to his honorable nature, Mike visits Joe at the police station and gives him his black belt in the locker room. In the tradition of Brazilian jiu-jitsu there are no tests for belt promotion: The rank is simply awarded in a non-

formal manner once the instructor believes the student is ready. As a bonus, Mike gives him the watch as well.

As the story continues to a predictable denouement, the screenwriter sews the previous developments together, which is an indelible component to his writing. Mamet stays faithful to the progression of the plot; his mantra is "what happens next?" He tends to eschew what he believes to be deviations and distractions by delving too much into a character's psychological makeup. In Mike's case, there are no intrinsic frailties, no rabbit corpse boiling in a stew pot. What the audience sees of his disposition at the beginning resonates throughout the course of the film.

Chet Frank could not be more different from Mike. We learn that Mike is a veteran of the war in Iraq when he visits Chet's film set. Chet only plays a military man, and is unfamiliar with the military jargon pervasive in his script. Later, during dinner at Chet's mansion, the non-Method actor offers Mike the title of coproducer on his film, while his wife courts Sondra by flattering her fashion acumen. Both Mike and Sondra are starry-eyed at the world of the glitterati.

Chet, it turns out, is a Judas Goat colluding with the architects of the open martial arts's competition, the IFC. The naïve couple discover that Chet and his wife's offers were a sham. When Joe commits suicide after being indicted for trying to pawn the Rolex, which turned out to be stolen, Mike finds himself being pulled into the corrupt and turbulent world surrounding the televised ring. The purse offered to the victor will help Joe's family as well as his own impoverished state of affairs. One betrayal is heaped on another as we learn that not only was Mike conned, but also the fight promoters stole his training technique of utilizing a "handicap" wherein one pupil is bound in some way before engaging in a match.

Waiting for his bout, Mike discovers that the fights are fixed and decides to remain honorable by bowing out. Competition is bad enough; scripted fights are verboten. It is the exchange between Mike and the troubled attorney-turned-student in the penultimate scene that gives the film a detour, and the climax is a graft from the *Rocky* series. Mike decides to intimate on live television that the fights are fraudulent. One man is there to stymie his effort: Bruno. The choreographed off-ring fight scene is true to form, highlighting the beauty of the grappling art of jiu-jitsu, with its trademark economy of motion between two combatants. The skilled fight between Ejiofor and Santoro is very convincing, and we see Mamet's admiration for the style. Mike prevails once he sees the "Professor" a deified figurehead of the Brazilian system. He makes it to the ring, and before he can make his proclamation, the suited Professor bestows Mike with the highest rank: his own red belt.

The red belt represents the highest level one can achieve while maintaining integrity and purity. No matter what the odds or temptations, Mike never compromises his true self. This perseverance earns him the red belt: He transcended. Mamet explains the merits of his tale to in an interview with Rebecca Murray: "As what happens in any hero journey, you start off saying, 'I'm not going to engage in the world. I'm going to live on my mountaintop. If I'm in my academy, everything is pure and I can teach purity.' Step two is that, 'I'm going to engage in the world. How can I live in a world full of stupid people?' And step three in the hero journey is, 'I'm one of them,' so that's what Mike has to go through."

David Metz Roberts

CREDITS

Mike Terry: Chiwetel Ejiofor
Sondra Terry: Alice Braga
Chet Frank: Tim Allen
Laura Black: Emily Mortimer
Bruno Silva: Rodrigo Santoro
Jerry Weiss: Joe Mantegna
Zena Frank: Rebecca Pidgeon
Richie: David Paymer
Marty Brown: Ricky Jay
Snowflake: Jose Pablo Cantillo
George: Ray Mancini
Joe Collins: Max Martini
Ricardo Silva: John Machado
Origin: USA
Language: English
Released: 2008
Production: Chrisann Verges; released by Sony Pictures Classics
Directed by: David Mamet
Written by: David Mamet
Cinematography by: Robert Elswit
Music by: Stephen Endelman
Sound: Paul Lewis
Editing: Barbara Tulliver
Art Direction: Ray Yamagata
Costumes: Debra McGuire
Production Design: David Wasco
MPAA rating: R
Running time: 99 minutes

REVIEWS

Boston Globe Online. April 30, 2008.
Entertainment Weekly Online. April 30, 2008.
Hollywood Reporter Online. April 25, 2008.
Los Angeles Times Online. May 2, 2008.
New York Times Online. May 2, 2008.
Rolling Stone Online. May 1, 2008.
Variety Online. April 25, 2008.
Village Voice Online. April 29, 2008.
Wall Street Journal. May 2, 2008, p. W1.

QUOTES

Chet Frank: "Everything has rules. The problem is sticking to them."

TRIVIA

David Mamet was inspired to write the script because of Ed O'Neill's practice of Brazilian Ju-Jitsu.

RELIGULOUS

Do you smell something burning?
—Movie tagline

Box Office: $13 million

Stand-up comedian turned political talk-show host Bill Maher takes his penchant for being an iconoclast into the genre of the docucomedy, a style of filmmaking perpetuated during the last decade by independent stalwarts Michael Moore and Morgan Spurlock. Partnering with *Borat* (2007) director Larry Charles, Maher wrote his op-ed work, *Religulous,* which is a portmanteau he coined from the words "religion" and "ridiculous." The film explores and satirizes many of the world's religions such as Christianity, Islam, and Mormonism, as well as a variety of cults. His travels were wide-ranging, bringing him to Florida, Utah, Missouri, the Vatican, and the Holy Land. (In one of the work's funnier scenes, Maher mimics a scientologist at Speaker's Corner in Hyde Park, London.)

Maher had George Carlin as a guest on his HBO show *Real Time with Bill Maher,* and admitted that the late comedian heavily influenced him to embark on his crusade against religion. Growing up in a Catholic household with a Jewish mother, Maher disdains any form of religion. Although humorous, witty, and intelligent, Maher lampoons religious adherents so acerbically that his likeability factor begins to wane early on in the film. It is due to his forte at ribaldry that his victims present as utterly incompetent buffoons; as commentator and interviewer, Maher comes across as a villainous Cyrano de Bergerac. His thesis is a simple one: Religions are the most portentous threat that humankind faces and their eradication is a necessity if humanity is to survive.

Maher travels abroad and admits to subverting his subjects by presenting himself as something other than he is (the *Borat* hoodwink technique). Jim Fletcher of *WorldNetDaily* reported that Maher openly admitted, "We never, ever, used my name. We never told anybody it was me who was going to do the interviews. We even had a fake title for the film. We called it *A Spiritual Journey*." (Moore also employed this guerrilla tactic for his film *Bowling for Columbine* (2002) in order to procure an interview with Charlton Heston.) Full of dexterous fluency, Maher frequently interrupts and talks over his interviewees. The editing process twists the knife as the interviews are often intercut with scenes from cinematic epics (such as the 1956 classic *The Ten Commandments*) or the Mel Brooks's 1974 spoof *Blazing Saddles*. Injecting clips of televangelists for comedic effect also highlights the inanity of the devotee.

The first half of the film lambasts Christianity. Among his exploits, Maher visits the Creation Museum in Hebron, Kentucky, where the Young Earth theory that dinosaurs and homo sapiens coexisted is exemplified by figures of dinosaurs nestled with children. Here he interviews Ken Ham, a prominent figure of the movement who believes, among other things, that the world is approximately 6,000 years old. Maher meets with an actor who stars in a live version of portions of the crucifixion scene as portrayed in *The Passion of the Christ* (2004) at the Christian theme park Holy Land Experience, located in Orlando, Florida. Venturing to Miami, he meets the cult leader José Luis de Jesus Miranda, founder of Creciendo en gracia (Growing in Grace International Ministry). Miranda, in a bizarre case of dissociative disorder, believes he is both the incarnation of Jesus Christ and the embodiment of the Antichrist, complete with a 666 tattoo inked on his forearm. Maher loses a golden opportunity at interviewing a man with a unique belief system, Dr. Francis S. Collins, the former director of the Human Genome Project. Author of the book *The Language of God: A Scientist Presents Evidence for Belief*, Collins is an evangelical Christian who believes that God exists and that evolution is a solvent theory, the mechanisms by which God utilized to form the living world. Unfortunately, Maher does not give the renowned scientist a chance to delineate his outlook. Maher is not interested in having a debate (or discussion) with a subject that dwarfs his own savvy intellect.

Interesting in its premise, and entertaining for agnostics and atheists (religious practitioners also would probably enjoy segments where their faith is not being scorched), *Religulous* has an alienating factor due to Maher's superimposing himself as mental giant walking among insipid lambs. His adroit silver-tongued manner causes the viewer to sympathize (if not emphasize) with his victims. It is this same arrogant glibness that caused

ABC to cancel his show *Politically Incorrect* when he said to the panel on September 17, 2001, regarding the terrorists who attacked the World Trade Center towers: "We have been cowards lobbing cruise missiles from 2,000 miles away. That's cowardly. Staying in the airplane when it hits the building, say what you want about it, it's not cowardly." Brett McCracken of *Christianity Today* conveys this insight regarding Maher's work: "*Religulous* is best seen as a comedy (and there are many funny moments) and not as a serious or measured examination of anything. It's a movie meant to make religious people look stupid, to 'prove' that religious belief and intelligence are mutually exclusive. If you are already prone to believe that, then this movie is for you. For everyone else, *Religulous* is a trifling and shoddy tirade that, ultimately, is not much of a threat."

David Metz Roberts

CREDITS

Himself: Bill Maher
Origin: USA
Language: English
Released: 2008
Production: Palmer West, Jonah Smith, Bill Maher; Thousand Words; released by Lionsgate
Directed by: Larry Charles
Cinematography by: Anthony Hardwick
Sound: Scott Harber
Editing: Jeff Werner, Jeff Groth, Christian Kinnard
MPAA rating: R
Running time: 101 minutes

REVIEWS

Boston Globe Online. October 3, 2008.
Chicago Sun-Times Online. October 2, 2008.
Entertainment Weekly Online. October 1, 2008.
Hollywood Reporter Online. September 4, 2008.
Los Angeles Times Online. October 3, 2008.
New York Times Online. October 3, 2008.
Rolling Stone Online. October 16, 2008.
San Francisco Chronicle. October 3, 2008, p. E7.
Variety Online. August 21, 2008.
Wall Street Journal Online. October 3, 2008.
Washington Post. October 3, 2008, p. C5.

QUOTES

Bill Maher: "Religion is dangerous because it allows human beings who don't have all the answers to think that they do. Most people would think it's wonderful when someone says, 'I'm willing Lord, I'll do whatever you want me to do.'

Except that since there are no gods actually talking to us, that void is filled in by people with their own corruptions and limitations and agendas."

TRIVIA

The production used the fake title "A Spiritual Journey" to obtain interviews with various religious leaders, many of whom did not know that Bill Maher was involved with the project until he arrived for the actual interviews.

REPO! THE GENETIC OPERA

Boasting the likes of British soprano sensation Sarah Brightman and the vapid American heiress Paris Hilton in the same cast, to call *Repo! The Genetic Opera* a puzzle would be an understatement. Producer/director Darren Lynn Bousman—director of *Saw II* (2005), *Saw III* (2006), and *Saw IV* (2007)—seems to be trying for a modern-day *Rocky Horror Picture Show* (1975), but his film lacks the upbeat, campy quality that made the horror of that earlier film so much fun for midnight audiences. *Repo! The Genetic Opera* takes its horror more seriously, eschewing self-satire for a political and social angle and droning, insipid musical numbers that mix as uneasily as its diverse cast.

Bousman, fresh from the easy, money-making machine that is the *Saw* franchise, perhaps saw an opportunity to pull in horror fans eager for something new and though that this futuristic horror musical might somehow fit the bill. The film is adapted from a stage production that Bousman directed in 2001, with a script from the play's authors Terrance Zdunich and Darren Smith. Unwisely, *Repo! The Genetic Opera* opened after Halloween (traditionally when the *Saw* films open) and, despite an $8.5 million budget and a host of stars, grossed a dismal $140,000 in its theatrical run. Only said horror fans will provide the film with a much-needed cult audience on DVD.

The dismal, Orwellian plot has organ transplants and body-part grafting as the biggest business going in 2056, when surgery scars are the new status symbol. GeneCo, led by the nasty Rotti Largo (Paul Sorvino), is the evil corporation at the root of it all, providing easy financing that comes with some pretty stiff terms: If you are late on a payment, you lose your shiny new limbs/internal organs courtesy of the "Repo Man," Nathan Wallace (Anthony Head).

The operatic drama involves Rotti and his relationship to Wallace, a respectable doctor by day who keeps his moonlighting a secret, and his daughter Shilo (Alexa Vega), a shut-in with a crippling blood disease. Harbor-

ing a mysterious hatred against the Repo Man, Rotti sets in motion a plan to ruin Wallace that will also involve Shilo, who just wants to get out from under her father's stifling restrictions, find a cure for her strange ailment, and look for answers to her family's secretive history. She soon finds herself in the clutches of the dying Rotti, who, amazingly, wants to leave GeneCo to her.

Spoiled siblings Luigi Largo (Bill Moseley), Pavi Largo (Nivek Ogre), and the surgery-obsessed Amber Sweet (Paris Hilton) make up Rotti's appalling clan that he suitably deems unworthy of his organ empire. Hilton's character provides a humorous and knowing nod and a wink to Hollywood, as her genetically engineered face falls off. Other main characters are played by cocreator Terrance Zdunich, who, reprising the role he originated as the Graverobber, serves as the film's narrator of sorts. Broadway and opera singer Sarah Brightman essentially plays herself as the blind opera singer, Blind Mag, who stars in the Genetic Opera.

The film deals in the darkest of topics, including genetic engineering, legalized murder, incest, and patricide. As in the *Saw* films, *Repo!* is heavy on the gore beloved by fans of the genre. The digitally shot, fast-paced musical packs in a mind-boggling fifty-six songs, which makes each song feel like a continuation of the last. Of the ensemble cast, Sorvino has both the lungs and the brio to compete with the film's nonstop bombast. Anthony Head, featured in "Nightsurgeon", and Sarah Brightman as the voice of GeneCo are also far and away the standouts.

In describing the film's dark, dystopian sets and visuals, more than one reviewer likened it to *Blade Runner* (1982) and *Sweeney Todd* (2007)—both much better films than the confused rock opera *Repo!* that will appeal to none but the staunchest horror seekers looking for a fresh thrill.

Hilary White

CREDITS

Nathan/Repo Man: Anthony Head
Shilo: Alexa Vega
Rotti Largo: Paul Sorvino
Luigi Rotti: Bill Moseley
Amber Rotti: Paris Hilton
Blind Mag: Sarah Brightman
Graverobber: Terrance Zdunich
Pavi Rotti: Nivek Ogre
Origin: USA
Language: English
Released: 2008

Production: Oren Koules, Mark Burg, Daniel Jason Heffner, Carl Mazzocone; Twisted Pictures; released by Lionsgate

Directed by: Darren Lynn Bousman

Written by: Darren Smith, Terrance Zdunich

Cinematography by: Joseph White

Music by: Darren Smith, Terrance Zdunich

Editing: Harvey Rosenstock

Costumes: Alex Kavanagh

Production Design: David Hackl

MPAA rating: R

Running time: 98 minutes

REVIEWS

Austin Chronicle Online. November 7, 2008.
Entertainment Weekly Online. November 4, 2008.
Hollywood Reporter Online. November 6, 2008.
Los Angeles Times Online. November 7, 2008.
New York Times Online. November 7, 2008.
Rolling Stone Online. November 13, 2008.
Variety Online. July 22, 2008.
Village Voice Online. November 4, 2008.

QUOTES

Shilo (to Nathan): "Stay with the dead, I'm joining the living!"

TRIVIA

Darren Lynn Bousman was the director of the second, third, and fourth installments of the "Saw" franchise and he directed the stage version of this film.

AWARDS

Golden Raspberries 2008: Worst Support. Actress (Hilton).

REVOLUTIONARY ROAD

How do you break free without breaking apart?
—Movie tagline

Box Office: $22.3 million

Director Sam Mendes takes the theme of suburban angst that he explored in *American Beauty* (1999) and transposes it to the 1950s, taking a far more realistic and ruthless tack. Based on the pitiless 1961 novel by Richard Yates, Justin Haythe's screenplay just as mercilessly chronicles an idealistic young couple's slow, downward trajectory into disillusioned and unhappily married strangers against the stifling, cigarette-smoke-tainted backdrop of the American midcentury.

Leonardo DiCaprio and Kate Winslet bring an added dimension of reality to the film, reteaming for the first time in more than a decade after portraying a very different pair of doomed lovers in the blockbuster, Oscar®-winning *Titanic* (1997). Looking only slightly older, DiCaprio and Winslet have a visceral, destructive chemistry and deliver two of the year's most riveting performances that drive this simple and punishingly gloomy marital drama.

April (Kate Winslet) is a talented New York actress who first meets the charming, charismatic Frank Wheeler (Leonardo DiCaprio) at a Manhattan party. Seven years later, the couple is living the American dream with two children in their comfortable suburban Connecticut home. Their dream life on the ironically named Revolutionary Road is very quickly revealed as a façade. Now a bored housewife, a distraught April sits in her dressing room after a disastrous community theater performance and receives little consolation from her bored, apathetic husband. Frank, meanwhile, is similarly frustrated by his dead-end job in the city selling office machines. The once limitless potential that they felt at the start of their relationship has fizzled into a monotonous, bourgeois existence that leaves them both feeling unfulfilled. Both April and Frank feel trapped in the marriage, a sentiment they internalize, and they are only able to express their unspoken resentment through constant prodding and bickering. A more serious symptom of their unhappy union is Frank's affair with his new secretary, Maureen Grube (Zoe Kazan).

Sensing at last the seriousness of the situation, April manages to rise out of the doldrums by hitting on an idea that will give a firm shape to the nebulous dreams of their youth and save their marriage and themselves in the process. She urges Frank to quit his job, leave Connecticut behind, and move the family to Paris, the bastion of bohemian freedom, where she will support the family by becoming a high-paid secretary and he will be free to explore his as-yet-undecided life's passion. In the film's single triumphant moment of hope, Frank agrees, and both April and the audience are filled with anticipation of their renewed enthusiasm for life and love.

Echoing the novel, the script is similarly unsympathetic, and April's radical plan for a fresh new start is in peril when Frank's formerly dead-end job at Knox Business Machines, where his father also worked, yields a glimmer of promise in the form a promotion and a raise. Frank faces an important crossroads, torn as he struggles to decide the course he should take that will irrevocably affect his life and marriage forever.

An ingenious contrast to the superficial trappings of 1955 suburban Connecticut takes the form of mental patient John (Michael Shannon). The son of the couple's friend Helen Givings (Kathy Bates), John meets the Wheelers, and far from acting insane, he ruthlessly unmasks the couple's self-deception and the society they live in. His is the sole voice of reason that injects the point of view of the author Yates that will also resonate with modern audiences.

Sadness engulfs the film, with characters that feel "special" railing against the fact that they are living lives expected of them instead of chosen by them. What could have easily come across as whiny suburban angst is given weight by the confinements of society of the day that offered limited options to both men and women, who were expected to mindlessly carry out traditional societal roles such as the male breadwinner and the female wife and mother. Sadder still is the fact that they themselves cannot figure out the way in which they are special— they know what they do not want, but have no clue as to what they actually need to fulfill them, which is why they glom on to the vague notion of freedom that Paris represents.

Winslet's performance is especially powerful, palpably conveying every disappointment and small hurts that add up to a lifetime of unhappiness. DiCaprio's role is more difficult, internalizing and deflecting his disappointments until the moment where he must choose his family's fate. At that critical juncture, DiCaprio unleashes an expressiveness that makes his somewhat unlikable character suddenly sympathetic. In a small role, Michael Shannon's memorable performance earned him an Oscar® nomination, one the film's three Academy Award® nominations that also included best art direction and best costumes.

Simple, but not simply told, this far-from-typical period film is infused with the same suffocating claustrophobia and sense of doom felt by the main characters, with several haunting images of conformity expertly captured by cinematographer Roger Deakins and an unnerving score by Thomas Newman.

It is hard to deny the unending gloominess of the film. The *Washington Post*'s Ann Hornaday described the depth of the film's darkness in terms such as "somber, almost dirgelike," "a chamber-piece of horrors," and "achingly sad" in the first paragraph of her review. The reason it succeeds, however, is the sensitivity of the direction, its unwavering unsentimentality, and the transcendent performances of DiCaprio, Winslet, and Shannon.

Hilary White

CREDITS

Frank Wheeler: Leonardo DiCaprio
April Wheeler: Kate Winslet
Helen Givings: Kathy Bates
Milly Campbell: Kathryn Hahn
John Givings: Michael Shannon
Shep Campbell: David Harbour
Jack Ordway: Dylan Baker
Howard Givings: Richard Easton
Maureen Grube: Zoe Kazan
Bart Pollack: Jay O. Sanders
Ed Small: Max Casella
Origin: USA
Language: English
Released: 2008
Production: John Hart, Scott Rudin, Sam Mendes, Bobby Cohen; BBC Films, Neal Street Productions, Dreamworks Pictures, Evamere Entertainment, Goldcrest Pictures; released by Paramount Vantage
Directed by: Sam Mendes
Written by: Justin Haythe
Cinematography by: Roger Deakins
Music by: Thomas Newman
Sound: Danny Michael
Music Supervisor: Randall Poster
Editing: Tariq Anwar
Art Direction: Teresa Carriker-Thayer
Costumes: Albert Wolsky
Production Design: Kristi Zea
MPAA rating: R
Running time: 119 minutes

REVIEWS

Entertainment Weekly Online. December 23, 2008.
Hollywood Reporter Online. November 17, 2008.
Los Angeles Times Online. December 26, 2008.
New York Times Online. December 26, 2008.
New Yorker Online. December 22, 2008.
Newsweek Online. November 28, 2008.
Rolling Stone Online. December 25, 2008.
Variety Online. November 17, 2008.
Village Voice Online. December 23, 2008.
Wall Street Journal Online. December 25, 2008.

QUOTES

Frank (on suburbia vs. Paris): "We're running from the hopeless emptiness of the life here."

TRIVIA

Unlike many features, this film was shot in sequence.

AWARDS

Golden Globes 2009: Actress—Drama (Winslet)
Nomination:
Oscars 2008: Art Dir./Set Dec., Costume Des., Support. Actor (Shannon)

British Acad. 2008: Actress (Winslet), Adapt. Screenplay, Costume Des., Production Des.

Golden Globes 2009: Actor—Drama (DiCaprio), Director (Mendes), Film—Drama

Screen Actors Guild 2008: Actress (Winslet).

RIGHTEOUS KILL

Most people respect the badge. Everybody respects the gun.
—Movie tagline

Box Office: $40 million

The first pairing of screen legends Robert De Niro and Al Pacino in Michael Mann's *Heat* (1995) was a treat for their fans, though some were disappointed that the two shared only two scenes. De Niro and Pacino appear together in many more scenes in *Righteous Kill*, yet while *Heat* is a one of the greatest crime films ever made, the actors' latest is far from a masterpiece.

Turk (Robert De Niro) and Rooster (Al Pacino) are two veteran Manhattan police detectives on the trail of a serial killer targeting those who get away with murder, rape, and drug peddling. Also on the case are two younger cops, Simon Perez (John Leguizamo) and Ted Riley (Donnie Wahlberg), who do not trust the thoroughness and competence of their colleagues' investigation, in part because Turk and Perez hate each other. When the younger investigators begin to suspect a policeman may be the killer, Rooster agrees, but Turk does not. *Righteous Kill* proceeds from one crime scene to another, while Lieutenant Hingis (Brian Dennehy), the detectives' boss, grows impatient and Turk continues his sadomasochistic relationship with Karen Corelli (Carla Gugino), another officer.

Screenwriter Russell Gewirtz wrote the much more accomplished *Inside Man,* whose intricate plotlines converged into a satisfactory conclusion. *Righteous Kill,* in comparison, lurches about. While the earlier film trusted the audience's intelligence, Gewirtz's latest assumes inattentiveness on the part of the viewers. The killer is clearly identified at the beginning of the film, but Gewirtz and director Jon Avnet, who was responsible for an even weaker Pacino vehicle, *88 Minutes* (2008), assume no one is paying attention. So strongly is the audience's attention directed toward one suspect that it becomes obvious this person is innocent. If he is not the murderer, there is only one other possibility. The trick ending of *Inside Man* works; this one does not.

Righteous Kill, finally, is of interest only to fans of De Niro and Pacino willing to see them in anything and not question how De Niro, sixty-five at the time of the film's release, Pacino, sixty-eight, and Dennehy, seventy,

could still be on the force. Since the days of *Heat,* De Niro has been criticized by reviewers and bloggers for choosing his projects unwisely and merely walking through them. As Turk he seems strangely unfocused, offering a blank stare interrupted occasionally by a sarcastic smile. Is he coasting, or has his face lost some of its expressiveness? Pacino, on the other hand, acquits himself fairly well. Often accused of also picking weak films, Pacino never walks through roles but sometimes shouts and struts a bit too much. As Rooster he varies his energy from scene to scene and is compelling to watch. His leathery face and intense eyes remain fascinating in ways De Niro's do not.

Ed Shearmur provides an effectively tense score, at times echoing Elliott Goldenthal's music for *Heat.* Cinematographer Denis Lenoir gives the film a moody steel-blue urban look. The supporting cast is good, especially Barry Primus as a supportive police psychologist, and the always wonderful Gugino, who warrants much better material.

Despite its many flaws *Righteous Kill* remains watchable as a gritty example of neo-noir and for Pacino's performance. Though they have only themselves to blame, the two superstars deserve better, as do their many fans.

Michael Adams

CREDITS

Turk: Robert De Niro
Rooster: Al Pacino
Lt. Hingis: Brian Dennehy
Karen Corelli: Carla Gugino
Det. Ted Riley: Donnie Wahlberg
Det. Simon Perez: John Leguizamo
Spider: Curtis "50 Cent" Jackson
Cheryl Brooks: Melissa Leo
Jessica: Trilby Glover
Stein: Alan Rosenberg
Prosky: Barry Primus
Martin Baum: Alan Blumenfeld
Yevgeny Mugalat: Oleg Taktarov
Natalya: Shirly Brener
Dr. Chadrabar: Ajay Naidu
Gwen Darvis: Saidah Arrika Ekulona
Origin: USA
Language: English
Released: 2008
Production: Avi Lerner, Rob Cowan, Randall Emmett, Jon Avnet; Millennium Films, Nu Image Films, Grosvenor Park; released by Overture Films
Directed by: Jon Avnet

Written by: Russell Gewirtz
Cinematography by: Denis Lenoir
Music by: Ed Shearmur
Sound: Matthew Price
Music Supervisor: Ashley Miller
Editing: Paul Hirsch
Art Direction: Christina Wilson
Costumes: Debra McGuire
Production Design: Tracey Gallacher
MPAA rating: R
Running time: 100 minutes

REVIEWS

Boston Globe Online. October 18, 2008.
Chicago Sun-Times Online. September 12, 2008.
Entertainment Weekly Online. September 17, 2008.
Hollywood Reporter Online. September 11, 2008.
Los Angeles Times Online. September 11, 2008.
New York Times Online. September 12, 2008.
San Francisco Chronicle. September 12, 2008.
Variety Online. September 11, 2008.
Washington Post. September 12, 2008.

QUOTES

Turk: "You don't become a cop because you want to serve and protect. You join the force because they let you carry a gun and a badge. You do it because you get respect."

AWARDS

Nomination:

Golden Raspberries 2008: Worst Actor (Pacino).

THE ROCKER

Opportunity rocks.
—Movie tagline
A comedy for the rockstar in all of us.
—Movie tagline

Box Office: $6.4 million

Rainn Wilson's *The Rocker* recalls another funnyman's foray into frustrated-rock-stardom-meets-adolescent-angst, *School of Rock* (2003). Despite its churlishly appealing lead performer and a technologically savvy script, this more uneven rock comedy did not fare well. One of the lowest grossing releases of 2008, *The Rocker* failed to parlay Wilson's television success on *The Office* into theaters, or to ignite the imagination of audiences in same way Jack Black's much more spirited and successful comedy did.

At the start of the film, Robert "Fish" Fishman (Rainn Wilson) is a drummer for the heavy metal rock band Vesuvius. On the verge of a lucrative record deal that will make the band rich and famous, the record executive adds a caveat that will replace Fish with the executive's nephew. Fast-forward twenty years, and Fish is a bitter failure, confronted everywhere by the enormous success of Vesuvius. He reaches an all-time low when he is forced to move into his sister Lisa's (Jane Lynch) attic when he loses yet another low-level office job.

His unlikely salvation comes in the form of Lisa's insecure, keyboard-playing son Matt (Josh Gad). Fish's nephew is in the deliciously named band A.D.D., along with gloomy vocalist Curtis (Teddy Geiger) and the sarcastic, punk-inspired bassist Amelia (Emma Stone). When A.D.D. loses their drummer, Matt suggests his uncle Fish, who reluctantly agrees.

After indulging in a grotesque ritual where he throws up and then puts the vomit in his pocket for luck, Fish takes the stage for the first time in two decades at Matt's prom. His crazed, hyperkinetic drum solo to Peter Gabriel's "In Your Eyes" causes a world of embarrassment for A.D.D., who threaten to kick him out. Fish is able to change their minds by telling the kids that he will get them an actual club gig.

The film offers a fresh, technology-driven plot turn when Robert, thrown out of his sister's attic, takes up residence in the basement of his favorite Chinese restaurant. The band comes up with the ingenious solution of rehearsing via iChat. Naturally, with Fish being a clueless middle-ager, he does not realize that everyone can see him playing the drums in the nude. They post the video of the "Naked Drummer" on YouTube and it quickly becomes a video viral sensation with million of hits. And, in an important piece of irony, it also attracts the attention of the same record company that signed Vesuvius all those years ago.

An agent (Jason Sudeikis) comes calling to sign A.D.D. and promptly sends them off on tour. Audiences across the country love the band and their quirky drummer, who begins to relive the rock star fantasy life he never actually had. Within the dynamics of the band, the film shows the generational clash of the television-tossing, groupie-groping wildness of the rock stars of yore that Fish aspired to, and the far tamer, wiser, rehabbed musicians that exist today. After they wind up in jail after a particularly wild party, Curtis's mother (Christina Applegate) joins the kids on tour to protect them from Fish's influence and provide a sweet, subplot romance.

Then, the unthinkable happens: A.D.D. is scheduled to open for Vesuvius at a concert in their hometown,

Cleveland. Setting the climactic concert there is a fitting tip of the hat to *This Is Spinal Tap* (1984), whose addled musicians get lost in the labyrinthine hallways on the way to the Cleveland stage.

An outraged Fish impulsively quits the band and gets a corporate job with the help of his brother-in-law. The distraught bandmates realize that Fish is the reason people come to see their show, and after they convince him to return, Fish is awarded his moment in the sun. Not only does the band play a triumphant gig, but Vesuvius gets their comeuppance when it is revealed that they have been lip-synching their entire career.

Directed by Peter Cattaneo with a script from Wallace Wolodarsky and Maya Forbes, the film is often funny and has its heart in the right place, but goes about it a bit too complacently, with well-worn 1980s references and a clichéd spandex and big hair wardrobe. The watery pop soundtrack is one of the main problems in a film that wants to glorify good old-fashioned rock and roll. Other than the always hilarious Jason Sudeikis as an obnoxious agent, the supporting performances are mostly third-rate, with Wilson forced to single-handedly carry the film, which he well might have done. Unfortunately, Fish is a role more suited to the bombastic Jack Black than to Wilson and the slyly subversive, pent-up-rage style of comedy he excels at.

Hilary White

CREDITS

Robert "Fish" Fishman: Rainn Wilson
Kim: Christina Applegate
Matt: Josh Gad
Amelia: Emma Stone
Curtis: Teddy Geiger
Lisa: Jane Lynch
Stan: Jeff Garlin
David Marshall: Jason Sudeikis
Gator: Howard Hesseman
Lex: Will Arnett
Trash: Bradley Cooper
Kerr: Fred Armisen
Sticks: Lonny Ross
Carol: Jane Krakowski
Origin: USA
Language: English
Released: 2008
Production: Shawn Levy, Tom McNulty; 21 Laps, Dune Entertainment III, Fox Atomic; released by 20th Century-Fox
Directed by: Peter Cattaneo
Written by: Maya Forbes, M. Wallace Wolodarsky

Cinematography by: Anthony B. Richmond
Music by: Chad Fischer
Sound: Bruce Carwardine
Music Supervisor: Patrick Houlihan
Editing: Brad E. Wilhite
Costumes: Christopher Hargadon
Production Design: Brandt Gordon
MPAA rating: PG-13
Running time: 102 minutes

REVIEWS

Boston Globe Online. August 20, 2008.
Chicago Sun-Times Online. August 20, 2008.
Entertainment Weekly Online. August 15, 2008.
Hollywood Reporter Online. July 25, 2008.
Los Angeles Times Online. August 20, 2008.
New York Times Online. August 20, 2008.
San Francisco Chronicle. August 20, 2008, p. E1.
Variety Online. July 23, 2008.
Washington Post. August 20, 2008, p. C3.

QUOTES

David Marshall: "John Lennon is rolling over in his grave to hide the giant boner you just gave him!"

ROCKNROLLA

A story of sex, thugs, and rock 'n roll.
—Movie tagline

Box Office: $5.7 million

Guy Ritchie's *RocknRolla* seems awfully familiar. It is peopled with London thugs who have *Pulp Fiction* (1994)style names (like a gangster named One Two), and some of them steal money or owe money to a crime boss, and all of them are unscrupulous and prone to violence, but they are funny in a goofy sort of way, and there is confusion as to which character is cheating which, and in the end they all blow one another away. In other words, it is a whole lot like Ritchie's *Lock, Stock and Two Smoking Barrels* (1998)—which was about poker players who owe money to gangsters—and Ritchie's *Snatch* (2000), which centered on boxers and thugs.

Compared to those two earlier Ritchie movies, and especially the first, which became something of a cult hit in the late 1990s, *RocknRolla* seems tired and worn. It is a little late to still be reprising the mood and spirit of *Pulp Fiction,* after all, and this movie feels like Ritchie is trying too hard to recapture a tone that now eludes him. The humor, the plot, and the characters in *RocknRolla* all seem forced.

It is not exactly clear who the protagonist of *Rockn-Rolla* is, and who we are supposed to be cheering for or against. At the outset of the film, the narrator is Archie (Mark Strong), the chief lieutenant for the crime boss Lenny Cole (Tom Wilkinson). In what amounts to an extended prologue, Archie quickly introduces the viewers to the main characters in the story and how they operate. With the camera lurching from one set of thugs to another, and Archie delivering the set-up in a rapid-fire manner, the opening sequences are among the film's best, setting a unique tone—a sort of pumped-up, hyperactive, comic-book, machine-gun style that lays out how Lenny Cole controls the booming real-estate market in London because he owns the city planning officials, lawyers, and judges who can make a project go or stall.

The problem is that after strong-arming the movie at the start, Archie and his narrator's voice virtually disappear and never return so forcefully, and Archie loses his place as the center of the movie. For awhile the focus shifts to Lenny, who is getting the opportunity to move up in class by greasing the skids for a Russian billionaire, Uri (Karel Roden), who has a mammoth housing project in the works. Uri is no-nonsense and cuts to the chase by asking Lenny to name his price for his services. Lenny boldly replies that he will expect to be paid seven million euros. In a contrived bit of plotting, Uri shows Lenny his "lucky painting" and tells him he can temporarily have it until the deal is completed.

If you watch Wilkinson in this scene of his first meeting with Roden's Uri, you can see the cunning way this accomplished actor inhabits a character. With his eyes covered by sunglasses in most of this film, Wilkinson cannot use facial expressions effectively. Watch how Wilkinson scrunches up his shoulders awkwardly when he walks in a manner that is almost affected. His body seems contorted into a sort of permanent controlled rage concealed beneath a veneer of civility, and that is how he employs his voice too. Wilkinson's Lenny is a man used to having his way, and completely confident in his own hegemony, yet his body seems stuck in a permanent flinch, as if it expects to be overruled by a forceful blow. When necessary, Wilkinson lets loose his holy wrath in a verge-of-mania anger, but most of the time he is like a jocular uncle holding court, preening a little but holding his power close. When Lenny gets his comeuppance, in a scene of a golf course kneecapping spoiled by its inclusion in the movie's preview trailer, it is as if his body had been coiled for this blow from the start. Wilkinson's Lenny is proud of operating as a self-proclaimed "old-school" crime boss, and by the time he realizes he is on new turf, it is too late.

The second most watchable character in the film is Stella, as played in catlike fashion by Thandie Newton.

Like Wilkinson, Newton is accomplished at disappearing into her roles, but here she is out in the open, coy and cool, a femme fatale who barely works up a sweat subduing her prey. Enmeshed in Stella's web are Uri, who sheepishly proposes marriage to her in a scene that shows the billionaire is easily under her control, and One Two (Gerard Butler), whom she corrals in her double-crossing scheme. Officially, Stella serves as Uri's "accountant," which means she is his money man. But she conceives a way to help One Two and his buddies repay a debt they owe to Lenny (a debt entirely engineered by Lenny) by having them steal the seven million euros she is delivering to Uri—not just once, but twice.

One Two emerges out of a gaggle of small-time crooks called the Wild Bunch who meet in their own sort of clubhouse and whose relationships are not crystal clear. These are the small-time operators who play cards and humor drop-in junkies and hangers-on, and they are heroic in this kind of film because they are regular guys who just happen to be violent and criminal. Butler's a fine actor too, and he gives One Two a bumbling sort of foolhardy courage that provides the film with some much-needed comic appeal. He does not seem to be trying as hard as the others to be over the top. But his character suffers from lack of delineation. If One Two is really the protagonist, it is only because he gradually is dragged into the role, but for a long time he is not sufficiently differentiated from the rest of the Wild Bunch.

With drug-addicted rock star Johnny Quid (Toby Kebbell) moving into the spotlight, and way too many minor characters, including an undeservedly small part for Chris Bridges (aka Ludacris), *RocknRolla* becomes an overpopulated mess. Kebbell is fine as the totally confused, spaced-out Quid, who somehow has a gentle soul beneath his persona. Quid is almost all pose and little substance, and he turns out to be Lenny's stepson, a connection that is fortuitous for some overwrought flashbacks, but otherwise seems forced.

Sorting out who is doing what to whom is not that difficult—Ritchie's screenplay is hardly that complex—but the bigger problem is working up an interest in the resolution. It is not too hard to figure that the bigger fish will end up gobbling up the smaller fish. But Ritchie, all engrossed in his histrionic style, seems himself to lose interest and focus concerning who is at the center of the plot and who is at the periphery. Characters move in and out of focus so much that all seem eventually to blur together. In a film like this, tone is everything, and the tone of *RocknRolla* is badly off compared to *Lock, Stock and Two Smoking Barrels*—it is as if Ritchie has lost his pitch and is trying too hard to make the same old music.

Michael Betzold

CREDITS

One Two: Gerard Butler
Lenny Cole: Tom Wilkinson
Stella: Thandie Newton
Archie: Mark Strong
Mumbles: Idris Elba
Handsome Bob: Thomas Hardy
Uri Omovich: Karel Roden
Johnny Quid: Toby Kebbell
Roman: Jeremy Piven
Mickey: Chris Ludacris Bridges
Councillor: Jimi Mistry
Origin: USA
Language: English
Released: 2008
Production: Joel Silver, Susan Downey, Steve Clark-Hall, Guy Ritchie; Castle Rock Entertainment, Tuff Guy Films; released by Warner Bros.
Directed by: Guy Ritchie
Written by: Guy Ritchie
Cinematography by: David Higgs
Music by: Steve Isles
Sound: John Hayes
Music Supervisor: Ian Neil
Editing: James Herbert
Art Direction: Andy Nicholson
Costumes: Suzie Hartman
Production Design: Richard Bridgland
MPAA rating: R
Running time: 114 minutes

REVIEWS

Boston Globe Online. October 31, 2008.
Chicago Sun-Times Online. October 29, 2008.
Entertainment Weekly Online. October 7, 2008.
Hollywood Reporter Online. September 4, 2008.
Los Angeles Times Online. October 8, 2008.
New York Times Online. October 8, 2008.
New Yorker Online. October 20, 2008.
Rolling Stone Online. October 16, 2008.
San Francisco Chronicle. October 31, 2008, p. E1.
Time Online. October 8, 2008.
Variety Online. September 4, 2008.
Washington Post Online. October 31, 2008.

QUOTES

Archie: "People ask the question…what's a RocknRolla? And I tell 'em—it's not about drums, drugs, and hospital drips, oh no. There's more there than that, my friend. We all like a bit of the good life—some the money, some the drugs, other the sex game, the glamour, or the fame. But a RocknRolla, oh, he's different. Why? Because a real RocknRolla wants the f**king lot."

TRIVIA

The band playing in the club scene are called The Subways.

ROLE MODELS

Danny and Wheeler were just sentenced to 150 hours mentoring kids. Worst idea ever.
 —Movie tagline

They're about to get more than they plea-bargained for.
 —Movie tagline

Box Office: $67.2 million

Underrated actors Paul Rudd and Seann William Scott are perfectly cast in *Role Models,* a comedy that takes full advantage of their on-screen comic personas and hits more often than it misses but wastes an opportunity with an undeveloped final act. From the unique mind of David Wain (*Wet Hot American Summer* [2001] and television's *The State*), *Role Models* features a fantastic set-up with a perfectly cast ensemble—two elements that go a long way in making a successful comedy—but misses the opportunity to truly develop those two. The first half hour of *Role Models* is as laugh-out-loud funny as anything produced in 2008, but it becomes clear about halfway through that the set-up is essentially the entire movie. Like a lot of supposed role models, sometimes first impressions fail to tell the entire story.

Paul Rudd and Seann William Scott are the surprisingly effective buddy team of the bitter Danny and the gregarious Wheeler, respectively. The two are pitchmen for the energy drink known as Minotaur, a take-off on the modern trend of obsession with energy drinks like Red Bull and Full Throttle. Wheeler dresses up as the mythical beast and Danny gives the sales routine to high schools around the greater Los Angeles area. The more rebellious half of the duo, Wheeler, seems content to be a salesman in horned beast's clothing for the rest of his life, but Danny is getting restless and bitter, particularly in his relationship with Beth (Elizabeth Banks). Danny has become restless hocking liquid energy for far too long a chunk of his youth, and lashes out in midlife-crisis fashion, awkwardly asking his girlfriend to marry him (she refuses) before getting into a scrape with a tow-truck guy and a cop that lands the comedic duo in some serious legal trouble.

Beth gets Wheeler and Danny out of doing jail time by committing them to 150 hours of community service at a big brother program known as Sturdy Wings headed by recovering drug addict Gayle Sweeny (the hysterical Jane Lynch). Danny is paired with an awkward teen named Augie (Christopher Mintz-Plasse), a young man who values live-action role-playing above all else, and Wheeler is lucky enough to mentor the raunchiest and most perverted preteen on the planet, Ronnie Shields (Bobb'e J. Thompson). There are lessons to be learned in *Role Models* about supporting individuality and bearing some responsibility for your actions, but it is largely just an excuse for Wain and his buddies to have some fun with Rudd's signature brand of sarcastic humor and Scott's vibrant on-screen personality.

In the set-up for *Role Models,* which simply allows Rudd and Scott to do what they do best, the combination of the former's intellectual energy and the physically driven comedy of the latter works nearly perfectly. Scott has a presence that serves as a great balance for Rudd's more cynical, intellectual brand of humor. In fact, the entire cast works throughout the piece, from the pitch-perfect work by Lynch to the lovely charisma of Banks to even the small roles from regular Wain-Rudd collaborators like Ken Marino and Joe Lo Truglio.

What holds *Role Models* back from comedy classic status is the barely-there final act. Once the audience realizes that Augie centers his whole world around role playing and that Ronnie is not as tough as his twisted vocabulary lets on, the movie has nowhere else to go. If Wain could have taken one more left turn instead of shuffling toward a relatively predictable finale (with some admittedly unpredictable KISS makeup), *Role Models* could have been a more refreshingly innovative movie. For a film about being whoever you want to be, *Role Models* ends up being surprisingly routine.

In the end, *Role Models* is an easy movie to summarize—funny but predictable; enjoyable but not quite as good as it could have or arguably should have been with the talent of its ensemble. One of the best comedy casts of 2008 and the comic timing of director/cowriter David Wain elevate the material above a lot of the genre offerings of the year, but the film hints at an undeveloped potential to be truly great. Like a lot of role models, Wain's film of the same name is not what it first appears.

Brian Tallerico

CREDITS

Danny: Paul Rudd
Wheeler: Seann William Scott
Beth: Elizabeth Banks
Gayle Sweeney: Jane Lynch
Jim: Ken Marino
Augie: Christopher Mintz-Plasse
Ronnie: Bobb'e J. Thompson
Origin: USA
Language: English
Released: 2008
Production: Mary Parent, Scott Stuber, Luke Greenfield; Relativity Media; released by Universal Pictures
Directed by: David Wain
Written by: Paul Rudd, Ken Marino, David Wain, Timothy Dowling
Cinematography by: Russ T. Alsobrook
Music by: Craig Wedren
Sound: Harrison D. Marsh
Music Supervisor: Kathy Nelson
Editing: Eric Kissack
Art Direction: Kevin Constant
Costumes: Molly Maginnis
Production Design: Steven Lineweaver
MPAA rating: R
Running time: 99 minutes

REVIEWS

Boston Globe Online. November 7, 2008.
Chicago Sun-Times Online. November 5, 2008.
Entertainment Weekly Online. November 4, 2008.
Hollywood Reporter Online. October 19, 2008.
Los Angeles Times Online. November 7, 2008.
New York Times Online. November 7, 2008.
Rolling Stone Online. November 13, 2008.
San Francisco Chronicle. November 7, 2008, p. E5.
Variety Online. October 19, 2008.
Wall Street Journal Online. November 7, 2008.

QUOTES

Wheeler: "This may be a stupid question. The 'Get Out of Jail Free' card, is that real?"

ROMAN DE GARE
(Crossed Tracks)

Box Office: $1.8 million

The beautifully shot, glossy mystery *Roman de gare* (also known as *Crossed Tracks*) blends intrigue, comedy, crime, and romance against a stunning backdrop of some of the most picturesque locations in France. It has the distinct stamp of its prolific Gallic director, Claude Lelouch. Stylistically complex, with flash-forwards, flashbacks, and the true identities of the main characters shrouded in mystery for most of the film, *Roman de gare* should be more engaging than it actually is. It is the too-complex structure and trickery-for-its-own-sake that undermines the story, bookending a more engrossing and believable narrative with characters the audience actually has time to get to know and become invested in. Critically well received, *Roman de gare* has been called a return to form for Lelouch, best known for his art-house sensation *A Man and a Woman* (1966).

The opening scene has a popular crime novelist, Judith Ralitzer (Fanny Ardant), being interrogated by police about two murders. It is revealed that a pedophile serial killer, Jacques Maury—known as "The Magician" because he uses magic to put his victims into a trance—has escaped from prison and may be on the outskirts of Paris.

The film then cuts to Huguette (Audrey Dana), a nervous, chain-smoking hairdresser, having what turns into a fierce argument with her fiancé Paul (Cyrille Eldin) while speeding down a highway outside Paris. When he cruelly abandons her in the wee hours of the morning at a service station without any money, she is quickly picked up by the humble Pierre (Dominique Pinon), who observes the scene from the station's café.

An engaging mystery thus begins. Pierre is not who he seems, and the film suggests that he may be any number of characters. During their journey, Pierre lets Huguette in on his secret identity, claiming to be the ghostwriter of the famous writer depicted in the film's flash-forward, Judith Ralitzer, who is also Huguette's idol. There is a brief scene showing a distraught wife telling police that she believes her husband, a schoolteacher, has abandoned her and their children. It may very likely be Pierre, given his unassuming nature. At Huguette's behest, Pierre feigns being her fiancé Paul to make a good impression on her country-dwelling parents and Huguette's young daughter, who also lives at the farmhouse. They family take to Pierre, especially her young daughter, who is impressed with his clever magic tricks. It is also possible that Pierre is several or all of these characters, and Lelouch does a fine job building suspense by letting the audience guess until late in the film.

As many will have suspected, Pierre's fondness for magic may reveal his true identity as the serial killer Jacques Maury, especially when Huguette naively allows the virtual stranger to go off fishing with her daughter.

Pierre reunites with his employer, Ralitzer, on a cruise in Cannes. The fact that he may have cut short his ghostwriting stint is perhaps why he is thought to have fallen overboard shortly thereafter, and, returning to the opening scene, the reason Ralitzer is being questioned in his murder. In this way Lelouch slyly suggests that, not just Pierre, but all the main characters may not be what they seem. Is Ralitzer actually a murderer? And is Huguette, in fact, a prostitute? The audience begins to sense that everything will be turned on its head at the conclusion.

As the film's mystery man, Dominique Pinon is deserving of the widespread praise given him by the majority of critics. Slight of build with a face more suited to the comedic roles he usually plays, his offbeat looks have not often put him in the role of romantic lead, but he is able to make his mysterious attraction plausible.

The title, *Roman de gare*, roughly translated, means pulp novel. Lelouch's film embodies that sort of guilty pleasure, having fun with this mystery, playing with audience expectations until the very end. In another mischievous move, Lelouch and longtime writing collaborator Pierre Uytterhoeven wrote and directed the film under a pseudonym, only revealing their hand when it played at the Cannes Film Festival. As is often the case in these elaborate, convoluted suspense pictures, however, the denouement is a letdown, revealing ample gaps in logic and requiring the audience to forgive a number of prior plot machinations that are simply red herrings.

Roman de gare makes ample use of the fine cast and luscious French scenery shot by Gérard de Battista, particularly in the pastoral settings framed by the Alps and the Mediterranean splendor of Cannes.

Hilary White

CREDITS

Louie: Dominique Pinon
Judith Ralitzer: Fanny Ardant
Commissioner: Zinedine Soualem
Huguette: Audrey Dana
Florence: Michèle Bernier
Origin: France
Language: French
Released: 2007
Production: Claude Lelouch; Les Films 13; released by Samuel Goldwyn Films
Directed by: Claude Lelouch
Written by: Claude Lelouch, Pierre Uytterhoeven
Cinematography by: Gérard de Battista
Music by: Alex Jaffray
Sound: Harald Maury, Pascal Chauvin
Editing: Stéphane Mazalaigue, Charlotte Lecoeur
Costumes: Marité Coutard
Production Design: François Chauvaud

MPAA rating: R
Running time: 103 minutes

REVIEWS

Hollywood Reporter Online. March 17, 2008.
New York Times Online. April 25, 2008.
New Yorker Online. April 28, 2008.
Variety Online. June 20, 2007.
Village Voice Online. April 22, 2008.

TRIVIA

Claude Lelouch originally wanted to release this self-financed film under the pseudonym Herve Picard, but the truth came out before its screening at the Cannes Film Festival.

ROMAN POLANSKI: WANTED AND DESIRED

The truth couldn't fit in the headlines.
—Movie tagline

This documentary film, directed by Marina Zenovich for Home Box Office but also intended for eventual theatrical release, tells the story of the European film director Roman Polanski by focusing on the legal difficulties the critically successful filmmaker had in California after the brutal murder of his wife, Sharon Tate, by members of the Charles Manson cult. At issue was Polanski's later relationship with a thirteen-year-old girl and what developed between them during a photo shoot at the house of Polanski's friend, the actor Jack Nicholson. Ultimately, Polanski was accused of having raped the girl, but the director pled not guilty, admitting only to having had consensual sex with Samantha Gailey Geimer. The trial became a cause célèbre, then a travesty of justice because of the unfortunate influence of a publicity seeking judge, Laurence J. Rittenband, who presided as ringmaster over the media circus.

Polanski had been assigned to shoot photos of young girls for *Vogue* magazine, and his credentials were impeccable: Because Polanski had done a similar photo shoot for Nastassja Kinski, he had made her a star. Knowing this, Samantha's mother had given her consent to the photo shoot. The shoot was scheduled to take place at Jack Nicholson's house on Mulholland Drive while Nicholson was out of town. Nicholson's caretaker let them in. Pictures were taken of Samantha in the jacuzzi and eventually she was asked to remove her top, which she did. Afterwards, there were drinks and caresses and a Quaalude pill was divided in three parts. On March 11, 1977, Polanski was arrested in Los Angeles and charged on several counts, including possession of a controlled substance, lewd acts, the use of drugs, having had sexual intercourse with a minor, perversion, and sodomy. Polanski's lawyer, Douglas Dalton, remarked: "I know the facts. I was there. People have the right to their own opinions, but they don't have the right to their own facts."

Attorney for the defense Douglas Dalton was considered a master of negotiations, but this sensationalistic rape trial involving a major celebrity who had made movies about perversion, corruption, and devil-worship put his talents to the test. The prosecuting attorney was Roger Gunsen, a straight-talking, thirty-seven-year-old Mormon. Before the trial was over, both attorneys would be cooperating to protect Polanski against the capriciousness of the court. As producer David Melnick notes in the documentary, "Roman was a perfect victim for them."

Polanski was no doubt psychologically vulnerable at the time of these accusations because of the tragedy of his wife's brutal murder. In terms of his career, Polanski was in top form. He had moved from Eastern Europe to Paris to London to Hollywood, making a number of successful and critically respected films, though some of them flirted with the irrational and the occult. The documentary points out that after *Rosemary's Baby* (1968), some people thought that Polanski was in league with the devil. Mia Farrow, the star of that horror film, remarks that Polanski thought "his future was made" in a new homeland, until everything collapsed. Producer Hank Koch thought that before the Sharon Tate murders "Roman was on top of the world." After agent Bill Tenant called Polanski in London with the horrible news, the director was devastated. "The only time of true happiness in my life," Polanski himself remarked, "was the time I spent with her." And yet, elements in the tabloid press blamed Polanski for Tate's murder. Despite such unfair allegations, Polanski "decided he was going to survive," according to his friend Anthea Slybert, but the survival was complicated by the charges of rape that were brought against him.

The documentary is of course sympathetic to Polanski. As assistant district attorney Jim Grodin remarks, "I'm not so sure that Mr. Polanski was aware of what being arrested in America meant." It is clear that during the confusion of his arrest Polanski did not understand why the authorities were so upset, since in his own mind, he had done nothing wrong. He might have considered the whole affair a cultural misunderstanding. He pleaded guilty only to the charge of "unlawful sexual intercourse," but that was not enough to satisfy Judge Rittenband, a publicity hound who had presided over a Cary Grant paternity suit and had litigated the divorce between Elvis and Priscilla Presley. He was clearly concerned about his own image, and boasted among friends that he would put Polanski away for the rest of his life.

Marina Zenovich could not interview the late Judge Rittenband, who died in 1993, nor would Polanski himself permit interviews for the film, but everyone else, including Samantha Geimer, was cooperative. Geimer, now married and living in Hawaii, told the *Wall Street Journal* that she thinks the case should be dropped. Of Polanski she said, "I'd be pleased if he was no longer a fugitive." The film was a hit at Sundance and at the Cannes Film Festival, and Polanski was quoted by the *Wall Street Journal,* saying "I've seen Marina Zenovich's film and, for the most part, it accurately depicts the facts as I understand them. In addition, there is important information which has not been disclosed before." Although Polanski did not sit for an interview for the documentary, he did meet with the director over lunch in Paris. When the film was made Polanski was seventy-four years old, married for the past eighteen years to the actress Emmanuelle Seigner and the father of two children. Polanski did allow interviews of his friends, both in France and in California, and his lawyer (who, more than anyone, steals the show), and Zenovich was assisted by Polanski's godson Adam Bardach.

In general the critics were sympathetic to Zenovich's treatment of the scandal, with the exception of John Leonard, writing for *New York* magazine, who wrote: "Yes, the minor seems to have had some sex previous to the European movie director. And yes, the media behaved throughout with a frenzy that would shame a shark. But none of this, spelled out in painful primer style in Marina Zenovich's sympathetic documentary, excuses Roman Polanski for feeding champagne and Quaaludes to a thirteen-year-old girl to get her into his bed." Nonetheless, Zenovich told William Booth of the *Washington Post* that "this isn't an apology project for Roman Polanski," adding: "But even people who think they recall the details of the case may be surprised." *Washington Post* television critic Tom Shales headlined his review "A Perversion of Justice," and predicted that even viewers who thought they remembered the facts of the case were likely to be hooked by this "bold and exhaustive new documentary." Shales disapproved of the film's innuendos concerning Judge Rittenband's own philandering, which are unnecessary and irrelevant, but was fully in sympathy with Polanski, who "belongs to a rarefied subculture [of] celebrities hounded by the state," putting him in company with Charlie Chaplin.

What happened to Polanski before the incident, the murder of his wife by members of the Charles Manson cult, was tragic, and is reported as such in the documentary. What happened after the alleged rape trial was farcical, as the showboating judge ordered Polanski to be held for ninety days of psychological evaluation.

Polanski was nervously incarcerated at Chino for forty-two days, then released on probation and allowed to travel to Europe to work on a forgettable Dino de Laurentiis film. While in Germany, Polanski attended Oktoberfest in Munich with friends and was photographed, apparently enjoying himself, flanked by two women. Judge Rittenband was incensed and ordered Polanski to return to prison to serve his remaining forty-eight days, even though the psychological evaluation had been completed. The judge had orchestrated the court proceedings that had sent Polanski to Chino for evaluation, instructing Duncan to argue for probation and Gunston to argue against it, even though both lawyers knew what the outcome would be.

The thirteen-year-old victim and her family had requested leniency for Roman Polanski, and the press had reported, "Sentencing Put Off Until He Finishes Film." The judge was criticized by the press because Polanski had not served the full ninety-day sentence, though one of Polanski's friends warned "Roman was not safe there," at the Chino facility. Judge Rittenband was determined to send Polanski back to prison, and all Dalton had to do was to trust the judge, who was demonstrably untrustworthy. So Polanski fled the country back to Paris, where he was safe from extradition because of his French citizenship. Toward the end of her film, as this court drama is being played out, Zenovich intercuts footage from one of Polanski's first, short, experimental films, *The Fat and the Lean* (1961), an absurdist allegory involving a master and his slave. The master beats a drum to keep the servile slave hopping, but finally the slave, played by a young Roman Polanski himself, discovers that he can escape from this fat tyrant, and that is exactly what he does. This forms an artistic context for the escape of Roman Polanski from a vain and unreasonable judge and a stacked court system.

Michael Cieply filed a follow-up story in the *New York Times* on July 17, 2008, reporting that Polanski and his lawyer "asked the Los Angeles district attorney's office to review a new documentary in which a former deputy district attorney claims to have coached the judge in the case," in order possibly to end the thirty-year warrant for Polanski's arrest for having fled the United States "on the eve of being sentenced for the statutory rape of a 13-year old girl." David Wells, the former prosecutor, was asked for his advice, even though he was not involved in the case, and Polanski's lawyer, Douglas Dalton, believed that such contacts with the judge "appeared to violate California law and legal ethics." Asked about these recent events in Paris, the seventy-four-year-old Polanski said, "I believe that closure of that entire matter is long overdue." Many Americans would no doubt agree.

James M. Welsh

CREDITS

Origin: USA
Language: English
Released: 2008
Production: Jeff Levy-Hinte, Lila Yacoub, Marina Zenovich; Antidote Film, Graceful Pictures; released by ThinkFilm
Directed by: Marina Zenovich
Written by: Marina Zenovich, Joe Bini, Peter G. Morgan
Cinematography by: Tanja Koop
Music by: Mark De Gli Antoni
Sound: Gary Tomaro
Editing: Joe Bini
MPAA rating: Unrated
Running time: 99 minutes

REVIEWS

Boston Globe Online. June 9, 2008.
Chicago Sun-Times Online. July 23, 2008.
Hollywood Reporter Online. January 20, 2008.
New York Times Online. March 31, 2008.
San Francisco Chronicle. July 25, 2008, p. E5.
Variety Online. January 19, 2008.
Village Voice Online. July 9, 2008.

THE ROMANCE OF ASTREE AND CELADON
(Les Amours d'Astrée et de Céladon)

Eric Rohmer has already announced that *The Romance of Astrea and Celadon* (*Les amours d'Astrée et de Céladon*) will be his last film and, at eighty-eight, he more than deserves a break. But it is a pity for the rest of us that the French director will no longer be making his wonderful films.

For this cinematic swan song, Rohmer again returns to his favorite theme: the follies of youth, specifically young lovers. In this case, *The Romance of Astrea and Celadon* is not a contemporary story, but a seventeenth-century verse novel set in fifth-century Gaul and written by Honoré d'Urfé.

In the story, as adapted by Rohmer, Astrea (Stéphanie Crayencour), a beautiful shepherd, is

heartbroken when she mistakenly believes her lover, Celadon (Andy Gillet), a handsome shepherd, has fallen for another. Likewise, Celadon mistakenly believes Astrea has found a new love. Though Celadon tries to convince Astrea there is no one else in his life, she refuses to listen and, in a fit of despair, Celadon tries to drown himself in a river. However, he saved by a group of nymphs.

Meanwhile, Astrea begins to regret rebuffing Celadon and fears he may be dead. Encouraged to woo Astrea without revealing himself, Celadon disguises himself as a woman, which leads to further misunderstandings. Ultimately, though, the lovers are reunited.

As usual, Rohmer tells a simple tale with both charm and depth of feeling. *The Romance of Astrea and Celadon* compares well to the director's *Tales of...* series, though it is deliberately more studied in its writing and acting style. It is still quite amazing how youthful the film feels, given Rohmer's age.

One of Rohmer's other rare period films, *Perceval le Gallois* (1978), was completely stylized and bound in studio settings. This time, as in *The Lady and the Duke* (2001), Rohmer combines the artifice of that early experiment with the cinéma vérité realism of his more celebrated works set in modern times.

The highlight for many will be the third "act," during which Celadon appears as young woman to get closer to his lady love. Echoing several Shakespearean comedies (as well as films like *Tootsie* [1982] and *Yentl* [1983]), this part of the story is an enjoyable gender-bending farce, though much of the rest of the film is imbued with Rohmer's bittersweet, even sorrowful, take on courtly love.

Rohmer's approach, allowing his actors to develop and build their own characters, must have been more limited this time, but he is blessed by his attractive, personable cast, including Crayencour and Gillet in the leading roles. Diane Baratier lends fluid camerawork, making the most of the Auvergne locations. And while Marie Dos Santos and Jérôme Pouvaret merely utilize nature as their production design, Pierre-Jean Larroque and Pu-Laï create stylish and pleasing period clothing. Finally, Jean-Louis Valéro contributes a sparingly used but lovely musical score.

A few critics embraced the film, but many more were disappointed. In the *New York Times* Stephen Holden wrote, "If the connections between this detached, dreamy fable and Mr. Rohmer's refined contemporary examinations of young love in *Six Moral Tales* are obvious, the characters in *The Romance of Astrea and Celadon,* pretty as they are, are historical phantoms with little flesh-and-blood substance. There are hugs and kisses galore but little actual desire."

Variety's Ronnie Scheib also had a mixed reaction: "Though less deliberately synthetic-looking than Rohmer's *The Lady and the Duke*, *Romance* often feels more artificial in its austerity. Each corner of nature appears to have been salvaged from some less bucolic landscape, and wandering shepherds might have been bussed in from Albania. On the other hand, the stilted language of courtly love feels absolutely natural."

The more enthusiastic responses included Andrew O'Hehir's review at *Salon*: "Rohmer never tries to modernize or sex up the antique plot conventions and stylized, poetic presentation of d'Urfé's story (and in fact this movie's a lot sexier than Woody Allen's allegedly erotic *Vicky Cristina Barcelona*). If anything, the film's charm lies in its journey in the other direction, into the mind-set and worldview of Renaissance yarn-spinning." Likewise, Sean Axmaker was highly positive in his *Seattle Post-Intelligencer* review: "There's a purity to the emotional turmoil of tormented lovers, but it's the rich simplicity of the filmmaking and the seductive sensuality of a bucolic Eden where maidens innocently fall out of their artfully revealing dresses that makes the romantic frolic so delicious."

The Romance of Astrea and Celadon is fitting coda for a filmmaker devoted to creating romantic tales that celebrate the innocence and frailty of young love.

Eric Monder

CREDITS

Adamas: Serge Renko
Hylas: Rodolphe Pauly
Celadon: Andy Gillet
Astrea: Stéphanie Crayencour
Galathée: Véronique Reymond
Léonide: Cécile Cassel
Lycidas: Jocelyn Quivrin
Origin: France, Italy, Spain
Language: French
Released: 2007
Production: Françoise Etchegaray, Philippe Liégeois, Jean-Michel Rey; Bim Distribuzione, Rezo Prods., Bim Distribuzione, Alta Produccion; released by Koch Lorber
Directed by: Eric Rohmer
Written by: Eric Rohmer
Cinematography by: Diane Baratier
Music by: Jean-Louis Valéro
Sound: Pascal Ribier
Editing: Mary Stephen
Costumes: Pierre-Jean Larroque, Pu-Laï
Production Design: Christian Paumier
MPAA rating: Unrated
Running time: 106 minutes

REVIEWS

The Independent Online. September 14, 2008.
New York Times Online. August 14, 2008.
San Francisco Chronicle. June 27, 2008, p. E6.
Variety Online. September 2, 2007.
Village Voice Online. August 12, 2008.

TRIVIA

Was chosen one of the ten best pictures of 2007 by *Les Cahiers du cinéma*.

ROMULUS, MY FATHER

In 1998 the Australian philosopher Raimond Gaita wrote an acclaimed memoir about the difficult circumstances of his childhood, growing up with an often absent mother and a struggling immigrant father. The movie version of the memoir, also titled *Romulus, My Father*, was written for the screen by musician/songwriter Nick Drake, but it relies more on iconic photography (by veteran cinematographer Geoffrey Simpson) and visually strong character portrayals than on spoken words. It seems an odd way of illustrating the early life of a man of language and ideas.

For Richard Roxburgh, an actor (*Moulin Rouge!* [2001]) and theater director, *Romulus, My Father* is a first foray into directing for the big screen. Roxburgh is a lover of scenes with striking images, and his film is full of luscious shots of the main characters set against stunning backdrops in rural Victoria. Nature and the land are never far away in this filmed version of Gaita's memoir, and they serve as powerful metaphors for the aching isolation and wonder of the boy's difficult childhood.

One repeated shot that is almost a signature for the film is that of Raimond (Kodi Smit-McPhee) riding behind Romulus (Eric Bana) on his father's motorcycle, along rural roads that cross the barren fields. Both are wearing old-fashioned goggles and leather hats, and they look like aviators. The film itself is a flight into a now-quaint era, a three-year period of Gaita's prepubescence in the early 1960s that coincided with a recession in Australia that made life very tough for immigrant farmers. Like almost everything else in the film, the economic situation is never clearly explained, but left to the viewer to surmise. At one point Romulus tries raising chickens, but later Hora (Marton Csokas) goes into a fit and hacks them up and buries them alive, claiming they are all diseased. (Are they? We never find out.) Another scene shows Romulus burning his fields with other farmers. Is this supposed to be clearing the land for new crops, or giving up on failed ones? Again, we have no idea.

We pick up the story when Romulus's German wife and Raimond's mother, Christina (Franka Potente), returns to the hardscrabble farm. We soon gather that Christina, who lives in Melbourne when she is not trying to restart her life with Romulus and Raimond, is estranged from her husband for reasons that have to do with her volatile mental condition and her habit of being faithless. Every time she returns, she expresses enthusiasm for Raimond and he clings to her, hoping for the best. Her intoxicating beauty entraps Romulus again and again, but each and every time they soon fight and she disappears.

That is exactly how scenes and characters come and go in *Romulus, My Father*—without explanation or connective tissue. Two Romanian brothers that Romulus met in a mining camp before moving to the farm also play murky roles in the film: Hora and Mitru (Russell Dykstra). One of them urges Romulus to shed Christina and get a new mail-order wife. One of them fights with Christina. One of them has a baby with Christina—or is it Romulus's baby? It is not clear, but Raimond apparently thinks of her as a sister.

If you are one of the few American viewers familiar with Gaita's memoir, what transpires might be very clear. If not, however, you'll have to try to make sense of the images that Roxburgh throws at you by connecting the dots. The characters have few actual conversations, and when they do, they are apt to be mumbled or whispered. They communicate more often by fighting or fornicating than by words.

There are some wrenching scenes that illustrate Raimond's strange education in the ways of his mother—most powerfully an eerie, disturbing scene in which, through peepholes in a barn, he witnesses his mother having rough sex. Later, when Raimond is sent away to boarding school, Christina comes to visit him. She takes him to a diner and puts a coin in the jukebox, and then tries to get her son to dance with her in the aisles, while the other customers glower. When Raimond refuses and then tells the school's headmaster he no longer wants to be called out of class when his mother visits, it is a turning point in their relationship. But are we meant to surmise that Christina ever touched him inappropriately? Or is her desire to dance just her odd way of trying to hold onto her son?

The memoir is set in a time and place where not much was known or done about mental illness. But there's little discussion about Christina's mental state in this movie; in fact, there's little discussion of anything at all. It is as if Roxburgh is determined to make a movie that is essentially a series of still paintings set into motion. The audience is given few clues as to what is happening between the characters or inside their heads.

Smit-McPhee gives an astoundingly moving performance as the child at the center of this maelstrom, and perhaps the purpose of Drake's sketchy screenplay and Roxburgh's minimalist directing is to cast audiences into the same sort of confusing stupefication that Raimond was undergoing as he struggled to make sense of the ill-fitting pieces of his family life. But Roxburgh takes the same approach to the economic and cultural framework of the era: He shows us Raimond watching a girl dancing to a Jerry Lee Lewis record, and then Raimond flailing away to the same rocker, with his father expressing disdain. But there's nothing else about incipient adolescent rebellion. At the beginning and end of the film, Romulus releases what appear to be dormant bees from his hand into the air, and they fly; there must be some meaning in this, but who can say what?

Roxburgh has spent most of his career as an actor, so how does he think you can make a movie by withholding verbal explanations, by merely compiling artsy, lovely scenes? Certainly it is realistic to suppose that Romulus and the others are not going to speak in polished, movie-star sentences—but is it too much to ask that they say enough to give viewers some clue about themselves? Given that most audiences are unaware of this philosopher and his memoir, it would have been better to have Raimond narrate the film and thus give the uninitiated a sense of who he became and how these events shaped him. Instead, we have a lovely tone poem that will cause most viewers to throw up their hands in utter frustration at its inscrutability.

Michael Betzold

CREDITS

Romulus Gaita: Eric Bana
Christina: Franka Potente
Mitru: Russell Dykstra
Hora: Marton Csokas
Raimond: Kodi Smit-McPhee
Vacek: Jacek Koman
Origin: Australia
Language: English
Released: 2007
Production: Robert Connolly, John Maynard; Arena Films, New South Wales Film & Television Office, Pick Up Truck Pictures; released by Magnolia Pictures
Directed by: Richard Roxburgh
Written by: Nick Drake
Cinematography by: Geoffrey Simpson
Music by: Basil Hogios
Sound: Gary Wilkins
Editing: Suresh Ayyar

Production Design: Robert Cousins
MPAA rating: R
Running time: 109 minutes

REVIEWS

Los Angeles Times Online. February 29, 2008.
San Francisco Chronicle. February 29, 2008, p. E6.
Variety Online. June 11, 2007.
Wall Street Journal. February 29, 2008, p. W1.

QUOTES

Mitru: "I wish it could be the way it used to be. When we were friends."

THE RUINS

Terror has evolved.
—Movie tagline

Box Office: $17.4 million

Scott B. Smith's brilliant debut novel, *A Simple Plan,* became an Oscar®-nominated smash critical hit and signaled the arrival of a major new talent. The novel was released in 1993; Smith himself wrote the screenplay for the 1998 Sam Raimi film adaptation and received a well-deserved Oscar® nomination. A nod from the Academy for his follow-up book and screenplay would be the most shocking in the history of the Oscars®. It took Smith thirteen years to write another novel, 2006's *The Ruins,* a book that Stephen King called "The best horror novel of the new century." Smith's sophomore fictional effort was very well received and a surprisingly effective slow-burn about a deadly tourist trap. The book was shocking in its dark, pessimistic nature, and offered readers little to no chance for anything positive. From the moment its characters got stuck in a deadly situation, readers knew in their hearts that not one of them was going to make it out alive. But the shocking lack of hope in Smith's novel was going to be a tough mood to sell to a studio and, from the minute it was announced, fans of the book worried about how it would look on the big screen. What worked so well on the page might collapse in a Ben Stiller-produced major motion picture. The worries of fans had some validity, and that may have been unavoidable. The film version of *The Ruins* proves that even the best horror novel of the new century can make for only a so-so movie because the media are so very different.

The Ruins opens with a group of college friends (Jonathan Tucker, Shawn Ashmore, Jena Malone, and Laura Ramsey) on a vacation in Mexico. The sexy quartet encounter a kindly German named Mathias (Joe Anderson) by the pool and listen to his interesting story of a brother who supposedly left for an archaeological dig and never came back. Either he is having so much fun that they should join him or he needs some help. The gang of Americans have been stuck in a resort their whole trip and decide to take the opportunity to look into a bit of the local flavor. If they had ever seen a horror movie before, they would know that this is a bad idea. If the genre has taught us anything, especially in recent years, it is that it is never a good idea to leave the hotel. Even leaving the country is usually a bad idea.

The group make it to the site of the archaeological dig and find Mathias's dead, vine-covered brother and a group of very angry locals, who instantly kill one member of the peaceful gang. Pushed back up to the top of the Mayan ruins by the bow-and-arrow-wielding men below, the friends soon discover that the Mayans are not trying to keep out the newcomers as much as make sure they never leave the vine-covered hill. Something ancient and deadly is alive on that hill. The next trauma comes when the group hears a ringing cell phone at the bottom of an abandoned shaft. They decide to tie Mathias to a flimsy rope and lower him down. The rope breaks and Mathias falls to the bottom, breaking his back. Rather than just leave him to die, the two girls fix the rope and head down to save him. Injured friends soon turn into a liability as the vines that cover the ruins start to come alive and seep their way into open wounds and broken legs. Paranoia plays a major role when the group starts to disagree about what to do next and it becomes clear that this battle between man and nature is going to be won by the latter.

Fiction allows for a lot of leeway when it comes to a story about killer plants. Cinema is not nearly as forgiving. What was creepy in the mind's eye has the tendency to look a little goofy on film. With that in mind, *The Ruins* actually has moments that work surprisingly well. Director Carter Smith (no relation to the writer) might have made the best possible version of Smith's book, simply because the limitations of the form make a film like this a really tough sell. The most fatal flaw, besides the hard-to-believe villain of the piece, is that Smith's novel allowed him time enough to develop each of the four characters so that the reader could identify with them and eventually mourn their deaths. They each played a different role in the piece. The director Smith simply does not have the time to develop his characters in a genre that demands instant horror gratification, which makes each member of the quartet a bit interchangeable. There are still elements of *The Ruins,* like the mimicking plants and the gory, paranoid end of the poor girl who believes the vines are inside her, that are very effective, but, as is usually the case, the movie only has half of the power of the novel. It may be a sign of the dearth of quality in the genre that even a half-effective version of a novel as great as *The Ruins* is still better than most of the derivative product horror fans have suffered through in recent years.

Brian Tallerico

CREDITS

Jeff: Jonathan Tucker
Amy: Jena Malone
Eric: Shawn Ashmore
Stacy: Laura Ramsey
Mathias: Joe Anderson
Dimitri: Dimitri Baveas
Origin: USA
Language: English
Released: 2008
Production: Stuart Cornfeld, Jeremy Kramer, Chris Bender; Red Hour, Spyglass Entertainment, Dreamworks Pictures; released by Paramount
Directed by: Carter Smith
Written by: Scott B. Smith
Cinematography by: Darius Khondji
Music by: Graeme Revell
Sound: Paul Brincat
Editing: Jeff Betancourt
Art Direction: Brian Edmonds
Costumes: Lizzy Gardiner
Production Design: Grant Major
MPAA rating: R
Running time: 90 minutes

REVIEWS

Boston Globe Online. April 5, 2008.
Entertainment Weekly Online. April 4, 2008.
Hollywood Reporter Online. April 7, 2008.
Los Angeles Times Online. April 5, 2008.
New York Times Online. April 5, 2008.
Variety Online. April 5, 2008.

QUOTES

Amy: "We're being quarantined here. We're being kept here to die."

RUN, FATBOY, RUN

Love. Commitment. Responsibility. There's nothing he can't run away from.
—Movie tagline

True love isn't a sprint. It's a marathon.
—Movie tagline

Box Office: $6 million

Run, Fatboy, Run is a mildly amusing romantic comedy that coasts on the irrepressible talents of its star (and cowriter) Simon Pegg of *Shaun of the Dead* (2004) and *Hot Fuzz* (2007) fame. Set in London and featuring a primarily English cast, the film offers flashes of warped, inspired humor, but unfortunately most of its jokes are obvious and juvenile. As a result, *Run, Fatboy, Run* has the stale flavor of an American sitcom overall—perhaps not surprisingly, given that it was directed by *Friends* alumnus David Schwimmer.

Five years after jilting his pregnant bride, Libby (Thandie Newton), at the altar, hapless London security guard Dennis Doyle (Simon Pegg) is still trying to wheedle himself back into her good graces. Much to his chagrin, Libby is also being wooed by a handsome and successful American businessman named Whit (Hank Azaria) who runs marathons for charity. Though he is out of shape, Dennis decides to toss aside his cigarettes and race in Whit's latest marathon in order to prove his follow-through to Libby. His landlord, Mr. Goshdashti-dar (Harish Patel), and best friend, Gordon (Dylan Moran), hop on board as spatula-wielding trainers. Dennis's resolve falters after Libby accepts Whit's proposal of marriage, but when Gordon and Mr. Goshdashtidar reject him for quitting—and more importantly, he realizes he is not setting a proper example for Jake (Matthew Fenton), his five-year-old son with Libby—Dennis shows up to run. During the marathon, a vexed Whit reveals his true colors by tripping Dennis, but Dennis finishes the race despite a badly sprained ankle. In the process, he becomes a media sensation in London and renews Libby's faith in him.

Whether he is preening in front of a mirror or adjusting his tiny, ill-fitting nylon running shorts, Pegg gamely squeezes yuks from every scene, and his ingratiating, high-energy performance is the main reason to see *Run, Fatboy, Run*. Pegg literally throws himself into the role of Dennis, tumbling from one pratfall to the next: He falls down stairs, trips over jump ropes, and (in a thirty-two-year-old joke) convulsively spits up a cocktail of raw eggs à la *Rocky* (1976). Despite his penchant for over-the-top antics, Pegg does rise above the silliness, adding enough vulnerability and earnestness to Dennis's quest for redemption that viewers will likely root for him to finish the marathon.

His hoped-for reunion with Libby may leave them cold, however. Newton, who seems uncomfortable when called on to be funny, has trouble selling the few humorous lines thrown her way. To be sure, she is one of the most ravishing actors working in cinema today, but with the scant material she is given here, the character registers as little more than a trophy. Compounding the problem, Whit's comeuppance in the third act is so cartoonish that Libby's reconciliation with Dennis after the race just feels empty.

Thankfully Moran is on hand to boost the material. As the deadpan rake Gordon, he serves as the perfect foil for Pegg. His bits of dialogue suggest the film had the potential to be better than it is. Poking a gigantic blister on Dennis's foot with a rusty nail, he wonders, "Maybe there is a little man inside of there who looks just like you but is really good at running." Though this type of character has become a staple in British romantic comedies of late (see Bill Nighy in *Love Actually* [2003], Rhys Ifans in *Notting Hill* [1999], and Darren Boyd in *Imagine Me & You* [2005]), Moran's effortless performance feels new.

If only the rest of the film were as fresh. To his credit, director Schwimmer keeps the tone light and engaging (at least until the overlong marathon sequence). His London looks crisp and colorful, and the film's soundtrack—while overwhelming at times—features lively songs from UK artists including Dirty Pretty Things, Air Traffic, Teenage Fanclub, and the Rumble Strips. The main problem is that he sabotages the film's pacing by telegraphing jokes from miles away; indeed, the viewer almost expects to hear a laugh track when each one hits its inevitable mark. For instance, after Whit congratulates Dennis for handling his budding relationship with Libby so maturely, the audience is primed for Dennis to behave immaturely—and surprise, surprise, he does, giving Whit the finger when the man turns away. Other childish gags abound, including requisite jokes about flatulence, jock itch, and erectile dysfunction. (Equally shameless are instances of Nike product placement. The company sponsors Dennis and Whit's marathon, and when Mr. Goshdashtidar treats Dennis to a new pair of trainers, the brand is Nike: "The man said they were the best you could buy.")

With its sitcomish rhythms, bright visuals, and poppy soundtrack, *Run, Fatboy, Run* seems destined to become one of those films repeatedly broadcast on cable television. It would have benefited from subtler comedic direction, a richly drawn female lead, and the courage to be original. But in light of its winning performances by Pegg and Moran, one could do worse on a rainy Saturday afternoon.

Marisa Carroll

CREDITS

Dennis: Simon Pegg
Libby: Thandie Newton
Whit: Hank Azaria
Gordon: Dylan Moran
Mr. Goshdashtidar: Harish Patel
Maya Goshdashtidar: India de Beaufort
Jake: Matthew Fenton
Origin: Great Britain
Language: English
Released: 2007
Production: Robert Jones, Sarah Curtis; Material Entertainment; released by Picturehouse
Directed by: David Schwimmer
Written by: Michael Ian Black, Simon Pegg
Cinematography by: Richard Greatrex
Music by: Alex Wurman
Sound: Alistair Crocker
Editing: Michael Parker
Art Direction: Julia Castle
Costumes: Annie Hardinge
Production Design: Sophie Becher
MPAA rating: PG-13
Running time: 100 minutes

REVIEWS

Boston Globe Online. March 28, 2008.
Chicago Sun-Times Online. March 28, 2008.
Entertainment Weekly Online. March 26, 2008.
Hollywood Reporter Online. September 11, 2007.
Los Angeles Times Online. March 28, 2008.
New York Times Online. March 28, 2008.
Rolling Stone Online. April 3, 2008.
San Francisco Chronicle. March 28, 2008, p. E9.
Variety Online. September 11, 2007.
Washington Post. March 28, 2008, p. C5.

QUOTES

Gordon: "The only serious relationship I've been in ended in a broken collarbone and a dead meerkat."

TRIVIA

Director David Schwimmer makes a brief cameo in the film as the man who hands Simon Pegg a beer during the marathon.

S

SAW V

You won't believe how it ends.
—Movie tagline

Box Office: $56.7 million

The unstoppable horror franchise that gave rise to the term "torture-porn" released its 2008 entry, *Saw V*, to the disdain of critics and a typically receptive audience. With its inventive debut in 2004, *Saw* was an intelligently crafted and unique addition to the horror genre that spawned two satisfying sequels. Critically and monetarily, *Saw IV* (2007) marked a slide in the series, which this latest effort continues. Familiar sequels director Darren Lynn Bousman steps aside for *Saw IV*'s production designer David Hackl, who makes his directorial debut but has difficulty breathing new life into the usual gory goings-on. Screenwriters Patrick Melton and Marcus Dunstan throw up a smokescreen to hide their uninspired script with their shameless attempt at drumming up interest in the aging franchise, obvious in the cut-to-the-chase tagline: "You won't believe how it ends." Viewers lured by the tagline might have thought they meant the end of the series, but they would be incorrect, with *Saw VI* dependably unspooling on Halloween 2009.

The typically convoluted plot depends much on viewers knowing what happened in the earlier *Saw* films, so it would be safe to say that *Saw V* is for those fans alone. With the death of the original Jigsaw Killer John Kramer (Tobin Bell) in *Saw III*, and his deranged protégé Amanda (Shawnee Smith) also deceased, Detective Mark Hoffman (Costas Mandylor) is alone left to mastermind inventive new devices to torture and kill new victims. Hoffman, however, is unaware that Agent Strahm (Scott Patterson) somehow escaped the trap Hoffman set for him. With its usual flashback sequences explaining the illogical twists in the plot, it is revealed how Hoffman came to work with Jigsaw in a scheme that initially involved blackmail. Strahm, meanwhile, is busy with his investigation as the police declare that the Jigsaw murders are officially over.

Free for the time being to get on with his murderous business, Hoffman targets five people who are somehow connected to one another and fit Jigsaw's criteria of ungrateful worms worthy of being gruesomely tested in ruthlessly medieval devices. Ashley (Laura Gordon), Charles (Carlo Rota), Brit (Julie Benz), Mallick (Greg Bryk), and Luba (Meagan Good) begin their torturous adventure chained in a sewer. Naturally, most do not pass the various tests they are forced to undergo, which usually involves a Sophie's Choice of mutilating oneself with a small chance of surviving or accepting the inevitable fate. They are disposed of one by one in the usual manner that the *Saw* films employ, including by means of all manner of bladed devices like saws and guillotines, and by electrocution.

The best of these torture scenes is also film's opening sequence, which has Seth Baxter (Joris Jarsky), chained to a table beneath a rusty pendulum blade. A convicted murderer, he was released from prison early because of a technicality. He learns via videotape that to save himself, he must put his hands into a press and willingly crush them. When he does so but is sliced in two by the blade anyway, it is actually somewhat surprising, and reveals Hoffman's marked departure from Jigsaw's signature style.

While the scene is virtually the only interesting, suspenseful one, it also notes the killer devolving from one who at least had a certain demented logic. Mandylor's Hoffman merely seems to derive a cheap thrill from it all. Mandylor as an actor also lacks the deranged brio of Tobin Bell, and is an especially subdued, dull-eyed killer who completely lacks believability and any trace of menace.

The script, however, will have it that Hoffman is nearly as ingenious as Jigsaw, and he craftily sets up Strahm to look like Jigsaw's accomplice. Of course, just as it seems Strahm has somehow outwitted Hoffman at the film's end, it turns out that Hoffman has set another trap for Strahm that he does not survive this time, while Hoffman safely escapes.

By now, the audience knows all the tricks and retroactive continuity that the *Saw* series lazily employs from film to film. That might have been forgiven if the script had devised new and inventive tortures to scream and squirm over. *Saw V*'s rehashed horror scenarios will disappoint fans as much as the marked lack of gore—which would have been the only reason to sit through an especially uninspired *Saw* retelling.

Hilary White

CREDITS

Jigsaw/John Kramer: Tobin Bell
Amanda Young: Shawnee Smith
Hoffman: Costas Mandylor
Brit: Julie Benz
Agent Strahm: Scott Patterson
Luba: Meagan Good
Jill Tuck: Betsy Russell
Charles: Carlo Rota
Origin: USA
Language: English
Released: 2008
Production: Oren Koules, Mark Berg; Twisted Pictures; released by Lionsgate
Directed by: David Hackl
Written by: Patrick Melton, Marcus Dunstan
Cinematography by: David Armstrong
Music by: Charlie Clouser
Sound: Mark Gingras, John Douglas Smith
Editing: Kevin Greutert
Costumes: Alex Kavanagh
Production Design: Anthony Ianni
MPAA rating: R
Running time: 92 minutes

REVIEWS

Entertainment Weekly Online. October 24, 2008.
Hollywood Reporter Online. October 24, 2008.
Los Angeles Times Online. October 25, 2008.
New York Times Online. October 25, 2008.
San Francisco Chronicle. October 27, 2008.
Variety Online. October 24, 2008.

QUOTES

Jigsaw: "Murder is distasteful."

TRIVIA

This is the first film of the franchise to fail to open at number one after opening weekend.

THE SECRET LIFE OF BEES

Bring your girlfriends, sisters, mothers, and daughters.
—Movie tagline

Box Office: $37.7 million

Gina Prince-Blythewood's drama set in the 1960s South, *The Secret Life of Bees,* based on the bestselling novel by Sue Monk Kidd, is a moving exploration of community, love, racial equality, and forgiveness. Although the film may occasionally dip into the well of melodrama and sentiment, the honesty of the performances by the appealing and skilled cast keep it from sinking.

During the summer of 1964, beekeeper August Boatwright (Queen Latifah) collects and sells honey and lives an idyllic life in the pleasant small town of Tiburon with her two sisters, June (Alicia Keys), a staunch civil rights activist, and May (Sophie Okonedo), empathetic in the extreme, a deeply feeling girl who may be unstable. In another, more troubled town, Lily Owens (Dakota Fanning), fourteen years old, suffers at the hands of her abusive father T. Ray (Paul Bettany) in the aftermath of her mother's death ten years before. When her housekeeper and protector Rosaleen (Jennifer Hudson) is attacked by racists and arrested, Lily helps her escape and, with nowhere else to go, heads to Tiburon. Lily found a strange-looking, quasi-religious image bearing the name of the town among her deceased mother's belongings, and they take it as a sign that that is the direction they should go.

They end up at the big-hearted August's gaily colored doorstep and she takes them in, despite objections from the radical June, after Lily weaves a tale that her parents have died and they are en route to an aunt's house. Sleeping on a cot in the bee house, Lily feels strangely at home and learns more about why as she bonds with June, May, and especially the motherly August while learning the art of beekeeping. For the first time in her young life, Lily experiences the comfort of home and family with the Boatwright sisters, and learns some important lessons in the way the sisters treat one another. August tells her that she and her sisters live with the embarrassment of a house painted a shocking pink simply because it brings joy to the troubled May. Lily learns not only through the Boatwrights' relationship with one another but also in the way August acted as a Good Samaritan by opening her door to strangers and sharing with them what little they had.

The film is also story of a white girl rescued from her white father and finding salvation with a family of black women in the highly charged racial atmosphere of 1960s, begging comparison with a now controversial classic set in a far more intolerant time. As *Chicago Sun-Times* critic Roger Ebert observed, "As Lily helps Rosaleen flee from virtual slavery, it's impossible not to think about Huck and Jim, unless political correctness has prevented you from reading that greatest of all novels about black and white in America." There are several scenes illustrating the outrageous racial inequality. When Lily sits in the "Coloreds Only" section at the movies with a black boy she likes, Zach (Tristan Wilds), he is beaten by two white men. As the film illuminates a turbulent and troubled time in American history, it simultaneously exhibits the ever-present seeds of understanding and tolerance.

Like several films of 2008, *The Secret Life of Bees* makes use of a plot device that has the main character killing a relative and then spending wasted years living with the grief and family tension that resulted. Unlike *Rachel Getting Married* and *I've Loved You So Long*, which slowly reveal this vital information late in the film, here the information is dispensed early on—in the first five minutes, in fact. When Lily was four years old, she accidentally shot and killed her mother, who had abandoned her and her father, T. Ray, months earlier. This adds to the drama by infusing both characters with sadness, loss, and more importantly, the guilt that drives a wedge between the two and which Lily must overcome to reclaim her life.

The film faithfully adapts the equally outstanding novel with a distaff ensemble that is one of the most impressive of the year. A more mature Fanning adroitly conveys all the nuances required to play such a complex teenage character who, despite of a lack of parental nurturing, is vulnerable enough to accept it from her adoptive family. Latifah's role as the matriarch is less of a stretch, but she is able to successfully transpose her radiant serenity and nurturing qualities to the 1960s and still be believable. The Oscar®-nominated Okonedo,

Oscar®-winning Hudson, and Keys also turn in strong performances.

Hilary White

CREDITS

August Boatwright: Queen Latifah
Lily Owens: Dakota Fanning
Rosaleen Daise: Jennifer Hudson
May Boatwright: Sophie Okonedo
Neil: Nate Parker
Deborah Owens: Hilarie Burton
T. Ray Owens: Paul Bettany
June Boatwright: Alicia Keyes
Zach Taylor: Tristan Wilds
Origin: USA
Language: English
Released: 2008
Production: James Lassiter, Will Smith, Lauren Schuler Donner, Ewan Leslie, Joe Pichirallo; Overbrook Entertainment; released by Fox Searchlight
Directed by: Gina Prince-Bythewood
Written by: Gina Prince-Bythewood
Cinematography by: Rogier Stoffers
Sound: Carl Rudisill
Music: Mark Isham
Editing: Terilyn Shropshire
Art Direction: William G. Davis, Alan Hook
Costumes: Sandra Hernandez
Production Design: Warren Alan Young
MPAA rating: PG-13
Running time: 110 minutes

REVIEWS

Boston Globe Online. October 17, 2008.
Chicago Sun-Times Online. October 15, 2008.
Entertainment Weekly Online. October 15, 2008.
Hollywood Reporter Online. September 5, 2008.
Los Angeles Times Online. October 17, 2008.
New York Times Online. October 17, 2008.
San Francisco Chronicle. October 17, 2008, p. E3.
Time Online. October 16, 2008.
Variety Online. September 8, 2008.
Washington Post. October 17, 2008, p. C3.

QUOTES

Lily: "I killed my mother when I was four years old. That's all I know about myself."

SEMI-PRO

Putting the funk into the dunk.
    —Movie tagline

The greatest fro on earth.
—Movie tagline

Box Office: $33.4 million

Will Ferrell has spent the better part of the past decade laying claim to a unique piece of cinematic turf: the bungling, egomaniacal man-child placed in any number of situations (race-car driver, figure skater, anchorman, et al.) mostly set either in the present day (*Talladega Nights: The Ballad of Ricky Bobby* [2006], *Blades of Glory* [2007]) or the 1970s (*Anchorman: The Legend of Ron Burgundy* [2004]). *Semi-Pro* builds on this legacy and expands it, with mixed results. With a plot that is straight out of the "any down-and-out sports team comeback" comedy playbook (think *Major League* [1989], *Slap Shot* [1977], or *Wildcats* [1986]), *Semi-Pro* plays as hard for audience laughs as it does for Will Ferrell's dominance as America's pre-eminent lovable, id-charged village idiot.

Occasionally, Ferrell tones down the egotism and channels an ingenuousness that can make his characters endearing (as in *Elf* [2003]) or even poignant (*Stranger than Fiction* [2006]), and a touch of that is on display in *Semi-Pro,* but for the most part, this film is Ron Burgundy meets Ricky Bobby—in an afro and short-shorts.

As with most Will Ferrell comedies, the plot is rather simple: Jackie Moon (Will Ferrell), coach and star forward of the American Basketball Association's Flint (Michigan) Tropics, attempts to ensure that his team is picked up by the National Basketball Association in a merger deal that stipulates that only four teams will make the cut. This, of course, is based on the actual ABA/NBA merger of 1976, in which the San Antonio Spurs, the New York Nets, the Denver Nuggets, and the Indiana Pacers were absorbed into the NBA and the rest of the league disbanded. Though the teams are chosen, Jackie, as one of the team owners, convinces the ABA board that the four best teams should move up to the NBA. He then endeavors to make certain that the Flint Tropics are one of those four best teams. In an effort to raise the Tropics's caliber of play, Jackie hires on one-time NBA benchwarmer Ed Monix (Woody Harrelson) to give the team a better chance of winning, and in doing so, launches the movie's second narrative thread—Monix's quest to win back his ex-wife Lynn (Maura Tierney), who happens to be romantically involved with Monix's number-one fan, Kyle (an almost unrecognizable, toupee-coiffed Rob Corddry). It turns out, however, that the deal Jackie struck with the ABA commissioner (David Koechner) has one more provision attached by the NBA: The NBA wants teams with major media markets, and the Flint Tropics have no fan base. In order to be seriously considered for inclusion in the NBA, the Tropics must have home game attendance of at least 2,000 fans for the remainder of the season. A man with infinite belief in his flair for promotion (despite a clear lack of results), Jackie embarks on a series of stunts to drum up attendance, including a free corndog night, a stunt in which Jackie attempts (and miraculously succeeds in) a jump over the Tropics's cheerleaders using nothing but skates and a giant ramp, and the most insane stunt of all time—trying to wrestle a bear. During the final game of the season, against the San Antonio Spurs, the Tropics are down and appear to be beaten until Jackie is knocked out by a foul toward the end of the second quarter and emerges from the half with the knowledge of a new method of scoring, the "Alleyoop." With this new weapon in their arsenal, the Tropics come back from a massive deficit to win the game. Though they are not subsumed into the NBA, the Tropics finish the season with a bit of pride, since they actually come in fourth in the league. Jackie, having proved himself to be a good promoter, is asked by the ABA commissioner to join him in the NBA as deputy commissioner of marketing—of course, before Jackie can accept, the commissioner is killed by the bear Jackie wrestled earlier in the movie, which had escaped and not been found.

Needless to say, the plot of the movie is really a loose framework on which to hang lots of funny bits, and *Semi-Pro* features a fantastic comedic cast, including Will Arnett as Lou Redwood and Andrew Daly as Dick Pepperfield, the Tropics's hilarious commentators, with bit parts and cameos played by the likes of Tim Meadows, Andy Richter, Matt Walsh, and Jackie Earle Haley—and André Benjamin (formerly of the hip-hop group OutKast) is absolutely fantastic as the Tropics's star player, Clarence "Coffee Black" Withers. Will Ferrell is a master of the comedy of excess, and a film about the flamboyant American Basketball Association set in the 1970s allows him and his cohorts to let things really rip. The very notion that Jackie purchased the Tropics using the proceeds from his one-hit-wonder single "Love Me Sexy," which is played several times throughout the film, is enough to elicit a guffaw. Sure, some moments are played for easy laughs—it is difficult not to chuckle with Will Ferrell and crew running around in short-shorts, sporting huge hair. What is truly interesting and unique about *Semi-Pro* in the Will Ferrell canon is that it takes profanity to a heretofore unexplored level. Various four-letter words and their many variants fly freely, which leads to some of the film's funniest moments, including some comments made by Jackie Moon to the Tropics's referee, Father Pat (Matt Walsh)—imagine an athlete saying all of the things an athlete might want to say to a referee, and then imagine that the referee in question is also a priest—and in things characters say to one another in the heat of the moment (Will Ferrell utters most of the cursing zingers on the court). The true genius of the power of the over-the-top swearing in *Semi-Pro,* however, is revealed in a profanity-laden poker game scene in which Jackie's friend Cornelius Banks (Tim Meadows) calls Lou Redwood a "jive turkey," Lou pulls a gun on Cornelius, and Jackie and the others attempt to defuse the situation by saying that Cornelius had really called Lou something much, much worse than a jive turkey. The scene has a completely ridiculous ending (of course), but it stands as one of the most memorable in the film. The cursing truly adds a new level of shock and surprise to the Ferrell oeuvre, which is not to say that *Semi-Pro*'s use of profanity does for sports comedies what television's *Deadwood* did for the western, but it certainly breaks some new ground for Ferrell and crew, who usually opt for more watered-down language to reach a wider audience. While the cursing may be a bit jarring (or even offensive) for some, it works in the piece—it seems entirely organic in this sporting world of man-boys set in the mid-1970s.

Semi-Pro, for all of its funny moments, is not a particularly funny film overall, nor is it by any measure a great film. Its split narrative of Jackie trying to save his team and Monix trying to rekindle his relationship with Lynn is formulaic to a fault, and, to be sure, *Semi-Pro*'s weakest attribute is its similarity to so many of Ferrell's previous films. Ferrell can certainly be accused of repeating himself here. However much the film may flounder in its totality, though, its bright spots generally outshine its flaws. Jackie Moon cares very much about his team, and not only for selfish reasons—he shares a genuine camaraderie with them, and the team's rapport is palpable. The motto on the Tropics's locker-room wall is "Everybody Love Everybody," or "E.L.E.," as Jackie admonishes his teammates in one locker-room scene, and that ultimately is what the viewer walks away with when *Semi-Pro* is over. The bottom line is that *Semi-Pro* is a flawed film with a good heart that has some decent laughs and a great deal of profanity in it, and it is difficult not to smile when Jackie Moon drives down the street in a tremendous car singing the Brothers Johnson hit "Get the Funk Out Ma Face."

John Boaz

CREDITS

Jackie Moon: Will Ferrell
Ed Monix: Woody Harrelson
Clarence 'Downtown' Withers: André Benjamin
Lynn: Maura Tierney
Lou Redwood: Will Arnett
Bobby Dee: Andy Richter

Commissioner: David Koechner
Kyle: Rob Corddry
Father Pat the Ref: Matt Walsh
Dukes: Jackie Earle Haley
Dick Pepperfield: Andrew Daly
Origin: USA
Language: English
Released: 2008
Production: Jimmy Miller; Mosaic Media Group; released by New Line Cinema
Directed by: Kent Alterman
Written by: Scot Armstrong
Cinematography by: Shane Hurlbut
Music by: Theodore Shapiro
Sound: Art Rochester
Editing: Debra Neil Fisher
Art Direction: Virginia L. Randolph, Jim Gloster
Costumes: Susan Matheson
Production Design: Clayton Hartley
MPAA rating: R
Running time: 90 minutes

REVIEWS

Boston Globe Online. February 29, 2008.
Chicago Sun-Times Online. February 29, 2008.
Hollywood Reporter Online. February 29, 2008.
Los Angeles Times Online. February 29, 2008.
New York Times Online. February 29, 2008.
Rolling Stone Online. March 20, 2008.
San Francisco Chronicle. February 29, 2008, p. E1.
Variety Online. February 28, 2008.
Washington Post. February 29, 2008, p. C1.

QUOTES

Jackie Moon: "If you see an opposum, kill it. It's not a pet."

TRIVIA

Save the Flint Tropics, all of the teams and uniforms are the same as they were in the actual ABA.

SEVEN POUNDS

Seven names. Seven strangers. One secret.
—Movie tagline

Box Office: $69.9 million

Few would expect a destructive tidal wave to arise from the waters of a bathtub, but that is what happens at the end of *Seven Pounds* as a tsunami of sentimentality wells up to bring down a story that was already quite soggy. The film's finale is akin to that of another numerically titled production, *The Sixth Sense* (1999), in which the pieces of a mysterious puzzle that have been gradually doled out suddenly snap together to make everything shockingly clear. Served up in a surgical bowl for viewers to see in close-up and then audibly beating during the last waterlogged ounces of *Seven Pounds* is a heart, and that is exclusively where the film is aimed. Some viewers were indeed powerfully moved, overcome by that climactic wave and its repercussions, while others reacted with a rising tide of incredulity.

Seven Pounds's protagonist, Ben Thomas (Will Smith), is at one point shown perched upon the craggy shores of the Pacific, which is appropriate since his life is clearly on the rocks. In glaring juxtaposition to his vibrant surroundings, including a lovely home from which one might enjoy such invigorating vistas, Ben appears drained, dispirited, and tuned in solely to something that is obviously gnawing voraciously at his soul. Viewers know for certain from the outset that something is troubling him terribly, as the film begins with an agonized Ben calling 911 to report his own impending suicide. *Seven Pounds* tells the tale of this shattered man in fragments, the bulk of it revealing what brought him to see the sense in self-annihilation, to feel that it is not only the right course of action but also a righteous one.

For a long time, it is exceedingly difficult to know what to make of Ben. Becoming irritated during a phone conversation with Ezra (Woody Harrelson), a meat distributor's customer-service representative whom he comes to realize is blind, Ben mercilessly berates and stingingly belittles the poor genial fellow who amazingly refrains from responding in kind despite being clearly wounded. However, it is Ben who inexplicably goes to pieces after the goading ends, clapping his hands over a mouth contorted from weeping and then dashing a chair to pieces. Then, representing the Internal Revenue Service, he goes to discuss a possible six-month extension on payment of overdue taxes owed by a nursing-home doctor, a man who is in great need of what is most likely a last-chance bone marrow transplant. Strangely, this IRS agent is more concerned with the physician's level of decency than debt, determined to learn whether or not Dr. Stewart Goodman (Tim Kelleher) lives up to his surname. As Ben gently approaches one of the home's wizened residents for her opinion, he flashes a charming, disarming smile previously visible only in flashbacks of infinitely happier, carefree times with a now-absent wife. With the elderly woman, he reveals a seemingly sincere warmth and appealing spark that an as-yet-unspecified trauma has failed to completely snuff out. Based solely upon this one woman's moving claims of Goodman's callousness, Ben vehemently and violently refuses to grant him more time, with words that extraordinarily but unmistakably sound like a dooming declaration deeming the man unworthy of life itself. Ben apparently has some sort of plan in the forefront of his deeply disquieted mind, and the volatility shown in his passionate pursuit of it is rather disconcerting.

Other intriguing purposeful interactions follow. There is the scared woman (Elpidia Carrillo) with small children and a big dilemma concerning domestic violence who is baffled about why Ben is there trying to help her, and she initially rebuffs him. Eventually, she accepts the haven of his fully furnished beach house, which he astonishingly hands over to her permanently. A goodhearted hockey coach (Bill Smitrovich) cannot figure out a total stranger's out-of-the-blue offering of a kidney. Ben also casts a caring glance in the direction of a downcast boy fighting cancer, eventually redirecting his bone marrow to this untarnished recipient. At one point, he even amiably passes on gardening knowledge that results with abundant symbolism in bountiful, beautiful flowers. It certainly seems humorously incongruous to have good tidings emanating from an employee of the dreaded and detested IRS.

Of all those Ben approaches, figuring most prominently in *Seven Pounds* is critically ill sweetheart Emily Posa (an engaging, affecting Rosario Dawson), whose congenitally defective heart and rare blood type make her future look decidedly grim. As portrayed by Dawson, however, Emily is still ravishing despite the ravages of her condition, and so it is not surprising that feelings of ardor add unanticipated complications to Ben's enigmatic agenda. While still intractably, impenetrably black and bleak in his walled-off cryptic core, Ben cannot help but brighten in this lovely person's presence. Like everyone else, Emily cannot fathom the reason behind the quirky, dogged personal attentiveness of an IRS man while apparently on the clock. Still, the mutually felt romantic regard that quickly develops provides her with a welcome source of light in the gathering darkness, enabling Emily to rather touchingly bloom for perhaps the last time. The two laugh. They dance. They make love. The scene in which Ben and Emily relax together in the fresh air of a sunlit field stands in stark contrast to the dimly lit, cold confines of her hospital room and the motel accommodations he has recently sought out, and serves as a visual representation of spirits symbiotically lifted out from under their respective crushing loads—at least temporarily.

Emily says that time with Ben enables her to "get out of her head, for once." What she fails to discern, however, is how he, in a far less healthy sense, is rather out of his own. Viewers, however, have seen and heard more than enough to be alarmed. A multitude of close-ups have lingered upon a face filled with excruciating torment, tears rolling down from profoundly preoccupied eyes. The audience has witnessed him rolling up the windows of his car so he can ragingly scream at the top of his lungs and beat the steering wheel. They have seen how what haunts Ben while he is awake also persistently plagues him with horrific vividness when he is asleep. Clearly he is in critical need of some professional help. How believable is it that his close, old friend Dan (Barry Pepper), the sole person Ben not only lets in on his plans but also asks to help facilitate them, never moves beyond anxious qualms to put an end to things before Ben puts an end to himself?

Even before Ben's ominous announcement to Dan that "it's time," many attentive viewers will at least guess the specifics of, and reasoning behind, what is about to transpire. There have been flashbacks throughout that reveal more and more of a horrendous traffic accident, and glimpses even early on of newspaper clippings reporting a number of dead equal to the seven names Ben cries out after hanging up with Ezra. There is the shot of a fully clothed Ben lying stiffly in an empty bathtub as if in the midst of a dress rehearsal for death, while a tank in the next room holds the recently purchased jellyfish he notes to be "the most deadly creature on Earth." There is undeniable foreshadowing in the scene where Ben lovingly restores the broken printing press belonging to the woman with the nearly out-of-order heart, providing Emily with something that works perfectly and clickety-clacks away with a rhythm reminiscent of a very healthy ticker. The man aims to attain peace for himself by literally giving away pieces of that self to others. Viewers learn later that Ben had already given a lung to his brother (Michael Ealy) and part of his liver to a friend (Judyann Elder). Once it is made clear that he was responsible for the crash that killed his wife and six others, it becomes an extreme scheme of expiation: Seven accidentally caused deaths will be atoned for through seven purposefully restored lives—at the expense of his own. (The film's title, then, refers to Shakespeare's *The Merchant of Venice* and the making good on a debt with "a pound of flesh" per Shylock's demands.)

The climactic spectacle, in which Ben thrashes about during a less-than-soothing final bath with no rubber ducky but a lot of organ-preserving ice and one very lethal jellyfish, led the *New York Times'* A.O. Scott to incredulously decry "what may be among the most transcendentally, eye-poppingly, call-your-friend-ranting-in-the-middle-of-the-night-just-to-go-over-it-one-more-time crazily awful motion pictures ever made." Water is often used to symbolize the washing-away of sins, and viewers should note how Ben has been thoroughly drenched in the film's final downpour before proceeding to redemptive death in a filled tub.

Ben's suicide triggers that wholehearted surge of mawkishness. The aforementioned heart transplantation scene is shot and scored with maximum tear-inducement as a goal, and includes a look at the couple's brief, precious happiness. The entire denouement's full-throttle sappiness veers unintentionally into ludicrousness on at least two counts. First, although actually there is no such thing as a whole-eye transplant, the bright blue eyes of lonely, blind Ezra (who also happens to be a pianist) are now Ben's dark brown ones. Emily gazes into them as if the peepers were still possessed by her now-departed paramour. Second, *Seven Pounds* lays it on awfully thick when a children's choir joyfully sings Herman's Hermits's "I'm Into Something Good," as if it is self-loathing Ben's heaven-sent expression of pleasure about having been placed into such thoroughly decent vessels.

Whether through egotism or a sincere desire to inspire (critics continue to debate), Smith yet again ably plays the role of savior as he did in *I Am Legend* (2007) and this year's *Hancock*. Interestingly, those of deep Christian faith seem to have been more likely to excuse *Seven Pounds*'s plot problems and excesses because they viewed him as an inspiring, self-sacrificing Christ figure, and director Gabriele Muccino, who collaborated with Smith on *The Pursuit of Happyness* (2006), definitely provides fodder to foster such a comparison. Viewers of any faith will surely not miss the blatancy of one particular shot in which the suffering character lays motionless upon his bed in a pose identical to the crucified Jesus.

Although it reportedly had the weakest opening of any Smith film since *Ali* (2001), *Seven Pounds* was able to gross more than its $55 million budget despite predominantly negative reviews of its plot but not the actors. *Variety*'s Todd McCarthy found it "off-putting for its manifest manipulations, as well as its pretentiousness and self-importance"; the *Wall Street Journal*'s Joe Morgenstern objected to "layers of sentimentality topped with indigestible grandiosity"; and *Entertainment Weekly*'s Lisa Schwarzbaum dismissed it outright as "unintentionally ludicrous."

David L. Boxerbaum

CREDITS

Ben Thomas: Will Smith
Emily: Rosario Dawson
Ezra: Woody Harrelson
Ben's brother: Michael Ealy

Dan: Barry Pepper
George: Bill Smitrovich
Connie Tepos: Elpidia Carrillo
Sarah: Robinne Lee
Stewart Goodman: Tim Kelleher
Dr. Briar: Gina Hecht
Larry: Joseph A. Nunez
Origin: USA
Language: English
Released: 2008
Production: Todd Black, James Lassiter, Will Smith, Steve Tisch, Jason Blumenthal; Columbia Pictures, Relativity Media, Overbrook Entertainment, Escape Artists; released by Sony Pictures
Directed by: Gabriele Muccino
Written by: Grant Nieporte
Cinematography by: Philippe Le Sourd
Music by: Angelo Milli
Sound: Jim Stuebe
Editing: Hughes Winborne
Art Direction: David Klassen
Costumes: Sharen Davis
Production Design: J. Michael Riva

REVIEWS

Boston Globe Online. December 19, 2008.
Chicago Sun-Times Online. December 18, 2008.
Entertainment Weekly Online. December 18, 2008.
Hollywood Reporter Online. December 17, 2008.
Los Angeles Times Online. December 19, 2008.
New York Times Online. December 19, 2008.
San Francisco Chronicle. December 19, 2008.
Variety Online. December 17, 2008.
Washington Post. December 18, 2008.

QUOTES

Ben Thomas: "I did something really bad once and I'm never gonna be the same!"

TRIVIA

The motel that Will Smith's character stays at is the same one that was used in the film *Mementon.*

SEX AND THE CITY: THE MOVIE

Get carried away.
—Movie tagline

Box Office: $152.6 million

Sex and the City: The Movie's tagline promises viewers the chance to "get carried away," a play on the first name of its main character, Carrie Bradshaw (Sarah Jessica Parker). But given her characterization in this film—as a helpless, shallow, self-pitying mope—it is hard to fathom how anyone, even diehard fans of the popular HBO television series, would enjoy going along for the ride. The TV show (especially in its first three seasons) was often a funny and observant portrayal of the quest to find romance in the modern world. The movie, on the other hand, is a pointless, overblown affair whose priorities are so confused, it eventually collapses under its own hypocrisy.

The film begins three years after the series left off. Writer Carrie Bradshaw has published several books about finding love in Manhattan and is in the process of writing another; PR pro extraordinaire Samantha Jones (Kim Cattrall) has relocated to Malibu, California, to manage the career of her actor boyfriend, Smith (Jason Lewis); lawyer Miranda Hobbes (Cynthia Nixon) has settled into Brooklyn with her husband, Steve (David Eigenberg), and their son; and homemaker Charlotte York Goldenblatt (Kristin Davis) and her husband, Harry (Evan Handler), are raising their adopted daughter on Park Avenue.

After ten years of dating off and on, Carrie and Mr. Big, a.k.a. John (Chris Noth), decide to purchase a penthouse apartment together and marry, but Carrie's wedding plans soon spiral out of control, and Big panics, leaving her at the altar. Samantha, Miranda, and Charlotte accompany a devastated Carrie on her aborted honeymoon in Mexico, and afterward, Carrie recovers from the breakup with their help and that of her new personal assistant, Louise (Jennifer Hudson). Meanwhile, troubled couple Miranda and Steve separate after his confession of a one-time infidelity, Samantha struggles with monogamy and a so-called weight problem, and "reproductively challenged" Charlotte learns she is pregnant and worries her good fortune will come to an end. The birth of Charlotte's baby serves as the catalyst for Carrie and Big's eventual reconciliation, and the two tie the knot in a modest civil ceremony—save those $525 Manolos, of course.

That Carrie Bradshaw likes her stuff is no revelation. From the pilot episode of the series, she counted herself among the great single New York women who pay their taxes, travel, and are willing to plunk down "$400 for a pair of strappy sandals." Fortunately, her materialism was at first tempered by other more relatable qualities: As she and her friends navigated New York's social scene and grappled with changing sexual mores, Carrie was by turns astute, vulnerable, sardonic, and optimistic. But as the series progressed—and the show's production values skyrocketed—Carrie grew more enamored with wealth, which she (and the writers) often misinterpreted as a sign of maturity and sophistication. The result, as *Salon* critic Stephanie Zacharek argues in her article "The Trouble With Carrie," was that the character lost some of her humanity along the way.

Zacharek, to borrow the show's parlance, could not help but wonder if "the 1998 Carrie Bradshaw [would] be able to stand the 2003 version"—and the 2008 incarnation is even more unlikable. In the film, Carrie seems to experience joy only when acquiring luxuries, like that Fifth Avenue apartment, or a couture wedding gown, or the walk-in closet custom-designed to house her strappy sandals. Furthermore, her sense of humor has been replaced by a "why me?" complex, as she spends most of the movie kvetching about her failed engagement while everyone around her picks up the pieces. "Will I ever laugh again?" she melodramatically asks Miranda. "When?" she presses. At one point, Carrie is so despondent that Samantha literally spoon-feeds her.

The desire of women to be rescued by a "white knight" was a fantasy the writers of the TV show interrogated. They recognized that a fairy-tale ending was a socially constructed delusion—but one that still exerts a powerful hold on modern women, no matter how savvy and self-sufficient they may be. In the film, the shape of the rescuer has shifted from a knight to four handmaidens. (That one of them, Carrie's personal assistant, is an African American woman "only underscores our heroine's oblivious entitlement," as *Slate* critic Dana Stevens has observed.) In the film, Carrie's expectation to be rescued is never examined; it is merely presented as her right.

Being left at the altar is undeniably a terrible experience. But most people who find themselves in such a situation do not have friends who drop everything to save them, or the means at their disposal to hire a personal assistant to reorganize their lives or an interior designer to redecorate their homes. And still, Carrie's whining continues. Perhaps her storyline would not be so maddening if it did not dominate most of the film. So much time is devoted to Carrie's narrative that the other characters receive short shrift. Miranda is granted some attention (probably because a remark she makes to Big has unforeseen consequences for Carrie), yet Charlotte's and Samantha's "problems" are introduced to be summarily resolved only minutes later.

Writer-director Michael Patrick King would have the audience believe that Carrie receives her comeuppance for forgoing "what really matters" in her quest for Style Section nuptials. But his point is undermined by the film's own fixation on extravagance: At least a dozen high-end designers are name-dropped, and scene after scene is saturated by product placements. As he conjures

up his frenzy of fabulousness, King loses sight of his characters just as Carrie loses sight of her relationship. King's money problem is mirrored by the Big character when he proposes for a second time. He begins by telling Carrie, "The way we decided to get married was all business, no romance. That's not the way you propose to someone." He gets down on one knee, but seems bereft after she accepts. "See, this is why there's a diamond," he explains, "you need to do something to close the deal." Even as Big tries his hand at romance, the language of the business world still creeps its way into his proposal. And when he does "close the deal," he does so by slipping a sequined Manolo Blahnik onto Carrie's awaiting foot, à la Prince Charming. With *Sex and the City*, it always comes down to the shoes.

Despite its shortcomings and lukewarm reviews, the movie exceeded industry expectations at the box office (pulling in $153 million) and challenged conventional Hollywood wisdom regarding the ticket-buying potential of adult women. As *Variety* reported, the film's strong opening weekend "shattered the decades-old thinking that females—particularly older ones—can't fuel the sort of big opening often enjoyed by a male-driven event pic or family movie." By the year's end, the actresses were in negotiations for an upcoming sequel. Hopefully, on the second go-round, King and company will provide *Sex and the City*'s fans with a film worthy of their devotion.

Marisa Carroll

CREDITS

Carrie Bradshaw: Sarah Jessica Parker
Samantha Jones: Kim Cattrall
Charlotte York: Kristin Davis
Miranda Hobbes: Cynthia Nixon
Mr. Big: Christopher Noth
Steve Brady: David Eigenberg
Smith Jerrod: Jason Lewis
Harry Goldenblatt: Evan Handler
Louise: Jennifer Hudson
Stanford Blatch: Willie Garson
Anthony Marentino: Mario Cantone
Magda: Lynn Cohen
Enid Frick: Candice Bergen
Magda: Lynn Cohen
Origin: USA
Language: English
Released: 2008
Production: Michael Patrick King, Sarah Jessica Parker, Darren Star, John Melfi, Eric M. Cyphers; Home Box Office; released by New Line Cinema
Directed by: Michael Patrick King

Written by: Michael Patrick King
Cinematography by: John Thomas
Music by: Aaron Zigman
Sound: William Sarokin
Editing: Michael Berenbaum
Art Direction: Ed Check
Costumes: Patricia Field
Production Design: Jeremy Conway
MPAA rating: R
Running time: 135 minutes

REVIEWS

Boston Globe Online. May 29, 2008.
Chicago Sun-Times Online. May 28, 2008.
Entertainment Weekly Online. May 27, 2008.
Hollywood Reporter Online. May 15, 2008.
Los Angeles Times Online. May 30, 2008.
New York Times Online. May 30, 2008.
Rolling Stone Online. June 12, 2008.
San Francisco Chronicle. May 29, 2008, p. E1.
Variety Online. May 15, 2008.
Village Voice Online. May 27, 2008.
Washington Post. May 29, 2008, p. C1.

QUOTES

Enid Frick: "Forty is the last age a woman can be photographed in a wedding dress without the unintended Diane Arbus subtext."

TRIVIA

More than 300 pieces of jewelry were loaned by H. Stern for use in the film.

SEX DRIVE

He's leaving virgin territory.
—Movie tagline

Box Office: $8.4 million

It is not too long a trip from the '80s glut of sex comedies like *Porky's* (1982) through the *American Pie* franchise to Sean Anders's *Sex Drive,* the latest in a long line of movies about the number-one priority of teenagers around the world—getting laid. All of them are essentially the same—horny, usually drunk kids, acting like idiots. Only the cast, level of gross-out humor, and loose plot details change from generation to generation. The kids just want to have a good time. The similarities can make it hard to qualify the good teen sex comedy from the bad one. Like most comedies, it comes down to cast and writing, and while there are some inspira-

tional casting choices and talented young actors in *Sex Drive,* the writing keeps these kids stuck in neutral.

Sex Drive features all of the standard writing cues of a teen sex comedy, but what is missing most from the final product is the all-important factor of characters to either relate to or root for. *Sex Drive* feels like an exercise in raunchy teen comedy, an example to other writers and directors of all the ingredients needed for this genre of film, instead of an original story with actually characters worth caring about. Admittedly, there are more laughs than the average lackluster teen sex movie due to some very original supporting performances, but there is a hollow center to *Sex Drive,* as if the characters in the movie exist only within their narrowly defined genre. Even with a few solid laughs, *Sex Drive* is not memorable enough to stand out in its time-tested genre.

The fatal flaw is that every single role in *Sex Drive,* except for one who completely steals the movie, is one that not only has been done before in the teen sex comedy but also has been done recently and done better. The common problem in the genre is that its writers underestimate the desire to see something new. In *Sex Drive* we have the classic character archetypes of the awkward virgin Ian (Josh Zuckerman), who is really in love with his sassy best friend Felicia (Amanda Crew), and the two are rounded out by the fast-talking cad Lance (Clark Duke). It was a clever move to cast Internet star Duke, half of the pair (with *Arrested Development* star Michael Cera) who turned *Clark and Michael* into a phenomenon, in a role that would typically be played by a young man with cookie-cutter good looks and style, but casting is not character, and Ian, Felicia, and Lance form a dynamic that audiences have seen a thousand times before. Duke makes the most of his material, but Zuckerman and Crew are dismally boring, making it hard to tell if it is the newcomers who are lackluster or just the characters they have been given.

Ian spends far too much of his life dressed up like a donut, trying to sell tasty treats at his mall stand. When he is not hocking sweets, he spends a lot of his time online, chatting up an allegedly beautiful woman with the user name Ms. Tasty. Even though he is unsure of the truthfulness of his online object of affection, Ian decides to take the plunge when she offers herself to him if her can make it down to Knoxville to see her. Ian, Felicia, and Lance steal Ian's brother Rex's (a hyperactive James Marsden) '69 GTO and hit the road for a series of very unusual encounters, including one with an angry hitchhiker (David Koechner), a sex-crazed redneck, and the most sarcastic Amish man on the planet (a movie-stealing Seth Green).

Writers Sean Anders and John Morris clearly understand that the basic set-up for *Sex Drive*—virgin, cad, and friend go on a road trip—is derivative and generic, so the success or failure from that point depends on writing that can separate this sex comedy from the countless ones before it. Anders and Morris make the mistake of thinking that the way to distinguish their film is to push the accelerator deep into the region of gross-out humor. The amount of bodily fluids on display in *Sex Drive* is remarkable, even for a movie of this genre. Nothing is safe. But it reeks of desperation, as if the only way to get attention is to be grosser than the comedy that came before. But that desperation and a level of gross-out humor that no one will be able to identify with is exactly what makes *Sex Drive* so disposable. Duke, Marsden, and Green do their best to keep *Sex Drive* from becoming a complete disaster, but the lackluster script and boring leads force this comedy car to break down long before it reaches its final destination.

Brian Tallerico

CREDITS

Ian: Josh Zuckerman
Felicia: Amanda Crew
Lance: Clark Duke
Rex: James Marsden
Ezekiel: Seth Green
Ms. Tasty: Katrina Bowden
Mary: Alice Greczyn
Origin: USA
Language: English
Released: 2008
Production: Leslie Morgenstein, Bob Levy, John Morris; Alloy Entertainment; released by Summit Entertainment
Directed by: Sean Anders
Written by: Sean Anders, John Morris
Cinematography by: Tim Orr
Music by: Stephen Trask
Sound: Mark Weber
Music Supervisor: Dave Jordan, Jojo Villanueva
Editing: George Folsey Jr.
Art Direction: Erin Cochran
Costumes: Kristen M. Burke
Production Design: Aaron Osborne
MPAA rating: R
Running time: 109 minutes

REVIEWS

Boston Globe Online. October 17, 2008.
Chicago Sun-Times Online. October 15, 2008.
Entertainment Weekly Online. October 10, 2008.
Hollywood Reporter Online. October 10, 2008.
Los Angeles Times Online. October 17, 2008.
New York Times Online. October 17, 2008.
San Francisco Chronicle. October 17, 2008, p. E3.
Variety Online. October 10, 2008.
Washington Post Online. October 17, 2008.

QUOTES

Lance: "I refuse to be embarrassed by a car that looks like a Trapper Keeper."

SHINE A LIGHT

Box Office: $5.5 million

Long considered the world's greatest rock-and-roll band, the Rolling Stones are also one of the longest-running popular-music acts, having been formed in 1962. Director Martin Scorsese has long been fascinated by the group, using its music on the soundtracks of his films from *Mean Streets* (1973), with "Jumpin' Jack Flash" and "Tell Me," to *The Departed* (2006), with "Gimme Shelter" and "Let It Loose." It is only natural that the filmmaker and the bad boys of rock and roll would eventually get together, and they did at New York's Beacon Theater in the fall of 2006. Scorsese filmed two concerts and wove the footage into a rousing film, which is shown in IMAX at some locations.

Shine a Light opens with a mostly black-and-white sequence showing Scorsese planning how to shoot the concert. When he tells Mick Jagger that several cameras, some remotely controlled, will be constantly swooping about the stage, the singer is concerned about the danger. A technician tells Scorsese that a planned lighting effect runs the risk of burning Jagger, and the director is alarmed. Many of these opening scenes involve Scorsese's efforts to obtain a list of the songs to be performed from Jagger. When the singer is presented with Scorsese-suggested titles, he peruses the list perfunctorily. Scorsese's purpose seems less to paint Jagger as difficult or eccentric than to provide humor.

Other humor in the opening sequence comes at the expense of Bill Clinton. Though never mentioned again after the concert proper begins, the event was a fundraiser for the Clinton Foundation as well as a belated sixtieth birthday party for the former president. Scorsese shows Clinton meeting the Rolling Stones and their being perturbed at having to meet everyone in his large party. Keith Richards, more amused by the proceedings than the rest, warmly greets Hillary Rodham Clinton's elderly mother by name. During the concert there are no cutaways to Clinton reactions, leaving the viewer to speculate about Dorothy Rodham's response to the frequent misogynism and profanity in the songs. The Stones are the complete focus in the concert, with few shots of the audience, as Scorsese eschews clichés of the concert genre. Bruce Willis can be spotted briefly, but his presence is never acknowledged.

When the band finally explodes into "Jumpin' Jack Flash," the screen, in the IMAX version, explodes with the music, filling the giant screen. The IMAX presentation is not only a thrilling visual experience; the increased sound capacity also makes *Shine a Light* one concert film that truly captures the experience of being in a theater with the musicians. Scorsese's *The Last Waltz* (1978), documenting the final performance by all the original members of The Band, is widely considered the best rock concert film ever, but it lacks the visual and aural intensity of *Shine a Light*. Scorsese, who edited *Woodstock* (1970), has clearly seen many concert films and realized that none, until *Shine a Light,* have come close enough to recreating being at the performance.

The Stones have been criticized by some for playing little but their greatest hits, especially on the 2005-2007 A Bigger Bang world tour, often changing only two or three songs from performance to performance. Jagger, with possible unseen influence by Scorsese, apparently tried to subdue this tendency in *Shine a Light*. While such favorites as "Shattered," "Start Me Up," and "Sympathy for the Devil" are performed, there are several less frequently performed numbers such as "All Down the Line," "Faraway Eyes," and "Some Girls." During his two-song solos in the middle of concerts, Richards almost always sings "Happy," but here he performs "You Got the Silver" and "Connection." At Scorsese's request the band plays the plaintive ballad "As Tears Go By," which Jagger says was first recorded by someone else (his then-girlfriend Marianne Faithfull) because he and Richards were embarrassed by the seriousness of their lyrics. Notably missing are such concert staples as "Gimme Shelter," "Honky Tonk Woman," and "It's Only Rock 'n' Rock." The Temptations's "Just My Imagination" made the cut, while Bobby Womack's "It's All Over Now," recommended by Scorsese and arguably the Stones' best rendition of a non-Jagger-Richards song, does not.

The three guest performers joining Jagger for duets also do relatively fresh material. Jack White tries to match Jagger's country twang on "Loving Cup," their voices melding smoothly. Christina Aguilera brings sexual energy to "Live with Me," turning Sir Mick into a leering old man. Best of all is Jagger and legendary bluesman Buddy Guy performing Muddy Waters's "Champagne and Reefer." Also the highlight of the Scorsese-produced blues concert film *Lightning in a Bottle*

(2004), the seventy-year-old Guy dominates the stage as singer, guitarist, and imposing physical presence.

Speaking of physicality, Scorsese calls attention to the aging features of Jagger, sixty-three at the time of the concert, Richards, sixty-two but looking much older, drummer Charlie Watts, sixty-five and frail, and Ronnie Wood, fifty-nine. In both the black-and-white footage and, especially, the IMAX images, their faces display creases associated with not only age but also proudly dissipated lives: very bad boys, indeed. Except for Watts, who exhales mightily following one number, the others remain quite energetic, especially Jagger, who prances about the stage with the gusto of a performer half his age. Scorsese presents the band not as relics but as oddly fascinating artifacts, musicians still excited by their art after all these years. Staging the concert at the art deco Beacon, actually a much seedier venue than it appears here, is fitting for the Stones.

Scorsese interrupts the music in *The Last Waltz* for interviews with members of The Band, who recount the group's history. While there are no new interviews in *Shine a Light,* Scorsese intersperses clips from throughout the Stones's long career, displaying Richards's guarded cockiness and Watts's reticence, making fun of the banality of questions asked by the press. In an early interview, Jagger says the band has been performing for two years and hoped to last another year. In a 1972 interview, Dick Cavett asks Jagger if he can see himself still performing at sixty, and the singer unhesitatingly says he can. Original Stones Brian Jones and Bill Wyman are glimpsed briefly in these clips but are never mentioned in the film.

Shine a Light is not a perfect film. Scorsese pays little attention to bass player Darryl Jones, Wyman's replacement, keyboardist Chuck Leavell, who has to remind Jagger of the correct lyrics during a rehearsal, the four-man wind section, and two of the three backup singers. The exception is the voluptuous Lisa Fischer, whom the director realizes has considerable camera presence. Too bad that she does not get to take center stage for "Gimme Shelter," which best displays her powerful voice. The film's title is from a minor, relatively benign Stones song heard partially only in the closing credits.

In addition to the Stones themselves, the real star of *Shine a Light* is its visual flair. Robert Richardson, who worked previously with Scorsese on *The Aviator* (2004), is the cinematographer, but his fine work is supported by having several other top directors of photography act as camera operators: Mitchell Amundsen, Stuart Dryburgh, David M. Dunlap, Robert Elswit, Ellen Kuras, Andrew Lesnie, Emmanuel Lubezki, Declan Quinn, and John Toll. David Tedeschi, who also edited Scorsese's brilliant documentary *No Direction Home: Bob Dylan*

(2005), cuts their footage to create the sensation of a seamless spectacle. Because the cameras and their personnel are visible only a few times, Tedeschi makes it appear as if the shots were captured by magic. *Shine a Light* is a magical musical and visual treat.

Michael Adams

CREDITS

Origin: USA

Language: English

Released: 2008

Production: Steve Bing, Michael Cohl, Victoria Pearman, Zane Weiner; Shangri-La Entertainment; released by Paramount Vantage

Directed by: Martin Scorsese

Cinematography by: Robert Richardson

Sound: Philip Stockton

Editing: David Tedeschi

MPAA rating: PG-13

Running time: 122 minutes

REVIEWS

Boston Globe Online. April 4, 2008.
Chicago Sun-Times Online. April 4, 2008.
Entertainment Weekly Online. April 1, 2008.
Hollywood Reporter Online. February 8, 2008.
Los Angeles Times Online. April 4, 2008.
New York Times Online. April 4, 2008.
New Yorker Online. April 14, 2008.
Rolling Stone Online. April 17, 2008.
San Francisco Chronicle. April 4, 2008, p. E7.
Variety Online. February 7, 2008.
Washington Post. April 4, 2008, p. C5.

QUOTES

Martin Scorsese: "We cannot set Mick Jagger on fire."

TRIVIA

The documentary is dedicated to music mogul Ahmet Ertegun, who suffered a fall at the concert and died shortly thereafter.

SHUTTER

> *The most terrifying images are the ones that are real.*
> —Movie tagline
> *Revenge never dies!*
> —Movie tagline

Box Office: $25.9 million

Moviemakers have used technology to provoke fear since the inception of cinema. Everyone has heard the story of the audience who first saw a train heading toward the camera and fled the theater for fear of being run down. Man's greatest fear is the unknown, and there will always be something about modern technology that remains mysterious for most people. No better proof of this exists than the phenomenon of Asian horror films about phones, televisions, cameras, and other modern devices used for evil. In the most successful of these films, *Ringu* (1998), a video tape starts the process, a phone call confirms it, and the climax features a ghost crawling from a television set. Those who never give in to the traps of the modern era would never have to worry. One of the best recent examples of this trend is 2004's *Shutter,* an effective and creepy ghost story from directors Banjong Pisanthanakun and Parkpoom Wongpoom that uses photography and a Polaroid camera as its devices of modern horror. Remade in 2008 by Masayuki Ochiai, the English-language version of *Shutter* had the most potential to finally break the trend of awful Asian horror remakes. Ochiai and his producers put together an interesting young cast, hired a brilliant director of photography, and had the strongest source material of any of the recent remakes. And yet *Shutter* falls victim to the same traps as *One Missed Call* (2008) and *The Eye* (2008), the other two pitches in the Asian remake strike-out of 2008—taking what worked about the source material and reducing it to derivative, predictable fare.

The well-cast Joshua Jackson and Rachael Taylor star in the *Shutter* remake as Ben, a photographer, and Jane, his loving wife. The pair head to Tokyo, where Ben used to live, for a job. Ben and Jane get into a car accident after hitting a mysterious woman standing in the middle of the road. When they wake from the crash, the girl is gone and Ben suspiciously denies that she ever existed. While on the new job and in their new city, Ben and Jane start to see ghostly images in their developed photos. At first, the images are just creepy, but they eventually become deadly as whatever is haunting their photography comes to life. Jane investigates and discovers a connection between the ghostly figure in her husband's photos and his old life in Tokyo. It turns out that Ben has a dark secret that ties together the girl on the road, the mysterious images in his photos, and the deadly future that may await both him and his innocent wife.

On paper, *Shutter* certainly has more going for it than *The Eye* or *One Missed Call.* The source material is strong, and Taylor and Jackson are more interesting actors than Edward Burns and Jessica Alba. And technically, *Shutter* looks vastly superior to the darkly lit failures that litter the genre. *Shutter* is lensed by the excellent Katsumi Yanagishima, who was also the cinematographer on *Battle Royale* (2000) and *Zatôichi* (2003). Considering how many of these Asian remakes forget that the originals were powerful in large part because of the imagery that they presented, it is notable that *Shutter* looks good.

The casting agent and producers may have hired some of the right people, but *Shutter* still falls apart at the feet of the person usually responsible for Asian remake failures—the screenwriter. Clearly, the producers of these films do not place much value on storytelling and dialogue, assuming that the concept of the original will be enough to make the remake a success. With *Shutter*, debut writer Luke Dawson makes the same mistake that many of his peers have—over-explanation. Asian horror movies place the emphasis on mood, and yet nearly every single one of their remakes has assumed that American audiences need to have everything explained to them. Subtlety is almost always the first victim when a hit Asian horror film gets green-lighted for an English-language remake. Dawson and Ochiai make the classic mistake of using too many jump cuts and sudden jolts of sound to scare their audience, mistaking volume for fear. There is still nothing scarier than a creaky door or a window that should be closed but somehow appears open. The original *Shutter* worked because audiences could relate to something unusual in the corner of a photograph. The remake misses its mark because it fails to understand that the technology of fear is there in the story itself, not something that needs to be overplayed in the editing room.

Brian Tallerico

CREDITS

Ben: Joshua Jackson
Jane: Rachael Taylor
Megumi: Megumi Okina
Bruno: David Denman
Adam: John Hensley
Seiko: Maya Hazen
Ritsuo: James Kyson Lee
Origin: USA
Language: English
Released: 2008
Production: Takashige Ichise, Roy Lee, Doug Davison; New Regency, Vertigo Entertainment, Ozla Pictures; released by 20th Century-Fox
Directed by: Masayuki Ochiai
Written by: Luke Dawson
Cinematography by: Katsumi Yanagishima
Music by: Nathan Barr

Sound: James Bolt
Music Supervisor: Dave Jordan, JoJo Villanueva
Editing: Michael N. Knue, Tim Alverson
Art Direction: Ayaki Takagi
Production Design: Norifumi Ataka
MPAA rating: PG-13
Running time: 85 minutes

REVIEWS

Boston Globe Online. March 22, 2008.
Hollywood Reporter Online. March 24, 2008.
Los Angeles Times Online. March 24, 2008.
New York Times Online. March 22, 2008.
San Francisco Chronicle. March 24, 2008, p. E5.
Variety Online. March 21, 2008.

QUOTES

Ben: "I'm not your f**king father!"

THE SISTERHOOD OF THE TRAVELING PANTS 2

Some friends just fit together.
—Movie tagline

Box Office: $44 million

Sisterhood of the Traveling Pants 2 catches up on the post-high school lives of the four life-long friends bound together by a revered pair of old jeans in the original *Sisterhood of the Traveling Pants* (2005), the first film based on Ann Brashares's best-selling series of novels for adolescent girls. Now, three years later, the girls—Carmen Lowell (America Ferrera), Tibby Tomko-Rollins (Amber Tamblyn), Lena Kaligaris (Alexis Bledel), and Bridget Vreeland (Blake Lively)—have become precocious young women and are making their separate ways in the adult world. Having just completed their first year apart at college, their friendships and past lives appear to be disintegrating along with their interest in maintaining the girlish quasi-mystical rituals surrounding the ragged pants that they continue to share by mail. Covered in patches, embroidery, writing, and other mementos, the miraculous jeans still manage to fit everyone despite differing body types and the passing of several years.

Taking advantage of the young characters' advancing maturity, screenwriter Elizabeth Chandler and director Sanaa Hamri latched onto a formula that, for better or worse, makes *Sisterhood of the Traveling Pants 2* feel like a PG-13 version of *Sex and the City* for girls. Much like the well-known HBO television series, *Sisterhood of the Traveling Pants 2* relies on a narrator (Carmen) to weave together four intertwining stories of love, lust, loss, and personal growth as each young woman ends up spending the summer away from home cultivating her particular talent in some interesting and enviable location. Also like the TV show, each of the four friends has a distinct personality based on a generic feminine archetype. Carmen is the serious, brainy one; Tibby is the edgy, punkish one; Lena is the artsy, romantic one; and Bridget is the tomboy.

Carmen, the central figure of the teen saga, is the character most troubled by the changing times. She is an only child, but her mother (Rachel Ticotin) has recently remarried and is now pregnant and about to move out of their long-time home. Feeling "lost," Carmen despairs over her friends' apparent indifference over drifting apart. The group had planned to spend the summer together back in Bethesda, but with everyone else having a change of plans, she decides to go with Julia (Rachel Nichols), a friend and fellow drama student from Yale, to attend a Shakespearean theater program in Vermont. Intending to just help out backstage, Carmen falls for a young British actor named Ian (Tom Wisdom) who tricks her into landing the lead female role opposite him in *The Winter's Tale*. Meanwhile, Tibby is stuck in New York City finishing an incomplete script for an NYU screenwriting class while working at a video store and experiencing an emotional crisis over her relationship with boyfriend Brian (Leonardo Nam). Broken-hearted Lena, who is attending a figure-drawing class at summer school at the Rhode Island School of Design, is embarking on a new relationship with a handsome nude model, Leo (Jesse Williams), and trying to forget her first love, Kostas (Michael Rady), a dashing young fisherman who lives in her grandmother's town in Greece and has recently married a woman whom he allegedly impregnated. Lastly, Bridget, following a year playing soccer at Brown University, goes on an archaeological dig in Turkey, but ends up at in Georgia at the house of her estranged grandmother Greta (Blythe Danner). Greta helps Bridget to finally understand her mother's suicide, which allows her to begin repairing a strained and painful relationship with her father (Ernie Lively, Blake Lively's real-life father). The final portion of the movie finds the four friends together in Greece, reunited by the pants, which, despite having been lost by Lena's younger sister Effie (Lucy Kate Hale), still help them rediscover the immeasurable value of friendship.

A chick flick with training wheels, *Sisterhood of the Traveling Pants 2* indoctrinates its intended audience of girls by offering up a hearty but overly simplified dose of inspiration for those who might think that they too can attend an Ivy League college or jet off to Turkey or Greece at a moment's notice. It also suffers a few shortcomings when it comes to promoting a completely positive message of female empowerment. As most feminist critics will probably agree, *Sisterhood of the Traveling Pants 2* focuses too strongly on the importance of having male approval and a boyfriend, and it sends a bad message when Tibby, faced with a pregnancy scare, just sits around and waits, doing nothing to help herself obtain professional advice or emergency birth control.

Jaye Furlonger

CREDITS

Bridget Vreeland: Blake Lively
Lena Kaligaris: Alexis Bledel
Carmen Lowell: America Ferrera
Tibby Tomko-Rollins: Amber Tamblyn
Julia: Rachel Nichols
Prof. Nasrin Mehani: Shohreh Aghdashloo
Greta: Blythe Danner
Bill Kerr: Kyle MacLachlan
Leo: Jesse Williams
Ian: Tom Wisdom
Kostos: Michael Rady
Bridget's father: Ernie Lively
Origin: USA
Language: English
Released: 2008
Production: Debra Martin Chase, Kira Davis, Denise Di Novi, Broderick Johnson, Andrew A. Kosove; Alcon Entertainment, Alloy Entertainment, DiNovi Pictures; released by Warner Bros.
Directed by: Sanaa Hamri
Written by: Elizabeth Chandler
Cinematography by: Jim Denault
Music by: Rachel Portman
Sound: Cameron Frankley
Music Supervisor: Julia Michels
Editing: Melissa Kent
Art Direction: Andrew Cahn
Costumes: Dona Granata
Production Design: Gae Buckley
MPAA rating: PG-13
Running time: 111 minutes

REVIEWS

Boston Globe Online. August 6, 2008.
Chicago Sun-Times Online. August 5, 2008.
Entertainment Weekly Online. August 5, 2008.
Hollywood Reporter Online. July 31, 2008.

Los Angeles Times Online. August 6, 2008.
New York Times Online. August 6, 2008.
San Francisco Chronicle. August 6, 2008, p. E1.
Variety Online. July 31, 2008.
Washington Post. August 6, 2008, p. C10.

QUOTES

Carmen Lowell: "Sometimes I like to think that the pants got lost on purpose. That this was their final gift to us. Bringing us back together. Back to a place of forgiveness, and love, and in understanding that what we shared was all the magic we could ever need. And as we spent those last few moments of summer, looking out at the blending of sea and sky, I realized it was a color I knew very well. The softly faded, essential blue of a well worn pair of pants. The pants had brought us together again. The rest is in our hands."

TRIVIA

The final cliff diving scene in the movie was suggested by Amber Tamblyn, Blake Lively, and America Ferrera after they saw some teenage boys performing the feat in Greece.

SLEEPWALKING

An unusually stark and fairly observant character study about child abandonment, *Sleepwalking* takes on a tough story about irresponsible adults but avoids moralisms about larger societal implications. Instead, it is an almost claustrophobic look at what happens to the dismal life of James "Speedy" Reedy (Nick Stahl), an unambitious and quiet young man, when his sister Joleen (Charlize Theron) arrives in desperate straits at his apartment with her thirteen-year-old daughter Tara (AnnaSophia Robb).

The movie opens with a series of loud arguments involving Joleen. She and Tara have been booted out of her boyfriend's house when he is arrested in the middle of the night, and she is seen arguing with a local police officer over her fitness to be a parent. While Tara is at school, Joleen enlists her brother to return to her boyfriend's place and retrieve her stuff. As police find marijuana plants in the yard, she grabs a wad of money and hides it in her boots.

The movie gives the accomplished Theron another chance to inhabit a working-class character, as she did so successfully in the Oscar®-winning *Monster* (2003) and in *North Country* (2005). Theron pulls back her hair and lets some of it dangle in her face, smokes cigarettes, and wears a haunted look. She is believable as a strung-out woman who has been abused by her father and has never recovered her integrity but keeps fighting back.

Her Joleen is so desperate for affection that she asks a guy whom she picks up for a one-night stand to tell her that he loves her before they have sex. She tells James he is too kind and lets people take advantage of him, then thanks him for taking her and Tara in.

The next morning, however, she is gone, and has left a note saying she has a plan and will return for Tara's birthday, in thirty days. James cannot fathom how he will handle this new responsibility thrust upon him. And neither can movie audiences; since Joleen does not return until movie's end, we miss Theron's magnetism. It turns out that "Speedy" is an ironic nickname. James is not so much a slacker—a person of some means who chooses to adopt a lifestyle devoid of striving—as a never-was. He is slow to catch on to each new day, and life seems continually to take him by surprise. We eventually find out that that Joleen and James have reacted in vastly different ways to the damage they have suffered at the hands of their abusive father.

The story of a man unprepared for parenting who is thrust into the role of a surrogate father is something of a movie staple. It is predictable that James will muff his first opportunity at forging a bond with his niece, lose Tara's trust, and then slowly regain it. There is nothing very interesting about this dully told part of the story, and Stahl seems determined to give us a character who is little more than a cipher. So quiet and withdrawn is his performance, so affectless, that it gives way too little information about James.

Robb, however, strikes just the right balance as a believable young teen who has seen plenty of hard knocks but still retains a cynical hope. She is sullen about the situation she has been thrust into, but seems to harbor no grudge against the mother who has abandoned her—Joleen, after all, has been the only consistent lifeline in Tara's existence. Tara is matter-of-fact about her situation but willing to give James plenty of chances.

When the two of them flee town together, it is another hackneyed device: after all, road trips are the favorite Hollywood device for any kind of bonding. And, true to the minimalist style of *Sleepwalking,* not much of interest happens on the road. The best scene involves Tara showing off her grown-up swagger to a couple of younger boys at a motel pool.

Only in the third act does the film start to grab the audience. That is when James brings Tara to meet her grandfather for the first time. Dennis Hopper plays the villainous Mr. Reedy in a creepy performance as a despotic patriarch who sneers at the weakness of his son. The story takes a sickening turn, revealing the reason for the brokenness of James and Joleen. It is an interesting method of understanding these characters' back stories, and of creating an opportunity for a few climactic thrills in a movie that could have used a lot more of them a lot sooner.

Hopper does a great job in his small role, as does Theron, and we even get a few scenes of Woody Harrelson playing a friend of James who is rather Woody-Harrelson-like: that is, a bit goofy around the edges. Robb is terrific and helps hold the film together, and Stahl has some splendid quiet moments. But overall, he, and the directing itself, by Bill Maher, are too quiet. The movie has some nicely observed moments but too few of them, and it is not exactly full of originality or fresh perspectives on dysfunctional families.

The plot is fine, but the writing suffers from clichés. When the key line of the movie is "this is the first day of the rest of your life," that reveals a lack of inspiration. The dialogue seems a bit wooden at times, and the directing does not give the characters much room to breathe. *Sleepwalking* is stark and sometimes sterile, as if the director and screenwriter are not confident enough of their story to give it a little air. And a bigger personality than Stahl would have given James more appeal, but perhaps at a cost to realism. Many people like James populate the landscape of the world, but few people will pay to watch them going nowhere fast. We never get a really plausible explanation, other than James's lack of ideas and imagination, for why he would bring Tara to the scene of his own childhood humiliation. But that, too, might be more realistic than most movie scenarios. *Sleepwalking* scores points for verisimilitude but still needs a better way of holding audience interest after Theron disappears from view.

Michael Betzold

CREDITS

Joleen: Charlize Theron
James: Nick Stahl
Tara: AnnaSophia Robb
Mr. Reedy: Dennis Hopper
Randall: Woody Harrelson
Danni: Deborra-Lee Furness
Origin: Canada, USA
Language: English
Released: 2008
Production: Charlize Theron, A.J. Dix, J.J. Harris, Beth Kono, Rob Merilees; Denver & Delilah Films, Icon Entertainment Media, Infinity Films, WJS Productions; released by Overture Films
Directed by: William Maher
Written by: Zac Stanford
Cinematography by: Juan Ruiz Anchia

Music by: Christopher Young
Sound: Chris Duesterdiek
Music Supervisor: Kevin J. Edelman
Editing: Stuart Levy
Art Direction: Sara McCudden
Costumes: Cathy McComb
Production Design: Paki Smith
MPAA rating: R
Running time: 101 minutes

REVIEWS

Boston Globe Online. March 14, 2008.
Entertainment Weekly Online. March 12, 2008.
Hollywood Reporter Online. January 22, 2008.
Los Angeles Times Online. March 14, 2008.
New York Times Online. March 14, 2008.
San Francisco Chronicle. March 14, 2008, p. E7.
Time Online. March 14, 2008.
Variety Online. January 22, 2008.
Village Voice Online. March 11, 2008.

QUOTES

James: "My whole life I feel like I've been sleepwalking. But you helped me. You woke me up."

TRIVIA

The working title for the film was "Ferris Wheel."

SLUMDOG MILLIONAIRE

Love and money...you have mixed them both.
—Movie tagline

Box Office: $125.8 million

Danny Boyle's *Slumdog Millionaire* is an emotional, vibrant, pulsating hymn to the value of life experience above all possible knowledge that can be obtained from the written word. It is a film about destiny, passion, luck, and, above all, the human will to triumph over adversity. Boyle's best work in an already accomplished career feels like a timeless fairy tale, a love letter to modern India, and more. Working from the best screenplay of 2008, Boyle and his team craft *Slumdog Millionaire* into one of the most beloved films of the last several years, a modern classic that taps into the human desire to believe that the human spirit can and will overcome any adversity. Perfectly conceived, expertly shot, and brilliantly edited, *Slumdog Millionaire* works on every level. It is one of the best films of 2008.

Based loosely on the book *Q&A* by Vikas Swarup, *Slumdog Millionaire* was adapted by Simon Beaufoy and directed by Danny Boyle. Beaufoy took a book that was essentially a series of short stories and constructed a concrete narrative around it—the story of Jamal Malik (Dev Patel), a street urchin in Mumbai who becomes an unlikely winner on the Hindi version of *Who Wants to Be a Millionaire?* The film opens with Malik being tortured and interrogated by a police force who believe he must have cheated to have proceeded as far as he has on the intellectually challenging game show—one question away from the ultimate prize. Prodded by a police inspector played by the great Irrfan Khan, Jamal tells the story of his life, making clear how the tragic and unusual experiences of his life have given him the knowledge needed to win on *Who Wants to Be a Millionaire?*

The narrative flashes back and forth between the game show filmed the night before Jamal's arrest, his telling of his life story to his captors, and the years that have brought him to that point. In the flashbacks, we meet a young Jamal and his brother Salim (played as an adult by Madhur Mittal) and learn that their mother died in an anti-Muslim riot, leaving the boys homeless orphans. On a rainy night, they meet Latika (played as an adult by Freida Pinto) and Jamal falls instantly in love with the young girl. Their romance serves as the backdrop for the rest of his complicated life.

Trying to survive the brutal streets of Mumbai sends the three children into the ugly world of men who use children to beg for money, and all the way to the grounds of the Taj Mahal, where the boys pretend to be tour guides for ignorant visitors. Salim eventually accepts a job with a crime lord, splitting Jamal from his brother and Latika, but fate will reunite them all before the end of this magical story.

The brilliance of what Danny Boyle has accomplished with *Slumdog Millionaire* is in the way he approaches the material with writer Simon Beaufoy and "codirector" Loveleen Tandan. The creative team behind the film blends multiple familiar genres into a beautiful, original vision. *Slumdog Millionaire* is part fairy tale, part Dickensian fable, part cultural examination, part travelogue for an area of the world rarely seen in Western films, part romantic drama, and part Bollywood musical. Like a lot of great movies, *Slumdog Millionaire* is a film that is constantly shifting and changing just as viewers think they have it figured out. Being simply an effective love story, cultural examination, or tale of triumph over adversity is enough for one movie, but *Slumdog Millionaire* is all three and more.

The ensemble, particularly newcomer Dev Patel and the lovely Freida Pinto, are effective in their roles, but *Slumdog Millionaire* excels primarily because of the accomplishments of its talented director and daring screenwriter. The script is a pitch-perfect blend of

suspense, romance, and drama that somehow balances all of its elements into a seamless whole. The structure, which bounces back and forth between the quiz show and stories that explain why Jamal knew the answers, never feels forced as it might have in the hands of so many other writers, and it becomes much more than just a storytelling device. The "destiny" aspect of Jamal's story also never feels melodramatically or manipulatively overplayed. Boyle and Beaufoy just let it sink in slowly that perhaps Jamal's life was fated to go this way. It is only one of many complex themes in *Slumdog Millionaire*—that destiny and knowledge are not opposites, and that unwavering love can sometimes be the only sustenance one needs to survive.

Ultimately, *Slumdog Millionaire* is one of the best films of 2008 for a simple reason—it is honestly joyful. So many movies try to be inspirational or moving but merely come off as manipulative. Much rarer is the movie that can touch the human spirit without telegraphing its creators' desire to do so. By eschewing genre and being comedy, drama, musical, thriller, and romance in one transcendent story, *Slumdog Millionaire* captures life in a way that so many movies have tried and failed.

Brian Tallerico

CREDITS

Prem: Anil Kapoor
Inspector: Irfan Khan
Jamal Malik: Dev Patel
Latika: Freida Pinto
Salim Malik: Madhur Mittal
Origin: USA, Great Britain
Language: English
Released: 2008
Production: Christian Colson; Celador Films, Warner Bros., Films 4; released by Fox Searchlight
Directed by: Danny Boyle
Written by: Simon Beaufoy
Cinematography by: Anthony Dod Mantle
Music by: A.R. Rahman
Sound: Resul Pookutty
Editing: Chris Dickens
Art Direction: Abhishek Redkar
Costumes: Suttirat Larlarb
Production Design: Mark Digby
MPAA rating: Unrated
Running time: 116 minutes

REVIEWS

Chicago Sun-Times Online. November 11, 2008.
Entertainment Weekly Online. November 12, 2008.

Hollywood Reporter Online. September 10, 2008.
Los Angeles Times Online. November 12, 2008.
New York Times Online. November 12, 2008.
Rolling Stone Online. November 13, 2008.
San Francisco Chronicle. November 12, 2008, p. E1.
Variety Online. September 1, 2008.
Village Voice Online. November 11, 2008.
Wall Street Journal Online. November 14, 2008.
Washington Post. November 12, 2008, p. C1.

QUOTES

Jamal Malike: "When somebody asks me a question, I tell them the answer."

TRIVIA

The actor whose autograph young Jamal receives is Amitabh Bachchan, who is the original host of the Indian version of *Who Wants To Be A Millionaire.*

AWARDS

Oscars 2008: Adapt. Screenplay, Cinematog., Director (Boyle), Film, Film Editing, Song ("Jai Ho"), Sound, Orig. Score
British Acad. 2008: Adapt. Screenplay, Cinematog., Director (Boyle), Film, Film Editing, Sound, Orig. Score
Golden Globes 2009: Director (Boyle), Film—Drama, Screenplay, Orig. Score
Screen Actors Guild 2008: Cast
Writers Guild 2008: Adapt. Screenplay

Nomination:

Oscars 2008: Song ("O Saya"), Sound FX Editing
British Acad. 2008: Actor (Patel), Support. Actress (Pinto), Production Des.
Directors Guild 2008: Director (Boyle)
Screen Actors Guild 2008: Support. Actor (Patel).

SMART PEOPLE

> *Sometimes the smartest people have the most to learn.*
> —Movie tagline

Box Office: $9.5 million

Dramas about dysfunctional families have always provided a rich territory for filmmakers to explore. *Smart People,* a small, cerebral film that revolves around a burnt-out academic and his family, is a worthy addition to the genre.

Set in Pittsburgh, *Smart People* marks the feature debut of director Noam Murro, a veteran director of landmark TV commercials. It is also a first for Mark Jude Poirier, a novelist and short story writer who makes his screenwriting debut with an intelligent and darkly witty script.

Dennis Quaid stars as Lawrence Wetherhold, a widowed, disillusioned college professor at Carnegie Mellon University who has been adrift since the death of his wife. Lawrence is so self-absorbed that he has managed to alienate his two kids—his son James (Ashton Holmes), an aspiring poet and student at Carnegie Mellon, and Vanessa (Ellen Page), a frighteningly precocious high school student.

When Lawrence suffers a seizure and can no longer legally drive, he invites his adoptive brother Chuck (Thomas Haden Church) to move into the family home and become his temporary chauffeur. Chuck, an unreliable, parasitic man-child is the complete opposite of Lawrence, which is precisely the reason he serves as the main catalyst for the depressed professor's renewal. Sarah Jessica Parker also lends support as Janet, a former student and now ER physician who offers Lawrence his first romantic relationship since his wife's death.

The entire cast of *Smart People* delivers strong performances throughout the film. In particular, Quaid plays the arrogant, sad-sack professor to perfection. His lovelorn academic is not exactly likeable, yet the viewer roots for his success nonetheless.

Church also gives a notable performance as the clownish buffoon who brings some much-needed life (and comic relief) to the Wetherhold household. However, the real revelation here is Page, and she easily steals every scene in the film with her whip-smart performance as the cool, acerbic, ultra-conservative daughter. Page's performance is even more astonishing when one learns that she made this movie before her star-making turn in *Juno* (2007).

Critics were mostly favorable in their reviews of *Smart People.* In his commentary for the *Wall Street Journal,* critic Joe Morgenstern wrote, "A good deal of the [film's] freshness comes from a grand, clownish slob played by Thomas Haden Church—he's actually the smartest person of the piece—while Dennis Quaid occupies the center with a mastery that's all the more notable for its humanity, because Lawrence Wetherhold is one refractory nut to crack…. This is some of the best work Mr. Quaid has done in an always interesting career."

William Arnold of the *Seattle Post-Intelligencer* remarked, "After its rough opening, *Smart People* settles down to be a funny, wryly enjoyable, effortlessly poignant parable of family life and a splendid showcase for its cast, especially Page, who handily steals the movie and proves that her *Juno* success was no fluke."

Entertainment Weekly's Owen Gleiberman thought the film's plot was a "little too rote," yet he praised the fine acting: "The actors in *Smart People* are such lively, offbeat company that you're happy to spend time with them. The movie is too savvy to let Lawrence shake off his curmudgeonly vibe. He doesn't 'grow,' he just emerges, and that's enough."

For viewers who are fans of intelligent, highly literate films, *Smart People* satisfies with superb acting and a smart script.

Beth A. Fhaner

CREDITS

Lawrence Wetherhold: Dennis Quaid
Dr. Janet Hartigan: Sarah Jessica Parker
Chuck: Thomas Haden Church
Vanessa: Ellen Page
James: Ashton Holmes
Origin: USA
Language: English
Released: 2008
Production: Bridget Johnson, Michael Costigan, Michael London, Bruna Papandrea; Corduroy Films, Groundswell Productions, Table Top Films; released by Miramax Films
Directed by: Noam Murro
Written by: Mark Jude Poirier
Cinematography by: Toby Irwin
Music by: Nuno Bettencourt
Sound: Sandy Gendler
Editing: Robert Frazen, Yana Gorskaya
Art Direction: Ron Mason
Costumes: Amy Westcott
Production Design: Patti Podesta
MPAA rating: R
Running time: 95 minutes

REVIEWS

Boston Globe Online. April 11, 2008.
Chicago Sun-Times Online. April 11, 2008.
Entertainment Weekly Online. April 9, 2008.
Hollywood Reporter Online. January 22, 2008.
Los Angeles Times Online. April 11, 2008.
New York Times Online. April 11, 2008.
San Francisco Chronicle. April 11, 2008, p. E9.
Variety Online. January 31, 2008.
Wall Street Journal. April 11, 2008, p. W1.
Washington Post. April 11, 2008, p. C1.

QUOTES

Chuck: "These children haven't been properly parented in many years. They're practically feral. That's why I was brought in."

SNOW ANGELS

Some will fall. Some will fly.
—Movie tagline

Quietly effective, *Snow Angels* brings Stewart O'Nan's prize-winning 1994 novel to the screen with an excellent and surprising cast and wintry melancholy to spare. The fourth feature from director David Gordon Green (*George Washington* [2000], *All The Real Girls* [2003]) is another feather in the distinguished cap of the young director. All of his previous efforts have been tonal variations on the rural or small town drama, and this is no exception. Thought there is less of the impressionistic editing style that made his previous works stand out from the pack, O'Nan's deliberate and meditative screenplay (which moves the proceedings from 1974 to the present) is a fine fit for the idiosyncratic Green.

The film opens with a small town Pennsylvania high school marching band practicing on a winter afternoon. As the band director (Tom Noonan) urges the band to put more passion into their performance of Peter Gabriel's "Sledgehammer," a gunshot rings out, causing everyone to pause. The narrative then shifts back several days to show us the events leading up to that day. Teenaged Arthur (Michael Angarano) buses tables at a Chinese restaurant with waitress Annie (Kate Beckinsale), who used to baby-sit him as a child. Annie, now a disillusioned woman, is raising her young daughter while recovering from a failed marriage to Glenn (Sam Rockwell), who has become born-again and moved back in with his parents as he tries to put his life back together. At the same time that shy Arthur feels the first stirrings of love toward new girl in school Lila (Olivia Thirlby), his parents (Griffin Dunne and Jeanetta Arnette) are splitting up. Glenn still harbors notions of making amends with Annie and continuing to raise their daughter, Tara, but when he discovers that Annie is having an affair with Nate (Nicky Katt), the husband of her friend and co-worker, Barb (Amy Sedaris), it sends Glenn into a violent, alcohol-fueled tailspin that will have serious consequences.

A simple small town tragedy in the vein of many autumnal/chilly dramas from the past, it is often easy to see where *Snow Angels* is going long before it gets there. At times it, feels like a blue-collar relative to *The Ice Storm* (1996), with lighter moments that recall the downbeats of Ted Demme's similarly snowy *Beautiful Girls* (1996), while the Glenn and Annie plot thread evokes comparisons Tim Blake Nelson's *Eye of God* (1997). In this case, though, familiarity is not a liability—*Snow Angels*'s many pleasures come from the rich atmosphere it conjures and the believable people who dwell within it.

The casting in the film is often surprising. Beckinsale, whose glamorous looks seemed to propel her from artier fare to bigger-budgeted Hollywood pictures early in her career, has not been seen in a small, character-driven film of this sort since *Laurel Canyon* (2002). Her work as Annie is a reminder of what she can do when not being relegated to a supporting role or drowned out by garish special effects. As Glenn, Rockwell allows us to feel sympathetic where the character could have easily come across as simply unlikable. Angarano's Arthur is the quiet center of the film. Obviously smitten with Annie, he is also the bridge between two marriages that have disintegrated in differing ways. While Glenn and Annie's situation bubbles with barely contained rage, Arthur's college professor father quietly and rationally moves out of the house at his mother's request. Angarano makes Arthur into a real teen—quiet, shy, and unsure of himself. Sedaris's Barb begins as a variation on one of her fast-talking, quick-quipping comic creations, but as Barb discovers that her husband is sleeping with Annie, Sedaris is allowed to add some dramatic shading to her likeable performance.

Opening the film with the climactic gunshot removes the mystery, allowing Green to backtrack and concentrate on creating an affinity for the characters, making the tragedy all the more weighty when it finally occurs. As the dramatic tension of the film increases considerably in the film's third act, the most appealing and believable aspect of the story is the blossoming relationship between Arthur and Lila. As Bruce Bennett writes in the *New York Sun,* "The growth of Arthur and Lila's burgeoning emotional and physical relationship is measured out in such unabashedly breathless doses that it almost seems like a wish-fulfillment vision of teenage lust and love bordering on Aristotelian perfection." Even with limited screen time, Thirlby colors Lila in with enough detail to make her exceptionally appealing and winning.

Green's storytelling is much more focused and to the point than in his previous works—according to the *Village Voice*'s Nathan Lee, "The film feels transitional for Green—one foot in the moody, interiorized indieverse of his previous work, the other taking a big step toward more conventional projects." Although, it avoids his trademark dreamlike montages and non-sequiturs, fans will notice more than a bit of him in the abrupt final shot. Still, his exceptional eye for detail remains—evidenced in things such as Arthur's ubiquitous pink knit cap and the unusual denizens at the bar that Glenn frequents—giving *Snow Angels* a lived-in authentic feel. Composer David Wingo, a usual Green collaborator hits all the right notes with a sparse, unobtrusive score. O'Nan creates a small, believable universe, showing how a tragedy affects even those on its periphery. The result is a low-key triumph, and a prime case of novelist and director collaborating to bring a story to the screen with their respective visions intact.

David Hodgson

CREDITS

Annie Marchand: Kate Beckinsale
Glen Marchand: Sam Rockwell
Arthur Parkinson: Michael Angarano
Louise Parkinson: Jeanetta Arnette
Don Parkinson: Griffin Dunne
Nate Petite: Nicky Katt
Lila Taybern: Olivia Thirlby
Barb Petite: Amy Sedaris
Mr. Chervenick: Tom Noonan
Warren Hardesty: Connor Paolo
Tara Marchand: Hudson Grace
Origin: USA
Language: English
Released: 2007
Production: Lisa Muskat, Dan Linau, Paul Miller, Cami Taylor; Crossroads Films, True Love Productions; released by Warner Independent
Directed by: David Gordon Green
Written by: David Gordon Green
Cinematography by: Tim Orr
Music by: Jeff McIlwain
Sound: Larry Blake
Music Supervisor: Janice Ginsberg
Editing: William Anderon
Art Direction: Terry Quennell
Costumes: Kate Rose
Production Design: Richard Wright
MPAA rating: R
Running time: 106 minutes

REVIEWS

Entertainment Weekly Online. March 5, 2008.
New York Times Online. March 7, 2008.
Variety Online. January 20, 2007.
Village Voice Online. March 4, 2008.

TRIVIA

Director David Gordon Green was originally hired to work on the script for the film but after several years, the original director moved onto another project and Green was enlisted to helm the project.

SON OF RAMBOW

Make Believe. Not War.
—Movie tagline

Box Office: $1.7 million

A thin, angel-faced young boy named Will Proudfoot (Bill Milner) reads the Bible sincerely for a small congregation of Christian zealots. Cut to a movie theater, where throngs of adults in the "Smoking" section are watching the Sylvester Stallone vigilante movie *Rambo: First Blood* (1982). Seated by himself in the "No Smoking" section is a devilish-looking boy, Lee Carter (Will Poulter), smoking a cigarette and staring at the fascinating movie through the lens of his camcorder. In an instant, we understand that the boy is a true cineaste, circa 1983, fascinated with this American exploitation flick.

In school, Will is dismissed from his classroom because his teacher is showing a documentary film, and the strict congregation his mother belongs to, the Brethren, does not permit its members to watch movies or listen to music. He has not been paying much attention anyway; at his desk he has been drawing fantastic creatures around the edges of his Bible—dragons, flying monsters, cartoon heroes. Sitting in the hallway, he gets up to take a large gulp from the drinking fountain, then spits it out into a fish tank. He is a dreamer and secretly a schemer. Down the hall, a teacher has pulled Lee from a classroom and is throttling him, yelling, but the miscreant is yelling back. The teacher stomps off in a rage, and Lee throws a ball down the hall; it hits Will, who has been peeking around a bookcase, in the face, and the fishbowl falls to the ground and shatters.

Both boys are waiting outside the headmaster's office when the diabolical Lee warns Will that they will be "tortured" mercilessly, hinting broadly of blows to their developing manhood. Lee offers to take all the blame in return for unspecified favors. Will offers him a watch he has taken from the table in his church where all the men set down their watches before services, presumably to abandon the worldly concept of time. Thus is a bizarre friendship struck up, beginning with a bribe.

In these fine opening scenes, writer/director Garth Jennings establishes the credentials of *Son of Rambow* as not your ordinary coming-of-age buddy flick. Instead of mawkish sentiment, we feel the heady rush of careless, thoughtless, youthful rebellion against a stifling world. But Jennings never lays that theme on so thick: instead, he shows us an inventive but credible world where motivations are immature and superficial. These two boys have been transported by movies, in particular one incredibly violent movie, and nothing in their world can hold a candle to their new dream of making a knockoff themselves.

The opening sequences proceed breathlessly, accompanied by stomping, discordant martial music interspersed with softer rhythms. Lee, faking serious injury from the headmaster's punishment, gets Will to pedal him back home in a cart attached to a bicycle, and we see the farm fields rush by. But not just farm fields: there are also the three towers of a nuclear plant near an area of abandoned industry, and the complete picture is that of a bygone, simpler bucolic life already ruined by greed and waste. Lee lives, with his older teenage brother, in the owner's portion of an old mansion that has become an old folks' home. It is run by his mother, nominally, but she spends most of her time abroad. Lee has a pirated copy of *First Blood,* and after Will sees it, his mind is overtaken by fantasies. These two are a perfect pair: the older, worldlier miscreant with ambitions of winning a BBC young filmmaker's contest, and the young, artistic dreamer awakened to life outside his semi-cloistered religious home.

On his nighttime pedal back home, Will's mind explodes into fantasy while he passes a scarecrow in a field, a singularly ridiculous scarecrow with an old oil barrel for a head. The scarecrow grabs Will, and in his fantasy the scarecrow is holding Rambo himself hostage, somehow aided in his cruelty by a flying dog. Will declares himself the son of Rambow and vows to get him back, and the next morning shows up at Lee's home determined to be the action star of their own movie, *Son of Rambow* (the boys are using the phonetic spelling as that is how they think it is spelled).

The boys' filmmaking is outrageous, silly, and hilarious, as they attempt a series of stunts that defy any mature assessment of danger. They are swept away by their own inventive pleasures and immature creativity. At first, Lee is still a bully, but soon they become blood brothers, and each reveals a secret about their missing fathers: Lee's ran away when Lee was a baby, and Will's succumbed to an aneurysm while mowing the lawn.

Everything about this movie is odd, but it gets odder still. Lee cooks for and kowtows to his older brother, who drives a snazzy sports car and talks on what to twenty-first-century eyes looks like an impossibly large mobile phone (the film is set in the early 1980s). Will worries his mother and a hovering male member of the church who's obviously looking to take Will's father's place—the boy's antics are causing not just dismay, but budding scandal. And into the school comes a busload of French exchange students, and a new rock star, a fabulously fashionable young boy named Didier (Jules Sitruk). He immediately acquires a fawning posse of wannabes, and an equally entranced coterie of girls who line up to kiss him. Didier pronounces them all unworthy of his attentions.

The Brethren are no match for Rambo. Jennings does not bother to create a moral dilemma in his protagonist, Will. One minute the boy seems genuine when promising his mother he will return to the straight-and-narrow path, but the next he is sneaking out of his bed to help direct an unauthorized movie scene. Jennings, who was born in 1972, wrote the story partly based on his own childhood experiences with a camcorder, and he gets everything right about the lure of the early technology, and the savage cliquishness of school culture, but thankfully without bothering to make us try to believe he has something profound to say. The satire, silliness, and movie scenes are all a romp, and a joy to watch for their own careless, uncalculated-seeming charm.

Alas, Jennings does eventually succumb to melodrama, but somehow that is fitting too, in the sense of life imitating art. And his is a smart, tough kind of redemption.

In this wonderfully appealing film about little kids wanting to make a movie, there are plenty of tossed-off movie references, but you do not have to get them all to enjoy what you are watching. *Son of Rambow* was an audience favorite at Sundance, and it is easy to see why. Jennings is not demanding we get some big message, and he is showing us childhood in all its immoral, contradictory messiness. These are kids acting like kids, and not cute Hollywood kids either, but like kids we know. The two young actors are superb. Milner keeps us believing in his innocence even when he has totally abandoned it. Poulter has eyebrows that look like Satanic daggers and eyes full of wild malevolence, but we understand immediately that, like most black sheep, he has fashioned his own brand of rough justice out of his beleaguered heart. In the end, we can take this story about betrayal and friendship easily, because there is so little pretension to it. It follows its own fantasy rules, and has oodles of knockabout charm.

Michael Betzold

CREDITS

Mary Proudfoot: Jessica Stevenson
Joshua: Neil Dudgeon
Will Proudfoot: Bill Milner
Lee Carter: Will Poulter
Didier: Jules Sitruk
Lawrence Carter: Ed Westwick
Origin: Great Britain
Language: English
Released: 2007
Production: Nick Goldsmith; Hammer and Tongs, Celluloid Dreams; released by Paramount Vantage
Directed by: Garth Jennings
Written by: Garth Jennings
Cinematography by: Jess Hall
Music by: Joby Talbot
Sound: Guillaume Sciama, Joseph Park-Stracey

Editing: Dominic Leung
Art Direction: Robyn Paiba
Costumes: Harriet Cawley
Production Design: Joel Collins
MPAA rating: PG-13
Running time: 96 minutes

REVIEWS

Boston Globe Online. April 30, 2008.
Entertainment Weekly Online. April 30, 2008.
The Guardian Online. April 4, 2008.
Hollywood Reporter Online. January 26, 2007.
Los Angeles Times Online. May 2, 2008.
New York Times Online. May 2, 2008.
The Observer Online. April 6, 2008.
Variety Online. January 25, 2007.
Village Voice Online. April 29, 2008.

QUOTES

Lee Carter: "I don't care what you and your so-called mates say about me, but don't you ever, ever call my brother a scab! You know, at least he's there for me! At least he cares about me, which is more than I can say for you, blood brother. You're a two-faced fake like the rest of them and I'm gutted it took me this long to work it out. I'm gutted I fell for it, Will. Lawrence is better than all of you and all that lot put together and he's all I've got, alright? He's all I've got."

TRIVIA

A member of Didier's entourage is wearing sunglasses because he could not stop looking into the camera.

SOUL MEN

Out of sync. Never out of style.
—Movie tagline

Box Office: $12 million

The soul music created by such performers as Aretha Franklin, Al Green, Wilson Pickett, Otis Redding, and Ike and Tina Turner during the 1960s and 1970s is one of the highpoints of American popular music. While these artists remain well known, many others faded into obscurity. *Soul Men* is a comic look at the messy lives of two such forgotten performers.

Floyd Henderson (Bernie Mac) and Louis Hinds (Samuel L. Jackson) got their starts as backup singers for Marcus Hooks (John Legend) as part of the Real Deal. When Marcus leaves the group to launch a successful solo career, Floyd and Louis try to continue as the Real Deal but break up after one hit. Floyd goes on to operate a chain of car washes, with skimpily dressed female employees, while Louis goes to prison for armed robbery.

As *Soul Men* opens, Floyd is living an uneasy retirement in an Arizona senior-citizens community, and Louis works as an auto mechanic. When Marcus dies the duo are invited by recording executive Danny Epstein (Sean Hayes) to come to New York to perform in a memorial tribute at Harlem's Apollo Theater. One problem is that Floyd and Louis hate each other because their breakup was precipitated by their falling in love with the same woman. Looking for any excuse to escape his moribund routine, however, Floyd is eager to go, and after he persuades the reluctant Louis to come along, the pair head off for New York in Floyd's vintage convertible.

Along the way, the initially rusty singers try to polish their act in lounges, resulting in two spirited performances in Amarillo and Memphis. They are joined en route by Cleo (Sharon Leal), the daughter of the woman who tore them apart. As the likely offspring of one of the two, Cleo has some singing talent and becomes part of the act. She also, unfortunately, has a sleazy, drug-dealing boyfriend, Lester (Affion Crockett), who creates havoc for Floyd and Louis.

Mac and Jackson have modest singing skills, while Leal, who appeared on Broadway in *Rent* (1996) and performs in *Dreamgirls* (2006), takes Cleo from a tentative to fully realized performer. The soundtrack, mixing classic soul and new tunes, is supplemented with songs by Legend, Eddie Floyd, Anthony Hamilton, Sharon Jones, Me'Shell Ndegeocello, Chris Pierce, Ryan Shaw, and Isaac Hayes, who appears briefly as himself.

Yet music plays a surprisingly small part in *Soul Men*. The emphasis is on the profane bickering between Floyd and Louis. The screenplay by Robert Ramsey and Matthew Stone may even set a record for obscenities. The biggest problem with *Soul Men* is that Ramsey and Stone, who co-wrote *Intolerable Cruelty* (2003) with Ethan and Joel Coen, and director Malcolm D. Lee, best known for *The Best Man* (1999), rely upon a mixture of tired gags and plot clichés. If Floyd's accidentally discharging Louis's handgun is funny once, think the filmmakers, twice is even more hilarious. The same goes for Floyd's sexual encounters with two enthusiastic older women (Vanessa del Rio and Jennifer Coolidge). As if to top the first, the second involves the woman's taking out her false teeth to perform oral sex. Lee, Ramsey, and Stone even feel compelled to provide some lame comic relief (in a comedy?) with Epstein's nerdy assistant (Adam Herschman), a short, rotund youth sporting a Jewish Afro. While the musical sequences are well done, there is a lot of dead air in the dialogue scenes.

Despite the general sloppiness of the proceedings, Mac and Jackson seem to be having a good time, especially when Louis leaves the Amarillo stage to join a group of line dancers. The two actors play well off each other, showing that Floyd and Louis use profanities to mask their affection for each other. Mac and Isaac Hayes died within a day of each other two months before the film's release. The closing credits of *Soul Men* pay tribute to the actors, with the highlight being the bawdy jokes Mac performed to warm up the Apollo audience. Fortunately, much more of Mac's verbal wit has been captured in Spike Lee's documentary *The Original Kings of Comedy* (2000).

Michael Adams

CREDITS

Louis: Samuel L. Jackson
Floyd: Bernie Mac
Himself: Isaac Hayes
Cleo: Sharon Leal
Philip: Adam Herschman
Danny Epstein: Sean Hayes
Marcus Hooks: John Legend
Rosalee: Jennifer Coolidge
Full-Figured Neighbor: Vanessa del Rio
Duane: Mike Epps
Lester: Affion Crockett
Origin: USA
Language: English
Released: 2008
Production: David T. Friendly, Charles Castaldi, Steve Greener; Dimension Films, Friendly Films; released by MGM
Directed by: Malcolm D. Lee
Written by: Robert Ramsey, Matthew Stone
Cinematography by: Matthew F. Leonetti
Music by: Stanley Clarke
Sound: Robert Eber
Music Supervisor: Alex Steyermark
Editing: William Henry, Paul Millspaugh
Art Direction: Meghan Rogers
Costumes: Danielle Hollowell
Production Design: Richard Hoover
MPAA rating: R
Running time: 100 minutes

REVIEWS

Boston Globe Online. November 7, 2008.
Chicago Sun-Times Online. November 5, 2008.
Entertainment Weekly Online. November 4, 2008.

Hollywood Reporter Online. November 3, 2008.
Los Angeles Times Online. November 7, 2008.
New York Times Online. November 7, 2008.
Rolling Stone Online. November 13, 2008.
San Francisco Chronicle. November 7, 2008, p. E5.
Variety Online. November 3, 2008.

QUOTES

Louis: "What money? It's a funeral! Don't nobody get paid to sing at no damn funeral!"

TRIVIA

There is a closing-credit tribute, including an interview, to Bernie Mac who died only months after he finished the film.

SPACE CHIMPS

Go Bananas!
—Movie tagline

Box Office: $30.1 million

Space Chimps is a playful tribute to classic science fiction adventure movies of the past, including *Star Wars* (1977), *Star Trek* (1979), *2001: A Space Odyssey* (1968), and *The Black Hole* (1979). Writer/director Kirk De Micco and co-writer Rob Moreland drew inspiration for this computer-animated, family-friendly comedy from the historic early years of the American space program as well as from films like *The Right Stuff* (1983). In 1961, prior to risking the first human astronauts, the United States launched a real chimpanzee named Ham on a rocket into outer space. Ham III, *Space Chimps'* unlikely hero, is the legendary ape's fictitious present-day grandson.

Compared to his valiant grandfather, Ham III (voice of Andy Samberg)—a circus performer known as "The Simian Satellite"— is an insufferable slacker. Due to his celebrated pedigree, however, Ham III is abducted by NASA to accompany two other chimps on a dangerous mission aboard the space shuttle Horizon. The objective is to retrieve a lost unmanned space probe, the Infinity, on a faraway planet showing possible signs of life. Unknown to the NASA scientists, the planet's evil overlord Zartog (voice of Jeff Daniels), bearing a passing resemblance to the Creature from the Black Lagoon, has discovered the Infinity and is using it to cruelly enslave the once carefree population.

Throughout much of *Space Chimps,* Titan (voice of Patrick Warburton), the Horizon's dignified, older, larger, and more experienced mission commander, butts heads with the immature goofball and interloper Ham III. The third crew member is the reluctant love-interest Lieutenant Luna (voice of Cheryl Hines), the brainy and attractive female chimp whom Ham III courts mercilessly until eventually winning her over with his persistent quick wit. The trio's mission is supported on the ground by two more chimps: Comet (voice of Zack Shada), a clever youngster disappointed to have been displaced by Ham III on the Horizon, and Houston (voice of Carlos Alazraqui), Ham III's show business manager who was taken along with him from the circus by NASA.

The Horizon crash-lands on its desired target after a hilariously bumpy flight through an intergalactic wormhole. Titan and Luna lose consciousness during entry into the planet's atmosphere while Ham III manages to stay alert. Despite his frenzied panicking, Ham III gives an early indication that he may have indeed inherited some of his grandfather's exceptional physical traits by remaining awake. While Titan is temporarily knocked out, Ham III and Luna venture naively outside the ship. Luna snaps photos of the bleak but seemingly safe desert landscape, documenting the unfamiliar environment for future scientific research purposes and trying to ignore the attention-grabbing Ham III as he mugs in front of her camera. In a sequence heavily reminiscent of *Star Wars,* the two are then harassed and driven away from the ship by some bizarre and hostile alien life-forms. After a long chase by flying manta ray-like creatures, they find themselves lost in a dense and inhospitable jungle. They go on to experience a variety of misadventures while attempting to reunite with the Horizon before it goes into automatic relaunch in less than twenty-four hours. They encounter some of the planet's unique inhabitants, including globhoppers—playful, colorful blobs that look like gumdrops—and Kilowatt (voice of Kristin Chenoweth)—a small and timid, bulbous-headed, androgynous doll-like character that is both cute and disturbingly creepy. The last of her unpronounceable kind, Kilowatt helps Ham III and Luna navigate through the unfamiliar territory. Having lived a life full of fear, she rises courageously to the occasion by sacrificing herself to the terrifying Flesh Devouring Beast in order to save their lives. Later, she happily emerges unscathed after making an unpleasant inner-journey through the beast. In the meantime, Titan has been discovered and captured by Zartog, who is forcing his minions to build a castle modeled after a Las Vegas-style casino featured in the Infinity's introductory slide show. Back in Florida, NASA having lost contact with the chimps, an overzealous senator (voice of Stanley Tucci) has declared the Horizon's mission a failure and has dismantled the entire space program, turning NASA into a ridiculous paint-your-own-plate retail establishment.

Over the course of their adventures, the chimps grapple with the indignity of being considered less than human. Despite the chimps' ability to speak to one another and be understood by the audience, the human scientists do not acknowledge their intelligence, seeing them as mere "space chimps," not as real and competent astronauts. Ham III, on a more personal level, also struggles with the notion of living in the shadow of his celebrated grandfather. Until he is ultimately forced into becoming a hero, he is resigned to being a clown and to taking the easy way out. In the end, although their human captors at NASA fail to recognize the chimps' intelligence and the incredible effort that contributed to their safe return to Earth, their genuine good nature and heroism are plainly felt.

A cast of Hollywood and Broadway celebrities lend their voices to *Space Chimps'* nonhuman and human characters, and some of the soundtrack music is provided by Blue Man Group. Although it was marketed primarily as a children's movie, without a doubt the film can be enjoyed by adults as well. Kids will find *Space Chimps* highly entertaining for its straightforward premise, stimulating and colorful visuals, cute and off-the-wall characters, mandatory physical gags, and goofy chimp-themed humor. If willing to overlook the inherent predictability and potty-jokes of any commercially made kids' flick, adults are likely to be impressed by the script's sophistication and abundance of historical and pop-culture references. They may also be amused, or even shocked, by the large handful of risqué jokes and double entendres boldly intended to fly over the heads of *Space Chimps'* youngest viewers.

Jaye Furlonger

CREDITS

Ham III: Andy Samberg (Voice)
Luna: Cheryl Hines (Voice)
Titan: Patrick Warburton (Voice)
Zartog: Jeff Daniels (Voice)
The Senator: Stanley Tucci (Voice)
Kilowatt: Kristin Chenoweth (Voice)
The Ringmaster: Kenan Thompson (Voice)
Houston: Carlos Alazraqui (Voice)
Dr. Jagu: Omid Abtahi (Voice)
Dr. Bob: Patrick Breen (Voice)
Dr. Smothers: Kath Soucie (Voice)
Dr. Poole: Jane Lynch (Voice)
Comet: Zack Shada (Voice)
Origin: USA
Language: English
Released: 2008

Production: Barry Sonnenfeld, John H. Williams; Odyssey Entertainment, Vanguard Animation, Starz Animation, Starz Media, Studiopolis; released by 20th Century-Fox
Directed by: Kirk De Micco
Written by: Kirk De Micco, Rob Moreland
Cinematography by: Jericca Cleland
Music by: David A. Stewart, Chris P. Bacon
Sound: Sean Garnhart, Keith Hodne
Editing: Debbie Berman
Art Direction: Matthias Lechner
MPAA rating: G
Running time: 81 minutes

REVIEWS

Boston Globe Online. July 18, 2008.
Chicago Sun-Times Online. July 17, 2008.
Entertainment Weekly Online. July 16, 2008.
Hollywood Reporter Online. July 18, 2008.
Los Angeles Times Online. July 18, 2008.
New York Times Online. July 18, 2008.
Variety Online. July 16, 2008.
Washington Post. July 18, 2008, p. C6.

QUOTES

Titan: "Commander's log, space...the final frontier."
Ham III: "Permission to speak commander."
Titan: "Permission granted."
Ham III: "You're a dork!"

SPEED RACER

Go.
—Movie tagline

Box Office: $43.9 million

On the May 5, 2008, broadcast of *The Colbert Report*, Stephen Colbert described the experience of seeing *Speed Racer* as follows: "Put eighty pounds of fireworks into an industrial dryer, crawl right in there with them, turn it on and then light the fuse. It'll give you a good idea of the visual onslaught you'll be enduring." He further described the plot as "the classic story of boy-meets-seizure-inducing-lights." As directed by the Wachowski brothers (Andy and Larry), the feature film adaptation of the Japanese cult classic cartoon show *Speed Racer* is little more than a blueprint for how to let special effects wizardry go horribly wrong. The visual style of the film is so overwhelming that it makes potentially redeeming elements—a decent (if conventional) story and some acting talent (particularly Emile Hirsch, John Goodman, and Susan Sarandon)—entirely secondary to the all-out visual assault, from the high-contrast colors to the energetic camera work to the computer-generated effects. A film that seems interested in visually conveying the thrill of racing (and in contrasting that excitement with the underbelly of corporate sponsorship) instead ends up drowning in a Technicolor computer-generated mess.

Speed Racer (Emile Hirsch) comes from a racing family. His father Pops (John Goodman) builds the cars. His brother Rex Racer (Scott Porter), the best driver in the world before having a falling out with Pops and apparently dying in the deadliest cross-country rally around, the Casa Cristo, was derided in the press for allegedly cheating in races. The rest of the Racer family, Mom (Susan Sarandon) and the youngest Racer boy, Spritle (Paulie Litt), along with his trusty chimpanzee Chim-Chim, also support Speed in his racing. When the head of Royalton Industries, E. P. Arnold Royalton (Roger Allam), makes Speed an offer he cannot refuse (wealth beyond imagining, access to Royalton Industries' vast resources, etc.), Speed refuses and soon finds himself having difficulty on and off the track as shadowy interests align against him. Royalton makes it clear to Speed that corporations fix the outcomes of the races for profit, so the only way to win in the big leagues is to play the corporate game. But Speed's love of the purity of racing leads him, along with his girlfriend Trixie (Christina Ricci), into an alliance with the mysterious Racer X (Matthew Fox) and Inspector Detector (Benno Fürmann). Together, they help another troubled racer, Taejo Togokhan (Korean pop singer Rain). But Speed is dismayed when he discovers that Taejo has used them to win so that he can drive up the stock value of his father's company, making its acquisition by Royalton more costly. This seems to confirm that racing is, in fact, purely a profit-making scheme for racing's corporate sponsors. Enraged, Speed hits the track, followed by Racer X, and takes the opportunity to confront the masked driver—they work so well as a team that Speed believes Racer X to be his long-lost brother, Rex. Racer X removes his mask, however, to reveal a stranger's face, and says that Speed's brother is truly dead. Meanwhile, Taejo's sister Horuko (Nan Yu) visits the Racers and presents Speed with an invitation to race in the Grand Prix—Speed was on the winning team, Taejo himself has no intention of racing anyway, and Horuko does not approve of her brother's deception. Speed races in the Prix, and Royalton's sponsored vehicle is shown to have been modified with illegal equipment, a revelation that causes Royalton's downfall. In winning the Prix, Speed reclaims the glory of racing from the cynical corporate sponsors. As an approving Racer X looks on, it is revealed to the audience that Racer X is, in fact, Rex Racer, who went undercover to help save the sport

he loved by fighting back against corrupt corporate interference. He opts to continue to live in hiding, as he feels it would do more harm than good to reveal himself to his family. Speed kisses Trixie as the cameras flash in the winner's circle and, as the closing credits sequence shows, Royalton is prosecuted for his crimes.

The main problem with *Speed Racer* is not necessarily its story or its slightly exaggerated acting, both of which are more or less fitting for this sort of epic race movie, but the fact that the visuals and design of the film are so completely overwhelming that they affect every aspect of the film, from the way the actors relate to their surroundings and each other to the audience's experience of the film. *Speed Racer* was shot entirely using green-screen technology, and most of its backgrounds and all of its action sequences are computer-generated. This is not necessarily a detriment on the face of it, but the design chosen for the look of the film—absolutely garish colors, outlandish cityscapes, and physics-defying automotive technology and action—serves only to undermine its apparent intentions: in the case of the action sequences, to translate the thrill of racing to the audience, and to give the overall film a sort of Japanese animation-like quality in homage to the source material. This emphasis on the artificial over the organic, however, leads to a trickle-down effect that allows the film's cartoonish aspects to permeate every facet of the picture. The real human actors must somehow try to communicate emotions, pursue goals, and build relationships through all of the visual noise. This sensibility may have worked in a low-budget Japanese cartoon from the 1960s, but it does not translate well to a major live-action film.

The one good thing *Speed Racer* manages to do, in the tradition of all thoughtful science fiction, is to examine the effect of, and express concerns about, whatever the issue of the day might be—in this case, the power and influence corporations exert on the workings of society. But by coupling this with the film's overbearing visual style and heavy reliance on the computer-generated action, the film takes on a bizarre hybrid quality. It is neither a serious film nor completely a cartoon, but some strange cross between *TRON* (1982) and *On the Waterfront* (1954), though lacking the pioneering visual dimension of the former and the emotional impact and gravitas of the latter. Interestingly, the movie's central theme—do what you love and what you want to do either with integrity or simply for the money—is apparently played out not only on the screen but behind the camera as well. *Speed Racer* is an attempt by the Wachowski brothers to reach a larger family audience; though they obviously love and respect the original *Speed Racer* series, and the process of filmmaking in general, their final product in this instance leads one to wonder if the film's overwrought design is the natural outgrowth of doing something for the money.

John Boaz

CREDITS

Speed: Emile Hirsch
Trixie: Christina Ricci
Racer X: Matthew Fox
Pops Racer: John Goodman
Mom Racer: Susan Sarandon
Royalton: Roger Allam
Mr. Musha: Hiroyuki Sanada
Ben Burns: Richard Roundtree
Spritle Racer: Paulie Litt
Inspector Detector: Benno Fürmann
Rex Racer: Scott Porter
Snake Oiler: Christian Oliver
Sparky: Kick Gurry
Grey Ghost: Moritz Bleibtreu
Cruncher Block: John Benfield
Taejo Togokahn: Rain
Horuko Togokahn: Nan Yu
Origin: USA
Language: English
Released: 2008
Production: Joel Silver, Grant Hill, Andy Wachowski, Larry Wachowski; Warner Bros. Pictures, Village Roadshow Pictures, Silver Pictures, Anarchos Prods., Velocity Productions Ltd., Sechste Babelsberg Film; released by Warner Bros.
Directed by: Andy Wachowski, Larry Wachowski
Written by: Andy Wachowski, Larry Wachowski
Cinematography by: David Tattersall
Music by: Michael Giacchino
Sound: Ivan Sharrock
Editing: Zach Staenberg, Roger Barton
Art Direction: Hugh Bateup, Sebastian Krawinkel, Marco Bittner Rosser
Costumes: Kym Barrett
Production Design: Owen Paterson
MPAA rating: PG
Running time: 129 minutes

REVIEWS

Boston Globe Online. May 9, 2008.
Chicago Sun-Times Online. May 8, 2008.
Entertainment Weekly Online. May 7, 2008.
Hollywood Reporter Online. May 1, 2008.
Los Angeles Times Online. May 9, 2008.
New York Times Online. May 9, 2008.
New Yorker Online. May 12, 2008.
San Francisco Chronicle. May 8, 2008, p. E1.
Variety Online. May 1, 2008.
Washington Post. May 9, 2008, p. C1.

QUOTES

Speed: "Racing's in our blood. Like for Pops, it isn't just a sport. It's way more important than that. It's like a religion. And in our house, the major sponsors are kind of like the devil. I don't mean to offend you, sir, and I do appreciate your offer, but after all we've been through, I don't think this kind of deal is for me."

TRIVIA

At one point, director Alfonso Cuarón was attached to direct the film and Johnny Depp was set to star as Speed.

AWARDS

Nomination:
Golden Raspberries 2008: Worst Sequel/Prequel.

THE SPIDERWICK CHRONICLES

Their world is closer than you think.
—Movie tagline

Box Office: $71.1 million

Based on the popular children's books by Holly Black and Tony DiTerlizzi, *The Spiderwick Chronicles* succeeds because the filmmakers behind it and the talented cast in front of the camera refuse to speak down to children, making an enjoyable fantasy movie that easily appeals to all generations. Far from a classic in the genre but also nowhere near the bottom of the family fantasy movie barrel, *The Spiderwick Chronicles* is a satisfactory adaptation, an enjoyable experience with an excellent ensemble that is still somehow not as memorable as it could have been, mostly due to some of the weaknesses of its source material and some failed special effects.

After Aunt Lucinda (Joan Plowright) passes away, she leaves the Spiderwick Estate to her recently separated niece (Mary-Louise Parker), who moves in with her three children—twins Jared and Simon Grace (Freddie Highmore, in a dual role) and their older sister Mallory (Sarah Bolger). The adventurous Jared finds a dumbwaiter system behind a wall and a secret room that leads him into a dusty study that shows him the way to an unseen world of monsters and fairies. It turns out the original owner of the estate, Arthur Spiderwick (David

Strathairn) had written a field guide to this other world and even placed a protective circle around the house to keep it safe. Jared meets a small creature named Thimbletack (voice of Martin Short), who warns him of the disaster that will come if the forces of evil get their hands on the guide and gives the young man a stone through which he can see the universe invisible to most mortals.

The powers trying to get their hands on the guide are led by an ogre named Mulgarath (voice of Nick Nolte). He leads a group of creatures who mistakenly kidnap Jared's identical twin, thinking that it is Simon. Trying to come to his rescue, Jared joins forces with a hobgoblin named Hogsqueal (voice of Seth Rogen), an enemy of Mulgarath, to save not only his family but the universe from the vast array of sprites, goblins, ogres, trolls, and fairies that it does not even know exists.

Director Mark Waters struggles a bit with the blending of the two worlds, designing creatures of an alternate universe that never feels completely a part of the real one. The creatures are nowhere near as interesting as the humans, something that most modern family fantasy films have also bungled. If audiences of all ages could more easily believe that Mulgarath and Thimbletack were real, the film would have significantly more power. The cinematography by the great Caleb Deschanel almost makes the visual aesthetic of *The Spiderwick Chronicles* more jarring because the remarkably lush, natural settings make the creatures placed against them look even less genuine.

What saves *The Spiderwick Chronicles* from devolving into another messy CGI extravaganza like the far inferior *The Golden Compass* (2007) or *Eragon* (2006) is, primarily, Waters's skill with his actors and, secondarily, the excellent dialogue by writers Karey Kirkpatrick, David Berenbaum, and John Sayles, who refuse to put stupid slang or inferior words into the mouths of the child characters. Highmore does great work playing two distinct characters. Building one of the more impressive resumes for an actor of any age with great work in *Finding Neverland* (2004), *August Rush* (2007), and *The Spiderwick Chronicles*, Highmore, not yet old enough to drive when this film was made, is likely to grow into a talented adult actor. Having supporting actors as talented as Mary-Louise Parker and David Strathairn in an ensemble is never a bad thing and the voice work by Nick Nolte and Seth Rogen is consistently entertaining.

Critics were kind to *The Spiderwick Chronicles*, with a large majority giving the film a positive review even if very few were effusive with their praise. Roger Ebert of the *Chicago Sun-Times* praised the film as "a well-crafted family thriller that is truly scary and doesn't wimp out." Rex Reed of the *New York Observer* noted that, "for a

story aimed at the moppet market, *The Spiderwick Chronicles* is one that holds the interest without unbalancing the I.Q." Finally, Justin Chang of *Variety* noted the film's thematic commonalities with the work of another director who has made a fortune blending the worlds of reality and fantasy, describing it as "a work of both modest enchantment and enchanting modesty, grounded in a classically Spielbergian realm where childlike wonderment crosses paths with the tough realities of young adulthood."

Brian Tallerico

CREDITS

Jared/Simon: Freddie Highmore
Mallory: Sarah Bolger
Helen: Mary-Louise Parker
Arthur Spiderwick: David Strathairn
Aunt Lucinda: Joan Plowright
Richard: Andrew McCarthy
Mulgarath: Nick Nolte (Voice)
Hogsqueal: Seth Rogen (Voice)
Thimbletack: Martin Short (Voice)
Origin: USA
Language: English
Released: 2008
Production: Mark Canton, Larry J. Franco, Ellen Goldsmith-Vein, Karey Kirkpatrick; Nickelodeon Movies; released by Paramount
Directed by: Mark S. Waters
Written by: Karey Kirkpatrick, David Berenbaum, John Sayles
Cinematography by: Caleb Deschanel
Music by: James Horner
Sound: Louis Marion
Editing: Michael Kahn
Art Direction: Isabelle Guay
Costumes: Joanna Johnston, Odette Gadoury
Production Design: James Bissell
MPAA rating: PG
Running time: 97 minutes

REVIEWS

Chicago Sun-Times Online. February 14, 2008.
Entertainment Weekly Online. February 13, 2008.
Hollywood Reporter Online. February 11, 2008.
Los Angeles Times Online. February 14, 2008.
New York Times Online. February 14, 2008.
San Francisco Chronicle. February 14, 2008, p. E1.
Variety Online. February 10, 2008.
Village Voice Online. February 12, 2008.

QUOTES

Thimbletack: "You don't see us, now you do, but only if we want you to."

TRIVIA

The fake title "Widow" was used on prints shipped to theaters.

THE SPIRIT

Down these mean streets a man must come. A hero born, murdered, and born again.
—Movie tagline

My city screams. She is my lover. And I am her spirit.
—Movie tagline

I'm gonna kill you all kinds of dead.
—Movie tagline

Box Office: $19.8 million

Will Eisner (1917–2005) is one of the most influential graphic artists, helping the medium make the slow transition from comic books to graphic novels. One of his most devout disciples is Frank Miller, who helped revitalize the flagging Batman franchise. To filmgoers Miller is best known as the writer and co-director, with Robert Rodriguez, of *Sin City* (2005), based on his graphic-novel series. For his first film as solo director, Miller has chosen *The Spirit,* inspired by the groundbreaking comics Eisner created from 1940 to 1952. Eisner's stories of his masked crimefighter mix mystery, horror, comedy, romance, and violence into a counterpart of the film noir genre evolving at the same time as the Spirit's adventures appeared. Miller's film struggles to blend these elements without much success.

After young policeman Denny Colt (Gabriel Macht) is shot to death, he is brought back to life, in an experiment, by the criminal scientist known as the Octopus (Samuel L. Jackson). Denny then becomes the Spirit who fights crime in Central City, occasionally butting heads with the dastardly Octopus. The plot, such as it is, of *The Spirit* has something to do with the Octopus's efforts to locate a vase of blood that will make him immortal, while the Spirit and Sand Saref (Eva Mendes), Denny's childhood sweetheart turned master criminal, try to stop him.

Miller keeps jumping back and forth between several characters in such a way that it is difficult to know how each element fits in with the others. For example, Plaster of Paris (Paz Vega), one of the Octopus's cohorts, rescues the Spirit from her boss only to try to kill him immediately for no obvious reason. While graphic novels may consist of long segments, such an endless stream of lengthy scenes, especially the flashbacks of the teenaged Denny (Johnny Simmons) and Sand (Seychelle Gabriel), grows wearing in a film. Like the artist he is, Miller knows how to compose shots but never establishes a rhythm for the film. The tone constantly shifts from action-packed to poignant, such as the scenes with Ellen Dolan (Sarah Paulson), the doctor filled with unrequited love for the hero, to camp, as the Octopus and his main aide, Silken Floss (Scarlett Johansson), attire themselves in different costumes, including Nazi regalia, for each appearance.

Macht does as well as he can, but Miller gives him little to do but grin, grimace, and fall. Some of the actors, especially Stana Katic as an enthusiastic rookie cop, seem to be deliberately bad. When she looks back on her career, Johansson, who delivers her lines in a monotonous drone, may want to expunge *The Spirit* from her resume. A true connoisseur of comic-book art, Miller appears interested in Mendes and Johansson primarily for their seam-straining pulchritude. Jackson, however, seems, as always, to be having a great time. Unfortunately, his sense of joy is missing from the rest of the film.

The main virtue of *The Spirit,* as with *Sin City,* is its monochromatic look. Beautifully shot by Bill Pope, who has dealt both with noir, in *Bound* (1996), and with superheroes, in *Spider-Man 2* (2004), the film blends sepia, white, and black with splotches of other colors, usually red, in each scene. Marvelous to behold, *The Spirit* is empty at its core.

Michael Adams

CREDITS

The Spirit/Denny Colt: Gabriel Macht
The Octopus: Samuel L. Jackson
Silken Floss: Scarlett Johansson
Sand Saref: Eva Mendes
Lorelei Rox: Jaime King
Plaster of Paris: Paz Vega
Ellen Dolan: Sarah Paulson
Morgenstern: Stana Katic
Mahmoud: Eric Balfour
Commissioner Dolan: Dan Lauria
Young Spirit: Johnny Simmons
Young Sand: Seychelle Gabriel
Origin: USA
Language: English
Released: 2008
Production: Deborah Del Prete, Gigi Pritzker, Michael Uslan; Odd Lot Entertainment; released by Lionsgate
Directed by: Frank Miller

Written by: Frank Miller
Cinematography by: Bill Pope
Music by: David Newman
Sound: David Brownlow
Music Supervisor: Dan Hubbert
Editing: Gregory Nussbaum
Art Direction: Rosario Provenza
Costumes: Michael Dennison
MPAA rating: PG-13
Running time: 102 minutes

REVIEWS

Boston Globe Online. December 25, 2008.
Chicago Sun-Times Online. December 23, 2008.
Entertainment Weekly Online. December 23, 2008.
Hollywood Reporter Online. December 18, 2008.
Los Angeles Times Online. December 25, 2008.
New York Times Online. December 25, 2008.
San Francisco Chronicle. December 25, 2008, p. E8.
Variety Online. December 18, 2008.
Washington Post. December 25, 2008, p. C5.

QUOTES

Ellen Dolan: "You're in love with every women you meet, Mr. Spirit. You say lovely things to all of us and you mean every word you say."

TRIVIA

The film was shot on green screen over 50 days.

STANDARD OPERATING PROCEDURE

> *The war on terror will be photographed.*
> —Movie tagline

Filmmaker Errol Morris, the recipient of a MacArthur "genius" grant, is the Academy Award®-winning director of *The Fog of War* (2003), a documentary focused on former defense secretary Robert McNamara and his attempt to come to grips with his own complicity in escalating the war in Vietnam, and other well-regarded documentaries. His breakthrough film, *The Thin Blue Line* (1989), was the first film ever to save a man from death row. Morris is an artist of conscience who takes very seriously the political responsibility of being a documentary filmmaker. For the documentary film *Standard Operating Procedure*, Morris collaborated with Philip Gourevitch, the award-winning author of *We Wish to Inform You That Tomorrow We Will Be Killed with our Families: Stories from Rwanda*, on the film's

companion book. Both men confront grim subjects without flinching. *Standard Operating Procedure* documents the abuse of prisoners in the Abu Ghraib military prison facility in Iraq by Military Police and generally anonymous CIA operatives. The film captures the grotesque laughter of the guards at the expense of the prisoners.

In the eyes of the world, America was defined by Guantánamo Bay after the invasion of Iraq, not only by the U.S. presence in Guantánamo, but by the U.S. military's activities and interrogations there. Since 2004, however, the obvious symbol of American arrogance and abuse shifted to a prison facility some twenty miles outside Baghdad called Abu Ghraib, where suspected terrorists and dissidents were held, interrogated, and tortured. Of course, this is not new information. The story of this prison scandal was originally written by the investigative journalist Seymour M. Hersh, first published in the *New Yorker* magazine, then in his 2004 book *Chain of Command: The Road from 9/11 to Abu Ghraib.* In the shocked aftermath, other books followed, including Mark Danner's *Torture and Truth: America, Abu Ghraib, and the War on Terror.* The military term used by one soldier in response to objections to the outrageous treatment of prisoners gives Morris's documentary film its title.

The scandal of Abu Ghraib and the allegations of torture used by the Central Intelligence Agency and the U.S. military in Iraq and elsewhere was one of the biggest news stories to have come out of the second American invasion and occupation of Iraq. The story is too big for one documentary film, as witnessed by the additional footage included in the DVD edition, and by the fact that Morris and Gourevitch also published a book to back up the documentary. There can be no doubt that prisoners were brutalized and tortured, many for no reason other than the fact that they were in the wrong place at the wrong time and were swept into prison without sufficient cause. The other message that the film makes clear is that low-ranking soldiers, totally underprepared for the responsibilities given them, were turned into scapegoats after the photographs of abused prisoners had been released and published. Obviously, somebody had to be punished, if not exactly brought to justice.

Morris's exposé of prisoner abuse at Iraq's Abu Ghraib facility takes its title from a statement by Pfc. Lynndie England and others, who told the camera what happened at Abu Ghraib was simply "standard operating procedure." Morris interviewed other soldiers besides England, including Cpl. Charles Graner, who fathered a child with England, and with other eyewitnesses, such as

Specialists Sabrina Harman and Megan Ambuhl, all of whom were eventually court-martialed. The companion book deplores the abuses and explores the context in greater detail, but as the film director told *Variety:* "The idea of the film came out of the photographs," captured by three cameras, each confirming the abuses documented by the others. "When we reflect on this war," Morris continued, "these photographs will be the iconic photographs of the war. The idea was to interview the people who are either in the photographs or took the photographs and to tell a story about that."

In 2003 the American military took over the running of prisons in Iraq, assigning this duty to combat units of the military police. Abu Ghraib was a logical prison site, built to American specifications by German contractors working for Saddam Hussein. Specialist Ambuhl was one of seven M.P.'s assigned to guard duty in a prison that housed over 1,000 prisoners. "They couldn't say we broke the rules because there were no rules," she told Morris. "We had no training, we were vastly outnumbered and we were given lots of responsibilities that we didn't have any knowledge about how to carry out," she added. When he arrived at Abu Ghraib, Maj. Gen. Geoffrey Miller told the guards, "You're treating the prisoners too well. You have to treat the prisoners like dogs." Guard dogs were used as instruments of terror to frighten and intimidate the prisoners. The military police were inventive in finding other ways to brutalize and humiliate the prisoners as well.

Morris and Gourevitch find precedence for prisoner abuse at the interrogation center of Bagram Air Force base in Afghanistan in 2003, where Army First Lt. Carolyn Wood established a policy that permitted prisoners to be held in solitary confinement for a month, stripped, shackled, and sleep-deprived. Even though three prisoners were beaten to death on her watch, she was awarded a Bronze Star, promoted to captain, and sent to Iraq. Miller came to Iraq following his command at the Guantánamo facility in Cuba, where military police did the bidding of military interrogators, C.I.A. operatives, and civilian contractors.

The tie-in book, *Standard Operating Procedure,* was also excerpted in the *New Yorker*, which featured a profile entitled "Exposure" of Specialist Sabrina Harman, "the woman behind the camera at Abu Ghraib." The disturbing photographs taken at the prison facility by Harman and others gave the torture story high definition and traction in even the mainstream media, but by the time the Morris documentary had been released, these pictures were old news, no less disturbing for all that, but embarrassing and shameful to the national honor. Perhaps for this reason the Morris documentary was generally ignored by the moviegoing public and the film sank at the box office, unable to compete with a huge summer serving of trivial, entertaining, cartoonish action-spectacles.

The film's reception by major film critics was generally good. After suggesting that Morris might deserve the Medal of Freedom, *Time* magazine critic Richard Corliss accurately predicted that *Standard Operating Procedure* "will reach only the art-house audience." *Washington Post* reviewer Stephen Hunter was among the naysayers, however, finding the film a disappointment, "full of inferences that higher-ups tacitly approved of the near-torture and extremely intensive ill-treatment meant to intimidate the prisoners into cooperation," but, he thought, lacking definitive proof of torture. Hunter was disappointed that Graner, the presumed ring-leader, was "the missing voice in this film, denied the latitude to contribute by the military that is holding him in prison for ten years." Oddly enough, for Hunter that prison sentence apparently "proved" nothing. Other criticism focused on the behind-the-scenes production techniques. In the *New York Times*, for example, Manohla Dargis noted that the film's credits included "a costume designer, a wardrobe stylist, six hair and make-up people, an action consultant, an armorer, five set designers, seven animal handlers [for the dogs used to intimidate prisoners], ten prop makers, thirty-three cast members, and Danny Elfman, the long-time composer for [director] Tim Burton"—an unusual number of supporting people in these particular tasks for a documentary production. Dargis concluded that the film's "costly-looking production values, special effects and elaborately choreographed re-enactments suggest that Mr. Morris has grown weary of working in the margins to which documentary filmmakers are still too often relegated." Dargis criticized the Morris method, however, for not really going anywhere. Lynndie England, for example, photographed with a naked prisoner on a dog-leash, was merely "like all the other low-ranking soldiers caught up in this film." In the filmed interviews, she says "next to nothing of interest, not only because she appears to have been a cog in a much larger military machine, but also because Mr. Morris's approach here is profoundly nondialectic," refusing "to challenge or engage her beyond a question about her age."

Another frequently interviewed soldier was Harman, who took many of the incriminating photographs, and most memorably had her own picture taken with the corpse of Manadel al-Jamadi, a prisoner killed while in CIA custody, flashing a smile and posing with her thumbs up. "Sabrina is not a monster," Morris told the magazine *Mother Jones,* refusing to pigeonhole this soldier who looks like an all-American girl involved in some very un-American antics. Morris warned that "it is easy to confuse photographs with reality." Morris described the photographs as "both an exposé and a cover-up," adding, "For the left, the photos [bear] the unmistakable fingerprints of Rumsfeld, Cheney, and Bush. For the right, it's these bad actors who acted on their own. Both interpretations fail to look beyond the photographs themselves to the reality of that place." Morris claimed that Harman, "under another set of circumstances," would have been given a Pulitzer Prize. Of course, *Standard Operating Procedure* is by no means an "objective" documentary. The editors of *Mother Jones* pointed out that in 2004, Morris "made dozens of brilliantly simple pro-Kerry, anti-Bush spots for MoveOn.org," but he found the experience of working with political consultants frustrating. Under better circumstances, Morris thought he could have improved the Kerry image, which seemed "robotic and wooden": "In fact, I think I could have turned him back into a person." But Morris never had the chance. *Standard Operating Procedure* gave him another opportunity to make a point about the Bush administration and its values.

James M. Welsh

CREDITS

Origin: USA

Language: English

Released: 2008

Production: Julie Bilson Ahlberg, Errol Morris; Participant Productions; released by Sony Pictures Classics

Directed by: Errol Morris

Written by: Errol Morris

Cinematography by: Robert Chappell, Robert Richardson

Music by: Danny Elfman

Sound: Jeremy Bowker, Pete Horner

Editing: Andrew Grieve, Daniel Mooney, Steven Hathaway

Costumes: Marina Draghici

Production Design: Steve Hardie

MPAA rating: R

Running time: 116 minutes

REVIEWS

Boston Globe Online. May 2, 2008.

Chicago Sun-Times Online. May 1, 2008.

Entertainment Weekly Online. April 17, 2008.

Hollywood Reporter Online. February 14, 2008.

Los Angeles Times Online. May 2, 2008.

New York Times Online. April 25, 2008.

San Francisco Chronicle. May 9, 2008, p. E8.

Variety Online. February 12, 2008.

Washington Post. May 23, 2008, p. C1.

TRIVIA

This is the first documentary to be nominated for the Golden Bear at the Berlin Film Festival.

STAR WARS: THE CLONE WARS

Box Office: $35.1 million

Something happened on the way to George Lucas's plan to do nine feature-length film episodes of his *Star Wars* saga. First, of course, he got interested in other projects after completing the first three films, which were actually episodes four through six. Then, when he returned to finish the three prequels, they met with mixed reviews, though they did great at the box office.

It is still not clear whether Lucas will ever attempt to do films seven through nine. It is much more likely now that if they are ever done, it will be as animated movies like the 2008 release *Star Wars: The Clone Wars*. This film covers a period of time that takes place between episodes two and three. The clone wars are often mentioned in the other episodes, but never fully explored.

The new feature movie was timed to coincide with the release of an identically named television series that will explore the same characters and the wars. The movie itself covers a period near the beginning of the wars and concerns itself with the battle between the Jedi and the Separatists (the members of the Dark Side who will eventually become the Empire) for the loyalty of the Hutts, the mercenaries who control some of the "key trade routes along the outer rim of the galaxy." Specifically, the plot involves the kidnapping of the son of Jabba the Hutt, a scheme by the Separatists who seek to pin the blame on the Jedi.

Lucas authorized and produced this project, concocting an instant animated franchise as part of his *Star Wars* empire. Dave Filoni, a former storyboard artist and fairly inexperienced director of animated television programs, directed. More experienced animation writer Henry Gilroy wrote the script. The only actors from the live-action *Star Wars* movies to return as voice talent in this version are Samuel L. Jackson as Mace Windu, Anthony Daniels as C-3P0, and Christopher Lee as the villain Count Dooku, but all three of them have relatively minor roles. Almost all the other voice talent is virtually unknown. As Padmé Amidala, who also has a small part, Catherine Taber tries to sound exactly like Natalie Portman, who portrayed her in the live-action feature films. Tom Kane makes a decent Yoda.

The film revolves around Anakin Skywalker (voice of Matt Lanter), Obi-Wan Kenobi (voice of James Arnold Taylor), and a new character, Ahsoka Tano (voice of Ashley Eckstein), who is Anakin's new Padawan, or apprentice. It is a big question whether Anakin is really ready to have an apprentice; Obi-Wan thinks not, Yoda assures that he is, and Anakin himself is unclear. Audiences will come to side with Kenobi.

A bigger question for *Star Wars* fans—and the subject of an intense debate—is whether the galaxy is ready for the beloved epic sagas to be turned into a cartoon aimed at a younger audience. Many *Star Wars* aficionados found the new film disappointing. Right from the start, as a narrator replaces the usual written prologue crawl explaining the background, this version diverges from the seriousness of the Lucas films. But perhaps that is a good thing; after all, some would say the main problem with the whole saga (and especially episodes one through three) is that Lucas takes his story and his characters much too seriously. In this version, there is not much chance of that.

In many ways, however, *Star Wars* works better as an animated film. The characters and the dialogue, not to mention the unnecessarily convoluted yet basically simplistic plots, have always been rather cartoonish. The outlandish creatures can be animated just as successfully as being created animatronically, although it is true they lack the gee-whiz factor. Rather than walking among live actors, cartoonlike figures like Yoda and Jabba the Hutt (voice of Kevin Michael Richardson) interact with other cartoon figures.

Still, it is disconcerting to see the noble Obi-Wan Kenobi reduced to an unimaginatively drawn figure whose hair and beard appear to be fashioned of wood paneling. The animation style here tends to incorporate the worst of retro and modern cartooning. Kenobi is bland and unremarkable, hardly someone with the kind of gravitas *Star Wars* fans would expect of the character. He is also inexplicably British; referring to an enemy defensive device, he exclaims, "That shield is certainly putting a crimp in my day!" Also, Anakin has lost his angst and ambivalence and is portrayed as a straightforward action hero.

The film is fine when there are typical *Star Wars* battles, though they lack the grandeur of the other films. And the animators do a serviceable job with most of the aliens. The film is a bit of a pastiche, with brief nods to all corners of the Lucas creation, even including a jazz band of aliens. Unimaginatively, however, *The Clone Wars* makes far too much use of communication through holography, as characters are beaming their images for face-to-face conversations almost constantly. These encounters must seem rather clunky to young audiences. After all, what might have been fabulous in the 1970s

(even though most of Lucas's original ideas were not all that original) now seems commonplace.

But where the film goes terribly wrong in terms of critical weight is exactly where it probably is dead-on right in terms of target audience appeal: giving Anakin the sidekick Ahsoka. Ahsoka is in every possible way a Disney creation: multiracial in appearance, sassy in her repartee with Anakin, and having a bizarre hint of sexiness. She has hair that is silver and gray and looks like a snake that is swallowing two ram's horns; her eyes are as big as saucers and her lips are full and gray; painted on her face are what look like Native American hieroglyphics, and she is wearing knee-high boots, white tights, and a leather miniskirt. She is Bratz meets Pocahontas with a nod to nonhuman species.

Half the movie is filled with annoying, repetitious, and entirely unsurprising banter between the smart, mouthy young apprentice and the confident, ready-for-anything hero who is teaching her how to be cool under fire. Ahsoka is by turns impetuous, smart, and heroic, but still, she learns how to obey. Anakin is by turns scolding and begrudgingly approving. In short, *Star Wars: The Clone Wars* is like almost every Disney movie of the last generation, pairing a spunky female character with a worthy verbal sparring partner. And together they triumph: youth over experience. It seems like a sure-fire recipe for a hit TV series, but it does not make for a thrilling movie experience. In fact, *Star Wars: The Clone Wars* is a dud: its special effects are not special at all, its animation is disappointingly middle-of-the-road, and the dialogue is as wooden as Obi-Wan's hair. Perhaps this is where the saga was meant to go all along: back to its roots but without the panache of newly recycled pleasure.

Michael Betzold

CREDITS

Anakin Skywalker: Matt Lanter (Voice)
Yoda/Narrator/Yularen: Tom Kane (Voice)
Chancellor Palpatine/Darth Sidious: Ian Abercrombie (Voice)
Jabba the Hutt: Kevin M. Richardson (Voice)
Ahsoka Tano: Ashley Eckstein (Voice)
Obi-Wan Kenobi: James Arnold Taylor (Voice)
Mace Windu: Samuel L. Jackson (Voice)
C-3PO: Anthony Daniels (Voice)
Count Dooku: Christopher Lee (Voice)
Gen. Loathsom/Ziro the Hutt: Corey Burton (Voice)
Padmé Amidala: Catherine Taber (Voice)
Origin: USA
Language: English
Released: 2008
Production: Catherine Winder; Lucasfilm Animation; released by Warner Bros.

Directed by: Dave Filoni
Written by: Henry Gilroy, Steven Melching, Scott Murphy
Music by: Kevin Kiner
Sound: Matthew Wood
Editing: Jason W. A. Tucker
MPAA rating: PG
Running time: 98 minutes

REVIEWS

Boston Globe Online. August 15, 2008.
Chicago Sun-Times Online. August 14, 2008.
Entertainment Weekly Online. August 15, 2008.
Hollywood Reporter Online. August 10, 2008.
Los Angeles Times Online. August 15, 2008.
New York Times Online. August 15, 2008.
San Francisco Chronicle. August 15, 2008, p. E1.
Variety Online. August 10, 2008.
Wall Street Journal. August 15, 2008, p. W1.
Washington Post. August 15, 2008, p. C1.

QUOTES

Anakin Skywalker: "The desert is merciless. It takes everything from you."

AWARDS

Nomination:

Golden Raspberries 2008: Worst Sequel/Prequel.

STEP BROTHERS

They grow up so fast.
—Movie tagline

Box Office: $100.4 million

Will Ferrell and John C. Reilly have made a mint playing men who simply refuse to grow up in films like *Semi-Pro* (2008) and *Walk Hard: The Dewey Cox Story* (2007). They struck box office gold together in *Talladega Nights: The Ballad of Ricky Bobby* (2006). Even their most mentally deficient characters might be turned off by the antics of Dale Doback and Brennan Huff, the two latest overgrown children that Ferrell and Reilly bring to the big screen in *Step Brothers,* a film that also reunites them with *Talladega Nights* director Adam McKay. Produced by the comedy king du jour, Judd Apatow, and co-written by McKay and Ferrell, *Step Brothers* is a sporadically funny but always original laughfest that succeeds because of its creative team's willingness to go to any end to make their audience laugh. McKay and Ferrell use such a rapid-fire, improvisational

style that every joke that misses its mark is matched by at least one that hits home. More widely hit-and-miss than nearly any comedy of 2008, *Step Brothers* features some material that hits the floor with a laugh-free thud, but also includes some of the more inspired humor of the year. Like most family relationships, *Step Brothers* is a love/hate affair with the former winning out in the comedic end.

Ferrell plays Brennan Huff, an overly emotional man-child who still lives with his mother, Nancy (Mary Steenburgen), even though he has only one year until the big four-zero. Before the credits have even finished rolling, Nancy has met the charming Robert (Richard Jenkins) and married him. It turns out that Robert has a homebound son of his own, the raunchy and unusual Dale (John C. Reilly), who now has a stepbrother as a rival for his dad's affection. Like ten-year-old boys given free license to swear and look at dirty magazines without hiding them from their parents, Dale and Brennan are every parent's nightmare—the child who will not only never leave home but never leave prolonged adolescence.

When Dale and Brennan first encounter one another they do so in the manner that most preteen boys would—with malice in their testosterone-driven hearts. Dale tries to lay down the law in his house, threatening Brennan against touching his coveted drum set. Of course, telling a preteen boy not to do something only starts the clock ticking until they eventually do, and these guys are nothing if not preteen boys in grown men's bodies. Dale and Brennan swear, fight, and threaten each other's lives as any stepbrothers would, if they were in the sixth grade. Only after Brennan's successful biological brother, Derek (Adam Scott), enters the picture do the step brothers bond in their hatred for the obnoxious other relative. The best way to get fighting brothers to unite is to give them a common enemy. After an unusual turn of events, Brennan and Dale are forced to try to keep their family together, even if that means going to therapy, getting a real job, and living a "normal" life.

Dale and Brennan come from a long line of cinematic man-children that includes Steve Martin's Navin Johnson in *The Jerk* (1979), Jim Carrey's Lloyd Christmas in *Dumb and Dumber* (1994), and more than one character already played by Ferrell and/or Reilly; but these guys go a step farther in the abrasiveness of their personalities. At first, the two actors push the envelope a bit too far, playing the brothers as guys who are not just a little unaware of the way the world works but possibly in need of some mental help. The opening act of *Step Brothers* is too in-your-face with its man-child themes and makes the pair too hard to root for. But writers Ferrell and McKay wisely turn Dale and Brennan from enemies to friends, and *Step Brothers* finds a more consistently enjoyable groove. They too often dip their comedic pen in the gross-out humor well (no one ever needs to see a grown man lick dog poop or wipe himself with the bathroom rug), but every moment of predictable lowbrow humor in *Step Brothers* is matched by something unexpected and very funny. There are jokes and improvised asides in *Step Brothers* that rank with some of the funniest scenes of the year, and the go-for-broke glee with which Ferrell and Reilly approach the material is infectious. Even the supporting cast (Jenkins and Kathryn Hahn, as Alice, nearly steal the movie) find moments of unexpected comic brilliance. Like any improv show, some of the jokes fall flat, but *Step Brothers* is a comedy that is never boring and more often funny than not, two things that have not been easy to say about most of the genre's offerings in 2008 and even much of the previous work of the people involved.

Brian Tallerico

CREDITS

Brennan Huff: Will Ferrell
Dale Doback: John C. Reilly
Nancy Huff: Mary Steenburgen
Dr. Robert Doback: Richard Jenkins
Derek: Adam Scott
Alice: Kathryn Hahn
Denise: Andrea Savage
Origin: USA
Language: English
Released: 2008
Production: Jimmy Miller, Judd Apatow; Columbia Pictures, Relativity Media, Mosaic Media Group; released by Sony Pictures Entertainment
Directed by: Adam McKay
Written by: Will Ferrell, Adam McKay
Cinematography by: Oliver Wood
Music by: Jon Brion
Sound: Art Rochester
Music Supervisor: Hal Willner
Editing: Brent White
Art Direction: Virginia Randolph Weaver
Costumes: Susan Matheson
Production Design: Clayton Hartley
MPAA rating: R
Running time: 95 minutes

REVIEWS

Boston Globe Online. July 25, 2008.
Chicago Sun-Times Online. July 24, 2008.
Entertainment Weekly Online. July 24, 2008.
Hollywood Reporter Online. July 24, 2008.
Los Angeles Times Online. July 25, 2008.
New York Times Online. July 25, 2008.
Rolling Stone Online. August 7, 2008.
San Francisco Chronicle. July 24, 2008, p. E1.
Variety Online. July 24, 2008.
Washington Post. July 25, 2008, p. C1.

QUOTES

Denise: "Brennan, I thought you were incredibly brave. And I mean that in strictly the most clinical and professional sense possible, with no emotional, intimate, sexual, or any other undertones that you could possibly infer."

TRIVIA

The bogus title "The Insane Team" was used when prints were shipped to theaters.

STEP UP 2 THE STREETS

It's not where you're from. It's where you're at.
—Movie tagline

Box Office: $58 million

Touchstone's *Step Up* was a shockingly big hit for the studio in the summer of 2006, which meant, especially considering the dance genre's growing popularity and relatively minuscule budget, that a sequel was inevitable. Despite the undeniable flaws of *Step Up,* the completely unexpected success of the film made it feel at least a little distinctive in a season of predictable teen sex movies. By the very fact that it is a sequel, *Step Up 2 the Streets* had an uphill battle when it came to originality, but it still feels entirely derivative and made solely to get fans of the original to open their wallet one more time. Without stars Jenna Dewan and Channing Tatum (except for a small cameo at the beginning by the latter that practically steals the movie), *Step Up 2 the Streets* almost feels like a cheap remake of the original with the genders reversed. The message, to quote the film's heroine—"It's not about what you got. It's what you make of what you got"— is essentially the same, but the stars are significantly less charismatic and the story is about as predictable as a paint-by-numbers picture. Dance thrives on its unpredictability, its ability to inspire by throwing something beautiful at the audience that they never thought they would see coming. *Step Up 2 the Streets* is as predictable a dance routine as Hollywood has released in years.

One of the few real changes from original to sequel made in the production of *Step Up 2 the Streets* was the switching of the gender roles. The first one was basically another modern take on *Romeo and Juliet*, with the blue-collar boy proving he could not only hold his own on the dance floor with the more refined female dancer but win her heart as well. This time, the streetwise character is a girl named Andie (Briana Evigan), who rolls with a group of street dancers called "The 410" in the streets of Baltimore. Her guardian gives her an ultimatum that leads her to audition for and surprisingly get accepted by the Maryland School of the Arts (MSA). There she meets Chase (Robert Hoffman), the more traditional modern dancer who is just looking for a way to break out of the MSA rut and do something more daring than a plié. After missing one rehearsal too many, Andie gets the boot from her group of street dancers and, after some convincing by Chase, forms her own crew with the outcasts of MSA. The new group of unlikely hoofers hopes to compete in the underground dancing competition known only as "the streets" but is thwarted by traditional teachers, angry competitors, and their own self-doubts. Outside of some energetic dance sequences, almost nothing that follows this set-up will come as a surprise to anyone who has ever seen a movie like *Step Up 2 the Streets* before, certainly not to fans of the original.

There is something to be said for doing something predictable well—dozens of good movies do it every year—but *Step Up 2 the Streets* does not even live up to that meager standard. The leads are, for lack of a kinder way to put it, annoyingly dull. Andie is supposed to be a firecracker, an inspiration to everyone she encounters, including her friends, crew, and love interest. When Andie steps up at the end to give a climactic speech, the part calls for an actress with screen presence to burn, one who will lift the audience over the derivative, predictable scenes to actual inspiration. Briana Evigan is an undeniable beauty and she can dance (or at least sell the scenes where her double stands in) with the best of recent genre stars, but as an actress she is disappointingly flat. The romance, the struggle of teenage years, the self-doubt—Evigan fails to give three-dimensional believability to a single element of this character. Her speech at the end is clearly supposed to be inspirational, but it comes off nearly laughable in its complete lack of energy. And her chemistry with Hoffman is nearly nonexistent.

Sequels often feel like an inferior version of their original, but rarely does it feel so much like that was nearly the intention of the production. The original director, writer, and cast refused to come back, making *Step Up 2 the Streets* nothing more than a blatant attempt to get fans of the original to pay for nearly the same film with less talented people making

it. They could have more accurately called it "Step Down."

Brian Tallerico

CREDITS

Andie: Briana Evigan
Chase Collins: Robert Hoffman
Blake Collins: Will Kemp
Sarah: Sonja Sohn
Tyler Gage: Channing Tatum
Moose: Adam G. Sevani
Sophie: Cassie Ventura
Origin: USA
Language: English
Released: 2008
Production: Patrick Waschsberger, Erik Feig, Adam Shankman, Jennifer Gibgot; Touchstone Pictures, Summit Entertainment, Offspring Entertainment; released by Walt Disney Studios
Directed by: John M. Chu
Written by: Toni Johnson, Karen Barna
Cinematography by: Max Malkin
Music by: Aaron Zigman
Sound: Jim Stuebe, Richard Van Dyke
Music Supervisor: Buck Damon
Editing: Andrew Marcus, Nicholas Erasmus
Art Direction: Paul D. Kelly
Costumes: Luca Mosca
Production Design: Devorah Herbert
MPAA rating: PG-13
Running time: 98 minutes

REVIEWS

Chicago Sun-Times Online. February 14, 2008.
Entertainment Weekly Online. February 13, 2008.
Hollywood Reporter Online. February 14, 2008.
Los Angeles Times Online. February 14, 2008.
New York Times Online. February 14, 2008.
San Francisco Chronicle Online. February 14, 2008.
Variety Online. February 13, 2008.

QUOTES

Andie: "Look, the streets is about where you're from. It's not some school talent show. There's no spring floors. There's no spotlights to use what you got and…what makes you think you got it, huh?"

TRIVIA

The director, Jon Chu, can be seen during the crew-recruiting montage rehearsing with a stunt double.

STOP-LOSS

The bravest place to stand is by each other's side.
—Movie tagline

Box Office: $10.9 million

Among the recent films dealing with the Iraq War, Kimberly Peirce's *Stop-Loss* is the first to concentrate on the delicate and little-publicized story of military personnel who want to get out of a return trip to Iraq but cannot do so legally. It is also one of the grittier, more realistic, and tougher movies about the controversial conflict and its effects on the people who have served in it.

The overlooked film *In the Valley of Elah* (2007) was the first major Hollywood production to examine the effects of the war on the behavior and psychology of returning American soldiers. The subject matter of *Stop-Loss* is similar but more complex, and this film also has a protagonist who suffers a stunning disillusionment with his country. In the former film, the character played by Tommy Lee Jones is a career military man who is awakened to the particularly devastating effects of service in Iraq when his son is at the center of a tragedy. In *Stop-Loss,* Sergeant Brandon King (Ryan Phillippe) experiences a similar arc, going from "gung-ho" to "hell-no."

Nobody in either film is a peacenik or in any sense softhearted about the conflict, and that adds to the intensity of the transformations of the protagonists. But *Stop-Loss* seems not a bit contrived. Peirce laces her depiction of the war in the opening scene with the hip-hop soundtrack and video camera vignettes one would expect from a movie produced by MTV Films. Peirce thrusts her viewers right into street fighting in Tikrit, where King and his men are guarding a checkpoint. When a vehicle provokes them by opening fire, King pursues the attackers through the streets of the town (the film was shot in a village in Morocco, but the locale is very convincing). Eventually, the Americans are ambushed in an alley, and one of King's squad is killed while another is seriously wounded.

This opening sequence is gripping and distressing, economically and brutally illustrating how difficult it is for the American soldiers to fight in the fog of a guerrilla street war. From there, the script by Peirce and Mark Richard rockets straight to a weekend leave as King and company return to their small rural Texas hometown. It is a veritable orgy of patriotism and barely restrained lust as girlfriends and townsfolk greet the returning heroes with very open arms. (Strangely, Peirce, who is best known for the gender-bending drama *Boys Don't Cry* [1999], does not acknowledge that a significant number of women are serving in the Iraq conflict; the American soldiers in the film are almost all male.)

But while their relatives and friends on the home front see the war as a great cause and their boys as unabashed heroes, the soldiers themselves are badly damaged. King is awarded a Purple Heart, but his ac-

ceptance speech to the assembled townsfolk starts to wander off. His best friend and comrade in arms, Steve Shriver (Channing Tatum) gets so drunk that he slaps around his fiancée Michelle (Abbie Cornish) and digs himself into a hole in her front yard, clutching his gun and thinking himself back in a combat zone. Another friend in the squad, Tommy Burgess (Joseph Gordon-Levitt), also drinks himself into a stupor and behaves so badly that his new bride jilts him. In the morning, the men assemble at a ranch and Tommy takes his heretofore unopened wedding gifts, unwraps them, and uses them for target practice. Expensive glassware explodes as the boys grunt in satisfaction.

For a while, Peirce is content to let the tensions simmer and use these incidents to illustrate how violent and disturbed the returning soldiers are. They seem barely capable of living in civilized society, even in as welcoming and gun-happy a milieu as rural Texas. Between fevered nightmares about the ambush he led his men into, Brandon is torn between remorse and anger, but he is clear-headed about one thing: He has done his duty for his country, and no one can deny that. Now he wants to get out.

There is only one problem with that plan: On the day he thinks he is going to be discharged, he is "stop-lossed" back for another tour of duty. Brandon argues that the president cannot do that to him, because he has already famously declared that the war was over in his "mission accomplished" statement. Convinced he is being unfairly treated, Brandon runs off the base and, to the horror of his buddy Steve, goes AWOL.

Brandon concocts an ill-conceived plan to go to Washington and see the congressman who promised him at the welcome-home reception that if Brandon ever needed anything, just ask. The politician has since flown back to D.C., but Brandon decides to drive there to meet him. Michelle volunteers to drive with him: she is sick of being mistreated by Steve and needs an escape of her own.

Thus unfolds a bleak and hopeless road trip that is the finest part of this brave movie. The cross-country saga is an American cinematic and literary tradition, but here it is transformed into a fugitive flight that symbolizes our national ambivalence about the war. The man so recently hailed as a hero is now a criminal at large, pursued by police and his own friends. His credibility as a fighter is secure, but he is on an emotional hair trigger: seeing shapes of his fallen buddies in a motel swimming pool, then lining up a couple of street thugs who have broken into his car and stolen a few things as if he were going to execute them for the assassination of his men. Michelle's tough-skinned acceptance of Brandon keeps him barely reined in and functioning.

Along the way to Washington, Brandon stops to see firsthand the results of his bad decisions in Iraq. He visits the parents of his deceased subordinate, explaining to them how he died, but while doing so he is ridiculed by the dead man's brother. Later, Brandon visits a military hospital and meets his wounded comrade Rico (Victor Rasuk), who has now lost two legs, an arm, half his face, and his vision. Rico is surprisingly upbeat and grateful for his visit. Rasuk's performance is stunning, and the entire scene, including a brief sequence in which Michelle plays pool against a wounded soldier with prosthetic legs, is unforgettable—and extremely difficult to watch. The matter-of-fact way in which the characters interact though they are so badly wounded captures a new reality of the Iraq war: the huge number of soldiers who have returned home disabled.

Brandon also encounters a fellow escapee who is tired of being on the run with his wife and child and, after fifteen months of wandering, being unwelcome in the land he defended, has decided to move to Canada. He gives Brandon the phone number of a New York lawyer who will help Brandon escape the same way, for a fee. By then it has become clear that the congressman will not help Brandon because he is a fugitive, so New York becomes the new destination.

This is a tough movie, and Peirce will not stop the pain for any romance. As played by Cornish, Michelle is as tough as the soldiers in her life, and will only admit to her unsuitability for being an army wife after chugging down several tequilas. It is clear that she and Brandon have the chance to form a new relationship, but it is as chancy and uncertain as Brandon's flight, which ends up having no viable exit.

If we compare this film to the films that came out in the 1970s about Vietnam, it is most apt to compare it to *The Deer Hunter* (1978), which was controversial because its take on the conflict at home was not one-sided. And neither does *Stop-Loss* allow its viewers the luxury of a satisfying solution. Peirce's film is uncompromising, brave, and instructive.

For anyone whose view of Ryan Phillippe was shaped by some of his earlier, flimsier roles, *Stop-Loss* should be another revelation, coming on the heels of other impressive performances in *Crash* (2004), *Flags of Our Fathers* (2006) and *Breach* (2007). His performance here is gritty, nuanced, and extremely compelling. His Brandon King is a genuine man of convictions set adrift and feeling betrayed, but he is also troubled and compromised. Like many war veterans, he is haunted by feelings of intense guilt for the actions he took and the mistakes he has made. Peirce's unique ending is not storybook, and when we last glimpse Phillippe as Brandon, our hearts and minds are straining to make sense out of

our own similar fog of war. And that is why *Stop-Loss* should be mandatory viewing. Except for its overindulgence of MTV-style techniques, Peirce's film is exceptionally realistic, courageous, and complex, as are her characters, and Phillippe's Brandon should rightly be one of modern cinema's most iconic and memorable heroes, broken but proud, a believable casualty of the Iraq adventure.

Michael Betzold

CREDITS

Brandon King: Ryan Phillippe
Michele: Abbie Cornish
Steve Shriver: Channing Tatum
Tommy Burgess: Joseph Gordon-Levitt
Roy King: Ciaran Hinds
Lt. Col. Boot Miller: Timothy Olyphant
Sen. Orton Worrell: Josef Sommer
Rico Rodriguez: Victor Rasuk
Isaac Butler: Rob Brown
Jeanie: Mamie Gummer
Origin: USA
Language: English
Released: 2008
Production: Scott Rudin, Gregory Goodman, Kimberly Peirce, Mark Roybal; MTV Films; released by Paramount
Directed by: Kimberly Peirce
Written by: Kimberly Peirce, Mark Richard
Cinematography by: Chris Menges
Music by: John Powell
Sound: Danny Michael
Music Supervisor: Randall Poster, Jim Dunbar
Editing: Claire Simpson
Art Direction: Peter Borck
Costumes: Marlene Stewart
Production Design: David Wasco
MPAA rating: R
Running time: 112 minutes

REVIEWS

Austin Chronicle Online. March 28, 2008.
Boston Globe Online. March 28, 2008.
Chicago Sun-Times Online. March 28, 2008.
Entertainment Weekly Online. March 26, 2008.
Hollywood Reporter Online. March 17, 2008.
Los Angeles Times Online. March 28, 2008.
New York Times Online. March 28, 2008.
Rolling Stone Online. April 3, 2008.
San Francisco Chronicle. March 28, 2008, p. E1.

Variety Online. March 14, 2008.
Washington Post. March 28, 2008, p. C5.

QUOTES

Brandon King: "With the shortage of guys and no draft, they're shipping back soldiers who's supposed to be getting' out."

TRIVIA

There were reportedly nearly sixty-five drafts of the script.

STRANGE WILDERNESS

> *This ain't March of the Penguins.*
> —Movie tagline
>
> *If you love nature, and the outdoors, don't watch their show!*
> —Movie tagline

Box Office: $6.5 million

Steve Zahn, Jonah Hill, and Justin Long all had great years in 2007, earning just praise for their work in *Rescue Dawn, Superbad,* and *Live Free or Die Hard* respectively. Their recent success is worth noting because it makes their involvement in *Strange Wilderness* all the more shocking. *Strange Wilderness* is the kind of comedy that almost always pops up on an actor's resume on the downside of the roller coaster of fame, rarely as they are climbing the hill. Even the involvement of Ernest Borgnine, Harry Hamlin, Robert Patrick, and a few of the incredibly unfunny Happy Madison Productions regulars (Allen Covert, Peter Dante) feels like a step down for nearly every actor involved. *Strange Wilderness* never quite breaches the wall of good taste where comedy goes from just bad to offensively awful but only because the entire affair is too instantly forgettable to do so. The entire team behind *Strange Wilderness,* particularly the writers Peter Gaulke and Fred Wolf (who also directs), give the clear impression that they might have taken the stoner attitude of their comedy too much to heart and actually penned the film in an altered state. It is the only rational explanation as to how anyone could find this script funny.

In a move that feels designed to make plots hard to recap for critics (or just a sign of the filmmakers' complete lack of ingenuity), the lead characters in *Strange Wilderness* are named Peter Gaulke (Steve Zahn) and Fred Wolf (Allen Covert), the same as the writers and director of the film. Who Cooker (Jonah Hill), Junior (Justin Long), Whitaker (Kevin Heffernan), and Cheryl (Ashley Scott) might be on the other side of the fourth wall is a little less clear. In the movie, they are the team

that is trying to keep a wildlife program called, of course, "Strange Wilderness" alive. Like the film itself, the show is half-conceived and horribly written (for example, the team suggests that bears were named after the football team in Chicago and note that while bear attacks on salmon are common, the other way around is pretty rare). Naturally, the ratings for the show-within-a-movie are in steep decline and Peter and Fred's boss, Ed Lawson (Jeff Garlin), tells them that the cancellation axe is about to fall. The team needs one big story to save the show, and their desperation puts them on the trail of one of the most elusive creatures known to man, Bigfoot. Finding the hairy monster could be the only way to save the show.

Happy Madison Productions has developed a pattern of low-budget comedies made with incredibly little effort, including *Dickie Roberts: Former Child Star* (2003), *Grandma's Boy* (2006), and *The Benchwarmers* (2006). There is clearly no concern at all for quality, with each film actually topping the next in terms of low quality and effort. It will be hard to find any room in the barrel below *Strange Wilderness*. The film earned a stunning 0 percent rating on Rotten Tomatoes, meaning that not one working critic gave the film a positive review, and it ranked on Metacritic's list of the worst films ever reviewed. Joe Leydon of *Variety* said, "Obviously the product of minimal effort by all parties involved, *Strange Wilderness* is a slovenly, slapped-together stoner comedy." He was definitely in the majority, with Michael Rechtshaffen echoing the complaint, "Laughter is definitely an endangered species where *Strange Wilderness* is concerned." Alonso Duralde of MSNBC went possibly the farthest, saying, "February may be too early to start thinking about year-end lists, but frankly, I'll be shocked if I see ten movies in 2008 that are worse than *Strange Wilderness.*"

In a weird way, it could be argued that *Strange Wilderness* is made in the spirit of the show within the film and its cast of characters. After all, it is the story of a team of people who work together regularly, usually stoned, and with no clear idea what it is they are doing. The fact that the co-writers of *Strange Wilderness* named the two lead characters after themselves makes the comparison all the more apt. The entire production gives off the feeling that the clear lack of effort on everyone's part was not just the byproduct of laziness but the actual intention to do as little actual writing, acting, or work as possible. Only Zahn seems like he is putting any heart into his role, but even an actor as good as he can be cannot possibly overcome the flaws of a half-written script and a barely conceived project. Actually, watching the show-within-a-movie, which is conceived as an awful program, would be more fun than watching *Strange Wilderness* again. Bigfoot deserved better.

Brian Tallerico

CREDITS

Peter Gaulke: Steve Zahn
Fred Wolf: Allen Covert
Cooker: Jonah Hill
Whitaker: Kevin Heffernan
Cheryl: Ashley Scott
Junior: Justin Long
Danny: Peter Dante
Sky: Harry Hamlin
Gus: Robert Patrick
Bill: Joe Don Baker
Ed: Jeff Garlin
Milas: Ernest Borgnine
Origin: USA
Language: English
Released: 2008
Production: Peter Gaulke; Level 1 Entertainment, Happy Madison Productions; released by Paramount
Directed by: Fred Wolf
Written by: Fred Wolf, Peter Gaulke
Cinematography by: David Hennings
Music by: Waddy Wachtel
Sound: David MacMillan
Music Supervisor: Michael Dilbeck, Bryan Bonwell
Editing: Tom Costain
Costumes: Maya Lieberman
Production Design: Perry Andelin Blake
MPAA rating: R
Running time: 85 minutes

REVIEWS

Boston Globe Online. February 2, 2008.
Hollywood Reporter Online. February 4, 2008.
Los Angeles Times Online. February 4, 2008.
New York Times Online. February 2, 2008.
Variety Online. February 1, 2008.

QUOTES

Peter Gaulke (voiceover): "No matter how many sea lions are killed each year by sharks, it never seems like enough."

TRIVIA

The film's two main characters are named after the film's screenwriters.

THE STRANGERS

Lock the door. Pretend you're safe.
—Movie tagline

We tell ourselves there's nothing to fear—but sometimes, we're wrong.
—Movie tagline

Box Office: $52.5 million

The Strangers is the first film of Bryan Bertino, who worked as a lighting technician in the film industry before his horror script was sold to Universal. The story concerns the night of terror endured by Kristen McKay (Liv Tyler) and James Hoyt (Scott Speedman), who arrive late at a remote country house owned by James's parents. They are coming from a wedding where James unexpectedly proposed to Kristen and, more unexpectedly, was refused by her. Their stay at the house thus begins with awkward silences and broken sentences brought about in part by the scattered rose petals and fluted champagne glasses James had earlier set out to mark what he thought would be a celebration. Soon three mask-wearing strangers begin to terrorize Kristen and James. From the moment the strangers pound on the front door, the personalities of the two main characters recede, and the remainder of the film becomes an increasingly predictable exercise in terror.

The script may have been sold simply on the geography of its premise: how might one cinematically exploit space and sound in a mostly enclosed area as two people are relentlessly terrorized in the fashion of a Manson-like home invasion? As a limited exercise for an aspiring director, this premise elicits a few good touches from Bertino. What is more surprising is the commercial success of such a conceptually remedial and formulaic film with a near absence of attention to human character and personality. *The Strangers* earned over ninety million dollars (against a budget of nine million), a popularity that has led to a sequel in the works. This success may be indicative of the control that video game plotting currently exerts on the film industry and also of the attempt to create a film that is virtually all climax. After the brief exposition described above, *The Strangers* develops like an arcade game. The first act utilizes the driveway and the outside of the house as a landscape for fright. The middle act brings the killers inside the house, along with one of James's friends, to increase the possibilities of danger. The last act shifts the action to the adjacent barn as hope for escape mixes with the increasing fear of violent death. Each segment is less compelling than the previous one.

Gadgets and objects figure prominently. These props are used primarily to elicit fear from the menaced characters rather than to reveal their personality or their ingenuity at battling their attackers. A record player, for example, signals the presence of the killers inside the house when Kristen and James hide upstairs. The phonograph needle sticks on a groove of a country song and provides repeating and eerie contrast to the thud of murderous boots trudging through the living room. Other props—a smoke alarm, a malfunctioning cell phone, a flickering flashlight, a two-way radio in the barn—become the means for attempting to create terror in other scenes, but the initial premise, good for a scene or two of shivers, cannot sustain the entire film. Even at eighty-five minutes, the movie comes to feel overlong.

The visual style is somewhat predictable and clichéd, employing the shaky, ever-drifting camera and swish pans of "punk-rock cinema," as defined recently by director Guillermo del Toro. In addition, Bryan Bertino makes little effort to employ subjective camera angles for the main characters, the approach famously favored by Alfred Hitchcock. The subjective approach (that of a character's point of view) tends to make the audience identify with the character and, from seeing what the character sees, to infer the character's thoughts and feelings. In contrast to this method, Bertino often takes an objective approach, which usually dehumanizes the protagonists or visually foreshadows their harm. For example, at one point James's friend Mike (Glenn Howerton) arrives, has his windshield immediately shattered by a brick, and warily enters the quiet house looking for his friends. His tiptoe trek to the second floor mixes shots from objective angles that show Mike in the foreground being followed silently by the ax-wielding killer behind him with shots that subjectively show Mike from the killer's view. Other scenes adopt this same visual design. The overall effect places the emphasis on the anticipation of violence, as in the splatter films *Friday the 13th* (1980) and *The Last House on the Left* (1972), rather than on the emotions and humanity of the characters, as in the classics of suspense cinema. Bertino chose the less ambitious movie models to follow, and it shows in the emotional shallowness of his film.

The carefully prepared effects track, however, stands out and gives the film some of its most atmospheric touches. The thuds on the door and the trudging feet come at the audience with a ripe resonance and from unpredictable directions. It is, in fact, easier for the viewer to sense the characters' dread from the richly orchestrated soundtrack than from the haphazard editing and camera moves. Musical knife chords, in the fashion of a drama from the golden age of radio, punctuate the soundtrack and signal either red herrings or real threats. Such aural melodrama may seem like nothing more than additional clichés, but the ambient sounds are so scrupulously assembled that every scratch of the phonograph needle and clatter on the countertop seem carefully crafted and purposely placed. The sound design becomes the most enjoyable aspect of the film.

It may or may not be unusual to see a film as artistically unambitious as *The Strangers* garner the commercial success that it did (though hardly any critical success). In what becomes essentially a characterless movie, Bryan Bertino maps out the escalating danger from one location to another in an initially creepy but ultimately empty film.

Glenn Hopp

CREDITS

Kristen: Liv Tyler
James: Scott Speedman
Mike: Glenn Howerton
Dollface: Gemma Ward
Man in the Mask: Kip Weeks
Pin-Up Girl: Laura Margolis
Origin: USA
Language: English
Released: 2008
Production: Doug Davison, Roy Lee, Nathan Kahane; Intrepid Pictures, Vertigo Entertainment, Mandate Pictures; released by Rogue Pictures
Directed by: Bryan Bertino
Written by: Bryan Bertino
Cinematography by: Peter Sova
Music by: Tomandandy
Sound: Jeffree Bloomer
Music Supervisor: Season Kent
Editing: Kevin Greutert
Art Direction: Linwood Taylor
Costumes: Susan Kaufmann
Production Design: John D. Kretschmer
MPAA rating: R
Running time: 90 minutes

REVIEWS

Chicago Sun-Times Online. May 29, 2008.
Entertainment Weekly Online. May 29, 2008.
Hollywood Reporter Online. May 29, 2008.
Los Angeles Times Online. May 30, 2008.
New York Times Online. May 30, 2008.
San Francisco Chronicle. May 30, 2008, p. E5.
Variety Online. May 29, 2008.
Village Voice Online. May 27, 2008.
Washington Post Online. May 30, 2008.

QUOTES

Kristen: "Why are you doing this to us?"
Dollface: "Because you were home."

TRIVIA

The film is purportedly inspired by the murders committed by the followers of Charlie Manson.

STREET KINGS

Their City. Their Rules. No Prisoners.
   —Movie tagline

Box Office: $26.4 million

Street Kings is a frenetic police procedural involving corrupt cops in a corrupt city that looks a lot like Los Angeles. Keanu Reeves plays Detective Tom Ludlow, an internal affairs cop embroiled in a complicated plot of police corruption that has more twists than a bag of pretzels. As the film begins we see Tom waking up. The first thing he does is to cock his pistol before going to the bathroom to throw up, then brush his teeth. This detective is paranoid cautious, but he has had a life of hard knocks, and the knocks just keep on coming. He lost his wife to a brain aneurysm while she was committing adultery. He has had a falling-out with his erstwhile partner, Detective Terrence Washington (Terry Crews), whom he suspects of being a "dirty" cop. He prefers to work alone, without back-up, when he single-handedly takes out two Korean thugs at the top of the film and rescues two frightened under-aged girls who are held hostage in a cage. He constantly lubricates himself with vodka, which he swigs from little "airline" bottles as he drives roaring (if not quite roaring drunk) through the streets. He seems to be unstoppable, and after the Korean shoot-out, he is lionized as a hero. Who would have expected Reeves to be playing a rough cop like Rambo? But maybe that is why the film works as well as it does. There is an element of surprise here.

It is hard to tell during the first half of the film who the dirtiest cop of them all might be, but the plot seems to be pointing at Captain James Biggs (Hugh Laurie). Clearly Detective Ludlow is being "played" by the system, and the system is as crooked as a warped corkscrew. Captain Jack Wander (Forest Whitaker) seems to head up a small squad of honest cops, including Ludlow, who seems to be the star performer. "When he was a rookie, I took him under my wing," Captain Wander says, and he repeatedly says that he's "got Tom's back." Meanwhile, Tom is facing an internal investigation because of his problems with his former partner, Detective Washington. He tails Washington into a convenience store that is invaded by two gang-bangers with machine guns. Their intent is not to rob the store, but to assassinate Washington. Ludlow is the only survivor of this shoot-out, and it looks as though he is being set up for the murder of Washington. But Wander has "got his back." Apparently planted evidence is suppressed—a shell casing from a third weapon at the shoot-out.

Ludlow knows something is wrong here, but he has to find out what. He meets the detective who is investigating him, Detective Paul Diskant (Chris Evans), and the two of them team up to find the gang-bangers who killed Washington. This is not as easy as it first seems, however, since Washington was in fact set up and killed by two undercover "deputies" in disguise. This search and pursuit is facilitated by a "snitch" named Scribble (played by Cedric the Entertainer in a red cap, driving a red Cadillac convertible) and leads to a second shoot-out, in which Diskant is killed. By this time Ludlow has figured out the mystery, but he finds himself a wanted man. So the improbable plot now has to serve up a Final Confrontation between Ludlow and his adversary.

Who is to blame for this train wreck of a plot? Not necessarily director David Ayer so much as the writers, Jamie Moss, Kurt Wimmer, and, especially, James Ellroy, who wrote the story on which the movie is based. According to *New York Times* reviewer Manohla Dargis, Ellroy, "the self-described 'demon dog' of American crime fiction, writes in a baroque, pulp prose style that hurries along the page like a speed freak in a rocket." Dargis observed that Ayer starts the film "in overdrive and keeps it there all the way to the exhausted, exhausting end." The Ellroy adaptation that worked best was probably *L.A. Confidential* (1997), directed by Curtis Hanson. The plot of this earlier adaptation did not move so obviously at warp speed.

Washington Post reviewer Desson Thomson objected to the clichéd nature of the plot set-up: "This just in," he wrote. "Cops take care of their own." He went on to criticize the filmmakers for failing to realize that this "conceit should be a starting point for deeper explorations and nuances about character, not the punch line to its own mystery." For Thomson, the plot is all too predictable: "We see the big picture way before the characters do," he claims, and he may be right, but Captain Biggs is set up to look like the villain of the piece, from the very start, when Tom Ludlow is taken to the hospital to be patched up after his derring-do with the Korean thugs by Nurse Garcia (Martha Higareda), who turns out to be his current squeeze.

Reeves is agreeable enough as Tom Ludlow, for the most part, until he kicks into paranoid overdrive. Cedric the Entertainer is, well, perhaps entertaining enough as a reluctant snitch. Forest Whitaker attempts to play Captain Jack with Idi Amin-like fury, a psychopath who wants to control the force and ultimately become mayor. Pointing out that Whitaker has never been a "quiet actor," the *New York Times* reviewer was amused by the way he "cuts crazy loose and starts popping his eyes" in the final confrontation. In fact, none of these star performers seems entirely at ease and comfortable, perhaps because of the jacked-up plot that captures them. No wonder, then, that the *Washington Post* reviewer complained that "the big-name casting brings no honor, or even fun, to the hackneyed roles." Sad, but true. A better film might have been made from this material with wiser direction.

James M. Welsh

CREDITS

Detective Tom Ludlow: Keanu Reeves
Capt. Jack Wander: Forest Whitaker
Capt. James Briggs: Hugh Laurie
Detective Paul Diskant: Chris Evans
Sgt. Mike Clady: Jay Mohr
Detective Dante Demille: John Corbett
Detective Cosmo Santos: Amaury Nolasco
Scribble: Cedric the Entertainer
Detective Terrence Washington: Terry Crews
Linda Washington: Naomie Harris
Coates: Common
Grill: The Game
Grace Garcia: Martha Higareda
Origin: USA
Language: English
Released: 2008
Production: Lucas Foster, Erwin Stoff, Alexandra Milchan; Regency Enterprises, Three Arts Entertainment Production; released by Fox Searchlight
Directed by: David Ayer
Written by: Kurt Wimmer, James Ellroy, Jamie Moss
Cinematography by: Gabriel Beristain
Music by: Graeme Revell
Sound: Piero Mura
Music Supervisor: John Houlihan, Season Kent
Editing: Jeffrey Ford
Costumes: Michele Michel
Production Design: Alec Hammond
MPAA rating: R
Running time: 109 minutes

REVIEWS

Boston Globe Online. April 11, 2008.
Chicago Sun-Times Online. April 11, 2008.
Entertainment Weekly Online. April 9, 2008.
Hollywood Reporter Online. April 4, 2008.
Los Angeles Times Online. April 11, 2008.
New York Times Online. April 11, 2008.
Rolling Stone Online. April 17, 2008.
San Francisco Chronicle. April 11, 2008, p. E1.
Variety Online. April 3, 008.
Washington Post Online. April 11, 2008.

QUOTES

Detective Cosmo Santos: "How can you shoot a guy taking a dump? I mean, seriously, that's sacred. That's like shooting a man in church."

TRIVIA

When James Ellroy write the screenplay in the early 1990s he was purportedly inspired by the O.J. Simpson trial.

SUMMER PALACE
(Yihe yuan)

Director Ye Lou was banned by the Chinese government from making movies for two years after the release of his 2000 film *Suzhou River*. But he never fell into compromising his art or his politics, and his film *Summer Palace* (*Yihe yuan*) attracted attention both for its depictions of student protests around the time of the Tiananmen Square upheavals and for its frank and explicit sexual scenes.

The film might have been scandalous to Chinese authorities, but to Western audiences this is difficult to comprehend. Ye Lou brings a raw power and gritty realism to many of his scenes, but this film also has a rather grandiose sense of its own scope and a tortured preciousness in its narration by a young woman from the countryside, Yu Hong (Lei Hao), who finds herself thrust into events when she goes to university in Beijing.

In the film's prologue, Yu Hong gets notice that she is accepted into college while hanging out with her motorcycle-riding boyfriend, Wang Bo (Xueyun Bai). That night, they make love on the outskirts of town in a field. Minutes of fevered coupling pass wordlessly, Yu Hong on her back, stretches of the lovers' skin gleaming in the dark. This is Ye Lou's favorite method of showing sex—it is naturalistic but hardly very erotic, and its main feature is that it lasts much longer than most non-porn-movie sex scenes. All his sex scenes are like that, a bit crude and raw, never gauzy.

Once Yu Hong gets to the university, she is befriended by a dorm mate, Li Ti (Ling Hu), and introduced eventually to a charismatic young man, Zhou Wei (Xiaodong Guo). Long scenes show the students dancing to outdated 1950s American pop music in what looks like a sock hop. Soon Zhou Wei becomes her lover, but to Yu Hong his love is from the start a dangerous kind of torture. She is buffeted by her desires, and her passion seems to threaten her independence. We know it is not easy for her to endure this lust-filled coupling because she tells us so, in narrated excerpts from her diary, filled with questions about the meaning of human desire. It seems like we have been thrust into one of those old-fashioned French movies where romantic love is a constant challenge to the soul. There is certainly plenty of inner ruminating about the meaning of it all.

We also know Yu Hong is troubled because she sometimes has episodes of self-doubt and suicidal thoughts while lying on the edge of a pool. And later, after she meets Zhou Wei again years after college, she runs her bicycle into a vehicle. Is she in a state of mental torment or just oblivious? It's hard to tell.

Eventually Yu Hong's circle of university friends is disrupted as protests sweep Beijing and the campus. By this time Yu Hong and Zhou Wei have tried to break up several times and betray each other with new lovers, but they are still caught in their own love trap. Concerned about her welfare, Wang Bo returns to Beijing, fights with Zhou Wei, and takes Yu Hong back home.

From here on the film becomes confusing. Titles on the screen take us rapidly through nearly a decade of time, in which Yu Hong moves several times and some of her best friends, including Li Ti and Zhou Wei, who have become sometime lovers, move to Germany. Rapid scenes of the former student friends are shot against the backdrop of world events, such as the fall of the Berlin Wall. With a pop tune blaring in the background, it is clear that Ye Lou is trying to connect with the events that shaped a generation that came of age with the growing democracy movements in China, Russia, and elsewhere; his movie is a soundtrack to the era, and Yu Hong's story is meant as a kind of iconic personal journey.

The trouble is, Yu Hong and her friends do not seem directly political. They are not so much swept up in protests as circling around them. They do not have much social consciousness nor do they ever espouse any clear goals. Their rebellion, such as it is, consists mostly of adopting some aspects of Western culture, like music. And Yu Hong is also drifting, rebelling against expectations by being an overtly sexual young woman, yet never escaping her own difficulties with desire.

Ten years after the college years that were at the center of *Summer Palace,* we pick up Yu Hong's story again as she reconnects with Zhou Wei, even though he is married. As they again couple passionately, we hear Yu Hong's voiceover narrative pondering the meaning of her love for Zhou Wei: "Humans yearn to be alone, and they long for death. Why else do we fight the ones we love?"

Why indeed? *Summer Palace* gives us a protagonist who is buffeted by life's events but clueless about how to piece together a way to join her desires to her goals. After making love to Zhou Wei, she finds another man, and says that the reason she keeps having sex with men is that it is the only way they can understand that she is really gentle, because she has the facade of a modern woman.

Confusingly, the film continues to follow the lives of its characters in China and in Berlin. There is plenty of wordless, raw sex, often performed to mournful strings. Ye Lou does manage to convey how desperately human beings can love one another, or at least make love, without commitment or understanding. Many of these scenes are poignant. It is certainly a kind of generational shorthand, this personal searching and rebellion, and *Summer Palace* is a lot like a typical American film of the 1960s. Only at the end, when we learn the film was based on the lives of real people, does it make any sense at all.

At its center, Lei Hao gives a mesmerizing performance as a young woman struggling to come to terms with her place in the modern world. She is beautiful in a quiet, mournful way, a frightening raw spirit who is both strong and fragile. But ultimately Ye Lou seems to lose his way and forget what and whose story he is telling. In the end, a disturbing scene of suicide grips the audience, but it is both under-motivated and inexplicable. It is hard to tell why the characters behave as they do, but it is clear that Ye Lou wants us to share in the haunted nature of this generation. He just has not found a way to make us connect to them.

Michael Betzold

CREDITS

Yu Hong: Lei Hao
Zhou Wei: Xiaodong Guo
Li Ti: Ling Hu
Ruo Gu: Xianmin Zhang
Origin: China, France
Language: Chinese, German, Korean
Released: 2006
Production: Sylvain Bursztejn, Li Fang, An Nai; Laurel Films, Dream Factory, Fantasty Pictures; released by Palm Pictures
Directed by: Ye Lou
Written by: Ye Lou, Feng Mei, Yingli Ma
Cinematography by: Qing Hua
Music by: Peyman Yazdanian
Sound: Kang FU
Editing: Ye Lou, Jian Zeng
Art Direction: Weixin Liu
Costumes: Katja Kirn
MPAA rating: Unrated
Running time: 140 minutes

REVIEWS

Hollywood Reporter Online. May 19, 2006.
New York Times Online. January 18, 2008.
New Yorker Online. January 21, 2008.
Variety Online. May 18, 2006.
Village Voice Online. January 15, 2008.

QUOTES

Yu Hong: "I want us to break up."
Zhou Wei: "Why?"
22Yu Hong: "Because I can't leave you."

TRIVIA

This was the only Asian films to compete for the Palme d'Or in 2006.

SUPERHERO MOVIE

The greatest superhero movie of all time! (not counting all the others)
—Movie tagline

Box Office: $25.8 million

Craig Mazin (producer and writer of the *Scary Movie* franchise) takes a stab at directing the superhero parody with the unambiguously titled *Superhero Movie*. Following the tradition of films such as *Date Movie* (2006), *Epic Movie* (2007), and the *Naked Gun* (1988–1994) series, Mazin spoofs the successful box office phenomenon of the superhero genre. Glutted with ribald humor (Marion Ross of *Happy Days* fame plays the lead's aunt, whose flatulence problem could be diagnosed as Mount St. Helen's Disease), *Superhero Movie* also appeals to the young, Internet-savvy crowd. Ty Burr of the *Boston Globe* clarifies this point: "Facebook, MySpace, YouTube and everything Apple come in for fond lumps, and when a character says 'You're no longer in my Five,' it's a giggle for anyone 20 or younger and crickets for everyone else. This could be the first icomedy."

The 1980 release of *Airplane!*, regarded as a classic for its over-the-top silliness and slapstick, was a runaway hit that spoofed the morbid *Airport* (1970–1979) series (which evolved into its own species of absurdity with each installment). This ingenious original became the blueprint for a genre-lampooning device. It is the template that subsequent imitators have overused to the point of inanity. *Superhero Movie*'s producer, David Zucker, one of the architects for this wacky, irreverent formula, was, along with Jim Abrahams, the producer/director/writer for *Airplane!* and a pioneer of cinematic satire. His resume also includes *The Kentucky Fried Movie* (1977) and *BASEketball* (1998) in addition to the aforementioned *Naked Gun* and *Scary Movie*. Zucker has been a heavy influence on Mazin, who provides his mentor with several salutary nods. Leslie Nielsen, who played Dr. Rumack in *Airplane!*, plays the clueless Uncle Albert. This character attempts to connect with his nephew by acting cyber-literate and offering avuncular advice despite always being three steps behind. Robert Hays (*Airplane!*'s Ted Striker) provides a cameo by way of a

flashback scene as the late father of Rick Riker (Drake Bell from Nickelodeon's *Drake and Josh*).

The story loosely follows the narrative framework of Sam Raimi's 2002 seminal work, *Spider-Man*. From this plot, several other films are mocked, including *Batman Begins* (2005), *Fantastic Four* (2005), *Superman Returns* (2006), and the *X-Men* trilogy (2000–2006). It also copies the comic book industry's habit of alliteration when naming heroes, villains, and ladies: Clark Kent, Lex Luthor, Peter Parker, Lois Lane, Lana Lang, ad infinitum. In this case Rick Riker is enamored of high school ingénue Jill Johnson (Sara Paxton). Christopher McDonald plays the film's villain, Lou Landers.

As with *Spider-Man*, Rick Riker was a timid teenage nerd who was inadvertently bit by a genetically spliced dragonfly that merged with his own DNA. Miraculously, Riker acquires the insect's abilities in a proportional sense with the exception of the ability to fly. He decides to dedicate his life to fighting crime with these newfound powers and adopts the alter ego "the Dragonfly." With the advent of a superhero, a villain of equal or superior power must coincide. *Superhero Movie* abides this tradition by having the wealthy evil industrialist Lou Landers become the victim of an experiment gone awry. An obvious Norman Osborn clone (who became the Green Goblin in *Spider-Man*), Landers discovers that he can absorb a person's life force and must do so daily in order to preserve his own life—thus the birth of "the Hourglass." After a plot trajectory rife with tedious, smutty crotch humor, the comedy reaches its climax with the Hourglass being thwarted and the Dragonfly growing wings in the nick of time.

In the movie's highlight, Miles Fisher performs a brilliant impersonation of Tom Cruise during an interview he gave regarding his Scientology faith. Fisher's skill at imitating subtle, and not so subtle, mannerisms during this mock cameo are without equal. He even looks like Cruise in the same sense that a good tribute band seems more genuine than the actual group. There is also a cameo by Pamela Anderson, who plays Invisible Girl, as well as a burlesque imitation of Dr. Stephen Hawking that should have had disability advocates livid. With a run time of seventy-five minutes, perhaps the biggest spoof is the movie's length. *The Dark Knight* (2008) alone lasted 155 minutes. For funnier spoofs of the superhero genre, one need look no farther than *Sky High* (2005) as well as 1999's *Mystery Men,* where the flatulence remained with Paul Reubens.

David Metz Roberts

CREDITS

Rick Riker/Dragonfly: Drake Bell
Aunt Lucille: Marion Ross

Jill Johnson: Sara Paxton
Lou Landers/Hourglass: Christopher McDonald
Uncle Albert: Leslie Nielsen
Lance: Ryan Hansen
Blaine Riker: Robert Hays
Tom Cruise: Miles Fisher
Invisible Girl: Pamela Anderson
Origin: USA
Language: English
Released: 2008
Production: Robert K. Weiss, David Zucker, Craig Mazin; Dimension Films; released by MGM
Directed by: Craig Mazin
Written by: Craig Mazin
Cinematography by: Thomas Ackerman
Music by: James L. Venable
Sound: David M. Kelson
Editing: Craig Mazin, Craig Herring, Daniel Schalk, Andrew S. Eisen
Art Direction: James Truesdale
Costumes: Carol Ramsey
Production Design: Bob Ziembicki
MPAA rating: PG-13
Running time: 75 minutes

REVIEWS

Boston Globe Online. March 29, 2008.
Entertainment Weekly Online. April 2, 2008.
Hollywood Reporter Online. March 28, 2008.
Los Angeles Times Online. March 31, 2008.
New York Times Online. March 29, 2008.
Variety Online. March 28, 2008.

QUOTES

Uncle Albert: "How can you say that? I've been like a father to you! I raised you, just like your father did! I believed in you, just like your father did! I slept with your mother, just like your father did!"

TRIVIA

This is the second film that Leslie Nielsen and Robert Hayes have appeared in together. The first was *Airplane!* (1980).

SURFWISE

Reject normal.
　　　—Movie tagline

Doug Pray's exceedingly well-made documentary examines a fascinating and enigmatic subject, Dorian "Doc" Paskowitz, and, in what seems almost like a sociological experiment, the manner in which he raised his eight sons and one daughter. A successful Stanford-educated physician and devout Jew, Paskowitz's love of surfing combined with his newly developed theories on life and love led him to leave conventional society to live a nomadic life, crisscrossing the country with his wife and brood of nine children in a twenty-four-foot camper van. The film is almost *Dateline*-like in its two-part approach: chronicling the idyllic aspects of such a life in the first half, then taking those notions and dashing them with some of the grim realities his children recall in the second half.

The film, beautifully shot in crisp digital by David Homcy, begins with Dorian, now in his mid-eighties, in his modest Oahu, Hawaii, home performing naked calisthenics while he rattles off a list of his health complaints but eschews any sort of medicine in favor of daily surfing and a healthy state of mind. Pray then moves to interviews with Dorian's family, who describe him as always being a bit different. Black-and-white photos show an earlier Dorian, already a study in contradictions: first as a strapping young man who was an avid surfer and lifeguard and later as a new graduate of Stanford Medical School in the 1940s. With his career firmly on track, Dorian followed a conventional path, but his two failed marriages and frequent panic attacks made him rethink his approach to life. He quit his job and took a trip to Israel, where he famously introduced the country to surfing. He began his quest to improve his sex life, which he pinpointed as the reason his marriages had failed, with a goal of sleeping with one hundred women and rating them on a scale from one to one hundred. He married one of the highest scoring, an attractive California native of Mexican and Indian descent, Juliette, who for the next ten years was either pregnant or breastfeeding their eights sons—David, Jonathan, Abraham, Israel, Moses, Adam, Salvador Daniel, and Joshua—and one daughter, Navah.

The majority of the film then deals with the period of raising their nine children during the 1960s and 1970s while traveling the country in a succession of three used camper vans. The children were to surf daily for healthy and spiritually beneficial exercise, chant and pray together, eat a lean, healthy, sugar-free diet, and were not to attend school, as Dorian postulated that education was not the equivalent of wisdom gotten by life experience. "Clean living, clean surfing" was Dorian's mantra. The family became well known in the 1970s as the "first family of surfing," and television footage shot of the family shows them lined up by height next to their surfboards. A sort of Von Trapp family of the waves, the children were the envy of children everywhere.

But Dorian ran the family with an iron fist. David, the eldest, recalls with bitterness his role as "the captain," making sure his siblings adhered to Doc's rigid program, which included physical violence when necessary. Daughter Navah, now a self-described "suburban Jewish soccer mom," is perhaps the most memorable interviewee in the film, and frequently likens herself and her youthful siblings to "puppies" and "monkeys," which is not far from what Dorian intended. He sometimes looked to the behavior of animals at the zoo as a guideline for how the family should live. Gorillas did not eat the skin of the apple, so neither did the Paskowitz children. Dorian, who supported his family with meager-paying medical positions in towns that could not otherwise afford it, taught his children to be distrustful of and shun the evils of the material world around them; the family had very little in the way of material possessions. The brothers, now all well into adulthood, recall how there was usually enough clothing for one complete outfit, with the rest of the brothers relegated to swim trunks and flip-flops. Children, rich and poor, whom they encountered in their travels all longed to be a part of the Paskowitz tribe and skip school to go surfing.

Pray draws the viewer into what seems an idyllic life for adults and a paradise for children, when the film turns to the practical realities that intruded into this world. Most, if not all, of the Paskowitz children resent not having had a formal education, which severely limited their career options. In one of the film's most touching moments, one of the brothers, while flipping burgers in a greasy spoon, recalls his dream at eighteen years of age of going to Stanford Medical School and becoming a doctor like his father, only to be told that he was ten years behind in school and would be thirty by the time he could even think of getting into college. Son Adam wryly notes that the way their father raised them groomed them for only three professions: bum, surfer, or rock star. A few of the boys are indeed musicians in Southern California rock bands. A few seem relatively content, like Israel ("Izzy"), who had a successful career in professional surfing and helped run the surf school Doc established in Mission Beach, California.

Pray's well-directed film, expertly edited by Lasse Jarvi, was produced by such notables as Mark Cuban and *Vanity Fair* editor Graydon Carter, as well as documentary subject Jonathan Paskowitz. The scene at the film's end showing the entire family gathering in Oahu after some ten years seems somewhat staged. However, what is real is the children's moving and emotional reunion with the father they love but do not understand.

Hilary White

CREDITS

Origin: USA
Language: English
Released: 2007
Production: Graydon Carter, Matthew Weaver, Tommy Means, Jonathan Paskowitz; HDNet Films, Consolidated Documentaries, Prospect Pictures, Mekanism; released by Magnolia Pictures
Directed by: Doug Pray
Written by: Doug Pray
Cinematography by: David Homcy
Music by: John Dragonetti
Sound: Kyle Schember
Music Supervisor: Janet Bilig Rich
Editing: Lasse Jarvi
MPAA rating: R
Running time: 93 minutes

REVIEWS

Boston Globe Online. May 23, 2008.
Chicago Sun-Times Online. June 20, 2008.
Entertainment Weekly Online. May 16, 2008.
Los Angeles Times Online. May 23, 2008.
New York Times Online. May 9, 2008.
San Francisco Chronicle. June 13, 2008, p. E5.
Variety Online. September 19, 2007.
Wall Street Journal. May 23, 2008, p. W1.
Washington Post. May 30, 2008, p. C5.

TRIVIA

The film premiered at the Toronto International Film Festival on September 11, 2007.

SWING VOTE

*One ordinary guy is giving the candidates a
reason to run.*
—Movie tagline

Box Office: $16.2 million

"This was funny when it started out, but it's not so funny any more." So pronounces Bud Johnson (Kevin Costner) as he is about to conduct a presidential debate to help him decide which candidate he will vote for as president of the United States. And he is absolutely right. The question is, did screenwriters Jason Richman and Joshua Michael Stern appreciate the irony of their own line? Because that is exactly what happens to *Swing Vote*—it is funny until it turns preachy.

Actually, the danger of preachiness lurks right from the opening scenes, when the sleeping, drunken Bud is prodded by his super-conscientious daughter Molly (Madeline Carroll) into driving her to school on time. Along the way, she lectures him about voting in the election that day, telling him it is his civic duty. Once in class, she delivers a stirring speech about the importance of voting, one that catches the attention of the ambitious local TV reporter Kate Madison (Paula Patton), who is tired of being stuck in Texico, New Mexico (do not ask how a purported town of 5,000 has its own TV station).

Unless you have seen no trailers and read nothing about the film and come to it completely cold, you already know that clueless, irresponsible Bud is going to cast the vote that decides the election. Through a cleverly contrived sequence of events, this impossible premise unfolds. Molly asks to meet him at the polling place after work and school are done. But Bud does not show up, because he got fired from the egg-packing plant that day, a victim of his own chronic tardiness and drunkenness and the availability of cheaper labor (illegal Mexican aliens), and has gone to the bar to drink away his sorrows. Molly finds him there, passed out, and then devises a scheme—she sneaks into the polling place and, while the senile poll workers are not looking, signs her father's name and inserts the ballot into the electronic machine. But one of the workers pulls a plug and the vote is never recorded.

The next morning, Bud awakens to find the world at the door of his ramshackle mobile home. It turns out that New Mexico will decide the election, with the candidates deadlocking in the electoral college elsewhere. The filmmakers (former television writer Stern is the director) hope you will accept this outcome as plausible given what happened in 2000 with Florida as the decisive state—though they also trust you will not recall all the weeks of recounts, suits, and counter-suits that year, which here magically do not occur, as everyone immediately accepts it is a statewide tie vote and no one asks for a recount. Under New Mexico Law—at least as presented in this script—Bud has the right to cast his vote ten days later.

That is the set-up, and you can imagine the reaction: the whole world watches as every political interest group, every media outlet, and both candidates' entourages descend on Bud's town. It is a situation a little reminiscent of a Frank Capra film, with Costner's drunken fool as the Everyman cast by democracy as the Decider. And what the candidates and their handlers initially do has the makings of sharp satire. President Andrew Boone (Kelsey Grammer), a vain, clueless country-club Republican, is handled by the film's own version of Karl Rove, campaign manager Martin Fox (an oily Stanley Tucci). Fox's scheme to woo Bud starts with sending racing legend Richard Petty, playing himself, to

pick up Bud and let him drive his race car to the encampment of the president, who is ensconced in his luxury plane on a runway out of town (and the media, puzzlingly, does not follow them there). There the president stoops to pretending to be a beer-drinking football fan and uses an extended analogy to lecture Bud on the importance of not letting the nuclear "football" (the suitcase with the launch codes for the country's atomic-weapons arsenal) be handled by an inexperienced "quarterback." The funniest part of this scene is when Fox, babysitting Molly in the war room, ends up squirming at her caustic questions.

The precocious girl is similarly unimpressed when the Democrats counter by having Willie Nelson issue an invitation to Bud and Molly to attend a soiree at which Bud will get to play with his old Willie Nelson tribute band. This is possible only because the challenger's manager, Art Crumb (Nathan Lane), has pulled some strings and gotten the rhythm section sprung from prison. After the concert, candidate Donald Greenleaf (Dennis Hopper), an effete liberal elitist, sits down to talk fishing with Bud (Greenleaf refers to cheat-sheet index cards when quizzing him about equipment and lures). Then Greenleaf drops the bombshell that the president is going to let unspecified sinister corporate interests build a dam that will destroy Bud's favorite fishing hole on the Pecos River. When the president counters by declaring the Pecos a national wildlife refuge, the satire starts to edge toward black comedy. It gets even closer when Greenleaf runs a tough ad against illegal immigrants after seeing Bud quoted as saying he blames Mexicans for taking jobs away from him and his friends.

Unfortunately, however, the filmmakers' ideas quickly run dry—and they lose their nerve. Instead of venturing farther down the road of lampooning to what lengths the candidates will go to sacrifice their principles for a victory, director Stern decides to provide everyone a moral awakening. This is much less plausible than what's occurred to that point, and it is excruciating to see Grammer, who is very effective in his role, have to play a scene where he balks at offering Bud a lobbying job, as if that would go beyond the moral pale of his character. Even Kate the reporter has her ethical test, and she aces it by passing up the story of a lifetime in the cause of helping Molly prep Bud on his civics test. By the time they spend an all-nighter getting Bud up to speed on all the stuff he never cared about but now suddenly does, the film has lurched into ridiculous sentimentality, with Bud as the champion of the forgotten working class.

The ending reveals what one suspected at the start: *Swing Vote* is not a rollicking swipe at the cravenness and distorted values of the American political process, it is a full-throated salute to the virtues of a citizen's right to vote. It is one big civics lesson from the insufferably upright Molly (one that even a fine performance from newcomer Carroll cannot salvage). Apparently, despite all the evidence to the contrary so convincingly laid out in the satiric middle of the movie, everything is just fine with American democracy, except that people like Bud do not make the time or effort to vote. It is a lecture aimed at the disaffected that pretends to be a paean to the suffering and steadfastness of the country's poor working class. As such, it is a little like Costner's performance, with his on-again, off-again cornpone accent—that is, totally affected. And along the way, there is the startling revelation that Bud is actually a good father, because the mother who abandoned Molly still has a substance-abuse problem (Bud apparently does too, but it seems the film's view is that alcoholism is somehow less problematic than other forms of drug addiction).

Capra would have had a sentimental ending, too, but it would have been earned by the integrity of the plot. Here, America is redeemed not by the virtues of the forgotten Everyman, but by the values of the elite imposed upon the Everyman, by the pretense that these candidates have somehow been transformed, like Bud, into honest, sincere folks. And Dennis Hopper running for president? The poor guy looks lost in his role as an uptight phony. As for Costner, it is yet another in his lifetime of pretentious, unctuous roles where he attempts to portray the soul of America but ends up acting more like a heel.

Michael Betzold

CREDITS

Bud Johnson: Kevin Costner
Molly Johnson: Madeline Carroll
Kate Madison: Paula Patton
President Andrew Boone: Kelsey Grammer
Donald Greenleaf: Dennis Hopper
Art Crumb: Nathan Lane
Martin Fox: Stanley Tucci
John Sweeney: George Lopez
Walter: Judge Reinhold
Larissa Johnson: Mare Winningham
Galena Greenleaf: Nana Visitor
Attorney General Wyatt: Mark Moses
Chief Running Bear: Floyd "Red Crow" Westerman
Himself: Richard Petty
Origin: USA
Language: English
Released: 2008

Production: Jim Wilson, Kevin Costner; Touchstone Pictures, Radar Pictures, 1821 Pictures, Treehouse Films; released by Walt Disney Studios
Directed by: Joshua Michael Stern
Written by: Joshua Michael Stern, Jason Richman
Cinematography by: Shane Hurlbut
Music by: John Debney
Sound: Matthew Nicolay
Editing: Jeff McEvoy
Art Direction: Mark Zuelzke
Costumes: Lisa Jensen
Production Design: Steve Saklad
MPAA rating: PG-13
Running time: 119 minutes

REVIEWS

Boston Globe Online. August 1, 2008.
Chicago Sun-Times Online. July 31, 2008.
Entertainment Weekly Online. July 30, 2008.
Hollywood Reporter Online. July 29, 2008.
Los Angeles Times Online. August 1, 2008.
New York Times Online. August 1, 2008.
San Francisco Chronicle. August 1, 2008, p. E1.
Time Online. July 31, 2008.
Variety Online. July 29, 2008.
Washington Post. August 1, 2008, p. C1.

QUOTES

Bud Johnson: "America needs someone who's bigger than their speeches."

SYNECDOCHE, NEW YORK

Box Office: $3 million

Charlie Kaufman is one of the most highly regarded American screenwriters because of the daring originality of such films as *Being John Malkovich* (1999), *Adaptation* (2002), and *Eternal Sunshine of the Spotless Mind* (2004). Kaufman creates unusual characters and places them in offbeat, unpredictable situations, with a thick layer of sadness running throughout his scripts. *Synecdoche, New York*, the first film directed by Kaufman, takes this melancholy quality and pushes it to its limits.

As the film opens, Caden Cotard (Philip Seymour Hoffman) is a theater director in Schenectady, New York, in 2005. He specializes in bringing offbeat approaches to traditional plays, such as by casting actors in their twenties as the leads in Arthur Miller's *Death of a Salesman* (1949). Kaufman's choice is hardly random because his film addresses themes similar to those of Miller: aging, death, success, failure, loneliness, and family tensions. Caden's artist wife, Adele (Catherine Keener), about to depart for an exhibition in Berlin, tells him she is leaving him and taking their young daughter, Olive (Sadie Goldstein), with her. Adele paints miniature portraits which must be viewed with magnifying glasses, a concept that ironically seems to inspire Caden.

When Caden receives a MacArthur Fellowship, the so-called genius grant, he moves to Manhattan and begins building a miniature version of the city inside an enormous warehouse. He hires actors to populate his set, including Claire (Michelle Williams), one of his *Death of a Salesman* stars, and they eventually marry and have a daughter, Ariel (Daisy Tahan). Caden's work in progress becomes a dramatization of his life, with Claire playing herself. Sammy (Tom Noonan), who has spent twenty years shadowing Caden, is hired to play the director.

One of the many themes of *Synecdoche, New York* is the nature of art and the artist, with Caden attempting to exert in his warehouse a level of control impossible in real life. Yet theater and reality begin to overlap in ways the director has never expected. Hazel (Samantha Morton), who ran the box office in his Schenectady theater, has long loved him from afar. When she comes to work for Caden again, Hazel has an affair with Sammy, while the director has a brief romance with Tammy (Emily Watson), who plays Hazel in Caden's production. The biggest problem with Caden's play, if it can be called that, is that as the years, perhaps as many as forty, pass, the production becomes more real than the reality it attempts to reflect.

Synecdoche, New York is also a view of modern neuroses, with all of the characters having personality quirks. The main neurotic is Caden himself, a hypochondriac with a difference: he has real ailments, including pustules on his face and body. He even pokes through his excrement looking for signs of blood. Most of the characters are quirky in different ways. In complete contrast with the morose Caden, Sammy is always smiling and upbeat, a demeanor which proves to be a misleading mask. Hazel's matter-of-fact approach to life is embodied by her living in a constantly burning house. Her casual acceptance of this fact makes her relative normalcy seem bizarre.

Kaufman's previous screenplays were essentially comedies with dramatic overtones, becoming progressively more serious up to *Eternal Sunshine of the Spotless Mind*. Some reviewers complained that *Synecdoche, New York* is humorless, but it has frequent comic moments, with Hazel's burning house being the most obvious

example. Yet the film is easily Kaufman's darkest, emphasizing the fragility of relationships and the hovering gloom of mortality. His characters die from disease, accident, mayhem, and suicide. Art is but a response to life, not a solution. Because Caden's production is never completed or seen by audiences, he cannot live on through his art.

Kaufman's direction is conservative, almost tentative, as if he was afraid any visual flourishes would distract from the power of his words. One exception is two shots of dirigibles crossing the skyline of the future Manhattan. He is, however, an excellent director of actors. Caden is in almost every scene, placing an enormous burden on Hoffman, who perfectly captures the character's conflicting emotions with small gestures. Caden speaks in a level monotone most of the time, making his few losses of control the more startling. Noonan, the playwright and director best known as the serial killer in Michael Mann's *Manhunter* (1986), is an inspired choice for Caden's double. Noonan and Hoffman look nothing alike, with Noonan almost a foot taller, and while Noonan has specialized in morose characters like Caden, he plays against type here, becoming buoyant, a rare ray of sunshine in Caden's overcast universe.

As with the director in Federico Fellini's *8½* (1963), an obvious influence, Caden's world is informed by his relationships with women. Morton gives her most fully developed performance as the loyal Hazel, using unusual timing to flesh out the character's eccentricities. Watson, a similar performer, makes Tammy/Hazel more assured and world-weary. Also notable are Jennifer Jason Leigh as Adele's lesbian friend, Dianne Wiest as a member of Caden's company whose change of roles shifts the momentum of the production, Robin Weigert as the adult Olive who speaks only German, and, especially, Hope Davis as a famous psychologist. A priceless throwaway joke involving the latter appears briefly during the final scenes.

Many have called *Synecdoche, New York* bleak, despairing, pretentious, and boring. Owen Gleiberman of *Entertainment Weekly* called it "a turgid challenge to sit through" and implied that anyone who thought otherwise was a phony. Roger Ebert, on the *Chicago Sun-Times* Web site, while calling Gleiberman's reaction reasonable and acknowledging he had considerable difficulties upon his first viewing, found the film comparable to great fiction. What is most notable, perhaps, about *Synecdoche, New York* is what Manohla Dargis of the *New York Times* called the film's "soaring ambitions." In an era of films based on comic books and video games, Kaufman is at least taking a big gamble, both on the possibility of maintaining control of his themes and upon audiences' grasping what he is trying to achieve.

Most American films, even serious ones, look at only a portion of the ways American lives are lived, but Kaufman struggles to show how the detritus of everyday life and larger philosophical issues can overlap.

The initially enthralling *Adaptation,* whose treatment of psychological doubles is a mere prelude for what Kaufman tries here, goes completely out of control as it limps to its conclusion. The final ten minutes or so of *Synecdoche, New York* are likewise not quite satisfactory. Perhaps taking his cue from T. S. Eliot's "The Hollow Men," in which the world ends not with a bang but a whimper, Kaufman's film stumbles gracelessly toward its conclusion, resembling the gait of the now aged, limping Caden himself. Thematically, it makes sense, but the ho-hum quality of the ending keeps the film from being the completely realized vision it might have been. Even with this and other minor flaws, Kaufman's creation is exhilarating because of the daring chances taken by the writer/director. Despite what happens in the film itself, *Synecdoche, New York* finally says less about life than about the potential of art.

Michael Adams

CREDITS

Caden Cotard: Philip Seymour Hoffman
Hazel: Samantha Morton
Claire Kent: Michelle Williams
Adele Lack: Catherine Keener
Tammy: Emily Watson
Ellen Bascomb/Millicent Weems: Dianne Wiest
Maria: Jennifer Jason Leigh
Madeleine Gravis: Hope Davis
Sammy Barnathan: Tom Noonan
Olive (child): Sadie Goldstein
Olive (adult): Robin Weigert
Ariel: Daisy Tahan
Origin: USA
Language: English

Released: 2008
Production: Anthony Bregman, Charlie Kaufman, Sidney Kimmel; Likely Story, Projective Testing Service, Russia, Inc.; released by Sony Pictures Classics
Directed by: Charlie Kaufman
Written by: Charlie Kaufman
Cinematography by: Frederick Elmes
Music by: Jon Brion
Sound: Drew Kunin
Music Supervisor: Bonnie Greenberg
Editing: Robert Frazen
Art Direction: Adam Stockhausen
Costumes: Melissa Toth
Production Design: Mark Friedberg
MPAA rating: R
Running time: 124 minutes

REVIEWS

Entertainment Weekly Online. October 22, 2008.
Hollywood Reporter Online. May 23, 2008.
Los Angeles Times Online. October 24, 2008.
New York Times Online. October 24, 2008.
Rolling Stone Online. November 13, 2008.
Time Online. October 23, 2008.
Variety Online. May 23, 2008.
Washington Post. November 7, 2008.

QUOTES

Sammy (to Caden): "I've been following you for 20 years. So cast me and see who you really are."

TRIVIA

The film's title is a play on Schenectady, New York, where the movie is set.

AWARDS

Ind. Spirit 2009: First Feature
Nomination:
Ind. Spirit 2009: Screenplay.

T

THE TALE OF DESPEREAUX

Small Hero. Big Heart.
—Movie tagline
Small Mouse. Big Dreams.
—Movie tagline

Box Office: $50.8 million

The Tale of Despereaux, adapted from the Kate Di-Camillo work which won the Newbery Medal as the outstanding children's book of 2003, suffers when compared to such animated films as *WALL-E* (2008) and, especially, *Ratatouille* (2007), to which it has many similarities. The computer animation, while striking at times, is not especially original, and the film lacks sufficient energy. It has enough virtues, mainly the performances of the voice actors, to make it a pleasant if unexceptional diversion.

Despereaux Tilling (voice of Matthew Broderick) is unlike the other mice in Mouseland, being much smaller except for his huge ears. More important, he lacks the fear that his father (voice of William H. Macy) feels is necessary for a mouse to survive. When the other inhabitants cower or scamper away from any threat, Despereaux charges forward. The individuality of the hero is nearly matched by that of Roscuro (voice of Dustin Hoffman), a seagoing rat who arrives in Despereaux's country seeking the gourmet soup that is the specialty of chef Andre (voice of Kevin Kline). When Roscuro accidentally falls into the soup as it is being served to the Queen (voice of Patricia Cullen), she dies of fright, leading to the banning of soup and a narrow escape from death for Roscuro.

Despereaux, already bursting for adventure, learns about the exploits of valiant knights from reading a book he is supposed to be eating and sets out to rescue Princess Pea (voice of Emma Watson), a damsel in distress. A subplot involving a porcine servant (voice of Tracey Ullman) determined to become a princess is awkwardly grafted onto the rest of the film just to create more conflict. Much more interesting is the villainy of Botticelli (voice of Ciarán Hinds), the despot who rules Ratworld like a Roman emperor, entertaining the masses by subjecting those who have displeased him to combat with a huge cat in a gladiatorial arena.

The Tale of Despereaux resembles a storybook, with seemingly two-dimensional figures in front of flat backgrounds. The visuals are serviceable if unremarkable except for the noirish gloom of Ratworld. Botticelli resembles Peter O'Toole's food critic from *Ratatouille*, and Hinds gives the ruler a stentorian authority similar to O'Toole's outstanding voice work in the earlier film. Despereaux himself is a tad too cute, and the princess too bland. Yet the animators, working for directors Sam Fell, who co-wrote and co-directed *Flushed Away* (2006), another rat tale, and Robert Stevenhagen, provide realistic eyes that convey significant emotions for the characters. A few allusions are tossed in for adult viewers, as with Andre's assistant, Boldo (voice of Stanley Tucci), a vegetable creature in the style of the Renaissance paintings of Giuseppe Arcimboldo. Another auteur of *The Tale of Despereaux* is screenwriter Gary Ross, who has written several films with overcoming-the-odds, finding-one's-true-self elements, including *Big* (1988), *Pleasantville* (1998), and *Seabiscuit* (2003).

In addition to Hinds, there is excellent vocal work by Tucci, Tony Hale (as Despereaux's timid brother), Frank Langella (as the solemn mayor), Richard Jenkins (as the perplexed principal of Despereaux's school), and Robbie Coltrane (as a forlorn dungeon guard). While Sigourney Weaver's narration is rather limp, Hoffman provides the film's biggest jolt of energy. Roscuro is the only character with any psychological depth, and the actor and the animators join in conveying the rat's conflicted emotions as he betrays his true nature only to see the error of his ways.

Too many scenes drag on a bit too long, with *The Tale of Despereaux* never establishing much narrative momentum. Yet the lessons it intends to impart are never presented didactically. It is difficult to say, however, who the film's ideal audience is. Too little of it is interesting enough to engage older viewers, and too much of it, as with the death of a mother, may unsettle younger ones. Fans of Hoffman, however, should be pleased with the nuances he manages to find in a lowly rat.

Michael Adams

CREDITS

Despereaux Tilling: Matthew Broderick (Voice)
Roscuro: Dustin Hoffman (Voice)
Princess Pea: Emma Watson (Voice)
Mig: Tracey Ullman (Voice)
Hovis: Christopher Lloyd (Voice)
Andre: Kevin Kline (Voice)
Lester: William H. Macy (Voice)
Boldo: Stanley Tucci (Voice)
Gregory: Robbie Coltrane (Voice)
Botticelli: Ciarán Hinds (Voice)
Furlough: Tony Hale (Voice)
Antoinette: Frances Conroy (Voice)
Principal: Richard Jenkins (Voice)
Mayor: Frank Langella (Voice)
Pietro: Charles Shaughnessy (Voice)
Narrator: Sigourney Weaver
Origin: USA
Language: English
Released: 2008
Production: Allison Thomas; Relativity Media, Larger Than Life, Framestore Animation; released by Universal
Directed by: Sam Fell, Robert Stevenhagen
Written by: Gary Ross
Cinematography by: Brad Blackbourn
Music by: William Ross
Sound: Jon Title
Music Supervisor: Kathy Nelson
Editing: Mark Solomon

Art Direction: Olivier Adam
Production Design: Evgeni Tomov
MPAA rating: G
Running time: 93 minutes

REVIEWS

Boston Globe Online. December 18, 2008.
Chicago Sun-Times Online. December 17, 2008.
Entertainment Weekly Online. December 17, 2008.
Hollywood Reporter Online. December 15, 2008.
Los Angeles Times Online. December 19, 2008.
New York Times Online. December 19, 2008.
San Francisco Chronicle. December 19, 2008, p. E1.
Variety Online. December 14, 2008.
Washington Post Online. December 19, 2008.

QUOTES

Narrator (voiceover): "Once upon a time, there was a brave, little mouse who loved honor and justice and always told the truth."

TRIVIA

The fruit and vegetable man is a nod to the work of Giuseppe Arcimboldo.

TAXI TO THE DARK SIDE

Alex Gibney's *Taxi to the Dark Side,* the 2008 Oscar® winner for Best Documentary Feature, is as harrowing and hard to take as any horror film released in years, but every bit of it is tragically real. Detailing not only the atrocities that took place at Abu Ghraib but the very concept of using torture to get information from prisoners, *Taxi to the Dark Side* should be required viewing for not only the soldiers on the ground but the people who govern them around the world. It is both the story of one tragic case of violence and torture and the story of all cases of abuse, both physical and of power in the years following 9/11. Gibney was allowed an amazing degree of access to the detainee structure of the United States, all the way to Guantanamo Bay, and he has returned with one of the best documentaries of the last few years, a definitive study of both the inhumanity and uselessness of torture.

The main focus of *Taxi to the Dark Side* is an Afghan taxi driver named Dilawar. The innocent man was beaten to death by American soldiers while he was being held and interrogated at the Bagram Air Base. But Dilawar is just the personal story that sheds light on a morally corrupt system that not only allowed a death like this to happen but made it an inevitability.

Dilawar was taken into custody in late 2002, as support for Americans and their actions abroad were at a fever pitch. Just a year after 9/11 and with Osama bin Laden still on the run and threats of another attack a regular occurrence both locally and abroad, the U.S. military could get away with nearly anything and were instructed to go to whatever means necessary to stop another attack. Dilawar was arrested simply because he had driven three men suspected in a terrorist attack in his taxi. Dilawar spent days deprived of sleep with his arms chained to a ceiling above him. Soldiers would regularly come in and beat him. All he did was cry and scream for days. He was murdered by a government policy that allowed his death to happen.

Only after his death was it learned that the poor man was completely innocent and knew nothing that the torture that killed him could have possibly gleaned. He lived for five hellish days in the prison at Bagram and died after blunt force trauma to his legs. As someone in *Taxi to the Dark Side* points out, Dilawar's injuries were so extreme, that if he had lived his legs would have been amputated.

Who beats a man's legs to the point that it kills him? Or that they would need to be cut off? And to what possible end? Pfc. Damien Corsetti of Military Intelligence says in the movie, "You put people in crazy situations and people do crazy things." The nearly unfathomable situation detailed by *Taxi to the Dark Side* features confused soldiers given poorly defined orders and investigations that always looked down the chain of command and never up it.

Gibney goes even further with *Taxi to the Dark Side* and suggests that the torture that took place at Bagram, Guantanamo, Abu Ghraib, and other places around the world is not only evil but ineffective. Interview subjects speak eloquently on the fact that even information gained from such techniques cannot be trusted. When torture subjects are in so much pain that they barely know their own name, it becomes impossible to trust what they might reveal about potential terrorist attacks.

In the end, the most terrifying thing about *Taxi to the Dark Side* is the answer to the question of whether or not torture inevitably leads to revenge. If an innocent man is killed, what stops his family or his peers from seeking revenge? Have we created a never-ending cycle of violence? When *Taxi to the Dark Side* was shot, there had been a total of 105 prisoner deaths and twenty-five had been labeled "homicides." To what end?

Taxi to the Dark Side looks at the provocative issue of torture during interrogation from so many angles that it starts to become overwhelming. Alex Gibney under-

stands the complexity of the issue more than any film on the subject has to date. He pulls no punches, tracing the chain of command all the way up to Vice President Dick Cheney and displaying shocking images of abuse. One would hope that Cheney himself has seen the film, but also that it will become required viewing for anyone with the power to take a life.

Brian Tallerico

CREDITS

Narrator: Alex Gibney
Origin: USA
Language: English
Released: 2007
Production: Alex Gibney, Susanna Shipman, Eva Orner; Jigsaw Productions, X-Ray Productions; released by ThinkFilm
Directed by: Alex Gibney
Written by: Alex Gibney
Cinematography by: Maryse Alberti, Greg Andracke
Music by: Ivor Guest
Sound: Felix Andrew
Editing: Sloane Klevin
MPAA rating: R
Running time: 106 minutes

REVIEWS

Boston Globe Online. February 8, 2008.
Chicago Sun-Times Online. February 7, 2008.
Entertainment Weekly Online. January 16, 2008.
Hollywood Reporter Online. May 11, 2007.
Los Angeles Times Online. January 18, 2008.
New York Times Online. January 18, 2008.
New Yorker Online. February 4, 2008.
San Francisco Chronicle. February 8, 2008, p. E7.
Variety Online. May 3, 2007.
Wall Street Journal. January 18, 2008, p. W1.
Washington Post. February 8, 2008, p. C6.

AWARDS

Oscars 2007: Feature Doc.

TEETH

Every rose has its thorns.
—Movie tagline

There is a ripe psychosexual comedy lurking somewhere in the idea of vagina dentata as a form of adolescent female empowerment and a tool of revenge against sex-obsessed, deceitful males. It is not difficult to imagine what Brian De Palma in his heyday could have concocted, a bloody yet teasingly sexy exploration of the messy crossover between the urges of the body and violence. *Teeth,* however, is not that movie.

The film's uneasy straddling between comedy and horror begins with the first scene, in which a soon-to-be-blended (albeit uneasily) family lazes in their suburban front yard, a smoke-belching power plant in the background. While mom Kim (Vivienne Benesch) and dad Bill (Lenny von Dohlen) recline in lawn chairs, young Dawn and Brad grudgingly share a wading pool. But when Brad escalates his bullying from water splashing to something more sinister, his offending finger is mysteriously pierced and bloodied. Flash-forward a dozen or so years, and the shivering, watchful little girl has grown into a lithe teenager.

As Dawn, the virginal heroine who has sworn to remain chaste until she is married and preaches abstinence to fellow students, Jess Weixler has a wide-eyed, giddy charm that is reminiscent of Drew Barrymore's, and she has a couple of double takes that are priceless. The camera is right to adore her, but she is poorly served by writer/director Mitchell Lichtenstein's tendency to prolong a scene until the humor has been drained from it and all that remains is an audience shifting in discomfort. When Dawn, panicked by the apparently deadly powers of her nether regions, goes to a clinic for her first gynecological exam, it is administered by a little-too-eager-to-probe doctor (Josh Pais). Lichtenstein drags out the punishment inflicted on the doctor until the scene loses any comic snap and the talented actors are stranded onscreen, shrieking and hollering.

Perhaps the biggest weakness of the movie lies in its treatment of the male characters. From round-faced boys to wrinkled elders, the Y-chromosome bearers of *Teeth* are only interested in one thing. Dawn's stepbrother, Brad (John Hensley), is such an ugly character that every time he appears, he yanks the movie in an unpleasant direction. (Lichtenstein has burdened Brad with every clichéd "bad boy" characteristic: tattoos, piercings, a fondness for pot, heavy metal, and anal sex, the last a result of his childhood encounter with the wrath of Dawn.) In fact, the only sympathetic male character in *Teeth* is Dawn's stepfather, Bill, and even he is presented as a weakling, unable to protect his stepdaughter from his son's advances. Tobey (Hale Appleman), the classmate of Dawn's with whom she shyly flirts, initially comes across as sweet and equally naïve and smitten. When he suddenly metamorphoses into a sex-driven brute who forces himself on a stunned Dawn, there is no setup or preparation for his transformation.

And there is an unfortunate resemblance between Tobey and Ryan (Ashley Springer), the classmate of Dawn's who has made a bet on his ability to bed her. It is hard to tell if the physical similarity was intentional on Lichtenstein's part when casting, or what purpose it serves. Is it meant to convey the message that all high school boys are really the same, and not just beneath the skin?

The best scenes in *Teeth* occur near the beginning. When Dawn starts the school day by running a gauntlet of jeering, taunting classmates, the movie shows promise. Striding to the school's entrance through a hail of thrown condoms, Dawn maintains a determinedly perky demeanor. She has a mission—to promote the power of chastity—and nothing will deter her, certainly not a minor unpleasantness like a sneered "cherry soda." "Purity, purity," she tells herself, repeating it like a mantra that will banish any and all unpleasantness from within and without.

Too often, however, Lichtenstein goes for the easy sight gag, letting the camera linger, for example, on the vulva-shaped hole in a tree when Dawn and Toby wander through a forest. Or he uses a motif—such as the power-plant stacks that ominously, continuously belch smoke—that has impact the first time it is shown, an impact that grows considerably less when it is repeated. Lichtenstein does not appear to trust the audience's intelligence. It is as though he wanted to make a sharp-witted satire but the adolescent male within, who thinks that the mere sight of a raw, waggling hot dog is hilarious, took over. "Some hero," Dawn mutters when stalking away from one predator turned victim. The same utterance could be made—more ruefully than disgustedly—by a viewer when Lichtenstein's credit rolls at the end of *Teeth*.

Heather L. Hughes

CREDITS

Dawn: Jess Weixler
Brad: John Hensley
Dr. Godfrey: Josh Pais
Bill: Lenny von Dohlen
Tobey: Hale Appleman
Kim: Vivienne Benesch
Ryan: Ashley Springer
Origin: USA
Language: English
Released: 2007
Production: Joyce Pierpoline, Mitchell Lichtenstein; released by Roadside Attractions
Directed by: Mitchell Lichtenstein

Written by: Mitchell Lichtenstein
Cinematography by: Wolfgang Held
Music by: Robert Miller
Sound: Benjamin Lowry
Music Supervisor: Beth Rosenblatt
Editing: Joe Landauer
Art Direction: Tom Cole
Costumes: Rita Ryack
Production Design: Paul Avery
MPAA rating: R
Running time: 94 minutes

REVIEWS

Boston Globe Online. January 25, 2008.
Hollywood Reporter Online. January 21, 2007.
Los Angeles Times Online. January 18, 2008.
New York Times Online. January 18, 2008.
San Francisco Chronicle. January 25, 2008, p. E10.
Variety Online. January 30, 2007.
Village Voice Online. January 15, 2008.
Wall Street Journal. January 18, 2008, p. W1.

QUOTES

Dawn: "The toothed vagina appears in the mythology of many and diverse cultures all over the world. In these myths, the story is always the same. The hero must do battle with the woman. The toothed creature can break her power."

TELL NO ONE
(Ne le dis à personne)

*8 years ago, Alex's wife was MURDERED.
Today...she e-mailed him.*
—Movie tagline

Box Office: $6.1 million

French filmmakers have long been drawn to American crime writers. Directors such as Jean-Jacques Beineix, Claude Chabrol, René Clément, Jean-Luc Godard, Bertrand Tavernier, and François Truffaut have made films drawn from such writers as Stanley Ellin, David Goodis, Patricia Highsmith, Ellery Queen, Jim Thompson, Lionel White, Charles Williams, and Cornell Woolrich. With the notable exception of Highsmith, these writers turned out pulp fiction, emphasizing plot over character, though the filmmakers often expanded their sources to give the resulting films greater philosophical and psychological depth.

The source of Guillaume Canet's *Tell No One* (also known as *Ne le dis à personne*) is a newer generation of American crime writer. After writing several mysteries featuring sports agent Myron Bolitar, Harlan Coben published a darker novel in 2001 in the vein of Ruth Rendell's psychological thrillers. In switching the setting of *Tell No One* from Manhattan and New Jersey to Paris and its suburbs, writer-director Canet takes an American tale and makes it his own.

Dr. Alexandre Beck (François Cluzet) and his wife, Margot (Marie-Josée Croze), are first seen swimming in a Rambouillet Forest lake they have visited since they were childhood sweethearts. Suddenly Margot is abducted and Alex knocked unconscious. Shortly afterward Margot's father, police inspector Jacques Laurentin (André Dussollier), identifies a brutally beaten and slashed corpse as his daughter.

Eight years later Alex, a pediatrician working with slum children, has still not recovered from the experience. Then a mysterious e-mail provides a live video of someone who appears to be Margot. With the help of his friend Hélène Perkins (Kristin Scott Thomas), also the lover of his sister, Anne (Marina Hands), Alex sets out to discover the truth. Though Margot's murder was suspected to have been committed by a serial killer, police inspector Eric Levkowitch (François Berléand) has never been convinced of Alex's innocence, and the police begin placing obstacles in his path, especially after another friend, photographer Charlotte Bertaud (Florence Thomassin), is murdered.

Not only are the police after Alex, but so are a gang of vicious thugs led by Bernard Valenti (Olivier Marchal), who also know Margot is alive and desperately want to find her, plunging Alex even deeper into a Kafkaesque nightmare. Lurking in the background is the unsolved murder of equestrian Philippe Neuville (played by Canet himself), whose wealthy father, Gilbert (Jean Rochefort), is friends with the Beck family. The complicated relations between these characters and their connections to several other events become clear only at the very end of *Tell No One*.

Although the plot of *Tell No One* is quite complicated, full of twists and turns in the tradition of Raymond Chandler, it remains a riveting entertainment thanks to outstanding performances and Canet's accomplished filmmaking. Canet, directing only his second film, and co-writer Philippe Lefebvre, who also appears in the film as a policeman, keep the numerous strands of the mystery in focus, and except for relying too much on close-ups, a notorious pitfall for actors turned directors, Canet gives the film considerable visual flare.

The highpoint of *Tell No One* comes when Alex flees the police by jumping out of his office window. The resulting chase takes the physician and his pursuers down several streets, across a busy highway, and into a filthy alley. What is most unusual about the chase is that when it seems to have ended, with Alex's narrow escape, it suddenly begins again. Much of the chase is shot with a jittery handheld camera to plunge the viewer even deeper into the action. Unlike most such sequences, in which the distance between the pursued and the pursuers fluctuates from cut to cut, this chase offers spatial logic to make it more realistic.

Speaking of realistic, Alex's run across the highway initiates a chain-reaction accident with a skidding truck narrowly missing the doctor, and no stunt double appears to have been substituted for Cluzet. This sequence, brilliantly edited by Hervé de Luze, has been compared by reviewers to a similar scene in John Schlesinger's *Marathon Man* (1976), partly because of Cluzet's startling resemblance to that film's star, Dustin Hoffman. Yet it is shot and edited more like the sequence of a car chasing Charles Denner on sidewalks in Costa-Gavras's *Z* (1969), in which Cluzet's father-in-law, Jean-Louis Trintignant, stars.

While many reviewers compared *Tell No One* to Alfred Hitchcock's *Vertigo* (1958) because of the superficial similarities in plot (man obsessed by dead woman), it more closely resembles Hitchcock's wrong-man films, most notably *North by Northwest* (1959), in which an ordinary man is falsely accused of a crime and must prove his innocence against great odds. As such, Cluzet is perfect casting for both his everyman looks and the haunted quality of his performance. When Alex sees the video of Margot, Cluzet offers a demonstration of minimal acting with subtle shifts between disbelief and hope. As the cop with a conscience, Berléand also stands out by giving an understated performance to display Levkowitch's slow realization that everything is not what it seems.

Its equestrian subplot makes Canet the perfect director for *Tell No One*. The son of horse breeders, he rode show horses, just as his character does in the film, before becoming an actor. Canet's father, Philippe, plays a small but significant role as Alex's father. In addition to Lefebvre, several other actors in *Tell No One* have writing and directing experience. Gilles Lellouche, as the criminal father of one of Alex's patients, co-wrote, with Lefebvre, and co-directed *Narc* (2004), which stars Canet, and Marchal wrote and directed the masterful noir *36 Quai des Orfèvres* (2004), which features Dussollier.

Tell No One was nominated for nine Césars, the French equivalent of the Academy Awards®, and won four: best director, best actor, best editing, and best original score (Mathieu Chedid). Much more than a complex mystery, *Tell No One* explores such themes as the impossibility of knowing the truth, the hold of the past on the present, and the ambiguity of good and evil while remaining an almost flawless entertainment.

Michael Adams

CREDITS

Alexandre Beck: François Cluzet
Jacques Laurentin: André Dussollier
Margot Beck: Marie-Josée Croze
Hélène Perkins: Kristin Scott Thomas
Elysabeth Feldman: Nathalie Baye
Eric Levkowitch: François Berléand
Gilbert Neuville: Jean Rochefort
Anne Beck: Marina Hands
Philippe Neuville: Guillaume Canet
Bruno: Gilles Lellouche
Charlotte Bertaud: Florence Thomassin
Bernard Valenti: Olivier Marchal
Origin: France
Language: French
Released: 2006
Production: Alain Attal; Europacorp, Les Prods. du Tresor, M6 Films; released by Music Box Films
Directed by: Guillaume Canet
Written by: Guillaume Canet, Philippe Lefebvre
Cinematography by: Christophe Offenstein
Music by: Mathieu Chedid
Sound: Pierre Gamet, Gérard Lamps, Jean Goudier
Editing: Hervé de Luze
Costumes: Carine Sarfati
Production Design: Philippe Chiffre
MPAA rating: Unrated
Running time: 125 minutes

REVIEWS

Chicago Sun-Times Online. July 10, 2008.
Entertainment Weekly Online. July 11, 2008.
Hollywood Reporter Online. April 24, 2007.
Los Angeles Times Online. July 2, 2008.
New York Times Online. July 2, 2008.
San Francisco Chronicle. July 11, 2008, p. E7.
Time Online. June 26, 2008.
Variety Online. November 6, 2006.
Wall Street Journal. July 2, 2008, p. D1.
Washington Post. July 18,2008, p. C6.

10,000 B.C.

It takes a hero to change the world.
—Movie tagline

The legend. The battle. The first hero.
   —Movie tagline

Box Office: $94.7 million

At the end of the Pleistocene Epoch, times were truly harsh for the Yagahl, a mountain tribe surviving the receding Ice Age by subsisting on a diet composed mainly of mammoth meat. The mammoth, or "mannak," was also a major influence on the development of their culture. Roland Emmerich's latest epic, *10,000 B.C.*, is a visually appealing account of the Yagahl with varied locations, including New Zealand, Thailand, South Africa, and Namibia, serving as the film's prehistoric setting. While robust in its panoramic sets, the film is lacking in story development and substitutes style with eye candy. The gems of the film, including the stampede of a herd of mammoths attempting to escape from Yagahl hunters along the northern tundra, are all too brief.

The plot is formulaic and bland: A young hunter is raised in a tribe of hunter-gatherers and subjected to undeserved regard as the son of a coward. D'Leh (Steven Strait) is attempting to renounce this reputation through a rite of passage, which involves killing a mammoth on a hunt. The Yagahl take one pachyderm at a time as they take from nature only that which is truly required for survival. When D'Leh makes a kill by accident, he earns the "White Spear," a status symbol which extinguishes his reputation as a coward. He also gains the hand of the ingénue, his beloved Evolet (Camilla Belle), an orphan who carries a mystique as the sole tribesperson to have blue eyes. Knowing his honor is undeserved, D'Leh returns the spear as he wishes to restore his family name by honorable means.

D'Leh is not consigned to live as the tribe's resident outcast for the duration of his life. Fate presents him with an opportunity to carry out the hero's journey that could easily be crafted after the Joseph Campbell book, *The Hero with a Thousand Faces*. Evolet is kidnapped by a neighboring tribe, who has harnessed the power of the horse, thus earning them the descriptive banner of "Four Legged Demons." D'Leh embarks on a rescue mission along with a small group including Tic'Tic (Cliff Curtis), who serves as his mentor. Their subsequent trials bring tragedy in Disney-like proportions, as does the film's second and last bit of visual intrigue, D'Leh's encounter with a "Spear-Tooth," the tribe's name for a saber-tooth tiger. The boy saves the prehistoric feline from drowning, and the tiger turns out to be a noble creature who returns the favor later in the plot.

D'Leh's party increases to a formidable force by the addition of various tribes whose people were also abducted by the enslavers that serve "the Almighty" (Affif Bed Badra), a powerful figurehead proclaiming to be a god. The mysterious leader's past is mired in mystery; it is believed he is a survivor of Atlantis and possibly an extraterrestrial. The Almighty, credited as the Warlord, is subjecting both a diverse range of people and mammoths to hard labor and sacrifice to construct the Great Pyramids. Beating the odds and escaping death, D'Leh misleads the Almighty by accepting his proposal that he will return Evolet to him in exchange for his noninterference and departure. As he approaches his nemesis, he comes within range to launch his spear at him. In this penultimate climax, it is learned that the Almighty is not a deity after all, but a frail old man consumed with grandiose dreams of wondrous tombs. The true climax occurs with Evolet's death, when a spurned warlord strikes her in the back with an arrow. The Yagahl's aged prophetess (Mona Hammond) knows of this, and as she exhales her last breath, she seems to span geography, breathing new life into the girl. The movie ends in a passionate kiss between the couple.

The filming of this project apparently took no risks. The initial mammoth stampede gave it promise but was only a tease, as the movie and its boring plot simply plod onward. The dialogue is spoken in perfect English and the cast sports dreadlocks and anachronistically flawless veneers. In the pre-CGI years of filmmaking, prehistoric dramas relied less on special effects and more on intrigue, such as *Quest for Fire* (1981), which had an enduring concept (preserving a fire during another long journey) and a dialogue composed solely of grunts. *One Million Years B.C.* (1966) took it one step farther by not relying either on effects or dialogue, but the ineffable talent of Raquel Welch.

David Metz Roberts

CREDITS

D'Leh: Steven Strait
Evolet: Camilla Belle
Tic'Tic: Clifford Curtis
Nakudu: Joel Virgel
Warlord: Ben Badra
Narrator: Omar Sharif
Origin: USA
Language: English
Released: 2008
Production: Roland Emmerich, Mark Gordon, Michael Wimer; Legendary Pictures, Centropolis Entertainment; released by Warner Bros.
Directed by: Roland Emmerich
Written by: Roland Emmerich, Harald Kloser
Cinematography by: Ueli Steiger
Music by: Harald Kloser, Thomas Wander

Sound: Nico Louw

Editing: Alexander Berner

Art Direction: Heather Cameron, Mark Homes, David Warren, Fleur Whitlock

Costumes: Odile Dicks-Mireaux, Renee April

Production Design: Jean-Vincent Puzos

MPAA rating: PG-13

Running time: 109 minutes

REVIEWS

Boston Globe Online. March 7, 2008.
Chicago Sun-Times Online. March 7, 2008.
Hollywood Reporter Online. March 7, 2008.
Los Angeles Times Online. March 7, 2008.
New York Times Online. March 7, 2008.
San Francisco Chronicle. March 7, 2008, p. E1.
Variety Online. March 6, 2008.
Washington Post. March 7, 2008, p. C4.

QUOTES

Tic'Tic: "A good man draws a circle around himself and cares for those within. His woman, his children."

TRIVIA

Prints were delivered to several theaters with the fake title "King Dinosurs" (misspelling intended).

THEN SHE FOUND ME

Life can change in a heartbeat.
　—Movie tagline

A thoroughly modern woman in a thoroughly modern crisis.
　—Movie tagline

Box Office: $3.7 million

With the good-intentioned but cluttered *Then She Found Me*, Helen Hunt continues the downward trajectory of a career that had her at the top of the actress ladder just a decade ago. Since 2001's *The Curse of the Jade Scorpion,* itself a complete disaster and one of Woody Allen's worst films, Hunt has appeared in only *A Good Woman* (2004), *Bobby* (2006), and this year's *Then She Found Me*. Despite Hunt's misguided casting decisions, she clearly has not lost any of her acting ability since she won the Oscar® for *As Good As It Gets* (1997). She seems to be picking the wrong projects or perhaps not being offered the parts she once got without audition. She is in that age group of actresses not as likely to be called by casting agents for the romantic lead but not yet old enough for the wise older woman

roles. Perhaps to offset the lack of good roles coming her way, Hunt decided to create a part for herself. She wrote, directed, and stars in *Then She Found Me*, a mixed bag of good performances and manipulative writing that never transcends the soap opera of its set-up and remains mired in the sentimentality and melodrama usually seen in Lifetime's TV movie-of-the-week.

In the opening of *Then She Found Me,* April (Helen Hunt), a teacher, and Ben (Matthew Broderick) are in the process of breaking up their marriage. Just before splitting for the last time, the cute couple decides to have passionate sex on the kitchen floor one final time and, as only happens in the movies, the not-so-young April, who has been long wanting and trying to have a baby, finally gets pregnant. Pregnancies in movies have a habit of happening at the worst time. Ben leaves and April falls for a sweet single father named Frank (Colin Firth), the proud pop of one of her students. Suddenly, April is looking at the possibility of going from a woman with no family at all, not even a loyal husband, to someone with a biological child and stepchild of her very own. The love triangle with themes of motherhood late in life could have made for an interesting film on its own, especially if it was played believably, but the novel by Elinor Lipman and the screenplay by Hunt add another plot, and the melodrama involved lessens both halves of the film.

While the relationship drama is unfolding in April's life, a family drama rears its head. April's adoptive mother dies, and a man who represents her birth mother comes to the funeral to tell our heroine that she wants to meet her. It turns out that April's real mother is a famous TV talk show host named Bernice (Bette Midler), who is looking to rekindle her relationship with her daughter after having some regretful women who gave up their kids for adoption on her show. But Bernice is hard to trust. She even claims that April's biological father is Steve McQueen, something that April can quickly and easily disprove. April is not even sure if she is Bernice's actual daughter or if it is not all just a stunt for the talk show queen's ratings.

The layering of increasingly ridiculous plots and coincidences in fiction is one thing, but it makes a film feel like soap opera. *Then She Found Me* simply has too much for one movie. Missing moms, single mothers, romantic interludes on linoleum and in the back seat of cars—it all feels like a script that was developed with TV movie intentions. Movies made for cable have a different structure. They need to give the audience a pop or a twist every fifteen minutes or so to keep them tuned in through the commercials. *Then She Found Me* has that kind of structure, where the coincidences of all these events happening in the same three months of April's life become too much to dramatically bear.

348

Hunt, Firth, Broderick, and Midler are never bad in the film, but they are overwhelmed by a story that demands that nearly every scene be plot-driven when a better movie would have focused on the characters. Hunt is a very good actress and does not make any significant mistakes as a writer (it is likely the source and not her adaptation of it that leads to the melodrama), but she does the overcrowded film no favors with some very dry direction. *Then She Found Me* not only feels like a TV movie structurally, it looks like one too. The Helen Hunt that was not long ago one of the best actresses working cannot be blamed for trying to write and direct herself a comeback role, but *Then She Found Me* is not it.

Brian Tallerico

CREDITS

April: Helen Hunt
Frank: Colin Firth
Bernice: Bette Midler
Ben: Matthew Broderick
Frank: Ben Shenkman
Trudy: Lynn Cohen
Dr. Masani: Salman Rushdie
Alan: John Benjamin
Origin: USA
Language: English
Released: 2007
Production: Pamela Koffler, Katie Roumel, Christine Vachon, Helen Hunt, Connie Tavel; Odyssey Entertainment, Killer Films, Blue Rider Pictures, John Wells Prods.; released by ThinkFilm
Directed by: Helen Hunt
Written by: Helen Hunt, Alice Arlen, Victor Levin
Cinematography by: Peter Donahue
Music by: David Mansfield
Sound: Ken Ishii
Editing: Pam Wise
Costumes: Donna Zakowska
Production Design: Stephen Beatrice
MPAA rating: R
Running time: 100 minutes

REVIEWS

Entertainment Weekly. April 25, 2008, p. 100.
Hollywood Reporter Online. September 8, 2007.
Los Angeles Times Online. April 25, 2008.
New York Times Online. April 25, 2008.
Newsweek Online. April 24, 2008.
Variety Online. September 30, 2007.

Village Voice Online. April 22, 2008.
Wall Street Journal. April 25, 2008, p. W1.

TRIVIA

Tim Robbins appears briefly as one of the interviewees on the Bernice's talk show.

TRAITOR

The only person he can trust is himself.
—Movie tagline

Box Office: $23.5 million

Traitor was a good, a necessary, and a courageous film to release during the summer of 2008, even though the movie-going public probably did not want to entertain any thoughts whatsoever about the continuing wars in Iraq or Afghanistan or about the widespread problem of terrorism in general. But then there was *Traitor,* going against the grain, making a point about Islam and fanatical Jihadists dedicated to striking out against the West in general and the United States in particular. The film starts with a flashback to Sudan in 1978, when a car bomb kills the father of the main character, Samir Horn, who later comes to Chicago with his mother, where he is educated, and then serves as a special forces operative. Samir is played by Don Cheadle, whose energy and charisma drive this picture. At first Samir, a devout Muslim, seems to be a terrorist himself, for he is first seen in Yemen, attempting to sell detonators to a Jihadist cell. The police sweep the area before the deal can be completed, however, and Samir finds himself in prison, where he is visited by two FBI operatives, Roy Clayton (Guy Pearce) and Max Archer (Neal McDonough), who work him over with a good cop/bad cop routine that apparently fails to get the desired result. Samir would rather stay in prison in Yemen than cooperate with these FBI bozos, a decision one fears he may later regret. But appearances may be deceptive here.

When Samir demonstrates his decency by attempting to help a prisoner who is being brutalized, he shows courage, but seems to be putting his life in danger, until a really tough Muslim named Omar (Saïd Taghmaoui) comes to his defense, threatening the lives of the prison thugs. Omar is a Swiss-educated Jihadist, who is smart enough to arrange a prison break that gets Samir out of prison and in cahoots with the Muslim brotherhood. Up to this point, for all the audience knows, Samir is simply a Jihadist, and one can sense the audience getting a bit queasy; the anxious should stay tuned, however, since all is not what it seems. Samir turns out to be a double agent, working deep cover for a CIA operative named Carter (Jeff Daniels), who seems to be the only one who knows about Samir's "mission." The plan begins with a terrorist bombing in Spain, then moves to France. Samir, a demolition expert, plants and then triggers a bomb at the U.S. Consulate in Nice that kills a half dozen people (unexpected consequences in the war against terror, it turns out). Samir is then spirited to London, where he rejoins terrorist kingpin Fareed Mansour (Alyy Khan), who then sends Samir to Toronto, then to British Columbia, then into the United States. The plan: to detonate a string of buses coast to coast in the U.S.A. to demonstrate that the country is not safe from terrorist attacks.

Samir turns out to be a counter-terrorist agent, but he is also expert at building bombs, and to make himself useful to the Jihadists, he has to cooperate with their schemes to achieve their goals, but, if possible, with minimal "collateral damage." Thus, the plot, constructed by director Jeffrey Nachmanoff and—amazingly enough—actor/writer Steve Martin, has to maneuver gingerly around that core complication. The conspirators harbor dreams of a hundred buses going up in flames all across America. Samir wants to prevent that, but he only has the names of ten suicide-bomber contacts. Will he be smart enough to pack all of them on the same bus; but if so, won't there still be collateral damage? The screenplay has too many loose ends to work perfectly, but at the heart of the tangle is the character of Samir, a man of divided nationalities and loyalties. In his *Variety* review, Todd McCarthy puzzled over the Samir Horn character, loaded with "extreme influences, life experiences and contradictions." McCarthy claimed that this "conflicted African-born Muslim-American" was an enigma and an impediment to the plot since the film "proves unable to really get inside its chameleon-like central character." Cheadle told *Entertainment Weekly* why he was drawn to the character of Samir Horn: "I've never seen a movie where a Muslim is the hero." Cheadle explained: "He gets caught up and has his allegiances, his Muslim faith, tested. It hopefully will serve as a good jumping-off point to examine this issue." As an actor, Cheadle has made several extremely good casting decisions, but even his talent could not save the film at the summer box-office or its relationship to the "war on terror." *Variety* predicted that "Commercial prospects look just OK." About Cheadle's performance, McCarthy complained that the "first things to go in Cheadle's portrayal of such a knotted, inward man are spontaneity and a sense of humor." And, in truth, the performance seems a little flat.

Variety compared *Traitor* to *Syriana* (2005) favorably because of Nachmanoff's "more conventional" and less complicated "straighter-line narrative," even though the action sprints from the Middle East to Spain, France,

and Britain, before crossing the Atlantic to Toronto, British Columbia, and Halifax for Samir, and Mexico for Omar, before both characters end up in Chicago. The plot works overtime to put a decent spin on Islam and its followers: the Jihadists are not merely presented as cartoon fanatics; but even so, innocent people die, a fact that bothers Samir and should bother the audience as well.

The lead FBI agent, Roy Clayton, develops thoughtfully into the soft-spoken son of a preacher who has studied religions and even learned Arabic, and so is more sympathetic to Samir, whom he is tracking. The tables turn when Samir sends Clayton an email that informs him that a mole has infiltrated FBI headquarters in Washington. Of course, this action-adventure plot leads to a final shootout, but Clayton somehow manages to save Samir's bacon, and the two part as friends after Samir has had a chance to heal in Chicago after the shootout at sea, offshore from Halifax, Nova Scotia. (The almost out-of-control plot is all over the map.) The other FBI agent seems to be little more than a reactive meathead. The Muslim characters are rather more interesting, especially Omar, Samir's prison friend who brings him into the Jihadist conspiracy, as intelligently played by Taghmaoui. Daniels is fine as the spooky CIA contact, Carter, but he only dodges in and out of the plot a few times, outside a London Tube station, for example, and next to a pay phone in Los Angeles, before being shot down by Omar, who thinks he is rescuing Samir. The plot is at times so murky that it seems possible that Samir may be discovered by the Muslim Brotherhood, but he is ultimately saved by his deeply religious faith in Islam. Despite its awkward moments (and there are rather too many), this film deserved better than it got.

James M. Welsh

CREDITS

Samir Horn: Don Cheadle
Roy Claxton: Guy Pearce
Max Archer: Neal McDonough
Omar: Saïd Taghmaoui
Chandra Dawkin: Archie Panjabi
Carter: Jeff Daniels
Fareed Mansour: Alyy Khan
Leyla: Mazhan Marno
Origin: USA
Language: English
Released: 2008
Production: David Hoberman, Todd Lieberman, Don Cheadle, Jeffrey Silver; Mandeville Films, Hyde Park Entertainment, Crescendo; released by Overture Films

Directed by: Jeffrey Nachmanoff
Written by: Jeffrey Nachmanoff
Cinematography by: J. Michael Muro
Music by: Mark Kilian
Sound: John Thomson
Editing: Billy Fox
Art Direction: Rocco Matteo
Costumes: Gersha Phillips
Production Design: Laurence Bennett
MPAA rating: PG-13
Running time: 113 minutes

REVIEWS

Boston Globe Online. August 27, 2008.
Chicago Sun-Times Online. August 26, 2008.
Entertainment Weekly Online. August 27, 2008.
Hollywood Reporter Online. August 16, 2008.
Los Angeles Times Online. August 27, 2008.
New York Times Online. August 27, 2008.
San Francisco Chronicle. August 27, 2008, p. E1.
Variety Online. August 16, 2008.
Washington Post. August 27, 2008, p. C1.

QUOTES

Samir Horn: "The truth is complicated."

TRIVIA

Steve Martin came up with the idea for the film while in production on *Bringing Down the House.*

TRANSPORTER 3

This time, the rules are the same. Except one.
—Movie tagline

Box Office: $31.7 million

As envisioned by their French filmmaker creator, Luc Besson, the *Transporter* movies are characterized by their charismatic hero, Jason Statham, stylish and elegant action sequences choreographed by Corey Yuen, a profusion of car chases, and mindlessly escapist but engaging plots that make for high-quality, testosterone-infused entertainment. *Transporter 3* delivers the goods just as reliably as the Transporter himself, who boasts an unblemished record of completed missions.

Opting instead to direct 2008's *The Incredible Hulk*, *Transporter 2* (2005) director Louis Leterrier is replaced by French filmmaker and former graffiti artist Olivier Megaton (his moniker derives from the bomb at Hiroshima, dropped on his birthday), who worked on the

Besson-produced *Hitman* (2007) as second unit director. The script, by Besson and Robert Mark Kamen, is a tad overly complex, with cuff bracelets rigged to explode in a *Speed* (1994)-like central plot device.

Frank Martin (Statham) is kidnapped by Johnson (Robert Knepper), part of an evil network that rigs a bomb to the Transporter's stripped-down Audi A8 that is set to explode if he ventures more than seventy-five feet from it. His mission is transport the comely Ukrainian Valentina (Natalya Rudakova), who along with Frank wears a bracelet linked to the Audi's bomb. Johnson and the rest need Valentina, the daughter of a Ukrainian government official, Leonid Vasilev (Jeroen Krabbé), as part of a larger scheme to smuggle ships full of toxic poisons into a Ukrainian harbor. Frank has no clue as to his ultimate destination. He must simply drive around with Valentina and await new GPS instructions.

The set up certainly allows ample room for the requisite car chases and fight sequences, many of which are surprisingly innovative and well executed. An early chase that ends on a bridge and continues underwater is one of the film's best, the tense underwater escape contrasted by tranquil, idyllic shots of Frank deep-sea fishing with friend Tarconi (François Berléand) while dissecting the comedic merits of Dean Martin and Jerry Lewis (a notable French favorite). And Megaton is not above playing the action film for comedy in a scene that has the laconic hero heatedly attempting to chase down his own car on a comically small bicycle. The film's cleverest fight scene, choreographed by the franchise's Corey Yuen, who also directed the original *The Transporter* (2002), involves Frank's simple white work shirt, which, à la James Bond, he employs as a deadly weapon. Many of the other martial arts fight scenes are sadly lost in the au courant, quick-cutting, virtually indecipherable camera style.

The journey takes them through Europe, from Marseilles to Odessa, with many more exciting but sometimes confusing action sequences along the way. One especially implausible one has Frank cartoonishly tilting his car up on two wheels at 120 miles an hour and driving between two Mack trucks.

The British Statham, seen earlier in his career in Guy Ritchie's films *Snatch* (2000) and *Lock, Stock and Two Smoking Barrels* (1998), is a former Olympic diver with a martial-arts background. This is evident in his still chiseled physique, showcased in several shirtless shots. In this latest addition to the franchise he proves that he has only improved on his natural talent with another effective and effortless performance. He works well pitted against the redheaded pixie Rudakova, in her film debut, especially in a scene where he rebuffs the advances of his sexy passenger, displaying a befuddled earnestness to comic effect. Valentina has an epiphany: "You're the gay!" "Nope! I am not 'the gay'," he firmly assures her. While his earlier 2008 release, *The Bank Job,* doubtless gave Statham more to sink his teeth into, it in no way lessens his contribution to the *Transporter* movies.

The *Speed*-like plot device that restricts Frank and Valentina to a narrow perimeter around the car makes for some interesting scenarios but could have been more fully and effectively explored. Mainly, though, the filmmakers use it as a handy way to bring these two disparate characters together and keep them together long enough to cultivate a necessary romance. The resulting love scenes are not among the action film's finest but are a worthy enough diversion from the car chases, fights, explosions, and daring escapes that are at the heart of *Transporter 3* and its two predecessors.

Hilary White

CREDITS

Frank Martin: Jason Statham
Tarconi: François Berléand
Johnson: Robert Knepper
Leonid Vasilev: Jeroen Krabbé
Valentina: Natalya Rudakova
Malcom Manville: David Atrakchi
Origin: France
Language: English
Released: 2008
Production: Luc Besson, Steve Chasman; TF-1 Films, Apipoulai Productions, Grive Prods., Current Entertainment; released by Lionsgate
Directed by: Olivier Megaton
Written by: Luc Besson, Robert Mark Kamen
Cinematography by: Giovanni Fiore Coltellacci
Music by: Alexandre Azaria
Sound: Yves-Marie Omnes
Editing: Carlo Rizzo, Camille Delamarre
Art Direction: Arnold Le Roch, Patrick Schmitt
Costumes: Olivier Bériot
Production Design: Patrick Durand
MPAA rating: PG-13
Running time: 104 minutes

REVIEWS

Boston Globe Online. November 26, 2008.
Chicago Sun-Times Online. November 25, 2008.
Entertainment Weekly Online. November 25, 2008.
Hollywood Reporter Online. November 18, 2008.
Los Angeles Times Online. November 26, 2008.

New York Times Online. November 26, 2008.
San Francisco Chronicle. November 26, 2008, p. E1.
Variety Online. November 18, 2008.
Washington Post. November 26, 2008, p. C10.

QUOTES

Frank Martin: "Do I look like a man who came half-way across Europe to die on a bridge?"

TRIVIA

All the stunts involving automobiles were performed in real time without the use of models and little CGI, which naturally resulted in numerous challenges for the stunt team.

TRANSSIBERIAN

Arrive on time.
—Movie tagline
You can't escape your lies.
—Movie tagline

Box Office: $2.2 million

Clearly inspired by Alfred Hitchcock greats like *Strangers on a Train* (1951) and *The Man Who Knew Too Much* (1956), writer/director Brad Anderson has crafted his own daring tale of a person caught in the very wrong place at the very wrong time in the thrilling *Transsiberian,* one of the best thrillers in years. Named after the rail line that shuttles a stunning variety of passengers from Beijing to Moscow across Russia's barren, frozen tundra, *Transsiberian* brilliantly plays with an odd dichotomy of train travel that contrasts the claustrophobia of spending days and nights in cabins that can barely fit one (much less sleep four), with the vast, unpopulated, open spaces that fly by the window. In that kind of mind-bending situation, people can make rash, uncalculated decisions, the kind that can get a nice American couple into some serious trouble and the kind that make for a riveting thriller in the hands of someone as talented as Anderson.

Transsiberian opens with the grisly discovery of a dead drug dealer and missing stash by Russian Officer Grinko (Ben Kingsley). After the intriguing prologue, Anderson and co-writer Will Conroy flash to Beijing and introduce the audience to the American couple, Roy (Woody Harrelson) and Jessie (Emily Mortimer), after a church trip and on their way to the Trans-Siberian rail line, leaving the audience to wonder how the missing drugs and our hapless heroes will eventually meet up. With little glimpses of character (and brilliant decisions by the talented Mortimer), we learn more about Roy and Jessie in those early scenes than most writers provide in an entire screenplay. Jessie is clearly the more rational of the two but could also be considered cold and sullen at times, while Roy has a wide-eyed innocence that could get them both in trouble in a place as unforgiving as Russia. A few marital problems are hinted at, as is the dark past of Jessie, who met her husband after she drunkenly crashed into him. Jessie does not drink a drop any more, which makes it all the more suspicious that their new cabin-mates on their Trans-Siberian train keep trying to hand her a shot. The drinkers are Carlos (Eduardo Noriega) and Abby (Kate Mara), an unusual pair who are clearly far more world-traveled than our hero and heroine. After Roy gets off the train to sightsee in a small Russian town and does not get back on when the locomotive pulls away, Jessie is left to make some very important decisions, almost none of which she makes correctly and almost all of which lead her deeper into a situation that would have made Hitchcock smile.

Like a lot of thrillers, *Transsiberian* is filled with twists that sometimes stretch the boundaries of disbelief. A solid argument can be made that most people would not make at least one, maybe two, of Jessie's crucial moves, but what sets *Transsiberian* apart is that Mortimer sells them as completely believable. In one of the best and most physically demanding performances of the year, this abundantly talented actress is completely convincing. She never hits a false note, never plays the eventual horror melodramatically, and always brings an authenticity to her character that few actresses could manage. Mortimer and Anderson realize that Jessie cannot just be a plot device, like so many thriller heroines. She needs to be 100 percent real for the audience to accept the many twists and turns that might seem ridiculous in the hands of a lesser actress or director.

Mortimer's excellent performance also seems to raise the game of everyone around her, with Harrelson seeming more genuine than he has in years and Noriega and Mara giving completely convincing performances. In particular, Mara has a complex, quiet role that feels more fully realized with fewer lines than most major lead turns of the year. Bad thriller writers forget that their genre is not just about the twist endings or the shocking death scenes. It has been and always will be about the characters. Anderson's focus on character in stand-out genre films like *Session 9* (2001) and *The Machinist* (2004) has made him one of the more interesting young directors working today.

By the time Kingsley returns in the final act (accompanied by the great character actor Thomas Kretschmann), this cinematic train may have taken one detour too many for viewers tempted to analyze the plot too closely. On reflection, *Transsiberian* has some gaps in the track, some places where the script could have used some tightening. But, more important, those flaws only barely register during the actual watching of the film, only coming to light upon serious critical reflection. *Transsiberian* is a thriller that is that rarest of things in today's derivative market—thrilling.

Brian Tallerico

CREDITS

Jessie: Emily Mortimer
Roy: Woody Harrelson
Grinko: Ben Kingsley
Abby: Kate Mara
Carlos: Eduardo Noriega
Kolzak: Thomas Kretschmann
Origin: Great Britain, Spain, Germany, Lithuania
Language: English, Russian
Released: 2008
Production: Julio Fernández, Carlos Fernández, Antonio Nava; Castelao Proucciones, Lithuanian Film Studios, Scout Productions; released by First Look Studios
Directed by: Brad Anderson
Written by: Brad Anderson, Will Conroy
Cinematography by: Xavi Giménez
Music by: Alfonso de Vilallonga
Sound: Rupert Ivey
Editing: Jaume Martí
Art Direction: Algis Garbaciauskas, Iñigo Navarro
Costumes: Thomas Oláh
Production Design: Alain Bainée
MPAA rating: R
Running time: 111 minutes

REVIEWS

Entertainment Weekly Online. July 16, 2008.
Hollywood Reporter Online. January 20, 2008.
New York Times Online. July 18, 2008.
Premiere Online. July 21, 2008.
Variety Online. January 19, 2008.
Village Voice Online. July 16, 2008.

QUOTES

Jessie: "Kill off all my demons, Roy, and my angels might die, too."

TROPIC THUNDER

The movie they think they're making...isn't a movie anymore.
—Movie tagline

Box Office: $110.5 million

It sure sounds like a ludicrous idea: Making a movie about the making of a movie about a Vietnam War rescue mission. Not only does the subject matter seem dated, it does not seem like a topic ripe for satire. And Ben Stiller directing Ben Stiller as a fading action star? And Robert Downey Jr. in blackface? All kinds of alarm bells seem to be going off.

Surprisingly, though, *Tropic Thunder* not only works, it is often hilarious. In a rare feat for this era, it is a punchy satire that keeps on punching. And the stars, including Jack Black, Steve Coogan, and Nick Nolte, are having plenty of fun making fun of Hollywood stars.

Vietnam is just an excuse, a convenient setting for this slashing, often silly roasting of moviedom egos, and the fact that the war is sufficiently distant to be a topic for humor keeps the movie, barely, from descending into difficult territory. Stiller the screenwriter (along with Justin Theroux) moves the story briskly along for at least the first half of the film and fills time with plenty of just-this-side-of-ridiculous dialogue. Stiller the director lacks subtlety, but he is good at delivering payoffs. And for once Stiller the actor puts his own hambone instincts to good use, playing a fading action hero, Tugg Speedman, with an oversized sense of his own thespian abilities. He has played this sort of self-satirizing character before, but never so convincingly.

The biggest gamble of all is that of inventing a character, Kirk Lazarus, to be Stiller's foil. Downey, stretching himself one again, takes on what seems to be more of a giant pitfall than a role. Lazarus is a serious, Oscar®-quality Australian actor (think Russell Crowe), who inexplicably takes on the role of a heroic black soldier in the film being shot on location in Vietnam. The film's director, played by Steve Coogan, is an ineffective lightweight trying to make the transition from British character studies to big-budget action movies, and as the movie opens, the film is already a disaster of Titanic proportions, leaching money and jeopardizing careers. He is threatened most alarmingly and profanely by a sadistic, domineering studio boss, played by a nearly unrecognizable Tom Cruise. And he is goaded into a new strategy by the phony disabled veteran, played by Nolte, whose falsified biography the movie is based on.

That strategy is to drop the five actors playing the heroes off the set and into the jungle, using the set's crazed pyrotechnics expert to scare the living daylights out of the men, as they are plunged into realistic dangers and forced to trade in their prissy characterizations for gutsy performances. The problem is, the director steps on a land mine and is exploded, and from there on only Stiller's Speedman thinks they are following a script. And, of course, it turns out there really are murderous

enemies in the jungle—not the Viet Cong, but a gang of heroin dealers run by a teenage dictator. And, not surprisingly, the actors must really transcend their roles.

Stiller keeps the plot from bogging down by throwing in plenty of silly diversions. It starts immediately and without warning when the movie opens with three fake trailers for coming attractions—introducing several of the characters, including Brandon T. Jackson as Alpa Chino, a rapper who hawks a popular energy drink, and Jack Black as Jeff Portnoy, the leading star of a television series about an obese family given to flatulence. And of course there is Speedman, whose franchise as a vigilante world-saving hero is slipping badly after a fifth sequel and an ill-advised foray into playing the serious role of a mentally challenged young man in a very maudlin movie.

Adding to the fun is Speedman's agent, played by Matthew McConaughey, whose obsession is making sure his star client has the TiVo® he has demanded in his contract. When he is tempted to make a devil's deal with the studio boss after Speedman is captured and held hostage, the film reaches a fever pitch of satire about the pettiness and greed of Hollywood.

Tropic Thunder is a rare instance in which top stars pull no punches in satirizing not only the business and some of their coworkers, but also themselves. The satire goes down easily because the film is awash in frivolity, but there are fascinating conversations about Hollywood's machinations and plenty of references to other films (in particular, of course, *Apocalypse Now* [1979] and *Hearts of Darkness* [1991], the documentary about its filming). It is all a mad, mad fling, but a fling with a point, and like all really good comedy, it zeroes in on its targets with laser precision wrapped in a sheath of good fun. In some senses it is like the live-action version of *Shrek* (2001) in that it is a vicious dissection of Hollywood's warped values but is also entertaining and hilarious on its face.

Eventually, and probably inevitably, the satire gets a little thin and creaky, but Stiller holds down the fort by playing one of those actors who has found his true self in the extremes of a challenging set, a hoary cliché that Hollywood actors like to recycle ad nauseum. It is certainly one of Stiller's most unfettered and satisfying performances. Nominated for an Oscar® for his role in this film, Downey pulls off this challenging part with a hugely entertaining performance that skates right on the edge of dangerous racial stereotyping and then rises above it with humor and valor. The scenes of Jackson ripping Downey's conceit to shreds are wonderfully written. Jay Baruchel as the fifth member of the platoon also carries his comic load with aplomb, but Black is miserably underused as a drug-addicted fathead and wimp. It is also nice to see Nolte's talents fully exploited as the phony at the heart of all the phoniness, with his crusty fake heroism blown to shreds by greed and pretension. It works because who can question the integrity of a Nick Nolte character? It is but one example of Stiller's ingenuity in the casting and filming of what might seem like an unfilmable story.

Michael Betzold

CREDITS

Tugg Speedman: Ben Stiller
Kirk Lazarus: Robert Downey Jr.
Jeff Portnoy: Jack Black
Kevin Sandusky: Jay Baruchel
Cody: Danny McBride
Studio Exec Ron Slolom: Bill Hader
Damien Cockburn: Steve Coogan
"Four Leaf" Tayback: Nick Nolte
Alpa Chino: Brandon T. Jackson
Les Grossman: Tom Cruise
Rick Peck: Matthew McConaughey
Rebecca: Christine Taylor
Script Supervisor: Amy Stiller
Tran: Brandon Soo Hoo
Himself: Tobey Maguire (Cameo)
Himself: Jon Voight (Cameo)
Herself: Tyra Banks (Cameo)
Herself: Jennifer Love Hewitt (Cameo)
Origin: USA
Language: English
Released: 2008
Production: Stuart Cornfeld, Eric McLeod, Ben Stiller, Justin Theroux; Goldcrest Films, Red Hour; released by DreamWorks
Directed by: Ben Stiller
Written by: Ben Stiller, Justin Theroux, Etan Cohen
Cinematography by: John Toll
Music by: Theodore Shapiro
Sound: Jim Brookshire, Craig Henighan
Editing: Greg Hayden
Art Direction: Raphael Gort, Richard L. Johnson, Dan Webster
Costumes: Marlene Stewart
Production Design: Jeff Mann
MPAA rating: R
Running time: 106 minutes

REVIEWS

Boston Globe Online. August 13, 2008.
Chicago Sun-Times Online. August 12, 2008.

Entertainment Weekly Online. August 12, 2008.
Hollywood Reporter Online. July 26, 2008.
Los Angeles Times Online. August 13, 2008.
New York Times Online. August 13, 2008.
Rolling Stone Online. August 21, 2008.
San Francisco Chronicle. August 13, 2008, p. E1.
Variety Online. July 25, 2008.
Washington Post. August 13, 2008, p. C1.

QUOTES

Kirk Lazarus: "I don't break character till the DVD commentary."
Kirk Lazarus: "I know who I am! I'm a dude playing a dude disguised as another dude!"

TRIVIA

The films was shipped to several theaters under the bogus name "Capricorn."

AWARDS

Nomination:

Oscars 2008: Support. Actor (Downey)
British Acad. 2008: Support. Actor (Downey)
Golden Globes 2009: Support. Actor (Cruise), Support. Actor (Downey)
Screen Actors Guild 2008: Support. Actor (Downey).

21

Inspired by the true story of five students who changed the game forever.
—Movie tagline
They proved the Vegas Blackjack System was beatable…by beating the hell out of it.
—Movie tagline

Box Office: $81.1 million

Charting the exploits of a group of math whiz kids who take Las Vegas casinos for a small fortune by counting cards at blackjack, *21* is loosely based on Ben Mezrich's best-selling *Bringing Down the House,* an inside look at a team of real-life MIT students who made millions beating the system. The film's screenplay, credited to Peter Steinfeld and Allan Loeb, takes many liberties with the book, such as streamlining the action and shaping it into a traditional narrative and creating a more clear-cut conflict by transforming a key character into a villain.

A movie, however, cannot simply replicate an episodic book composed mainly of a series of trips to casinos where enormous winnings are accumulated before the system inevitably catches up with the players. By using the source material's basic premise while smoothing out the rough edges and giving the whole package a Hollywood sheen, director Robert Luketic has succeeded in turning the book into a fast-moving, entertaining film. He conveys what life was like for these young superstars of blackjack while making their story work as a movie with a strong arc for the protagonist and some thrilling plot twists and turns.

Jim Sturgess stars as Ben Campbell, a brilliant MIT undergrad who is financially strapped and thus in danger of seeing his dreams of attending Harvard Medical School vanish. But math professor Micky Rosa (Kevin Spacey) recognizes Ben's gift with numbers and recruits him for a secret club that masters card-counting techniques and makes clandestine trips to Las Vegas. Also prominent on the team is the pretty Jill (Kate Bosworth), who is just one more incentive for the straight-arrow Ben to take a chance on the world of big-time blackjack. Rounding out the group are Choi (Aaron Yoo), Kianna (Liza Lapira), and Fisher (Jacob Pitts), who grows increasingly jealous as Ben quickly assumes a leadership position on the team.

Where the book delved a bit into the protagonist's inner conflict of leading a double life as he becomes more and more enamored of Vegas glitz, the movie's Ben very quickly takes to his new life and abandons his old, nerdy friends. The screenplay is shrewd in giving Ben motivations, not just the financial incentive but the fun and freedom that Las Vegas brings to his dull world. As someone who has been a serious student all of his life, Ben happily takes to the fantasy of being someone different—a high roller whom the casino personnel treat with respect.

In the scenes of casino play, Luketic excels in drawing us into the team dynamics—how members give each other secret hand and verbal signals to alert the designated "Big Player" of the group when a table's count favors the players and when he should therefore raise his bet. Blackjack itself is not inherently cinematic, but Russell Carpenter's cinematography zeroes in on cards flying through the air and flipping over, close-ups of thousands of dollars of chips being played, and the use of fast motion and slow motion to simulate the heady feeling of being in a casino for long periods of time.

Ben's character arc, the rise and fall of a good kid who is seduced by the high life and loses control, is recognizable. Initially attracted to the idea of winning $300,000 to cover medical school costs, he cannot help but keep going. But when he lets his emotions get the better of him—something that a seasoned player should never do—and loses, it drives a wedge between him and Micky, who ransacks Ben's dorm room and takes thousands of dollars to compensate for his losses.

Meanwhile, a casino security man named Cole Williams (Laurence Fishburne) is monitoring the team's play and gradually closing in. This character could have been the standard casino heavy, but he is given extra dimension. As technology gradually supplants the need for security men, he is in danger of becoming a dinosaur, which becomes part of his motivation for personally bringing down the team.

In what may be too much of a coincidence, Cole and Micky just happen to have an old rivalry, which becomes the backstory for the climax as the team reassembles with Micky to take the casino for one last big score—a sequence punctuated by double crosses and an exhilarating, unpredictable finish. It is, admittedly, much more a Hollywood ending than what is found in the book, in which some questions are left unanswered, the various plot threads do not work themselves out as neatly, and the bad guys remain shadowy casino employees.

The screenplay also takes a more conventional moral stance by not letting the hero directly profit from his card counting, whereas the film's real-life inspiration, Jeffrey Ma (who, incidentally, has a cameo in the film as a card dealer), raked in a small fortune. But the film nonetheless ends on a bright note with Ben using the tale of his fantastic adventures to impress a Harvard professor and win a scholarship. Still, it is hard not to notice that the story loses some richness in not immersing us, as the book does, in the background of Vegas history, the utter madness of casino life, and all the minutiae of team play.

Nonetheless, while *21* deviates from Mezrich's more realistic depiction of the MIT team's adventures, the changes make for a satisfying film that captures the essence of the story. And turning Micky Rosa into a duplicitous figure lets Spacey tap into the smarmy operator persona that he assumes so well. He is a natural for this role, and, as a producer who shepherded the project to the screen, knew immediately that he wanted to play the part.

Like Las Vegas itself, *21* offers great escapist pleasures. Luketic takes us on a swift, exciting ride that most audiences can relate to because, on some level, it would be a dream come true. The idea of beating the casinos at their own game has an intrinsic appeal, and the film cheerfully revels in the glamour and high-stakes action of this irresistible fantasy.

Peter N. Chumo II

CREDITS

Ben Campbell: Jim Sturgess
Micky Rosa: Kevin Spacey

Jill: Kate Bosworth
Choi: Aaron Yoo
Jimmy Fisher: Jacob Pitts
Cole Williams: Laurence Fishburne
Kianna: Liza Lapira
Cam: Sam Golzari
Bob Phillips: Jack Gilpin
Ellen Campbell: Helen Carey
Miles Connoly: Josh Gad
Stemple: Spencer Garrett
Terry: Jack McGee
Origin: USA
Language: English
Released: 2008
Production: Dana Brunetti, Kevin Spacey, Michael De Luca; Relativity Media, Trigger Street, Columbia Pictures; released by Sony Pictures Entertainment
Directed by: Robert Luketic
Written by: Peter Steinfeld, Allan Loeb
Cinematography by: Russell Carpenter
Music by: David Sardy
Sound: Mike Wilhoit
Editing: Elliot Graham
Art Direction: James Truesdale
Costumes: Luca Mosca
Production Design: Missy Stewart
MPAA rating: PG-13
Running time: 123 minutes

REVIEWS

Boston Globe Online. March 28, 2008.
Chicago Sun-Times Online. March 27, 2008.
Entertainment Weekly Online. March 26, 2008.
Hollywood Reporter Online. March 13, 2008.
Los Angeles Times Online. March 28, 2008.
New York Times Online. March 28, 2008.
Rolling Stone Online. April 3, 2008.
San Francisco Chronicle. March 28, 2008, p. E1.
Variety Online. March 7, 2008.
Washington Post. March 28, 2008, p. C5.

QUOTES

Cole Williams: "If I see you in here again, I will break your cheekbone with a small hammer. And then I will kill you."
Micky Rosa: "You are only ever as good to me as the money you make!"

TRIVIA

Since MIT would not allow filming on campus, the movie was actually on the Boston University campus.

27 DRESSES

Always a bridesmaid, never a bride.
—Movie tagline

Box Office: $76.8 million

Katherine Heigl is the charming center of this fairly routine, albeit quite likable, romantic comedy, directed by Anne Fletcher from a script by Aline Brosh McKenna. As the good-hearted Jane Nichols, who organizes all of her friends' weddings down to the last detail while pining away for her boss, George (Edward Burns), Heigl is the classic woman living for others instead of herself, someone very easy for us to root for. If the film contains all of the genre's reliable elements, including a love triangle, a handsome love interest whose initial antagonism to Jane can only mean that he is ultimately the man meant for her, and a wisecracking best friend, the tried and true plot conventions do not get in the way of the film's overall geniality.

At an early age, Jane fell in love with weddings and, as an adult, is so obsessed that she seems to cultivate friendships just so she can play the part of wedding planner. A very funny opening has her scurrying back and forth between two receptions in one night and constantly alternating her bridesmaid outfits in the back seat of a cab. At one of the receptions, she meets Kevin (James Marsden), a reporter who covers nuptials for the *New York Journal* (a thinly veiled stand-in for the *New York Times*) even though he is cynical about marriage and thus Jane's polar opposite. In true romantic-comedy fashion, the cynic and the idealist are, of course, meant for each other, and, while their chemistry may not have the pizzazz of the classic screen couples, their banter is pleasant and the rivalry fun to watch.

The plot takes a turn when Jane's younger sister, Tess (Malin Akerman), arrives for an extended visit and, not knowing that Jane has had a longstanding crush on George, instantaneously steals his heart. Meanwhile, Kevin begins to ingratiate himself with Jane because he believes that her almost obsessive devotion to all things matrimonial would make a great story, which would be his ticket to more interesting assignments. Because he uses a pen name, Jane does not realize that Kevin is really her favorite newspaper writer. It is just one more well-used device of the genre—if Jane can fall for the cynical reporter while already being in love with the sensitive writer, they are obviously meant to end up together.

While Jane embodies an appealing combination of selflessness and intelligence, Tess acts like a complete phony, claiming to be a vegetarian and lover of the outdoors so that her tastes will seem to align with George's. But when they get engaged after a whirlwind romance and Jane's father gives Tess their late mother's wedding dress, it is almost too much for Jane. And when Tess essentially mutilates the dress to suit her, the hurt is so great that we wonder if this light entertainment has gone too far, if it has treaded into such a dicey area that it cannot recover its light spirit, especially when Jane retaliates by exposing all of her sister's lies. But in this idealized world, nothing can permanently come between the sisters, and, true to formula, these seemingly rough patches can be gently smoothed over without taking too much of a toll on the film's believability.

It is hard to imagine *27 Dresses* without Heigl, an actress who radiates such goodness that it is easy to picture Jane moving on to a fresh start and getting her own happy ending with Kevin, which means, ultimately, her own wedding attended by the twenty-seven brides for whom she had served as bridesmaid. Heigl also brings an appealing combination of warmth, heart, and a knack for physical comedy that heralds her as the next big romantic-comedy star. Just a roll of the eyes or throwaway remark generates a laugh. At the same time, she also subtly reveals the depths of a woman who is often hurt or disappointed but must cover up her true feelings and smile through her pain.

And even within the formulas—including an over-reliance on montages to fill in plot—there are bursts of creativity. When we are treated to a montage of Jane modeling her 27 bridesmaid dresses for Kevin, the sequence may feel obligatory, but the wide range of dresses, from the silly to the downright weird, makes the sequence very engaging. Jane and Kevin falling for each other while drunkenly singing Elton John's "Bennie and the Jets" at a bar may not be inspired filmmaking, but the actors bring a buoyancy and sense of fun to the familiar scene.

While Burns is so bland as the object of Jane's affection that we can see almost immediately that George is not the right man for her, Marsden matches Heigl in charm and intelligence. And Judy Greer makes an impression as Casey, the sarcastic, promiscuous best friend who must constantly bring Jane down to earth from her flighty notions.

27 Dresses is, admittedly, predictable fare, ending with Jane's own happily ever after, but fans of the genre will enjoy it even as they check off all the requisite plot ingredients. The real discovery, though, is Heigl, whose twin successes with 2007's *Knocked Up* and now *27 Dresses* confirm that a new romantic-comedy heroine has arrived.

Peter N. Chumo II

CREDITS

Jane Nichols: Katherine Heigl
Kevin: James Marsden
Tess: Malin Akerman
Casey: Judy Greer
George: Edward Burns

Maureen: Melora Hardin
Hal: Brian Kerwin
Trent: Maulik Pancholy
Origin: USA
Language: English
Released: 2008
Production: Roger Birnbaum, Gary Barber, Jonathan Glickman; Fox 2000 Pictures, Spyglass Entertainment; released by 20th Century-Fox
Directed by: Anne Fletcher
Written by: Aline Brosh McKenna
Cinematography by: Peter James
Music by: Randy Edelman
Sound: Tom Nelson
Music Supervisor: Buck Damon
Editing: Priscilla Nedd Friendly
Art Direction: Jonathan Arkin, Miguel Lopez-Castillo
Costumes: Catherine Thomas
Production Design: Shepherd Frankel
MPAA rating: PG-13
Running time: 107 minutes

REVIEWS

Boston Globe Online. January 18, 2008.
Chicago Sun-Times Online. January 18, 2008.
Entertainment Weekly. January 18, 2008, p. 62.
Hollywood Reporter Online. January 1, 2008.
Los Angeles Times Online. January 18, 2008.
New York Times Online. January 18, 2008.
San Francisco Chronicle. January 18, 2008, p. E1.
Variety Online. December 28, 2007.
Washington Post. January 18, 2008, p. C5.

QUOTES

Jane: "I feel like I just found out my favorite love song was written about a sandwich."

TRIVIA

The fake title "Wardrobe" was used when prints were shipped to theaters.

TWILIGHT

When you can live forever, what do you live for?
—Movie tagline

Box Office: $190.6 million

Moviegoers have long loved to cower in the dark and dread the undead, ravenous for thrills as delicious to them as a corpseful of primo plasma would be to any vampire. Even before the motion picture was old enough to talk, audiences were being filled with a mixture of delight and disgust by Max Schreck looming horrifically upon the screen as *Nosferatu* (1922), a terrifying treat of a performance that has caused more nights of tormented sleep than could ever be counted on the character's claw-like fingers.

Such nightmarish grotesquery is a far cry from the bloodsucking dreamboat that made scores of swooning adolescent girls do anything but avert their eyes during *Twilight*, the fervently anticipated, fairly faithful adaptation of Stephenie Meyer's 2005 gusher of a bestseller. Many initial screenings of the film had the aura of a pajama party, packed with hordes of girls emitting high-pitched squeals of anticipatory excitement as they bonded over a shared ardor for Meyer's love story between seventeen-year-old Bella Swan and eternally seventeen-year-old Edward Cullen. Adults present had to chuckle during the film at the size of the young ladies' sighs, along with all the other forms of audible adoration elicited by Robert Pattinson, portrayer of the icy-skinned protagonist whom they decisively declared to be exceedingly hot. While many of their male peers would likely find this vampire film anemic, bored by the lack of gore and derisive of all the mushiness, one can see how *Twilight* successfully struck a romantic chord within young women who, like Bella, are simultaneously titillated and terrified as they teeter on the verge of adulthood.

Anyone of school age or beyond can understand what an anxiety-inducing challenge it would be to not only have to fit in at a new school in a new town but also do so some six months after classes have started and cliques have solidified. That is what high school junior Bella (Kristen Stewart) does when she makes a March move from the parched tan-colored surroundings of sweltering Phoenix, Arizona, to the cool, cloud-enshrouded lush greens of a tiny Pacific Northwest town. There she takes up residence with her police chief father (Billy Burke), after her mother (Sarah Clarke) goes on the road with her new, baseball-playing husband. There is an authentic, brave-faced, awkward tentativeness to the way this teen plugs into her new surroundings. She worries about knowing no one at school and yet warily puts up her guard upon entering, characterizing herself when approached by a welcoming student as the "suffer-in-silence type" in order to maintain a protective unobtrusiveness.

While this attractive, bright, rather dark young lady soon has a bubbly group of companions warmly coalesce around her, she craves the attentions of one extraordinarily intriguing classmate whose eyes keep boring into her soul from a distance, and who possesses a good excuse for initially giving her such an inexplicably cold shoulder. Powerfully alluring, mysterious, and brooding Edward

(Robert Pattinson) certainly stands out in the crowded cafeteria, with his impressively contoured shock of black hair, expression-punctuating heavy eyebrows above equally inky eyes, and blood-red lips, all about a face as strikingly handsome as it is chalky white. He is one of the foster children of Dr. Carlisle Cullen (Peter Facinelli) and his wife, Esme (Elizabeth Reaser), a sun-averse, unusually pasty-looking bunch. They look like they could use blood transfusions but actually get them on a regular basis—orally. The family is a cut above your average vampires, vowing to eschew the human arteries they would still prefer to bite deep down. Thus the aptly-named Cullens go about culling the area's deer population, calling themselves "vegetarians" and comparing their morally restricted diet to eating tofu: it "never really satisfies." Only local Native Americans like Billy Black (Gil Birmingham) and his son, Jacob (Taylor Lautner), have knowledge based upon legend about what the Cullens really are.

Thus Edward initially endeavors not to get too temptingly close to this new girl who singularly stirs his reined-in vampiric longings. Maintaining not only a safe physical but also emotional distance is an increasingly challenging task, however, as Bella inspires heartfelt adoration on top of salivation. Of course, every time the unmistakably captivated hunk inexplicably backs off, she is all the more intrigued and in need of answers. Especially after Edward repeatedly steps in to save Bella from harm with amazing abilities that both baffle and impress, the young lady he is attracted to like "my own personal brand of heroin" comes to view him with even deeper adoration as her magnificent, trusty hero. So much for Bella's expressed aversion to anything cold.

If a potent stare could cause pregnancy, Bella would have been shopping for maternity clothes shortly after Edward first laid eyes upon her. Meyer, a Mormon, wrote a book that was charged with a chaste eroticism, and the film carries this forward with incessant penetrating eye contact as opposed to any physical sexual communion. (Those pressing for teenage abstinence must have gotten very excited by a hit movie featuring a glorious and meritorious bridling of teenaged ardor.) Yet *Twilight*'s vampirism is undeniably just a metaphor for powerful, all-consuming primal passions, ones that, in this case, could literally destroy a girl who has quickly become far too smitten to worry about being bitten. For Edward, the mere whiff of Bella's scent rather comically drives him into a frenzy perhaps only slightly beyond that experienced by the average hormonally propelled high school guy struggling with self-control.

What especially appealed to *Twilight*'s legion of ardent female fans is Edward's chivalrous refusal to ever risk ravaging and ruining Bella, steadfastly thinking about his soul mate's welfare even after she has realized what he is and lets him know how perfectly willing she is to succumb. Sure he feels a compulsion to "go all the way" in his way and change her forever, but, despite being eternally and painfully stuck in an especially angst-ridden and often lonely time of life that he could permanently improve with one bite, Edward selflessly refrains. (Noting glimpses of the vampire's self-loathing, such as the way he swipes aside her rhapsodic praise of him at one point with the clearer-eyed rebuttal that he is a cursed "monster," will allow viewers to fully understand his choice.) Edward basically makes two stirring assertions at the same time that powerfully combine to make susceptible hearts flutter: his desire for Bella is grandly immense and ferociously intense, and yet his love and respect for her is greater still. Thus, in vampire terms, he would give his eyeteeth to claim her, but will not sink them in. So with Edward's devastating good looks, gallant restraint, unwavering thoughtfulness and unfailing protectiveness, impeccable manners, tormented bad-boy angst that needs soothing, and a lack of pressure to do anything beyond adore Bella, is it any wonder girls watching *Twilight* said they would leap at their chance if she ever decided to dump him?

It is ironic how *Twilight* loses electricity during a thunderstorm baseball game, which sets up a moderately suspenseful climactic battle for Bella fought by Edward and the other good vampires against an ominous roving band of the traditional kind who had been guzzling from the locals of late. After brutal and relentlessly bloodthirsty James (standout Cam Gigandet) succeeds in biting her, Edward can either let her be damned to their ranks or keep her just as he loves her by sucking out only enough of her blood to remove the venom. Of course he does the latter, and as the two sway slowly in each other's arms at their prom, the film ends with the door left wide open for a sequel, which was given the go-ahead immediately after *Twilight*'s bonanza of an opening weekend. (Not surprisingly, there are already tentative plans to film the final two books in Meyer's rabidly devoured series.) Made on a budget of $37 million, *Twilight*'s domestic theatrical gross alone surpassed $150 million.

Catherine Hardwicke was chosen to direct *Twilight* primarily because of her first film, *Thirteen* (2003), in which she was able to convincingly convey the sometimes questionable choices and confused paths girls can be drawn to take while navigating through the challenges of adolescence. Ed Stern, Hardwicke's director of photography on both that film and this, uses a highly mobile camera that floats and twirls at will around the lovers, emphasizing the headiness of it all. He beautifully captures Washington's misty, moody climate, with turbulent ocean views and stormy skies meant to reflect the characters' dramatic emotions. Both Stewart and

Pattinson do well in roles that require them to convey depths of stringently restricted emotion, the former's words cascading forth at times like water through the break in a dam. Nice flashes of warm humor are added by Burke, with both deaths and dates bringing on recommendations of pepper spray for Bella. There are problems with pacing, scenes that do not quite pan out, and special effects that sometimes look a little cheesy. However, none of this will matter a whit to the film's target audience, who left *Twilight* with a pleasant afterglow.

David L. Boxerbaum

CREDITS

Bella Swan: Kristen Stewart
Edward Cullen: Robert Pattinson
Jacob Black: Taylor Lautner
Charlie Swan: Billy Burke
Dr. Carlisle Cullen: Peter Facinelli
Esme Cullen: Elizabeth Reaser
Rosalie Hale: Nikki Reed
Jasper Cullen: Jackson Rathbone
Alice Cullen: Ashley Greene
Emmett Cullen: Kellan Lutz
James: Cam Gigandet
Victoria: Rachel Lefevre
Laurent: Edi Gathegi
Jessica Stanley: Anna Kendrick
Mike Newton: Michael Welch
Billy Black: Gil Birmingham
Origin: USA
Language: English
Released: 2008
Production: Mark Morgan, Wyck Godfrey, Greg Mooradian; Temple Hill, Maverick Films, Imprint Entertainment; released by Summit Entertainment
Directed by: Catherine Hardwicke
Written by: Melissa Rosenberg
Cinematography by: Elliot Davis
Music by: Carter Burwell
Sound: Glenn Micallef
Music Supervisor: Alexandra Patsavas
Editing: Nancy Richardson
Costumes: Wendy Chuck
Production Design: Dan Bishop
MPAA rating: PG-13
Running time: 121 minutes

REVIEWS

Boston Globe Online. November 21, 2008.
Chicago Sun-Times Online. November 19, 2008.

Entertainment Weekly Online. November 19, 2008.
Hollywood Reporter Online. November 20, 2008.
Los Angeles Times Online. November 21, 2008.
New York Times Online. November 21, 2008.
San Francisco Chronicle. November 20, 2008, p. E1.
Time Online. November 20, 2008.
Variety Online. November 19, 2008.
Wall Street Journal Online. November 21, 2008.
Washington Post. November 20, 2008, p. C1.

QUOTES

Edward Cullen (to Bella): "I feel very protective of you."

Edward Cullen: "I'm the world's most dangerous predator. Everything about me invites you in. My voice, my face, even my smell. As if I would need any of that. As if you could outrun me. As if you could fight me off. I'm designed to kill."

TRIVIA

The author of the original books the film is based on, Stephenie Meyer, has a cameo in the diner scene where Charlie asks Bella if she likes the boys in town (she is ordering a vegetarian sandwich).

TYLER PERRY'S MEET THE BROWNS

(Meet the Browns)

Check your baggage at the door.
—Movie tagline

You can't choose your family, you can only pack accordingly.
—Movie tagline

Box Office: $41.9 million

Tyler Perry has created one of the more fascinating cinematic empires of the last decade and has done so with not just a lack of critical support but outright damnation of his product by the community that judges motion pictures. After a very successful theatrical career, Perry moved on to make the films *Madea's Family Reunion* (2006) and *Diary of a Mad Black Woman* (2005). An interesting thing happened—critics hated them at the same time that audiences fell in love. The debate over whether or not critics were out of touch with the tastes of the public had found one of its most interesting talking points, but things started to change with 2007's *Why Did I Get Married,* a film to which nearly half of the nation's critics gave a positive review. Either critics had started to give in to what Perry had accomplished with his demographic or, more likely, Perry

had actually improved his filmmaking skills. Sadly, Perry slid back with the abysmal *Daddy's Little Girls* (2007), but the inclusion of the great Angela Bassett at the forefront of *Meet the Browns,* an adaptation of Perry's own play, gave the critical community hope that they would finally be on the same page with the American public on a Perry film. *Meet the Browns* is still a significant improvement over Perry's first two films, largely helped by Bassett's ability to turn even the most clichéd role into something interesting, but an intriguing set-up is deflated by Perry's continued reliance on physical comedy and melodrama in the second two acts.

Brenda (Angela Bassett) is a single mother living in inner-city Chicago who has been struggling for years to keep her son on the straight and narrow while she makes ends meet. At the beginning of *Meet the Browns,* Brenda is laid off unexpectedly and takes her two daughters and her teenage son Michael (Lance Gross) to Georgia for a funeral. The opening act of *Meet the Browns,* as Bassett takes front and center as a believably struggling mother, is Perry's best filmmaking yet. He still dips into melodrama far too easily, but Bassett is the best actress he has ever had in front of his camera and her skill shines through the soap opera. Sadly, Bassett gets buried by Perry's screenwriting flaws when Brenda goes to Georgia and meets the Browns, a stereotypical Southern clan of two-dimensional characters headed by the flamboyant Mr. Leroy Brown (David Mann). *Meet the Browns* is another "city mouse in the country" comedy that lays on the lessons about the importance of family and Southern morality with all the subtlety of a punch to the face. Brenda gets an interesting romantic lead (Rick Fox) and Sofía Vergara steals some scenes as her best friend, but nearly everything that happens with the Brown family feels written by a computer designed to pen stereotypes, clichés, and melodrama. Perry the director is getting more accomplished at the basics—*Meet the Browns* looks better than his other films, most of which had a "filmed play" sensation—but Perry the screenwriter still feels the need to swing wildly from melodrama to cartoonish comedy and back again.

Meet the Browns was another success for Perry, making more than double its meager budget before it even left domestic theaters, but critics were back in line to point out this popular filmmaker's flaws. Frank Scheck of the *Hollywood Reporter* noted, "The film demonstrates all too vividly its creator's penchant for soap opera-style melodramatic, absurdly broad comedy and offensively stereotypical characterizations." Joe Leydon of *Variety* went a step further by saying that "*Tyler Perry's Meet the Browns* often plays more like Tyler Perry's Greatest Hits as it recycles various elements from the writer-director's earlier works." Perry may have improved his directorial skills but critics still correctly bemoaned his lack of screenwriting ability. Even an actress as talented as Bassett could not get Perry's fan base and the critical community on the same page.

Perry clearly prides himself on giving his audience some of everything. His films contain some of the most wildly inconsistent tone shifts of the last decade, and *Meet the Browns* is no exception. Gritty realism in Chicago is followed by broad, theatrical humor in the South. Emotional scenes are followed by odd physical humor. Like all of his movies, *Meet the Browns* jams moral lessons in between the broad comedy, lessening the impact of both. There is a good chance, especially with the improvement of his last few films over his first two, that there will be one day that critics and audiences will get on the same page regarding a Tyler Perry film. *Meet the Browns* is not that day.

Brian Tallerico

CREDITS

Brenda: Angela Bassett
Harry: Rick Fox
Sarah: Margaret Avery
L.B.: Frankie Faison
Vera: Jenifer Lewis
Cheryl: Sofía Vergara
Will: Lamman Rucker
Mildred: Irma P. Hall
Joe/Madea: Tyler Perry
Michael: Lance Gross
Mr. Brown: David Mann
Cora Brown: Tamela Mann

Judy Rhee: Judy Rhee
Origin: USA
Language: English
Released: 2008
Production: Tyler Perry, Reuben Cannon; released by Lionsgate
Directed by: Tyler Perry
Written by: Tyler Perry
Cinematography by: Sandi Sissel
Music by: Aaron Zigman
Sound: Shirley Libby
Music Supervisor: Joel High
Editing: Maysie Hoy
Costumes: Keith Lewis
Production Design: Ina Mayhew
MPAA rating: PG-13
Running time: 101 minutes

REVIEWS

Boston Globe Online. March 22, 2008.
Entertainment Weekly Online. March 25, 2008.
Hollywood Reporter Online. March 24, 2008.
Los Angeles Times Online. March 24, 2008.
New York Times Online. March 22, 2008.
San Francisco Chronicle. March 24, 2008, p. E5.
Variety Online. March 21, 2008.

QUOTES

Brenda: "Hey, what if I told you I love you too? But, I got scared for a second. But I'd rather be scared and with you, than be not scared and not have you."
Harry: "Why would I scare you?"
Brenda: "'Cause you're everything I always wanted in a man."
Harry: "Then let me be that for you."

U-V

UNDER THE SAME MOON
(La misma luna)

The love between a mother and a son knows no boundaries.
—Movie tagline

Box Office: $12.5 million

There are hundreds of fascinating stories of immigration, about both the danger of actually crossing over and the sad way foreigners are treated once they make it to the United States. Politics aside, the immigration crisis in the United States is ripe for dramatic potential in screenwriting. Thousands of people put their lives at risk to flee poverty from south of the border only to find themselves working jobs that no one else would take in the United States. Coming here is difficult enough, but living here can be even harder. Patricia Riggen's heartfelt *Under the Same Moon* (*La misma luna*) tries to tell one of those stories, but ends up feeling manipulative and overreaching in its themes. Riggen and screenwriter Ligiah Villalobos clearly are not satisfied telling a single story of the rough passage of immigration. They want to tell them all in one movie and overcrowd what could have been a heartwarming tale with enough story that it becomes melodramatic. *Under the Same Moon* is about important issues and contains plot details and imagery pertaining to things that happen every day and yet it never feels like anything more than a movie.

The main problem with *Under the Same Moon* starts with the very age of its protagonist, poor young Carlitos (Adrian Alonso) with his wide, tear-filled eyes and pained frown. Kids in danger, even just of the emotionally scarring variety, are a tough line for a screenwriter to walk. Showing the repeated suffering of a child automatically makes a film feel manipulative, and overcoming that foundation takes some serious skill with realism. Carlitos cries through the majority of the first fifteen minutes of *Under the Same Moon*, and it becomes difficult to shake the feeling that Riggen and Villalobos are using a sobbing child to provoke emotions in their audience, not to tell a story. That feeling never goes away. Carlitos is crying because his mother Rosario (Kate del Castillo) has already made the trip across the border to Los Angeles, and he misses her madly. She too dreams of the day they will be reunited, as the only contact they have had in the last four years has been a weekly phone call. Rosario works multiple jobs, and Carlitos assists a kindly woman in setting up passage for people to cross the border illegally. Just before Carlitos's guardian, his grandmother, passes away, an American couple (America Ferrera and Jesse Garcia, in cameo roles) offers to ferry Carlitos across the border illegally in a compartment in their car in exchange for payment. The child who will do anything to see his mother again, so he accepts the offer. Of course, things go very wrong at the border, and Carlitos finds himself on the run, trying in whatever way he can to get back to his mother.

Del Castillo and Alonso are good at making the audience believe that they are actually mother and son, and their emotionally believable bond holds *Under the Same Moon* together through some of its rough patches (and adds power to the strong ending). But their acting is not nearly enough to tie the whole film together.

Everyone but Carlitos and, to a small extent, Enrique (Eugenio Derbez), a man he encounters along the way, feels like a plot device. For example, Ferrera and Garcia's characters could not be more awkward or suspicious at the border, and the man Carlitos runs into after that might as well be wearing a neon sign that says "untrustworthy junkie." On the other side, the obnoxious socialite who fires Rosario just because she has to work more than one job to make ends meet could not be more stereotypically two-dimensional. Everyone but the two leads feels like a movie character instead of the genuine people needed to make a story like *Under the Same Moon* effective. Villalobos and Riggen do too little by trying to do too much. The death of a loved one, the bond between mother and child, the plight of immigrants in L.A., border crossing, I.N.S. raids, even the love life of Rosario—it is all too much for one movie to take without crossing the boundaries between realism and melodrama. All of these issues are important to the story of immigration in the new millennium, but forcing them all into the same manipulative movie only drains them of their dramatic power.

Brian Tallerico

CREDITS

Carlitos: Adrian Alonso
Alicia: Maya Zapata
Rosario: Kate del Castillo
Enrique: Eugenio Derbez
Paco: Gabriel Porras
Marta: America Ferrera
David: Jesse Garcia
Origin: USA
Language: English, Spanish
Released: 2007
Production: Patricia Riggen, Gerardo Barrera, Lorenzo O'Brien; Potomac Productions, Creando Films; released by Fox Searchlight, Weinstein Co.
Directed by: Patricia Riggen
Written by: Ligiah Villalobos
Cinematography by: Checco Varese
Music by: Carlo Siliotto
Sound: Santiago Núñz, Leonel Pedraza
Music Supervisor: Lynn Fainchtein
Editing: Aleshka Ferrero
Production Design: Carmen Giminéz-Cacho, Gloria Carrasco
MPAA rating: PG-13
Running time: 109 minutes

REVIEWS

Boston Globe Online. April 4, 2008.
Christian Science Monitor Online. March 21, 2008.

Entertainment Weekly Online. March 19, 2008.
Los Angeles Times Online. March 19, 2008.
New York Times Online. March 19, 2008.
San Francisco Chronicle. March 19, 2008, p. E8.
Variety Online. January 23, 2007.
Wall Street Journal. March 21, 2008, p. W1.
Washington Post. March 21, 2008, p. C1.

UNTRACEABLE

The FBI Cyber Crimes Division hunts down vicious criminals online...but the most dangerous one is hunting them.
—Movie tagline

A cyber killer has finally found the perfect accomplice: You.
—Movie tagline

Box Office: $28.6 million

"It's a jungle in there."

That's the one good line from *Untraceable*—a fairly standard cops-versus-lone-lunatic thriller, with the not-so-original idea that the Internet can be a playground for the criminally minded. Writer/director Gregory Hoblit postures the film as if this were groundbreaking turf. Really, it is just a slightly bolder version of the cyber-cops-and-robbers drama that has become a staple of Hollywood trash-thriller films.

In this case, the bold idea is that the criminal kills people online, devising ingenious ways that ensure that the more people who log onto the Web site, the faster the victim dies. Or at least a few ingenious ways: the first is bleeding to death hastened by an anticoagulation IV drug drip, the second burning to death by heat lamps powered by Internet traffic, and then there is a guy in a tank of water into which leaks sulfuric acid. By the end, however, the writers have run out of fresh ideas, and we get a more standard horror motif: victim suspended upside down above a thrashing nest of spinning metal blades.

The ingenious part is that the killer gets to blame the voyeurs—after all, if no one were watching, the poison would not drip, because it is activated by user traffic, or something to that effect. As his "Watch Me Kill" Web site's viewership expands exponentially, however, there seems to be a self-defeating point: if the idea is that people love to watch someone being tortured to death, wouldn't they want the torture to be slower, rather than faster?

The scheme also depends on having dumb cops— and *Untraceable* has plenty of those. The local authorities keep calling press conferences to publicize the ongoing tortures, even though the deaths would not happen if people did not watch. Roomfuls of FBI cyber spies keep gathering, mouths agape, around big-screen TVs in police conference rooms watching the horrors unfold, while seemingly having no coherent plan to stop them. And even the gutsy heroine and obvious ultimate target, Jennifer Marsh (Diane Lane), stupidly climbs blithely into the driver's seat of an SUV in the back seat of which every sentient being in the audience knows the killer (Colin Hanks) is hiding.

Critics roasted *Untraceable* for exploiting the very kind of torture voyeurism its plot decries, and certainly the camera does seem to linger a little too long on many of the gruesome murder scenes. But compared with other blood-drenched horror movies of this day and age, *Untraceable* seems relatively tame. It is not the exploitation that is this film's biggest problem anyway—it is actually lack of imagination and logic. The killer's spree is motivated by the fact that his father's tragic suicide was broadcast by a local TV station and then viewed repeatedly on the Internet. But for some reason his greatest wrath is reserved for Marsh and her crew, because even though they are trying to crack down on cyber crime, apparently they are somehow complicit because they do not stop people from watching horrible things online—as if they could. And while the criminal behind these sick displays at first seems like a mastermind, the sleuthing required to identify him is not very interesting, and the climactic confrontation is rather disappointing.

The creepy feel of *Untraceable* is actually one of its pluses. So is the reliable Lane. In this film she is almost continually distraught and disheveled. She sports badly chopped brown hair streaked with blonde, uncertain makeup and a blotchy face—almost the antithesis of the glamorous bad-ass heroine of recent years. Lane lets her character look sleep-deprived, stressed, and all too realistic, but still her beauty shines through. With her deep, sometimes growly voice and her penetrating eyes, Lane makes her too-glib character credible enough to carry the day. Marsh has already lost a husband to the job of pursuing ruthless criminals, and after the tragedies mount and get closer to her, she confesses: "I'm not good at losing people." All her grief fills the screen, but the camera quickly gets on to its more mundane tasks. Lane is much too good to be in this mediocre movie.

While the other cops are bland and underwritten—one of them seems to be a candidate for a flirtation with Lane's character that never develops—her ill-fated partner Richard, played by Peter Lewis, provides some needed comic relief and speaks the film's one memorable line. It is cheesy but perceptive. Yet the problem is that too many movies do not seem to know how to change the standard cop-versus-creep motifs to fit the Internet age. Compare this movie to the vastly superior *Zodiac* (2007), in essence a very similar tale about a taunting criminal who thrives on cat-and-mouse publicity games, and you can easily see what is lacking: cleverness and atmosphere. In *Untraceable* we even get a little preaching about the special dangers of "the jungle in there," but no special insights into it.

It is perverse fun to see a face that reminds you of Tom Hanks play another creepy villain, and we even get the killer as devil—shot from above, with high forehead. Hoblit likes vertical shots, and they are sometimes successful, particularly one of a grieving, distraught Lane leaning over a balcony in the police building. The visual architecture of the film is fine, and for once in a Hollywood movie the computer screens even seem mildly plausible, rather than filled with fake graphics and commands that do not exist on real computers. It might be damning with faint praise to point out also that while the plot toys with doing awful things to Marsh's eight-year-old daughter, it does not actually go there. The killer even congratulates himself for having the decency not to kidnap her! It almost proceeds like a plot point written out. And as Marsh's mother, Mary Beth Hurt may have the fewest words ever spoken by a protective mother on screen. The film and the script are fairly economical, with not too much fat, but in the end we are short on substance and long on wallowing in a belated insight: Look what criminals could do online! Somebody had better stop them!

Michael Betzold

CREDITS

Jennifer Marsh: Diane Lane
Detective Eric Box: Billy Burke
Griffin Dowd: Colin Hanks
Owen Riley: Joseph Cross
Stella Marsh: Mary Beth Hurt
Tim Wilks: Tyrone Giordano
Annie Haskins: Perla Haney-Jardine
Richard Brooks: Peter Lewis
Herbert Miller: Tim De Zarn
Origin: USA
Language: English
Released: 2008
Production: Tom Rosenberg, Gary Lucchesi, Hawk Koch, Steven Pearl, Andy Cohen; Lakeshore Entertainment, Screen Gems; released by Sony Pictures Entertainment
Directed by: Gregory Hoblit
Written by: Allison Burnett, Robert Fyvolent, Mark R. Brinker
Cinematography by: Anastas Michos
Music by: Christopher Young

Sound: Steve Morrow
Editing: David Rosenbloom, Gregory Plotkin
Art Direction: Michael Mayer
Costumes: Elisabetta Beraldo
Production Design: Paul Eads
MPAA rating: R
Running time: 100 minutes

REVIEWS

Boston Globe Online. January 25, 2008.
Chicago Sun-Times Online. January 24, 2008.
Entertainment Weekly Online. January 23, 2008.
Hollywood Reporter Online. January 18, 2008.
Los Angeles Times Online. January 25, 2008.
New York Times Online. January 25, 2008.
San Francisco Chronicle. January 25, 2008, p. E11.
Variety Online. January 17, 2008.
Washington Post. January 26, 2008, p. C6.

QUOTES

Owen Reilly (speaking to a victim in a tub slowly filling with battery acid): "You know if no one was watching right now, you'd just be sitting in water. But the whole world wants to watch you die, and they don't even know you."

TRIVIA

The site used by the killer in the film (www.killwithme.com) actually exists and is owned by the studio and was used to promote the movie.

VALKYRIE

Many saw evil. They dared to stop it.
  —Movie tagline

Box Office: $82.8 million

In July of 1944, with the Allies putting pressure on their western holdings and the war all but lost for Germany, a group of officers within the German army attempted to assassinate Adolf Hitler, initiate a coup to overthrow the Nazi Party, and seize control of Berlin in order to negotiate peace with the Allies and bring the war to an end before Germany was utterly defeated. These officers had seen the brutality of the Nazi regime firsthand and knew that the army's personal oath to Hitler all but ensured that the horrible atrocities carried out by the Nazis would continue unless Hitler was killed. *Valkyrie* is about a contingent of high-ranking military officers and politicians who quietly opposed Hitler from within and sought an opportunity to assassinate him. Directed by Bryan Singer and written by Christopher

McQuarrie, the same team that created the well-regarded film *The Usual Suspects* (1994), *Valkyrie* stars Tom Cruise as the chief conspirator, Colonel Claus von Stauffenberg (a casting choice which occasionally proved problematic for the production), with a truly excellent supporting cast (many of whom are screen luminaries in their own right). At times intriguing, at others merely technically proficient, *Valkyrie* manages to be a well-wrought if not spectacular or particularly illuminating historical drama.

The film opens with von Stauffenberg stationed in Tunisia, writing in his journal that most of the officer corps in the German army finds what Hitler and the Nazis doing to be destructive to Germany—he writes, "We can fight for Hitler or Germany, but not both." Shortly thereafter, von Stauffenberg is severely wounded in an Allied air raid, losing his left eye, his right hand, and two fingers on his left hand. Upon returning to Berlin, von Stauffenberg, now a well-placed and highly regarded combat hero, is recruited into the German resistance by General Olbricht (Bill Nighy), second in command of the German reserve army. Von Stauffenberg meets with a secret committee which has coordinated several botched attempts on Hitler's life. The committee is composed of several high-ranking German political and military officials, including General Ludwig Beck (Terrence Stamp), Major General Henning von Tresckow (Kenneth Branagh)—whose failed attempt to blow up a plane carrying Hitler is seen early in the film—and Dr. Carl Goerdeler (Kevin McNally), who is slated to become chancellor in the event of a coup. All of them agree, ultimately, that Hitler must die (because the army has sworn a personal oath to him—the man must be destroyed to topple the Nazi regime), but they have no plan for the aftermath of the assassination. Von Stauffenberg realizes that the resistance can rewrite Operation Valkyrie, Hitler's plan to mobilize the reserve army to seize control of Berlin in the event of a coup, to ensure stability once Hitler is dead and the resistance puts a new government in place. In his rank of colonel, von Stauffenberg uses his direct access to Hitler not only to have the Führer himself sign off on his rewritten Valkyrie plan (which Hitler does without reading the revisions), but also to position himself as Hitler's assassin. On July 16, 1944, the resistance begins to put a coup in motion—von Stauffenberg is to try to kill Hitler at a strategy meeting with a bomb placed inside Hitler's bunker, the Wolf's Lair—but Goerdeler refuses at the last minute to give von Stauffenberg permission to proceed when it is realized that Himmler, the head of the SS (the Nazi Party's paramilitary force and fiercely loyal to Hitler personally), is not at the meeting. Upon returning to Berlin, von Stauffenberg blames the failure on Goerdeler's indecisiveness, and though Goerdeler demands that von Stauffenberg be relieved, Beck tells him that the Gestapo has orders for his arrest, leaving von Stauffenberg in place while Goerdeler is forced into hiding. Freed from Goerdeler's waffling, von Stauffenberg tries to assassinate Hitler again on July 20, 1944, but several factors are against him—he is able to arm only one of the two bombs he is carrying, the meeting is moved to a wooden hut (the blast would be more deadly if unleashed in a reinforced, sealed structure like the bunker), and the bomb must be placed under a heavy oak table, potentially shielding the target from the blast. Seeing the considerable explosion from outside the hut, however, von Stauffenberg assumes Hitler to be dead and quickly manages to talk his way out of the Wolf's Lair compound. When he returns to Berlin a few hours later, von Stauffenberg discovers that General Olbricht has not put Valkyrie in motion because of conflicting reports about Hitler's death. Von Stauffenberg admonishes him and Valkyrie is quickly executed, but the still-living Hitler manages to issue orders to several officials in Berlin faithful to the Nazis and they begin to halt the coup. Once Hitler goes on the radio and addresses the German people, it is clear that the plot has failed, and the reserve army quickly turns on the conspirators. Colonel General Friedrich Fromm, the head of the German reserve army and a peripheral conspirator (in the sense that he was sympathetic to the resistance but not active in it, and acquiesced to their machinations), orders the immediate execution of von Stauffenberg and Olbricht among others in an effort to cover up his foreknowledge of the coup plot. Just before von Stauffenberg is shot, he yells, "Long live sacred Germany!"

Valkyrie is by no means a bad film—it works as historical drama. Assertions that the outcome of the history is known and therefore undermines the suspense miss the point entirely. Indeed, such arguments have not stopped any number of fact-based dramas from being box office or artistic successes. In fact, the film has been promoted as being a thriller, when really it is more a conventional war film with suspense elements. The subject of the film is a military operation (albeit against the German military's own government), not unlike *The Longest Day* (1962) or portions of *Patton* (1970); the outcomes of the battles and operations depicted and discussed therein are all a matter of historical record, available to anyone with a mind to look them up. But such films are about the human details that underlie the facts, and in this way *Valkyrie* works as drama—the degree of its power as a cinematic experience may be the subject of considerable debate, but *Valkyrie* abides by its own rules and delivers taut action while simultaneously examining the culpability of individuals in relation to the actions of the state (and the attendant responsibility of the individual to take action if he or she knows that the state is acting immorally in the name of the people).

As he also managed to do in the *X-Men* films, Bryan Singer delivers a very good genre film that uses its high profile to examine social issues. In the case of *X-Men* (2000), it was the experience of the outcast, and the status quo's fear and distrust of the different and the unknown (which can be broadly applied to the examination of the treatment of illegal immigrants, people of various religions, homosexuals, etc.—any group that might not be part of what is perceived to be the mainstream). *Valkyrie* looks at the responsibility of individuals who know that they serve a society based on an invalid social contract at best, and at worst one that has thrown ethics and morality completely out the window for the whims of one man (a man to whom the armed forces were personally loyal by virtue of swearing an oath directly to Hitler). The film is satisfying on an intellectual level (the subject matter is interesting, the performances are solid, the camerawork is deftly executed, the pacing is brisk), rather than an emotional one. *Valkyrie* is well made, but it is neither genre-defining nor radical. Any viewer hoping for the next *The Usual Suspects* or *X-Men* is likely to be disappointed, though this is not entirely fair. *Valkyrie* is a testament to Singer's proficiency, not his inventiveness.

Something noteworthy about the production of *Valkyrie* is that the casting of Tom Cruise as Claus von Stauffenberg caused a bit of controversy in Germany, and one of von Stauffenberg's surviving sons also aired concerns publicly over Cruise's portrayal of the German hero, going so far as to say that he hoped Cruise would drop the role. The German defense ministry at one point even blocked filming at the Benderblock memorial, the site of von Stauffenberg's execution. The controversy arose over Cruise's adherence to Scientology, which German authorities have denounced as a cult (though von Stauffenberg's son seems to have been more concerned about his father being portrayed by a lightweight American matinee idol). Several German film artists, however, both inside and outside Germany, viewed Cruise's participation as an opportunity to bring this largely unknown story from history to a broad audience. The latter view ultimately prevailed, and the defense ministry relented, allowing the film crew access to the memorial.

John Boaz

CREDITS

Claus von Stauffenberg: Tom Cruise
Adolf Hitler: David Bamber
Heinrich Himmler: Matthias Freihof
Nina von Stauffenberg: Carice van Houten
Henning von Tresckow: Kenneth Branagh

Erich Fellgiebel: Eddie Izzard
Otto Ernst Remer: Thomas Kretschmann
Friedrich Olbricht: Bill Nighy
Ludwig Beck: Terence Stamp
Dr. Carl Goerdeler: Kevin McNally
Mertz von Quirnheim: Christian Berkel
Heinz Brandt: Tom Hollander
Wilhelm Keitel: Kenneth Cranham
Origin: USA, Germany
Language: English
Released: 2008
Production: Bryan Singer, Gilbert Adler, Christopher McQuarrie; United Artists, Bad Hat Harry, Achte Babelsberg Film; released by MGM
Directed by: Bryan Singer
Written by: Christopher McQuarrie, Nathan Alexander
Cinematography by: Newton Thomas Sigel
Music by: John Ottman
Sound: Chris Munro
Editing: John Ottman
Art Direction: Cornelia Ott
Costumes: Joanna Johnston
Production Design: Lilly Kilvert, Patrick Lumb
MPAA rating: PG-13
Running time: 120 minutes

REVIEWS

Boston Globe Online. December 25, 2008.
Chicago Sun-Times Online. December 23, 2008.
Entertainment Weekly Online. December 23, 2008.
Hollywood Reporter Online. December 10, 2008.
Los Angeles Times Online. December 25, 2008.
New York Times Online. December 25, 2008.
Rolling Stone Online. December 25, 2008.
San Francisco Chronicle. December 25, 2008, p. E1.
Variety Online. December 10, 2008.
Washington Post. December 25, 2008, p. C1.

QUOTES

Col. Von Stauffenberg: "In serving my country I have betrayed my conscience."
Henning von Tresckow: "We have to show the world that not all of us are like him. Otherwise, this will always be Hitler's Germany."

TRIVIA

The only non-German cast member who actually speaks in a German accent is David Bamber (Adolf Hitler).

VANTAGE POINT

8 Strangers. 8 Points of View. 1 Truth.
—Movie tagline

If you think you've seen it all…look again.
—Movie tagline

Box Office: $72.2 million

As the title suggests, *Vantage Point* is a film about seeing an incident from a particular point of view, but it is also, oddly, not necessarily interested in offering much perspective about the event unfolding before the characters and the audience. Starring a top-notch cast and driven by a somewhat interesting premise, *Vantage Point* fails to maintain the excitement generated by its initial incident or to live up to the far superior 1950 Akira Kurosawa film *Rashômon*, the influence of which was noted in several reviews. Though it is unfair to expect a film on the level of *Rashômon*, one cannot help noting that Kurosawa's piece about the dodgy and self-serving nature of memory is specifically invoked as an inspiration for, at the very least, the film's structure. But compared to the earlier film, *Vantage Point* lacks cathartic power and coherence. While first-time feature film director Pete Travis certainly displays some technical skill and ambition with this labyrinthine project, he fails to deliver as rich and complex a storytelling experience as the film promises.

The plot of *Vantage Point* can be stated simply as follows: a terrorist organization attempts an assassination of the president of the United States and fails, though it comes very close to succeeding. Such a description does not do justice to the film's plotting—events unfold in segments, each going over roughly the same period of time while revealing another facet of the story from the perspective of a different character. The movie begins from the viewpoint of a news crew covering the president's appearance at an antiterrorism summit in Salamanca, Spain. Within moments of commencing coverage, the president is shot, and bombs explode, killing one of the news correspondents. The film then jumps back in time and shifts to the president's security detail. Agents Thomas Barnes (Dennis Quaid) and Kent Taylor (Matthew Fox) guard the president on the Plaza Mayor. After the shooting, chaos reigns: Barnes tackles a man attempting to storm the stage; Taylor offers to check out a window that Barnes thinks may have been the shooter's perch; Barnes notices a man on the plaza with a video camera, Howard Lewis (Forest Whitaker), and in reviewing the footage notices that a woman tossed a bag under the stage; and then the stage explodes. In the aftermath, Barnes makes his way out to the GNN (Global News Network) mobile studio and demands to see their footage. As he talks to Taylor on his cell phone, he sees something shocking on the GNN live feed and runs out. The film then switches to Enrique (Eduardo Noriega), a Salamanca cop, assigned to protect the mayor (the opening speaker for the president) and reveals his largely involuntary role in the events (he delivers a bag to his girlfriend which, unbeknownst to him, contains the bomb that destroys the president's stage). The film moves to Howard Lewis's viewpoint and shows him not only filming the shooting and the bombing, but also befriending a Spanish girl and her mother (who become separated in the confusion), and chasing down Enrique after he flees the Secret Service. Then the film takes something of a departure—it shifts away from the plaza that has been the scene of most of the action, to a hotel where the real president Ashton is very much alive. It turns out he had caught wind of the plot and sent a double to the Plaza—but the terrorists have someone on the inside and manage to capture him anyway. The final segment is dedicated to the viewpoint of the terrorist plotters, whose plan unravels, apparently in the face of the film's own complexity: Barnes chases down Taylor, who turns out to be one of the conspirators, and the ambulance carrying the abducted president crashes when the driver swerves to avoid none other than the girl Howard Lewis befriended on the Plaza, who runs into the middle of the street in pursuit of her mother.

The story of *Vantage Point* is really quite intriguing at first, and the opening scene is expertly structured to draw the viewer in. As Rex Brooks (Sigourney Weaver), the producer in GNN's mobile newsroom, barks out orders to her correspondent and to the camera operators to catch key figures on the Plaza, the president is shot, a distant explosion is heard (coming from somewhere outside the Plaza) and shortly thereafter, another explosion destroys a portion of the stage, killing the GNN correspondent. The film establishes a particular frame of reference for the audience—the exciting yet clockwork world of journalism in action, with all of its carefully chosen moments and angles, obliterated by unforeseen catastrophe and horror. The scene does an effective job of disposing with some exposition (this is the opening ceremony for a summit on terrorism, agent Barnes was wounded protecting the president recently, and it is a surprise to see him back in action so soon) and lulling the audience into a false sense of security (the audience is in the room with all video feeds, separated from events, yet with seeming omniscience over the proceedings) and then ripping the audience into the tense action of the movie. Unfortunately, the film fails to sustain that tension, or to fulfill its promise as a tense mystery thriller with a political edge. As the plot unfolds (both that of the film and that of the terrorist organization behind the assassination attempt) in ever-widening circles, it loses momentum as it moves away from the happenings on the Plaza out into Salamanca at large. The revelation of the depth of not only the conspiracy (a Secret Service agent is one of the terrorists) but also of the attempt to thwart the plot (President Ashton's *double* is assassinated on the Plaza, not Ashton himself) lends *Vantage Point* an unnecessary level of complication that dissipates the film's intensity, and undermines audience interest and sympathy by introducing these elements ham-handedly, making them seem all the more implausible. The implied early promise of the films is, "Watch carefully and all will be revealed"; once *Vantage Point* leaves the incidents at the Plaza, what to that point has been one film about the pitfalls of perception becomes another, rather rote mystery film à la Agatha Christie with key, deliberately withheld information introduced in the eleventh hour.

Also, the film's structure, though initially effective in creating *Vantage Point*'s sense of tension, ultimately serves to undermine its narrative and thematic power. *Vantage Point* is told in fifteen-minute screen-time segments that translate to approximately twenty-three minutes each in the world of the film, and each such segment is roughly congruent to the perspective of a different character in the story (the idea apparently being that no single character is privy to the full story). The events progress to a certain point with one character, then roll back twenty-three minutes (or so) and switch to another character's perspective. While this does have the advantage of gradually revealing information to the audience, keeping it hooked (for a while), it has the side effect, again, of implying that the mystery/conspiracy will be revealed in reviewing what has taken place on the Plaza (the first four segments are mostly about events on the Plaza). When the film abruptly leaves the Plaza to show the perspective of the "real" President Ashton, "secured" in his hotel room, the effect is jarring. Adding a new location and introducing a decoy/real president plotline creates too large a leap in venue and plausibility for the film to maintain any credibility as a *Rashômon*-inspired thriller, attempts to rewrite the movie's own rules, and loses its audience along the way. The film ends, fittingly enough, in a mish-mash of perspectives that shows the full extent of the terrorist conspiracy and makes no effort to maintain itself as a thriller, devolving into little more than a series of car chases and revelations that attempt to tie up loose ends.

Finally, it must be noted that although *Vantage Point*'s structure is clearly inspired by *Rashômon*, the comparison ends there. Like *Rashômon*, *Vantage Point* reviews the same event from multiple perspectives, but *Vantage Point* does so in an objective fashion—each of *Vantage Point*'s segments unfold in real time, and the movie as a whole is a culmination of those various points of view, giving the distinct impression that, despite the complexity of what has gone before, the viewer has witnessed the actual events. *Rashômon*, however, is specifically concerned with the unreliable, self-serving nature of memory and the apparent impossibility of knowing the whole truth about a past event, even if one has participated in it. At the end of *Vantage Point,* a GNN anchor announces that the president is out of intensive care, that the antiterrorism summit will continue, and that the lone assassin was shot (all falsehoods). In doing this, *Vantage Point* may be suggesting that the public at large cannot possibly know the truth of events, even those that are seemingly objective, recorded events, because powerful interests will inevitably endeavor to conceal the truth or warp the outcome for their own ends. But a quick footnote in the form of a lying newscast cannot override the ninety minutes that have preceded it. By showing the audience the events as they occurred, it closes the question of obfuscation—the reality of events are knowable in *Vantage Point,* if only to a chosen few. *Rashômon* would reject this outright. Certain facts may be knowable, but the truths of why, how, and to what end are largely obscured by perspective and personal motivation.

John Boaz

CREDITS

Thomas Barnes: Dennis Quaid
Kent Taylor: Matthew Fox
Howard Lewis: Forest Whitaker
President Ashton: William Hurt
Rex Brooks: Sigourney Weaver
Phil McCullogh: Bruce McGill
Javier: Edgar Ramirez
Suarez: Saïd Taghmaoui
Veronica: Ayelet Zurer
Angie Jones: Zoë Saldana
Enrique: Eduardo Noriega
Holden: Richard T. Jones
Ron Matthews: Holt McCallany
Kevin Cross: Leonardo Nam
Ted Heinkin: James LeGros
Origin: USA
Language: English
Released: 2008
Production: Neal H. Moritz; Relativity Media, Original Film; released by Sony Pictures Entertainment
Directed by: Stuart Baird, Pete Travis
Written by: Barry L. Levy
Cinematography by: Amir M. Mokri
Music by: Atli Örvarsson
Sound: Nicolas Santiago Nuñez Rojo
Editing: Stuart Baird
Art Direction: Hania Robledo Richards, Marcelo Del Rio Galnares
Costumes: Luca Mosca

Production Design: Brigitte Broch
MPAA rating: PG-13
Running time: 90 minutes

REVIEWS

Boston Globe Online. February 22, 2008.
Entertainment Weekly Online. February 20, 2008.
Los Angeles Times Online. February 22, 2008.
New York Times Online. February 22, 2008.
Rolling Stone Online. March 6, 2008.
San Francisco Chronicle. February 22, 2008, p. E1.
Variety Online. February 21, 2008.
Wall Street Journal. February 22, 2008, p. W1.
Washington Post. February 22, 2008, p. C1.

QUOTES

Suarez: "The beauty of American arrogance is that they can't imagine a world where they're not a step ahead."

TRIVIA

Although the film was originally supposed to be released in October 2007 it was unexplicably delayed until February 2008.

VICKY CRISTINA BARCELONA

Life is the ultimate work of art.
—Movie tagline

Box Office: $23.2 million

Ever since the drama *Interiors* (1978), Woody Allen has alternated between comedies and more serious films, often combining elements of both approaches, most notably in *Match Point* (2005). Following the critical praise for the latter, Allen stumbled somewhat with *Scoop* (2006), seen as too fluffy, despite its serial-killer plot, and *Cassandra's Dream* (2008), considered too dark and dreary. The writer-director bounces back with *Vicky Cristina Barcelona,* a contemplation on the vagaries of love that smoothly balances its comedic and serious elements.

Vicky (Rebecca Hall), a student of Catalan culture, and Cristina (Scarlett Johansson), an actress and filmmaker dissatisfied with her first, twelve-minute film, come to Barcelona for a stay with acquaintances Judy (Patricia Clarkson) and Mark (Kevin Dunn). Vicky wants to experience the language, music, and architecture of Barcelona, while Cristina simply wants a break from her recent failure. When painter Juan Antonio (Javier

Bardem) invites the pair for a romantic weekend in Oviedo, Cristina is enthusiastic and Vicky reluctant. While Cristina is sidetracked by food poisoning, Vicky, though engaged to Doug (Chris Messina), allows herself to be seduced by Juan Antonio.

Vicky initially regrets her rash act, and Cristina drifts into a ménage a trois with Juan Antonio and his jealous, impetuous ex-wife, Maria Elena (Penélope Cruz), also a painter. While Allen has borrowed extensively in the past from European directors such as Ingmar Bergman and Federico Fellini, he has never displayed much influence by the French new wave directors. The first of the two romantic triangles, however, recalls François Truffaut's *Jules and Jim* (1962), with Juan Antonio standing in for the impulsive character played by Jeanne Moreau. With the appearance of Maria Elena, the dynamics shift, and she becomes the unstable center of another triangle. Allen acknowledges his debt to Truffaut by using, in a picnic scene, an old-fashioned iris shot as in *Jules and Jim.*

Allen keeps offering variations of the traditional triangle, especially after Doug appears and a fellow language student (Pablo Schreiber) begins flirting with Vicky. It becomes increasingly clear that none of the four protagonists knows what he or she wants out of love or life. For all the comedy in Allen's films and his dark musings on death, his true subject is love. Can people truly choose the ones with whom they fall in love? Does love cause more pleasure or pain? Is sex love or vice versa? Does love last? Is love enough? *Vicky Cristina Barcelona* can be seen as a distillation of Allen's views on romance. Love is messy and illogical, but it is all there is—until death.

Vicky Cristina Barcelona has a slickness missing from Allen's two previous films, moving gracefully from one state of confusion to the next. While some of Allen's narrative lurches about, editor Alisa Lepselter makes the film move smoothly from scene to scene. Notable both for its effectiveness and for being unlike Allen's usual conservative style is an intimate scene between Vicky and Juan Antonio in which, instead of cutting from face to face, their images dissolve into each other. Cinematographer Javier Aguirresarobe, whose impressive credits include Alejandro Amenábar's *The Others* (2001) and Pedro Almodóvar's *Talk to Her* (2002), bathes Barcelona in a golden, late-afternoon glow to heighten the romantic intensity of the proceedings. Allen abandons his usual jazz and classical music for Spanish guitar pieces that add another layer of romance.

Vicky Cristina Barcelona can be faulted for stacking the deck by making Doug such a stiff, selfish prig. As seen in the flawed relationship between Judy and Mark, Doug's work will always be more important to him.

Vicky's falling for Juan Antonio seems less the result of passion than as a protest against the conventional life she is destined to lead. As in too many of his films, Allen never questions the privileged lives of characters who can cavalierly travel to exotic places with no thoughts about expense or obligations. As with the fiction of F. Scott Fitzgerald, Allen only seems to condemn the rich while gazing longingly at their recklessness.

As in the novels and stories of Henry James, Allen's Europe offers its American visitors a depth of feeling missing from their comparatively bland existences back home. Juan Antonio remains enigmatic because he seems to have an understanding of life of which Vicky and Cristina are incapable. The two American women are used to calm, orderly relationships and are dazzled by the ferocity of Maria Elena's feelings.

Johansson's only fully realized performance occurs in *Match Point,* yet Allen gives her little to work with here. Cristina is more a concept than a fully realized character. Though the mostly positive reviews focused on the Cristina-Juan Antonio-Maria Elena triangle, the main character, also representing Allen's viewpoint, is Vicky. She would be content to observe life from the sidelines, again like a Henry James protagonist, but finds herself unwillingly drawn into the chaos of life. As Allen places a burden on Hall, with many shots of Vicky's reactions to the others, she ably conveys the character's mixed emotions. While Juan Antonio could have been a cliché hunk, the astonishingly versatile Bardem imbues him with a layer of mystery. Though some of Juan Antonio's actions are questionable, Bardem makes them seem logical. The painter always appears to be considering his next step. Cruz, equally versatile, is capable of both subtlety and passion and emphasizes the latter here, unafraid of how foolish Maria Elena may appear. While some reviewers compared Cruz's performance to those of Sophia Loren, her approach most closely resembles the no-holds-barred style of Anna Magnani.

Because of the presence of Bardem and Cruz and the setting, reviewers compared *Vicky Cristina Barcelona* to the films of Pedro Almodóvar. Allen works with a simpler palette than Almodóvar, both stylistically and thematically. If Almodóvar's films are lush operas, Allen's are melancholy Tin Pan Alley tunes.

Michael Adams

CREDITS

Juan Antonio: Javier Bardem
Vicky: Rebecca Hall
Cristina: Scarlett Johansson
Maria Elena: Penélope Cruz

Judy Nash: Patricia Clarkson
Mark Nash: Kevin Dunn
Doug: Chris Messina
Ben: Pablo Schreiber
Narrator: Christopher Evan Welch (Voice)
Origin: USA, Spain
Language: English, Spanish
Released: 2008
Production: Letty Aronson, Stephen Tenenbaum, Gareth Wiley; MediaPro, Gravier Productions, Antena 3; released by Weinstein Company
Directed by: Woody Allen
Written by: Woody Allen
Cinematography by: Javier Aguirresarobe
Editing: Alisa Lepselter
Art Direction: Iñigo Navarro
Costumes: Sonia Grande
Production Design: Alain Bainée
MPAA rating: PG-13
Running time: 96 minutes

REVIEWS

Boston Globe Online. August 15, 2008.
Chicago Sun-Times Online. August 14, 2008.
Entertainment Weekly Online. August 15, 2008.
Los Angeles Times Online. August 15, 2008.
New York Times Online. August 15, 2008.
New Yorker Online. August 11, 2008.
Rolling Stone Online. August 21, 2008.
San Francisco Chronicle. August 15, 2008, p. E1.
Variety Online. May 16, 2008.
Wall Street Journal. August 15, 2008, p. W1.
Washington Post. August 15, 2008, p. C1.

QUOTES

Cristina: "I'll go to your room, but you'll have to seduce me."

TRIVIA

This is the fourth consecutive film that Woody Allen had shot outside of the United States.

AWARDS

Oscars 2008: Support. Actress (Cruz)
British Acad. 2008: Support. Actress (Cruz)
Golden Globes 2009: Film—Mus./Comedy
Ind. Spirit 2009: Screenplay, Support. Actress (Cruz)
Nomination:
Golden Globes 2009: Actor—Mus./Comedy (Bardem), Actress—Mus./Comedy (Hall), Support. Actress (Cruz)
Ind. Spirit 2009: Actor (Bardem)

Screen Actors Guild 2008: Support. Actress (Cruz)
Writers Guild 2008: Orig. Screenplay.

VINCE VAUGHN'S WILD WEST COMEDY SHOW: 30 DAYS & 30 NIGHTS — HOLLYWOOD TO THE HEARTLAND
(Wild West Comedy Show)

Despite some undeniable laughs and the introduction of a group of comedians worth watching, *Vince Vaughn's Wild West Comedy Show: 30 Days & 30 Nights — Hollywood to the Heartland* is more memorable for the inappropriate length of its title than anything in the film itself. The actual comedy documentary is surprisingly inert and inconsequential, failing to take the opportunity to illuminate anything about the world of sleeping on a tour bus during the day and telling jokes at night. Vaughn, the star of *Swingers* (1996) and *Wedding Crashers* (2005), reportedly hand-picked four comedians from the Comedy Store in Los Angeles and took them on a thirty-day tour across the United States. The movie, directed by Ari Sandel, intercuts footage of the four new jokesters and their star host with their own biographical interviews and behind-the-scenes antics. The small problem is that none of the four are remarkable enough to hold their own film and Vaughn is not the first person that most people would associate with the art of stand-up comedy. When *Wild West Comedy Show* focuses on the art of stand-up, as in an interesting sequence where one of the young men clearly rocks a set but is convinced he bombed and another when his co-comedian describes a standing ovation as the highlight of his career, it works. But Sandel and Vaughn are only half-interested in the new quartet, making a film with an identity crisis—part star vehicle, part concert film, part documentary, part biography of young talent, with none of these aspects really that engaging.

The lack of focus in *Wild West Comedy Show* is most pronounced in the opening scenes. Vaughn himself compares what he and his foursome will attempt to the spirit of the Wild West shows, which might indicate some variety acts and unusual material, but it quickly becomes clear that what traveled the country for thirty days was basically just a stand-up show with four comedians and a superstar host. And Vaughn and Sandel put the focus too heavily and too quickly on Vince and his friends. The first extended bit on-stage in *Wild West Comedy Show* features Vaughn with special guests Jon Favreau and Justin Long. Other special guests along the way include Peter Billingsley and Dwight Yoakam.

The quartet of young comedians should be the focus of *Wild West Comedy Show* from minute one, but they feel like second billing in their own movie.

Eventually, the film starts to focus on the quartet at the heart of the tour, and only then does *Wild West Comedy Show* get interesting. All four of the comedians—Ahmed Ahmed, John Caparulo, Bret Ernst, and Sebastian Maniscalco—show promise and deliver some excellent sets, and they are all guys that are very easy to root for. Like a lot of young men, these comedians are working day and night to hone their craft, praying that they do not have to go back to day jobs, and it is always rewarding to watch ambitious people succeed at what they have dreamed about and worked hard to accomplish. All four of them take what they do very seriously and clearly value the opportunity that was given to them by Vaughn. At least one of them is likely to "make it big," which should make *Wild West Comedy Show* an interesting time capsule, and it would not be shocking if more than just one found widespread success—Bret Ernst and John Caparulo clearly have a way with a crowd and could become stars someday.

Having said that, what sinks *Wild West Comedy Show* is that this foursome is far from alone. There are talented stand-up comedians on Comedy Central, HBO, and playing in small clubs around the world at this very minute. Even Ahmed, Caparulo, Ernst, and Maniscalco would probably agree that they are just a sampling of the world of stand-up comedy and probably not the best quartet working the circuit. So, if *Wild West Comedy Show* does not feature the best of the best, it would have worked better as the story of "average comedians" trying to make it work in an era when stand-up is harder than ever. Sandel could have made a great documentary about the modern art of stand-up and people who bust their backs to make people laugh, but he never focuses long enough on that to give his film any sort of impact. The best stand-up acts are determined in their focus, leading the audience by the nose exactly where the comedian wants to take them. *Wild West Comedy Show* is all over the map and loses the crowd by doing so.

Brian Tallerico

CREDITS

Himself: Vince Vaughn
Himself: Ahmed Ahmed
Himself: John Caparulo
Himself: Bret Ernst
Himself: Sebastian Maniscalco
Himself: Jon Favreau
Himself: Dwight Yoakam
Himself: Peter Billingsley
Himself: Justin Long
Origin: USA
Language: English
Released: 2006
Production: Vince Vaughn; Wild West Picture Show; released by Picturehouse
Directed by: Ari Sandel
Music by: John O'Brien
Sound: Greg Morgenstein
Editing: Dan Lebental, Jim Kelly
MPAA rating: R
Running time: 100 minutes

REVIEWS

Boston Globe Online. February 8, 2008.
Entertainment Weekly. February 15, 2008, p. 48.
Hollywood Reporter Online. September 11, 2006.
Los Angeles Times Online. February 8, 2008.
New York Times Online. February 8, 2008.
Rolling Stone Online. February 7, 2007.
San Francisco Chronicle. February 8, 2008, p. E1.
Variety Online. September 11, 2006.
Washington Post Online. February 8, 2008.

QUOTES

Sebastian Mansicalco: "One day your name is up in lights and the next day it's on a nametag."

THE VISITOR

Connection is everything.
—Movie tagline

Box Office: $9.4 million

The Visitor achieves great results without calling attention to its elements. By no means a mundane or commonplace affair—either in its content or as an overall piece of filmmaking—this understated film is nothing short of extraordinary. The film manages to take a subject which could easily inspire Hollywood bombast—the deportation of foreigners living illegally in the United States—and makes it not only plausible but poetic by linking that storyline to the deep human need for connection and the underlying truth of existence: that everyone is a visitor, each occupying a little time and space with one another, until it is time to go. As directed by actor/director Tom McCarthy, the creative force behind the equally marvelous *The Station Agent* (2003), *The Visitor* is a testament to what filmmaking can achieve in the hands of gifted, committed people who trust their material, their skill, and their audience.

The Visitor opens with Walter Vale (Richard Jenkins), a college economics professor, doing poorly at a piano lesson. It is apparent that he has lost interest in teaching; he has only one class, ostensibly so that he can author a book, but his disenchantment is obvious. He is asked by his dean to present a paper in New York City, despite Walter's protestations that he put his name on the paper only to help a colleague of his and did not really contribute to it. He leaves his Connecticut home to stay in his long-vacated apartment in New York, and discovers a young immigrant couple squatting in it (it turns out the couple thought they had legally sublet it, but were in fact conned). Their names are Tarek (Haaz Sleiman), a drummer from Syria, and Zainab (Danai Jekesai Gurira), a jewelry maker and seller from Senegal. They do not wish to upset Walter or cause trouble because they are living in the United State illegally, but to their surprise Walter allows them to stay in the apartment. Over time, Tarek and Walter become friends. Tarek teaches Walter to play the drum, Walter accompanies the couple to one of Tarek's gigs in a jazz club. Walter and Tarek also play together in a drum circle in Central Park. Tarek is arrested in a subway station, though, while he and Walter are heading back to the apartment. Walter visits Tarek at a detention center for illegal immigrants in Queens, and tells Tarek that he will pay for an immigration lawyer (which he does) to fight Tarek's possible deportation. Tarek's mother Mouna (Hiam Abbass) eventually comes to New York from Michigan after not hearing from Tarek for a few days. Walter offers to let Mouna stay with him (Zainab opts to stay elsewhere when Tarek is arrested), and she reluctantly agrees. Walter and Mouna begin to develop a relationship. Mouna finds out that Tarek was living with Zainab and meets her, asking if they can do something that Zainab liked to do with Tarek. They all take the ferry to Staten Island, looking at the Statue of Liberty on the way. Walter finds out that he must return to Connecticut to take care of some things, but asks Mouna to remain in the apartment in his absence. She agrees, and Walter leaves. Back at his regular residence, he sells his piano to the teacher who gave him the lesson at the beginning of the film. When Walter returns to New York, he visits Tarek, who is clearly beginning to become very concerned about what is going to happen to him. That night, Walter and Mouna have a night out in Manhattan and at dinner Walter announces that he is taking a leave of absence, confessing that he has not done any real work in a very long time but only pretends to be busy while not doing anything. They agree that their night out together is the most fun either one of them have had in a long time. The following day, Walter discovers that Tarek has been deported to Syria. Mouna chooses to leave for Syria to be with her son, knowing

that she cannot return. She also confesses that long ago she received a letter warning of Tarek's deportation but she threw it away and never told him. She tells Walter, "After a time, you forget—you think that you really belong." Walter says that he does not want her to go, but she must. The film ends with Walter playing Tarek's drum alone in the subway.

The Visitor is the sort of independent cinematic surprise that comes along only occasionally. Often, independent films are hobbled by their intent to be so quirky and contrarian that they neglect storytelling and relationships entirely. No so with *The Visitor*. To begin with, information is delivered subtly. Certain details imply character or relationship and must be discovered by the viewer, which makes the film engaging on a sublimely deep level—not only does the viewer get to take an active role in the unfolding of the movie, the filmmakers, by setting up the film in this way, communicate their implicit trust in the audience to see, hear, remember, and comprehend. For instance, when the piano instructor first arrives at Walter's home in Connecticut, the relationships are unclear, as are the motives of both Walter and the instructor; but as the film progresses, it seems that Walter connects with other people through music. It is revealed that his late wife was a classical pianist, and the gateway to Walter's friendship with Tarek is through Tarek's drum lessons. Through that awkward opening scene, though the audience is hardly aware of it until much later in the movie, Walter's past and his way forward are revealed. That is excellent filmmaking. In fact, the themes that run throughout *The Visitor* are the difficulty of and the need for fruitful communication and the immediacy of music. (Walter and Mouna see the musical *The Phantom of the Opera* on Broadway, the themes of which are loss and the power of music). Music transcends language and opens the listener to new sounds, new images, and new ways of thinking. Walter may be closed off and trapped in his ways, but he knows this and is open to new experiences though he does not initially seek them out. *The Visitor* is a testament to the power of being open and facing new situations and unfamiliar things in good faith.

What makes *The Visitor* such a transcendent film experienceis its refusal to confine itself to the internal journey of one man or the specifics of a single character's development. The film wrestles, admirably, with real-world social justice issues and their attendant moral and existential implications. The larger story in *The Visitor* is, of course, that of people who live in the United States illegally and the constant threat they face that they might be deported, regardless of how long they have lived here, their moral character, or their standing in the community. When Tarek is arrested, the threat becomes very real, and because the audience has seen Tarek through Walter's eyes, it is as concerned for Tarek as Walter is. As Tarek's plight progresses, the more terrifying the faceless power of the government becomes. Not to consider the specifics of the individual runs against Walter's approach to the world and the ethos of *The Visitor*, yet it is the operating principle for the U.S. Immigration Service. The film suggests that the government treats all detainees as if they were criminals. "I am not a criminal," Tarek says. "Terrorists have money, they have support...I just want to live my life and play my music." The horrible irony is that Tarek's father was a Syrian journalist who died after being unjustly incarcerated in a Syrian jail; Tarek came to the United States to find hope and instead finds himself imprisoned. Through Walter's journey of the self and through the wrenching trials of Tarek (and thus his mother, Mouna, and his girlfriend, Zainab), the "visitor" in *The Visitor* is shown to refer not only to those who are physically displaced (or to Walter visiting Tarek in the detention center), but to the transient nature of living—that all people are passing through this life and get to know each other, perhaps touch each other's lives, only briefly, and that it is everyone's responsibility to remain open to the possibilities of human connection, because to allow oneself to be closed off leads to detention centers, distrust of others, and unfulfilled and unrealized lives. The magic of *The Visitor* is that it manages to communicate these things not by stating them outright, but by trusting that the audience will be open to them.

John Boaz

CREDITS

Walter Vale: Richard Jenkins
Mouna: Hiam Abbass
Tarek: Haaz Sleiman
Zainab: Danai Gurira
Origin: USA
Language: English
Released: 2007
Production: Mary Jane Skalski, Michael London; Participant Productions, Groundswell Productions; released by Overture Films

Directed by: Tom McCarthy
Written by: Tom McCarthy
Cinematography by: Oliver Bokelberg
Music by: Jan A.P. Kaczmarek
Sound: Damian Canelos
Editing: Tom McArdle
Art Direction: Len X. Clayton
Costumes: Melissa Toth
Production Design: John Paino
MPAA rating: PG-13
Running time: 108 minutes

REVIEWS

Boston Globe Online. April 18, 2008.
Entertainment Weekly Online. April 9, 2008.
Hollywood Reporter Online. September 12, 2007.
Los Angeles Times Online. April 11, 2008.
New York Times Online. April 11, 2008.
Rolling Stone Online. April 17, 2008.
San Francisco Chronicle. April 18, 2008, p. E5.
Variety Online. September 9, 2007.
Wall Street Journal. April 18, 2008, p. C1.
Washington Post. April 18, 2008, p. C1.

QUOTES

Walter Vale: "You can't just take people away like that. Do you hear me? He was a good man, a good person. It's not fair! We are not just helpless children! He had a life! Do you hear me? I mean, do YOU hear ME? What's the matter with you?"

AWARDS

Ind. Spirit 2009: Director (McCarthy)

Nomination:

Oscars 2008: Actor (Jenkins)
Ind. Spirit 2009: Actor (Jenkins), Support. Actor (Sleiman)
Screen Actors Guild 2008: Actor (Jenkins)
Writers Guild 2008: Screenplay.

W

W.
───────■───────

W.

A life misunderestimated.
—Movie tagline

Box Office: $25.5 million

If your name is Oliver Stone and you are releasing a movie about President George W. Bush a month before the election that will determine who is his successor, the expectation is that it will be a scathing satire, or a deeply disturbing and wild conspiracy ride à la *JFK*. When it turns out instead to be neither of these things, but a comparatively restrained examination of the family tensions that accompanied Bush the younger's rise to the White House, critics shake their heads in confusion.

Actually, Stone's *W.* is commendable for rarely seeming too preachy or overly provocative or polemical. In fact, it is more persuasive this way, as a selective biopic that zeroes in on George W. Bush's lifelong quest to win the attention and approval of his father, George Herbert Walker Bush.

It is dangerous—some might even say foolhardy—to make a non-propaganda movie about a president while he is still in office, even if, like Bush, the subject is on his way out the door of the White House. There are so many possible ways to see Bush, whose terms were history-making and controversial, and trying to capture the sweep of his accomplishments and notable failures without the vantage point of a few years' breathing space would be a gargantuan task. Stone's choice is not to be all-inclusive but instead to home in on one of the more intriguing theories about why W. took the country to war against Iraq: that in so doing he was trying to settle a score with his domineering father.

The explanation was a popular one, widely circulating around the liberal blogosphere in the beginning years of the war. What is odd is not that Stone has chosen to make that viewpoint the centerpiece of his film, but that he waited so long to release a film with such an ax to grind. No doubt partisan audiences who believe in such a theory, as at least one plausible explanation for the decision to launch a pre-emptive attack against the regime of Saddam Hussein, will find the story justifies their presumptions—though some of these same folks might find the film insufficiently broad in its indictment. However, even the more rabid critics are thrown some meat too, in a Dr. Strangelove-style lecture by Dick Cheney (Richard Dreyfuss) that makes it clear that the war was about controlling oil, and nothing else, and that he and others duped the president into following their agenda.

Stone does a neat job of focusing on the manner in which Bush's upbringing and career arc dovetail with his policy positions. He juxtaposes scenes that chronologically lead up to Bush's inauguration with scenes that lead up to his decision to invade Iraq. Despite the film's naysayers, it is actually quite effective propagandizing for an Iraq war critic's point of view. And while Stone, uncharacteristically, does not pound home the point, at the end the viewer can take home the disturbing question about whether this war, with all its death and destruction and tremendous monetary cost, was merely a way of advancing W.'s position in a family feud.

Certainly, critics who thought Stone's film was too timid had to ignore its fairly consistent, and rarely sympathetic, depiction of the forty-third president as an unambitious, incurious black sheep of a family led by a prestigious but difficult-to-satisfy father. We first meet George W. Bush in college, already a drinker and clearly a slacker, soon to be chewed out by his father for seeming to show no real interest in any of the options laid out for him. Eventually, though, the younger Bush gets excited about owning the Texas Rangers. Stone uses that as a frame for the film—a recurring dream sequence in which Bush walks onto a baseball field in front of empty stands, imagines he hears cheers, and has the chance to make a big game-saving catch of a fly ball. But the ball never returns to earth. It is a nice metaphor for Bush's simplistic incompetence, except that it does not fit well into the rest of the story—and we never learn anything about Bush's actual tenure as a baseball owner; Stone is not interested in any part of the story that shows Bush as a successful businessman.

Instead, we get plenty of scenes of Bush (Josh Brolin) being slighted and insulted by his father (James Cromwell) and mother (Ellen Burstyn), who constantly compare him unfavorably to his brother Jeb (Jason Ritter). It rings true enough, as every family has members who are assigned roles and personalities whose traits can become ossified. The family dynamics are believable enough, even if a little one-dimensional, and they are spiced up by the later presence of Laura Bush (Elizabeth Banks), who in this film shines with a sexy down-home luster as the wife who believes in her man.

Brolin gets by portraying the future president as an unremarkable guy with a chip on his shoulder and a rather unconvincing bluster. It is not a grandstanding performance and it is a rather thankless one, but Brolin succeeds without excess. Cromwell is more all-controlling and patrician than the real George H. W. Bush seemed in public—but in a wise and avuncular rather than mean-spirited way. It is perhaps this quality about the characters that drove some of George W. Bush's strongest critics a little mad; these are not despicable people, even if they can be petty.

The same cannot be said, however, for the characters in Bush's cabinet who push him to war. They are more like caricatures than the well-rounded figures in the Bush family. Cheney, done to a deliciously skulking tee by Dreyfuss, is monstrously menacing. But when he sketches out his plan for how the Iraq invasion will allow the United States to get a geopolitical stranglehold on the Middle East's oil resources, the lecture is implausibly barefaced, and the realism of the film veers hopelessly toward *Dr. Strangelove* (1964) spoof territory. Everyone else in the run-up to the war gets a turn to speak in what passes for believable character, including a nerdish Karl Rove (Toby Jones), a hectoring but mostly silent Condoleezza Rice (Thandie Newton), a wrong-headed Donald Rumsfeld (Scott Glenn), and other figures that will not be instantly identifiable to the politi-

cally inattentive. As Colin Powell, Jeffrey Wright appears headed for sainthood—Powell is portrayed as the ignored conscience of the cabinet and the hero of the resistance to the war effort. The conversations of these characters propel Bush to war in a way that makes sense for the plot but hardly rings true—it is a *Cliff's Notes* condensation of the actual events and arguments.

It is not true that *W.* is sympathetic to Bush. It does make a nod toward understanding what might have been his personal and political motivations, but it is the kind of film that starts from a premise (in this case, that *W.* went to war to upstage and impress his daddy) and thus musters every available stratagem to prove its already assumed hypothesis. The film is neither fair nor balanced, but it is certainly no tirade, and its central character seems paltry and petty enough without Stone feeling the need to lampoon him mercilessly. The trouble with a satire of Bush is that the truth might be stranger than satire, and for once Stone, recognizing this fact, plays it straight.

Michael Betzold

CREDITS

George W. Bush: Josh Brolin
Laura Bush: Elizabeth Banks
Condoleezza Rice: Thandie Newton
Dick Cheney: Richard Dreyfuss
Donald Rumsfeld: Scott Glenn
Tony Blair: Ioan Gruffudd
George Herbert Walker Bush: James Cromwell
Barbara Bush: Ellen Burstyn
Don Evans: Noah Wyle
Jeb Bush: Jason Ritter
Gen. Colin Powell: Jeffrey Wright
Thatcher: Jesse Bradford
Ari Fleischer: Rob Corddry
Karl Rove: Toby Jones
Saddam Hussein: Sayed Badreya
Gen. Tommy Franks: Michael Gaston
Origin: USA
Language: English
Released: 2008
Production: Bill Block, Moritz Borman, Eric Kopeloff, Paul Hanson; QED International, Ixtlan Corporation, Omnilab Media; released by Lionsgate
Directed by: Oliver Stone
Written by: Stanley Weiser
Cinematography by: Phedon Papamichael
Music by: Paul Cantelon
Sound: John Pritchett
Editing: Julie Monroe

Art Direction: John Richardson, Alex Hajdu
Costumes: Michael Dennison
Production Design: Derek R. Hill
MPAA rating: PG-13
Running time: 131 minutes

REVIEWS

Boston Globe Online. October 17, 2008.
Chicago Sun-Times Online. October 15, 2008.
Entertainment Weekly Online. October 15, 2008.
Hollywood Reporter Online. October 7, 2008.
Los Angeles Times Online. October 17, 2008.
New York Times Online. October 17, 2008.
Newsweek Online. October 11, 2008.
San Francisco Chronicle. October 17, 2008, p. E1.
Variety Online. October 7, 2008.
Washington Post. October 17, 2008, p. C1.

QUOTES

George Herbert Walker Bush: "Who do you think you are…a Kennedy? You're a Bush! Act like one!"

TRIVIA

Christian Bale was originally cast as George W. Bush but quit the project at the last minute prompting the casting of Josh Brolin.

THE WACKNESS

Sometimes it's right to do the wrong things.
—Movie tagline

Box Office: $2 million

Imagine a world without cell phones, Google, and DVDs. Jonathan Levine plunges his audience into that distant era—actually, 1994—in *The Wackness,* a comic yet affectionate look at young and not-so-young love in Manhattan. Reminiscent of other coming-of-age films, such as *The Graduate* (1967) and *Tadpole* (2002), *The Wackness* takes its time unveiling its charms.

Luke Shapiro (Josh Peck), about to graduate from a private high school, needs some guidance and goes to the psychiatrist Jeffrey Squires (Ben Kingsley), the stepfather of a classmate, Stephanie (Olivia Thirlby). Dr. Squires dispenses half-hearted advice in exchange for marijuana. Luke is an honest, upstanding, all-American drug dealer, an occupation Levine treats with a casualness that may annoy some.

In addition to their fondness for marijuana, Luke and Squires have something else in common. Luke pines

for Stephanie's attention, while the psychiatrist's marriage to Kristin (Famke Janssen) is collapsing. He still loves her, yet she all but ignores his existence. Although the teenager and the doctor are unaware of each other's problems, they slowly bond. Bored with his existence, Squires begins hanging out with Luke, desperately trying to recapture a youth that has long since faded.

As Luke and Squires grow closer, the drug dealer also becomes friendlier with Stephanie. When her mother and stepfather dash off to Barbados to try to rekindle their romance, Luke and Stephanie head for the Squires beach house on Fire Island and become lovers. Further complicating matters is economic turmoil in the Shapiro household. Luke's bumbling father (David Wohl) has lost most of the family's money, much to the chagrin of his wife (Talia Balsam), and they may have to move. Luke cannot imagine life anywhere but the Upper East Side.

Writer-director Levine, in his first feature, shows Luke maturing, slowly, often painfully, over the summer of 1994, while Squires becomes increasingly infantile. Luke is an obnoxious jerk in the opening scene but gradually becomes more likable. Levine seems aware that viewers need not immediately identify with the protagonist of a film, that audience sympathy must be earned, an insight many beginning filmmakers fail to grasp. Squires is stiff and unresponsive in this first scene but loosens up considerably, as the characters almost switch personalities. Matters are brought to a resolution of sorts in a purification-by-water scene, providing the film's deepest pathos.

As with mouth-breathing Luke himself, Peck, star of the Nickelodeon series *Drake & Josh* (2004–2007), is initially off-putting but eventually softens the character's brash façade to reveal his vulnerability. Occasionally guilty of overacting, Kingsley throws himself completely into his frantic role, risking appearing ridiculous several times, especially when Squires begins making out with one of Luke's flaky customers (Mary-Kate Olsen). While some reviewers found fault with Kingsley's performance, he is riveting because of Squires's unpredictability. Kingsley's best moment comes when Squires meets another of Luke's customers, a middle-aged, former rock musician played by Jane Adams. The two actors make the instant, unspoken attraction between the characters both comic and tender.

Visually, Levine is a conservative director, never doing anything flashy, almost always keeping characters in the center of the frame in medium shots. Cinematographer Petra Korner gives *The Wackness* a surprisingly dark look for a comedy. The scenes in Squires's office have a brown somberness like Gordon Willis's work in *The Godfather* films (1972–1990). For a Barbados bedroom scene, Korner allows the light streaming in from a window behind the characters to obliterate their faces, robbing Janssen of her big moment.

Despite the self-obsession of the characters and the questionable morality of the drug-dealing angle, Levine keeps *The Wackness* fresh and entertaining by providing numerous offbeat touches. Luke and his friends are devoted to hip hop and work lyrics of their favorite songs into conversations, totally unaware of how ridiculous they sound. Squires has named his Scottish terrier Jesus Christ, creating a double meaning when the dog suddenly urinates. A running joke shared by several characters involves complaining about how Mayor Rudolph Giuliani is ruining New York City by cleaning it up. Like the city in transition, *The Wackness* has an odd blend of seediness and charm.

Michael Adams

CREDITS

Luke Shapiro: Josh Peck
Dr. Jeffrey Squires: Ben Kingsley
Kristin Squires: Famke Janssen
Stephanie: Olivia Thirlby
Union: Mary-Kate Olsen
Eleanor: Jane Adams
Percy: Method Man
Mrs. Shapiro: Talia Balsam
Mr. Shapiro: David Wohl
Grandpa Shapiro: Bob Dishy
Origin: USA
Language: English
Released: 2008
Production: Keith Calder, Felipe Marino, Joe Neurauter; Occupant Films, SBK Ent.; released by Sony Pictures Classics
Directed by: Jonathan Levine
Written by: Jonathan Levine
Cinematography by: Petra Korner
Music by: David Torn
Music Supervisor: Jim Black
Editing: Josh Noyes
Sound: Ken Ishii
Art Direction: Beth Kuhn
Costumes: Michael Clancy
Production Design: Annie Spitz
MPAA rating: R
Running time: 95 minutes

REVIEWS

Boston Globe Online. July 11, 2008.
Chicago Sun-Times Online. July 10, 2008.
Entertainment Weekly. July 11, 2008, p. 48.
Hollywood Reporter Online. January 22, 2008.
Los Angeles Times Online. July 3, 2008.
New York Times Online. July 3, 2008.
Rolling Stone Online. June 25, 2008.
San Francisco Chronicle. July 11, 2008, p. E7.
Variety Online. January 19, 2008.
Village Voice Online. July 2, 2008.
Washington Post Online. July 11, 2008.

QUOTES

Dr. Squires (to Luke): "You don't need medication, you need to get laid."

TRIVIA

Ben Kingsley provided the hat that his character wears in the film.

AWARDS

Nomination:

Ind. Spirit 2009: First Screenplay
Golden Raspberries 2008: Worst Support. Actor (Kingsley).

WALL-E

*After 700 years of doing what he was built for—
he'll discover what he's meant for.*
—Movie tagline

An adventure beyond the Ordinar-E.
—Movie tagline

Box Office: $223.8 million

WALL-E continues Pixar's winning streak, not merely in financial terms but in consistently producing rich, engaging, meaningful, and thoroughly enjoyable films that just happen to be animated. Set in a distant future when Earth has been polluted and seemingly rendered incapable of supporting life, *WALL-E* is darker and perhaps sadder than prior Pixar films, yet at the same time it succeeds in telling a poignant, touching, funny, and hopeful story that should entertain children and move adults.

The movie is set 700 years in the future and reveals that our planet has become a wasteland of garbage piled sky-high and cluttering the atmosphere. There is no life to be seen, other than a cockroach who has befriended the sole functioning robot left on the planet, a waste collector known as WALL-E (an acronym for Waste Allocation Load Lifter-Earth-class). Little WALL-E (voice of Ben Burtt) has apparently been doing his job for hundreds of years, gathering trash, compacting it in squares, and stacking it in formations that from a distance appear to be skyscrapers. Over the years, the robot has collected artifacts from the garbage around him, ranging from a Rubik's cube to a VHS tape of *Hello, Dolly!*, which he watches longingly. Clearly the lonely little guy has developed a sentimental and romantic personality.

One day WALL-E's routine is interrupted by the arrival of a spacecraft bearing a sleek, obviously more advanced robot that immediately sets out on some sort of search mission. WALL-E becomes fascinated with the female robot right away and eventually she warms up to him, amused by his antics. She tells WALL-E her name is EVE (voice of Elissa Knight), but WALL-E seems only able to pronounce it as "Eva." Before long, the purpose of EVE's visit to Earth becomes clear when WALL-E shows her a small plant he had found growing amidst the garbage. When EVE's sensors identify the plant as living vegetation, she goes into "auto" mode, tucks the plant away inside her, and shuts down. Soon the spacecraft returns to Earth to retrieve her, and WALL-E—determined not to lose his newfound friend—latches onto the craft and is carried away with it as the ship heads out into space.

The ship takes EVE and WALL-E to an enormous city-sized spaceship called the Axiom, occupied by Earth's human refugees and maintained by countless robots of all kinds and sizes. The humans had left the Earth hundreds of years earlier when the planet became uninhabitable. Now, having spent several centuries in the resort-like Axiom, their needs attended to by the robots, humans have evolved into fat, baby-like people who spend all their time in hovering chairs, wearing the same clothes (and even the same colors) and following the same routine every day. Once onboard the Axiom, WALL-E follows EVE to the captain (voice of Jeff Garlin), who is shocked to see the small plant. The plant is evidence that the Earth can support life, so the captain determines that it is time to return to the planet. Conflict arises, however, when the ship's autopilot, appropriately called AUTO (MacIn Talk), refuses to obey the captain, having been given a secret directive hundreds of years before when the last humans on Earth determined that the planet could not be saved. Ultimately the captain, with help from EVE and of course WALL-E, takes control away from AUTO and pilots the Axiom back to Earth.

The film carries a fairly obvious but worthwhile ecological message about the need for taking better care of our planet, a message that is not hammered over the head of the viewer but one that simply arises out of the context of the setting. The environmental theme also plays well across age groups, equally accessible to children and adults. Yet alongside the straightforward ecological implications, *WALL-E* offers some commentary on the role of corporate responsibility with regard to protecting the environment (or contributing to its destruction). In the wasteland that WALL-E inhabits, billboards and logos for a huge corporation called Buy N Large seem to be everywhere, and it was in fact Buy N Large that constructed the WALL-E robots and later the Axiom and all its technology. Interestingly, it was this corporation that spearheaded the attempt to clean up the planet—after evidently being a major contributor to the pollution that made it uninhabitable. On board the Axiom, the video messages from the past, explaining what happened so many years before, are delivered by the corporation's CEO, Shelby Forthright (Fred Willard in the film's only live action role). Forthright stands behind a podium that makes him appear almost presidential, suggesting that perhaps corporate power had ascended to a kind of governing level, swallowing up everything in society.

The story of WALL-E and EVE is an endearing one, a touching portrait of two individuals that truly develop a special love for each other, and what makes the success of this story so interesting is that the characters are robots. The human characters in the film are secondary (the most fully developed and dynamic character is the captain), even though ultimately it is they who must restore a more responsible civilization on Earth. Even more fascinating is the sparse dialogue in the film. WALL-E and EVE speak, but they do not have long conversations, and much of the first half of the film passes without significant speech. The friendship and love that develop between the two robots occur through their interactions. The fact that the film succeeds so well with this character development is a testament to its narrative artistry, which also contributes to the movie's universality.

Not surprisingly, given Pixar's achievements with its previous films, *WALL-E* is visually compelling. With rich colors and dynamic lighting, realistic CG animation, and a kinetic landscape that draws the audience into the imaginary world of the film, the movie straddles the line between mimetic realism and fantastical artistry. Indeed, the visuals predominantly tell the story, and a memorable and touching story it is. Many critics proclaimed it one of the best movies of the year, and it is very likely *WALL-E* will long be counted as a triumphant achievement in animated film.

David Flanagin

CREDITS

Shelby Forthright/BnL CEO: Fred Willard
Captain McCrea: Jeff Garlin (Voice)

WALL-E/M-O: Ben Burtt (Voice)
Ship's Computer: Sigourney Weaver (Voice)
Mary: Kathy Najimy (Voice)
John: John Ratzenberger (Voice)
EVE: Elissa Knight (Voice)
Origin: USA
Language: English
Released: 2008
Production: Jim Morris; Pixar; released by Walt Disney Studios
Directed by: Andrew Stanton
Written by: Andrew Stanton, Jim Reardon
Cinematography by: Jeremy Lasky
Music by: Thomas Newman
Sound: Ben Burtt
Editing: Stephen R. Schaffer
Production Design: Ralph Eggleston
MPAA rating: G
Running time: 97 minutes

REVIEWS

Boston Globe Online. June 27, 2008.
Chicago Sun-Times Online. June 26, 2008.
Entertainment Weekly Online. June 26, 2008.
Hollywood Reporter Online. June 25, 2008.
Los Angeles Times Online. June 27, 2008.
New York Times Online. June 27, 2008.
San Francisco Chronicle. June 27, 2008, p. E1.
Variety Online. June 26, 2008.
Wall Street Journal. June 27, 2008, p. W1.
Washington Post. June 27, 2008, p. C1.

QUOTES

EVE: "WALL-E."
WALL-E: "Eeeee...va."

TRIVIA

This is the first instance of live-action footage being used in a feature-length Pixar film.

AWARDS

Oscars 2008: Animated Film
British Acad. 2008: Animated Film
Golden Globes 2009: Animated Film
Nomination:
Oscars 2008: Orig. Screenplay, Song ("Down to Earth"), Sound, Sound FX Editing, Orig. Score
British Acad. 2008: Sound, Orig. Score
Golden Globes 2009: Song ("Down to Earth").

WALTZ WITH BASHIR
(Vals Im Bashir)

Box Office: $2 million

Ari Folman's searing, evocative *Waltz with Bashir* (*Vals Im Bashir*) is mind-bending proof that limitations of genre are only set by the filmmakers themselves. The idea that animation could or should be one thing or another or that a documentary needs to be made a certain way to satisfy its form has stifled creative voices for years, but Folman and his collaborators clearly see things differently. Their daring film is not what audiences typically expect from either animation or nonfiction film, but it has shattered expectations worldwide, from the acclaim it received at the 2008 Cannes Film Festival to the critical plaudits and awards that greeted the film at the end of the year. Harrowing, emotional, dreamlike, and unique, *Waltz with Bashir* is easily one of the best films of 2008 and arguably one of the best of the last few years.

Waltz with Bashir is essentially a cinematic window into the mind and memory of its creator. Ari Folman was a nineteen-year-old infantry soldier for the Israel Defense Forces in 1982 when they were involved in the 1982 Lebanon War. After a friend who also served in that conflict tells Folman of a recurring nightmare about the twenty-six dogs that he remembers shooting in that war, the filmmaker himself starts to have confusing flashbacks and dreams, all mesmerizingly brought to life through animation in the film. In one recurring dream, he and his fellow soldiers are bathing when they see flares, walk through an abandoned city, and encounter dozens of screaming women. He has no memory of these events happening in real life. To try and answer questions raised by his memories and nightmarish visions, Folman speaks to people who served in Lebanon and who may have some insight into what he is remembering and what he is repressing. He speaks with soldiers, a psychologist, friends, and a reporter who all help him shine light on a very dark corner of his mind, the one that was involved with the massacre at Sabra and Shatila.

Instead of merely intercutting footage of the interviews that helped Folman on his personal journey of remembrance and regret, the filmmaker chose to animate the talking heads, giving *Waltz with Bashir* a dreamlike quality that has an amazing emotional impact. Just as memories often come back to people in surreal, nearly animated form, the visual aesthetic of *Waltz with Bashir* allows Folman to come to terms with what he has repressed from his time in Lebanon, especially during the period when Christian Phalangists massacred hundreds of Palestinians in the camps at Sabra and Shatila. Pulling absolutely no punches, Folman questions not only his involvement in those atrocities but the cyclical nature of violence and revenge, even going as far as to compare what happened there to what the Nazis did during World War II.

To call *Waltz with Bashir* a visual masterpiece would not be an understatement in the slightest. Folman does not merely animate his own memories and those of his interview subjects, he makes daring musical choices and segues smoothly and brilliantly from surreal to realistic and back again, until he finally uses actual footage in the finale, giving his ending a visceral power that is impossible to put into words. *Waltz with Bashir* walks that amazing line, feeling both like a memory or dream and a horrifying account of the inhumanity of which men are capable in their darkest times. *Waltz with Bashir* is both a brutally honest portrait of a man dealing with his own repression and self-loathing and a daring, shockingly vibrant piece of work that proves that labels like animation, documentary, or even war movie are merely words and that talented filmmakers can find ways to breathe new meanings into them that viewers dared not even imagine.

Very few films of the last several years, much less 2008, were as unforgettable as *Waltz with Bashir*. The winner of the Golden Globe® for Best Foreign Language Film appeared on several high-profile top ten lists at the end of 2008 and even won the National Society of Film Critics prize for the best picture of the year. *Waltz with Bashir* was deemed one of the best by major publications including the *Hollywood Reporter*, the *Chicago Reader*, *Entertainment Weekly*, the *Village Voice*, *New York*, magazine, *Newsweek*, the *Wall Street Journal*, and the *Los Angeles Times*. Easily one of the most critically acclaimed films of 2008, *Waltz with Bashir* was widely hailed as a masterpiece. It is a film about repressed memories that itself will not soon be forgotten by all who see it.

Brian Tallerico

CREDITS

Origin: France, Israel, Germany
Language: Hebrew
Released: 2008
Production: Serge Lalou, Ari Folman, Yael Nahlieli, Gerhard Meixner, Roman Paul; Les Films d'Ici, Razor Film, Bridget Folman Film Gang; released by Sony Pictures Classics
Directed by: Ari Folman
Written by: Ari Folman
Music by: Max Richter
Sound: Aviv Aldema
Editing: Nili Feller
Art Direction: David Polonsky
MPAA rating: R
Running time: 87 minutes

REVIEWS

Hollywood Reporter Online. May 15, 2008.
Los Angeles Times Online. December 25, 2008.

New York Times Online. December 26, 2008.
Newsweek Online. November 28, 2008.
Rolling Stone Online. January 22, 2009.
Variety Online. May 15, 2008.
Village Voice Online. December 23, 2008.
Wall Street Journal Online. December 25, 2008.
Washington Post. January 23, 2008.

QUOTES

Boaz Rein-Buskila: "Do you ever have flashbacks from Lebanon?"
Ari Folman: "No. No, not really."

AWARDS

Directors Guild 2008: Feature Doc.
Golden Globes 2009: Foreign Film
Writers Guild 2008: Doc. Screenplay
Nomination:
Oscars 2008: Foreign Film
British Acad. 2008: Animated Film, Foreign Film.

WANTED

Choose your destiny.
—Movie tagline
Their world. Her rules. His destiny.
—Movie tagline

Box Office: $134.5 million

While many action-packed thrillers have brought viewers to the edges of their seats, *Wanted* is an ultra-intense, ultra-lurid, hyperbolic roar of a film that blasted audiences against the backs of those seats and endeavored to keep them pinned there for the duration. It is a thunderously raging spectacle that rarely stops to take a breath or let the audience catch theirs, bombarding viewers with not only CGI-tweaked images that make jaws drop but also savagery so potent that moviegoers likely felt the need to count their teeth on their way back up the aisle. *Wanted* rivals even the best-stocked Red Cross center with the ample blood it contains. The film also boasts the loony story of a Loom of Fate, which has been encoding murder decrees into its textiles for a full millennium. These assassination orders have been reverently obeyed by a secret fraternity of weavers dedicated to preserving the very fabric of our lives. (To maintain societal order, their justifying rationale is, "kill one, maybe save a thousand.") What is certain is that audiences should refrain from examining the threads of *Wanted*'s plot too closely, the most cerebral thing about it being its over-fondness for graphic head shots triggered by bullets that do aerodynamically impossible acrobatics on their way from barrel to brain. Yet, despite all the full-tilt, blood-spattered, hurricane-force excess and head-scratching preposterousness, *Wanted* works.

The main reason it does, besides the film's special effects, is its increasingly noteworthy lead, James McAvoy, who heretofore had not been envisioned by anyone as the formidable central figure of a film in this genre. After all, he neither towers nor seems extraordinarily likely to make the brawniest and most powerful cower. However, he is perfectly cast here as an anxiety-ridden, cuckolded, and generally miserable victim who goes from feeling like something to be scraped off the bottom of someone's shoe to kicking ass as an eminently skilled executioner. McAvoy's Wesley comes across as Everyman, an accountant slogging like so many people through a drab, discontented life, wondering how long he can successfully keep his soul-corroding woe hidden, and starting not to care one way or the other.

The character's effective voiceover succinctly conveys Wesley's angst, as do scenes which enumerate his crushing mountain of troubles. Wesley's father disappeared from his life back when he was just a week old, and he surmises that the man had already been able to recognize his progeny as an embarrassing disappointment. Wesley's girlfriend, Cathy (Kristen Hager), commands and complains when she is not enjoying tabletop trysts with his best friend and coworker, Barry (Chris Pratt in an enjoyable performance). Wesley does not even put his foot down when Barry asks him to pay for a box of fruit-flavored condoms, despite knowing full well who will be enjoying them with his two-faced friend. Further emasculation is accomplished by his shrew of a boss (Lorna Scott), especially bigmouthed but also plus-sized in every other way, who gets perverse pleasure out of grinding him down. (For fun, she sneaks up and unnervingly snaps a stapler by his ears.) Even an ATM machine cruelly but humorously mocks Wesley for deficiencies beyond an almost-depleted bank account. McAvoy skillfully expresses the way his character feels inside, with nearly-dead eyes and a face, both reddened and scrunched up in palpable agony, that he clutches in the excruciating throes of a panic attack. Wesley is a sorry sort indeed, and so it is highly appropriate that he is incessantly apologizing. He relates to the audience that he desperately yearns to be someone else somewhere else, but does not hold out much hope that things will ever change.

However, change beyond what he ever could have imagined soon arrives in the fetching, tattooed form of the aptly named Fox (Angelina Jolie), who will take him from impotence to omnipotence. She startles and confounds him in a convenience store line with the following calmly stated claim: his father was the aforemen-

tioned Fraternity's greatest gunman until being snuffed out the day before by the man presently pointing a firearm directly at Wesley. As a gun battle begins between Fox and rogue assassin Cross (Thomas Kretschmann), an immediate and comical contrast is made between her sleek, cool surety and lethal finesse and Wesley's fumbling, fear-fueled urge to escape. With her slender arms, Fox wields hefty-looking weapons with apparent ease. Viewers hear the quickening beat of Wesley's pounding heart as one of *Wanted*'s most exciting, humorous, überkinetic, and cacophonous sequences unfolds. The film itself seems destined to hyperventilate as much as Wesley as he and Fox race off in a flaming red Viper to try to outmaneuver and outdistance their relentless pursuer. Along with a soundtrack likely frowned upon by ear specialists everywhere, the breakneck speed and chaotic nature of the suspenseful chase are enhanced by both crosscutting and jerky camera images that make viewers feel as if they too are being tossed around within the ever-careening car. Jolie makes quite an impression when her character bashes out the windshield to recline on the front of her speeding vehicle, guns blazing.

It is comical to observe Wesley's bewildered struggle to process the information about the Fraternity and how his own destiny is to follow in the footsteps of his father. He is told he possesses unstoppable, peerless powers, and must use them to avenge his father's death. He thinks it is all hooey, especially the idea that he could carry out such a mission against a killer possessing skills second only to those of his late father. Yet it is intriguing to see how the pathetic, put-upon nobody cannot help but respond to ego-inflating assertions that he is not only somebody but somebody special. Feeling empowered for the first time and sporting a new, peppy smile, Wesley explodes (verbally) at his boss and (physically) at Barry, leaving what had passed for a life behind.

Wesley's metamorphosis from intimidated easy mark to confident, unparalleled marksman turns out to be alarmingly difficult—both for him to go through and for viewers to watch. After he meets the Fraternity's sagacious leader, Sloan (Morgan Freeman), and other members with ominous-sounding names like the Exterminator (Konstantin Khabensky) and the Butcher (Dato Bakhtadze), poor Wesley's grueling and gruesome training includes his being endlessly bullied, knifed, and beaten to a bloody pulp by Fox and her comrades, breaking him down and then building him up. In between the bloodlettings, Wesley is seen lying eerily submerged in a milky paraffin bath that speeds healing. Topsy-turvy camerawork and unusual angles purposely add to the discomfort the viewer feels in witnessing such horrors.

Wesley is soon jumping onto the tops of Chicago's El trains in anticipation of a practice kill, but he has a harder time taking the leap of faith that will enable him to obey the Loom and kill strangers who, unlike Cross, have done nothing to him personally. Viewers will feel uneasy as they watch him follow through with several murders with increasing aplomb, convinced that what they are doing is for the best. In a telling shot that gives one pause, Wesley and Sloan are viewed through the myriad threads of the Loom of Fate, visually underscoring how the young man has been ensnared. Ready to go after Cross, Wesley's chest is now puffed up both figuratively and to some extent literally (McAvoy underwent a demanding training regimen for the part), and the new steely-eyed determination of this man on a mission is impossible to miss. McAvoy's Wesley resolves to make Cross pay for killing his father.

Wanted's most raucous, chaotic, eye-popping action sequence is also the one in which Wesley's mind is especially disquieted and confused and his eyes are opened to some vital facts. This devastating letdown happens just seconds before he plummets into water hundreds of feet below. Before learning that the man he has just made pay for his father's death is his actual father, and that everything else the Fraternity told him was a lie, viewers get bullets whizzing, cars crashing, and a spectacular, screeching, sparking derailment and downward, dizzying plunge of a passenger-filled train traversing a deep gorge. As a stunned Wesley strains to digest truths capable of eating him alive, the character's inner turmoil is clearly expressed in McAvoy's eyes.

How many films can boast a climactic scene featuring a retributive detonation of scores of peanut butter-loving rats? *Wanted* can, and before the lengthy credits roll, Wesley performs a sort of blood-soaked ballistic ballet (which includes blasting additional victims with a gun still lodged in an initial victim's shattered forehead), Fox sends a single bullet on a circular trajectory through her cohorts' craniums and then finally her own, and Sloan meets his maker.

Wanted is the English-language debut for the Kazakhstan-born director Timur Bekmambetov, continuing the intensity and visual flair of his *Night Watch* (2004) and *Day Watch* (2006), the two highest-grossing films in the history of Russian cinema. (The vampires in those films would likely adore all the gore in *Wanted*.) His latest is based upon the series of comic books by Mark Millar and J. G. Jones, to which changes were especially made to keep Wesley from committing a lot of sympathy-suppressing heinous acts. It will surprise few that those who crafted this adaptation were responsible for films in the *Fast and Furious* franchise. Made on a budget between $75 and $100 million, *Wanted* surpassed both figures in domestic box office, with high hopes for foreign markets. Critical reaction was quite positive, praising the film as an enjoyable summer popcorn flick. With its interesting (if not exactly

resolved) character arc and bullets that improbably but amazingly do the same, the film's unrelenting concussive force will likely blow away fans of the genre in a much happier sense than experienced by so many of the characters in *Wanted*.

David L. Boxerbaum

CREDITS

Wesley Gibson: James McAvoy
Fox: Angelina Jolie
Sloan: Morgan Freeman
Pekwarsky: Terence Stamp
Cross: Thomas Kretschmann
The Gunsmith: Common
The Repairman: Marc Warren
Mr. X: David O'Hara
Cathy: Kristen Hager
The Exterminator: Konstantin Khabenskiy
The Butcher: Dato Bakhtadze
Janice: Lorna Scott
Origin: USA
Language: English
Released: 2008
Production: Marc E. Platt, Iain Smith, Jim Lemley, Jason Netter; Spyglass Entertainment, Relativity Media, Kickstart; released by Universal
Directed by: Timur Bekmambetov
Written by: Michael Brandt, Derek Haas, Chris Morgan
Cinematography by: Mitchell Amundsen
Music by: Danny Elfman
Sound: Petr Forejt, Chris Jenkins, Frank A. Montaño
Music Supervisor: Kathy Nelson
Editing: David Brenner
Art Direction: Tomas Voth
Costumes: Varvara Avdyushko
Production Design: John Myhre
MPAA rating: R
Running time: 110 minutes

REVIEWS

Boston Globe Online. June 27, 2008.
Chicago Sun-Times Online. June 26, 2008.
Entertainment Weekly Online. June 26, 2008.
Hollywood Reporter Online. June 19, 2008.
Los Angeles Times Online. June 27, 2008.
New York Times Online. June 27, 2008.
New Yorker Online. June 30, 2008.
Rolling Stone Online. June 27, 2008.
San Francisco Chronicle. June 27, 2008, p. E1.
Variety Online. June 19, 2008.

Wall Street Journal. June 27, 2008, p. W1.
Washington Post. June 27, 2008, p. C1.

QUOTES

Sloan (to Wesley): "Let your instincts guide you."

TRIVIA

According to Angelina Jolie, she patterned her character after Clint Eastwood.

AWARDS

Nomination:

Oscars 2008: Sound, Sound FX Editing
Screen Actors Guild 2008: Outstanding Performance by a Stunt Ensemble.

WAR, INC.

When it comes to war...America means business.
—Movie tagline

It would be heartening to report that *War, Inc.* is the antiwar movie of the decade, the film everyone disenchanted with the war in Iraq has been waiting for, a *Dr. Strangelove* (1964) for our times, a brilliant satirical allegory that will change minds and make a difference. But it would be a lie. Iraq was poison at the box office during the summer of 2008, and anything remotely evoking the war was destined to fail. Certainly, *War, Inc.* was not about to turn that trend around. A far better film, *Standard Operating Procedure* (2008), surely one of the year's best documentary films, played for only a few weeks. Reasonably good and intelligent films about the war on terror emerged along with *War, Inc.*. Tommy Lee Jones won critical recognition for his portrayal of a dead soldier's father in *In the Valley of Elah* (2007), for example, and in 2008 Kimberly Pearce directed Ryan Phillippe flawlessly in *Stop-Loss*. Brian De Palma told the story of the rape and murder of a fourteen-year-old Iraqi girl by American soldiers in his film *Redacted*. But these films were not box-office hits. Many speculated that viewers did not want to be reminded of disturbing subjects; those with summer release dates faced audiences that just wanted to be entertained. As John Cusack, who co-wrote, produced, and acted in the film, which was made on a budget of $8 million and distributed by a small independent studio, told the *New York Times*, "We wanted to make something and not just talk about it, and we were aware of the challenges that went with it."

Cusack produced and co-wrote *War, Inc.* (with Mark Leyner and Jeremy Pikser, whose screenwriting credits include *Bulworth* [1998]), apparently inspired by Naomi Klein's reporting on the war for the *Nation* magazine, and he therefore has to take much of the blame for its mistakes and excesses. In the film the government is no longer in the business of waging war. Instead, a Haliburton-like contractor called Tamerlane (named after the ruthless barbarian despot celebrated in drama by Christopher Marlowe) is at the helm. Cusack plays an operative named Brand Hauser, who is given his orders by a demented ex-vice president (Dan Aykroyd plays this Cheneyesque cameo; we first see him sitting on a commode, pants down). Hauser's first assignment is to assassinate some uncooperative Germans in the Canadian Arctic, dispatched with consummate shock effect, in order to begin this wretched movie with a bang. His second mission is to run a loony trade show in the fictional Middle Eastern country of Turaqistan and to assassinate its leader, who, due to the screenplay's terminal cuteness, is named Omar Sharif (Lyubomir Neikov). The problem is, Hauser seems halfway fond of the guy. Sharif, a Middle Eastern oil minister, plans to build a pipeline that might jeopardize Tamerlane's conspiracy to monopolize Turaqistan's oil resources. Mr. Vice-President is on the case. Sharif must die. Hardly the stuff of comedy.

Cusack told the left-of-center magazine *Mother Jones* (July/August 2008) that his character was based on Paul Bremer, the American diplomat assigned to oversee the reconstruction of post-invasion Iraq: "As Iraq was still on fire, literally, Paul Bremer rode in, dressed like my character in his Brooks Brothers suit with his military boots, the uniform of the disaster capitalist. It was a messianic fantasy where Iraq was going to be a free-market utopia." When asked how this satire of where America is in the world came about, Cusack answered: "I don't think people knew that the Bush agenda was going to be as radical as it was in implementing the Milton Friedman playbook of radical privatization—what Naomi Klein calls 'disaster capitalism.'" There is a Naomi Klein surrogate in the film, a journalist named Natalie Hegalhuzen (Marisa Tomei). But, as Ann Hornaday wrote in the *Washington Post*, the film's biggest surprise was Hilary Duff, playing "a Turaqi pop tart named Yonica Babyyeah," who just might be the daughter of Brand Hauser, we learn later, as this trainwreck of a film goes way off track. By this time, all the characters have lost all sense of reality, so such astonishing disclosures can be little more than tiresome. Nothing is believable here.

Cusack's sister Joan Cusack puts in an amusingly over-the-top portrayal of Marsha Dillon, Hauser's assistant in charge of coordinating the trade show and its entertainments, which tastelessly includes a chorus line of female amputees doing high steps in flexible prosthetic legs. Stephen Holden of the *New York Times* called her "an enraged sourpuss who suggests an exponentially more disagreeable Mary Matalin." But, then, everything is over the top here. Nothing makes much sense, since the universe is utterly absurd. Hauser is given instructions by a Wizard of Oz-type mandarin (leaving one to wonder how Sir Ben Kingsley could have been talked into taking such a demeaning role), confined to a wheelchair because he had been physically damaged and disabled by Hauser in a trash compactor in an earlier encounter that is provided in flash-back for the viewer's disgust. But *The Wizard of Oz* (1939) had a better, and arguably more realistic plot. Cue the flying monkeys!

Everything in this mess of a movie is derivative. One begins with the Green Zone in Baghdad, which the *Washington Post* journalist Rajiv Chandrasekaran magically transformed into metaphor in his award-winning book *Imperial Life in the Emerald City: Inside Iraq's Green Zone*. As the plot of *War, Inc.* flits from one ridiculous detail to the next, the viewer begins to harbor thoughts of escape before the whole 106 minutes of the film are up. The movie is dumbly derivative and sadly lacks basic nuances of comic timing. As David Carr wrote in the *New York Times*, *War, Inc.* "is a satire that goes over the top and stays there."

James M. Welsh

CREDITS

Brand Hauser: John Cusack
Yonica Babyyeah: Hilary Duff
Natalie Hegalhuzen: Marisa Tomei
Marsha Dillon: Joan Cusack
Walken: Ben Kingsley
Mr. Vice President: Dan Aykroyd
Omar Sharif: Lubomir Neikov
Medusa Hair: Ben Cross
Zubleh/Ooq-Yu-Fay Taqnufmini: Ned Bellamy
Hauser's Wife: Shirly Brener
Origin: USA
Language: English
Released: 2008
Production: Danny Lerner, John Cusack, Grace Loh, Les Weldon; Millennium Films, New Crimes; released by First Look Studios
Directed by: Joshua Seftel
Written by: John Cusack, Jeremy Pikser, Mark Leyner
Cinematography by: Zoran Popovic
Music by: David Robbins
Editing: Michael Berenbaum
Sound: Vladimir Kaloyanov
Costumes: Vicki Graef

Production Design: Miljen Kreka Kljakovic
MPAA rating: R
Running time: 107 minutes

REVIEWS

Christian Science Monitor Online. May 23, 2008.
Hollywood Reporter Online. April 28, 2008.
Los Angeles Times Online. May 23, 2008.
New York Times Online. May 23, 2008.
Variety Online. April 30, 2008.
Village Voice Online. May 20, 2008.
Wall Street Journal. May 23, 2008, p. W1.

QUOTES

Brand Hauser: "But the way I look at it is this: the day we can actually feel and hear all the suffering of mankind, that's the day when 'The Christ' will come back! So we got that going for us."

TRIVIA

The Tamerlane corporate gift bag contains an autobiography attributed to "Oh, you know who," called *How I Conquered the World and Dealt with Issues with my Father.*

AWARDS

Nomination:

Golden Raspberries 2008: Worst Support. Actor (Kingsley).

WELCOME HOME ROSCOE JENKINS

Going home is no vacation.
—Movie tagline

Box Office: $42.4 million

Welcome Home Roscoe Jenkins is merely further cinematic proof that spending two hours at someone else's family barbecue can never sustain the running time of a feature film. Just more evidence that another person's family reunion is not going to be interesting to anyone but that individual, *Roscoe Jenkins* falls into the overused "wacky relatives" genre of comedy and ends up low-ranked even in that ignominious crowd. Once an edgy comedian, Martin Lawrence has found a new career in low-brow family comedies that do the bare minimum in terms of comedy and character. His old self, the one that shocked audiences and filled arenas with screaming fans, would rip his new self, the one that has completely sold out in comedies like *Wild Hogs* (2007), *College Road Trip* (2008), and *Welcome Home Roscoe Jenkins,* into pieces. Actually, his old self probably would not even bother to see his new one's movies.

Written and directed by Malcolm D. Lee, the cousin of Spike Lee and director of *Undercover Brother* (2002), *The Best Man* (1999), and *Roll Bounce* (2005), *Welcome Home Roscoe Jenkins* opens with the introduction of its title character (Martin Lawrence) and his vain fiancée Bianca Kittles (Joy Bryant). Jenkins has taken on the more TV-friendly appellation of Dr. R.J. Stevens and become a talk-show sensation with his motivational speeches. Roscoe may have changed his name, found himself a gorgeous, reality-show-winning girlfriend, and a ton of cash, but he can only run so far from his Southern roots in Dry Springs, Georgia.

R.J. Stevens gets dragged back into the persona of Roscoe Jenkins when his parents (James Earl Jones and Margaret Avery) ask their distant son to come home for their fiftieth wedding anniversary. He may be heading home with his gorgeous girlfriend and impressive career to show his relatives and hometown friends just how far he has come, but *Welcome Home Roscoe Jenkins* illustrates just how easy it is for a grown man to become a whiny child when he is surrounded by the people who have known him the longest. An accomplished cast, including Michael Clarke Duncan, Cedric the Entertainer, Mike Epps, and Mo'Nique, co-star as the down-home folks who bring Roscoe down to size.

A comedy about the power that family has to shrink even the biggest egos, with a cast this talented and a director who has proven to have good comic timing in his earlier films, should have made for a successful formula, but *Welcome Home Roscoe Jenkins* is far from a success. Alternating between grating characters that are impossible to care about, moments of family wisdom that are more boring than moving, and bizarre gross-out humor, *Welcome Home Roscoe Jenkins* is a complete mess. The wildly inconsistent tone that fluctuates from a grown man getting sprayed in the face by a skunk to awkward scenes of lessons learned about the importance of family and friends might not be so unbearable if the movie had even a few moments of true laughter. *Welcome Home* is not a hit-and-miss comedy as much as miss-and-miss. There is nothing to like here and the only reason to even see it is to marvel at how actors as talented as Jones, Bryant, and Duncan could get suckered into doing something so forgettable. Even Cedric the Entertainer may have to change his name after this one.

Critics were not kind to *Welcome Home Roscoe Jenkins*. Walter Addiego of the *San Francisco Chronicle* observed that the filmmaker's efforts are "undermined with crass humor, mugging and slapstick." Even the notoriously agreeable Peter Travers of *Rolling Stone* noted

that "nothing the skunk does can begin to match the stench of this movie." When the comedic peak of a film includes the unusual positioning of a small dog on top of a big canine during copulation, it is going to be very hard to get the critical community on-board for a trip to Dry Springs, Georgia.

Unlike other comedies of the "down-home family lesson" ilk, *Welcome Home Roscoe Jenkins* is not even mercifully short. Perhaps afraid he would never work with an ensemble this impressive again, and hoping to get the most bang for his buck, Lee wrote and directed a film that goes on for 114 minutes. Even fans of *Welcome Home Roscoe Jenkins* will get restless when the film crosses the ninety-minute mark and still has a little ways to go. How a producer could approve a film that runs around thirty minutes longer than it should remains a mystery, but the very low user rating—below four—on the Internet Movie Database (IMDB.com) proves that it may not have been the wisest move and that not only critics were dissatisfied. You can go home again, but if home is this boring, why would you want to?

Brian Tallerico

CREDITS

R.J.: Martin Lawrence
Mama Jenkins: Margaret Avery
Papa Jenkins: James Earl Jones
Bianca Kittles: Joy Bryant
Otis: Michael Clarke Duncan
Clyde: Cedric the Entertainer
Reggie: Mike Epps
Betty: Mo'Nique
Marty: Louis C.K.
Lucinda: Nicole Ari Parker
Jamaal: Damani Roberts
Origin: USA
Language: English
Released: 2008
Production: Scott Stuber, Mary Parent, Charles Castaldi; Spyglass Entertainment; released by Universal
Directed by: Malcolm D. Lee
Written by: Malcolm D. Lee
Cinematography by: Greg Gardiner
Music by: David Newman
Sound: Pud Cusack
Music Supervisor: Bonnie Greenberg
Editing: George Bowers, Paul Millspaugh
Art Direction: Gary Baugh
Costumes: Danielle Hollowell
Production Design: William A. Elliott

MPAA rating: PG-13
Running time: 114 minutes

REVIEWS

Boston Globe Online. February 8, 2008.
Entertainment Weekly Online. February 6, 2008.
Hollywood Reporter Online. February 8, 2008.
Los Angeles Times Online. February 8, 2008.
New York Times Online. February 8, 2008.
San Francisco Chronicle. February 8, 2008, p. E6.
Variety Online. February 7, 2008.
Washington Post. February 8, 2008, p. C6.

WENDY AND LUCY

Not quite a distaff *Harry and Tonto* (1974), *Wendy and Lucy* is a perceptive and heartfelt drama about a homeless woman who loses the only thing she cherishes in a world where humanity is also lost.

Michelle Williams plays the hapless heroine Wendy in Kelly Reichardt's screenplay, co-written with Jonathan Raymond, based on Raymond's short story, "Train Choir." Wendy is a young Indiana woman of little means who starts a new life for herself and her dog, Lucy, by securing a lucrative fish cannery job in Alaska.

Along the way, Wendy's plan is upended when her car breaks down in Oregon and she finds she does not have enough funds to get it fixed. Trying to save a few dollars to pay for a mechanic (Will Patton) to repair the car, Wendy shoplifts some dog food at a local market. When she is caught by a clerk, she is sent to jail, leaving behind her beloved Lucy tied to a post near the store.

By the time Wendy is released from jail, Lucy is missing. For the next several days, Wendy tries to find the dog—walking around the town, visiting the pound, posting Lucy's picture, and asking anyone if they have seen her. The only one who gives Wendy even the slightest bit of help is an elderly Walgreens guard (Wally Dalton, in a realistic performance), who lets Wendy use his cell phone to make some much-needed calls.

Frustrated by the lack of news about Lucy, Wendy decides to try sleeping in a park on her dog's favorite blanket, hoping she will show up. Instead, a homeless man (Larry Fessenden) scares her and she runs away.

The next day, thanks to the security guard, Wendy receives a call from a man who says he has found Lucy and has been keeping her at his house. Relieved, Wendy plans to get her but discovers her car at the shop is not even worth repairing. So Wendy gets a lift to the house and reunites at last with Lucy. During the reunion, however, Wendy realizes she does not have the resources to take Lucy with her (as she is now on foot), and makes an emotionally painful decision before heading off to a very uncertain future.

As with her previous film, *Old Joy* (2006), Reichardt keenly observes a small slice-of-life. In that film, two buddies meet after some time apart only to discover they have gone separate ways in life and that their friendship cannot be renewed. In *Wendy and Lucy*, most of the narrative focus is on just a single character and her search for her dog. Yet, despite the slight storylines and minimal plotting, both films are emotionally gripping and even (at times) suspenseful.

Though reminiscent of Allison Anders's *Gas Food Lodging* (1992), *Wendy and Lucy* seems more piercingly honest about the feminization of poverty and the under-reported fact that so many homeless people are women. While we never really know Wendy's backstory, it turns out just as well: she becomes a sort of Everywoman (or everyperson, given her androgynous look). Our identification is due, in part, to how we project our own life challenges on this generally stoic character. Though she gets angry and upset and (in the climax) very sad, most of Wendy's thoughts are not readable since she acts resigned to and unfazed by life's injustices.

As Wendy, Williams strikes the perfect balance between vulnerability and self-sufficiency. Made up to look pixieish and sad-sack, the usually attractive actress does a commendable job of immersing herself in her character—a role with similarities to her Oscar®-nominated performance in *Brokeback Mountain* (2005) but worlds apart from her role in *Deception* (2008). Her work in this film demonstrates her talent.

Though only eighty minutes long, *Wendy and Lucy* captures a modern-day form of naturalism through its minute focus and well-executed attention to details. Reichardt is ably assisted in this sage approach by Sam Levy's cinematography, Ryan Smith's production design, and Amanda Needham's costume design. The nighttime park scene is the only one that does not work very well, partly because the lighting is so dark that it is hard to tell what is going on (is the homeless man attacking Wendy or just trying to scare her?).

From beginning to end, *Wendy and Lucy* is touching and believable. The film movingly conveys the relevant message that economic turmoil hurts the underclass the most, and shows the results of social anomie and a failure of empathy.

Eric Monder

CREDITS
Wendy: Michelle Williams
Icky: Will Oldham

Andy: John Robinson
Mechanic: Will Patton
Hobo in Park: Larry Fessenden
Security Guard: Wally Dalton
Origin: USA
Language: English
Released: 2008
Production: Neil Kopp, Anish Savjani, Larry Fessenden; Glass Eye Pix, FilmScience; released by Oscilloscope Pictures, Inc.
Directed by: Kelly Reichardt
Written by: Kelly Reichardt, Jonathan Raymond
Cinematography by: Sam Levy
Editing: Mike Burchett, Kelly Reichardt
Sound: Javier Bennassar
Costumes: Amanda Needham
Production Design: Ryan Smith
MPAA rating: R
Running time: 80 minutes

REVIEWS

Christian Science Monitor Online. December 5, 2008.
Entertainment Weekly. December 12, 2008, p. 55.
Hollywood Reporter Online. May 27, 2008.
Los Angeles Times Online. December 12, 2008.
New York Times Online. December 10, 2008.
Rolling Stone Online. December 25, 2008.
Variety Online. June 2, 2008.
Village Voice Online. December 9, 2008.
Wall Street Journal. December 12, 2008.

TRIVIA

Writer/director Kelly Reichardt's own dog is Lucy.

AWARDS

Nomination:

Ind. Spirit 2009: Actress (Williams), Film.

WHAT HAPPENS IN VEGAS

Get lucky.
—Movie tagline
It's a battle of the sexes and they're playing dirty.
—Movie tagline

Box Office: $80.2 million

What Happens in Vegas, a romantic comedy that is neither romantic nor comedic, stretches the boundaries of how far an audience is willing to root for protagonists to succeed at romance when the hero and heroine are so shallow and grating that it would be much easier to root for them to get hit by a crosstown bus. Ashton Kutcher and Cameron Diaz play lead characters whose only redeeming quality as human beings seems to be their good looks, and the supporting cast in the film is so poorly written and directed that the entire vain, shallow attempt at humor collapses under the weight of its own superficiality. Like the city from which it takes its title, *What Happens in Vegas* may look good but is ultimately hollow.

The female lead, Joy McNally (Cameron Diaz), is a perfectionist stockbroker who gets dumped by her fiancée (Jason Sudeikis) just outside of the surprise birthday party she has thrown for him, making the embarrassment of their break-up all the more painful. Meanwhile, Jack Fuller (Ashton Kutcher) discovers that he is the kind of slacker who cannot hold a job even when his boss is his father (Treat Williams). To lick their personal and professional wounds, Jack and Joy head to Las Vegas, the town where problems drift away on a current of slot machines, showgirl numbers, and mixed drinks.

In the city of sin, Jack meets Joy and the two drunkenly decide to get married before the clarity of a hangover brings the realization that they would rather not spend another minute together, much less a lifetime. Just before they can get the quickie divorce to balance out the quickie marriage, Joy gives Jack a quarter that he uses in a giant slot machine, winning three million dollars. Joy thinks she is entitled to some of the winnings not only because it was her spare change but because of their marital status, setting the stage for a financial showdown in divorce court.

Back in New York City, Jack and Joy attempt to get a divorce, but a judge (Dennis Miller) orders that they go to marriage counseling and try to make it work for six months. Knowing that if one of them gives in and refuses to make it work during the six-month period then they will lose their share of the money, Jack and Joy begin domestic warfare, doing everything they can to push the other out of the marriage. Joy invites girls over to entice Jack to cheat. Jack urinates in the sink and shoves popcorn down his pants. Of course, it is all just a physical comedy set-up for an inevitable romance.

The problem with *What Happens in Vegas* is that the romantic union that will naturally take up the final act of the film comes way too late. By that time, Jack and Joy have been such awful, despicable people to each other that the only conceivable way to root for them to get together is so they will not inflict their brand of narcissistic romance on anyone else. When the two leads stretch the boundaries of what any decent people would do to each other for money, including messing with family, careers, and broken hearts, *What Happens in Vegas* completely falls apart. Screenwriter Dana Fox assumes that an audience will care about romantic leads or want to see them lucky in love as well as slot machines just because they are beautiful on the outside. Jack and Joy are too ugly on the inside for us to care about what happens to them anywhere.

As if to balance out the grating personalities of Jack and Joy, director Tom Vaughan surrounds them with some of the least interesting supporting actors in film. Rob Corddry occasionally works in the right material, but he plays his best friend role to Jack as obnoxiously as one of Kutcher's buddies from *Punk'd*, and Lake Bell is simply awful as Joy's friend Toni. Even the smaller roles, like Miller's judge or the marriage counselor played by Queen Latifah, feel miscast.

The inherent flaw in the concept of *What Happens in Vegas* might not be such a serious problem for director Vaughan if Diaz and Kutcher had an ounce of romantic chemistry. Their eventual union and the big kiss that comes with it is one of the least sexy or romantic of 2008. Ultimately, *What Happens in Vegas* is kind of like a night in the city of sin itself—loud, superficial, and full of regrets.

Brian Tallerico

CREDITS

Joy McNally: Cameron Diaz
Jack Fuller: Ashton Kutcher
Tipper: Lake Bell
Hater: Rob Corddry
Dr. Twitchell: Queen Latifah
Mr. Fuller: Treat Williams
Judge Whopper: Dennis Miller
Banger: Dennis Farina
Dave the Bear: Zach Galifianakis
Mason: Jason Sudeikis
Chong: Michelle Krusiec
Kelly: Krysten Ritter
Mrs. Fuller: Deirdre O'Connell
Origin: USA
Language: English
Released: 2008
Production: Michael Aguilar, Shawn Levy, Jimmy Miller; Regency Enterprises, 21 Laps, Mosaic Media Group; released by 20th Century-Fox
Directed by: Tom Vaughan
Written by: Dana Fox
Cinematography by: Matthew F. Leonetti
Music by: Christophe Beck
Sound: Christopher Newman

Music Supervisor: Deva Anderson
Editing: Matthew Friedman
Art Direction: W. Steven Graham
Costumes: Renee Ehrlich Kalfus
Production Design: Stuart Wurtzel
MPAA rating: PG-13
Running time: 99 minutes

REVIEWS

Boston Globe Online. May 9, 2008.
Chicago Sun-Times Online. May 9, 2008.
Entertainment Weekly Online. May 7, 2008.
Hollywood Reporter Online. May 7, 2008.
Los Angeles Times Online. May 9, 2008.
New York Times Online. May 9, 2008.
San Francisco Chronicle. May 9, 2008, p. E1.
Variety Online. May 4, 2008.
Washington Post. May 9, 2008, p. C1.

QUOTES

Judge Whopper: "Listen, I've been married for twenty five years to the same wonderful, infuriating woman. And granted there are days when I want to light her on fire but I don't, because I love her. And that would be illegal. And you know something, and I might be old fashioned but when I said those vows, I meant them."

AWARDS

Nomination:

Golden Raspberries 2008: Worst Actress (Diaz), Worst Screen Couple (Diaz and Kutcher).

WHAT JUST HAPPENED

In Hollywood, everybody can hear you scream.
—Movie tagline

Box Office: $1 million

It can be frustrating for a director when critics say his new satire is not very good, especially when he not only thinks it is a good film but also did not mean it as a satire. That was the reaction Oscar®-winner Barry Levinson had to many reviews of his *What Just Happened*, which was based on the 2002 Art Linson memoir that bore the subtitle, *Bitter Hollywood Tales from the Front Line*. In that book, the producer of memorable films like *Fast Times at Ridgemont High* (1982), *Fight Club* (1999), and *Into the Wild* (2007) provided a frank and deliciously wicked insider's take on the amazing inanities of the motion picture business. For example, he told of how beautiful and talented up-and-comer Gwyneth Paltrow almost lost out on being cast in *Great Expectations* (1997) due to what was considered her too-small chin, one deemed not befitting of an actress in a lead role. An even more startling and peculiar tale recounted the behavior of the recalcitrant, overly hairy and paunchy Alec Baldwin, who seemed hell-bent on emulating costar Bart the Bear (who was actually better behaved) as filming was about to get under way on *The Edge* (1997). In adapting his work for the screen, Linson distilled a thinly veiled account of Baldwin's volatility into a work of fiction, informed by a career's-worth of complications and hard-won realizations. What intrigued Levinson about the story Linson came up with was that, rather than being another rapier-witted lampooning of the entire industry, it was a comedic but fairly realistic slice-of-life portrait of a middle-aged producer struggling like crazy amid Tinseltown's madness.

Ben (a thoroughly-present Robert De Niro), the producer upon which *What Just Happened* focuses, talks repeatedly about the desire of his former wife Kelly (Robin Wright Penn) to recover what was his favorite chair in their home, a change from the comfortable dark green fabric he knew and loved to a bright red less to his liking but more to her own. She has every right to do so, after all, as both the chair and the house are now hers as a result of their divorce settlement, but it still clearly irks him. It seems to be symbolic in his mind of all the things in his personal and professional lives over which he has had an unsettling lack of control of late, as well as the underlying dread of getting cast aside and replaced by life in general as he grows increasingly longer in the tooth.

Judging by the size and décor of the homes now owned by Kelly and the other ex who preceded her, producer Ben has done quite well. What is clearly conveyed to viewers, however, is the desperate, never-ending necessity to continue succeeding, with even the prospect of a noteworthy flop causing profound flop sweat. As *What Just Happened* begins, Ben is poised to shine during a validating, career-sustaining *Vanity Fair* photo shoot touting a select group deemed the most powerful producers in the business. By the film's end, however, following the devastating unveiling of a bomb at the prestigious Cannes Film Festival, something that was all about puffing up has turned into something that he now needs to prop him up, where he stands in both the industry and the photo spread now nearly marginalized out of sight. Levinson's film deals with what happened in the intervening two weeks that strenuously tested Ben's "power credential."

It is said in the film that a producer is like the mayonnaise in a sandwich, the cohesive ingredient that ensures everything comes together to create a satisfying whole. As *What Just Happened* successfully makes clear,

that mayonnaise comes into contact with more than a little baloney. Ben first has to deal with wildly temperamental and substance-imbued British director Jeremy Brunell (Michael Wincott), who comes unhinged in his defense as art of what is actually ill-conceived dreck. Jeremy strenuously insists that *Fiercely*, his hard-hitting, provocative crime drama starring Sean Penn (who plays himself and has fun with his image), absolutely must end with a gunshot to a dog's head that revoltingly causes blood to splash upon the camera's lens. After a test audience is jolted out of apparent boredom by this profoundly off-putting sanguinary spectacle, steely studio exec Lou Tarnow (a glacial Catherine Keener) is none too pleased overall, and hopes to lessen her losses by at least having the ending changed. Ben is given the daunting task of convincing proud artiste Jeremy to alter his beloved creation so it will be much more palatable and, most important, more profitable.

At the same time, Ben also has the pressing duty of grabbing the reins on a seethingly defiant Bruce Willis, who, looking less like a leading man and more like a portly far-north lumberjack, is unfortunately staking his artistic integrity on the retention of a wholly inappropriate, bountiful beard. (Willis plays either an unflattering version of himself or Alec Baldwin, depending on how one wants to look at it.) The studio will pull the plug on the film if the facial hair fails to disappear, the actor's outsized ego costing everyone on down to the lowest grip their expected income. Willis's nebbish of an agent, Dick Bell (John Turturro), is of little help, so thoroughly intimidated by his bullheaded cash cow of a client that he is seized by fits of retching.

While struggling mightily to keep his head above such choppy, uncertain waters, Ben is not only torn by his unresolved feelings for Kelly, but is also racked with jealous anger at his colleague and Kelly's current bedmate, writer Scott Solomon (Stanley Tucci), and further thrown by the eye-opening realization that his underage daughter, Zoë (Kristen Stewart), was involved with a promising member of the film community who just blew his brains out. In an earlier scene Ben shares with the girl, De Niro skillfully reveals a tenderness that shows his character to be a wistfully loving father, one who probably realizes he too often failed to have time for a daughter who is now teenaged and inexorably pulling away. This small scene continues to resonate, helping those watching to, if not exactly warmly embrace or enthusiastically root for him, feel at least a sense of compassion for the man.

It is a close shave, but Willis does use a razor at the very last minute to everyone's relief. Jeremy, however, stabs Ben in the back, removing and then surreptitiously replacing his original hound homicide ending for Cannes. As a result, Lou expresses her displeasure by stranding beleaguered Ben on the airport tarmac, and yet he seems determined to press on, a screen capital survivor.

The film emphasizes the relentless, dizzying pressures under which a producer must strive to make what hangs in the balance tip in a lucrative direction. As Ben ricochets from place to place, he seems like a pinball in the midst of a high-stakes game, and he knows the score all too well. To visually underscore the on-the-fly, rapid-fire pace of a producer's deadline-punctuated existence, Levinson uses fast-motion sequences, periodically notes the time of day in the bottom of the shot, and continually shows Ben conversing on his ever-present Bluetooth while in transit through LA traffic. The movie's variously flawed but universally stressed characters resort to booze, pills, cigarettes, yoga, and therapists as crucial pressure-release valves.

Is much of this news? No. Furthermore, too many attempts at humor fall flat, a word unfortunately apropos of the production as a whole. (Especially impotent is a cemetery scene in which inattentive shoveling by Ben sends a sputtering Dick tumbling atop a lowered casket.) Many critics felt that *What Just Happened* would likely be of interest only to those who know firsthand about the trials and tribulations of toiling within the industry, and there is likely truth to that. However, some agreed with Levinson that most people can probably relate to the strenuous but vital struggle to juggle multiple aspects of life while also trying to keep up appearances.

After being shown at the Sundance Film Festival, *What Just Happened* took a while to find a distributor. When finally released late in the year, the film, reportedly made on a budget of $25 million, took a month to gross $1 million. It is understandable that those who thought the aim was for biting commentary found Levinson's film surprisingly, disappointingly toothless. *What Just Happened*—flaccid, unremarkable, and meandering—just happens.

David L. Boxerbaum

CREDITS

Ben: Robert De Niro
Actor: Bruce Willis
Himself: Sean Penn
Scott Solomon: Stanley Tucci
Dick Bell: John Turturro
Kelly: Robin Wright Penn
Jeremy Brunell: Michael Wincott
Lou Tarnow: Catherine Keener
Zoe: Kristen Stewart
Dawn: Lily Rabe

Origin: USA
Language: English
Released: 2008
Production: Jane Rosenthal, Mark Cuban, Art Linson, Robert De Niro, Barry Levinson; 2929 Productions, Tribeca Productions; released by Magnolia Pictures
Directed by: Barry Levinson
Written by: Art Linson
Cinematography by: Stéphane Fontaine
Music by: Marcelo Zarvos
Sound: Steve Cantamessa
Editing: Hank Corwin
Art Direction: Anthony Parrillo
Costumes: Ann Roth
Production Design: Stefania Cella
MPAA rating: R
Running time: 113 minutes

REVIEWS

Boston Globe Online. October 17, 2008.
Chicago Sun-Times Online. October 15, 2008.
Entertainment Weekly Online. October 15, 2008.
Hollywood Reporter Online. January 20, 2008.
Los Angeles Times Online. October 17, 2008.
New York Times Online. October 17, 2008.
New Yorker Online. October 20, 2008.
San Francisco Chronicle. October 17, 2008, p. E3.
Variety Online. January 22, 2008.
Washington Post. October 17, 2008, p. C2.

WHEN DID YOU LAST SEE YOUR FATHER?

Between every father and his son there is a story to be told.
—Movie tagline

Box Office: $1 million

Based on the award-winning 1993 novel by English poet Blake Morrison, *When Did You Last See Your Father?* (alternately titled *And When Did You Last See Your Father?*) explores the universally complex relationship between sons and fathers through the examination of the life and the death of the author's own charismatic but overbearing father, Arthur Morrison, a man described as "infallible, invincible and immortal." Morrison, who returned home to help his mother and sister care for Arthur during his final weeks of battling cancer, kept a journal as a form of therapy and rediscovered many lost childhood memories as he wrote. Director Anand Tucker and screenwriter David Nicholls transformed Morrison's impressionistic text into motion picture by attempting to capture his internal process while recording his memories in his journal. Boasting a very strong cast of accomplished actors, the movie adaptation was filmed in various picturesque locations throughout England by cinematographer Howard Atherton. A gorgeous musical score composed by Barrington Pheloung works exceptionally well with the often breathtaking scenery and the serious subject matter.

When Did You Last See Your Father? takes place in the 1980s, with flashbacks to the 1950s and 1960s exposing the history of a tense but occasionally heartwarming, normal father-son relationship. Forty-year-old Blake (Colin Firth), who is also the narrator, is an established writer with a wife, Kathy (Gina McKee), and two children. In the portions of the film that are set in the present, Arthur (Jim Broadbent) still dominates his grown-up son as though he were an inept child. The film follows Blake's psychological development from his initial anger directed at Arthur's pomposity, self-righteousness, and need to be the center of attention, to his resignation to playing the role of dutiful son in response to learning of his father's terminal illness, and his eventual reconciliation with events of the past. Frank scenes depicting Arthur's rapidly declining health are interspersed with juxtaposing recollections showing him in the prime of his life.

The movie begins in the 1950s with the Morrison family snarled in a traffic jam on their way to a car racing event. Arthur and his wife Kim (Juliet Stevenson, who, like Broadbent, ages throughout the course of the movie) are rural doctors working for the same medical practice. In addition to Blake, the couple has a younger daughter named Gillian (played as an adult by Claire Skinner). The opening scenes—in which Arthur embarrasses his family by brazenly using his doctor's privileges to bypass the long line of stopped cars, then bluffs their entrance to a higher-priced section of the spectators' field by claiming to have been sent the wrong level of tickets—serves as an early introduction to Arthur's questionable moral character, audacity, and sense of entitlement. Blake's adult narration further sets the tone for the movie to come: "This is the way it was with my father: Minor duplicities. Little fiddles. My childhood a web of little scams and triumphs. Parking where you shouldn't. Drinking after hours. The goods off the back of a lorry. He was lost if he couldn't cheat in a small way. My father could talk his way into and out of anything." The following scene flashes forward to the present, to a prestigious awards reception in honor of Blake in which an aging Arthur manages to steal the spotlight and belittle him in front of his peers—a pattern that repeats throughout the film.

Flashbacks to the 1950s, in which Blake (Bradley Johnson) is still a young boy, importantly serve to implicate Arthur as a philanderer, hinting that his close relationship with a family friend, "Aunt" Beaty (Sarah Lancashire), is less than proper and that he might even be the father of Beaty's daughter Sophie. Later, adult Blake attempts to gain an understanding of his parents' unconventional marriage through confronting his long-suffering mother about the affair. At the film's conclusion, Beaty and Sophie reappear at Arthur's memorial, giving Blake the opportunity to face the situation head on and achieve a degree of closure to one of the most unsettling aspects of his father's life.

Set to period British rock music, the 1960s episodes establish the nature of the frustrated relationship between Blake and Arthur. Arthur, a self-absorbed extrovert, is unwittingly antagonistic toward the introverted and awkward teenage Blake (Matthew Beard), who to his father's dismay is inclined toward studying literature over medicine at college. While the majority of these scenes highlight the growing sense of inferiority, discomfort, and shame being imposed on Blake by his father, glimmers of tenderness surface between the two in instances such as Arthur's teaching him how to drive and in Blake's send-off to university. Other flashbacks digress to memories of family vacations—with the shamelessly flirtatious Arthur in his glory—and to Blake's first love, Sandra (Elaine Cassidy), the Morrisons' housekeeper, who reappears near the end of the movie to share an intimate fling with the adult Blake and to provide him with some valuable insight into his father's character. It is only after Arthur's death, when Blake's tears come, that he is finally able to fully understand their relationship and to make peace with the memory of his father.

Jaye Furlonger

CREDITS

Arthur Morrison: Jim Broadbent
Blake Morrison: Colin Firth
Kim Morrison: Juliet Stevenson
Kathy Morrison: Gina McKee
Teenaged Blake: Matthew "Stymie" Beard
Beaty: Sarah Lancashire
Sandra: Elaine Cassidy
Gillian Morrison: Claire Skinner
Blake (teen): Matthew Beard
Blake (child): Bradley Johnson
Origin: Great Britain
Language: English
Released: 2007
Production: Elizabeth Karlsen, Stephen Woolley; Number 9 Films, Audley Films; released by Sony Pictures Classics

Directed by: Anand Tucker
Written by: David Nicholls
Cinematography by: Howard Atherton
Music by: Barrington Pheloung
Sound: Jim Greenhorn
Editing: Trevor Waite
Art Direction: Lynne Huitson
Costumes: Caroline Harris
Production Design: Alice Normington
MPAA rating: PG-13
Running time: 92 minutes

REVIEWS

The Guardian Online. October 5, 2007.
Hollywood Reporter Online. September 21, 2007.
Los Angeles Times Online. June 6, 2008.
New York Times Online. June 6, 2008.
The Observer Online. October 7, 2007.
Variety Online. August 21, 2007.
Village Voice Online. June 6, 2008.
Wall Street Journal Online. June 6, 2008.

QUOTES

Blake Morrison: "And at the risk of getting sentimental I'd just like to say a quick thanks to my wife, Kathy, not only for her encouragement and support but also because she especificly asked me to mention her."

TRIVIA

In order to better resember Colin Firth, Matthew Beard wore borw contact lenses.

WITLESS PROTECTION

Protecting America's assets.
    —Movie tagline

Box Office: $4.1 million

There are certain basic foundations of filmmaking that are usually followed even in the worst films of the year. The actors will be adequately lit. The shot will be accurately framed by the director of photography. The director will call action before his actors start speaking and cut when they are done. The screenplay will have three acts, characters, a beginning and an ending. It is truly rare to see a film so awful that it completely misses these basics of filmmaking, but *Witless Protection* is that rarity and one of the most shockingly horrible films in a long time. Charles Robert Carner's "comedy" is so misguided and poorly made that it is not out of the question to ask if it should even be called a "film."

Larry the Cable Guy has a devoted fan base, but even they should be shocked at how little effort has been put into *Witless Protection*. The stand-up comedian stars as, of course, a dimwitted fool named Larry, a small-town deputy in Mississippi (although the film was shot in Illinois and looks nothing like the South). Larry believes that he has witnessed a kidnapping and that this will be his moment to shine as a true enforcer of the law instead of just a small-town hick. It turns out that the kidnappers are actually FBI agents who are trying to protect the woman in question, Madeleine Dimkowski (Ivana Milicevic)—her childish pun of a name being the most interesting thing about her. Things get more complicated when Larry discovers that the agents who are going to deliver the woman, led by the slumming Yaphet Kotto, to a corruption trial in Chicago are actually on the take and are planning to kill the star witness themselves because they work for the corrupt tycoon played by a miscast Peter Stormare. Jenny McCarthy plays Larry's girlfriend Connie and Joe Mantegna pops up in a role that is easily one of the most baffling of the year. How the notable Mantegna agreed to be involved with this worthless picture is impossible to understand. An excessive amount of scatological humor that would fail to make a six-year-old boy chuckle fills in the gaps in the plot.

There are many, many bad comedies released in a year (and the amount seems to be increasing), but very few are as truly inept as *Witless Protection*. Not only does the film not contain one single laugh, it is almost jaw-dropping in the laziness of its production. Shots are not framed well. Punchlines are hit and then actors stand around as if there were no director to call "cut" or editor to trim the fat. No one would ever turn to *Witless Protection* for believability, but there are films being directed by high school students that are more competently produced. It is as if Carner, who both wrote and directed this train wreck, purposefuy tried to see how little he could deliver and still get fans of Larry the Cable Guy to open their wallet. There is literally not one single thing about *Witless Protection* worth even a minute of a discerning filmgoer's time.

Witless Protection was loathed by fans and critics alike when it was released in February 2008. As of fall 2008, the film held a spot on the worst 100 movies of all time, as voted on by users of the Internet Movie Database (IMDB.com). Of the poor twenty-three souls who paid to see the film (it was not screened in advance) and then reviewed it, according to Rotten Tomatoes, not one had a good word to say. Tod Goldberg of *E! Online* accurately said, "You have what might very well be the worst movie of 2008. And 2009. And probably 2010, too." Steven Hyden of *The Onion* pulled no punches when he wrote "Larry the Cable Guy is a cancerous boil on the ass of comedy, but it's still sort of shocking how little effort he puts into his movies." Frank Scheck of the *Hollywood Reporter* noted that the film "makes his previous effort, *Delta Farce*, seem a classic by comparison."

Bad movies are as common as Fridays, but *Witless Protection* goes a significant step lower on the cinematic totem pole. The film reeks of crass commercialism and desperation, trying to milk a fan base for their dollar with as little effort as possible. It is undeniably one of the worst movies of the new millennium.

Brian Tallerico

CREDITS

Deputy Larry Stalder: Larry the Cable Guy
Madeleine Dimkowski: Ivana Milicevic
Alonzo Moseley: Yaphet Kotto
Arthur Grimsley: Peter Stormare
Connie: Jenny McCarthy
Wilford Duvall: Eric Roberts
Dr. Rondog 'Doc' Savage: Joe Mantegna
Origin: USA
Language: English
Released: 2008
Production: J. P. Williams, Alan Blomquist; Parallel Entertainment Pictures, Samwilla, Shale Entertainment; released by Lionsgate
Directed by: Charles Robert Carner
Written by: Charles Robert Carner
Cinematography by: Michael Goi
Music by: Eric Allaman
Sound: Scott D. Smith
Editing: Marc Leif
Art Direction: David Tennanbaum
Costumes: Susan Kaufmann
Production Design: Cabot McMullen
MPAA rating: PG-13
Running time: 97 minutes

REVIEWS

Boston Globe Online. February 23, 2008.
Hollywood Reporter Online. February 25, 2008.
Los Angeles Times Online. February 25, 2008.
New York Times Online. February 23, 2008.
San Francisco Chronicle. February 25, 2008, p. E2.
Variety Online. February 22, 2008.

QUOTES

Larry: "Dang, my hand hasn't been this sore since the first episode of *Baywatch*!"

AWARDS

Nomination:

Golden Raspberries 2008: Worst Actor (Larry the Cable Guy), Worst Support. Actress (McCarthy), Worst Screen Couple (Larry the Cable Guy and McCarthy).

THE WITNESSES
(Les Témoins)

The Witnesses (also known as *Les Témoins*) charts France's earliest responses to the AIDS epidemic through the experiences of five friends. André Téchiné's elegiac drama never quite recreates the early 1980s atmosphere convincingly but becomes touching nonetheless.

As with so many of his films, writer/director Téchiné shows his skill at developing character and mood. His narrative, however, is less than compelling, in part because *The Witnesses* feels more like a microcosmic study of an era than a realistic recreation.

Téchiné's story (co-written with Laurent Guyot and Viviane Zingg) begins in Paris during the "innocent" summer of 1984 when Mehdi (Sami Bouajila), a police inspector, and his wife Sarah (Emmanuelle Béart), a children's book author, argue over who should care for their newborn baby. Meanwhile, the couple's friend, Adrien (Michel Blanc), a gay doctor, picks up Manu (Johan Libéreau) in a park and falls in love with the gangly, fresh-faced teenager (despite the fact that he refuses to sleep with Adrien).

Manu lives with his sister Julie (Julie Depardieu), an aspiring opera singer, but gladly accepts an invitation from Adrien to spend the summer with his friends, Mehdi and Sarah. During a trip to the French Riviera, Mehdi saves Manu from drowning. Soon after, Mehdi starts and affair with the young man. When Adrien finds out, he is furious, though Sarah is less so since she and Mehdi had agreed to an open marriage.

Manu eventually becomes very ill, which overwhelms the news of the affair. But while Mehdi drifts away from Manu, Adrien becomes more attached than ever—and does all he can as a doctor to study and cure this mysterious new disease affecting his friend. As it turns out, Manu has contracted an HIV infection. When Mehdi and Sarah learn this, Sarah becomes obsessed with finding out the details of the affair, which she decides to incorporate into a new book. She and Mehdi get an AIDS test and anxiously await the results. In the end, the surviving friends sadly but wisely appreciate life for the better.

Téchiné and his co-scenarists divide the story into three parts: the carefree days before the epidemic; the first days of discovery; and the sober post-mortems. Though episodic, *The Witnesses* moves along briskly. As in his better films (*Wild Reeds* [1994], *Changing Times* [2004]), the director creates flawed but appealing characters and casts them extremely well. The best performances come from the men: Bouajila as the caring yet conflicted Mehdi, Blanc as the volatile, pathetic Adrien, and newcomer Libéreau as the fun-loving if selfish Manu. Béart does what she can with another selfish character, though Sarah is less well-defined than the others; and Depardieu's Julie seems to drift in from another movie.

The only major problem with *The Witnesses* is that, while the characters are believable, it never quite captures the look or sounds of the 1980s. The production is handsome (thanks to Michèle Abbé's production design, Radija Zeggai's costume design, and Julien Hirsch's elegant widescreen cinematography) but does not evoke the period very well (it is not helpful that there are several anachronistic bloopers, including a hospital bed pillow branded with the year 2006). Two other minor issues are the overextended ending and the casting of an "American" character with an actor who does not seem American.

Most critics liked *The Witnesses*. Deborah Young in *Variety* called the film a "fast-moving, engrossing multiple-character drama...one of Téchiné's best..." Stephen Holden wrote in the *New York Times*: "*The Witnesses* may frustrate those who prefer movies that tell clear-cut stories in which hard lessons are learned. But in the director's farsighted vision of life, the ground under our feet is always shifting. As time pulls us forward, the shocks of the past are absorbed and the pain recedes. In its light-handed way, *The Witnesses* is profound."

Roger Ebert of the *Chicago Sun-Times* was also impressed: "Téchiné tells the story with comic intensity for the first hour, and then aching drama. The possibility of having a disease of this sort, especially when you are married, allegedly straight and even an anti-gay enforcer for the cops, creates secrecy and shame, and can lead to much worse than simply facing the truth. And it is that pain of the double life that concerns Téchiné in his later scenes."

The Witnesses is an engrossing film that addresses an issue that was and continues to be of great importance.

Eric Monder

CREDITS

Sarah: Emmanuelle Béart
Adrien: Michel Blanc
Manu: Johan Libéreau
Julie: Julie Depardieu

Mehdi: Sami Bouajila
Origin: France
Language: French
Released: 2007
Directed by: André Techine
Written by: André Techine, Laurent Guyot, Viviane Zingg
Cinematography by: Julien Hirsch
Music by: Philippe Sarde
Sound: Cyril Holtz
Editing: Martine Giordano
Costumes: Radija Zeggai
Production Design: Michèle Abbé
MPAA rating: Unrated
Running time: 115 minutes

REVIEWS

Chicago Sun-Times Online. May 6, 2008.
Entertainment Weekly Online. February 20, 2008.
Los Angeles Times Online. February 15, 2008.
New York Times Online. January 31, 2008.
San Francisco Chronicle. February 1, 2008.
Variety Online. July 14, 2007.
Washington Post. March 13, 2008.

THE WOMEN

It's all about...the Women
—Movie tagline

Box Office: $26.9 million

With the highly anticipated 2008 release of *Sex and the City*, the filmmakers behind *The Women*—another film about four urban female friends and fashion—certainly had reason to believe that middle-aged women were a viable audience seeking more films of that ilk. *The Women* also boasts a cast of actresses nearly as high-profile as George Cukor's 1939 original—which starred Joan Crawford, Rosalind Russell, Paulette Goddard, Joan Fontaine, and Norma Shearer—and features one of America's best-liked romantic comedy stars, Meg Ryan. This indolent remake by writer/director Diane English (creator of television's *Murphy Brown*), however, calls neither of the aforementioned films to mind. In a film that purports to be about modern women, it is oddly old-fashioned. The caricatured representation of the female sex, the screwball comedy, the precisely timed banter and fast-talking wisecracks seem forced and out of place in this modern-day chick flick.

Ryan, her natural good looks from the days of *When Harry Met Sally...*(1989) replaced by a more artificial-looking visage, plays Mary Haines, the film's central character. To be fair, Ryan is hardly aided by the film stylists, who fit her with a frizzy looking mop to wear on her head for the first two reels. Mary has all but derailed her dreams of being a clothing designer to become the perfect Connecticut wife—fundraising and gardening—and the doting mother of Molly (India Ennenga). Her friend Sylvie (Annette Bening) is a busy professional, trying to be the next Anna Wintour by creating a thinking woman's fashion magazine. Edie (Debra Messing)—clownishly dressed like a modern-day Raggedy Ann—is Mary's ditsy, earth mother friend with a gaggle of daughters and pregnant again. Author Alex (Jada Pinkett Smith) is the token lesbian character—too militant and too obvious a symbol for a "liberated" woman. It is this circle of friends who help Mary cope after finding out that her husband is cheating on her with the vampish Saks Fifth Avenue perfume girl, Crystal Allen (Eva Mendes).

The Women is shameless in the amount of corny, trite film tricks it uses. It borrows from the original in not having any male characters appear onscreen, but what was clever in Cukor's, film just feels plagiarized here. The films shows Sylvie literally having "shopping radar vision," and a particularly stagy scene involves Sylvie and Grace conversing while looking into the camera-as-mirror. There is studied dialogue and an abundance of theatricality in every scene. Until Candice Bergen shows up as Mary's mother, Catherine, it all seems like a bad dream. She does not play by the film's rules—she actually speaks like a real person and is a much-needed injection of normalcy. Then Ryan's Mary utters the fateful line, "What do you think this is? Some kind of 1930s movie?" and we are plunged right back in.

The self-referential in-jokes do not stop there. The gossipy manicurist Tanya (Debi Mazar), who first blabbed about Crystal's affair with Mary's husband, also recounts a story about meeting Madonna and how it propelled her to fame as a manicurist. In real life, Mazar was Madonna's makeup artist. *The Women* is so busy trying to pull you out of its stagey, carefully crafted reality, one barely has time to acknowledge any at all.

The movie's fine actresses must work with a flat script. When Edie's passengers hear a female voice in her car, she explains who it is: "The navigation lady. She's always calm. She never talks back. My husband's in love with her." Alex sums up Mary's personality with a line that must have sounded better on the page: "Our girl's all blue sky."

Like its premise and style, what the film has to say about the sexes is equally dated. Women should put up with men having affairs for the sake of the children and scheme how to win them back from their mistresses as

though it were a competition. The mistress in *The Women* is a stereotypically heartless, manipulative, hip-shaking vixen. There is even a winking, 1950s-style saleswoman who calls Mr. Haines to get the credit card number to charge Crystal's lingerie even though she knows his wife is in the next dressing room. The ensuing confrontation between Mary and Crystal in lingerie is humiliating for both Meg Ryan and the audience. Even more embarrassing is the scene when she tells the help—her nosy housekeeper Maggie (Cloris Leachman) and au pair Uta (Tilly Scott Pedersen)—that her husband should stay with her because she can "suck the nails out of a board." That we never see said husband or any man at all does nothing to empower this impotent female film.

With the help of Bette Midler's character Leah, Mary finds being cheated on is all for the best. It gives her the opportunity to find herself, start a promising fashion design career that also wins her back Molly's approval, and perhaps most important, straighten her hair. The film concludes with a sloppy and chaotic childbirth scene with all the requisite screaming that gathers all the women together for the arrival of Edie's first baby boy. That this film that attempts to be all things female ends with a childbirth is not surprising, given that the film also includes an earlier scene where the aging Catherine sits with her head heavily bandaged in a roomful of other facelift patients and another where teenage Molly burns her tampons.

Perhaps the worst scenes in the film, though, are at the expense of Bening. She seems supremely constrained in her role, and it is no wonder, since her character is so oddly written. She is at first utterly confident, pitching smart, novel ideas at work, showing off her shopping prowess at Saks, and helping Mary confront her husband's mistress. Then, the minute one of her young editors comes up with a decent idea for an upcoming issue, she is cripplingly intimidated and crumbles. That scene, involving the upstart young editor "outshining" Sylvie, is also horribly acted and completely unconvincing. It is followed by a better-acted but equally unconvincing scene with Carrie Fisher, which prompts Sylvie's betrayal of her best friend Mary for the sake of her career. "C'mon. Messy divorces sell more papers than presidential campaigns," Fisher's character says. Not necessarily true in 2008.

The film suggests that female betrayal is worse than marital betrayal. Perhaps, but not many female buddy films are worse than *The Women*.

Hilary White

CREDITS

Mary Haines: Meg Ryan
Sylvie Fowler: Annette Bening

Crystal Allen: Eva Mendes
Edie Cohen: Debra Messing
Alex Fisher: Jada Pinkett Smith
Leah Miller: Bette Midler
Catherine Frazier: Candice Bergen
Bailey Smith: Carrie Fisher
Maggie: Cloris Leachman
Tanya: Debi Mazar
Barbara Delacorte: Joanna Gleason
Pat: Ana Gasteyer
Molly Haines: India Ennenga
Glenda Hill: Lynn Whitfield
Origin: USA
Language: English
Released: 2008
Production: Diane English, Victoria Pearman, Mick Jagger, Bill Johnson; Jagged Films, Inferno Distribution, Double Edge Entertainment; released by Picturehouse
Directed by: Diane English
Written by: Diane English
Cinematography by: Anastas Michos
Music by: Mark Isham
Sound: Tom Williams
Music Supervisor: Chris Douridas
Editing: Tia Nolan
Art Direction: Mario R. Ventenilla
Costumes: John A. Dunn
Production Design: Jane Musky
MPAA rating: PG-13
Running time: 114 minutes

REVIEWS

Boston Globe Online. September 12, 2008.
Chicago Sun-Times Online. September 12, 2008.
Entertainment Weekly Online. September 10, 2008.
Hollywood Reporter Online. September 9, 2008.
Los Angeles Times Online. September 11, 2008.
New York Times Online. September 12, 2008.
San Francisco Chronicle. September 12, 2008.
Variety Online. September 9, 2008.
Washington Post. September 12, 2008.

QUOTES

Mary: "I admit I underestimated the value of the slut factor in the bedroom."

AWARDS

Nomination:
Golden Raspberries 2008: Worst Actress (Bening, Mendes, Messing, Pinkett Smith, Ryan).

THE WRESTLER

Love. Pain. Glory.
—Movie tagline

Box Office: $24.7 million

Professional wrestling, that choreographed performance art, has corralled many gaudily resplendent personalities in its long history, most famously Andre the Giant, Hulk Hogan, The Rock, and Cold Stone Steve Austin. Suspension of disbelief is a prerequisite to fully enjoy the contrived spectacle. Most do not confuse the theatrical events of the ECW or the WWE with Greco-Roman and Freestyle wrestling, which have the Olympic stamp of approval and are bona fide competitions. Enjoying the over-the-top feuds and story arcs where Jurassic men strut around the ring as king divas is part of the fun. Darren Aronofsky's fourth film, *The Wrestler*, creates one more wrestling star, the Ram, a rugged wreck of a man who looks like he has been hit with an iron skillet one too many times. The film takes the audience behind the ring away from the florid dramas and tells the absorbing story of a prominent performer.

The beginning of the film displays a mélange of promotional posters featuring Randy "The Ram" Robinson (Mickey Rourke), who has enjoyed a lucrative, fame-filled wrestling career. The Quiet Riot song "Metal Health" adds to the tone and pace and captures the overall ambience. The song becomes the Ram's anthem as it reappears several times throughout the movie. Randy has been past his prime for over a decade and a half, and his current matches, which once sold out Madison Square Garden, have been consigned to venues in elementary school gymnasiums and bleak amphitheaters. He is an eighties relic, flaunting his curly blond mane and bronzed skin by way of a tanning salon. It is a downward spiraling career and one he can no longer subsist on as a weekend warrior. During the weekdays, Randy unloads produce at a supermarket warehouse.

There is a gentleness and sincerity about Randy that gleams in his doleful brown eyes and soft voice. Rourke, who bulked up for this part, overshadows his last truly brilliant performance, the semiautobiographical film about Charles Bukowski, *Barfly* (1987). Rourke adds vulnerability to the Ram by having him don reading glasses and a hearing aid, which brings nuance to the character. Away from the ring's antics, the wrestlers share a camaraderie (often referring to each other as "Brother") and respect for each other. Randy offers a young, up-and-coming, Mohawk-wearing grappler avuncular compliments and advice: "You looked good, you really brought it. You hang in there, you've got a lot of ability." Randy is admired by his peers but is shown contempt by his manager at the supermarket. When Randy asks for more work, the manager retorts, "All I got is weekends. Isn't that when you sit on other dudes' faces?" Late on rent, Randy often must endure the cold, slushy New Jersey winter nights in his run-down gray van (a

Dodge Ram). He is portrayed as a lonely man, beloved by the children in his neighborhood, who finds solace in booze and painkillers. However, he remains true to his craft, perhaps his one true passion.

Aronofsky does not show Randy's face immediately, and the camera often follows the Ram from behind as he lumbers through the corridors of his daily life. Following a hardcore match with Necro Butcher (Dylan Summers), in which the combatants tackle, leap, and trip, each other in a ring strewn with barbed wire, glass, and thumb tacks (the Ram's tattoo of Jesus wearing a crown of thorns is a subtle reflection of his occupation), Randy has a wakeup call: he suffers a heart attack and must have a bypass operation. He is told by his doctor that wrestling and his drug use must cease if he wants to live. At a true crossroad, Randy has a personal day of reckoning and cancels all his upcoming bouts, including his twentieth-anniversary rematch with his old nemesis, the Ayatollah (Ernest Miller), which Randy believed would return him to the top of his game.

He decides to pursue what is important to him, to win the heart of an aging stripper he is infatuated with, Cassidy (Marisa Tomei), and to reunite with his estranged daughter, Stephanie (Evan Rachel Wood). Although Wood and Rourke share a convincing chemistry with each other, the scenes between absent father and neglected daughter are too predictable as far as subplots go. Randy's pursuit of Cassidy radiates more interest and poignancy as well as entertainment value as the pair mirror each other in so many ways. Both are parents of children of the opposite sex, both are on the waning edge of their respective careers, both wax hopelessly nostalgic about the eighties. Meeting Ram at a bar, Pam (Cassidy's civilian name) breaks her cardinal rule of never seeing customers aside from lap dances. The two name their favorite eightees glitter-metal bands—Mötley Crüe, Cinderella, Guns N' Roses—and Randy complains, "…and then that Cobain had to come around and ruin it all." They agree that "Nineties sucked." Despite Pam's affection for Randy, she decides to adhere to her professional standard of not getting involved with clients.

In another poignant scene underscoring the chasm of Randy's life outside the ring, he plays an antiquated Nintendo Entertainment System video game featuring himself during his hey-day, "Wrestle Jam: The Ram vs. The Ayatollah," with a neighborhood kid. The boy expresses boredom with the laughingly outdated system, comparing it negatively to a state of the art game Randy has never heard of, "Call of Duty 4."

Randy attends a wrestling showcase and is invited to party with his former colleagues. Following a night of debauchery, complete with a one-night stand, Randy

slumbers the day away recovering from a hangover. He misses the dinner date he promised his daughter, who has finally warmed up to him. In the emotionally charged aftermath, Stephanie calls him a loser and tells him that she wants him out of her life permanently. This begins Randy's nosedive. He concludes that, with his failure to gain the affection of Pam and once again being severed from his daughter, all is for naught. His health no longer a concern, he proceeds to return to wrestling and the rematch with the Ayatollah is back on. His world is the ring, the wrestlers and its fans, his family. Abruptly quitting the strip club for Randy, Pam pleads with him to step away and to share a life with her. But Randy has reached the tipping point. As he takes a last backward glance at a possible life, for him it is already a memory. Despite the Ayatollah's concerns about Randy, the match reaches its peak when Randy leaps from atop the ropes, initiating his signature "Ram Jam." It is this defeatist, self-martyring ending, similar in essence to the final scene of *Thelma & Louise* (1991), that compromises the film's plausibility. Aside from that, *The Wrestler*'s stellar acting and heartrending script made it one of the year's finest films and Mr. Rourke's triumphant comeback.

David Metz Roberts

CREDITS

Randy 'the Ram' Robinson: Mickey Rourke
Cassidy/Pam: Marisa Tomei
Stephanie: Evan Rachel Wood
Necro Butcher: Dylan Summers
The Ayatollah: Ernest Miller
Origin: USA
Language: English
Released: 2008
Production: Darren Aronofsky, Scott Franklin; Wild Bunch, Protozoa Pictures; released by Fox Searchlight Pictures
Directed by: Darren Aronofsky
Written by: Robert Siegel
Cinematography by: Maryse Alberti
Music by: Clint Mansell
Sound: Ken Ishii
Music Supervisor: Jim Black, Gabe Hilfer
Editing: Andrew Weisblum
Art Direction: Matthew Munn
Costumes: Amy Westcott
Production Design: Tim Grimes
MPAA rating: R
Running time: 109 minutes

REVIEWS

Entertainment Weekly Online. December 10, 2008.
Hollywood Reporter Online. September 4, 2008.

Los Angeles Times Online. December 17, 2008.
New York Times Online. December 17, 2008.
New Yorker Online. December 15, 2008.
Rolling Stone Online. December 11, 2008.
Time Online. December 15, 2008.
Variety Online. September 4, 2008.
Village Voice Online. December 16, 2008.
Wall Street Journal Online. December 19, 2008.

QUOTES

Randy 'the Ram' Robinson: "I'm an old broken down piece of meat and I deserve to be all alone, I just don't want you to hate me."

TRIVIA

Director Darren Aronofsky states that Mickey Rourke was the first choice to play the lead in the film but the studio wanted Nicolas Cage, feeling he was more bankable. Aronofsky fought for Rourke and eventually convinced the studio.

AWARDS

British Acad. 2008: Actor (Rourke)

Golden Globes 2009: Actor—Drama (Rourke), Song ("The Wrestler")

Ind. Spirit 2009: Actor (Rourke), Cinematog., Film

Nomination:

Oscars 2008: Actor (Rourke), Support. Actress (Tomei)

British Acad. 2008: Support. Actress (Tomei)

Golden Globes 2009: Support. Actress (Tomei)

Screen Actors Guild 2008: Actor (Rourke)

Writers Guild 2008: Orig. Screenplay.

X-Z

THE X FILES: I WANT TO BELIEVE

Believe Again.
—Movie tagline

To find the truth, you must believe.
—Movie tagline

Box Office: $20.9 million

At the peak of its popularity, *The X-Files* (1993–2002), starring David Duchovny and Gillian Anderson, could boast a devoted fan following and a mostly positive critical response. The television series was often compared to both the mystery-science fiction gold standard in television, *The Twilight Zone* (1959–1964) and the groundbreaking cult series tinged with the paranormal, *Twin Peaks* (1990–1991), which, interestingly, featured Duchovny in a recurring role. It might be reasonable to assume that only a spectacular script or some other burning necessity (such as timely subject matter) would drag the venerated series, often listed as one of the greatest cult television shows of the last twenty-five years, out of mothballs for a feature film sequel six years after it went off the air. *The X-Files: I Want to Believe,* though a well-structured and for the most part a finely acted film, lacks a true impetus for being. Divorced from the series' central (and in the opinion of some followers of the show, vexing) mythology about U.S. government collusion in an alien invasion of the earth, *The X-Files: I Want to Believe* is a throwback to the freak-of-the-week structure of the show's first couple of seasons, presumably so as not to alienate potential viewers interested in having an *X-Files*

experience but intimidated by the prospect of not knowing nine seasons' worth of show history. The resultant film by director, co-writer, and series creator Chris Carter is an ably constructed mystery-thriller that lacks a compelling story.

The film opens with a shadowy late-night abduction of a woman just outside what appears to be her garage, interspersed with footage of an FBI team headed by Father Joseph Crissman (Billy Connolly), a defrocked priest, searching for what turns out to be a severed arm in a snow-covered field. The film cuts to former FBI agent Dana Scully (Gillian Anderson), a medical doctor, working at Our Lady of Sorrows Catholic hospital treating a boy named Christian with a mysterious brain condition. She is approached by the FBI to find Fox Mulder (David Duchovny), who is Scully's ex-partner and the fugitive former head of the X-Files division. The FBI will call off its manhunt for him if he will help investigate the disappearances of several women, including a young FBI agent. Scully convinces Mulder to help, though Mulder believes that this may be a pretext for luring him out of hiding. In Washington, D.C., Agent Dakota Whitney (Amanda Peet) explains that Mulder's expertise with the paranormal is needed because their leads were obtained as a result of visions seen by a priest, Father Joe, a convicted pedophile, who believes that his visions of the crimes come from God. Mulder wants to believe the man, but Scully is disgusted by Father Joe's past and questions both his motivations and the legitimacy of his visions. Whitney takes Father Joe and Mulder to the kidnapped FBI agent's home, and the former priest accurately describes the abduction in accordance with the physical evidence, and begins bleeding from his eyes. A short time later, a second woman, who is driving home after swimming at an indoor pool, is run off the road by a man (Callum Keith Rennie) who then smashes the window of her wrecked car and kidnaps her. The film jumps to Mulder and Scully in bed together looking quite comfy, and they talk about an assortment of things, not the least of which is that the severed arm found by Father Joe's search team at the beginning of the film contained animal tranquilizer. Mulder along with Father Joe and another FBI team scour the same snowy field and discover many other body parts, all containing traces of the same tranquilizer. This leads Mulder to Dacyshyn, the Russian who abducted the woman from her car, and Franz Tomczeszyn (Fagin Woodcock), who happens to have been one of the altar boys Father Joe molested several years earlier. Meanwhile, Scully battles with the head priest at her hospital, Father Ybarra (Adam Godley), over what should be done with young Christian—Scully wishes to pursue a radical new stem cell treatment, and the priest recommends hospice, as the boy's condition is thought to be incurable. During an FBI raid on the organ-donor facility where Dacyshyn works, he escapes, and Mulder and Whitney chase him to a construction site. Whitney is killed when Dacyshyn knocks her down an elevator shaft several stories high. Dacyshyn flees shortly thereafter. Eventually, Mulder borrows Scully's car to continue investigating the animal tranquilizer lead. At a feed store in a small town near the abductions, he learns Dacyshyn has purchased animal tranquilizer there. Dacyshyn arrives moments later, and Mulder manages to follow his snowplow. On an isolated road, Mulder attempts to call Scully to tell her about his discoveries, but Dacyshyn crashes into the car and pushes it down an embankment with Mulder still inside. Dacyshyn leaves and Mulder crawls from the wreck, starts down the road, and stops at a compound where many dogs are barking—a major detail of Father Joe's visions. As Scully researches radical stem cell treatments for Christian, she comes across Russian studies that attempted to graft the heads of dying subjects onto new bodies—the Russians had experimented with dogs (one photograph shows a dog with two heads), and suddenly the significance of the animal tranquilizer is clear to Scully. Mulder infiltrates the compound after nearly being attacked by a two-headed dog, and finds a rag-tag Russian medical team about to attempt to graft Tomczeszyn's severed living head onto the body of the second abducted woman, but he is injected with animal tranquilizer before he can act. Fortunately, Scully, using Mulder's cell phone to triangulate the location of her wrecked car along with some details gleaned from Father Joe, is able to find the compound. With Mulder's and Scully's old boss Walter Skinner (Mitch Pileggi) along, they break into the

compound and save Mulder from being murdered by Dacyshyn. Mulder later receives word that Father Joe died and realizes that it happened at about the same moment that Tomczeszyn's severed head died, leading him to believe that the two men were, in fact, connected. Scully returns to the hospital to continue Christian's treatments, both wary of and driven by Father Joe's admonition, "Don't give up."

The major problem with *The X-Files: I Want to Believe* is that there is nothing truly compelling about the content, so much so that it is nearly impossible to find any genuine tension in the film's structure or execution. Everything about the movie feels rote (at least for *The X-Files*), from the glib treatment of the relationships to the handling of the subject matter. Divorced from the original show's UFO/extraterrestrial mythology, *The X-Files: I Want to Believe* may have been a good forty-two minute episode in 1998 but in 2008 feels more like an exercise than a fully realized effort. The film's elements add up, they just do not manage to make the film feel necessary or interesting; it is built on a hodge-podge of issues that, though still certainly unresolved in public discourse (the molestation of boys in the Catholic Church by priests, the use of controversial methods in medical treatment, and a shadowy unease about homosexuality), are hardly the burning issues of the moment. This may be an effort to move science fiction away from the issues that the genre has dealt with predominantly of late—perhaps best exemplified by the re-imagined series *Battlestar Galactica*, which in its more allegorical moments explores such topics as preemptive war, the rule of law, the clash of civilizations, and all of the various attendant moral and ethical problems that follow—to spotlight unresolved problems that dog Western society. If so, this is a failed effort. The resurrected *X-Files* franchise proves to be a poor platform for stoking smoldering social problems. Moreover, the core that made the *X-Files* so fascinating, namely the tension between Mulder and Scully (not simply the underlying sexual tension, but the more overt struggle between Mulder's willingness to dive into the unexplained based on faith and Scully's unyielding insistence on evidence—a dynamic that would seem to be suitable for a movie that has the subtitle *I Want to Believe*), is simply not here. In other words, the film is not only built on issues that had much more resonance in the broader culture five to ten years ago, but it is also hobbled by its refusal to rely on the strongest assets of its lead players. Though Duchovny and Anderson obviously have some on-screen chemistry and manage to strike an appropriate tone for where their characters are in their lives and in their relationship as things stand in the world of the film, this clear tweaking of the Mulder-Scully formula only serves to underscore how much the filmmakers have chosen to handicap themselves.

Structurally, the film is well-executed in terms of parallelism—the search for the missing FBI agent, and Scully's quest to cure young Christian offer some startling (and, once detected, satisfying) comparisons. For instance: in both investigations, Scully clashes with priests, Father Joe in the abduction case and the head priest at her hospital in Christian's treatment; Mulder is compelled to seek out the missing and the unexplained because of his missing sister, and Scully seems so drawn to helping Christian at least in part because her son is gone; in both the abductions and in Christian's treatment, radical stem cell procedures are used to help the patients and, indeed, it is Scully's unyielding pursuit of information about these procedures that leads her to the tips that help her and Mulder locate the abducted women and the perpetrators. Yet despite this very well-wrought structure, *The X-Files: I Want to Believe* utterly fails in marrying this proficiency in construction to worthwhile content—the film cannot create sufficient suspense or intriguing character development, and does not provide riveting subject matter or plotting. That the superbly executed parallelism is not mirrored in the quality of the content makes the the film's architecture come off as little more than an exercise. If only Carter and his co-writers had bothered to put the same effort into creating a great story as they obviously put into the final story's framework, the movie might have been something grand, and truly worthy of *The X-Files*.

John Boaz

CREDITS

Fox Mulder: David Duchovny
Dana Scully: Gillian Anderson
Father Joseph Crissman: Billy Connolly
Agent Mosley Drummy: Alvin "Xzibit" Joiner
ASAC Dakota Whitney: Amanda Peet
Janke Dacyshyn: Callum Keith Rennie
Father Ybarra: Adam Godley
Walter Skinner: Mitch Pileggi
Franz Tomczeszyn: Fagin Woodcock
Origin: USA
Language: English
Released: 2008
Production: Chris Carter, Frank Spotnitz; Ten Thirteen; released by 20th Century-Fox
Directed by: Chris Carter
Written by: Chris Carter, Frank Spotnitz
Cinematography by: Bill Roe
Music by: Mark Snow

Sound: Michael Williamson
Editing: Richard Harris
Art Direction: Tony Wohlgemuth
Costumes: Lisa Tomczeszyn
Production Design: Mark Freeborn
MPAA rating: PG-13
Running time: 104 minutes

REVIEWS

Boston Globe Online. July 25, 2008.
Chicago Sun-Times Online. July 24, 2008.
Hollywood Reporter Online. July 24, 2008.
Los Angeles Times Online. July 25, 2008.
New York Times Online. July 25, 2008.
San Francisco Chronicle. July 25, 2008, p. E1.
Time Online. July 24, 2008.
Variety Online. July 23, 2008.
Washington Post. July 25, 2008, p. C1.

QUOTES

Dana Scully: "What are you doing?"
Fox Mulder: "Trying to ignore you."

TRIVIA

When Scully is on her way into her office, director Chris Carter can be seen sitting on a bench.

YELLA

A Germanic *Twilight Zone?* A cautionary allegory about cold war Germany? Christian Petzold's *Yella* is as enigmatic as it is entertaining. Though an art house release in 2008, this metaphysical thriller should be appreciated beyond its initial audience.

Yella is Petzold's third film in the "Gespenster" trilogy that includes *The State I Am In* (2000) and *Wolfsburg* (2003), and may be the best of all three. According to the German-born director, the idea for this final entry came (in part) from the Herk Harvey 1961 cult horror classic, *Carnival of Souls,* and it compares favorably. There are at least a few other influences, including Krzysztof Kieslowski's *Double Life of Veronique* (1991) and even Peter Howitt's *Sliding Doors* (1998), though *Yella* is neither as heavy as the former nor as slick as the latter. In addition, the lead character's name, Yella, is a direct reference to the star of another German director's work—Yella Rottlander in Wim Wenders's *Alice in the Cities* (1974).

In Petzold's screenplay (co-written with Simone Bär), Yella (Nina Hoss) is an East German business executive who is being stalked by her dangerous former husband, Ben (Hinnerk Schönemann). Nonetheless, she accepts a ride from him to get to a new job in Hamburg. They end up driving into the Elbe River, barely escaping to shore.

Later, at her new place of employment in the former West Germany, Yella sees her boss has been locked out of his office and a colleague, Philipp (Devid Striesow), shows her the ropes and then some. Eventually, Yella starts a romance with Philipp and begins to excel at her job, using a more ruthless approach than in the past, but she is still followed by Ben. Suddenly, Yella's life swirls out of control due to strange and ghostly events—climaxing in the most unexpected of occurrences.

The mixture of the real and unreal is well balanced by Petzold, thanks to the director's control of the various elements. Compared to Tom Tykwer's overrated *Run, Lola, Run* (1999), *Yella* is downright Bressonian. Though the low-budget quality of *Carnival of Souls* made that film oddly creepy and atmospheric, *Yella*, by comparison, seems closer to a Hollywood production—yet it still works.

Much of the credit goes to Petzold's rigorous scene-building and attention to detail, Hoss's impressive, sharply etched performance (she is in every scene and deservedly won the Silver Bear for Best Actress in 2007 at the Berlin International Film Festival), and the technical aspects, from Hans Fromm's elegant photography to Kade Gruber's imaginative though minimal art direction that makes use of a bold color scheme. The costumers contribute an interesting (and symbolically red) dress for the heroine.

What is most opaque about *Yella* is not so much the literal story but its meaning. Could Petzold be echoing Rainer Werner Fassbinder's critique of Germany's post-World War II boom in *The Marriage of Maria Braun* (1978), with its slash-and-burn capitalist-style business practices, or is he saying something more universal about self-identity in an uncertain and chaotic postindustrial age? If the earlier films in the trilogy are any guide, it is probably a combination of both themes—and a successful exercise in style to boot.

The critics were generally enthusiastic. *Variety's* Derek Elley said, "Petzold returns to top form…[with a] precision-helmed, tightly wound, metaphysical thriller that confirms him as one of Germany's finest middle-generation directors." In the *New York Times* Stephen Holden wrote, "*Yella* is the kind of movie that tantalizes the mind with possibilities without solving the puzzle…[It] offers a surreal X-ray vision of cutthroat capitalism in 21st-century Germany."

A few critics complained about the ending. Walter Addiegio of the *San Francisco Chronicle* wrote, "As good

as the movie is, it's saddled with a tacked-on twist ending that is simply a mistake on Petzold's part. The concluding scene doesn't exactly undo everything that's gone before, but it does end things on a disappointing note." Roger Ebert echoed this sentiment in the *Chicago Sun-Times:* "Another surprise I will not even hint at, except to say that I could happily have done without it. It has all the value of the prize in a box of Cracker Jack: Worthless, but working your way down to it is a lot of fun." (Oddly and ironically, Ebert was one of the mainstream critics who championed the long-neglected *Carnival of Souls*, which has a similar ending and was the reported inspiration for this film.)

Some American viewers may have stayed away from *Yella* because its title sounds silly in English, but fans of thrillers and well-crafted stories should give the film a try.

Eric Monder

CREDITS

Ben: Hinnerk Schönemann
Philipp: Devid Striesow
Yella's Father: Christian Redl
Schmidt-Ott: Michael Wittenborn
Origin: Germany
Language: German
Released: 2007
Production: Florian Koerner von Gustorf, Michael Weber; Schramm Film; released by The Cinema Guild
Directed by: Christian Petzold
Written by: Christian Petzold, Simone Bär
Cinematography by: Hans Fromm
Sound: Andreas Mücke-Niesytka
Editing: Bettina Böhler
Production Design: Kade Gruber
Costumes: Anette Guther, Charlotte Sawatzki
MPAA rating: Unrated
Running time: 89 minutes

REVIEWS

The Guardian Online. September 21, 2007.
New York Times Online. May 16, 2008.
The Observer Online. September 23, 2007.
Variety Online. February 14, 2007.
Village Voice Online. May 13, 2008.

YES MAN

One word can change everything.
—Movie tagline

Box Office: $97.4 million

Jim Carrey's *Yes Man* is a blatant attempt on the actor's part to return to the physical brand of comedy that made him a star in movies like *Ace Ventura: Pet Detective* (1994) and *Liar Liar* (1997). But repetition is the death of humor, and the routine is not nearly as effective as it was over a decade ago, especially with a team behind the camera not talented enough to lift the material above the generic and the familiar. Carrey's shtick has not only grown tired, but the ineffective screenplay and lackluster direction of *Yes Man* seem almost completely reliant on it, as if watching this talented actor resort to his least interesting skills would carry an entire film. Only Zooey Deschanel, giving a vibrant, far more interesting performance than her leading man or anyone else in the cast, makes it out of *Yes Man* with anything positive to say about her work. Dull direction by Peyton Reed, and a generic, boring screenplay by Nicholas Stoller, Jarrad Paul, and Andrew Mogel (based on Danny Wallace's book) are not nearly as lucky.

Carl Allen (Jim Carrey) is the type of cynical, bitter soul that says "no" to everything before he even considers the alternative. Ignoring plans even as important as his best friend Peter's (Bradley Cooper) engagement party and trying his hardest to ignore his awkward boss Norman (Rhys Darby) even if his lack of involvement costs him a promotion, Carl is what could politely be called a loner. One day, outside of the bank he grudgingly works at, Carl runs into Nick (John Michael Higgins), who introduces him to the concept of "Yes." Carl reluctantly attends a seminar presided over by a motivational speaker named Terrence Bundley (Terence Stamp). The philosophy is simple—say "yes" instead of "no" and you will find eternal bliss.

After the seminar, Carl gives a homeless man a ride, money, and use of his cell phone, unable to say no to any of the requests, and finds himself stuck in Elysian Park, out of gas, with a dead battery, and no easy way home. This comedy of errors forces him to cross paths with the lovely Allison (Zooey Deschanel), to whom Carl is instantly attracted, something he has not been quick to welcome since his wife Stephanie (Molly Sims) left him. Thinking that it was the string of positive answers that led him into the life of Allison, an adventurous soul herself, Carl begins to say "yes" to every single opportunity that presents itself to him. This means Korean lessons, guitar classes, skydiving, bungee jumping, and anything else the writers could cram into a funny montage. Of course, there are some things that should be turned down, and if Carl wants to win Allison's heart, he is going to have to prove that he actually wants to be with her and does not just have to say yes every time she calls.

To be fair, Jim Carrey is far from awful in *Yes Man*. He shows a bit more life than he has in recent disasters like *Fun with Dick and Jane* (2005) and *The Number 23* (2007). And his chemistry with Deschanel is surprisingly believable. The energy produced by his comic timing and her massive amount of charisma when the two are on screen together is easily the best thing about *Yes Man*.

The problem with *Yes Man* is behind the screen— most notably, the team hired to adapt the nonfiction book it is loosely based on. The writers of *Fun With Dick and Jane* and *Bewitched* (2005) clearly do not have the comic talent befitting a cast like Carrey, Deschanel, Higgins, Stamp, or even Cooper. They have an incredibly difficult time finding a balanced tone, as if every scene that drives the plot forward is just an excuse to get to the next goofy montage. Every bit that they write away from the central love story, including everything to do with Norman's obsession with Harry Potter and a horrendous recurring joke about oral sex with an old lady, falls completely flat. If actors as talented as the folks who signed on to *Yes Man* had not responded in the affirmative to the casting offer, it could have been a lot worse.

Just as bad is the lackluster direction by Peyton Reed, who made the similarly sitcom-ish *The Break-Up* (2006). He seems intent merely on pushing the story forward instead of injecting it with any comic energy, not to mention that his work is visually flat. With a different director and better writers, *Yes Man* could have ended up more than a maybe.

Brian Tallerico

CREDITS

Carl Allen: Jim Carrey
Allison: Zooey Deschanel
Terrence Bundley: Terence Stamp
Lucy: Sasha Alexander
Peter: Bradley Cooper
Rooney: Danny Masterson
Stephanie: Molly Sims
Norman: Rhys Darby
Tillie: Fionnula Flanagan
Nick: John Michael Higgins
Origin: USA
Language: English
Released: 2008
Production: Richard D. Zanuck, David Heyman; Heyday Films, Village Roadshow Pictures; released by Warner Bros.
Directed by: Peyton Reed
Written by: Nicholas Stoller, Jarrad Paul, Andrew Mogel

Cinematography by: Robert Yeoman
Music by: Lyle Workman, Mark Oliver Everett
Sound: William B. Kaplan
Music Supervisor: Jonathan Karp
Editing: Craig Alpert
Art Direction: Eric Sundahl
Costumes: Mark Bridges
Production Design: Andrew Laws
MPAA rating: PG-13
Running time: 104 minutes

REVIEWS

Boston Globe Online. December 18, 2008.
Chicago Sun-Times Online. December 17, 2008.
Entertainment Weekly Online. December 17, 2008.
Hollywood Reporter Online. December 15, 2008.
Los Angeles Times Online. December 19, 2008.
New York Times Online. December 19, 2008.
San Francisco Chronicle. December 19, 2008, p. E7.
Variety Online. December 14, 2008.
Wall Street Journal Online. December 19, 2008.
Washington Post Online. December 19, 2008.

QUOTES

Carl Allen: "You ever had a Red Bull? Ive never had a Red Bull before, but I had a Red Bull last night—I really like Red Bull."

TRIVIA

Jim Carrey did not receive a salary for his work in the film but instead opted for a percentage of the film's profits.

YOU DON'T MESS WITH THE ZOHAN

> *Lather. Rinse. Save the World.*
> —Movie tagline

Box Office: $100 million

You Don't Mess with the Zohan is further proof that Adam Sandler has the power in Hollywood to get any concept he can possibly dream up approved, funded, and brought to the big screen without anyone asking if it can really sustain a feature film. If anyone else had taken the concept of *Zohan* to a major studio, they would have been ridiculed and escorted out by security. The very idea of a comedy about an Israeli Special Forces soldier who wants to be a hairdresser—never mind that it has the worst title of the year—has the ring of something that a satirical look at Hollywood would

include as a movie-within-a-movie to highlight Hollywood's continuing love affair with stupidity. Arguably the most bulletproof actor in Hollywood, Adam Sandler has produced a string of comedy hits that have been nothing but ridiculed by critics and, even more remarkably, largely disliked by his own fan base. The Internet is strewn with complaints about *I Now Pronounce You Chuck and Larry* (2007), *Little Nicky* (2000), *Anger Management* (2003), and more of Sandler's awful career decisions but he continues to amass a significant fortune doing ridiculous variations on the same man-child routine that made him a star on *Saturday Night Live*. His latest, *You Don't Mess with the Zohan*, is far from his worst film but continues a depressing pattern of lazy humor that fails to recapture the energetic performer on display in his first few films, his *SNL* days, or even his more dramatic work in films like *Punch-Drunk Love* (2002) and *Spanglish* (2004). Its very existence is the most memorable thing about the entire production.

The Zohan (Adam Sandler) is a legendary Israeli soldier who dreams of the day that he can put down his hand grenades and pick up a pair of hair clippers. The Zohan's nemesis is the Phantom (John Turturro), an equally deadly assassin of Palestinian descent who presents the hero of this odd comedy a way out when he gives him an opportunity to fake his own death at the end of a battle. Freed from the "hilarity" of the Middle East crisis, *You Don't Mess with the Zohan* moves to one of those great communities in New York City where Palestinians and Jews just happen to live on the same block. In the center of the biggest melting pot in the world, the Big Apple, the Zohan is forced to hide his identity and work in a Palestinian hair salon with the cute Dahlia (Emmanuelle Chriqui) after he gets turned away from his hairdressing idol, Paul Mitchell. Zohan pretends to be Australian and moves in with an awkward young man (Nick Swardson), whom he saves from a fight between bike rider and car driver, and his mother. Zohan becomes a huge hit in Dahlia's hair salon by not only giving his clients sexy new hairdos, but providing even his most elderly female clients with a quickie in the storage room at the back of the salon. Zohan soon learns that flings with his elderly clients will not fill the hole in his heart and that Dahlia is his true love, but when an Arabic taxi driver (Rob Schneider) spots the infamous killer, a plot gets set in motion that could not only bring down the salon but everything around it. A subplot involving a corporation trying to gentrify the ethnic communities of New York City and the return of the the Phantom fill out the final act of this way-too-long comedy.

The problem with *You Don't Mess with the Zohan* is a simple and common one for Sandler—it is only occasionally funny. The reason Sandler drives so many critics to reserve an annual spot for him on their year-end worst lists is because nearly everything he does reeks of laziness. There is little effort in *Zohan* to do anything interesting beyond the concept, and critics argue that an extended *Saturday Night Live* sketch does not justify a film's running time. Some of Sandler's comedies are lazier than others, and *Zohan* does represent a little more effort than total failures like *Little Nicky* or *I Now Pronounce You Chuck and Larry*. There are moments, especially in the physical comedy of the first act, where the film has a cartoonish creativity that is often lacking from Sandler's other work. Sandler also makes the smart decision to only rarely allow *Zohan* to take itself remotely seriously, so the film avoids the awkward life lessons of junk like *Big Daddy* (1999) or *50 First Dates* (2004). The serious moments, mostly in the zero-chemistry romance between Sandler and Chriqui, represent the low points of the film, but there is some physical comedy that ranks among Sandler's best in years. It is tempting to say that with the low expectations brought to mind by the words "Adam Sandler summer comedy," *You Don't Mess with the Zohan* almost works. One would hope that does not give the most powerful man in comedy even more validation that selling his ridiculously lazy brand of humor is something worthy of praise.

Brian Tallerico

CREDITS

Zohan Dvir: Adam Sandler
The Phantom/Fartoshi: John Turturro
Dahlia: Emmanuelle Chriqui
Michael: Nick Swardson
Salim: Rob Schneider
Gail: Lainie Kazan
James: Dave Matthews
Oori: Ido Mosseri
Walbridge: Michael Buffer
Gray Kleibolt: Barry Livingston
Zohan's father: Shelley Berman
Origin: USA
Language: English
Released: 2008
Production: Adam Sandler, Jack Giarraputo; Columbia Pictures, Relativity Media, Happy Madison Productions; released by Sony Pictures Entertainment
Directed by: Dennis Dugan
Written by: Adam Sandler, Robert Smigel, Judd Apatow
Cinematography by: Michael Barrett
Music by: Rupert Gregson-Williams
Sound: Greg Orloff, Gary C. Bourgeois
Music Supervisor: Michael Dilbeck, Brooks Arthur

Editing: Tom Costain
Art Direction: Alan Au, John Collins
Costumes: Ellen Lutter
Production Design: Perry Andelin Blake
MPAA rating: PG-13
Running time: 113 minutes

REVIEWS

Boston Globe Online. June 6, 2008.
Chicago Sun-Times Online. June 6, 2008.
Entertainment Weekly Online. June 4, 2008.
Hollywood Reporter Online. June 4, 2008.
Los Angeles Times Online. June 6, 2008.
New York Times Online. June 6, 2008.
San Francisco Chronicle. June 6, 2008, p. E5.
Variety Online. June 4, 2008.
Wall Street Journal Online. June 6, 2008.
Washington Post. June 6, 2008, p. C5.

QUOTES

Zohan: "I just want to make people silky-smooth!"

TRIVIA

Although the film was written in 2000, production was postponed following the events on September 11 due to the film's terrorist themes.

YOUNG@HEART

Rock 'n Roll Will Never Die.
　　—Movie tagline

Box Office: $3.9 million

The cliché that age is more clearly defined by state of mind or passion of heart than actual years is brilliantly brought to life in Stephen Walker's documentary *Young@Heart,* a film about the chorus of the same name. *Young@Heart* is a crowd-pleaser in the best sense of the overused phrase. Walker's documentary and the men and women that it chronicles have the power to make hardened criminals smile and the most cynical movie watchers sob. The idea that people can do whatever they set out to do and find something they love in the most unique and unexpected places has rarely been as perfectly captured in a documentary. Walker does find gold for documentary filmmakers in the endearing human beings that he chooses as his subject, but he also expertly weaves together a film that could have fallen apart in another director's hands.

Young@Heart the film is titled after a chorus composed of about two dozen senior citizens with an average age of eighty. One of the unique things about Young@Heart is that the group sings not the expected choir material for any age, much less octogenarians. These singers put their heart and souls into songs by OutKast, Radiohead, Jimi Hendrix, Sonic Youth, Sinead O'Connor, Coldplay, and more. Walker follows the chorus as they rehearse for their annual concert in Northampton, Massachusetts. From the introduction of new songs to the members to the actual show, Walker was allowed access into the details and emotional ups and downs of Young@Heart's life. It would not be spoiling anything about the movie to reveal that the lives of an octogenarian choir must deal with death and illness on a regular, daily basis. Members of the band talk about living a couple more years just so they can play a few more shows, and some of them seem to be holding on to this mortal coil for their next solo.

On a traditional scale, most of them cannot really sing—rehearsal is more about getting the timing and the words down than the notes—and a couple of the members are not even sure which side of the CD goes up in the player. But Young@Heart brings something to the stage that has never been captured before in quite the same way. It has long been said that with age comes wisdom, but there is something remarkable about hearing life experience channeled through modern music. For example, a member of the group has, quite literally, cheated death because of his love for the chorus and singing in it. He was so close to passing away that he was read his Last Rites. After pulling through, his family reported that he sang every single song that he knew from the chorus in his recovery room and dreamed of being on stage again. Hearing him rehearse Coldplay's "Fix You" brings an element to the song that even Chris Martin could never have imagined. Just the look on the faces of the prisoners who see a *Young@Heart* show says it all. Watching convicts listen to the elderly sing Bob Dylan's "Forever Young" is one of the most remarkable things a documentary filmmaker has gotten on celluloid in quite some time. This is no ordinary community choir.

There is more than enough story in the lives of the people who make up *Young@Heart*, but there was still room for failure in a documentary about them. A lot of directors would have gone down manipulative roads, focusing on health problems and tragedy, but Walker shines light on the positive nature as much as the negative. There is a reason that one of the songs heard most in the film is "I Feel Good" (and it is not just because the folks it was assigned to seem to have the most trouble with the words). At the same time, a lot of filmmakers would have made *Young@Heart* too dry or repetitive. It is easy to imagine a movie about an elderly choir getting slow or depressing, but just as those feel-

ings creep in, Walker cuts to what will be a series of music videos that he shot with the chorus. From "I Want to Be Sedated" to "Stayin' Alive," they are all fantastically clever.

Truly uplifting movies are few and far between and yet there is no better way to describe *Young@Heart*. Walker conveys the dignity and beauty of people dealing with not only their own impending mortality but the regular loss of the people close to them. He dares the audience not only to find some perspective on what they might have deemed a problem in what is very likely a much easier existence than that of these wonderful people, but he makes the remarkable case that if one has only a few breaths left, one should use them to sing.

Brian Tallerico

CREDITS

Narrator: Stephen Walker
Origin: USA
Language: English
Released: 2007
Production: Sally George; Channel Four Films, Walter George Films; released by Fox Searchlight
Directed by: Stephen Walker
Cinematography by: Ed Marritz, Simon Poulter
Sound: Mark Mandler
Editing: Chris King
MPAA rating: PG
Running time: 107 minutes

REVIEWS

Boston Globe Online. April 18, 2008.
Christian Science Monitor Online. April 11, 2008.
Entertainment Weekly Online. April 11, 2008.
Los Angeles Times Online. April 9, 2008.
New York Times Online. April 9, 2008.
San Francisco Chronicle. April 18, 2008, p. E4.
Variety Online. June 28, 2007.
Washington Post. April 18, 2008, p. C6.

ZACK AND MIRI MAKE A PORNO

What would you do to get out of debt?
    —Movie tagline

Box Office: $31.4 million

Kevin Smith came to prominence with *Clerks* (1994) and has been making variations on the profane-but-likable-slacker-themed film ever since. *Zack and Miri Make a Porno* is a return to the themes of *Clerks*, with both films following the day-to-day exploits of workers in low-wage jobs and the often outlandish things they do, combined with witty and tangential banter. *Zack and Miri* goes one step further, melding elements not only of Smith's signature film but also drawing loosely on his own personal history of making it. Smith seeks to place this latest film in the context of a genre of twenty-first century romantic comedy, best exemplified by the Judd Apatow films *The 40 Year Old Virgin* (2005) and *Knocked Up* (2007). Whether he has mellowed by some combination of age and fatherhood, or whether he is seeking to make a more commercially viable film (though still infused with his trademark mix of vulgarity-plus-intelligence), *Zack and Miri Make a Porno*, despite its title and subject matter, finds Kevin Smith wallowing unabashedly in sentimentality and decidedly conventional romance territory. Though *Zack and Miri* sports a solid and able cast as well as some good laughs, the movie is ultimately, in spite of its title, a rather conventional, uninspired romantic comedy posing as cutting-edge. The film is further undermined by Smith's (either deliberate or subconscious) invocation of Apatow, the new master of the genre.

The plot of *Zack and Miri* is a variation on Smith's own story behind the making of *Clerks* (a low-wage worker makes a film at his workplace late at night), with some obvious changes and embellishments. Lifelong friends and longtime roommates Zack Brown (Seth Rogen) and Miri Linky (Elizabeth Banks) cannot seem to make ends meet. Their rent is overdue, their utility bills have not been paid, and to make matters worse, they have a high school reunion to attend. At the reunion, Miri attempts to throw herself at her old high school crush Bobby Long (Brandon Routh, who played Superman in 2006's *Superman Returns*), only to discover along with Zack, that Bobby is in attendance with his lover, gay porn star Brandon St. Randy (Justin Long). Faced with the loss of electricity, heat, and water in their apartment, as well as the threat of eviction, Zack and Miri take a cue from their encounter with Bobby and Brandon at the reunion and realize that people might actually pay to see them have sex with each other, so making a porno could solve all of their financial problems. After pondering several possible porno projects, they settle on a *Star Wars* parody entitled *Star Whores*. They hire a crew of friends and acquaintances, including Zack's coworker Delaney (Craig Robinson, who plays Darryl on the American version of the sitcom *The Office*) as a producer, and they rent a dilapidated warehouse as a soundstage. The warehouse and most of the sets and costumes are destroyed the night before shooting is to commence; it turns out that the person

who rented the inexpensive space to them had no right to do so. Desperate to keep the project moving, Zack convinces the group to change the plot and setting to the coffeehouse where he holds down a soul-crushing, low-wage job, and they decide to film late at night after the place closes.

As filming progresses, eventually it comes time for Zack and Miri to have sex on camera, a moment they have talked about and prepared for. When it happens they are unexpectedly and deeply affected by it. They are unable to contend with their feelings, and jealousy over pending scenes with other actors threatens their relationship. Zack ultimately confesses to Miri that he loves her, but when she does not reciprocate, Zack quits the film and his job and moves out of the apartment. Months later, Delaney finds Zack and shows him footage of the film. During the screening, Zack discovers that Miri never shot a scene with another actor after he left. He goes to their old apartment and makes it clear to Miri that he never slept with a particular actress; in fact they spent all of their time together talking about his relationship with Miri. The credits roll as the couple reconciles, and a segment during the credits reveals that Zack and Miri marry and start a business called Zack and Miri Make Your Porno, an amateur video service for couples.

Take out the pornography, and what is left is essentially a fairly run-of-the-mill romantic comedy with a few good laughs along the way, but utterly lacking in surprise or innovative character or plot development. Smith is at his best and funniest writing witty banter, and some of the exchanges between Bobby and Brandon at Zack and Miri's high school reunion are easily some of the funniest stand-alone material in the film, especially Brandon's penchant for speaking explicitly about their sex life. Many of the discarded titles for porno projects are not only comic gold, but they also tie this movie ever more strongly to *Clerks*, which featured a scene consisting of a long list of zany porno titles. A few of the tamer yet still funny titles considered are *Edward Penis-hands* and *Lawrence of a Labia* (the funniest title involves a play on a movie about gay cowboys). Some of Smith's humor is simply juvenile, though that should probably be expected in a romantic comedy that centers on making a pornographic movie. If only Smith's wit extended beyond the occasionally funny things his characters say, there might be more to *Zack and Miri*. But between jokes the film feels labored and stale.

Kevin Smith is a fine filmmaker who obviously has a good sense of humor—his specialties are finding the profane in the mundane and poking fun at the drudgery of working in a low-wage service job—but his major problem as a storyteller is that he does not trust his audience or his material. *Zack and Miri* has entered the scene a bit late. This is a post-Apatow world, which would not necessarily be such a bad thing for Smith had Apatow not laid claim to Smith's territory and changed the landscape of the screwball, relationship-driven sex comedy so completely. Smith himself appears to recognize this fact, given that *Zack and Miri* is populated by one major Apatow player (Rogen) and two actors from *The 40 Year Old Virgin* (Banks and Gerry Bednob). Many of the characters in this film seem to be playing derivatives of themselves from something else. In the case of Rogen and Banks, they are reprising characters they have played in other films. Rogen has imported a slightly more vulgar version of his character from *Knocked Up*, and Banks seems to be doing the same character she played in *The 40 Year Old Virgin*, without the overt sexual perversion. Robinson seems to have transplanted Darryl wholesale from *The Office*. Bednob, who played Mooj in *The 40 Year Old Virgin*, has a cameo as Zack's and Delaney's boss at the coffeehouse, and it is almost as if they are working for Mooj's equally foul-mouthed twin brother. Old Kevin Smith standby actors Jason Mewes and Jeff Anderson (Jay and Randall, respectively, from *Clerks*) do their best to keep the film firmly rooted in the Kevin Smith universe, but their peripheral status simply ensures that they provide a sense of local color instead of informing the core identity of the movie. Given the recycled sentiments and the menagerie of recycled characters, *Zack and Miri Make a Porno,* for all its apparent promise of novelty or shock value, delivers a pretty standard romantic comedy in a slightly more perverse but all-too-familiar package.

Zack and Miri Make a Porno, for all its passing laughs, knowing winks, and attempts at being either refreshingly profane or ingratiatingly cute, tends to fall squarely in the shadow of Judd Apatow's recent films. The movie certainly has its moments, but it fails to transcend its genre, or to add anything of significance to the Kevin Smith canon.

John Boaz

CREDITS

Zack Brown: Seth Rogen
Miriam Linky: Elizabeth Banks
Delaney: Craig Robinson

Lester: Jason Mewes
Deacon: Jeff Anderson
Bubbles: Traci Lords
Barry: Ricky Mabe
Bobby Long: Brandon Routh
Stacey: Katie Morgan
Brandon St. Randy: Justin Long
Mr. Surya: Gerry Bednob
Origin: USA
Language: English
Released: 2008
Production: Scott Mosier; View Askew, Weinstein Company; released by MGM
Directed by: Kevin Smith
Written by: Kevin Smith
Cinematography by: David Klein
Music by: James L. Venable, Chris Ward
Sound: Whit Norris
Editing: Kevin Smith
Art Direction: Elise G. Viola
Costumes: Salvador Pérez Jr.
Production Design: Robert Holtzman
MPAA rating: R
Running time: 101 minutes

REVIEWS

Boston Globe Online. October 31, 2008.
Chicago Sun-Times Online. October 29, 2008.
Entertainment Weekly Online. October 29, 2008.
Hollywood Reporter Online. September 7, 2008.
Los Angeles Times Online. October 31, 2008.
New York Times Online. October 31, 2008.
Rolling Stone Online. November 13, 2008.
San Francisco Chronicle. October 31, 2008, p. E5.
Variety Online. September 7, 2008.
Washington Post. October 31, 2008, p. C1.

QUOTES

Delaney: "Han Solo ain't never had no sex with Princess Leia in the Star War!"

TRIVIA

The controversial title was abbreviated in numerous advertisements as simply *Zack and Miri.*

List of Awards

Academy Awards

Film: *Slumdog Millionaire*
Animated Film: *WALL-E*
Director: Danny Boyle (*Slumdog Millionaire*)
Actor: Sean Penn (*Milk*)
Actress: Kate Winslet (*The Reader*)
Supporting Actor: Heath Ledger (*The Dark Knight*)
Supporting Actress: Penélope Cruz (*Vicky Cristina Barcelona*)
Original Screenplay: Dustin Lance Black (*Milk*)
Adapted Screenplay: Simon Beaufoy (*Slumdog Millionaire*)
Cinematography: Anthony Dod Mantle (*Slumdog Millionaire*)
Editing: Chris Dickens (*Slumdog Millionaire*)
Art Direction: Donald Graham Burt and Victor J. Zolfo (*The Curious Case of Benjamin Button*)
Visual Effects: Eric Barba, Steve Preeg, Burt Dalton, and Craig Barron (*The Curious Case of Benjamin Button*)
Sound: Ian Tapp, Richard Pryke, and Resul Pookutty (*Slumdog Millionaire*)
Sound Editing: Richard King (*The Dark Knight*)
Makeup: Greg Cannom (*The Curious Case of Benjamin Button*)
Costume Design: Michael O'Connor (*The Duchess*)
Original Score: A. R. Rahman (*Slumdog Millionaire*)
Original Song: "Jai Ho" (A. R. Rahman and Gulzar *Slumdog Millionaire*)
Foreign Language Film: *Okuribito*
Documentary, Feature: *Man on Wire*
Best Documentary, Short Subject: *Smile Pinki*
Best Short Film, Animated: *Tsumiki no ie*
Best Short Film, Live Action: *Spielzeugland*

British Academy of Film & Television Awards

Animated Film: *WALL-E*
Film: *Slumdog Millionaire*
Director: Danny Boyle (*Slumdog Millionaire*)
Original Screenplay: Martin McDonagh (*In Bruges*)
Adapted Screenplay: Simon Beaufoy (*Slumdog Millionaire*)
Actor: Mickey Rourke (*The Wrestler*)
Actress: Kate Winslet (*The Reader*)
Supporting Actor: Heath Ledger (*The Dark Knight*)
Supporting Actress: Penélope Cruz (*Vicky Cristina Barcelona*)
Chris Dickens (*Slumdog Millionaire*)
Cinematography: Anthony Dod Mantle (*Slumdog Millionaire*)

Production Design: Donald Graham Burt and Victor J. Zolfo (*The Curious Case of Benjamin Button*)
Costume Design: Michael O'Connor (*The Duchess*)
Makeup: Jeann Ann Black and Colleen Callaghan (*The Curious Case of Benjamin Button*)
Sound: Ian Tapp, Richard Pryke, Glenn Freemantle, Tom Sayers, and Resul Pookutty (*Slumdog Millionaire*)
Visual Effects: Eric Barba, Craig Barron, Nathan McGuinness, and Edson Williams (*The Curious Case of Benjamin Button*)
Music: A. R. Rahman (*Slumdog Millionaire*)
Foreign Film: *Il y a longtemps que je t'aime*
Short Animation: *Wallace and Gromit in "A Matter of Loaf and Death"*
Short Film: *September*

Directors Guild of America Awards

Outstanding Directorial Achievement in Motion Pictures: Danny Boyle (*Slumdog Millionaire*)
Outstanding Directorial Achievement in Documentary: Ari Folman (*Vals Im Bashir*)

Golden Globes

Film, Drama: *Slumdog Millionaire*

Film, Musical or Comedy: *Vicky Cristina Barcelona*
Animated Film: *WALL-E*
Director: Danny Boyle (*Slumdog Miollionaire*)
Actor, Drama: Mickey Rourke (*The Wrestler*)
Actor, Musical or Comedy: Colin Farrell (*In Bruges*)
Actress, Drama: Kate Winslet (*Revolutionary Road*)
Actress, Musical or Comedy: Sally Hawkins (*Happy-Go-Lucky*)
Supporting Actor: Heath Ledger (*The Dark Knight*)
Supporting Actress: Kate Winslet (*The Reader*)
Screenplay: Simon Beaufoy (*Slumdog Millionaire*)
Score: A. R. Rahram (*Slumdog Millionaire*)
Song: "The Werstler" (Bruce Springsteen, *The Wrestler*)
Foreign Language Film: *Vals Im Bashir*

Golden Raspberry Awards

Worst Picture: *The Love Guru*
Worst Director: Uwe Boll (*Tunnel Rats* and *In the Name of the King: A Dungeon Siege Tale*)

Worst Actor: Mike Myers (*The Love Guru*)
Worst Actress: Paris Hilton (*The Hottie & the Nottie*)
Worst Supporting Actor: Pierce Brosnan (*Mamma Mia!*)
Worst Supporting Actress: Paris Hilton (*Repo! The Genetic Opera*)
Worst Screenplay: Mike Myers and Aaron Seltzer (*The Love Guru*)
Worst Screen Couple: Paris Hilton, Christine Lakin, and Joel Moore (*The Hottie & the Nottie*)
Worst Prequel, Remake, Rip-Off or Sequel: *Indiana Jones and the Kingdom of the Crystal Skull*

Independent Spirit Awards

Film: *The Wrestler*
First Film: Charlie Kaufman *Synechdoche, New York*
Director: Thomas McCarthy (*The Visitor*)
Actor: Mickey Rourke (*The Wrestler*)
Actress: Melissa Leo (*Frozen River*)
Supporting Actor: James Franco (*Milk*)

Supporting Actress: Penélope Cruz (*Vicky Cristina Barcelona*)
Screenplay: Woody Allen (*Vicky Cristina Barcelona*)
First Screenplay: Dustin Lance Black (*Milk*)
Cinematography: Maryse Alberti (*The Wrestler*)
Foreign Language Film: *Entre les murs*
Documentary: *Man on Wire*

Screen Actors Guild Awards

Actor: Sean Penn (*Milk*)
Actress: Meryl Streep (*Doubt*)
Supporting Actor: Heath Ledger (*The Dark Knight*)
Supporting Actress: Kate Winslet (*The Reader*)
Ensemble Cast: *Slumdog Millionaire*
Stunt Ensemble: *The Dark Knight*

Writers Guild of America Awards

Original Screenplay: Dustin Lance Black (*Milk*)
Adapted Screenplay: Simon Beaufoy (*Slumdog Millionaire*)
Documentary Screenplay Award: Ari Folman (*Vals Im Bashir*)

Obituaries

Edie Adams (April 16, 1927–October 15, 2008). The singer and actress was born Edith Elizabeth Enke in Kingston, Pennsylvania. A classically trained singer who graduated from Juilliard, Adams used her mother's maiden name professionally. A beauty pageant win led to her appearing with Milton Berle and meeting comedian Ernie Kovacs, whom she married in 1954 (he died in 1962) with Adams becoming a regular on Kovacs' television show. Adams made her Broadway debut in 1953's *Wonderful Town* and won a Tony award for her portrayal of Daisy Mae in the 1956 musical *Li'l Abner*. She was also the flirtatious spokesperson for the Muriel Cigars brand for nineteen years. Adams was a frequent guest-star on television and she played a series of supporting roles in such films as *The Apartment* (1960), *Lover Come Back* (1961), *Under the Yum Yum Tree* (1963), *It's a Mad, Mad, Mad, Mad World* (1963), and *The Best Man* (1964).

Jill Adams (July 22, 1930–May 13, 2008). Born Jill Siggins in London, England, supporting actress Adams was the daughter of silent-screen actress Molly Adair. She took the surname of her first husband and began her career as a model before getting bit parts in movies beginning in 1953. Among her films were *The Young Lovers* (1954), *The Constant Husband* (1955), *One Jump Ahead* (1955), *Brothers in Law* (1956), *The Green Man* (1956), *Privates' Progress* (1956), *The Scamp* (1957), *Dust in the Sun* (1958), *Death on My Shoulder* (1958), *Carry on Constable* (1960), *Crosstrap* (1960), *Doctor in Distress* (1963), *Yellow Teddy Bears* (1963), *The Comedy Man* (1964), and *Promise Her Anything* (1965). When her career faded, Adams moved to Portugal and became a restaurateur.

Robert J. Anderson (March 6, 1933–June 6, 2008). Anderson, whose father Gene was an assistant director and production manager at Columbia Pictures, had a brief career as a child actor. His best-known role was as the young George Bailey in *It's a Wonderful Life* (1946). Other films included *Young People* (1940), *A Tree Grows in Brooklyn* (1945), and *The Bishop's Wife* (1947). After serving in the Navy, Anderson worked as an assistant director, production manager, and producer for various studios.

Rafael Azcona (October 24, 1926–March 24, 2008). The screenwriter and novelist was born in Logorno, Spain, and began writing novels after moving to Madrid in 1951. Azcona was approached by Italian director Marco Ferreri, who adapted two of these novels into films: *El Pisito/The Little Flat* (1958) and *El Cochecito/The Wheelchair* (1958). The two also worked together on *The Conjugal Bed* (1963), *The Ape Woman* (1964), *The Audience* (1971), *La Grande Bouffe* (1973), and *The Last Woman* (1976) among other films. Among Azcona's other screenplays were *Placido* (1961), *The Executioner* (1962), *Peppermint Frappe* (1968), *Life Size* (1973), *Ay, Carmela!* (1990), *Belle Epoque* (1992), and *The Butterfly Tongue* (1999).

Sam Bottoms (October 17, 1955–December 16, 2008). Samuel John Bottoms was born in Santa Barbara, California and began acting in youth theater at the age of ten. His brothers Timothy, Joseph, and Ben are also actors and Sam got his film break at the age of fifteen when he went to Texas to watch brother Timothy film *The Last Picture Show* (1971). Director Peter Bogdonovich cast Sam in the role of mute innocent Billy. Bottoms also made a memorable impression in 1979's *Apocalypse Now* as soldier/surfer Lance B. Johnson. Other credits included *The Outlaw Josey Wales* (1976), *Bronco Billy* (1980), *East of Eden* (1981), *Gardens of Stone* (1987), *Seabiscuit* (2003), *Havoc* (2005), *Shopgirl* (2005), and *Sherrybaby* (2006).

Irving Brecher (January 17, 1914–November 17, 2008). Born in New York, the writer, director, and producer started his career as a teenager, sending one-line gags to various columnists such as Ed Sullivan and Walter Winchell. Comedian Milton Berle hired Brecher to write material for his 1936 radio program, *The Gillette Original Community Sing,* and then took Brecher to Hollywood with him to write for the movie *New Faces of 1937* in which Berle co-starred. Brecher was then signed to a contract by Mervyn

LeRoy and worked at MGM, co-writing the Marx Brothers' comedies *At the Circus* (1939) and *Go West* (1940). Other MGM credits included *Shadow of a Thin Man* (1941), *Best Foot Forward* (1943), *DuBarry Was a Lady* (1943), *Meet Me in St. Louis* (1944), for which Brecher received an Oscar® nomination, *Yolanda and the Thief* (1945), and *Summer Holiday* (1948). Brecher then asked to be released from his contract and worked independently in radio, television, and film, including *Cry for Happy* (1961) and *Bye Bye Birdie* (1963). He also revamped an idea intended for Groucho Marx into the radio show *The Life of Riley*, which ran from 1944 to 1951 (and later transferred to television) as well as directing the 1949 film version. Brecher also directed *Somebody Loves Me* (1952) and *Sail a Crooked Ship* (1961). Brecher's memoir, *The Wicked Wit of the West*, was published in 2009.

Bernie Brillstein (April 26, 1931–August 7, 2008). Born Bernard J. Brillstein in New York City, the manager and producer graduated from New York University with an advertising degree and got a job (in the mailroom) at the William Morris Agency. He moved to Los Angeles in 1967 and formed the Brillstein Company in 1969 with such clients as Jim Henson, Gilda Radner, Dan Aykroyd, John Belushi, and Lorne Michaels. In 1991, Brillstein partnered with protégé Brad Grey on the production company Brillstein-Grey Entertainment and later formed Brillstein Entertainment Partners. Brillstein was also the executive producer on a number of movies and television shows. His memoir, *Where Did I Go Right?: You're No One in Hollywood Unless Someone Wants You Dead*, was published in 1999.

Chris Bryant (June 7, 1936–October 27, 2008). Born Christopher Brian Spencer Dobson in Bolton, Lancashire, England, he was a writer and lawyer. Bryant was a law lecturer at McGill University in Montreal when he met his writing partner Allan Shiach. They started as comedy writers on Canadian television with Dobson using "Chris Bryant" professionally while Shiach wrote as Allan Scott. Their first screen credit was 1970's *The Man Who Had Power Over Women* and they went on to write *Don't Look Now* (1973), *The Girl from Petrovka* (1974), *The Spiral Staircase* (1975), *Golden Rendezvous* (1977), *Joseph Andrews* (1977), *The Awakening* (1980), and *Martin's Day* (1984). Bryant's solo work included *Sword of Gideon* (1986), *Stealing Heaven* (1988), *One Against the Wind* (1991), *Young Catherine* (1991), *Foreign Affairs* (1993), and *Miracle at Midnight* (1998).

George Carlin (May 12, 1937–June 22, 2008). The award-winning comedian was born in New York City and began his stand-up career after teaming up with Jack Burns in the late 1950s. Carlin began his solo career in 1962 and first appeared on television in 1965 on *The Merv Griffin Show*. Carlin's first comedy album *Take-Offs and Put-Ons* was released in 1967 (he made twenty-three albums) and he had a recurring role on the sitcom *That Girl* (1966–67). The direction of his career changed in 1970 when Carlin turned to anti-establishment humor for a younger audience, eventually with his controversial routine "Seven Words You Can Never Say on Television," which appeared on his 1972 album *Class Clown*. He was the host of the first episode of *Saturday Night Live* in 1975 and made fourteen comedy specials for HBO from 1977 to 2005. Carlin was also a

best-selling author, works included *Brain Droppings* (1997) and *When Will Jesus Bring the Pork Chops?* (2004). Carlin's films included *With Six You Get Eggroll* (1968), *Car Wash* (1976), *Bill and Ted's Excellent Adventure* (1989), *The Prince of Tides* (1991), *Dogma* (1999), and the voice role of Volkswagen bus Fillmore in *Cars* (2006). He was named the recipient of the 2008 Mark Twain Prize for American Humor, which was awarded posthumously.

Youssef Chahine (January 25, 1926–July 27, 2008). Born in Alexandria, Egypt, the director, screenwriter, and actor studied engineering at Alexandria University before persuading his parents to send him to study acting at the Pasadena (California) Institute. Upon his return to Egypt, Chahine directed his first film, *Daddy Amin*, in 1950. His work was often controversial and Chahine was frequently censured by both the Egyptian government and religious fundamentalists. Among his films were *Son of the Nile* (1951), *The Blazing Sun* (1954), *Cairo Station* (1958), *Saladin* (1963), *The Land* (1969), *Alexandria, Why?* (1978), *An Egyptian Story* (1982), *Adieu Bonaparte* (1985), *Alexandria Again and Forever* (1989), *The Emigrant* (1994), *Destiny* (1997), *Silence...We Are Rolling* (2001), *Alexandria...New York* (2004), and *This Is Chaos* (2007). Chahine received a lifetime achievement award at Cannes in 1997.

Kim Chan (1917–October 5, 2008). Born in the province of Canton, China, Chan emigrated to New York as a boy, working at his family's restaurant. Always interested in acting, Chan picked up walk-on roles and bit parts on stage and in the movies, making his film debut in 1957's *A Face in the Crowd*. The character actor was a familiar face, frequently cast in stereotypical Asian roles. Chan was also a regular on the television series *Kung Fu: The Legend Continues* from 1993 to 1997. Screen credits included *The Owl and the Pussycat* (1970), *The King of Comedy* (1982), *The Cotton Club* (1984), *Jumpin' Jack Flash* (1986), *Cadillac Man* (1990), *American Shaolin* (1991), *Thousand Pieces of Gold* (1991), *The Fifth Element* (1997), *Lethal Weapon 4* (1998), *Shanghai Knights* (2003), *Zen Noir* (2004), and *The Honeymooners* (2005).

Ben Chapman (October 29, 1928–February 21, 2008). Born in Oakland, California (where his Tahitian parents temporarily lived), the one-time actor grew up in Tahiti before returning to California in 1940. He served as a Marine in the Korean War and was briefly a contract player at Universal where he achieved cult fame in a role with no dialogue and that never showed his face: the Gill Man in the 1954 3-D monster movie, *The Creature From the Black Lagoon*. When his option was not picked up by the studio, Chapman began a career in real estate.

Cyd Charisse (March 8, 1922–June 17, 2008). Born Tula Ellice Finklea in Amarillo, Texas, the dancer and actress started ballet lessons as a child after a mild case of polio. Charisse later enrolled in dance school in Los Angeles and became a member of the touring Ballet Russe de Monte Carlo (using fake Russian names). She married dancer Nico Charisse in 1939 and started her film career in bit parts under the name Lily Norwood. She finally became Cyd (a variation of family nickname Sid) Charisse when MGM signed her to a contract in 1946. She had specialty spots in the films *Till the Clouds Roll By* (1946), *The Kissing Bandit*

(1948), and *Words and Music* (1948) before dancing with Gene Kelly in the ballet sequence in *Singin' in the Rain* (1952). She was also paired with Kelly in *Brigadoon* (1954) and *It's Always Fair Weather* (1955). Charisse danced with Fred Astaire in *The Band Wagon* (1953) and *Silk Stockings* (1957). Other films included *Fiesta* (1947), *Deep in My Heart* (1954), *Party Girl* (1958), *Two Weeks in Another Town* (1962), and *The Silencers* (1966). Charisse later performed on television and the stage as well as in a nightclub revue with second husband, singer Tony Martin, with whom she wrote a double autobiography, *The Two of Us*, published in 1976.

B(aldev) R(aj) Chopra (April 22, 1914–November 5, 2008). The Bollywood producer and director was born in Ludiana, Punjab, working as a film reviewer and editor of the magazine *Cine Herald* after graduating from Lahore University. Chopra turned to film production in the late 1940s and turned to directing with 1951's *Afsana*. Chopra formed his own production company, B.R. Films, in 1955. Credits included *Shole* (1953), *Chandni Chowk* (1954), *Ek Hi Raasta* (1956), *Naya Daur* (1957), *Sadhana* (1958), and *Kanoon* (1960). In the late 1980s, Chopra turned to television, producing the popular series *Mahabharat*, which was directed by his son Ravi.

Arthur C. Clarke (December 16, 1917–March 19, 2008). The visionary science fiction writer was born in Minehead, England. He wrote more than 100 short stories as well as numerous fiction and nonfiction books and hundreds of articles. Clarke's collaboration with director Stanley Kubrick began in 1964 over Clark's short story "The Sentinel," which they used as the idea for *2001: A Space Odyssey*. Clarke wrote that they worked on the screenplay and novel simultaneously, with both coming out in 1968. The duo received an Oscar® nomination for their screenplay; Clarke later wrote three sequels to the original novel.

Peter Copley (May 15, 1915–October 7, 2008). The prolific character actor was born in Bushey, England, and trained at London's Old Vic Theatre, joining the company in 1932. Copley's first film appearance was the 1934 short *Tell Me If It Hurts* and he made some 150 screen appearances over his seventy year career. He alternated between stage, television, and film throughout his life. Credits included *Farewell Again* (1937), *The Elusive Pimpernel* (1950), *The Sword and the Rose* (1953), *Foreign Intrigue* (1956), *Just My Luck* (1957), *Help!* (1965), *The Knack* (1965), *Anna Karenina* (1978), *Empire of the Sun* (1987), and *Wives and Daughters* (1999).

Alexander Courage (December 10, 1919–May 15, 2008). The orchestrator, arranger, and composer was born in Philadelphia, Pennsylvania and raised in New Jersey. He graduated from the Eastman School of Music in 1941 and was a bandleader in the Army Air Corp during World War II. Courage started as a composer for CBS Radio in 1946 and became an orchestrator with MGM in 1948, working on such musicals as *Showboat* (1951), *The Band Wagon* (1953), *Guys and Dolls* (1955), *Funny Face* (1957), and *Gigi* (1958). Courage and partner Lionel Newman were nominated for Oscars® for their adapted scores for *The Pleasure Seekers* (1963) and *Doctor Doolittle* (1968). He began

composing for television in 1959, including the main fanfare for the *Star Trek* series, which can also be heard in the *Star Trek* movies.

Hazel Court (February 10, 1926–April 15, 2008). The actress was born in Birmingham, England and had her first role (one-line) in 1944's *Champagne Charlie*. Larger roles followed in *Dreaming* (1944), *Carnival* (1946), *Gaiety George* (1946), and *The Root of All Evil* (1947) before Court got her first starring role in *Meet Me at Dawn* (1947) and a lead in *Holiday Camp* (1947). Other films included *Bond Street* (1948), *My Sister and I* (1948), *Forbidden* (1948), *Ghost Ship* (1952), *Counterspy* (1953), and *Devil Girl From Mars* (1954). Then Court began her stint as the "Queen of Scream" in such Hammer horror films as *The Curse of Frankenstein* (1957), *The Man Who Could Cheat Death* (1959), *Dr. Blood's Coffin* (1960), *The Premature Burial* (1962), *The Raven* (1963), and *Masque of the Red Death* (1964). Shortly after her second marriage to actor/director Don Taylor, Court retired from acting and began a career as an artist. Court also wrote an autobiography, *Hazel Court: Horror Queen*, published in England in 2008.

Fred Crane (March 22, 1918–August 21, 2008). Born Herman Frederick Crane in New Orleans, Louisiana, the actor became part of cinema history when his character, Brent Tarleton, uttered the first line heard in 1939's *Gone With the Wind*. He had accompanied his cousin, actress Leatrice Gilbert, to Selznick studios for her audition for the role of Suellen. Crane's southern accent won him his part (his cousin lost out to Evelyn Keyes) and he was put under contract. He appeared in the 1949 film *The Gay Amigo* and acted on television in the 1960s. Crane also worked as a disc jockey for Los Angeles classical radio station KFAC until 1987. Crane and his wife Terry later opened a bed-and-breakfast in an antebellum mansion outside Atlanta, Georgia that he named Tarleton Oaks after his character.

Michael Crichton (October 23, 1942–November 4, 2008). Born John Michael Crichton in Chicago, Illinois, the writer graduated with a degree in anthropology from Harvard University in 1964. In 1966, he entered Harvard Medical School and wrote fiction to help pay his tuition, using such pseudonyms as John Lange and Jeffrey Hudson. In 1969, Crichton earned his medical degree and published his first thriller under his own name, *The Andromeda Strain*, which was filmed in 1971. Crichton wrote the novel *Dealing* with his brother Douglas in 1970 (published under the name Michael Douglas), which was filmed in 1972. His next novel, *The Terminal Man* (1972), was filmed in 1974. Crichton made his own directorial debut with 1973's *Westworld* for which he also wrote the screenplay. Crichton's other directorial efforts included *Coma* (1978), *The Great Train Robbery* (1979), *Looker* (1981), *Runaway* (1984), and *Physical Evidence* (1989). Among Crichton's other novels to be made into films were *Jurassic Park* (1993), *Rising Sun* (1993), *Disclosure* (1994), *Congo* (1995), *The Lost World* (1997), *Sphere* (1998), *The 13th Warrior* (1999), and *Timeline* (2003). Crichton also created the television series *ER* (1994–2009).

Eva Dahlbeck (March 8, 1920–February 8, 2008). Born in Saltsjo-Duvnas, Sweden, the actress starred in five of Ingmar Bergman's early films. Dahlbeck studied at the

Royal Dramatic Theatre School and made her stage debut in 1941's *Ride Tonight*, playing the same role in the 1942 film version. Her first Bergman film was *Waiting Woman* (1952), followed by *Lesson in Love* (1954), *Smiles of a Summer Night* (1955), *So Close to Life* (1958), and *Now About These Women* (1964). Other screen appearances included *Eva* (1948), *Only a Mother* (1949), *Barabbas* (1953), *A Matter of Morals* (1961), *The Counterfeit Traitor* (1962), *Loving Couples* (1964), and *Les Creatures* (1966). Dahlbeck retired from acting in the 1970s and became a writer.

John Daly (July 16, 1937–October 31, 2008). The film producer was born in London, England and worked a variety of jobs (including insurance salesman) before meeting actor David Hemmings. In 1967, they formed Hemdale Film Corporation, which began as a talent agency before moving into film and television production and distribution. Daly bought Hemmings' share of the business in 1971 and the company released more than 100 movies between 1970 and 1995 with Daly serving as executive producer on the majority. In 1995, Hemdale was taken over by Orion Pictures and Daly moved on to other production ventures. He also directed two films: *The Petersburg-Cannes Express* (2003) and *The Aryan Couple* (2004).

Jules Dassin (December 8, 1911–March 31, 2008). Born in Middletown, Connecticut, the director was the son of Russian Jewish immigrants and grew up in Harlem. Dassin started as an actor in the Yiddish Theater in the 1930s before switching to directing and he went to Hollywood in the early 1940s, working for MGM, Universal, and 20th Century Fox. Among his studio pictures was *Nazi Agent* (1942), *The Canterville Ghost* (1944), *A Letter for Evie* (1946), *Brute Force* (1947), *Naked City* (1948), *Thieves' Highway* (1949), and *Night and the City* (1950). In 1951, Dassin, who had been a Communist Party member in the 1930s, was blacklisted and he moved to France in 1953; his first French film was 1955's *Rififi*, which earned Dassin the best director award at the Cannes Film Festival. (He also played the thief Cesar under the pseudonym Perlo Vita.) Dassin directed his second wife Melinda Mercouri in *He Who Must Die* (1957), *La Legge* (1959), *Never on Sunday* (1960), for which he received Oscar® nominations for direction and screenplay, as well as *Phaedra* (1962), *Topkapi* (1964), and *A Dream of Passion* (1978). His last film was *Circle of Two* (1980).

Luther Davis (August 29, 1916–July 29, 2008). The writer was born in Brooklyn, New York, graduating from Yale University and serving as an intelligence officer in World War II. Davis began writing for the stage and screen in the 1940s. Davis and Charles Lederer wrote the book for the 1953 Broadway musical, *Kismet*, for which they won a Tony Award, and then did the film version in 1955. Among his screenplays were *The Hucksters* (1947), *A Lion in the Streets* (1953), *Lady in a Cage* (1964), and *Across 110th Street* (1972).

Ennio De Concini (December 6, 1923–November 17, 2008). The screenwriter was born in Rome, Italy and began his career working as an assistant on Vittorio De Sica's *Shoeshine* (1946). De Concini shared a best original screenplay Academy Award® for 1961's *Divorce—Italian Style*. Other credits included *Outlaw Girl* (1950), *Three Corsairs*

(1952), *She Wolf* (1953), *Ulysses* (1954), *The Queen of Babylon* (1955), *The Railway Man* (1956), *The Cry* (1957), *The Wide Blue Road* (1957), *European Nights* (1959), *Hercules Unchained* (1959), *The Ugly Mess* (1959), and *Black Sunday* (1960). De Concini also wrote and directed 1952's *The Eleven Musketeers* and directed *Daniele & Maria* (1973) and *Hitler: The Last Ten Days* (1973).

Jean Delannoy (January 12, 1908–June 19, 2008). The director was born in Noisy-le-Sec, near Paris, and joined his sister Henriette acting in silent films in the 1920s. Delannoy switched to film editing and began directing shorts in the 1930s. His first feature was 1934's *Paris-Deauville* and his last, 1995's *Marie de Nazareth*. Films included *Gambling Hell* (1939), *Pontcarrel* (1942), *Love Eternal* (1943), *The Pastoral Symphony* (1946), *The Chips Are Down* (1947), *God Needs Men* (1950), *Obsession* (1954), *The Little Rebels* (1955), *Notre Dame du Paris* (1956), *Maigret Lays a Trap* (1958), *Maigret and the St. Fiacre Case* (1959), *The Princess of Cleves* (1961), *This Special Friendship* (1964), *Bernadette* (1988), and *The Passion of Bernadette* (1989).

Guillaume Depardieu (April 7, 1971–October 13, 2008). Born in Paris, France, the son of actors Gerard Depardieu and Elisabeth Guignot died suddenly of complications from pneumonia. The younger Depardieu's life was marred by heroin addiction, two prison stints, and a motorcycle accident that eventually led to the amputation of his right leg. He acted several times with his father, including his first film, 1991's *All the Mornings of the World* as well as *The Count of Monte Cristo* (1998), *Les Miserables* (2000), *Honor Your Father* (2002), *Napoleon* (2002), and *A Cursed Monarchy* (2005). Depardieu received a Cesar award as the most promising young actor for *The Apprentices* (1995). Other credits included *Pola X* (1999), *The Aquarium* (2001), *Once Upon an Angel* (2002), *The Pharmacist* (2003), *Milady* (2004), *The Duchess of Langeais* (2007), and *Versailles* (2008). The actor had a frequently combative relationship with his father, denouncing him in his 2004 autobiography *Tout Donner (Giving Everything)*, although they later reconciled.

Tamara Desni (October 22, 1911–February 7, 2008). Born Tamara Bodsky in Berlin, Germany, the actress got her start in 1931's *Terror of the Garrison*, the same year she also appeared on stage in London for the operetta *White Horse Inn*. Desni remained in England, working on such films as *Falling for You* (1933), *Forbidden Territory* (1934), *How's Chances?* (1934), *Blue Smoke* (1935), *Dark World* (1935), *His Brother's Keeper* (1939), *Flight from Folly* (1945), *Send for Paul Temple* (1946), *The Hills of Donegal* (1947), and *Dick Barton at Bay* (1950). After her acting career ended, Desni moved to France and opened an inn.

Ivan Dixon (April 6, 1931–March 16, 2008). Born in New York City, the actor, director, and producer studied drama and graduated from North Carolina Central University. Dixon began his career in the theater and later served as Sidney Poitier's stunt double in *The Defiant Ones* before working opposite the star in *Porgy and Bess* (1959) and *A Raisin in the Sun* (1961). Dixon also worked frequently on television in the 1960s and played the role of Sgt. Kinchloe on *Hogan's Heroes* (1965–70) as well as directing episodes of a number of series, including *The Bill Cosby Show*, *The Rockford Files*, and *The Waltons*. Dixon also produced and directed the independent feature *The Spook Who Sat by the Door* (1973). Among his other screen appearances were *Nothing but a Man* (1964), *A Patch of Blue* (1965), and *Car Wash* (1976).

Jack Douglas (April 26, 1927–December 18, 2008). The comic actor was born Jack Robertson in Newcastle upon Tyne, England and got his start in the theater and as a stand-up comedian, including a successful double act with Joe Baker Jr. Douglas' cameo role in 1972's *Carry On Matron* lead to his appearing in eight *Carry On* films, including the 1992 revival *Carry On Columbus*, as well as TV specials, spin-offs, and a stage version. Douglas continued his stage and television work and wrote several books, including an autobiography entitled *A Twitch in Time*.

Julie Ege (November 12, 1943–April 29, 2008). Born Julie Dzuli in Sandnes, Norway, the actress started her career as a model, winning the Miss Norway contest, which sent her to the Miss Universe pageant in 1962. She started her film career in 1967's *The Sky and the Ocean* and had a brief appearance in the 1969 Bond film *On Her Majesty's Secret Service*. Frequently cast as a seductress in various low-budget productions, Ege's other films included *Every Home Should Have One* (1970), *Creatures the World Forgot* (1971), *The Magnificent Seven Deadly Sins* (1971), *Up Pompeii* (1971), *Rentadick* (1972), *Not Now Darling* (1973), *Legend of the Seven Golden Vampires* (1974), *The Mutations* (1974), *Percy's Progress* (1974), and *The Amorous Milkman* (1975). Ege then returned to Norway where she gave up acting and became a nurse. Her autobiography, *Naked*, was published in 2002.

Mel Ferrer (August 25, 1917–June 2, 2008). The actor and director was born Melchior Gaston Ferrer in Elberon, New Jersey and began his Broadway career as a chorus dancer, later working as a disc jockey, and as a director for NBC. Ferrer signed a directing contract with Columbia in 1945 and his first effort was the low-budget *The Girl of the Limberlost* (1945) before he returned to act on Broadway in *Strange Fruit* (1945); he then directed *Cyrano de Bergerac* (1946). He returned to Hollywood and made his screen acting debut in *Lost Boundaries* (1949), followed by *Born to Be Bad* (1950), *The Brave Bulls* (1951), *Rancho Notorious* (1952), *Scaramouche* (1952), *Lili* (1953), and *Knights of the Round Table* (1954). Ferrer appeared on Broadway with Audrey Hepburn in 1954's *Ondine* and they married that year. They also starred together in *War and Peace* (1956) and Ferrer directed Hepburn in 1959's *Green Mansions*; they divorced in 1968. Later acting credits included *The Sun Also Rises* (1957), *The World, the Flesh and the Devil* (1959), *The Longest Day* (1962), *Sex and the Single Girl* (1964), *El Greco* (1966), *Brannigan* (1975), *Eaten Alive* (1977), and *Lili Marleen* (1981).

William Finnegan (June 29, 1928–November 28, 2008). The film and television producer was born in Kansas City, Missouri. After serving in the Navy, Finnegan began his career as a journalist in 1950, writing for the Associated Press, CBS, and other organizations before moving into television and films as an assistant director and production manager. Finnegan, his wife Patricia, and partner Sheldon Pinchuk formed the production firm, Finnegan-Pinchuk Co. Credits included *Support Your Local Gunfighter* (1971), *The Ordeal of Patty Hearst* (1979), *The $5.20 an Hour*

Dream (1980), *World War III* (1982), *The Dollmaker* (1984), *Amos* (1985), *The Atlanta Child Murders* (1985), *Hoover* (1987), *North Shore* (1987), *The Fabulous Baker Boys* (1989), *White Palace* (1990), *The Babe* (1992), *Criss-Cross* (1992), *Reality Bites* (1994), and *Ed* (1996). Finnegan retired in 2003.

Nina Foch (April 20, 1924–December 5, 2008). The actress was born Nina Consuelo Maud Fock in Leyden, the Netherlands. She and her parents, orchestral conductor Dirk Fock and actress Consuelo Flowerton, moved to New York in 1928. Foch attended the American Academy of Dramatic Arts and made her first screen appearance in the 1943 short *Wagon Wheels West* for Columbia Pictures, who modified her last name. Her feature film debut came in 1944's *The Return of the Vampire*. She then appeared in a series of B-movies, including *The Cry of the Werewolf* (1944), *Shadows in the Night* (1944), *Boston Blackie's Rendezvous* (1945), *My Name Is Julia Ross* (1945), *A Song to Remember* (1945), *The Dark Past* (1948), *Johnny Allegro* (1949), and *The Undercover Man* (1949). Foch's fortunes changed after she left Columbia for MGM and she was cast as socialite Milo Roberts in *An American in Paris* (1951). Other film credits included *Scaramouche* (1952), *Sombrero* (1952), *Executive Suite* (1954) for which she earned an Oscar® nomination as best supporting actress, *Illegal* (1955), *The Ten Commandments* (1956), *Cash McCall* (1960), *Spartacus* (1960), *Mahogany* (1975), *It's My Party* (1996), and *How to Deal* (2003). Foch also appeared on stage, starting with 1947's *John Loves Mary*, and on television, beginning in 1949, including a recurring role on the CBS series, *NCIS*. Foch also taught film and drama at the University of Southern California's School of Cinematic Arts and the American Film Institute.

John Forbes-Robertson (May 10, 1928–May 14, 2008). Born in Worthing, England, his parents were both actors and Forbes-Robertson began his career on stage and did a number of television roles. His credits included *Casino Royale* (1967), *The Vampire Lovers* (1970), *Nicholas and Alexandra* (1971), *The Legend of the Seven Golden Vampires* (1974), *QB VII* (1974), *The Naked Civil Servant* (1975), *The Rise and Fall of Reginald Perrin* (1976), *Venom* (1981), and *Number 36* (2004).

John Furlong (April 14, 1933–June 23, 2008). The actor was born in Albany, New York and frequently worked with exploitation director Russ Meyer, both as an actor and narrator, after moving to California in the early 1960s. Films included *Mudhoney* (1965), *Faster, Pussycat! Kill! Kill!* (1965), *Mondo Topless* (1966), *Common-Law Cabin* (1967), *Finders Keepers, Lovers Weepers!* (1968), *Vixen!* (1968), *Supervixens* (1975), and *Beneath the Valley of the Ultra-Vixens* (1979). Furlong also did character roles in other films and on television; he retired in 2001.

George Furth (December 14, 1932–August 11, 2008). The character actor and playwright was born George Schweinfurth in Chicago, Illinois and majored in drama at Northwestern University. Furth wrote the book for *Company* (1970), which won him a Tony Award, and also collaborated with Stephen Sondheim on *Merrily We Roll Along* (1981) and *Getting Away with Murder* (1996). Other plays included *Twigs* (1971), *The Supporting Cast* (1981), and *Precious Sons* (1996). He made his acting debut on Broadway in *A Cook for the General* (1961) and had a long list of television credits from the 1960s to the 1990s. Furth's screen appearances included *The Best Man* (1964), *Butch Cassidy and the Sundance Kid* (1969), *Blazing Saddles* (1974), *Shampoo* (1975), and *Bulworth* (1998).

Beverly Garland (October 17, 1926–December 5, 2008). The actress was born Beverly Fessenden in Santa Cruz, California and studied acting in high school. Under the name Beverly Campbell (from a brief teenage marriage), she made her screen debut in 1950's *D.O.A.* She became Beverly Garland from a second marriage to actor Richard Garland. Garland starred in a number of B-movies in the 1950s and frequently guest-starred on television. She had recurring roles in the TV series' *Decoy* (1957–59), *My Three Sons* (1969–72), *Mary Hartman, Mary Hartman* (1976–77), and *Scarecrow and Mrs. King* (1983–87). Screen credits included *Killer Leopard* (1954), *The Rocket Man* (1954), *Swamp Women* (1955), *Gunslinger* (1956), *It Conquered the World* (1956), *The Joker Is Wild* (1957), *Not of This Earth* (1957), *Naked Paradise* (1957), *The Alligator People* (1959), *Pretty Poison* (1968), *Airport 1975* (1974), *Where the Red Fern Grows* (1974), and *Roller Boogie* (1979).

Irving Gertz (May 19, 1915–November 14, 2008). The composer was born in Providence, Rhode Island, and studied at the Providence College of Music. Gertz was hired by Columbia Pictures in 1938 and went on to compose music for more than 200 western, horror, and science fiction films, though his work frequently went uncredited since the studios often used multiple composers and only the head of the studio's music department received screen credit. Besides Columbia, Gertz worked for Universal, United Artists, RKO, 20th Century Fox, and a number of independent producers. Gertz also composed music for such television series as *Daniel Boone, Voyage to the Bottom of the Sea, Land of the Giants,* and *The Invaders.*

Erwin Geschonneck (December 27, 1906–March 12, 2008). Born in Bartenstein in East Prussia (now Poland), the actor joined the Communist Party in 1919 and became a member of one of the many workers' theater groups in Berlin. Geschonneck fled the country in 1933 when Hitler came to power, going into exile in the Soviet Union. When he was expelled from the country in 1938, he went to Prague where he was arrested by the Gestapo in 1939 and spent the next six years in concentration camps. In 1949, Geschonneck moved to East Berlin and became a staple in films made by D.E.F.A., the East Germany state-run film agency. Films included *The Axe of Wandsbek* (1951), *Carbide and Sorrel* (1963), *Naked Among Wolves* (1963), *Jacob the Liar* (1974), *The Man of the Cap Arcona* (1982), and *Matulla and Busch* (1985).

Estelle Getty (July 23, 1923–July 22, 2008). The character actress was born Estelle Scheer in New York City, working as a teenager in Yiddish theater and doing comedy at Catskill resorts. She took her stage name from her husband Arthur Gettleman, whom she married in 1947. Getty's first success came on stage in *Torch Song Trilogy* (1981). The touring production took her to Los Angeles where she auditioned for the octogenarian role of Sophia Petrillo on television's *Golden Girls* (1985–92), which she also played in the spinoffs *The Empty Nest* and *The Golden Palace.* Getty was nominated seven times for Emmy awards for the role but only won in 1988. Screen credits included *Copacabana* (1985), *Mask* (1985), *Stop! Or My Mom Will Shoot* (1992), and *Stuart Little* (1999). Getty's autobiography, *If I Knew Then What I Know Now, So What?,* was published in 1988.

William Gibson (November 13, 1914–November 25, 2008). The writer was born in the Bronx, New York and began his literary career writing prize-winning poetry. Gibson's first novel, *The Cobweb,* was filmed in 1955 and the money allowed Gibson to write his first successful stage show, *Two for the Seesaw,* which was filmed in 1962. The 1958 Broadway show had starred Anne Bancroft for whom Gibson wrote 1959's *The Miracle Worker* (also filmed in 1962); Gibson received an Oscar® nomination for his screenplay adaptation. Gibson won Tony awards for both stage productions as well as 1964's *The Golden Boy.*

David Groh (May 21, 1939–February 12, 2008). The actor was born in Brooklyn, New York and graduated from Brown University, also studying at the London Academy of Music and Dramatic Art. After his Army service, Groh studied at the Actors Studio and began his stage career. He is best-known for this television role as Joe, who married the title character in the sitcom *Rhoda* (1974–77) and as D.L. Brock on the soap opera *General Hospital* (1983–85). His stage work included *Hot L Baltimore* (1973), *Chapter Two* (1978), and *The Twilight of the Golds* (1993). Film credits included *Two-Minute Warning* (1976), *Victory at Entebbe* (1976), *A Hero Ain't Nothing but a Sandwich* (1978), and *Get Shorty* (1995). Groh also taught acting at the Strasberg Institute.

Earle Hagen (July 9, 1919–May 26, 2008). The composer was born in Chicago, Illinois but grew up in Los Angeles. He played trombone with several big band orchestras, composing the jazz standard "Harlem Nocturne" in 1939, which he later used as the theme song for the television detective series *Mickey Spillane's Mike Hammer.* After serving in World War II, Hagen joined 20th Century Fox as an arranger and orchestrator for dozens of movies and received a 1960 Oscar® nomination (along with Lionel Newman) for *Let's Make Love.* Hagen did original scores for more than 3,000 episodes during his television career, which lasted from 1953 until his retirement in 1986. These included *The Andy Griffith Show, The Dick Van Dyke Show, Make Room for Daddy, I Spy, That Girl, The Mod Squad, Eight Is Enough,* and *The Dukes of Hazzard.* Hagen was also the author of three books on scoring and published his autobiography, *Memoirs of a Famous Composer—Nobody Ever Heard Of,* in 2002.

Fred Haines (February 27, 1936–May 4, 2008). The writer and director was born in Los Angeles, eventually graduating from the University of California Berkeley. While working as a radio station manger for KPFK in Los Angeles, Haines met director Joseph Strick, who helped him get a job with the story department at Columbia Pictures. The two adapted the James Joyce novel *Ulysses* for a 1968 film and were nominated for an Academy Award® for their screenplay. Haines also adapted the Herman Hesse novel *Steppenwolf* and directed the 1974 film version.

Bernie Hamilton (June 12, 1928–December 30, 2008). Bernard Hamilton was born in Los Angeles and got involved in acting while attending Oakland Technical High

School. He made a number of television appearances, including the role of Captain Harold Dobey on the series *Starsky and Hutch* (1975–79). Film credits included *Mysterious Island* (1951), *The Young One* (1960), *The Devil at 4 O'Clock* (1961), *Synanon* (1965), *The Swimmer* (1968), *Lost Man* (1969), *Walk the Walk* (1970), *The Organization* (1971), *Hammer* (1972), *Scream Blacula Scream* (1973), and *Bucktown* (1975). In the 1980s, Hamilton turned from acting to producing R&B and gospel records under the record label Chocolate Snowman.

Isaac Hayes (August 20, 1942–August 10, 2008). The baritone singer/songwriter, known for his soul sound, was born in Covington, Tennessee. Raised by his grandparents, who eventually moved to Memphis, Hayes performed in local clubs and made his first recording in 1962. He joined Stax Records as a session musician in 1964 and composed some 200 songs for the label with partner David Porter. Hayes released his first solo album in 1968. In 1971, he scored the film *Shaft* and became the first African-American composer to win an Oscar® for Best Song; he was also nominated for Best Score. Hayes scored two more soundtracks in 1974, *Tough Guys* and *Truck Turner* in which he also played the lead role. Hayes continued both his music and acting careers and was elected to the Rock and Roll Hall of Fame in 2002. He voiced the role of "Chef" on the television show *South Park* from 1997 to 2006. Film credits included *Escape From New York* (1981), *I'm Gonna Git You Sucka* (1988), *Robin Hood: Men in Tights* (1992), *Reindeer Games* (2000), *Hustle & Flow* (2005), and *Soul Men* (2008).

John Michael Hayes (May 11, 1919–November 19, 2008). The screenwriter was born in Worcester, Massachusetts, beginning his career as a journalist before writing for radio. Hayes moved to Hollywood in the mid-1940s to try screenwriting, receiving his first credits for the 1953 films *Thunder Bay* and *Torch Song*. Hayes met director Alfred Hitchcock (they were both clients of MCA) and worked with him on *Rear Window* (1954), *To Catch a Thief* (1955), *The Trouble With Harry* (1955), and *The Man Who Knew Too Much* (1956) during which the two fell out over the screenwriter's credit. Hayes' later credits included *Peyton Place* (1957), *Butterfield 8* (1960), *The Children's Hour* (1961), *The Carpetbaggers* (1964), *The Chalk Garden* (1964), *Where Love Has Gone* (1964), *Harlow* (1965), and *Nevada Smith* (1966). Hayes then turned to writing for television although his last screen credit was for the Disney film *Iron Will* (1994). Hayes received Oscar® nominations for *Rear Window* and *Peyton Place*.

William L. Hayward (March 27, 1941–March 9, 2008). Producer William Leland Hayward III was born in Los Angeles, the son of agent and producer Leland Hayward and actress Margaret Sullivan. He produced the television movie *Haywire* (1980), based on his sister Brooke's family memoir. Hayward's production credits included *Easy Rider* (1969), *The Hired Hand* (1971), *High-Ballin'* (1978), and *Wanda Nevada* (1979).

Neal Hefti (October 29, 1922–October 11, 2008). The composer and arranger was born in Hastings, Nebraska, and played trumpet as a teenager in local bands as well as writing arrangements. Hefti joined the tours of several big bands, including Woody Herman, and he worked with

Count Basie in the 1950s. Hefti composed the theme music for the television series *Batman* in 1966, for which he won a Grammy Award for best instrumental theme. Credits as a film composer included *Sex and the Single Girl* (1964), *Boeing Boeing* (1965), *Harlow* (1965), *Duel at Diablo* (1966), *Barefoot in the Park* (1967), *A New Leaf* (1971), and *Last of the Red Hot Lovers* (1972). His theme for *The Odd Couple* (1968) was later used in the 1970s television series. Hefti retired in 1976.

Eileen Herlie (March 8, 1918–October 8, 2008). Born Eileen Herlihy in Glasgow, Scotland, the actress was educated at Shawlands Academy and joined the Scottish National Players at the age of eighteen. In 1942, Herlie joined the Old Vic in London. She opened at the Haymarket in *The Matchmaker* in 1954 and then made her Broadway debut in the role in 1955. Herlie was nominated for a Tony Award for her role in *Take Me Along* (1959). In 1976, the red-haired actress joined the cast of the ABC soap opera *All My Children*, playing the role of Myrtle Fargate until her death. Screen credits included *Hamlet* (1948 and 1964), *The Story of Gilbert and Sullivan* (1953), *She Didn't Say No!* (1958), *Freud* (1962), *The Sea Gull* (1968), and *The Woman I Love* (1972).

Charlton Heston (October 4, 1924–April 5, 2008). The actor, who gained fame starring in epic roles, was born John Charlton Carter in Evanston, Illinois before his family moved to St. Helen, Michigan. When his mother remarried after a divorce, they moved back to Illinois and the boy took his stepfather's surname of Heston. He studied acting at Northwestern University and served in the Army Air Corps during World War II. Heston then went to New York and eventually got a break on Broadway with 1947's *Antony and Cleopatra*. Heston then appeared on a number of live television dramas and came to Los Angeles after getting a contract from producer Hal B. Wallis; he made his film debut with 1950's *Dark City*. His work at the Paramount studio brought him to the attention of director Cecil B. DeMille, who cast Heston in *The Greatest Show on Earth* (1952). In 1956, DeMille cast Heston as Moses in *The Ten Commandments*. The actor received a Best Actor Oscar® for the title role of *Ben Hur* (1959). Other screen credits included *Ruby Gentry* (1953), *The President's Lady* (1954), *Touch of Evil* (1957), *The Big Country* (1958), *The Buccaneer* (1958), *El Cid* (1961), *55 Days at Peking* (1963), *The Agony and the Ecstasy* (1965), *The Greatest Story Ever Told* (1965), *Major Dundee* (1965), *Khartoum* (1966), *Will Penny* (1967), *The Planet of the Apes* (1968), *Beneath the Planet of the Apes* (1970), *The Hawaiians* (1970), *The Omega Man* (1971), *Skyjacked* (1972), *Soylent Green* (1973), *Airport 1975* (1974), *True Lies* (1994), *Any Given Sunday* (1999), and his last appearance in the Michael Moore documentary *Bowling for Columbine* (2002). Heston published his autobiography, *In the Arena*, in 1995. He was diagnosed with Alzheimer's in 2002 and withdrew from public life.

Leonard Hirschfield (1928–August 15, 2008). Born in Pittsburgh, Pennsylvania, the filmmaker spent most of his career as a cinematographer, director, and producer of television commercials. Hirschfield was the cinematographer on two independent films from director Frank Perry:

1962's *David and Lisa* and 1963's *Ladybug, Ladybug*. He also wrote and directed the 1966 film *Steps*.

Jun Ichikawa (November 25, 1948–September 19, 2008). The director was born and raised in Tokyo, Japan. After failing to get into art school, Ichikawa drew advertising storyboards and began directing commercials. He made his film debut with the 1987 youth feature, *Bu Su*. Other films included *Dying at a Hospital* (1993), *Tokyo Siblings* (1994), *Tokyo Lullaby* (1997), *Tokyo Marigold* (2001), *Tony Takitani* (2004), and *How to Become Myself* (2007). Ichikawa died of a brain hemorrhage while editing his film *Buy a Suit*.

Kon Ichikawa (November 20, 1915–February 13, 2008). Born in Uji-Yamada, in the Mie prefecture of western Japan, the director graduated from Tokyo University in 1933. He began his career as an animator for the studio that eventually became Toho Motion Picture Company, directing feature cartoon films beginning in 1945. Ichikawa's early films were popular in Japan but it was 1956's *The Burmese Harp* that first won him international acclaim, a prize at the Venice Film Festival, and an Oscar® nomination for best foreign language film. Other films included *Conflagration* (1958), *Fires on the Plain* (1959), *Her Brother* (1960), *Odd Obsession* (1960), *Being Two Isn't Easy* (1962), *An Actor's Revenge* (1963), *Alone on the Pacific* (1963), *Tokyo Olympiad* (1965), *To Love Again* (1971), *I Am a Cat* (1975), *The Makioka Sisters* (1983), *Princess From the Moon* (1987), *47 Ronin* (1994), *Alley Cat* (2000), *Big Mama* (2001), and *The Inugamis* (2006).

Charles Joffe (July 16, 1929–July 9, 2008). The agent and producer was born in Brooklyn, New York, graduating from Syracuse University. He joined MCA as a junior agent, which is where he met Jack Rollins; the duo formed their own agency in 1953. Early clients included Harry Belafonte, Mike Nichols, Elaine May, and Woody Allen. Joffe got Allen his first contract as writer and actor on *What's New Pussycat?* (1965) and brokered his first directorial effort with *Take the Money and Run* (1969). Joffe was also able to guarantee Allen complete artistic control of his films. Rollins and Joffe remained partners until the late 1980s when each decided to focus on a single client: Rollins became an executive producer for David Letterman while Joffe continued to produce Allen's films. Allen's 2008 release, *Vicky Cristina Barcelona*, was Joffe's 42nd project with the filmmaker.

Van Johnson (August 25, 1916–December 12, 2008). The actor was born Charles Van Dell Johnson in Newport, Rhode Island and started his career on Broadway as a chorus boy after graduating from high school. Johnson made his unbilled screen debut in 1940's *Too Many Girls* (he'd first worked in the stage musical) and then had a small role on Broadway in *Pal Joey*, which lead him back to Hollywood. Warner Bros. offered Johnson a six-month contract and cast him in 1942's *Murder in the Big House* but dropped him. Johnson's friend Lucille Ball then introduced him to MGM casting director Billy Grady. His first film for the studio was *Somewhere I'll Find You* (1942) and he worked for MGM for twelve years, frequently cast in All-American, boy-next-door roles. Screen credits included *The War Against Mrs. Hadley* (1942), *A Guy Named Joe* (1943), *Human Comedy* (1943), *Madame Curie* (1943), *Pilot No. 5* (1943), *Thirty Seconds Over Tokyo* (1944), *Two Girls and a Sailor* (1944), *Thrill of a Romance* (1945), *Weekend at the Waldorf* (1945), *The Romance of Rosy Ridge* (1947), *Command Decision* (1948), *Battleground* (1949), *In the Good Old Summertime* (1949), *Go for Broke* (1951), *Brigadoon* (1954), *The Caine Mutiny* (1954), *The Last Time I Saw Paris* (1954), *The End of the Affair* (1955), *Wives and Lovers* (1963), *Divorce American Style* (1967), *Yours, Mine and Ours* (1968), and *The Purple Rose of Cairo* (1985). Later in his career Johnson frequently appeared on television and on stage.

Ollie Johnston (October 31, 1912–April 14, 2008). Born Oliver Martin Johnston Jr. in Palo Alto, California, the animator was the last surviving member of the team Walt Disney nicknamed the "Nine Old Men." Johnston met his best friend—and fellow animator—Frank Thomas while studying art at Stanford University. Thomas joined the Disney studio in 1934 and Johnston followed the next year. Johnston's first major feature was assisting on *Snow White and the Seven Dwarfs* (1937) and he drew key scenes for *Fantasia* and *Pinocchio* (both 1940) and *Dumbo* (1941). Johnston and Thomas then became the supervising animators on 1942's *Bambi*. Other Disney features included *Song of the South* (1946), *Cinderella* (1950), *Alice in Wonderland* (1951), *Peter Pan* (1953), *101 Dalmatians* (1961), *Mary Poppins* (1964), *The Jungle Book* (1967), *Aristocats* (1970), *Robin Hood* (1973), *The Rescuers* (1977), and *Winnie the Pooh* (1977). Both Johnston and Thomas retired in 1978, collaborating on the book *Disney Animation: The Illusion of Life*, published in 1981, as well as *Too Funny for Words* (1987), *Bambi: The Story and the Film* (1990), and *The Disney Villains* (1993). In 1995, Thomas' son, Theodore, produced the film *Frank and Ollie* with the duo reminiscing about their careers. Johnston was the first animator to be honored with the National Medal of Arts in 2005.

David Jones (February 19, 1934–September 19, 2008). The film and theater director was born in Poole, Dorset, England, graduating from Christ's College, Cambridge. Jones joined the BBC in 1958, working on various arts programs, and began a long association with the Royal Shakespeare Company. Among his films were *Langrishe, Go Down* (1978), *Betrayal* (1983), *84 Charing Cross Road* (1987), and *The Trial* (1993).

Evelyn Keyes (November 20, 1916–July 4, 2008). Born in Port Arthur, Texas, the actress gained lasting fan recognition for her role of Suellen, Scarlett O'Hara's younger sister, in *Gone With the Wind* (1939). Her family moved to Atlanta, Georgia when she was a child and Keyes studied dance and voice. After moving to Hollywood, the actress was signed to a Paramount contract by Cecil B. DeMille, who cast her in *The Buccaneer* (1938). When Paramount didn't renew her contract, Keyes then signed with Columbia. Screen credits included *Before I Hang* (1940), *The Lady in Question* (1940), *The Face Behind the Mask* (1941), *Here Comes Mr. Jordan* (1941), *Ladies in Retirement* (1941), *The Desperadoes* (1943), *Dangerous Blondes* (1943), *Nine Girls* (1944), *A Thousand and One Nights* (1945), *Renegades* (1945), *The Jolson Story* (1946), *Thrill of Brazil* (1947), *Johnny O'Clock* (1947), *The Mating of Millie* (1948), *Mrs. Mike* (1949), *The Prowler* (1951), *It Happened in Paris* (1952), *Rough Shoot* (1953), *99 River Street* (1953), *The Seven Year Itch* (1955), and *Wicked Stepmother* (1989). Keyes also worked on the stage and guest starred on television as well as writing two memoirs: *Scarlett O'Hara's Younger Sister* (1977) and *I'll Think About That Tomorrow* (1991) in which she candidly described her romances and marriages, including those to directors Charles Vidor and John Huston and her last marriage to bandleader Artie Shaw.

Eartha Kitt (January 17, 1927–December 25, 2008). The self-proclaimed "sex kitten" singer and actress was born Eartha Mae Keith in North, South Carolina to a black Cherokee mother and a white father. Her mixed-race heritage was a problem and the child was sent to live with her aunt, Marnie Kitt, in Harlem. Growing up in poverty, Kitt auditioned for the Katherine Dunham Dance Company on a dare and joined the company in 1946. She sang in cabaret and Broadway revues and released her first album, *RCA Victor Presents Eartha Kitt*, in 1952; it included the hit songs "C'est Si Bon" and "Santa Baby." Kitt had the lead female role in the 1958 film *St. Louis Blues* and was the second Catwoman (after Julie Newmar) on the *Batman* television series in the 1960s. Kitt publicly protested the Vietnam War while a guest at a White House luncheon in 1968 and was effectively blacklisted in the U.S., but she successfully worked overseas. She later earned Tony nominations for the musical *Timbuktu!* (1978) and *The Wild Party* (2000). Other film credits included *The Mark of the Hawk* (1957), *Anna Lucasta* (1959), *Saint of Devil's Island* (1961), *Friday Foster* (1975), *Dragonard* (1987), *Erik the Viking* (1989), *Boomerang* (1992), *Harriet the Spy* (1996), *The Emperor's New Groove* (2000), *Holes* (2003), and *And Then Came Love* (2007). Kitt also wrote three autobiographies and a guide to staying fit.

Edward Klosinski (January 2, 1943–January 5, 2008). The cinematographer was born in Warsaw, Poland and graduated from the National Film and Theatre School in 1967. Klosinski got his first job as director of photography on Andrzej Wajda's *The Birch Wood* (1970) and the duo worked together eight times. Screen credits included *Illumination* (1973), *Camouflage* (1977), *Man of Marble* (1977), *Rough Treatment* (1978), *Man of Iron* (1981), *Decalogue* (1988), *Europa* (1991), and *Three Colors: White* (1994).

Harvey Korman (February 15, 1927–May 20, 2008). Comedian Korman was born in Chicago, Illinois and studied at the Goodman School of Drama at the Chicago Art Institute. Korman moved to New York in the 1950s and struggled for years before moving to Hollywood, eventually joining the cast of *The Danny Kaye Show* in 1964. After the show ended in 1967, Korman joined *The Carol Burnett Show,* winning four Emmys out of seven nominations, until his departure in 1977 for his own (brief) series. From 1983 to 1985, Korman appeared on the sitcom *Mama's Family.* Film credits included *Blazing Saddles* (1974), *High Anxiety* (1977), *Bud and Lou* (1978), *Herbie Goes Bananas* (1980), *History of the World: Part 1* (1981), *Trail of the Pink Panther* (1982), *Curse of the Pink Panther* (1983), *The Flintstones* (1994), *Dracula: Dead and Loving It* (1995), and *The Flintstones in Viva Rock Vegas* (2000).

Don LaFontaine (August 26, 1940–September 1, 2008). Born in Duluth, Minnesota, LaFontaine, a baritone, was known in the industry as "the king of voiceovers" and "the voice of God," recording more than 5000 movie trailers in his decades-long career. He started as a recording engineer in the Army and then worked on producing radio commercials in New York. LaFontaine and partner Floyd Petersen started a company that specialized in film advertising and he recorded his first trailer for 1964's *Gunfighters of Casa Grande.* He launched his own company, then joined Paramount Pictures, but later resumed his career as an independent producer. LaFontaine also voiced an estimated 350,000 radio and television commercials.

Harry Lange (December 7, 1930–May 22, 2008). Hans-Kurt Lange was born in Eisenbach, Germany and studied art, later moving to New York to work in advertising. During the Korean War he illustrated training manuals, which led to his work with NASA, creating illustrations of space vehicles. Eventually, Lange met Arthur C. Clarke and began to work as a production designer with Clarke and director Stanley Kubrick on *2001: A Space Odyssey* (1968), for which he received an Oscar® nomination. Lange continued his cinema career, working on such films as *ZPG* (1972), *Star Wars* (1977), *Moonraker* (1979), *The Empire Strikes Back* (1980), *The Great Muppet Caper* (1981), *The Dark Crystal* (1982), and *Return of the Jedi* (1983).

John Phillip Law (September 7, 1937–May 13, 2008). The actor was born in Los Angeles and decided on an acting career after taking drama classes in college. He moved to New York and landed bit parts on Broadway before traveling to Italy where Law got film work. His striking looks (tall, blonde, blue-eyed) brought him to the attention of director Norman Jewison who cast him as the juvenile lead in *The Russians Are Coming, the Russians Are Coming* (1965). Law's co-star in *Hurry Sundown* (1967), Jane Fonda, introduced him to her then-husband Roger Vadim who cast Law as the blind angel Pygar in 1968's *Barbarella.* Other credits included *Smog* (1962), *High Fidelity* (1964), *Three Nights of Love* (1964), *The Devil Rides a Horse* (1967), *Danger Diabolik* (1968), *The Sergeant* (1968), *Skidoo* (1968), *The Hawaiians* (1970), *The Red Baron* (1970), *The Love Machine* (1971), *The Golden Voyage of Sinbad* (1974), *The Cassandra Crossing* (1977), and *Tarzan the Ape Man* (1981).

Heath Ledger (April 4, 1979–January 22, 2008). Born Heathcliff Andrew Ledger in Perth, Australia, the actor was named after the character in Emily Bronte's *Wuthering Heights.* He started acting professionally as a teenager, moving to Sydney and beginning his career on television, including roles on Australian soap operas and the 1997 series *Roar.* Ledger was then cast in the 1999 Australian film *Two Hands* before moving to Los Angeles for his first American film, *10 Things I Hate About You* (1999), which was followed by *The Patriot* (2000) and *A Knight's Tale* (2001). Later roles included *Monster's Ball* (2001), *The Four Feathers* (2002), *Ned Kelly* (2003), *The Brothers Grimm* (2005), *Casanova* (2005), *The Lords of Dogtown* (2005), *Candy* (2006), and *I'm Not There* (2007). He earned a best actor Oscar® nomination for 2005's *Brokeback Mountain* and played Batman's nemesis The Joker in 2008's *The Dark Knight* for which he received several posthumous awards. Ledger was filming Terry Gilliam's *The Imaginarium of Doctor Parnassus* at the time of his death from an accidental drug overdose and his scenes are expected to remain when the film is released in 2009.

Bruce Lester (June 6, 1912–June 13, 2008). Born Bruce Somerset Lister in Johannesburg, South Africa, the dapper actor began his career on the London stage before finding film work in low-budget "quota quickies," beginning with *The Girl in the Flat*, followed by *Badger's Green*, *To Be a Lady*, and *Death at Broadcasting House* (all 1934). Lister made over twenty films in five years, including *Old Faithful* (1935), *Crime Over London* (1936), *Mayfair Melody* (1937), *Quiet Please* (1938), and *Thistledown* (1938). The actor then went to Hollywood (where his name was changed to Lester) with a Warner Bros. contract and he had roles in *Boy Meets Girl* and *If I Were King* (both 1938) and *The Invisible Man Returns*, *The Letter*, and *Pride and Prejudice* (all 1940). Lester was then cast in several World War II-related films, including *Man Hunt* (1941), *A Yank in the RAF* (1941), *Eagle Squadron* (1942), *Desperate Journey* (1942), and *Above Suspicion* (1943). His career slowed down in the late 1940s, although he appeared in *Without Reservations* (1946), *Golden Earrings* (1947), and *The Sinister Affair of Poor Aunt Nora* (1948). Lester then became a story analyst at Paramount and Columbia studios. He retired from acting with 1958's *Tarzan and the Trappers*.

Russell Lloyd (January 16, 1916–January 21, 2008). The film editor was born Hugh Russell Lloyd in Swansea, Wales, and worked as a film projectionist before getting a job in the editing room at London Films. During World War II, Lloyd was commissioned by the Crown Film Unit to edit the submarine documentary *Close Quarters* (1943) before producing, directing, and writing *A Harbour Goes to France* (1944) for the Army Film Unit. After the war, Lloyd went back to commercial film work. He worked with director John Huston on eleven films: *Moby Dick* (1956), *Heaven Knows, Mr. Allison* (1957), *The Roots of Heaven* (1958), *The Unforgiven* (1960), *Reflections in a Golden Eye* (1967), *Sinful Davey* (1969), *A Walk with Love and Death* (1969), *The Kremlin Letter* (1970), *The Last Run* (1971), *The MacKintosh Man* (1973), and *The Man Who Would Be King* (1975) for which Lloyd received an Academy Award® nomination.

Bernie Mac (October 5, 1957–August 9, 2008). The comedian and actor was born Bernard Jeffery McCullough in Chicago, Illinois, growing up with his single mother and then with his grandparents after his mother's death when he was sixteen. He worked a series of day jobs while honing his material in small comedy clubs. Mac won the Miller Lite Comedy Search contest in 1990 and then did some shows with the Def Comedy Jam tour. He also started getting small film roles in *Mo' Money* (1992), *Who's the Man?* (1993), and *House Party 3* (1994) as well as the HBO variety series *Midnight Mac* and the Original Kings of Comedy tour, which Spike Lee filmed in 2000. He had a recurring role on *Moesha* beginning in 1996 and then had his own series, *The Bernie Mac Show*, from 2001 to 2006. Other films included *Friday* (1995), *Get on the Bus* (1996), *Booty Call* (1997), *Life* (1999), *Ocean's Eleven* (2001), *Bad Santa* (2003), *Charlie's Angels: Full Throttle* (2003), *Head of State* (2003), *Mr. 3000* (2004), *Ocean's Twelve* (2004), *Guess Who* (2005), *Ocean's Thirteen* (2007), *Pride* (2007), *Madagascar: Escape 2 Africa* (2008), and *Soul Men* (2008). Mac published his memoir, *Maybe You Never Cry Again,* in 2004; he died from complications of pneumonia.

Abby Mann (December 1, 1927–March 25, 2008). The writer, director, and producer was born Abraham Goodman in Philadelphia, Pennsylvania, growing up in a working-class neighborhood in East Pittsburgh. He studied at New York University and began his career writing for television in the early 1950s. Mann won a best adapted screenplay Academy Award® for 1961's *Judgment at Nuremberg* from a script he had written in 1959 for CBS's *Playhouse 90*. He received an Oscar® nomination for 1965's *Ship of Fools*. Mann also won three Emmy awards for his television movies: *The Marcus-Nelson Murders* (1973), *Murderers Among Us: The Simon Wiesenthal Story* (1989), and *Indictment: The McMartin Trial* (1995). Other credits included *A Child Is Waiting* (1963), *The Detective* (1968), *Report to the Commissioner* (1974), *King* (1978), *Sinatra* (1992), and *Whitewash: The Clarence Bradley Story* (2002).

Dick Martin (January 30, 1922—May 24, 2008). Comedian and director Thomas Richard Martin was born in Battle Creek, Michigan. He moved to Los Angeles at age twenty, working as a comic, actor, and writer for radio shows. His partnership with Dan Rowan began in 1952 and they starred in the low-budget western comedy *Once Upon a Horse* (1958) although they had greater success in nightclubs and on television, eventually becoming the writers and hosts of NBC's *Rowan & Martin's Laugh-In* (1968–73). The duo also appeared in the 1968 film *The Maltese Bippy*. After Rowan retired in 1977, Martin pursued a solo career as a comedian and television director with an occasional film role, including *Air Bud 2: Golden Receiver* (1998), which was directed by his son, Richard Martin.

Bill Melendez (November 15, 1916–September 2, 2008). Born Jose Cuautemoc Melendez in Hermosillo, Sonora, Mexico, the animator, director, and producer earned eight Emmy Awards (out of seventeen nominations), two Peabody Awards, and an Oscar® nomination for his work featuring Charles Schulz's Peanuts characters, including the 1965 holiday classic *A Charlie Brown Christmas*. (Melendez also supplied the various sounds made by Snoopy and Woodstock.) Features included *A Boy Named Charlie Brown* (1969), *Snoopy, Come Home* (1972), *Race for Your Life, Charlie Brown* (1977), and *Bon Voyage, Charlie Brown* (1980). His family had moved to Arizona in 1928 and then to Los Angeles where he attended the Chouinard Art Institute. He began his career at the Walt Disney Studios in 1939 but left in 1941 for Schlesinger Cartoons. In 1948, Melendez joined United Productions of America (UPA), working on shorts and commercials. He met Schulz in 1959 while creating Ford Motor Co. commercials that featured the Peanuts gang. Melendez become the only person Schulz authorized to animate his characters. Melendez established his own company in 1964 and with his partner Lee Medelsohn produced, directed, and animated some seventy Peanuts specials as well as numerous commercials.

Marisa Merlini (August 6, 1923–July 27, 2008). Born in Rome, Italy, the actress grew up in poverty and worked at a perfume counter before her pin-up girl figure got her parts in comedy stage revues. Merlini made her screen debut in 1942's *Stasera Niente di Nuovo* and appeared in some 100 films, largely playing warm-hearted but comedic figures. Among her films were *The Emperor of Capri* (1949), *Bread,*

Love and Dreams (1953), *Bread, Love and Jealousy* (1954), *Fathers and Sons* (1956), *The Traffic Policeman* (1960), *Destination Rome* (1963), and her last screen role in *The Second Wedding Night* (2005).

Anthony Minghella (January 6, 1954–March 18, 2008). The playwright, screenwriter, and director was born on the Isle of Wight. He studied and later taught drama at Hull University before finding work in television, eventually becoming a script editor and writer. Minghella wrote and directed *Truly Madly Deeply* (1990), which was made by the BBC but was released as a feature film. He received an Oscar® as best director for *The English Patient* (1996) as well as a nomination for best adapted screenplay. His other films included *Mr. Wonderful* (1993), *The Talented Mr. Ripley* (1999, an Oscar® nomination for best adapted screenplay), *Cold Mountain* (2003), and *Breaking and Entering* (2006). Minghella also produced the films *Iris* (2001), *The Quiet American* (2002), *Michael Clayton* (2007), and *Revolutionary Road* (2008). He died from post-operative complications following surgery for tonsil cancer.

Rudy Ray Moore (March 17, 1927–October 19, 2008). The comedian was born Rudolph Frank Moore in Fort Smith, Arkansas. He moved to Cleveland, Ohio as a teenager, studying tap dancing and eventually joined a travelling black variety show. Moving to Los Angeles in 1959, Moore began releasing explicit underground comedy albums, including material that featured a character called Dolemite. In 1975, Moore made a successful blaxploitation movie of the same name, followed by the sequels *The Human Tornado* (1976), and *The Return of Dolemite* (2002). Moore's rhymed storytelling was a precursor to hip-hop and rap and his influence has been cited by a number of rappers, including Dr. Dre and Snoop Dogg.

Nonna Mordyukova (November 25, 1925–July 6, 2008). Born in Konstantinovskaya, USSR, Noyabrina Mordyukova was one of the country's most popular actresses. She entered Moscow's state film school in 1946 and made her debut in 1948's *The Young Guard*. Other films included *The Return of Vasili Bortnikov* (1952), *A Simple Story* (1960), *The Chairman* (1962), *Balzaminov's Wedding* (1965), *The Commissar* (1967), *Diamond Arm* (1968), *Kinfolk* (1981), and her last film, *After Mama* (1999).

Barry Morse (June 10, 1918–February 2, 2008). Born Herbert Morse in London, England, the actor was best known for his television role as Lt. Philip Gerard, who relentlessly chased Richard Kimble in *The Fugitive* (1963–67), though he actually appeared in only thirty-eight episodes. Morse trained at the Royal Academy of Dramatic Arts and played in repertory and in the West End, also appearing in such films as *The Goose Steps Out* (1942), *Thunder Rock* (1942), *When We Are Married* (1943), and *Mrs. Fitzherbert* (1947) . He and his wife moved to Canada in 1951 and Morse got a job with the Canadian Broadcasting Corporation working on radio and television while continuing his theater work. Morse later had roles in the television series *The Adventurer* (1972–73) and *Space:1999* (1975–76). His autobiography, *Remember With Advantages: Chasing "The Fugitive" and Other Stories From an Actor's Life,* was published in 2007.

Robert Mulligan (August 23, 1925–December 20, 2008). The director was born in the Bronx, New York, served in the Navy during World War II, and graduated from Fordham University in 1948. Mulligan's messenger job at CBS led to television directing for such series as *Playhouse 90, Studio One,* and *The Philco Television Playhouse.* He also won an 1960 Emmy award for the television film *The Moon and Sixpence.* Mulligan's first film credit was 1957's *Fear Strikes Out.* He received an Academy Award® nomination for *To Kill a Mockingbird* (1962). Other credits included *Come September* (1961), *The Great Imposter* (1961), *The Spiral Road* (1962), *Love With the Proper Stranger* (1963), *Baby the Rain Must Fall* (1965), *Inside Daisy Clover* (1965), *Up the Down Staircase* (1967), *The Stalking Moon* (1969), *The Pursuit of Happiness* (1971), *Summer of '42* (1971), *The Other* (1972), *The Nickel Ride* (1974), *Bloodbrothers* (1978), *Same Time, Next Year* (1978), *Kiss Me Goodbye* (1982), and *Clara's Heart* (1988). Mulligan's last film was 1991's *The Man in the Moon.*

Lois Nettleton (August 16, 1927–January 18, 2008). The actress was born in Oak Park, Illinois, studying at the Goodman Theatre before moving to New York where she joined the Actors Studio. Nettleton made her Broadway debut in 1949 in *The Biggest Thief in Town.* She began working in television in the 1950s and made her film debut in 1962's *Period of Adjustment* as one of the last contract players at MGM. Other screen credits included *Mail Order Bride* (1964), *The Man in the Glass Booth* (1975), and *The Best Little Whorehouse in Texas* (1982).

Paul Newman (January 26, 1925–September 26, 2008). The actor was born in Cleveland, Ohio but grew up in the suburb of Shaker Heights. He acted in high school (as well as playing football) and served in the Navy before entering Kenyon College on an athletic scholarship. Newman briefly attended Yale Drama School, but moved to New York to study at the Actors Studio. He made his Broadway debut in *Picnic* (1953); Joanne Woodward was an understudy in the production. They married in 1958 and appeared in eleven films together, with Newman directing Woodward in four films. His film debut came with the 1954 costume drama *The Silver Chalice,* a film for which he would publicly apologize. He returned to Broadway as well as acting on television. Newman acted in some sixty-five films and received Oscar® nominations for *Cat on a Hot Tin Roof* (1958), *The Hustler* (1961), *Hud* (1963), *Cool Hand Luke* (1967), *Absence of Malice* (1981), *The Verdict* (1982), *Nobody's Fool* (1994), and *Road to Perdition* (2003); he won the best actor award in 1986 for *The Color of Money.* The Academy also bestowed a lifetime achievement award in 1985 and the Jean Hersholt award for his philanthropic work in 1993. Other screen credits included *Somebody Up There Likes Me* (1956), *The Left-Handed Gun* (1958), *The Long Hot Summer* (1958), *Exodus* (1960), *From the Terrace* (1960), *Sweet Bird of Youth* (1962), *Harper* (1966), *Torn Curtain* (1966), *Hombre* (1967), *Butch Cassidy and the Sundance Kid* (1969), *The Sting* (1973), *The Towering Inferno* (1974), *The Drowning Pool* (1975), *Buffalo Bill and the Indians* (1976), *Slap Shot* (1977), *Fort Apache the Bronx* (1981), *Mr. & Mrs. Bridge* (1990), *The Hudsucker Proxy* (1994), *Twilight* (1998), and as the voice of Doc Hudson in *Cars* (2006); he effectively retired in 2007. Newman directed *Rachel, Rachel* (1968), *Sometimes a Great Notion* (1971), *Effect on Gamma Rays on Man-in-the-Moon Marigolds* (1972), *The Shadow Box* (1980), *Harry & Son* (1984), and *The Glass Menagerie* (1987). Newman had become intrigued with automobile racing after starring in the 1969 film *Winning* and raced professionally as well as becoming a team owner. In 1982, Newman and A.E. Hotchner started the Newman's Own food brand and the company's profits were donated to charity, including the Hole in the Wall Gang Camps for seriously ill children. Previously, he had founded the Scott Newman Center to publicize the dangers of alcohol and drug abuse, named after his only son who died of an overdose in 1978.

Ken Ogata (July 20, 1937–October 5, 2008). Born in Tokyo, Japan, the actor joined the Shinkokugeki drama troupe in 1958 and his television roles in period dramas brought him national attention. Screen credits included *The Castle of Sand* (1974), *The Last Samurai* (1974), *The Demon* (1978), *Vengeance Is Mine* (1979), *Eijanaika* (1981), *Ballad of Narayama* (1983), *Mishima: A Life in Four Chapters* (1985), *House on Fire* (1986), *Zegen* (1987), and *The Pillow Book* (1996).

Stig Olin (September 11, 1920–June 28, 2008). The actor was born Stig Hogberg in Stockholm, Sweden and began his association with Ingmar Bergman in the 1940s, appearing in some early Bergman-written films (beginning with 1944's *Frenzy*) as well as those he directed. Olin began writing and directing films in the 1950s although he left the film industry by the early 1960s to work in radio and directing theater productions. Credits included *Crisis* (1946), *To Joy* (1950), *Summer Interlude* (1951), and *The Yellow Squadron* (1954).

Anita Page (August 4, 1910–September 6, 2008). Born Anita Pomares in Flushing, New York, the actress found success as a teenager in silent films, first working for Paramount Studios in New York before signing a contract with MGM (who changed her last name). Page had debuted as an extra in 1925's *A Kiss for Cinderella* but became a star opposite Joan Crawford in *Our Dancing Daughters* (1928). She successfully transitioned to sound films with the musical *The Broadway Melody* in 1929. Other films included *Telling the World* (1928), *While the City Sleeps* (1928), *The Flying Fleet* (1929), *Navy Blues* (1929), *Our Modern Maidens* (1929), *Speedway* (1929), *Free and Easy* (1930), *Our Blushing Brides* (1930), *The Easiest Way* (1931), *Sidewalks of New York* (1931), *Are You Listening?* (1932), *Night Court* (1932), *Skyscraper Souls* (1932), and *Jungle Bride* (1933). Her contract with MGM expired and Page made a last appearance in 1936's *Hitchhike to Heaven* before retiring to married life. After a sixty-year sabbatical, Page appeared in several low-budget films, including *Sunset After Dark* (1996), *Witchcraft XI* (2000), and *The Crawling Brain* (2002).

Joy Page (November 9, 1924–April 18, 2008). The actress was born Joy Paige in Los Angeles, the daughter of silent screen actor Jose Paige who acted under the name Don Alvarado. Warner Bros. studio chief Jack L. Warner was her stepfather, but he refused to sign her to a studio contract although Page was allowed to take acting classes. This lead to her auditioning and winning the role of Annina Brandel in *Casablanca* (1942). Other credits included *Kismet*

(1944), *Man-Eater of Kumaon* (1948), *The Bullfighter and the Lady* (1951), *Conquest of Cochise* (1953), *Fighter Attack* (1953), *The Shrike* (1955), and *Tonka* (1958). Page later worked on television before retiring in 1962.

Michael Pate (February 16, 1920–September 1, 2008). The actor was born Edward John Pate in Drummoyne, Australia. Pate acted in radio plays and onstage before getting cast in bit film parts beginning in 1940. His first significant role was in 1949's *Sons of Matthew*. Pate moved to Hollywood in 1951 to reprise his stage role in *Thunder on the Hill*. He was frequently cast in westerns, including *Hondo* (1953), *Curse of the Undead* (1959), *McLintock!* (1963), and *Major Dundee* (1965), and worked on numerous television series. Pate returned to Australia in 1968, producing the 1969 film *Age of Consent*. He wrote and produced *The Mango Tree* (1977) and adapted, directed, and produced *Tim* (1979). Pate retired from acting in 2001.

House Peters Jr. (January 12, 1916–October 1, 2008). The son of a silent screen actor, he was born Robert House Peters Jr. in New Rochelle, New York, studying drama in high school. Although his career lasted from 1935 to 1967, Peters' roles were generally as the brawny support or henchman, both in film and on television. The actor was also cast as the original Mr. Clean in Proctor & Gamble's commercials from the late 1950s to the early 1960s. Credits included *Flash Gordon* (1936), *Public Cowboy No. 1* (1937), *Under California Stars* (1948), *Outlaw Country* (1949), *Batman and Robin* (1949), *Over the Border* (1950), *Oklahoma Annie* (1952), *Black Patch* (1957), *Big Night* (1960), and *Rio Conchos* (1964). Peters' autobiography is entitled *Another Side of Hollywood*.

Joseph Pevney (September 15, 1911–May 18, 2008). The film and television director was born in New York City and began his career as a boy soprano in vaudeville. He played character roles on stage, also working as a director, and had several film roles, including *Nocturne* (1946), *Body and Soul* (1947), *The Street With No Name* (1948), and *Thieves' Highway* (1949). Pevney also gave himself a cameo in the first film he directed, *Shakedown* (1950), and he built a solid career with such films as *Iron Man* (1951), *Because of You* (1952), *Desert Legion* (1953), *Female on the Beach* (1955), *Foxfire* (1955), *Away All Boats* (1956), *Man of a Thousand Faces* (1957), *Tammy and the Bachelor* (1957), *Torpedo Run* (1958), and *The Plunderers* (1960). Pevney then turned from film to television, directing episodes of *Wagon Train, The Virginian, The Munsters, Bonanza, Adam-12, Emergency, Fantasy Island,* and *The Incredible Hulk* among other shows. Pevney's best-known television work were the fourteen episodes he directed of the original *Star Trek* series, including "The City on the Edge of Forever," "Amok Time," "Journey to Babel," and "The Trouble With Tribbles." Pevney retired in 1985.

Kate Phillips (July 19, 1913–April 18, 2008). The supporting actress was born Mary Katherine Linaker in Pine Bluffs, Arkansas. She studied at the American Academy of Dramatic Arts in New York, graduating from New York University. She signed a film contract with Warner Bros., appearing onscreen under the name Kay Linaker in such films as *The Girl from Mandalay* (1936), *Charlie Chan in Monte Carlo* (1937), *Charlie Chan in Reno* (1939), *Drums Along the Mohawk* (1939), *Charlie Chan at Treasure Island*

(1939), *Charlie Chan's Murder Cruise* (1940), *Kitty Foyle* (1940), *Blood and Sand* (1941), *Charlie Chan in Rio* (1941), *Two Weeks to Live* (1943), and *Men on Her Mind* (1944). After marrying Howard Phillips (who was an executive at NBC), she turned to teaching and co-wrote (with Theodore Simonson) the screenplay for the cult classic *The Blob* (1958).

Harold Pinter (October 10, 1930–December 24, 2008). The writer, poet, director, actor, and political activist was born in the east London borough of Hackney. He acted in school plays and briefly attended drama school before joining a touring company in 1951. Pinter also started writing and his debut effort was 1957's *The Room*, which was followed by his first full-length play, *The Birthday Party*, in 1958. Pinter wrote some thirty plays, including *The Caretaker*, *The Dumb Waiter*, *The Homecoming*, *Old Times*, *The Trial*, and *Celebration* as well as a number of screenplays. He was nominated for an Oscar® for the 1983 film version of his 1978 play *Betrayal*. Other screenplays included *The Servant* (1963), *The Pumpkin Eater* (1964), *The Quiller Memorandum* (1966), *Accident* (1967), *The Go-Between* (1970), *The Last Tycoon* (1976), *The French Lieutenant's Woman* (1981), *The Turtle Diary* (1985), *The Comfort of Strangers* (1990), *The Handmaid's Tale* (1990), and *Sleuth* (2007). Pinter was awarded the Nobel Prize for Literature in 2005 but was too ill to attend the ceremony and videotaped his acceptance speech.

Ugo Pirro (April 24, 1920–January 18, 2008). Born Ugo Mattone in Salerno, Italy, the novelist and screenwriter moved to Rome and worked as a journalist. His first script was for 1951's *Achtung! Banditti!* He received two Academy Award® nominations in 1971: best original screenplay for *Investigation of a Citizen Above Suspicion* and best adapted screenplay for *The Garden of the Finzi-Continis*. Credits included *Men and Wolves* (1956), *The Hunchback* (1960), *The Verona Trial* (1963), *To Each His Own* (1967), *The Working Class Goes to Heaven* (1971), *Property Is No Longer a Robbery* (1973), *Blood Brothers* (1974), *Ogro* (1979), and *Plebian Nymph* (1996). Pirro published his autobiography, *Just a Name On the Credit Titles,* in 1998.

Suzanne Pleshette (January 31, 1937–January 19, 2008). Born in Brooklyn Heights, New York, the husky-voiced actress was known for her sitcom role as Emily Hartley on *The Bob Newhart Show* (1972–78). Pleshette attended the New York High School for the Performing Arts and spent two years at the Neighborhood Playhouse School of the Theatre. She made both her television and stage debuts in 1957 and her film debut in 1958's *The Geisha Boy.* Other credits included *Rome Adventure* (1962), *The Birds* (1963), *40 Pounds of Trouble* (1963), *A Distant Trumpet* (1964), *Fate Is the Hunter* (1964), *Youngblood Hawke* (1964), *A Rage to Live* (1965), *Nevada Smith* (1966), *The Ugly Dachshund* (1966), *The Adventures of Bullwhip Griffin* (1967), *Blackbeard's Ghost* (1968), *If It's Tuesday, This Must Be Belgium* (1969), *The Shaggy D.A.* (1976), and *Leona Helmsley: The Queen of Mean* (1991).

Sydney Pollack (July 1, 1934–May 26, 2008). The film director, producer, and actor was born in Lafayette, Indiana and moved to New York after high school to attend the Neighborhood Playhouse School of the Theatre. After his Army service, Pollack began acting and directing for television in the 1950s. He made his directorial film debut with 1965's *The Slender Thread.* Other directorial credits included *The Scalphunters* (1968), *They Shoot Horses, Don't They?* (1969), *The Yakuza* (1975), *Bobby Deerfield* (1977), *Absence of Malice* (1981), *Tootsie* (1982, Pollack also played the part of the agent), *The Firm* (1993), *Sabrina* (1995), *Random Hearts* (1999), and *The Interpreter* (2005). Pollack met his friend and collaborator Robert Redford when Pollack made his screen-acting debut in 1962's *War Hunt.* Pollack directed Redford in *This Property Is Condemned* (1966), *Jeremiah Johnson* (1972), *The Way We Were* (1973), *Three Days of the Condor* (1975), *The Electric Horseman* (1979), *Out of Africa* (1985, Pollack won the best director Oscar®), and *Havana* (1990). Among his acting credits were *Husbands and Wives* (1992), *The Player* (1992), *Eyes Wide Shut* (1999), *Michael Clayton* (2007), and *Made of Honor* (2008).

Robert Prosky (December 13, 1930–December 8, 2008). The character actor was born Robert Porzuczek in Philadelphia, Pennsylvania. Prosky worked as a bookkeeper but also studied at the American Theater Wing in New York. His acting break came in 1958 with the Arena Stage in Washington, DC and he played some 130 roles over twenty-three seasons at the theater. He also received Tony nominations for *Glengarry Glen Ross* (1984) and *A Walk in the Woods* (1988). Prosky made his screen debut in 1981's *Thief.* Other screen credits included *Christine* (1983), *The Natural* (1984), *Broadcast News* (1987), *Things Change* (1988), *Hoffa* (1992), *Mrs. Doubtfire* (1993), *Rudy* (1993), *Miracle on 34th Street* (1994), *Dead Man Walking* (1995), and *Mad City* (1997). Prosky also frequently appeared on television and played the role of desk sergeant Stan Jablonski on *Hill Street Blues* from 1984 to 1987.

Jerry Reed (March 20, 1937–September 1, 2008). The singer, songwriter, and actor was born Jerry Reed Hubbard in Atlanta, Georgia. He received his first recording contract with Capitol Records in 1955 and they dropped his surname for promotional purposes, but he found his greatest recording success after signing with RCA in 1965. Burt Reynolds offered Reed a role in his 1975 film *WW and the Dixie Kings* and Reed would also appear with the actor in *Gator* (1976), *Smokey and the Bandit* (1977) and its 1980 and 1983 sequels. Other films included *The Concrete Cowboys* (1979), *Hot Stuff* (1980), *Survivors* (1983), *Bat 21* (1988), and *The Waterboy* (1998).

Brad Renfro (July 25, 1982–January 15, 2008). Born in Knoxville, Tennessee, the actor made an impressive debut at the age of twelve in 1994's *The Client,* but Renfro's later life would be marred by reckless behavior, arrests, and alcohol and drug addiction, and he died of a drug overdose. Screen credits included *The Cure* (1995), *Sleepers* (1996), *Apt Pupil* (1998), *Bully* (2001), *Ghost World* (2001), *The Jacket* (2005), and *The Informers* (2008).

Terence Rigby (January 2, 1937–August 10, 2008). The character actor was born in Birmingham, England and was best-known for his stage performances although he also frequently worked on television and had some film roles. Rigby studied at the Royal Academy of Dramatic Arts before going into repertory theater. Credits included *Get Carter* (1971), *The Dogs of War* (1980), *Tinker, Tailor, Solider, Spy* (1980), *The Hound of the Baskervilles* (1982),

Scandal (1989), *Tomorrow Never Dies* (1997), *Mona Lisa Smile* (2003), and *Flick* (2007).

Dino Risi (December 23, 1916–June 7, 2008). Born in Milan, Italy, the director and writer first studied medicine (his father was a doctor at the La Scala opera house). During World War II, his family took refuge in Geneva, Switzerland and Risi began writing film criticism, which lead to some work as an assistant director after his move to Rome. Risi directed several documentaries before directing (and co-writing) his first feature, 1951's *Vacation With a Gangster*. Risi made fifteen films with actor Vittorio Gassman, including 1974's *Profumo di Donna (Scent of a Woman)*, which received Oscar® nominations for best foreign language film and best adapted screenplay. Their other work together included *Love and Larceny* (1959), *Behind Closed Doors* (1960), *The Easy Life* (1962), *The March to Rome* (1962), *The Monsters* (1963), *The Tiger and the Pussycat* (1967), *In the Name of the Italian People* (1972), and *Dear Dad* (1979). Other films included *Scandal in Sorrento* (1955), *Poor But Beautiful* (1956), *A Difficult Life* (1961), *The Priest's Wife* (1970), and *Dirty Weekend* (1973). Risi retired in 2002 and published his autobiography, *I Miei Mostri (My Monsters)* in 2004.

Lawrence Roman (May 30, 1921–May 18, 2008). The screenwriter was born in Jersey City, New Jersey although his family moved to Los Angeles in the early 1930s. Roman graduated from UCLA in 1942 and, after his Army service, became a writer at CBS Radio before turning to plays and films. Roman adapted his 1960 Broadway hit *Under the Yum Yum Tree* for the 1963 film version. Other credits included *Vice Squad* (1953), *A Kiss Before Dying* (1956), *Paper Lion* (1968), *A Warm December* (1973), *McQ* (1974), *Anatomy of an Illness* (1984), and *The Ernest Green Story* (1993).

Leonard Rosenman (September 7, 1924–March 4, 2008). The composer was born in Brooklyn, New York and he earned a music degree from the University of California, Berkeley. Rosenman returned to New York, intending to be a concert composer, but supported himself teaching music. Actor James Dean became a friend and student and he introduced Rosenman to director Elia Kazan who hired him to write the score for the film *East of Eden* (1955). Rosenman won two Oscars® for best musical adaptation for *Barry Lyndon* (1975) and *Bound for Glory* (1976) and received nominations for *Cross Creek* (1983) and *Star Trek IV: The Voyage Home* (1986). Other work included *The Cobweb* (1955), *Rebel Without a Cause* (1955), *The Rise and Fall of Legs Diamond* (1960), *Hell Is for Heroes* (1962), *Fantastic Voyage* (1966), *Beneath the Planet of the Apes* (1970), *A Man Called Horse* (1970), *Battle for the Planet of the Apes* (1973), *Sybil* (1976), *The Lord of the Rings* (1978), *Friendly Fire* (1979), and *RoboCop 2* (1990).

Cirio Santiago (January 18, 1936–September 26, 2008). The writer, producer, and director was born in Manila, the Philippines and worked on more than 100 films. His father founded the film company Premiere Productions in 1936 and Santiago got his start working on action films. He made some twenty movies for Roger Corman, including *The Big Doll House* (1971), *Women in Cages* (1971), *The Big Bird Cage* (1972), *Hell Cats* (1972), and *Fly Me* (1973). Santiago worked in various exploitation genres; films included *Savage!* (1973), *TNT Jackson* (1975), *Ebony, Ivory and Jade* (1976), *Vampire Hookers* (1978), *Stryker* (1983), *Naked Vengeance* (1985), *Equalizer 2000* (1986), *The Sisterhood* (1988), *Nam Angels* (1989), *Dune Warriors* (1990), *The Call of Duty* (1992), *Caged Heat 2: Stripped of Freedom* (1994), *Vulcan* (1997), and *Aladdin and the Adventure of All Time* (1999). At the time of his death, Santiago has finished the movie *Road Raiders*.

Ann Savage (February 19, 1921–December 25, 2008). The B-movie actress was born Bernice Maxine Lyon in Columbia, South Carolina. Savage's family later moved to Los Angeles and she enrolled in acting school, which lead to a contract at Columbia Pictures. Her first credit was in 1943's *One Dangerous Night* and that same year she also appeared in *After Midnight With Boston Blackie, Saddles and Sagebrush, Two Senoritas from Chicago, Passport to Suez, Dangerous Blondes, Footlight Glamour, Klondike Kate,* and *What a Woman!* Savage was often cast as the bad girl and she won acclaim for 1945's *Detour* but was unimpressed by most of her roles. After her marriage to agent Bert D' Armand in 1947, Savage did some television work and commercials, later working as a legal secretary. She returned to acting for the 1986 film *Fire With Fire* and her last role was as the mother in 2007's *My Winnipeg*. Other screen credits included *Two-Man Submarine, Ever Since Venus, The Unwritten Code,* and *Dancing In Manhattan* (all 1944), *Scared Stiff, Midnight Manhunt, Apology for Murder,* and *The Spider* (all 1945), *The Dark Horse, The Last Crooked Mile, Lady Chaser,* and *Renegade Girl* (all 1946), *Jungle Flight* (1947), *Satan's Cradle* (1949), *Pier 23* (1951), and *The Woman They Almost Lynched* (1953).

Roy Scheider (November 10, 1932–February 10, 2008). Born in Orange, New Jersey, the actor took drama classes at Franklin and Marshall College and worked in the theater before making his film debut in the low-budget horror film *The Curse of the Living Corpse* (1964). Scheider received Oscar® nominations for best supporting actor for *The French Connection* (1971) and best actor for *All That Jazz* (1979). Credits included *Stiletto* (1969), *Puzzle of a Downfall Child* (1970), *Klute* (1971), *The Seven-Ups* (1973), *Jaws* (1975), *The Marathon Man* (1976), *Sorcerer* (1977), *Jaws 2* (1978), *The Last Embrace* (1979), *Still of the Night* (1982), *Blue Thunder* (1983), *The Fourth War* (1990), *The Russia House* (1990), *Naked Lunch* (1991), *Romeo Is Bleeding* (1993), and *The Punisher* (2004).

Paul Scofield (January 21, 1922–March 19, 2008). The actor was born David Paul Scofield in Hurstpierpoint, England and made his career in the theater, beginning in repertory theater in the 1940s and working regularly with the Royal Shakespeare company and the National Theatre. His best-known film role was as Sir Thomas More in *A Man for All Seasons*, which he first played on the London stage in 1960 before reprising it for the 1966 film for which he won a best actor Academy Award®. Screen credits included *That Lady* (1955), *A Delicate Balance* (1974), *Henry V* (1988), *When the Whales Came* (1989), *Hamlet* (1990), *Utz* (1991), *Quiz Show* (1995), and *The Crucible* (1996).

Leopoldo Serran (May 6, 1942–August 20, 2008). The screenwriter was born in Rio de Janeiro, Brazil. While studying to become a lawyer at the Pontificia Universidade Catolica, Serran met several filmmakers, including Carlos

Diegues with whom he would make his first film, *Ganga Zumba* (1963). Other credits included *The Big City* (1966), *Dona Flor and Her Two Husbands* (1976), *Bye, Bye Brazil* (1979), *Gabriela, Clove and Cinnamon* (1983), *O Quatrilho* (1996), *Four Days in September* (1997), and *Where You Walk* (2004).

Bob Spiers (September 27, 1945–December 9, 2008). The director was born in Glasgow, Scotland but his family moved to London when Spiers was thirteen. He worked in amateur theatricals before joining the BBC in 1967 where he worked as a production assistant before turning to directing with such television comedies as *Dad's Army, Are You Being Served?, Fawlty Towers,* and *Absolutely Fabulous* among other series. Spiers also directed three films: *Spice World* (1997), *That Darn Cat* (1997), and *Kevin of the North* (2001).

Elizabeth Spriggs (September 18, 1929–July 2, 2008). The character actress was born in Buxton, England and taught speech and drama before working in a number of repertory theaters until gaining national recognition after joining the Royal Shakespeare Company in 1962. Spriggs also worked frequently on television and had a recurring role in the series *Shine on Harvey Moon* (1982–85). Credits included *Work Is a Four-Letter Word* (1968), *Three Into Two Won't Go* (1969), *Oranges Are Not the Only Fruit* (1989), *Middlemarch* (1994), *Sense and Sensibility* (1996), *Harry Potter and the Sorcerer's Stone* (2001), *Victoria and Albert* (2001), and *Shackleton* (2002).

Malvin Wald (August 8, 1917–March 6, 2008). Born in Brooklyn, New York, the screenwriter graduated from Brooklyn College in 1936 and followed his older brother Jerry (a screenwriter and producer) to Hollywood. During World War II, Wald was assigned to the First Motion Picture Unit of the Army Air Corp and wrote military training and recruitment films. Wald was nominated for an Academy Award® for *The Naked City* (1948), which concluded with the line, "There are eight million stories in the naked city. This has been one of them." (A television show of the same name aired from 1958 to 1963.) Other credits included *Jive Junction* (1943), *Behind Locked Doors* (1948), *Outrage* (1950), and *Battle Taxi* (1955). Wald wrote frequently for television and taught screenwriting at the University of Southern California.

David Watkin (March 23, 1925–February 19, 2008). The cinematographer was born in Margate, England. His father was a lawyer for the railways and Watkin worked with the film unit of British Railways and British Transport Films making travelogues. Beginning in 1960, he freelanced on a number of television commercials before shooting his first feature, 1965's *The Knack*, directed by Richard Lester. Lester and Watkin then worked together on *Help!* (1965) as well as *How I Won the War* (1967), *The Bed Sitting Room* (1969), *The Three Musketeers* (1973), *The Four Musketeers* (1975), *Robin and Marian* (1976), and *Return of the Musketeers* (1989). Watkin received a cinematography Oscar® for *Out of Africa* (1985). Other credits included *The Charge of the Light Brigade* (1968), *Catch-22* (1970), *The Devils* (1971), *Jesus of Nazareth* (1977), *Chariots of Fire* (1981), *Yentl* (1983), *Hotel New Hampshire* (1984), *Moonstruck* (1987), *Masquerade* (1988), *Journey to the Center of the Earth* (1989), *Hamlet* (1990), *Memphis Belle* (1990),

and *Tea with Mussolini* (1999). Watkin wrote two volumes of memoirs: *Why Is There Only One Word for Thesaurus?* and *Was Clara Schumann a Fag Hag?*

Donald E(dwin) Westlake (July 12, 1933–December 31, 2008). The prolific writer was born in Brooklyn, New York and attended several colleges although he did not graduate. Westlake wrote more than 100 books and used a number of pseudonyms, including Richard Stark, Tucker Coe, Samuel Holt, and Edwin West. His first novel, *The Mercenaries*, was published in 1960 and his last novel, *Get Real*, was published in 2009. Under the Westlake name, he wrote a series of books featuring comic criminal character John Dortmunder and as Richard Stark he wrote about an anti-hero criminal named Parker, which were adapted for the films *Point Blank* (1967) and *Payback* (1999). More than fifteen of his novels were adapted for film, including *The Split* (1968), *The Hot Rock* (1972), *The Outfit* (1973), *Bank Shot* (1974), *Slayground* (1983), *The Hook* (2004), and *The Ax* (2005). Westlake also wrote several screenplays and was nominated for an Academy Award® for *The Grifters* (1990). Other screenplays included *The Stepfather* (1987), *Why Me?* (1990), and *Ripley Under Ground* (2005). Westlake was awarded the title of Grand Master from the Mystery Writers of America in 1993.

Claude Whatham (December 7, 1927–January 4, 2008). Born in Manchester, England, the director first studied stage and costume design and worked as a set designer in the theater before joining the BBC. Deciding to try directing, Whatham took a training course with Granada Television and began directing programs in 1956. Among his notable television productions were *A Voyage Round My Father* (1969), *Cider with Rosie* (1971), *Elizabeth R* (1971), and *Disraeli* (1978). Whatham made his film debut with 1973's *That'll Be the Day*; other credits included *All Creatures Great and Small* (1974), *Swallows and Amazons* (1974), and *Buddy's Song* (1990).

Christopher Wicking (January 10, 1943–October 13, 2008). Born in London, England, the screenwriter began his career as a film critic, working for *Cahiers du Cinema, Positif, Time Out,* and *Monthly Film Bulletin*. Wicking also worked as a film booker and an assistant film editor before receiving his first screenwriting credit for 1969's *The Oblong Box* for director Gordon Hessler. They then went on to collaborate on *Cry of the Banshee* (1970), *Scream and Scream Again* (1970), *Murders in the Rue Morgue* (1971), and *Medusa* (1973). Wicking's other credits included *Blood from the Mummy's Tomb* (1971), *Venom* (1971), *Demons of the Mind* (1972), *To the Devil a Daughter* (1976), *Lady Chatterley's Lover* (1981), *Absolute Beginners* (1986), *Dream Demon* (1988), *The Way to Dusty Death* (1995), and *On Dangerous Ground* (1996).

Richard Widmark (December 26, 1914–March 24, 2008). The actor was born in Sunrise, Minnesota and was active in the drama department in high school and at Lake Forest College. Widmark moved to New York in 1938 and started working in radio; he made his Broadway debut in 1943. He made a notable screen debut as sadistic gangster Tommy Udo in 1947's *Kiss of Death* for which he received his only Oscar® nomination (for best supporting actor). Widmark was signed to a contract with 20th Century Fox, who promptly typecast him as a heavy. After his contract expired, Widmark decided to work independently and formed his own company, Heath Productions. Credits included *Street With No Name* (1948), *Road House* (1948), *Yellow Sky* (1948), *Down to the Sea in Ships* (1949), *Halls of Montezuma* (1950), *Night and the City* (1950), *No Way Out* (1950), *Panic in the Streets* (1950), *Red Skies of Montana* (1952), *Pickup on South Street* (1953), *Broken Lance* (1954), *Time Limit* (1957), *The Alamo* (1960), *Judgment at Nuremberg* (1961), *The Secret Ways* (1961), *Two Rode Together* (1961), *Cheyenne Autumn* (1964), *The Long Ships* (1964), *The Bedford Incident* (1965), *Alvarez Kelly* (1966), *The Way West* (1967), *Madigan* (1968; he played the same role in the 1972 television series), *Murder on the Orient Express* (1974), *Twilight's Last Gleaming* (1977), *Coma* (1978), *Against All Odds* (1984), *Cold Sassy Tree* (1989), and *True Colors* (1991).

Stan Winston (April 7, 1946–June 15, 008). Born in Arlington, Virginia, Winston was a film creature and makeup designer and a special-effects expert. He won Oscars® for his work on *Aliens* (1986), *Terminator 2: Judgment Day* (1991), and *Jurassic Park* (1993), and received nominations for *Heartbeeps* (1981), *Predator* (1987), *Edward Scissorhands* (1990), *Batman Returns* (1992), *The Lost World: Jurassic Park* (1997), and *AI: Artificial Intelligence* (2001). Winston also won Emmys for *Gargoyles* (1972) and *The Autobiography of Miss Jane Pittman* (1974). He studied at the University of Virginia, and then moved to Hollywood in 1969 for an acting career. When that failed, Winston joined an apprenticeship program at Walt Disney Studios as a makeup artist for three years. He started his own company, Stan Winston Studios, in 1972. Credits included *WC Fields and Me* (1976), *The Wiz* (1978), *The Terminator* (1984), *Interview With the Vampire* (1994), *Congo* (1995), *End of Days* (1999), *Pearl Harbor* (2001), *Big Fish* (2003), *Terminator 3: Rise of the Machines* (2003), *Constantine* (2005), and *Iron Man* (2008). Winston also wrote and directed the 1988 horror film *Pumpkinhead.*

Jin Xie (November 21, 1923–October 18, 2008). The director was born in Shaoxing, China and attended the Jiang-an school of dramatic art. Xie joined the Datong film studio in 1949 and directed his first film, *A Crisis,* in 1953. During the cultural revolution, Xie was under house arrest and in a labor camp from which he was released to direct propaganda films, including the 1970 remake of his 1961 film *The Red Detachment of Women.* Other credits included *Woman Basketball Player Number Five* (1957), *Two Stage Sisters* (1965), *Legend of the Tianyun Mountain* (1980), *Hibiscus Town* (1986), *The Last Aristocrats* (1989), *The Opium War* (1997), and *Woman Soccer Player Number Nine* (2001).

Selected Film Books of 2007

Albright, Brian. *Wild Beyond Belief! Interviews with Exploitation Filmmakers of the 1960s and 1970s.* McFarland, 2008. Interviews with sixteen directors, performers, screenwriters, and stuntmen of independent, low-budget western, biker, horror, and other genre releases.

Andersen, Christopher. *Somewhere in Heaven: The Remarkable Love Story of Dana and Christopher Reeve.* Hyperion, 2008. A portrait of the couple that includes both their public and private lives and struggles.

Anderson, John, and David Sterritt. *The B List: The National Society of Film Critics on the Low-Budget Beauties, Genre-Bending Mavericks, and Cult Classics We Love.* Da Capo Press, 2008. Collection of idiosyncratic film titles that fall outside the mainstream.

Andrews, Julie. *Home: A Memoir of My Early Years.* Hyperion, 2008. The actress covers her difficult childhood and her career touring the English music halls beginning at the age of nine as well as her theater work and stage success in *My Fair Lady*. This volume concludes in 1963 with Andrews about to film Disney's *Mary Poppins*.

Baker, Brian. *Masculinity in Fiction and Film: Representing Men in Popular Genres, 1945–2000.* Continuum, 2008. Analyzes the way masculinity has been depicted in popular culture in Britain and the United States in various genres, including spy fiction, science fiction, westerns, and police thrillers.

Bapis, Elaine M. *Camera and Action: American Film as Agent of Social Change, 1965–1975.* McFarland, 2008. Study examines the changes in the industry, audiences, and feature films, including the rise of independent filmmaking.

Barsan, Michael. *True West: An Illustrated Guide to the Heyday of the Western.* Texas Christian University Press, 2008. Showcases classic western films, novels, comics, soundtracks, television shows, toys, and other western memorabilia.

Bean, Shawn C. *The First Hollywood: Florida and the Golden Age of Silent Filmmaking.* University Press of Florida, 2008. Looks at the rise and fall of Jacksonville, Florida's film industry and the fifteen film companies that worked in the area from 1908 to 1928.

Borgnine, Ernest. *Ernie: The Autobiography.* Kensington/Citadel, 2008. Borgnine reflects on a career that spans six decades and includes more than 190 film and television roles as well as his childhood and naval career.

Briley, Ron, Michael K. Schoenecke, and Deborah A. Carmichael, editors. *All-Stars and Movie Stars: Sports in Film and History.* University Press of Kentucky, 2008. Examines the interplay between sports films and such defining cultural characteristics as race, gender, and sexuality.

Brody, Richard. *Everything Is Cinema: The Working Life of Jean-Luc Godard.* Metropolitan, 2008. Critical biography of one of the leading innovators of French New Wave includes interviews with colleagues, friends, and family.

Carroll, Diahann, with Bob Morris. *The Legs Are the Last to Go: Aging, Acting, Marrying, and Other Things I Learned the Hard Way.* Amistad, 2008. Autobiography of the actress/singer, who astutely analyzes the highs and lows of her career and personal struggles.

Carter, David. *The Western.* Oldcastle Books/Kamera Books, 2008. A basic reference work to the major directors and noteworthy films of the genre as well as the writers and folk heroes associated with the western.

Chandler, Charlotte. *Not the Girl Next Door—Joan Crawford, a Personal Biography.* Simon & Schuster, 2008. Offers brief descriptions of Crawford's films and her studio work and a discreet view of her personal life with interviews from Crawford and other film personages.

Cohen, David S. *Screen Plays: How 25 Scripts Made It to a Theater Near You—For Better or Worse.* HarperEntertainment, 2008. *Variety* reporter Cohen reveals how twenty-five films went from the script stage to film release, including *American Beauty, Black Hawk Down, Lost in Translation,* and *Troy.*

Conley, Kevin. *The Full Burn: On the Set, At the Bar, Behind the Wheel and Over the Edge with Hollywood Stuntmen.* Bloomsbury, 2008. Describes the physical skills, preparation, and cinematic challenges behind a stuntman's work; includes numerous interviews.

Cox, Alex. *X Films: True Confessions of a Radical Filmmaker.* Soft Skull Press, 2008. Autobiography of the independent filmmaker that discusses the ten films he's made as well as his thoughts on the filmmaking process.

Cox, Stephen, and Kevin Marhanka. *The Incredible Mr. Don Knotts.* Cumberland House Publishing, 2008. The authors discuss Knotts' forty feature-film career, which began in 1958 and lasted until 1998. Includes interviews with Knotts as well as many of his co-stars.

Crane, Cheryl. *Lana: The Memories, the Myths, the Movies.* Running Press, 2008. The actress's daughter talks about her mother's career and life, including her marriages and trial for murder.

Curtis, Tony, and Peter Golenbock. *American Prince: A Memoir.* Harmony Books, 2008. Curtis offers a no-holds-barred look at his career, friends, and personal life, including his marriages and recovery from addictions.

Dalle Vacche, Angela. *Diva: Defiance and Passion in Early Italian Cinema.* University of Texas Press, 2008. Analyzes some seventy films made prior to World War I that explore the persona of the modern Italian woman.

Dance, Robert, and John Russell Taylor. *Glamour of the Gods.* Steidl & Partners, 2008. Survey of Hollywood photo-portraiture from 1920–1960, drawn from the archive of the John Kobal Foundation.

De Winter, Helen. *What I Really Want to Do Is Produce: Top Producers Talk Movies and Money.* Macmillan, 2008. Looks at what a producer actually does on a film, including raising money and publicizing the production.

Detweiler, Craig. *Into the Dark: Seeing the Sacred in the Top Films of the 21ˢᵗ Century.* Baker Academic, 2008. Offers theological interpretations of contemporary movies and how they provide spiritual meaning.

Dixon, Wheeler Winston, and Gwendolyn Audrey Foster. *A Short History of Film.* Rutgers University Press, 2008. A detailed overview of the major movements, directors, studios, and genres from the 1880s to the present in Hollywood and world cinema.

Dobrenko, Evgeny. *Stalinist Cinema and the Production of History.* Yale University Press, 2008. Looks at Stalinist historical films and novels as an effective form of propaganda.

Donovan, Barna William. *The Asian Influence on Hollywood Action Films.* McFarland, 2008. Showcases the influence of Eastern popular culture on American cinema from low-budget martial arts movies to blockbusters.

Dubas, Rita. *Shirley Temple: A Pictorial History of the World's Greatest Child Star.* Applause, 2008. Heavily illustrated art book offers a concise history of the child star as well as the collectibles bearing her image.

Ebert, Roger. *Scorsese by Ebert.* University of Chicago Press, 2008. The film critic compiles his reviews of every Scorsese film from 1967 to 2008 as well as his interviews with the director over a twenty-five year period.

Eliot, Marc. *Reagan: The Hollywood Years.* Harmony, 2008. Examines Ronald Reagan's thirty-year film and television career, his personal life, and his transition into politics.

Epstein, Joseph. *Fred Astaire.* Yale University Press, 2008. Biography of the dancer/actor, including his early career with his sister Adele, Astaire's work habits, and his movie dance partners.

Fojas, Camilla. *Border Bandits: Hollywood on the Southern Frontier.* University of Texas Press, 2008. An analysis of how Hollywood films depict the border between the United States and Mexico to tell their stories, including westerns, drug-trafficking and immigration films, and Latino cinema.

Forrest, Jennifer, editor. *The Legend Returns and Dies Harder Another Day: Essays on Film Series.* McFarland, 2008. Examines a selection of film series from the silent era, Classic Hollywood cinema, and New Hollywood cinema.

Fujiwara, Chris. *The World and Its Doubts: The Life and Work of Otto Preminger.* Faber and Faber, 2008. Biography of the director (and sometime actor) and his volatile personality and work methods with each chapter covering a single movie.

Fuller-Seeley, Kathryn, editor. *Hollywood in the Neighborhood: Historical Case Studies of Local Moviegoing.* University of California Press, 2008. Essays on the social and cultural changes wrought by motion picture cinemas opening in America's small cities and towns.

Galbraith, Stuart, IV. *The Toho Studios Story: A History and Complete Filmography.* Scarecrow Press, 2008. A chronological presentation of the films produced and/or distributed by the Japanese company since its inception in 1933.

Gallagher, Gary W. *Causes Won, Lost, and Forgotten: How Hollywood and Popular Art Shape What We Know About the Civil War.* University of North Carolina Press, 2008. Civil War historian Gallagher surveys how the popular media has reflected and influenced the political, social, and racial ideas of their times about the war.

Galloway, Patrick. *Warring Clans, Flashing Blades: A Samurai Film Companion.* Stone Bridge Press, 2008. Looks at fifty martial arts films and such spin-off genres as yakuza, ninja, and matatabi.

Gans, Eric. *Carole Landis: A Most Beautiful Girl.* University Press of Mississippi, 2008. Biography of the actress covers her Hollywood career and WWII USO performances to her suicide in 1948.

Giesen, Rolf. *Special Effects Artists: A Worldwide Biographical Dictionary of the Pre-Digital Era.* McFarland, 2008. Offers career synopses and movie credits for special effects artists from the early years of cinematography to the end of the mechanical age of filmmaking.

Graham, Don. *State Fare: An Irreverent Guide to Texas Movies.* Texas Christian University Press, 2008. Offers an overview of Texas in the movies and a detailed commentary on films about the Lone Star State.

Graver, Gary, with Andrew J. Rausch. *Making Movies with Orson Welles: A Memoir.* Scarecrow Press, 2008. Graver recounts offering his services as a cinematographer to Welles in 1970 and their subsequent collaboration on more than a dozen projects until Welles' death in 1995.

Hamilton, George, and William Stadiem. *Don't Mind If I Do.* Touchstone, 2008. Self-deprecating memoir about the well-tanned actor's Hollywood film career to his appearance on *Dancing with the Stars.*

Haydock, Nickolas. *Movie Medievalism: The Imaginary Middle Ages.* McFarland, 2008. Explores how life in the Middle Ages has been depicted in films.

Herzberg, Bob. *Savages and Saints: The Changing Image of American Indians in Westerns.* McFarland, 2008. Contrasts the fictionalized images of Native Americans portrayed in western films against the historical reality of life on the frontier.

Herzogenrath, Bernd, editor. *The Cinema of Tod Browning: Essays of the Macabre and Grotesque.* McFarland, 2008. Film scholars study the major themes apparent in Browning's films, including parenthood, disability, masochism, surrealism, and the occult.

Hill, Derek. *Charlie Kaufman and Hollywood's Merry Band of Pranksters, Fabulists and Dreamers: An Excursion into the American New Wave.* Kamera Books, 2008. Looks at the filmmakers and filmmaking provocateur movement of the 1990s and beyond, including Sofia Coppola, Wes Anderson, Spike Jonze, David O. Russell, and others.

Hogan, Patrick Colm. *Understanding Indian Movies: Culture, Cognition, and Cinematic Imagination.* University of Texas Press, 2008. Presents cultural contexts for understanding Indian films, including religions and history.

Hughes, Howard. *Stagecoach to Tombstone: The Filmgoers' Guide to Great Westerns.* Macmillan, 2008. An exploration of twenty-seven key western films from well-known blockbusters to B-movies.

Jacobs, Lea. *The Decline of Sentiment: American Films in the 1920s.* University of California Press, 2008. Documents the modernization of Hollywood film style and narrative form in films from the Jazz Age.

Jordan, Leslie. *My Trip Down the Pink Carpet.* Simon Spotlight Entertainment, 2008. The diminutive actor discusses his southern childhood and growing up gay, his move to Hollywood and his career as a supporting actor as well as dealing with his alcohol addiction.

Jordan, Stephen C. *Hollywood's Original Rat Pack: The Bards of Bundy Drive.* Scarecrow Press, 2008. Jordan revisits antics and scandals of the actors, writers, and artists (John Barrymore, Errol Flynn, Ben Hecht, John Decker, and others) who made up the group known as the Bundy Drive Boys.

Kanin, Dan. *The Comedy of Charlie Chaplin: Artistry in Motion.* Scarecrow Press, 2008. Examines how Chaplin combined his talents in mime, dance, acting, music, writing, and directing to the medium of film.

Kaufman, David. *Doris Day: The Untold Story of the Girl Next Door.* Virgin, 2008. Biography of the actress includes interviews with more than 150 people on her career and private life.

Kay, Glenn. *Zombie Movies: The Ultimate Guide.* Chicago Review Press, 2008. Traces the evolution of the zombie genre, reviews nearly 300 zombie films, and includes interviews with actors, directors, makeup people, and others.

Keaney, Michael F. *British Film Noir Guide.* McFarland, 2008. Presents 369 British films produced between 1937 and 1964 that conform to the film noir canon.

Kelly, Richard, editor. *10 Bad Dates with De Niro: A Book of Alternative Movie Lists.* Rookery Press, 2008. A collection of eighty essays that offer ten best lists on arcane movie topics such as great movie endings, poetry in films, animal performances, cross-dressing, and worst wigs.

Kimmel, Daniel M. *I'll Have What She's Having: Behind the Scenes of the Great Romantic Comedies.* Ivan R. Dee, 2008. Kimmel looks at fifteen romantic comedies to see what makes them classics of the genre, from 1932's *Trouble in Paradise* to 2003's *Love, Actually.*

King, Rob. *The Fun Factory: The Keystone Film Company and the Emergence of Mass Culture.* University of California Press, 2008. Explores how the Keystone Film Company, founded in 1912, brought popular working-class ideas to its comic shorts.

Knight, Timothy. *Great Kisses…and Famous Lines Right Out of the Movies.* HarperCollins, 2008. Features photos of fifty notable screen kisses and reprints the dialogue that preceded the moment.

Koszarski, Richard. *Hollywood on the Hudson: Film and Television in New York from Griffith to Sarnoff.* Rutgers University Press, 2008. Examines how the East Coast continued to play a significant role in film and television production in the first half of the 20th century even after major studio production moved to Southern California.

Koven, Mikel J. *Film, Folklore and Urban Legends.* Scarecrow Press, 2008. An analysis of film and television narratives that utilize pop culture folklore, including *Candyman, Urban Legend, I Know What You Did Last Summer, Halloween,* and others.

Kowalski, Dean A., editor. *Steven Spielberg and Philosophy: We're Gonna Need a Bigger Book.* University Press of Kentucky, 2008. Philosophers explore such Spielberg themes as moral character, human rights, family ethics, and religion.

Lamberson, Gregory. *Cheap Scares! Low Budget Horror Filmmakers Share Their Secrets.* McFarland, 2008. The author draws on his own experience creating low-budget movies from outlines to distribution.

Lanzoni, Remi Fournier. *Comedy Italian Style: The Golden Age of Italian Film Comedies.* Continuum, 2008. Explores the commedia all'italiana genre from the late 1950s through the 1970s.

Lee, Nathan. *From Star Wars to Jackass: 101 Movies for the Whatever Generation.* Alyson Books, 2008. A survey of 101 films from the 1980s to the present that have importance to a generation raised with multiple media technologies.

Lindlof, Thomas R. *Hollywood Under Siege: Martin Scorsese, the Religious Right, and the Culture Wars.* University Press of

Kentucky, 2008. Chronicles the production and release of Scorsese's film *The Last Temptation of Christ* and the strong protests that were organized by conservative Christian groups.

Lisanti, Tom. *Glamour Girls of Sixties Hollywood: Seventy-Five Profiles.* McFarland, 2008. Offers biographical profiles of the models, centerfolds, beauty queens, and showgirls who provided decoration to film and television series.

Louvish, Simon. *Cecil B. DeMille: A Life in Art.* St. Martin's/Dunne, 2008. This unauthorized survey of the career of the pioneering director received no help from the DeMille estate so the author focuses primarily on the films and not DeMille's personal life.

Lovell, Glenn. *Escape Artist: The Life and Films of John Sturges.* University of Wisconsin Press, 2008. Biography of one of the first independent producer-directors in Hollywood as well as critical analyses of his films.

Lowenstein, Stephen, editor. *My First Movie: Take Two.* Pantheon, 2008. Candid interviews from such directors as Richard Linklater, Terry Gilliam, Shekhar Kapur, Takeshi Kitano, Sam Mendes, and others on making their first feature films.

MacDonald, Scott. *Canyon Cinema: The Life and Times of an Independent Film Distributor.* University of California Press, 2008. Chronicles the film exhibition and distribution collective that began in the San Francisco Bay Area in the 1960s.

Maren, Jerry. *Short and Sweet: The Life and Times of the Lollipop Munchkin.* Cumberland House Press, 2008. Illustrated discussion by Maren of his sixty-year career, including his films, television, and commercial work.

Mark, Mary Ellen. *Seen Behind the Scene.* Phaidon Press, 2008. Covers the best images from more than 100 film sets from the 1960s to the present of Mark's work as a special stills photographer.

McCarty, Michael. *Modern Mythmakers: Interviews with Horror, Science Fiction and Fantasy Writers and Filmmakers.* McFarland, 2008. Original interviews from Herschell Gordon Lewis, Elvira, Ray Bradbury, Laurell K. Hamilton, and many others.

McIntosh, Shawn, and Marc Leverette, editors. *Zombie Culture: Autopsies of the Living Dead.* Scarecrow Press, 2008. Essays on how zombies have been depicted in film and popular culture in the 20th century.

McLean, Adrienne L. *Dying Swans and Madmen: Ballet, the Body, and Narrative Cinema.* Rutgers University Press, 2008. Explores how ballet and its dancers have been depicted in commercial films.

McNally, Peter. *Bette Davis: The Performances That Made Her Great.* McFarland, 2008. Detailed analyses of the actress' top twelve films from 1938 to 1987.

Meehan, Paul. *Tech-Noir: The Fusion of Science Fiction and Film Noir.* McFarland, 2008. Examines more than 100 movies from the 1920s to the present that combine common noir elements with the technology of science fiction to form a distinctive film subgenre.

Mirisch, Walter. *I Thought We Were Making Movies, Not History.* University of Wisconsin Press, 2008. Film producer Mirisch reflects on his career and his company's production of more than 100 films, which garnered eighty-seven nominations and twenty-eight Oscars®.

Moore, Roger. *My Word is My Bond: A Memoir.* Collins, 2008. The actor recalls his friends, film career (including his role as James Bond), and his battle with prostate cancer.

Nama, Adilifu. *Black Space: Imagining Race in Science Fiction Film.* University of Texas Press, 2008. Analyzes more than thirty science fiction films from the 1950s to the present and how they represent African Americans within the genre.

Olson, Greg. *David Lynch: Beautiful Dark.* Scarecrow Press, 2008. Explores the director's life and work, including his art, short films, features, and television show *Twin Peaks*.

Osbourne, Robert. *80 Years of the Oscar: The Official History of the Academy Awards.* Abbeville Press, 2008. A year-by-year chronicle of the ceremony, films, trends, speeches, and other information.

Pando, Leo. *An Illustrated History of Trigger: The Lives and Legend of Roy Rogers' Palomino.* McFarland, 2008. Detailed look at the original movie horse and the look-alikes as well as a filmography of all film and television appearances.

Patterson, Eric. *On Brokeback Mountain: Meditations About Masculinity, Fear, and Love in the Story and the Film.* Lexington Books, 2008. A comparative discussion on the movie and the short story on which it was based.

Paul, Louis. *Tales from the Cult Film Trenches: Interviews with 36 Actors from Horror, Science Fiction and Exploitation Cinema.* McFarland, 2008. Interviews with actors and actresses of sixties and seventies cult cinema.

Peri, Don. *Working with Walt: Interviews with Disney Artists.* University Press of Mississippi, 2008. Includes fifteen interviews with animators, voice actors, and designers who worked at the Disney studio during its animation heyday.

Pitts, Michael R. *Western Film Series of the Sound Era.* McFarland, 2008. Covers thirty western film series produced from the mid-1930s to the early 1950s.

Plummer, Christopher. *In Spite of Myself: A Memoir.* Knopf, 2008. The actor breezily reflects on his six-decade career on television, the stage, and in the movies as well as his private life.

Price, David A. *The Pixar Touch: The Making of a Company.* Knopf Publishing Group, 2008. Covers the company's money-losing beginnings at the New York Institute of Technology and with George Lucas, how Steve Jobs took the company public, and its sale to Disney.

Pykett, Derek. *British Horror Film Locations.* McFarland, 2008. Lists the shooting locations (both in-studio and on-site) for more than 100 British horror films released between 1932 and 2006 as well as credit information and a brief plot synopsis.

Pyne, Robert. *Long Ago and Far Away: Hollywood and the Second World War.* Scarecrow Press, 2008. A study of World War II films from 1941 to the present and how they paralleled the national mores and politics of their times.

Raw, Laurence. *Adapting Nathaniel Hawthorne to the Screen: Forging New Worlds.* Scarecrow Press, 2008. Shows how filmmakers have depicted the writings (both novels and short stories) of the early 19th-century American author onscreen.

Rege, Philippe. *An Encyclopedia of French Film Directors.* Scarecrow Press, 2008. Cites nearly 3,000 French directors who have made at least one feature film since 1895.

Rhodes, Gary D., editor. *Edgar G. Ulmer: Detour on Poverty Row.* Lexington Books, 2008. Offers twenty-one essays on the German immigrant who became one of the reigning directors of Poverty Row B-movies in Hollywood.

Ricci, Steven. *Cinema and Fascism: Italian Film and Society, 1922–1943.* University of California Press, 2008. Investigates the relationship between the totalitarian regime and the film industry, looking at the films and the role of cinema in daily life.

Richards, Jeffrey. *Hollywood's Ancient Worlds.* Continuum, 2008. Examines the cyclical rise and fall in production of historical epics that depict the ancient world from the silent film era to the present.

Robb, Brian J. *Heath Ledger: Hollywood's Dark Star.* Plexus Publishing, 2008. Biography of the young Australian actor, who died in 2008, which includes the making of *Brokeback Mountain* and the film's impact as well as his personal relationships.

Rollins, Peter C., and John E. O'Connor, editors. *Why We Fought: America's Wars in Film and History.* University Press of Kentucky, 2008. Comprehensive look at war films, from depictions of the American Revolution to September 11 and its aftermath.

St. Romain, Theresa. *Margarita Fischer: A Biography of the Silent Film Star.* McFarland, 2008. Examines Fischer's life and career, her marriage to fellow performer Harry Pollard, and Pollard Picture Plays, the production company founded by the couple.

Sandford, Christopher. *Polanski: A Biography.* Palgrave Macmillan, 2008. A superficial biography of scandal-plagued director Roman Polanski includes his American career, the murder of his wife Sharon Tate by members of the Manson Family, and his 1977 arrest for statutory rape.

Santopietro, Tom. *Sinatra in Hollywood.* St. Martin's/Dunne, 2008. A career assessment of the singer/actor that begins with Sinatra's 1935 short subjects and blends his work with his public persona and personal life.

Schickel, Richard. *Film on Paper: The Inner Life of Movies.* Ivan R. Dee, 2008. Schickel compiles his own reviews of books covering the film industry that were published in the *Los Angeles Times* from 1989 to 2007.

Schickel, Richard, and George Perry. *You Must Remember This: The Warner Bros. Story.* Running Press, 2008. Authorized look at the eighty-five-year history of the studio.

Schifrin, Lalo. *Mission Impossible: My Life in Music.* Scarecrow Press, 2008. Autobiography of the musician, conductor, and composer of more than 100 film and television scores as well as numerous classical and jazz compositions.

Schoell, William. *Creature Features: Nature Turned Nasty in the Movies.* McFarland, 2008. An examination of movie monsters, including dragons, dinosaurs, giant insects and animals, and other creatures, from the silent era to the present.

Schwartz, Ronald. *Great Spanish Films Since 1950.* Scarecrow Press, 2008. A compendium of more than 120 Spanish films and directors from the pre-Francoist era through the Spanish New Wave to the present.

Schwartz, Vanessa R. *It's So French! Hollywood, Paris, and the Making of Cosmopolitan Film Culture.* University of Chicago Press, 2008. A sociological analysis of the influence of French culture on American movies, the Cannes Film Festival, the career of Brigitte Bardot as a French icon, and the globalization of filmmaking.

Scivally, Bruce. *Superman on Film, Television, Radio and Broadway.* McFarland, 2008. History of the superhero from the first cartoon in 1941 to the 2006 live-action movie.

Shatner, William, with David Fisher. *Up Till Now: My Autobiography.* St. Martin's/Dunne, 2008. The actor, writer, and director, who is not afraid to document his humiliations as well as his successes, covers his work in theatre, television, and movies.

Sheward, David. *Rage and Glory: The Volatile Life and Career of George C. Scott.* Applause Books, 2008. Documents the life and career of the actor, including his work on stage and television, and in film, including *Patton*.

Silver, Alain, and James Ursini, editors. *Gangster Film Reader.* Limelight Editions, 2008. Contains essays that provide an overview of the genre and the evolution of the gangster film, including reprints of seminal articles and new works written for this volume.

Singer, Irving. *Cinematic Mythmaking: Philosophy in Film.* MIT Press, 2008. Explores the hidden and overt use of mythological themes in films.

Skal, David J., with Jessica Rains. *Claude Rains: An Actor's Voice.* University Press of Kentucky, 2008. Biography of the English-born actor who emigrated to America in 1926 to work in Hollywood and his career within the studio system.

Spoto, Donald. *Spellbound by Beauty: Hitchcock and His Leading Ladies.* Harmony, 2008. Spoto's third book about the director examines each Hitchcock film in terms of its leading lady, especially Ingrid Bergman, Grace Kelly, and Tippi Hedren.

Sragow, Michael. *Victor Fleming: An American Movie Master.* Pantheon, 2008. Film critic Sragow has written a flattering biography of the Old Hollywood studio director known for such films as *Gone With the Wind, The Wizard of Oz, The Virginian,* and *Bombshell.*

Starr, Michael Seth. *Hiding in Plain Sight: The Secret Life of Raymond Burr.* Applause, 2008. Details the actor's career in movies and on television while Burr managed to keep his homosexuality and long-term relationship private.

Stirling, Richard. *Julie Andrews: An Intimate Biography.* St. Martin's, 2008. The London-based actor, who has known Andrews since 1986, traces her career from her post-WWII work on radio and stage to her arrival in America, detailing the professional and personal highlights of her life.

Stoehr, Kevin L., and Michael C. Connolly, editors. *John Ford in Focus: Essays on the Filmmaker's Life and Work.* McFarland, 2008. Examines the intersections between Ford's personal life and artistic vision.

Streible, Dan. *Fight Pictures: A History of Boxing and Early Cinema.* University of California Press, 2008. Chronicles the development of prizefights in films from legitimate bouts to comic sparring matches.

Thomson, David. *"Have You Seen...?" A Personal Introduction to 1,000 Films.* Knopf, 2008. The film critic offers an alphabetically arranged selection of must-see movies from *Abbott and Costello Meet Frankenstein* to *Zabriskie Point* and why you too should see them.

Tropiano, Stephen. *Obscene, Indecent, Immoral & Offensive: 100+ Years of Censored, Banned, and Controversial Films.* Limelight Editions, 2008. Analyzes films that contained controversial adult themes and material, including explicit language, nudity, sex, and violence.

Tucker, David C. *Shirley Booth: A Biography and Career Record.* McFarland, 2008. Provides coverage of the actress' six decade career in theater, film, radio, and television.

Tucker, Ken. *Scarface Nation: The Ultimate Gangster Movie and How It Changed America.* St. Martin's Griffin, 2008. Marks the twenty-fifth anniversary of Brian de Palma's gangster film.

Turner, Kathleen, with Gloria Feldt. *Send Yourself Roses: Thoughts on My Life, Love, and Leading Roles.* Springboard, 2008. The actress discusses her film and theatrical roles, her personal life, and her battles with rheumatoid arthritis and alcohol.

Vance, Jeffrey. *Douglas Fairbanks.* University of California Press, 2008. Biography, film history, and analysis of the star's personal and professional lives.

Vermilye, Jerry. *Buster Crabbe: A Biofilmography.* McFarland, 2008. Details the work of the actor who made 103 feature films and serials, including his roles as Tarzan, Buck Rogers, and Flash Gordon.

Vick, Tom. *Asian Cinema: A Field Guide.* HarperCollins, 2008. Offers an overview of movies produced in Asian nations, including a discussion of history and themes.

Wagner, Robert, with Scott Eyman. *Pieces of My Heart: A Life.* Harper Entertainment, 2008. The actor discusses his childhood fascination with movies, long career on stage and in film and television, and his personal life, including his marriages to Natalie Wood and her tragic drowning death.

Waldman, Harry. *Nazi Films in America, 1933–1942.* McFarland, 2008. Details the nearly 500 German-language films that were imported and shown in the United States.

Walker, Elsie M., and David T. Johnson, editors. *Conversations with Directors: An Anthology of Interviews from Literature/Film Quarterly.* Scarecrow Press, 2008. Chronologically arranged interviews cover thirty-five years, beginning with the journal's founding in 1973.

Weaver, Tom. *I Talked with a Zombie: Interviews with 23 Veterans of Horror and Sci-Fi Films and Television.* McFarland, 2008. Weaver's latest compilation of interviews has an increased emphasis on genre television series.

Weissman, Stephen M. *Chaplin: A Life.* Arcade Publishing, 2008. Traces Chaplin's life from his tragic childhood and how it shaped his personality and work.

White, Timothy. *Hollywood Pinups.* CollinsDesign, 2008. Collection of color photographs of today's female stars taken by the celebrity photographer.

Wilkinson, Simon A. *Hollywood Horror from the Director's Chair: Six Filmmakers in the Franchise of Fear.* McFarland, 2008. Examines the work of such directors as Wes Craven and Don Coscarelli.

Williams, Linda. *Screening Sex.* Duke University Press, 2008. Investigates how sex acts have been represented onscreen from the silent era to the present.

Director Index

Sunny Abberton
  Bra Boys *37*

Marc Abraham
  Flash of Genius *117*

Andrew Adamson (1966-)
  The Chronicles of Narnia: Prince
    Caspian *58*

Alexandre Aja (1978-)
  Mirrors *218*

Fatih Akin
  The Edge of Heaven *103*

Woody Allen (1935-)
  Cassandra's Dream *46*
  Vicky Cristina Barcelona *370*

Kent Alterman
  Semi-Pro *293*

Sean Anders
  Sex Drive *300*

Brad Anderson (1964-)
  Transsiberian *354*

Paul W.S. Anderson (1965-)
  Death Race *79*

Darren Aronofsky (1969-)
  The Wrestler *401*

Jon Avnet (1949-)
  88 Minutes *105*
  Righteous Kill *274*

David Ayer (1972-)
  Street Kings *333*

Stuart Baird (1947-)
  Vantage Point *368*

Juan Antonio Bayona
  The Orphanage *238*

Timur Bekmambetov
  Wanted *385*

Peter Berg (1964-)
  Hancock *146*

Bryan Bertino
  The Strangers *331*

Larry Bishop (1947-)
  Hell Ride *153*

Sergei Bodrov (1948-)
  Mongol *222*

Uwe Boll (1965-)
  In the Name of the King: A
    Dungeon Siege Tale *169*

Darren Lynn Bousman (1979-)
  Repo! The Genetic Opera *271*

Danny Boyle (1956-)
  Slumdog Millionaire *307*

Eric Brevig (1957-)
  Journey to the Center of the
    Earth *179*

Steven Brill (1962-)
  Drillbit Taylor *95*

Adam Brooks (1956-)
  Definitely, Maybe *83*

Neil Burger
  The Lucky Ones *198*

Nanette Burstein
  American Teen *4*

Guillaume Canet (1973-)
  Tell No One *345*

Charles Robert Carner (1957-)
  Witless Protection *397*

Chris Carter
  The X Files: I Want to Be-
    lieve *405*

D.J. Caruso (1965-)
  Eagle Eye *101*

Peter Cattaneo (1964-)
  The Rocker *275*

Joseph Cedar
  Beaufort *24*

Claude Chabrol (1930-)
  A Girl Cut in Two *141*

Justin Chadwick
  The Other Boleyn Girl *239*

Larry Charles (1956-)
  Religulous *269*

John M. Chu
  Step Up 2 the Streets *326*

Philippe Claudel
  I've Loved You So Long *177*

Ethan Coen (1957-)
  Burn After Reading *40*

Joel Coen (1954-)
  Burn After Reading *40*

Rob Cohen (1949-)
  The Mummy: Tomb of the
    Dragon Emperor *224*

Isabel Coixet (1960-)
  Elegy *107*

Steve Conrad (1968-)
  The Promotion *256*

Stephen Daldry (1960-)
  The Reader *265*

Eric Darnell
  Madagascar: Escape 2 Af-
    rica *202*

Kirk De Micco
  Space Chimps *315*

Guillermo del Toro (1964-)
  Hellboy II: The Golden
    Army *155*

Mitchell Lichtenstein (1956-)
Teeth *343*

Doug Liman (1965-)
Jumper *180*

Phyllida Lloyd (1957-)
Mamma Mia! *205*

Ye Lou
Summer Palace *334*

Jeff Lowell
Over Her Dead Body *241*

Baz Luhrmann (1962-)
Australia *8*

Robert Luketic (1973-)
21 *357*

Kent Mackenzie
The Exiles *108*

William Maher
Sleepwalking *306*

David Mamet (1947-)
Redbelt *267*

Neil Marshall (1970-)
Doomsday *91*

Darnell Martin
Cadillac Records *43*

Steve Martino
Dr. Seuss' Horton Hears a
Who! *90*

Craig Mazin
Superhero Movie *336*

Tom McCarthy (1969-)
The Visitor *373*

Nelson McCormick
Prom Night *255*

Michael McCullers
Baby Mama *13*

Martin McDonagh
In Bruges *168*

Tom McGrath
Madagascar: Escape 2 Af-
rica *202*

Adam McKay (1968-)
Step Brothers *325*

Olivier Megaton
Transporter 3 *353*

Fernando Meirelles (1955-)
Blindness *29*

Sam Mendes (1965-)
Revolutionary Road *272*

Jiri Menzel (1938-)
I Served the King of En-
gland *165*

Frank Miller
The Spirit *320*

Randall Miller
Bottle Shock *34*

Rob Minkoff
The Forbidden Kingdom *124*

John Moore (1970-)
Max Payne *210*

David Moreau
The Eye *111*

Paulo Morelli
City of Men *63*

Brett Morgen
Chicago 10 *54*

Errol Morris (1948-)
Standard Operating Proce-
dure *321*

Gabriele Muccino (1967-)
Seven Pounds *295*

Cristian Mungiu
4 Months, 3 Weeks and 2
Days *129*

Noam Murro
Smart People *309*

Jeffrey Nachmanoff
Traitor *351*

Bharat Nalluri (1965-)
Miss Pettigrew Lives for a
Day *220*

Erik Nelson
Dreams with Sharp Teeth *94*

Morgan Neville
The Cool School *68*

Christopher Nolan (1970-)
The Dark Knight *75*

Masayuki Ochiai
Shutter *303*

Gavin O'Connor
Pride and Glory *253*

Kenny Ortega (1950-)
High School Musical 3: Senior
Year *158*

Mark Osborne
Kung Fu Panda *185*

Mark Palansky
Penelope *246*

Xavier Palud
The Eye *111*

Danny Pang (1965-)
Bangkok Dangerous *18*

Oxide Pang (1965-)
Bangkok Dangerous *18*

Vincent Paronnaud
Persepolis *247*

Kimberly Peirce
Stop-Loss *327*

Mark Pellington (1965-)
Henry Poole Is Here *156*

Vadim Perelman
The Life Before Her Eyes *192*

Tyler Perry (1969-)
Tyler Perry's Meet the
Browns *363*

Christian Petzold
Yella *407*

Andrew Piddington
The Killing of John Len-
non *182*

Jon Poll
Charlie Bartlett *51*

Doug Pray
Surfwise *337*

Gina Prince-Bythewood (1969-)
The Secret Life of Bees *292*

Michael Radford (1946-)
Flawless *118*

Ian Iqbal Rashid
How She Move *161*

Peyton Reed (1964-)
Yes Man *408*

Matt Reeves (1966-)
Cloverfield *64*

Kelly Reichardt
Wendy and Lucy *389*

Rob Reiner (1945-)
The Bucket List *39*

Patricia Riggen
Under the Same Moon *365*

Guy Ritchie (1968-)
RocknRolla *276*

Jacques Rivette (1928-)
The Duchess of Langeais *98*

Brian Robbins (1964-)
Meet Dave *211*

Eric Rohmer (1920-)
The Romance of Astree and Celadon *283*

George A. Romero (1940-)
Diary of the Dead *86*

Richard Roxburgh (1962-)
Romulus, My Father *284*

Patricia Rozema (1958-)
Kit Kittredge: An American
Girl *184*

Stefan Ruzowitzky (1961-)
The Counterfeiters *70*

Ira Sachs (1965-)
Married Life *208*

Pierre Salvadori (1964-)
Priceless *252*

Screenwriter Index

Sunny Abberton
Bra Boys *37*

Andrew Adamson (1966-)
The Chronicles of Narnia: Prince
Caspian *58*

Jonathan Aibel
Kung Fu Panda *185*

Alexandre Aja (1978-)
Mirrors *218*

Fatih Akin
The Edge of Heaven *103*

Rodney Al Haddad
Caramel *45*

Nathan Alexander
Valkyrie *366*

Arif Aliyev
Mongol *222*

Matt R. Allen
Four Christmases *127*

Woody Allen (1935-)
Cassandra's Dream *46*
Vicky Cristina Barcelona *370*

Sean Anders
Sex Drive *300*

Brad Anderson
Transsiberian *354*

Edward A. Anderson
Flawless *118*

Paul W.S. Anderson (1965-)
Death Race *79*

Judd Apatow (1968-)
You Don't Mess with the Zohan *410*

Alice Arlen
Then She Found Me *350*

Scot Armstrong (1970-)
Semi-Pro *293*

Tom J. Astle
Get Smart *137*

Doug Atchison
The Longshots *194*

Simone Bär
Yella *407*

Karen Barna
Step Up 2 the Streets *326*

Peter Barsocchini
High School Musical 3: Senior
Year *158*

Stuart Beattie
Australia *8*

Simon Beaufoy (1967-)
Miss Pettigrew Lives for a
Day *220*
Slumdog Millionaire *307*

David Berenbaum
The Spiderwick
Chronicles *318*

Glenn Berger
Kung Fu Panda *185*

Bryan Bertino
The Strangers *331*

Eric Besnard
Babylon A.D. *14*

Luc Besson (1959-)
Transporter 3 *353*

Joe Bini
Roman Polanski: Wanted and
Desired *281*

Larry Bishop (1947-)
Hell Ride *153*

Dustin Lance Black
Milk *214*

Michael Ian Black (1971-)
Run, Fatboy, Run *287*

Lawrence Block (1943-)
My Blueberry Nights *227*

Sergei Bodrov (1948-)
Mongol *222*

Mark Bomback
Deception *80*

Pascal Bonitzer (1946-)
The Duchess of Langeais *98*

Doug Bost
Diminished Capacity *87*

Emmanuel Bourdieu
A Christmas Tale *57*

Pam Brady
Hamlet 2 *145*

Michael Brandt (1968-)
Wanted *385*

Duncan Brantley
Leatherheads *190*

Mark R. Brinker
Untraceable *366*

Jeremy Brock (1959-)
Brideshead Revisited *38*

Adam Brooks (1956-)
Definitely, Maybe *83*

Kristofor Brown
Drillbit Taylor *95*

Neil Burger
The Lucky Ones *198*

Allison Burnett
Untraceable *366*

Paul Haggis (1953-)
Quantum of Solace *259*

Lance Hammer
Ballast *16*

Michael Haneke (1942-)
Funny Games *134*

David Hare (1947-)
The Reader *265*

Ed Harris (1949-)
Appaloosa *5*

Ronald Harwood (1934-)
Australia *8*

Jeffrey Hatcher
The Duchess *96*

Chris Hauty
Never Back Down *229*

Justin Haythe
Revolutionary Road *272*

Brad Hennegan
The First Saturday in May *114*

John Hennegan
The First Saturday in May *114*

Tim Herlihy (1966-)
Bedtime Stories *26*

Mark Herman (1954-)
The Boy in the Striped Pajamas *35*

Jihad Hojeily
Caramel *45*

Mat Holloway
Iron Man *175*

Christophe Honoré (1970-)
Love Songs *197*

Hou Hsiao-Hsien (1947-)
Flight of the Red Balloon *120*

Courtney Hunt
Frozen River *133*

Helen Hunt (1963-)
Then She Found Me *350*

Jon Hurwitz
Harold & Kumar Escape from Guantanamo Bay *152*

Garth Jennings
Son of Rambow *311*

Anders Thomas Jensen (1972-)
The Duchess *96*

Catherine Johnson (1957-)
Mamma Mia! *205*

Toni Johnson
Step Up 2 the Streets *326*

Robert Mark Kamen
Transporter 3 *353*

John Kamps
Ghost Town *139*

Deborah Kaplan
Made of Honor *204*

Wong Kar-wai (1958-)
Ashes of Time Redux *7*
My Blueberry Nights *227*

Mathieu Kassovitz (1967-)
Babylon A.D. *14*

Charlie Kaufman (1958-)
Synecdoche, New York *340*

Alex Kendrick
Fireproof *113*

Stephen Kendrick
Fireproof *113*

Simon Kinberg (1973-)
Jumper *180*

Michael Patrick King
Sex and the City: The Movie *298*

Sherwood Kiraly
Diminished Capacity *87*

Karey Kirkpatrick
The Spiderwick Chronicles *318*

Andrew Klavan
One Missed Call *237*

Harald Kloser (1956-)
10,000 B.C. *346*

Robert Knott
Appaloosa *5*

David Koepp (1964-)
Ghost Town *139*
Indiana Jones and the Kingdom of the Crystal Skull *173*

Eran Kolirin
The Band's Visit *17*

Howard Korder (1957-)
Lakeview Terrace *189*

Joseph Kwong
Nim's Island *233*

Ian La Frenais (1937-)
The Bank Job *19*

Nadine Labaki
Caramel *45*

Analisa LaBianco
Beverly Hills Chihuahua *27*

Ian LaFrenais
See Ian La Frenais

Christine Laurent
The Duchess of Langeais *98*

Charles Leavitt
The Express *110*

Jieho Lee
The Air I Breathe *1*

Malcolm D. Lee (1970-)
Welcome Home Roscoe Jenkins *389*

Philippe Lefebvre
Tell No One *345*

Mike Leigh (1943-)
Happy-Go-Lucky *150*

Claude Lelouch (1937-)
Roman de gare *279*

Gregory Lévasseur
Mirrors *218*

Marc Levin
Journey to the Center of the Earth *179*
Nim's Island *233*

Victor Levin
Then She Found Me *350*

Jonathan Levine
The Wackness *381*

Barry L. Levy
Vantage Point *368*

Mark Leyner
War, Inc. *388*

Mitchell Lichtenstein (1956-)
Teeth *343*

Art Linson (1942-)
What Just Happened *393*

Allan Loeb
21 *357

Matt Lopez
Bedtime Stories *26*

Ye Lou
Summer Palace *334*

David Loughery
Lakeview Terrace *189*

Jeff Lowell
Over Her Dead Body *241*

Jon Lucas
Four Christmases *127*

Baz Luhrmann (1962-)
Australia *8*

Jenny Lumet (1967-)
Rachel Getting Married *262*

Karen McCullah Lutz
The House Bunny *159*

Kent Mackenzie
The Exiles *108*

Yingli Ma
Summer Palace *334*

David Magee (1962-)
Miss Pettigrew Lives for a Day *220*

Cecile Maistre (1967-)
A Girl Cut in Two *141*

David Mamet (1947-)
Redbelt *267*

Cinematographer Index

Thomas Ackerman
  Superhero Movie *336*

Barry Ackroyd (1954-)
  Battle in Seattle *21*

Javier Aguirresarobe (1948-)
  Vicky Cristina Barcelona *370*

Maryse Alberti
  Taxi to the Dark Side *342*
  The Wrestler *401*

Maxime Alexandre (1971-)
  Mirrors *218*

Jerome Almeras
  I've Loved You So Long *177*

Russ T. Alsobrook (1946-)
  Forgetting Sarah Marshall *125*
  Role Models *278*

Michel Amathieu
  Penelope *246*

Mitchell Amundsen (1958-)
  Wanted *385*

Juan Ruiz Anchia
  Sleepwalking *306*

Greg Andracke
  Taxi to the Dark Side *342*

Daniel Aranyo
  High School Musical 3: Senior
    Year *158*

Thierry Arbogast
  Babylon A.D. *14*

David Armstrong
  Saw V *289*

Howard Atherton
  When Did You Last See Your
    Father? *395*

John Bailey (1942-)
  Mad Money *201*
  Over Her Dead Body *241*

Florian Ballhaus (1965-)
  Definitely, Maybe *83*
  Marley & Me *207*

Diane Baratier
  The Romance of Astree and Cela-
    don *283*

Michael Barrett (1970-)
  Bedtime Stories *26*
  You Don't Mess with the Zo-
    han *410*

Brian Baugh
  An American Carol *2*

Affonso Beato
  Nights in Rodanthe *231*

Gabriel Beristain (1955-)
  Street Kings *333*

Brad Blackbourn
  The Tale of Despereaux *341*

Oliver Bokelberg (1964-)
  The Visitor *373*

Michael Bonvillain
  Cloverfield *64*

David Boyd
  Kit Kittredge: An American
    Girl *184*

Eigil Bryld
  In Bruges *168*

Don Burgess (1956-)
  Fool's Gold *123*

Russell Carpenter (1950-)
  21 *357*

Alan Caso
  First Sunday *116*

Vanja Cernjul (1968-)
  Diminished Capacity *87*

Robert Chappell
  Standard Operating Proce-
    dure *321*

Cesar Charlone (1958-)
  Blindness *29*

Remy Chevrin
  Love Songs *197*

Jerica Cleland
  Space Chimps *315*

Giovanni Fiore Coltellacci
  Transporter 3 *353*

Michael Coulter
  The Bank Job *19*

Lol Crawley
  Ballast *16*

Erik Daarstad
  The Exiles *108*

Elliot Davis
  Twilight *360*

Gerard de Battista
  Roman de gare *279*

John de Borman (1954-)
  Miss Pettigrew Lives for a
    Day *220*

Macario De Souza
  Bra Boys *37*

Roger Deakins (1949-)
  Doubt *92*
  The Reader *265*
  Revolutionary Road *272*

Benoit Delhomme (1961-)
  The Boy in the Striped Pajamas *35*

Peter Deming (1957-)
  The Love Guru *195*
  Married Life *208*

Jim Denault (1960-)
  The Sisterhood of the Traveling Pants 2 *302*

Caleb Deschanel (1941-)
  The Spiderwick Chronicles *318*

Peter Donahue
  Then She Found Me *350*

Wes Dorman
  Dreams with Sharp Teeth *94*

Christopher Doyle (1952-)
  Ashes of Time Redux *7*
  Paranoid Park *243*

Stuart Dryburgh (1952-)
  Nim's Island *233*

Simon Duggan (1959-)
  The Mummy: Tomb of the Dragon Emperor *224*

Roger Eaton
  The Killing of John Lennon *182*

Pawel Edelman (1958-)
  The Life Before Her Eyes *192*

Frederick Elmes
  Synecdoche, New York *340*

Robert Elswit (1950-)
  Redbelt *267*

Lukas Ettlin
  Never Back Down *229*

Óscar Faura
  The Orphanage *238*

Stéphane Fontaine
  What Just Happened *393*

Hans Fromm
  Yella *407*

Tak Fujimoto
  The Happening *149*

Greg Gardiner
  Welcome Home Roscoe Jenkins *389*

Eric Gautier (1961-)
  A Christmas Tale *57*

Xavi Giménez (1970-)
  Transsiberian *354*

Michael Goi (1959-)
  Witless Protection *397*

Adriano Goldman
  City of Men *63*

Shai Goldman
  The Band's Visit *17*

Richard Greatrex
  Flawless *118*
  Run, Fatboy, Run *287*

Jack N. Green (1946-)
  My Best Friend's Girl *225*

Xavier Perez Grobet
  City of Ember *61*

Alexander Grusynski (1950-)
  Hamlet 2 *145*

Conrad W. Hall (1958-)
  The Longshots *194*

Jess Hall
  Brideshead Revisited *38*
  Son of Rambow *311*

Robert Hanna
  American Teen *4*

Anthony Hardwick
  Religulous *269*

Wolfgang Held
  American Teen *4*
  Teeth *343*

Brad Hennegan
  The First Saturday in May *114*

John Hennegan
  The First Saturday in May *114*

David Hennings
  Strange Wilderness *330*

Gilles Henry
  Priceless *252*

David Higgs
  RocknRolla *276*

Julien Hirsch (1964-)
  The Witnesses *398*

David Homcy
  Surfwise *337*

Qing Hua
  Summer Palace *334*

Shane Hurlbut
  Semi-Pro *293*
  Swing Vote *338*

Ofer Inov
  Beaufort *24*

Toby Irwin
  Smart People *309*

Peter James (1947-)
  27 Dresses *359*

Yong Duk Jhun
  Kung Fu Panda *185*

Shelly Johnson
  The House Bunny *159*

Jeffrey Jur
  The Eye *111*

Janusz Kaminski (1959-)
  Indiana Jones and the Kingdom of the Crystal Skull *173*

Robert Kaufman
  The Exiles *108*

Scott Kevan (1972-)
  Death Race *79*
  Hell Ride *153*

Darius Khondji (1955-)
  Funny Games *134*
  My Blueberry Nights *227*
  The Ruins *286*

Laela Kilbourn
  American Teen *4*

Jeffrey L. Kimball (1943-)
  Four Christmases *127*

Rainer Klausmann (1949-)
  The Edge of Heaven *103*

David Klein (1972-)
  Zack and Miri Make a Porno *412*

Tanja Koop
  Roman Polanski: Wanted and Desired *281*

Petra Korner
  The Wackness *381*

Ellen Kuras (1959-)
  Be Kind Rewind *22*

Jean-Claude Larrieu
  Elegy *107*

Jeremy Lasky
  WALL-E *382*

Philippe Le Sourd
  Seven Pounds *295*

Pin Bing Lee
  See Mark Lee Ping-Bin

Denis Lenoir
  88 Minutes *105*
  Righteous Kill *274*

Matthew F. Leonetti (1941-)
  Soul Men *313*
  What Happens in Vegas *392*

Sam Levy
  Wendy and Lucy *389*

Rain Kathy Li
  Paranoid Park *243*

Matthew Libatique (1969-)
  Iron Man *175*
  Miracle at St. Anna *217*

Karl Walter Lindenlaub (1957-)
  The Chronicles of Narnia: Prince Caspian *58*

Walt Lloyd
  The Air I Breathe *1*

Emmanuel Lubezki (1964-)
  Burn After Reading *40*

William Lubtchansky (1937-)
  The Duchess of Langeais *98*

Glen MacPherson (1957-)
  One Missed Call *237*
  Rambo *264*

Max Malkin
  Step Up 2 the Streets *326*

Anthony Dod Mantle (1955-)
  Slumdog Millionaire *307*

Ed Marritz
  Young@Heart *411*

J. Clark Mathis
  Meet Dave *211*

Shawn Maurer
  Disaster Movie *88*
  Meet the Spartans *213*

Sam McCurdy
  Doomsday *91*

Kieran McGuigan
  The Other Boleyn Girl *239*

Glen McPherson
  See Glen MacPherson

Chris Menges (1940-)
  The Reader *265*
  Stop-Loss *327*

Peter Menzies, Jr.
  The Incredible Hulk *171*

Phil Mereaux
  Beverly Hills Chihuahua *27*

Anastas Michos
  Cadillac Records *43*
  Untraceable *366*
  The Women *399*

Claudio Miranda
  The Curious Case of Benjamin
    Button *71*

Amir M. Mokri (1956-)
  Vantage Point *368*

Reed Dawson Morano
  Frozen River *133*

Kramer Morgenthau
  The Express *110*

John Morrill
  The Exiles *108*

J. Michael Muro
  Traitor *351*

Fred Murphy (1942-)
  Drillbit Taylor *95*
  Ghost Town *139*

Oleg Mutu
  4 Months, 3 Weeks and 2
    Days *129*

Guillermo Navarro (1955-)
  Hellboy II: The Golden
    Army *155*

Benedict Neuenfels
  The Counterfeiters *70*

Mathias Neumann (1965-)
  In the Name of the King: A
    Dungeon Siege Tale *169*

Morgan Neville
  The Cool School *68*

Ramsay Nickell (1963-)
  Chaos Theory *50*

Christophe Offenstein
  Tell No One *345*

Daryn Okada (1960-)
  Baby Mama *13*
  Harold & Kumar Escape from
    Guantanamo Bay *152*

Tim Orr (1968-)
  Choke *55*
  Pineapple Express *249*
  Sex Drive *300*
  Snow Angels *310*

Michael Ozier
  Bottle Shock *34*

Gyula Pados (1969-)
  The Duchess *96*

Phedon Papamichael (1962-)
  W. *377*

Peter Pau (1952-)
  The Forbidden Kingdom *124*

Chris Perkel
  The Cool School *68*

Barry Peterson
  Jumper *180*

Wally Pfister
  The Dark Knight *75*

Andre Pienaar
  How She Move *161*

Tony Pierce-Roberts (1945-)
  Made of Honor *204*

Mark Lee Ping-Bin (1954-)
  Flight of the Red Balloon *120*

Ekkehart Pollack
  Pathology *244*

Bill Pope (1952-)
  The Spirit *320*

Dick Pope (1947-)
  Happy-Go-Lucky *150*

Zoran Popovic
  War, Inc. *388*

Simon Poulter
  Young@Heart *411*

Declan Quinn (1957-)
  The Lucky Ones *198*
  Pride and Glory *253*
  Rachel Getting Married *262*

Robert Richardson (1955-)
  Shine a Light *301*
  Standard Operating Proce-
    dure *321*

Anthony B. Richmond (1942-)
  The Rocker *275*

Tom Richmond
  Nick & Norah's Infinite Playl-
    ist *230*

Dylan Robertson
  The Cool School *68*

Bill Roe
  The X Files: I Want to Be-
    lieve *405*

Julie Rogers
  Kit Kittredge: An American
    Girl *184*

Paul Sarossy (1963-)
  Charlie Bartlett *51*

Harris Savides (1957-)
  Milk *214*

Roberto Schaefer
  Quantum of Solace *259*

Tobias Schliessler
  Hancock *146*

Eric Schmidt (1966-)
  Henry Poole Is Here *156*

Yves Schnaoui
  Caramel *45*

John Schwartzman (1960-)
  The Bucket List *39*

Bob Scott
  Fireproof *113*

Jonathan Sela
  Max Payne *210*

Dean Semler (1943-)
  Appaloosa *5*
  Get Smart *137*

Ken Seng
  Quarantine *260*

Eduardo Serra (1943-)
  Defiance *82*
  A Girl Cut in Two *141*

Lawrence Sher (1970-)
  The Promotion *256*

Chuck Shuman
  Journey to the Center of the
    Earth *179*

Newton Thomas Sigel (1961-)
  Leatherheads *190*
  Valkyrie *366*

Brooke Silvester
  Bra Boys *37*

Geoffrey Simpson
  Romulus, My Father *284*

Editor Index

Sean Albertson
   Rambo *264*

Craig Alpert
   Pineapple Express *249*
   Yes Man *408*

Tim Alverson
   Shutter *303*

William Anderon
   Snow Angels *310*

Tariq Anwar
   Revolutionary Road *272*

Suresh Ayyar
   Romulus, My Father *284*

Stuart Baird
   Vantage Point *368*

Jason Ballantine
   Prom Night *255*

Roger Barton
   Speed Racer *316*

Ned Bastille
   Meet Dave *211*

Alan Baumgarten
   Charlie Bartlett *51*

Baxter
   Mirrors *218*

David Baxter
   The Life Before Her Eyes *192*

Kirk Baxter
   The Curious Case of Benjamin
      Button *71*

Michael Berenbaum
   Sex and the City: The
      Movie *298*
   War, Inc. *388*

Peter E. Berger
   88 Minutes *105*

Debbie Berman
   Space Chimps *315*

Alexander Berner
   10,000 B.C. *346*

Jeff Betancourt
   The Ruins *286*

Joe Bini
   Roman Polanski: Wanted and
      Desired *281*

Andrew Bird
   The Edge of Heaven *103*

Bettina Böhler
   Yella *407*

Roger Bondelli
   College Road Trip *67*

George Bowers (1944-)
   Welcome Home Roscoe Jen-
      kins *389*

Randall Boyd
   Dreams with Sharp Teeth *94*

Peter Boyle
   Flawless *118*

David Brenner
   Wanted *385*

Laurence Briaud
   A Christmas Tale *57*

Wendy Greene Bricmont
   Mad Money *201*

Don Brochu
   High School Musical 3: Senior
      Year *158*

Barry Alexander Brown (1960-)
   Miracle at St. Anna *217*

Virginie Bruant
   I've Loved You So Long *177*

Jeff Buchanan
   Be Kind Rewind *22*

Conrad Buff
   The Happening *149*

Dana Bunescu
   4 Months, 3 Weeks and 2
      Days *129*

Mike Burchett
   Wendy and Lucy *389*

Nanette Burstein
   American Teen *4*

William Chang
   My Blueberry Nights *227*

Matt Chesse
   Quantum of Solace *259*

Debra Chiate
   The House Bunny *159*

Lisa Zeno Churgin
   Henry Poole Is Here *156*
   Pride and Glory *253*

Jim Clark (1931-)
   Happy-Go-Lucky *150*

Ethan Coen (1957-)
   Burn After Reading *40*

Joel Coen (1954-)
   Burn After Reading *40*

Hank Corwin
   What Just Happened *393*

Tom Costain
   Bedtime Stories *26*
   Strange Wilderness *330*
   You Don't Mess with the Zo-
      han *410*

H. Lee Peterson
Madagascar: Escape 2 Africa *202*

Barney Pilling
Miss Pettigrew Lives for a Day *220*

Sabrina Plisco
Beverly Hills Chihuahua *27*

Joel Plotch
Lakeview Terrace *189*

Gregory Plotkin
Untraceable *366*

Peck Prior
Disaster Movie *88*
Meet the Spartans *213*

Kelly Reichardt
Wendy and Lucy *389*

Daniel Rezende
Blindness *29*
City of Men *63*

David Richardson
In the Name of the King: A Dungeon Siege Tale *169*

Nancy Richardson
Twilight *360*

Carlo Rizzo
Transporter 3 *353*

Gary D. Roach
Changeling *47*
Gran Torino *142*

Dylan Robertson
The Cool School *68*

Stéphane Roche
Persepolis *247*

David Rosenbloom
Untraceable *366*

Steven Rosenblum
Defiance *82*
Journey to the Center of the Earth *179*

Harvey Rosenstock
Repo! The Genetic Opera *271*

Paul Rubell
Hancock *146*

Elena Ruiz
The Orphanage *238*

Jill Savitt
Flash of Genius *117*

Pietro Scalia
Body of Lies *30*

Stephen R. Schaffer
WALL-E *382*

Daniel Schalk
Superhero Movie *336*

Herve Schneid
Igor *166*

Adam P. Scott
City of Ember *61*

Sam Seig
Ghost Town *139*

Zohar M. Sela
Beaufort *24*

Rick Shaine
The Incredible Hulk *171*

Terilyn Shropshire
The Secret Life of Bees *292*

Claire Simpson
The Reader *265*
Stop-Loss *327*

Kevin Smith (1970-)
Zack and Miri Make a Porno *412*

Lee Smith
The Dark Knight *75*

Paul Martin Smith
Journey to the Center of the Earth *179*

Mark Solomon
The Tale of Despereaux *341*

Tim Squyres
Rachel Getting Married *262*

Zach Staenberg
Mongol *222*
Speed Racer *316*

William Steinkamp
The Express *110*

Mary Stephen
The Romance of Astree and Celadon *283*

Kevin Stitt
Cloverfield *64*

Eric Strand
The Forbidden Kingdom *124*

Tim Streeto
Diminished Capacity *87*
The Promotion *256*

Liao Ching Sung
Flight of the Red Balloon *120*

Vincent Tabaillon
The Incredible Hulk *171*

Troy Takaki
Fool's Gold *123*

Patrick Tam (1968-)
Ashes of Time Redux *7*

David Tedeschi
Shine a Light *301*

Peter Teschner
Definitely, Maybe *83*

Dylan Tichenor
Doubt *92*

Michael Tronick
Bedtime Stories *26*

Jason W. A. Tucker
Star Wars: The Clone Wars *323*

Barbara Tulliver
Redbelt *267*

Gus Van Sant (1952-)
Paranoid Park *243*

Bernat Vilaplana
Hellboy II: The Golden Army *155*

Fernando Villena
Battle in Seattle *21*

Tracey Wadmore-Smith
Fool's Gold *123*

Christian Wagner
Deception *80*

John Wahba
The Pirates Who Don't Do Anything: A VeggieTales Movie *251*

Wayne Wahrman
The Day the Earth Stood Still *77*

Trevor Waite
When Did You Last See Your Father? *395*

Lesley Walker
Mamma Mia! *205*

Angus Wall
The Curious Case of Benjamin Button *71*

Billy Weber
The Love Guru *195*

Benjamin Weill
Babylon A.D. *14*

Debra Weinfeld
Never Back Down *229*

Andrew Weisblum
The Wrestler *401*

Jeff Werner
Religulous *269*

Blake West
Hell Ride *153*

Dirk Westervelt
Journey to the Center of the Earth *179*

Brent White
Step Brothers *325*

Brad E. Wilhite
The Rocker *275*

Monika Willi
  Funny Games *134*

Kate Williams
  Frozen River *133*

Hughes Winborne
  Seven Pounds *295*

Pam Wise
  Then She Found Me *350*

Jeffrey Wolf
  First Sunday *116*
  The Longshots *194*

John Wright
  The Incredible Hulk *171*

William Yeh
  Hell Ride *153*

Jian Zeng
  Summer Palace *334*

Dan Zimmerman
  Max Payne *210*

Dean Zimmerman
  Jumper *180*

Don Zimmerman
  Jumper *180*

Art Director Index

Olivier Adam
    The Tale of Despereaux *341*

David Allday
    The Other Boleyn Girl *239*

Jonathan Arkin
    27 Dresses *359*

Steve Arnold
    Appaloosa *5*

Michael Atwell (1943-2006)
    Four Christmases *127*

Alan Au
    You Don't Mess with the Zo-
    han *410*

Patrick Banister
    Flash of Genius *117*

Guy Barnes
    Hamlet 2 *145*

Hugh Bateup
    Speed Racer *316*

Gary Baugh
    Welcome Home Roscoe Jen-
    kins *389*

Charley Beal
    Milk *214*

Olivier Besson
    Igor *166*

Dan Bevan
    A Christmas Tale *57*

Jon Billington
    City of Ember *61*

Oana Bogdan
    Four Christmases *127*

Peter Borck
    Stop-Loss *327*

Simon Bowles
    Doomsday *91*

Sirma Bradley
    The Edge of Heaven *103*

Michele Brady
    Kit Kittredge: An American
    Girl *184*

Stephen Bream
    Mirrors *218*

Gerard Bryan
    Penelope *246*

Chris Burian-Mohr
    Bedtime Stories *26*

Andrew Cahn
    The Sisterhood of the Traveling
    Pants 2 *302*

Heather Cameron
    10,000 B.C. *346*

Thomas Cardone
    Dr. Seuss' Horton Hears a
    Who! *90*

Teresa Carriker-Thayer
    Revolutionary Road *272*

Stephen Carter
    Doomsday *91*

Julia Castle
    Run, Fatboy, Run *287*

Raymond Chan
    Fool's Gold *123*
    How to Lose Friends & Alienate
    People *162*

Sue Chan
    Made of Honor *204*

Ed Check
    Sex and the City: The
    Movie *298*

John Chichester
    The House Bunny *159*

Len X. Clayton
    The Visitor *373*

Erin Cochran
    Sex Drive *300*

Tom Cole (1933-2009)
    Teeth *343*

John Collins
    You Don't Mess with the Zo-
    han *410*

Kevin Constant
    Role Models *278*

Chris Cornwell
    Prom Night *255*
    Quarantine *260*

Emmanuelle Cuillery
    Love Songs *197*

Marc Dabe
    Pineapple Express *249*

Dennis Davenport
    The Love Guru *195*

William G. Davis
    Nights in Rodanthe *231*
    The Secret Life of Bees *292*

Joshu de Cartier
    Blindness *29*

Matteo De Cosmo
    Choke *55*

Jeremie Degruson
    Fly Me to the Moon *121*

Music Director Index

Ishai Adar
  Beaufort *24*

Mark Adler
  Bottle Shock *34*

Eric Allaman
  Witless Protection *397*

Pierre Allio
  The Duchess of Langeais *98*

Stig Anderson (1931-97)
  Mamma Mia! *205*

Benny Andersson
  Mamma Mia! *205*

Mar De Gli Antoni
  Roman Polanski: Wanted and
    Desired *281*

Craig Armstrong (1959-)
  The Incredible Hulk *171*

David Arnold (1962-)
  How to Lose Friends & Alienate
    People *162*
  Quantum of Solace *259*

Jean-Louis Aubert
  I've Loved You So Long *177*

Alexandre Azaria
  Transporter 3 *353*

Chris P. Bacon
  Space Chimps *315*

Nathan Barr
  Shutter *303*

Tyler Bates
  The Day the Earth Stood
    Still *77*
  Doomsday *91*

Camille Bazbaz
  Priceless *252*

Jeff Beal (1963-)
  Appaloosa *5*

Alexandre Beaupain (1974-)
  Love Songs *197*

Gilbert Becaud
  Roman de gare *279*

Christophe Beck (1972-)
  Charlie Bartlett *51*
  Drillbit Taylor *95*
  What Happens in Vegas *392*

Marco Beltrami (1966-)
  The Eye *111*
  Max Payne *210*

Gilad Benamram
  Chaos Theory *50*

Robert Berger
  Diminished Capacity *87*

Jean-Michel Bernard
  Be Kind Rewind *22*

Olivier Bernet
  Persepolis *247*

Terence Blanchard (1962-)
  Cadillac Records *43*
  Miracle at St. Anna *217*

Ales Brezina (1965-)
  I Served the King of En-
    gland *165*

Jon Brion (1963-)
  Step Brothers *325*
  Synecdoche, New York *340*

Ryan Brothers
  The First Saturday in May *114*

Lisa Brown
  College Road Trip *67*

David Buckley
  The Forbidden Kingdom *124*

Carter Burwell (1955-)
  Burn After Reading *40*
  In Bruges *168*
  Twilight *360*

Paul Cantelon
  The Other Boleyn Girl *239*
  W. *377*

Teddy Castellucci
  The Longshots *194*

Matthieu Chabrol (1956-)
  A Girl Cut in Two *141*

Mathieu Chedid
  Tell No One *345*

Stanley Clarke (1951-)
  First Sunday *116*
  Soul Men *313*

George S. Clinton (1947-)
  Harold & Kumar Escape from
    Guantanamo Bay *152*
  The Love Guru *195*

Charlie Clouser (1963-)
  Saw V *289*

Ry Cooder (1947-)
  My Blueberry Nights *227*

Dan Crane
  The Cool School *68*

Jeff Danna (1964-)
  Chicago 10 *54*
  Lakeview Terrace *189*

Mychael Danna (1958-)
  Lakeview Terrace *189*

Martin Davich
  Mad Money *201*

Jeff McIlwain
    Snow Angels *310*
Ashley Miller
    Rambo *264*
Robert Miller
    Teeth *343*
Angelo Milli
    Seven Pounds *295*
Mark Mothersbaugh (1950-)
    Nick & Norah's Infinite Playlist *230*
Khaled Mouzanar
    Caramel *45*
Nico Muhly
    The Reader *265*
Javier Navarrete (1956-)
    Mirrors *218*
David Newman (1954-)
    The Spirit *320*
    Welcome Home Roscoe Jenkins *389*
Randy Newman (1943-)
    Leatherheads *190*
Thomas Newman (1955-)
    Revolutionary Road *272*
    WALL-E *382*
John O'Brien (1962-)
    Vince Vaughn's Wild West Comedy Show: 30 Days & 30 Nights —Hollywood to the Heartland *372*
One Point Six
    Battle in Seattle *21*
Norman Orenstein
    Diary of the Dead *86*
Atli Örvarsson
    Babylon A.D. *14*
    Vantage Point *368*
John Ottman (1964-)
    Valkyrie *366*
Michael Penn (1958-)
    American Teen *4*
Hector Pereira
    Beverly Hills Chihuahua *27*
Barrington Pheloung (1954-)
    When Did You Last See Your Father? *395*
Antonio Pinto
    City of Men *63*
Rachel Portman (1960-)
    The Duchess *96*
    The Sisterhood of the Traveling Pants 2 *302*
John Powell (1963-)
    Bolt *32*
    Dr. Seuss' Horton Hears a Who! *90*

Hancock *146*
Jumper *180*
Kung Fu Panda *185*
Stop-Loss *327*
Trevor Rabin (1954-)
    Get Smart *137*
A.R. Rahman (1966-)
    Slumdog Millionaire *307*
Graeme Revell (1955-)
    Pineapple Express *249*
    The Ruins *286*
    Street Kings *333*
Griffin Richardson
    Diminished Capacity *87*
Jeff Richmond
    Baby Mama *13*
Max Richter
    Waltz with Bashir *384*
David Robbins (1955-)
    War, Inc. *388*
J. Peter Robinson
    The Bank Job *19*
William Ross
    The Tale of Despereaux *341*
Marius Ruhland
    The Counterfeiters *70*
Ralph Sall
    Hamlet 2 *145*
Buck Sanders
    Max Payne *210*
Philippe Sarde (1945-)
    The Witnesses *398*
David Sardy
    21 *357*
Marc Shaiman (1959-)
    The Bucket List *39*
Shantel
    The Edge of Heaven *103*
Theodore Shapiro (1971-)
    Marley & Me *207*
    Semi-Pro *293*
    Tropic Thunder *355*
Ed Shearmur (1966-)
    College Road Trip *67*
    88 Minutes *105*
    Righteous Kill *274*
Howard Shore (1946-)
    Doubt *92*
Carlo Siliotto (1950-)
    Under the Same Moon *365*
Darren Smith
    Repo! The Genetic Opera *271*
Mark Snow (1946-)
    The X Files: I Want to Believe *405*

Michael Stevens
    Gran Torino *142*
David A. Stewart (1952-)
    Space Chimps *315*
Marc Streitenfeld
    Body of Lies *30*
Eddie Sunrise
    The Exiles *108*
John Swihart
    The Longshots *194*
Joby Talbot
    Penelope *246*
    Son of Rambow *311*
Zafer Tawil
    Rachel Getting Married *262*
Jeanine Tesori
    Nights in Rodanthe *231*
Richard Thompson (1949-)
    Dreams with Sharp Teeth *94*
Tomandandy
    The Strangers *331*
Wu Tong
    Ashes of Time Redux *7*
David Torn (1953-)
    The Wackness *381*
Stephen Trask
    Sex Drive *300*
Brian Tyler
    Bangkok Dangerous *18*
    Eagle Eye *101*
    Rambo *264*
Bjorn Ulvaes
    Mamma Mia! *205*
William Ungerman
    The Cool School *68*
Jean-Louis Valéro
    The Romance of Astree and Celadon *283*
Fernando Velázquez
    The Orphanage *238*
James L. Venable
    An American Carol *2*
    Superhero Movie *336*
    Zack and Miri Make a Porno *412*
Joseph Vitarelli
    Kit Kittredge: An American Girl *184*
Waddy Wachtel
    The House Bunny *159*
    Strange Wilderness *330*
Thomas Wander
    10,000 B.C. *346*
Michael Wandmacher (1967-)
    Never Back Down *229*

Performer Index

Hiam Abbass (1960-)
The Visitor *373*

Jake Abel
Flash of Genius *117*

Ian Abercrombie (1933-)
Star Wars: The Clone Wars
(V) *323*

Simon Abkarian (1962-)
Persepolis (V) *247*

Alon Aboutboul
Body of Lies *30*

Josef Abrham (1939-)
I Served the King of En-
gland *165*

Omid Abtahi
Space Chimps (V) *315*

Alon Abutbul (1965-)
Beaufort *24*

Joss Ackland (1928-)
Flawless *118*

Marie-Christine Adam
Priceless *252*

Amy Adams (1974-)
Doubt *92*
Miss Pettigrew Lives for a
Day *220*

Jane Adams (1965-)
The Wackness *381*

Tunde Adebimpe
Rachel Getting Married *262*

Trace Adkins
An American Carol *2*

James Adomian
Harold & Kumar Escape from
Guantanamo Bay *152*

Shohreh Aghdashloo (1952-)
The Sisterhood of the Traveling
Pants 2 *302*

Ahmed Ahmed
Iron Man *175*
Vince Vaughn's Wild West Com-
edy Show: 30 Days & 30
Nights—Hollywood to the
Heartland *372*

Malin Akerman (1978-)
27 Dresses *359*

Yasmine Al Masri
Caramel *45*

Carlos Alazraqui
Space Chimps (V) *315*

Jessica Alba (1981-)
The Eye *111*
The Love Guru *195*

Kate Albrecht
My Best Friend's Girl *225*

Alan Alda (1936-)
Diminished Capacity *87*
Flash of Genius *117*

Eddie Alderson
Changeling *47*

Buzz Aldrin
Fly Me to the Moon (V) *121*

Sasha Alexander (1973-)
Yes Man *408*

Mahershalhashbaz Ali
The Curious Case of Benjamin
Button *71*

Roger Allam (1953-)
Speed Racer *316*

Joan Allen (1956-)
Death Race *79*

Karen Allen (1951-)
Indiana Jones and the Kingdom
of the Crystal Skull *173*

Tim Allen (1953-)
Redbelt *267*

Adrian Alonso
Under the Same Moon *365*

Laz Alonso
Miracle at St. Anna *217*

Mathieu Amalric (1965-)
A Christmas Tale *57*
Quantum of Solace *259*

Eva Amurri (1985-)
The Life Before Her Eyes *192*

Ronni Ancona
Penelope *246*

Mini Anden (1978-)
My Best Friend's Girl *225*

Gillian Anderson (1968-)
How to Lose Friends & Alienate
People *162*
The X Files: I Want to Be-
lieve *405*

Jeff Anderson (1970-)
Zack and Miri Make a
Porno *412*

Joe Anderson
The Ruins *286*

Pamela Anderson
Superhero Movie *336*

Andre 3000
See Andre Benjamin

Michael Angarano (1987-)
  The Forbidden Kingdom *124*
  Snow Angels *310*

Chriss Anglin
  An American Carol *2*

Jennifer Aniston (1969-)
  Marley & Me *207*

Gisele Aouad
  Caramel *45*

Christina Applegate (1971-)
  The Rocker *275*

Hale Appleman (1986-)
  Teeth *343*

Tomas Arana (1959-)
  Defiance *82*

Fanny Ardant (1949-)
  Roman de gare *279*

Alan Arkin (1934-)
  Get Smart *137*
  Marley & Me *207*

Fred Armisen (1966-)
  The Promotion *256*
  The Rocker *275*

Tre Armstrong
  How She Move *161*

Jean-Claude Arnaud
  I've Loved You So Long *177*

Will Arnett (1970-)
  Dr. Seuss' Horton Hears a Who!
    (V) *90*
  The Rocker *275*
  Semi-Pro *293*

Jeanetta Arnette (1954-)
  Snow Angels *310*

David Arquette (1971-)
  Hamlet 2 *145*

Richmond Arquette (1964-)
  Made of Honor *204*

Gemma Arterton
  Quantum of Solace *259*

Tadanobu Asano (1973-)
  Mongol *222*

Shawn Ashmore (1979-)
  The Ruins *286*

Skylar Astin
  Hamlet 2 *145*

Ted Atherton
  Max Payne *210*

David Atrakchi
  Transporter 3 *353*

Hayley Atwell
  Brideshead Revisited *38*
  Cassandra's Dream *46*
  The Duchess *96*

Margaret Avery
  Tyler Perry's Meet the
    Browns *363*
  Welcome Home Roscoe Jen-
    kins *389*

Shlomi Avraham
  The Band's Visit *17*

Dan Aykroyd (1952-)
  War, Inc. *388*

Hank Azaria (1964-)
  Chicago 10 (V) *54*
  Run, Fatboy, Run *287*

Anthony Azizi
  Eagle Eye *101*

Obba Babatunde (1951-)
  The Eye *111*

Kevin Bacon (1958-)
  The Air I Breathe *1*
  Frost/Nixon *131*

Diedrich Bader (1966-)
  Meet the Spartans *213*

Ben Badra
  10,000 B.C. *346*

Sayed Badreya
  Iron Man *175*
  W. *377*

Robert Bailey, Jr.
  The Happening *149*

Diora Baird (1983-)
  My Best Friend's Girl *225*

Becky Ann Baker
  Nights in Rodanthe *231*

Dylan Baker (1958-)
  Chicago 10 (V) *54*
  Diminished Capacity *87*
  Revolutionary Road *272*

Joe Don Baker (1936-)
  Strange Wilderness *330*

Dato Bakhtadze
  Wanted *385*

Saleh Bakri
  The Band's Visit *17*

Liane Balaban (1980-)
  Definitely, Maybe *83*

Alec Baldwin (1958-)
  Madagascar: Escape 2 Africa
    (V) *202*
  My Best Friend's Girl *225*

William Baldwin (1963-)
  Forgetting Sarah Marshall *125*

Christian Bale (1974-)
  The Dark Knight *75*

Eric Balfour
  Hell Ride *153*
  The Spirit *320*

Jeanne Balibar (1968-)
  The Duchess of Langeais *98*

Jonas Ball
  The Killing of John Len-
    non *182*

Talia Balsam (1960-)
  The Wackness *381*

David Bamber (1954-)
  Valkyrie *366*

Eric Bana (1968-)
  The Other Boleyn Girl *239*
  Romulus, My Father *284*

Elizabeth Banks (1974-)
  Definitely, Maybe *83*
  Meet Dave *211*
  Role Models *278*
  W. *377*
  Zack and Miri Make a
    Porno *412*

Tyra Banks (1973-)
  Tropic Thunder *355*

Christine Baranski (1952-)
  Mamma Mia! *205*

Javier Bardem (1969-)
  Vicky Cristina Barcelona *370*

Ike Barinholtz
  Disaster Movie *88*

Ben Barnes
  The Chronicles of Narnia: Prince
    Caspian *58*

Ivan Barnev
  I Served the King of En-
    gland *165*

Adriana Barraza (1956-)
  Henry Poole Is Here *156*

Drew Barrymore (1975-)
  Beverly Hills Chihuahua
    (V) *27*

Roger Bart (1962-)
  Harold & Kumar Escape from
    Guantanamo Bay *152*

Jay Baruchel (1982-)
  Nick & Norah's Infinite Playl-
    ist *230*
  Tropic Thunder *355*

Angela Bassett (1958-)
  Tyler Perry's Meet the
    Browns *363*

Jason Bateman (1969-)
  Forgetting Sarah Marshall *125*
  Hancock *146*

Kathy Bates (1948-)
  The Day the Earth Stood
    Still *77*
  Revolutionary Road *272*

Marie Baumer
  The Counterfeiters *70*

Dimitri Baveas
The Ruins *286*

Nathalie Baye (1948-)
Tell No One *345*

Michael Beach (1963-)
First Sunday *116*

Matthew Beard (1925-81)
When Did You Last See Your
Father? *395*

Emmanuelle Béart (1965-)
The Witnesses *398*

Amber Beattie
The Boy in the Striped Pajamas *35*

Madisen Beaty
Bedtime Stories *26*
The Curious Case of Benjamin
Button *71*

Kate Beckinsale (1974-)
Snow Angels *310*

Gerry Bednob
Zack and Miri Make a
Porno *412*

Jason Beghe (1960-)
One Missed Call *237*

Ed Begley, Jr. (1949-)
Pineapple Express *249*

Drake Bell (1986-)
Superhero Movie *336*

Jamie Bell (1986-)
Defiance *82*
Jumper *180*

Kristen Bell (1980-)
Forgetting Sarah Marshall *125*

Lake Bell
Over Her Dead Body *241*
Pride and Glory *253*
What Happens in Vegas *392*

Marshall Bell (1944-)
Hamlet 2 *145*

Tobin Bell (1942-)
Saw V *289*

Ned Bellamy (1960-)
War, Inc. *388*

Camilla Belle (1986-)
10,000 B.C. *346*

Maria Bello (1967-)
The Mummy: Tomb of the
Dragon Emperor *224*

Gil Bellows (1967-)
The Promotion *256*

Vivienne Benesch
Teeth *343*

John Benfield
Cassandra's Dream *46*
Speed Racer *316*

Annette Bening (1958-)
The Women *399*

Gabrielle Lopes Benites
Persepolis *(V)* *247*

André Benjamin (1975-)
Battle in Seattle *21*
Semi-Pro *293*

John Benjamin
Then She Found Me *350*

Richard Benjamin (1938-)
Henry Poole Is Here *156*

Haley Bennett
Marley & Me *207*

Jimmy Bennett (1996-)
Diminished Capacity *87*

Sonja Bennett (1980-)
Elegy *107*

Morgan Benoit
The Forbidden Kingdom *124*

Julie Benz (1972-)
Rambo *264*
Saw V *289*

Candice Bergen (1946-)
Sex and the City: The
Movie *298*
The Women *399*

Christian Berkel (1957-)
Valkyrie *366*

François Berléand (1952-)
A Girl Cut in Two *141*
Tell No One *345*
Transporter 3 *353*

Emile Berling
A Christmas Tale *57*

Shelley Berman (1926-)
You Don't Mess with the Zohan *410*

Gael Garcia Bernal (1978-)
Blindness *29*

Michele Bernier
Roman de gare *279*

Francoise Bertin
A Christmas Tale *57*

Erin Bethea
Fireproof *113*

Paul Bettany (1971-)
Iron Man *(V)* *175*
The Secret Life of Bees *292*

Ken Bevel
Fireproof *113*

Dante Beze
See Mos Def

Leslie Bibb (1974-)
Iron Man *175*

Jason Biggs (1978-)
My Best Friend's Girl *225*
Over Her Dead Body *241*

Peter Billingsley (1971-)
Iron Man *175*
Vince Vaughn's Wild West Com-
edy Show: 30 Days & 30
Nights—Hollywood to the
Heartland *372*

Rachel Bilson
Jumper *180*

Juliette Binoche (1964-)
Flight of the Red Balloon *120*

Gil Birmingham
Twilight *360*

Larry Bishop (1947-)
Hell Ride *153*

Jack Black (1969-)
Be Kind Rewind *22*
Kung Fu Panda *(V)* *185*
Tropic Thunder *355*

Selma Blair (1972-)
Hellboy II: The Golden
Army *155*

Michel Blanc (1952-)
The Witnesses *398*

Tammy Blanchard (1976-)
Cadillac Records *43*

Cate Blanchett (1969-)
The Curious Case of Benjamin
Button *71*
Indiana Jones and the Kingdom
of the Crystal Skull *173*

Kelly Blatz
Prom Night *255*

Alexis Bledel (1981-)
The Sisterhood of the Traveling
Pants 2 *302*

Moritz Bleibtreu (1971-)
Speed Racer *316*

Corbin Bleu (1989-)
High School Musical 3: Senior
Year *158*

Marc Blucas (1972-)
Meet Dave *211*

Alan Blumenfeld
Righteous Kill *274*

Eric Bogosian (1953-)
Cadillac Records *43*

Philip Daniel Bolden (1995-)
Fly Me to the Moon *(V)* *121*

Sarah Bolger (1991-)
The Spiderwick
Chronicles *318*

Mark Boone, Jr. (1955-)
Frozen River *133*

Bobby Cannavale (1971-)
Diminished Capacity *87*
The Promotion *256*

John Canoe
Frozen River *133*

Jose Pablo Cantillo (1979-)
Redbelt *267*

Mario Cantone (1959-)
Sex and the City: The
Movie *298*

John Caparulo
Vince Vaughn's Wild West Comedy Show: 30 Days & 30 Nights—Hollywood to the Heartland *372*

Laurent Capelluto
A Christmas Tale *57*

Lizzy Caplan (1982-)
Cloverfield *64*
My Best Friend's Girl *225*

Nestor Carbonell (1967-)
The Dark Knight *75*

Manolo Cardona
Beverly Hills Chihuahua *27*

Steven Carell (1963-)
Dr. Seuss' Horton Hears a Who!
(V) *90*
Get Smart *137*

Helen Carey
21 *357*

Christopher Carley
Gran Torino *142*

Kelly Carlson (1976-)
Made of Honor *204*

Jennifer Carpenter (1979-)
Battle in Seattle *21*
Quarantine *260*

David Carradine (1936-)
Hell Ride *153*

Jim Carrey (1962-)
Dr. Seuss' Horton Hears a Who!
(V) *90*
Yes Man *408*

Elpidia Carrillo (1963-)
Seven Pounds *295*

Madeline Carroll (1996-)
Swing Vote *338*

Montserrat Carulla
The Orphanage *238*

Max Casella (1967-)
Revolutionary Road *272*

Cécile Cassel
The Romance of Astree and Celadon *283*

Elaine Cassidy (1979-)
When Did You Last See Your Father? *395*

Sergio Castellitto (1953-)
The Chronicles of Narnia: Prince Caspian *58*

Kim Cattrall (1956-)
Sex and the City: The Movie *298*

Valeria Cavalli
A Girl Cut in Two *141*

Fernando Cayo
The Orphanage *238*

Cedric the Entertainer (1964-)
Cadillac Records *43*
Madagascar: Escape 2 Africa (V) *202*
Street Kings *333*
Welcome Home Roscoe Jenkins *389*

Michael Cera (1988-)
Nick & Norah's Infinite Playlist *230*

Valentina Cervi
Miracle at St. Anna *217*

Sarah Chalke (1977-)
Chaos Theory *50*

Jackie Chan (1954-)
The Forbidden Kingdom *124*
Kung Fu Panda (V) *185*

Kyle Chandler (1965-)
The Day the Earth Stood Still *77*

Miles Chandler
The Longshots *194*

Dolores Chaplin
The Counterfeiters *70*

Geraldine Chaplin (1944-)
The Orphanage *238*

Maury Chaykin (1949-)
Blindness *29*

Don Cheadle (1964-)
Traitor *351*

Kristin Chenoweth (1968-)
Four Christmases *127*
Space Chimps (V) *315*

Jacky Cheung (1961-)
Ashes of Time Redux *7*

Leslie Cheung (1956-2003)
Ashes of Time Redux *7*

Maggie Cheung (1964-)
Ashes of Time Redux *7*

Michael Chiklis (1963-)
Eagle Eye *101*

John Cho (1972-)
Harold & Kumar Escape from Guantanamo Bay *152*

Margaret Cho (1969-)
One Missed Call *237*

Deepak Chopra
The Love Guru *195*

Collin Chou (1967-)
The Forbidden Kingdom *124*

Emmanuelle Chriqui (1977-)
Cadillac Records *43*
You Don't Mess with the Zohan *410*

Hayden Christensen (1981-)
Jumper *180*

Jesper Christensen (1948-)
Quantum of Solace *259*

Shawn Christian
Meet Dave *211*

Khulan Chuluun
Mongol *222*

Thomas Haden Church (1960-)
Smart People *309*

Louis CK (1967-)
Diminished Capacity *87*

Cam Clarke (1957-)
The Pirates Who Don't Do Anything: A VeggieTales Movie (V) *251*

Jason Clarke
Death Race *79*

Patricia Clarkson (1960-)
Elegy *107*
Married Life *208*
Vicky Cristina Barcelona *370*

John Cleese (1939-)
The Day the Earth Stood Still *77*
Igor (V) *166*

George Clooney (1961-)
Burn After Reading *40*
Leatherheads *190*

Joshua Close (1981-)
Diary of the Dead *86*

François Cluzet (1955-)
Tell No One *345*

Lynn Cohen
Eagle Eye *101*
Sex and the City: The Movie *298*
Then She Found Me *350*

Oshri Cohen
Beaufort *24*

Sacha Baron Cohen (1971-)
Madagascar: Escape 2 Africa (V) *202*

Stephen Colbert (1964-)
The Love Guru *195*

Christina Cole (1982-)
Miss Pettigrew Lives for a Day *220*

Eric Dane (1972-)
   Marley & Me *207*

Beverly D'Angelo (1953-)
   Harold & Kumar Escape from
      Guantanamo Bay *152*
   The House Bunny *159*

Anthony Daniels (1946-)
   Star Wars: The Clone Wars
      (V) *323*

Jeff Daniels (1955-)
   Space Chimps (V) *315*
   Traitor *351*

Blythe Danner (1944-)
   The Sisterhood of the Traveling
      Pants 2 *302*

Ted Danson (1947-)
   Mad Money *201*

Peter Dante (1968-)
   Strange Wilderness *330*

Rhys Darby
   Yes Man *408*

Danielle Darrieux (1917-)
   Persepolis (V) *247*

Darrin Dewitt, Henson
   The Express *110*

Jareb Dauplaise
   Meet the Spartans *213*

Alexa Davalos (1982-)
   Defiance *82*

Ishan Dave
   Charlie Bartlett *51*

Madison Davenport (1996-)
   Kit Kittredge: An American
      Girl *184*

Robert Davi (1953-)
   An American Carol *2*

Keith David (1954-)
   First Sunday *116*

Brianne Davis
   Prom Night *255*

Dana Davis
   Prom Night *255*

Hope Davis (1964-)
   Charlie Bartlett *51*
   Synecdoche, New York *340*

Kristin Davis (1965-)
   Sex and the City: The
      Movie *298*

Viola Davis (1952-)
   Doubt *92*
   Nights in Rodanthe *231*

Warwick Davis (1970-)
   The Chronicles of Narnia: Prince
      Caspian *58*

Ken Davitian
   Get Smart *137*
   Meet the Spartans *213*

Baki Davrak
   The Edge of Heaven *103*

Rosario Dawson (1979-)
   Eagle Eye *101*
   Seven Pounds *295*

Isaach de Bankole (1957-)
   Battle in Seattle *21*

India de Beaufort
   Run, Fatboy, Run *287*

Joel de la Fuente
   The Happening *149*

Paz de la Huerta (1984-)
   Deception *80*

John de Lancie (1948-)
   Pathology *244*

Robert De Niro (1943-)
   Righteous Kill *274*
   What Just Happened *393*

Tim De Zarn
   Untraceable *366*

Ron Dean
   The Dark Knight *75*

Kate del Castillo
   Under the Same Moon *365*

Shaun Delaney
   Bangkok Dangerous *18*

Julie Delpy (1969-)
   The Air I Breathe *1*

Vanessa del Rio
   Soul Men *313*

Patrick Dempsey (1966-)
   Made of Honor *204*

Jeffrey DeMunn (1947-)
   Burn After Reading *40*

Judi Dench (1934-)
   Quantum of Solace *259*

Catherine Deneuve (1943-)
   A Christmas Tale *57*
   Persepolis (V) *247*

David Denman (1973-)
   Shutter *303*

Brian Dennehy (1939-)
   Righteous Kill *274*

Kat Dennings (1986-)
   Charlie Bartlett *51*
   The House Bunny *159*
   Nick & Norah's Infinite Playl-
      ist *230*

Gerard Depardieu (1948-)
   Babylon A.D. *14*

Guillaume Depardieu (1971-2008)
   The Duchess of Langeais *98*

Julie Depardieu (1973-)
   The Witnesses *398*

Eugenio Derbez
   Under the Same Moon *365*

Debi Derryberry
   Dr. Seuss' Horton Hears a Who!
      (V) *90*

Zooey Deschanel (1980-)
   The Happening *149*
   Yes Man *408*

Shawn Desman
   How She Move *161*

Loretta Devine (1949-)
   Beverly Hills Chihuahua
      (V) *27*
   First Sunday *116*

Emmanuelle Devos (1964-)
   A Christmas Tale *57*

Rosemarie DeWitt
   Rachel Getting Married *262*

Cameron Diaz (1972-)
   What Happens in Vegas *392*

Melonie Diaz (1984-)
   Be Kind Rewind *22*
   Hamlet 2 *145*

Leonardo DiCaprio (1974-)
   Body of Lies *30*
   Revolutionary Road *272*

August Diehl (1976-)
   The Counterfeiters *70*

John Diehl (1958-)
   The Lucky Ones *198*

Vin Diesel (1967-)
   Babylon A.D. *14*

Joe Dinicol
   Diary of the Dead *86*

Peter Dinklage (1969-)
   The Chronicles of Narnia: Prince
      Caspian *58*
   Penelope *246*

Bob Dishy (1943-)
   The Wackness *381*

Andrew Divoff (1955-)
   Indiana Jones and the Kingdom
      of the Crystal Skull *173*

Omid Djalili (1965-)
   The Love Guru *195*

Vernon Dobtcheff (1934-)
   Priceless *252*

Placido Domingo
   Beverly Hills Chihuahua
      (V) *27*

Jeffrey Donovan (1968-)
   Changeling *47*

Mike Dopud
   In the Name of the King: A
      Dungeon Siege Tale *169*

David Dorfman (1993-)
Drillbit Taylor *95*

Rodrigo dos Santos
City of Men *63*

Roy Dotrice (1925-)
Hellboy II: The Golden
Army *155*

Ann Dowd
Marley & Me *207*

Robert Downey, Jr. (1965-)
Charlie Bartlett *51*
The Incredible Hulk *171*
Iron Man *175*
Tropic Thunder *355*

Ashley Drane
See Ashley Eckstein

Eshaya Draper
College Road Trip *67*

Richard Dreyfuss (1947-)
W. *377*

Alice Drummond (1929-)
Doubt *92*

David Duchovny (1960-)
The X Files: I Want to Believe *405*

Neil Dudgeon
Son of Rambow *311*

Hilary Duff (1987-)
War, Inc. *388*

Kevin Duhaney
How She Move *161*

Clark Duke
Sex Drive *300*

Jaromir Dulava
I Served the King of En-
gland *165*

Michael Clarke Duncan (1957-)
Kung Fu Panda (V) *185*
Welcome Home Roscoe Jen-
kins *389*

Kevin Dunn (1956-)
Vicky Cristina Barcelona *370*

Nora Dunn (1952-)
Pineapple Express *249*

Griffin Dunne (1955-)
Snow Angels *310*

Kirsten Dunst (1982-)
How to Lose Friends & Alienate
People *162*

Eliza Dushku (1980-)
Bottle Shock *34*

André Dussollier (1946-)
Tell No One *345*

Charles S. Dutton (1951-)

The Express *110*

Robert Duvall (1931-)
Four Christmases *127*

Wayne Duvall (1958-)
Leatherheads *190*
Pride and Glory *253*

Russell Dykstra
Romulus, My Father *284*

Alexis Dziena (1984-)
Fool's Gold *123*
Nick & Norah's Infinite Playl-
ist *230*

Michael Ealy (1973-)
Miracle at St. Anna *217*
Seven Pounds *295*

Richard Easton (1933-)
Revolutionary Road *272*

Clint Eastwood (1930-)
Gran Torino *142*

Aaron Eckhart (1968-)
The Dark Knight *75*

Ashley Eckstein (1981-)
Star Wars: The Clone Wars
(V) *323*

Zac Efron (1987-)
High School Musical 3: Senior
Year *158*

Jennifer Ehle (1969-)
Pride and Glory *253*

David Eigenberg (1964-)
Sex and the City: The
Movie *298*

Debra Eisenstadt
Chicago 10 (V) *54*

Chiwetel Ejiofor (1976-)
Redbelt *267*

Carmen Ejogo (1975-)
Pride and Glory *253*

Saidah Arrika Ekulona
Righteous Kill *274*

Idris Elba (1972-)
Prom Night *255*
RocknRolla *276*

Carmen Electra (1972-)
Disaster Movie *88*
Meet the Spartans *213*

Ronit Elkabetz (1966-)
The Band's Visit *17*

Gad Elmaleh (1971-)
Priceless *252*

Eli Eltonyo
Beaufort *24*

Noah Emmerich (1965-)
Pride and Glory *253*

India Ennenga (1994-)
The Women *399*

Mike Epps (1970-)
Soul Men *313*
Welcome Home Roscoe Jen-
kins *389*

Jake Epstein
Charlie Bartlett *51*

Bayartsetseg Erdenebat
Mongol *222*

Bret Ernst
Vince Vaughn's Wild West Com-
edy Show: 30 Days & 30
Nights—Hollywood to the
Heartland *372*

Mike Erwin (1978-)
Chaos Theory *50*

Susie Essman
Bolt (V) *32*

Chris Evans (1981-)
Street Kings *333*

Briana Evigan
Step Up 2 the Streets *326*

Peter Facinelli (1973-)
Twilight *360*

Krisha Fairchild
The Killing of John Len-
non *182*

Frankie Faison (1949-)
Tyler Perry's Meet the
Browns *363*

Dakota Fanning (1994-)
The Secret Life of Bees *292*

Elle Fanning (1998-)
The Curious Case of Benjamin
Button *71*

Golshifteh Farahani
Body of Lies *30*

Dennis Farina (1944-)
Bottle Shock *34*
What Happens in Vegas *392*

Pierfrancesco Favino
The Chronicles of Narnia: Prince
Caspian *58*
Miracle at St. Anna *217*

Anna Faris (1976-)
The House Bunny *159*

Sean Faris (1982-)
Never Back Down *229*

Kevin Farley
An American Carol *2*

Vera Farmiga (1973-)
The Boy in the Striped Pajamas *35*

Colin Farrell (1976-)
Cassandra's Dream *46*

In Bruges *168*
Pride and Glory *253*

Mia Farrow (1945-)
Be Kind Rewind *22*

James Faulkner (1948-)
The Bank Job *19*

Jon Favreau (1966-)
Four Christmases *127*
Iron Man *175*
Vince Vaughn's Wild West Comedy Show: 30 Days & 30 Nights—Hollywood to the Heartland *372*

Michael Feast (1946-)
Penelope *246*

Matthew Fenton
Run, Fatboy, Run *287*

Colm Feore (1958-)
Changeling *47*

Karina Fernandez
Happy-Go-Lucky *150*

Adam Ferrara
Definitely, Maybe *83*

Will Ferrell (1968-)
Semi-Pro *293*
Step Brothers *325*

America Ferrera (1984-)
The Sisterhood of the Traveling Pants 2 *302*
Under the Same Moon *365*

Larry Fessenden (1963-)
Wendy and Lucy *389*

Mark Feuerstein (1971-)
Defiance *82*

Tina Fey (1970-)
Baby Mama *13*

William Fichtner (1956-)
The Dark Knight *75*

Ralph Fiennes (1962-)
The Duchess *96*
In Bruges *168*
The Reader *265*

Colin Firth (1961-)
Mamma Mia! *205*
Then She Found Me *350*
When Did You Last See Your Father? *395*

Jenna Fischer (1974-)
The Promotion *256*

Laurence Fishburne (1963-)
21 *357*

Carrie Fisher (1956-)
The Women *399*

Isla Fisher (1976-)
Definitely, Maybe *83*

Dr. Seuss' Horton Hears a Who! (V) *90*

Jaishon Fisher (1996-)
Lakeview Terrace *189*

Miles Fisher
Superhero Movie *336*

Tom Fisher
Cassandra's Dream *46*

Crista Flanagan
Disaster Movie *88*

Fionnula Flanagan (1941-)
Yes Man *408*

Jason Flemyng (1966-)
The Curious Case of Benjamin Button *71*

Josh Flitter (1994-)
Dr. Seuss' Horton Hears a Who! (V) *90*

Neil Flynn (1960-)
Indiana Jones and the Kingdom of the Crystal Skull *173*

Dan Fogler
Dr. Seuss' Horton Hears a Who! (V) *90*
Kung Fu Panda (V) *185*

Harrison Ford (1942-)
Indiana Jones and the Kingdom of the Crystal Skull *173*

Luke Ford (1981-)
The Mummy: Tomb of the Dragon Emperor *224*

Claire Forlani (1972-)
In the Name of the King: A Dungeon Siege Tale *169*

William Forsythe (1955-)
88 Minutes *105*

Jodie Foster (1963-)
Nim's Island *233*

Joseph Foster II
Doubt *92*

Matthew Fox (1966-)
Speed Racer *316*
Vantage Point *368*

Megan Fox (1986-)
How to Lose Friends & Alienate People *162*

Rick Fox (1969-)
Tyler Perry's Meet the Browns *363*

James Franco (1978-)
Milk *214*
Nights in Rodanthe *231*
Pineapple Express *249*

Brendan Fraser (1968-)
The Air I Breathe *1*

Journey to the Center of the Earth *179*
The Mummy: Tomb of the Dragon Emperor *224*

Alfonso Freeman
The Bucket List *39*

Morgan Freeman (1937-)
The Bucket List *39*
The Dark Knight *75*
Wanted *385*

Matthias Freihof
Valkyrie *366*

Judah Friedlander (1969-)
Meet Dave *211*

Gal Friedman (1963-)
Beaufort *24*

Rupert Friend (1981-)
The Boy in the Striped Pajamas *35*

Alex Frost
Drillbit Taylor *95*

Benno Fürmann (1972-)
Speed Racer *316*

Deborra-Lee Furness (1960-)
Sleepwalking *306*

Sasson Gabai
The Band's Visit *17*

Seychelle Gabriel
The Spirit *320*

Elisa Gabrielli
Madagascar: Escape 2 Africa (V) *202*

Josh Gad
The Rocker *275*
21 *357*

Brennan Gademans
How She Move *161*

Jim Gaffigan (1966-)
The Love Guru *195*

Trevor Gagnon
Fly Me to the Moon (V) *121*

Johnny Galecki (1975-)
Hancock *146*

Zach Galifianakis (1969-)
What Happens in Vegas *392*

Rey Gallegos
Rambo *264*

Nathan Gamble
The Dark Knight *75*
Marley & Me *207*

Michael Gambon (1940-)
Brideshead Revisited *38*

The Game (1979-)
Street Kings *333*

James Gammon (1940-)
Appaloosa *5*

Bruno Ganz (1941-)
The Reader *265*

Victor Garber (1949-)
Milk *214*

Paula Garcés (1974-)
Harold & Kumar Escape from
Guantanamo Bay *152*

Andy Garcia (1956-)
The Air I Breathe *1*
Beverly Hills Chihuahua
(V) *27*

Jesse Garcia
Under the Same Moon *365*

Jeff Garlin (1962-)
The Rocker *275*
Strange Wilderness *330*
WALL-E (V) *382*

Louis Garrel (1983-)
Love Songs *197*

Beau Garrett
Made of Honor *204*

Spencer Garrett (1963-)
21 *357*

Willie Garson (1964-)
Sex and the City: The
Movie *298*

Ana Gasteyer (1967-)
The Women *399*

Michael Gaston
Body of Lies *30*
W. *377*

Edi Gathegi
Twilight *360*

Rafi Gavron
Nick & Norah's Infinite Playlist *230*

Devon Gearhart (1995-)
Funny Games *134*

Teddy Geiger
The Rocker *275*

Sarah Michelle Gellar (1977-)
The Air I Breathe *1*

Troy Gentile
Drillbit Taylor *95*

Anisa George
Rachel Getting Married *262*

Richard Gere (1949-)
Nights in Rodanthe *231*

Peter Gerety (1940-)
Changeling *47*
Leatherheads *190*

Greg Germann (1962-)
Bolt (V) *32*
Quarantine *260*

Laura Gerow
The Pirates Who Don't Do Any-
thing: A VeggieTales Movie
(V) *251*

Ricky Gervais (1961-)
Ghost Town *139*

Giancarlo Giannini (1942-)
Quantum of Solace *259*

Alex Gibney
Taxi to the Dark Side (N) *342*

Tyrese Gibson (1978-)
Death Race *79*

Cam Gigandet
Never Back Down *229*
Twilight *360*

Ariadna Gil (1969-)
Appaloosa *5*

Andy Gillet
The Romance of Astree and Celadon *283*

Jack Gilpin (1951-)
The Life Before Her Eyes *192*
21 *357*

Tyrone Giordano (1976-)
Untraceable *366*

Hippolyte Girardot (1955-)
A Christmas Tale *57*
Flight of the Red Balloon *120*

Ron Glass (1945-)
Lakeview Terrace *189*

Joanna Gleason (1950-)
The Women *399*

Brendan Gleeson (1954-)
In Bruges *168*

Scott Glenn (1942-)
Nights in Rodanthe *231*
W. *377*

Danny Glover (1947-)
Be Kind Rewind *22*
Blindness *29*

Julian Glover (1935-)
Mirrors *218*

Trilby Glover
Righteous Kill *274*

Erica Gluck
Mirrors *218*

Adam Godley
The X Files: I Want to Believe *405*

Walton Goggins (1971-)
Miracle at St. Anna *217*

Sadie Goldstein
Synecdoche, New York *340*

Sam Golzari
21 *357*

Rick Gonzalez (1979-)
Pride and Glory *253*
The Promotion *256*

Irv Gooch
Be Kind Rewind *22*

Meagan Good (1981-)
The Love Guru *195*
One Missed Call *237*
Saw V *289*

Matthew Goode (1978-)
Brideshead Revisited *38*

Dana Min Goodman
The House Bunny *159*

John Goodman (1952-)
Speed Racer *316*

Malcolm Goodwin
The Longshots *194*
Miracle at St. Anna *217*

Joel Gordon
Max Payne *210*

Joseph Gordon-Levitt (1981-)
Miracle at St. Anna *217*
Stop-Loss *327*

David Gore
Fly Me to the Moon (V) *121*

Luke Goss (1968-)
Hellboy II: The Golden
Army *155*

Jenn Gotzon
Frost/Nixon *131*

Lucas Grabeel
College Road Trip *67*
High School Musical 3: Senior
Year *158*
Milk *214*

Hudson Grace
Snow Angels *310*

Lauren Graham (1967-)
Flash of Genius *117*

Kelsey Grammer (1954-)
An American Carol *2*
Swing Vote *338*

Beth Grant (1949-)
Henry Poole Is Here *156*

Faye Grant (1957-)
My Best Friend's Girl *225*

Richard E. Grant (1957-)
Penelope *246*

Ari Graynor (1983-)
Nick & Norah's Infinite Playlist *230*

Alice Greczyn (1986-)
Sex Drive *300*

Scott Green
Paranoid Park *243*

Seth Green (1974-)
    Sex Drive *300*

Ashley Greene
    Twilight *360*

Judy Greer (1971-)
    27 Dresses *359*

Clark Gregg (1964-)
    Choke *55*
    Iron Man *175*

Laurent Grevill (1961-)
    I've Loved You So Long *177*

Gattlin Griffith
    Changeling *47*

Richard Griffiths (1947-)
    Bedtime Stories *26*

Frank Grillo
    The Express *110*
    Pride and Glory *253*

Lance Gross
    Tyler Perry's Meet the
        Browns *363*

Ioan Gruffudd (1974-)
    W. *377*

Carla Gugino (1971-)
    Righteous Kill *274*

Tim Guinee (1962-)
    Iron Man *175*

David Gulpilil (1954-)
    Australia *8*

Mamie Gummer
    Stop-Loss *327*

Xiaodong Guo
    Summer Palace *334*

Danai Gurira
    The Visitor *373*

Kick Gurry
    Speed Racer *316*

Luis Guzman (1956-)
    Beverly Hills Chihuahua
        (V) *27*

Maggie Gyllenhaal (1977-)
    The Dark Knight *75*

Johnathan Haagensen
    City of Men *63*

Matthias Habich (1940-)
    The Reader *265*

Sihame Haddad
    Caramel *45*

Bill Hader (1978-)
    Forgetting Sarah Marshall *125*
    Pineapple Express *249*
    Tropic Thunder *355*

Molly Hagan (1962-)
    The Lucky Ones *198*

Kristen Hager
    Wanted *385*

Kathryn Hahn (1974-)
    Revolutionary Road *272*
    Step Brothers *325*

Tony Hale (1970-)
    The Tale of Despereaux
        (V) *341*

Brian Haley (1963-)
    Gran Torino *142*

Jackie Earle Haley (1961-)
    Semi-Pro *293*

Anthony Michael Hall (1968-)
    The Dark Knight *75*

Arsenio Hall (1956-)
    Igor (V) *166*

Irma P. Hall (1937-)
    Tyler Perry's Meet the
        Browns *363*

Rebecca Hall (1982-)
    Frost/Nixon *131*
    Vicky Cristina Barcelona *370*

Regina Hall (1971-)
    First Sunday *116*

Lisa Gay Hamilton (1964-)
    Deception *80*

Harry Hamlin (1951-)
    Strange Wilderness *330*

Jon Hamm
    The Day the Earth Stood
        Still *77*

Chin Han (1969-)
    The Dark Knight *75*

Sheila Hancock (1933-)
    The Boy in the Striped Paja-
        mas *35*

Evan Handler (1961-)
    Sex and the City: The
        Movie *298*

Marina Hands
    Tell No One *345*

Perla Haney-Jardine
    Untraceable *366*

Colin Hanks (1977-)
    The House Bunny *159*
    Untraceable *366*

John Hannah (1962-)
    The Mummy: Tomb of the
        Dragon Emperor *224*

Ryan Hansen
    Superhero Movie *336*

Lei Hao
    Summer Palace *334*

David Harbour
    Quantum of Solace *259*
    Revolutionary Road *272*

Melora Hardin (1967-)
    27 Dresses *359*

Kadeem Hardison (1965-)
    Made of Honor *204*

Omari Hardwick (1974-)
    Miracle at St. Anna *217*

Thomas Hardy (1977-)
    RocknRolla *276*

Jason Butler Harner
    Changeling *47*

Elisabeth Harnois (1979-)
    Chaos Theory *50*

Woody Harrelson (1962-)
    Battle in Seattle *21*
    Semi-Pro *293*
    Seven Pounds *295*
    Sleepwalking *306*
    Transsiberian *354*

Danneel Harris (1979-)
    Harold & Kumar Escape from
        Guantanamo Bay *152*

Ed Harris (1949-)
    Appaloosa *5*

Jared Harris (1961-)
    The Curious Case of Benjamin
        Button *71*

Naomie Harris (1976-)
    Street Kings *333*

Neil Patrick Harris (1973-)
    Harold & Kumar Escape from
        Guantanamo Bay *152*

Steve Harris (1965-)
    Quarantine *260*

Deborah Harry (1945-)
    Elegy *107*

Margo Harshman (1986-)
    College Road Trip *67*

Kevin Hart (1980-)
    Fool's Gold *123*
    Meet Dave *211*

Nate Hartley
    Drillbit Taylor *95*

Joshua Harto (1979-)
    The Dark Knight *75*
    Iron Man *175*

Anne Hathaway (1982-)
    Get Smart *137*
    Rachel Getting Married *262*

Nigel Havers (1949-)
    Penelope *246*

Sally Hawkins (1976-)
    Cassandra's Dream *46*
    Happy-Go-Lucky *150*

Salma Hayek (1966-)
    Beverly Hills Chihuahua
        (V) *27*

Isaac Hayes (1942-2008)
Soul Men *313*

Sean Hayes (1970-)
The Bucket List *39*
Igor *(V)* *166*
Soul Men *313*

David Hayman (1950-)
The Boy in the Striped Pajamas *35*

Robert Hays
Superhero Movie *336*

Serge Hazanavicius
I've Loved You So Long *177*

Maya Hazen
Shutter *303*

Anthony Head (1954-)
Repo! The Genetic Opera *271*

Jae Head
Hancock *146*

Glenne Headley
Kit Kittredge: An American
Girl *184*

Amber Heard
Never Back Down *229*
Pineapple Express *249*

John Heard (1946-)
The Lucky Ones *198*

Gina Hecht
Seven Pounds *295*

Jamie Hector
Max Payne *210*

Kevin Heffernan (1968-)
Strange Wilderness *330*

Hugh Hefner (1926-)
The House Bunny *159*

Katherine Heigl (1978-)
27 Dresses *359*

Ed Helms
Harold & Kumar Escape from
Guantanamo Bay *152*
Meet Dave *211*

Panward Hemmanee
Bangkok Dangerous *18*

Martin Henderson (1974-)
Battle in Seattle *21*

Shirley Henderson (1966-)
Miss Pettigrew Lives for a
Day *220*

Brad William Henke (1971-)
Choke *55*

Georgie Henley
The Chronicles of Narnia: Prince
Caspian *58*

Lance Henriksen (1940-)
Appaloosa *5*

Lenny Henry (1958-)
Penelope *246*

John Hensley
Shutter *303*
Teeth *343*

Taraji P. Henson (1970-)
The Curious Case of Benjamin
Button *71*

Natasha Henstridge (1974-)
Deception *80*

Ahney Her
Gran Torino *142*

Karoline Herforth
The Reader *265*

Jay Hernandez (1978-)
Lakeview Terrace *189*
Quarantine *260*

Adam Herschman
Soul Men *313*

Annelise Hesme (1976-)
Priceless *252*

Howard Hesseman (1940-)
The Rocker *275*

Dom Hetrakul
Bangkok Dangerous *18*

Jennifer Love Hewitt (1979-)
Tropic Thunder *355*

Martha Higareda
Street Kings *333*

Clare Higgins (1955-)
Cassandra's Dream *46*

John Michael Higgins (1962-)
Yes Man *408*

Freddie Highmore (1992-)
The Spiderwick
Chronicles *318*

Tad Hilgenbrink
Disaster Movie *88*

Jonah Hill (1983-)
Dr. Seuss' Horton Hears a Who!
(V) *90*
Forgetting Sarah Marshall *125*
Strange Wilderness *330*

Paris Hilton (1981-)
Repo! The Genetic Opera *271*

Tyler Hilton (1983-)
Charlie Bartlett *51*

Ciarán Hinds (1953-)
Miss Pettigrew Lives for a
Day *220*
Stop-Loss *327*
The Tale of Despereaux
(V) *341*

Cheryl Hines (1965-)
Henry Poole Is Here *156*
Space Chimps *(V)* *315*

Marin Hinkle (1966-)
Quarantine *260*

Emile Hirsch (1985-)
The Air I Breathe *1*
Milk *214*
Speed Racer *316*

Iben Hjejle (1971-)
Defiance *82*

Dustin Hoffman (1937-)
Kung Fu Panda *(V)* *185*
The Tale of Despereaux
(V) *341*

Philip Seymour Hoffman (1967-)
Doubt *92*
Synecdoche, New York *340*

Robert Hoffman
Step Up 2 the Streets *326*

Siobhan Fallon Hogan (1972-)
Baby Mama *13*

Tom Hollander (1969-)
Valkyrie *366*

Ashton Holmes (1978-)
Smart People *309*

Katie Holmes (1978-)
Mad Money *201*

James Hong (1929-)
The Day the Earth Stood
Still *77*
Kung Fu Panda *(V)* *185*

Brian Hooks (1973-)
Fool's Gold *123*

Leslie Hope (1965-)
Never Back Down *229*

Telma Hopkins (1948-)
The Love Guru *195*

Dennis Hopper (1936-)
Elegy *107*
Hell Ride *153*
Sleepwalking *306*
Swing Vote *338*

Chelah Horsdal (1973-)
Elegy *107*

Bob Hoskins (1942-)
Doomsday *91*

Djimon Hounsou (1964-)
Never Back Down *229*

Ken Howard (1944-)
Rambo *264*

Terrence Howard (1969-)
Iron Man *175*

Brian Howe
Gran Torino *142*

Glen Howerton (1978-)
The Strangers *331*

Brigitte Lin Ching Hsia
See Brigitte Lin

Ling Hu
　Summer Palace *334*

Marin Huba
　I Served the King of En-
　　gland *165*

Vanessa Anne Hudgens (1988-)
　High School Musical 3: Senior
　　Year *158*

Jennifer Hudson
　The Secret Life of Bees *292*
　Sex and the City: The
　　Movie *298*

Kate Hudson (1979-)
　Fool's Gold *123*
　My Best Friend's Girl *225*

Geraldine Hughes
　Gran Torino *142*

Helen Hunt (1963-)
　Then She Found Me *350*

John Hurt (1940-)
　Hellboy II: The Golden
　　Army *155*
　Indiana Jones and the Kingdom
　　of the Crystal Skull *173*

Mary Beth Hurt (1948-)
　Untraceable *366*

William Hurt (1950-)
　The Incredible Hulk *171*
　Vantage Point *368*

Anjelica Huston (1951-)
　Choke *55*

Danny Huston (1962-)
　How to Lose Friends & Alienate
　　People *162*

Josh Hutcherson (1992-)
　Journey to the Center of the
　　Earth *179*

Ice Cube (1969-)
　First Sunday *116*
　The Longshots *194*

Jeremy Irons (1948-)
　Appaloosa *5*

Bill Irwin (1950-)
　Rachel Getting Married *262*

Oscar Isaac
　Body of Lies *30*

Simon Iteanu
　Flight of the Red Balloon *120*

Vlad Ivanov
　4 Months, 3 Weeks and 2
　　Days *129*

Dana Ivey (1942-)
　Ghost Town *139*

Eddie Izzard (1962-)
　The Chronicles of Narnia: Prince
　　Caspian (V) *58*

Igor (V) *166*
　Valkyrie *366*

Hugh Jackman (1968-)
　Australia *8*
　Deception *80*

Brandon T. Jackson
　Tropic Thunder *355*

Curtis "50 Cent" Jackson (1975-)
　Righteous Kill *274*

Joshua Jackson (1978-)
　Battle in Seattle *21*
　Shutter *303*

Samuel L. Jackson (1948-)
　Iron Man *175*
　Jumper *180*
　Lakeview Terrace *189*
　Soul Men *313*
　The Spirit *320*
　Star Wars: The Clone Wars
　　(V) *323*

Gillian Jacobs
　Choke *55*

Famke Janssen (1964-)
　The Wackness *381*

Ricky Jay (1948-)
　Redbelt *267*

Marianne Jean-Baptiste (1967-)
　City of Ember *61*

Richard Jenkins (1953-)
　Burn After Reading *40*
　Step Brothers *325*
　The Tale of Despereaux
　　(V) *341*
　The Visitor *373*

Julia Jentsch (1978-)
　I Served the King of En-
　　gland *165*

Ken Jeong
　Pineapple Express *249*

François Jerosme
　Persepolis (V) *247*

Igor Jijikine
　Indiana Jones and the Kingdom
　　of the Crystal Skull *173*

Scarlett Johansson (1984-)
　The Other Boleyn Girl *239*
　The Spirit *320*
　Vicky Cristina Barcelona *370*

Bart Johnson
　High School Musical 3: Senior
　　Year *158*

Bradley Johnson
　When Did You Last See Your
　　Father? *395*

Dwayne "The Rock" Johnson (1972-)
　Get Smart *137*

Gary 'G-Thang' Johnson
　Disaster Movie *88*

Richard Johnson (1927-)
　The Boy in the Striped Paja-
　　mas *35*

Alvin "Xzibit" Joiner (1974-)
　The X Files: I Want to Be-
　　lieve *405*

Angelina Jolie (1975-)
　Changeling *47*
　Kung Fu Panda (V) *185*
　Wanted *385*

Doug Jones (1960-)
　Hellboy II: The Golden
　　Army *155*

James Earl Jones (1931-)
　Welcome Home Roscoe Jen-
　　kins *389*

Jill Marie Jones (1975-)
　The Longshots *194*

Norah Jones
　My Blueberry Nights *227*

Richard T. Jones (1972-)
　Vantage Point *368*

Toby Jones (1967-)
　City of Ember *61*
　Frost/Nixon *131*
　W. *377*

Vinnie Jones (1965-)
　Hell Ride *153*

Oldrich Kaiser
　I Served the King of En-
　　gland *165*

Tom Kane (1962-)
　Star Wars: The Clone Wars
　　(V) *323*

Tim Kang
　Rambo *264*

Anil Kapoor (1959-)
　Slumdog Millionaire *307*

Kim Kardashian
　Disaster Movie *88*

Stana Katic
　Quantum of Solace *259*
　The Spirit *320*

Nicky Katt (1970-)
　Snow Angels *310*

Lainie Kazan (1942-)
　You Don't Mess with the Zo-
　　han *410*

Zoe Kazan
　Revolutionary Road *272*

Diane Keaton (1946-)
　Mad Money *201*

Toby Kebbell
　RocknRolla *276*

Catherine Keener (1961-)
  Hamlet 2 *145*
  Synecdoche, New York *340*
  What Just Happened *393*

Jack Kehler
  Pineapple Express *249*

Tim Kelleher
  Flash of Genius *117*
  Seven Pounds *295*

Michael Kelly (1969-)
  Changeling *47*

Will Kemp (1977-)
  Step Up 2 the Streets *326*

Anna Kendrick
  Twilight *360*

Brian Kerwin (1949-)
  27 Dresses *359*

Laura Ann Kesling
  Bedtime Stories *26*

Alicia Keyes
  The Secret Life of Bees *292*

Skander Keynes
  The Chronicles of Narnia: Prince
    Caspian *58*

Konstantin Khabenskiy
  Wanted *385*

Alyy Khan
  Traitor *351*

Irfan Khan
  Slumdog Millionaire *307*

Maung Maung Khin
  Rambo *264*

Nicole Kidman (1966-)
  Australia *8*

Pat Kilbane (1969-)
  Meet Dave *211*

Taran Killam (1982-)
  My Best Friend's Girl *225*

Randall Duk Kim (1943-)
  Kung Fu Panda (V) *185*

Nevo Kimchi
  Beaufort *24*

Georgia King
  The Duchess *96*

Jaime King (1979-)
  The Spirit *320*

Joey King (1999-)
  Dr. Seuss' Horton Hears a Who!
    (V) *90*

Rowena King
  The Bucket List *39*

Ben Kingsley (1943-)
  Elegy *107*
  The Love Guru *195*

Transsiberian *354*
The Wackness *381*
War, Inc. *388*

Greg Kinnear (1963-)
  Baby Mama *13*
  Flash of Genius *117*
  Ghost Town *139*

Robert Kirk
  The Killing of John Len-
    non *182*

Jay Klaitz
  Frozen River *133*

Kevin Kline (1947-)
  Definitely, Maybe *83*
  The Tale of Despereaux
    (V) *341*

Robert Knepper (1959-)
  The Day the Earth Stood
    Still *77*
  Transporter 3 *353*

Christopher Knight (1957-)
  Madagascar: Escape 2 Africa
    (V) *202*

Elissa Knight
  WALL-E (V) *382*

Keira Knightley (1985-)
  The Duchess *96*

Ohad Knoller (1976-)
  Beaufort *24*

Beyonce Knowles (1981-)
  Cadillac Records *43*

David Koechner (1962-)
  Get Smart *137*
  Semi-Pro *293*

Frederick Koehler (1975-)
  Death Race *79*

Jacek Koman
  Romulus, My Father *284*

Jeff Koons
  Milk *214*

Bernie Kopell (1933-)
  Get Smart *137*

Nursel Kose
  The Edge of Heaven *103*

Elias Koteas (1961-)
  The Curious Case of Benjamin
    Button *71*

Yaphet Kotto (1937-)
  Witless Protection *397*

Jeroen Krabbé (1944-)
  Transporter 3 *353*

Jane Krakowski (1966-)
  Kit Kittredge: An American
    Girl *184*
  The Rocker *275*

John Krasinski (1979-)
  Leatherheads *190*

Thomas Kretschmann (1962-)
  Transsiberian *354*
  Valkyrie *366*
  Wanted *385*

David Kross
  The Reader *265*

David Krumholtz (1978-)
  Harold & Kumar Escape from
    Guantanamo Bay *152*

Olek Krupa (1955-)
  Burn After Reading *40*

Michelle Krusiec (1974-)
  What Happens in Vegas *392*

Mila Kunis (1983-)
  Forgetting Sarah Marshall *125*
  Max Payne *210*

Tuncel Kurtiz
  The Edge of Heaven *103*

Olga Kurylenko
  Max Payne *210*
  Quantum of Solace *259*

Clyde Kusatsu (1948-)
  Harold & Kumar Escape from
    Guantanamo Bay *152*

Ashton Kutcher (1978-)
  What Happens in Vegas *392*

Jake La Botz
  Rambo *264*

Nadine Labaki
  Caramel *45*

Shia LaBeouf (1986-)
  Eagle Eye *101*
  Indiana Jones and the Kingdom
    of the Crystal Skull *173*

Jiri Labus
  I Served the King of En-
    gland *165*

Amy Lalonde
  Diary of the Dead *86*

Sarah Lancashire (1964-)
  When Did You Last See Your
    Father? *395*

Martin Landau (1931-)
  City of Ember *61*

Steve Landesberg (1945-)
  Forgetting Sarah Marshall *125*

Diane Lane (1965-)
  Jumper *180*
  Nights in Rodanthe *231*
  Untraceable *366*

Nathan Lane (1956-)
  Swing Vote *338*

Frank Langella (1940-)
  Frost/Nixon *131*
  The Tale of Despereaux
    (V) *341*

George Lopez (1961-)
    Beverly Hills Chihuahua
        (V) *27*
    Henry Poole Is Here *156*
    Swing Vote *338*

Traci Lords (1968-)
    Zack and Miri Make a
        Porno *412*

Susanne Lothar (1960-)
    The Reader *265*

Jonathan Loughran (1966-)
    The House Bunny *159*

Louis C.K.
    Welcome Home Roscoe Jen-
        kins *389*

Yuri Lowenthal
    The Pirates Who Don't Do Any-
        thing: A VeggieTales Movie
        (V) *251*

Richard Lu
    Paranoid Park *243*

Jessica Lucas
    Cloverfield *64*

Derek Luke (1974-)
    Definitely, Maybe *83*
    Miracle at St. Anna *217*

Diego Luna (1979-)
    Milk *214*

Kellan Lutz
    Twilight *360*

Jane Lynch (1960-)
    The Rocker *275*
    Role Models *278*
    Space Chimps (V) *315*

John Carroll Lynch (1963-)
    Gran Torino *142*

Ricky Mabe (1983-)
    Zack and Miri Make a
        Porno *412*

Bernie Mac (1958-2008)
    Madagascar: Escape 2 Africa
        (V) *202*
    Soul Men *313*

Kelly Macdonald (1977-)
    Choke *55*

Seth MacFarlane
    Hellboy II: The Golden Army
        (V) *155*

Matthew Macfayden
    Frost/Nixon *131*

John Machado
    Redbelt *267*

Gabriel Macht (1972-)
    The Spirit *320*

Anthony Mackie (1979-)
    Eagle Eye *101*

Kyle MacLachlan (1959-)
    The Sisterhood of the Traveling
        Pants 2 *302*

William H. Macy (1950-)
    The Tale of Despereaux
        (V) *341*

Justin Mader
    Death Race *79*

Michael Madsen (1959-)
    Hell Ride *153*

Virginia Madsen (1963-)
    Diminished Capacity *87*

Benoit Magimel (1974-)
    A Girl Cut in Two *141*

Sean Maguire
    Meet the Spartans *213*

Tobey Maguire (1975-)
    Tropic Thunder *355*

Bill Maher (1956-)
    Religulous *269*

Kimberly Makkouk
    The House Bunny *159*

Patrick Malahide (1945-)
    Brideshead Revisited *38*

Romany Malco (1968-)
    Baby Mama *13*
    The Love Guru *195*

Harris Malcom
    Fireproof *113*

Phyllis Malcom
    Fireproof *113*

Jonathan Malen (1987-)
    Charlie Bartlett *51*

John Malkovich (1953-)
    Burn After Reading *40*
    Changeling *47*

Jena Malone (1984-)
    The Ruins *286*

Method Man
    The Wackness *381*

Ray Mancini (1961-)
    Redbelt *267*

Costas Mandylor (1965-)
    Saw V *289*

David Mann
    Tyler Perry's Meet the
        Browns *363*

Leslie Mann (1972-)
    Drillbit Taylor *95*

Tamela Mann
    Tyler Perry's Meet the
        Browns *363*

Sebastian Mansicalco
    Vince Vaughn's Wild West Com-
        edy Show: 30 Days & 30

Nights—Hollywood to the
    Heartland *372*

Joe Mantegna (1947-)
    Redbelt *267*
    Witless Protection *397*

Kate Mara (1983-)
    Transsiberian *354*

Olivier Marchal
    Tell No One *345*

Oscar Marcus
    The Life Before Her Eyes *192*

Louise Margolin
    Flight of the Red Balloon *120*

Laura Margolis
    The Strangers *331*

Miriam Margolyes (1941-)
    How to Lose Friends & Alienate
        People *162*

Cheech Marin (1946-)
    Beverly Hills Chihuahua
        (V) *27*

Anamaria Marinca
    4 Months, 3 Weeks and 2
        Days *129*

Ken Marino (1968-)
    Role Models *278*

Karl Markovics (1963-)
    The Counterfeiters *70*

Mazhan Marno
    Traitor *351*

Eddie Marsan (1968-)
    Hancock *146*
    Happy-Go-Lucky *150*

James Marsden (1973-)
    Sex Drive *300*
    27 Dresses *359*

Chan Marshall
    My Blueberry Nights *227*

Chris Martin
    Chaos Theory *50*

Steve Martin (1945-)
    Baby Mama *13*

Nathalia Martinez
    Death Race *79*

Max Martini (1969-)
    Redbelt *267*

Elizabeth Marvel
    Burn After Reading *40*

Danny Masterson (1976-)
    Yes Man *408*

Chiara Mastroianni (1972-)
    A Christmas Tale *57*
    Love Songs *197*
    Persepolis (V) *247*

Radha Mitchell (1973-)
Henry Poole Is Here *156*

Rhona Mitra (1976-)
Doomsday *91*

Madhur Mittal
Slumdog Millionaire *307*

Katy Mixon
Four Christmases *127*

Colin Mochrie
Kit Kittredge: An American
Girl *184*

Jay Mohr (1970-)
Street Kings *333*

Jenny Mollen (1979-)
My Best Friend's Girl *225*

Taylor Momsen (1993-)
Paranoid Park *243*

Michelle Monaghan (1976-)
Eagle Eye *101*
Made of Honor *204*

Mo'Nique (1968-)
Welcome Home Roscoe Jen-
kins *389*

Camila Monteiro
City of Men *63*

Demi Moore (1962-)
Flawless *118*

Julianne Moore (1961-)
Blindness *29*

Danny Mora
The Eye *111*

Dylan Moran (1971-)
Run, Fatboy, Run *287*

Marguerite Moreau (1977-)
Beverly Hills Chihuahua
(V) *27*

Chloe Grace Moretz (1997-)
The Eye *111*

Katie Morgan
Zack and Miri Make a
Porno *412*

Michelle Morgan
Diary of the Dead *86*

Tracy Morgan (1968-)
First Sunday *116*

Phil Morris (1959-)
Meet the Spartans *213*

David Morrissey (1963-)
The Other Boleyn Girl *239*

Rob Morrow (1962-)
The Bucket List *39*

Viggo Mortensen (1958-)
Appaloosa *5*

Emily Mortimer (1971-)
Chaos Theory *50*

Redbelt *267*
Transsiberian *354*

Samantha Morton (1977-)
Synecdoche, New York *340*

Mos Def (1973-)
Be Kind Rewind *22*
Cadillac Records *43*

Bill Moseley (1957-)
Repo! The Genetic Opera *271*

William Moseley
The Chronicles of Narnia: Prince
Caspian *58*

Mark Moses (1958-)
Swing Vote *338*

Ido Mosseri
You Don't Mess with the Zohan *410*

Joanna Moukarzel
Caramel *45*

Stephen Moyer (1971-)
88 Minutes *105*

Dermot Mulroney (1963-)
Flash of Genius *117*

Cillian Murphy (1974-)
The Dark Knight *75*

Dwain Murphy
How She Move *161*

Eddie Murphy (1961-)
Meet Dave *211*

Bill Murray (1950-)
City of Ember *61*
Get Smart *137*

Rubi Muscovich
The Band's Visit *17*

Austin Lind Myers
Meet Dave *211*

Mike Myers (1963-)
The Love Guru *195*

Ajay Naidu (1972-)
Righteous Kill *274*

Kathy Najimy (1957-)
WALL-E (V) *382*

Leonardo Nam (1979-)
Vantage Point *368*

Manu Narayan
The Love Guru *195*

Khalifa Natour
The Band's Visit *17*

Mike Nawrocki
The Pirates Who Don't Do Any-
thing: A VeggieTales Movie
(V) *251*

Audrie Neenan
Doubt *92*

Liam Neeson (1952-)
The Chronicles of Narnia: Prince
Caspian (V) *58*

Regine Nehy
Lakeview Terrace *189*

Lubomir Neikov
War, Inc. *388*

Nelsan, Ellis
The Express *110*

Emily Nelson
Made of Honor *204*

Tim Blake Nelson (1965-)
The Incredible Hulk *171*

Gabe Nevins
Paranoid Park *243*

Laraine Newman (1952-)
Dr. Seuss' Horton Hears a Who!
(V) *90*

Thandie Newton (1972-)
RocknRolla *276*
Run, Fatboy, Run *287*
W. *377*

David Ngoombujarra (1967-)
Australia *8*

Melanie Nicholls-King
How She Move *161*

Rachel Nichols (1980-)
The Sisterhood of the Traveling
Pants 2 *302*

Jack Nicholson (1937-)
The Bucket List *39*

Connie Nielsen (1965-)
Battle in Seattle *21*

Leslie Nielsen (1926-)
An American Carol *2*
Superhero Movie *336*

Bill Nighy (1949-)
Valkyrie *366*

Sarah Niles
Happy-Go-Lucky *150*

Homer Nish
The Exiles *108*

Alessandro Nivola (1972-)
The Eye *111*

Cynthia Nixon (1966-)
Sex and the City: The
Movie *298*

Amaury Nolasco (1970-)
Max Payne *210*
Street Kings *333*

Nick Nolte (1941-)
Chicago 10 (V) *54*
The Spiderwick Chronicles
(V) *318*
Tropic Thunder *355*

Tom Noonan (1951-)
Snow Angels *310*
Synecdoche, New York *340*

Laura Ramsey (1982-)
The Ruins *286*

David Rasche (1944-)
Burn After Reading *40*

Victor Rasuk (1984-)
Stop-Loss *327*

Jackson Rathbone
Twilight *360*

John Ratzenberger (1947-)
WALL-E *(V)* *382*

Raven-Symoné
College Road Trip *67*

Elizabeth Reaser (1975-)
Twilight *360*

Christian Redl (1948-)
Yella *407*

Eddie Redmayne
The Other Boleyn Girl *239*

Nikki Reed (1988-)
Twilight *360*

Keanu Reeves (1964-)
The Day the Earth Stood
Still *77*
Street Kings *333*

Joe Regalbuto (1949-)
Bottle Shock *34*

James Reilly
Frozen River *133*

John C. Reilly (1965-)
The Promotion *256*
Step Brothers *325*

Judge Reinhold (1958-)
Swing Vote *338*

James Remar (1953-)
Pineapple Express *249*

Mark Rendall (1988-)
Charlie Bartlett *51*

Jérémie Renier (1981-)
In Bruges *168*

Yannick Renier
Love Songs *197*

Serge Renko
The Romance of Astree and Celadon *283*

Callum Keith Rennie (1960-)
The X Files: I Want to Believe *405*

Thekla Reuten (1975-)
In Bruges *168*

Ernie Reyes, Jr. (1972-)
Indiana Jones and the Kingdom
of the Crystal Skull *173*

Véronique Reymond
The Romance of Astree and Celadon *283*

Burt Reynolds (1936-)
In the Name of the King: A
Dungeon Siege Tale *169*

Ryan Reynolds (1976-)
Chaos Theory *50*
Definitely, Maybe *83*

Tommy Reynolds
The Exiles *108*

Judy Rhee
Tyler Perry's Meet the
Browns *363*

John Rhys-Davies (1944-)
In the Name of the King: A
Dungeon Siege Tale *169*

Christina Ricci (1980-)
Penelope *246*
Speed Racer *316*

Philip Riccio
Diary of the Dead *86*

Kevin M. Richardson (1964-)
Star Wars: The Clone Wars
(V) *323*

Andy Richter (1966-)
Madagascar: Escape 2 Africa
(V) *202*
Semi-Pro *293*

Alan Rickman (1946-)
Bottle Shock *34*

Tarra Riggs
Ballast *16*

Kelly Ripa (1970-)
Fly Me to the Moon *(V)* *121*

Jason Ritter (1980-)
W. *377*

Krysten Ritter
What Happens in Vegas *392*

Tyson Ritter (1984-)
The House Bunny *159*

Mabel Rivera
The Orphanage *238*

AnnaSophia Robb (1993-)
Jumper *180*
Sleepwalking *306*

Tim Robbins (1958-)
City of Ember *61*
The Lucky Ones *198*

Damani Roberts
Welcome Home Roscoe Jen-
kins *389*

David Roberts
Fool's Gold *123*

Eric Roberts (1956-)
The Dark Knight *75*
Witless Protection *397*

Shawn Roberts
Diary of the Dead *86*

Charles Robinson (1945-)
The House Bunny *159*

Craig Robinson (1971-)
Pineapple Express *249*
Zack and Miri Make a
Porno *412*

John Robinson (1985-)
Wendy and Lucy *389*

Jean Rochefort (1930-)
Tell No One *345*

Chris Rock (1966-)
Madagascar: Escape 2 Africa
(V) *202*

Rock, The
See Dwayne "The Rock" Johnson

Sam Rockwell (1968-)
Choke *55*
Frost/Nixon *131*
Snow Angels *310*

Karel Roden (1962-)
RocknRolla *276*

Freddy Rodriguez (1975-)
Bottle Shock *34*

Marco Rodriguez
Hamlet 2 *145*

Mel Rodriguez
Lakeview Terrace *189*

Michelle Rodriguez (1978-)
Battle in Seattle *21*

Paul Rodriguez (1955-)
Beverly Hills Chihuahua
(V) *27*

Daniel Roebuck (1963-)
Flash of Genius *117*

Seth Rogen (1982-)
Dr. Seuss' Horton Hears a Who!
(V) *90*
Kung Fu Panda *(V)* *185*
Pineapple Express *249*
The Spiderwick Chronicles
(V) *318*
Zack and Miri Make a
Porno *412*

Fernanda Romero
The Eye *111*

Saoirse Ronan (1994-)
City of Ember *61*

Michael Rooker (1956-)
Jumper *180*

Stephen Root (1951-)
Leatherheads *190*
Mad Money *201*
Over Her Dead Body *241*

Alan Rosenberg (1950-)
Righteous Kill *274*

Howard Rosenman
Milk *214*

JimMyron Ross
Ballast *16*

Lonny Ross
The Rocker *275*

Marion Ross (1928-)
Superhero Movie *336*

Carlo Rota
Saw V *289*

Tim Roth (1961-)
Funny Games *134*
The Incredible Hulk *171*

Adam Rothenberg
Mad Money *201*

Brigitte Rouan (1965-)
Love Songs *197*

Samuel Roukin
Happy-Go-Lucky *150*

Richard Roundtree (1942-)
Speed Racer *316*

Mickey Rourke (1955-)
The Wrestler *401*

Jean-Paul Roussillon (1931-)
A Christmas Tale *57*

Brandon Routh (1979-)
Zack and Miri Make a
Porno *412*

Alan Ruck (1960-)
Ghost Town *139*

Lamman Rucker
Tyler Perry's Meet the
Browns *363*

Natalya Rudakova
Transporter 3 *353*

Paul Rudd (1969-)
Forgetting Sarah Marshall *125*
Over Her Dead Body *241*
Role Models *278*

Belén Rueda
The Orphanage *238*

Mark Ruffalo (1967-)
Blindness *29*
Chicago 10 (V) *54*

Olesya Rulin
High School Musical 3: Senior
Year *158*

Salman Rushdie
Then She Found Me *350*

Betsy Russell (1964-)
Saw V *289*

Keri Russell (1976-)
Bedtime Stories *26*

Amy Ryan (1970-)
Changeling *47*
Chicago 10 (V) *54*

Max Ryan (1967-)
Death Race *79*

Meg Ryan (1961-)
The Women *399*

Mark Rylance (1960-)
The Other Boleyn Girl *239*

Ludivine Sagnier (1979-)
A Girl Cut in Two *141*
Love Songs *197*

Zoë Saldana (1978-)
Vantage Point *368*

Andy Samberg (1978-)
Space Chimps (V) *315*

Hiroyuki Sanada (1960-)
Speed Racer *316*

Ashlyn Sanchez
The Happening *149*

Jay O. Sanders (1953-)
Revolutionary Road *272*

Will Sanderson (1980-)
In the Name of the King: A
Dungeon Siege Tale *169*

Adam Sandler (1966-)
Bedtime Stories *26*
You Don't Mess with the Zo-
han *410*

Miguel Sandoval (1951-)
Bottle Shock *34*

Rodrigo Santoro (1975-)
Redbelt *267*

Susan Sarandon (1946-)
Speed Racer *316*

Peter Sarsgaard (1971-)
Elegy *107*

Will Sasso (1975-)
College Road Trip *67*

Andrea Savage
Step Brothers *325*

Greta Scacchi (1960-)
Brideshead Revisited *38*

Johnathon Schaech (1969-)
Prom Night *255*
Quarantine *260*

Jack Scanlon
The Boy in the Striped Pajamas *35*

Roy Scheider (1932-2008)
Chicago 10 (V) *54*

Rob Schneider (1963-)
You Don't Mess with the Zohan *410*

Hinnerk Schönemann
Yella *407*

Liev Schreiber (1967-)
Chicago 10 (V) *54*
Defiance *82*

Pablo Schreiber (1978-)
Nights in Rodanthe *231*
Vicky Cristina Barcelona *370*

Barbet Schroeder (1941-)
The Duchess of Langeais *98*

Paul Schulze
Rambo *264*

David Schwimmer (1966-)
Madagascar: Escape 2 Africa
(V) *202*

Hanna Schygulla (1943-)
The Edge of Heaven *103*

Matteo Sciabordi
Miracle at St. Anna *217*

Adam Scott (1973-)
Step Brothers *325*

Ashley Scott (1977-)
Strange Wilderness *330*

Seann William Scott (1976-)
The Promotion *256*
Role Models *278*

Lorna Scott
Wanted *385*

Kristin Scott Thomas (1960-)
I've Loved You So Long *177*
The Other Boleyn Girl *239*
Tell No One *345*

Nick Searcy (1959-)
Eagle Eye *101*

Amy Sedaris (1961-)
Snow Angels *310*

Jason Segel (1980-)
Forgetting Sarah Marshall *125*

Lise Segur
I've Loved You So Long *177*

Rachel Seiferth
Henry Poole Is Here *156*

Aziza Semaan
Caramel *45*

Ba Sen
Mongol *222*

Rade Serbedzija (1946-)
Battle in Seattle *21*
The Eye *111*
Quarantine *260*

Nestor Serrano (1957-)
Definitely, Maybe *83*

Adam G. Sevani
Step Up 2 the Streets *326*

Amanda Seyfried (1985-)
Mamma Mia! *205*

Zack Shada
Space Chimps (V) *315*

Michael Shannon (1974-)
Revolutionary Road *272*

Molly Shannon (1964-)
Igor *(V)* *166*

Omar Sharif (1932-)
10,000 B.C. *(N)* *346*

Charles Shaughnessy (1955-)
The Tale of Despereaux
(V) *341*

Wallace Shawn (1943-)
Kit Kittredge: An American
Girl *184*

Michael Sheen (1969-)
Frost/Nixon *131*

Ben Shenkman (1968-)
Then She Found Me *350*

Dax Shepard (1975-)
Baby Mama *13*

Sherri Shepherd (1970-)
Madagascar: Escape 2 Africa
(V) *202*

William Morgan Sheppard (1932-)
Over Her Dead Body *241*

Rade Sherbedgia
See Rade Serbedzija

Nicolette Sheridan (1963-)
Fly Me to the Moon *(V)* *121*

Shmuel
The Boy in the Striped Pajamas *35*

Columbus Short (1982-)
Cadillac Records *43*
Quarantine *260*

Martin Short (1950-)
The Spiderwick Chronicles
(V) *318*

John Shrapnel (1942-)
Mirrors *218*

Elisabeth Shue (1963-)
Hamlet 2 *145*

Alexander Siddig (1965-)
Doomsday *91*

Anna Sigalevitch
Flight of the Red Balloon *120*

Caroline Sihol (1949-)
A Girl Cut in Two *141*

James B. Sikking (1934-)
Made of Honor *204*

Caroline Silhol
See Caroline Sihol

Douglas Silva
City of Men *63*

J.K. Simmons (1955-)
Burn After Reading *40*

Johnny Simmons
The Spirit *320*

Rico Simonini
Max Payne *210*

Molly Sims (1973-)
Yes Man *408*

Ngai Sing
See Collin Chou

Marc Singer (1948-)
Eagle Eye *101*

Karolin Siol
See Caroline Sihol

Jules Sitruk
Son of Rambow *311*

Stellan Skarsgard (1951-)
Mamma Mia! *205*

Claire Skinner (1965-)
When Did You Last See Your
Father? *395*

Azura Skye (1981-)
One Missed Call *237*

Christian Slater (1969-)
Igor *(V)* *166*

Haaz Sleiman
The Visitor *373*

Lindsay Sloane (1977-)
Over Her Dead Body *241*

Amy Smart (1976-)
Mirrors *218*

Kodi Smit-McPhee
Romulus, My Father *284*

Anna Deavere Smith (1950-)
Rachel Getting Married *262*

Arjay Smith (1983-)
Be Kind Rewind *22*

Jaden Smith
The Day the Earth Stood
Still *77*

Lauren Lee Smith
Pathology *244*

Lois Smith (1930-)
Diminished Capacity *87*

Michael J. Smith, Sr.
Ballast *16*

Shawnee Smith (1970-)
Saw V *289*

Tasha Smith (1971-)
The Longshots *194*

Will Smith (1968-)
Hancock *146*
Seven Pounds *295*

Willow Smith
Kit Kittredge: An American
Girl *184*

Wyatt Smith
Never Back Down *229*

Bill Smitrovich (1947-)
Eagle Eye *101*
Flash of Genius *117*
Iron Man *175*
Seven Pounds *295*

Brittany Snow (1986-)
Prom Night *255*

Leelee Sobieski (1982-)
88 Minutes *105*
In the Name of the King: A
Dungeon Siege Tale *169*

Sonja Sohn
Step Up 2 the Streets *326*

Phyllis Somerville
The Curious Case of Benjamin
Button *71*

Josef Sommer (1934-)
Stop-Loss *327*

Brenda Song (1988-)
College Road Trip *67*

Fang Song
Flight of the Red Balloon *120*

Brandon Soo Hoo
Tropic Thunder *355*

Kevin Sorbo (1958-)
Meet the Spartans *213*

Joseph Julian Soria
Hamlet 2 *145*

Lodovico Sorret
See Tom Noonan

Paul Sorvino (1939-)
Repo! The Genetic Opera *271*

Shannyn Sossamon (1979-)
One Missed Call *237*

Zinedine Soualem
Roman de gare *279*

Kath Soucie (1967-)
Space Chimps *(V)* *315*

Sissy Spacek (1949-)
Four Christmases *127*

Kevin Spacey (1959-)
21 *357*

Timothy Spall (1957-)
Appaloosa *5*

Scott Speedman (1975-)
The Strangers *331*

Bruce Spence (1945-)
Australia *8*

Jacques Spiesser (1947-)
Priceless *252*

Stephen Spinella (1956-)
Milk *214*

Ashley Springer
Teeth *343*

Nick Stahl (1979-)
  Sleepwalking *306*

Michael Stahl-David
  Cloverfield *64*

Sylvester Stallone (1946-)
  Rambo *264*

Terence Stamp (1940-)
  Get Smart *137*
  Valkyrie *366*
  Wanted *385*
  Yes Man *408*

Jason Statham (1972-)
  The Bank Job *19*
  Death Race *79*
  In the Name of the King: A
    Dungeon Siege Tale *169*
  Transporter 3 *353*

Brian Steele
  Hellboy II: The Golden
    Army *155*

Mary Steenburgen (1952-)
  Four Christmases *127*
  Step Brothers *325*

Selma Stern
  Made of Honor *204*

Jessica Stevenson (1972-)
  Son of Rambow *311*

Juliet Stevenson (1956-)
  When Did You Last See Your
    Father? *395*

Kristen Stewart (1990-)
  Twilight *360*
  What Just Happened *393*

Amy Stiller (1961-)
  Tropic Thunder *355*

Ben Stiller (1965-)
  Madagascar: Escape 2 Africa
    (V) *202*
  Tropic Thunder *355*

Emma Stone (1988-)
  The House Bunny *159*
  The Rocker *275*

Peter Stormare (1953-)
  Witless Protection *397*

Steven Strait (1986-)
  10,000 B.C. *346*

David Strathairn (1949-)
  My Blueberry Nights *227*
  The Spiderwick
    Chronicles *318*

Meryl Streep (1949-)
  Doubt *92*
  Mamma Mia! *205*

Devid Striesow
  The Counterfeiters *70*
  Yella *407*

Phoebe Strole
  Hamlet 2 *145*

Mark Strong (1963-)
  Babylon A.D. *14*
  Body of Lies *30*
  Miss Pettigrew Lives for a
    Day *220*
  RocknRolla *276*

Jessica Stroup
  Prom Night *255*

Geoff Stults (1977-)
  The Express *110*

Jim Sturgess
  The Other Boleyn Girl *239*
  21 *357*

David Suchet (1946-)
  The Bank Job *19*

Jason Sudeikis
  The Rocker *275*
  What Happens in Vegas *392*

Dylan Summers
  The Wrestler *401*

Honglei Sun (1970-)
  Mongol *222*

Kevin Sussman (1970-)
  Made of Honor *204*

Donald Sutherland (1934-)
  Fool's Gold *123*

Kiefer Sutherland (1966-)
  Mirrors *218*

Nick Swardson (1976-)
  You Don't Mess with the Zo-
    han *410*

D.B. Sweeney (1961-)
  Miracle at St. Anna *217*

Tilda Swinton (1961-)
  Burn After Reading *40*
  The Chronicles of Narnia: Prince
    Caspian *58*
  The Curious Case of Benjamin
    Button *71*

Catherine Taber
  Star Wars: The Clone Wars
    (V) *323*

Saïd Taghmaoui (1973-)
  Traitor *351*
  Vantage Point *368*

Charlie Tahan
  Nights in Rodanthe *231*

Daisy Tahan
  Synecdoche, New York *340*

Faran Tahir
  Iron Man *175*

Oleg Taktarov (1967-)
  Righteous Kill *274*

Ana Claudia Talancón (1980-)
  One Missed Call *237*

Amber Tamblyn (1983-)
  The Sisterhood of the Traveling
    Pants 2 *302*

Jeffrey Tambor (1944-)
  Hellboy II: The Golden
    Army *155*

Channing Tatum (1980-)
  Battle in Seattle *21*
  Step Up 2 the Streets *326*
  Stop-Loss *327*

Audrey Tautou (1978-)
  Priceless *252*

Christine Taylor (1971-)
  Tropic Thunder *355*

Holland Taylor (1943-)
  Baby Mama *13*

James Arnold Taylor (1969-)
  Star Wars: The Clone Wars
    (V) *323*

Jayceon Taylor
  See The Game

Lili Taylor (1967-)
  The Promotion *256*

Rachael Taylor (1984-)
  Bottle Shock *34*
  Deception *80*
  Shutter *303*

Juno Temple
  The Other Boleyn Girl *239*

Maria Thayer (1975-)
  Forgetting Sarah Marshall *125*

Charlize Theron (1975-)
  Battle in Seattle *21*
  Hancock *146*
  Sleepwalking *306*

David Thewlis (1963-)
  The Boy in the Striped Paja-
    mas *35*

Max Thieriot (1988-)
  Jumper *180*
  Kit Kittredge: An American
    Girl *184*

Melanie Thierry
  Babylon A.D. *14*

Olivia Thirlby
  Snow Angels *310*
  The Wackness *381*

Eddie Kaye Thomas (1980-)
  Harold & Kumar Escape from
    Guantanamo Bay *152*

Florence Thomassin
  Tell No One *345*

Bobb'e J. Thompson
  Role Models *278*

Marc Warren (1967-)
Wanted *385*

Kerry Washington (1977-)
Lakeview Terrace *189*
Miracle at St. Anna *217*

Mia Wasikowska
Defiance *82*

Gedde Watanabe (1955-)
Forgetting Sarah Marshall *125*

Emily Watson (1967-)
Synecdoche, New York *340*

Emma Watson (1990-)
The Tale of Despereaux
(V) *341*

Naomi Watts (1968-)
Funny Games *134*

Sigourney Weaver (1949-)
Baby Mama *13*
Be Kind Rewind *22*
The Tale of Despereaux
(N) *341*
Vantage Point *368*
WALL-E (V) *382*

Kip Weeks
The Strangers *331*

Robin Weigert
Synecdoche, New York *340*

Rachel Weisz (1971-)
Definitely, Maybe *83*
My Blueberry Nights *227*

Jess Weixler
Teeth *343*

Christopher Evan Welch
Vicky Cristina Barcelona
(V) *370*

Michael Welch (1987-)
Twilight *360*

David Wenham (1965-)
Australia *8*
Married Life *208*

Scott Wentworth
Diary of the Dead *86*

Rutina Wesley
How She Move *161*

Floyd "Red Crow" Westerman (1936-2007)
Swing Vote *338*

Michael Weston (1973-)
Pathology *244*

Ed Westwick
Son of Rambow *311*

Shea Whigham (1969-)
Pride and Glory *253*

Ben Whishaw (1980-)
Brideshead Revisited *38*

Forest Whitaker (1961-)
The Air I Breathe *1*
Street Kings *333*
Vantage Point *368*

Brian White (1973-)
In the Name of the King: A
Dungeon Siege Tale *169*

Michael Jai White (1967-)
The Dark Knight *75*

Lynn Whitfield (1953-)
The Women *399*

Bradley Whitford (1959-)
Bottle Shock *34*

Kym E. Whitley (1961-)
College Road Trip *67*

Mae Whitman (1988-)
Nights in Rodanthe *231*

Daniel Lawrence Whitney
See Larry the Cable Guy

Johnny Whitworth (1975-)
Pathology *244*

Dianne Wiest (1948-)
Synecdoche, New York *340*

Kristen Wiig (1973-)
Ghost Town *139*

Tristan Wilds
The Secret Life of Bees *292*

Tom Wilkinson (1948-)
Cassandra's Dream *46*
RocknRolla *276*

Fred Willard (1939-)
WALL-E *382*

will.i.am
Madagascar: Escape 2 Africa
(V) *202*

Jesse Williams
The Sisterhood of the Traveling
Pants 2 *302*

Katt Williams (1973-)
First Sunday *116*

Kiely Williams
The House Bunny *159*

Malinda Williams (1975-)
First Sunday *116*

Michelle Williams (1980-)
Deception *80*
Synecdoche, New York *340*
Wendy and Lucy *389*

Treat Williams (1952-)
What Happens in Vegas *392*

Yvonne Williams
The Exiles *108*

Bruce Willis (1955-)
What Just Happened *393*

Rumer Willis (1988-)
The House Bunny *159*

Lambert Wilson (1959-)
Babylon A.D. *14*
Flawless *118*

Luke Wilson (1971-)
Henry Poole Is Here *156*

Owen Wilson (1968-)
Drillbit Taylor *95*
Marley & Me *207*

Patrick Wilson (1973-)
Lakeview Terrace *189*

Rainn Wilson (1968-)
The Rocker *275*

Michael Wincott (1959-)
What Just Happened *393*

Debra Winger (1955-)
Rachel Getting Married *262*

Mare Winningham (1959-)
Swing Vote *338*

Kate Winslet (1975-)
The Reader *265*
Revolutionary Road *272*

Ray Winstone (1957-)
Fool's Gold *123*
Indiana Jones and the Kingdom
of the Crystal Skull *173*

Eric Winter (1976-)
Harold & Kumar Escape from
Guantanamo Bay *152*

Tom Wisdom (1973-)
The Sisterhood of the Traveling
Pants 2 *302*

Ray Wise (1947-)
One Missed Call *237*

James With
Bangkok Dangerous *18*

Reese Witherspoon (1976-)
Four Christmases *127*
Penelope *246*

Alicia Witt (1975-)
88 Minutes *105*

Michael Wittenborn
Yella *407*

David Wohl (1953-)
The Wackness *381*

Chau Sang Anthony Wong (1961-)
The Mummy: Tomb of the
Dragon Emperor *224*

Russell Wong (1963-)
The Mummy: Tomb of the
Dragon Emperor *224*

Evan Rachel Wood (1987-)
The Life Before Her Eyes *192*
The Wrestler *401*

Fagin Woodcock
    The X Files: I Want to Believe *405*

Simon Woods (1980-)
    Penelope *246*

Jeffrey Wright (1965-)
    Cadillac Records *43*
    Chicago 10 *(V)* *54*
    Quantum of Solace *259*
    W. *377*

Noah Wyle (1971-)
    W. *377*

Shahkrit Yamnarm
    Bangkok Dangerous *18*

Jose Maria Yazpik (1970-)
    Beverly Hills Chihuahua *27*

Anton Yelchin (1989-)
    Charlie Bartlett *51*

Michelle Yeoh (1962-)
    Babylon A.D. *14*
    The Mummy: Tomb of the
        Dragon Emperor *224*

Nurgul Yesilcay
    The Edge of Heaven *103*

Charlie Yeung
    Bangkok Dangerous *18*

Dwight Yoakam (1956-)
    Four Christmases *127*
    Vince Vaughn's Wild West Comedy Show: 30 Days & 30
        Nights—Hollywood to the
        Heartland *372*

Aaron Yoo
    Nick & Norah's Infinite Playlist *230*
    21 *357*

Mark L. Young
    The Lucky Ones *198*

Kelvin Yu
    Milk *214*

Nan Yu
    Speed Racer *316*

Odette Yustman
    Cloverfield *64*

Steve Zahn (1968-)
    Strange Wilderness *330*

Nick Zano
    Beverly Hills Chihuahua *27*

Maya Zapata
    Under the Same Moon *365*

Terrance Zdunich
    Repo! The Genetic Opera *271*

Alexis Zegerman
    Happy-Go-Lucky *150*

Renee Zellweger (1969-)
    Appaloosa *5*
    Leatherheads *190*

Xianmin Zhang
    Summer Palace *334*

Mather Zickel
    Rachel Getting Married *262*

Constance Zimmer (1970-)
    Chaos Theory *50*

Patrycia Ziolkowska
    The Edge of Heaven *103*

August Zirner (1956-)
    The Counterfeiters *70*

Martin Zirner
    The Counterfeiters *70*

Mouss Zouheyri
    I've Loved You So Long *177*

Josh Zuckerman
    Sex Drive *300*

Ayelet Zurer
    Vantage Point *368*

Elsa Zylberstein (1969-)
    I've Loved You So Long *177*

Subject Index

Photography or Photographers

Shutter *303*

Pigs

College Road Trip *67*

Pirates

The Pirates Who Don't Do Anything: A VeggieTales Movie *251*

Pittsburgh

Smart People *309*
Zack and Miri Make a Porno *412*

Police

Mirrors *218*
Redbelt *267*
The Spirit *320*
Street Kings *333*

Political Campaigns

Definitely, Maybe *83*
Swing Vote *338*

Politics and/or Government

Battle in Seattle *21*
Burn After Reading *40*
Chicago 10 *54*
The Duchess *96*
Get Smart *137*
Stop-Loss *327*
W. *377*

Pornography or Pornographers

Zack and Miri Make a Porno *412*

Post-Apocalypse

Babylon A.D. *14*
Doomsday *91*

Postwar Era

The Reader *265*

Poverty

Ballast *16*
Frozen River *133*
Slumdog Millionaire *307*
Wendy and Lucy *389*

Pregnancy

Baby Mama *13*
Babylon A.D. *14*
The Exiles *108*

Hellboy II: The Golden Army *155*

Sex and the City: The Movie *298*
Then She Found Me *350*

Prehistory

10,000 B.C. *346*

Presidency

Frost/Nixon *131*
Swing Vote *338*
Vantage Point *368*
W. *377*

Prison or Jail

Death Race *79*
Standard Operating Procedure *321*
Traitor *351*

Prostitution

The Edge of Heaven *103*

Psychiatry or Psychiatrists

Charlie Bartlett *51*
88 Minutes *105*
The Wackness *381*

Psychotics or Sociopaths

The Dark Knight *75*
Funny Games *134*
Prom Night *255*

Race Against Time

Eagle Eye *101*
88 Minutes *105*

Radio

Cadillac Records *43*

Real Estate

RocknRolla *276*

Rebels

Charlie Bartlett *51*

Religious Themes

Henry Poole Is Here *156*
Religulous *269*
Son of Rambow *311*

Rescue Missions

Beverly Hills Chihuahua *27*
Bolt *32*
The Tale of Despereaux *341*

The Resistance

Defiance *82*

Restored Footage

Ashes of Time Redux *7*

Revenge

Hell Ride *153*
Max Payne *210*
Quantum of Solace *259*
Wanted *385*

Rio de Janiero

City of Men *63*

Rise from Poverty

Slumdog Millionaire *307*

Road Trips

Babylon A.D. *14*
The Bucket List *39*
College Road Trip *67*
Diminished Capacity *87*
The Happening *149*
The Lucky Ones *198*
My Blueberry Nights *227*
The Rocker *275*
Sex Drive *300*
Soul Men *313*
Speed Racer *316*
Stop-Loss *327*
Surfwise *337*
Under the Same Moon *365*
Vince Vaughn's Wild West Comedy Show: 30 Days & 30 Nights—Hollywood to the Heartland *372*

Robots or Androids

Meet Dave *211*
Star Wars: The Clone Wars *323*
WALL-E *382*

Romance

Fool's Gold *123*
A Girl Cut in Two *141*
High School Musical 3: Senior Year *158*
Love Songs *197*
Made of Honor *204*
Married Life *208*
My Best Friend's Girl *225*
The Other Boleyn Girl *239*
Snow Angels *310*
Twilight *360*
Vicky Cristina Barcelona *370*
The Wackness *381*

Romantic Comedy

Chaos Theory *50*
Definitely, Maybe *83*
Forgetting Sarah Marshall *125*

Title Index

This cumulative index is an alphabetical list of all films covered in the volumes of the *Magill's Cinema Annual.* Film titles are indexed on a word-by-word basis, including articles and prepositions. English leading articles (A, An, The) are ignored, as are foreign leading articles (El, Il, La, Las, Le, Les, Los). Acronyms appear alphabetically as if regular words. Common abbreviations in titles file as if they are spelled out. Proper names in titles are alphabetized beginning with the individual's first name. Titles with numbers are alphabetized as if the numbers were spelled out. When numeric titles gather in close proximity to each other, the titles will be arranged in a low-to-high numeric sequence. Films reviewed in this volume are cited in bold with an Arabic number indicating the page number on which the review begins; films reviewed in past volumes are cited with the *Annual* year in which the review was published. Original and alternate titles are cross-referenced to the American release title. Titles of retrospective films are followed by the year, in brackets, of their original release.

A

A corps perdu. *See* Straight for the Heart.

A. I.: Artificial Intelligence 2002

A la Mode (Fausto) 1995

A Lot Like Love 2006

A Ma Soeur. *See* Fat Girl.

A nos amours 1984

Abandon 2003

ABCD 2002

Abgeschminkt! *See* Making Up!.

About a Boy 2003

About Adam 2002

About Last Night... 1986

About Schmidt 2003

Above the Law 1988

Above the Rim 1995

Abre Los Ojos. *See* Open Your Eyes.

Abril Despedacado. *See* Behind the Sun.

Absence of Malice 1981

Absolute Beginners 1986

Absolute Power 1997

Absolution 1988

Abyss, The 1989

Accepted 2007

Accidental Tourist, The 1988

Accompanist, The 1993

Accordeur de tremblements de terre, L'. *See* Piano Tuner of Earthquakes, The.

Accused, The 1988

Ace in the Hole [1951] 1986, 1991

Ace Ventura: Pet Detective 1995

Ace Ventura: When Nature Calls 1996

Aces: Iron Eagle III 1992

Acid House, The 2000

Acqua e sapone. *See* Water and Soap.

Across the Tracks 1991

Across the Universe 2008

Acting on Impulse 1995

Action Jackson 1988

Actress 1988

Adam Sandler's 8 Crazy Nights 2003

Adam's Rib [1950] 1992

Adaptation 2003

Addams Family, The 1991

Addams Family Values 1993

Addicted to Love 1997

Addiction, The 1995

Addition, L'. *See* Patsy, The.

Adjo, Solidaritet. *See* Farewell Illusion.

Adjuster, The 1992

Adolescente, L' 1982

Adventure of Huck Finn, The 1993

Adventures in Babysitting 1987

Adventures of Baron Munchausen, The 1989

Adventures of Buckaroo Banzai, The 1984

Adventures of Elmo in Grouchland, The 2000

Adventures of Felix, The 2002

Best Man, The 1999

Best Man, The 2000

Best of the Best 1989

Best of the Best II 1993

Best of Times, The 1986

Best of Youth, The 2006

Best Revenge, The 1996

Best Seller 1987

Best Years of Our Lives, The [1946] 1981

Bestia nel cuore, La. *See* Don't Tell.

Betrayal 1983

Betrayed 1988

Betsy's Wedding 1990

Better Luck Tomorrow 2004

Better Off Dead 1985

Better Than Chocolate 2000

Better Than Sex 2002

Betty 1993

Betty Blue 1986

Between the Teeth 1995

Beverly Hillbillies, The 1993

Beverly Hills Brats 1989

Beverly Hills Chihuahua pg. 27

Beverly Hills Cop 1984

Beverly Hills Cop II 1987

Beverly Hills Cop III 1995

Beverly Hills Ninja 1997

Bewitched 2006

Beyond Borders 2004

Beyond Rangoon 1995

Beyond Reasonable Doubt 1983

Beyond Silence 1999

Beyond the Gates 2008

Beyond the Limit 1983

Beyond the Mat 2001

Beyond the Rocks 2006

Beyond the Sea 2005

Beyond Therapy 1987

Bhaji on the Beach 1995

Bian Lian. *See* The King of Masks.

Bicentennial Man 2000

Big 1988

Big Bad Mama II 1988

Big Bang, The 1990

Big Blue, The (Besson) 1988

Big Blue, The (Horn) 1988

Big Bounce, The 2005

Big Bully 1996

Big Business 1988

Big Chill, The 1983

Big Daddy 2000

Big Easy, The 1987

Big Fat Liar 2003

Big Fish 2004

Big Girls Don't Cry, They Get Even 1992

Big Green, The 1995

Big Hit, The 1999

Big Kahuna, The 2001

Big Lebowski, The 1999

Big Man on Campus 1989

Big Momma's House 2001

Big Momma's House 2 2007

Big Night 1996

Big One, The 1999

Big Picture, The 1989

Big Shots 1987

Big Squeeze, The 1996

Big Tease, The 2001

Big Time 1988

Big Top Pee-Wee 1988

Big Town, The 1987

Big Trouble (Cassavetes) 1986

Big Trouble (Sonnenfeld) 2003

Big Trouble in Little China 1986

Biker Boyz 2004

Bikur Ha-Tizmoret. *See* Band's Visit, The.

Bill and Ted's Bogus Journey 1991

Bill and Ted's Excellent Adventure 1989

Billy Bathgate 1991

Billy Budd [1962] 1981

Billy Elliot 2001

Billy Madison 1995

Billy's Hollywood Screen Kiss 1999

Biloxi Blues 1988

Bin-jip. *See* 3-Iron.

Bingo 1991

BINGO 2000

Bio-Dome 1996

Bird 1988

Bird on a Wire 1990

Birdcage, The 1996

Birdy 1984

Birth 2005

Birth of a Nation, The [1915] 1982, 1992

Birthday Girl 2003

Bitter Moon 1995

Bittere Ernte. *See* Angry Harvest.

Bix (1990) 1995

Bix (1991) 1995

Bizet's Carmen 1984

Black and White 2001

Black Beauty 1995

Black Book 2008

Black Cat, The (Fulci) 1984

Black Cat (Shin) 1993

Black Cat, White Cat 2000

Black Cauldron, The 1985

Black Christmas 2007

Black Dahlia, The 2007

Black Dog 1999

Black Harvest 1995

Black Hawk Down 2002

Black Joy 1986

Black Knight 2002

Black Lizard 1995

Black Mask 2000

Black Moon Rising 1986

Black Peter [1964] 1985

Black Rain (Imamura) 1990

Black Rain (Scott) 1989

Black Robe 1991

Black Sheep 1996

Black Snake Moan 2008

Black Stallion Returns, The 1983

Black Widow 1987

Blackboard Jungle [1955] 1986, 1992

Blackout 1988

Blackout. *See* I Like It Like That.

Blade 1999

Blade II 2003

Blade Runner 1982

Grindhouse 2008

Gringo 1985

Grizzly Man 2006

Grizzly Mountain 1997

Groomsmen, The 2007

Groove 2001

Gross Anatomy 1989

Grosse Fatigue 1995

Grosse Pointe Blank 1997

Ground Truth, The 2008

Ground Zero 1987, 1988

Groundhog Day 1993

Grudge, The 2005

Grudge 2, The 2007

Grumpier Old Men 1995

Grumpy Old Men 1993

Grune Wuste. *See* Green Desert.

Guardian, The 1990

Guardian, The 2007

Guarding Tess 1995

Guatanamera 1997

Guelwaar 1995

Guerre du Feu, La. *See* Quest for Fire.

Guess Who 2006

Guess Who's Coming to Dinner? [1967] 1992

Guest, The 1984

Guests of Hotel Astoria, The 1989

Guilty as Charged 1992

Guilty as Sin 1993

Guilty by Suspicion 1991

Guinevere 2000

Gummo 1997

Gun in Betty Lou's Handbag, The 1992

Gun Shy 2001

Gunbus. *See* Sky Bandits.

Guncrazy 1993

Gunfighter, The [1950] 1989

Gung Ho 1986

Gunmen 1995

Gunner Palace 2006

Guru, The 2004

Guy Named Joe, A [1943] 1981

Guy Thing, A 2004

Guys, The 2003

Gwendoline 1984

Gwoemul. *See* Host, The.

Gyakufunsha Kazoku. *See* Crazy Family, The.

Gymkata 1985

H

H. M. Pulham, Esq. [1941] 1981

Hable con Ella. *See* Talk to Her.

Hackers 1995

Hadesae: The Final Incident 1992

Hadley's Rebellion 1984

Hail Mary 1985

Hairdresser's Husband, The 1992

Hairspray 1988

Hairspray 2008

Haizi wang. *See* King of the Children.

Hak hap. *See* Black Mask

Hak mau. *See* Black Cat.

Half-Baked 1999

Half Moon Street 1986

Half of Heaven 1988

Halfmoon 1996

Hall of Fire [1941] 1986

Halloween (Zombie) 2008

Halloween III: Season of the Witch 1982

Halloween IV 1988

Halloween V 1989

Halloween VI: the Curse of Michael Myers 1995

Halloween H20 1999

Halloween: Resurrection 2003

Hamburger 1986

Hamburger Hill 1987

Hamlet (Zeffirelli) 1990

Hamlet (Branagh) 1996

Hamlet (Almereyda) 2001

Hamlet 2 pg. 145

Hammett 1983

Hana-Bi. *See* Fireworks.

Hancock pg. 146

Hand That Rocks the Cradle, The 1992

Handful of Dust, A 1988

Handmaid's Tale, The 1990

Hangfire 1991

Hanging Garden, The 1999

Hanging Up 2001

Hangin' with the Homeboys 1991

Hanky Panky 1982

Hanna K. 1983

Hannah and Her Sisters 1986

Hannibal 2002

Hannibal Rising 2008

Hanoi Hilton, The 1987

Hans Christian Andersen's Thumbelina 1995

Hansel and Gretel 1987

Hanussen 1988, 1989

Happening, The pg. 149

Happenstance 2002

Happily Ever After 1993

Happily Ever After 2006

Happily N'Ever After 2008

Happiness 1999

Happy Accidents 2002

Happy End 2001

Happy Endings 2006

Happy Feet 2007

Happy '49 1987

Happy Gilmore 1996

Happy Hour 1987

Happy New Year 1987

Happy, Texas 2000

Happy Times 2003

Happy Together 1990

Happy Together 1997

Happy-Go-Lucky pg. 150

Hard Candy 2007

Hard Choices 1986

Hard Core Logo 1999

Hard Eight 1997

Hard Hunted 1995

Hard Promises 1992

Hard Rain 1999

Hard Target 1993

Hard Ticket to Hawaii 1987

Hard Times 1988

Hard to Hold 1984

Henry and June 1990

Henry IV 1985

Henry V 1989

Henry Fool 1999

Henry Poole in Here pg. 156

Her Alibi 1989

Her Name Is Lisa 1987

Herbie: Fully Loaded 2006

Hercules 1983

Hercules II 1985

Herdsmen of the Sun 1995

Here Come the Littles 1985

Here On Earth 2001

Here's to Life 2002

Hero 1992

Hero 2004

Hero 2005

Hero and the Terror 1988

He's My Girl 1987

Hey Arnold! The Movie 2003

Hexed 1993

Hibiscus Town 1988

Hidalgo 2005

Hidden. *See* Cache.

Hidden, The 1987

Hidden Agenda 1990

Hidden Hawaii 1995

Hide and Seek 2006

Hideaway 1995

Hideous Kinky 2000

Hiding Out 1987

Hifazaat. *See* In Custody.

High Art 1999

High Crimes 2003

High Fidelity 2001

High Heels 1991

High Heels and Low Lives 2002

High Hopes 1988, 1989

High Lonesome: The Story of Blue-grass Music 258

High Risk 1995

High Road to China 1983

High School High 1996

High School Musical 3: Senior Year pg. 158

High Season 1988

High Spirits 1988

High Tension 2006

High Tide 1987

Higher Learning 1995

Highlander 1986

Highlander 2: The Quickening 1991

Highlander 3: The Final Dimension 1995

Highlander: Endgame 2001

Highway Patrolman 1995

Highway 61 1992

Highway to Hell 1992

Hijacking Hollywood

Hijo se la Novia, El. *See* Son of the Bride.

Hi-Lo Country, The 2000

Hilary and Jackie 1999

Hills Have Eyes, The 2007

Hills Have Eyes II, The 2008

Himmel uber Berlin, Der. *See* Wings of Desire.

Histories d'amerique. *See* American Stories.

History Boys, The 2007

History Is Made at Night [1937] 1983

History of Violence, A 2006

Hit, The 1985

Hit and Runway 2002

Hit List 1989

Hit the Dutchman 1995

Hitch 2006

Hitcher, The 1986

Hitcher, The (Meyers) 2008

Hitchhiker's Guide to the Galaxy, The 2006

Hitman 2008

Hitman, The 1991

Hoax, The 2008

Hocus Pocus 1993

Hoffa 1992

Holcroft Covenant, The 1985

Hold Back the Dawn [1941] 1986

Hold Me, Thrill Me, Kiss Me 1993

Holes 2004

Holiday [1938] 1985

Holiday, The 2007

Holiday Inn [1942] 1981

Hollow Man 2001

Hollow Reed 1997

Hollywood Ending 2003

Hollywood Homicide 2004

Hollywood in Trouble 1986

Hollywood Mavericks 1990

Hollywood Shuffle 1987

Hollywood Vice Squad 1986

Hollywoodland 2007

Holy Blood. *See* Santa Sangre.

Holy Innocents, The 1985

Holy Man 1999

Holy Smoke 2000

Holy Tongue, The 2002

Hombre [1967] 1983

Home Alone 1990

Home Alone II: Lost in New York 1992

Home Alone III 1997

Home and the World, The 1985

Home at the End of the World, A 2005

Home for the Holidays 1995

Home Free All 1984

Home Fries 1999

Home Is Where the Heart Is 1987

Home of Our Own, A 1993

Home of the Brave 1986

Home on the Range 2005

Home Remedy 1987

Homeboy 1988

Homegrown 1999

Homer and Eddie 1990

Homeward Bound 1993

Homeward Bound II: Lost in San Francisco 1996

Homework 1982

Homicide 1991

Homme et une femme, Un. *See* Man and a Woman, A.

Hondo [1953] 1982

Honey 2004

Honey, I Blew Up the Kid 1992

Hurricane, The 2000

Hurricane Streets 1999

Husbands and Wives 1992

Hush (Darby) 1999

Hush! (Hashiguchi) 2003

Hustle & Flow 2006

Hyenas 1995

Hypnotic. *See* Close Your Eyes.

I

I Am David 2005

I Am Legend 2008

I Am My Own Woman 1995

I Am Sam 2002

I Can't Sleep 1995

I Capture the Castle 2004

I Come in Peace 1990

I Demoni. *See* Demons.

I Don't Buy Kisses Anymore 1992

I Don't Want to Talk About It 1995

I Dreamed of Africa 2001

I Got the Hook-Up 1999

"I Hate Actors!" 1988

I Heart Huckabees 2005

I Know What You Did Last Summer 1997

I Know Where I'm Going [1945] 1982

I Know Who Killed Me 2008

I Like It Like That 1995

I Love Trouble 1995

I Love You 1982

I Love You, Don't Touch Me 1999

I Love You, I Love You Not 1997

I Love You to Death 1990

I, Madman 1989

I Married a Shadow 1983

I Now Pronounce You Chuck and Larry 2008

I Only Want You to Love Me 1995

I Ought to Be in Pictures 1982

I Remember Mama [1948] 1981

I, Robot 2005

I Sent a Letter to My Love 1981

I Served the King of England pg. 165

I Shot Andy Warhol 1996

I Spy 2003

I Stand Alone 2000

I Still Know What You Did Last Summer 1999

I, the Jury 1982

I Think I Do 2000

I Think I Love My Wife 2008

I Want to Go Home 1989

I Want Someone to Eat Cheese With 2008

I Was a Teenage Zombie 1987

I Went Down 1999

I Woke Up Early the Day I Died 2000

Ice Age 2003

Ice Age: The Meltdown 2007

Ice Harvest, The 2006

Ice House 1989

Ice Pirates, The 1984

Ice Princess 2006

Ice Rink, The 2001

Ice Runner, The 1993

Ice Storm, The 1997

Iceman 1984

Icicle Thief, The 1990

Ideal Husband, An 2000

Identity 2004

Identity Crisis 1989

Idiocracy 2007

Idiots, The [1999] 2001

Idle Hands 2000

Idlewild 2007

Iedereen Beroemd! *See* Everybody's Famous!

If Looks Could Kill 1991

If Lucy Fell 1996

If You Could See What I Hear 1982

Igby Goes Down 2003

Ignorant Fairies 2002

Igor pg. 166

Iklimler. *See* Climates.

Il y a longtemps que je t'aime. *See* I've Loved You So Long.

Ill Testimone dello Sposo. *See* Best Man, The.

I'll Be Home for Christmas 1999

I'll Do Anything 1995

I'll Sleep When I'm Dead 2005

Illtown 1999

Illuminata 2000

Illusionist, The 2007

Illustrious Energy 1988

Ils se Marient et Eurent Beaucoup D'Enfants. *See* Happily Ever After.

I'm Dancing as Fast as I Can 1982

I'm Going Home 2003

I'm No Angel [1933] 1984

I'm Not There 2008

I'm Not Rappaport 1997

I'm the One That I Want 2001

Imagemaker, The 1986

Imaginary Crimes 1995

Imaginary Heroes 2006

Imagine 1988

Imagine Me & You 2007

Immediate Family 1989

Immortal Beloved 1995

Imperative 1985

Importance of Being Earnest, The 1995

Importance of Being Earnest, The (Parker) 2003

Imported Bridegroom, The 1991

Impostor 2003

Impostors 1999

Impromptu 1991

Impulse (Baker) 1984

Impulse (Locke) 1990

In a Shallow Grave 1988

In America 2004

In and Out 1997

In Bloom. *See* Life Before Her Eyes, The.

In Bruges pg. 168

In Country 1989

In Crowd, The 2001

In Custody 1995

In Dangerous Company 1988

In Dreams 2000

In Fashion. *See* A la Mode.

In God's Hands 1999

Island of Dr. Moreau, The 1996

Isn't She Great 2001

Istoriya As-Klyachimol. *See* Asya's Happiness.

It Could Happen to You 1995

It Couldn't Happen Here 1988

It Had to Be You 1989

It Happened One Night [1934] 1982

It Happened Tomorrow [1944] 1983

It Runs in the Family 2004

It Takes Two 1988

It Takes Two 1995

Italian for Beginners 2002

Italian Job, The 2004

Italiensk for Begyndere. *See* Italian for Beginners.

It's a Wonderful Life [1946] 1982

It's Alive III 1987

It's All About Love 2005

It's All Gone Pete Tong 2006

It's All True 1993

It's My Party 1996

It's Pat 1995

It's the Rage 2001

Ivan and Abraham 1995

I've Heard the Mermaids Singing 1987

I've Loved You So Long pg. 177

J

Jack 1996

Jack and His Friends 1993

Jack and Sarah 1996

Jack Frost 1999

Jack the Bear 1993

Jackal, The 1997

Jackass Number Two 2007

Jacket, The 2006

Jackie Brown 1997

Jackie Chan's First Strike 1997

Jacknife 1989

Jackpot 2002

Jack's Back 1988

Jacob 1988

Jacob's Ladder 1990

Jacquot of Nantes 1993

Jade 1995

Jagged Edge 1985

J'ai epouse une ombre. *See* I Married a Shadow.

Jailhouse Rock [1957] 1986

Jake Speed 1986

Jakob the Liar 2000

James and the Giant Peach 1996

James' Journey to Jerusalem 2005

James Joyce's Women 1985

Jamon, Jamon 1993

Jane Austen Book Club, The 2008

Jane Eyre 1996

January Man, The 1989

Japanese Story 2005

Jarhead 2006

Jason Goes to Hell 1993

Jason X 2003

Jason's Lyric 1995

Jawbreaker 2000

Jaws: The Revenge 1987

Jaws 3-D 1983

Jay and Silent Bob Strike Back 2002

Jazzman 1984

Je Rentre a la Maison. *See* I'm Going Home.

Je tu il elle [1974] 1985

Je vous salue, Marie. *See* Hail Mary.

Jean de Florette 1987

Jeanne Dielman, 23 Quai du Commerce, 1080 Bruxelles [1976] 1981

Jeepers Creepers 2002

Jeepers Creepers 2 2004

Jefferson in Paris 1995

Jeffrey 1995

Jekyll and Hyde…Together Again 1982

Jennifer Eight 1992

Jerky Boys 1995

Jerome 2001

Jerry Maguire 1996

Jersey Girl 2005

Jerusalem 1996

Jesus of Montreal 1989

Jesus' Son 2000

Jet Lag 2004

Jet Li's Fearless 2007

Jetsons 1990

Jewel of the Nile, The 1985

JFK 1991

Jigsaw Man, The 1984

Jim and Piraterna Blom. *See* Jim and the Pirates.

Jim and the Pirates 1987

Jiminy Glick in Lalawood 2006

Jimmy Hollywood 1995

Jimmy Neutron: Boy Genius 2002

Jimmy the Kid 1983

Jindabyne 2008

Jingle All the Way 1996

Jinxed 1982

Jit 1995

Jo-Jo at the Gate of Lions 1995

Jo Jo Dancer, Your Life Is Calling 1986

Joan the Mad. *See* Mad Love.

Jocks 1987

Joe Dirt 2002

Joe Gould's Secret 2001

Joe Somebody 2002

Joe the King 2000

Joe Versus the Volcano 1990

Joe's Apartment 1996

Joey 1985

Joey Takes a Cab 1991

John and the Missus 1987

John Carpenter's Ghosts of Mars 2002

John Carpenter's Vampires 1999

John Grisham's the Rainmaker 1998

John Huston 1988

John Huston and the Dubliners 1987

John Q 2003

John Tucker Must Die 2007

Johnny Be Good 1988

Johnny Dangerously 1984

Johnny English 2004

Johnny Handsome 1989

Johnny Mnemonic 1995

Johnny Stecchino 1992

Johnny Suede 1992

johns 1997

Killer Instinct 1995

Killer Klowns from Outer Space 1988

Killer of Sheep 2008

Killer Party 1986

Killing Affair, A 1988

Klling Fields, The 1984

Killing Floor, The 1995

Killing of a Chinese Bookie, The [1976] 1986

Killing of John Lennon, The pg. 182

Killing Time 1999

Killing Time, The, 1987

Killing Zoe 1995

Killpoint 1984

Kindergarten Cop 1990

Kindred, The 1987

King, The 2007

King Arthur 2005

King and I, The 2000

King David 1985

King Is Alive, The 2002

King Is Dancing, The 2002

King James Version 1988

King Kong [1933] 1981

King Kong 2006

King Kong Lives 1986

King Lear 1987

King of Comedy, The 1983

King of Jazz [1930] 1985

King of Kong: A Fistful of Quarters, The 2008

King of Masks, The 2000

King of New York 1990

King of the Children 1988

King of the Hill 1993

King Ralph 1991

King Solomon's Mines 1985

Kingdom, Part 2, The 1999

Kingdom, The 1995

Kingdom, The 2008

Kingdom Come 2002

Kingdom of Heaven 2006

Kingpin 1996

Kings and Queen 2006

King's Ransom 2006

Kinjite 1989

Kinky Boots 2007

Kinsey 2005

Kipperbang 1984

Kippur 2001

Kiss Before Dying, A 1991

Kiss Daddy Good Night 1987

Kiss Kiss Bang Bang 2006

Kiss Me a Killer 1991

Kiss Me Goodbye 1982

Kiss Me, Guido 1997

Kiss Me, Stupid [1964] 1986

Kiss of Death 1995

Kiss of the Dragon 2002

Kiss of the Spider Woman 1985

Kiss or Kill 1997

Kiss, The 1988

Kiss the Girls 1997

Kissed 1997

Kissing a Fool 1999

Kissing Jessica Stein 2003

Kit Kittredge: An American Girl pg. 184

Kitchen Party 1999

Kitchen Stories 2005

Kitchen Toto, The 1987

Kite Runner, The 2008

Kitty and the Bagman 1983

Klynham Summer 1983

Knafayim Shvurot. *See* Broken Wings.

Knight's Tale, A 2002

Knights of the City 1986

Knock Off 1999

Knockaround Guys 2003

Knocked Up 2008

Kolya 1997

Korczak 1991

Koyaanisqatsi 1983

Krampack. *See* Nico and Dani.

Krays, The 1990

Krieger und die Kaiserin, Der. *See* Princess and the Warrior, The.

Krippendorf's Tribe 1999

Krotki film o zabijaniu. *See* Thou Shalt Not Kill.

Krull 1983

Krush Groove 1985

K2 1992

Kuffs 1992

Kull The Conqueror 1997

Kundun 1997

Kung Fu Hustle 2006

Kung Fu Panda pg. 185

Kuroi ame. *See* Black Rain.

Kurt and Courtney 1999

L

L. I.. E. 2002

L.627 1995

L.A. Confidential 1997

La Meglio Gioventu. *See* Best of Youth, The.

La Sorgente del fiume. *See* Weeping Meadow.

L.A. Story 1991

La Terre qui pleure. *See* Weeping Meadow.

Laberinto del Fauno, El. *See* Pan's Labyrinth.

Labyrinth 1986

Labyrinth of Passion 1990

Ladder 49 2005

Ladies Club, The 1986

Ladies' Man, The 2001

Ladri di saponette. *See* Icicle Thief, The.

Ladro Di Bambini, Il 1993

Lady and the Duke, The 2003

Lady Beware 1987

Lady Chatterley 2008

Lady Eve, The [1941] 1987

Lady in the Water 2007

Lady in White 1988

Lady Jane 1986

Lady Sings the Blues [1972] 1984

Ladybird, Ladybird 1995

Ladybugs 1992

Ladyhawke 1985

Ladykillers, The 2005

Lagaan: Once Upon a Time in India 2003

Lair of the White Worm, The 1988

Laissez-Passer. *See* Safe Conduct.

Leopard Son, The 1996

Leprechaun 1993

Leprechaun II 1995

Les Patterson Saves the World 1987

Less Than Zero 1987

Let Him Have It 1991

Let It Come Down: The Life of Paul Bowles 2000

Let It Ride 1989

Let's Fall in Love. *See* New York in Short: The Shvitz and Let's Fall in Love.

Let's Get Lost 1988

Let's Spend the Night Together 1983

Lethal Weapon 1987

Lethal Weapon 2 1989

Lethal Weapon 3 1992

Lethal Weapon 4 1999

Letter to Brezhnev 1986

Letters from Iwo Jima 2007

Leviathan 1989

Levity 2004

Levy and Goliath 1988

Ley del deseo, La. *See* Law of Desire, The.

Liaison Pornographique, Une. *See* Affair of Love, An.

Liam 2002

Lianna 1983

Liar, Liar 1997

Liar's Moon 1982

Libertine, The 2007

Liberty Heights 2000

Licence to Kill 1989

License to Drive 1988

License to Wed 2008

Lie Down With Dogs 1995

Liebestraum 1991

Lies 1986

Life 2000

Life After Love 2002

Life and Nothing But 1989

Life and Times of Allen Ginsberg, The 1995

Life and Times of Judge Roy Bean, The [1972] 1983

Life Aquatic with Steve Zissou, The 2005

Life as a House 2002

Life Before Her Eyes, The pg. 192

Life Classes 1987

Life in the Food Chain. *See* Age Isn't Everything.

Life in the Theater, A 1995

Life Is a Long Quiet River 1990

Life Is Beautiful 1999

Life Is Cheap 1989

Life Is Sweet 1991

Life Less Ordinary, A 1997

Life Lessons. *See* New York Stories.

Life of David Gale, The 2004

Life on a String 1992

Life on the Edge 1995

Life or Something Like It 2003

Life Stinks 1991

Life with Father [1947] 1993

Life with Mikey 1993

Life Without Zoe. *See* New York Stories.

Lifeforce 1985

Lift 2002

Light Ahead, The [1939] 1982

Light It Up 2000

Light Keeps Me Company 2001

Light of Day 1987

Light Sleeper 1992

Lighthorsemen, The 1987

Lightning in a Bottle 2005

Lightning Jack 1995

Lightship, The 1986

Like Father Like Son 1987

Like Mike 2003

Like Water for Chocolate 1993

Lili Marleen 1981

Lilies 1997

Lilies of the Field [1963] 1992

Lillian 1995

Lilo & Stitch 2003

Lily in Love 1985

Limbo 2000

Limey, The 2000

Line One 1988

Lingua del Santo, La. *See* Holy Tongue, The.

Linguini Incident, The 1992

Linie Eins. *See* Line One.

Link 1986

Lion King, The 1995

Lionheart (Lettich) 1991

Lionheart (Shaffner) 1987

Lions for Lambs 2008

Liquid Dreams 1992

Liquid Sky 1983

Lisa 1990

Listen to Me 1989

Listen Up 1990

Little Big League 1995

Little Black Book 2005

Little Buddha 1995

Little Children 2007

Little Devil, the 1988

Little Dorrit 1988

Little Drummer Girl, The 1984

Little Giants 1995

Little Indian, Big City 1996

Little Jerk 1985

Little Man 2007

Little Man Tate 1991

Little Men 1999

Little Mermaid, The 1989

Little Miss Sunshine 2007

Little Monsters 1989

Little Nemo: Adventures in Slumberland 1992

Little Nicky 2001

Little Nikita 1988

Little Noises 1992

Little Odessa 1995

Little Princess, A 1995

Little Rascals, The 1995

Little Secrets 1995

Little Secrets (Treu) 2003

Little Sex, A 1982

Little Shop of Horrors [1960] 1986

Little Stiff, A 1995

Little Sweetheart 1988

Little Thief, The 1989

Major Payne 1995

Make Way for Tomorrow [1937] 1981

Making Love (Hiller) 1982

Making Love (Tognazzi) 2002

Making Mr. Right 1987

Making the Grade 1984

Making Up! 1995

Makioka Sisters, The 1985

Mal d'aimer, Le. *See* Malady of Love, The.

Mala education, La. *See* Bad Education

Malady of Love, The 1987

Malcolm 1986

Malcolm X 1992

Malena 2001

Malibu Bikini Shop, The 1987

Malibu's Most Wanted 2004

Malice 1993

Mallrats 1995

Malone 1987

Maltese Falcon, The [1941] 1983

Mama, There's a Man in Your Bed 1990

Mamba 1988

Mambo Italiano 2004

Mambo Kings, The 1992

Mamma Mia! pg. 205

Man, The 2006

Man and a Woman, A 1986

Man Apart, A 2004

Man Bites Dog 1993

Man Called Sarge, A 1990

Man cheng jin dai huang jin jia. *See* Curse of the Golden Flower.

Man from Elysian Fields, The 2003

Man from Snowy River, The 1982

Man Hunt [1941] 1984

Man I Love, The [1946] 1986

Man in Love, A 1987

Man in the Iron Mask, The 1999

Man in the Moon, The 1991

Man in Uniform, A 1995

Man Inside, The 1990

Man of Iron 1981

Man of Marble [1977] 1981

Man of No Importance, A 1995

Man of the Century 2000

Man of the House (Orr) 1995

Man of the House 2006

Man of the Year 1996

Man of the Year 2007

Man on Fire 2005

Man on the Moon 2000

Man on the Train, The 2004

Man Outside 1988

Man Trouble 1992

Man Who Cried, The 2002

Man Who Fell to Earth, The [1975] 1982

Man Who Knew Too Little, The 1997

Man Who Loved Women, The 1983

Man Who Wasn't There, The 1983

Man Who Wasn't There, The 2002

Man Who Would Be King, The [1975] 1983

Man with One Red Shoe, The 1985

Man with Three Coffins, The 1988

Man with Two Brains, The 1983

Man Without a Face, The 1993

Man Without a Past, The 2003

Man Without a World, The 1992

Man, Woman and Child 1983

Manchurian Candidate, The 2005

Manderlay 2007

Maneuvers 1988

Mangler, The 1995

Manhattan by Numbers 1995

Manhattan Murder Mystery 1993

Manhattan Project, The 1986

Manhunter 1986

Maniac Cop 1988

Manic 2004

Manifesto 1989

Manito 2004

Mannequin 1987

Mannequin Two 1991

Manny & Lo 1996

Manon des sources. *See* Manon of the Spring.

Manon of the Spring 1987

Man's Best Friend 1993

Mansfield Park 2000

Map of the Human Heart 1993

Mapantsula 1988

Mar Adentro. *See* Sea Inside, The.

March of the Penguins 2006

Marci X 2004

Margaret's Museum 1997

Margarita Happy Hour 2003

Margot at the Wedding 2008

Maria Full of Grace 2005

Maria's Lovers 1985

Mariachi, El 1993

Mariages 2003

Marie 1985

Marie Antoinette 2007

Marie Baie des Anges. *See* Marie from the Bay Angels.

Marie from the Bay Angels 1999

Marilyn Monroe 1987

Marine, The 2007

Marine Life 2001

Marius and Jeannette 1999

Marius et Jeannette: Un Conte de L'Estaque. *See* Marius and Jeannette.

Marked for Death 1990

Marlene 1986

Marley & Me pg. 207

Marooned in Iraq 2004

Marquis 1995

Marriages. *See* Mariages.

Married Life pg. 208

Married to It 1993

Married to the Mob 1988

Marrying Man, The 1991

Mars Attacks! 1996

Marsupials, The 1987

Martha and Ethel 1995

Martha and I 1995

Martha, Ruth, and Edie 1988

Martian Child 2008

Martians Go Home 1990

Marusa No Onna. *See* Taxing Woman, A.

Nuts 1987

Nutty Professor, The 1996

Nutty Professor 2: The Klumps 2001

O

O 2002

O Brother, Where Art Thou? 2001

O' Despair. *See* Long Weekend, The.

Oak, The 1995

Oasis, The 1984

Obecna Skola. *See* Elementary School, The.

Oberst Redl. *See* Colonel Redl.

Object of Beauty, The 1991

Object of My Affection, The 1999

Oblivion 1995

Obsessed 1988

Obsluhoval jsem anglického krále. *See* I Served the King of England.

O.C. and Stiggs 1987

Ocean's Eleven 2002

Ocean's Thirteen 2008

Ocean's Twelve 2005

Oci Ciornie. *See* Dark Eyes.

October Sky 2000

Octopussy 1983

Odd Man Out [1947] 1985

Oedipus Rex 1995

Oedipus Rex [1967] 1984

Oedipus Wrecks. *See* New York Stories.

Of Human Bondage [1946] 1986

Of Love and Shadows 1996

Of Mice and Men 1992

Of Unknown Origin 1983

Off Beat 1986

Off Limits 1988

Off the Menu: The Last Days of Chasen's 1999

Office Killer 1997

Office Party 1989

Office Space 2000

Officer and a Gentleman, An 1982

Official Story, The 1985

Offret. *See* Sacrifice, The.

Oh God, You Devil 1984

O'Hara's Wife 1982

Old Explorers 1991

Old Gringo 1989

Old Joy 2007

Old Lady Who Walked in the Sea, The 1995

Old School 2004

Oldboy 2006

Oleanna 1995

Oliver and Company 1988

Oliver Twist 2006

Olivier Olivier 1993

Omen, The 2007

On Deadly Ground 1995

On Golden Pond 1981

On Guard! 2004

On the Edge 1986

On the Line 2002

On the Other Side. *See* Edge of Heaven, The.

On the Town [1949] 1985

On Valentine's Day 1986

Once 2008

Once Around 1991

Once Bitten 1985

Once More 1988

Once Were Warriors 1995

Once Upon a Crime 1992

Once Upon A Forest 1993

Once Upon a Time in America 1984

Once Upon a Time in Mexico 2004

Once Upon a Time in the Midlands 2004

Once Upon a Time...When We Were Colored 1996

Once We Were Dreamers 1987

One 2001

One, The 2002

One and a Two, A. *See* Yi Yi.

One Crazy Summer 1986

One Day in September 2001

One False Move 1992

One Fine Day 1996

One Flew over the Cuckoo's Nest [1975] 1985, 1991

One from the Heart 1982

One Good Cop 1991

One Hour Photo 2003

101 Dalmatians 1996

101 Reykjavik 2002

102 Dalmatians 2001

187 1997

112th and Central 1993

One Magic Christmas 1985

One Missed Call pg. 237

One More Saturday 1986

One More Tomorrow [1946] 1986

One Nation Under God 1995

One Night at McCool's 2002

One Night Stand 1997

One Tough Cop 1999

One True Thing 1999

Onegin 2000

Onimaru. *See* Arashi Ga Oka.

Only Emptiness Remains 1985

Only the Lonely 1991

Only the Strong 1993

Only the Strong Survive 2004

Only Thrill, The 1999

Only When I Laugh 1981

Only You 1995

Open Doors 1991

Open Range 2004

Open Season 2007

Open Water 2005

Open Your Eyes 2000

Opening Night 1988

Opera 1987

Operation Condor 1997

Operation Dumbo Drop 1995

Opportunists, The 2001

Opportunity Knocks 1990

Opposite of Sex, The 1999

Opposite Sex, The 1993

Orange County 2003

Orchestra Seats. *See* Avenue Montaigne.

Ordeal by Innocence 1985

Order, The 2004

Orfanato, El. *See* Orphanage, The.

Orgazmo 1999

Original Gangstas 1996

Original Kings of Comedy, The 2001

Original Sin 2002

Orlando 1993

Orphan Muses, The 2002

Orphanage, The pg. 238

Orphans 1987

Orphans of the Storm 1984

Osama 2005

Oscar 1991

Oscar & Lucinda 1997

Osmosis Jones 2002

Ososhiki. *See* Funeral, The.

Osterman Weekend, The 1983

Otac Na Sluzbenom Putu. *See* When Father Was Away on Business.

Otello 1986

Othello 1995

Other Boleyn Girl, The pg. 239

Other People's Money 1991

Other Side of Heaven, The 2003

Other Sister, The 2000

Other Voices, Other Rooms 1997

Others, The 2002

Our Lady of the Assassins 2002

Our Relations [1936] 1985

Our Song 2002

Out Cold 1989

Out for Justice 1991

Out in the World. *See* Among People.

Out of Africa 1985

Out of Bounds 1986

Out of Control 1985

Out of Life. *See* Hors la Vie.

Out of Order 1985

Out of Sight 1999

Out of Sync 1995

Out of the Dark 1989

Out of the Past [1947] 1991

Out of Time 2004

Out-of-Towners, The 2000

Out on a Limb 1992

Out to Sea 1997

Outbreak 1995

Outfoxed: Rupert Murdoch's War on Journalism 2005

Outing, The 1987

Outland 1981

Outrageous Fortune 1987

Outside Providence 2000

Outsiders, The 1983

Over Her Dead Body 1995

Over Her Dead Body pg. 241

Over the Edge [1979] 1987

Over the Hedge 2007

Over the Hill 1995

Over the Ocean 1995

Over the Top 1987

Overboard 1987

Overexposed 1990

Overseas 1991

Owning Mahowny 2004

Ox, The 1992

Oxford, Blues 1984

Oxygen 2000

P

P.O.W. the Escape 1986

P.S. 2005

Pacific Heights 1990

Pacifier, The 2006

Package, The 1989

Pacte des Loups, Le. *See* Brotherhood of the Wolf.

Pagemaster, The 1995

Paint Job, The 1995

Painted Desert, The 1995

Painted Veil, The 2008

Palais Royale 1988

Pale Rider 1985

Palindromes 2006

Pallbearer, The 1996

Palmetto 1999

Palombella Rossa. *See* Redwood Pigeon.

Palookaville 1996

Panama Deception, The 1992

Pane e Tulipani. *See* Bread and Tulips.

Panic 2001

Panic Room, The 2003

Pan's Labyrinth 2007

Panther 1995

Papa's Song 2001

Paparazzi 2005

Paper, The 1995

Paper Hearts 1995

Paper Mask 1991

Paper Wedding, A 1991

Paperback Romance 1997

Paperhouse 1988

Paprika 2008

Paradise (Donoghue) 1991

Paradise (Gillard) 1982

Paradise Lost 1996

Paradise Now 2006

Paradise Road 1997

Paranoid Park pg. 243

Parasite 1982

Parde-ye akhar. *See* Last Act, The.

Parent Trap, The 1999

Parenthood 1989

Parents 1989

Paris, I Love You. *See* Paris, je t'aime.

Paris, Texas 1984

Paris Blues [1961] 1992

Paris Is Burning 1991

Paris je t'aime 2008

Parsifal 1983

Parsley Days 2001

Parting Glances 1986

Partisans of Vilna 1986

Partners 1982

Party Animal 1985

Party Girl 1995

Party Line 1988

Party Monster 2004

Pascali's Island 1988

Pass the Ammo 1988

Passage, The 1988

Passage to India, A 1984, 1990

Passages 1995

Passed Away 1992

Passenger 57 1992

Passion (Duncan) 2001

Passion (Godard) 1983

Passion d'amore 1984

Passion Fish 1992

Passion in the Desert 1999
Passion of Martin, The 1991
Passion of Mind 2001
Passion of the Christ, The 2005
Passion to Kill, A 1995
Passionada 2003
Pastime 1991
Patch Adams 1999
Patch of Blue, A [1965] 1986
Pathfinder 1990
Pathfinder 2008
Pathology pg. 244
Paths of Glory [1957] 1991
Patinoire, La. *See* Ice Rink, The.
Patriot, The 2001
Patriot Games 1992
Patsy, The 1985
Patti Rocks 1987
Patty Hearst 1988
Paul Bowles: The Complete Outsider 1995
Paulie 1999
Pauline a la plage. *See* Pauline at the Beach.
Pauline and Paulette 2003
Pauline at the Beach 1983
Paura e amore. *See* Three Sisters.
Pavilion of Women 2002
Pay It Forward 2001
Payback 2000
Paycheck 2004
PCU 1995
Peace, Propaganda & The Promised Land 2006
Peaceful Air of the West 1995
Peacemaker, The 1997
Pearl Harbor 2002
Pebble and the Penguin, The 1995
Pecker 1999
Pee-wee's Big Adventure 1985
Peggy Sue Got Married 1986
Pelican Brief, The 1993
Pelle Erobreren. *See* Pelle the Conqueror.
Pelle the Conquered 1988
Pelle the Conqueror 1987

Penelope pg. 246
Penitent, The 1988
Penitentiary II 1982
Penitentiary III 1987
Penn and Teller Get Killed 1989
Pennies from Heaven 1981
People I Know 2004
People on Sunday [1929] 1986
People Under the Stairs, The 1991
People vs. Larry Flynt, The 1996
Pepi, Luci, Bom 1992
Perez Family, The 1995
Perfect 1985
Perfect Candidate, A 1996
Perfect Man, The 2006
Perfect Match, The 1987
Perfect Model, The 1989
Perfect Murder, A 1999
Perfect Murder, The 1988
Perfect Score, The 2005
Perfect Son, The 2002
Perfect Storm, The 2001
Perfect Stranger 2008
Perfect Weapon, The 1991
Perfect World, A 1993
Perfectly Normal 1991
Perfume: The Story of a Murderer 2008
Perhaps Some Other Time 1992
Peril 1985
Peril en la demeure. *See* Peril.
Permanent Midnight 1999
Permanent Record 1988
Persepolis pg. 247
Personal Best 1982
Personal Choice 1989
Personal Services 1987
Personal Velocity 2003
Personals, The 1983
Persuasion 1995
Pervola, Sporen in die Sneeuw. *See* Tracks in the Snow.
Pest, The 1997
Pet Sematary 1989
Pet Sematary II 1992

Pete Kelly's Blues [1955] 1982
Peter Ibbetson [1935] 1985
Peter Pan 2004
Peter Von Scholten 1987
Peter's Friends 1992
Petit, Con. *See* Little Jerk.
Petite Bande, Le 1984
Petite Veleuse, La. *See* Little Thief, The.
Peyote Road, The 1995
Phantasm II 1988
Phantom, The 1996
Phantom of the Opera, The (Little) 1989
Phantom of the Opera, The (Schumacher) 2005
Phantoms 1999
Phar Lap 1984
Phat Beach 1996
Phat Girlz 2007
Phenomenon 1996
Philadelphia 1993
Philadelphia Experiment, The 1984
Philadelphia Experiment II, The 1995
Phobia 1988
Phone Booth 2004
Phorpa. *See* Cup, The.
Physical Evidence 1989
Pi 1999
Piaf 1982
Pianist, The 2003
Pianiste, La. *See* Piano Teacher, The.
Piano, The 1993
Piano Piano Kid 1992
Piano Teacher, The 2003
Piano Tuner of Earthquakes, The 2007
Picasso Trigger 1988
Piccolo diavolo, II. *See* Little Devil, The.
Pick-Up Artist, The 1987
Pickle, The 1993
Picture Bride 1995
Picture Perfect 1997
Picture This: The Life and Times of Peter Bogdanovich in Archer City, Texas 1995

Running Brave 1983

Running Free 2001

Running Hot 1984

Running Man, The 1987

Running on Empty 1988

Running Scared 1986

Running Scared 2007

Running with Scissors 2007

Rupert's Land 2001

Rush 1991

Rush Hour 1999

Rush Hour 2 2002

Rush Hour 3 2008

Rushmore 1999

Russia House, The 1990

Russian Dolls 2007

Russia's Wonder Children 2001

Russkies 1987

Russlands Wunderkinder. *See* Russia's Wonder Children.

Rustler's Rhapsody 1985

Rustling of Leaves, A 1990

Ruthless People 1986

RV 2007

Ryan's Daughter [1970] 1990

S

S.F.W. 1995

Sabrina [1954] 1986

Sabrina 1995

Sacrifice, The 1986

Saddest Music in the World, The 2005

Sade 2004

Safe 1995

Safe Conduct 2003

Safe Journey. *See* Latcho Drom.

Safe Passage 1995

Safety of Objects, The 2003

Sahara 2006

Sahara (McLaglen) 1984

St. Elmo's Fire 1985

Saint, The 1997

Saint Clara 1997

Saint of Fort Washington, The 1993

Saison des Hommes, La. *See* Season of Men, The.

Salaam Bombay! 1988

Salmer fra Kjokkenet. *See* Kitchen Stories.

Salmonberries 1995

Salome's Last Dance 1988

Salsa 1988

Salt of the Earth [1954] 1986

Salt on Our Skin. *See* Desire.

Salton Sea, The 2003

Saltwater 2002

Salvador 1986

Sam and Sarah 1991

Samantha 1995

Sam's Son 1984

Samba Traore 1995

Same Old Song 2000

Sammy and Rosie Get Laid 1987

Sandlot, The 1993

Sandwich Years, The 1988

Sang for Martin, En. *See* Song for Martin, A.

Sans toit ni loi. *See* Vagabond.

Santa Claus 1985

Santa Clause, The 1995

Santa Clause 2, The 2003

Santa Clause 3: The Escape Clause, The 2007

Santa Fe 1988

Santa Sangre 1990

Sara 1995

Saraband 2006

Sarafina! 1992

Satan 1995

Satisfaction 1988

Saturday Night at the Palace 1987

Saturday Night, Sunday Morning: The Travels of Gatemouth Moore 1995

Sauve qui peut (La Vie). *See* Every Man for Himself.

Savage Beach 1989

Savage Island 1985

Savage Nights 1995

Savages, The 2008

Savannah Smiles 1983

Save the Last Dance 2002

Save the Tiger [1973] 1988

Saved! 2005

Saving Grace (Young) 1986

Saving Grace (Cole) 2001

Saving Private Ryan 1999

Saving Silverman 2002

Savior 1999

Saw 2005

Saw V pg. 289

Saw IV 2008

Saw III 2007

Saw II 2006

Say Anything 1989

Say It Isn't So 2002

Say Yes 1986

Scandal 1989

Scandalous 1984

Scanner Darkly, A 2007

Scanners III: The Takeover 1995

Scaphandre et le papillon, Le. *See* Diving Bell and the Butterfly, The.

Scarface 1983

Scarlet Letter, The [1926] 1982, 1984

Scarlet Letter, The 1995

Scarlet Street [1946] 1982

Scary Movie 2001

Scary Movie 2 2002

Scary Movie 3 2004

Scary Movie 4 2007

Scavengers 1988

Scenes from a Mall 1991

Scenes from the Class Struggle in Beverly Hills 1989

Scent of a Woman 1992

Scent of Green Papaya, The (Mui du du Xanh) 1995

Scherzo del destino agguato dietro l'angelo come un brigante di strada. *See* Joke of Destiny, A.

Schindler's List 1993

Schizo 2006

Schizopolis 1997

School Daze 1988

School for Scoundrels 2007

School of Flesh, 432

Shadow of the Vampire 2001

Shadow of the Wolf 1993

Shadowboxer 2007

Shadowlands 1993

Shadows and Fog 1992

Shadrach 1999

Shaft 2001

Shag 1988

Shaggy Dog, The 2007

Shakedown 1988

Shakes the Clown 1992

Shakespeare in Love 1999

Shaking the Tree 1992

Shall We Dance? 1997

Shall We Dance? 2005

Shallow Grave 1995

Shallow Hal 2002

Shame 1988

Shanghai Knights 2004

Shanghai Noon 2001

Shanghai Surprise 1986

Shanghai Triad 1995

Shaolin Soccer 2005

Shape of Things, The 2004

Shark Tale 2005

Sharky's Machine 1981

Sharma and Beyond 1986

Shatterbrain. *See* Resurrected, The.

Shattered 1991

Shattered Glass 2004

Shaun of the Dead 2005

Shaunglong Hui. *See* Twin Dragons.

Shawshank Redemption, The 1995

She Hate Me 2005

She Must Be Seeing Things 1987

Sherrybaby 2007

She-Devil 1989

Sheena 1984

Sheer Madness 1985

Shelf Life 1995

Sheltering Sky, The 1990

Sherlock Holmes [1922] 1982

Sherman's March 1986

She's All That 2000

She's De Lovely. *See* De-Lovely.

She's Gotta Have It 1986

She's Having a Baby 1988

She's Out of Control 1989

She's So Lovely 1997

She's the Man 2007

She's the One 1996

Shiloh 2: Shiloh Season 2000

Shimian Maifu. *See* House of Flying Daggers.

Shine 1996

Shine a Light pg. 299

Shining, The [1980]

Shining Through 1992

Shipping News, The 2002

Shipwrecked 1991

Shiqisuide Danche. *See* Beijing Bicycle.

Shirley Valentine 1989

Shiza. *See* Shizo.

Shoah 1985

Shock to the System, A 1990

Shocker 1989

Shoot 'Em Up 2008

Shoot the Moon 1982

Shoot to Kill 1988

Shooter 2008

Shooting, The [1966] 1995

Shooting Dogs. *See* Beyond the Gates.

Shooting Fish 1999

Shooting Party, The 1985

Shootist, The [1976] 1982

Shopgirl 2006

Short Circuit 1986

Short Circuit II 1988

Short Cuts 1993

Short Film About Love, A 1995

Short Time 1990

Shot, The 1996

Shout 1991

Show, The 1995

Show Me Love 2000

Show of Force, A 1990

Showdown in Little Tokyo 1991

Shower, The 2001

Showgirls 1995

Showtime 2003

Shrek 2002

Shrek the Third 2008

Shrek 2 2005

Shrimp on the Barbie, The 1990

Shutter pg. 301

Shvitz, The. *See* New York in Short: The Shvitz and Let's Fall in Love.

Shy People 1987

Siberiade 1982

Sibling Rivalry 1990

Sicilian, The 1987

Sick: The Life and Death of Bob Flanagan, Supermasochist 1997

Sicko 2008

Sid and Nancy 1986

Side Out 1990

Sidekicks 1993

Sidewalk Stories 1989

Sidewalks of New York, The 2002

Sideways 2005

Siege, The 1999

Siesta 1987

Sign o' the Times 1987

Sign of the Cross, The [1932] 1984

Signal Seven 1986

Signs 2003

Signs & Wonders 2002

Signs of Life 1989

Silence, The 2001

Silence After the Shot, The. *See* Legend of Rita, The.

Silence at Bethany, The 1988

Silence of the Lambs, The 1991

Silencer, The 1995

Silent Fall 1995

Silent Hill 2007

Silent Madness, The 1984

Silent Night 1988

Silent Night, Deadly Night 1984

Silent Night, Deadly Night II 1987

Silent Night, Deadly Night III 1989

Silent Rage 1982

Silent Tongue 1995

Silent Touch, The 1995

Silent Victim 1995

Sunset Boulevard [1950] 1986

Sunset Park 1996

Sunshine 2001

Sunshine (Boyle) 2008

Sunshine State 2003

Super, The 1991

Super Mario Bros. 1993

Super Size Me 2005

Superbad 2008

Supercop 1997

Superfantagenio. *See* Aladdin.

Supergirl 1984

Superhero Movie pg. 334

Superman II 1981

Superman III 1983

Superman IV 1987

Superman Returns 2007

Supernova 2001

Superstar 1991

Superstar 2000

Sur 1988

Sur Mes Levres. *See* Read My Lips.

Sure Fire 1993

Sure Thing, The 1985

Surf II 1984

Surf Nazis Must Die 1987

Surf Ninjas 1993

Surf's Up 2008

Surfwise pg. 335

Surrender 1987

Survival Quest 1990

Surviving Christmas 2005

Surviving the Game 1995

Surviving Picasso 1996

Survivors, The 1983

Suspect 1987

Suspect Zero 2005

Suspended Animation 2004

Suspicious River 2002

Suture 1995

Swamp, The. *See* Cienaga, La.

Swamp Thing 1982

Swan Lake 1991

Swan Princess, The 1995

Swann in Love 1984

S.W.A.T. 2004

Sweeney Todd: The Demon Barber of Fleet Street 2008

Sweet and Lowdown 2000

Sweet Country 1987

Sweet Dreams 1985

Sweet Emma, Dear Bobe: Sketches, Nudes 1995

Sweet Hearts Dance 1988

Sweet Hereafter, The 1997

Sweet Home Alabama 2003

Sweet Liberty 1986

Sweet Lorraine 1987

Sweet Nothing 1996

Sweet November 2002

Sweet Revenge 1987

Sweet Sixteen 1984

Sweet Sixteen 2004

Sweet Talker 1991

Sweetest Thing, The 2003

Sweetie 1990

Sweetwater 1988

Swept Away 2003

Swept from the Sea 1999

Swimfan 2003

Swimming Pool 2004

Swimming to Cambodia 1987

Swimming Upstream 2006

Swimming With Sharks 1995

Swindle, The 2000

Swing Kids 1993

Swing Shift 1984

Swing Vote pg. 336

Swingers 1996

Switch 1991

Switchback 1997

Switching Channels 1988

Swoon 1992

Sword and the Sorcerer, The 1982

Swordfish 2002

Swordsman III. *See* East is Red, The.

Sydney White 2008

Sylvester V 1987

Sylvia 1985

Sylvia 2004

Synecdoche, New York pg. 338

Syriana 2006

T

Table for Five 1983

Taboo 2001

Tacones lejanos. *See* High Heels.

Tadpole 2003

Tadpole and the Whale 1988

Tag 1982

Tai-pan 1986

Tailor of Panama, The 2002

Take a Letter, Darling [1942] 1984

Take the Lead 2007

Take Two 1988

Taking Care of Business 1990

Taking Lives 2005

Taking of Beverly Hills, The 1991

Taking Off [1971] 1985

Taking Sides 2004

Tale of Despereaux, The pg. 341

Tale of Ruby Rose, The 1987

Tale of Springtime, A 1992

Tale of Winter, A 1995

Talented Mr. Ripley, The 2000

Tales from the Crypt: Bordello of Blood 1996

Tales from the Crypt Presents Demon Knight 1995

Tales from the Darkside 1990

Tales from the Hood 1995

Tales of Ordinary Madness 1983

Talk 1995

Talk of Angels 1999

Talk Radio 1988

Talk to Her 2003

Talk to Me 2008

Talkin' Dirty After Dark 1991

Tall Guy, The 1990

Tall Tale: The Unbelievable Adventures of Pecos Bill 1995

Talladega Nights: The Ballad of Ricky Bobby 2007

Talons of the Eagle 1995

Talvisota 1989

Taming of the Shrew, The [1967] 1993

Tampopo 1987

Tango and Cash 1989

Tango Bar 1988, 1989

Tango Lesson, The 1998

Tank 1984

Tank Girl 1995

Tao of Steve, The 2001

Tap 1989

Tape 2002

Tapeheads 1988

Taps 1981

Target 1985

Target 1996

Tarnation 2005

Tarzan 2000

Tarzan and the Lost City 1999

Tasogare Seibei. *See* Twilight Samurai, The.

Taste of Others, The 2002

Tatie Danielle 1991

Taxi 2005

Taxi Blues 1991

Taxi nach Kairo. *See* Taxi to Cairo.

Taxi to Cairo 1988

Taxi to the Dark Side pg. 342

Taxi to the Toilet. *See* Taxi Zum Klo.

Taxi Zum Klo 1981

Taxing Woman, A 1988

Taxing Woman's Return, A 1989

Tea in the Harem 1986

Tea With Mussolini 2000

Teachers 1984

Teacher's Pet: The Movie. *See* Disney's Teacher's Pet.

Teaching Mrs. Tingle 2000

Team America: World Police 2005

Tears of the Sun 2004

Ted and Venus 1991

Teen Witch 1989

Teen Wolf 1985

Teenage Mutant Ninja Turtles 1990

Teenage Mutant Ninja Turtles (2007). *See* TMNT.

Teenage Mutant Ninja Turtles II 1991

Teenage Mutant Ninja Turtles III 1993

Teeth pg. 343

Telephone, The 1988

Tell No One pg. 345

Telling Lies in America 1997

Témoins, Les. *See* Witnesses, The.

Temp, The 1993

Tempest 1982

Temporada de patos. *See* Duck Season.

Temps qui changent, Les. *See* Changing Times.

Temps qui reste, Les. *See* Time to Leave.

Temps Retrouve. *See* Time Regained.

Temptress Moon 1997

Ten 2004

Ten Things I Hate About You 2000

10,000 B.C. pg. 346

10 to Midnight 1983

Tenacious D in the Pick of Destiny 2007

Tender Mercies 1983

Tenebrae. *See* Unsane.

Tenue de soiree. *See* Menage.

Tequila Sunrise 1988

Terminal, The 2005

Terminal Bliss 1992

Terminal Velocity 1995

Terminator, The 1984

Terminator 2 1991

Terminator 3: Rise of the Machines 2004

Termini Station 1991

Terminus. *See* End of the Line.

Terms of Endearment 1983

Terror Within, The 1989

Terrorvision 1986

Tess 1981

Test of Love 1985

Testament 1983

Testimony 1987

Tetsuo: The Iron Man 1992

Tex 1982, 1987

Texas Chainsaw Massacre, The (Nispel) 2004

Texas Chainsaw Massacre, Part II, The 1986

Texas Chainsaw Massacre: The Beginning, The 2007

Texas Comedy Massacre, The 1988

Texas Rangers 2003

Texas Tenor: The Illinois Jacquet Story 1995

Texasville 1990

Thank You and Good Night 1992

Thank You for Smoking 2007

That Championship Season 1982

That Darn Cat 1997

That Night 1993

That Old Feeling 1997

That Sinking Feeling 1984

That Thing You Do! 1996

That Was Then…This Is Now 1985

That's Entertainment! III 1995

That's Life! 1986, 1988

The au harem d'Archi Ahmed, Le. *See* Tea in the Harem.

Thelma and Louise 1991

Thelonious Monk 1988

Then She Found Me pg. 348

Theory of Flight, The 1999

There Goes My Baby 1995

There Goes the Neighborhood 1995

There Will Be Blood 2008

There's Nothing Out There 1992

There's Something About Mary 1999

Theremin: An Electronic Odyssey 1995

They All Laughed 1981

They Call Me Bruce 1982

They Drive by Night [1940] 1982

They Live 1988

They Live by Night [1949] 1981

They Might Be Giants [1971] 1982

They Still Call Me Bruce 1987

They Won't Believe Me [1947] 1987

They're Playing with Fire 1984

Thiassos, O. *See* Traveling Players, The.

Thief 1981

Thief, The 1999

Welcome in Vienna 1988

Welcome to Collinwood 2003

Welcome to Mooseport 2005

Welcome to the Dollhouse 1996

Welcome to Sarajevo 1997

Welcome to Woop Woop 1999

Wendigo 2003

Wendy and Lucy pg. 389

We're Back 1993

We're No Angels [1955] (Curtiz) 1982

We're No Angels (Jordan) 1989

We're Talkin' Serious Merry 1992

Wes Craven Presents: Dracula 2000 2001

Wes Craven Presents: They 2003

Wes Craven's New Nightmare 1995

West Beirut 2000

West Beyrouth. *See* West Beirut.

Western 1999

Wet and Wild Summer. *See* Exchange Lifeguards.

Wet Hot American Summer 2002

Wetherby 1985

Whale Rider 2004

Whales of August, The 1987

What a Girl Wants 2004

What About Bob? 1991

What Dreams May Come 1999

What Happened to Kerouse? 1986

What Happened Was... 1995

What Happens in Vegas pg. 390

What Just Happened pg. 391

What Lies Beneath 2001

What Planet Are You From? 2001

What the (Bleep) Do We Know? 2005

What Time Is It There? 2002

What Women Want 2001

Whatever 1999

Whatever It Takes (Demchuk) 1986

Whatever It Takes (Raynr) 2001

What's Cooking? 2001

What's Eating Gilbert Grape 1993

What's Love Got To Do With It 1993

What's the Worst That Could Happen? 2002

When a Man Loves a Woman 1995

When a Stranger Calls 2007

When Brendan Met Trudy 2002

When Did You Last See Your Father? pg. 393

When Father Was Away on Business 1985

When Harry Met Sally 1989

When Love Comes 2000

When Nature Calls 1985

When Night is Falling 1995

When the Cat's Away 1997

When the Party's Over 1993

When the Whales Came 1989

When the Wind Blows 1987

When We Were Kings 1997

When Will I Be Loved 2005

Where Angels Fear to Tread 1992

Where Are the Children? 1986

Where Spring Comes Late 1988

Where the Boys are '84 1984

Where the Day Takes You 1992

Where the Green Ants Dream 1985

Where the Heart Is (Boorman) 1990

Where the Heart Is (Williams) 2001

Where the Heart Roams 1987

Where the Money Is 2001

Where the Outback Ends 1988

Where the River Runs Black 1986

Where The Rivers Flow North 1995

Where the Truth Lies 2006

Wherever You Are 1988

While You Were Sleeping 1995

Whispers in the Dark 1992

Whistle Blower, The 1987

White 1995

White Badge 1995

White Balloon, The 1996

White Boys 2000

White Chicks 2005

White Countess, The 2006

White Dog 1995

White Fang 1991

White Fang II: Myth of the White Wolf 1995

White Girl, The 1990

White Hunter, Black Heart 1990

White Man's Burden 1995

White Men Can't Jump 1992

White Mischief 1988

White Nights 1985

White Noise 2006

White of the Eye 1987, 1988

White Oleander 2003

White Palace 1990

White Rose, The 1983

White Sands 1992

White Sister, The [1923] 1982

White Squall 1996

White Trash 1992

White Winter Heat 1987

Who Framed Roger Rabbit 1988

Who Killed the Electric Car? 2007

Who Killed Vincent Chin? 1988

Who Knows? *See* Va Savoir.

Who Shot Pat? 1992

Whole Nine Yards, The 2001

Whole Ten Yards, The 2005

Whole Wide World, The 1997

Whoopee Boys, The 1986

Whore 1991

Who's Afraid of Virginia Wolf? [1966] 1993

Who's Harry Crumb? 1989

Who's That Girl 1987

Who's the Man? 1993

Whose Life Is It Anyway? 1981

Why Did I Get Married? 2008

Why Do Fools Fall In Love 1999

Why Has Bodhi-Dharma Left for the East? 1995

Why Me? 1990

Why We Fight 2007

Wicked Lady, The 1983

Wicked Stepmother 1989

Wicker Man, The [1974] 1985

Wicker Man, The 2007

Wicker Park 2005

Wide Awake 1999

Wide Sargasso Sea 1993

Widow of Saint-Pierre, The 2002

Widows' Peak 1995

Wife, The 1996

Wigstock: the Movie 1995

Wilbur Wants to Kill Himself 2005

Wild, The 2007

Wild America 1997

Wild at Heart 1990

Wild Bill 1995

Wild Bunch, The [1969] 1995

Wild Duck, The 1985

Wild Geese II 1985

Wild Hearts Can't Be Broken 1991

Wild Hogs 2008

Wild Horses 1984

Wild Life, The 1984

Wild Man Blues 1999

Wild Orchid 1990

Wild Orchid II: Two Shades of Blue 1992

Wild Pair, The 1987

Wild Parrots of Telegraph Hill, The 2006

Wild Reeds 1995

Wild Thing 1987

Wild Things 1999

Wild Thornberrrys Movie, The 2003

Wild West 1993

Wild West Comedy Show. *See* Vince Vaughn's Wild West Comedy Show: 30 Days & 30 Nights—Hollywood to the Heartland.

Wild Wild West 2000

Wildcats 1986

Wilde 1999

Wilder Napalm 1993

Wildfire 1988

Willard 2004

William Shakespeare's A Midsummer's Night Dream 2000

William Shakespeare's Romeo & Juliet 1996

William Shakespeare's The Merchant of Venice. *See* Merchant of Venice, The.

Willow 1988

Wilt. *See* Misadventures of Mr. Wilt, The.

Wimbledon 2005

Win a Date with Tad Hamilton 2005

Wind 1992

Wind, The [1928] 1984

Wind in the Willows, The 1997

Wind the Shakes the Barley, The 2008

Wind Will Carry Us, The 2001

Window Shopping 1995

Window to Paris 1995

Windtalkers 2003

Windy City 1984

Wing Commanders 2000

Winged Migration 2004

Wings of Desire 1988

Wings of the Dove 1997

Winner, The 1997

Winners, The 2000

Winners Take All 1987

Winslow Boy, The 2000

Winter Guest, The 1997

Winter Meeting [1948] 1986

Winter of Our Dreams 1982

Winter Passing 2007

Winter People 1989

Winter Solstice 2006

Winter Tan, A 1988

Winter War, The. *See* Talvison.

Wiping the Tears of Seven Generations 1995

Wired 1989

Wired to Kill 1986

Wirey Spindell 2001

Wisdom 1986

Wise Guys 1986

Wisecracks 1992

Wish You Were Here 1987

Wishmaster 1997

Witchboard 1987

Witches, The 1990

Witches of Eastwick, The 1987

With a Friend Like Harry 2002

With Friends Like These... 2006

With Honors 1995

With Love to the Person Next to Me 1987

Withnail and I 1987

Without a Clue 1988

Without a Paddle 2005

Without a Trace 1983

Without Evidence 1996

Without Limits 1999

Without You I'm Nothing 1990

Witless Protection pg. 395

Witness 1985

Witness for the Prosecution 1986

Witness to a Killing 1987

Witnesses, The pg. 396

Wittgenstein 1995

Wizard, The 1989

Wizard of Loneliness, The 1988

Wizard of Oz, The [1939], 1999

Wo De Fu Qin Mu Qin. *See* Road Home, The.

Wo Die Gruenen Ameisen Traeumen. *See* Where the Green Ants Dream.

Wo Hu Zang Long. *See* Crouching Tiger, Hidden Dragon.

Wolf 1995

Wolfen 1981

Woman, Her Men, and Her Futon, A 1992

Woman in Flames, A 1984

Woman in Red, The 1984

Woman in the Moon 1988

Woman in the Window, The [1944] 1982

Woman Next Door, The 1982

Woman on the Beach, The [1947] 1982

Woman's Pale Blue Handwriting, A 1988

Woman's Tale, A 1991

Wombling Free [1979] 1984

Women, The pg. 397

Women on the Verge of a Nervous Breakdown 1988

Women's Affair 1988

Wonder Boys 2001

Wonderful Days. *See* Sky Blue.

Wonderful, Horrible Life of Leni Riefenstahl, The 1995